WOMEN'S AMERICA
Refocusing the Past

WOMEN'S AMERICA

Refocusing the Past

VOLUME 2

EIGHTH EDITION

Edited by

Linda K. Kerber
University of Iowa

Jane Sherron De Hart
University of California, Santa Barbara

Cornelia Hughes Dayton
University of Connecticut

Judy Tzu-Chun Wu
University of California, Irvine

New York   Oxford
Oxford University Press

Oxford University Press is a department of the University of Oxford.
It furthers the University's objective of excellence in research,
scholarship, and education by publishing worldwide.

Oxford   New York
Auckland   Cape Town   Dar es Salaam   Hong Kong   Karachi
Kuala Lumpur   Madrid   Melbourne   Mexico City   Nairobi
New Delhi   Shanghai   Taipei   Toronto

With offices in
Argentina   Austria   Brazil   Chile   Czech Republic   France   Greece
Guatemala   Hungary   Italy   Japan   Poland   Portugal   Singapore
South Korea   Switzerland   Thailand   Turkey   Ukraine   Vietnam

For titles covered by Section 112 of the US Higher Education
Opportunity Act, please visit www.oup.com/us/he for the
latest information about pricing and alternate formats.

Published by Oxford University Press
198 Madison Avenue, New York, New York 10016
http://www.oup.com

Library of Congress Cataloging-in-Publication Data
Women's America / edited by Linda K. Kerber, University of Iowa, Jane Sherron
De Hart, University of California, Santa Barbara, Cornelia Hughes Dayton, University
of Connecticut, Judy Tzu-Chun Wu, Ohio State University. -- Eighth edition.
    pages cm
  ISBN 978-0-19-934936-4
  1. Women--United States--History--Sources. 2. Women--Employment--United States--
History--Sources. 3. Women--Political activity--United States--History--Sources.
4. Women--Health and hygiene--United States--History--Sources. 5. Feminism--United
States--History--Sources. I. Kerber, Linda K.
  HQ1426.W663 2015
  305.40973--dc23
                                                                        2014033991

Printing number: 9 8 7 6 5 4 3 2 1

Printed in the United States of America
on acid-free paper

For our teachers

Annette Kar Baxter (1926–1984)

Mary Maples Dunn

Lilia Fernández

Estelle Freedman

Susan Hartmann

John Atlee Kouwenhoven (1909–1990)

Gerda Lerner (1920–2013)

Peggy Pascoe (1954–2010)

Susan Porter Benson (1943–2005)

Leila J. Rupp

Anne Firor Scott

Christine Stansell

Eleanor M. Tilton (1913–1994)

Teaching Workshop in Women's History (UCLA)

and

our own cohorts of pioneering women's historians

and, of course,

the present and future generations of women's and gender history scholars

ILLUSTRATIONS

CONTENTS

PREFACE

To our readers:

Twenty-seven years ago, writing the preface for the second edition of *Women's America*, we observed that in the few years since the first edition, "an extraordinary amount of new scholarship has appeared, changing the way in which professional historians address the major issues in the field. . . . The pace of scholarly development is so rapid that comparisons can appropriately be made to scientific fields, which are expected to change overnight, rather than to the leisured pace of traditional history." That observation is even truer today, as the history of women in the United States reaches out to embrace changing understandings of gender and to engage comparisons with other national histories.

Recognizing the wider range of new scholarship, this eighth edition of *Women's America* includes some 23 new items, many on subjects new to these volumes, with enhanced coverage of women's transnational contacts and activities; sexual choices and dilemmas, including transsexuality; and women's lives in the West, the Midwest, and the South. Even more than all previous editions, *Women's America* gives fresh attention to the challenges of citizenship and its grounding in the law, now in global context.

We have written a new, more succinct Introduction, reflecting on the book's purposes and its readers' questions in the 32 years since *Women's America* was first published. We continue to offer an account of different stages in historians' inquiries into the history of women and gender in the United States. In it, we explain key terms and concepts, such as feminism, the social construction of gender, and intersectionality (the understanding that categories of difference, of race, ethnicity, class, able-bodiedness, sexual expression, culture, nationality, religion, and historical memory intersect and define one another). We give a few examples of how mainstream ideas about proper gender roles and women's and men's differing sexual drives have changed dramatically over the four centuries of U.S. history. For example, today, sex (male/female) is increasingly seen as a spectrum. We stress that varied activism aimed at improving women's lives, expanding rights, and fulfilling goals of liberation occurred continuously throughout the nation's history—and sometimes in unexpected places and ways. The introduction contains tips on using the book and a roadmap in terms of the book's major themes. Here and throughout the book, we invite students to join us in asking how we can find equality in an American society shaped, like all human societies, by differences. Repeatedly we encourage students to ask their own questions and to embark on their own research, especially by doing local and oral histories.

Recognizing the richness of new scholarship on the twentieth century, and wanting to accommodate the different shapes of upper-division courses, *Women's America* now gathers its essays, documents, and images into five chronological sections. Part I: Early America, 1600–1820, and Part II: America's Many Frontiers, 1820–1880, retain the same temporal bounds as previous editions, although new readings have been added. We introduce a new bridge section, Part III: Modern America Emerges, 1880–1920. In the two-volume version, Part III appears in each volume. Instructors of *early* U.S. women's history can use Part III to extend their course to the passage of women's suffrage, if they wish to. Instructors of *modern* U.S. women's history can extend their course back to the late nineteenth century. A new Part IV: A Transforming World, 1920–1945, focuses on women's history from suffrage to the end of World War II. Part V: A Transforming World, 1945–2014, includes emerging scholarship along with some key primary sources on the decades since World War II.

For instructors perhaps the most salient innovation is that that the materials in each Part are now arranged in thematic clusters, such as Workplace and Household Scenes, Sexuality and the Body, Gender and the Armed Forces. These vary in each part, but reflect six core themes of *Women's America*: *family/household/sexuality, labor/economy/class, race/ethnicity/religion, law and citizenship, women's activism*, and the *global context of U.S. women's history*. And don't forget the two Photo Essays, each of which ranges over the full sweep of U.S. history, offering a running commentary on visual materials relating to the broad themes of Women in Public and Adorning the Body. These images and text can serve as independent readings and as supplements to other items in *Women's America*. We have also added a list of illustrations to the volume's table of contents so that all visual materials can be better identified by readers.

ACKNOWLEDGMENTS

We are delighted to welcome Judy Tzu-Chun Wu to our quartet of editors. And although the best part of the collaboration is meeting in person, we are grateful for the many means of electronic communication that carry our daily exchanges—Dropbox, e-mail, SKYPE—that enable the rich, three- and four-way conversations among us.

We are lucky to have had the advice of nearly seven users of previous editions, who offered their advice anonymously to Oxford University Press.

We are grateful for the good counsel of friends and colleagues as we prepared this edition. Among them are Alexis Boylan, Judith Carney, Catherine Denial, Estelle Freedman, Allison Horrocks, Omar Jimenez-Valerio, Katherine Marino, Stephanie McCurry, Micki McElya, Tracy McQueen, Daniel Rivers, Terri Snyder, Amy Sopcak-Joseph, Lisa Wilson, and Sharon Wood. Karissa Haugeberg shared her deep knowledge of the history of reproductive rights and pitched in at crucial moments. We benefitted from the ideas and advice of students in Lisa Wilson's classes at Connecticut College and Dayton's at the University of Connecticut. We are especially grateful to Mike Limberg and Philip Moore, who assisted Nina Dayton at the University of Connecticut, and to law librarians Druet Cameron Klughmand and Noëlle Sinclair at the University of Iowa College of Law.

James Boster unflaggingly cheered us on and was a fount of invaluable computer know-how. We are grateful to archivist Jenny Gotwals at the Schlesinger Library for the History of Women in America at the Radcliffe Institute. We thank Brian Wheel, Brianna Provenzano, and Taylor Pilkington of Oxford University Press; India Gray and Christian Holdener for shepherding the manuscript through copy-editing; and our thoughtful agent, Anne Borchardt.

Linda K. Kerber
Jane Sherron De Hart
Cornelia Hughes Dayton
Judy Tzu-Chun Wu

III

MODERN AMERICA EMERGES

1880–1920

GENDER AND THE
JIM CROW SOUTH

GLENDA GILMORE
Forging Interracial Links
in the Jim Crow South

Anna Julia Cooper—an extraordinary woman in her own right—wrote in 1892, "the colored woman of today ... is confronted by a woman question and a race problem."* Equality of the sexes, Cooper insisted, would mean that black women should not be passive and subordinate in their relationships with black men; and black men should not criticize women's efforts to obtain equal rights. Equality of the sexes, Cooper continued, meant sharing the leadership burden in the struggle against racism. A remarkable group of African American women did just that.

Part of a small but growing black middle class in the South, they were prepared by education, professional training, and voluntary work to be the vanguard of their race. Following the disfranchisement of black men in the 1890s, they emerged not only as community activists but also as ambassadors to the white community and astute political strategists. Their political skills were put to the test when, during the most racist era in U.S. history, these black women attempted to forge links with elite white women in an interracial movement. At the forefront of the effort was a remarkable North Carolinian, Charlotte Hawkins Brown.

With sensitivity and insight, Glenda Gilmore illuminates Brown's search for fault lines in the system of white supremacy. She also demonstrates just how Brown manipulated class, gender, and even her own identity in the interests of racial justice. In the end, Brown's generation fell short of their goal of racial and sexual equality. The odds against them were overwhelming. In the process, however, they created and nourished a tradition of activism that would emerge with new force and greater success in the 1960s.

Consider Brown's strategy. What were her options? What were the personal costs? Do you agree with Gilmore's characterization of her as a "political genius"?

---

*Anna Julia Cooper, *A Voice from the South by a Black Woman of the South* (Xenia, Ohio: Aldine, 1892), p. 135.

Excerpted from "Forging Interracial Links," ch. 7 of *Gender and Jim Crow: Women and the Politics of White Supremacy in North Carolina, 1896–1920,* by Glenda Elizabeth Gilmore (Chapel Hill: University of North Carolina Press, 1996). Reprinted by permission of the author and publisher. The author has supplied new paragraphs, and renumbered and edited the notes.

In the segregated world of the Jim Crow South, laws told black and white people where to eat and where to sit. Undergirding those laws lay a complex web of custom. Its strands separated the races in places beyond the reach of legislation. Custom dictated, for example, which part of the sidewalk belonged to whites and which to blacks. When whites and blacks sometimes occupied the same space, custom demanded that African Americans behave in a subservient manner. Any breach of these codes by a black person could bring an instant response from a white person: a reprimand, a beating, a jail sentence, or even death at the end of a lyncher's rope.

Whites held two unshakable beliefs that gave them the courage and energy to structure such a complicated society, making good on its rules with violence and even murder. First, whites thought that they acted to protect white women from black men's sexual desires. Second, they firmly believed that African Americans should be excluded from the American democratic system. They spoke freely and acted openly against any extension of political rights to blacks. After the turn of the century, restrictive legislation prevented most southern black men from voting and segregation laws crowded the books. White men considered their work done. Henceforth, they thought, African Americans would be a permanent lower caste in southern society: physically separated and politically powerless.

But the white supremacists did not reckon with black women. From behind the borders of segregation and disfranchisement, African American women became diplomats to the white community. They built social service and civic structures that wrested some recognition and meager services from the expanding welfare state. Ironically, as black men were forced from the political sphere, the functions of government expanded, opening a new space for black women to approach officials as good citizens intent on civic betterment.

One of their political strategies was to build contacts with white women. Meager and unequal as they were, these interracial connections often provided black women access to resources for their families, students, and neighbors. Charlotte Hawkins Brown personified such black women across the South who forged invisible careers in interracial politics.

As president of the North Carolina Association of Colored Women's Clubs, Charlotte Hawkins Brown began to direct African American women's formal civic experiences in the state in 1912 and continued to do so for twenty-five years.... No black man could claim prominence to equal hers in ... the state during the period. Brown's work and racialist ideologies illustrate that the decade before woman suffrage constituted a critical period in defining the boundaries of race relations that would remain in place until the post–World War II era.

Charlotte Hawkins Brown's life also provides a parable of the possibilities and the personal costs of interracial cooperation. Her story is so interwoven with myth—fiction that she fashioned to outmaneuver racism—that it is difficult to separate the reality of her experience from the result of her self-creation. The difference between her lived life and her public persona reveals a great deal about her perception of southern whites' racial ideologies and the points at which she saw possibility. Charlotte Hawkins Brown invented herself, repeatedly and with brilliance, but at great personal cost.[1]

According to her account, she was born in Henderson, North Carolina, in 1883 to Caroline Frances Hawkins, the daughter of Rebecca and Mingo Hawkins. Her father was Edmund H. Hight, from "whom fate separated me at birth" and who "belonged to a family that had grown up on the adjoining plantation."[2] Brown characterized her grandmother, Rebecca Hawkins, as a "fair" woman "with blue eyes," the African American sister of her white master, "a great railroad captain whose vision and foresight built up the great Southern Railroad." Brown cast the white master as the Hawkins family's "protector."[3] About the time of my birth, colored people in large numbers were leaving for parts north," she remembered. Charlotte moved with her mother and brother to Cambridge, Massachusetts, where her mother married and the family lived in a large, handsome house near Harvard University.[4] Caroline Hawkins managed a hand laundry in the basement, and Charlotte attended the public schools of Cambridge. Whisked away from the South at an early age, Charlotte was "not conscious of the difference in color and took part in all the activities of my class."[5] She acquired a New England accent, which she kept all of her life.

Charlotte Hawkins's family insisted that she get a practical education and sent her to

Massachusetts State Normal School in Salem. Alice Freeman Palmer, the wife of a Harvard professor and the first female president of Wellesley College, was a member of the state board of education that oversaw the school. One day a few months before she entered the normal school, as Charlotte Hawkins was pushing a baby carriage while reading a high school Latin textbook, she chanced to meet Palmer on the street. Hawkins was babysitting to raise money for a silk slip to wear under her new organdy graduation dress, but Palmer assumed that she was an impoverished student, overcoming all odds to get an education. Palmer mentioned Hawkins favorably to the principal of her high school when they next met, and the incident ended. Now, when Hawkins realized that Palmer was an overseer of her normal school, she wrote to her and reminded her of their chance meeting. Palmer responded by paying Hawkins's tuition.[6]

Several months before graduation, Charlotte Hawkins met a supervisor from the American Missionary Association (AMA) on a train. The AMA representative impressed upon Hawkins the needs of the South, and Hawkins left school to accept a position at a one-teacher school in Sedalia, North Carolina, near Greensboro in 1901.[7] The AMA funded the school for two years, then withdrew support. For a year, Hawkins drew no salary, and she and the students survived on what they grew, the produce their parents donated, and a $100 county appropriation. Charlotte Hawkins returned to Cambridge and approached Alice Freeman Palmer for financial help, which Palmer promised to consider when she returned from Europe some months later. Palmer died in Europe, however, and Hawkins decided to name the school in her memory. With continuing county support and private contributions, Palmer Memorial Institute taught practical vocational skills to its students, and Hawkins became active in the North Carolina Teachers Association and in women's club work. In 1911, Hawkins married Edward S. Brown. But the marriage lasted only a few months since Edward said he could not remain in Sedalia and be "Miss Hawkins's husband."[8]

In the South, Brown tells us, she demanded the respect of whites and received it from the "quality people." She insisted upon being addressed as "Miss," "Mrs.," or, after she gained honorary degrees, "Doctor."[9] She refused to be Jim Crowed and reported that several times she was "put out of Pullman berths and seats during all hours of the night." . . . By 1920, with the support of prominent Greensboro whites, Brown built Palmer Memorial Institute into a sprawling complex. She was proud that the most powerful whites in Greensboro served on the Palmer board, including Lula McIver and Julius Cone, head of the huge Cone Mills.[10]

As Brown rendered it, the theme of her life story is challenge met through interracial cooperation. Brown shaped the narrative in two critical ways: she minimized the restrictions of race in her daily life and exaggerated whites' helpfulness at every critical juncture. She obscured the fact that she was illegitimate by making it seem as if her father, Edmund Hight, was separated from the family by slavery. Brown was born in 1883 and had an older brother, demonstrating that her mother had a long-term relationship with Hight. The Hight family continued to live near Henderson throughout the twentieth century. Brown's grandmother, Rebecca Hawkins, may have been the sister of railroad magnate Captain John Hawkins, Jr., but, far from acting as the family's protector, he retained no contact with his black relatives and was a Democrat of the white supremacist persuasion.[11]

Brown mythologized her birth to remind southern whites of slavery's legacy: their shared kinship with African Americans. At the same time, she drew whites as sympathetic figures, the "protectors" of their African American relatives. Such circumstances did exist in the South; they just did not happen to exist within Charlotte's immediate family. As whites created the fictional "good darky" who treasured the interpersonal relationships that sprang from the close association of whites and blacks during slavery, Brown created a fictional "good master" who realized the responsibilities of miscegenation and loved his family, white and black. She used this good master to assuage whites' guilt about slavery and to argue that even slaves and masters achieved interracial understanding. She did not have to fight whites who melded ancestral ties to romantic class mythologies; she could simply join them. She shared their aristocratic roots.

Brown had moved to Cambridge not "about the time of my birth" but at the age of six. Yet she claimed to have no memory of her early life in North Carolina, no first-hand recollection of discrimination against blacks in the South, indeed no racial consciousness while growing up, even though she spent a great deal of time in the South during her childhood, even entire summers. Brown remade herself as a New Englander. When asked how her name should appear on her high school diploma, she instantly dropped her North Carolina name—Lottie Hawkins—for the more genteel sounding "Charlotte Eugenia Hawkins," which she made up on the spot. She spoke in a manner that "combine[d] the mellow tones of the southern Negro and the quick clipped qualities of New England—people turn[ed] around to see who [was] speaking."[12]

By casting herself as a New Englander, Brown attempted to remain above the southern racial structure. In Greensboro, she occupied a place much like that of African diplomats to the United States—she was an exotic but North Carolina's own exotic. If whites accused her of being an outside agitator, Brown could fall back on her North Carolina roots. Then she presented herself as native stock, a female, black Ulysses who fought her way back to the South and to her own people, where she belonged.

The story of the AMA's dispatch of Charlotte Hawkins to the South to save her people competes with another, more complicated parable that Brown merely hinted at and may have consciously avoided dwelling upon. Rather than seeing herself as a New England missionary to a foreign place, Brown may have construed her return to North Carolina as coming to terms with the realities of race in her own life. One night at a Cambridge meeting, she watched magic lantern slides of the race work being done by African Americans in the South. She was particularly struck by two educators, Joseph Price, the founder of Livingstone College, and Lucy Laney, the founder of Haines Institute in Augusta, Georgia. She noted that both Price and Laney were, like herself, very dark skinned. Price and Laney were also brilliant, and their faces on the screen moved Brown to feel that there was a place where she might belong: the South.[13] Brown never acknowledged publicly that she had any personal reason for wanting to leave New England, choosing rather to emphasize the missionary aspect of her return.

As the years passed, accounts of the relationship between Alice Freeman Palmer and Brown made it seem as if Palmer had sent Brown to the South to found the school and that they had enjoyed a close friendship. . . . Contemporary newspaper accounts, which relied on Brown's own promotional material, reported that Palmer's "efforts" had made the school possible and "until her death she was an ardent supporter of her namesake."[14]

Although Brown did not actually lie about Palmer's interest in her and the school, she embroidered the truth. Brown and Palmer spent less than fifteen minutes together in their lifetimes, and Palmer never promised that she would personally contribute to the school. Instead, Palmer had told Brown upon their second meeting that she was too busy at the moment but that after her return from Europe she would contact friends in Boston to encourage them to support the school. Why, then, when Palmer never returned, did Brown name the school Palmer Memorial Institute? Actually, Brown originally named the school Alice Freeman Palmer Settlement in order to gain support from Palmer's friends in Boston.[15] Palmer, after a brilliant career, had died at a young age and was mourned by her friends, and a memorial to her could prompt contributions. . . .

Around 1910, Brown cannily began to play southern pride against northern dollars when she inspired white leaders in Greensboro to challenge their community to take over the financial support of Palmer.[16] In soliciting southern white support, Brown . . . most often called the school Sedalia rather than Palmer. For example, Brown named the group of students who sang African American spirituals the Sedalia Singers.[17] She understood the white southerners' sense of place, and since her school was the only thing in the crossroads of Sedalia, she did not encroach upon white territory in appropriating the name. The location of Palmer at Sedalia facilitated support from Greensboro whites. It was ten miles outside of the city, surrounded by sparsely populated farmland. Brown never permitted Palmer students to travel alone to Greensboro but instead brought them as a group, with the boys clad in coats and ties and the girls wearing hats and white gloves. Once in the city, they did not mingle with Greensboro's African Americans; rather, Brown negotiated special seating sections for her students at public events.[18]

Although Brown cloaked the curriculum at Palmer in vocational disguises and portrayed it to the press as an industrial school until the late 1930s, the institute offered mostly academic courses from its inception.[19] Booker T. Washington met Brown on a trip to Boston while she was still a student there and pronounced her "the only convert that he made in New England." If he believed her to be a convert, she outfoxed the Wizard himself.[20] . . . Brown never embraced Washington's vocational philosophy past the point of providing for the school's basic needs, but she portrayed the school as industrial, detailing "farm yields" in fund-raising letters.[21] An unidentified Palmer teacher explained the ruse this way: "[Brown] always had a college preparatory class . . . a cultural academic school. All the Negroes had to have that in order to get along in the South." Even though this teacher believed, along with Brown, that African Americans profited most from classical knowledge coupled with reinforcement of middle-class values, support for that sort of training did not exist. So Brown and her teachers positioned Palmer as a "vocational" school. Funding for industrial education "could always get through," the teacher recalled. Despite the vocational exterior, she continued, "you could teach anything you wanted when you got in your school. You came inside your class room and you taught them Latin and French and all the things you knew."[22] Although initially Brown's students were the poor children of the neighborhood, by 1920, Palmer functioned as an academic boarding school that drew students from counties across the state and included secondary grades.[23]

Notwithstanding her vocal cover, at times Brown argued that her approach to "cultural" instruction benefited whites as well as African Americans. She explained, "Recognizing the need of a cultural approach to life, believing absolutely in education through racial contacts, I have devoted my whole life to establish for Negro youth something superior to Jim Crowism." She tried to accomplish this "by bringing the two races together under the highest cultural environment that will increase race pride, mutual respect, confidence, sympathetic understanding, and interracial goodwill."[24]

Why did Brown repeatedly overdraw white understanding and support and minimize the restrictions that her color placed on her? Throughout her life, she operated by a simple rule: it is better to overestimate possibility than to underestimate it. Charlotte Hawkins Brown created a fictional mirror of civility in race relations and held it up to whites as a reflection of their better selves. From slavery, she drew compassion; from the loneliness of Cambridge, racial liberality among her schoolmates; from Alice Freeman Palmer's deferral, a legacy; and from frightened, pinched southern whites, chivalry of a sort. Brown was a political genius, especially suited for interracial work. Her renderings served her own purposes, but she did not . . . delude herself into thinking that they were true. Immune to her own romantic stories, Brown was the consummate pragmatist. So convinced was she of her mission and of her opponent's rigid character, that she could risk the heartbreak of gilding the lily. She expected nothing, received little, and turned that pittance into bounty.

But Charlotte Hawkins Brown was a double agent. When she refused to turn her head toward the "colored" waiting room, she must have felt the stares of its patrons burn into her consciousness. In the decade preceding 1920, Brown immersed herself in social welfare projects and political activity that she kept hidden from whites. After 1920, Brown acquired a national reputation for her interracial work and landed official positions in interracial organizations, success that brought her activities under public scrutiny. Until then, and thereafter when she could, Brown generally said one thing to whites and then did another if it suited her purposes.

Brown's double life left its mark on her. . . . Living her life as a diplomat to the white community, Brown could never be just Lottie Hawkins. African American women who chose to take up interracial work walked a tightrope that required them to be forever careful, tense, and calculating. One slip would end their careers; they worked without nets.

In Lula Martin McIver, Brown found an exception to her belief that the southern white woman stood at the center of the race "problem." Their first meeting represents a classic case of the Brown treatment. Constantly seeking funds for Palmer Memorial Institute, Brown decided in the spring of 1905 that she must approach prominent white men in Greensboro for support. In Greensboro, Brown had no magic key such as Alice Freeman Palmer's name. Sedalia was a crossroads, Palmer Institute tiny, and Brown unknown. She had no historic connections to white North Carolinians there, no reputation in the black community, no denominational bridge since she had converted to Congregationalism, a faith rare in the South among either African Americans or whites. She had only herself—the New England persona she so carefully cultivated—and courage.

In 1904, she had written a poignant letter to Charles McIver, president of the white women's normal college in Greensboro. It began, "This letter may come to you from a strange source, but it comes from one whose heart is in the educational and moral uplift of our people." It concluded by begging McIver to come to Palmer for a visit. A year later, Brown was still imploring him to the same end, touting the ease of the train ride and signing herself "Very Anxiously Yours."[25] Still McIver did not come. One morning Brown dressed carefully in her customary ankle-length dress, hat, and white gloves and set out to call on him in Greensboro. She had no appointment. Most often Brown did not write or telephone ahead and risk refusal from those she wished to meet but simply appeared on their doorstep. That morning she knocked on the front door of the president's residence and found that he was away. His wife, Lula Martin McIver, invited Brown in, an unusual act in itself. Lula McIver was stunned by Brown's appearance at the door. "Her daring, her enthusiasm, her faith intrigued me," McIver recalled. The two women talked for over an hour and warmed toward each other. Soon, McIver was advising Brown on "the best way to win friends" and on how to raise money among the Greensboro elite for the school.[26]

When Lula McIver opened the door, Brown chanced upon a valuable connection that would prove enduring. Brown sat in the parlor of the state's foremost white female educational advocate. Graduated from the Moravian academy in Salem, Lula Martin had longed to become a doctor like her father. After she learned that the profession was virtually closed to women, she became an outspoken feminist. As an adolescent, she abandoned the Moravians for the Methodists upon reading that the early Moravian settlers chose wives by lottery. In 1885, strong-willed Lula Martin met Charles Duncan McIver, a dedicated young teacher, who supported her feminist ideas and called her a "most sensible" woman. They married in a ceremony that omitted the word "obey," and Lula refused a wedding ring, which she regarded as a "badge of slavery."[27]

The McIvers worked to build North Carolina's white public educational system one school at a time. While Charles traveled throughout the state promoting grade school education, Lula served as his advance team, preceding him to scrub courthouse venues speckled with tobacco juice, to set up chairs, to post flyers, and to raise a crowd. She was delighted when Charles became first president of the state-supported normal school for white women since both felt that educating women would be the key to building an effective public school system. She helped to found the Woman's Association for the Betterment of Public School Houses, and after Charles's death, she accepted a paying position as its field secretary.[28]

The subtleties of Lula McIver's racial ideology are elusive, but at the center of her thinking about race lay the strongly held belief that African Americans deserved a good education. For nearly a half century after they met, McIver continually raised money for Palmer Memorial Institute. Lula McIver attended meetings of black women's clubs in Greensboro. After the early death of Charles McIver in 1909, and to the eternal perplexity of Greensboro whites, each semester Lula McIver invited a male African American student from nearby North Carolina Agricultural and Technical College to board in the president's residence where she lived until her death. There, surrounded by young white women students, Lula McIver offered an object lesson in race relations.[29]

Both Brown and McIver realized the restrictions on their relationship in the Jim Crow South. For starters, McIver was a woman and thus not powerful in her own right. Moreover, as the normal school's maternal figurehead, she had to act circumspectly since all of her actions reflected upon the school, which was still in the minds of some a dangerous experiment that wasted state money to educate women. Given these restrictions, McIver could do three concrete things for Brown: influence prominent white Greensboro men to support her, introduce leading club women to Palmer's mission, and raise money. She did another intangible and invaluable thing for Brown: Lula McIver publicly referred to Charlotte Hawkins Brown as her friend.[30]

It appears that Lula McIver realized that her husband's influence would be more valuable than her own, and she urged Charles to write an "open letter of endorsement" for Palmer Memorial Institute shortly after she met Brown. Since Charles McIver served on the Southern Education Board, his vote of confidence carried weight in the North as well as the South. The letter went out in June 1905, but Charles McIver admitted in it that he had never been to Palmer.[31] He died four years later. Long after that, Brown named Charles D. McIver as her "first friend" in North Carolina.[32] There is no record that McIver ever made the trip to Sedalia or that Brown ever met him. With Lula McIver's help, Brown appropriated the memory of Charles McIver as she had that of Alice Freeman Palmer.

Local support of Palmer flowered around 1914 when Lula McIver brought a delegation of white women from across the state to visit the school. A member of the delegation wrote an account of the visit that appeared in the *Greensboro Daily Record* and encouraged white women to take an interest in Brown's work. Brown struck just the right note in her solicitation letter: Palmer, she said, "has conducted its work for the past 13 years without seeking very much help from our southern friends." She claimed friendship and a debt come due in the same breath.[33] The 1914 campaign was the beginning of a steady stream of white visitors to the school and financial support from white North Carolinians.[34] In 1917, Lula McIver conducted some of Greensboro's leading white businessmen on a tour of the school. Many of the men who had ignored Brown's previous appeals converted after that visit. E. P. Wharton recalled that Charlotte Brown had called on him around 1903 to obtain support for Palmer and that he was "ashamed of [him]self for losing sight" of Brown's work. He subsequently served for decades as a Palmer trustee. By 1920, the board of Palmer Memorial Institute included a Greensboro attorney, a banker, and an industrial magnate.[35] McIver sought no publicity for a trip she made to Boston with Charlotte Hawkins Brown two years later. There McIver called upon prominent white women, vouched for Brown's success, and asked for contributions to Palmer. When northern white women visited Palmer, they would not spend the night at the black school but stayed instead with Lula McIver.[36]

In 1919, Charlotte Hawkins Brown, with the endorsement of Lula McIver, published a remarkable novel, *Mammy*. On its face, the appearance of *Mammy* places Brown squarely in the accommodationist camp of African Americans, currying favor from whites by invoking the ties of slavery. The story tells of a loving black woman who nurses a white family and raises its children. Then, when the woman becomes old and ill, the family provides no help beyond an occasional visit to her drafty log cabin. Ultimately, they stand by as Mammy goes to the county home. Brown dedicated the book to "my good friend, Mrs. Charles Duncan McIver." She continued, "It is with gratitude I acknowledge her personal interest in the colored members of her household."[37]

What could Brown have hoped to accomplish by the publication of *Mammy*? At the time, she served as president of the statewide Association of Colored Women's Clubs, refused Jim Crow seating, and was secretly organizing a campaign to interest the state's black women in woman suffrage. She had spent almost twenty years building her dignity in North Carolina. It was amazing that she would play the *Mammy* card now. A close reading of Brown's introduction and McIver's response to the dedication indicates that both saw *Mammy* as a tool to promote their agenda: interracial cooperation among women. Mammies represented the one point of contact between southern black and white women, and white women continually bragged about their love for their Mammies. But Brown's *Mammy* is not a tale of love rewarded; it is an indictment of white neglect of African Americans. Brown calls upon white women to remember their duty to black women and redefines that duty in new ways. It is no longer enough to be fond of ol' Mammy; white women must act on that affection.

McIver framed her endorsement of *Mammy* carefully. She said that today's white woman was not the person her mother was, for in her mother's day, there was "understanding and sympathy" between the races. The problem was the separation of the races since there could be no racial harmony without "knowledge of each other's problems and an active interest in solving them." McIver endorsed the concept of "racial integrity" but reminded white southerners that their "task [was the] training of the uncivilized African." Brown must have winced at that remark, but it preceded McIver's most important statement: "I verily believe that to the most intelligent southern white women we must look for leadership in keeping our 'ship of state' off the rocks of racial antagonism." She signed the piece, "Your friend, Lula Martin McIver."[38]

Interracial cooperation, association among black and white women to solve mutual problems, was the solution that *Mammy* endorsed. McIver did not propose that white women individually care for their mammies but that they enter the public sphere and provide leadership. Male sailors had steered the ship of state onto rocky racial shores. It was time for women to man the lifeboats and rescue government from the oppressive racial politics of the white supremacists. In the same month that *Mammy* appeared, the state's white and black women began to do just that by traveling to Memphis, Tennessee, for a formal interracial summit. The state associations of women's clubs and the YWCAs sent forth those first intrepid female navigators.

Most of the black women who traveled to the Memphis interracial summit learned leadership skills in the National Association of Colored Women, but their experience in working with white women had come from two other sources as well: heretofore racially segregated groups that came together on the homefront in World War I and the interracial work of the Young Women's Christian Association (YWCA). During World War I organizational lines between women's groups of both races blurred when the Council of National Defense chose white women from each southern state to head committees to coordinate work on the homefront. In North Carolina, white women set up integrated county councils that included African American and white women, carefully chosen to represent clubs, YWCAs, and denominational social service programs.[39]

The work of the black YWCA centered on another upheaval of the time: African American migration from farm to town. Southern black women believed strongly in the YWCA's ability to reach poor young women who had moved to the city to find work. The national YWCA board determined that any southern African American branch must be supervised by an existing "central" YWCA. "Central" meant white. Once founded, the black YWCA must be overseen by a management committee of three white women and two black women. The rules mandated interracial "cooperation" of a sort. Despite these humiliating restrictions, two southern black women, Mary McCrorey of Charlotte, North Carolina, and Lugenia Burns Hope of Atlanta, founded Ys in their cities.[40]

On the train to Memphis, a group of white men pulled Brown out of the Pullman car and marched her past "southern white women passing for Christians" who were on their way to the Memphis meeting. The white women sat silent as the men forced Brown to the Jim Crow car.[41] Brown probably recognized among the fellow Memphis delegates North Carolina white women whom she had come to know over the past decade. Among them was the wife of the governor, Fanny Bickett. . . .

When Brown rose to address the white women, the frustration of a decade of interracial work erupted, and she shared the humiliation of being ousted from the Pullman car two nights before. She exhorted white women to fight lynching, to recognize the dignity of the African American woman, and to help black women. Brown ended on an ominous note: "You are going to reach out for the same hand that I am reaching out for but I know that the dear Lord will not receive it if you are crushing me beneath your feet."[42] Most of the white women were profoundly moved.

As it happened, the women's Memphis interracial meeting foundered on the spot that Lula McIver had warned of in *Mammy:* the shoal of politics. Two months before the meeting, a federal amendment had mandated woman suffrage and a month after the meeting women would vote for the first time. Just before Brown left for Tennessee, she had been secretly organizing black women in North Carolina to register to vote. One faction of black women would not budge on the issue of suffrage at the Memphis meeting. A full year later, the white and black women still had not agreed on a statement of goals for an interracial movement. Brown, McCrorey, and Hope favored a version that included the controversial demand for protection of African American voting rights. Their language was blunt: "We believe that the ballot is the safe-guard of the Nation and that every citizen in the Nation should have the right to use it. We believe that if there is ever to be any justice before the law, the Negro must have the right to exercise the vote."[43] But the white women balked at the suffrage statement and the condemnation of lynching, both points "which the Negro women dared not leave out."[44] Whites suggested the wording, "We believe that the ballot is the safe-guard of the Nation, and that every *qualified* citizen in the Nation should have the right to use it."[45]

Interracial cooperation led straight into politics. As black and white women inched toward cooperation on a grass roots level, they came face-to-face with larger political forces. With a decade of women's interracial experience behind them, many African American women believed that the time had come to take a firm stand on suffrage. Black women looked to their white allies to support their right to vote, a gesture that underscores the success of interracial cooperation. Yet white women's confusion over black women's suffrage reveals the limits of voluntary interracial work. Upon the passage of woman suffrage, white women involved with interracial social service projects had to chose between gender and race. They could support black women's right to vote as women, or oppose their right to vote as *black* women. Charlotte Hawkins Brown called the question when she used the NACW to organize black women's voter registration drives in urban areas in the fall of 1920. Across the South, other black women did the same thing, reporting back to the National Association for the Advancement of Colored People (NAACP).

In Mobile, Alabama, registrars told black women that they must own property to vote, and when the black juvenile court officer challenged them, court officials fired her.[46] From Birmingham came the news that when a black teacher attempted to register, the registrar "called her an ugly name and ordered her out." Another teacher "answered every question asked her—ex post facto law, habeas corpus proceedings, etc." The frustrated registrar still would not yield and "tore up her card and threw it in her face."[47] Ultimately, in Birmingham, 225 black women succeeded in registering, although 4,500 made the attempt.[48]

It is impossible to judge Charlotte Hawkins Brown's success in the North Carolina registration campaign. Most registration books failed to survive, but those that exist show not only that black women succeeded in urban areas, but that voter registration increased for black men as well. Probably less than 1,000 black women registered in North Carolina that fall.[49] To judge the results of black women's drive for suffrage, however, one must look not just at the few thousand who managed to register in 1920, but at the heritage of interracial work upon which they built and at the example they set for those who followed. The number of black women who voted in 1920 may have

been small, but their significance in the South's racial politics was large. For the first time since the nineteenth century in the South, black voters approached the registrars en masse. They assembled as the result of a coordinated, subversive campaign that crossed over the boundaries of voluntary interracial work to reintroduce black civil rights in electoral politics. By their presence at the polls, black women dared whites to use violence and won the dare. In 1921, white supremacy still stood, but black women had found faultlines in its foundations.

NOTES

1. Ceci Jenkins, incomplete notes for "The Twig Bender of Sedalia" ([1946]), unpublished biography of Charlotte Hawkins Brown, reel 1, #12, Brown Collection, Manuscript Collection, Schlesinger Library (SL). See also Stephen Birmingham, *Certain People: America's Black Elite* (Boston: Little, Brown, 1977).

2. "A Biography," reel 1, and "Some Incidents in the Life and Career of Charlotte Hawkins Brown Growing out of Racial Situations, at the Request of Dr. Ralph Bunche," reel 1, #2, both in Brown Collection, SL.

3. "Some Incidents," 1–2, reel 1, #2, ibid.

4. "A Biography," reel 1, ibid. The language of "A Biography" is closely echoed in Sadie L. Daniel, *Women Builders* (Washington, D.C.: Associated Publishers, 1970), 133–63.

5. "A Biography," 13, reel 1, Brown Collection, SL.

6. On Palmer, see Ruth B. Bordin, *Alice Freeman Palmer: The Evolution of a New Woman* (Ann Arbor: University of Michigan Press, 1993). On the Brown/Palmer relationship, see "A Biography," 16–18, reel 1, and Jenkins, "Twig Bender of Sedalia," reel 1, #7, both in Brown Collection, SL.

7. Daniel, *Women Builders*, 139; "A Biography," 19, reel 1, Brown Collection, SL.

8. Charlotte E. Hawkins to Dr. Buttrick, 31 Aug. 1904, folder 1005, box 111, series 1, subseries 1, General Education Board Collection, RAC. Mary Grinnell to Charlotte Hawkins Brown, 4 Oct. 1910, 8 Feb. 1911; H. F. Kimball to Charlotte Hawkins Brown, 12 June 1911; and J. G. Bright to Charlotte Hawkins Brown, 1 Aug. 1911, all on reel 2, #33; Mary T. Grinnell to Charlotte Hawkins Brown, 6 Aug. 1912, 17 Feb. 1913, reel 2, #34; and Charlotte Hawkins Brown Ebony Questionnaire, 16, reel 1, #11, all in Brown Collection, SL.

9. Brown wrote that it was a "big surprise" that the white people in the South refused to "use the term 'Miss'" when they addressed black women. She continued, "Naturally I was constantly being insulting and insulted which merited for me the name 'Yankee Huzzy.'" See "Some Incidents," 5, reel 1, #2, Brown Collection, SL. Leading whites in Greensboro referred to her as "Dr. Brown" after she received honorary degrees from Wilberforce, Lincoln, and Howard universities. See Junius Scales to Glenda Gilmore, 4 Jan. 1990, in author's possession.

10. Letterhead, Palmer Memorial Institute, C. Hawkins Brown to W. E. B. Dubois [sic], to June 1930, W. E. B. Du Bois Papers, reel 33, University of Massachusetts, Amherst.

11. Ruth Anita Hawkins Hughes, *Contributions of Vance County People of Color* (Raleigh: Sparks Press, 1988).

12. Jenkins, "Twig Bender of Sedalia," 1, reel 1, #7, Brown Collection, SL.

13. Ibid., insert B; "Some Incidents," 9, reel 1, #2, Brown Collection, SL.

14. Eva M. Young, "Palmer Memorial Institute Unique," *Charlotte Observer*, 10 Mar. 1940, folder 51, box 94–3, ibid.

15. Jenkins, "Twig Bender of Sedalia," E.F. 16, reel 1, #7, Brown Collection, SL.

16. Ibid., E.F. 16, E.F. 17; "Some Incidents," reel 1, #2, Brown Collection, SL.

17. For an example of the conflation of Sedalia and Palmer Institute, see *Palmer Memorial Institute: The Mission and the Legacy* (Greensboro: Women of Greensboro, [1981]).

18. The description here is from interviews and conversations with Dawn Gilmore, Brooks Gilmore, and Lois MacKenzie, the author's aunt, uncle, and mother, respectively. The author's grandfather, Clyde Manly Gilmore, was Brown's physician, and the author's mother, MacKenzie, was her attorney's secretary in the 1950s.

19. Brown transformed the institute in the late 1930s into a preparatory school for upper-class African Americans. By 1940, the school letterhead read: "The Charm School Idea of the Palmer Memorial Institute, Charlotte Hawkins Brown, President and Promoter." See C. Hawkins Brown to My Dear Friend, 20 Mar. 1940, folder 124, box 112–4, Washington Conservatory of Music Records, Moorland-Spingarn Research Center, Howard University (MRSC).

20. Jenkins, "Twig Bender of Sedalia," insert G, reel 1, #7, Brown Collection, SL.

21. Charlotte Hawkins Brown to Wallace Buttrick, 19 Dec. 1912, folder 1005, box 111, series 1, subseries 1, General Education Board Collection, Rockefeller Archive Center (RAC).

22. "Charlotte Hawkins Brown," Dannett Collection, uncataloged, LC. See also Sylvia G. L. Dannett, *Profiles of Negro Womanhood* (New York: M. W. Lads, 1964–66), 59–63. The notes for Dannett's biographical sketches often do not identify the interviewee and are fragmentary.

23. Map, "Palmer Memorial Institute—Sedalia—Enrol[l]ment—1920–1921," folder 1006, box 111, series 1, subseries 1, General Education Board Collection, RAC.

24. "Some Incidents," reel 1, #2, Brown Collection, SL.

25. Board, 1904, Correspondence G-M, box 14, and C. E. Hawkins to Dr. McIver, 13 Apr. 1905, file Southern Education Board, 1905, Correspondence, E-L, box 15, both in Charles D. McIver Collection, University Archives, Walter Clinton Jackson Library, University of North Carolina, Greensboro (WCJL).

26. Mrs. Charles D. McIver to editor of *Greensboro Daily News*, [ca. 1940], reel 1, #13, and Jenkins, "Twig Bender of Sedalia," reel 1, #7, both in Brown Collection, SL.

27. Rose Howell Holder, *McIver of North Carolina* (Chapel Hill: University of North Carolina Press, 1917), 63–67. See also Virginia T. Lathrop, "Mrs. McIver Believes Greatness of the Past Holds State's Hope for Present and Future," *News and Observer*, 6 Oct. 1940, Clipping File, vol. 94, reel 24, 371–72, North Carolina Collection, University of North Carolina, Chapel Hill (NCC).

28. James Leloudis, "'A More Certain Means of Grace': Pedagogy, Self, and Society in North Carolina, 1880–1920" (Ph.D. diss., University of North Carolina at Chapel Hill, 1989), and Pamela Dean, "Covert Curriculum: Class and Gender in a New South Women's College" (Ph.D. diss., University of North Carolina at Chapel Hill, 1995). On the association, see James Leloudis, "School Reform in the New South: The Woman's Association for the Betterment of Public School Houses in North Carolina, 1902–1919," *Journal of American History* 69 (March 1983): 886–909. See also Lula Martin McIver to Charles L. Coon, 4 Feb. 1909, folder 28, box 2, and Lula Martin McIver to Charles L. Coon, 25 Jan. 1910, folder 29, box 2, both in Coon Papers, Southern Historical Collection, University of North Carolina, Chapel Hill (SHC).

29. Sallie Waugh McBryan to Mrs. McIver, 22 Nov. 1913, file Correspondence, 1909–44, box 141, Lula Martin McIver Collection, WCJL; "Famous Landmark at WCUNC Razed," *Durham Morning Herald*, 26 Oct. 1952, Clipping File, vol. 94, reel 24, 343–44, NCC.

30. Lula Martin McIver to Charlotte Hawkins Brown, 6 Apr. 1920, reel 2, #41, Brown Collection, SL.

31. Charles D. McIver letter, 5 June 1905, reel 2, #30, Correspondence, 1902–6, ibid.

32. "Award Will Go to Dr. Brown," *Greensboro Daily News*, 10 Apr. 1947, Clipping File, vol. 18, reel 5, 239, NCC.

33. C. Hawkins Brown to My dear Sir [Professor Julius I. Foust], 25 May 1914, file General Correspondence, 1913–15, box 57, Foust Collection, WCJL.

34. Jenkins, "Twig Bender of Sedalia," 77, reel 1, #12, Brown Collection, SL.

35. E. P. Wharton to Charlotte Hawkins Brown, 12 Jan. 1917, reel 2, #37, Jan.–Apr. 1917; Mrs. Charles D. McIver to editor of *Greensboro Daily News*, n.d., reel 1 #13; and Jenkins, "Twig Bender of Sedalia," 78, reel 1, #12, all in Brown Collection, SL.

36. H. F. Kimball to Charlotte Hawkins Brown, 6 Nov. 1916, reel 2, #36, 1916, and "Notes," copy of notebook maintained by Charlotte Hawkins Brown, reel 1, #8, both in Brown Collection, SL; Annie L. Vickery to My Dear Mrs. McIver, 7 Mar. 1917, file Correspondence, 1909–44, box 141, Lula Martin McIver Collection, WCJL.

37. Charlotte Hawkins Brown, *Mammy* (Boston: Pilgrim Press, 1919).

38. Lula Martin McIver to Charlotte Hawkins Brown, 6 Apr. 1920, reel 2, #41, Brown Collection, SL.

39. Laura Holmes Reilley to D. H. Hill, 18 Oct. 1917, file Women's Committee, box 30, North Carolina Council of Defense, World War I Papers, 1903–33, pt. 2, Military Collection, North Carolina Department of Archives and History.

40. Mary J. McCrorey to Mrs. Hope, 7 May 1920; "Mrs. Hope of the Cleveland Meeting, 1920," 29 May 1920; "What the Colored Women Are Asking of the

Y.W.C.A."; "To the National Board of the Young Women's Christian Association"; Minutes of the Cleveland Meeting, 1920; "Minutes of the meeting held in the offices of the South Atlantic Field Committee, Richmond, Virginia, 3 July 1920"; and Mary J. McCrorey to Mrs. Hope, 27 Jan. 1921, all in box 5, NU 14-C-5, Y.W.C.A., Neighborhood Union Papers, Special Collections, Robert Woodruff Library, Atlanta University, Atlanta, Georgia. Mary J. McCrorey to Charlotte Hawkins Brown, 2 Apr. 1920, reel 2, #41, Brown Collection, SL.

41. Jacquelyn Dowd Hall, *Revolt against Chivalry: Jessie Daniel Ames and the Women's Campaign against Lynching*, rev. ed. (New York: Columbia University Press, 1987), 93; "Some Incidents," reel 1, #2, Brown Collection, SL.

42. Brown address, folder 1, box 1, ibid.; Hall, *Revolt against Chivalry*, 93–94.

43. "First Draft," section 2, folder 1, box 1, ibid.

44. "Statement of Negro Women in Session, Mar. 26, 1921," folder 1, box 1.

45. Folder 1, box 1, ibid. (emphasis added).

46. W. E. Morton to NAACP, file Voting, 10–30 Nov. 1920, C284, National Association for the Advancement of Colored People Papers, Library of Congress.

47. H. M. Kingsley to NAACP, 9 Nov. 1920, file Voting, 1–9 Nov. 1920, C284, NAACP Papers.

48. Charles McPerson to NAACP, file Voting, 1–9 Nov. 1920, C284, NAACP Papers. For a summary of reports from across the South, see "Disfranchisement of Colored Americans in the Presidential Election of 1920" ([1920]), file Voting, Dec. 1920, C284, NAACP Papers.

49. Glenda E. Gilmore, *Gender and Jim Crow: Women and the Politics of White Supremacy in North Carolina, 1896–1920* (Chapel Hill: University of North Carolina Press, 1996), 219–224.

KIM E. NIELSEN
The Southern Identity of Helen Keller

Although Helen Keller is widely regarded as a "national icon representing the triumphs of the disabled," Kim E. Nielsen urges us to understand Keller in a more complex way by acknowledging that her regional background and racial identity shaped her life. In other words, Nielsen offers an intersectional analysis, analyzing how being white, southern, middle-class, and gendered female affected Keller's experience with disability. The author keeps in play many dimensions of Keller's life: her spirituality, her relationships with her parents, her activism (national and international), her geographic comings and goings, and her reading. Nielsen also helps us imagine what it might have been like for a displaced southerner like Keller to read *Gone with the Wind* the year it came out. Compare this with your own encounters with Margaret Mitchell's novel and the movie based on it.

Does Nielsen's portrayal of Keller change the ways you think about her? What do you see as the significance of her southern background? Why is Keller's whiteness important to understanding her identity?

Though Helen Keller left her parents' home in Tuscumbia, Alabama, at the young age of eight, the culture, people, and sensory adventures of her native state were essential to her outlook throughout her life. The deaf-blind activist, author, and world traveler, born in 1880, considered Ivy Green, her family's Tuscumbia home, as her own. Beginning in her lifetime and continuing today, Tuscumbia and Alabama have similarly regarded her as their own—even featuring her on the 2003 state quarter. Keller was also a child of the broader South. Though after her initial departure she always lived outside the region, her southern childhood and

Excerpted from "The Southern Ties of Helen Keller," *Journal of Southern History* 73:4 (November 2007): 783–806, by Kim E. Nielsen. Reprinted by permission of the author and publisher. Notes have been edited and renumbered.

family ties formed and constituted vital elements of her public and private identity. She claimed this identity fondly but frequently labeled as shameful the dominant southern racial ideologies and practices.

Paradoxically, it was perhaps Keller's disability that provided the opportunities that most frequently caused her to question southern gender and racial traditions. Her disability took her physically away from the South, as she and her family turned to northern educational institutions with historical ties to abolitionism. Her disability and her politics as an adult separated her from her family ideologically and geographically. Once she became world famous and increasingly active politically, those commenting upon or questioning her political ideas used her southern identity to either praise or deride her and her principles. As she traveled more, claiming global citizenship and analyzing national and world politics, she naturally did so from a base of knowledge and culture built on her southern background. Today, however, Keller is embraced as a national icon representing the triumphs of the disabled. Her image is now divorced from her southern identity. She is viewed as an American, devoid of regional affiliations or associations. In contrast, this essay positions Keller as a southerner of a Confederate family whose background and beliefs helped shape her worldview and her life as a white, southern woman with a disability.[1]

Keller and her family embraced an esteemed southern heritage, which they perhaps regarded as being more illustrious than it really had been. When Keller wrote her autobiography, *The Story of My Life,* in 1903, she described her lineage according to both geography and the Civil War. In this narrative the men served and the women sired. Helen's father, Arthur H. Keller, served as a captain and her maternal grandfather as a brigadier general for the Confederacy. Her paternal grandmother, she noted, was second cousin to Robert E. Lee. Captain Keller edited the Tuscumbia *North Alabamian* for many years and served in the mid-1880s as U.S. marshal for the northern district of Alabama. Through him, the young Helen claimed Alexander Spotswood, a lieutenant governor (and de facto governor) in early-eighteenth-century Virginia, as her great-great-grandfather.[2]

Captain Arthur Keller considered his family to be part of the deserving upper-class white elite. . . . Like many other southern landholding and formerly slaveholding whites, they had lost much of their wealth between 1860 and 1880. At the time of Helen Keller's birth, her family lived on the homestead her grandfather had built and named Ivy Green decades earlier due to the "beautiful English ivy" covering trees and fences. The Kellers were, however, no longer the wealthy family they once were. Moreover, the daily physical labor demanded to sustain the household, even with the aid of the formerly enslaved and their descendants, had surprised and exhausted Helen's young mother, Kate, after she became the second wife of the much older man whom all called Captain Keller.[3]

The young toddler Helen, Kate's first child, became blind and deaf due to an illness at the age of nineteen months. From Ivy Green, Arthur and Kate Keller sought assistance with the child whom they loved but, as she grew older, felt increasingly incapable of parenting. Family members encouraged placing the girl in an asylum or institution.

Talladega, only about 170 miles away from Tuscumbia, hosted both the Alabama School for the Deaf (founded in 1858) and the Alabama School for the Blind (founded in 1867). While technically separate, the schools had at one point shared a campus and were only blocks apart. Keller would not have been the first deaf-blind student, for another had enrolled as early as 1867. Neither school admitted African Americans.[4] Apparently neither Keller parent considered sending Helen to either of these schools, likely because both institutions had few resources and floundering reputations, having emerged from the Civil War damaged and inadequately funded.

Kate Keller initially refused to send her young child away from home. Like most Americans at that time, she doubted that a deaf-blind child could be educated. As a parent, however, she clearly had hopes for her daughter's life. In the mid-1880s the obviously literate Mrs. Keller read Charles Dickens's *American Notes* (1842) and in it his reference to Laura Bridgman and abolitionist Samuel Gridley Howe, the founder of Boston's Perkins Institution. Bridgman also had lost her sight and hearing at a fairly young age due to illness. Howe's successful effort to teach Bridgman to use the manual alphabet to communicate and perhaps his even greater success at publicizing her had made Howe, Perkins, and Bridgman nearly world famous.[5] Mrs. Keller reasoned that if Bridgman had learned such communication, so might Helen.

Kate Keller's first effort ended after she learned that Howe had died in 1876, but the mother of the young deaf-blind girl persisted. She and her husband tried again, contacting Baltimore oculist Dr. Julian Chisholm. He encouraged them to contact Alexander Graham Bell. . . . Captain Keller traveled by train first to Baltimore and then to Washington, D.C., with the six-year-old and apparently very unruly Helen in order to consult with both doctors personally. Bell recommended that the Kellers seek assistance for their daughter from the Perkins Institution, . . . [then directed by Howe's] son-in-law, Michael Anagnos. For Bell the school where the by-then-elderly Laura Bridgman still lived was the only logical place to seek an education for Helen.[6]

Southerners often looked at educational institutions for deaf and blind children with suspicion because of the linkage between educational reformers and abolitionism. Despite this source of doubt, Keller's parents were not alone as they turned to northern educational institutions. Southern whites with resources tended to send deaf or blind children to schools in the North. Northern educational institutions had stronger reputations, greater fiscal resources, enhanced international ties, and more highly educated teachers than did those in the South.[7]

In July 1886 Arthur Keller allowed his concern for his daughter to trump his hesitancy about northern educational institutions, and he wrote to Perkins's director. . . . Keller sought a skilled teacher willing to travel to Tuscumbia in order to care for young Helen. Anagnos said his thoughts "almost instinctively turned towards Miss Annie M. Sullivan," who was then summering in Brewster, Massachusetts. He recommended her "most highly and without any reservation." After exchanges of letters in numerous directions, Captain Keller agreed to Sullivan as an appropriate teacher and assured Anagnos that she would be treated "as one of our immediate family." He would pay her twenty-five dollars per month, a significant salary.[8]

The Keller family knew relatively little about Anne Sullivan. As the 1886 valedictorian of Perkins, she had given an address described . . . as "a beautiful original production, teeming with felicitous thoughts clothed in a graceful style."[10] Anagnos likely thought of her as a teaching candidate because of her intellectual skills, but he also considered her because she needed employment direly. Sullivan had arrived at Perkins via the almshouse. After the death of her mother and subsequently being deserted by her father, the blind, ten-year-old child of poor Irish immigrants had entered the almshouse of the Massachusetts State Infirmary at Tewksbury. Only by begging an education from touring philanthropists was the child able to enroll at Perkins. Numerous eye operations temporarily improved her eyesight; but her eyes frequently caused her pain, and her vision fluctuated. Despite graduating from Perkins, few respectable or viable employment opportunities existed for the twenty-year-old woman. . . .[9]

In March 1887 Anne Sullivan entered the gardens of Ivy Green with a northern viewpoint as firm as the Keller family's southern identity. . . . Sullivan grew up valorizing several sworn enemies of slavery and the Confederacy. Both Franklin B. Sanborn, who as general state inspector of charities in Massachusetts had enabled her escape from the Tewksbury almshouse, and Samuel Gridley Howe, founder of the Perkins Institution, had conspired as part of John Brown's so-called secret six [Bostonians who funded Brown's plan to start a slave insurrection in Virginia]. In the almshouse and at Perkins she had pored over the Boston *Pilot* (a weekly Irish American newspaper), particularly drawn to its coverage of abolitionist and orator Wendell Phillips. And to what must have been the horror of Captain Keller if he ever found out, Sullivan most favored Major General Benjamin Butler—the (in)famous Union "Beast" of New Orleans, supporter of black military regiments in the Civil War, female suffragist, punisher of the Confederacy, and Massachusetts advocate for the poor. As governor of Massachusetts from 1882 to 1886, he had rigorously investigated the ill treatment of residents at Tewksbury, and Sullivan adored him for it. Though many northerners increasingly "overlooked the history of American slavery" by the 1880s, Sullivan did not do so.[10] . . .

Sullivan purportedly hesitated to even accept employment in the Keller household for fear (correctly) that the family had once owned slaves. Friends warned her that she should "hold my peace while [in the] south, that any reference to conditions before or during the

Civil War would cause my instant dismissal." . . . As Sullivan later put it, she "did not like the idea of going south to live in a family that had probably been slave-holders."[11]

The arrival at the segregated Tuscumbia train station of the twenty-one-year-old Boston girl with a lingering Irish accent was novel enough for it to be a community event. A crowd gathered alongside Kate Keller, eagerly awaiting a glimpse of "the Yankee girl who was going to teach the Keller child." And just as the Tuscumbia community had never before encountered anyone like Anne Sullivan, she in turn had never before been to a place like Tuscumbia.[12]

Sullivan's descriptions of her life in Tuscumbia focus almost exclusively either on Helen or on the characteristics that made the region both southern and disagreeable (in her opinion). Her criticisms ranged widely, including the "untidy, shiftless manner of keeping house," "the shabbiness of the grounds and out-houses," and the muddy state of country roads. "Finding it very difficult not to air my righteous indignation," she ignored the advice of her friends and argued the war vigorously with Keller family members, particularly Captain Keller's brother Frank. After one bitter argument with "Uncle Frank"—in which "all the torrents of my wrath broke restraint, and I opened fire, and I did not cease until I had my say out to the last bitter word"—she temporarily packed her carpetbag to leave.[13]

The household in which young Helen grew up and in which Sullivan struggled held a strong Confederate identity. By the time of Keller's birth in 1880, white Alabamians had brutally silenced the discussions of racial equality and freedom formulated during the Civil War. As Sullivan arrived in 1887, white Alabamians were building and observing Lost Cause mythology via memoirs, memorials, parades, the glorification of veterans such as Keller's father, and a widely celebrated statewide public tour by Jefferson Davis. In the words of historian David W. Blight, it was the "diehard era" of the Lost Cause, in which Civil War remembrance became "a lucrative industry."[14] . . .

Keller thus grew up embedded in stories of the Old South and shared in the privileges of the Jim Crow "New" South. The household's daily schedule, labor divisions, and balances of power maintained the privileges of whiteness and patriarchy. Like other family members,

Helen Keller, young and disabled though she was, benefited from the system of racial inequalities.

Though deaf-blind and young, by 1887 the seven-year-old girl had already learned how to reinforce racial hierarchies. For example, the child Helen expected her nurse Viny and the household's cook, both African American servants, to serve her. This expectation is reflected unquestioningly in Keller's 1903 autobiography, *The Story of My Life*. Many of her childhood memories centered [on] Martha Washington, "a little coloured girl . . . the child of our cook," who accompanied, entertained, and monitored the difficult child. . . . As Keller put it unself-consciously, "I seldom had any difficulty in making her do just as I wished. It pleased me to domineer over her, and she generally submitted to my tyranny rather than risk a hand-to-hand encounter." In 1903 Keller attributed her successful dominance to the fact that she was "strong, active, indifferent to consequences," and willing "to fight tooth and nail"—not to her whiteness. Her biographers have generally attributed her violent behavior as a child to her frustration at being unable to communicate. Clearly, however, the young Keller directed her "tyranny" most often at Washington, for whom responding with physical violence held great consequence. Most likely Washington, two or three years older than Keller, respected the violence that the young white child could and did frequently accomplish. Yet Washington also undoubtedly knew that most African American boys and girls like herself were expected to serve white children. For whites, it was a way to care for their own children while indoctrinating black children in service and racial obsequiousness. Keller maintained her tyranny with the threat of personal violence, [an] . . . aggression [that] was a part of and enabled by the much larger racial realities of post-Redemption Alabama.[15]

As Keller's knowledge of the world rapidly expanded after Sullivan arrived in 1887, the child also learned more about race and southern racial mores. Early in the educational process Sullivan explained to Keller, in a lesson the teacher considered to be about colors, that Keller was white and the servants black. Keller quickly "concluded that all who occupied a similar menial position were of the same hue." Race determined status. It humored Sullivan that Keller hesitantly replied "blue" when questioned about the "colour of some one whose occupation she did not know."[16]

The contradictory, changing, and sometimes uneasy nature of the lessons of race provided challenges to all involved. By Christmas 1892 the then-twelve-year-old had received substantial monetary gifts and publishing earnings from an article in the magazine *Youth's Companion*. She desired, at least according to Sullivan, to spend some of that money on Christmas presents for "two darkey namesakes." Her father prohibited it. Sullivan, apparently considering herself more racially enlightened (despite the "darkey" language she used), defied Mr. Keller and used her own funds to buy the presents. Sullivan proudly believed that "The servants, and indeed the Negroes generally, are devoted to Helen. Several of them have learned to talk to her and it is touching to see how patient and gentle she is with them always—ever ready with an excuse in explanation of their faults."[17] . . .

Keller's education included not only race but also the more formalized topics of literature, history, science, and religion. Everyone assumed that as a child Helen should learn of God in some way. . . . Sullivan, an alienated and angry Catholic, had little but scorn for religiosity during her early years with Helen in Tuscumbia, but Sullivan felt a . . . responsibility toward responding to Helen's questions truthfully.[18] . . . Keller's parents held other priorities.

Thus, though the daughter of a Presbyterian father and an Episcopalian mother, as a child Keller learned of religion primarily through Sullivan. The overwhelming cultural presence of religion and religiosity made it a topic impossible to avoid. In 1888 a group of Presbyterian clergy, meeting in Tuscumbia, encountered the increasingly famous child. When asked "What do ministers do?" Keller knew enough about organized religion to reply, "They read and talk loud for people to be good." Sullivan wrote privately of the ministers, presumably reflecting her larger attitudes and beliefs about religion, "And thirty such stupid and homely men I have never met before. If they had only been moderately good looking one might excuse the length, logic and nonsense of their fire and brimstone sermons. But being as ugly as it was possible for them to be one felt like saying very disagreeable things about them."[19]

The teacher did her best, but the literature and history she and Helen read, the discussions they had of creation and science, and the people around Keller prompted question after question from the inquisitive child. By early 1890 Sullivan found Keller's questions too much to handle and turned to the assistance of a major Bostonian religious figure, the Reverend Phillips Brooks, the rector of Trinity Church and an Episcopalian preacher at Harvard. . . . Keller and Brooks began a lengthy correspondence, and while in Boston she often met with him. Her parents left no record of their thoughts on their young child's religious inquiry, though it tied her to Boston and New England religiosity. Helen grew extremely fond and appreciative of Brooks. Her parents approved enough of the relationship to bend to eleven-year-old Helen's desire in 1891 to name her new baby brother Phillips Brooks Keller—likely one of the few white Alabamians of the late nineteenth century named after a Boston preacher.[20]

Within a year of her arrival in Tuscumbia, the forceful Sullivan persuaded Keller's reluctant parents to allow the pair to visit Boston and the Perkins Institution. She insisted to them that Keller needed to be removed from her overly protective family circle and that Perkins was the sensible educational choice. Privately she acknowledged her personal, almost desperate wish to return to Boston.[21] For the rest of the 1880s and 1890s Keller and Sullivan moved back and forth between Boston, Tuscumbia, and New York, though nearly always summering in Tuscumbia. After 1900, however, except for periods in the summers of 1916, 1919, and 1922, Keller spent little time in either Tuscumbia or the larger South. Anne Sullivan became the dominant and most consistent guide in her life. After her initial breakthrough in comprehending finger spelling, Keller also learned to write, to read lips by touch, and to speak. As an adolescent and adult, Keller reveled in the cultural and intellectual life of Boston—Harvard University and Radcliffe College specifically—and then New York.

Keller's conversion to the Christian faith tradition of Swedenborgianism further removed her from southern culture and society. . . . As a teenager, she had been unable to find all the answers she desired in the teachings and Christianity of Phillips Brooks. Guided by John Hitz, the secretary of Alexander Graham Bell who provided Emanuel Swedenborg's writings in Braille, she embraced Swedenborgianism in 1896 and followed it for the rest of her life. Many New England reformers, radicals, and spiritualists adopted the belief system, which was built on the eighteenth-century Christian mysticism of the Swedish Lutheran Swedenborg. He argued for the permeability of the veil between the physical and spiritual worlds. His writings taught Keller that her blindness and deafness mattered nil; her spiritual senses, her internal life, enabled her to access God. The faith also resonated with Keller's growing dedication toward action and service. Swedenborg equated love with service, but he believed that living a "life of the spirit" exemplified active service. Whatever form Keller's service took, again regardless of her disability, when done in a "life of the spirit" it qualified as vital and genuine Christian service.[22]

As an adult, Keller consistently sought a life of active public citizenship synonymous with her theological and political conceptualization of service. She first became familiar with radical and progressive analyses of hierarchy, oppression, and exploitation while a student at Boston's Radcliffe College (1900–1904), the prestigious female counterpart to Harvard. There she read, argued, listened, and was thrilled by the intellectual debates. Perhaps she attended services at the Swedenborgian congregation not far from Harvard Square. For the first time she testified before a state legislature. She began to realize that political efficacy was possible, even for a woman deaf, blind, and from Alabama.

Keller thus embraced a wide-ranging, enduring, and intensely active public life based on a commitment to compassion, justice, and equality. Like her mother, she embraced female suffrage (though Kate Keller likely did not endorse Alice Paul's National Woman's Party, as her daughter did). Helen went on to endorse birth control, the radical Industrial Workers of the World, racial equality, and the causes of striking workers, and she joined the Socialist Party of America in 1909. She advocated for people with disabilities but blamed the inequalities of capitalism for causing disability among a disproportionately high number of working-class people. She criticized World War I as a profit-making venture and later condemned the U.S. use of atomic weapons in World War II. For the American Foundation for the Blind she became an incredibly effective fund-raiser and lobbyist. International politics fascinated her, as did world travel and other cultures, and she became one of the nation's most successful unofficial ambassadors in the cold war era.[23]

Despite the intellectual life of her mother, as an adult Keller seems to have fallen prey to the stereotypical belief that all southern white women were apolitical and subservient. All evidence indicates that throughout her life she remained largely unaware of the various streams of reform and progressive activism percolating among some southern white women. Keller was simply one of a number of white women, liberals and radicals, who in varying ways sought to remake southern white womanhood throughout the decades of the twentieth century. . . . [Yet] throughout her lifetime Keller had very little contact with those engaged in similar efforts. Perhaps her disability, the viciousness of antiradical attacks on activists for racial equality, or simply her northern residency deterred this contact.[24]

Keller had become a displaced southerner. Her regional background, however, constituted a widely known part of her even more widely known personal story. She was a deafblind woman from a region frequently considered inferior: economically, socially, politically disabled. Northerners taught her oral language, while the South lacked the institutions and faculty to do so.[25] She became an uprooted southerner reconstructed by the North, but still always southern.

Throughout this transformation, what it meant to Keller and others for her to be southern was often unclear and contradictory. She left behind little reflective analysis of her southern identity, most likely because of her complicated uneasiness with that heritage. Some of her childhood memories brought her joy; southern racial inequalities made her "ashamed in my very soul." She knew that her own intellectual and personal renewal had come from northern reformers and their followers. She seemingly was unaware of homegrown efforts to refigure southern identity and cultural memories.[26] . . . Her most common acknowledgment of her southern identity was in superficial, and stereotypical, reflections on the beauty and sensuality of southern flowers and trees.

Keller's complicated relationship with her southern background often became entangled with another aspect of her identity—the essential question of her intellectual capacity and abilities, of her humanity. From childhood through old age, others frequently questioned whether she, as a person with a disability, had the capacity to genuinely know anything. As an adult attempting to shape an active political and intellectual life, she regularly encountered the belief that her disability disqualified her from such an undertaking. Because politics and political participation interested her intensely, this dismissal of her as unfit frustrated and enraged her.[27] Detractors made her battle for a public identity even more problematic when they voiced their criticisms in regional terms, as they frequently did.

For example, when as a young adult Keller expressed political opinions considered radical in the early 1900s, opponents from her home state of Alabama blamed it on the Yankee influence of her by-then-married teacher Anne Sullivan Macy and her husband John Macy. These criticisms became very explicit after Keller sent a hundred dollars and a statement of vigorous support—including an expression of shame in her southern heritage—to the National Association for the Advancement of Colored People (NAACP) in 1916. Her views became public after W. E. B. Du Bois printed the letter in the NAACP's newspaper, the *Crisis*. "I warmly endorse your efforts," she had written, "to bring before the country the facts about the unfair treatment of the colored people in some parts of the United States. What a comment upon our social justice is the need of an association like yours!" She felt that "It should bring the blush of shame to the face of every true American to know that ten millions of his countrymen are denied the equal protection of the laws." The Alabama daughter of a Confederate captain confessed, "Ashamed in my very soul I behold in my own beloved southland the tears of those who are oppressed, those who must bring up their sons and daughters in bondage, to be servants because others have their fields and vineyards, and on the side of the oppressor is power." She insisted, drawing on her own theological beliefs, that "The outrages against the colored people are a denial of Christ."[28]

Keller's sentiments did not go unnoticed. The Selma (Ala.) *Journal* reprinted the NAACP letter and accompanied it with an editorial that described the letter as "full of untruths, full of fawning and bootlicking phrases." Implying that Keller could not have generated such beliefs herself, the editorial blamed her teachers: "The people who did such wonderful work in training Miss Keller must have belonged to

the old Abolition Gang for they seemed to have thoroughly poisoned her mind against her own people."[29] Her disability and resulting education supposedly left her politically pliable, especially vulnerable to northern educators and abolitionists, and incapable of intentional deliberation. It caused her to be a disloyal southerner.

Though her father was by then dead, Keller's family pressured her to retreat from her public stance in support of the NAACP. Her mother appealed for her to consider the reputations of extended family members living in Selma. Acquiescing, Keller wrote to the Selma *Times*, the competing newspaper of the Selma *Journal*, that the *Journal* had misinterpreted her letter to the NAACP. With unclear differentiation, she insisted that she had advocated "equality of all men before the law," rather than "the social equality of white people and Negroes."[30]

In early 1917 Keller's personal life fell into chaos that sent her southward into the fray. Perhaps this is one reason she resisted her family's pressure so halfheartedly. Anne Macy suffered ill health, tuberculosis, undoubtedly made worse by the deterioration of her marriage to John Macy and a relatively unsuccessful 1916 Chautauqua tour for the student and teacher duo. Doctors advised that Anne Macy have a rest, which she took, away from Keller, in Lake Placid and then Puerto Rico. Separated from her friend for one of the first times in decades, Keller planned to spend several months with her widowed mother in Alabama, perhaps smoothing over their relationship. Before leaving the North, however, she fell in love and made secret plans to marry a finger-spelling fellow socialist, Peter Fagan. The remaining members of Keller's nuclear family, already angry at Helen, drew the line. Purportedly sneaking her away on a forced midnight train trip and chasing Fagan away with a gun, they insisted to her that her disability rendered her ineligible for marriage and childbearing.[31]

Keller submitted and cut off contact with Fagan. . . . Presumably she grieved the close of her relationship with Fagan and the normality he represented in her life. She expressed constant concern to Anne Macy about the possibility of the war in Europe enveloping the United States. Keller complained that in Montgomery "[p]arties, dresses, babies, weddings—and obesity are the topics of conversation." In turn, Macy wrote with little cheer of her failed marriage to John and made preparations that assumed her death would come soon. She tried unconvincingly to reassure Helen. "Yes, it is true that most people you meet in Montgomery lack individuality," Macy wrote. "It is equally true of most places."[32]

As Keller understood and experienced her family relationships, both departure from the geographic South and her departure from the traditional gender and racial politics of the white South went hand in hand with emotional separation from her mother. Her fond but often uneasy adult relationship with her mother reflected these concerns. Contemplating their relationship eight years after her mother's death, she wrote in 1929, "My mother talked intelligently, brilliantly, about current events, and she had a Southerner's interest in politics. But after my mind took a radical turn she could never get over the feeling that we had drifted apart. It grieves me that I should have added to the sadness that weighed upon her."[33] To be a disloyal southerner, as her family understood it and as Keller often experienced it, meant geographical and familial exile.

Southerners sometimes questioned her southern identity, but people living in the North frequently defined Keller as inherently southern even though she lived most of her life in the northeastern United States. It was an identity she could not escape. In 1929 she spoke "as a representative of the South" at the monthly meeting of the group "Alabamians in New York." Along with a representative of the American Federation of Labor she there urged study of the working conditions of southern textile mill hands. . . . In 1938 publisher H. E. Maule approached her about writing a biography of Clara Barton. He picked her, he said, because "As a woman interested in social work and aid to the handicapped, and as a Southerner by birth, it occurred to me that you would be sympathetic to her great voice."[34] . . .

The 1937 publication of Margaret Mitchell's *Gone with the Wind* prompted Keller, like many other Americans, to reflect on the Old South, its meanings for United States race relations, and the implications for her personal identity. She read the twelve-volume Braille version . . . while sailing for Japan in April 1937. Anne Macy had died in October 1936. As an escape, and seeking new purpose, Keller seized the opportunity to advocate for blind people in other countries. Friends offered her the chance in Japan. She thus read the book while grieving the loss of Macy, pondering her past and better times, and attempting to determine the future course of her life.[35]

In many ways Mitchell's work enchanted Keller. "How charmingly the book opens," she wrote, "with a placid life on a Georgia plantation!" It was a sensual delight that drew to her memories of home. "It stirs in me a nostalgia for the drowsy, sweet spring and early summer days in Tuscumbia, the red earth, the huge old magnolia trees and live oaks. Again I smell Mother's royal wealth of roses, the masses of tangled honeysuckle and paulownia blossoms heavy in the afternoon heat. Again the air about me vibrates with excitement as the men fulminate against some political group or refight the Civil War." It caused her to remember, in terms and imagery paralleling Mitchell's images of slavery, "the Negroes" who gathered water at the spring. "Picturesque in bright-colored bandanas, barefooted, always singing or dancing or performing a cakewalk, they warm my heart, and I long for the joyous pickaninnies who so good-naturedly played with the insatiate tomboy I was."[36]

Mitchell's romanticization of white supremacy and her mythic Old South captivated Keller, just as it did many other readers. By the book's completion, Keller had even adopted Mitchell's historical analysis of Reconstruction. "For the first time," Keller proclaimed, "I am beginning to form a clear picture of the dreadful Reconstruction Period in the South. . . . The criminally stupid descent of the North upon prostrate states with a deluge of carpetbaggers and scalawags turns into a mockery the bloody Civil War fought to emancipate the slaves." Perhaps her embrace of Mitchell's version of history reflected her own yearnings for a happier time. *Gone with the Wind* offered examples of men and women struggling valiantly against economic depression, just as many Americans were doing in the late 1930s. It also offered solace in a false but idyllic past while Keller's own future grew increasingly uncertain. She yearned for Macy. As she wrote in March 1937, "from the moment I wake in the morning until I lie down at night there is an ache at my heart which never stops."[37] Mitchell's myth offered personal comfort and reflection that tomorrow would always come. It offered female models who survived. And . . . it "offered a nostalgic depiction of the Old South but did not advocate its return."[38]

Keller uncomfortably recognized the contradictions between her personal memories, the cultural memories reinforced by *Gone with the Wind*, and the personal knowledge she had garnered over the previous decades. She clearly enjoyed the book, but that pleasure discomforted her: she variably exclaimed passionate opinions about the actions and characters of Rhett, Scarlett, and Melanie and then disavowed her interest with calmer political analyses. The contradictions increased her discomfort and guilt. Despite her fervor for the book, she wrote that "time's disillusioning searchlight" forced her to realize that all may not have been happy in the Old South. "Sadly I recall the degrading poverty, the ignorance and superstition into which those little ones were born and the bitterness of the Negro problem through which many of them are still living."[39] . . . Luckily for her, perhaps, the intoxicating effects of *Gone with the Wind* did not last long. Confronting her personal shame and identity could be once more avoided. After her initial read in 1937, she never mentioned the book again.

U.S. politics, however, forced Keller to pay increasing attention to racial inequalities in both North and South as civil rights campaigns developed in the post–World War II period. . . . In 1946 she attended and spoke at a Danbury, Connecticut, rally "to urge justice to negroes of Connecticut." There she met black and white activists, including opera singer Marian Anderson.[40] Events such as these allowed her to acknowledge racial inequalities and her own shame about them, but in a context that spread responsibility for racial inequalities and shame over both the North and the South. . . . As she became more open with herself and others about racial inequalities, she also grew to realize those inequities went far beyond the geography of the American South.

After the Danbury rally, enthused and contemplative, Keller wrote to a friend that she felt "unquenchable shame" over the social, political, and economic conditions of African Americans. "This revolt has never slumbered within me since I began to notice for myself how they are degraded, and with what cold-blooded deliberation the keys of knowledge, self-reliance and well paid employment are taken from them, so that they may not enter the gate of social competence." She detailed a long list of incidents large and small that infuriated her. She remembered when a "colored

teacher of high culture and noble dignity" visited her and was forced to take the southern hotel's freight elevator. Continued lynching and violence "augur[ed] ill for America's future." The blinding of an African American veteran by a police officer who acted in supposed self-defense was "another abyss of evil . . . moral infection by traitors to Christianity and to the whole democratic spirit in the best traditions of America." She compared her "concentrated horror and fury" to that she had felt when reading Shakespeare's *King Lear* for the first time.[41]

Keller also began to draw connections between racism, the discrimination faced by people with disabilities, and the additive discrimination confronted by African Americans with disabilities. In her 1944 testimony to the House Labor Committee urging expansion of the Social Security Act, she highlighted the circumstances of "the colored blind" and "the deaf-blind." These were, she said, "the hardest pressed and least cared-for" among her "blind fellows." After the 1946 Danbury rally she continued: "It stabs me to the soul to recall my visits to schools for the colored blind which were shockingly backward, and what a hard struggle it was for them to obtain worth while instruction and profitable work because of race prejudice." . . . Her disability activism and the opportunities created by her fame as a person with a disability provided her with the tools necessary to begin to analyze southern racial mores. It did not, however, provide her with instant answers.[42]

A 1951 trip to South Africa pushed Keller to a deeper examination of racial inequalities globally and of the relationship between racism and discrimination against people with disabilities. The journey thrilled the seventy-one-year-old global adventurer. She traveled with the blessings and assistance of the U.S. State Department and the American Foundation for the Blind (an international educational, lobbying, and research group she had worked for since 1921). The State Department found her global travels extremely beneficial because of the positive press and goodwill she elicited. An invitation from the Reverend Arthur Blaxall, a white member of the South African National Council for the Blind and an acquaintance of hers since 1931, initiated the visit. Again her analyses began with memories of her childhood in Alabama. She wrote that she "was the more ready to accept Mr. Blaxall's invitation because I remembered the earliest years when little Afroamericans were my playmates."[43]

Keller's preparations for the trip pushed her further into national and international racial politics and into closer contact with African American and African activists. She read Alan Paton's *Cry the Beloved Country* and Mohandas Gandhi's *Autobiography* to learn more about South Africa's racial apartheid. She gleaned all she could about South African people, plants, and animals from an acquaintance. . . . In Harlem, perhaps for the first time, she attended a "colored debutantes' cotillion" as a guest of the Reverend Dr. Adam Clayton Powell Sr., famed race man and minister at Harlem's Abyssinian Baptist Church. There she met guest of honor Ralph Bunche, from whom she learned "the historic point of view." Only months previously, Bunche had been awarded the Nobel Peace Prize (for which Keller would later be nominated) for his powerful advocacy of civil rights and decolonization. The eloquence, charisma, and dynamism with which he critiqued South African racial injustices appealed to her sense of service. Energized, she committed herself to confronting South African racism.[44]

Keller sought to do so directly but proceeded cautiously. She knew that disregard and lack of social support made the lives of many blind people across the world difficult, but racism compounded the problem for "the colored blind" in South Africa. Her goal, as she described it to her host Arthur Blaxall before departure, was to use "skill and tact as well as enthusiasm to obtain the right help for the colored blind, who, owing to their handicap are more subject to the arbitrary will of white society than their seeing fellows."[45] . . .

Once in South Africa, Keller found the country's beauty contrasted sharply with its brutality and racial inequality. She could not deny her enjoyment at being covered with the spray of Victoria Falls or the awesomeness of Kruger National Park. Once, looking for hippopotami, she stood alone: "the tall grasses rustled against me, and I drank in the sweet, clean air and the sense of four hundred miles where wild animals were free to roam." And, as wherever she went when she traveled, she attracted immense attention. As her host described it, "for two months she was the center of interests, and a subject of conversation, eclipsing even the parliamentary news of the day."[46]

In spite of the warm welcome she and her companion Polly Thomson received at the twenty-eight schools and institutions she visited and the forty-eight meetings and receptions she addressed, "the bitter sense of racial discrimination and injustice" soured her visit. Racism even compounded her schedule, as the laws and attitudes of apartheid required separate assemblies for "the whites, the colored people, the natives and the Indians."[47]

Despite efforts to "keep watch over our mutinous lips" around powerful and wealthy donors, Keller did criticize apartheid publicly. She acknowledged, however, that it took "all the courage and fortitude Polly and I could command" to do so. Her insistence on addressing and visiting assemblies of nonwhites forced acknowledgment of their existence and needs. On at least one occasion her address to a white audience included "concern about the thousands of natives who were as yet untaught and unbefriended." She wrote to one dear friend, "Many times my heart sank as I observed how apathetic many of the public had been toward those unfortunates ["the natives blind or deaf"], and occasionally in my dreams I banged my head against an impenetrable wall trying to discover a break-through." . . . Nothing, she wrote privately, "made me more ashamed of my own race" than the ideology of "Afrikaaners."[48] Just as in the United States, racism compounded the discrimination and limited options of people of African descent who had disabilities.

In the years following Keller's return from South Africa, . . . the United States civil rights movement grew in activism and success. Evidence indicates that she followed and approved of its course, but she was never actively involved (perhaps partly due to her age). In response to Emmett Till's death in 1955 she sought to give financial assistance to the NAACP.[49] No evidence remains of ties to other white female dissidents [and advocates of racial equality] from the South, like Anne Braden or Katharine Lumpkin. . . .

Examining Keller's southern identity reveals the important role of region in forming personal identity. Keller never questioned the region's uniqueness and its influence on her. Though geographically separated from the South and often in conflict with her family (which to her sometimes seems to have become synonymous with the region) because of her politics, she retained a personal identification as a southerner. Her southern roots also shaped how others defined her. For some, it caused pride, for others derision, and it led many to expect or demand political stances from her that reflected dominant southern hierarchies of race, gender, and class.

Keller both savored and resented this southern identification. At times it gave her pleasure, at other times discomfort. In either case, however, she could not shed the collective cultural memories and regional identity integral to forming her personal outlook. As an adult, she struggled to separate regional identity from acceptance of Lost Cause mythology.

Examining Keller as a southerner provides an example of the historical and personal evolution of white shame, the term she frequently used in the latter half of her life. As Tara McPherson has written, "guilt emerges as a central aspect of twentieth-century southern feeling, and a variety of approaches to managing guilt are tracked across the southern landscape."[50] Racial politics remained central to a southern white identity in the late-nineteenth- and twentieth-century United States, even for one who had moved far away from her Alabama childhood. Race and the South's regionally focused politics based on maintaining the color line lingered omnipresent in her analyses, her sense of home, and her exploration of world politics. While claiming her southern ties fondly, Keller tended to do so only by linking them with accompanying statements of shame and disavowal.

As an adult Keller increasingly drew connections between racism, the discrimination faced by people with disabilities, and the additive discrimination confronted by African Americans with disabilities. Examining her as a southerner provides clues as to how, unaided by other intellectual theorists, she grew to comprehend that systems of hierarchy—whether based upon race, class, gender, or the abilities of one's body—were inherently linked and intertwined. Like others, she struggled to clarify and articulate the connections between efforts to end discrimination and stereotyping. Keller did not, however, connect with the organizations and people of the rapidly growing disability rights movement, just as she failed to do so during her earlier years.[51] Even today, activists in the racial freedom movements, the disability rights movement, and the feminist movement seek to fully theorize these connections.

Finally, examining Helen Keller as a southerner expands the realization that southern womanhood is not monolithic. . . . Keller's experience of southern white womanhood—and her attempts to reformulate it—was influenced equally by factors as disparate as family tales of the glory days of the Old South, her disability, and her northern education. While Keller studied at Radcliffe and walked the streets of Cambridge, Massachusetts, between 1900 and 1904, she wrote, "Never have I found in the greenhouses of the North such heart-satisfying roses as the climbing roses of my southern home. They used to hang in long festoons from our porch, filling the whole air with their fragrance, untainted by any earthly smell; and in the early morning, washed in the dew, they felt so soft, so pure, I could not help wondering if they did not resemble the asphodels of God's garden."[52] To her, though she never again lived for a long period in the South, the region always remained an idyllic and sensual geography. The physicality of place became the easiest way, or perhaps simply the least complicated way, for her to feel southern.

Notes

1. For more on Helen Keller see Kim E. Nielsen, "Was Helen Keller Deaf? Blindness, Deafness, and Multiple Identities," in Brenda Jo Brueggemann and Susan Burch, eds., *Women and Deafness: Double Visions* (Washington, D.C., 2006); Kim E. Nielsen, ed., *Helen Keller: Selected Writings* (New York, 2005); Kim E. Nielsen, *The Radical Lives of Helen Keller* (New York, 2004); Joseph P. Lash, *Helen and Teacher: The Story of Helen Keller and Anne Sullivan Macy* (New York, 1980); and Dorothy Herrmann, *Helen Keller: A Life* (New York, 1998).

2. Helen Keller, *The Story of My Life: With Supplementary Accounts by Anne Sullivan and John Albert Macy*, edited by Roger Shattuck and Dorothy Herrmann (1903; new ed., New York, 2003), 12–13; Herrmann, *Helen Keller*, 8.

3. Keller, *Story of My Life*, 14.

4. In 1892 educators founded the Alabama School for the Negro Deaf and Blind, also in Talladega. See the website of the Alabama Institute for Deaf and Blind at http://www.aidb.org/aidb-story-overview/.

5. See Ernest Freeberg, *The Education of Laura Bridgman: First Deaf and Blind Person to Learn Language* (Cambridge, Mass., 2001); and Elisabeth Gitter, *The Imprisoned Guest: Samuel Howe and Laura Bridgman, the Original Deaf-Blind Girl* (New York, 2001).

6. Keller described this trip in *Story of My Life*, 23–24.

7. See Hannah Joyner, "'This Unnatural and Fratricidal Strife': A Family's Negotiation of the Civil War, Deafness, and Independence," in Paul K. Longmore and Lauri Umansky, eds., *The New Disability*

History: American Perspectives (New York, 2001), 83–106; Hannah Joyner, From Pity to Pride: Growing Up Deaf in the Old South (Washington, D.C., 2004); and Steven Noll, Feeble-Minded in Our Midst: Institutions for the Mentally Retarded in the South, 1900–1940 (Chapel Hill, 1995).

8. Fifty-Sixth Annual Report of the Trustees of the Perkins Institution, 79, 81; Arthur Keller to Michael Anagnos, January 28, 1887 (Samuel P. Hayes Research Library, Perkins School for the Blind, Watertown, Mass.).

9. Fifty-Sixth Annual Report of the Trustees of the Perkins Institution, 79; Herrmann, Helen Keller, chap. 3.

10. "Teacher's Life, Tewksbury," undated and unnumbered notes by Anne Sullivan Macy, Notes of Nella Braddy Henney, Nella Braddy Henney Collection (Hayes Research Library, Perkins School for the Blind); Nella Braddy Henney, Anne Sullivan Macy: The Story Behind Helen Keller (Garden City, N.Y., 1933), 34; Nina Silber, The Romance of Reunion: Northerners and the South, 1865–1900 (Chapel Hill, 1993), 124.

11. "The South," undated and unnumbered notes by Anne Sullivan Macy, Notes of Nella Braddy Henney, Henney Collection.

12. "Going to Tuscumbia," undated and unnumbered notes by Anne Sullivan Macy, ibid.

13. "The South," undated and unnumbered notes by Anne Sullivan Macy, ibid.

14. David W. Blight, Race and Reunion: The Civil War in American Memory (Cambridge, Mass., 2001), 171, 260. See also Gaines M. Foster, Ghosts of the Confederacy: Defeat, the Lost Cause, and the Emergence of the New South, 1865 to 1913 (New York, 1987).

15. Keller, Story of My Life, 18, 163–64. The enslaved girl's name, Martha Washington, clearly begs for analysis. Whether the name Keller used in her autobiography was indeed the girl's name—or a pseudonym—is unclear.

16. Ibid., 174.

17. Anne Sullivan to Michael Anagnos, January 23, 1893, Annie Sullivan Letters (Manuscript Department, American Antiquarian Society, Worcester, Mass.).

18. Nielsen, Radical Lives, 20.

19. Ibid., 182; Anne Sullivan to Michael Anagnos, April 20, 1888, Sullivan Letters.

20. Anne Sullivan to Michael Anagnos, July 7, 1890, Sullivan Letters; Lash, Helen and Teacher, 780.

21. For example, see Annie M. Sullivan to Michael Anagnos, April 22, 1888, Sullivan Letters.

22. Helen Keller, "A Vision of Service," quoted in Keller, Light in My Darkness, edited by Ray Silverman (1994; 2nd ed., New York, 2000), 107. Keller's most lengthy explanation of her faith is in Keller, My Religion (New York, 1927).

23. Nielsen, Radical Lives.

24. On southern women's activism, see, for example, Elna C. Green, Southern Strategies: Southern Women and the Woman Suffrage Question (Chapel Hill, 1997); Anastatia Sims, The Power of Femininity in the New South: Women's Organizations and Politics in North Carolina, 1880–1930 (Columbia, S.C., 1997); Elizabeth Hayes Turner, Women, Culture, and Community: Religion and Reform in Galveston, 1880–1920 (New York, 1997); Jane Turner Censer, The Reconstruction of White Southern Womanhood, 1865–1895 (Baton Rouge, 2003); Jacquelyn Dowd Hall, "Open

Secrets: Memory, Imagination, and the Refashioning of Southern Identity," American Quarterly, 50 (March 1998), 109–24; Catherine Fosl, Subversive Southerner: Anne Braden and the Struggle for Racial Justice in the Cold War South (New York, 2002); and Jacquelyn Dowd Hall, "Women Writers, the 'Southern Front,' and the Dialectical Imagination," Journal of Southern History, 69 (February 2003), 3–38.

25. Educators generally considered northern educational institutions for deaf people superior because of their post–Civil War switch to oralism rather than sign language. Southern institutions remained signing institutions largely because of funding shortages that made hiring and training new oralist teachers difficult. See Douglas C. Baynton, Forbidden Signs: American Culture and the Campaign against Sign Language (Chicago, 1996).

26. Nielsen, Radical Lives, 38–39 (quotation on p. 38), 42. After 1924 Keller primarily expressed her interest in radical politics privately, but her interest remained.

27. Kim Nielsen, "Helen Keller and the Politics of Civic Fitness," in Longmore and Umansky, eds., New Disability History, 268–90.

28. New York Crisis, April 1916, pp. 305–6; Nielsen, Radical Lives, 38–39, 42; Lash, Helen and Teacher, 454–56; Herrmann, Helen Keller, 204.

29. Lash, Helen and Teacher, 454; Herrmann, Helen Keller, 205.

30. Herrmann, Helen Keller, 205; Lash, Helen and Teacher, 454–55.

31. Nielsen, Radical Lives, 40–41. Keller's mother, Kate Keller, was particularly opposed to a possible marriage and any form of a sexual life for her daughter. Not only did Keller's family and Anne Sullivan Macy hold eugenic fears about Helen's possible reproduction and sexuality, but also many state laws prohibited women with disabilities from marriage and children. For information on eugenics and disability see Wendy Kline, Building a Better Race: Gender, Sexuality, and Eugenics from the Turn of the Century to the Baby Boom (Berkeley, 2001); Martin S. Pernick, The Black Stork: Eugenics and the Death of "Defective" Babies in American Medicine and Motion Pictures Since 1915 (New York, 1996); and Steven Selden, "Eugenics and the Social Construction of Merit, Race and Disability," Journal of Curriculum Studies, 32 (March 2000), 235–52.

32. Lash, Helen and Teacher, 452; Anne Sullivan Macy to Helen Keller, undated letter from 1917, Folder 5, Box 69, Helen Keller Archives (American Foundation for the Blind, New York).

33. Helen Keller, Midstream: My Later Life (1929; reprint, New York, 1968), 220.

34. "Sees Much Poverty in Trade Centres," New York Times, November 13, 1929, p. 46; H. E. Maule to Helen Keller, June 16, 1938 (copy to Nella Braddy Henney), Henney Collection.

35. For more on Keller's travels to Japan, see Nielsen, Radical Lives, chaps. 3 and 4.

36. Helen Keller, Helen Keller's Journal, 1936–1937 (Garden City, N.Y., 1938), 281, 298.

37. Ibid., 305; Keller, Helen Keller's Journal, 231.

38. However, the female models who survived [in the book] were white women whose survival became racially defined. On this point, see Tara

McPherson, *Reconstructing Dixie: Race, Gender, and Nostalgia in the Imagined South* (Durham, N.C., 2003), 47–64. Nostalgic depiction: Sarah E. Gardner, *Blood and Irony: Southern White Women's Narratives of the Civil War, 1861–1937* (Chapel Hill, 2004), 239. See also Marian J. Morton, "'My Dear, I Don't Give A Damn': Scarlett O'Hara and the Great Depression," *Frontiers* 5 (Autmun 1980), 52–56; Drew Gilpin Faust, "Clutching the Chains that Bind: Margaret Mitchell and *Gone with the Wind*," *Southern Cultures* 5 (Spring 1999), 6–20; Elizabeth Fox-Genovese, "Scarlett O'Hara: The Southern Lady as New Woman," *American Quarterly* 33 (Autumn 1981), 391–41.

39. Keller, *Helen Keller's Journal,* 298–99.

40. Helen Keller to Nella Braddy Henney, September 22, 1946, Henney Collection.

41. Ibid.

42. Helen Keller's speech before the House Labor Committee Investigating Aid to the Handicapped. October 3, 1944. Legislation-Federal Folder, Social Security Act—Title X, Folder 4, Box 36, Helen Keller Archives. See also "Helen Keller Urges More Help to Blind," *New York Times,* October 4, 1944, p. 25. Helen Keller to Nella Braddy Henney, September 22, 1946, Henney Collection.

43. Arthur William Blaxall, *Helen Keller Under the Southern Cross* (Cape Town, 1952), 32. For more on Keller's travels to South Africa see Nielsen, *Radical Lives,* 102–5.

44. Blaxall, *Helen Keller Under the Southern Cross,* 32; Nielsen, *Radical Lives,* 102–5; Helen Keller to Jo Davidson, January 24, 1951, Jo Davidson File, Folder 9, Box 52, Helen Keller Archives (quotations).

45. Lash, *Helen and Teacher,* 724.

46. Helen Keller to Jo Davidson, August 1, 1951, Box 11, Papers of Jo Davidson (Manuscript Division, Library of Congress, Washington, D.C.). Blaxall, *Helen Keller Under the Southern Cross,* 25.

47. Helen Keller to Jo Davidson, August 1, 1951, Box 11, Papers of Jo Davidson.

48. Undated newspaper clipping from 1951, Nella Braddy Henney Journal, Henney Collection; Blaxall, *Helen Keller Under the Southern Cross,* 36; Helen Keller to Jo Davidson, August 1, 1951, Box 11, Papers of Jo Davidson.

49. Nella Braddy Henney to Polly Thomson, October 23, 1955, Nella Braddy Henney File, Folder 7, Box 58, Helen Keller Archives.

50. McPherson, *Reconstructing Dixie,* 6.

51. For further information on the disability rights movement, see Joseph P. Shapiro, *No Pity: People with Disabilities Forging a New Civil Rights Movement* (New York, 1993); Paul K. Longmore and David Goldberger, "The League of the Physically Handicapped and the Great Depression: A Case Study in the New Disability History," *Journal of American History* 87 (December 2000), 888–922; and Doris Zames Fleischer and Frieda Zames, *The Disability Rights Movement: From Charity to Confrontation* (Philadelphia, 2001). For more on Keller's relationship with the disability rights movement, see Nielsen, *Radical Lives,* chap. 5.

52. Keller, *Story of My Life,* 14–15.

Ida B. Wells, Southern Horrors (with an introduction
by Patricia A. Schechter)

Ida B. Wells's 1892 pamphlet *Southern Horrors: Lynch Law in All Its Phases* launched a critical phase of the African American struggle for civil rights. Its statistical refutation of the rape charge against black men that was used to justify lynching is a sociological breakthrough that has stood the test of time and study. Wells also demonstrates how the concepts of "race" and "rape" were tied to power relations in the administration of justice, in the media, and in everyday life. Finally, Wells expounds the racial and class dimensions of the sexual double standard in ways that connect to contemporary feminist concerns with violence against all women, communities of color, and the poor in the United States and globally.

The insights expressed in *Southern Horrors* reflect Wells's personal and community survival strategy in the New South. Her situation was shaped by both new opportunities and new oppressions facing the first generation of free African Americans who came of age after the Civil War. Wells's parents, who had been slaves in Mississippi, bequeathed to their children a legacy of strong religious faith, pride in wage-earning, and a commitment to education that echoes through the many projects their daughter undertook over her lifetime. Wells's father, James Wells, was a skilled carpenter and a member of the Masons who, after the war, served on the board of Holly Springs local American Missionary Association school, Rust College, which his daughter attended. Wells's mother, "Lizzie" Warrenton Wells, worked as a cook and was a devout Methodist who made sure her children attended church, where she herself learned to read the Bible. After James and Lizzie's untimely deaths in 1878 from a yellow fever epidemic that swept the Delta, sixteen-year-old Ida B. Wells was left to care for her five siblings, earning money by teaching school.

The prospect of better wages and the presence of extended family soon drew Wells to Memphis, Tennessee. There, her intellectual, social, and political horizons expanded in a burgeoning black community notable for its highly accomplished middle-class and elite members. Aspirations for equality nourished community institutions like schools, newspapers, social clubs, literary lyceums, and churches, especially the Baptist and African Methodist Episcopal denominations. In Memphis, Wells found encouragement to turn her intellectual talents into leadership by teaching Sunday school and by pursuing literary activities, especially journalism. Her first newspaper article appeared in 1883 in a Baptist weekly. It explained how Wells had been unfairly ejected from a first-class "ladies" railroad coach and how she fought racial discrimination by taking her case to court. While tens of thousands of educated women joined the paid labor force as school "ma'ams," religious educators, and journalists in the late nineteenth century, these social roles had particular significance for African American women, whose personal, family, and community well-being was intimately bound up with their wage-earning, educational activities, and community-betterment work.

As *Southern Horrors* emphatically argues, a white racist backlash followed closely upon the achievements of African Americans after Reconstruction. The result of this backlash was "Jim Crow" segregation, a set of laws designed for the economic deprivation, social marginalization, and political disfranchisement of black people. Jim Crow was established and enforced through systematic violence and terror. Ida B. Wells's eight pamphlets, written between 1892 and 1920, painstakingly document the ways in which African Americans were deprived of their rights through mob and police violence, through negative propaganda campaigns in the media, and through the elimination of economic opportunity and political rights.* Few aspects of Jim Crow escaped Wells's sharp scrutiny in the press and eventually, while in Memphis, she caught the negative attention of critics. As the following excerpt explains, she was forced to leave the South as a kind of political exile, first traveling to New York, then to Great Britain, and finally settling in Chicago in 1895. There, she married lawyer and fellow activist Ferdinand L. Barnett (hyphenating her name to Wells-Barnett) and raised a family of four children.

Post-exile, Wells-Barnett's writing and activism were sustained through African American community networks and by organizations shared by black and white women reformers, such as the Woman's Christian Temperance Union. Her work with black women's church and club networks nurtured her into a powerful public speaker and political organizer. Between 1892 and 1895, Wells-Barnett organized scores of antilynching committees and women's clubs all over the United States and abroad, and helped inaugurate the National Association of Colored Women (NACW), a group that functioned as the preeminent civil rights organization up to World War I. In 1909, Wells-Barnett cofounded the National Association for the Advancement of Colored People (NAACP), which, in 1917, assumed principal leadership of the antilynching fight in the United States.

The trajectory of Wells-Barnett's civil rights agitation was neither simple nor smooth. Controversy followed her and her work, especially during its first decade. White supremacists in the North and South vilified her in the press, slandering her morals and threatening her with violence for speaking out against lynching. While most African American communities embraced Wells-Barnett as a heroine, there was little consensus about how, exactly, to end lynching or resist Jim Crow. Black leaders were a diverse group ideologically and generationally; regional considerations also came into play as black southerners found themselves more circumscribed than their northern peers. Women's roles were also fundamental to the building of black communities and to resistance work. Though black women's families and communities were dependent upon their contributions, any move on their part into official political and intellectual leadership—especially where interactions with whites were concerned—usually sparked controversy. Whether in

---

*Besides *Southern Horrors*, the pamphlets were *The Reason Why the Colored American Is Not in the World's Columbian Exposition: The Afro-American's Contribution to Columbian Literature* (Chicago: Ida B. Wells, 1893); *United States Atrocities: Lynch Law* (London: Lux Publishing, 1894); *A Red Record: Tabulated Statistics and Alleged Causes of Lynchings in the United States, 1892–1893–1894* (Chicago: Donahue & Henneberry, 1895); *Lynch Law in Georgia* (Chicago: Ida B. Wells-Barnett, 1899); *Mob Rule in New Orleans: Robert Charles and His Fight to the Death* (Chicago: Ida B. Wells-Barnett, 1900); *The East St. Louis Massacre: The Greatest Outrage of the Century* (Chicago: The Negro Fellowship Herald Press, 1917); *The Arkansas Race Riot* (Chicago: Ida B. Wells-Barnett, 1920).

journalism, public speaking, or institutional leadership—as with her Chicago social settlement, the Negro Fellowship League (1909–1919)—Wells-Barnett's initiatives were always double-edged, affording new spaces for community defense and activism while potentially exposing black men as somehow deficient in their protective or leadership roles. For every celebration of her hard work and successes, there were always powerful voices affirming the propriety of male ministers, business leaders, and elected officials leading the civil rights agenda for African Americans. Wells-Barnett remained staunchly committed to equality for black women, however, fighting hard for suffrage rights in Illinois and nationally. After the passage of the Nineteenth Amendment, she eventually ran for public office herself, in 1930.

Wells-Barnett's steadfast commitment to full equality not just for lynching victims but for "every citizen" rings through *Southern Horrors*, lending the text its prophetic, visionary quality; hers is a plea, to quote further from the pamphlet's preface, that "justice be done though the heavens fall." *Southern Horrors* draws on a number of powerful currents in American thought and style to make its case. As a graphic exposé, *Southern Horrors* shares kinship with muckraking journalism, a hallmark of the U.S. press at the turn of the century. Its empirical bent draws on statistical work to be found in the nascent academic field of sociology. *Southern Horrors* also stands in a tradition of radical pamphleteering in U.S. history that includes Tom Paine's *Common Sense* (1776) and David Walker's *Appeal to the Colored People of the Americas* (1829). Like these texts, *Southern Horrors* is peppered with wilting sarcasm and theatrical asides designed to provoke, starting with its title, a mocking send up of "southern honor." Instead of the neat closure of genteel fiction, *Southern Horrors* is full of questions and commands in a kind of call-and-response engagement with the reader, a pattern of expression at the heart of black worship traditions and one designed to work a deep transformation in participants. Finally, *Southern Horrors* ends with a practical list of strategies for "self-help," including education, boycotts, migration, agitation for protective legislation, suing through the courts, and even armed self-defense, to be "used to give that protection which the law refuses to give." Nearly five thousand Americans, almost three-fourths of them black, were lynched in Wells-Barnett's lifetime. Repeated efforts of African American activists to pass federal legislation making lynching a crime were defeated in Congress in 1922, 1937, and 1940.

What are the different kinds of violence or threats of violence that Wells documents in *Southern Horrors*? How is violence linked to issues of sexual, racial, and class privilege? How does Wells compare the social and sexual experiences of black and white women under Jim Crow? In what ways does class shape the social behavior and political strategies of the historical actors Wells describes?

CHAPTER I: THE OFFENSE

Wednesday evening May 24th, 1892, the city of Memphis was filled with excitement. Editorials in the daily papers of that date caused a meeting to be held in the Cotton Exchange Building; a committee was sent for the editors of the *Free Speech*, an Afro-American journal published in that city, and the only reason the open threats of lynching that were made were not carried out was because they could not be found. The cause of all this commotion was the following editorial published in the *Free Speech* May 21st, 1892, the Saturday previous.

> Eight negroes lynched since last issue of the *Free Speech*, one at Little Rock, Ark., last Saturday morning where the citizens broke (?) into the

Excerpted from Ida B. Wells, *Southern Horrors: Lynch Law in All Its Phases* (New York: New York Age, 1892).

penitentiary and got their man; three near Anniston, Ala., one near New Orleans; and three at Clarksville, Ga., the last three for killing a white man, and five on the same old racket—the new alarm about raping white women. The same programme of hanging, then shooting bullets into the lifeless bodies was carried out to the letter.

Nobody in this section of the country believes the old threadbare lie that Negro men rape white women. If Southern white men are not careful, they will over-reach themselves and public sentiment will have a reaction; a conclusion will then be reached which will be very damaging to the moral reputation of their women.

The Daily Commercial of Wednesday following, May 25th, contained the following leader:

Those negroes who are attempting to make the lynching of individuals of their race a means for arousing the worst passions of their kind are playing with a dangerous sentiment. The negroes may as well understand that there is no mercy for the negro rapist and little patience with his defenders. A negro organ printed in this city, in a recent issue publishes the following atrocious paragraph: "Nobody in this section of the country believes the old thread-bare lie that negro men rape white women. If Southern white men are not careful they will over-reach themselves, and public sentiment will have a reaction; and a conclusion will be reached which will be very damaging to the moral reputation of their women."

The fact that a black scoundrel is allowed to live and utter such loathsome and repulsive calumnies is a volume of evidence as to the wonderful patience of Southern whites. But we have had enough of it.

There are some things that the Southern white man will not tolerate, and the obscene intimations of the foregoing have brought the writer to the very outermost limit of public patience. We hope we have said enough.

The *Evening Scimitar* of same date, copied the *Commercial's* editorial with these words of comment: "Patience under such circumstances is not a virtue. If the negroes themselves do not apply the remedy without delay it will be the duty of those whom he has attacked to tie the wretch who utters these calumnies to a stake at the intersection of Main and Madison Sts., brand him in the forehead with a hot iron and perform upon him a surgical operation with a pair of tailor's shears."

Acting upon this advice, the leading citizens met in the Cotton Exchange Building the same evening, and threats of lynching were freely indulged, not by the lawless element upon which the deviltry of the South is usually saddled—but by the leading business men, in their leading business centre. Mr. Fleming, the business manager and owning a half interest the *Free Speech*, had to leave town to escape the mob, and was afterwards ordered not to return; letters and telegrams sent me in New York where I was spending my vacation advised me that bodily harm awaited my return. Creditors took possession of the office and sold the outfit, and the *Free Speech* was as if it had never been.

The editorial in question was prompted by the many inhuman and fiendish lynchings of Afro-Americans which have recently taken place and was meant as a warning. Eight lynched in one week and five of them charged with rape! The thinking public will not easily believe freedom and education more brutalizing than slavery, and the world knows that the crime of rape was unknown during four years of civil war, when the white women of the South were at the mercy of the race which is all at once charged with being a bestial one.

Since my business has been destroyed and I am an exile from home because of that editorial, the issue has been forced, and as the writer of it I feel that the race and the public generally should have a statement of the facts as they exist. They will serve at the same time as a defense for the Afro-American Sampsons who suffer themselves to be betrayed by white Delilahs.

The whites of Montgomery, Ala., knew J. C. Duke sounded the keynote of the situation—which they would gladly hide from the world, when he said in his paper, *The Herald*, five years ago: "Why is it that white women attract negro men now more than in former days? There was a time when such a thing was unheard of. There is a secret to this thing, and we greatly suspect it is the growing appreciation of white Juliets for colored Romeos." Mr. Duke, like the *Free Speech* proprietors, was forced to leave the city for reflecting on the "honah" of white women and his paper suppressed; but the truth remains that Afro-American men do not always rape (?) white women without their consent.

Mr. Duke, before leaving Montgomery, signed a card disclaiming any intention of slandering Southern white women. The editor of the *Free Speech* has no disclaimer to enter, but asserts instead that there are many white women in the South who would marry colored men if such an act would not place them at once beyond the pale of society and within the clutches of the law. The miscegenation laws of the South only operate against the legitimate union of the races; they leave the white man free to seduce all the colored girls he can, but it is death to the colored man who yields to the force and advances of a similar attraction in white women. White men lynch the offending Afro-American, not because he is a de-spoiler of virtue, but because he succumbs to the smiles of white women.

CHAPTER II: THE BLACK AND WHITE OF IT

The *Cleveland Gazette* of January 16, 1892, publishes a case in point. *Mrs. J. S. Underwood*, the wife of a minister of Elyria, Ohio, accused an Afro-American of rape. She told her husband that during his absence in 1888, stumping the State for the Prohibition Party, the man came to the kitchen door, forced his way in the house and insulted her. She tried to drive him out with a heavy poker, but he overpowered and chloroformed her, and when she revived her clothing was torn and she was in a horrible condition. She did not know the man but could identify him. She pointed out William Offett, a married man, who was arrested and, being in Ohio, was granted a trial.

The prisoner vehemently denied the charge of rape, but confessed he went to Mrs. Underwood's residence at her invitation and was criminally intimate with her at her request. This availed him nothing against the sworn testimony of a minister's wife, a lady of the highest respectability. He was found guilty, and entered the penitentiary, December 14, 1888, for fifteen years. Some time afterwards the woman's remorse led her to confess to her husband that the man was innocent.

These are her words: "I met Offett at the Post Office. It was raining. He was polite to me, and as I had several bundles in my arms he offered to carry them home for me, which he did. He had a strange fascination for me, and I invited him to call on me. He called, bringing chestnuts and candy for the children. By this means we got them to leave us alone in the room. Then I sat on his lap. He made a proposal to me and I readily consented. Why I did so, I do not know, but that I did is true. He visited me several times after that and each time I was indiscreet. I did not care after the first

time. In fact I could not have resisted, and had no desire to resist."

When asked by her husband why she told him she had been outraged, she said: "I had several reasons for telling you. One was the neighbors saw the fellow here, another was, I was afraid I had contracted a loathsome disease, and still another was that I feared I might give birth to a Negro baby. I hoped to save my reputation by telling you a deliberate lie." Her husband horrified by the confession had Offett, who had already served four years, released and secured a divorce.

There are thousands of such cases throughout the South, with the difference that the Southern white men in insatiate fury wreak their vengeance without intervention of law upon the Afro-Americans who consort with their women. A few instances to substantiate the assertion that some white women love the company of the Afro-American will not be out of place. Most of these cases were reported by the daily papers of the South.

In the winter of 1885–6 the wife of a practicing physician in Memphis, in good social standing whose name has escaped me, left home, husband and children, and ran away with her black coachman. She was with him a month before her husband found and brought her home. The coachman could not be found. The doctor moved his family away from Memphis, and is living in another city under an assumed name. . . .

Sarah Clark of Memphis loved a black man and lived openly with him. When she was indicted last spring for miscegenation, she swore in court that she was *not* a white woman. This she did to escape the penitentiary and continued her illicit relation undisturbed. That she is of the lower class of whites, does not disturb the fact that she is a white woman. "The leading citizens" of Memphis are defending the "honor" of *all* white women, *demi-monde* included.

Since the manager of the *Free Speech* has been run away from Memphis by the guardians of the honor of Southern white women, a young girl living on Poplar St., who was discovered in intimate relations with a handsome mulatto young colored man, Will Morgan by name, stole her father's money to send the young fellow away from that father's wrath. She has since joined him in Chicago. . . .

The very week the "leading citizens" of Memphis were making a spectacle of themselves in defense of all white women of every kind, an Afro-American, M. Stricklin, was found in a white woman's room in that city. Although she made no outcry of rape, he was jailed and would have been lynched, but the woman stated she bought curtains of him (he was a furniture dealer) and his business in her room that night was to put them up. A white woman's word was taken as absolutely in this case as when the cry of rape is made, and he was freed.

What is true of Memphis is true of the entire South. . . . Frank Weems of Chattanooga who was not lynched in May only because the prominent citizens became his body guard until the doors of the penitentiary closed on him, had letters in his pocket from the white woman in the case, making the appointment with him. Edward Coy who was burned alive in Texarkana, January 1, 1892, died protesting his innocence. Investigation since as given by the Bystander in the *Chicago Inter-Ocean*, October 1, proves: . . . The woman who was paraded as a victim of violence was of bad character; her husband was a drunkard and a gambler. . . . She was compelled by threats, if not by violence, to make the charge against the victim. . . . When she came to apply the match Coy asked her if she would burn him after they had "been sweethearting" so long. . . .

Hundreds of such cases might be cited, but enough have been given to prove the assertion that there are white women in the South who love the Afro-American's company even as there are white men notorious for their preference for Afro-American women.

There is hardly a town in the South which has not an instance of the kind which is well-known, and hence the assertion is reiterated that "nobody in the South believes the old thread-bare lie that negro men rape white women." Hence there is a growing demand among Afro-Americans that the guilt or innocence of parties accused of rape be fully established. They know the men of the section of the country who refuse this are not so desirous of punishing rapists as they pretend. The utterances of the leading white men show that with them it is not the crime but the *class*, Bishop Fitzgerald has become apologist for lynchers of the rapists of *white* women only. . . . But when the victim is a colored woman it is different.

Last winter in Baltimore, Md., three white ruffians assaulted a Miss Camphor, a young Afro-American girl, while out walking with a young man of her own race. They held her

escort and outraged the girl. It was a deed dastardly enough to arouse Southern blood, which gives its horror of rape as excuse for lawlessness, but she was an Afro-American. The case went to the courts, an Afro-American lawyer defended the men and they were acquitted.

In Nashville, Tenn., there is a white man, Pat Hanifan, who outraged a little Afro-American girl, and, from the physical injuries received, she has been ruined for life. He was jailed for six months, discharged, and is now a detective in that city. . . . Only two weeks before Eph. Grizzard, who had only been *charged* with rape upon a white woman, had been taken from the jail, with Governor Buchanan and the police and militia standing by, dragged through the streets in broad daylight, knives plunged into him at every step, and with every fiendish cruelty a frenzied mob could devise, he was at last swung out on the bridge with hands cut to pieces as he tried to climb up the stanchions. . . .

At the very moment these civilized whites were announcing their determination "to protect their wives and daughters," by murdering Grizzard, a white man was in the same jail for raping eight-year-old Maggie Reese, an Afro-American girl. He was not harmed. The "honor" of grown women who were glad enough to be supported by the Grizzard boys and Ed Coy, as long as the liasion was not known, needed protection; they were white. The outrage upon helpless childhood needed no avenging in this case; she was black. . . .

CHAPTER III: THE NEW CRY

. . . Thoughtful Afro-Americans with the strong arm of the government withdrawn and with the hope to stop such wholesale massacres urged the race to sacrifice its political rights for the sake of peace. They honestly believed the race should fit itself for government, and when that should be done, the objection to race participation in politics would be removed.

But the sacrifice did not remove the trouble, nor move the South to justice. One by one the Southern States have legally (?) disfranchised the Afro-American, and since the repeal of the Civil Rights Bill nearly every Southern State has passed separate car laws with a penalty against their infringement. The race regardless of advancement is penned into filthy, stifling partitions cut off from smoking cars. . . . The dark and bloody record of the

South shows 728 Afro-Americans lynched during the past eight years; ... and not less than 150 have been known to have met violent death at the hands of cruel bloodthirsty mobs during the past nine months.

To palliate this record (which grows worse as the Afro-American becomes intelligent) and excuse some of the most heinous crimes that ever stained the history of a country, the South is shielding itself behind the plausible screen of defending the honor of its women. This, too, in the face of the fact that only *one-third* of the 728 victims to mobs have been *charged* with rape, to say nothing of those of that one-third who were innocent of the charge. . . .

Even to the better class of Afro-Americans the crime of rape is so revolting they have too often taken the white man's word and given lynch law neither the investigation nor condemnation it deserved.

They forget that a concession of the right to lynch a man for a certain crime, not only concedes the right to lynch any person for any crime, but (so frequently is the cry of rape now raised) it is in a fair way to stamp us a race of rapists and desperadoes. They have gone on hoping and believing that general education and financial strength would solve the difficulty, and are devoting their energies to the accumulation of both. . . .

Mary McLeod Bethune,
"How the Bethune-Cookman College Campus Started"

Mary McLeod Bethune was one of the most distinguished educators of her generation. The daughter of slaves, she received her early education from missionary teachers. Like others of her race who saw education as a key to racial advancement at a time when the white South was indifferent if not hostile to the aspirations of African-Americans, Bethune faced extraordinary obstacles. When she began a little school at Daytona Beach, Florida, in 1904, America was entering an era of reform. Yet even most northern progressives—with the notable exception of women such as Mary White Ovington, one of the founders of the NAACP— shared the racist assumptions of that era, believing that the future of black women, like immigrant women, lay in domestic service. Bethune had larger dreams. Because of her courage, energy, and vision, she was able to keep her school afloat with her intrepid fund-raising, guiding its growth from grammar school to high school and to what finally became an accredited four-year college. President of the institution from its founding until her resignation in 1942, she remained a trustee of Bethune-Cookman College until her death in 1955. She was an activist and held many important posts within the black community, founding such organizations as the National Association of Colored Women's Clubs and the National Council of Negro Women. A national figure as well, she served in the Roosevelt administration during the 1930s, advising the president on minority affairs. She was also involved in early efforts on behalf of the United Nations. Her many offices and honors, however, never diverted her from her primary purpose—the pursuit of full citizenship rights for all black Americans.*

*See Joyce A. Hanson, *Mary McLeod Bethune and Black Women's Political Activism* (Columbia: University of Missouri Press, 2003).

Excerpted from "Faith That Moved a Dump Heap" by Mary McLeod Bethune, in *Who, The Magazine about People* 1, no. 3 (June 1941): 31–35, 54.

Soon after opening the Daytona Educational and Industrial Institute for Negro Girls, its founder, Mary McLeod Bethune, posed with pupils lining the road leading to its first Daytona Beach building—a four-room cottage. One of the fields nearby, nicknamed Hell's Hole, would soon be purchased by Bethune as the foundation of a genuine campus. At the time, Florida's handful of state-supported public "high" schools for blacks operated only five months a year, in contrast to nine for whites' schools. Bethune, a tireless fundraiser, chose Daytona Beach, despite the fact that it was home to a Ku Klux Klan chapter, because of two primary factors: it had a fast-growing black population attracted by relatively good jobs, and its wealthy whites, both year-round and summer residents, included some who supported her efforts. (Courtesy of the State Archives of Florida.)

On October 3, 1904, I opened the doors of my school, with an enrollment of five little girls, aged from eight to twelve, whose parents paid me fifty cents' weekly tuition. My own child was the only boy in the school. Though I hadn't a penny left, I considered cash money as the smallest part of my resources. I had faith in a living God, faith in myself, and a desire to serve. . . .

We burned logs and used the charred splinters as pencils, and mashed elderberries for ink. I begged strangers for a broom, a lamp, a bit of cretonne to put around the packing case which served as my desk. I haunted the city dump and the trash piles behind hotels, retrieving discarded linen and kitchenware, cracked dishes, broken chairs, pieces of old lumber. Everything was scoured and mended. This was part of the training to salvage, to reconstruct, to

make bricks without straw. As parents began gradually to leave their children overnight, I had to provide sleeping accommodations. I took corn sacks for mattresses. Then I picked Spanish moss from trees, dried and cured it, and used it as a substitute for mattress hair.

The school expanded fast. In less than two years I had 250 pupils. In desperation I hired a large hall next to my original little cottage, and used it as a combined dormitory and classroom. I concentrated more and more on girls, as I felt they especially were hampered by lack of educational opportunities. . . .

I had many volunteer workers and a few regular teachers, who were paid from fifteen to twenty-five dollars a month and board. I was supposed to keep the balance of the funds for my own pocket, but there was never any balance—only a yawning hole. I wore old clothes sent me by mission boards, recut and redesigned for me in our dress-making classes. At last I saw that our only solution was to stop renting space, and to buy and build our own college.

Near by was a field, popularly called Hell's Hole, which was used as a dumping ground. I approached the owner, determined to buy it. The price was $250. In a daze, he finally agreed to take five dollars down, and the balance in two years. I promised to be back in a few days with the initial payment. He never knew it, but I didn't have five dollars. I raised this sum selling ice cream and sweet-potato pies to the workmen on construction jobs, and I took the owner his money in small change wrapped in my handkerchief.

That's how the Bethune-Cookman college campus started. . . .

As the school expanded, whenever I saw a need for some training or service we did not supply, I schemed to add it to our curriculum. Sometimes that took years. When I came to Florida, there were no hospitals where a Negro could go. A student became critically ill with appendicitis, so I went to a local hospital and begged a white physician to take her in and operate. My pleas were so desperate he finally agreed. A few days after the operation, I visited my pupil.

When I appeared at the front door of the hospital, the nurse ordered me around to the back way. I thrust her aside—and found my little girl segregated in a corner of the porch behind the kitchen. Even my toes clenched with rage.

That decided me. I called on three of my faithful friends, asking them to buy a little cottage behind our school as a hospital. They agreed, and we started with two beds.

From this humble start grew a fully equipped twenty-bed hospital—our college infirmary and a refuge for the needy throughout the state. It was staffed by white and black physicians and by our own student nurses. We ran this hospital for twenty years as part of our contribution to community life; but a short time ago, to ease our financial burden, the city took it over.

Gradually, as educational facilities expanded and there were other places where small children could go, we put the emphasis on high-school and junior-college training. In 1922, Cookman College, a men's school, the first in the state for the higher education of Negroes, amalgamated with us. The combined coeducational college, now run under the auspices of the Methodist Episcopal Church, is called Bethune-Cookman College. We have fourteen modern buildings, a beautiful campus of thirty-two acres, an enrollment in regular and summer sessions of 600 students, a faculty and staff of thirty-two, and 1,800 graduates. The college property, now valued at more than $800,000, is entirely unencumbered.

When I walk through the campus, with its stately palms and well-kept lawns, and think back to the dump-heap foundation, I rub my eyes and pinch myself. And I remember my childish visions in the cotton fields.

But values cannot be calculated in ledger figures and property. More than all else the college has fulfilled my ideals of distinctive training and service. Extending far beyond the immediate sphere of its graduates and students, it has already enriched the lives of 100,000 Negroes.

In 1934, President Franklin D. Roosevelt appointed me director of the division of Negro affairs of the National Youth Administration. My main task now is to supervise the training provided for 600,000 Negro children, and I have to run the college by remote control. Every few weeks, however, I snatch a day or so and return to my beloved home.

This is a strenuous program. The doctor shakes his head and says, "Mrs. Bethune, slow down a little. Relax! Take it just a little easier." I promise to reform, but in an hour the promise is forgotten.

For I am my mother's daughter, and the drums of Africa still beat in my heart. They will not let me rest while there is a single Negro boy or girl without a chance to prove his worth.

WOMEN IN THE WEST

PEGGY PASCOE
Ophelia Paquet, a Tillamook of Oregon, Challenges Miscegenation Laws

When Ophelia Paquet's husband died in 1919, the county court recognized her as his widow—the Paquets had been married for thirty years—and appointed Ophelia to administer his estate. As there were no children, Ophelia stood to inherit her late husband's property. It was a just arrangement inasmuch as it was her money that had been used to purchase the land and pay taxes on it. John Paquet, Fred's disreputable brother, thought otherwise. Ultimately the court awarded the estate to him, leaving the sixty-five-year-old widow destitute.

Ophelia's story is a complicated one. It illuminates many issues: the purpose of miscegenation laws, the role of marriage in the transmission of property, the "invisibility" of married women's economic contributions, and the way race can compound gender disadvantage.

In what respects does John Paquet's victory illuminate the convergence of race and class? What parallels does Pascoe draw between the Paquet case and contemporary debates over same-sex marriage? How is the failure to count Ophelia's economic contribution to the marriage related to the "pastoralization" of housework that Jeanne Boydston discusses on pages 128–139?

Although miscegenation laws are usually remembered (when they are remembered at all) as a Southern development aimed at African Americans, they were actually a much broader phenomenon. Adopted in both the North and the South in the colonial period and extended to western states in the nineteenth century, miscegenation laws grew up with slavery but became even more significant after the Civil War, for it was then that they came to form the crucial "bottom line" of the system of white supremacy embodied in segregation.

The earliest miscegenation laws, passed in the South, forbade whites to marry African Americans, but the list of groups prohibited from marrying whites was gradually expanded, especially in western states, by adding first American Indians, then Chinese and Japanese (both often referred to by the catchall term "Mongolians"), and then Malays (or Filipinos). And even this didn't exhaust the list. Oregon prohibited whites from marrying "Kanakas" (or native Hawaiians); South Dakota proscribed "Coreans"; Arizona singled out Hindus; and

From "On the Significance of Miscegenation Law in United State History," in *New Viewpoints in Women's History: Working Papers from the Schlesinger Library 50th Anniversary Conference, March 4–5, 1994,* ed. Susan Ware (Cambridge, Mass.: Arthur and Elizabeth Schlesinger Library on the History of Women in America, Radcliffe College, [1994]). Condensed and reprinted by permission of the author. Notes have been renumbered and edited. We mourn Peggy Pascoe's death on July 23, 2010. For Estelle Freedman's remembrance, see http://www.historians.org/publications-and-directories/perspectives-on-history/november-2010/in-memoriam-peggy-pascoe.

Georgia prohibited whites from marrying "West" and "Asiatic" Indians.

Many states packed their miscegenation laws with multiple categories and quasi-mathematical definitions of "race." Oregon, for example, declared that "it shall not be lawful within this state for any white person, male or female, to intermarry with any negro, Chinese, or any person having one fourth or more negro, Chinese, or Kanaka blood, or any person having more than one half Indian blood." Altogether, miscegenation laws covered forty-one states and colonies. They spanned three centuries of American history: the first ones were enacted in the 1660s, and the last ones were not declared unconstitutional until 1967.

Although it is their sexual taboos that have attracted most recent attention, the structure and function of miscegenation laws were . . . more fundamentally related to the institution of marriage than to sexual behavior itself. In sheer numbers, many more laws prohibited interracial marriage than interracial sex. And in an even deeper sense, all miscegenation laws were designed to privilege marriage as a social and economic unit. Couples who challenged the laws knew that the right to marry translated into social respectability and economic benefits, including inheritance rights and legitimacy for children, that were denied to sexual liaisons outside marriage. Miscegenation laws were designed to patrol this border by making so-called "miscegenous marriage" a legal impossibility. Thus criminal courts treated offenders as if they had never been married at all; that is, prosecutors charged interracial couples with the moral offense of fornication or other illicit sex crimes, then denied them the use of marriage as a defense.

Civil courts guarded the junction between marriage and economic privilege. From Reconstruction to the 1930s, most miscegenation cases heard in civil courts were ex post facto attempts to invalidate relationships that had already lasted for a long time. They were brought by relatives or, sometimes, by the state, after the death of one partner, almost always a white man. Many of them were specifically designed to take property or inheritances away from the surviving partner, almost always an African American or American Indian woman. By looking at civil law suits like these (which were, at least in appeals court records, more common than criminal cases), we can begin to trace the links between white patriarchal privilege and property that sustained miscegenation laws.

Let me illustrate the point by describing [a] sample case, *In re Paquet's Estate*, decided by the Oregon Supreme Court in 1921.[1] The Paquet case, like most of the civil miscegenation cases of this period, was fought over the estate of a white man. The man in question, Fred Paquet, died in 1919, survived by his 63-year-old Tillamook Indian wife, named Ophelia. The Paquet estate included 22 acres of land, some farm animals, tools, and a buggy, altogether worth perhaps $2500.[2] Fred and Ophelia's relationship had a long history. In the 1880s, Fred had already begun to visit Ophelia frequently and openly enough that he had become one of many targets of a local grand jury which periodically threatened to indict white men who lived with Indian women.[3] Seeking to formalize the relationship—and, presumably, end this harrassment—Fred consulted a lawyer, who advised him to make sure to hold a ceremony which would meet the legal requirements for an "Indian custom" marriage. Accordingly, in 1889, Fred not only reached the customary agreement with Ophelia's Tillamook relatives, paying them $50 in gifts, but also sought the formal sanction of Tillamook tribal chief Betsy Fuller (who was herself married to a white man); Fuller arranged for a tribal council to consider and confirm the marriage.[4] Afterwards Fred and Ophelia lived together until his death, for more than thirty years. Fred clearly considered Ophelia his wife, and his neighbors, too, recognized their relationship, but because Fred died without leaving a formal will, administration of the estate was subject to state laws which provided for the distribution of property to surviving family members.

When Fred Paquet died, the county court recognized Ophelia as his widow and promptly appointed her administrator of the estate. Because the couple had no children, all the property, including the land, which Ophelia lived on and the Paquets had owned for more than two decades, would ordinarily have gone to her. Two days later, though, Fred's brother John came forward to contest Ophelia for control over the property.[5] John Paquet had little to recommend him to the court. Some of his neighbors accused him of raping native women, and he had such an unsavory reputation in the community that at one point the county judge declared him "a man of immoral habits ... incompetent to transact ordinary business affairs and generally untrustworthy."[6] He was, however, a "white" man, and under Oregon's miscegenation law, that was enough to ensure that he won his case against Ophelia, an Indian woman.

The case eventually ended up in the Oregon Supreme Court. In making its decision, the key issue for the court was whether or not to recognize Fred and Ophelia's marriage, which violated Oregon's miscegenation law.[7] The Court listened to—and then dismissed—Ophelia's argument that the marriage met the requirements for an Indian custom marriage and so should have been recognized as valid out of routine courtesy to the authority of another jurisdiction (that of the Tillamook tribe).[8] The Court also heard and dismissed Ophelia's claim that Oregon's miscegenation law discriminated against Indians and was therefore an unconstitutional denial of the Fourteenth Amendment guarantee of equal protection. The Court ingenuously explained its reasoning; it held that the Oregon miscegenation law did not discriminate because it "applied alike to all persons, either white, negroes, Chinese, Kanaka, or Indians."[9] Following this logic, the Court declared Fred and Ophelia's marriage void because it violated Oregon's miscegenation law; it ordered that the estate and all its property be transferred to "the only relative in the state," John Paquet, to be distributed among him, his siblings and their heirs.[10]

As the Paquet case demonstrates, miscegenation law did not always prevent the formation of interracial relationships, sexual or otherwise. Fred and Ophelia had, after all, lived together for more than thirty years and had apparently won recognition as a couple from many of those around them; their perseverance had even allowed them to elude grand jury crackdowns. They did not, however, manage to escape the really crucial power of miscegenation law: the role it played in connecting white supremacy to the transmission of property. In American law, marriage provided the glue which allowed for the transmission of property from husbands to wives and their children; miscegenation law kept property within racial boundaries by invalidating marriages between white men and women of color whenever ancillary white relatives like John Paquet contested them.[11] ... Property, so often described in legal sources as simple economic assets (like land and capital) was

actually a much more expansive phenomenon, one which took various forms and structured crucial relationships. ... Race is in and of itself a kind of property.[12] As [legal scholar] Derrick Bell ... explains, most whites did—and still do—"expect the society to recognize an unspoken but no less vested property right in their 'whiteness.'" "This right," Bell maintains, "is recognized and upheld by courts and the society like all property rights under a government created and sustained primarily for that purpose."[13]

As applied to the Paquet case, this theme is easy to trace, for, in a sense, the victorious John Paquet had turned his "whiteness" (the best—and perhaps the only—asset he had) into property, and did so at Ophelia's expense. This transformation happened not once but repeatedly. One instance occurred shortly after the county judge had branded John Paquet immoral and unreliable. Dismissing these charges as the opinions of "a few scalawags and Garibaldi Indians," John Paquet's lawyers rallied enough white witnesses who would speak in his defense to mount an appeal which convinced a circuit court judge to declare Paquet competent to administer the estate.[14] Another example of the transformation of "whiteness" into property came when the Oregon Supreme Court ruled that Ophelia Paquet's "Indianness" disqualified her from legal marriage to a white man; with Ophelia thus out of the way, John and his siblings won the right to inherit the property.

The second property relationship [is] illuminated by the etymological connection between the words "property" and "propriety." Miscegenation law played on this connection by drawing a sharp line between "legitimate marriage" on the one hand and "illicit sex" on the other, then defining all interracial relationships as illicit sex. The distinction was a crucial one, for husbands were legally obligated to provide for legitimate wives and children, but men owed nothing to "mere" sexual partners: neither inheritance rights nor the legitimacy of children accompanied illicit relationships.

By defining all interracial relationships as illicit, miscegenation law did not so much prohibit or punish illicit sex as it did create and reproduce it. Conditioned by stereotypes which associated women of color with hypersexuality, judges routinely branded long-term settled relationships as "mere" sex rather than marriage. Lawyers played to these assumptions by reducing interracial relationships to inter-racial sex, then distinguishing interracial sex from marriage by associating it with prostitution. Describing the relationship between Fred and Ophelia Paquet, for example, John Paquet's lawyers claimed that "the alleged 'marriage' was a mere commercial affair" that did not deserve legal recognition because "the relations were entirely meretricious from their inception."[15]

It was all but impossible for women of color to escape the legacy of these associations. Ophelia Paquet's lawyers tried to find a way out by changing the subject. Rather than refuting the association between women of color and illicit sexuality, they highlighted its flip side, the supposed connection between white women and legitimate marriage. Ophelia Paquet, they told the judge, "had been to the man as good a wife as any white woman could have been."[16] In its final decision, the Oregon Supreme Court came as close as any court of that time did to accepting this line of argument. Taking the unusual step of admitting that "the record is conclusive that [Ophelia] lived with [Fred] as a good and faithful wife for more than 30 years," the judges admitted that they felt some sympathy for Ophelia, enough to recommend—but not require—that John Paquet offer her what they called "a fair and reasonable settlement."[17] But in the Paquet case, as in other miscegenation cases, sexual morality, important as it was, was nonetheless still subordinate to channelling the transmission of property along racial . . . lines. Ophelia got a judicial pat on the head for good behavior, but John and his siblings got the property.

Which brings me to the third form of property relationship structured by miscegenation laws—and, for that matter, marriage laws in general—and that is women's economic dependence on men. Here the problems started long before the final decision gave John Paquet control of the Paquet estate. One of the most intriguing facts about the Paquet case is that everyone acted as if the estate in question belonged solely to Fred Paquet. In fact, however, throughout the Paquet marriage, Fred had whiled away most of his time; it was Ophelia's basket-making, fruit-picking, milk-selling, and wage work that had provided the income they needed to sustain themselves. And although the deed to their land was made out in Fred Paquet's name, the couple had used Ophelia's earnings, combined with her proceeds from

government payments to Tillamook tribal members, both to purchase the property and to pay the yearly taxes on it. It is significant . . . that, although lawyers on both sides of the case knew this, neither they nor the Oregon Supreme Court judges considered it a key issue at the trial in which Ophelia lost all legal right to what the courts considered "Fred's" estate.

Indeed, Ophelia's economic contribution might never have been taken into account if it were not for the fact that in the wake of the Oregon Supreme Court decision, United States Indian officials found themselves responsible for the care of the now impoverished Ophelia. Apparently hoping both to defend Ophelia and to relieve themselves of the burden of her support, they sued John Paquet on Ophelia's behalf. Working through the federal courts that covered Indian relations and equity claims, rather than the state courts that enforced miscegenation laws, they eventually won a partial settlement. Yet their argument, too, reflected the assumption that men were better suited than women to the ownership of what the legal system referred to as "real" property. Although their brief claimed that "Fred Paquet had practically no income aside from the income he received through the labor and efforts of the said Ophelia Paquet," they asked the Court to grant Ophelia the right to only half of the Paquet land.[18] In the end, the Court ordered that Ophelia should receive a cash settlement (the amount was figured at half the value of the land), but only if she agreed to make her award contingent on its sale.[19] To get any settlement at all, Ophelia Paquet had to relinquish all claims to actual ownership of the land, although such a claim might have given her legal grounds to prevent its sale and so allow her to spend her final years on the property.

It is not even clear that she received any payment on the settlement ordered by the court. As late as 1928, John Paquet's major creditor complained to a judge that Paquet had repeatedly turned down acceptable offers to sell the land; perhaps he had chosen to live on it himself.[20]

Like any single example, the Paquet case captures miscegenation law as it stood at one moment, and a very particular moment at that, one that might be considered the high water mark of American courts' determination to structure both family formation and property transmission along racial dividing lines.

Today, most Americans have trouble remembering that miscegenation laws ever existed ... [and] are incredulous at the injustice and the arbitrariness of the racial classifications that stand out in [such] ... cases. [Yet] few ... notice that one of the themes raised in the Paquet case—the significance of marriage in structuring property transmission—not only remains alive and well, but has, in fact, outlived both the erosion of traditional patriarchy and the rise and fall of racial classifications in marriage law.

More than a generation after the demise of miscegenation laws ... the drawing of exclusionary lines around marriage [continues]. ... The most prominent—though hardly the only—victims are lesbian and gay couples, who point out that the sex classifications currently embedded in marriage law operate in much the same way that the race classifications embedded in miscegenation laws once did: that is, they allow courts to categorize same-sex relationships as illicit sex rather than legitimate marriage and they allow courts to exclude same-sex couples from the property benefits of marriage, which now include everything from tax advantages to medical insurance coverage.

Both these modern legal battles and the earlier ones fought by couples like Fred and Ophelia Paquet suggest ... that focusing on the connections between property and the political economy of marriage ... offer a revealing vantage point from which to study both the form and power of analogies between race and sex classifications in American law and the relationships between race and gender hierarchies in American history.

Notes

1. The Paquet case can be followed not only by reading the text of the appeals court decision, In re Paquet's Estate, 200 P 911 (Oregon 1921), but also in the following archival case files: *Paquet v. Paquet*, file No. 4268, Oregon Supreme Court, 1920; *Paquet v. Henkle*, file No. 4267, Oregon Supreme Court, 1920; and Tillamook County Probate file #605, all in the Oregon State Archives; and in *U.S. v. John B. Paquet*, Judgment Roll 11409, Register No. 8-8665, March 1925, National Archives and Records Administration, Pacific Northwest Branch.

2. Initial estimates of the value of the estate were much higher, ranging from $4500 to $12,500. I have relied on the figure of $2528.50 provided by court-appointed assessors. See Tillamook Country Probate file #605, Inventory and Appraisement, June 15, 1920.

3. *Paquet v. Paquet*, Respondent's brief, November 1, 1920, pp. 2–5.

4. Tillamook County Probate file #605, Judge A.M. Hare, Findings of Facts and Conclusions of Law, February 3, 1920; *Paquet v. Paquet*, Appellants Abstract of Record, September 3, 1920, pp. 10–16.

5. *Paquet v. Paquet*, Appellants Abstract of Record, September 3, 1920, p. 3.

6. Tillamook County Probate file #605, Judge A. M. Hare, Findings of Fact and Conclusions of Law, February 3, 1920.

7. Court records identify Fred Paquet as being of French Canadian origin. Both sides agreed that Fred was a "pure" or "full-blooded" "white" man and Ophelia was a "pure" or "full-blooded" "Indian" woman. *Paquet* v. *Paquet*, Appellant's First Brief, October 8, 1920, p. 1; *Paquet v. Paquet*; Respondent's brief, November 1, 1920, p. 2.

8. The question of legal jurisdiction over Indian tribes was—and is—a very thorny issue. Relations with Indians were generally a responsibility of the U.S. federal government, which, although it advocated assimilating Indian families into white middle-class molds, had little practical choice but to grant general recognition to tribally-determined marriages performed according to Indian custom. In the U.S. legal system, however, jurisdiction over marriage rested with the states rather than the federal government. States could, therefore, use their control over marriage as a wedge to exert some power over Indians by claiming that Indian-white marriages, especially those performed outside recognized reservations, were subject to state jurisdiction. In the Paquet case, for example, the court insisted that, because the Tillamook had never been assigned to a reservation and because Fred and Ophelia lived in a mixed settlement, Ophelia could not be considered part of a recognized tribe nor a "ward" of the federal government. As events would later show, both contentions were inaccurate: Ophelia was an enrolled member of the Tillamook tribe, which was under the supervision of the Siletz Indian Agency; the federal government claimed her as "a ward of the United States." See *U.S. v. John B. Paquet*, Bill of Complaint in Equity, September 21, 1923, p. 3.

9. In re Paquet's Estate, 200 P 911 at 913 (Oregon 1921).

10. In re Paquet's Estate, 200 P 911 at 914 (Oregon 1921).

11. Although the issue did not come up in the Paquet case, ... in miscegenation cases, not only the wife but also the children might lose their legal standing, for one effect of invalidating an interracial marriage was to make the children technically illegitimate. According to the law of most states, illegitimate children automatically inherited from their mothers, but they could inherit from their fathers only if their father had taken legal steps to formally recognize or adopt them. Since plaintiffs could rarely convince judges that fathers had done so, the children of interracial marriages were often disinherited along with their mothers.

12. Derrick Bell, "Remembrances of Racism Past," in Hill and Jones, *Race in America: The Struggle for Equality* (Madison: University of Wisconsin Press, 1992), 78. See also Bell, "White Superiority in America: Its Legal Legacy, Its Economic Costs," *Villanova Law Review* 33 (1988), 767–779.

13. *Paquet v. Henkle,* Respondent's brief, March 14, 1920, p. 6; *Paquet v. Henkle,* Index to Transcript, August 25, 1920, p. 3.

14. *Paquet v. Paquet,* Respondent's brief, November 1, 1920, p. 7. Using typical imagery, they added that the Paquet relationship was "a case where a white man and a full blooded Indian woman have chosen to cohabit together illictly [sic], to agree to a relation of concubinage, which is not only a violation of the law of Oregon, but a transgression against the law of morality and the law of nature" (p. 16).

15. *Paquet v. Paquet,* Appellant's First Brief, October 8, 1920, p. 2.

16. In re Paquet's Estate, 200 P 911 at 914 (Oregon 1921).

17. *U.S. v. John B. Paquet,* Bill of Complaint in Equity, September 21, 1923, pp. 4, 6–7.

18. *U.S. v. John B. Paquet,* Stipulation, June 2, 1924; *U.S. v. John B. Paquet,* Decree, June 2, 1924.

19. Tillamook County Probate file #605, J. S. Cole, Petition, June 7, 1928. Cole was president of the Tillamook-Lincoln County Credit Association.

20. For a particularly insightful analysis of the historical connections between concepts of "race" and "family," see Liu, "Teaching the Differences among Women in a Historical Perspective," *Women's Studies International Forum* 14 (1991): 265–276.

JUDY YUNG

Unbound Feet: From China to San Francisco's Chinatown

The imbalance of men and women in the largest Chinese community on the West Coast was a source of immense frustration, especially after the Immigration Act of 1924 effectively barred Chinese wives, even those married to U.S. citizens, from entering the country. Pany Lowe, an American-born Chinese man, expressed the feelings of men: "I think most Chinese in this country like have their son go to China get married. Under this new law ... can't do this. No allowed marry white girl. Not enough American-born Chinese to go around. China only place to get wife. Not allowed to bring them back. For Chinaman, very unjust."* Although the act was amended in 1930 to allow the entry of women who had been married to U.S. citizens prior to May 26, 1924, the process of gaining entrance was lengthy, costly, and humiliating for most Chinese women. Many men, like Pany Lowe, chose to visit their wives in China rather than subject them to the ordeal of immigration.

Judy Yung's essay traces the experiences of three women from Guangdong Province who arrived in San Francisco in 1922. Two, Wong Ah So and Law Shee Low, came from impoverished villages to join their husbands in arranged marriages. Wong Ah So was in for a major surprise when she discovered her "marriage" was part of a system of enslaving women in forced prostitution to fill what was perceived to be a pressing need in a Chinese bachelor society. The third woman came from a different background with different expectations. Jane Kwong Lee was an urbanized, unmarried "new woman" who came to the

*Quoted in Judy Yung, *Unbound Feet: A Social History of Chinese Women in San Francisco* (Berkeley: University of California Press, 1995), p. 58.

United States to further her education. While she would endure many of the same gender and racial restrictions as the other two women, differences in her class and education made her experience—and the opportunities available to her—significantly different from that of other immigrant Chinese women in the 1920s.

Women's emancipation was heralded in San Francisco's Chinatown on the afternoon of November 2, 1902, when Sieh King King, an eighteen-year-old student from China and an ardent reformer, stood before a theater full of men and women and, according to newspaper accounts, "boldly condemned the slave girl system, raged at the horrors of foot-binding and, with all the vehemence of aroused youth, declared that men and women were equal and should enjoy the privileges of equals."[1] Her talk and her views on women's rights were inextricably linked with Chinese nationalism and the 1898 Reform Movement, which advocated that China emulate the West and modernize in order to throw off the yoke of foreign domination. Elevating the status of women to the extent that they could become "new women"—educated mothers and productive citizens—was part of this nationalist effort to strengthen and defend China against further encroachment.

What Sieh King King advocated on behalf of Chinese women—unbound feet, education, equal rights, and public participation—remained at the heart of social change for Chinese women for the next three decades. This was due largely to the continuous influence of nationalism and women's emancipation in China, the reform work of Protestant missionary women in Chinatown, and Chinese women's entry into the urban economy. By 1929, immigrant women had made considerable progress toward freeing themselves of social restrictions and moving into the public arena. Footbinding was no longer practiced, prostitution had been eradicated, and a substantial number of women were working outside the home, educating themselves and their daughters, and playing a more visible role in community affairs. This discussion of the lives of Chinese immigrant women from 1902, when Sieh King King introduced her feminist views in San Francisco, to 1929, the beginnings of the Great Depression, will illustrate how socioeconomic developments in China and the United States

facilitated the unbinding of their feet and of their lives.

JOURNEY TO GOLD MOUNTAIN

At the time of Sieh King King's speech, China was still suffering under the stranglehold of Western imperialism and the inept rule of the Manchus. Life for the ordinary Chinese remained disrupted; survival was precarious. Consequently, many able-bodied peasants in Southeast China continued to emigrate overseas where kinfolk had already settled. Despite the Chinese Exclusion Acts and anti-Chinese hostilities, a good number went to California, the Gold Mountain. As increased numbers of Chinese sojourners became settlers, some found the economic means by which to get married or send for their wives and children from China. American immigration laws and the process of chain migration determined that most Chinese women would continue to come from the rural villages of Guangdong Province, where traditional gender roles still prevailed. Among these women were Wong Ah So and Law Shee Low, who both emigrated as obedient daughters in 1922 to escape poverty at home. Jane Kwong Lee, who also came the same year, was among the small number of urbanized "new women" who emigrated on their own for educational reasons. Together, these three women's stories provide insights into the gender roles and immigration experiences of Chinese women in the early twentieth century.

"I was born in Guangdong Province," begins Wong Ah So's story. "My father was sometimes a sailor and sometimes he worked on the docks, for we were very poor."[2] Patriarchal cultural values often put the daughter at risk when poverty strikes: From among the five children in the family, her mother chose to betroth her, the eldest daughter, to a Gold Mountain man in exchange for a bride price of 450 Mexican dollars.

> I was 19 when this man came to my mother and said that in America there was a great deal of gold. Even if I just peeled potatoes there, he told my

mother I would earn seven or eight dollars a day, and if I was willing to do any work at all I would earn lots of money. He was a laundryman, but said he earned plenty of money. He was very nice to me, and my mother liked him, so my mother was glad to have me go with him as his wife.

Out of filial duty and economic necessity, Ah So agreed to sail to the United States with this laundryman, Huey Yow. He had a marriage certificate prepared and told her to claim him as her husband to the immigration officials in San Francisco, although as she admitted later, "I claimed to be the wife of Huey Yow, but in truth had not at any time lived with him as his wife."

In Law Shee Low's case, her family succumbed to poverty after repeated raids by roving bandits in the Chungshan District of Guangdong Province. Conditions became so bad that the family had to sell their land and give up their three servants; all four daughters had to quit school and help at home. Speaking of her arranged marriage to a Gold Mountain man, she said, "I had no choice; we were so poor. We had no food to go with rice, not even soy sauce or black bean paste. Some of our neighbors even had to go begging or sell their daughters, times were so bad. So my parents thought I would have a better future in Gold Mountain."[3] Her fiancé said he was a clothing salesman in San Francisco and a Christian. He had a minister from Canton preside over the first "modern" wedding in his village. Law was eighteen and her husband, thirty-four. Nine months after the wedding, they sailed for America.

Born in 1902 to wealthy parents of the Toishan District, Guangdong Province (her family owned land and her father and uncle were successful businessmen in Australia), Jane Kwong Lee was able to acquire a Western education in the treaty port of Canton. There she was first exposed to American ideas of democracy and women's emancipation. During her last year in school, she was swept up by the May Fourth Movement, in which students agitated for political and cultural reforms in response to continuing foreign domination. At the time of her graduation from middle school, she observed that classmates were either entering technical institutions or getting married. "I thought otherwise," she said. "I enjoyed studying and I wanted to be economically independent. In that sense, it was clear in my mind that I had to have as much formal education as possible."[4]

Although she wanted to become a doctor, medical school was out of the question, as her father's remittances from Australia could no longer support both her and her younger brother's education. Arguing that graduates trained in American colleges and universities were drawing higher salaries in China than local graduates, Jane convinced her mother to sell some of their land in order to pay her passage to the United States. She then obtained a student's visa and sailed for America, planning to earn a doctorate and return home to a prestigious academic post. Jane Kwong Lee's class background, education, and early exposure to Western ideas would lead her to a different life experience in America than Law Shee Low and Wong Ah So, who came as obedient wives from sheltered and impoverished families.

The San Francisco Chinatown that the three women came to call home was different from the slum of "filth and depravity" of bygone days. After the 1906 earthquake and fire destroyed Chinatown, Chinese community leaders seized the opportunity to create a new "Oriental City" on the original site. The new Chinatown, in stark contrast to the old, was by appearance cleaner, healthier, and more modern with its wider paved streets, brick buildings, glass-plated storefronts, and pseudo-Chinese architecture. In an effort to establish order in the community, nurture business, and protect the growing numbers of families, the merchant elite and middle-class bourgeoisie established new institutions: Chinese schools, churches, a hospital, newspapers, and a flurry of civic and political organizations. Soon after the 1911 Revolution in China, queues and footbinding were eliminated, tong wars and prostitution reduced, and more of Chinatown's residents were dressing in Western clothing and adopting democratic ideas. Arriving in San Francisco's Chinatown at this juncture in time gave immigrant women such as Wong Ah So, Law Shee Low, and Jane Kwong Lee unprecedented opportunities to become "new women" in the modern era of Chinatown.

ESCAPING "A FATE WORSE THAN DEATH"

Upon landing in America, Wong Ah So's dreams of wealth and happiness vanished when she found out that her husband, Huey

Yow, had in fact been paid $500 by a madam to procure her as a slave.

> When we first landed in San Francisco we lived in a hotel in Chinatown, a nice place, but one day, after I had been there for about two weeks, a woman came to see me. She was young, very pretty, and all dressed in silk. She told me that I was not really Huey Yow's wife, but that she had asked him to buy her a slave, that I belonged to her, and must go with her, but she would treat me well, and I could buy back my freedom, if I was willing to please, and be agreeable, and she would let me off in two years, instead of four if I did not make a fuss.

For the next year, Wong Ah So worked as a prostitute for the madam in various small towns. She was also forced to borrow $1,000 to pay off Huey Yow, who was harassing her and threatening her life. Soon after, she was sold to another madam in Fresno for $2,500. Meanwhile, her family in China continued to write her, asking for money. Even as her debts piled up and she became ill, she fulfilled her filial obligation by sending $300 home to her mother, enclosed with a letter that read in part:

> Every day I have to be treated by the doctor. My private parts pain me so that I cannot have intercourse with men. It is very hard. . . . Next year I certainly will be able to pay off all the debts. Your daughter is even more anxious than her mother to do this. Your daughter will do her part so that the world will not look down upon us.

Then one evening at a tong banquet where she was working, Wong Ah So was recognized by a friend of her father's, who sought help from the Presbyterian Mission Home on her behalf. Ten days later, she was rescued and placed in the care of Donaldina Cameron, the director of the home. As she wrote, "I don't know just how it happened because it was all very sudden. I just know that it happened. I am learning English and to weave, and I am going to send money to my mother when I can. I can't help but cry, but it is going to be better. I will do what Miss Cameron says." A year later, after learning how to read Chinese and speak English and becoming a Christian, Ah So agreed to marry Louie Kwong, a merchant in Boise, Idaho.

Wong Ah So's story harks back to the plight of the many Chinese women who were brought to the United States as prostitutes to fill a specific need in the Chinese bachelor society. By the 1920s, however, the traffic had gone underground and was on the decline due to the Chinese exclusion laws, antiprostitution legislation, and the efforts of Protestant missionaries. In 1870, the peak year of prostitution, 1,426 or 71 percent of Chinese women in San Francisco were listed as prostitutes. By 1900 the number had dropped to 339 or 16 percent; and by 1910, 92 or 7 percent. No prostitutes could be found in the 1920 census, although English- and Chinese-language newspaper accounts and the records of the Presbyterian Mission Home indicate that organized prostitution continued through the 1920s.[5]

Most well known for her rescue work in Chinatown, Donaldina Cameron was a product of the Social Gospel and Progressive movements, which sought to uplift the "uncivilized" throughout the world and eradicate political corruption and social vices in the nation's cities. Unable to work effectively among Chinatown bachelors and spurned by white prostitutes, Cameron found her calling among Chinese prostitutes and slave girls. In turn, some Chinese prostitutes, calculating their chances in an oppressive environment with few options for improvement, saw the Mission Home as a way out of their problems. Cameron made it her crusade to free them from "a fate worse than death" by first rescuing them, and then inculcating them with Christian moral values. Numerous accounts in newspapers and religious publications describe in vivid detail the dangerous raids led by Cameron, who was credited with rescuing hundreds of Chinese slave girls during her forty years of service at the Presbyterian Mission Home.[6]

Once rescued, the young women were brought back to the Mission Home to be educated, trained in the domestic arts and industrial skills, and, most importantly, indoctrinated with Victorian moral values. The goal was to regroom them to enter society as Christian women. While some women chose to return to China under Christian escort, others opted to enter companionate marriages, pursue higher education, or become missionary workers. Wong Ah So—a direct beneficiary of the efforts of Protestant missionary women—was among the last to be rescued, Christianized, and married to a Chinese Christian.

Newly-arrived Chinese women and children awaiting interrogation at the Immigration Station on Angel Island, near San Francisco, sometime after 1910. (Courtesy of California Historical Society, FN-18240.)

IMMIGRANT WIVES AS INDISPENSABLE PARTNERS

Immigrant wives like Law Shee Low also found their lives transformed by the socioeconomic conditions in Chinatown. They did not find streets paved with gold, but practically speaking, they at least had food on the table and hope that through their hard work conditions might improve for themselves and their families. Although women were confined to the domestic sphere within the borders of Chinatown, their contributions as homemakers, wage earners, and culture bearers made them indispensable partners to their husbands in their struggle for economic survival. Their indispensability, combined with changing social attitudes toward women in Chinatown, gave some women leverage to shape gender arrangements within their homes and in the community.

Upon arrival in San Francisco, Law Shee Low moved into a one-room tenement apartment in Chinatown with her husband, where she lived, worked, and gave birth to eleven children, eight of whom survived. While her husband worked in a restaurant that catered to black customers on the outskirts of Chinatown, Law stayed home and took in sewing. Like other immigrant women who followed traditional gender roles, Law believed that the proper place for a woman was at home. As she recalls those days,

> There was no time to feel imprisoned; there was so much to do. We had to cook, wash the clothes and diapers by hand, the floors, and sew whenever we had a chance to sit still. It was the same for all my neighbors. We were all good, obedient, and diligent wives. All sewed; all had six or seven children. Who had time to go out?

Fortunately for Law Shee Low, her husband turned out to be cooperative, supportive, and devoted. Until he developed a heart condition in the 1950s, he remained the chief breadwinner, first cooking at a restaurant, then picking fruit in Suisun [California], sewing at home during the depression, and finally working in the shipyards during World War II. Although he refused to help with housecleaning or childcare, he did all the shopping, cooked the rice, and hung out the wash. In his own way, he showed concern for his wife. "When he was afraid I wasn't eating, he would tell me to eat more. Even though it was an arranged marriage, we got along well. I didn't complain that he went out every day. We hardly talked. Good or bad, we just struggled along as we had work to do."

As far as children were concerned Law Shee Low, like her neighbors, had not known how to interfere with nature. "We didn't know about birth control. We would become pregnant every year without realizing it. Even if we didn't want it, we didn't have the money to go see the doctor." All of Law's children were born at home, with the help of neighbors or the local midwife. Fortunately, her husband wanted children and was more than willing to provide for them all regardless of sex. "Other men would scold their children and beat them. One woman who had four children told me her husband would drag her out of bed and beat her because she didn't want to have any more children. We heard all kinds of sad stories like that, but my husband never picked on me like that."

It was not until her children were older that Law Shee Low went out to work in the sewing factories and to the Chinese movies on Saturdays, but she still did not leave the confines of Chinatown. Prior to that, she went out so seldom that one pair of shoes lasted her ten years. Since their first responsibility was to their families, many immigrant wives like Law found themselves housebound, with no time to learn English or to participate in social activities outside the home. Their husbands continued to be the chief breadwinner, to hold the purse strings, and to be their liaison to the outside world. But in the absence of the mother-in-law, immigrant wives usually ruled the household and assumed the responsibility of disciplinarian, culture-bearer, and of maintaining the integrity of their families. With few exceptions, they were hardworking, frugal, and tolerant, faithful and respectful to their husbands, and self-sacrificing toward their children. As such, they were indispensable partners to their husbands in their efforts to establish and sustain family life in America. And although they presented a submissive image in public, many immigrant women were known to "wear the pants" at home.

Overall, as compared to their predecessors, immigrant women in the early twentieth century were less tolerant of abuses to their persons and more resourceful in upgrading their status, thanks to the influence of the press, the support of Protestant organizations in the community, and a legal system that was sympathetic toward abused women. Although most immigrant wives like Law Shee Low could not read the Chinese newspapers, they were affected by public opinion as filtered through their husbands, neighbors, and social reformers looking after their interests. Law noted that after the 1911 Revolution it was no longer considered "fashionable" to have bound feet, concubines, or slave girls. And as housebound as Law was, she was aware of the mission homes that rescued prostitutes, helped abused women, and provided education for children and immigrant women.

CHINESE WOMEN IN THE LABOR MARKET

Compared to Wong Ah So and Law Shee Low, Jane Kwong Lee had an easier time acclimating to life in America. Not only was she educated, Westernized, English-speaking, and unencumbered by family responsibilities, but she also had the help of affluent relatives who provided her with room and board, financial support, and important contacts that enabled her eventually to strike out on her own.

Arriving in the middle of a school semester and therefore unable to enroll in a college, she decided to look for a job. In spite of her educational background and qualifications, she found that only menial jobs and domestic service were opened to her. "At heart I was sorry for myself; I wished I were a boy," she wrote in her autobiography. "If I were a boy, I could have gone out into the community, finding a job somewhere as many newcomers from China had done." But as a Chinese woman, she had to bide her time and look for work appropriate for her race and gender. Thus, until she could be admitted to college, and during the summers after she enrolled at Mills College, Jane took whatever jobs were open to Chinese women. She tried embroidery work at a Chinatown factory, sorting vegetables in the wholesale district, working as a live-in domestic for a white family, peeling shrimp, sorting fruit at a local cannery, and sewing flannel nightgowns at home.

As was true for European immigrant women, the patterns of work for Chinese women were shaped by the intersection of the local economy, ethnic traditions, language and job skills, and family and child-care needs, but in addition, race was an influential factor. At the time of Jane's arrival, San Francisco was experiencing a period of growth and prosperity. Ranked the eighth largest city in the country, it was the major port of trade for the Pacific Coast and touted as the financial and corporate capital of the West. Jobs were plentiful in the city's three largest economic sectors—domestic and personal service, trade and transportation, and manufacturing and mechanical industries—but they were filled according to a labor market stratified by race and gender, with Chinese men occupying the lowest tier as laborers, servants, factory workers, laundrymen, and small merchants, while Chinese women, handicapped further by gender, worked primarily in garment and food-processing factories for low piece-rate wages. With inadequate child-care services in the community, most seamstresses worked with their children close by or had their babies strapped to their backs.

For Jane Kwong Lee, being Chinese and a woman was a liability in the job market, but because she spoke English, was educated, and had good contacts among Chinese Christians, she was better off than most other immigrant women. She eventually got a scholarship at Mills College and part-time work teaching Chinese school and tutoring Chinese adults in English at the Chinese Episcopal Church in Oakland. After earning her bachelor's degree in sociology, she married, had two children, and returned to Mills College, where she received a master's degree in sociology and economics in 1933. She then dedicated herself to community service, working many years as coordinator of the Chinese YWCA and as a journalist and translator for a number of Chinatown newspapers.

For most immigrant women, joining the labor market proved to be a double-edged sword: On the one hand, their earnings helped to support their families and elevate their socioeconomic status; on the other hand, they became exploited laborers in the factory system, adding work and stress to their already burdensome lives. On the positive side, however, working outside the home offered women social rewards—a new sense of freedom, accomplishment, and camaraderie. They were no longer confined to the home, they were earning money for themselves or the family, and they were making new acquaintances and becoming exposed to new ideas. As Jane Kwong Lee observed, having money to spend made the women feel more liberated in America than in China: "They can buy things for themselves, go out to department stores to choose their own clothes instead of sewing them."

FIRST STEPS TOWARD SOCIAL ACTIVISM

For working-class women like Law Shee Low, family and work responsibilities consumed all their time and energy, leaving little left over for self-improvement or leisure activities, and even less for community involvement. This was not the case for a growing group of educated and professional women like Jane Kwong Lee, who, inspired by Christianity, Chinese nationalism, and Progressivism, took the first steps toward social activism. Prior to the 1911 Revolution in their homeland, Chinese women in America followed the tradition of remaining publicly invisible. They seldom ventured out of their homes except perhaps to shop or go to the Chinese opera, where they sat in a segregated section apart from the men.

The Protestant churches and Chinese YWCA were the first to encourage Chinese women's participation in organized activities outside the home, as evidenced by the small but visible number of them at Sunday services, English classes, meetings, outings, and other church-sponsored programs. Some of the churches also helped organize Chinese women's societies to encourage involvement in Christian activities. Members of these groups met regularly to have lunch or socialize, and paid dues to help support the work of Bible women in their home villages in China.[7]

Aside from Christianity, the intense nationalistic spirit that took hold in the early twentieth century also affected Chinese women in far-reaching ways. Not only did the call for modernization include the need to improve conditions for Chinese women, but reformers also solicited women's active participation in national salvation work. Fundraising for disaster relief and the revolution in China opened up opportunities for women to become involved in the community, develop leadership abilities, and move into the male-dominated public sphere. The Tongmenghui, the revolutionary party founded by Dr. Sun Yat-sen to overthrow the Qing dynasty and establish a republic in China, was the earliest organization to accept women into its ranks. While women in China participated in benefit performances, enlisted in the army, and engaged in dangerous undercover work, women in San Francisco also did their share for the revolutionary effort—making patriotic speeches, donating money and jewelry for the cause, and helping with Red Cross work—sometimes under the auspices of Protestant churches, other times under the banner of the Women's Young China Society.

Although the success of the revolution and the establishment of a republic in China failed to bring peace and prosperity to the country, it did have a lasting impact on the lives of Chinese American women. As Jane Kwong Lee observed, "After the establishment of the Republic of China, Chinese women in this country picked up the forward-looking trend for equality with men. They could go to school, speak in public places, have their feet free from binding, and go out to work in stores and small factories if they needed to work."[8]

Arriving as a liberated woman at the time when she did, Jane did not hesitate to join other women in becoming socially active in the Chinatown community. In her capacity as a community worker at the Chinese YWCA, she made house visits, wrote articles that were published in the local newspapers, and implemented programs that benefited Chinese women in the community. She was particularly known for her loud and forceful speeches that she delivered in Chinese at churches and street corners in support of Christianity and nationalist causes, and before Chinatown organizations on behalf of the Chinese YWCA. Jane also made presentations in English to groups interested in learning more about Chinese culture, and traveled as a Chinese delegate to YWCA functions outside of Chinatown. On one of these occasions, she was so moved by a discussion on racial discrimination that she surprised herself and African Americans at a YWCA meeting by speaking up for them. "I said, you are all equal; nobody is inferior to another."[9]

CONCLUSION

As Sieh King King had advocated in 1902, Chinese women unbound their feet and began to unbind their lives in America during the first three decades of the twentieth century. Most, like Law Shee Low and Wong Ah So, had immigrated for a better livelihood but found themselves exploited as prostitutes or working wives at the bottom of a labor market stratified by race and gender. Some, like Jane Kwong Lee, had come from a privileged background yet still encountered discrimination in the workplace and in the larger American society. But like many other immigrant women before them, they not only persevered and survived, but took advantage of new circumstances to improve their lives and contribute to the well-being of their families and community. Even as immigrant women began to enjoy their new roles as emancipated women, economic depression set in and war loomed large in their homeland. The challenges of the 1930s and 1940s—economic survival and the war effort on two fronts—would lead to even greater dramatic changes in their lives, allowing them to take the first steps toward fuller participation in American society.

NOTES

1. *San Francisco Chronicle,* November 3, 1902, p. 7.

2. Wong Ah So's story is taken from "Story of Wong Ah So—Experiences as a Prostitute," *Orientals and Their Cultural Adjustment,* Social Science Source Documents, no. 4 (Nashville: Social Science Institute, Fisk University, 1946), pp. 31–35; and Donaldina Cameron, "The Story of Wong So," *Women and Missions* 2, no. 5 (August 1925):169–72.

3. Law Shee Low's story is based on her interview with Sandy Lee, May 2, 1982; and interview with author, October 20, 1988.

4. Jane Kwong Lee's story is based on her unpublished autobiography, "A Chinese American," in the possession of her daughter Priscilla Holmes.

5. See Lucie Cheng Hirata, "Free, Indentured, Enslaved: Chinese Prostitutes in Nineteenth-Century California," *Signs: Journal of Women in Culture and Society* 5, no. 1 (autumn 1979):3–29. The figures for 1900, 1910, and 1920 are based on my computations from the U.S. National Archives, Record Group 29, "Census of U.S. Population" (manuscript), San Francisco, California.

6. See Peggy Pascoe, *Relations of Rescue: The Search for Female Moral Authority in the American West, 1874–1939* (New York: Oxford University Press, 1990).

7. See Wesley Woo, "Protestant Work among the Chinese in the San Francisco Bay Area, 1850–1920," Ph.D. dissertation, University of California, Berkeley, 1983.

8. Jane Kwong Lee, "Chinese Women in San Francisco," *Chinese Digest* (June 1938):8.

9. Jane Kwong Lee, interview with author, November 2, 1988.

DOCUMENT

Zitkala-Ša (Gertrude Simmons Bonnin), ". . . this semblance of civilization . . ."

Z itkala-Ša (1876–1938), whose mother was Sioux and father was Anglo-American, sought throughout her life to bridge the cultures of Native Americans and the United States. She was one of the first American Indian women who built an independent career as a writer; her voice, as the following selection from her early writing shows, could be simultaneously eloquent, sentimental, and bitter. Zitkala-Ša was eight years old when she left her home on the Yankton Sioux Agency in South Dakota for White's Indiana Manual Labor Institute in Wabash, Indiana, a training school funded by Quakers. She continued her education first at a teacher training school close to her home, then at Earlham College, and finally at the New England Conservatory of Music in Boston where she studied the violin.

After her marriage in 1901, Zitkala-Ša worked with her husband, Raymond Bonnin, who was an employee of the Bureau of Indian Affairs (BIA), advocating citizenship for Indians, exposing corruption in the BIA, and insisting on the dignity of Indian religions. In this stage of her life, she used her anglicized married name, Gertrude Simmons Bonnin. Bonnin lobbied for the Indian Citizenship Act of 1924; she founded the National Council of American Indians; and she sought to shape the Indian policy of the New Deal years.

When she wrote this memoir of her childhood in 1900 at age twenty-four, Zitkala-Ša had not yet taught at the Carlisle Indian School in Pennsylvania. The experience would strengthen her criticism of the practice of removing native children from their homes. It would also lead her to expose the corruption she found among the school's directors, who received federal money for each child they boarded and whose promotion of "Americanization" could be harsh and cruel. To what extent did her mother anticipate that the experience at the mission school would be difficult? What advantage did the educators think would result from cutting girls' hair? What evidence is there to suggest that she herself was involved in the process of acculturation? Compare Bonnin's education and geographic mobility to that of Sarah Winemucca (see Rose Stremlau's essay, pp. 227–237) and Wilma Mankiller (pp. 785–790).

The first turning away from the easy, natural flow of my life occurred in an early spring. It was in my eighth year; in the month of March, I afterward learned. At this age I knew but one language, and that was my mother's native tongue.

From some of my playmates I heard that two paleface missionaries were in our village. They were from that class of white men who wore big hats and carried large hearts, they said. Running direct to my mother, I began to question her why these two

Excerpted from "Impressions of an Indian Childhood," "The School Days of an Indian Girl," and "An Indian Teacher among Indians," by Zitkala-Ša, *Atlantic Monthly* 85 (January, February, March 1900): 45–47, 186–87, 386.

Zitkala-Ša, ca. 1898, posed in traditional dress.
This photograph is one in a series taken by the professional photographer Gertrude Käsebier, who had a studio on Fifth Avenue in New York City. In other images taken at the same sitting, Zitkala-Ša is in western dress (a white gown), and in some she holds in her lap a book, her violin, or an Indian basket. For interpretations of Käsebier's portraits of Zitkala-Ša and other Indians, see Laura Wexler, Tender Violence: Domestic Visions in an Age of U.S. Imperialism *(Chapel Hill: University of North Carolina Press, 2000), pp. 115–124, 177–208; and Elizabeth Hutchinson, "When the 'Sioux Chief's Party Calls': Käsebier's Indian Portraits and the Gendering of the Artist's Studio,"* American Art *16 (Summer 2002), 40-65. (Courtesy of the Smithsonian Institution.)*

strangers were among us. She told me, after I had teased much, that they had come to take away Indian boys and girls to the East. My mother did not seem to want me to talk about them. But in a day or two, I gleaned many wonderful stories from my playfellows concerning the strangers.

"Mother, my friend Judéwin is going home with the missionaries. She is going to a more beautiful country than ours; the palefaces told her so!" I said wistfully, wishing in my heart that I too might go.

Mother sat in a chair, and I was hanging on her knee. Within the last two seasons my big brother Dawée had returned from a three years' education in the East, and his coming back influenced my mother to take a farther step from her native way of living. First it was a change from the buffalo skin to the white man's canvas that covered our wigwam. Now she had given up her wigwam of slender poles, to live, a foreigner, in a home of clumsy logs.

Judéwin had told me of the great tree where grew red, red apples; and how we could reach out our hands and pick all the red apples we could eat. I had never seen apple trees. I had never tasted more than a dozen red apples in my life; and when I heard of the orchards of the East, I was eager to roam among them. The missionaries smiled into my eyes, and patted my head. I wondered how mother could say such hard words against them.

"Mother, ask them if little girls may have all the red apples they want, when they go East," I whispered aloud, in my excitement.

The interpreter heard me, and answered: "Yes, little girl, the nice red apples are for those who pick them; and you will have a ride on the iron horse if you go with these good people."

I had never seen a train, and he knew it.

"Mother, I'm going East! I like big red apples, and I want to ride on the iron horse! Mother, say yes!" I pleaded.

My mother said nothing. The missionaries waited in silence; and my eyes began to blur with tears, though I struggled to choke them back. The corners of my mouth twitched, and my mother saw me.

"I am not ready to give you any word," she said to them. "Tomorrow I shall send you my answer by my son."

With this they left us. Alone with my mother, I yielded to my tears, and cried aloud, shaking my head so as not to hear what she was saying to me. This was the first time I had ever been so unwilling to give up my own desire that I refused to harken to my mother's voice.

There was a solemn silence in our home that night. Before I went to bed I begged the Great Spirit to make my mother willing I should go with the missionaries.

The next morning came, and my mother called me to her side. "My daughter, do you still persist in wishing to leave your mother?" she asked.

"Oh, mother, it is not that I wish to leave you, but I want to see the wonderful Eastern land," I answered. . . .

. . . My brother Dawée came for mother's decision. I dropped my play, and crept close to my aunt.

"Yes, Dawée, my daughter, though she does not understand what it all means, is anxious to go. She will need an education when she is grown, for then there will be fewer real Dakotas, and many more palefaces. This tearing her away, so young, from her mother is necessary, if I would have her an educated woman. The palefaces, who owe us a large debt for stolen lands, have begun to pay a tardy justice in offering some education to our children. But I know my daughter must suffer keenly in this experiment. For her sake, I dread to tell you my reply to the missionaries. Go, tell them that they may take my little daughter, and that the Great Spirit shall not fail to reward them according to their hearts."

Wrapped in my heavy blanket, I walked with my mother to the carriage that was soon to take us to the iron horse. I was happy. I met my playmates, who were also wearing their best thick blankets. We showed one another our new beaded moccasins, and the width of the belts that girdled our new dresses. Soon we were being drawn rapidly away by the white man's horses. When I saw the lonely figure of my mother vanish in the distance, a sense of regret settled heavily upon me. I felt suddenly weak, as if I might fall limp to the ground. I was in the hands of strangers whom my mother did not fully trust. I no longer felt free to be myself, or to voice my own feelings. The tears trickled down my cheeks, and I buried my face in the folds of my blanket. Now the first step, parting me from my mother, was taken, and all my belated tears availed nothing.

Having driven thirty miles to the ferry-boat, we crossed the Missouri in the evening.

Then riding again a few miles eastward, we stopped before a massive brick building. I looked at it in amazement, and with a vague misgiving, for in our village I had never seen so large a house. Trembling with fear and distrust of the palefaces, my teeth chattering from the chilly ride, I crept noiselessly in my soft moccasins along the narrow hall, keeping very close to the bare wall. I was as frightened and bewildered as the captured young of a wild creature.

The first day in the land of apples was a bitter-cold one; for the snow still covered the ground, and the trees were bare. A large bell rang for breakfast, its loud metallic voice crashing through the belfry overhead and into our sensitive ears. The annoying clatter of shoes on bare floors gave us no peace. The constant clash of harsh noises, with an undercurrent of many voices murmuring an unknown tongue, made a bedlam within which I was securely tied. And though my spirit tore itself in struggling for its lost freedom, all was useless.

A paleface woman, with white hair, came up after us. We were placed in a line of girls who were marching into the dining room. These were Indian girls, in stiff shoes and closely clinging dresses. The small girls wore sleeved aprons and shingled hair. As I walked noiselessly in my soft moccasins, I felt like sinking to the floor, for my blanket had been stripped from my shoulders. I looked hard at the Indian girls, who seemed not to care that they were even more immodestly dressed than I, in their tightly fitting clothes. While we marched in, the boys entered at an opposite door. I watched for the three young braves who came in our party. I spied them in the rear ranks, looking as uncomfortable as I felt. . . .

. . . Late in the morning, my friend Judéwin gave me a terrible warning. Judéwin knew a few words of English; and she had overheard the paleface woman talk about cutting our long, heavy hair. Our mothers had taught us that only unskilled warriors who were captured had their hair shingled by the enemy. Among our people, short hair was worn by mourners, and shingled hair by cowards!

We discussed our fate some moments, and when Judéwin said, "We have to submit, because they are strong," I rebelled.

"No, I will not submit! I will struggle first!" I answered.

I watched my chance, and when no one noticed I disappeared. I crept up the stairs as quietly as I could in my squeaking shoes—my moccasins had been exchanged for shoes. Along the hall I passed, without knowing whither I was going. Turning aside to an open door, I found a large room with three white beds in it. The windows were covered with dark green curtains, which made the room very dim. Thankful that no one was there, I directed my steps toward the corner farthest from the door. On my hands and knees I crawled under the bed, and cuddled myself in the dark corner.

From my hiding place I peered out, shuddering with fear whenever I heard footsteps near by. Though in the hall loud voices were calling my name, and I knew that even Judéwin was searching for me, I did not open my mouth to answer. Then the steps were quickened and the voices became excited. The sounds came nearer and nearer. Women and girls entered the room. I held my breath, and watched them open closet doors and peep behind large trunks. Some one threw up the curtains, and the room was filled with sudden light. What caused them to stoop and look under the bed I do not know. I remember being dragged out, though I resisted by kicking and scratching wildly. In spite of myself, I was carried downstairs and tied fast in a chair.

I cried aloud, shaking my head all the while until I felt the cold blades of the scissors against my neck, and heard them gnaw off one of my thick braids. Then I lost my spirit. Since the day I was taken from my mother I had suffered extreme indignities. People had stared at me. I had been tossed about in the air like a wooden puppet. And now my long hair was shingled like a coward's! In my anguish I moaned for my mother, but no one came to comfort me. Not a soul reasoned quietly with me, as my own mother used to do; for now I was only one of many little animals driven by a herder. . . .

. . . Now, as I look back upon the recent past, I see it from a distance, as a whole. I remember how, from morning till evening, many specimens of civilized peoples visited the Indian school. The city folks with canes and eyeglasses, the countrymen with sunburnt cheeks and clumsy feet, forgot their relative social ranks in an ignorant curiosity. Both sorts of these Christian palefaces were alike astounded at seeing the children of savage warriors so docile and industrious.

As answers to their shallow inquiries they received the students' sample work to look upon. Examining the neatly figured pages, and gazing upon the Indian girls and boys bending over their books, the white visitors walked out of the schoolhouse well satisfied: They were educating the children of the red man! They were paying a liberal fee to the government employees in whose able hands lay the small forest of Indian timber.

In this fashion many have passed idly through the Indian schools during the last decade, afterward to boast of their charity to the North American Indian. But few there are who have paused to question whether real life or long-lasting death lies beneath this semblance of civilization.

CHANGE AGENTS

KATHRYN KISH SKLAR
Florence Kelley and Women's Activism in the Progressive Era

Florence Kelley was a remarkable woman who lived in a period when attempts to address the problems created by industrialization and urbanization generated both the early social sciences and the foundation of the welfare state. Kathryn Sklar, Kelley's biographer, provides in this authoritative and highly informative essay an account of a single individual that also illuminates the pursuit of social justice in which many progressive women of Kelley's generation were involved. Sklar reveals the factors that made it possible for these women to influence public policy even before they were allowed to vote. She also describes the changing political context that limited their influence following the Red Scare at the end of World War I.

What were the influences, personal and intellectual, that shaped Kelley's vision of social reform? What strategies did she employ in pursuit of that vision? What does Sklar mean when she says that Kelley used gender-specific legislation as a surrogate for class legislation? Precisely how did the Red Scare affect the political agenda of women's organizations? In what respects were at least three of the four significant features of women's power in the Progressive era that Sklar identified highly gendered? As we move into reading about the 1930s and beyond, think about which of the features persist and which do not.

One of the most powerful women in American history deserves to be better known today. Florence Kelley (1859–1932) was well known to her contemporaries as a leading champion of social justice legislation. For most of the 1890s she lived in the nation's leading reform institution, Hull House, a social settlement founded in Chicago by Jane Addams in 1889. Between 1899 and 1932 she served as head of the National Consumers' League in New York City.

Living collectively with other women reformers in Chicago and New York, Florence Kelley was able to make the most of her talents; for four decades she occupied the vanguard of social reform. Her forceful personality flourished in the combative atmosphere generated by her struggles for social justice. Jane Addams's nephew, who resided with Kelley at Hull House, was awed by the way she "hurled the spears of her thought with such apparent carelessness of what breasts they pierced." He thought her "the toughest customer in the reform riot, the finest rough-and-tumble fighter for the good life for others, that Hull House ever knew: Any weapon was a good weapon in her hand—evidence, argument, irony or invective." Nevertheless, he said, those who were close to her knew she was "full of love."[1]

Kelley's career, like that of many of her reform contemporaries, was responding to

Written expressly for *Women's America*. A revised version of this essay appears in Rima Lunin Schultz and Adele Hast, eds., *Women Building Chicago, 1790–1990: A Biographical Dictionary* (Bloomington: Indiana University Press, 2001.) Copyright © by Kathryn Kish Sklar.

profound changes in American social and economic life. Rapid industrialization was recasting the economy, massive immigration was reconstituting the working class, and sustained urbanization was making cities the focus of social change.[2] In this context, college-educated women reformers often achieved what men and male-dominated organizations could not.

Florence Kelley's life helps us understand how women reformers accomplished their goals. Her reform career exemplified four significant features of women's power in the Progressive era: their access to higher education; their prominence in early social science; the political autonomy of their separate institutions; and their ability to challenge American traditions of limited government. Having experienced these ingredients of women's power in her own life before 1899, thereafter, as the General Secretary of the National Consumers' League, she integrated them into her strategies for pursuing social justice.[3]

WOMEN'S ACCESS
TO HIGHER EDUCATION

When she graduated from Cornell University in 1882, Florence Kelley joined thousands of other young women in her generation who received college educations. Two changes in the 1860s and 1870s enabled white, middle-class women to attend college in sufficient numbers to become a sociological phenomenon. Elite women's colleges, such as Vassar, Smith, and Wellesley, began accepting students between 1865 and 1875, providing equivalents to elite men's colleges such as Harvard, Yale, and Princeton. And state universities, established through the allocation of public lands in the Morrill Act of 1862 and required to be "open for all," gradually made college educations accessible for the first time to large numbers of women in the nation's central and western states. By 1880 women, numbering forty thousand, constituted 33 percent of all enrolled students in higher education.[4] Though a small percentage of all women, they exercised an influence disproportionate to their numbers.

To Cornell Kelley brought a social conscience shaped by her family. Born into an elite Philadelphia family with Quaker and Unitarian political traditions, she grew up against the background of the Civil War and Reconstruction—dramas in which her father and her mother's aunt played major roles. Her father,

William Durrah Kelley, one of the founders of the Republican Party, was reelected to fifteen consecutive terms in the U.S. Congress between 1860 and 1890. As a Radical Republican, he advanced the cause of black suffrage and tried to forge a biracial Republican Party in the South. Her mother's aunt, Sarah Pugh, served as president of the Philadelphia Female Anti-Slavery Society almost every year between 1838 and 1870. In the 1860s and 1870s, Pugh accompanied her close friend, Lucretia Mott, to early woman suffrage conventions. To young "Florrie," Sarah Pugh was conscience incarnate, a full-time reformer who lived her beliefs, never wearing slave-made cotton or eating slave-produced sugar.[5]

During six mostly schoolless years before she entered Cornell, Florence systematically read through her father's library, imbibing the fiction of Dickens and Thackeray, Louisa May Alcott and Horatio Alger; the poetry of Shakespeare, Milton, Byron, and Goldsmith; the writings of James Madison; histories by Bancroft, Prescott, and Parkman; and the moral and political philosophy of Emerson, Channing, Burke, Carlyle, Godwin, and Spencer. These readings helped her reach out to her moody and distant father. For that purpose she also began reading government reports at the age of ten and, on trips to Washington, began using the Library of Congress by the time she was twelve.

A darker side of Kelley's childhood was shaped by her mother's permanent depression—caused by the death of five of her eight children before they had reached the age of six. Caroline Bonsall Kelley was a descendant of John Bartram, the Quaker botanist. Orphaned at the age of nine, she was raised in the Pugh family. With the death of her infants, Caroline developed a "settled, gentle melancholy" that threatened to envelop her daughter as long as she lived at home.[6] Florence grew up with two brothers, but no sisters survived. Keenly aware of the high social cost of infant mortality to nineteenth-century families, she developed a rage against human suffering that formed her lifelong career as a reformer.

WOMEN'S PROMINENCE
IN EARLY SOCIAL SCIENCE

Like higher education, the newly emerging field of social science served as a critical vehicle by which middle-class women expanded the space they occupied within American civic life between 1860 and 1890. Social science leveled the playing field on which women interacted with men in public life. It offered tools of analysis that enhanced women's ability to investigate economic and social change, speak for the welfare of the whole society, devise policy initiatives, and oversee their implementation. Yet at the same time, social science also deepened women's gender identity in public life and attached their civic activism even more securely to gender-specific issues.[7]

Kelley's early commitment to social science as a tool for social reform built on a generation of women's presence in American social science. Women came with the civic territory that social science embraced. Caroline Dall had been a cofounder of the association in 1865, and other women were especially active in the American Social Science Association's (ASSA) department of education, public health, and social economy, which gave them clear but limited mandates for leadership.

The question of "After college, what?" was as pertinent to Florence Kelley as it was to other women graduates.[8] Barred from admission to graduate study at the University of Pennsylvania because she was a woman, she faced a very limited set of opportunities. First she threw her energies into the New Century Working Women's Guild, an organization that fostered middle-class aid for self-supporting women. She helped found the Guild, taught classes in history, and assembled the group's library. Then, remaining a dutiful daughter, in 1882 she accompanied her brother when his doctor prescribed a winter of European travel to cure temporary blindness. In Europe she encountered M. Carey Thomas, a Cornell acquaintance, who had just completed a Ph.D. at the University of Zurich, the only European university that granted degrees to women. Thomas recommended that Kelley go to Zurich for graduate study.

Initially accompanied by her mother and younger brother, Kelley studied government and law at Zurich between 1883 and 1886. There she promptly befriended exiled socialist students from Russia and Germany. To the shocked amazement of her family and friends, in 1885 she married Lazare Wischnewetzky, a Russian, Jewish, socialist, medical student. She then gave birth to three children in three years.

Cloaked with her new personal identity as a European married woman, she stopped communicating with her family and began to forge a new political identity. Rejecting American public culture because it limited her opportunities for social service and because her father's career revealed so starkly that culture's tolerance of social injustice, she underwent a dramatic conversion to socialism, joined the German Social Democratic Party (SPD), and began to translate the writings of Friedrich Engels and Karl Marx. Outlawed in Germany, the SPD maintained its European headquarters in Zurich, where Kelley met many of its leaders. Since the death of Marx in 1885, Engels had become the chief theoretician of German socialism. Kelley's translation of his 1845 book, *The Condition of the Working Class in England*, is still the preferred scholarly version of that now-classic social science study. This project launched a close but troubled relationship with Engels that persisted until his death in 1895.[9]

When Kelley returned to the United States in 1886 with her small family, she searched without success for a political context capable of sustaining her newfound radicalism. Settling in New York City, within a year she was expelled from the Socialist Labor Party, predominantly a German-speaking immigrant group, for "incessant slander" against party leaders, whom she denounced for failing to recognize the importance of the writings of Marx and Engels.[10] Having reached a political dead-end, Kelley reoriented her use of social science as a vehicle for her activism. She resumed contact with her Philadelphia family and became a self-taught authority on child labor in the United States, as well as a sharp critic of state bureaus of labor, the agencies responsible for monitoring child labor. Writing articles on child labor that deployed both statistical and rhetorical power, she discovered that her most responsive publisher was the Woman's Temperance Publication Association, which printed her lengthy, hard-hitting pamphlet, *Our Toiling Children*, in 1889.

Lazare Wischnewetzky, meanwhile, never having managed to establish a medical practice, began battering her. After enduring this for more than a year, she borrowed money from a friend and fled with her children to Chicago. There she headed for the Woman's Temple, a twelve-story office building and hotel constructed by the Woman's Christian Temperance Union, where she was directed to an even more congenial place—Hull House, the nation's preeminent social settlement founded by Jane Addams and Ellen Gates Starr in 1889.

THE POLITICAL AUTONOMY OF WOMEN'S SEPARATE INSTITUTIONS

"We were welcomed as though we had been invited," Kelley later wrote about her arrival at Hull House. "We stayed."[11] Addams arranged for Kelley's children, Nicholas, Margaret, and John, age seven, six, and five, to live with the family of Henry Demarest Lloyd and his wife, Jessie Bross Lloyd. That winter Kelley cast her lot with Addams and Hull House, remaining until May 1, 1899, when she returned to New York as a figure who had achieved national renown as a reformer of working conditions for women and children.

Chicago and the remarkable political culture of the city's women opened opportunities to Kelley that she had sought in vain in Philadelphia, Germany, and New York. Exploiting those opportunities to the fullest, she drew on the strength of three overlapping circles of politically active women. The core of her support lay with the community of women at Hull House. This remarkable group helped her reconstruct her political identity within women's class-bridging activism, and provided her with an economic and emotional alternative to married family life. Partly overlapping with this nucleus were women trade unionists. By drawing women and men trade unionists into the settlement community, she achieved the passage of pathbreaking legislation. Toward the end of her years in Chicago, she worked with the circle of middle-class and upper-middle-class women who supported Hull House and labor reform.

Florence Kelley's life in Chicago began with her relationship with Jane Addams. Julia Lathrop, another Hull House resident, reported that Kelley and Addams "understood each other's powers" instantly and worked together in a "wonderfully effective way."[12] Addams, the philosopher with a deep appreciation of the unity of life, was better able to construct a vehicle for expressing that unity in day-to-day living than she was capable of devising a diagram for charting the future. And Kelley, the politician with a thorough understanding of what the future should look like, was better able to invoke that future than to express it in her day-to-day existence. Addams

taught Kelley how to live and have faith in an imperfect world, and Kelley taught Addams how to make demands on the future.

At Hull House Kelley joined a community of college-educated women reformers who, like Addams and herself, sought work commensurate with their talents. Julia Lathrop, almost twenty years later the first director of the U.S. Children's Bureau, had joined the settlement before Kelley. Alice Hamilton, who arrived in 1897, developed the field of industrial medicine. These four, with Mary Rozet Smith, Jane Addams's life partner, became the settlement's main leaders. In addition to these women, Kelley forged close ties with Mary Kenney, a trade union organizer affiliated with the settlement, who lived nearby with her mother.

Since her father had lost most of his money before his death in 1890, Kelley had to support herself and her children. She first did so by working for the Illinois Bureau of Labor Statistics and the U.S. Department of Labor, collecting data for governmental studies of working conditions. A good example of the empowerment of her Hull House residence lay in her use of data collected for the U.S. Department of Labor, which in 1895 formed the basis of the maps published in *Hull House Maps and Papers*. She and four government "schedule men" collected responses to sixty-four questions on printed schedules from "each house, tenement, and room" in the ward surrounding Hull House.[13] From this data Carroll Wright, head of the Department of Labor, constructed scores of tables. But Kelley and Hull House associates, using only data about nationalities and wages in conjunction with residential information, created color-coded maps that displayed geographic patterns that told more than Wright's charts. Because the maps defined spatial relationships among human groups, they vividly depicted social and economic relationships: the concentration of certain ethnic groups in certain blocks; the relationship between poverty and race; the distances between the isolated brothel district and the rest of the ward; the very poor who lived in crowded, airless rooms in the rear of tenements and those with more resources in the front; and the omniscient observer and the observed. Expressing the democratic relationship among Hull House residents, *Hull House Maps and Papers* listed only "Residents of Hull House" as the volume's editors.

Kelley described the transformative effect of the Hull House community on her personal life in a letter to her mother a few weeks after her arrival. "In the few weeks of my stay here I have won for the children and myself many and dear friends whose generous hospitality astonishes me. It is understood that I am to resume the maiden name and that the children are to have it."[14] By joining a community of women, she had achieved a new degree of personal autonomy.

CHALLENGING TRADITIONS OF LIMITED GOVERNMENT

In the spring of 1892, Kelley used Hull House as a base to exert leadership within an anti-sweatshop campaign that had been launched in 1888 by the Illinois Woman's Alliance, a class-bridging coalition of women's organizations. At mass meetings that attacked the sweatshop system, Kelley shared the podium with Mary Kenney, Henry Demarest Lloyd, and other Chicago notables such as Reverend Jenkin Lloyd Jones, minister at All Souls' Unitarian Church, the most liberal pulpit in Chicago, and with young trade union organizers in the clothing industry such as Abraham Bisno.

Campaigns against sweatshops were widespread in American cities in the 1890s. These efforts targeted "predatory management" and "parasitic manufacturers" who paid such low wages to their workers as to require them to seek support from relief or charity, thereby indirectly providing employers with subsidies that enabled them to lower wages further.[15] Supported by trade unions, these campaigns used a variety of strategies to shift work from tenement sweatshops to factories. In factories, union organizing could more easily succeed in improving working conditions and raising wages to levels necessary to sustain life.

Outcries raised by anti-sweatshop campaigns prompted government inquiries, and in 1893, after intense lobbying in Springfield by Hull House residents and other well-known Chicago women, the passage of pathbreaking legislation drafted by Florence Kelley. That year Governor John Peter Altgeld appointed Kelley to a position the new statute created: Chief Factory Inspector of Illinois. Nowhere else in the Western world was a woman trusted to enforce the labor legislation of a city, let

alone of a large industrial region the size of Illinois. With eleven deputies, five of whom were required to be women, and a budget of $28,000, for the next three years Kelley enforced the act's chief clauses. The act banned the labor of children under fourteen years of age; it regulated the labor of children age fourteen to sixteen; it outlawed the production of garments in tenements; it prohibited the employment of women and minors for more than eight hours a day; and it created a state office of factory inspection.

The statute's eight-hour clause made it the most advanced in the United States, equaled only by an eight-hour law for all workers in Australia. The limitation of hours, whether through statutes or union negotiations with employers, was the second most important goal of the labor movement between 1870 and 1910, the first being the recognition of the right of workers to form unions. Skilled workers had acquired the eight-hour day for themselves in many trades by the 1890s, but since women were not admitted to most skilled occupations, their hours remained long, often extending to twelve or even fourteen hours a day. In the late 1880s more than 85 percent of female wage earners were between the ages of fourteen and twenty-five and only about 5 percent were married.[16] Excluded from access to skilled jobs and presumed to leave the paid labor force upon marriage, they were crowded into a few unskilled occupations, where they were easily replaced, and employers exploited them by requiring long hours and paying low wages. Statutes that limited women's hours limited this exploitation. How to achieve such reduction of hours without reducing wages was a challenge that Kelley's office met by promoting the formation of unions among affected women workers, thereby helping them negotiate better wages for the hours they worked.

But the reduction of women's hours by statute had other beneficial effects: in many occupations it also reduced the hours of unskilled men, as was the case in garment-making sweatshops. In this and many other occupations, it proved impossible to keep men working longer than the legal limit of the working day for women. Therefore, hours statutes drove sweatshops out of business, since their profits could only be achieved through long hours. In the United States more than in other industrializing nations, the union movement consisted with few exceptions (miners being the chief exception) of skilled workers who shunned responsibility for the welfare of unskilled workers. Therefore, in the United States more than in elsewhere, gender-specific reforms like Kelley's 1893 legislation—undertaken by women for women—also had the effect of aiding all unskilled workers, men as well as women and children. In the United States, where labor movements were not as strong as they were elsewhere, gender-specific reforms accomplished goals that elsewhere were achieved under the auspices of class-specific efforts.[17]

In an era when courts nullified legislative attempts to intervene in the laissez-faire relationship between capital and labor, Kelley's enforcement of this new eight-hour law was inevitably challenged in the courts. In 1895 the Illinois Supreme Court found the eight-hour clause of the 1893 law unconstitutional because it violated women's right to contract their labor on any terms set by their employer. This setback made Kelley determined to change the power of state courts to overturn hours laws for women.

The high tide of Kelley's achievements between 1893 and 1896 ebbed quickly when Altgeld lost the election of 1896. His successor replaced her with a person who did not challenge the economic status quo, and she was unable to find work commensurate with her talents. German admirers came to her rescue. For fifty dollars a month she provided a leading German reform periodical with assessments of recent American social legislation. She also worked in the Crerar Library, a reference library specializing in economic, scientific, and medical topics.

Needing to reach beyond the limits of Hull House activities, Kelley began to work more closely with Ellen Henrotin. Wife of a leading Chicago banker, Henrotin had supported Kelley's legislation in 1892, and spoke vigorously at a rally to defend the law in 1894, urging those in attendance to "agitate for shorter hours for women because it means in the end shorter hours for all workers, men and women."[18] Henrotin's organization in 1893 of thirty women's congresses at the Chicago World's Fair catapulted her into the presidency of the General Federation of Women's Clubs (GFWC; founded 1890) from 1894 to 1898. By 1897 the GFWC served as an umbrella organization for more than five hundred women's

clubs, including the powerful Chicago Women's Club. Fostering the creation of over twenty state federations to coordinate those clubs, Henrotin moved the GFWC in progressive directions by establishing national committees on industrial working conditions and national health. In this way she directed the path of what was to become one of the largest grass-roots organizations of American women beyond the minimal goals of good government and civil service reform to the more challenging issues of social inequalities and social justice.

Reflecting her growing awareness of the potential power of women's organizations as a vehicle for her social justice agenda, in 1897 Kelley began to work closely with Henrotin in organizing an Illinois Consumers' League. They built on the example of the New York Consumers' League, which had been founded in 1891 to channel consumers' consciousness toward political action on behalf of workers who made the goods that consumers purchased.

THE NATIONAL CONSUMERS' LEAGUE AND NEW STRATEGIES FOR SOCIAL JUSTICE

Kelley's work with Henrotin helped her make the biggest career step of her life when, in 1899, she agreed to serve as Secretary of the newly formed National Consumers' League, a position she held until her death in 1932. With a salary of $1,500 plus traveling and other expenses, the job offered financial stability and a chance to develop a more radical and more focused women's organization than the GFWC.

When she carried her formidable talents into the National Consumers' League in 1899, women's political culture gained a warrior with formidable rhetorical and organizational skills. She quickly made the National Consumers' League (NCL) into the nation's leading promoter of protective labor legislation for women and children. Between 1900 and 1904 she built sixty-four local consumer leagues—one in nearly every large city outside the South. Through a demanding travel schedule, which required her to spend one day on the road for every day she worked at her desk, Kelley maintained close contact with local leagues, urging them to implement the national organization's agenda and inspiring them to greater action within their states and municipalities. At the age of forty she had finally found a platform that matched her talents and goals.

In New York she lived until 1926 at Lillian Wald's nurses' settlement on Henry Street on Manhattan's Lower East Side. Her children moved east with her. Supported by aid from Jane Addams's life partner, Mary Rozet Smith, Nicholas Kelley graduated from Harvard in 1905 and then from Harvard Law School. Living in Manhattan, he became his mother's closest advisor. In a blow that caused Kelley to spend the rest of that year in retirement in Maine, her daughter Margaret died of heart failure during her first week at Smith College in 1905. After this bereavement Kelley maintained a summer home on Penobscot Bay, Maine, where she retreated for periods of intense work with a secretary each summer. John Kelley never found a professional niche, but remained close to his mother and joined her in Maine each summer.

THE WHITE LABEL CAMPAIGN: NEW WAYS OF EDUCATING MIDDLE-CLASS WOMEN ABOUT INDUSTRIAL WORKING CONDITIONS

The national branch of the Consumers' League was formed in 1898 to coordinate the efforts of previously existing leagues in New York, Brooklyn, Philadelphia, Boston, and Chicago, all of which had conducted campaigns against sweatshops. At a convention of the local leagues called to coordinate their anti-sweatshop efforts, Kelley proposed the creation of a consumers' label as a way of identifying goods made under fair conditions. Her proposal galvanized the convention into creating a national organization "for the express purpose of offering a Consumers' League Label" nationally, recognizing that local efforts against sweatshops could never succeed until all producers were "compelled to compete on a higher level," and agreeing that the label could be a means of achieving that goal.[19] The NCL awarded its label to manufacturers who obeyed state factory laws, produced goods only on their own premises, did not require employees to work overtime, and did not employ children under sixteen years of age. To enforce the label, however, factories had to be inspected. Local leagues had employed their own factory inspectors; Kelley became the league's national inspector.

In determining whether local factories qualified for the label, local league members had to educate themselves about local working conditions. They had to pose and answer questions new to middle-class women, though painfully familiar to union organizers: Did the manufacturer subcontract to home workers in tenements? Were children employed? Were state factory laws violated? Could workers live on their wages, or were they forced to augment their pay with relief or charitable donations? How far below the standard set by the consumers' label were their own state laws? Even more technical questions arose when leagues came into contact with factory inspectors, bureaus of labor statistics, state legislatures, and courts. Should the state issue licenses for home workers? What was the relationship between illiteracy in child workers and the enforcement of effective child labor laws? Was their own state high or low on the NCL's ranked list showing the number of illiterate child workers in each? Should laws prohibit the labor of children at age fourteen or sixteen? Should exceptions be made for the children of widows? How energetically were state factory laws enforced? How could local factory standards be improved? These questions, recently quite alien to middle-class women, now held the interest of thousands of the most politically active among them. This was no small accomplishment. State leagues differed in the degree to which they worked with state officials, but wherever they existed they created new civic space in which women used their new knowledge and power to expand state responsibility for the welfare of women and children workers.

On the road steadily between 1900 and 1907, Kelley inspected workshops, awarded the label to qualified manufacturers, and strengthened local leagues. Her efforts were rewarded by the spectacular growth of NCL locals, both in number and location. The NCL's 1901 report mentioned thirty leagues in eleven states; by 1906 they numbered sixty-three in twenty states.

Flourishing local leagues sustained the national's existence, channeling money, ideas, and the support of other local groups into the national office. At the same time, locals implemented the national's agenda at the state level. Most league members were white, urban, northern, middle-class Protestants, but Jewish women held important positions of leadership. Catholic women became more visible after Cardinal James Gibbons of Baltimore consented to serve as vice president of a Maryland league and Bishop J. Regis Canevin of Pittsburgh encouraged members of that city's Ladies Catholic Benevolent Association to join. Two important reasons for the absence of black women from the NCL's membership and agenda were the league's focus on Northern urban manufacturing, and the residence of 90 percent of the nation's black population in the South, employed primarily in agriculture, in 1900.

10-HOUR LAWS FOR WOMEN: NEW USES OF SOCIAL SCIENCE

The work of educating her constituency being achieved by 1907, Kelley implemented a second stage of league work. With the use of social science data, the NCL overcame legal obstacles to the passage of state laws limiting women's hours. The overturning of Illinois's 1893 law by Illinois's Supreme Court in 1895 made Kelley determined to defend such laws before the U.S. Supreme Court. When an Oregon ten-hour law came before the court in 1907, she threw the resources of the NCL into its defense. This case, *Muller v. Oregon,* pitted the NCL and its Oregon branch against a laundry owner who disputed the state's ability to regulate working hours in non-hazardous occupations. For what became known as the "Brandeis Brief," Kelley's Research Director, Josephine Goldmark, gathered printed evidence from medical and other authorities (most of whom were British or European) to demonstrate that workdays longer than ten hours were hazardous to the health of women. Goldmark obtained the services of her brother-in-law, Louis D. Brandeis, a leading Boston attorney, who successfully argued the case on sociological rather than legal grounds, using the evidence that Goldmark had compiled. Thus at the same time that this case cleared the way for state hours laws for women, it also established the court's recognition of sociological evidence, a strategy that sustained the court's ruling against segregated schools in *Brown v. Board of Education* in 1954.

In the years immediately following the *Muller* decision, inspired by Kelley's leadership, and supported by other groups, local consumer leagues gained the passage in twenty states of the first laws limiting women's working hours. Also responding to the decision, nineteen other states revised and expanded their laws governing women's working hours.

The Supreme Court's 1908 opinion tried to block the possibility of extending such protections to men by emphasizing women's special legal status (they did not possess the same contractual rights as men) and their physiological difference from men (their health affected the health of their future children). Nevertheless, in 1917 Kelley and the NCL again cooperated successfully with the Oregon league in arguing another case on sociological grounds before the U.S. Supreme Court, *Bunting v. Oregon,* in which the Court upheld the constitutionality of hours laws for men in non-hazardous occupations. Viewing laws for women as an entering wedge for improving conditions for all working people, Kelley achieved that goal in the progression from *Muller* to *Bunting.* In this as in other aspects of her work with the League, though nominally focused on gender, her reforms had class-wide effects.

THE MINIMUM WAGE CAMPAIGN: NEW USES OF THE POWER OF WOMEN'S ORGANIZATIONS

As early as 1899, Florence Kelley had hoped "to include a requirement as to minimal wages" in the NCL's White Label. Australia and New Zealand had already organized wage boards as part of compulsory arbitration, but the path to an American equivalent did not seem clear until she and other Consumers' League members in 1908 attended the First International Conference of Consumers' Leagues, in Geneva, where they learned about the proposed British wage law of 1909, which that year implemented minimum wages for all workers in certain poorly paid occupations.

Almost immediately on her return, Kelley established her leadership in what became an enormously successful campaign for minimum wage laws for women in the United States. In her campaign she denounced the large profits made in three industries: retail stores, sweatshop garment making, and textile manufacturers. "Low wages produce more poverty than all other causes together," she insisted, urging that "goods and profits are not ends in themselves to which human welfare may continue to be sacrificed."[20]

Kelley argued that minimum wages would raise the standards in women's employment by recognizing their need to support themselves. "So long as women's wages rest upon the assumption that every woman has a husband, father, brother, or lover contributing to her support, so long these sinister incidents of women's industrial employment (tuberculosis, insanity, vice) are inevitable." She urged that "society itself must build the floor beneath their feet."[21]

Minimum wage legislation was much more difficult to achieve than maximum hours laws because, as one of Kelley's allies put it, wage legislation "pierces to the heart the classic claim that industry is a purely private affair."[22] For this reason, Kelley and the NCL were unaided in their efforts by their male-dominated equivalent, the American Association for Labor Legislation (AALL). When Kelley appealed in 1910 to their executive director, John Andrews, he loftily replied: "I question very seriously the wisdom of injecting the minimum wage proposal into the legislative campaign of this year, because I do not believe our courts would at the present time uphold such legislation, and I am afraid it would seriously jeopardize the splendid progress now being made to establish maximum working hours."[23] Two years later the AALL still opposed wage legislation as premature.

Kelley and the NCL were able to move ahead with this pathbreaking legislation because they could mobilize grass-roots support for it at local and state levels. The AALL had no local branches; instead, their power flowed from a network of male academic experts who advised politicians about legislation. If politicians were not ready to move, neither was the AALL. The NCL, by contrast, had in its sixty-four local branches enough political muscle to take the initiative and lead politicians where they otherwise wouldn't have gone.

In 1912 Massachusetts passed the first minimum wage law for women, followed in 1913 by eight additional states: California, Colorado, Minnesota, Nebraska, Oregon, Utah, Washington, and Wisconsin. By 1919 fourteen states and the District of Columbia and Puerto Rico had enacted minimum wage statutes for women. The success of these laws influenced the inclusion of a minimum wage for men *and* women in the Fair Labor Standards Act (FLSA) of 1938. In 1942, when the U.S. Supreme Court approved the constitutionality of the FLSA, the eight-hour day and the minimum wage became part of the social contract for most American workers. The class-bridging activism of middle-class women

in the NCL forged the way with these fundamental reforms.

GAINS AND SETBACKS IN THE 1920S

At Henry Street, Kelley continued to benefit from the same consolidation of female reform talents that had sustained her efforts at Hull House in Chicago. The creation of the U.S. Children's Bureau in 1911 sprang from her discussions with Lillian Wald. The Children's Bureau was the only governmental agency in any industrial society that was headed and run by women. Kelley thought that her most important contribution to social change was the passage in 1921 of the Sheppard-Towner Maternity and Infancy Protection Act, which first allocated federal funds to health care. She was instrumental in the creation of the coalition that backed the act's passage, the Women's Joint Congressional Committee, and in the coalition's successful campaign for the bill in Congress. Although limited to a program administered by the Children's Bureau to combat infant and maternal mortality, Kelley thought the Sheppard-Towner Act marked the beginning of a national health care program.[24]

After this high point in 1921, however, the decade brought a series of reversals that threatened to undo most of her achievements. In 1923 the U.S. Supreme Court in *Adkins* v. *Children's Hospital* found Washington, D.C.'s wage law for women unconstitutional. Many state wage boards continued to function during the 1920s and 1930s, however, providing ample evidence of the benefits of the law, but no new wage laws were passed. In 1926, Congress refused to allocate new funds for Sheppard-Towner programs, and responsibility for maternal and infant health returned to state and county levels.[25]

Just as important, by 1922 Kelley's strategy of using gender-specific legislation as a surrogate for class legislation had generated opposition from a new quarter—women who did not themselves benefit from gendered laws. The National Woman's Party (NWP), formed in 1916 by the charismatic leadership of Alice Paul and funded almost entirely by Alva Belmont, created a small coalition consisting primarily of professional women with some wage-earning women who worked in male-dominated occupations. Despite Kelley's strong objections over the damage they would do to gender-specific legislation, including the Sheppard-Towner Act, in 1921 the NWP proposed an Equal Rights Amendment to the U.S. Constitution (ERA). Although mainstream organizations such as the General Federation of Women's Clubs and the League of Women Voters continued to support gender-specific legislation, the NWP's proposed amendment undercut the momentum of such gendered strategies. In the 1920s most wage-earning women opposed the ERA because they stood to lose rather than benefit from it. By the 1970s changes in working conditions and protective labor laws meant that most wage-earning women stood to benefit from the amendment, and many more supported it.[26]

Even more damaging than these reversals, however, were the right-wing attacks launched by hyperpatriots against Kelley and other women reformers during the "red scare" of the 1920s. *The Woman Patriot* exemplified these attacks. Launched in 1916 and published twice a month, before the enactment of the woman suffrage amendment this newsletter was subtitled *Dedicated to the Defense of Womanhood, Motherhood, the Family and the State AGAINST Suffragism, Feminism and Socialism.* After 1920 the newsletter dropped its reference to suffrage, but continued its virulent attacks on the social agenda of women reformers. "SHALL BOLSHEVIST-FEMINISTS SECRETLY GOVERN AMERICA?" their headlines screamed, referring to the Sheppard-Towner Act. When *The Woman Patriot* referred to Kelley as "Mrs. Wischnewtzky" and called her "Moscow's chief conspirator," Kelley urged Addams to join her in a libel suit against them. Addams gently persuaded her to ignore the attacks. Kelley then wrote an impassioned series of autobiographical articles that established her lineage as an inheritor of American ideals and a dedicated promoter of American values.[27]

Attacks on women reformers in the 1920s were in part generated by supporters of American military expansion in the aftermath of World War I, when Kelley and many other women reformers were actively promoting peace and disarmament. For example, *The Woman Patriot* characterized the support that women reformers were giving to disarmament as "an organized internationalist Bolshevist-Feminist plot to embarrass the Limitation of Armaments Conference." Government employees joined the attack in 1924, when Lucia Maxwell of the Chemical

Warfare Department of the Department of War issued a "Spider Web Chart" entitled "The Socialist-Pacifist Movement in America Is an Absolutely Fundamental and Integral Part of International Socialism." Depicting the connections between women's organizations and Congressional lobbying for social legislation and for disarmament, the chart sought to characterize as "pacifist-socialist" most women's organizations in the United States, including the National Consumers' League, the National League of Women Voters, the General Federation of Women's Clubs, the Woman's Christian Temperance Union, the National Congress of Mothers and Parent-Teachers Association, the National Women's Trade Union League, the American Home Economics Association, the American Association of University Women, the National Council of Jewish Women, the Girls' Friendly Society, the Young Women's Christian Association, and the National Federation of Business and Professional Women.[28]

Historians have not measured the effect of these attacks on the political agendas of women's organizations, but after these attacks the agendas of many women's organizations, for example that of the League for Women Voters, shifted from social justice to good government projects, from support for a Child Labor Amendment to the U.S. Constitution to advocacy for a city manager form of governance.[29] Such a shift was in keeping with the demise of the Progressive movement after World War I. But that demise was hastened by the rise of "red scare" tactics in American political culture.

Florence Kelley did not live to see many of her initiatives incorporated into federal legislation in the 1930s. Faced with the collapse of the American economy in the Great Depression of 1929–1939, policymakers drew heavily on the legacy of Progressive reforms initiated between 1890 and 1920. Florence Kelley's legacies, including the minimum wage and maximum hours legislation incorporated in the Fair Labor Standards Act of 1938, were strong enough to survive the reversals of the 1920s. In 1933, with the inauguration of Franklin Delano Roosevelt, Kelley's protégée Frances Perkins became the first woman to serve as a cabinet member. Reflecting the power of women's organizations in shaping a new social contract for American working people, Perkins was appointed Secretary of Labor.[30]

But Kelley's legacy reaches beyond any specific policies. U.S. Supreme Court Justice Felix Frankfurter said in 1953 that the nation owed Kelley an "enduring debt for the continuing process she so largely helped to initiate, by which social legislation is promoted and eventually gets on the statute books."[31] As Kelley shaped it during her long reform career between 1890 and 1930, that process relied heavily on women's organizations and their ability to act independently of the political status quo.

NOTES

1. James Weber Linn, *Jane Addams: A Biography* (New York, 1938), 138.

2. For an overview of social change in the Progressive era, see Steven J. Diner, *A Very Different Age: Americans of the Progressive Era* (New York, 1998).

3. For more on Kelley before 1900, see Kathryn Kish Sklar, *Florence Kelley and the Nation's Work: The Rise of Women's Political Culture, 1830–1900* (New Haven, 1995). Specific page references are provided for quotations used below.

4. Mabel Newcomer, *A Century of Higher Education for American Women* (New York, 1959), 37, 46. See also Barbara Miller Solomon, *"In the Company of Educated Women": A History of Women and Higher Education in America* (New Haven, 1985), 62–77.

5. For Kelley's childhood, see Kathryn Kish Sklar, ed., *The Autobiography of Florence Kelley: Notes of Sixty Years* (Chicago, 1986).

6. Sklar, *Autobiography of Florence Kelley*, 30.

7. Kathryn Kish Sklar, "Hull House Maps and Papers: Social Science as Women's Work in the 1890s," in Helene Silverberg, ed., *Gender and American Social Science: The Formative Years* (Princeton, 1998).

8. See Joyce Antler, "After College, What?: New Graduates and the Family Claim," *American Quarterly* 32 (Fall 1980):409–34.

9. See Dorothy Rose Blumberg, "'Dear Mr. Engels': Unpublished Letters, 1884–1894, of Florence Kelley (Wischnewetzky) to Friedrich Engels," *Labor History* 5 (Spring 1964), 103–33.

10. Sklar, *Florence Kelley*, 129.

11. Sklar, *Autobiography of Florence Kelley*, 77.

12. Jane Addams, *My Friend Julia Lathrop* (New York, 1935), 77.

13. Residents of Hull House, *Hull House Maps and Papers* (New York, 1895).

14. FK to Caroline B. Kelley, Chicago, Feb. 24, 1892, Nicholas Kelley Papers, New York Public Library.

15. Kathryn Kish Sklar, "Two Political Cultures in the Progressive Era: The National Consumers' League and the American Association for Labor Legislation," in Linda K. Kerber, Alice Kessler-Harris and Kathryn Kish Sklar, eds., *U.S. History as Women's History: New Feminist Essays* (Chapel Hill, N.C., 1995), 58.

16. U.S. Commissioner of Labor, *Fourth Annual Report, Working Women in Large Cities* (Washington, D.C., 1889), 62–64.

17. For a full argument of this point, see Kathryn Kish Sklar, "The Historical Foundations of Women's Power in the Creation of the American Welfare State, 1830–1930," in Seth Koven and Sonya Michel, eds., *Mothers of a New World: Maternalist Politics and the Origins of Welfare States* (New York, 1993).

18. "Hit at Sweat Shops," *Chicago Tribune*, April 23, 1894; Sklar, *Florence Kelley*, 261.

19. Sklar, *Florence Kelley*, 309.

20. Florence Kelley, "Minimum Wage Boards," *American Journal of Sociology* 17 (Nov. 1911), 303–14.

21. Florence Kelley, "Ten Years from Now," *Survey*, March 26, 1910, 978–81.

22. Sklar, "Two Political Cultures," 60.

23. See, for example, John B. Andrews to Erich Stern, New York, Dec. 14, 1910, American Association for Labor Legislation Papers, Cornell University.

24. See Molly Ladd-Taylor, *Mother-Work: Women, Child Welfare, and the State, 1890–1930* (Urbana, Ill., 1994), 167–96.

25. See J. Stanley Lemons, *The Woman Citizen: Social Feminism in the 1920s* (Urbana, Ill., 1973), 169–76.

26. For the opposition of the progressive mainstream of the women's movement, see Kathryn Kish Sklar, "Why Did Most Politically Active Women Oppose the ERA in the 1920s?" in Joan Hoff-Wilson, ed., *Rights of Passage: the Past and Future of the ERA* (Bloomington, Ind., 1986).

27. *The Woman Patriot*, Vol. 5, no. 29, Nov. 1, 1921, 1. For the complete documents of this correspondence between Kelley and Addams, see Anissa Harper, "Pacifism vs. Patriotism in Women's Organizations in the 1920s: How Was the Debate Shaped by the Expansion of the American Military," in *Women and Social Movements in the United States, 1830–1930*, an Internet website edited by Kathryn Kish Sklar and Thomas Dublin, http://womhist .binghamton.edu. See also Nancy F. Cott, *The Grounding of Modern Feminism* (New Haven, 1987), 243–67.

28. The Spider Web Chart is reproduced in Helen Baker, "How Did the Women's International League for Peace and Freedom Respond to Right Wing Attacks in the 1920s?" in *Women and Social Movements* at http://womhist.binghamton.edu.

29. For example, see the furor aroused within the League of Women Voters over the proposed Child Labor Amendment to the U.S. Constitution in 1924, in Louise M. Young, *In the Public Interest: The League of Women Voters, 1920–1970* (New York, 1989), 97–98.

30. For Perkins see Susan Ware, *Beyond Suffrage: Women in the New Deal* (Cambridge, Mass., 1981), *passim*.

31. Felix Frankfurter, "Foreword," in Josephine Goldmark, *Impatient Crusader: Florence Kelley's Life Story* (Urbana, Ill., 1953), v.

ANNELISE ORLECK

From the Russian Pale to Labor Organizing in New York City

The pale of Jewish settlement was a territory within Russia to which Jews were restricted during the eighteenth and nineteenth centuries and where they were frequently subjected to ferocious outbursts of anti-Semitic violence. Crossing from the pale to the teeming streets of Manhattan's Lower East Side was a frontier crossing of major proportions. Yet two million European Jews who came to the United States between 1880 and 1924 made it across, among them the remarkable young women who are the subjects of Annelise Orleck's lively and informative essay.

Like so many of their fellow immigrants, Rose Schneiderman, Fannia Cohn, Clara Lemlich, and Pauline Newman gravitated to one of the earliest industries to employ women—the garment industry. Based in New York City, the industry had long provided countless married women with piecework to take back to dimly lit tenements, where they often enlisted the help of grandmothers and children. By the turn of the century, much of the work had been transferred to sweatshops and factories that were notorious for their low wages and squalid working conditions. Because so many of the female employees were young single women who presumably regarded their work as a temporary necessity until rescued by marriage, labor leaders usually assumed that the women were virtually unorganizable. Yet between 1909 and 1915, women garment workers in New York as well as in other cities exploded in labor militancy. By 1919, half of all women garment workers belonged to trade unions and many had joined the suffrage struggle as well. The role these four young women played in this process is the focus of Orleck's essay.

What experiences shaped their political consciousness and propelled their activism? As young girls forced to work and forego school and college, how did they educate themselves and for what purpose? Who were their allies and why were these alliances so necessary, yet so unstable? How was the balancing act required of the four with respect to male trade unionists and elite female reformers similar to that required of Charlotte Hawkins Brown, albeit in a different context (see Glenda Gilmore's essay, pp. 300–310)? What attracted these young working women to suffrage? What is meant by the term "industrial feminists"? You will find Pauline Newman's reminiscence of garment work in the documents that accompany this cluster of essays.

During the summer of 1907, when New York City was gripped by a severe economic depression, a group of young women workers who had been laid off and were facing eviction took tents and sleeping rolls to the verdant Palisades overlooking the Hudson River. While rising rents and unemployment spread panic among the poor immigrants of Manhattan's Lower East Side, these teenagers lived in a makeshift summer camp, getting work where they could

Excerpted from the prologue, and chs. 1 and 2 of *Common Sense and a Little Fire: Women and Working-Class Politics in the United States, 1900–1965,* by Annelise Orleck (Chapel Hill: University of North Carolina Press, 1995). Used by permission of the author and publisher. Notes have been edited and renumbered.

find it, sharing whatever food and drink they could afford, reading, hiking, and gathering around a campfire at night to sing Russian and Yiddish songs. "Thus we avoided paying rent or, worse still, being evicted," Pauline Newman later recalled. "Besides which, we liked living in the open—plenty of fresh air, sunshine and the lovely Hudson for which there was no charge."[1]

Away from the clatter of the shops and the filth of Lower East Side streets, the young women talked into the night, refreshed by what Newman called "the cool of the evening, glorious sunsets, the moon and stars." They shared personal concerns as well as shop-floor gripes—worries about love, about the future, and about the pressing problems of housing and food.

Their cliffside village meant more to Newman and her friends than a summer escape. They had created a vibrant alternative to the tenement life they found so oppressive, and their experience of it had set them to wondering. Perhaps the same sense of joy and comradeship could help workers transcend the drudgery of the garment shops and form the basis for effective organizing.[2]

At season's end, they emerged with strengthened bonds and renewed resolve to organize their communities around issues that the recent depression had brought into sharp relief: the need for stabilized rent and food prices, improved working conditions, and housing for the poor.[3]

The spirit of intimacy and solidarity that pervaded the summer of 1907 would inspire much of Pauline Newman's later organizing. Indeed, it became a model for the vision of change that Newman shared with her fellow Jewish immigrant radicals Fannia Cohn, Rose Schneiderman and Clara Lemlich. The four women moved to political struggle not simply by the need for better wages, hours and working conditions but also, in Newman's words, by a need to ensure that "poverty did not deprive us from finding joy and satisfaction in things of the spirit."[4] This essay examines the early careers of these four remarkable organizers and the role they played in building a militant working women's movement during the first decades of the twentieth century.

For even as girls, these marginally educated immigrants wanted to be more than . . . shop-floor drudges. They wanted lives filled with beauty—with friendships, books, art,

music, dance, fresh air, and clean water. "A working girl is a human being," Newman would later tell a legislative committee investigating factory conditions, "with a heart, with desires, with aspirations, with ideas and ideals." That image nourished Newman, Schneiderman, Lemlich, and Cohn throughout their long careers. And it focused them on a single goal: to reshape U.S. society so that "working girls" like themselves could fulfill some of their dreams.[5]

The four women moved through strikingly different cultural milieus over the course of long careers that would carry them in different directions. Still, they each bore the imprint of the shared culture in which they were raised, first in Eastern Europe and then in New York City. That common experience gave them a particular understanding of gender, class, and ethnicity that shaped their later activism and political thought.

All four were born in the Russian-dominated pale of Jewish settlement during the last two decades of the nineteenth century. Rose Schneiderman was born in the Polish village of Saven in 1882; Fannia Cohn was born in Kletsk, Poland, in 1885; Clara Lemlich was born in the Ukrainian village of Gorodok in 1886; and Pauline Newman was born in Kovno, Lithuania, around 1890.[6]

They were ushered into a world swept by a firestorm of new ideas, where the contrasting but equally messianic visions of orthodox Judaism and revolutionary Socialism competed for young minds. The excitement of living in a revolutionary era imbued these young women with a faith in progress and a belief that political commitment gave life meaning. It also taught them, at an early age, that gender, class, and ethnicity were fundamental social categories and essential building blocks for political change. Being born into turbulence does not in itself make a child into a political activist. But the changes sweeping the Russian Empire toward the end of the nineteenth century shaped the consciousness of a generation of Eastern European Jews who contributed, in wildly disproportionate numbers, to revolutionary movements in Russia and to the labor and radical movements in the United States.[7]

The four were exposed to Marxist ideas at a tender age. As Eastern Europe shifted uneasily from feudalism to capitalism in the latter part of the nineteenth century, class analysis became part of the common parlance of young people in Jewish towns and villages. "Behind every other volume of Talmud in those years, there was a volume of Marx," one union organizer recalled of his small Polish town. Clara Lemlich grew up on revolutionary tracts and songs; Fannia Cohn considered herself a committed Socialist by the age of sixteen.[8]

Their awareness of ethnicity was even more keen. As Jews in Eastern Europe, the four learned young that ethnic identity was a double-edged sword. It was a source of strength and solace in their bitterly poor communities, but it also enabled Tsarist authorities to single Jews out and sow seeds of suspicion among their peasant neighbors. Jews living under Russian rule were made painfully aware of their status as permanent "others" in the land where they had lived for centuries. Clara Lemlich's family lived not far from Kishinev, where in 1903 the Tsar's government openly and unabashedly directed an orgy of anti-Jewish violence that shocked the world. In cosmopolitan Minsk, where she had gone to study, Fannia Cohn watched with dismay as the revolutionary populist organization she had joined began mouthing the same anti-Semitic conspiracy theories spewed by the government they despised. Frustration turned to fear when her brother was almost killed in yet another pogrom.[9]

Sex was just as distinct a dividing line as class and ethnicity. Eastern European Jews had observed a strict sexual division of labor for more than a thousand years. But by the late nineteenth century, as political and economic upheaval jolted long-accepted ways of thinking, sex roles too were being questioned. And so the four girls' understandings of gender were informed both by traditional Jewish conceptions of womanhood and by the challenges issued by new political movements.

In traditional Jewish society, mothers were also entrepreneurs. Clara Lemlich, Pauline Newman, and Rose Schneiderman were all raised by mothers who were skilled businesswomen. Jewish mothers' success in this role grew out of and reinforced a belief that women were innately suited to competition in the economic sphere. In contrast to the image of the sheltered middle-class housewife then dominant in the United States, Eastern European Jewish religious tradition glorified strong, economically sophisticated wives and mothers.

But as much as women's entrepreneurship was respected, a far higher premium was placed on study and prayer. And that, religious tradition dictated, could be performed only by men. A woman was expected to be pious, to read the vernacular Yiddish—rather than ancient Hebrew—translation of the Bible, and perhaps to attend women's services at the synagogue. But her primary religious role was as keeper of the home. Formal religious education was offered only to males.[10] Because Eastern European Jewish women had to fight for every scrap of education they received, many began to see education as the key to independence from all masters. This view would strongly influence their political organizing once in the United States.

The four emigrated as part of the mass movement that brought two million Jews from Eastern Europe to the United States between 1881 and 1924. Schneiderman came in 1890, Newman in 1901, Lemlich in 1903, and Cohn in 1904. Like most of their compatriots, they arrived in New York Harbor and settled on Manhattan's Lower East Side, the largest settlement of Eastern European Jews in the United States.[11] The newcomers were tantalized by the exciting diversions that New York life promised: libraries, theater, music, department stores, and amusement parks. But they had neither time nor money to indulge in such pleasures, for all of them soon found themselves laboring long hours to support their families.

At an age when most girls in the United States were still in grade school, immigrant working girls like Newman spent twelve- to fourteen-hour days in the harshest of atmospheres. Their bodies and minds reeled from the shock of the shops: the deafening noise, the brutal pace, and the rebukes of foremen. Some children were able to slough off the hardship with jokes and games. Others, realizing that they were destined to spend their youth in dank factories rather than in classrooms or schoolyards, grew sullen and withdrawn.

Clara Lemlich, like so many others, was quickly disillusioned by her first job in a New York garment shop: "I went to work two weeks after landing in this country. We worked from sunrise to set seven days a week. . . . Those who worked on machines had to carry the machines on their back both to and from work. . . . The shop we worked in had no central heating, no electric power. . . . The hissing of the machines, the yelling of the foreman, made life unbearable."[12]

Newly arrived European women undergoing medical examinations at Ellis Island, ca. 1900.
"The day of the emigrant's arrival in New York was the nearest earthly likeness to the final day of Judgement, when we have to prove our fitness to enter Heaven." The words are those of a sympathetic journalist who shared the anxiety-ridden experience awaiting the immigrants at the port of entry. Failing the medical test could mean deportation. (Courtesy of Brown Brothers, Sterling, Pennsylvania.)

Anger drove young women workers like Lemlich and Newman to band together. Untrained and largely unschooled, these young women were drawn to Socialism and trade unionism not because they felt an ideological affinity but because they had a desperate need to improve their working conditions. "I knew very little about Socialism," Lemlich recalled. "[But] the girls, whether Socialist or not, had many stoppages and strikes." Newman too found that for most young women workers, political understanding followed action rather than precipitating it: "We of the 1909 vintage knew nothing about the economics of . . . industry or for that matter about economics in general. All we knew was the bitter fact that, after working seventy and eighty hours in a seven day week, we did not earn enough to keep body and soul together." These assertions reveal much about the political development of the tens of thousands of women garment workers who would soon amaze New York and the nation with their militancy.[13]

Shop-floor culture fed the young women's emerging sense of political identity. Working alongside older men and women who discussed Socialism daily, they began to feel a sense of belonging to a distinct class of people in the world: workers. This allegiance would soon become as important to them as their Judaism. The shops also provided an opportunity for bonding with other women. Slowly, out of their workplace experiences, they began to develop a complex political identity in which class, gender and ethnicity overlapped. Young women workers were moved by the idea of sisterhood. It captured their own experiences in the sex-segregated shops where they worked. The majority of New York's garment workers were little more than girls, and the relationships they forged with factory friends were similar to those of schoolgirls—intense, melodramatic, and deeply loyal. They were teenage confidantes as well as fellow workers, and they relied on shop-floor rapport to soften the harshness of factory life.[14] For young immigrant women trying to build lives in a new land, such bonds were powerful and lasting. From these shop-floor friendships would soon evolve the ties of union sisterhood.[15]

Pauline Newman and her co-workers at the Triangle Shirtwaist Factory literally grew up together. Only twelve when she first came to Triangle, Newman was assigned to a corner known as "the kindergarten," where workers as young as eight, nine, or ten years old trimmed threads from finished garments. They labored, Newman later recalled, "from 7:30 A.M. to 6:30 at night when it wasn't busy. When the season was on we worked till 9 o'clock. No overtime pay." Their only taste of a normal childhood came through the songs and games they invented to help pass the time, the stories they told and the secrets they shared.[16]

By the early twentieth century, New York State had passed laws prohibiting night work for children. But little attempt was made to enforce them. On the rare occasions when an inspector showed up at her factory, Newman remembered, "the employers were always tipped off.... 'Quick,' they'd say, 'Into the boxes!' And we children would climb into the big box the finished shirts were stored in. Then some shirts were piled on top of us and when the inspector came—No children." In a way it was fun, Newman remembered. They thought they were playing a game like hide and seek.[17]

But it wasn't really a game. Children who had to help support their parents grew up quickly. Rose Schneiderman was thirteen when her mother begged United Hebrew Charities, an organization run by middle-class German Jews, to find her daughter a "respectable job" at a department store. Retail jobs were deemed more respectable than factory work because the environment was more pleasant and sexual harassment was thought to be less common. Deborah Schneiderman worried that factory work would sully Rose's reputation and make her less marriageable. A job as a fashionable salesgirl, she hoped, would usher Rose into the middle class. The single mother who had fed her children on charity food baskets and had been forced to place them in orphanages was grimly determined to help them escape poverty.

But then as now, pink-collar jobs paid significantly less than industrial work. Anxious to free her mother from the rigors of maintaining their tenement building, Schneiderman left her job in Ridley's department store for the harsher and more morally suspect conditions of an industrial shop. Making linings for caps and hats, she immediately raised her weekly income from $2.75 to $6. As the sole supporter of her family, the sixteen-year-old hoped to work her way up quickly to a skilled job in the cap trade.[18]

Clara Lemlich's family also relied on her wages, particularly because her father was unemployed. She aspired to the skilled position of draper, one of the highest-paid positions a woman could attain in the dressmaking trade. Despite terrible working conditions, many ambitious young women chose garment work over other jobs because it seemed to offer their greatest chance to acquire skills and command high wages. When these hopes were dashed, some young workers grew angry. That anger was fanned and channeled by older women in the shops who were itching to challenge the authority of the bosses.[19]

That is what happened to Rose Schneiderman, who, like many skilled women garment workers, was blocked from advancement by the unofficial gender hierarchy at her factory. Finding that all the highest-paid jobs in her capmaking shop were reserved for men, Schneiderman asked around about ways to break through those barriers. When she approached fellow worker Bessie Braut with her concerns, Schneiderman was initiated simultaneously into trade unionism, Socialism, and feminism. Schneiderman recalled, "Bessie was an unusual person. Her beautiful eyes shone out of a badly pockmarked face and the effect was startling. An outspoken anarchist, she made a strong impression on us. She wasted no time in giving us the facts of life—that the men in our trade belonged to a union and were, therefore, able to better their conditions. She added pointedly that it would be a good thing for the lining-makers to join a union along with the trimmers, who were all women."[20]

Schneiderman, Braut, and several other workers called on the secretary-treasurer of the United Cloth Hat and Cap Makers to request union recognition for their fledgling local of trimmers and lining makers. Within a few days they had enough signatures to win a charter for their local, and Schneiderman was elected secretary.[21]

Surprising even herself, the once-shy red-head soon found she could be an eloquent and fierce advocate for her fellow workers. In recognition of her growing reputation, the capmakers elected her to the Central Labor Union of New York. Deborah Schneiderman was disturbed by the turn Rose's life was taking. She warned Rose that if she pursued a public life she would never find a husband. No man wants a woman with a big mouth, her mother said.[22]

In the flush of excitement at the praise and warmth suddenly coming her way, young Rose did not stop to worry. In organizing, she had found both a calling and a world of friends. She had no intention of turning back. "It was such an exciting time," she wrote later. "A new life opened up for me. All of a sudden I was not lonely anymore. . . . It was the beginning of a period that molded all my subsequent life."[23]

Fannia Cohn, too, chose garment work as her path to a career. And like Schneiderman, Lemlich, and Newman, she found a community there. Unlike the others, however, she did not enter a garment factory looking for work that paid well. She was a comfortable middle-class woman in search of a trade ripe for unionizing.

Cohn arrived in New York in 1904 and moved in with her affluent cousins. There was little about her early days in the United States that was comparable to the hard-pressed scrambling for a living that the Schneidermans, Lemlichs, and Newmans experienced. "My family suggested that I complete my studies and then join the labor movement but I rejected this as I did not want to come into it from 'without' but from 'within.' I realized then that if I wanted to really understand the mind, the aspirations of the workers, I should experience the life of the worker in a shop."[24] In 1905, Fannia Cohn became a sleevemaker. For a year she moved from shop to shop until, in the "white goods" trade, she found the organizing challenge she was looking for.

Shops that manufactured white goods—underwear, kimonos, and robes—were considered particularly hard to organize. Production took place in tiny sweatshops, not large factories, and the manufacturing process had been broken down into small tasks that required little skill. The majority of white goods workers were immigrant girls under the age of fifteen. And because they came from a wide range of backgrounds—Jewish, Italian, Syrian, Turkish, and Greek—it was difficult for them to communicate with each other, let alone organize. As a result, these workers were among the lowest paid in the garment trades.

At twenty, Cohn was an elder in the trade. With her high school education and fluency in three languages, she was seen as a mother figure by many of the adolescents in the shops. She and a handful of older women workers began to operate as mentors, meeting with the girls in each shop and identifying potential leaders. Cohn taught her co-workers to read, write, and speak in public, hoping they would channel those skills into the union struggle. Cohn had already created the role that she would play throughout her career: an educator of younger workers.[25]

Education was a primary driving force in the metamorphosis of all four young women from shop workers to union organizers. From the isolated towns and restive cities of Eastern Europe, where gender, class, and ethnicity stymied Jewish girls' hopes for education, the lure of free public schooling in the United States beckoned powerfully. Having to drop out of school to work was more than a disappointment for many Jewish immigrant girls; it was their first great disillusionment with the dream of America. And they did not give that dream up easily.

"When I went to work," Rose Schneiderman remembered, "I was determined to continue my studies." Her only option was to attend one of the many night schools then open to immigrant workers in New York. Having carried with her from Poland the ideal of education as an exalted, liberating process, she was disgusted by the mediocre instruction she encountered and felt betrayed by teachers who seemed to be patronizing her. "I enrolled and went faithfully every evening for about four weeks. But I found that . . . the instructor seemed more interested in getting one-hundred-percent attendance than in giving one-hundred-percent instruction. He would joke and tell silly stories. . . . I soon realized I was wasting my time." Schneiderman left the evening school but did not stop studying. She asked older co-workers if she could borrow books that she had discussed with them in the shop. In the evenings, she read with her mother at home. Serializations of Emile Zola's *J'Accuse* and other contemporary writings in the Yiddish evening paper *Abendblatt* gave Rose a taste for literature. "I devoured everything I could get my hands on."[26]

Clara Lemlich was an equally avid reader. At the end of each twelve-hour day stitching shirtwaists, she would walk from her factory to the East Broadway branch of the New York Public Library. There she read the library's entire collection of Russian classics. "I was so eager to learn things," she later recalled. When she tired of solitary study, Lemlich joined a free night school on Grand Street. She returned home late each night, ate the dinner her mother had kept warm for her, then slept for just a few hours before rising again for work.[27]

Not surprisingly, young women like Schneiderman, Newman, and Lemlich turned to radical politics to fulfill their desire for a life of the mind. If no other school was available, then what Pauline Newman called "the school of solidarity" would have to do. Membership in the Socialist Party and in unions, tenant organizations, and benevolent societies provided immigrant women with an opportunity to learn and study that most would never have gotten otherwise. And as Newman put it, "Because they were hitherto deprived of any tutorship, they at once became ardent students."[28]

Pauline Newman was just fifteen when she first knocked on the doors of the Socialist Literary Society. Although women were not yet allowed to join, she was permitted to attend classes. The Literary Society was a revelation to the young worker. There she was introduced to the writings of Shakespeare, George Eliot, and Thomas Hardy and personally met writers like Jack London and Charlotte Perkins Gilman, who came to speak there. Gratitude, however, didn't stop her from joining a successful petition drive to admit women to the society.

For Newman—as for Clara Lemlich, who attended Marxist theory classes at the Socialist Party's Rand School—studying was more than a distraction from work. The "desire to get out of the shop," Newman wrote later, "to learn, to understand, became the dominant force in my life." But unlike many immigrants, who saw schooling as a ladder out of the working class, both she and Lemlich were committed to helping others rise with them. So Newman and Lemlich formed study groups that met during lunch hours and after work to share what they were learning with their friends.[29]

"We tried to educate ourselves," Newman remembered of her co-workers at the Triangle Shirtwaist Factory. "I would invite the girls to my room and we took turns reading poetry in English to improve our understanding of the language." Because they had to steal the time to study, the young women approached everything they read with a heightened sensitivity. And when something they were reading struck a chord of recognition, seemed to reflect on their own lives, the catharsis was not only emotional; it was political.[30]

The evolution of Lemlich's study group illustrates how study often led to union activity. Older workers, who were teaching Lemlich the craft of draping, invited her to join their lunchtime discussion groups to learn more about trade unionism. Soon Lemlich and a group of young women waistmakers formed their own study group. Discussion quickly escalated to action, and they decided to form a union.[31]

Skilled male workers in the shirtwaist trade had been trying to establish a union since 1900. But after five years the union had managed to attract only ten members. The problem, Lemlich told her male colleagues, was that women workers had to be approached by an organizer who understood their particular needs as women. They bristled at the suggestion that this young girl might know more about their business than they did. But years later, one conceded that the failure of the first waistmakers' union was due at least in part to their ham-fisted tactics: "We would issue a circular reading somewhat as follows: 'Murder the exploiters, the blood-suckers, the manufacturers. . . . Pay your dues. . . . Down with the Capitalists!'" Few women or men showed up at their meetings.[32]

During the spring of 1905 the union disbanded and reorganized as Local 25 of the ILGWU, with Clara Lemlich and a group of six young women from her waistmaking shop on the executive board. Taking their cue from Lemlich, the new union used women organizers to attract women workers. Lemlich addressed street-corner meetings in English and Yiddish and found Italian women to address the Italian workers. Soon, like Schneiderman, Newman, and Cohn, she realized that she had found a calling.[33]

In the progressive atmosphere of early-twentieth-century New York City, influential people quickly noticed the militant young working women. Older Socialists, trade unionists, and middle-class reformers offered their assistance. These benefactors helped the young organizers sharpen their arguments, provided

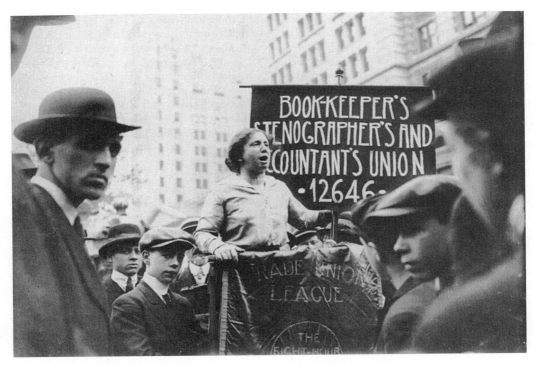

Rose Schneiderman addresses a street rally in New York City, probably 1910s. (Courtesy of Brown Brothers, Sterling, Pennsylvania.)

financial assistance, and introduced them to politicians and public officials. The protégés recognized the importance of this informal mentoring and would later work to recreate such networks in the unions, schools, and training programs they built for young women workers. Schneiderman, Newman, Lemlich, and Cohn were keenly aware that young working women needed help from more experienced and more powerful allies. But they also worried that the voices of women workers might be outshouted in the clamorous process of building alliances. From these early days, they battled to preserve the integrity of their vision.

Pauline Newman found her first mentors in the Socialist Party, which she joined in 1906 at the age of fifteen. Older women, including former garment worker Theresa Serber Malkiel, took her on as a protégé. Newman quickly blossomed under their tutelage. Before long she was running street-corner meetings. Armed with a sonorous voice and the certitude of youth, she would take "an American flag and a soapbox and go from corner to corner," exhorting the gospel of Socialism in Yiddish and English. "I, like many of my friends and comrades, thought that socialism and socialism alone could and would someday fill the gap between rich and poor," Newman recalled. In a neighborhood crowded with sidewalk proselytizers, this child evangelist became one of the party's most popular streetcorner attractions.[34]

In 1908, nine years before New York State gave women the vote, seventeen-year-old Newman was nominated by the Socialist Party to run for New York's Secretary of State. Newman used her campaign as a platform for suffrage. Her speeches were heckled by some Socialist men, and her candidacy provoked amused commentaries in New York City newspapers; some writers snickered at the prospect of a "skirted Secretary of State." It was a largely symbolic crusade, but Newman felt that she got people talking about the idea of women in government. The highlight of the campaign was her whistlestop tour with presidential candidate and Socialist leader Eugene V. Debs on his "Red Special" train.

The Socialist Party opened up a new world to Newman, who, after all, had never graduated from elementary school. Along with Debs, she met future Congressmen Meyer Berger and Morris Hillquit and leading Socialist intellectuals. Newman later wrote about the excitement of discussions that carried over from meetings and went into the night as she and her friends walked through Central Park, arguing till the sun came up. Those nights made her feel part of a historic moment.[35]

While Newman was being nurtured by the Socialist Party, Rose Schneiderman found her mentors in the United Cloth Hat and Cap Makers. At the union's 1904 convention she was elected to the General Executive Board; she was the first woman to win such a high-level post in the American labor movement. During the winter of 1904–5, Schneiderman's leadership skills were tested when owners tried to open up union shops to nonunion workers. The largely immigrant capmaker's union called for a general strike. The 1905 strike was a watershed event in Schneiderman's emerging career. Her role as the only woman leader in the union won attention from the press and lasting respect from male capmakers, including the future president of the union, Max Zaritsky, who became a lifelong friend and admirer.[36]

It also brought her to the attention of the newly formed Women's Trade Union League (WTUL), an organization of progressive middle- and upper-class women reformers founded in 1903 to help working women organize. Schneiderman had misgivings about the group because she "could not believe that men and women who were not wage earners themselves understood the problems that workers faced." But she trusted the League's best-known working-class member, Irish shirtmaker Leonora O'Reilly. And she could not ignore the favorable publicity that the WTUL won for the strikers. By March 1905, Schneiderman had been elected to the executive board of the New York WTUL. In 1906, the group elected her vice president.[37]

Schneiderman's entrance into the New York WTUL was an important turning point for both her and the organization. Three years after its founding, the WTUL remained dominated by affluent reformers who had dubbed themselves "allies" of the working class. Despite their genuine commitment to trade unionism, League leaders had credibility problems among women workers. Schneiderman had joined the League recognizing that working women lacked the education, the

money, and the political clout to organize effectively without powerful allies. Still, she remained ambivalent for a variety of reasons.[38]

The progressive reformers who dominated the League tried to steer workers away from radical influences, particularly the Socialist Party. Yet Schneiderman and O'Reilly, the League's leading working-class organizers, were Socialist Party members and saw unionism as a potentially revolutionary tool. As a result, the pair often felt torn by competing loyalties. Socialists distrusted their work with upper-crust women reformers. Union men were either indifferent or openly hostile to working women's attempts to become leaders in the labor movement. And the League women often seemed to Schneiderman and O'Reilly to act out of a patronizing benevolence that had little to do with real coalition building. The two grew angry at what they saw as attempts by wealthy allies to manipulate them. In January 1906, Leonora O'Reilly announced the first of her many resignations from the League, claiming "an overdose of allies."[39]

There were a few deep friendships between affluent WTUL leaders and working women like Schneiderman, O'Reilly, and Pauline Newman, who joined the League in 1909. Such bonds created hope that intimacy was possible between women of different classes; but cross-class friendships were the exception rather than the rule. Working women like Newman never lost sight of the ways their class background separated them from wealthy reformers. Sisterhood was exhilarating, but outside the WTUL, their lives and political agendas diverged sharply.[40]

Consequently, these women's relations with most wealthy League supporters were marked by deep ambivalence inasmuch as WTUL backers wanted to distance the League from radical working-class activism and to stake out a decidedly middle ground in the struggle for women's rights that was then gathering steam.

Schneiderman tried to counterbalance such influences by encouraging male union leaders to play a more active role in the League, but she had little success. She told them that the WTUL could help the labor movement by successfully organizing women workers, whose low wages might otherwise exert a downward pressure on unionized male wages. A *women's* trade union league was needed, she insisted, because women workers responded to different arguments than did men workers. The League could focus on the particular concerns of women, such as the double shift—having to perform household chores after coming home from long days in the factory. Her suggestions were greeted with indifference.

Addressing the First Convention of American Women Trade Unionists, held in New York on July 14, 1907, Schneiderman reported that she "was very much surprised and not a little disappointed that the attention of men unionists was so small." The truth is, she told her audience, working women needed more than unions. They needed political power. "The time has come," she said firmly, "when working women of the State of New York must be enfranchised and so secure political power to shape their own labor conditions." The convention passed a suffrage resolution, one of the first prosuffrage statements by any organization representing American working-class women.[41]

Schneiderman confronted middle- and upper-class allies with equal frankness. She told the NYWTUL executive board that they were having little success organizing women workers because they approached their task like scholars, not trade unionists. They surveyed conditions in the women's trades, noting which had the lowest salaries, the longest hours, and the worst hygienic conditions. Then they established committees to study the possibilities for unionizing each trade. Finally they went into the shops to explain their findings to the working women. Schneiderman suggested a simpler alternative: take their lead from women workers and respond to requests for aid from women workers who were already trying to organize. It was something they had never thought to do.[42]

Before long, requests for help were pouring in, mostly from immigrant Jewish women. In the dress trade, where Clara Lemlich was working, and in the white goods trade, where Fannia Cohn was organizing, women workers had launched a series of wildcat strikes. "It was not unusual for unorganized workers to walk out without having any direct union affiliation," Schneiderman later recalled.[43]

By 1907, long-simmering anger over speedups, wage cuts, and the requirement that employees pay for their own thread reached a boiling point. Foreshadowing its role in the decades to come, the Women's Trade Union League decided to champion women workers ignored by the male unions. The strike fever soon engulfed Brooklyn, where for two years Fannia Cohn had been struggling against male union leaders' indifference to organize white goods workers. So when three hundred workers in one shop decided to strike in 1908, they bypassed the UGW and called for help from Schneiderman and the WTUL.

Since the ethnic makeup of the Brooklyn white goods trade was far more diverse than any other in the garment industry, this strike raised a new challenge for Schneiderman: how to forge a sense of solidarity between working-class women of many religions and nationalities. Schneiderman decided that the best way to reach immigrant workers was through organizers who literally spoke their language.[44]

She decided to focus first on Italian workers because, after Jews, they comprised the single largest ethnic group in the garment trades. Recognizing the cultural as well as linguistic differences that separated her from Italian immigrant women, Schneiderman tried a strategy she would employ many times over the years to come: to identify and cultivate a leader from within the ranks of the workers. She began working with a Brooklyn priest on ways to approach young Italian women. She also got the League to hire an Italian-speaking organizer who assembled a committee of progressive New York Italians—including prominent women professionals and the editor of a popular evening paper *Bolatino de la Sera*—to popularize trade unionism among Italian women workers.[45]

The strategy proved successful. By 1909 enough workers had enlisted that the ILGWU finally recognized the Brooklyn white goods workers' union. The vast majority of its members were teenage girls; these young women elected their mentor, Fannia Cohn, then twenty-four, to the union's first executive board. Cohn, who stepped off the shop floor to a policy-making position, would remain a paid union official for the rest of her life.[46]

In 1909, Clara Lemlich—then in her twenties and on the executive board of ILGWU Local 25—enlisted Schneiderman's aid in her drive to organize shirt-waist makers. For the past three years, Lemlich had been zigzagging between small shops, stirring up trouble. Her first full-scale strike was at Weisen and Goldstein's Manhattan factory. Like the Triangle Shirtwaist Factory, where Newman worked, Weisen and Goldstein's was considered a model shop. The workrooms were modern and airy—a pleasant contrast to the dark basement rooms where most white goods workers labored. However, the advantages of working in a clean, new factory were offset by the strains of mechanization. In 1907 the workers at Weisen and Goldstein's went on strike to protest speedups.

Older male strikers proved critical to Lemlich's political education. Confused by an argument between workers at a strike meeting, Lemlich asked one to explain the difference between Socialist unionism and the "pure and simple trade unionism" of the American Federation of Labor (AFL). When the meeting ended, the man took Lemlich for a long walk. He explained Socialism in terms she could use with her fellow workers. "He started with a bottle of milk—how it was made, who made the money from it through every stage of its production. Not only did the boss take the profits, he said, but not a drop of that milk did you drink unless he allowed you to. It was funny, you know, because I'd been saying things like that to the girls before. But now I understood it better and I began to use it more often—only with shirtwaists."[47]

Lemlich returned to the picket line with a more sophisticated view of organizing. She became a regular at Socialist Party meetings and began attending classes at the Rand School. Through the Socialist Party she became friends with Rose Schneiderman, Pauline Newman, and other young women organizers. Both individually and in tandem, this group of radical young women organized strikes across the Lower East Side.

In 1909, after being fired from two more shops for leading strikes, Lemlich began working at the Leiserson shop. Brazenly, she marched uninvited into a strike meeting that had been called by the shop's older male elite— the skilled cutters and drapers. Warning them that they would lose if they attempted to strike without organizing the shop's unskilled women, Lemlich demanded their help in organizing women workers. They bridled at her nerve, but ultimately they helped her unionize the women.[48]

Lemlich's reputation as a leader grew rapidly during the fall of 1909 as stories of her bravery spread. During the Leiserson strike, which began that September, she was arrested seventeen times and had six ribs broken by

club-wielding police and company guards. Without complaint, she tended to her bruises and returned to the line. By November 1909, when she stepped onto the stage in Cooper Union's Great Hall of the People to deliver the speech that would spark the largest women's strike the nation had yet seen, Lemlich was not the anonymous "wisp of a girl" that news accounts described. She was a battle-scarred veteran of the labor movement, well known among her fellow workers.[49]

Still, it is worth remembering that in this period, the four women activists were just barely adults. Newman, Schneiderman, and Lemlich still lived with their parents. During the Leiserson strike, Lemlich was so fearful that her parents would try to keep her home if they knew about her injuries that she hid her escapades and bruises from them. Later she explained the events to her grandson: "Like rain the blows fell on me. The gangsters hit me. . . . The boys and girls invented themselves how to give back what they got from the scabs, with stones and whatnot, with sticks. . . . Sometimes when I came home I wouldn't tell because if I would tell they wouldn't want me to go anymore. Yes, my boy, it's not easy. Unions aren't built easy."[50]

On November 23, 1909, New York City awoke to a general strike of shirtwaist makers, the largest strike by women workers the United States had ever seen. Overnight, between 20,000 and 40,000 workers—most of them teenage girls—silenced their sewing machines to protest the low wages, long hours, and dangerous working conditions. Though the magnitude of the strike amazed nearly everyone, including Schneiderman, Newman, Cohn, and Lemlich, the four knew that this was no spontaneous uprising: they had been organizing feverishly for almost three years and had noted a transformation in the working women they talked to, a growing sense of collective identity matched by an increasing militancy. They had laid the groundwork through a series of smaller strikes and had trained fellow workers to expect and respond to the violent and divisive tactics used by bosses to break the strike.

Despite their effectiveness, the strike was threatened by the escalation of police violence against the young women picketers. Two weeks after the strike call, Schneiderman and Dreier led ten thousand young waistmakers on a march to city hall to demand that Mayor

George McClellan rein in the police. He promised an investigation but did little. One month into the strike, there had been 771 arrests, many made with undue force.[51]

WTUL leaders decided to try a different tack. They called a mass meeting of all the young women who had been attacked by police. The press and wealthy supporters were invited. One after another, adolescent girls rose to the stage to tell their stories. Mollie Weingast told a cheering crowd that when an officer tried to arrest her, she informed him that she had a constitutional right to picket. Minnie Margolis demanded that a policeman protect her from physical attack by her boss. When he refused, she took down his badge and precinct numbers. It was, she told the audience, an officer's job to protect her right to protest peacefully. Celie Newman, sixteen, said that police had manhandled her and dragged her into court, where her boss told a judge that she was an anarchist and should be deported. At another meeting earlier that week, seventeen-year-old Etta Ruth said that police had taunted her with lewd suggestions.[52]

Implying that picketers were little better than streetwalkers, employers often resorted to sexual innuendos to discredit the strikers. The workers clearly resented the manner in which middle-class standards of acceptable feminine behavior were used to manipulate them even though they enjoyed none of the advantages of middle-class birth. Then as now, society offered a limited range of cultural images of working-class women. They were either "good" girls who listened docilely to fathers, employers, and policemen, or "bad" women whose aggressive behavior made them akin to prostitutes. By walking on picket lines and going public with their demands, they'd forfeited their claims to femininity and respectability—and thus to protection.[53]

Such women were shown little deference by police and company thugs, who attacked them with iron bars, sticks, and billy clubs. And they received little sympathy in court when they attempted to press charges. One young woman appeared in court with a broken nose, a bruised face, and a head swathed in bandages. Yet the judge dropped her assault charge against police. "You are on strike against God and nature," one magistrate told a worker. Only the League's decision to invite college students and wealthy women onto the picket lines ended the violence. Alva Belmont

and Anne Morgan led a contingent of New York's wealthiest women in what newspapers dubbed "mink brigades," which patrolled the dirty sidewalks of the Lower East Side. Fearful of clubbing someone on the Social Register, police grew more restrained.[54]

The socialites' presence generated both money and press for the strikers. The move proved politically wise for the suffrage cause as well, because the constant proselytizing of suffrage zealot Alva Belmont, who often bailed strikers out of jail, got young workers talking about the vote. But rubbing elbows with the mink brigade did not blind workers to the class-determined limits of sisterhood. How far they were from the protected status of more affluent women was made abundantly clear by the violence they encountered at the hands of police and company guards and by the fact that the mink brigades were able to end police brutality simply by joining the picket lines.

Encounters in court and with feminist allies speeded the growth of group consciousness. Telling their stories in court, to reporters, and to sympathetic audiences of college and society women, the strikers grew more confident of their speaking abilities and of their capacity to interpret their world. They became more aware of the distribution of power in the United States. And finally, the violence directed against them intensified their bonds with one another.

For Schneiderman, Newman, and Lemlich, the 1909 shirtwaist uprising sped their maturation as organizers and political leaders. The strike breathed new life into a struggling immigrant labor movement and transformed the tiny ILGWU into a union of national significance. Still, it ended with mixed success for workers. Many won pay increases and union recognition; others did not. And the contracts hammered out by ILGWU negotiators left a devastating legacy, for without consulting the strikers, male union negotiators decided that safety conditions were less important than other issues. Their concessions would come back to haunt the entire labor movement two years later, when the Triangle Shirtwaist Factory burned.[55]

Flames from the volcanic 1909 uprising licked industrial cities from New York to Michigan. Within a matter of weeks, 15,000 women waistmakers in Philadelphia walked off their jobs. The spirit of militancy soon touched the Midwest. In 1910, Chicago women led a strike of 41,000 men's clothing makers. The following year, women workers and the wives of male workers played key roles in a bitter cloakmakers' strike in Cleveland. Meanwhile, in Muscatine, Iowa, young women button makers waged and won a long battle for union recognition. In 1912, corset makers in Kalamazoo, Michigan, launched a campaign for better working conditions that polarized their city and won national press attention. In 1913, a strike of underwear and kimono makers swept up 35,000 young Brooklyn girls and women. Finally, in 1915, Chicago dressmakers capped this period of women's labor militancy by winning recognition of their local union after years of struggle. They elected their organizer, Fannia Cohn, as the first woman vice president of a major American labor union.[56]

Cohn, Rose Schneiderman, Pauline Newman, and Clara Lemlich were at the center of a storm that by 1919 had brought half of all women garment workers into trade unions. Individually and in tandem, the four women participated in all of the major women's strikes between 1909 and 1915, arguably the most intense period of women's labor militancy in U.S. history. This wave of "uprisings" seemed to herald the birth of a working women's movement on a scale never before seen. And it catapulted the four young women into positions of leadership, forcing them, in conjunction with colleagues, to articulate a clearly defined set of goals for the new movement.[57] In the passion and excitement of the years that followed, Schneiderman, Newman, Lemlich, and Cohn would begin to mature as political leaders and to forge a vision of political change that originated in their years on the shop floor. Pauline Newman would later describe this new brand of activism as politics of the 1909 vintage, fermented during a brief era of young women's mass protest. That description expresses the importance of the 1909 strike as both symbol and catalyst for a new working women's politics.

"Industrial feminism," the phrase coined in 1915 by scholar Mildred Moore to describe working women's militancy over the previous six years, evokes the same spirit but focuses more broadly. It simultaneously captures the interaction between women workers and feminist activists and recognizes the profound influence that the shop floor had on shaping working women's political consciousness. Industrial feminism accurately depicts the contours of an emerging political movement that by decade's end would propel the problems and concerns of industrial working women to the center of U.S. political discourse and make them players in the Socialist Party, the suffrage movement, and the politics of progressive reform.[58]

Industrial feminism was not a carefully delineated code of political thought. It was a vision of change forged in an atmosphere of crisis and awakening, as women workers in one city after another "laid down their scissors, shook the threads off their clothes and calmly left the place that stood between them and starvation." These were the words of former cloakmaker, journalist, and Socialist Party activist Theresa Malkiel, a partisan chronicler of women's labor militancy. Once an organizer, later a mentor for Newman, Lemlich, and Schneiderman, Malkiel told readers of the *New York Call* that they should not be surprised by the seemingly sudden explosion of young women workers' discontent. As hard as they might find it to take seriously the notion of a "girl's strike," she warned them, this was no outburst of female hysteria. "It was not . . . a woman's fancy that drove them to it," she wrote, "but an eruption of a long smoldering volcano, an overflow of suffering, abuse and exhaustion."[59]

Common sense, Pauline Newman would later say, dictated the most immediate goals of industrial feminists in the era of women's strikes. Given the dire realities of garment workers' lives, the first order of business had to be to improve their wages, hours, and working conditions. Toward that end the "girl strikers" of 1909–15 followed the most basic tenets of unionism. They organized, struck, and negotiated through their labor unions. But the "long-smoldering volcano" that Malkiel cautioned her readers to heed had been stirred to life by more than dissatisfaction over low wages and poor conditions.

The nascent political philosophy that began to take shape after the 1909 strike was more complex than the bread-and-butter unionism of AFL president Samuel Gompers. Why, young working women reasoned, should unions only negotiate hours and wages? They wanted to build unions that would also offer workers educational and cultural activities, health care, and maybe even a chance to leave the city and enjoy the open countryside.

Such ambitious goals derived largely from the personal experiences of industrial feminist leaders like Cohn, Schneiderman, Lemlich, and Newman. Political activism had enriched the four young women's lives, exposing them to more interesting people than they would have met had they stayed on the shop floor: writers, artists, professors, people with ideas. Through politics they had found their voices and a forum in which to raise them. The personal excitement and satisfaction they found in activism in turn shaped the evolution of their political vision: they wanted to create institutions that would provide some of the same satisfactions to any working woman who joined.

But alone, working women had none of the political or economic clout needed to open up such doors of opportunity. To build a successful movement, the four knew that they would have to win the support of more powerful allies. So they learned to build coalitions. From the time they left the shop floor until the end of their careers, they operated within a tense nexus of union men, progressive middle- and upper-class women, and the working women they sought to organize. These alliances shifted continuously, requiring the four women to perform a draining and politically hazardous balancing act. But each core group contributed an important dimension to the political education of the four organizers.

With their male counterparts and older women in the labor movement, they shared a class solidarity that would always remain at the heart of their politics. Traveling around the country, they met coal miners, loggers, and railroad workers who shared both their experiences of exploitation as laborers and their exhilaration in the economic and political strength that trade unions gave them.

From the middle- and upper-class women who joined them on the picket lines and lent them both financial and strategic support, they learned that trade union activism was not the only way to fight for improved work conditions. These allies would expose Newman, Cohn, Schneiderman, and Lemlich to a world of power and political influence, encouraging them to believe that through suffrage and lobbying, government could be put to work for their benefit.

Finally, as they began to think in terms of forging a national movement, they were forced to develop new techniques to reach women workers of different races, religions, and ethnicities. They learned from the women they sought to organize that just as women workers were best reached by women organizers, so Italian, Polish, and Hispanic immigrants and native-born black and white Protestant women were better reached by one of their own than by Jewish women steeped in the political culture of Eastern Europe and the Lower East Side. Though each of the four women had some success in bridging racial and ethnic divisions, they were forced to acknowledge their limitations. They could not do it all themselves; they had to nurture women shop-floor leaders from different backgrounds.

The work required to remain politically effective in this nexus of often-conflicting relationships yielded some real rewards, both strategically and personally. But sometimes the constant struggling wore on them. Conflicts and tensions were brought into sharp relief as the four exhausted themselves making speeches and giving pep talks to weary workers, when they themselves needed reassurance: although they had achieved recognition by the end of the 1909 strike, Schneiderman, Cohn, Newman, and Lemlich were still poor, uneducated, and young. Newman was only eighteen years old when the strike began, and Lemlich twenty-three. Even the elders in the circle, Cohn and Schneiderman, were only twenty-five and twenty-eight, respectively.

Letters between Newman and Schneiderman from that era reveal their vulnerability to slights and criticisms by male union leaders and female reformers. Life on "the battlefield," as Newman referred to it, was lonely. At an age when other women were contemplating marriage and family, they spent their nights in smoky union halls or the cheap, dingy hotel rooms that unions rented for their organizers. They sometimes questioned their life choices, for the reality of union work was far less glamorous than it had seemed in their shop-floor days. Indeed, Newman would quit several times before decade's end. Ultimately, though, their disillusionment did not drive the four women from the union movement. Instead, it fueled their desire to broaden the vision of U.S. trade unionism. When Schneiderman said "The working woman needs bread, but she needs roses, too," she was speaking from personal experience.[60]

NOTES

1. Pauline Newman, "Letters to Hugh and Michael" (1951–69), Box 1, Folder 3, Pauline M. Newman Papers, Schlesinger Library, Radcliffe College, Cambridge, Mass. (hereafter cited as Newman Papers).

2. Ibid.

3. Ibid.; *New York Times,* November 2, 25, December 3, 26, 1907.

4. Newman, "Letters to Hugh and Michael."

5. "The Testimony of Miss Pauline M. Newman," in *Hearings of the New York State Factory Investigating Commission* (Albany: J. B. Lyons Printers, 1915), 2868–71.

6. My estimate of Newman's age is based on evidence suggesting that she was around eighteen years old at the time of the 1909 shirtwaist strike. Newman, like many Jews of her generation, never knew for sure how old she was. Her birthdate was recorded only on the flyleaf of the family Bible. After the Bible was lost in transit, she could only guess at her age.

7. For analyses of the position of Jews in Russian society at the turn of the century, see S. Ettinger, "The Jews at the Outbreak of the Revolution," in *The Jews in Soviet Russia since 1917,* ed. Lionel Kochan, 3d ed. (Oxford: Oxford University Press, 1978), 15–30; see also Salo Baron, *The Russian Jew under Tsars and Soviets* (New York: Macmillan, 1976).

8. Sidney Jonas, interview by author, Brooklyn, N.Y., August 10, 1980; Paula Scheier, "Clara Lemlich Shavelson: Fifty Years in Labor's Front Line," *Jewish Life,* November 1954; Ricki Carole Myers Cohen, "Fannia Cohn and the International Ladies' Garment Workers' Union" (Ph.D. diss., University of Southern California, 1976), 5.

9. Newman, "Letters to Hugh and Michael"; Cohen, "Fannia Cohn," chap. 1; Scheier, "Clara Lemlich Shavelson"; Fannia M. Cohn to "Dear Emma," May 15, 1953, Fannia M. Cohn Papers, Astor, Lenox, and Tilden Foundations, Rare Books and Manuscripts Division, New York Public Library (hereafter cited as Cohn Papers).

In March 1903, gangs organized by Russian police rampaged through the Ukrainian town of Kishinev, killing 51 Jewish men, women, and children, and wounding at least 495 others. Edward H. Judge, *Eastern Kishinev: Anatomy of a Pogrom* (New York: New York University Press, 1992).

10. See Charlotte Baum, Paula Hyman, and Sonya Michel, *The Jewish Woman in America* (New York: NAL/Dutton, 1977), 55–91; Mark Zborowski and Elizabeth Herzog, *Life Is with People* (New York: Schocken, 1962); Jack Kugelmass and Jonathan Bayarin, *From a Ruined Garden: The Memorial Books of Polish Jewry* (New York: Schocken Books, 1985).

11. The Lower East Side continued to receive Jewish immigrants from Eastern Europe into the 1920s. See Ettinger, "Jews at the Outbreak of the Revolution," 19–22; Celia Heller, *On the Edge of Destruction* (New York: Schocken, 1980), 45–55; and Irving Howe, *World of Our Fathers* (New York: Harcourt Brace & Jovanovich, 1976), xix.

12. Clara Lemlich Shavelson to Morris Schappes, March 15, 1965, published in *Jewish Currents* 36, no. 10 (November 1982): 9–11.

13. Clara Lemlich, "Remembering the Waistmakers' General Strike, 1909," *Jewish Currents,* November 1982; Newman, "Letters to Hugh and Michael."

14. Much has been written about the importance of women's colleges to the various social reform movements of the Progressive Era. Stephen Norwood makes a similar argument for high schools. Norwood, *Labor's Flaming Youth: Telephone Workers and Labor Militancy, 1878–1923* (Urbana: University of Illinois Press, 1990).

15. Newman, "Letters to Hugh and Michael"; Pauline Newman, interview by Barbara Wertheimer, New York, N.Y., November 1976; Pauline Newman résumé, n.d., Newman Papers.

16. Pauline Newman, interview by author, New York, N.Y., February 9, 1984; Newman, interview by Wertheimer.

17. Joan Morrison and Charlotte Fox Zabusky, eds., *American Mosaic* (New York: E. P. Dutton, 1980).

18. See Rose Schneiderman, *All for One* (New York: Paul S. Eriksson, 1967), 35–42, and Susan Porter Benson, "The Customers Ain't God: The Work Culture of Department Store Saleswomen, 1890–1940," in *Working Class America,* ed. Michael Frisch and Daniel J. Walkowitz (Urbana: University of Illinois Press, 1983), 185–212.

19. Scheier, "Clara Lemlich Shavelson." See also Susan Glenn, *Daughters of the Shtetl: Work, Unionism and the Immigrant Generation* (Ithaca: Cornell University Press, 1990), 122–31.

20. Schneiderman, *All for One,* 48.

21. Ibid., 48–50.

22. Ibid.

23. Ibid.

24. FMC to Selig Perlman, December 26, 1951, Box 5, Cohn Papers.

25. Information on the problems of organizing the white goods trade is located in Minutes of the Executive Board of the NYWTUL, February 28, August 22, and November 26, 27, 1907, Reel 1, Papers of the New York Women's Trade Union League, Tamiment Institute Library, New York University (hereafter cited as NYWTUL Papers); information on Cohn comes from Cohen, "Fannia Cohn," 11–21.

26. Schneiderman, *All for One,* 39–40.

27. Scheier, "Clara Lemlich Shavelson."

28. Pauline Newman, "The White Goods Workers' Strike," *Ladies' Garment Worker* 4, no. 3 (March 1913): 1–4.

29. Scheier, "Clara Lemlich Shavelson"; Pauline Newman, Fragments 1958–61, Box 1, Newman Papers.

30. Newman, interview by Wertheimer; Newman, interview in Morrison and Zabusky, *American Mosaic.*

31. Scheier, "Clara Lemlich Shavelson."

32. Louis Levine [Lewis Lorwin], *The Women's Garment Workers: A History of the International Ladies' Garment Workers' Union* (New York: B. W. Huebsch, 1924), 148–49.

33. This information is pieced together from Scheier, "Clara Lemlich Shavelson"; Dora Smorodin, interview by author, Maplewood, N.J., March 12, 1991; and Levine, *Women's Garment Workers,* 148–49.

34. Newman, interview by Wertheimer; Newman, "Letters to Hugh and Michael."

35. Ibid.

36. Schneiderman, *All for One,* 58–60.

37. Ibid., 73–77; Minutes of the NYWTUL Executive Board, February 24, March 24, 1905. Reel 1, NYWTUL Papers.

38. Nancy Schrom Dye, *As Equals and as Sisters: Feminism, Unionism and the Women's Trade Union League of New York* (Columbia: University of Missouri Press, 1980), 110–22.

39. Ibid.; Minutes of the NYWTUL Executive Board, January 25, 1906, Reel 1, NYWTUL Papers.

40. Newman, interview by Wertheimer; Newman, interview by author, February 9, 1984, New York.

41. See also Alice Kessler-Harris, "Rose Schnei-derman," in *American Labor Leaders*, ed. Warren Van Tine and Melvyn Dubofsky (Urbana: University of Illinois Press, 1987), 160–84.

42. Minutes of the NYWTUL Executive Board, February 24, 1905-February 1, 1909, Reel 1, NYWTUL Papers.

43. Schneiderman, *All for One*, 84.

44. Minutes of the NYWTUL Executive Board, February 28, August 22, November 26, 27, 1907, Reel 1, NYWTUL, Papers; Levine, *Women's Garment Workers*, 220.

45. Minutes of the NYWTUL Executive Commit-tee, November 26, 27, 1907, Reel 1, NYWTUL Papers.

46. Levine, *Women's Garment Workers*, 220; Cohen, "Fannia Cohn," 36–43.

47. Scheier, "Clara Lemlich Shavelson."

48. Martha Schaffer, telephone interview by author, March 11, 1989; Joel Schaffer, Evelyn Velson, and Julia Velson, interview by author, Oakland, Calif., September 9, 1992.

49. Scheier, "Clara Lemlich Shavelson."

50. Clara Lemlich Shavelson, interview by Martha and Joel Schaffer, Los Angeles, Calif., February 2, 1974.

51. *New York Call*, November 30, December 4, 5, 6, 7, 8, 29, 1909.

52. *New York Call*, December 5, 7, 8, 1909.

53. *New York Call*, December 29, 1909. For com-plete coverage of day-to-day events on the picket line, see the *New York Times*, November 5, 6, and 14, 1909, and almost daily from November 23, 1909, through January 28, 1910.

54. Minutes of the New York Women's Trade Union League Membership Meeting, April 20, June 15, 1910, Reel 1, NYWTUL Papers.

55. See Meredith Tax, *The Rising of the Women: Feminist Solidarity and Class Conflict, 1880–1917* (New York: Monthly Review Press, 1980), pp. 230–240. Tax discusses the hierarchical union structure and the ways that union-appointed arbitrators undermined the women workers' control of the strike.

56. For information on the many women's strikes of the period, read the WTUL publication *Life and Labor*, which covered them all in some detail. The progressive magazine *The Survey* (1909–1914) also has good coverage of most of the strikes. See too, Pauline Newman, "The White Goods Workers' Strike," *Ladies' Garment Worker* 4, number 3 (March 1913): 1–4; on the Chicago strike see Mari Jo Buhle, *Women and American Socialism, 1870–1920* (Urbana: University of Illinois Press, 1981), 194–198. On the Kalamazoo strike see Karen Mason, "Feeling the Pinch: The Kalamazoo Corset Makers' Strike of 1912," in *To Toil the Livelong Day: America's Women at Work*, ed. Carol Groneman and Mary Beth Norton (Ithaca: Cornell University Press, 1987), 141–60. On the 1915 strike see *Chicago Day Book* cited in Wini-fred Carsel, *A History of the Chicago Ladies' Garment Workers' Union* (Chicago: Normandie House, 1940).

57. Gladys Boone, *The Women's Trade Union Leagues* (New York: Columbia University Press, 1942), 112–14.

58. Mildred Moore, "A History of the Women's Trade Union League of Chicago" (M.A. thesis, Uni-versity of Chicago, 1915), cited in Diane Kirkby, "The Wage-Earning Woman and the State: The National Women's Trade Union League and Protective Labor Legislation, 1903–1923," *Labor History* 28, no. 1 (Winter 1987): 58–74.

59. Theresa Malkiel, "The Uprising of the 40,000," *New York Call*, December 29, 1909.

60. Pauline Newman, "From the Battlefield—Some Phases of the Cloakmakers' Strike in Cleve-land," *Life and Labor*, October 1911.

Pauline Newman, "We fought and we bled and we died . . ."

One of the four young garment industry workers whose organizing activities emerged so vividly from the pages of Annelise Orleck's account, Pauline Newman had started out at the Triangle Shirtwaist Factory, which became the scene of one of the great industrial tragedies in New York City's history. Although the factory contained several elevators and two staircases, the eight-story wooden building had no sprinkler system; the doors to the fire escapes were locked to prevent outdoor relaxation. When fire broke out in 1911, 500 employees—many of them young Jewish and Italian women—were trapped behind locked doors. Some on the upper floors jumped to their deaths; others burned or asphyxiated while trapped inside. Altogether, the fire claimed the lives of 146 women. Viewing their charred bodies on the street, one reporter recalled that some of these same women had gone on strike only the year before to demand decent wages, more sanitary working conditions, and safety precautions.

The young women who died at the Triangle fire were buried together under a single monument. Hundreds of thousands of New Yorkers walked in the funeral procession in a driving rain. Not until 2011, a hundred years later, were they identified. The last living survivor of the fire, Rose Freedman, died in 2001 at the age of 107. She had saved herself by asking: what are the executives doing? She headed for their offices on the tenth floor, and then to the roof by way of the freight elevator, from which firefighters pulled them to safety. She never forgave the executives for saving themselves but leaving the doors locked, or, later, attempting to bribe her to testify that the doors were unlocked.

Unsafe buildings, blocked exits, and inadequate sprinkler systems threaten garment workers again today. The mass-market clothes that American women wear are often made in substandard conditions—in the United States when minimum wage, maximum hour, and occupational health and safety laws are unenforced, and abroad, in places where such standards barely exist. In an eerie reprise of the Triangle Fire, almost exactly 102 years later, in April 2013, the Rana Plaza factory in Dhaka, Bangladesh, collapsed, killing 1,129 workers, mostly women, who made cheap clothes for Western markets. (The United States suspended trade preferences for Bangladesh in recognition of labor rights violations and the persistence of safety problems, but unsafe factories continue to be used in that country and elsewhere.)*

---

*"100 Years Later, the Roll of the Dead in a Factory Fire is Complete," *New York Times*, Feb. 20, 2011; "Rose Freedman, Last Survivor of Triangle Fire, Dies at 107," ibid., Feb. 17, 2001; "Manufacturers in Bangladesh Resist Closing Garment Factories," ibid., June 26, 2014, pp. B1, B7.

Adapted from "Pauline Newman," in *American Mosaic: The Immigrant Experience in the Words of Those Who Lived It*, ed. Joan Morrison and Charlotte Fox Zabusky (New York: E. P. Dutton, 1980), pp. 9–14. Copyright © 1980 by Joan Morrison and Charlotte Fox Zabusky. Reprinted by permission of the publisher.

Educational director for the International Ladies' Garment Workers' Union until her death in 1986, Newman conveys in her own words what it was like to be a garment worker in the early twentieth century. What does she feel has been gained by organized labor? What does she feel has been lost over the years?

A cousin of mine worked for the Triangle Shirtwaist Company and she got me on there in October of 1901. It was probably the largest shirtwaist factory in the city of New York then. They had more than two hundred operators, cutters, examiners, finishers. Altogether more than four hundred people on two floors. The fire took place on one floor, the floor where we worked. You've probably heard about that. But that was years later.

We started work at seven-thirty in the morning, and during the busy season we worked until nine in the evening. They didn't pay you any overtime and they didn't give you anything for supper money. Sometimes they'd give you a little apple pie if you had to work very late. That was all. Very generous.

What I had to do was not really very difficult. It was just monotonous. When the shirtwaists were finished at the machine there were some threads that were left, and all the youngsters—we had a corner on the floor that resembled a kindergarten—we were given little scissors to cut the threads off. It wasn't heavy work, but it was monotonous, because you did the same thing from seven-thirty in the morning till nine at night.

Well, of course, there were [child labor] laws on the books, but no one bothered to enforce them. The employers were always tipped off if there was going to be an inspection. "Quick," they'd say, "into the boxes!" And we children would climb into the big boxes the finished shirts were stored in. Then some shirts were piled on top of us, and when the inspector came—no children. The factory always got an okay from the inspector, and I suppose someone at City Hall got a little something, too.

The employers didn't recognize anyone working for them as a human being. You were not allowed to sing. Operators would have liked to have sung, because they, too, had the same thing to do and weren't allowed to sing. We weren't allowed to talk to each other. Oh, no, they would sneak up behind if you were found talking to your next colleague. You were admonished: "If you keep on you'll be fired." If

you went to the toilet and you were there longer than the floor lady thought you should be, you would be laid off for half a day and sent home. And, of course, that meant no pay. You were not allowed to have your lunch on the fire escape in the summertime. The door was locked to keep us in. That's why so many people were trapped when the fire broke out.

My pay was $1.50 a week no matter how many hours I worked. My sisters made $6.00 a week; and the cutters, they were skilled workers, they might get as much as $12.00. The employers had a sign in the elevator that said: "If you don't come in on Sunday, don't come in on Monday." You were expected to work every day if they needed you and the pay was the same whether you worked extra or not. You had to be there at seven-thirty, so you got up at five-thirty, took the horse car, then the electric trolley to Greene Street, to be there on time. . . .

I stopped working at the Triangle Factory during the strike in 1909 and I didn't go back. The union sent me out to raise money for the strikers. I apparently was able to articulate my feelings and opinions about the criminal conditions, and they didn't have anyone else who could do better, so they assigned me. And I was successful getting money. After my first speech before the Central Trade and Labor Council I got front-page publicity, including my picture. I was only about fifteen then. Everybody saw it. Wealthy women were curious and they asked me if I would speak to them in their homes. I said I would if they would contribute to the strike, and they agreed. So I spent my time from November to the end of March upstate in New York, speaking to the ladies of the Four Hundred [the elite of New York's society] and sending money back. . . .

We didn't gain very much at the end of the strike. I think the hours were reduced to fifty-six a week or something like that. We got a 10 percent increase in wages. I think that the best thing that the strike did was to lay a foundation on which to build a union. There was so much feeling against unions then. The judge, when one of our girls came before him,

There was no morgue in New York City large enough to hold the bodies of the young women who had jumped from the burning buildings of the Triangle Shirtwaist Company in 1911. They were laid out on a pier for families to identify. Six of the victims were so badly burned that even relatives could not recognize them. (Courtesy of UNITE Archives, Kheel Center for Labor-Management Documentation and Archives, School of Industrial and Labor Relations, Cornell University, Ithaca, New York.)

said to her: "You're not striking against your employer, you know, young lady. You're striking against God," and sentenced her to two weeks on Blackwell's Island, which is now Welfare Island. And a lot of them got a taste of the club. . . .

After the 1909 strike I worked with the union, organizing in Philadelphia and Cleveland and other places, so I wasn't at the Triangle Shirtwaist Factory when the fire broke out, but a lot of my friends were. I was in Philadelphia for the union and, of course, someone from here called me immediately and I came back. It's very difficult to describe the feeling because I knew the place and I knew so many of the girls. The thing that bothered me was the employers got a lawyer. How anyone could have *defended* them!—because I'm quite sure that the fire was planned for insurance purposes. And no one is going to convince me

otherwise. And when they testified that the door to the fire escape was open, it was a lie! It was never open. Locked all the time. One hundred and forty-six people were sacrificed, and the judge fined Blank and Harris seventy-five dollars!

Conditions were dreadful in those days. But there was something that is lacking today and I think it was the devotion and the belief. We *believed* in what we were doing. We fought and we bled and we died. Today they don't have to.

You sit down at the table, you negotiate with the employers, you ask for 20 percent, they say 15, but the girls are working. People are working. They're not disturbed, and when the negotiations are over they get the increases. They don't really have to fight. Of course, they'll belong to the union and they'll go on strike if you tell them to, but it's the inner faith that people had in those days that I don't see today. It was a terrible time, but it was interesting. I'm glad I lived then.

Even when things were terrible, I always had that faith. . . . Only now, I'm a little discouraged sometimes when I see the workers spending their free hours watching television—trash. We fought so hard for those hours and they waste them. We used to read Tolstoy, Dickens, Shelley, by candlelight, and they watch the *Hollywood Squares*. Well, they're free to do what they want. That's what we fought for.

Crystal Eastman, Now We Can Begin

Crystal Eastman charts an agenda for feminists after the achievement of suffrage. For all humankind, what should we think of as being embraced by her observation that "freedom is a large word"? Most of her short essay focuses on how to achieve "woman's freedom" as she saw it through her particular early twentieth-century feminist frame. Do you agree that the issues she identifies needed to be prioritized in the 1920s? Are these issues still relevant today?

We invite you to do background research on Crystal Eastman and *The Liberator*, a magazine published in New York City starting in 1918 and named for William Lloyd Garrison's legendary abolitionist newspaper of the early nineteenth century. What things do you find most striking about Eastman's life? Who published *The Liberator* and for how long? Take a moment to open up the link to the digitized December 1920 issue so that you can see her short essay alongside other essays, artwork, and advertisements, imagining yourself as someone who moved in Eastman's circles in the 1920s.

Most women will agree that August 23, the day when the Tennessee legislature finally enacted the Federal suffrage amendment, is a day to begin with, not a day to end with. Men are saying perhaps "Thank God, this everlasting woman's fight is over!" But women, if I know them, are saying, "Now at last we can begin." In fighting for the right to vote most women have tried to be either non-committal or thoroughly respectable on every other subject. Now they can say what they are really after; and what they are after, in common with all the rest of the struggling world, is *freedom*.

Freedom is a large word.

Many feminists are socialists, many are communists, not a few are active leaders in these movements. But the true feminist, no matter how far to the left she may be in the revolutionary movement, sees the woman's battle as distinct in its objects and different in its methods from the workers' battle for industrial freedom. She knows, of course, that the vast majority of women as well as men are without property, and are of necessity bread and butter slaves under a system of society which allows the very sources of life to be privately owned by a few, and she counts herself a loyal soldier in the working-class army that is marching to overthrow that system. But as a feminist she also knows that the whole of woman's slavery is not summed up in the profit system, nor her complete emancipation assured by the downfall of capitalism.

Woman's freedom, in the feminist sense, can be fought for and conceivably won before the gates open into industrial democracy. On

Crystal Eastman, "Now We Can Begin," *The Liberator*, 3, no. 12 (December 1920), 23–4. For an open-access, digitized copy of the magazine issue, go to http://www.marxists.org/history/usa/culture/pubs/liberator/1920/12/v3n12-w33-dec-1920-liberator.pdf.

the other hand, woman's freedom, in the feminist sense, is not inherent in the communist ideal. All feminists are familiar with the revolutionary leader who "can't see" the woman's movement. "What's the matter with the women? My wife's all right," he says. And his wife, one usually finds, is raising his children in a Bronx flat or a dreary suburb, to which he returns occasionally for food and sleep when all possible excitement and stimulus have been wrung from the fight. If we should graduate into communism tomorrow this man's attitude to his wife would not be changed. The proletarian dictatorship may or may not free women. We must begin now to enlighten the future dictators.

What, then, is "the matter with women"? What is the problem of women's freedom? It seems to me to be this: how to arrange the world so that women can be human beings, with a chance to exercise their infinitely varied gifts in infinitely varied ways, instead of being destined by the accident of their sex to one field of activity—housework and child-raising. And second, if and when they choose housework and child-raising, to have that occupation recognized by the world as work, requiring a definite economic reward and not merely entitling the performer to be dependent on some man.

This is not the whole of feminism, of course, but it is enough to begin with. "Oh, don't begin with economics," my friends often protest, "Woman does not live by bread alone. What she needs first of all is a free soul." And I can agree that women will never be great until they achieve a certain emotional freedom, a strong healthy egotism, and some unpersonal sources of joy—that in this inner sense we cannot make woman free by changing her economic status. What we can do, however, is to create conditions of outward freedom in which a free woman's soul can be born and grow. It is these outward conditions with which an organized feminist movement must concern itself.

Freedom of choice in occupation and individual economic independence for women: How shall we approach this next feminist objective? First, by breaking down all remaining barriers, actual as well as legal, which make it difficult for women to enter or succeed in the various professions, to go into and get on in business, to learn trades and practice them, to join trades unions. Chief among these remaining

barriers is inequality in pay. Here the ground is already broken. This is the easiest part of our program.

Second, we must institute a revolution in the early training and education of both boys and girls. It must be womanly as well as manly to earn your own living, to stand on your own feet. And it must be manly as well as womanly to know how to cook and sew and clean and take care of yourself in the ordinary exigencies of life. I need not add that the second part of this revolution will be more passionately resisted than the first. Men will not give up their privilege of helplessness without a struggle. The average man has a carefully cultivated ignorance about household matters—from what to do with the crumbs to the grocer's telephone number—a sort of cheerful inefficiency which protects him better than the reputation for having a violent temper. It was his mother's fault in the beginning, but even as a boy he was quick to see how a general reputation for being "no good around the house" would serve him throughout life, and half-consciously he began to cultivate that helplessness until today it is the despair of feminist wives.

A growing number of men admire the woman who has a job, and, especially since the cost of living doubled, rather like the idea of their own wives contributing to the family income by outside work. And of course for generations there have been whole towns full of wives who are forced by the bitterest necessity to spend the same hours at the factory that their husbands spend. But these bread-winning wives have not yet developed home-making husbands. When the two come home from the factory the man sits down while his wife gets supper, and he does so with exactly the same sense of fore-ordained right as if he were "supporting her." Higher up in the economic scale the same thing is true. The business or professional woman who is married, perhaps engages a cook, but the responsibility is not shifted, it is still hers. She "hires and fires," she orders meals, she does the buying, she meets and resolves all domestic crises, she takes charge of moving, furnishing, settling. She may be, like her husband, a busy executive at her office all day, but unlike him, she is also an executive in a small way every night and morning at home. Her noon hour is spent in planning, and too often her Sundays and holidays are spent in "catching up."

Two business women can "make a home" together without either one being over-burdened or over-bored. It is because they both know how and both feel responsible. But it is a rare man who can marry one of them and continue the homemaking partnership. Yet if there are no children, there is nothing essentially different in the combination. Two self-supporting adults decide to make a home together: if both are women it is a pleasant partnership, more fun than work; if one is a man, it is almost never a partnership—the woman simply adds running the home to her regular outside job. Unless she is very strong, it is too much for her, she gets tired and bitter over it, and finally perhaps gives up her outside work and condemns herself to the tiresome half-job of housekeeping for two.

Cooperative schemes and electrical devices will simplify the business of homemaking, but they will not get rid of it entirely. As far as we can see ahead people will always want homes, and a happy home cannot be had without a certain amount of rather monotonous work and responsibility. How can we change the nature of man so that he will honorably share that work and responsibility and thus make the home-making enterprise a song instead of a burden? Most assuredly not by laws or revolutionary decrees. Perhaps we must cultivate or simulate a little of that highly prized helplessness ourselves. But fundamentally it is a problem of education, of early training—we must bring up feminist sons.

Sons? Daughters? They are born of women—how can women be free to choose their occupation, at all times cherishing their economic independence, unless they stop having children? This is a further question for feminism. If the feminist program goes to pieces on the arrival of the first baby, it is false and useless. For ninety-nine out of every hundred women want children, and seventy-five out of every hundred want to take care of their own children, or at any rate so closely superintend their care as to make any other full-time occupation impossible for at least ten or fifteen years. Is there any such thing then as freedom of choice in occupation for

women? And is not the family the inevitable economic unit and woman's individual economic independence, at least during that period, out of the question?

The feminist must have an answer to these questions, and she has. The immediate feminist program must include voluntary motherhood. Freedom of any kind for women is hardly worth considering unless it is assumed that they will know how to control the size of their families. "Birth control" is just as elementary an essential in our propaganda as "equal pay." Women are to have children when they want them, that's the first thing. That ensures some freedom of occupational choice; those who do not wish to be mothers will not have an undesired occupation thrust upon them by accident, and those who do wish to be mothers may choose in a general way how many years of their lives they will devote to the occupation of child-raising.

But is there any way of insuring a woman's economic independence while child-raising is her chosen occupation? Or must she sink into that dependent state from which, as we all know, it is so hard to rise again? That brings us to the fourth feature of our program—motherhood endowment. It seems that the only way we can keep mothers free, at least in a capitalist society, is by the establishment of a principle that the occupation of raising children is peculiarly and directly a service to society, and that the mother upon whom the necessity and privilege of performing this service naturally falls is entitled to an adequate economic reward from the political government. It is idle to talk of real economic independence for women unless this principle is accepted. But with a generous endowment of motherhood provided by legislation, with all laws against voluntary motherhood and education in its methods repealed, with the feminist ideal of education accepted in home and school, and with all special barriers removed in every field of human activity, there is no reason why woman should not become almost a human thing.

It will be time enough then to consider whether she has a soul.

EMPIRE AND INTERNATIONALISM

LAURA WEXLER
A Lady Photojournalist Goes to the 1904 St. Louis World's Fair

How might *you* stage a world's fair, organizing the grounds, pavilions, and interior displays? With numerous nations and peoples showcased, there is inevitably a politics to how the various groups are represented. Laura Wexler's essay explores the gender, racial, and imperial politics of the 1904 World's Fair in St. Louis. Let's note two things about the timing of this fair.

First, many white Americans felt they were at a crossroads. At the previous world's fair, held in 1893 in Chicago, historian Frederick Jackson Turner had given a speech that quickly became famous, entitled "The Significance of the Frontier for American History."* He argued that the existence of a frontier, "a meeting place between savagery and civilization," and the availability of "free land" had been the crucial elements in shaping American society. The frontier experience of free land shaped the American people, particularly Euro-American men, fostering democratic and independent values. As much as his talk celebrated Anglo-American westward expansion, it also mourned what he understood to be the end of the frontier, as the 1890 census reported that pockets of settlement interrupted what had once been clear lines of division between Anglo-American and aboriginal settlement. Without the frontier, what would happen to democracy in the United States?

Second, during the last decade of the nineteenth century, the U.S. government engaged in a series of economic, political, and military endeavors to extend the American frontier beyond the continent. During this decade, the United States fought the Spanish-American War, thereby acquiring control over islands in the Caribbean. It also incorporated islands in the Pacific Ocean—Hawaii, Guam, Samoa, and the Philippines—that could serve as stepping stones or way stations for commercial and military endeavors. Nationalists in the Philippines, a colony of Spain, had supported the United States during the war, anticipating their own independence. However, once Spain was vanquished, the United States occupied and controlled the islands, refusing to recognize Filipino demands for independence. Filipino nationalists resisted; the United States responded with force. The three-year

---

* Frederick Jackson Turner, "The Significance of the Frontier in American History," Paper presented at the American Historical Association, Chicago, 1893; excerpts are available at http://nationalhumanitiescenter .org/pds/gilded/empire/text1/turner.pdf.

Excerpted from the introduction and ch. 7 of *Tender Violence: Domestic Visions in an Age of U.S. Imperialism* by Laura Wexler (Chapel Hill: University of North Carolina Press, 2000). Reprinted by permission of the author and publisher. Notes have been edited and renumbered.

guerrilla war that ensued resulted in the death of hundreds of thousands of Filipinos (some 20 percent of the population) and 4,000 Americans.[†]

The 1904 World's Fair in St. Louis provided an opportunity for the United States to display its new imperial possessions. Wexler's essay focuses on one of the white, middle-class female photographers who frequented and worked at the fair, Jessie Tarbox Beals. Becoming a lady photographer allowed a woman to travel and document (and hence interpret) the world around her. Wexler complicates this narrative of gender liberation, however, by emphasizing the racial impact of privileged white women's photography, especially given its embeddedness in an "Age of Imperialism" for the United States.

The first cohort of American women photographers to achieve serious public careers as photojournalists at the turn of the century often used the "innocent eye" attributed to them by white domestic sentiment to construct images of war as peace, images that were, in turn, a constitutive element of the social relations of United States imperialism during the era's annexation and consolidation of colonies. My term, "the innocent eye," designates a deeply problematic practice of representation that developed within the private domain of family photography at midcentury in the United States. At that time, white middle-class women, in both the North and the South, were regularly portrayed in family photographs as if looking out from within, without seeing the race and class dynamics of the household. [The "innocent eye"] . . . of domestic sentiment functioned to normalize . . . raced and classed relations of dominance during slavery and to reinscribe them after its legal end. As a representational practice, this private gaze took on a new national significance when in the late 1890s and early 1900s a certain group of American "New Women" photographers—among them Frances Benjamin Johnston; Gertrude Käsebier; Alice Austen; the Gerhard sisters, Emme and Mamie; and Jessie Tarbox Beals . . . —learned to turn it to their professional advantage by ensuring that from the panorama of foreign wars fought by white American men, white American women would construct visions of domestic peace.

When the World's Fair opened in St. Louis, Missouri, in 1904, thirty-four-year-old photojournalist Jessie Tarbox Beals was there—along with many other white, middle-class, American women photographers. The spectacle of the nineteenth century's great fairs and expositions held strong attractions for them,

and they often went to great lengths to photograph them. For the World's Columbian Exposition of 1893, for instance, Jessie (then Tarbox), a single, twenty-three-year-old, Canadian-born schoolteacher, had taken the train to Chicago from her home in Greenfield, Massachusetts. She stayed for twenty-five days in the women's dormitory, shooting photographs with her new little Kodak (she could not get a permit for a larger view camera with tripod) and developing her own film in the public darkroom facilities that the Exposition's photography department provided. After Chicago, no longer would her own life look the same to her.

She returned to small-town existence in western Massachusetts and to schoolteaching, writes her biographer Alexander Alland, "consumed with the desire to visit the foreign places whose makeshift villages she had seen and photographed at the exposition."[1] When she then discovered that she could make more money in one summer of selling freelance pictures than she could in a year of teaching school, she was spoiled for "protected" feminine domestic gentility for ever. Within seven years, Jessie Tarbox had married Alfred Beals, an Amherst College graduate who was working as a machinist in Greenfield, quit schoolteaching, and persuaded Alfred to give up his job, become her darkroom assistant, and set off to see what possibilities there were in earning their living as itinerant photographers. They started in Vermont, traveled for a year through Florida, and regrouped to upstate New York. Alfred, it turned out, had married a "lady" photographer. At the time, neither he nor she quite knew what that was going to mean. . . .

To the photographing woman, the fairs and expositions offered congenial stimulation and a way to gain recognition and make some money selling photographs. Simultaneously,

[†]This war was an early occasion in which U.S. military forces used waterboarding; see Paul Kramer, "The Water Cure: Debating Torture and Counterinsurgency—A Century Ago," *The New Yorker*, February 25, 2008.

they offered a way to construct a larger identity as a "lady photographer." If, as many scholars have proposed, the fairs performed the public function of remaking a national self-definition for a United States reunited a generation after the Civil War and newly emerging as an industrial world power, they also served the private purpose of self-making for white women photographers of the era. The fairs encouraged them to emerge from domestic confinement and to test just how far the designation "lady with a camera" would go.

St. Louis was very much a southern city at the start of the nineteenth century. From the time of the Missouri Compromise in 1820, through the 1857 *Dred Scott v. Sanford* decision, which ruled that a slave who lived in a free state or territory was still a slave, debates over slavery and abolition gave a veneer of political debate to St. Louis; meanwhile, slave auctions took place on the steps of the very courthouse where these decisions were handed down. The citizens of St. Louis defiantly elected a Secessionist governor before the Civil War, although the state of Missouri stayed in the Union. Because of strong economic ties to the north, St. Louis eventually became a center of Union support and a staging ground for Union troops, but many there never altered their allegiance to the South.

And now, at the turn of the century, the St. Louis World's Fair of 1904 invited the city and the world to contemplate the triumph of yet another new formulation of United States power. America's recent victory in the war with Spain highlighted the global ambitions of the new American state. More than 1,270 acres of Forest Park had been given over to display the nationalist fervor of a new imperial order. The fair transformed both the resistant sectionalism of the Old South and the resilient commercialism of the New beyond all possibilities of imagining earlier in the century.

Not that the voices of the Old South were stilled, by any means. Widespread Democratic anti-imperialist agitation built heavily upon the racist presumptions of men like Thomas Nelson Page, author of *Red Rock* (1898), and Thomas Dixon, author of *The Leopard's Spots* (1902), *The Clansman* (1905), and *The Traitor* (1907). Both these men argued against annexation of the Philippines on the grounds that imperial acquisition was unconstitutional and anti-republican and that Filipino self government was the only way to avoid burdening the United States with what Mrs. Jefferson Davis

called "fresh millions of foreign negroes, even more ignorant and more degraded . . . than those at home."[2]

However, the thrust of the times was against them. Pro-annexation arguments were neither more egalitarian nor necessarily less racist. They simply alleged that in the Philippines "Caucasians were ushering in a new era in human history," an era in which "human culture is become unified, not only through diffusion but through the extinction of lower grades."[3] The cotton plantations of the Old South were a model for prospective fruit, sugar, and hemp plantations in Hawaii and the Philippines. Nineteen hundred four was one of the peak years of immigration to the United States by whites from western and eastern Europe, most of them poorly educated peasants looking for ways to better themselves and escape from lives of unremitting manual labor. Many blacks were also arriving from the West Indies, not all of whom were fully indoctrinated into the culture of American race relations. Nativist sentiment had not yet pushed Congress toward immigration restriction and overall quotas—that would take another twenty years—but its organization was growing. . . .

Above all else, then, the St. Louis World's Fair was advancing an argument for the vigor of the Caucasian culture of the Unites States and its capacity to incorporate the labor of such immigrants, since it had been able so successfully to discipline and assimilate its former slaves and aboriginal Others into a seemingly credible domestic "peace." In exemplifying how the United States had already dealt with similar tasks, the St. Louis World's Fair was addressing the greatest anxieties of its day, to indicate where and how white Americans could and would prevail. Industrial leaders believed that "the burden of humanity is already in large measure the White Man's burden—for, viewing the human world as it is, white and strong are synonymous terms."[4] They looked forward to shouldering America's load.

These particular views on race and national destiny were, in fact, the sentiments of Mr. W. J. McGee, one of the chief officers of the St. Louis Fair. McGee, the head of the Anthropology Department of the fair, reasoned that it was precisely the new global industrial opportunities that rationalized the horrific cost of the Civil War and the preservation of the Union. In the south, Reconstruction was over; its demise left a growing ambition to explore these new opportunities. McGee portrayed the field for action as nearly limitless: "It is the duty of the strong man to subjugate lower nature, to extirpate the bad and cultivate the good among living things, to delve in earth below and cleave the air above in search of fresh resources, to transform the seas into paths for ships and pastures for food-fishes, . . . and in all ways to enslave the world for the support of humanity and the increase of human intelligence."[5]

McGee and the rest of the team designed the St. Louis World's Fair to make the perspective of scientific racism and the imperative of United States imperialism seem equally valid and inevitable. . . . The St. Louis World's Fair was also the Louisiana Purchase Centenary Celebration. It commemorated the treaty which in 1803 had more than doubled the geographical size of the United States and simultaneously transformed the old Creole town of St. Louis into a booming American city, "the gateway to the West." It also celebrated a potent analogy constructed between pacification of "domestic" tribes of Native Americans and "foreign" tribes of Filipinos. As one of the official publications of the Exposition explained, "The time is coming when the purchase and retention of the Philippine Islands will seem as wise to our descendants as does the Louisiana Purchase seem to us who live today."[6]

In the brief nine months that it was open, St. Louis World's Fair of 1904 formulated for almost 19 million people who participated in its construction or visited its grounds a vision not only of the fruits of the past hundred years of expansion and conquest but also of the promising connection between that past and future acquisitions. The intertwined notions of imperialism and progress that the fair projected captured the spirit of the twentieth century as "The American Century," at its very moment of inception. . . .

Beals and her husband Alfred traveled to St. Louis from Albany, New York, where Jessie had been working as the "first official woman" staff photographer for the *Buffalo Courier*, with Alfred as her darkroom assistant. Beals regularly photographed suicides, murder trials, and fires for the paper when she could. When times were slow, she showed up where work crews met, or lingered at factory doors, or rode door-to-door on her bicycle, balancing twenty- to thirty-odd pounds of camera

equipment and soliciting the chance to take portraits. Business was good. Her photographer's diary from the time is peppered with phrases such as "got a fine list of orders" and "Work has been booming–16 to 30 pictures taken daily. Poor Beals is kept busy developing and printing." When they left Albany on April 4, 1904, her departure was mourned in the Buffalo newspapers as the loss not simply of a newspaper photographer but of a *woman* newspaper photographer: "Buffalo lost one of its best professional women today when Mrs. Jessie Tarbox Beals, staff camera artist, departed on an early morning train for St. Louis." At the farewell party they hosted for her, . . . "the staffs of the two dailies Jessie worked for presented her with a parting gift—a gold enameled pin studied with pearls."[7] It was a gift particularly appropriate for the "woman" part of the equation, and it must have encouraged Beals about the viability of her plans to go to St. Louis as a "professional woman." . . .

"Lady" photographers had a larger official role at St. Louis . . . than at any other fair. . . . But what the presence of these [other] women meant in practice for Jessie Tarbox Beals was that when she arrived at St. Louis, at first all the doors were closed to her: "She had hoped her reputation in Buffalo would warrant an official press card. But officials at the exposition said that the Buffalo newspapers were regional and of no value to the national promotion of the fair. She applied to the St. Louis newspapers; they were fully staffed. She kept overhearing remarks that working on the crowded fairgrounds was too much for a woman to tackle."[8] This was the problem of tokenism. . . .

Beals solved this problem in a characteristic way. She transformed the fair officials' anxiety that a woman was of "no value to the national promotion of the fair" into evidence that the "nation" could be promoted by a women. First, she wrangled a "Pre-Exhibition Permit," which allowed her into the fair but limited her to making photographs "prior to the opening of the fair" and prevented her from selling any of the images or using them "in any other way except as ordinary illustrations . . . every negative made under the permit and not accepted as an illustration is to be destroyed."[9] The fair's officials were so eager to marshal all the images of the fair into the

Jessie Tarbox Beals taking pictures from a ladder at the St. Louis World's Fair, 1904, photographer unknown. The ladder is supported by her assistant, "Pumpkin." (Courtesy of the Schlesinger Library, Radcliffe Institute, Harvard University.)

grand educational (and commercial) scheme that Beals worked on pain of expulsion from the fairgrounds if she was found to violate these conditions.

If they were used to controlling the access of women photographers, the officials apparently didn't figure on Beals's next step: "Undaunted by the rules, Jessie roamed the fairgrounds as she saw fit, photographing what interested her. Most of the other photographers there concentrated on the sumptuous exhibits of the industrial nations; Jessie was drawn instead to the scenes of the daily lives of exotic, little-known peoples in their native habitats. She took pictures of the Igorots, the Bogobos, the Zulus, the Hottentots, the Eskimos, the Filipinos and other defenseless recipients of missionary barrels," writes Alland. Her multicultural pictures of domesticity read much like a precursor to [photographer Edward] Steichen's famous *Family of Man* exhibit.[10]

And then came some good luck. Regular hard work photographing the daily lives of "exotic, little-known peoples" happened to put Beals at the scene when some "Patagonian Giants" of South America arrived at the "village" next door to the "Ainus of Japan." At first, she was the only photographer there. By the time the other photographers arrived, Beals had already made her interpretation of the event. As Alland reports, "An old Patagonian woman issued an edict that no black boxes were to be pointed at her people and she chased the camera men over a barbed wire fence. But Jessie had already made her images, and they were exclusives."[11]

What Beals had done was to show "Patagonian Giants" next to "pygmies," in a comparison by size that imaged the anthropometric premise of the fair—the belief that the essential information about where a group of people fell on the evolutionary ladder could be gleaned from their physical characteristics. Her pictures sold all over the country—providing the "national exposure" the Fair's officials craved—not only because they were positioned as "exclusive images" but [also] because they were images of

"Pygmy and Patagonian Giant," Jessie Tarbox Beals, photographer. (Courtesy of St. Louis Public Library.)

an "exclusive" position that white Americans were constructing for themselves—as the physical golden mean and the evolutionary model.

Beals was rewarded for this work of making material the abstract racial premise of the anthropological "display." The next day's headlines trumpeted the news: "Woman Gets Permit to Take Pictures at the Fair." The story read, "The first permit to be issued to a woman authorizing the taking of photographs in the World's Fair Grounds has been given to Mrs. T. Beals. Mrs. Beals secured notice through her work in obtaining photographs of the double suicide of Mr. and Mrs. Pennell of Buffalo, who rode their automobile over a cliff into a quarry." The pygmy/Patagonian comparison showed the fair officials that Beals's eye was ... good. ... With it, Beals had become the "First Pictorial Journalist of Her Sex," even though she was not, as we have seen, the first woman licensed to take photographs in the "World's Fair Grounds."[12]

What really made Beals "first" ... was that she had understood ... that in St. Louis, juxtaposition was the clearest signifier of American size and strength. The St. Louis World's Fair was the largest international exposition ever yet presented. Its total exhibition space exceeded that of the Chicago Exposition of 1893

by more than one-third. The fair cost $15 million to produce, the same amount of money originally paid for the entire Louisiana Territory. The fair was so big that medical advisers warned "neurasthenic" patients to avoid the fair entirely, for fear of mental collapse, and "brain-fagged businessmen" and "men of affairs" were encouraged to spend "at least several weeks or months in order to avoid the almost certain breakdown that would result from a hurried visit."[13] It took a week merely to view the agricultural display. However, the real core ... was the Department of Anthropology, ... and the "exposition within an exposition," the U.S. government's Philippine Reservation. Other world's fairs, notably the one in Chicago, had featured anthropological divisions, but St. Louis's was by far the largest and the most central.

On the Anthropology Department's grounds and at the Philippine Reservation were displayed "specimens" of the peoples that American civilization had conquered and was now in the process of "educating," "disciplining," and "converting." The Philippine Reservation consisted of almost twelve hundred Filipinos living in villages on a 47-acre site that was deliberately called a "reservation" to make plain the parallel between the subjugation of the Native Americans and the domestication of the Philippines. The grounds were carefully laid out to represent "a sequential synopsis of the developments that have marked man's progress." In an essay entitled "The Trend of Human Progress," McGee explained that process as . . . "a trend of vital development from low toward the high, from dullness toward brightness, from idleness groveling toward intellectual uprightness. . . . It is a matter of common observation that the white man can do more and better than the yellow, the yellow man more and better than the red or black. . . . Classed in terms of blood, the peoples of the world may be grouped in several races; classed in terms of what they do rather than what they merely are, they are conveniently grouped in the four culture grades of savagery, barbarism, civilization, and enlightenment." McGee believed that at the turn of the century "perfected man is over-spreading the world." "Perfected man," in McGee's terms, meant "the two higher culture-grades—especially the Caucasian race, and (during recent decades) the budded enlightenment of Britain and full-blown enlightenment of America."[14]

To illustrate these "common observations," the Anthropology Department portrayed a "logical arrangement" of ethnological displays of "villages" of "non-white types" and "culture grades." Besides the twelve hundred Filipinos, these "types" included pygmies from the Congo, Japanese Ainu, Patagonian "giants," Kwakiutl Indians from Vancouver Island, and several groupings of Native Americans. Also on exhibit were the Apache leader Geronimo (under armed guard as a military prisoner), Chief Joseph of the Nez Percé, and Quanah Parker of the Comanche. The Indian School Building and the Philippine Reservation were carefully placed to make the instrumental relation between the two as plain as possible. Calling the Indian School building "designed not merely as a consummation, but as a prophecy," McGee explained the rationale behind its inclusion at the Fair: "now that other primitive peoples are passing under the beneficent influence and protection of the Stars and Stripes, it is needful to take stock of past progress as a guide to the future."[15] . . .

Beals played the woman's angle for all it was worth, which was considerable. She made many sets of "sympathetic" pictures of domestic life in the anthropology exhibits. Seen as "ethnological studies," they were eagerly bought by Harvard and Yale Universities and by natural history museums all over the country. Perhaps her most famous set of pictures was *Mother and Babe at the Exhibition;* but Beals made other sets of photographs as well, such as the *The Children of the Fair, Musical Instruments, Native Habitations, Strange Wedding Ceremonies, Head Dress, Dances of All Nations, Cooking Methods,* and *The Mutilation Practices.* In fact, Beals's work at St. Louis was taken as so good a model for ethnographic photography that in 1906 she was invited to exhibit some of it at a "women photographers" exhibition (the first ever in New England) at the Camera Club of Hartford, Connecticut, where confused critics singled out her work as "one of the best exhibits," crediting her with having "furnished several scenes in Japan (taken at the St. Louis World's Fair)."[16] . . .

As if all this were not recognition enough, Beal's photographs of the Philippine reservation were met with such consummate delight by the organizers of that exhibit that they brought them to the notice of Secretary of War William Howard Taft, previously governor-general of the Philippines. Much impressed, Taft offered Beals "a passport and a free round-trip to the islands . . . to bring back, as a contribution to science, pictorial records of the daily life of the little-known wild tribes."[17] Beals was elated, but unfortunately Alfred didn't want to go, quite possibly because he was aware that the fighting still continued in the Philippines.

Beals also exploited her angle of vision in a literal way, by choosing dramatic vantage points from which to photograph and allowing herself to be photographed and written about "as a woman" while in such stances. For instance, she climbed a twenty-foot ladder to photograph a parade. And just before the beginning of the International Balloon Race she climbed into one of the [balloon] baskets with her camera. One newspaper years later memorialized the event this way: "Just as one of the balloons was being set free, the huge crowd was thunderstruck to see a woman, a camera slung over her shoulder, grip the top of a basket and pull herself aboard. The balloon was off, and with it the intrepid woman photographer." Dr. David Francis, president of the Exposition, published the resulting panoramas of the fairgrounds, which Beals made from 900 feet aloft, in the official *Louisiana Purchase Exposition Bulletin.* Her bird's-eye view photographs were, he

"As the Lady Managers wanted to have them" Pierre Chouteau.

"As the Lady Managers wanted to have them—Prime Christians," Jessie Tarbox Beals's satiric photograph of Filipinos (mis)representing their customary dress and lifeways, on the Philippine Reservation at the St. Louis World's Fair, 1904. (Courtesy of Missouri History Museum.)

wrote, "a view which I wish to remember."[18] This is perhaps not surprising, since, like the eye of the American eagle, they dominated what they surveyed.

But what exactly *was* the point of view of the "intrepid woman photographer"? The people in Beals's photographs were neither given derogatory names nor photographed as fetishes for the contemplation of nude bodily display. Her images are therefore less overtly racist than the productions of [other women's photographers such as] the Gerhard Sisters [Emme and Mamie]. Indeed, Beals made a photograph that explicitly mocked the sanctimonious (and highly publicized) efforts of the Board of Lady Managers to make the Igorots wear full sets of clothes rather than the loincloths that were their accustomed dress because it seemed to them that the male nudity was drawing

prurient looks, especially from "lady" visitors. In her hilarious but sharply pointed image, the Filipinos cooperate with Beals in performing a satiric pantomime of "'As the Lady Managers wanted to have them'—Prime Christians," which is how she captioned the photograph. Fully and awkwardly covered in heavy robes, coats, and wearing hats, but still barefoot, five Philippine Reservation inhabitants walk in a line, evidently performing one of their ceremonial dances the "Prime Christian" way.

Nor do Beals's images reproduce the sensational stereotypes of turn-of-the-century primitivism's imaginary [created by other women photographers at the fair] .... On the contrary, Beals felt that she had made "many new friends" among the "foreign" people she photographed and "would treasure their many parting gifts, particularly the pina fiber dress presented by the Filipino villagers and the exquisite bolt of Chinese silk given to her by Prince Pu Lun of China."[19] Given the American occupation of the Philippines, such "friendships" must have had a considerable component of fantasy.

Nonetheless, Beals seems to have been personally affected by the racial vision of the fair. The photographs she made are complexly complicit in keeping offstage any vision of the violence of the pacification of a people. While she was still at the fair, Beals made a collage of her photographs from the anthropological villages. The pictures are uniformly gracious and dignified domestic scenes, with their grass-rooted huts, their pastoral waterways, their smiling children, and their graceful young mothers. . . . [T]hey argue for the unharmed humanity of those they picture but without challenging the violent framework in which that humanity was concurrently differentiated, primitivized, and separated from the "higher" domestic forms of the "white race."

Thus, Beals's pictures extended sympathy, but they also fully eradicated any traces of the military surveillance that had accompanied the Filipinos to St. Louis. That is to say, first, they normalized the presence among the fair's Filipino delegation of several hundred members of the Philippine constabulary, a paramilitary force of Philippine collaborators set in place by the American occupation; one of them, photographed with an "innocent eye" by Beals, was included in the upper right-hand corner of her collage. Second, they remained oblivious to the fact that the Philippine villages were surrounded by high board fences and their inhabitants monitored by curfews, in a direct quotation of the so-called "relocation camps" in which thousands of their countrymen were being interned back in the Philippines at that very moment. And third, they avoided any view of the outer perimeter of the Philippine "reservation" itself, which was designed as a model of the old Spanish defense of the city of Manila. When walking through it to the ethnic villages, every visitor–and every Filipino inhabitant–re-created the heroic story of [Commodore George] Dewey's conquest and penetration of the city [in 1898] to gain access to the nation of "primitives" that supposedly lay beyond.[20] Even though during the whole time the fair was open in

St. Louis, Filipino insurgents were continuing to battle the United States occupation, and the United States was continuing to execute Filipino patriots as "outlaws," there is no sign of this activity in Beals's images. Her collage of domestic life in the Anthropological Department so completely illustrates the present success and bright future of the American rule of peace that it is no wonder that Taft himself, the author of the concept of "benevolent assimilation," longed to send her to the Philippines. . . .

Beals photographed the virtual geography of the fair by moving freely between the obviously "fake" Manila and the "obviously" real St. Louis, but it is difficult to distinguish the two in her photographs. This was, of course, the desired effect. The fact that Harvard and Yale Universities bought Beals's exposition images as ethnographic studies is one result of this confusion. . . . But the most significant reality effect of this simulacrum was that in construing the Philippine present as coterminous with the Southern past, the fair was portraying that past as the progressive and inevitable future of the American empire. Conversely, it was erasing actual Philippine history in order to rescript it as naturally consonant with the context of the American South.

In an essay entitled "The Sign as a Site of Class Struggle," Jo Spence identifies the ideological work of photographs as the production of an "imaginary coherence," one in which "images from . . . photography . . . are immediate yet appear to be retrospective," and in which "their presence confirms the absence of what appears to have been previously present."[21] This elegant formulation exactly describes what Beals's photographs accomplished. Their normalization of [the ethnic villages of the] St. Louis [Fair] as the Philippine future confirms the influence of the Southern past as constitutive of the Philippine's immediate reality. Never mind that it was a coherence that was patently corrupt; the conjuncture was made potent by Jim Crow—and rendered invisible by Jessie Beals.

However, the experience of working at the fair, with its emphasis on racial "diversity" and racial "progress," not only translated into photographs that configured the way that viewers were to see the coming American Century; it also prophesied a new Beals. After her work in St. Louis, Beals evolved into an even more ambitious photographer and an even less conventional woman. Beals was aware of its importance to herself. Some years after returning from St. Louis, Beals made another photographic collage, this time a narrative of her own life. The two panels document changes in a small-town girl's experience as she discovers photography. The world in the pictures steadily expands. In them, Beals and her camera conquer obstacles, travel, go to parties, and meet interesting and famous people. There are more photographs of Beals at the fair than at any other period of her life. In the photographs of St. Louis we see Beals in the balloon, Beals on the twenty-foot ladder, Beals working at the fair with her camera assistant named "Pumpkin," and Beals's hard-won press pass and photo ID card. Functioning as the fulcrum of Beals's autobiography, the fair separates her own experience into a "before," and "after." The collage demonstrates that as a sentimental indoctrination, the fair had apparently fulfilled an inner, as well as an ideological mission.

Indeed, life "before" was one thing, but life "after" was something else again. For a long time after St. Louis, nothing measured up for Jessie to the intensity of the nine months she had spent photographing the fair. Perhaps it was that Alfred Beals had dragged his feet about the trip to the Philippines and prevented her accepting the assignment from Taft. Perhaps it was that Jessie Beals was nearing forty and after many years of marriage she and Alfred still had no children. Her only infant, a girl born in 1901, had died only a few hours after birth. Perhaps it was simply that Beals had grown weary of the concept of "woman photographer" that juxtaposed her solely to Alfred or to other photographing women, when she had seemed in St. Louis to have the whole world as her counterpart.

NOTES

1. Alexander Alland, Sr., *Jessie Tarbox Beals: First Woman News Photographer* (New York: Camera/Graphic Press, 1978), 22. Other published sources of information on Beals include Jane Cutler, *Song of the Molimo* (New York: Farrar Straus Giroux, 1998).

2. Mrs. Jefferson Davis is quoted in Walter Benn Michaels, "Anti-Imperial Americanism," in *Cultures of U.S. Imperialism,* ed. Amy Kaplan and Donald Pease (Durham, N.C.: Duke University Press, 1993), 387 n. 1.

3. Robert W. Rydell, *All the World's a Fair: Visions of American Empire at American International Expositions, 1876–1916* (Chicago: University of Chicago Press, 1987), 161.

4. W. J. McGee, "Trend of Human Progress," quoted in Rydell, *All the World's a Fair,* 161.

5. W. J. McGee, "National Growth and National Character," quoted in ibid., 161.

6. W. J. McGee, quoted in ibid., 167.

7. Alland, *Beals,* 26, 40-41.

8. Ibid., 43.

9. Ibid.

10. Ibid. [In 1955 Steichen, as the director of photography at the Museum of Modern Art in New York, organized a monumental show of 503 photographs taken by 273 artists from 68 nations. The exhibit aimed to show life experiences and emotions shared across cultures. It went on a worldwide tour and became a best-selling book.]

11. Ibid.

12. Ibid., 43, 45.

13. Rydell, *All the World's a Fair,* 157.

14. McGee quoted in Ibid., 160, 161.

15. Ibid., 167.

16. Camera Club of Hartford, Conn., April 1906, quoted in Alland, *Beals,* 62.

17. Ibid., 52.

18. *Philadelphia Public Ledger,* January 26, 1921, and David Francis, both quoted in Alland, *Beals,* 48.

19. Ibid.

20. Beverly K. Grindstaff, "Creating Identity: Exhibiting the Philippines at the 1904 Louisiana Purchase Exhibition," in Donald Preziosi and Claire J. Farago, eds., *Grasping the World: The Idea of the Museum* (Aldershot, UK: Ashgate, 2003), 298–320.

21. Jo Spence, "The Sign as a Site of Class Struggle," in *Photography/Politics: Two,* ed. Patricia Holland, Jo Spence, and S. Watney (London: Commedia, 1986), 176.

LEILA J. RUPP

Sexuality and Politics in the Early Twentieth-Century International Women's Movement

We often imagine that in U.S. history "the sexual revolution" took place in the 1960s. Historians, however, perceive what they sometimes call a first sexual revolution, occurring early in the twentieth century (although this ignores changing ideas about sexual expression and gender roles in the 1700s and 1800s*). Two broad shifts were at work in mainstream American culture after the turn of the twentieth century, most notably in the 1920s. The first concerned homosociality, or the extent to which persons of one perceived sex spend most of their time with members of the same sex. For decades prior to 1920, women and men were expected largely to occupy different social realms. Around the period of the "roaring twenties," some Europeans and Americans began to pursue and celebrate heterosocial patterns of engagement, both in informal social activities and the organizations they joined. At the same time, heterosexual experimentation prior to and outside of marriage became more acceptable in some circles. One consequence of these shifts was that same-sex emotional and physical intimacy became increasingly stigmatized and labeled (pejoratively) as homosexuality.

Leila J. Rupp's essay tells us about the political alliances forged across national borders by women in Europe and the Americas, with the sexual revolution of the early twentieth century as a backdrop. These activists could afford to travel overseas and to devote themselves full-time to volunteer or paid work on the behalf of organizations such as the International Council of Women. They were often fluent in several languages. Some lived openly as same-sex couples. Others gloried in their heterosexual marriages or did not do much to hide their many affairs with men. Rupp reads personal correspondence and organizational records to find out how much sexual (or "affectional," as in where you place your most important affections) life choices factored in the political differences among the activists—such as over the issue of woman-only gatherings. She finds that national, class, and generational differences were just as important.

How do you think her insights about sexuality and politics might apply to activists today? Rupp's study focuses on transnational connections among women in the West. How might issues relating to sexual politics be similar or different if we examined transnational women's activism today between the global North and global South?

---

*For arguments about major shifts prior to 1830, see Richard Godbeer, *Sexual Revolution in Early America* (Baltimore: Johns Hopkins University Press, 2002); and Clare A. Lyons, *Sex Among the Rabble: An Intimate History of Gender and Power in the Age of Revolution, Philadelphia, 1730-1830* (Chapel Hill: University of North Carolina Press, 2006).

Excerpted from "Sexuality and Politics in the Early Twentieth Century: The Case of the International Women's Movement," by Leila J. Rupp, in *Feminist Studies* 23, no. 3 (Fall 1997): 577–605. Reprinted by permission of the author and publisher. Notes have been renumbered and edited.

In her autobiography, Lena Madesin Phillips, U.S. founder of the International Federation of Business and Professional Women, who lived for thirty-three years with a woman to whom she "lost her heart," reported that an Austrian colleague had once asked her about the large number of unmarried women in the organization. "You women seem quite content to have meetings without men present; to be happy though unmarried. . . . American women told us they had a splendid banquet where women had a fine meal, some speeches, and no men," the Austrian woman remarked with evident astonishment. Within the same international women's movement circles, Brazilian International Alliance of Women member Bertha Lutz expressed her disgust at the lobbying tactics of Inter-American Commission of Women head Doris Stevens, an American "emancipated woman" who worked for an international equal rights treaty by seeking the support of male government representatives to the Pan American Union. Lutz called Stevens a "nymphomaniac" and accused her of "paying the mexican delegates in kisses . . . [and] luring the haitians with a french secretary she has."[1]

These contrasting observations—about a surprisingly happy female world and a disturbingly (hetero)sexual one—alert us to some of the tensions that simmered beneath the seemingly placid surface of early-twentieth-century international women's organizations. In the industrialized societies of the Euroamerican arena, the first decades of the century marked a critical transition, sometimes graced with the label of "sexual revolution," from a world of privatized to a world of more public and commercialized sexuality. As the barriers between women's and men's public worlds began to break down in the decades on either side of 1900 and young women in Chicago and Harlem, London, and Copenhagen, laid assertive new claims to their own sexuality, increasingly rigid definitions of heterosexuality and homosexuality cast more and more suspicion on a whole range of women's relationships and forms of organizing.[2] Women might step over the line of respectable heterosexuality by cavorting with men outside of marriage, but women without men—whether "spinsters" or women in same-sex couples—came more frequently to earn the label "deviant." And, as I argue here, these moves had consequences for the politics of women's single-sex organizing.

Sexual respectability was not a new concern in the women's movement of the early twentieth century—one has only to think of the scandals that surrounded Mary Wollstonecraft or Victoria Woodhull [for Woodhull, see pp. 258–259]. But heightened attention to the deviant lesbian subject did transform the context in which women gathered in single-sex organizations. Before the categorization of the "female invert" or "lesbian" at the end of the nineteenth century, women in the women's movement could more easily form intense and passionate relationships as "romantic friends" or choose to live out their lives as single women without a diagnosis of abnormality.[3] Scholarship has long emphasized the importance of supportive relationships among women for the strength of the women's movement.[4] Although recent work has opened our eyes to the ease with which romantic friends in the nineteenth century and earlier could transgress what the counsel for the defense in a famous [Scottish] case called "ordinary female friendship," there is no question that coupled women had to trod ever more carefully as time wore on.[5]

The organizations making up the international women's movement provide a particularly interesting case study of such tensions, because these bodies came to life as shifts in the conceptualization of women's relationships proceeded. They also brought together women from a variety of cultures, if primarily middle-and upper-class women of European origin from the countries of Western Europe and North America. As we shall see, not only affectional but generational, class, and national differences—and their complex interplay in the lives of women—shaped responses to the practice of single-sex organizing.

My research concentrates on the three major transnational women's groups—the International Council of Women, the International Alliance of Women, and the Women's International League for Peace and Freedom—and the more narrowly focused bodies with which they interacted on a regular basis in the years between the emergence of international organizing in the 1880s and the conclusion of the Second World War, which marked the end of the first wave of the international women's movement (and the lull before the swell of the second). In this period all three organizations remained heavily elite and Euroamerican in composition and leadership. Not only did Europe and what have been called the "neo-Europes" contribute

Farewell banquet, International Council of Women, Quinquennial Congress at the Mayflower Hotel, May 13, 1925.
Reproduced from the Report on the Quinquennial Meeting, *Washington, D.C., 1925. (Image courtesy of Leila Rupp.)*

all but one of the national sections until 1923 but women from the United States, Great Britain, and Western and Northern Europe also served as the founders and leaders. This pattern perpetuated itself through the choice of official languages—English, French, and German—and the location of congresses primarily in Europe, with a few excursions to North America. Although women from Latin America, the Middle East, Asia, and Africa increasingly found their voices within the international organizations after the First World War undermined European dominance of the world system, their relative silence in the recorded debate about sexuality is testimony to their marginality in the organizational friendship circles.[6]

The International Council of Women (ICW), the most vaguely defined group, came together in 1888 and welcomed all women's organizations with whatever purposes, bringing in a huge number of members but forestalling commitment to controversial goals. The International Woman Suffrage Alliance (IWSA), later known as the International Alliance of Women (IAW), split off from the ICW in 1904 in order to take a position in favor of suffrage and remained a strongly feminist-identified

body, even after the increasing extension of the vote to women in the years after the First World War undermined the group's original rationale. The Women's International League for Peace and Freedom (WILPF), founded in 1915 by IWSA members who insisted on meeting despite wartime hostilities, consistently took quite radical positions on a range of issues.[7] These three groups, in conjunction with a wide array of bodies organized on a regional basis, or comprised of particular constituencies of women, or devoted to single issues, formed coalitions in the years between the wars to coordinate international collective action, especially lobbying at the League of Nations.

The transnational women's groups focused on issues of women's rights, peace, and women's work, paying minimal attention to questions of sexuality, with the exception of what they called "the traffic in women." The dialogue about sexuality and politics, then, must be ferreted out of the sources, read from assumptions and associations. As I explored discussions of difference between women and men, arguments about the appropriateness of single-sex organizing, and correspondence about personal relationships, I began to perceive tensions within the international organizations and patterns linking women's personal lives and cultural contexts to their political choices.

SAME-SEX LOVE, HOMOSOCIALITY, AND SEPARATISM

Within the international women's organizations, some women coupled with women in what seem to have been "lesbian" relationships or as "romantic friends," sometimes in relationships in which one woman served as a kind of caretaker for the other. Some women never formed intimate relationships with either women or men. None of these women can be easily categorized, but in one way or another all made their lives with other women.

We have no direct evidence that any of the women involved in the international women's movement identified as lesbians, but the concept of lesbianism was not unknown in their intellectual world. As early as 1904, in a speech to the Scientific Humanitarian Committee, the pioneering German homosexual rights group, Anna Ruhling associated lesbians ("Uranian women" in the terminology of the time) with the international women's movement, asserting that

> the homosexual woman is particularly capable of playing a leading role in the international women's rights movement for equality. And indeed, from the beginning of the women's movement until the present day, a significant number of homosexual women assumed the leadership in the numerous struggles and, through their energy, awakened the naturally indifferent and submissive average women to an awareness of their human dignity and rights.[8]

. . . That women in the international women's movement had some familiarity with the discourse of "homosexuality" as it emerged in the late nineteenth century is clear. . . . Discussion within international women's movement circles of "fairies," use of the terms "queer" and "perverse from a sexual point of view," [and] references to "Manly-Looking" women and women who "went about together at the Hague, hair cropped short and rather mannish in dress," . . . suggest that at least the European women had some familiarity with the work of the sexologists [such as Havelock Ellis].[9]

Despite such derogatory usages, women within the movement accepted women's couple relationships, conceptualizing them as romantic friendships or "Boston marriages" rather than lesbian love affairs. Anita Augspurg and Lida Gustava Heymann formed one such couple within the circle of internationally organized women. Augspurg, leading member of the radical wing of the German women's movement and the country's first woman lawyer, met Heymann, who had freed herself from the life of a daughter of a rich Hamburg merchant to become a social worker and trade union organizer, at an 1896 international women's conference in Berlin. In their memoirs, Heymann described her first vision of the woman she came to live with for over forty years. Arrested by Augspurg's powerful voice, she saw her at the lectern, dressed in a brown velvet dress. "Already graying short hair framed a high forehead, under which two clear-sighted eyes sparkled. A sharp profile contrasted markedly but not unharmoniously with a delightful small mouth, chin, and small ears."[10] Obviously it was a momentous meeting, and the physical description smacks of a "love at first sight" genre.

Although early on the two women decided not to live together, they happily broke that promise. "Every year brought us closer," Heymann wrote, "deepened our friendship, let us know that not only in questions of Weltanschauung [worldview] . . . but also in all the events of daily life . . . we stood in exquisite harmony." They moved to the country where they launched a series of ambitious, and successful, agricultural enterprises, a quite unusual undertaking for two women. As a result, they reported that their Upper Bavarian peasant neighbors viewed them with some suspicion. In the section of their memoirs entitled "Private Life," Heymann recounted that "it excited the envy and anger of the farmers that two 'vagabonds in petticoats' were successful, creative, and happy to organize their lives according to their own desires and inclinations." One day a cattle dealer came to call with proposals of marriage for both women, explaining that the farm was splendid and lacked only a man. "It took all our effort to remain serious and make clear to the man the hopelessness of his desire. As he left, we shook with laughter," Heymann commented.[11]

As such descriptions make clear, Heymann and Augspurg presented themselves in public, in their daily lives, and unselfconsciously as a couple, and that is certainly how they were treated within the international women's movement. Correspondents regularly sent messages to and received them from both women. Heymann sent "Heartfelt greetings from us both" to Rosika Schwimmer in 1919. . . . Augspurg and Heymann stayed in double rooms when they attended congresses, entertained movement friends at their home, and described a happy family life: "I had a very good journey home and found Anita and our dog in good health," Heymann wrote [to the French WILPF leader] on her return from a trip to Paris. When Heymann planned to travel to Geneva for a meeting in 1930, a WILPF staff member reported that "she is coming without Dr. Augspurg which is scarcely believable!"[12]

Heymann and Augspurg were enjoying a Mediterranean vacation in March of 1933 when Hitler came to power in Germany. As pacifists and feminists they had made themselves enemies of the Nazis, so they never returned to the land of their birth. Although in this way they stayed out of the Nazis' clutches, the regime seized all their property, including their books and personal papers, prompting WILPF friends to try to help them. Swiss WILPF cochair Clara Ragaz, hoping to arrange hospitality at headquarters in Geneva, commented about Augspurg, who suffered from heart disease, that "it is a very hard time for her friend—and of course for herself." When Heymann died in June of 1943, American Emily Greene Balch worked to raise money to support Heymann's "life-long friend and co-worker . . . , for whom she had cared so devotedly." But as it turned out, Augspurg did not survive long. "Did you notice that Lida Gustava Heymann and Dr. Anita Augspurg died within a few short weeks of each other?" Rosika Schwimmer asked a friend.[13]

Augspurg and Heymann made the acquaintance of another well-known couple, Hull House founder and WILPF president Jane Addams and Mary Rozet Smith, in the course of their work in the international women's movement. The German women enjoyed the hospitality of Addams and Smith when they came to the United States for the WILPF congress in 1924. . . . Like the German couple, Addams and Smith sent and received messages for one another, made arrangements for double-bedded rooms when they traveled, and took care of each other, although that responsibility fell more heavily on [the younger] Smith. . . .[14]

. . . Such relationships between older and younger, or more and less powerful, women [like Smith's devoted service to her more prominent partner] seemed to obscure the bond of love from the vision of outsiders. The relationship between Anna Howard Shaw, American minister, charismatic orator, and international leader, and Lucy Anthony, a niece of . . . Susan B. Anthony, falls into this category. Shaw had a reputation within suffrage circles for her "strong and passionate attachments to other women," some of which "have broken up in some such tempestuous fashion." Shaw described her "abiding love for home and home life" at her country house, Moylan, which she shared with Anthony. When Shaw fell and broke her foot and Anthony, at the same time, fractured her elbow, Shaw ruefully labeled them "rather a broken up couple." Yet Aletta Jacobs [Dutch IWSA leader and WILPF founder] saw Anthony as Shaw's "secretary, friend, and housekeeper," since Shaw paid her a salary. Anthony herself called Shaw, after her death, "my Precious Love," "the joy of my life."[15]

The same confusion greeted the relationship of International Woman Suffrage Alliance president Carrie Chapman Catt and New York suffrage leader Mary Garrett Hay. Catt's reserve and distaste for emotional display—one intimate friend likened her to "cold boiled halibut"—may have obscured the reality of her relationships, or the fact that Catt married twice may have led observers—as it has scholars—to undervalue her ties to women.[16] But Catt did not even live full time with her husband when he was alive, and when he died she and Hay set up housekeeping together. . . . Apparently rather authoritarian, Hay was not popular in international circles. Shaw, who detested her, ... did "not think there is any hope of breaking that affair off." . . . [W]hen Catt died in 1947, she was buried, at her request, not with either of her two husbands but next to her "unforgettable friend and comrade" Hay.[17]

More ambivalent, but following a similar pattern, was the relationship of Emily Greene Balch, Wellesley professor, WILPF leader, and winner of the Nobel Peace Prize, and her childhood friend Helen Cheever. Balch, like Catt, was a reserved woman; she described her Yankee background as one that valued "restraint not only of expression of emotion but of emotion itself." Cheever was a wealthy woman who financially supported Balch and wanted to live with her on a permanent basis. But Balch, who admitted that she both loved and was irritated by Cheever, balked. Perhaps, she wrote her sister, it was a result of Cheever's "giving me more love than I can quite digest." Yet when Balch was in Geneva as international secretary of WILPF, her coworkers eagerly anticipated, on Balch's behalf, a visit from Cheever. "I think she is homesick and it would be very good if her friend from America came soon to keep her company and also attend a bit to her physical health," Heymann confided to Jane Addams. Three years later Cheever wanted to resign her offices in the U.S. section of WILPF in order to go to Geneva where "my usefulness to the W.I.L. will be confined to being with Miss Balch." . . . [In the end] Balch resisted becoming part of a female couple and identified [instead] as an unmarried woman. . . . Unmarried women [found it] strange, [she later explained to Jane Addams, that] . . . "everything that is not concerned with the play of desire between men and women [is seen] as without adventure."[18]

The public defensiveness of single women may have originated in the awakened suspicion that women living without men might have perverse desires or it might simply have been provoked by popular assumptions that such women had no intimate ties. In a 1931 German anthology on the modern single career woman, Elisabeth Busse explained that such women were not "amazonian," "inverts," or "homosexuals," although "they lived in women's unions." So it is not surprising that ICW secretary Alice Salomon, a German Jewish pioneer in the world of social work who never married, apologized in her autobiography that "this book may sometimes seem as much a book about women as though I had lived in a harem." Actually, she assured her readers, "I always had men and women, old and young, rich and poor, and sometimes whole families as my friends." But, in fact, Salomon made her life in the female world of social reform and the women's movement. She apparently felt compelled to discuss why she never married, explaining that her work . . . "made me reluctant to form a union which could not combine love with common interests and convictions."[19]

In the ICW *Bulletin* of October 1932, Salomon published a defense of unmarried women, the first generation of independent women who pursued careers. She recognized that the discipline of psychology had changed attitudes toward single women—that they were reputed to be warped by celibacy—but quoted a woman of "international fame" to the effect that "they are alive, active, and they fully participate in present-day life by means of a thousand interests." Similarly, Lena Madesin Phillips recognized: "To live an old maid was . . . considered something to be greatly deplored"; but she insisted that she had "no complaints, no regrets, no fears" about her own unmarried, but woman-coupled life. Helen Archdale, a British equal rights advocate active in the international arena, reacted testily to a paean to marriage penned [by a friend] . . . . "What you say about the beneficial effects of marriage on one's life rather puzzles me. Why should 'spinsterhood' be gray?" Archdale shared a London flat and country home with Lady Margaret Rhondda, another international activist, in the 1920s, after which they "personally drifted very far apart."[20] Such defensiveness and defiance about living apart from men reflects the power of the intensified vision of married life as the only healthy alternative for women.

In the first decades of the twentieth century, then, overlapping frames of lesbianism, romantic friendship, devoted service, and singleness existed for women's choices in their personal lives. Women-only organizations offered an appealing haven for those who made their lives with other women, whatever the nature of their ties. But in a context in which homosociality often cast a pall of deviance, the desire to work apart from men grew more complex.

Almost all participants in the major international women's organizations accepted—or did not raise public objections to—an ideology of fundamental difference between women and men. The notion of difference underlay . . . "maternalist politics"—the construction of public positions on the foundation of women's biological and social roles as mothers.[21] But among women not involved in intimate relationships with men, belief in female values—read superior values—also led in a different direction: to the regular expression of anti-male sentiments in both private and public life. Heymann and Augspurg tried as far as possible to hire only women to manage their farm, and Heymann contrasted their satisfaction with their women employees to their displeasure with a male manager: "Vanity, thy name is man!" she proclaimed. "The customary judgment maintains, of course, that the female sex is the one enslaved by vanity, but this customary assertion is only a diversion and contradicts the law of nature among humans and animals."[22]

Similarly, Anna Howard Shaw had little use for men in her private life. When Lucy Anthony's broken arm failed to heal properly, Shaw announced that if a woman physician had treated Anthony everything would have been all right. During the First World War, Shaw complained about "male experts" wasting "millions of dollars on smoke and drink" while advising housewives to tighten their belts. "Men, I am convinced, never grow up and of all the animal creation are the least capable of reason."[23]

Such views spilled over into work in the international women's movement, merging especially with the common association of men with war and women with peace. The outbreak of the First World War unleashed a veritable barrage of anti-male proclamations. Shaw found men's "war madness and barbarism" "unthinkable" and claimed, despite her already low opinion of men, that "I have not half the respect for man's judgment or common sense that I used to have, that they are such fools as to go out and kill and be killed without knowing why." Heymann condemned men's "lies and hatred and violence" at the WILPF congress in 1919, proclaiming that the war would "never have come to pass had we women, the mothers of the world, been given the opportunity of helping to govern the people and join in the social life of nations." At the 1934 WILPF congress, Augspurg denounced the "world of men" as "built up on profit and power, on gaining material wealth and oppressing other people." Women "would be able to build a new world which would produce enough for all." According to Carrie Chapman Catt, "All wars are men's wars. Peace has been made by women but war never."[24]

Advocacy of separatist organizing logically flowed from such assumptions about women's moral superiority and potential efficacy in creating a peaceful world. It is not that women who built lives apart from men never associated or worked with them—both Heymann and Addams, for example, participated in political parties—but that they seemed particularly to value the women's world of the women's movement. Yet few women in the international women's movement explicitly defended the practice

of separatism. Emily Greene Balch seemed to prefer work with women but to feel that WILPF had to consider admitting men. In the first year after the [1915] Hague congress, she wrote that "my interest and belief in our woman's organization is as strong as ever." WILPF debated its commitment to separatism in the early 1920s but decided to remain a woman-only organization on the international level, in the process putting out a pamphlet that explained the reasons for keeping out men, one of the only public documents to defend the practice of separatism. . . .[25]

Given the persistence of all-female groups, the lack of vigorous defense of the principle of separatism is curious. Yet such silence speaks. It is possible that the need never occurred to those long committed to organizing in woman-only groups. But because the question of admitting men did arise, perhaps the silence was a sign of uneasiness over the old-fashioned associations of single-sex organizing in an increasingly heterosocial world. That separatist inclinations remained strong is clear from the apology of Eva Fichet, member of the mixed-gender Tunis section of WILPF, who planned to bring her member husband to the 1934 international congress. Noting that "his presence will offend some of our collaborators," she promised that "he will only make an appearance at public meetings, if there are any." Still, the comments of British suffragist and WILPF member Catherine E. Marshall, who never married, stand out in the records of the international women's movement: "It is always a pleasure to meet Women fellow workers. . . . I do like women best! Who was it said: The more I see of men the better I think of women!"[26] Such sentiments expressed the conviction that women had more in common with one another than with men and underlay the inclination to make both a personal and work life with other women.

HETEROSEXUALITY AND WORK WITH MEN

Some women within the international women's movement lived traditional married lives, while others engaged in more unconventional forms of heterosexual relationships. The model of the woman leader married to a supportive husband received a great deal of praise, but unorthodox heterosexuality crossed the line of respectability in a way that women's same-sex relationships did not and as a result met with disapproval. This difference probably reflects the generational divide that separated the predominantly older women of the international women's movement from younger cohorts more blasé about heterosexual expressiveness and more attuned to the sexual possibilities between women.

Lady and Lord Aberdeen, Scottish aristocrats, were without doubt the most lauded couple in international women's movement circles. The ICW regularly held them up as an exemplar of a couple committed to the same work, even though Lord Aberdeen in fact played no role in the organization.... Lady Aberdeen's devoted friend Alice Salomon described the Aberdeen marriage as modern and ideal and insisted that the ICW was as much a matter of concern to Lord Aberdeen as to Lady Aberdeen. The ICW president herself appreciated her husband's "never wavering support and ... belief in the I.C.W." that had made possible everything she had accomplished. Emma Ender, the president of the German section of the ICW, responded that she knew from her own experience "what it means, to live at the side of a man who totally understands and supports the life work that we have taken on." Even after Lord Aberdeen's death, Lady Aberdeen referred to "the inestimable blessing of husbands who wish us to enter into all the fullness of life in service and responsibility."[27]

Aletta Jacobs, the first woman physician in the Netherlands and an international leader, and her husband, Carel Victor Gerritsen, also attracted favorable attention as a model couple within the international women's movement. Jacobs entered into [the] marriage, despite her perception of the institution's injustice, in deference to her husband's political career and their mutual desire to have a child. She described Gerritsen as "a feminist from the start," and when they married she kept her own name and they maintained separate quarters within the house they shared. Gerritsen actually took up Jacobs's cause by not only supporting her but by also speaking himself in favor of women's suffrage.[28] ...

[Some] married women leaders [spoke] out on behalf of cooperation across the lines of gender. In her 1899 presidential address, Lady Aberdeen referred to separate women's organizations as a "temporary expedient to meet a temporary need" and hoped that they would not be allowed "to crystallise into a permanent element in social life." Her successor as [ICW] president, American May Wright Sewall, also a married woman, agreed: "the Council idea does not stand for the separation of women from men, but rather for the reunion of women with men in the consideration of great general principles and large public interests." In a 1976 interview, Margery Corbett Ashby [president of the IWSA/IAW from 1923 to 1946] explained that the goal of women's organizations was to eliminate the need for women's organizations, although she admitted that it could be difficult for devoted members to accept this.[29]

... [Tension arose in the case of] women perceived as too involved—or in improper relationships-with men attracted harsh criticism. Martina Kramers, who maintained a long-term but unconventional liaison with a man, faced the censure of Carrie Chapman Catt in 1913. Bobbie, whom Kramers called her "left-handed husband," was a socialist and married man whose wife refused to divorce him. As president of the IWSA, Catt wrote to Kramers to recommend that she resign as editor of the organization's journal, *Jus Suffragii*, because her "moral transgressions" had provoked "horror and repugnance" among U.S. IWSA members. Kramers reacted with incredulity and defiance, refusing to give up either her man or her work and insisting to Catt that she was not a "propagandist of free love." She also implicitly equated the unconventionality but acceptability of her relationship with same-sex sexuality by comparing her situation to "the cases of Anita Augspurg [and] Kathe Schirmacher ... accused by many gossipers of homosexual intercourse." ... But to no avail. Catt managed, as Kramers put it, "to throw me out of the whole movement" by moving the office of *Jus Suffragii* to London and appointing a new editor....[30]

[Controversy also swirled around Doris Stevens's work at] the Inter-American Commission of Women, as seen [in this essay's opening paragraph]. Stevens struck Bertha Lutz, a single woman who called herself Catt's "daughter," ... as a "sex-mad psychopath" and a "mentally deranged woman." In fact, Stevens did engage in heterosexual activities outside of marriage, and in her work for the Inter-American Commission of Women she pursued flirtatious relationships with several Latin American diplomats. Far from [being] ashamed of such interactions, she remarked that women and men active in politics together were likely to find that the "deep personal bond takes the form of heterosexual love." . . . [But heterosexually active women like Stevens drew from some female comrades] strong criticism of [not only their allegedly] disreputable behavior but also [their] political [alliances] with men.[31] . . .

I do not mean to imply that the lines on the question of separatism ran strictly in accordance with sexuality or that no other factors shaped the political practices of separatist organizing. As the evidence presented here makes clear, women within the international women's movement in the first half of the twentieth century formed a variety of relationships, with both women and men, and cannot easily be categorized as "homosexual" and "heterosexual" in any case. There were married women such as Carrie Chapman Catt who lived with and loved women, and single women such as Alice Salomon who lavished devoted admiration on Lord and Lady Aberdeen. Coupled women's relationships might be characterized as lesbian partnerships, romantic friendships, loving caretaking, or some combination. In fact, given the variety of bonds, we might wonder whether internationally organized women managed to cross the boundaries of sexuality more easily than those of class, religion, and nationality.[32] Certainly the conflicts over sexuality within the movement tended to pit "respectable" against unconventional behavior rather than same-sex against heterosexual relationships.

And even if we could divide women into neat categories, the association would not be perfect. Rosika Schwimmer, who was married briefly in her youth but lived most of her life in close association with women, grew disgusted with separatist organizing in the 1930s. Mildred Scott Olmstead, a U.S. WILPF leader who maintained an intimate relationship with a woman throughout her married life, proposed in 1934 that the international organization admit men.[33] And the married women leaders and heterosexual renegades all continued to commit themselves to all-female groups, whatever their ideas about the proper way to organize.

Furthermore, affectional choices alone did not fashion the politics of separatism. National and generational differences, which helped to construct interpretations of sexuality, are particularly striking. European women seemed both more open to sexual expression and less interested in single-sex organizing than their Anglo-American colleagues. . . . [European women tended to associate separatism, like sexual prudery,] with the "New World." Danish women responded to the announcement of the Woman's Peace Party in the United States and a call for the formation of similar groups in other countries by asserting that "we preferred to work together, men and women, in the same organisation." At the 1915 Hague congress, Dutch women called for the concentration of all forces, female and male, working for peace. They noted that "a special women's movement is not necessary and therefore undesired. The force of a movement where two sexes cooperate will come to better results than an organisation of one sex only." Women trade unionists from Germany and Austria refused to send representatives to the second congress of the International Federation of Working Women in 1921, because they were "opposed to taking part in a separate women's trade union organisation" in the American fashion. . . .[34]

Similarly, women struggling side by side with men of their class or national group for justice or independence had reason to look critically at separatist organizing. . . . In 1935, Margery Corbett Ashby reported that the enormous difficulties facing the nationalist struggle in Egypt "bring the men and women nearer together" and found the leading Egyptian nationalist movement, the Wafd, "quite progressive as regards women's position." A Syrian woman, speaking at the Istanbul congress of the IAW in the same year, asserted her belief in the necessity of working shoulder to shoulder with men in her country for prosperity and freedom. "The economic and political situation of my country is so desperate that it is extremely difficult for us women to give our wholehearted energies to the cause of feminism alone."[35]

Generational differences on the question of separatism are also striking. Young women experiencing firsthand the breakdown between female and male social spheres in the twentieth-century world challenged women-only groups more readily than their older colleagues who clung to separatist organizing. . . . In 1931, Canadian Dorothy Heneker pointed out that young European women thought that women should work with men, and the IAW Youth Committee reported in 1938 that the general feeling favored a mixed organization of young women and men.[36] Generational, like national, differences on the question of separatism grew from distinctive patterns of homosocial versus heterosocial interaction, and so resistance to all-female groups came from both traditional and progressive sources.

The case of the international women's movement in this period illuminates the paradoxes of a women's world in an era undergoing profound change in the relations between the sexes. Internationally organized women, or at least some of them, knew about lesbianism but chose to view the same-sex relationships of their coworkers in an older frame, [not as pathologized]. Single women alternated between defiance and defensiveness, suggesting that the declining social segregation of the sexes in the industrialized Western world and the more insistent labeling of women without men as lesbians or old maids made a woman's choice of a female—or no—partner more suspicious and thus the women's world of separatist organizations more precarious. The . . . reservation of the strongest condemnation for women who challenged respectability through their sexual liaisons with men hints at the unease that spilled over from the transformation of social and sexual relations to the process of political organizing.

The story of the international women's movement also reveals how important it is to attend to the interaction of sexuality and politics. Conflict over sexuality and separatism added to the national, class, and generational tensions already bubbling within the international organizations and foreshadowed some of the contemporary critiques of lesbian separatism in the United States by working-class women and women of color.[37] At the same time, the silencing of the defenders of separatist organizing may have helped to undermine the potential power of a global women's movement in these years by questioning the validity of gathering apart from men in an increasingly heterosocial world. Whatever the case, the dynamics within the first wave of international organizing among women make clear that our contemporary struggles over sexuality and politics have a longer and more complex history than we sometimes think.

NOTES

1. Marjory Lacey-Baker, "Chronological Record of Events and Activities for the Biography of Lena Madesin Phillips, 1881–1955"; Lena Madesin Phillips,

"Unfinished History of the International Federation of Business and Professional Women," Phillips Papers, cartons 7 and 9, Schlesinger Library, Radcliffe College, Cambridge, Mass.; Lutz to Carrie Chapman Catt, 12 Feb. 1934, 7 July 1936, National American Woman Suffrage Association (NAWSA) Papers, reel 12, Library of Congress, Washington, D.C.

2. See Joanne J. Meyerowitz, *Women Adrift: Independent Wage Earners in Chicago, 1880–1930* (Chicago: University of Chicago Press, 1988); Kathy Peiss, *Cheap Amusements: Working Women and Leisure in Turn-of-the-Century New York* (Philadelphia: Temple University Press, 1986); Hazel V. Carby, "'It Jus Be's Dat Way Sometime': The Sexual Politics of Women's Blues," in *Unequal Sisters: A Multicultural Reader in U.S. Women's History*, ed. Ellen Carol DuBois and Vicki L. Ruiz (New York: Routledge, 1990), 238–49; Judith R. Walkowitz, *City of Dreadful Delight: Narratives of Sexual Danger in Late-Victorian London* (Chicago: University of Chicago Press, 1992); Birgitte Søland, *Becoming Modern: Young Women and the Reconstruction of Womanhood in the 1920s* (Princeton, N.J.: Princeton University Press, 2000).

3. On the emergence of the category and identity "lesbian" at the turn of the century, see George Chauncey Jr., "From Inversion to Homosexuality: Medicine and the Changing Conceptualization of Female Deviance," *Salmagundi*, nos. 58–59 (Fall 1982–Winter 1983): 114–46; and Lisa Duggan, "The Trials of Alice Mitchell: Sensationalism, Sexology, and the Lesbian Subject in Turn-of-the-Century America," *Signs* 18 (Summer 1993): 791–814.

4. See, for example, Mineke Bosch with Annemarie Kloosterman, *Politics and Friendship: Letters from the International Woman Suffrage Alliance, 1902–1942* (Columbus: Ohio State University Press, 1990); Ian Tyrrell, *Woman's World, Woman's Empire: The Woman's Christian Temperance Union in International Perspective, 1880–1930* (Chapel Hill: University of North Carolina Press, 1991), which discusses couples within the World Woman's Christian Temperance Union; and Johanna Alberti, *Beyond Suffrage: Feminists in War and Peace, 1914–1928* (London: Macmillan, 1989), which describes women's love for other women within the British women's movement; and Leila J. Rupp and Verta Taylor, *Survival in the Doldrums: The American Women's Rights Movement, 1945 to the 1960s* (New York: Oxford University Press, 1987), which emphasizes the centrality of coupled women in the U.S. women's rights movement.

5. In this early-nineteenth-century case, a well-connected girl accused her two schoolmistresses of engaging in sexual behavior, causing the ruin of the school; see Lillian Faderman, *Scotch Verdict* (New York: William Morrow, 1983). For more on the acceptability issue, see Martha Vicinus, "'They Wonder to Which Sex I Belong': The Historical Roots of the Modern Lesbian Identity," *Feminist Studies* 18 (Fall 1992): 467–97; Lisa Moore, "'Something More Tender Still than Friendship': Romantic Friendship in Early-Nineteenth-Century England," ibid., 499–520; and Marylynne Diggs, "Romantic Friends or a 'Different Race of Creatures'? The Representation of Lesbian Pathology in Nineteenth-Century America," *Feminist Studies* 21 (Summer 1995): 317–40.

6. The neo-Europes included Australia, New Zealand, the United States, and Canada. See Leila J.

Rupp, "Constructing Internationalism: The Case of Transnational Women's Organizations, 1888–1945," *American Historical Review* 99 (Dec. 1994): 1571–1600, and Rupp, "Challenging Imperialism in International Women's Organizations," *NWSA Journal* 8 (Spring 1996): 8–27.

7. *Women in a Changing World: The Dynamic Story of the International Council of Women since 1888* (London: Routledge and Kegan Paul, 1966); Arnold Whittick, *Woman into Citizen* (London: Athenaeum with Frederick Muller, 1976), on the International Alliance of Women; and Bosch, *Politics and Friendship*. On WILPF, see, for example, Gertrude Bussey and Margaret Tims, *Women's International League for Peace and Freedom, 1915–1965* (London: George Allen and Unwin, 1965); Lela B. Costin, "Feminism, Pacifism, Internationalism, and the 1915 International Congress of Women," *Women's Studies International Forum* 5, no. 3/4 (1982): 301–15; Catherine Foster, *Women for All Seasons: The Story of the Women's International League for Peace and Freedom* (Athens: University of Georgia Press, 1989).

8. Anna Ruhling, "Welches Interesse hat die Frauenbewegung an der Losing des homosexuellen problems?" [What interest does the women's movement have in the homosexual question?], in *Lesbian-Feminism in Turn-of-the-Century Germany*, ed. and trans. Lillian Faderman and Brigitte Eriksson ([Weatherby Lake, Mo.]: Naiad Press, 1980), 81–91 (quotation on 88).

9. Rosika Schwimmer to Wilhelmina van Wulfften Palthe, 29 July 1917, Schwimmer-Lloyd Collection, box A-90, Rare Books and Manuscripts Division, New York Public Library, Astor, Lenox, and Tilden Foundations; Marguerite Gobat to Vilma Glucklich [French], 27 Oct. 1924, Women's International League for Peace and Freedom Papers, reel 1; Aletta Jacobs to Rosika Schwimmer, 3 May 1909, Schwimmer-Lloyd Collection, box A-20; Helen Archdale to Anna Nilsson, 17 May 1933, Equal Rights International Papers, box 331, Fawcett Library, London Guildhall University.

10. Lida Gustava Heymann with Anita Augspurg, *Erlebtes-Erschautes: Deutsche Frauen kampfen fur Freiheit, Recht und Frieden 1850–1940*, ed. Margrit Twellman (Meisenheim am Glan: Anton Hain, 1972), 62. See also Regina Braker, "Bertha von Suttner's Spiritual Daughters: The Feminist Pacifism of Anita Augspurg, Lida Gustava Heymann, and Helene Stocker at the International Congress of Women at The Hague, 1915," *Women's Studies International Forum* 18, no. 2 (1995): 103–11.

11. Heymann with Augspurg, *Erlebtes-Erschautes*, 64, 74, 76.

12. Heymann to Schwimmer [in German], 3 Oct. 1919, Schwimmer-Lloyd Collection, box A-119; Emily Balch to Aletta Jacobs, 15 Nov. 1916, Jacobs Papers, box 2, Internationaal Informatiecentrum en Archief voor de Vrouwenbeweging, Amsterdam (hereafter, IIAV); Emily Hobhouse to Aletta Jacobs, 24 Apr. 1920, ibid., box 1; "List of individuals expected in Innsbruck" [German], [1925], WILPF Papers, reel 2; Heymann to Gabrielle Duchene, 17 Feb. 1926, Dossiers Gabrielle Duchene, Fol Res. 206, Bibliotheque de Documentation Internationale Contemporaine, University of Paris, Nanterre; Anne Zueblin to Jane Addams, 17 Jan. 1930,

Addams Papers, reel 21 (University Microfilms International).

13. Clara Ragaz to K.E. Innes and Gertrud Baer, 18 Apr. 1940, WILPF Papers, reel 4; Rosika Schwimmer to Alice Park, 7 Jan. 1944, Alice Park Papers, box 1, Hoover Institution, Stanford, California.

14. Heymann to Mary Rozet Smith [in German and English], 5 June 1924, Addams Papers, reel 16; Anne Zueblin to M. Illova, 10 June 1929, WILPF Papers, reel 19. On Addams and Smith, see Blanche W. Cook, "Female Support Networks and Political Activism: Lillian Wald, Crystal Eastman, Emma Goldman," *Chrysalis* 3 (Autumn 1977): 43–61. Addams described Smith as her "most intimate friend"; Addams to Heymann, 23 Feb. 1924, Addams Papers, reel 16.

15. For the theme of devoted service in these relationships, see Karin Lutzen, *Was das Herz begehrt: Liebe und Freundschaft zwischen Frauen*, translated from Danish by Gabriele Haefs (Hamburg: Ernst Kabel Verlag, 1990), 110–38. Shaw: Rachel Foster Avery to Aletta Jacobs, 14 July 1910, Jacobs Papers; Biography of Anna Howard Shaw, Dillon Collection, box 18, Schlesinger Library; Anna Howard Shaw to Aletta Jacobs, 19 Mar. 1914, Jacobs Papers; Aletta H. Jacobs, *Uithet leven van merkwaardige vrouwen* (Amsterdam: F. van Rossen, 1905), 37, quoted in Bosch, *Politics and Friendship*, 25; Barbara R. Finn, "Anna Howard Shaw and Women's Work," *Frontiers* 4 (Fall 1979): 21–25, quoted in ibid., 26.

16. Mary G. Peck to Carrie Chapman Catt, 6 Feb. 1929, quoted in Robert Booth Fowler, *Carrie Catt: Feminist Politician* (Boston: Northeastern University Press, 1986), 42. Catt also carried on a romantic relationship with Peck, who herself lived with another woman; see Catt to Frances Squire Potter, n.d., quoted in Bosch, *Politics and Friendship*, 38.

17. Anna Howard Shaw to Aletta Jacobs, 8 Feb. 1909, 7 Apr. 1911, and 14 Dec. 1908, Jacobs Papers, box 2; Rachel Foster Avery to Aletta Jacobs, 14 July 1910, ibid.; Anna Manus-Jacobi, tribute to Carrie Chapman Catt [in German], 11 Mar. 1947, Manus Papers, IIAV.

18. Quoted in Mercedes Randall, *Improper Bostonian: Emily Greene Balch* (New York: Twayne Publishers, 1964), 397, 299; Heymann to Addams [in German], 16 Sept. 1919, and Helen Cheever to Jane Addams, 13 Sept. 1922, both in Addams Papers, reel 12 and 15; Jane Addams, *Second Twenty Years at Hull House*, 197–98, quoted in Randall, *Improper Bostonian*, 399.

19. Elisabeth Busse, "Das moralische Dilemma in der modernen Madchenerziehung," in Ada Schmidt-Beil, *Die Kultur der Frau* (Berlin: Verlag fur Kultur und Wissenschaft, 1931), 594; Alice Salomon, "Character Is Destiny," 218 and 39–42, Alice Salomon Papers, Memoir Collection, Leo Baeck Institute, New York.

20. Alice Salomon, "The Unmarried Woman of Yesterday and Today," *ICW Bulletin* 11 (October 1932); Lena Madesin Phillips to Carrie Probst, 28 May 1935, Phillips Papers, carton 4, Schlesinger Library (on Phillips's relationship, see Rupp and Taylor, *Survival in the Doldrums*, 121–24); Archdale to Doris Stevens, 14 Feb. 1936, and Lady Rhondda to Doris Stevens [May 1928], both in Stevens Papers, cartons 4 and 5, Schlesinger Library. On Lady

Rhondda's relationships with women, see Shirley M. Eoff, *Viscountess Rhondda: Equalitarian Feminist* (Columbus: Ohio State University Press, 1991), 107–16.

21. See Rupp, "Constructing Internationalism." On maternalist politics, see the various contributions to Lynn Y. Weiner et al., "Maternalism as a Paradigm," *Journal of Women's History* 5 (fall 1993): 95–131; Seth Koven and Sonya Michel, "Womanly Duties: Maternalist Politics and the Origins of the Welfare States in France, Germany, Great Britain, and the United States, 1880–1920," *American Historical Review* 95 (October 1990): 1076–1108; and Karen Offen, "Defining Feminism: A Comparative Historical Approach," *Signs* 14 (Autumn 1988): 119–57.

22. Heymann with Augspurg, *Erlebtes-Erschautes*, 70.

23. Lucy Anthony to Aletta Jacobs, 10 Jan. 1915, and Anna Howard Shaw to Aletta Jacobs, 30 Aug. 1917, both in Jacobs Papers, box 2.

24. Anna Howard Shaw to Aletta Jacobs, 22 Aug. 1915 and 18 Apr. 1916, Jacobs Papers, box 2; speech of Lida Gustava Heymann, WILPF Zurich Congress, [1919], WILPF Papers, reel 17; Minutes, WILPF International Congress, 3–8 Sept. 1934, WILPF Papers, reel 20; "Man Made Wars," *Pax* 6 (May 1931).

25. Emily Greene Balch to Aletta Jacobs, 15 Nov. 1916, Jacobs Papers, reel 9.

26. Eva Fichet to Emily Balch [French], 19 Aug. 1934, WILPF Papers, reel 20; Catherine E. Marshall to Vilma Glucklich, 14 May [1923], Addams Papers, reel 15. On Marshall, see Jo Vellacott, *From Liberal to Labour with Women's Suffrage: The Story of Catherine Marshall* (Buffalo, N.Y.: McGill-Queen's University Press, 1993).

27. Alice Salomon, "To Lord and Lady Aberdeen on the Occasion of Their Golden Wedding, November 7th, 1927," ICW *Bulletin* 6 (November 1927); Lady Aberdeen to Emma Ender [in German], 31 Jan. 1928, Helene-Lange-Archiv, 78–315 (1), Landesarchiv Berlin; Emma Ender to Lady Aberdeen [German], 13 Feb. 1928, Helene-Lange-Archiv, 85–333 (2), Landesarchiv Berlin; "Lady Aberdeen's Response to Toast Proposed by Baroness Boel . . .," 13 July 1938, ICW, *President's Memorandum Regarding the Council Meeting of the ICW held at Edinburgh, (Scotland), July 11th to 21st 1938*, 15–17.

28. Aletta Jacobs to Rosika Schwimmer [in German], 18 Nov. 1903, Schwimmer-Lloyd Collection, box A-4; see Bosch, *Politics and Friendship*, 9–12, 53–55. Jacobs's reminiscences have been translated and published as *Memories: My Life as an International Leader in Health, Suffrage, and Peace*, ed. Harriet Feinberg, trans. Annie Wright (New York: Feminist Press, 1996).

29. Lady Aberdeen, "Presidential Address," ICW, *Report of Transactions of Second Quinquennial Meeting Held in London July 1899*, ed. Countess of Aberdeen (London: T. Fisher Unwin, 1900), v. 1, 49;

ICW, *Report of Transactions*, 1899, v. 1, 56; Margery Corbett Ashby interview, 21 Sept. 1976, conducted by Brian Harrison, Corbett Ashby Papers, cassette #6, Fawcett Library, London.

30. Catt to Kramers, 21 May 1913, box A-33; Kramers to Schwimmer [in German], 27 May 1913 and 2 June 1913, box A-32 and box A-33; Kramers to Schwimmer [in German], 31 May 1907 and 7 Oct. 1908, box A-12 and box A-17, all in Schwimmer-Lloyd Collection.

31. Lutz to Carrie Chapman Catt, 7 July 1936, 12 Feb. 1934, 15 July 1936, NAWSA Papers, reel 12; Doris Stevens, transcription of taped reminiscences, Stevens Papers, carton 3, Schlesinger Library. See Leila J. Rupp, "Feminism and the Sexual Revolution in the Early Twentieth Century: The Case of Doris Stevens," *Feminist Studies* 15 (Summer 1989): 289–309.

32. I am indebted to Susan Hartmann for this insight.

33. Rosika Schwimmer to Gabrielle Duchene, [1934], WILPF Papers, reel 20; Minutes, Eighth International Congress, 3–8 Sept. 1934, WILPF Papers, reel 20. On Mildred Scott Olmstead's complex personal life, see Margaret Hope Bacon, *One Woman's Passion for Peace and Freedom: The Life of Mildred Scott Olmstead* (Syracuse: Syracuse University Press, 1993).

34. Elizabeth Baelde, "Impressions of the Visit of the I.C.W. to Canada," in *Our Lady of the Sunshine*, ed. Countess of Aberdeen (London: Constable, 1909), 310–34; Eline Hansen to Rosika Schwimmer, 12 Mar. 1915, and Edna Munch to Schwimmer, 18 Mar. 1915, both in Schwimmer-Lloyd Collection, box A-55 and A-57; "Report of Business Sessions," 29 Apr. and 1 May [1915], International Committee of Women for Permanent Peace, *International Congress of Women, The Hague—April 28th to May 1st 1915: Report*, 111–17, 162–63; "Stenographic Report of Second Congress," 17 Oct. 1921, International Federation of Working Women Papers, Schlesinger Library.

35. Margery Corbett Ashby to Josephine Schain, 5 Feb. 1935, Schain Papers, box 4 [Mrs. Bader Dimeschquie], "Delegates and Friends," 1935, International Alliance of Women Papers, box 1, both in Sophia Smith Collection, Smith College, Northampton, Mass.

36. Idola Saint-Jean to Helen Archdale, 15 Sept. 1931, Equal Rights International Papers, box 334; Minutes, Meeting of the International Alliance of Women for Suffrage and Equal Citizenship Board, Paris, 6–9 Dec. 1938, International Alliance of Women Papers, both at Fawcett Library.

37. For more on the national, ethnic, class, and generational tensions within the international women's movement, see Leila J. Rupp, *Worlds of Women: The Making of an International Women's Movement* (Princeton, N.J.: Princeton University Press, 1997).

SUFFRAGE AND CITIZENSHIP

ELLEN CAROL DUBOIS

The Next Generation of Suffragists: Harriot Stanton Blatch and Grassroots Politics

Campaigns to expand suffrage require that voters who are reasonably content with the status quo be persuaded to welcome new and unpredictable constituencies into the political arena. It is perhaps no surprise that the expansion of suffrage met severe resistance, in the North where there were considerable doubts about the immigrant vote and especially in the South where the franchise had been restricted (through literacy tests and poll taxes) to exclude African Americans and, in the process, many poor whites.

The campaign for woman suffrage presented a formidable challenge to established political theory that held a married woman's political interests were represented by her husband. It proceeded with a successful national mass mobilization at a time when even presidential campaigns hardly met that criteria. And it required brilliant street theater on a massive scale and, simultaneously, clever and delicate political maneuvering for which women were not noted. Although the accomplishment of woman suffrage in 1920 is well known, the complexity of the work that was required and the high level of political skill that women had to acquire is less appreciated than it deserves to be.

Harriot Blatch, the daughter of Elizabeth Cady Stanton, led the efforts of the Women's Political Union (WPU) to win suffrage for the women of New York State. From 1910 to 1915, the WPU lobbied state legislators to support the suffrage bill. They also targeted public support with parades, suffrage shops, and films. (See Photo Essay: "Women in Public," pp. 255–266.)

Ironically, many suffragists who demanded the vote were deeply skeptical about politics. Believing that women were more pure than men and that politics were corrupt, they insisted that if women had the vote, they would put an end to partisanship. In fact, their views were not so far apart from antisuffragists who resisted the vote precisely because they felt partisan politics would corrupt American womanhood. To their credit, Harriot Blatch and her colleagues understood that acquiring political skills and understanding partisanship were essential to acquiring the vote and, once acquired, using it effectively.

The battle for women's rights had begun in the state of New York, the birthplace of Elizabeth Cady Stanton and the longtime home of Susan B. Anthony. In Seneca Falls, New York, the Declaration of Rights and Sentiments had been rousingly proclaimed in 1848. In Albany, both Stanton and Anthony testified in the 1850s before the New York Senate's Judiciary Committee. There they argued, with some success, for changes in state law to establish women's guardianship rights over their children, grant property and earnings rights to married women, and deliver woman suffrage. In 1915, nearly seventy years later, the struggle, now led by a new generation, had come to focus on woman suffrage. Fittingly, Harriot Stanton Blatch, Elizabeth Cady Stanton's daughter, led this major effort to win woman suffrage in its home state. But even in the early twentieth century, success was uncertain.

Harriot Stanton, the second daughter and sixth child of Elizabeth Cady and Henry Brewster Stanton, inherited her role as defender of her sex from her mother. She was born in Seneca Falls in 1856, during a period when Elizabeth Cady Stanton was immersed in women's issues and the development of a convention movement to publicize concerns as revolutionary as liberalizing divorce.... While other Victorian girls followed their mothers into quiet lives based on family service, Harriot was taught to be assertive and independent.... Her mother prepared her daughters to go out into the world not only to make their individual marks on it but also to embody her convictions about women's untapped capacities....

... In 1874, [Harriot] enrolled at Vassar, the first all-female college established in the United States. There, she elected an unconventional course of study focused on science, politics, and history. Upon graduation, she became a member of the first generation of women college graduates, one of only a few thousand women in the United States who held a bachelor's degree....

[In 1882,] she met William Blatch, the handsome, accommodating son of a wealthy brewer from Basingstoke, Hampshire, England. Harriot and William married in 1882, and the couple's first child Nora (named after the heroine of Ibsen's *A Doll's House*) was born in England the next year. A second child, Helen, born in 1892, died of whooping cough in 1896. Like her mother but with fewer children, more money,

and a compliant husband, Harriot Blatch managed to combine marriage and motherhood with an energetic commitment to reform activities. She joined with veteran British women activists to revive the British suffrage movement.... In 1890, she joined the socialist Fabian Society, where she fought for, but failed to win, strong support for women's rights. For two decades as an [expatriate] in Edwardian England, she honed her political skills and updated her mother's feminist convictions, speaking at meetings, writing for suffrage journals, and becoming involved in local politics as a member of the Women's Local Government Society.

In 1902, with her daughter Nora grown and studying engineering at Cornell, and her husband Henry able to retire, Harriot Blatch moved permanently to New York to take up the task she had inherited—leadership of the American suffrage movement. She joined the Women's Trade Union League, a pioneering effort of elite settlement house women and female wage earners joined together to empower, not patronize, working women. There she came to see that to be modern and effective the suffrage movement in the United States must unite women across the classes in a militant effort. She also saw, as other women activists did not, that women's growing interest in electoral politics was crucial to the reinvigoration of the suffrage movement. Like the English suffragist Emmeline Pankhurst, she was committed to forcing the political parties to address the suffrage issue and winning from them the political support necessary to gain victory....

To enact her vision of a militant, democratic suffrage organization based on a coalition of working-class and middle-class working women, Harriot Blatch organized the Equality League of Self-Supporting Women in 1907, renamed the Women's Political Union (WPU) in 1910. Although it gradually moved away from reliance on wage-earning women for its most active participants, the WPU went on to spearhead a political effort to force the New York legislature to pass a bill authorizing a referendum to amend the state constitution to grant women suffrage.

The WPU suffrage campaign, which ran from 1910 to 1915, involved an exhausting and elaborate two-pronged effort: First, both houses of the state legislature had to pass a bill authorizing a referendum on woman suffrage, and then the state's all-male electorate had to approve the referendum.... [S]uffragists in New York took hope from a narrowly won suffrage victory in California in October 1911.... By 1912, California was the sixth state in which women were voting in the presidential election. Blatch and her followers were determined that New York women would do the same in the next presidential election....

Harriot Blatch had a talent and taste for partisan politics that was unusual in the movement. Although many of the new generation of suffragists were college-trained professionals, Mary Beard, the historian and a close friend, wrote of Blatch that more than others, "she worked steadfastly to root the suffrage movement in politics, where alone it could reach its goal."[1] She certainly had the lineage. Her mother and Susan B. Anthony had immersed themselves in party politics. From them, from her father, and from her years in England, Harriot had come to see that if suffragists were ever to win, they would have to go behind the scenes and engage in precisely the political maneuvering and lobbying that women had traditionally repudiated as the unhappy consequence of the male monopoly of public life. While such openly political methods distressed many older women reformers, they invigorated Harriot.

In one episode, which became a staple of suffrage legend, Harriot and other WPU leaders tracked down a particularly elusive senator. By this time, opposition to suffrage had moved from ridicule to avoidance. "The chase led up and down elevators in and out of the Senate chamber and committee rooms." Finally, they ferreted out his hiding place and cornered him; he could no longer avoid the issue. The WPU account reversed the standard metaphors of gender to emphasize the senator's humiliation at the hands of women. "Of slight build," he was literally overpowered by the suffragists. "With Mrs. Blatch walking on one side with her hand resting ever so slightly on his sleeve [sic]," the women led him into the committee room and got his vote. "I'll never forgive this," he told Blatch. "Oh yes, you will," she responded, "some day you will be declaring with pride how your vote advanced the suffrage resolution."[2]

The WPU won a similar battle with Robert Wagner, the new Democratic majority leader of the state Senate and one of the most determined opponents of suffrage in the New York legislature. To prevent Wagner from once again employing the delaying legislative tactics of moving to table or returning the referendum resolution to committee for another year, Harriot arranged for three hundred New York City suffragists to go to Albany to pressure him to set a date for a vote. Some fifty or sixty women crowded into the committee room, with the rest gathered in the corridor outside. When Wagner moved to take his place in the chair at the front of the room, the aisle filled with suffragists. "There were no antisuffragists to rescue him," wrote Harriot later. "There were only all about him, the convinced and ruthless members of the Women's Political Union." He grudgingly agreed to set a date for the state Senate to vote on the suffrage resolution.[3]

In both episodes, the WPU's power rested not only in numbers but also in its willingness to exploit the gendered meanings of power. Wagner yielded because he could not afford to let it be known that he had been physically and politically outmaneuvered by women. The newspapers predictably reported what the women requested, and Wagner graciously granted a date for the Senate vote. But at a time in which accounts of British militant suffragists smashing windows were prominently featured in American papers, the sense of sexual warfare, of women besting men, was close to the surface and hard to overlook.

The Senate debate and vote took place on the date Wagner had guaranteed. Harriot and her followers watched from the gallery. Like good politicians, they had carefully counted their supporters, knew that they had just the right number of votes with not one to spare, and "were full of confidence" that the referendum would carry.[4] Across the hall, the lower house was giving them an unanticipated victory. It looked like the legislative battle might actually be won. But at the last moment a perfidious senator abandoned the public pledge he had given the WPU, shifted his vote, and denied them their victory.

With this undeserved defeat uppermost in her mind, Blatch went to the people. The WPU had organized parades twice before, but the 1912 New York City parade was by far the most carefully organized street demonstration in U.S. suffrage history. The WPU spared no effort at recruiting and educating a large number of marchers and alerting the public to the meaning and significance of the parade. Pledge cards were circulated, committing marchers to take to the streets. Newspapers eagerly covered the clever "stunts" that suffragists devised to advertise the parade: suffragists at the circus, "suffragette hats" for sale at department stores, recruitment booths behind the Public Library.

Harriot was determined that the parade give evidence of a massive, disciplined army of women with which politicians would have to come to terms. She paid great attention to the details of the march, the numbers of marching columns, and the spacing of the lines of marchers. Women were instructed to dress simply, walk erectly, and keep their eyes forward. The spectacle was to be an emotional and sensual evocation of women's power. Opponents, according to Blatch, should be converted through their eyes. "The enemy must see women, marching in increasing numbers year by year out on the public avenues, holding high their banner, Votes For Women." On the appointed day, more than ten thousand took to the streets: women college graduates in their academic gowns, working women by trades and industries, prominent wealthy women, even some men. The president of the national suffrage society marched with a banner that read "Catching Up with China"—a reference to reports that insurgent nationalists in one of China's provincial legislatures had declared women enfranchised. Public demonstrations of this sort were new and a bit daunting to many women. "I marched the whole length," one demonstrator proudly reported to a friend.[5]

In 1912, the emergence of a third national political party, the Progressives, affected the task of getting a suffrage referendum. While Progressive leaders begged women for their support, Blatch was disappointed with the tepid role the party had played in a woman suffrage referendum in Ohio earlier in that year. And former president Theodore Roosevelt, the party's candidate for president in 1912, repeatedly embarrassed himself and his party by sexist declarations that suffragists were "indirectly encouraging immorality."[6] Still, the Progressive Party's support was crucial for the WPU's plans in New York because of the leverage it gave in prying support out of the Republicans, who were struggling to keep voters from bolting to the new party. First the Progressives and then the Republicans endorsed the submission of the suffrage referendum to New York voters at their state conventions. . . .

[T]he Democrats followed the other two parties in urging submission of the referendum. Victory, at least in the legislature, was assured. The election of 1912 swept the Democrats . . . into power in the state, and, under the leadership of Woodrow Wilson, into the presidency as well.

There was a last-minute complication when the Republicans added a clause to the referendum subjecting immigrant women, who were citizens by marriage, to special requirements for voting, and the Democrats objected. The issue was a difficult one for Blatch. On the one hand, she had lost her American citizenship by virtue of her marriage to an Englishman and was sympathetic to women whose citizenship was altered by marriage. On the other hand, like her mother decades before, she had her own nativist prejudices, as did many of her middle-class followers. In the end, she decided the issue politically: Keeping the clause would gain the referendum more upstate Republican votes than it would lose downstate Democrats.

Party leaders followed her lead, and in January 1913, both houses passed legislation proposing an amendment to the state constitution striking out the word male and enfranchising citizens over twenty-one "provided that a citizen by marriage should have been an inhabitant of the United States for five years."[7] Blatch had worked three years for this moment, a long time for a single bill. And even with this victory, the most difficult task lay ahead—the winning of the referendum itself. Now the suffrage leaders would have to convince a majority of New York men to vote for woman suffrage.

Harriot Blatch and the leaders of the WPU had no illusions about how difficult this might be. "The task we must accomplish between now and election day 1915 [when the referendum would appear on the ballot] is a Herculean one, compared to that we have just completed," the Executive Committee of the Women's Political Union declared. Harriot had her misgivings about immigrant voters, with their "Germanic and Hebraic attitude toward women," but she counted on the democratic logic of the situation, believing that men who were being allowed to exercise the franchise could be convinced to vote in favor of women's demand to share it. [But a great deal was riding on the New York referendum. "If we win the Empire State all the states will come tumbling down like a deck of cards," she promised.[8]]

To cultivate the voters, the WPU played on its strengths. It based its suffrage advocacy on the proliferating devices of modern mass culture—forms of commercial recreation, methods of advertising, and the pleasures of consumerism. Californians had used billboards, automobile caravans, and suffrage postcards to bring their cause before the electorate in their successful campaign of 1911. New York women had to do the same. ["If we are to reap a victory in 1915, we must cultivate every inch of soil and sow our suffrage seed broadcast in the Empire state," Harriot declared.[9]]

Such an approach conformed to Harriot's view of democracy which, she believed, should be based on the heart rather than the head. Emotions were the key to popular democracy, not reason. "We learned . . . as we toiled in our campaign," she later wrote, "that sermons and logic would never convince. . . . Human beings move because they feel, not because they think."[10] This was not an expression of any special contempt for either women or working-class voters; on the contrary, she considered men (especially politicians) more irrational than women and the rich more prejudiced and conservative than the poor. She believed particularly that changes in women's status and in power relations between the sexes could never be reduced to rational arguments and dispassionate appeals, even to venerable principles of American democracy such as equality and civic virtue.

"Democracy was the keynote" of the grand suffrage ball that the WPU sponsored in January 1913 to inaugurate the referendum campaign. Extensively advertised, it took place in New York City's Seventy-First Street Armory, which was barely large enough for the eight thousand men and women who attended. Rich and poor, working-class and society women alike paid fifty cents to dance the turkey trot and other popular new dances. The event proved, as the WPU put it, "that love of liberty and democracy did not belong to one class or one sex but is deeply rooted in human nature itself."[11] . . .

Given Harriot's appreciation for the role of emotions in mass politics, she was especially intrigued by new technologies of mass communication. "I stand for the achievements of the twentieth century," she declared. "I will make use of . . . anything which civilization places at my command."[12] Lee de Forest, her

former son-in-law (Nora's brief marriage to him had ended after a year), was one of the pioneers of modern radio broadcasting. . . . At his invitation, she delivered a radio talk on woman suffrage from the newly opened broadcasting station in downtown Manhattan.

Moving pictures represented another new technology with political possibilities. The WPU arranged for a commercial movie company to produce *The Suffragette and the Man,* a romantic comedy in which the beautiful young heroine, forced to choose between her suffrage principles and her fiancé, first picks principles and then overcomes an anti-suffrage competitor and wins back her lover.

In 1913, the WPU collaborated on a second movie entitled *What 8,000,000 Women Want.* This time the romantic triangle did not involve good and bad men fighting for a heroine's heart but good and bad politics fighting for the hero's soul. Newsreel footage of actual suffrage parades was interspersed with the dramatic action. Harriot played herself and brought to the screen her self-confident authority and her genuine pleasure at conducting the struggle. . . .

[In 1913, as in previous years, the most spectacular suffrage event was the parade organized by the WPU. Each year, the parades had become more stunning affairs, symbolically conveying both the diversity and the unity of modern women.] The 1913 parade was one of the high points of Harriot's suffrage leadership. "We will muster an army fifty thousand strong this year," she predicted. The marchers were arranged by divisions. At the head were two dozen female marshals mounted on horseback and dressed in stylish adaptations of men's evening wear, black cutaways and silk hats with streamers of green, purple, and white, the WPU's colors and those of the movement in England. Leading them, dressed in white and astride a white horse, was Inez Millholland, "the official beauty of the parade." The intention was to provide unforgettable visual images of all kinds of women marching shoulder to shoulder together. "In these times of class wars," Harriot observed, could men really afford "to shut out from public affairs that fine spirit of fellowship" that suffragism represented?[13]

The effectiveness of the parade as political propaganda infuriated antisuffragists, for whom the spectacular aspect of the movement was proof positive of the social and cultural upheaval that votes for women threatened. The antisuffragists charged that the bold stance of the marchers smacked of the deliberate exploitation of "sex appeal." . . . Harriot Blatch found the charges amusing. "Funny idea of sex appeal. Twenty thousand women turn out on a hot day. 87 degrees and march up Fifth Avenue to the blaring music of thirty-five bands; eyes straight to the front; faces red with the hot sun. . . . If it had been mellow moonlight. . . . But a sex appeal set to brass bands! That certainly is a new one."[14] The WPU was determined to finesse the conventional notions of female beauty that had so long restrained women's public activities. . . .

During the legislative lobbying years from 1910 to 1913, Harriot and the WPU had not faced much organizational opposition within the New York suffrage movement. The state suffrage organization was small and ineffective. But once the referendum campaigning began in earnest, the Woman's Political Union, led by the blunt, sometimes undiplomatic Blatch, came into direct conflict with the other great figure of New York suffragism, the moderate, circumspect Carrie Chapman Catt. Within the women's movement, Catt embodied the progressive faith in organizational structure and administrative centralization. In contrast, Harriot celebrated individual initiative, modern invention, and personal freedom. Notwithstanding lofty suffrage rhetoric about the unity of all womanhood and the solidarity of the sex, these two were bound to clash. . . . Catt was always more concerned to unify and reconcile all existing suffragists than to reach out and create new ones. While some activists believed that Blatch was autocratic and high-handed, the ever-diplomatic Catt prized harmony within the movement above all things. Catt's efforts went to creating internal order rather than tackling external obstacles. Unlike Blatch, Catt had little skill or interest in the intricacies of partisan politics and legislative maneuvers.

Catt's plan was to bring all the suffrage societies in New York . . . under one wing, but the Women's Political Union [crucial to her efforts and the richest organization in the state] refused to subsume itself under Catt's leadership. . . . By 1914, it was clear that two parallel suffrage campaigns would be conducted in New York, one by Catt's Empire State Campaign Committee and the other by Harriot Blatch's Women's Political Union. Both raised money for the referendum effort; both sent paid agents around the state; both set up separate offices, sometimes generating considerable conflict among activists in smaller communities in upstate New York. The suffrage movement had survived previous internal divisions and would face others in the future. . . .

In the last six months of the campaign, the WPU flooded the state with publicity-generating gimmicks and stunts. Suffragists played both ends of the gender divide to demonstrate that they could join in traditional male activities as good fellows and at the same time retain their female virtue. On Suffrage Day at the Polo Grounds, New York suffrage organizations competed with each other to sell tickets to a benefit baseball game between the New York Giants and the Chicago Cubs. . . . To counter the anti-suffrage claims that they were bitter women who wanted the ballot as compensation for their inability to find husbands, they even held a series of "married couple days," in which husbands and wives declared their mutual happiness and support of votes for women. . . .

Ten weeks before the end of the campaign, Harriot's single-minded attention to the cause was shattered by the sudden death of her husband, William Blatch, who was accidentally electrocuted. . . . Before leaving [for England to tend to her husband's estate], she took advantage of one benefit of widowhood and resumed her U.S. citizenship. Harriot's decision to leave the country so close to the end of the 1915 campaign is something of a puzzle. She could have postponed the trip a few months. Moreover, England was already at war with Germany, and the transatlantic trip was dangerous. Perhaps she was growing weary of the unrelenting labor of trying to convert New York voters, or perhaps she sensed that she was losing her position as New York's foremost suffragist to Carrie Chapman Catt. . . . By the time she returned in mid-October, the Empire State Campaign Committee . . . had taken over organization of the final suffrage parade. . . .

November 2, 1915, the day toward which Harriot Blatch, Carrie Catt, and thousands of other New York women had been working for years, was the kind of warm, sunny day for which hard-working campaigners pray. When the polls opened at 6 A.M., several thousand suffrage activists were in their places as poll-watchers, guarding against any effort to cheat them of their victory. . . .

By midnight, it was clear that the woman suffrage amendment had been defeated. Out of 1,200,000 votes cast across the state, woman suffrage had been defeated by 190,000 votes, about 16 percent of the total. All the boroughs of New York City voted against woman suffrage as well as fifty-six of the state's sixty-one counties.

Most New York suffragists kept the bitter disappointment they felt to themselves and declared the referendum a moral triumph. "On the whole we have achieved a wonderful victory," Carrie Chapman Catt proclaimed. "It was short of our hopes but the most contemptuous opponents speak with newly acquired respect for our movement."[15] Catt's wing of the campaign announced the day after the election that a second referendum campaign would begin as soon as state law permitted. . . .

Harriot Blatch was one of the few suffrage leaders who dared to react with open anger. She was "disgusted at the conditions which had forced women to campaign in the streets" and humiliated at having to appeal to immigrant men to gain her native-born rights as an American citizen.[16] She vowed she would never make another street-corner speech. Her retreat into this outraged elitism recalled her mother's reaction to her own crushing disappointment at the failure of the Reconstruction constitutional amendments to include women. Blatch also blamed the suffrage forces themselves for the defeat, at least the Catt wing of the movement, which she thought had neglected upstate New York. She believed a second referendum would be a mistake because the antisuffragists would be even better organized for the next round.

In this she was wrong. In 1917, a second voters' referendum was victorious in New York, thus winning an incalculably important political prize in the battle that was intensifying nationwide. Yet Harriot was correct in a larger way. The era of state suffrage referenda was over; with the exception of New York, no other state was won by this method after 1915. From this point on, attention, energy, and political initiative shifted to the federal arena, to the constitutional amendment Elizabeth Cady Stanton and Susan B. Anthony had first introduced and

which had been stalled in congressional committee for almost fifty years. In less than five years, the amendment was moved onto the floor, secured a two-thirds vote in the House and three years later in the Senate, and was ratified by three-quarters of the state legislatures to become the law of the land. . . .

NOTES

1. "Foreword" by Mary Beard, in Harriot Stanton Blatch and Alma Lutz, *Challenging Years: The Memoirs of Harriot Stanton Blatch* (New York: G. P. Putnam's Sons, 1940), p. vii.

2. Nora de Forest, "Political History of Women's Political Union," reel 1, Harriot Stanton Blatch Papers, Library of Congress, pp. 13–14; *Challenging Years,* pp. 162–63.

3. *Challenging Years,* pp. 163–64.

4. Ibid., pp. 169–70; Women's Political Union 1912–1913 Annual Report, pp. 7–8.

5. *Challenging Years,* p. 180; "Chinese Women Parade for Suffrage," *New York Times,* April 14, 1912, pt. 7, p. 5; Katherine Devereux Blake to Alice Park, n.d., Susan B. Anthony Memorial Collection, Huntington Library, San Marino, CA.

6. "Roosevelt Is for Woman Suffrage," *New York Times,* February 3, 1912, p. 7.

7. "Official Copy of Proposed Amendment," November 2, 1915, Blatch Papers, Library of Congress.

8. "The Referendum Policy of the Women's Political Union," p. 19, reel 1, Blatch Papers, Library of Congress. "Mrs. Blatch Plans Hot Fight to Win New York to Suffrage," *Chicago Tribune,* March 16, 1913. Blatch to Alice Paul, August 26, 1913, reel 4, National Woman's Party Papers: Suffrage Years.

9. Blatch, "Seed Time and Harvest," *Women's Political World,* June 16, 1913, p. 2.

10. *Challenging Years,* p. 192.

11. "Suffragists Tour City to Boom Ball," *New York Daily Mail,* January 11, 1913; "Charity Versus Votes," *Women's Political World,* January 15, 1913, p. 7.

12. "Barnard Girls Test Wireless Phones," *New York Times,* February 26, 1909, p. 7.

13. ". . . with Suffrage Workers," *New York Post,* March 7, 1913; "Eyes to the Front," *New York Tribune,* May 3, 1913; Blatch, "A Reviewing Stand," *Women's Political World,* May 15, 1913, p. 1.

14. "Answers Anti Attack," *New York Times,* May 13, 1913, p. 3.

15. Catt to Mary Grey Peck, December 12, 1912, Catt Papers, Library of Congress.

16. "Mrs. Blatch Pours Out Wrath . . . ," *New York Times,* November 4, 1915, p. 3.

Chinese Exclusion: The Page Act and Its Aftermath

Named for the California congressman Horace F. Page, who was its most ardent supporter, the Page Act of 1875 was the nation's first federal exclusion of certain kinds of immigrants. Public and congressional debate on expanding the statute continued, and within seven years, the much more expansive Chinese Exclusion Act of 1882 barred virtually all but elite Chinese from entering the United States and reiterated the exclusion of women. "The Exclusion Act is clearly the pivot on which all American immigration policy turned," writes historian Roger Daniels, "the hinge on which Emma Lazarus's 'Golden Door' began to swing toward a closed position. It initiated an era of steadily increasing restrictions on immigration of all kinds that lasted until 1943."* Not until our alliance with China in World War II was the Chinese exclusion law repealed.

The Page Act, like the more capacious legislation that followed, was fueled by a mixture of policies: racist hostility to Asians; hostility to unscrupulous entrepreneurs who recruited unskilled workers, pressured them into multiyear contracts, brought them to the United States, and then undercut established wages; and authentic fears of prostitution rings. Knowledge that Chinese families practiced polygamy and foot-binding fueled generalizations about immorality and sexual exploitation. One San Francisco politician conceded that "as a class Chinese are intelligent," but insisted that among "the multitudes of Chinese women in our state there is not a wife or virtuous female in their number."[†]

The Page Act gestured in the direction of outlawing contract labor but actually focused on trafficking in women. It made the American consular officers in Chinese ports responsible for interrogating all prospective immigrants; in practice, any woman who wished to travel to the United States had first to persuade the consul that she was not a prostitute. Memories of this humiliating experience have been passed down over many generations in some Chinese-American families.

The impact of the law was quickly felt. In the two years between 1880 and 1882, some 50,000 Chinese men entered the United States, but only 220 Chinese women did so. In 1910 the gender ratio among Chinese in the United States was 14:1. The principle that prospective immigrant women had the additional burden of proving their morality persisted. The 1891 Immigration Act required all incoming pregnant women to prove that they were married. It also provided for the

---

*Roger Daniels, *Guarding the Golden Door: American Immigration Policy and Immigrants since 1882* (New York: Hill and Wang, 2004), p. 19.
†For a helpful overview, see Martha Gardner, *The Qualities of a Citizen: Women, Immigration, and Citizenship, 1870–1965* (Princeton, N.J.: Princeton University Press, 2005).

Page Act of 1875, 43rd Cong., 2nd sess., ch. 141.

expulsion of immigrants who became a public charge within a year of entry. That time limit was gradually expanded—to two years, then three, then five. In 1910, a new statute provided that alien women who turned to sex work could be deported at any time. In the debates over immigration policy in the early twenty-first century, shrill accusations against pregnant women seeking entry are again heard. Why do you think immigration officials and the American public are so concerned about female sexuality and reproductive capabilities?

The second gatekeeping mechanism in the Page Act (see the final paragraph) took on renewed vigor in later acts and with the construction of immigrant receiving stations—Ellis Island in New York Harbor in 1892 and Angel Island in San Francisco Bay in 1910. At the latter, Asian immigrant women tended to be detained longer than men, as well as grilled about their sexual character, plans to marry (if single), and ability to support themselves in the United States. See photograph on p. 341.

Be it enacted . . . that in determining whether the immigration of any subject of China, Japan, or any Oriental country, to the United States, is free and voluntary . . . it shall be the duty of the . . . consul of the United States residing at the port from which it is proposed to convey such subjects, in any vessels enrolled or licensed in the United States . . . to ascertain whether such immigrant has entered into a contract or agreement for a term of service within the United States, for lewd and immoral purposes; and if there be such contract or agreement, the said . . . consul shall not deliver the required permit or certificate . . .

. . . That the importation into the United States of women for the purposes of prostitution is hereby forbidden; and all contracts and agreements in relation thereto, made in advance or in pursuance of such illegal importation and purposes, are hereby declared void; and whoever shall knowingly and willfully import, or cause any importation of, women into the United States for the purposes of prostitution, or shall knowingly or willfully hold, or attempt to hold, any woman to such purposes, in pursuance of such illegal importation and contract or agreement, shall be deemed guilty of a felony, and, on conviction thereof, shall be imprisoned not exceeding five years and pay a fine not exceeding five thousand dollars . . .

. . . That it shall be unlawful for aliens of the following [two] classes to immigrate into the United States, namely, persons who are undergoing a sentence for conviction in their own country of felonious crimes other than political . . . and women "imported for the purposes of prostitution." Every vessel arriving in the United States may be inspected under the direction of the collector of the port at which it arrives, if he shall have reason to believe that any such obnoxious persons are on board. . . .

Mackenzie v. Hare, 1915

The persistent expansion of married women's property acts and the increasing popularity of woman suffrage make it tempting to conclude that the practice of coverture—women's legal and civic subordination to men—steadily dissolved over the course of the nineteenth and early twentieth centuries. But although it is true that some aspects of coverture eroded, others were sustained and even strengthened.

Mackenzie v. Hare, 239 U.S. 299 (1915).

Although Chief Justice Morrison R. Waite had been right when he observed in *Minor v. Happersett* (1874) (pp. 294–295) that "[t]here is no doubt that women may be citizens," he was wrong when he went on to claim that "sex has never been made one of the elements of citizenship. . . . [M]en have never had an advantage over women." According to the common law and early American practice, white women, like men, became citizens either by birth or by their own choice to be naturalized. But in 1855, following practices established in France by the conservative Code Napoleon (1804) and in Britain in 1844, the U.S. Congress extended the principle of marital unity to provide that "any woman who might lawfully be naturalized under the existing laws, married, or shall be married to a citizen of the United States shall be deemed and taken to be a citizen." That is, foreign women who married male citizens did not need to go through a naturalization process or even take an oath of allegiance. The law did not explain what should happen when a woman with U.S. citizenship married a noncitizen man. For the next fifty years, there was little consistency in how courts dealt with related cases that came before them. Often the principle of "marital unity" prevailed, meaning that women who were American citizens lost their citizenship by marrying a foreign national. In 1907, Congress passed a statute explicitly providing that women take the nationality of their husbands when they marry.

Expatriation—the loss of citizenship—traditionally has been a very severe punishment, usually reserved for cases of treason. If a married woman had to assume the nationality of her husband, she might become the subject of a king or czar in a political system that offered her even less protection than did the United States. She might even become stateless. If Americans claimed to base their political system on the "consent of the governed," could women's "consent" be arbitrarily denied? In time of war, the American woman who married, say, a German national could change her status overnight from a citizen to an alien enemy. President Ulysses S. Grant's daughter lost her citizenship when she married an Englishman in 1874; it required a special act of Congress to reinstate her citizenship when she returned from England as a widow in 1898.

Ethel Mackenzie, who had been born in California, married Gordon Mackenzie, a British subject, in 1909—two years after the passage of the Citizenship Act of 1907. She was active in the woman suffrage movement in California, and when it was successful in 1911 she worked in the San Francisco voter registration drive. It is not surprising that she herself should try to register to vote. When the Board of Election Commissioners denied her application, holding that upon her marriage to a British subject she had "ceased to be a citizen of the United States," she refused to let her husband apply for citizenship and instead challenged the law, claiming that Congress had exceeded its authority. She could not believe that Congress had actually *intended* to deprive her of the citizenship she understood to be her birthright. Why did the Supreme Court deny her claim? What "ancient principle of jurisprudence" did they rely on? Why did the Court think that the marriage of an American woman to a foreign man should be treated differently from the marriage of an American man to a foreign woman?

MR. JUSTICE MCKENNA:

. . . The question . . . is, Did [Ethel Mackenzie] cease to be a citizen by her marriage? . . . [Mackenzie contends] that it was not the intention [of Congress] to deprive an American-born woman, remaining within the jurisdiction of the United States, of her citizenship by reason of her marriage to a resident foreigner. . . . [She is trying to persuade the Court that the citizenship statute was] beyond the authority of

Congress. . . . [She offered the] earnest argument . . . that . . . under the Constitution and laws of the United States, [citizenship] became a right, privilege and immunity which could not be taken away from her except as a punishment for crime or by her voluntary expatriation. . . .

[But the Court concludes:] . . . The identity of husband and wife is an ancient principle of our jurisprudence. It was neither accidental nor arbitrary and worked in many instances for her protection. There has been, it is true, much relaxation of it but in its retention as in its origin it is determined by their intimate relation and unity of interests, and this relation and unity may make it of public concern in many instances to merge their identity, and give dominance to the husband. It has purpose, if not necessity, in purely

domestic policy; it has greater purpose and, it may be, necessity, in international policy. . . . Having this purpose, has it not the sanction of power?

. . . The law in controversy deals with a condition voluntarily entered into. . . . The marriage of an American woman with a foreigner has consequences . . . [similar to] her physical expatriation. . . . Therefore, as long as the relation lasts it is made tantamount to expatriation. This is no arbitrary exercise of government. . . . It is the conception of the legislation under review that such an act [marriage to a foreign man] may bring the Government into embarrassments and, it may be, into controversies. . . . [Marriage to a foreign man] is as voluntary and distinctive as expatriation and its consequence must be considered as elected.

The decision in *Mackenzie* angered suffragists and energized them; American women needed suffrage to protect themselves against involuntary expatriation and statelessness. The repeal of the Citizenship Act of 1907 was high on the suffragists' agenda, and they returned to it as soon as suffrage was accomplished (see Equal Suffrage [Nineteenth] Amendment). The Cable Act of 1922 provided that "the right of a person to become a naturalized citizen shall not be denied to a person on account of sex or because she is a married woman," but it permitted American women who married foreigners to retain their citizenship only if they married men from countries whose subjects were eligible for U.S. citizenship—that is, not from China or Japan. American-born women who married aliens from China or Japan still lost their citizenship. American-born women who married aliens not from China or Japan were treated as naturalized citizens who would lose their citizenship should they reside abroad for two years.

The Cable Act was extended by amendments well into the 1930s, but some exclusions remained, and the improvements were generally not retroactive. Thus, as late as the 1950s, some American-born women were denied passports because they had married foreign men before 1922. In 1998, 2001, and again in 2011, the U.S. Supreme Court upheld a practice of different rules for non-marital children born abroad. The child born to an unmarried citizen mother and a noncitizen man is a citizen at birth (so long as the mother has lived in the United States for at least one year). The child born to an unmarried citizen father and a noncitizen woman can be a citizen only if the father has met a number of requirements. Among them are that he must have lived in the United States for a specified number of years after he reached the age of fourteen. (The number of years changed when Congress revised the statute: until 1986 it was five years; then it was reduced to two years.) The father must also formally legitimize and financially support the child before the child reaches the age of eighteen.*

*Miller v. Albright , 523 U.S. 420 (1998); *Nguyen v. Immigration and Naturalization Service*, 533 U.S. 53 (2001); *Flores-Villar v. United States*, 131 S. Ct 2312 (2011). This note draws on Candice Lewis Bredbenner, *A Nationality of Her Own: Women, Marriage and the Law of Citizenship* (Berkeley: University of California Press, 1998).

In sustaining different rules for mothers and fathers, the Supreme Court majority emphasized the possibility of fraudulent claims of citizenship by unmarried noncitizen mothers and their children; the dissenting minority emphasized the ease with which men could avoid responsibility for the nonmarital children they had fathered.

Equal Suffrage (Nineteenth) Amendment, 1920

When the Fourteenth and Fifteenth Amendments (see p. 289) failed to provide for universal suffrage, a federal amendment was introduced into the Senate by S. C. Pomeroy of Kansas in 1868 and into the House by George W. Julian of Indiana in March 1869. Historian Ellen DuBois has observed, "Previously the case for suffrage had consistently been put in terms of the individual rights of all persons, regardless of their sex and race. Angered by their exclusion from the Fifteenth Amendment, women's rights advocates began to develop fundamentally different arguments for their cause. They claimed their right to the ballot not as individuals but as a sex. . . . The reason women should vote was not that they were the same as men but that they were different. That made for a rather thorough reversal of classic women's rights premises."*

Arguing for the vote on the basis of women's *difference* from men could be effective in strengthening women's sense of group consciousness, but it also was compatible with racist and nativist arguments that white women needed the vote to counteract the suffrage of black and immigrant men. The old alliance of woman suffrage and abolitionist activism eroded, even though voting rights for black men were under siege after Reconstruction. The suffrage efforts of 1870 to 1920 continued to display arguments on the basis of equality, but younger generations of activists were increasingly likely to emphasize difference—what one activist called "the mother instinct for government."

Woman suffrage was not accomplished easily. One scholar has counted 480 suffrage campaigns waged at the state level between 1870 and 1910, but in the end only seventeen referenda were held, with only two successes (in Colorado and Idaho).** Stanton died in 1902; Anthony in 1906. But a new, younger generation adopted new strategies. Americans were inspired by the militancy of the British suffrage movement. In 1902 Carrie Chapman Catt was simultaneously president of the International Woman Suffrage Alliance and the National American Woman Suffrage Association (NAWSA). By 1910 it was clear that a reinvigorated movement was under way, using door-to-door campaigns, street-corner speakers, and poll watchers on Election Day. For the first time, cross-class suffrage organizations, like New York's Equality League of Independent Women, were mobilizing

---

*Ellen Carol DuBois, "Outgrowing the Compact of the Fathers: Equal Rights, Woman Suffrage, and the United States Constitution, 1820–1878," *Journal of American History* 74 (December 1987): 848.

**Eleanor Flexner, *Century of Struggle* (Cambridge, Mass.: Belknap Press of Harvard University Press, 1959), 13; Rebecca Edwards, "Pioneers at the Polls: Woman Suffrage in the West," in *Votes for Women: The Struggle for Suffrage Revisited*, ed. Jean H. Baker (New York: Oxford University Press, 2002), pp. 90–101.

support for suffrage. Suffragists staged public parades that attracted tens of thousands of supporters.

Although many suffragists had claimed that when women got the vote, there would be no more American endorsements of war, Catt swung NAWSA behind Woodrow Wilson, American support for the allies, and, eventually, the nation's entry into World War I in April 1917. The more radical National Women's Party (NWP), under the leadership of Alice Paul, staked out a very public position protesting Wilson's failure to explicitly endorse a federal guarantee for women's suffrage. (For an image and more on the story of the NWP's picketing of the White House in 1917, see p. 261) Putting aside his states' rights approach, the president publicly endorsed a constitutional amendment in early 1918. One day later, the House of Representatives passed the suffrage amendment, barely achieving the required two-thirds majority. But despite a personal appearance from Wilson, it failed by only two votes to carry the Senate.

As state after state enacted woman suffrage for statewide elections, the number of members of Congress dependent on women's votes increased. With the federal suffrage amendment slated to come before Congress again and again, these men were likely to believe that they had no choice but to support it. In the fall 1918 elections, NAWSA targeted four senators for defeat; two of them failed to be reelected. Moreover, energetic campaigns in the states to elect prosuffrage candidates to Congress worked. When the amendment came up in the new Congress, according to Anne F. Scott and Andrew Scott, "224 of those voting yes came from suffrage states, and eighty from nonsuffrage states."[†] It squeaked by in the Senate. It was ratified by thirty-five states by August 1920; the final state was Tennessee, where, after a bitter struggle, it was ratified by a single vote, just in time to permit women to vote in the elections of 1920.

When Puerto Rican women attempted to register to vote in 1920, however, the U.S. Bureau of Insular Affairs decided that the Nineteenth Amendment did not automatically apply to U.S. territories. Suffragist groups mobilized in Puerto Rico, lobbying throughout the next decade both on the island and in Washington, D.C., with support from the NWP. In 1929 the territorial legislature granted suffrage to women restricted by a literacy requirement; not until 1935 was universal suffrage established in Puerto Rico.

Many southern states had excluded African American men from voting by using literacy tests, poll taxes, and intimidation; in those states black women could vote no more easily than black men, and suffrage was an empty victory. The state of Georgia effectively discouraged white women from voting as well by providing that any woman who did not choose to register to vote did not have to pay the poll tax. This law, which encouraged women—and their husbands—to see voting as an expensive extravagance, was upheld by the U.S. Supreme Court in 1937 (*Breedlove v. Suttles*, 302 U.S. 277).

Section 1. The right of the citizens of the United States to vote shall not be denied or abridged by the United States or by any State on account of sex.

Section 2. Congress shall have power to enforce this article by appropriate legislation.

[†]Anne F. Scott and Andrew MacKay Scott, *One Half the People: The Fight for Woman Suffrage* (Urbana: University of Illinois Press, 1982; orig. publ. Philadelphia: Lippincott, 1975), p. 45.

I V

STORMS ON MANY FRONTS

1920–1945

SEXUALITY AND THE BODY

JOAN JACOBS BRUMBERG
Fasting Girls: The Emerging Ideal of Slenderness in American Culture

---

A lthough anorexia nervosa is generally considered a modern disease, appetite control has long been an important dimension of female experience. Joan Jacobs Brumberg's pioneering study of anorexia nervosa traces changing cultural pressure on women to control their appetite. Exploring the links between food and femininity in the nineteenth century, Brumberg found that by 1890 thinness had become a way in which young privileged women could distance themselves from their working-class counterparts. More important, food preferences and thin bodies also sent moral and aesthetic messages. The young woman whose frail, delicate frame demonstrated her rejection of all carnal appetites more closely approached the Victorian ideal of femininity than did her more robust counterpart whose heavier physique signaled sexual craving. The twentieth century brought additional pressures to control body weight, according to Brumberg, with the development of scientific nutrition and the standard sizing of clothes. By 1920, fat had become a moral issue. Combined with social changes having to do with food and sexuality occurring in the 1960s, the stage was set for the epidemic of eating disorders evident in the 1980s and 1990s. What evidence is there of the persistence of these disorders in the twenty-first century? What is it that we expect our bodies to convey?

Within the first two decades of the twentieth century, even before the advent of the flapper, the voice of American women revealed that the female struggle with weight was under way and was becoming intensely personal. As early as 1907 an *Atlantic Monthly* article described the reaction of a woman trying on a dress she had not worn for over a year: "The gown was neither more [n]or less than anticipated. But I . . . *the fault was on me* . . . I was more! Gasping I hooked it together. The gown was hopeless, and I . . . I am fat."[1] . . . By the twentieth century . . . overweight in women was not only a physical liability, it was a character flaw and a social impediment.

Early in the century elite American women began to take body weight seriously as fat became an aesthetic liability for those who followed the world of haute couture. Since the mid-nineteenth century wealthy Americans— the wives of J. P. Morgan, Cornelius Vanderbilt, and Harry Harkness Flagler, for instance—had traveled to Paris to purchase the latest creations from couturier collections such as those on view at Maison Worth on the famed rue de la Paix. The couturier was not just a dressmaker who made clothes for an individual woman; rather, the couturier fashioned "a look" or a collection of dresses for an abstraction—the stylish woman. In order to be stylish and wear

Excerpted from *Fasting Girls: The Emergence of Anorexia Nervosa as a Modern Disease* by Joan Jacobs Brumberg (Cambridge, Mass.: Harvard University Press, 1988). Reprinted by permission of the author and publisher. Notes have been edited and renumbered.

couturier clothes, a woman's body had to conform to the dress rather than the dress to the body, as had been the case when the traditional dressmaker fitted each garment.[2] . . .

In 1908 the world of women's fashion was revolutionized by Paul Poiret, whose new silhouette was slim and straight. . . . Almost immediately women of style began to purchase new kinds of undergarments that would make Poiret's look possible; for example, the traditional hourglass corset was cast aside for a rubber girdle to retract the hips.

After World War I the French continued to set the fashion standard for style-conscious American women. In 1922 Jeanne Lanvin's chemise, a straight frock with a simple bateau neckline, was transformed by Gabrielle Chanel into the uniform of the flapper. Chanel dropped the waistline to the hips and began to expose more of the leg: in 1922 she moved her hemlines to midcalf, and in 1926–27 the ideal hem was raised to just below the knee. In order to look good in Chanel's fashionable little dress, its wearer had to think not only about the appearance of her legs but about the smoothness of her form.[3] Women who wore the flapper uniform turned to flattening brassieres constructed of shoulder straps and a single band of material that encased the body from chest to waist. In 1914 a French physician commented on the revised dimensions of women's bodies: "Nowadays it is not the fashion to be corpulent; the proper thing is to have a slight, graceful figure far removed from embonpoint, and *a fortiori* from obesity. For once, the physician is called upon to interest himself in the question of feminine aesthetics."[4]

The slenderized fashion image of the French was picked up and promoted by America's burgeoning ready-to-wear garment industry.[5] Stimulated by the popularity of the Gibson girl and the shirtwaist craze of the 1890s, ready-to-wear production in the United States accelerated in the first two decades of the twentieth century. Chanel's chemise dress was a further boon to the garment industry. Because of its simple cut, the chemise was easy to copy and produce, realities that explain its quick adoption as the uniform of the 1920s. According to a 1923 *Vogue*, the American ready-to-wear industry successfully democratized French fashion: "Today, the mode which originates in Paris is a factor in the lives of women of every rank, from the highest to the lowest."[6]

In order to market ready-to-wear clothing, the industry turned in the 1920s to standard sizing, an innovation that put increased emphasis on personal body size and gave legitimacy to the idea of a normative size range. For women, shopping for ready-to-wear clothes in the bustling department stores of the early twentieth century fostered heightened concern about body size.[7] With a dressmaker, every style was theoretically available to every body; with standard sizing, items of clothing could be identified as desirable, only to be rejected on the grounds of fit. (For women the cost of altering a ready-made garment was an "add-on"; for men it was not.) Female figure flaws became a source of frustration and embarrassment, not easily hidden from those who accompanied the shopper or from salesclerks. Experiences in department-store dressing rooms created a host of new anxieties for women and girls who could not fit into stylish clothing. . . .

Ironically, standard sizing created an unexpected experience of frustration in a marketplace that otherwise was offering a continually expansive opportunity for gratification via purchasable goods. Because many manufacturers of stylish women's garments did not make clothing in large sizes, heavy women were at the greatest disadvantage. In addition to the moral [disgrace] of overweight, the standardization of garment production precluded fat women's participation in the mainstream of fashion. This situation became worse as the century progressed. Fashion photography was professionalized, a development that paralleled the growth of modern advertising, and models became slimmer both to compensate for the distortions of the camera and to accommodate the new merchandising canon—modern fashion was best displayed on a lean body.[8]

The appearance in 1918 of America's first best-selling weight-control book confirmed that weight was a source of anxiety among women and that fat was out of fashion. *Diet and Health with a Key to the Calories* by Lulu Hunt Peters was directed at a female audience and based on the assumption that most readers wanted to lose rather than gain weight. . . . "You should know and also use the word calorie as frequently, or more frequently, than you use the words foot, yard, quart, gallon and so forth. . . . Hereafter you are going to eat calories of food. Instead of saying one slice of bread, or a piece of pie, you will say 100 calories of bread, 350 calories of pie."[9]

Peters' book was popular because it was personal and timely. Her 1918 appeal was related to food shortages caused by the exigencies of the war in Europe. Peters told her readers that it was "more important than ever to reduce" and recommended the formation of local Watch Your Weight Anti-Kaiser Classes. "There are hundreds of thousands of individuals all over America who are hoarding food," she wrote. "They have vast amounts of this valuable commodity stored away in their own anatomy." In good-humored fashion Peters portrayed her own calories counting as both an act of patriotism and humanitarianism:

> I am reducing and the money that I can save will help keep a child from starving . . . [I am explaining to my friends] that for every pang of hunger we feel we can have a double joy, that of knowing we are saving worse pangs in some little children, and that of knowing that for every pang we feel we lose a pound. A pang's a pound the world around we'll say.[10]

But Peters showed herself to be more than simply an informative and patriotic physician. Confessing that she once weighed as much as 200 pounds, the author also understood that heavy women were ashamed of their bulk and unlikely to reveal their actual weight. Peters observed that it was not a happy situation for fat women. "You are viewed with distrust, suspicion, and even aversion," she told her overweight readers. . . .

Peters' book was among the first to articulate the new secular credo of physical denial: modern women suffered to be beautiful (thin) rather than pious. Peters' language and thinking reverberated with references to religious ideas of temptation and sin. For the modern female dieter, sweets, particularly chocolate, were the ultimate temptation. Eating chocolate violated the morality of the dieter and her dedication to her ideal, a slim body. Peters joked about her cravings ("My idea of heaven is a place with me and mine on a cloud of whipped cream") but she was adamant about the fact that indulgence must ultimately be paid for. "If you think you will die unless you have some chocolate creams [go on a] *debauch,*" she advised. "'Eat 10 or so' but then *repent* with a 50-calorie dinner of bouillon and crackers." (Italics added.)[11]

Although the damage done by chocolate creams could be mediated by either fasting or more rigid dieting, Peters explained that there was a psychological cost in yielding to the temptation of candy or rich desserts. Like so many modern dieters, Peters wrote about the issue of guilt followed by redemption through parsimonious eating: "Every supposed pleasure in sin [eating] will furnish more than its equivalent of pain [dieting]." But appetite control was not only a question of learning to delay gratification, it was also an issue of self-esteem. "You will be tempted quite frequently, and you will have to choose whether you will enjoy yourself hugely in the twenty minutes or so that you will be consuming the excess calories, or whether you will dislike yourself cordially for the two or three days you lose by your lack of will power." For Peters dieting had as much to do with the mind as with the body. "There is a great deal of psychology to reducing," she wrote astutely.[12] In fact, with the popularization of the concept of calorie counting, physical features once regarded as natural—such as appetite and body weight—were designated as objects of conscious control. The notion of weight control through restriction of calories implied that . . . overweight resulted solely from lack of control; to be a fat woman constituted a failure of personal morality.

The tendency to talk about female dieting as a moral issue was particularly strong among the popular beauty experts, that is, those in the fashion and cosmetics industry who sold scientific advice on how to become and stay beautiful. Many early-twentieth-century beauty culturists, including Grace Peckham Murray, Helena Rubenstein, and Hazel Bishop, studied chemistry and medical specialties such as dermatology. The creams and lotions they created, as well as the electrical gadgets they promoted, were intended to bring the findings of modern chemistry and physiology to the problem of female beauty. Nevertheless, women could not rely entirely on scientifically achieved results. The beauty experts also preached the credo of self-denial: to be beautiful, most women must suffer.

Because they regarded fat women as an affront to their faith, some were willing to criminalize as well as medicalize obesity. In 1902 *Vogue* speculated, "To judge by the efforts of the majority of women to attain slender and sylphlike proportions, one would fancy it a crime to be fat." By 1918 the message was more distinct: "There is one crime against the modern ethics of beauty which is unpardonable; far better it is to commit any number of petty crimes than to be guilty of the sin of growing fat." By 1930 there was no turning back. Helena Rubenstein, a high priestess of the faith, articulated in *The Art of Feminine Beauty* the moral and aesthetic dictum that would govern the lives of subsequent generations of women: "An abundance of fat is something repulsive and not in accord with the principles that rule our conception of the beautiful.[13] . . .

In adolescence fat was considered a particular liability because of the social strains associated with that stage of life. In the 1940s articles with titles such as "What to Do about the Fat Child at Puberty," "Reducing the Adolescent," and "Should the Teens Diet?" captured the rising interest in adolescent weight control.[14] Women's magazines, reflecting the concerns of mothers anxious to save their daughters from social ostracism, for the first time promoted diets for young girls. According to the *Ladies' Home Journal*: "Appearance plays too important a part in a girl's life not to have her grow up to be beauty-conscious. Girls should be encouraged to take an interest in their appearance when they are very young."[15] . . . Adolescent weight control was also promoted by popular magazines hoping to sell products to young women. . . . *Seventeen's* adoption of the cause of weight control confirmed that slimness was a critical dimension of adolescent beauty and that a new constituency, high school girls, was learning how to diet. From 1944 [when it was founded] to 1948, *Seventeen* had published a full complement of articles on nutrition but almost nothing on weight control. Following the mode of earlier home economists and scientific nutritionists, the magazine had presented basic information about food groups and the importance of each in the daily diet; balance but not calories had been the initial focus. In 1948, however, *Seventeen* proclaimed overweight a medical problem and began educating its young readers about calories and the psychology of eating. Adolescent girls were warned against using eating as a form of emotional expression (do not "pamper your blues" with food) and were given practical tips on how to avoid food bingeing. No mention was made of the new "diet pills" (amphetamines) introduced in the 1930s for clinical treatment of obesity. Instead, teenagers were encouraged to go on "sensible" and "well-rounded" diets of between 1,200 and 1,800 calories. By the 1950s advertisements for "diet foods" such as Ry-Krisp were offering assistance as they told the readership "Nobody Loves a Fat Girl."[16] Girls,

much as adult women, were expected to tame the natural appetite.

Although adolescent girls were consistently warned against weight reduction without medical supervision, dieting was always cast as a worthwhile endeavor with transforming powers. "Diets can do wonderful things. When dispensed or approved by your physician . . . all you have to do is follow whither the chart leads."[17] The process of metamorphosis from fat to thin always provided a narrative of uplift and interest. "The Fattest Girl in the Class" was the autobiographical account of Jane, an obese girl who, after suffering the social stigma associated with teenage overweight, went on a diet and found happiness.[18] Being thin was tied to attractiveness, popularity with the opposite sex, and self-esteem—all primary ingredients in adolescent culture. Nonfiction accounts of "make-overs" became a popular formula in all the beauty magazines of the postwar period and provided a tantalizing fantasy of psychological and spiritual transformation for mature and adolescent women alike.[19]

The popularization of adolescent female weight control in the postwar era is a prime component of the modern dieting story and a critical factor in explaining anorexia nervosa as we know it today. . . . Since the 1960s the dieting imperative has intensified in two noticeable and important ways. . . . First, the ideal female body size has become considerably slimmer. After a brief flirtation with full-breasted, curvaceous female figures in the politically conservative postwar recovery of the 1950s, our collective taste returned to an ideal of extreme thinness and an androgynous, if not childlike, figure.[20] A series of well-known studies point to the declining weight since the 1950s of fashion models, Miss America contestants, and *Playboy* centerfolds.[21] Neither bosoms, hips, nor buttocks are currently in fashion as young and old alike attempt to meet the new aesthetic standard. A Bloomingdale's ad posits, "Bean lean, slender as the night, narrow as an arrow, pencil thin, get the point?"[22] It is appropriate to recall Annette Kellerman who, at 5 feet 3¾ inches and 137 pounds, epitomized the body beautiful of 1918. Obviously, our cultural tolerance for body fat has diminished over the intervening years.

Second, notably since the middle to late 1970s, a new emphasis on physical fitness and athleticism has intensified cultural pressures on the individual for control and mastery of the body. For women this means that fitness has been added to slimness as a criterion of perfection.[23] Experts on the subject, such as Jane Fonda, encourage women to strive for a lean body with musculature. The incredible popularity among women of aerobics, conditioning programs, and jogging does testify to the satisfactions that come with gaining physical strength through self-discipline, but it also expresses our current urgency about the physical body. Many who are caught up in the exercise cult equate physical fitness and slimness with a higher moral state. . . . Compulsive exercising and chronic dieting have [thus] been joined as twin obsessions. . . . [In the] 1980s clinical reports and autobiographical statements show a clear-cut pattern of anorexic patients who exercise with ritualistic intensity. How much one runs and how little one eats is the prevailing moral calculus in present-day anorexia nervosa. . . .

The proliferation of diet and exercise regimens in the past decade, although an important context for understanding the increase in anorexia nervosa, is not the whole story. For a more complete explanation we must turn to some other recent social changes, keeping in mind that no one factor has caused the contemporary problem. Rather, it is the nature of our economic and cultural environment, interacting with individual and family characteristics, which exacerbates the social and emotional insecurities that put today's young women at increasing risk for anorexia nervosa. Two very basic social transformations are relevant to the problem: one has to do with food; the other, with new expectations between the sexes.

Since World War II, and especially in the last two decades, middle-class Americans have experienced a veritable revolution in terms of how and what we eat, as well as how we think about eating.[24] The imperatives of an expanding capitalist society have generated extraordinary technological and marketing innovations, which in turn have transformed food itself, expanded our repertoire of foods, and affected the ways in which we consume them. Even though much contemporary food is characterized by elaborate processing and conservation techniques that actually reduce and flatten distinctive textures and flavors, the current array of food choices seems to constitute an endless smorgasbord of new and different tastes. [Since] the 1980s an individual in an

urban center looking for a quick lunch [has been] able to choose from tacos with guacamole and salsa, hummus and falafel in pita, sushi, tortellini, quiche, and pad thai—along with more traditional "American" fare such as hamburgers. Thirty years ago this diversified international menu was as unknown to most Americans as were many of the food products used to create it. . . . As a consequence of [the expansion of our food repertoire], we are faced with an abundance of food which, in our obesophobic society, necessitates ever greater self-control. . . . It is no wonder, then, that we talk so incessantly about food and dieting.

The food revolution is a matter of ideas and manners as much as technology and markets. . . . In our society food is chosen and eaten not merely on the basis of hunger. It is a commonplace to observe that contemporary advertising connects food to sociability, status, and sexuality. In an affluent society, in particular, where eating appears to involve considerable individual choice, food is regarded as an important analogue of the self.

In the 1960s, for example, many young people in the counterculture gave up goods associated with their bourgeois upbringing and turned instead to a diet of whole grains, unprocessed foods, and no meat. This new diet made a statement about personal and political values and became a way of separating one generation from another. . . . In the 1980s, the extent to which the choice of cuisine dominates and defines the sophisticated life-style [among well-to-do urbanites] is reflected in a recent *New Yorker* cartoon, which shows a young professional couple after a dinner party given by friends. In complete seriousness they say to each other, "We could get close with David and Elizabeth if they didn't put béarnaise sauce on everything."[25] The anorectic is obviously not alone in her use of food and eating as a means of self-definition. There are many others who internalize the dictum "You are what you eat"— or, for that matter, what you don't eat.[26]

Along with the expansion of our food repertoire and our extraordinary attention to food selection, the eating context has changed. Eating is being desocialized. In American society today, more and more food is being consumed away from the family table or any other fixed center of sociability. This process began in the postwar period with the introduction of convenience foods and drive-in restaurants, precursors of the fast-food chains that now constitute a $45-billion-a-year industry. . . . Americans [now] eat everywhere—in the classroom; in theaters, libraries, and museums; on the street; at their desks; on the phone; in hot tubs; in cars while driving. . . . Signs saying "no food and drink," infrequent in other parts of the world, adorn our public buildings, a clear sign of our pattern of vagabond eating.[27]

On college and university campuses, where eating disorders are rampant, the situation is exaggerated. By the early 1970s most undergraduate students were no longer required to take any sit-down meals at fixed times in college dormitories. . . . Typically, students frequent a series of university cafeterias or commercial off-campus restaurants where they can obtain breakfast, lunch, or dinner at any time of the day. Some campus food plans allow unlimited amounts, a policy that fuels the behavior of the bulimic: "I used to go to Contract, eat a whole bunch of stuff, go to the bathroom, throw it up, come back, eat again, throw it up, eat again."[28] In addition, the availability of nearly any kind of food at any time contributes to a pattern of indiscriminate eating. Traditions of food appropriateness—that is, that certain foods are eaten at particular times of the day or in a certain sequence—disappear in this unstructured climate. Thus, an ice-cream cone, a carbonated soft drink, and a bagel constitute an easy popular "meal" that may be eaten at any time of day. Most colleges and the surrounding communities have made provisions to gratify student appetites no matter what the hour. Snack bars and vending machines adorn nearly every free alcove in classroom buildings and residence halls; pizza and Chinese food are delivered hot in the middle of the night.

In a setting where eating is so promiscuous, it is no wonder that food habits become problematic. This is not to say that our universities, on their own, generate eating-disordered students. They do, however, provide fertile ground for those who carry the seeds of disorder with them from home. In the permissive and highly individualized food environment of the post-1970 college or university, overeating and undereating become distinct possibilities.[29]

For those young women with either incipient or pronounced anorexia nervosa, the unstructured college life . . . often accentuates the anorectic's physical and emotional problems. [As one young anorectic explained]:

I don't know any limits here at all. At home, I have my mom dishing out my food . . . But when I'm here it's a totally different story—I can't tell portion size at all. I always get so afraid afterwards, after eating. Oh my God did I eat that much or this much? So I just pass things up altogether and don't eat.[30]

The anorectic's preoccupation with appetite control is fueled by incessant talk about dieting and weight even among friends and associates who eat regularly. Diet-conscious female students report that fasting, weight control, and binge eating are a normal part of life on American college campuses.[31] . . . In our obesophobic society women struggle with food because, among other things, food represents fat and loss of control. For a contemporary woman to eat heartily, energetically, and happily is usually problematic (and, at best, occasional). As a result, some come to fear and hate their own appetite; eating becomes a shameful and disgusting act, and denial of hunger becomes a central facet of identity and personality. . . .

Among adolescents concerned with the transition to adulthood, an intense concern with appetite control and the body [also] operates in tandem with increasing anxiety over sexuality and the implications of changing sex roles. For sex is the second important arena of social change that may contribute to the rising number of anorectics. There are, in fact, some justifiable social reasons why contemporary young women fear adult womanhood. The "anorexic generations," particularly those born since 1960, have been subject to a set of insecurities that make heterosexuality an anxious rather than a pleasant prospect. Family insecurity, reflected in the frequency of divorce, and changing sex and gender roles became facts of life for this group in their childhood. . . . Although there is no positive correlation between divorced families and anorexia nervosa, family disruption is part of the world view of the anorexic generations. Its members understand implicitly that not all heterosexual relationships have happy endings.

As a consequence of these social changes, some young women are ambivalent about commitments to men and have adopted an ideal of womanhood that reflects the impact of post-1960 feminism. Although they generally draw back from an explicitly feminist vocabulary, most undergraduate women today desire professional careers of their own without forsaking the idea of marriage and a family. A 1985 study of college women by sociologist Mirra Komarovsky reveals that finding one's place in the world of work has become essential for personal dignity in this generation—yet a career without marriage was the choice of only 2 percent of the sample.[32] Convinced that individuality can be accommodated in marriage, these young women are interested in heterosexuality, but admit that "relationships with guys" are difficult even in college. Komarovsky describes conflict over dating rituals (who takes the initiative and who pays), decision making as a couple, intellectual rivalries, and competition for entrance into graduate school. Unlike Mother, who followed Dad to graduate school and supported him along the way, today's undergraduate—whether she is a declared feminist or not—wants her own professional career both as a ticket to the good life and as a protection for herself in case of divorce.

Sexual activity also requires an extraordinary degree of self-protection in the modern world of AIDS. While premarital sex is acceptable (if not desirable), it is an understandable source of worry among female undergraduates. An advertisement in a 1986 issue of *Ms.*, aimed at selling condoms to young women, captured the current ambivalence about the physical side of heterosexuality: "Let's face it, sex these days can be risky business, and you need all the protection you can get. Between the fear of unplanned pregnancy, sexually transmitted diseases, and the potential side effects of many forms of contraception, it may seem like sex is hardly worth the risk anymore."[33] For some students the unprecedented privacy and freedom of modern university life generates as much fear as pleasure. It bears repeating that clinical materials suggest an *absence* [emphasis is the editors'] of sexual activity on the part of anorectics.

Even though feminine dependency is no longer in fashion, these same young women combine traditional expectations with a quest for equity and power. To be brainy and beautiful; to have an exciting $75,000-a-year job; to nurture two wonderful children in consort with a supportive but equally high-powered husband—these are the personal ambitions of many in the present college generation. In order to achieve this level of personal and social perfection, young women must be extremely demanding of themselves: there can be no distracting personal or avocational detours— they must be unrelenting in the pursuit of goals. The kind of personal control required to become the new Superwoman (a term popularized by

columnist Ellen Goodman)[34] parallels the single-mindedness that characterizes the anorectic. In sum, the golden ideal of this generation of privileged young women and their most distinctive pathology appear to be flip sides of the same record.

My assertion that the post-1960 epidemic of anorexia nervosa can be related to recent social change in the realm of sexuality [and gender roles] is not an argument for turning back the clock. . . . [H]istorical investigation demonstrates that anorexia nervosa was latent in the economic and emotional milieu of the bourgeois family as early as the 1950s. It makes little sense to think a cure will be achieved by putting women back in the kitchen, reinstituting sit-down meals on the nation's campuses, or limiting personal and professional choices to what they were in the Victorian era. On the basis of the best current research on anorexia nervosa, we must conclude that the disease develops as a result of the intersection of external and internal forces in the life of an individual. External forces such as those described here do not, by themselves, generate psychopathologies, but they do give them shape and influence their frequency.

In the confusion of this transitional moment, when a new future is being tentatively charted for women but gender roles and sexuality are still constrained by tradition, young women on the brink of adulthood are feeling the pain of social change most acutely.[35] They look about for direction, but find little in the way of useful experiential guides. What parts of women's tradition do they want to carry into the future? What parts should be left behind? These are difficult personal and political decisions, and most young women are being asked to make them without benefit of substantive education in the history and experience of their sex. In effect, our young women are being challenged and their expectations raised without a simultaneous level of support for either their specific aspirations or for female creativity in general.

Sadly, the cult of diet and exercise is the closest thing our secular society offers women in terms of a coherent philosophy of the self.[36] This being the case, anorexia nervosa is not a quirk and the symptom choice is not surprising. When personal and social difficulties arise, a substantial number of our young women become preoccupied with their bodies and control of appetite. Of all the messages they hear, the imperative to be beautiful and good, by being thin, is still the strongest and most familiar. Moreover, they are caught, often at a very early age, in a deceptive cognitive trap that has them believing that body weight is entirely subject to their conscious control. Despite feminist influences on the career aspirations of the present college-age generation, little has transpired to dilute the basic strength of this powerful cultural prescription that plays on both individualism and conformity. The unfortunate truth is that even when she wants more than beauty and understands its limitations as a life goal, the bourgeois woman still expends an enormous amount of psychic energy on appetite control as well as on other aspects of presentation of the physical self.

And what of the future? . . .

We can expect to see eating disorders continue, if not increase, among young women in those postindustrial societies where adolescents tend to be under stress. For both young men and young women, vast technological and cultural changes have made the transition to adulthood particularly difficult by transforming the nature of the family and community and rendering the future unpredictable. According to psychologist Urie Bronfenbrenner and others, American adolescents are in the worst trouble: we have the highest incidence of alcohol and drug abuse among adolescents of any country in the world; we also have the highest rate of teenage pregnancy of any industrialized nation; and we appear to have the most anorexia nervosa.[37]

Although the sexually active adolescent mother and the sexually inactive adolescent anorectic may seem to be light-years apart, they are linked by a common, though unarticulated, understanding. For adolescent women the body is still the most powerful paradigm regardless of social class. Unfortunately, a sizable number of our young women—poor and privileged alike—regard their body as the best vehicle for making a statement about their identity and personal dreams. This is what unprotected sexual intercourse and prolonged starvation have in common. Taken together, our unenviable preeminence in these two domains suggests the enormous difficulty involved in making the transition to adult womanhood in a society where women are still evaluated primarily in terms of the body rather than the mind.

NOTES

1. "On Growing Fat," *Atlantic Monthly* (Mar. 1907):430–31.

2. Jo Ann Olian, *The House of Worth: The Gilded Age, 1860–1918* (New York: Museum of the City of New York, 1982); Jane Beth Abrams, "The Thinning of America: The Emergence of the Ideal of Slenderness in American Popular Culture, 1870–1930" (B.A. thesis, Harvard University, 1983), chap. 2.

3. Michael Batterberry and Ariane Batterberry, *Mirror Mirror: A Social History of Fashion* (New York: Holt, Rinehart and Winston, 1977), pp. 289–97; Diane DeMarly, *The History of Haute Couture, 1850–1950* (New York: Holmes & Meier, 1980), pp. 81–83.

4. P. Rostaine, "How to Get Thin," *Medical Press and Circular* 149 (Dec. 23, 1914):643–44.

5. Stuart Ewen and Elizabeth Ewen, *Channels of Desire: Mass Images and the Shaping of American Consciousness* (New York: McGraw-Hill, 1982), pt. 4; Claudia Kidwell and Margaret C. Christman, *Suiting Everyone: The Democratization of Clothing in America* (Washington, D.C.: Smithsonian Institution Press, 1974).

6. *Vogue* (Jan. 1, 1923):63.

7. Lois W. Banner, *American Beauty* (New York: Random House, 1983), p. 262; Ewen and Ewen, *Channels of Desire*, pp. 193–98.

8. Banner, *American Beauty*, p. 287; Anne Hollander, *Seeing through Clothes* (New York: Viking Press, 1975).

9. Lulu Hunt Peters, *Diet and Health with a Key to the Calories* (Chicago: The Reilly & Britton Company, 1918), pp. 24, 39.

10. Ibid., pp. 12, 104, 110.

11. Ibid., pp. 85, 94.

12. Ibid., pp. 85, 93, 94.

13. "On Her Dressing Table," *Vogue* (Apr. 24, 1902):413; ibid. (July 1, 1918):78.

14. Mildred H. Bryan, "Don't Let Your Child Get Fat!" *Hygeia* 15 (1937):801–3; G. D. Schultz, "Forget That Clean-Plate Bogey!" *Better Homes and Gardens* 21 (Sept. 1942):24.

15. Louise Paine Benjamin, "I Have Three Daughters," *Ladies Homes Journal* 57 (June 1940):74.

16. "You'll Eat It Up at Noon," *Seventeen* (Sept. 1946):21–22; Irma M. Phorylles, "The Lost Waistline," ibid. (Mar. 1948):124; "Overweight?" ibid. (Aug. 1948):184.

17. Ibid.

18. "Fattest Girl in the Class," ibid. (Jan. 1948): 21–22.

19. "Psychology of Dieting," *Ladies' Home Journal* (Jan. 1965):66.

20. Banner, *American Beauty*, pp. 283–85.

21. David M. Garner et al., "Cultural Expectations of Thinness in Women," *Psychology Reports* 47 (1980):483–91.

22. Rita Freedman, *Beauty Bound* (Lexington: Lexington Books, 1986), p. 150.

23. "Coming on Strong: The New Ideal of Beauty," *Time* (Aug. 30, 1983):71–77.

24. William Chafe, *The Unfinished Journey: America since World War II* (New York: Oxford University Press, 1986).

25. *New Yorker* (July 21, 1986):71.

26. "What's Your Food Status Because the Way You Live Has a Lot to Do with the Way You Eat," *Mademoiselle* (Sept. 1985):224–26; "Food as Well as

Clothes, Today, Make the Man—As a Matter of Life and Style," *Vogue* (June 1985):271–73.

27. "Severe Growing Pains for Fast Food," *Business Week* (Mar. 22, 1985):225.

28. Greg Foster and Susan Howerin, "The Quest for Perfection: An Interview with a Former Bulimic," *Iris: A Journal about Women* [Charlottesville, Va.] (1986):21.

29. Before they even arrive on campus, during their senior year in high school and the summer before entering college, many girls began to talk about the "freshmen 10 or 15." This is the weight gain predicted as a result of eating starchy institutional food and participating in late-night food forays with friends.

30. Elizabeth Greene, "Support Groups Forming for Students with Eating Disorders," *Chronicle of Higher Education* (Mar. 5, 1986):1, 30.

31. K. A. Halmi, J. R. Falk, and E. Schwartz, "Binge-Eating and Vomiting: A Survey of a College Population," *Psychological Medicine* 11 (1981): 697–706; R. L. Pyle et al., "The Incident of Bulimia in Freshman College Students," *International Journal of Eating Disorders* 2, 3 (1983):75–86.

32. Mirra Komarovsky, *Women in College: Shaping the New Feminine Identities* (New York: Basic Books, 1985), pp. 89–92, 225–300.

33. *Ms.* (Sept. 1986):n.p. The condom is called Mentor.

34. Ellen Goodman, *Close to Home* (New York: Fawcett Crest, 1979).

35. In *Theories of Adolescence* (New York: Random House, 1962), R. E. Muuss wrote: "Societies in a period of rapid transition create a particular adolescent period; the adolescent has not only the society's problem to adjust to but his [or her] own as well" (p. 164).

36. My view of this issue complements ideas presented in Robert Bellah et al., *Habits of the Heart: Individualism and Commitment in American Life* (New York: Harper & Row, 1986).

37. These data are synthesized in Urie Bronfenbrenner, "Alienation and the Four Worlds of Childhood," *Phi Delta Kappan* (Feb. 1986):434.

VICKI L. RUIZ

The Flapper and the Chaperone: Mexican American Teenagers in the Southwest

Over one million Mexicans immigrated to the United States between 1900 and 1930, forming new communities or settling alongside families whose descendants had migrated north decades and centuries before. This essay plunges us into the decisions to be made about dating, dancing, and dressing up by young women growing up Mexican American in western cities and farm towns from the 1920s to the 1940s. Focusing on first-generation teenagers, Vicki L. Ruiz insists that we see them not as caught between the mores of their Mexican-born Catholic parents and the freedoms of modern America, but rather as navigating "across multiple terrains" simultaneously. Home for most if not all of these young women was located in the *barrios*, dense neighborhoods where Mexican and Mexican American families, businesses, and parishes were clustered.

Ruiz's goal is to uncover the dreams and strategies of young women rather than those of *pachucos*, or zoot-suiters, the youthful male subculture that has drawn scholarly attention. What range of sources and methods does she employ? If you were conducting such a study of teenage girls in the 1970s, or during the past decade, what research techniques and documents would be available to you?

Excerpted from "The Flapper and the Chaperone," ch. 3 of *From Out of the Shadows: Mexican Women in Twentieth-Century America* by Vicki L. Ruiz (New York: Oxford University Press, 1998). Reprinted by permission of the author and publisher. Notes have been edited and renumbered.

In the interwar years, a central figure in cross-sex socializing was the chaperone—*la dueña*. Why do you think adult women and not men were called on to fill the role in Mexican American culture? What cultural messages would be sent if chaperones dogged youthful men's activities, not young women's? Ruiz finds that second-generation women, once married with their own children, tended not to continue the chaperoning tradition. In the 1960s, activist women of Mexican descent embraced the identity of Chicana and, as Ruiz indicates at the close of her essay, issued new challenges to conventional expectations shaped by popular culture, family oligarchy, and men's demands. (See Jennie V. Chávez's 1972 activist statement, pp. 733–735.)

Imagine a gathering in a barrio hall, a group of young people dressed "to the nines" trying their best to replicate the dance steps of Fred Astaire and Ginger Rogers. This convivial heterosocial scene was a typical one in the lives of teenagers during the interwar period. But along the walls, a sharp difference was apparent in the barrios. Mothers, fathers, and older relatives chatted with one another as they kept one eye trained on the dance floor. They were the chaperones—the ubiquitous companions of unmarried Mexican-American women. Chaperonage was a traditional instrument of social control. Indeed, the presence of *la dueña* was the prerequisite for attendance at a dance, a movie, or even church-related events. "When we would go to town, I would want to say something to a guy. I couldn't because my mother was always there," remembered Maria Ybarra. "She would always stick to us girls like glue. . . . She never let us out of her sight."[1]

An examination of events like this one reveals the ways in which young Mexican women in the United States between the wars rationalized, resisted, and evaded parental supervision. It offers a glimpse into generational conflict that goes beyond the more general differences in acculturation between immigrants and their children. Chaperonage existed for centuries on both sides of the political border separating Mexico and the United States. While conjuring images of patriarchal domination, chaperonage is best understood as a manifestation of familial oligarchy whereby elders attempted to dictate the activities of youth for the sake of family honor. A family's standing in the community depended, in part, on women's purity. Loss of virginity not only tainted the reputation of an individual, but of her kin as well. For Mexicano immigrants living in a new, bewildering environment filled with temptations, the enforcement of chaperonage assumed a particular urgency.[2] . . .

Confronting "America" began at an early age. Throughout the Southwest, Spanish-speaking children had to sink or swim in an English-only environment. Even on the playground, students were punished for conversing in Spanish. Admonishments, such as "Don't speak that ugly language, you are an American now," not only reflected a strong belief in Anglo conformity but denigrated the self-esteem of Mexican-American children. As Mary Luna stated: "It was rough because I didn't know English. The teacher wouldn't let us talk Spanish. How can you talk to anybody? If you can't talk Spanish and you can't talk English. . . . It wasn't until maybe the fourth or fifth grade that I started catching up. And all that time I just felt I was stupid." Yet Luna credited her love of reading to a Euro-American educator who had converted a small barrio house into a makeshift community center and library. Her words underscore the dual thrust of Americanization—education and consumerism. "To this day I just love going into libraries . . . there are two places that I can go in and get a real warm, happy feeling; that is, the library and Bullock's in the perfume and make-up department."[3] . . .

For Mexican Americans, second-generation women as teenagers have received scant scholarly attention. Among Chicano historians and writers, there appears a fascination with the sons of immigrants, especially as *pachucos*.[4] Young women, however, may have experienced deeper generational tensions as they blended elements of Americanization with Mexican expectations and values. . . .

. . . The recollections of seventeen women serve as the basis for my reconstruction of adolescent aspirations and experiences (or dreams and routines). The women themselves, . . . with two [major] exceptions, . . . are U.S. citizens by birth and attended southwestern schools. All the interviewees were born between 1908 and 1926. Although three came from families once considered middle class in Mexico, most can be considered working class in the United States. Their fathers' typical occupations included farm worker, miner, day laborer, and railroad hand. These women usually characterized their mothers as homemakers, although several remembered that their mothers took seasonal jobs in area factories and fields. The most economically privileged woman in the sample, Ruby Estrada, helped out in her family-owned hardware and furniture store. She is also the only interviewee who attended college. It should be noted that seven of the seventeen narrators married Euro-Americans. Although intermarriage was uncommon, these oral histories give us insight into the lives of those who negotiated across cultures in a deeply personal way and who felt the impact of acculturation most keenly. Rich in emotion and detail, these interviews reveal women's conscious decision-making in the production of culture. In creating their own cultural spaces, the interwar generation challenged the trappings of familial oligarchy.[5]

... Within families, young women, perhaps more than their brothers, were expected to uphold certain standards. Parents, therefore, often assumed what they perceived as their unquestionable prerogative to regulate the actions and attitudes of their adolescent daughters. Teenagers, on the other hand, did not always acquiesce in the boundaries set down for them by their elders. Intergenerational tension flared along several fronts.

Like U.S. teenagers, in general, the first area of disagreement between an adolescent and her family would be over her personal appearance.... [T]he length of a young woman's tresses was a hot issue spanning class, region, and ethnic lines. During the 1920s, a woman's decision "to bob or not bob" her hair assumed classic proportions within Mexican families. After considerable pleading, Belen Martinez Mason was permitted to cut her hair, though she soon regretted the decision. "Oh, I cried for a month." Differing opinions over fashions often caused ill feelings. One Mexican American woman recalled that as a young girl, her mother dressed her "like a nun" and she could wear "no make-up, no cream, no nothing" on her face. Swimwear, bloomers, and short skirts also became sources of controversy. Some teenagers left home in one outfit and changed into another at school. Once María Fierro arrived home in her bloomers. Her father inquired, "Where have you been dressed like that, like a clown?" "I told him the truth," Fierro explained

"He whipped me anyway.... So from then on whenever I went to the track meet, I used to change my bloomers so that he wouldn't see that I had gone again."[6] ... [A] popular ballad chastised Mexican women for applying makeup so heavily as to resemble a piñata. [7]

The use of cosmetics, however, cannot be blamed entirely on Madison Avenue ad campaigns. The innumerable barrio beauty pageants, sponsored by *mutualistas*, patriotic societies, churches, the Mexican Chamber of Commerce, newspapers, and even progressive labor unions, encouraged young women to accentuate their physical attributes. Carefully chaperoned, many teenagers did participate in community contests from La Reina de Cinco de Mayo to Orange Queen. They modeled evening gowns, rode on parade floats, and sold raffle tickets.[8] ...

The commercialization of personal grooming made additional inroads into the Mexican community with the appearance of barrio beauty parlors. Working as a beautician conferred a certain degree of status—"a nice, clean job"—in comparison to factory or domestic work. As one woman related:

> I always wanted to be a beauty operator. I loved makeup; I loved to dress up and fix up. I used to set my sisters' hair. So I had that in the back of my mind for a long time, and my mom pushed the fact that she wanted me to have a profession—seeing that I wasn't thinking of getting married.[9]

While further research is needed, one can speculate that neighborhood beauty shops reinforced women's networks and became places where they could relax, exchange *chisme* (gossip), and enjoy the company of other women.

During the 1920s, the ethic of consumption became inextricably linked to making it in America. The message of affluence attainable through hard work and a bit of luck was reinforced in English and Spanish-language publications. Mexican barrios were not immune from the burgeoning consumer culture. The society pages of the influential Los Angeles-based *La Opinion*, for example, featured advice columns, horoscopes, and celebrity gossip. Advertisements for makeup, clothing, even feminine hygiene products reminded teenagers of an awaiting world of consumption.[10] ...

Advertisements aimed at women promised status and affection if the proper bleaching cream, hair coloring, and cosmetics were purchased. Or, as one company boldly claimed, "Those with lighter, more healthy skin tones will become much more successful in business, love, and society." A print ad [in English] for Camay Soap carried by *Hispano America* in 1932 reminded women readers that "Life Is a Beauty Contest." Flapper fashions and celebrity testimonials further fused the connections between gendered identity and consumer culture. Another promotion encouraged readers to "SIGA LAS ESTRELLAS" (FOLLOW THE STARS) and use Max Factor cosmetics.[11] . . .

. . . Mexican women interpreted these visual representations in a myriad of ways. Some ignored them, some redefined their messages, and other internalized them. The popularity of bleaching creams offers a poignant testament to color consciousness in Mexican communities, a historical consciousness accentuated by Americanization through education and popular culture.

Reflecting the coalescence of Mexican and U.S. cultures, Spanish-language publications promoted pride in Latino theater and music while at the same time celebrated the icons of Americanization and consumption. Because of its proximity to Hollywood, *La Opinion* ran contests in which the lucky winner would receive a screen test. On the one hand, *La Opinion* nurtured the dreams of "success" through entertainment and consumption while, on the other, the newspaper railed against the deportations and repatriations of the 1930s. Sparked by manufactured fantasies and clinging to youthful hopes, many Mexican women teenagers avidly read celebrity gossip columns, attended Saturday matinees, cruised Hollywood and Vine, and nurtured their visions of stardom. A handful of Latina actresses, especially Dolores del Rio and Lupe Velez, whetted these aspirations and served as public role models of the "American dream." As a *La Opinion* article on Lupe Velez idealistically claimed, "Art has neither nationalities nor borders".[12]

. . . Mexican-American women teenagers . . . positioned themselves within the cultural messages they gleaned from English and Spanish-language publications, afternoon matinees, and popular radio programs. Their shifting conceptions of acceptable heterosocial behavior, including their desire "to date," heightened existing generational tensions between parents and daughters.

Obviously, the most serious point of contention between an adolescent daughter and her Mexican parents regarded her behavior toward young men. In both cities and rural towns, close chaperonage was a way of life.

Recalling the supervisory role played by her "old maid" aunt, María Fierro laughingly explained, "She'd check up on us all the time. I used to get so mad at her." Ruby Estrada recalled that in her small southern Arizona community, "all the mothers" escorted their daughters to the local dances. Estrada's mother was no exception when it came to chaperoning her daughters. "She went especially for us. She'd just sit there and take care of our coats and watch us." Even talking to male peers in broad daylight could be grounds for discipline. Adele Hernández Milligan, a resident of Los Angeles for over fifty years, elaborated: "I remember the first time that I walked home with a boy from school. Anyway, my mother saw me and she was mad. I must have been sixteen or seventeen. She slapped my face because I was walking home with a boy" [13] . . .

Faced with this type of situation, young women had three options: they could accept the rules set down for them; they could rebel; or they could find ways to compromise or circumvent traditional standards. "I was *never* allowed to go out by myself in the evening; it just was not done," related Carmen Bernal Escobar. In rural communities, where restrictions were perhaps even more stringent, "nice" teenagers could not even swim with male peers. According to Ruby Estrada, "We were ladies and wouldn't go swimming out there with a bunch of boys." Yet many seemed to accept these limits with equanimity. Remembering her mother as her chaperone, Lucy Acosta insisted, "I could care less as long as I danced." "It wasn't devastating at all," echoed Ruby Estrada. "We took it in stride. We never thought of it as cruel or mean. . . . It was taken for granted that that's the way it was."[14] . . .

Women in cities had a distinct advantage over their rural peers in that they could venture miles from their neighborhood into the anonymity of dance halls, amusement parks, and other forms of commercialized leisure. With carnival rides and the Cinderella Ballroom, the Nu-Pike amusement park of Long Beach proved a popular hangout for Mexican youth in Los Angeles. It was more difficult to abide by traditional norms when excitement loomed just on the other side of the streetcar line.

Some women openly rebelled. They moved out of their family homes and into apartments. Considering themselves freewheeling single women, they could go out with men unsupervised as was the practice among their Anglo peers. Others challenged parental and cultural standards even further by living with their boy-friends. In his field notes, University of Califor-nia economist Paul Taylor recorded an incident in which a young woman had moved in with her Anglo boyfriend after he had convinced her that such arrangements were common among Americans. "This terrible freedom in the United States," one Mexicana lamented. "I do not have to worry because I have no daughters, but the poor *señoras* with many girls, they worry".[15]

Those teenagers who did not wish to defy their parents openly would "sneak out" of the house to meet their dates or attend dances with female friends. Whether meeting some-one at a drugstore, roller rink, or theater, this practice involved the invention of elaborate stories to mask traditionally inappropriate be-havior. In other words, they lied.[16] . . .

. . . [W]hat other tactics did teenagers devise? . . . Alicia Mendeola Shelit recalled that one of her older brothers would accompany her to dances ostensibly as a chaperone. "But then my oldest brother would always have a blind date for me." Carmen Bernal Escobar was per-mitted to entertain her boyfriends at home, but only under the supervision of her brother or mother. The practice of "going out with the girls," though not [generally] accepted until the 1940s, was fairly common. Several Mexican-American women, often related, would escort one another to an event (such as a dance), so-cialize with the men in attendance, and then walk home together. In the sample of seven-teen interviews, daughters negotiated their ac-tivities with their parents. Older siblings and extended kin appeared in the background as either chaperones or accomplices. . . .

. . . [M]any teenage women knew little about sex other than what they picked up from friends, romance magazines, and the local theater. As Mary Luna remembered, "I thought that if somebody kissed you, you could get pregnant." In *Singing for My Echo*, New Mexico native Gregorita Rodríguez confided that on her wedding night, she knelt down and said her rosary until her husband gently asked, "Gregorita, *mi esposa*, are you afraid of me?" At times this naiveté persisted beyond the wed-ding. "It took four days for my husband to touch me," one woman revealed. "I slept with dress and all. We were both greenhorns, I guess."[17] . . .

Chaperonage . . . exacerbated conflict not only between generations but within individu-als as well. In gaily recounting tales of ditching the *dueña* or sneaking down the stairwell, the laughter of the interviewees fails to hide the painful memories of breaking away from fa-milial expectations. Their words resonate with the dilemma of reconciling their search for au-tonomy with their desire for parental affirma-tion. . . . [E]very informant who challenged or circumvented chaperonage held a fulltime job, as either a factory or service worker. In contrast, most women who accepted constant supervi-sion did not work for wages. Perhaps because they labored for long hours, for little pay, and frequently under hazardous conditions, factory and service workers were determined to exer-cise some control over their leisure time.[18] . . .

It may also be significant that none of the employed teenagers had attended high school. They entered the labor market directly after or even before the completion of the eighth grade. Like many female factory workers in the United States, most Mexican operatives were young, unmarried daughters whose wage labor was essential to the economic survival of their fami-lies. As members of a "family wage economy," they relinquished all or part of their wages to their elders. According to a 1933 University of California study, of the Mexican families sur-veyed with working children, the children's monetary contributions constituted 35 percent of total household income. Cognizant of their earning power, they resented the lack of per-sonal autonomy.[19]

Delicate negotiations ensued as both par-ents and daughters struggled over questions of leisure activities and discretionary income. Could a young woman retain a portion of her wages for her own use? If elders demanded every penny, daughters might be more in-clined to splurge on a new outfit or other per-sonal item on their way home from work or, even more extreme, they might choose to move out, taking their paychecks with them. Recog-nizing their dependence on their children's income, some parents compromised. Their concessions, however, generally took the form of allocating spending money rather than re-laxing traditional supervision. Still, women's earning power could be an important bargain-ing chip. . . .

To complete the picture, we also have to consider the perspective of Mexican immigrant parents who encountered a youth culture very different from that of their generation. For them, courtship had occurred in the plaza; young women and men promenaded under the watch-ful eyes of town elders, an atmosphere in which an exchange of meaningful glances could well portend engagement. One can understand their consternation as they watched their daughters apply cosmetics and adopt the apparel advertised in fashion magazines. In other words, "If she dresses like a flapper, will she then act like one?" Seeds of suspicion reaffirmed the penchant for traditional supervision. . . .

. . . [P]arents in the barrios of major cities fought a losing battle against urban anonymity and commercialized leisure. The Catholic Church was quick to point out the "dangerous amusement" inherent in dancing, theatergoing, dressing fashionably, and reading pulp fiction. Under the section, "The Enemy in the Ballroom," a Catholic advice book warned of the hidden temptations of dance. "I know that some persons can indulge in it without harm; but sometimes even the coldest temperaments are heated by it." Therefore, the author offered the following rules:

(1) If you know nothing at all . . . about dancing do not trouble yourself to learn (2) Be watchful. . . . and see that your pleasure in dancing does not grow into a passion. . . . (3) Never frequent fairs, picnics, carnivals, or public dancing halls where Heaven only knows what sorts of people congregate. (4) Dance only at private parties where your father or mother is present.

Pious pronouncements such as these had little impact on those adolescents who cherished the opportunity to look and act like vamps and flappers.[20]

Attempting to regulate the social life of young parishioners, barrio priests organized gender-segregated teen groups. In Los Angeles, Juventud Católica Feminina Mexicana (JCFM) had over fifty chapters. In her autobiography *Hoyt Street*, Mary Helen Ponce remembered the group as one organized for "nice" girls with the navy blue uniform as its most appealing feature. . . .

Ponce enjoyed going to "*las vistas*," usually singing cowboy movies shown in the church hall after Sunday evening rosary. . . . The cut-rate features . . . raised money for local activities. . . . In an era of segregated theaters, church halls tendered an environment where Mexicanos and their children could enjoy inexpensive entertainment and sit wherever they pleased.[21] . . .

[P]opular culture offered an alternative vision to parental and church expectations complete with its own aura of legitimacy. . . . Even the Spanish-language press fanned youthful passions. On May 9, 1927, *La Opinion*

ran an article entitled; "How do you kiss?" Informing readers that "el beso no es un arte sino una ciencia" [kissing is not an art but rather a science], this short piece outlined the three components of a kiss: quality, quantity, and topography. The modern kiss, furthermore, should last three minutes.[22] Though certainly shocking older Mexicanos, such titillating fare catered to a youth market. . . .

Mexican-American women were not caught between two worlds. They navigated across multiple terrains at home, at work, and at play. They engaged in cultural coalescence. The Mexican-American generation selected, retained, borrowed, and created their own cultural forms. Or as one woman informed anthropologist Ruth Tuck, "Fusion is what we want—the best of both ways."[23] These children of immigrants may have been captivated by consumerism, but few would attain its promises of affluence. Race and gender prejudice as well as socioeconomic segmentation constrained the possibilities of choice. . . .

. . . [W]hat seems most striking is that the struggle over chaperonage occurred against a background of persistent discrimination. During the early 1930s, Mexicans were routinely rounded up and deported and even when deportations diminished, segregation remained. Historian Albert Camarillo has demonstrated that in Los Angeles restrictive real estate covenants and segregated schools increased dramatically between 1920 and 1950. The proportion of Los Angeles area municipalities with covenants prohibiting Mexicans and other people of color from purchasing residences in certain neighborhoods climbed from 20 percent in 1920 to 80 percent in 1946. Many restaurants, theaters, and public swimming pools discriminated against their Spanish-surnamed clientele. In southern California, for example, Mexicans could swim at the public plunges only one day out of the week (just before they drained the pool). Small-town merchants frequently refused to admit Spanish-speaking people into their places of business. "White Trade Only" signs served as bitter reminders of their second-class citizenship.[24]

Individual acts of discrimination could also blunt youthful aspirations. Erminia Ruiz recalled that from the ages of thirteen to fifteen, she worked full-time to support her sisters and widowed mother as a doughnut maker. "They could get me for lower wages." When health officials would stop in to check the premises, the underage employee would hide in the flour bins. At the age of sixteen, she became the proud recipient of a Social Security card and was thrilled to become the first Mexican hired by a downtown Denver cafeteria. Her delight as a "salad girl" proved short-lived. A co-worker reported that $200 had been stolen from her purse. In Erminia's words:

> Immediately they wanted to know what I did with the $200.00. I didn't know what they were talking about so they got . . . a policewoman and they took me in the restroom and undressed me. [Later they would discover that the co-worker's friend had taken the money.] I felt awful. I didn't go back to work.

Though deeply humiliated, Erminia scanned the classified ads the next day and soon combined work with night classes at a storefront business college.[25] . . .

Mexican-American adolescents felt the lure of Hollywood and the threat of deportation, the barbs of discrimination, and the reins of constant supervision. In dealing with all the contradictions in their lives, many young women focused their attention on chaperonage, an area where they could make decisions. The inner conflicts expressed in the oral histories reveal that such decisions were not made impetuously. Hard as it was for young heterosexual women to carve out their own sexual boundaries, imagine the greater difficulty for lesbians coming of age in the Southwest barrios. . . .

. . . Although still practiced in some areas, chaperonage appeared less frequently after World War II. By the 1950s, chaperonage had become more of a generational marker. Typically only the daughters of recent immigrants had to contend with constant supervision. Mexican Americans relegated chaperonage to their own past, a custom that, as parents, they chose not to inflict on their children. Family honor also became less intertwined with female virginity; but the preservation of one's "reputation" was still a major concern.[26] In the poem "Pueblo, 1950," Bernice Zamora captures the consequences of a kiss:

> I remember you, Fred Montoya
> You were the first *vato* to ever kiss me
> I was twelve years old.
> My mother said shame on you,
>
> my teacher said shame on you, and
> I said shame on me, and nobody
> said a word to you.[27] . . .

In challenging chaperonage, Mexican-American teenagers did not attack the foundation of familial oligarchy—only its more obvious manifestation. It would take later generations of Chicana feminists to take on this task.

NOTES

1. Interview with Maria Ybarra, December 1, 1990, conducted by David Pérez.

2. For colonial New Mexico, Ramón Gutiérrez convincingly demonstrates how family honor was tied, in part, to women's *vergüenza* (literally, shame or virginity). See Ramón Gutiérrez, "Honor, Ideology, and Class Gender Domination in New Mexico, 1690–1846," *Latin American Perspectives* 12 (Winter 1985): 81–104.

3. Ruth D. Tuck, *Not with the Fist: Mexican-Americans in a Southwest City* (New York: Harcourt, Brace and Co., 1946; rpt. Arno Press, 1974), 185–88; Vicki L. Ruiz, "Oral History and La Mujer: The Rosa Guerrero Story," in *Women on the U.S.-Mexico Border: Responses to Change* (Boston: Allen and Unwin, 1987), 226–27; interview with Mary Luna, Volume 20 of *Rosie the Riveter Revisited: Women and the World War I Work Experience*, ed. Sherna Berger Gluck (Long Beach: CSULB Foundation, 1983), 9–10. Bullock's was a major department store in the West. During the 1940s, bilingual education appeared as an exciting experiment in curriculum reform.

4. Mauricio Mazón's *The Zoot Suit Riots* (Austin: University of Texas Press, 1984) and the Luis Valdez play and feature film, *Zoot Suit*, provide examples of the literature on *pachucos*.

5. María Fierro, Rose Escheverria Mulligan, Adele Hernández Milligan, Beatrice Morales Clifton, Mary Luna, Alicia Mendeola Shelit, Carmen Bernal Escobar, Belen Martínez Mason, and Julia Luna Mount grew up in Los Angeles. Lucy Acosta and Alma Araiza García came of age in El Paso and Erminia Ruiz in Denver. Representing the rural experience are María Arredondo and Jesusita Torres (California), María Ybarra (Texas), and Ruby Estrada (Arizona). As a teenager, Eusebia Buriel moved with her family from Silvis, Illinois, to Riverside, California. Nine of these women were born between 1908 and 1919, and eight between 1920 and 1926. This sample includes some who were chaperoned during the 1920s and others who were chaperoned during the thirties and forties. Nine interviews are housed in university archives, seven are part of the *Rosie the Riveter* collection at California State University, Long Beach, California.

6. F. Scott Fitzgerald, "Bernice Bobs Her Hair," *Flappers and Philosophers* (London: W. Collins Sons and Co., Ltd., 1922), 209–46; Martínez Mason interview, 44; interview with Alicia Mendeola Shelit, Volume 37 of *Rosie the Riveter*, 18; Paul S. Taylor, *Mexican Labor in the United States, Volume II* (Berkeley: University of California Press, 1932), 199–200; interview with María Fierro, Volume 12 of *Rosie the Riveter*, 10. [Vicki Ruiz Writes:] Changing clothes at school is not peculiar to our mothers and grandmothers. As a high school student in the early 1970s, I was not allowed to wear the fashionable micromini skirts. But I bought one anyway. I left home in a full dirndl skirt with a flowing peasant blouse, but once I arrived at school, I would untie the skirt

(which I would then dump in my locker) to reveal the mini-skirt I had worn underneath.

7. Taylor, *Mexican Labor, Vol. II*, vi–vii.

8. Rodolfo F. Acuña, *Community Under Siege: A Chronicle of Chicanos East of the Los Angeles River, 1945–1975* (Los Angeles: UCLA Chicano Studies Publications, 1984), 278, 407–408, 413–414, 418, 422.

9. Sherna B. Gluck, *Rosie the Riveter Revisited: Women, The War and Social Change* (Boston: Twayne Publishers, 1987), 81, 85.

10. For examples, *see La Opinion*, September 26, 1926; May 14, 1927; June 5, 1927; September 9, 1929; January 15, 1933; January 29, 1938.

11. *La Opinion*, September 29, 1929; *Hispano-America*, July 2, 1932.

12. For examples, *sec La Opinion*, September 23, 24, 27, and 30, 1926; March 2, 1927.

13. Interview with Adele Hernández Milligan, Volume 26 of *Rosie the Riveter*, 17.

14. Escobar interview, 1986; Estrada interview, 11, 13; interview no. 653 with Lucy Acosta conducted by Mario T. García, October 28, 1982 (on file at the Institute of Oral History, University of Texas, El Paso), 17.

15. Paul S. Taylor, "Women in Industry," field notes for his book, *Mexican Labor in the United States, 1927–1930*, Bancroft Library, University of California, 1 box; Richard G. Thurston, "Urbanization and Sociocultural Change in a Mexican-American Enclave" (Ph.D. dissertation, University of California, Los Angeles, 1957).

16. Martínez Mason interview, 30; Ruiz interviews (1990, 1993); Thomas Sheridan, *Los Tucsonenses* (Tucson: University of Arizona Press, 1986), 131–32.

17. Interview with Julia Luna Mount, November 17, 1983, by the author; Fierro interview, 18; Luna interview, 29; Ruiz interview (1993); Gregorita Rodríguez, *Singing for My Echo* (Santa Fe: Cota Editions, 1987), 52; Martínez Mason interview, 62.

18. See Douglas Monroy, "An Essay on Understanding the Work Experiences of Mexicans in Southern California, 1900–1939," *Aztlán* 12 (Spring 1981): 70. Feminist historians have also documented this push for autonomy among the daughters of European immigrants.

19. Heller Committee for Research in Social Economics of the University of California and Constantine Panuzio, *How Mexicans Earn and Live*, University of California Publications in Economics, XIII, No. 1, Cost of Living Studies V (Berkeley: University of California, 1933), 11, 14, 17; Taylor notes; Luna Mount interview; Ruiz interviews (1990, 1993); Shelit interview, 9.

20. Rev. F. X. Lasance, *The Catholic Girl's Guide and Sunday Missal* (New York: Benziger Brothers, 1905), 249–75. I have a 1946 reprint edition passed down to me by my older sister who had received it from our mother.

21. George J. Sanchez, *Becoming Mexican American: Ethnicity, Culture, and Identity in Chicano Los Angeles, 1900–1945* (New York: Oxford University Press, 1993), 167; Mary Helen Ponce, *Hoyt Street* (Albuquerque: University of New Mexico Press, 1993), 258, 266–71.

22. *La Opinion*, May 9, 1927.

23. Tuck, *Not with the Fist*, 134.

24. Rodolfo Acuña, *Occupied America: A History of Chicanos*, 2nd ed. (New York: Harper & Row, 1981), 310, 318, 323, 330–31; Shelit interview, 15; Paul S. Taylor, *Mexican Labor in the United States*, Vol. I (Berkeley: University of California Press, 1930; rpt. Arno Press, 1970), 221–24; Arredondo interview; Ruiz interviews (1990, 1993).

25. Ruiz interview (1993).

26. Acosta interview: Tuck, *Not with the Fist*, 126–27; Thurston, "Urbanization," 109, 117–119; Ruiz interviews (1990, 1993).

27. Bernice Zamora, "Pueblo, 1950," in *Infinite Divisions: An Anthology of Chicana Literature*, eds. Tey Diana Rebolledo and Eliana Rivero (Tucson: University of Arizona Press, 1993), 315.

CHERYL D. HICKS
Mabel Hampton in Harlem: Regulating Black Women's Sexuality in the 1920s

It can be very difficult for historians to unearth how people in the past experienced sexuality. Not only might sexuality be a taboo topic, but some women resist telling the truth about their experiences, fantasies, and desires as a form of self-protection. Darlene Clark Hine calls this practice among black women "a culture

Excerpted from ch. 7 of *Talk with You Like a Woman: African American Women, Justice, and Reform in New York, 1890–1935* by Cheryl D. Hicks (Chapel Hill: University of North Carolina Press, 2010). Reprinted by permission of the author and publisher. Notes have been edited and renumbered.

of dissemblance." Because black women have been stereotyped as hypersexual, some shield their sexual lives from public scrutiny.

Cheryl D. Hicks takes us behind this veil of silence to explore the sexual lives of some working-class residents of Harlem, New York, in the 1920s. The black population of the neighborhood was growing by leaps and bounds. In what is called the Great Migration, approximately one million African Americans in the South relocated to the North during World War I, seeking jobs in the wartime economy and fleeing the Jim Crow (segregated) South. They came mostly to the largest cities, where, to their disappointment, they met with racial discrimination in workplaces and in the housing market. Many who came to New York ended up living in a 48-block area centered on West 134th Street in Manhattan. Nonresidents often referred to this part of Harlem as a "slum," given its dilapidated and crowded housing. Yet Harlem had also become a commercial and tourist destination associated with jazz and sex. White New Yorkers, as well as visitors from around the world, went to Harlem to sample the nightlife—to go "slumming."

Hicks shows us that sexual repression and policy were very much present during this supposed era of sexual liberation. After arrest and conviction on charges like vagrancy and soliciting sex, Hicks's subjects found themselves detained in the New York State Reformatory for Women in rural Bedford, about 50 miles north of the city. The admission interview, Hicks argues, was one of the few times in their lives some girls and women spoke about their sexual desires, practices, and histories (including sexual abuse). What emerges in these accounts of "sex and the city"? Why do you think surveillance goes hand in hand with liberation?

Mabel Hampton's experiences in Harlem never quite measured up to the popular image of the black neighborhood. Visitors from other parts of the city would go to "the night-clubs . . . and dance to such jazz music as can be heard nowhere else." Elite and middle-class white voyeurs, finding confirmation for their own ideas about the authenticity of primitive black culture, enjoyed Harlem's "'hot' and 'barbaric' jazz, the risqué lyrics and the 'junglelike' dancing of its cabaret floor shows, and all its other 'wicked' delights." As the black writer and activist James Weldon Johnson put it, after "a visit to Harlem at night," partygoers who practiced slumming believed that the town "never sleeps and that the inhabitants . . . jazz through existence."[1] Hampton's everyday life was strikingly different from the romanticized image of Harlem. In 1924, the twenty-one-year-old southern migrant was doing domestic work by day and occasionally dancing in a chorus line at night. She learned to navigate Harlem's social and cultural complexities as she encountered its opportunities and hardships and faced its pleasures and dangers. The fact that she was sexually attracted to women, rather than to men, intensified the paradox: Harlem offered her real freedoms, but also significant constraints.

At the same historical moment when Harlem was touted by white New Yorkers as one of the most sexually liberated spaces in the city, women experienced critical surveillance and their romantic attachments came under intense scrutiny. With the growing popularity of movies, dance halls, and amusement parks, families and community members became more and more concerned about how and with whom young women were spending their leisure time. Reformers and the police attempted to regulate working-class women's social lives, especially their sexuality. During World War I, the federal government showed particular concern because of the fear that women would spread venereal disease to soldiers, weakening the armed forces and endangering the war effort. Anxieties about working-class women's sexual behavior influenced the passing of numerous state laws that were proposed by reformers, approved by legislatures, and enforced by police officers. During the period that scholars have noted as the early-twentieth-century sexual revolution, the active pursuit of romance and sex by young working-class women caused their elders unease, in part because these women failed to conform to traditional courtship practices. . . . [2]

Race and ethnicity influenced reformers' and criminal justice administrators' interactions with their charges. Reformers and the police targeted white immigrant and native-born working-class women for questionable moral behavior, but they generally believed these women could be reformed. Black women, whom whites characterized as innately promiscuous because of their African ancestry and the legacy of American enslavement, were seen as less amenable to rehabilitation. The fact that many African American women lived in Harlem, which was seen as a center of social and sexual abandon, reinforced their libidinous image and inflected police officers' and criminal justice administrators' assessments of their culpability in sexual offenses.

Young black women, incarcerated primarily for sex-related offenses on charges that included vagrancy, disorderly conduct, and prostitution, usually rejected reformers' concerns and believed they were unfairly targeted. Mabel Hampton contended that her imprisonment at the New York State Reformatory for Women at Bedford for solicitation stemmed from a false arrest. Other inmates recounted their problems with law enforcement and disagreed with the verdict that their behavior was criminal. For the years between 1917 and 1928, one hundred black women appear in Bedford's case files. Fifty-one were New York natives, immigrants, or migrants from New England or the Midwest. Forty-nine were southern migrants who embraced a social and political freedom that had been unavailable in the South but found themselves on the wrong side of the law. During this time period, many young working-class women grappled with the relentless surveillance of concerned relatives, community members, police officers, and urban reformers as they pursued personal autonomy and sexual expression.

During admission interviews and throughout their association with Bedford, black women revealed personal experiences that were far more complex than public perceptions of their sexual behavior suggested. Most importantly, their varying responses provide a lens through which we can understand how working-class black women dealt with sex in the city. Like their white counterparts, they experimented with courting, treating, and the sex trade, but what Evelyn Brooks Higginbotham calls the "metalanguage of race," especially "racial constructions of sexuality,"

influenced the distinct reactions of authority figures. Racial stereotypes led the police and Bedford administrators to view black women's "sexual delinquency" as natural, rather than judging the conduct of individuals.[3] Essentialized renderings of black women's sexuality, coupled with black reformers' concerted efforts to counter these negative images by repressing discussions of sexual desire, have obscured ordinary black women's decisions and dilemmas regarding sex. While black women enjoyed a greater range of choices regarding the conduct of their social lives, they faced more restrictive treatment by public officials and higher expectations from their community. The stories of black women offer a window into how they remembered and decided to describe past sexual encounters. This [essay] focuses on the ways in which working-class black women constructed their own narratives and the kinds of details they chose to reveal about their sexual experiences. In early-twentieth-century New York, a moral panic about working-class female sexuality shaped the agenda of urban reformers and the criminal justice system. Local and state officials' racialized conceptions of women's sexual behavior influenced the dynamics of reform in black communities as well as the tenor of Bedford's institutional policies.

Incarcerated women offer a perspective that places black working-class women's own ideas about and experiences with sexuality at the center of the discussion. While historians have explored the sexuality of white working-class women, the sexual experiences of black working-class and poor women have rarely been examined. Female offenders' viewpoints vividly underscore the complexity of the black working class. Black women understood, experienced, and expressed heterosexual and same-sex desire at the same time that they had to deal with others' perceptions of and attempts to regulate their sexuality.[4] Looking at this dynamic from the perspective of a specific group of working-class women responds to Evelynn Hammonds's call to consider "how differently located black women engaged in reclaiming the body and expressing desire." Scholarship on black women's sexuality at the turn of the twentieth century has emphasized that black women refrained from discussing sexual desire and advocated behavior that rejected stereotypes that defined them as sexually promiscuous or deviant. Black female activists promoted what Evelyn Brooks Higginbotham calls the "politics of respectability"; decorous behavior was a defensive response to gendered images of black immorality as well as to civil and political inequalities.[5] Black women enacted what Darlene Clark Hine calls a "culture of dissemblance," creating "the appearance of openness and disclosure but actually" fashioning a silence about their personal and sexual lives that protected them "from their oppressors." Hammonds argues that the "politics of silence" worked so successfully that black women eventually "lost the ability to articulate any conception of their sexuality." The most significant exception was the blues singer, who expressed sexual desire through explicit lyrics and performance.[6]

Black women confined at Bedford include both those who practiced a "politics of silence" and those who openly expressed an identity as sexual beings. Answering the explicit questions that Bedford administrators asked all women during the admissions process, black domestics, laundresses, factory workers, and children's nurses between the ages of sixteen and twenty-eight revealed a range of sexual experiences that occurred as a result of desire, ignorance, or abuse. In some cases, administrators became frustrated when black women acknowledged their involvement in the sex trade but were reticent about conveying further details. For example, a twenty-year-old Virginia native was characterized as "pleasant" and "truthful" but provided officials with "little information about herself."[7] White female administrators (and one white male superintendent) documented black inmates' sense of propriety when they refused to talk about their sexual experiences or said they complied with moral proscriptions by rejecting premarital sex.

Female offenders' responses to prison administrators might be seen as evidence of the state's intrusion into black women's lives and an attempt to construct and reinforce derogatory racialized images. Yet black women understood administrators' skepticism when what they recounted did not coincide with long-standing stereotypes. Consider, for instance, the sexual history of one inmate who revealed that she had been raped and had prostituted herself twice but adamantly denied that she was promiscuous. The administrator seemed to dismiss the woman's difficult circumstances by focusing solely on her demeanor,

noting that the woman's "better education" had given her a "superior manner" and her "distant and haughty" attitude kept her from having an "attractive personality." Indeed, what administrators thought, as well as what they observed and chose to hear from black women, shaped the information recorded in all the case files.[8] But these partial transcripts also show how inmates challenged the public discourse that characterized all black women as pathologically promiscuous. These women's responses were particularly influenced by their attempts to negotiate Bedford's indeterminate sentencing; depending on how an administrator assessed an inmate's behavioral improvement, she could be given a minimum sentence of several months or a maximum sentence of three years.

... [B]lack women who felt compelled to silence outside the prison walls may have seen the admission interview as an opportunity to articulate their desires as well as to reveal sexual abuse. Some women described experiences that ranged from romance to participation in the sex trade. Others revealed the dangers encountered by young women alone in a large city. Understanding that white society believed that black women were complicit in their rapes, these inmates may have viewed administrators' direct question about whether their first "sexual offense" was consensual or rape as a chance to address their abuse in ways that may not have been possible with friends, family members, community leaders, or the police. Administrators' decision to label young women's first sexual encounters as criminal offenses reminds us of their moral position on premarital sex and makes clear their preconceived notions about working-class women.

Officials also observed and documented what they called "harmful intimacy": interracial relationships among the women incarcerated at Bedford. In 1917, "the disciplinary records of 175 women were studied for information as to the amount of harmful intimacy reported of officers ... and it was found that these inmates were frequently punished for such offenses." While acknowledging the prevalence of same-sex desire among white inmates, administrators were most concerned with attachments between black and white women. Records of conduct violations in white women's files, described variously as "fond of colored girls" or "seen passing notes to black inmates," provide evidence of these relationships.[9] Black women also received conduct violations, which indicates that they actively participated in inter-racial liaisons. Administrators, however, por-trayed "harmful intimacy" as white women's heterosexual attraction to black women whose dark skin color represented masculine virility rather than same-sex desire.[10] Officials attempted to ignore black women's participation in roman-tic relationships with other black women.

Prison officials overlooked their own evi-dence of black women's varied sexual experi-ences and instead based many of their evaluations on powerful racial stereotypes. Centuries-old preconceptions that defined black women as immoral and pathological deeply influenced their perceptions. As histori-ans Deborah Gray White and Jennifer Morgan have shown, seventeenth-century male Euro-peans depicted African women's bodies as savage, lewd, and unfeminine, and unleashed Christian condemnations of "uncivil" cultural practices, such as semi-nudity, polygamy, and dancing, that eventually justified the slave trade. (See Morgan's essay, pp. 24–33.) The as-sociation of lasciviousness with Africans shaped the development of slavery, [with] . . . Europeans view[ing] black men and women's bodies as "icon[s] for deviant sexuality." South-ern slaveholders accepted the notion that en-slaved women were sexually insatiable and depicted white men as victims of dark tempt-resses. The direct connections that southerners made between black women, immorality, and promiscuity remained vivid in popular culture long after slavery's demise. In 1904, when one southern white woman commented that she could not "imagine such a creation as a virtuous black woman," she articulated the sentiments of many late-nineteenth- and early-twentieth-century white Americans.[11]

When black women were imprisoned for sex-related and other minor offenses, prevail-ing stereotypes influenced Bedford prison of-ficials' assessment of their culpability. . . . Such written comments as "true African type . . . inclined to be somewhat vicious looking" and "a typical African cunning calculating eyes" indicate the depth of their prejudices in evalu-ating individual women. Observations were always qualified by race, ranging from "re-fined looking pretty colored girl" to "very infe-rior looking colored girl."[12] More positive appraisals, such as "appears intelligent for one of her race and station" and "has little moral sense but appears more decent than the aver-age colored girl," reveal officials' belief in black

inferiority. Regional biases are also apparent in initial interviews. Administrators observed the marks of southern origins—"peculiar way of speaking, a drawl and a typically Southern way of pronouncing words"—and questioned migrants' level of intelligence, fitness for urban life, and predisposition to criminality based on their diction.[13]

In 1924, Mabel Hampton, described by Bedford superintendent Amos Baker as a "small, rather bright and good looking colored girl," complicated Bedford officials' assump-tions. Administrators never questioned the va-lidity of her arrest, despite her fervent denials of solicitation. Yet they acknowledged that Hampton seemed unique. . . . They found her "alert" and "composed," with a "pleasant voice and manner of speaking." In another interview, they noted that Hampton's "attitude and manner seem truthful" and that she talked "freely and frankly conceal[ing] nothing." Al-though administrators found Hampton per-sonable and honest, they still imprisoned her. Ignoring their own observations regarding her credibility, officials judged Hampton based on their preconception that, even when black women had not violated the law, their sexual misconduct could be attributed to their innate susceptibility to "bad company." Hampton ex-plained her altercation with the police quite dif-ferently, calling her arrest a "put up job."[14]

The "ill-feeling" that Hampton expressed "toward her accuser" mirrored the sentiments of many black women and community mem-bers who contended that police corruption rather than women's behavior accounted for high numbers of prostitution arrests. Caught in a house raid when her employer of two years took an extended European trip, Hampton was most likely arrested because she was "between jobs." The fact that Hampton had access to her employer's home shows that she was trusted, but Hampton had no one to vouch for her repu-tation in court.[15] Her arrest resulted from the fact that the legislature and the courts had ex-panded the legal definition of vagrancy, which had applied only to public drunkards and per-sons "with no visible means of support," to in-clude anyone who "in any way, aids and abets or participates" in the sex trade. A plainclothes detective charged Hampton with being an ac-cessory to a sex crime by alleging that she per-mitted a female friend to use her employer's apartment for the "purposes of prostitution." According to Hampton, on the night of the arrest, she and a friend were waiting for their dates, "who promised to take them to a cabaret." Shortly after the men arrived, the police raided her employer's home and arrested both women. Hampton denied ever prostituting herself, contending that she had been seeing her date for a month and he "wanted to marry her." Hampton's perception of her boyfriend changed when she surmised that her date worked as a stool pigeon or police accomplice and arranged for her arrest. Hampton's evening excursion led to her imprisonment because in court, the police officer's word was deemed more legitimate than a young black domestic's.[16]

Young black working women who sought entertainment and companionship found themselves exposed to myriad danger. Not only could they be harassed by men at cabarets and dance halls, but they also could be arrested in a police set-up. In 1923, Harriet Holmes, a laundress making $15 a week, argued that she was falsely arrested when leaving a popular dance hall. It is not clear whether she arrived at the function with friends, but when she left at half past one o'clock in the morning she was alone. The twenty-three-year-old said that when she was walking to her apartment on West 133rd Street, a car stopped at the curb and four men claiming to be police officers pulled her into the car "without any reason . . . [and] declared that she was guilty of prostitution."[41] In a similar case, a twenty-two-year-old left a cabaret alone at half past one o'clock in the morning but followed her sister's advice to "always take a taxi" home after dark. When she got in the cab, "two men stepped in with her." She fought them, thinking they were robbers. Instead, they were policemen, who took her to the police station and arrested her for prostitution.[17]

Young black women found that the cheap and pleasurable practice of visiting friends' homes could also be a dangerous form of leisure. A number of women were arrested for solicitation while enjoying the company of friends in their tenement or boardinghouse rooms. Twenty-four-year-old Millie Hodges, for example, had separated from her husband of nine years and decided to leave Chicago and come to New York. She was visiting her friend's boardinghouse on 132nd Street when it was raided and its occupants were charged with "being disorderly."[18] Her denial that she had been soliciting and her assertion that she had

never been arrested did nothing to change her fate; she was convicted and sent to Bedford simply for visiting her friend's home at the wrong time. Young black women in Harlem enjoyed the freedom to partake of commercial and informal amusements, but the stigmas attached to working-class and black communities meant that their behavior was regulated on a discriminatory basis. . . .

Twenty-two-year-old Wanda Harding, a native of the British West Indies, acknowledged her misconduct in terms drawn from her Pentecostal background, recognizing her "great weakness and craving for the attractions of this world" and remarking that "everybody . . . is a born a sinner." Harding was acutely aware of her mistakes and struggled to face their consequences. Stating that "her father and mother were devout Christians" and concerned about her moral quandary, Harding's minister concluded that "through bad company she went astray [and] through good company she will be brought back again to the narrow way."[19] Relatives and black community members believed that young women should socialize only with respectable people and under appropriate circumstances.

While black people were aware of rampant police corruption, they expressed serious concerns about young women's naive or wayward behavior. Even though they sympathized with those who had been falsely arrested for prostitution, they also questioned these young women's decisions to attend unsupervised dances, associate with unsavory people, or walk unaccompanied late at night. The families of young women were especially anxious. The mother of an eighteen-year-old Long Island native declared: "Her going to the bad was going to dances and then being led by others older than herself." This mother protested that she worked diligently to safeguard her children: "I have tried to bring my children up in a [C]hristian way [and] have done the best I knew of, but you know the world has to[o] many charms for young people of today." Working-class parents shared reformers' belief that "silk and electric lights" and other "evil influences" such as dance halls and saloons caused young women to go astray.[20]

Although they were acutely aware of black people's second-class citizenship and of racial discrimination, many young women simply wanted to enjoy Harlem's social life. While they understood their relatives' anxieties about its temptations, they sought diversion after they had worked all day. Many had been employed since they were twelve or thirteen years old. As a nineteen-year-old domestic from Washington, DC, asked: "Why shouldn't I go out some times if I worked?" These women hoped that the easy pleasure of commercial leisure would temporarily transport them from their everyday drudgery and the constant struggle to make ends meet. When they had extra money or they had a date, they spent their time in dance halls, gyrating enthusiastically to popular tunes. To the horror of most of their parents and community members, young women quickly learned popular dances, such as the "turkey trot" in the early 1910s and the "black bottom," the "mess around," and the "Charleston" in the 1920s. In 1914, Rev. Adam Clayton Powell noted that young blacks' fascination with music and dancing was evident "not only in their conversations but in the movement of their bodies about the home and on the street." This anxiety about the unrestrained black female body epitomized the black community's concerns about individual women's welfare, in addition to their belief that respectability was essential for a stable family life and a viable strategy for racial advancement.[21] Attending dances, cabarets, and movie theaters was not the most pressing problem or seductive inducement, however. Socializing within smaller, unsupervised, mixed-sex groups and the concomitant romantic and sexual interests alarmed adults and excited young women. Young women in prison disclosed the reasons why they rejected or became involved in premarital sexual relationships. Some were seduced by the promise of marriage, were led astray by curiosity, were too ignorant to understand the situation, or were willing to barter sex for nice things; others were subject to coercion.

Relatives constantly sought to prevent young women from acting independently and hoped to guide their moral lives. They chaperoned their young women, set up strict curfews, and encouraged them to devote their leisure time to church activities. In some instances, their efforts were successful, as a number of women prisoners adamantly denied ever having premarital intercourse. Relatives dealt directly with the consequences of young women's disobedient behavior. A twenty-three-year-old Cuban immigrant, for example, explained that after she became pregnant at the age of

fifteen, her aunt forced her to marry the baby's father.[22]

Miranda Edmonds's experience illustrates the tensions within families over leisure activities and sexuality. When recalling her first sexual encounter, the seventeen-year-old North Carolina migrant said that she was "partly forced" to have intercourse with her boyfriend. While she blamed the troubling experience on her "ignorance," she was "clear in opinion" that her parents were also at fault because the incident "would not have happened if she had had sex instruction." Edmonds raises a critical point that suggests how the "politics of silence" could injure young women even though their relatives believed that they were protecting their kin. Moreover, many working-class black parents agreed with the tenets of racial uplift's concern about sexual purity and reproduction but, in certain instances, chose not to be as open or explicit about "sex instruction" as the etiquette, sex, and home manuals that black leaders provided for black community members. Edmonds's position also highlights the complex consequences of her inexperience and her disregard for family rules regarding respectability: she was sent to Bedford by her mother as an incorrigible case because she stayed away from home for two consecutive days with her boyfriend.[23] Edmonds suffered from the gap between the adult behavior young women thought they exhibited when they dated and became sexually active and the maturity they actually needed to live as independent adults.

Many black women acknowledged that ignorance and curiosity fueled their sexual encounters. One twenty-five-year-old divulged that she had sex at fifteen but still "had no idea why." A twenty-year-old noted that her first encounter occurred because "she was [simply] foolish." A number of women admitted that they had intercourse because they "saw other girls do it" or that they were "curious to know what sex experience was." In another case, a nineteen-year-old revealed that she consented to sex with a boy because he was someone "she had known for some time," suggesting a degree of trust. These accounts convey these women's youthful lack of forethought about the physical and moral dangers of sexual relationships.[24]

The promise of marriage prompted a number of single women to engage in premarital sex. As romantic relationships transitioned into more intimate contact, young men, whether they were sincere or not, negotiated with girlfriends about the meaning of sex in relation to the couple's courtship and future commitment. For example, a nineteen-year-old baby nurse explained that she consented to sex because she "liked the man" and he "promised to marry her." In another case, a twenty-one-year-old unmarried waitress noted that she had her first sexual relationship at eighteen because she was "engaged." These women's expectation that marriage would follow their decision to have premarital sex was quite conventional. A boyfriend's refusal to marry a young woman in the wake of an unplanned pregnancy challenged her beliefs about courtship. . . . [25]

In the early twentieth century, young women's sexual activity was becoming more than a precursor to marriage. Some working women engaged in consensual and noncommercial sexual relationships outside of serious courtships. Scholars have highlighted the phenomenon known as "treating," in which women bartered sex or sexual favors for goods or commercial amusements rather than accepting money for intercourse. A nineteen-year-old black domestic, for example, emphasized that she took "presents from the men she went with but . . . never accepted money." Evelyn Pitts, who was also nineteen, claimed that she never prostituted herself but did have sex "off and on with two or three different men since she was 17." Like many other young women, she stressed that she "never [took] . . . money for it." The terms some women used to refer to their sexual partners, such as friend, sweetheart, or lover, suggest these women's distinct perceptions of acceptable heterosexual relationships. . . . [26]

. . . Relatives, reformers, and prison administrators viewed these women's situations quite differently; for them, treating represented a new form of female sexual delinquency. Young women's frequent admissions to being "immoral" suggest how they responded to administrators' specific questions about their premarital sexual practices. Like the twenty-three-year-old who disclosed that she had been "immoral" but denied that she had "ever practiced prostitution," these working women insisted that they had made an independent choice to engage in sex solely for the enjoyment it provided, not for income. [27]

Not all black women's sexual relationships were consensual, however. Young women recounted experiences of sexual harassment, rape, and abuse by employers as well as within their families. Mabel Hampton, for example, recalled that when she was eight years old her uncle had raped her; and when she was working as a domestic, men in the household "would try to touch" her inappropriately. [28] Like most women, Hampton understood that in any disclosure of sexual harassment, her credibility, not her assailant's would be questioned.

Some black women were abused by men they knew. A twenty-one-year-old told how she was raped by "the husband of her foster parent," and a twenty-four-year-old disclosed that she was raped by a "friend who was visiting her sister's house." Even seemingly innocent interactions between young women and men could lead to horrific consequences. A twenty-three-year-old domestic recalled that she was forced into intercourse at fifteen when she and a boy "were playing school" and then a game called "Mama and Papa," which she "did not understand" until it was too late. [29]

Even as they were indicted for sexual offenses themselves, these women disclosed that rape committed by a family member, friend, or neighbor had made a huge impact on their lives. In this forum with prison administrators, where they knew their stories would be recorded, black women revealed their harrowing experiences. They understood that administrators would not take legal action against their abusers, but they believed that speaking of their trauma was important enough to provide details about it. Some may have sought to mitigate administrators' negative view of them as well. Twenty-three-year-old domestic and Colorado native Sally Bruce seems to have blamed herself for her abuse when she explained how she dealt with her rape. She revealed that her "first time was at 20 years [old] without her consent" but decided to continue with the relationship, rationalizing that "she was a woman, no longer a child and intended to marry" her abuser. Indeed, Bruce's belief that she had no other options highlights the difficult choices working women made when negotiating their sexuality in light of the long-standing pernicious belief that black women could not be raped. [30]

Black women's decision to enter the sex trade represented a difficult choice for those who did so to supplement their paltry salaries as personal-service laborers. Highlighting the contrast between the inadequate wages paid for menial labor work and the higher earnings brought by solicitation, Heather Hayes, a twenty-six-year-old New York native who toiled as a cook and chambermaid, acknowledged that she had "practiced prostitution off and on since she was seventeen" to supplement her income. This sort of testimony was corroborated by a 1914 Women's Court investigation that concluded that black women's "meager salaries and uncongenial surroundings tend to produce a state of dissatisfaction which sometimes leads . . . to prostitution." Unlike the twenty-two-year-old laundress who admitted to being a "habitual prostitute," many black women claimed that they solicited only infrequently. For instance, a twenty-three-year-old acknowledged that she "prostituted with 2 men in 3 years" but, while conceding that she had been "immoral," denied "being promiscuous."[31]

Black women's behavior after arrest suggests that they struggled with the psychological consequences of their decision to solicit. The 1914 Women's Court study indicated that when questioned during admission interviews, twenty-four out of fifty-six women stated that they were single and alone in the city "without near relatives." At least eight of these women "admitted having mothers" in New York but refused to provide their addresses to court administrators because they did not want their relatives "to know where they were." The investigation concluded that most of the women came from "poor but respectable homes" but eventually buckled under the pressures of inadequate wages and bad company. . . . [32]

The lure of easy money led some young women to enter the sex trade full time. A seventeen-year-old domestic earning $7 a month claimed she was able to make "about $10 a week" as a prostitute. A few women needed money to support their drug habit. And a small group of women claimed that they solicited because they enjoyed sex and needed money for material possessions. The same year that one sixteen-year-old domestic consented to have sex with her "boy-sweetheart," she also began prostituting herself for "money and pleasure." Another woman entered the sex trade because "she saw other girls with nice things and wanted them too." . . . [33]

Poor black women who made a difficult but definite choice to work in legitimate jobs understood the impact of prostitution on their lives all too well. Often living in the same neighborhoods where the trade thrived, they negotiated their moral stance against the sex trade on a daily basis and contended with the generally accepted notion that black women were its natural participants. Although most black reformers expressed their frustration with prostitution in a public forum and incorporated their concerns in their work, likeminded working women must have also talked with one another and their families about their anxieties. One twenty-four-year-old domestic told prison administrators that "prostitution is . . . the worst crime anybody can . . . commit because you have to do things that take away your self-respect." Women like her made a conscious choice not to prostitute and were frustrated that they were consistently mistaken for and often arrested as sex workers. Relatedly, they made specific distinctions between immorality and promiscuity. During the period of what scholars have defined as the early-twentieth-century sexual revolution, where working-class women "self-consciously rejected Victorian mores," they understood their elders' condemnation of premarital sex and would agree that having sex before marriage and with men they did not intend to marry was immoral.[34] Their making a choice to engage in premarital intercourse, whether they considered themselves promiscuous or not, was quite different than their being innately drawn to sex because of their racial and socioeconomic status. Indeed, black working women were in a tenuous position as they negotiated their perceived as well as actual sexual identities. These women's concerns about prostitution reflected the negative consequences they feared and experienced when they exposed their sexual desires within their community.

During the 1920s, Harlem was the site not only of a renaissance in black cultural production but also for the open expression of various forms of sexuality. Many black residents and community leaders expressed grave concerns about the confluence of popular entertainment and nonmarital sex. They were particularly concerned about the growing visibility of same-sex relationships. Many were aware of the lesbian references in songs like Gertrude Ma Rainey's "Prove It on Me Blues" and the popular, sexually explicit parties held in Harlem.[35] Within many working-class communities, however, the public expression of sexual desire—of heterosexual desire, not to mention same-sex desire—was discouraged. With relatively few exceptions, black churches enunciated and attempted to enforce conservative gender and sexual norms.[36]

Ironically, some black ministers were discovering, or rather exposing, their own gay congregants during this time. Denunciation of these relationships conflated two distinct issues: same-sex desire and ministers who preyed on young male congregants. Rev. Adam Clayton Powell of the Abyssinian Baptist Church lamented that young women were increasingly involved in same-sex relationships, although he did not distinguish consensual from predatory relationships. "Homosexuality and sex-perversion among women," he thundered, "has grown into one of the most horrible debasing, alarming and damning vices of present day civilization." According to Powell, homosexuality was "prevalent to an unbelievable degree" and "increasing day by day." Powell's conflation of same-sex desire with the sexual abuse of children gained strong support from his colleagues as well as his congregation, whose responses on the day of his sermon indicated that his "opinions were endorsed and approved without limitations."[37] Mabel Hampton would have understood the minister's sentiments as representing the views of most Harlem residents, since she hid her sexual orientation in her neighborhood but participated in private rent parties. Many Harlemites gladly paid to enjoy a night of food, bootleg liquor, music, and dancing while helping a neighbor pay the rent. According to Hampton, partygoers might eat "chicken and potato salad," "pig feet, chittlins," and black-eyed peas and "dance and have fun" until the wee hours. But Hampton partied exclusively with other women, which some black Harlemites would not have accepted. Explaining her predicament in retrospect, Hampton revealed that as a young woman in Harlem she experienced a "free life" where she "could do anything she wanted," but publicly expressing her desire for women was out of the question. "When I was coming along everything was hush-hush," she recalled. She and women like her felt safer meeting at house parties, "private things where you'd go with" a woman without fear of reprisals.[38]

Hampton's recollections indicate that black women who desired women usually disguised their feelings in public, in order to avoid both the police and other black Harlemites. When women attended all-female parties, "very seldom did any of them [wear] . . . slacks . . . because they had to come through the streets." Instead, they played it safe and dressed in women's suits. "You couldn't go out there with

too many pants on because the men was ready to see . . . and that was no good," Hampton stated. "You had to protect yourself and protect the woman that you was with." . . . Hampton's case . . . suggests that lesbians were less accepted in black neighborhoods than gay men, regardless of the residents' socioeconomic status.[39]

Hampton did not reveal whether she had experienced repercussions from exposing her attraction to women, but her fear prompted her to take precautions. She managed by limiting her contact with people who were not "in the life." Much later, she told a friend that even during the height of the Harlem Renaissance "you had to be very careful," which meant that Hampton and her friends "had fun behind closed doors."[40] Going out to bars was too much of a hassle because, as she recalled, "too many men was [tangled] up with it; . . . they didn't know you was a lesbian . . . [and] they didn't care. . . . You was a woman . . . [so] you had the public [and] you had the men to tolerate." Although she met a number of girlfriends when she was working as a dancer in Harlem cabarets such as the Garden of Joy, she eventually stopped dancing because, in her experience, it required exchanges with men. "I gave up the stage," she explained, "because unless you go with men you don't eat." As a gay rights activist later in life, Hampton spoke about herself as having embraced lesbianism directly and publicly as a young adult, yet when she was arrested for prostitution in 1924 she was not forthcoming about her sexual orientation. . . . [41]

Hampton's same-sex inclinations were shared by other women, black and white, but urban reformers and criminal justice administrators focused on regulating the behavior of heterosexual working-class women. During World War I, the federal government attempted to prevent the spread of venereal disease, not only by distributing condoms to the troops, but also by appropriating funds for at least forty-three reformatories and houses of detention that confined and treated "women and girls who, as actual and potential carriers of venereal diseases, were a menace to the health of the Military Establishment of the United States."[42] . . .

Bedford's goal was to reform young women by instilling morality and restraining sexual conduct. The institution opened in 1901, just when perceptions of aberrant female behavior were changing from the nineteenth-century idea of the "fallen woman" to the twentieth-century notion of the sexual delinquent. During the 1870s, reformers concerned about the growing number of young women in custodial prisons pushed for segregating women under thirty from older women because they believed that young first offenders had the capacity to be reformed. During Bedford's initial years, administrators believed that working-class women's delinquent behavior could be addressed and even eliminated through proper training. Bedford's first superintendent, Katharine Bement Davis, stated that the women who entered the institution were "capable of . . . education and industrial training" that "would restore them to society, self-respecting and self-supporting."[43] City magistrates and some state legislators, however, found the reformatory's operation too expensive, and it was consistently underfunded. Reformers argued that expenses related to rehabilitation far outweighed the consequences of being apathetic about urban crime. Bedford officials agreed. "The cost to the State of allowing [young women] to lead dishonorable, and perhaps criminal lives, . . . [perpetuating] their kind in succeeding generations in an ever-increasing propensity to evil," they declared, "is so very great [that] reformation . . . is the cheapest means of securing the public welfare."[44]

Reformers advocated practical programs of reform with varying degrees of success. Over the years, the institution ensured that inmates were constantly occupied, through industrial classes, religious services, or extracurricular activities. Instead of prison cells, women resided in individual cottages with matrons who encouraged family-style relationships. Some inmates seemed to enjoy this arrangement, as a number of paroled women wrote Bedford for permission to return to visit their friends. Inmates were separated by age in 1901. By 1924, when Ruby Brooks and Mabel Hampton were admitted, Bedford was segregated according to inmates' psychological diagnosis and race, with cottages designated for a range of inmates from "feeble-minded" white girls to newly admitted black girls.[45] . . .

Administrators agreed that the advent of probation, in which a woman was supervised in her community rather than being imprisoned, changed the type of inmate they received. Introduced in 1901, probation slowly parceled out the most redeemable female offenders and left the institution populated with probation violators, recidivists, and uncontrollable women. Katharine Bement Davis identified these inmates as the major impediment to Bedford's rehabilitation process. In 1906, Davis argued that if Bedford was to "receive so large a proportion of 'difficult' young women, whom probation and private institutions . . . have failed to help, the public must recognize the task" Bedford had before it. Since black women had more difficulty obtaining probation, their disproportionate representation in the institution's population increased as its reputation as a model reformatory declined. Black women who were first-time offenders, like Brooks and Hampton, were admitted along with white women whose behavior failed to warrant probation or who had violated probation. More young women were also being committed to Bedford, which led to overcrowding.[46]

Bedford's problems led to a 1914 State Commission of Prisons inspection and a scathing report, followed by public hearings a year later. While inspector Rudolph Diedling's report noted myriad problems with Bedford, ranging from its rural location to the fact that it could be more self-sustaining because it held "several hundred able-bodied young women delinquents whose labors should suffice for their maintenance," the report focused on the institution's inability to maintain discipline. During the public hearings, investigators noted that the most troubling issue involved same-sex romances between black and white inmates. Bedford's administrators publicly disclosed that the institution's primary disciplinary quandary stemmed from "harmful intimacy," or, rather, interracial sex.[47]

When the State Board of Charities' special investigative committee addressed Bedford's "harmful intimacy," it focused on the fact that, unlike most women's prisons in the North or the South, Bedford was racially integrated. When questioned about this policy, former superintendent Katharine Davis explained that she did "not believe in segregation by color in principle and [had] not found it to work well in practice." The committee strongly recommended segregation. With Davis no longer the superintendent, Bedford's Board of Managers agreed with the committee's final recommendations, which pronounced segregation to be the most viable solution to inappropriate interracial relationships. Denying any accusation of racism, the board declared that "most undesirable sex relations grow out of . . . mingling of the two races." The board defended its right to segregate inmates against the protests of those who argued that racial segregation was "contrary to the equal rights of all citizens under the Constitution." Explaining the discretionary power given to them by the State Charities Law, the Board of Managers argued that "individual rights are not disturbed by the separation of delinquents into groups when such segregation is likely to promote reformation and prevent undesirable relations."[48] In 1917, Bedford institutionalized racial segregation with two cottages "set apart" for black women. Superintendent Helen Cobb explained that, in addition to disciplinary concerns, the separate cottages were established as a result of written requests by black inmates. . . . Ironically, even after racial segregation was established, administrators failed to acknowledge publicly that "harmful intimacy" persisted as inmates continued to pursue relationships across the color line.[49]

The actions of Bedford administrators and state officials coincided with the views of psychiatrists and prison reformers. Generally, psychiatrists and prison reformers addressed the issue of female homosexuality by emphasizing, to the virtual exclusion of other romantic or sexual attachments, the problem of developing relationships between white and black inmates. They portrayed white women's participation in same-sex, interracial relationships within the confines of the prison as a longing for masculinity. The psychologist Margaret Otis voiced the opinions of many scientific observers when she argued in the *Journal of Abnormal Psychology* in 1913 that whether viewed as "an affair simply for fun and . . . lack of anything more interesting to take up their attention" or as a relationship of "serious fascination and . . . [an] intensely sexual nature," this kind of association had a racial and gendered character. "The difference in color," she added, "takes the place of difference in sex." Much like Cesare Lombroso's 1895 linkage of black women's color and physical features with masculinity and criminality, Otis's explanation of same-sex desire equated black women's darker skin color with virility. Moreover, these relationships could be described as an example of what Regina Kunzel calls "racialized gender inversion." For example, a white woman to whom Otis referred in her article "admitted that the colored girl she loved seemed the man." In 1921, a Bedford official explained that black women's "abandon and virility . . . offered" white women "the nearest

substitute" for the opposite sex. According to her, black women functioned as masculine substitutes who fulfilled white women's heterosexual desire. Psychologists and prison administrators characterized white inmates' attraction to one another as nothing more than crushes. In their courtships, according to one report, women "vow that they will be friends forever, dream and plan together, confide their deepest secrets," and there is no serious connection to homosexuality. White inmates, whether or not they were aggressors in these affairs, maintained a normative heterosexual status. In this sense, administrators failed to address same-sex desire directly, but rather constructed their explanations so that, as Kunzel remarks, "homosexuality was heterosexuality; the unnatural was natural." In contrast to white inmates, black women at Bedford were rarely portrayed as initiating relationships, although they may have done so. Administrators did not characterize black women as responding in like manner to the attentions of white women, or as experiencing crushes among themselves. By and large, black women's romantic attachments, whether heterosexual or homosexual, were ignored.[50] . . .

The attraction that white inmates expressed for black women . . . was usually diagnosed by administrators as mental deficiency, which they described variously in terms that ranged from feeblemindedness to psychopathology. When defending Bedford from charges that the institution fomented interracial, same-sex relationships, the president of the Board of Managers, James Woods, conflated women's working-class status with deviant sexual behavior, arguing that women initiated these kinds of associations before they entered the reformatory. Addressing the problem without direct reference to black women, Woods remarked that this behavior was "not uncommon among the people of this class and character in the outside world, and when inmates addicted to these practices come into the institution it is practically impossible to prevent them finding an opportunity in some way or other to continue them." Woods's assessment shows how administrators attempted to deflect responsibility for an escalating disciplinary problem by suggesting that these relationships should not be solely defined as "situational homosexuality," that is, the consequence of incarceration among women. Indeed, Woods's perspective highlighted what administrators had already discovered: that homoerotic relationships were also emerging in the larger society, both black and white.[51] . . .

[Lynette] Moore's case illustrates the fluid nature of sexuality: some women desired men as well as women. . . . Moore married and became pregnant after being discharged, but she stayed in contact with Connie Carlson, the white inmate with whom she developed an "undesirable friendship" in Bedford. After Moore became estranged from her husband, the two women began living together. At some point, an anonymous letter was sent to a charitable agency informing it that Moore had become a beggar and Carlson was "usually with her." In contrast to Mabel Hampton, who attempted to keep her romantic relationships private, Moore did not conceal her romance— and suffered the consequences. Five years later, Moore was arrested for gun possession and again sent to Bedford. Bedford officials refused to keep her, but they did interview her. Moore explained that while working as a nightclub hostess she had continued to experience relationship problems, as she wanted to marry her boyfriend but had not divorced her first husband. Her second case file documents her continuing tie to Carlson. Although neither woman could support the other or Moore's infant and they stopped living together, Moore acknowledged her continued connection with Carlson.[52] Moore's reference to Carlson as a friend indicates that she boldly defied Bedford's continual attempts to keep the women apart. Yet the institution was simply another conduit for enforcing a respectable domesticity and de facto racial segregation. Both women were married with children; Moore lived in Manhattan while Carlson resided in Long Island. Moore's simple but bold actions provide us with a hint of the struggle that she and Carlson faced as they attempted to maintain a connection with one another.

Mabel Hampton's experience complicates prison officials' essentialized portraits of homoerotic relationships. The story of her lesbianism, which was never directly mentioned in her case file but revealed through her subsequent social activism, challenges Bedford administrators' premise about "harmful intimacy" and highlights many of the institution's evaluative discrepancies. In Hampton's brief account of her Bedford experience, she openly acknowledged the prevalence of same-sex relationships and affirmed her participation in them, though she did not indicate whether they were interracial or intraracial. She remembered these relationships as comforting. After she and another prisoner revealed their attraction to one another, Hampton recalled, the woman "took me in her bed and held me in her arms and I went to sleep." Although Hampton was attracted to women and dated men before her imprisonment, her Bedford experience may have provided her with an opportunity to embrace her same-sex desire more fully. . . . Hampton's case [also] suggests the extent of administrators' indifference to black women's sexuality within the prison. Yet Hampton's post-Bedford life as a lesbian was in some ways an open secret: she and her black partner, Lillian Foster, who met in 1932 and remained together until Foster's death in 1978, "negotiated the public world as 'sisters.'" . . . Referring to themselves as sisters protected them from unwanted attention and allowed "expressions of affection" that "demanded a recognition of their intimacy."[53]

Mabel Hampton's experiences in Harlem and at Bedford as recorded by prison administrators and her subsequent reflections upon her life provide a unique lens through which we can view black women's sexuality. She was neither a reformer advocating the "politics of respectability" nor a blues singer expressing sexual desire through performance. Rather, her life shows the complex ways that young women acknowledged the importance of decorum at the same time that they participated in consumer culture and popular amusements. Women faced enormous challenges as they sought to establish their independence in a society that simultaneously offered uninhibited opportunities for pleasure and was threatened by working-class women's sexual behavior. Relatives, community members, and the police monitored young women's sexual expression and generally supported the rehabilitative objectives of state institutions like Bedford.

The case files of black women at Bedford give us a sense of the language that ordinary black women used to describe their sexual experiences. Although the information found in prisoners' case files has been mediated through prison administrators' biases, we can discern the stories that black women chose to impart behind officials' responses to those narratives. The sexual experiences that are documented in Bedford's records range from premarital heterosexual intercourse and same-sex desire to rape and prostitution. The concerns of black women's relatives and community members often conflicted with what black women wanted for themselves. In their interactions with the community residents black women acted as cautiously as they did around representatives of the state. Mabel Hampton's reflections about Harlem highlight how she dissembled in her neighborhood. Black women who were attracted to women "had to be careful" and "had fun behind closed doors."[54]

Although Hampton seems to have hidden her relationships with women when she was incarcerated, other women, black and white, flaunted their attachments. Bedford claimed that the majority of their disciplinary problems stemmed not simply from same-sex relationships but from "harmful intimacy," that is, intimacy that crossed the color line. Prison administrators' anxieties about interracial relationships mirrored the national preoccupation with interracial social and sexual relationships. Instituting racial segregation did more to assuage their racial anxieties than to address the issue of "harmful intimacy." When some officials acknowledged that young women brought same-sex romance into the institution and that same-sex relationships might not be a consequence of imprisonment, they illuminated the fact that sexual expression took many forms both within and outside Bedford. . . .

NOTES

1. James Weldon Johnson, *Black Manhattan* (New York: Da Capo Press, 1991; orig. publ., New York, 1930), 160–61; Jervis Anderson, *This Was Harlem: A Cultural Portrait, 1900-1950* (New York: Farrar, Straus, and Giroux, 1982), 139. Regarding the practice of slumming, see Kevin J. Mumford, *Interzones: Black/White Districts in Chicago in the Early Twentieth Century* (New York: Columbia University Press, 1997), 133-56; and Chad Heap, *Slumming: Sexual and Racial Encounters in American Nightlife, 1885–1940* (Chicago: University of Chicago Press, 2009).

2. Allan M. Brandt, *No Magic Bullet: A Social History of Venereal Disease in the United States since 1880* (New York: Oxford University Press, 1985); Elizabeth Alice Clement, *Love for Sale: Courting, Treating, and Prostitution in New York City, 1900–1945* (New York: Basic Books, 1994), esp. chs. 4 and 7; Estelle Freedman, *Their Sisters's Keepers: Women's Prison Reform in America, 1830–1930* (Ann Arbor: University of Michigan Press, 1981), 109–142; Mary Odem, *Delinquent Daughters: Protecting and Policing Adolescent Female Sexuality in the United States, 1885–1920* (Chapel Hill: University of North Carolina Press, 1985), 1–7, 95–127; Ruth Alexander, *The "Girls Problem": Female Sexual Delinquency in New York, 1890–1930* (Ithaca, N.Y.: Cornell University Press,

1995), 1–7, 33–66; Joanne Meyerowitz, "Sexual Geography and Gender Economy: The Furnished-Room Districts of Chicago, 1890–1930," in *Unequal Sisters: A Multi-Cultural Reader in U.S. Women's History*, 3rd ed., ed. Vicki L. Ruiz and Ellen Carol DuBois (New York: Routledge, 2000), 307–23.

3. Evelyn Brooks Higginbotham, "African-American Women's History and the Metalanguage of Race," *Signs* 17 (Winter 1992), 262.

4. My thinking about working-class women's sexuality has been influenced by Kathy Peiss, "'Charity Girls' and City Pleasures: Historical Notes on Working-Class Sexuality, 1880–1920," in *Passion and Power: Sexuality in History*, ed. Kathy Peiss and Christina Simmons with Robert A. Padgug (Philadelphia: Temple University Press, 1989), 57–69; Peiss, *Cheap Amusements: Working Women and Leisure in Turn-of-the-Century New York* (Philadelphia: Temple University Press, 1986); and Christine Stansell, *City of Women: Sex and Class in New York, 1789–1860* (Urbana: University of Illinois Press, 1987). Examples of black women expressing same-sex desire are found Hansen, "'No Kisses Like Youres': An Erotic Friendship between Two African-American Women during the Mid-Nineteenth Century," *Gender & History* 7 (August 1995), 153–82; Farah Jasmine Griffin, ed., *Beloved Sisters and Loving Friends: Letters from Rebecca Primus of Royal Oak, Maryland, and Addie Brown of Hartford, Connecticut, 1854–1868* (New York: Knopf, 1999); and Elizabeth Lapovsky Kennedy and Madeline D. Davis, *Boots of Leather, Slippers of Gold: The History of a Lesbian Community* (New York: Routledge, 1993).

5. Evelynn M. Hammonds, "Black (W)holes and the Geometry of Black Female Sexuality," *differences: A Journal of Feminist Cultural Studies* 6, nos. 2–3 (Summer 1994), 138; Higginbotham, *Righteous Discontent, The Women's Movement in the Black Baptist Church, 1880–1920* (Cambridge, MA: Harvard University Press, 1993), 185–229. Elsa Barkley Brown has pointed out that "the struggle to present Black women and the Black community as 'respectable' eventually led to repression within the community"; "Imaging Lynching: African American Women, Communist Struggle, and Collective Memory," in *African American Women Speak Out on Anita Hill-Clarence Thomas*, ed. Geneva Smitherman (Detroit: Wayne State University Press, 1995), 108.

6. On black women's sexuality in relation to the blues, see Hazel V. Carby, "'It Jus Be's Dat Way Sometime': The Sexual Politics of Black Women's Blues," in *Unequal Sisters*, 330–41. See also Angela Davis, *Blues Legacies and Black Feminism: Gertrude "Ma" Rainey, Bessie Smith and Billie Holiday* (New York: Vintage Books, 1998), 40; Ann Ducille, "Blue Notes on Black Sexuality: Sex and the Texts of Jessie Fauset and Nella Larsen," *Journal of the History of Sexuality* 3, no. 3 (1993), 418–44; Hortense J. Spillers, "Interstices: A Small Drama of Words," in *Pleasure and Danger: Exploring Female Sexuality*, edited by Carole S. Vance (Boston: Routledge and Kegan Paul, 1984), 74.

7. All women who entered Bedford were asked who told them about sex, when and at what age they had their first sexual encounter, and whether that encounter was consensual. Finally, they were asked whether they practiced prostitution and, if they did,

at what age they entered the trade as well as how much money they earned; Inmate #3724, Admission Record, August 1924; and Recommendation for Parole, March 10, 1925, Bedford Hills Correctional Facility, 14610–77B Inmate Case Files, ca. 1915–30, 1955–65, Records of the Dept. of Correctional Services, New York State Archives, State Education Dept., Albany, NY (hereafter, BH). [I have used a pseudonym for inmates' names but have retained original case numbers.]

8. Inmate #3706, History Blank, July 8, 1924, BH. For some issues of interpretation, see Regina Kunzel, "Pulp Fictions and Problem Girls: Reading and Rewriting Single Pregnancy in the Postwar United States," *American Historical Review* 100 (Dec. 1995), 1468–69, and Timothy Gilfoyle, "Prostitutes in History: From Parables of Pornography to Metaphors of Modernity," *American Historical Review* 104 (Feb. 1999), 139–40.

9. State of New York, State Board of Charities, *Report of the Special Committee*, 7; Inmate #2475, Conduct Record, Oct.–Dec. 1918; and Inmate #4044, Conduct Record, June 13, 1926, BH.

10. Margaret Otis, "A Perversion Not Commonly Noted," *Journal of Abnormal Psychology* 3, no. 2 (June–July 1913), 113.

11. Jennifer L. Morgan, "'Some Could Suckle over Their Shoulder': Male Travelers, Female Bodies, and the Gendering of Racial Ideology, 1500–1770," *William and Mary Quarterly*, 3rd ser., 54 (Jan. 1997) 167–92; Deborah Gray White, *Ar'n't I a Woman? Female Slaves in the Plantation South*, rev. ed. (New York: W.W. Norton, 1999), 29–34; Sander L. Gilman, "Black Bodies, White Bodies: Toward and Iconography of Female Sexuality in Late Nineteenth-Century Art, Medicine, and Literature," *Critical Inquiry* 12, no. 1 (Autumn 1985), 209 (quotation); "Experiences of the Race Problem: By a Southern White Woman," *Independent* 56 (Mar. 17, 1904): 46 (quotation).

12. Inmate #3533, History Blank, Oct. 24, 1923; Inmate #3521, History Blank, Sept. 20, 1923; Inmate #3333, History Blank, Dec. 26, 1922; Inmate #3728, Admission Record, Aug. 19, 1924, BH.

13. Inmate #3699, Admission Record, July 10, 1924; Inmate #3502, History Blank, Aug. 22, 1923; Inmate #4477, Escape Description Record, July 19, 1928, BH.

14. Inmate #3696, History Blank, July 10, 1924; Recommendation for Parole, Jan. 1925; and History blank, July 10, 1924, BH. I have revealed this inmate's name and case file in accordance with the Freedom of Information Act of 1966, 5 USC Sec. 552, Part I, Subchapter II.

15. After returning from Europe, Hampton's employer was apparently so "indignant at the idea of her apartment having been used for purposes of prostitution that she refused to appear" in court to vouch for Hampton's character, although Hampton had been in "faithful service" for at least two years. See Inmate #3696, letter from Amy M. Prevost to Dr. Amos T. Baker, Nov. 13, 1924, BH.

16. Arthur B. Springarn, *Laws Relating to Sex Morality in New York City* (New York: Century Co., 1915 (revised by W. Bruce Cobb in 1926), 32–33; Joan Nestle, "'I Lift My Eyes to the Hill': The Life of Mabel Hampton as Told by a White Woman," in Nestle, *A Fragile Union: New and Selected Writings*

(San Francisco: Cleis Press, 1998), 34; Inmate #3696, Recommendation for Parole, Jan. 13, 1925, BH.

17. Inmate, 3474, History Blank, July 1923; Inmate #3489, History Blank, Aug. 1, 1923; and Preliminary Investigation, ca. June 1923, BH.

18. Inmate #3535, History Blank, Oct. 18, 1923, BH. On visiting, see William Fielding Ogburn, "The Richmond Negro in New York City: His Social Mind as Seen in His Pleasures" (Master's thesis, Columbia University, 1909), 60–61.

19. Inmate #3377, History Blank, Feb. 16, 1923 and letter from Minister to Bedford Reformatory, Aug. 13, 1923, BH.

20. Inmate #4058, letter of Inmate's Mother to Superintendent Baker, April 26, 1926, BH; "Silk and Lights Blamed for Harlem Girls' Delinquency," *Baltimore Afro-American*, May 19, 1928, Reel 31, Tuskegee Institute Clippings File (hereafter, TNCF).

21. Inmate #2505, Mental Examination, Attitude Toward Offense, Sept. 18, 1917, BH; "Race is Dancing Itself to Death," *New York Age*, Jan. 8, 1914. See Higginbotham, *Righteous Discontent*, 194–204; Kevin K. Gaines, *Uplifting the Race: Uplifting the Race: Black Leadership, Politics, and Culture in the Twentieth Century* (Chapel Hill: University of North Carolina Press, 1996), 152–78; and Michele Mitchell, *Righteous Propagation: African Americans and the Politics of Racial Destiny after Reconstruction*, 76–140.

22. Inmates #3696, 3389, 4058, 2796; Cuban immigrant: Inmate #3501, History Blank, Aug. 21, 1923, BH.

23. Inmate #4028, History Blank, ca. Feb. 1926, BH. On manuals, see Mitchell, *Righteous Propagation*, chs. 3 and 4.

24. Inmate #3722, History Blank, Aug. 26, 1924; Inmate #3721, History Blank, Oct. 10, 1924; Inmate #2760, History Blank, ca. Dec. 7, 1925; Inmate #3699, History Blank, July 19, 1924; Inmate #2504, Statement of Girl, Aug. 8, 1917, BH.

25. Inmate #3705, History Blank, July 18, 1924; and Inmate #4498, History Blank, ca. Mar. 30, 1926, BH; see Clement, *Love for Sale*, 18–25.

26. Inmate #2505, Statement of Girl, Aug. 2, 1917; Inmate #2504, Statement of Girl, Aug. 8, 1917; Inmates #3367, 3386, 2505, BH. On treating, see Peiss, *Cheap Amusements*, 108–14; and Clement, *Love for Sale*, 45–75.

27. Inmate #3718; also see Inmates #3533, 3474, 4498, BH.

28. Rape: Nestle, "Excerpts from the Oral History of Mabel Hampton," 930; see also Nestle, *Fragile Union*, 32. Touching: excerpt from tape-recorded oral history interviews with Mabel Hampton, by Joan Nestle, MH-2 Box 3, Mabel Hampton Special Collection, Lesbian Herstory Archives, Brooklyn, NY (hereafter, MHSC).

29. Inmate #4501, Summary Report on Application for Parole, ca. 1928; Inmate #2480, Statement of Girl, June 23, 1917; Inmate #4078, History Blank, ca. May 1, 1926, BH.

30. Inmate #3706, History Blank, July 18, 1924, BH; see Melton A. McLaurin, *Celia, A Slave* (New York: Bard, 1991).

31. Inmate #3494, Recommendation for Parole, ca. 1924, BH; Carietta V. Owens, "Investigation of Colored Women at Night Court. From June 8th to August 8th 1914," Folder-Women's Court-Negro Cases, Box 63, p. 7, Committee of Fourteen Collection,

New York Public Library, Rare Books and Manuscripts Division, Astor, Lenox, and Tilden Foundations, New York, NY (hereafter, COF); Inmate #3497, History Blank, Aug. 13, 1923; Inmate #3706, History Blank, July 18, 1924, BH.

32. Owens, "Investigation of Colored Women at Night Court," p. 7. For background on reformers' argument about the relationship between women's low wages and prostitution, see Freedman, *Their Sisters' Keepers*, 114, 123–24.

33. Inmate #2497, Verified History, July 26, 1917; Inmate #3365, History Blank, Feb. 8, 1923; Inmate #4063, History Blank, ca. April 23, 1926, BH.

34. Inmate #2480, Information Concerning the Patient, June 23, 1917, BH. See Meyerowitz, "Sexual Geography," 307.

35. Kevin J. Mumford, "Homosex Changes: Race, Cultural Geography, and the Emergence of the Gay," *American Quarterly* 48 (Sept. 1996): 400, 402–405; Angela Davis, *Blues Legacies and Black Feminism: Gertrude "Ma" Rainey, Bessie Smith and Billie Holiday* (New York: Vintage Books, 1998), 39–40; and Carby, "'It Jus Be's Dat Way Sometime,'" 337.

36. Evelyn Brooks Higginbotham, "Rethinking Vernacular Culture: Black Religion and Race Records in the 1920s and 1930s," in *The House That Race Built: Black Americans, U.S. Terrain*, ed. Wahneema Lubiano (New York: Pantheon Books, 1997), 157–77. In his discussion of Chicago minister Clarence Cobbs, Wallace D. Best argues that the black working class seemed more accepting of gay black men than the black middle class; see Best, *Passionately Human, No Less Divine: Religion and Culture in Black Chicago* (Princeton, N.J.: Princeton University Press, 2005), 188–89.

37. Eric Garber, "A Spectacle in Color: The Lesbian and Gay Subculture of Jazz Age Harlem," in *Hidden from History: Reclaiming the Gay and Lesbian Past*, ed. Martin Baumal Duberman, Martha Vicinus, and George Chauncey, Jr. (New York: New American Library, 1989), 318–31. See also, "Dr. A. C. Powell Scores Pulpit Evils," *New York Age*, Nov. 16, 1929, p. 1; "Dr. Powell's Crusade against Abnormal Vice Is Approved," ibid., Nov. 23, 1929; and "Corruption in the Pulpit," *New York Amsterdam News*, Dec. 11, 1929, p. 20. George Chauncey, Jr., discusses this issue in *Gay New York: Gender, Urban Culture, and the Making of the Gay Male World, 1890–1940* (New York: Basic Books, 1994), 254–57.

38. Mabel Hampton interview by Joan Nestle, May 21, 1981, Hampton tape, 10, 11, MHSC.

39. Mabel Hampton interview by Joan Nestle, *LFL Coming Out Stories*, June 21, 1981, 8, Box 3, MHSC. Another version is in Nestle, *Fragile Union*, 36.

40. Hampton interview by Nestle, May 21, 1981, Hampton tape, 9, MHSC. The statements quoted in the text came in response to Nestle's question: "How would you describe the twenties? Was it a good period to be gay?"

41. Hampton interview by Nestle, *LFL Coming Out Stories*, June 21, 1981, 9, Box 3, MHSC.

42. Mary Macey Dietzler, *Detention Houses and Reformatories as Protective Social Agencies in the Campaign of the United States against Venereal Diseases* (Washington, D.C.: U.S. Government Printing Office, 1922), 27. See also Allan M. Brandt, *No Magic Bullet: A Social History of Venereal Disease in the United States since 1880* (New York: Oxford University Press), 52–121; and Clement, *Love for Sale*, 114–43.

43. Katharine Bement Davis, "A Plan for the Conversion of the Laboratory of Social Hygiene at Bedford Hills to a State Clearing House . . . ," Bureau of Social Hygiene General Material 1911-16, Box 6, Record Group 2, Rockefeller Boards, Rockefeller Archive Center, Tarrytown, NY.

44. New York State Reformatory for Women at Bedford Hills, *Annual Report of the New York State Reformatory for Women at Bedford for the Year Ending September 30, 1901* (Albany, N.Y.: J. B. Lyon, 1902), 7, New York State Library, Cultural Education Center, Albany, NY (hereafter, NYSL). For the trajectory of women's prison reform from private benevolence to state control, see Gunja Sen-Gupta, *From Slavery to Poverty: The Racial Origins of Welfare in New York, 1840–1918* (New York: New York University Press, 2009).

45. See, for example, Inmate #2507, letter from Inmate to Superintendent Cobb, March 1, 1920, BH. New York State Reformatory for Women at Bedford, *Annual Report . . . for the Year Ending September 30, 1901*, 17–18. Expectant mothers and inmates who had children no older than two years were also housed in a separate cottage.

46. Freedman, *Their Sisters' Keepers*, 138–39; Charles L. Chute, "Probation and Suspended Sentence," *Journal of Criminal Law and Criminology* 12 (Feb. 1922), 559; State of New York, *New York State Reformatory for Women at Bedford, Sixth Annual Report . . .* (Albany: J. B. Lyon, 1906), 17, NYSL. According to Davis, administrators noticed the change in the type of inmate committed to Bedford in 1905.

47. State of New York, State Commission of Prisons, *Twentieth Annual Report of the State Commission of Prisons* (Albany, N.Y.: The Commission, 1914), 116–19, NYSL; State of New York, State Board of Charities, *Report of the Special Committee, Consisting of Commissioner Kevin, Smith, and Mulry, Appointed to Investigate Charges Made against the New York State Reformatory for Women at Bedford Hills* (Albany, N.Y.: J. B. Lyon, 1915), 3–29 ("harmful intimacy," 7).

48. "Miss Davis Stands by Bedford Home," *New York Herald*, Dec. 24, 1914, p. 8; State of New York, State Board of Charities, *Report of the Special Committee*, 26–27; State of New York, State Board of Charities, *Annual Report for the Year* (Albany, N.Y.: J. B. Lyon, 1915), 96, NYSL.

49. State of New York, New York State Reformatory for Women at Bedford, *Seventeenth Annual Report . . .* (Albany, N.Y.: J. B. Lyon, 1918,) 8, 16, NYSL; Inmate #4044, Conduct Record, June 13, 1926, BH.

50. Otis, "A Perversion Not Commonly Noted," 114; Estelle Freedman, "The Prison Lesbian: Race, Class, and the Construction of the Aggressive Female Homosexual, 1915–1965," *Feminist Studies* 22 (Summer 1996): 400–401; Regina G. Kunzel, "Situating Sex: Prison Sexual Culture in the Mid-Twentieth-Century United States," *GLQ: Journal of Lesbian and Gay Studies* 8 (May 2002): 262; Moreno, *Who Shall Survive?*, 229, 230. See also Anne Meis Knupfer, "'To Become Good, Self-Supporting Women': The State Industrial School for Delinquent Girls at Geneva, Illinois, 1900–1935," *Journal of the History of Sexuality* 9 (Oct. 2000): 437–41.

51. State of New York, State Board of Charities, *Report of the Special Committee*, 8. See also Sarah

Potter, "'Undesirable Relations': Same-Sex Relationships and the Meaning of Sexual Desire at a Women's Reformatory during the Progressive Era," *Feminist Studies* 30 (Summer 2004): 400; Kunzel, "Situating Sex," 253–70, esp. 256–56.

52. Inmate #2503, letter from Church Mission of Help to Bedford, June 9, 1921, and letter from Church Mission of Help to Superintendent Baker, ca. June 1921, BH; Inmate #4092, Family History, ca. 1926, BH.

53. Joan Nestle, "Lesbians and Prostitutes: An Historical Sisterhood," in Nestle, *A Restricted Country* (New York: Firebrand Books, 1987), 169; Nestle, *Fragile Union*, 34–35, 40–41, 43. Billie Holiday noted the prevalence of same-sex relations when she was an inmate in the Federal Women's Reformatory at Alderson, Virginia; see Holiday, with William Duffy, *Lady Sings the Blues* (New York: Lancer Books, 1969), 132.

54. Mabel Hampton interview by Joan Nestle, May 21, 1981, Hampton tape, 9, MHSC.

LESLIE J. REAGAN
When Abortion Was a Crime: Reproduction and the Economy in the Great Depression

The frequency with which women—especially those who were married, native-born Protestant, and middle- or upper-middle-class—resorted to abortion fueled a movement to criminalize the practice, as James Mohr discussed in Part II. Motivated by a variety of factors that had little to do with the protection of women's health, which was the primary reason advanced by the physicians who led the movement, antiabortionists succeeded in making the practice illegal in the post–Civil War era. Some states did allow physicians to perform therapeutic abortions if the woman's life was threatened by carrying the pregnancy to term. In many states, however, the requirements for getting clearance to perform a therapeutic abortion in a hospital setting made this loophole virtually meaningless, especially when a vigilant district attorney was prepared to pit his interpretation against the physician's.

Leslie Reagan's prizewinning study of the practice and policing of abortion during the century it was criminalized (1867–1973) reveals that, despite the law, millions of abortions were performed during those years—and by no means all by "back-alley" butchers.

"My husband has been out of work for over six months and no help is in sight," wrote one mother to Margaret Sanger and the American Birth Control League; "I can't afford more children." Every year she performed two abortions upon herself, and she reported, "I have just now gotten up from an abortion and I don't want to repeat it again."[1] The disaster of the Great Depression touched all aspects of women's lives, including the most intimate ones, and brought about a new high in the incidence of abortion. As jobs evaporated and wages fell, families found themselves living on insecure and scanty funds. Many working people lost their homes; tenants had their belongings put out on the street. Married couples gave up children to orphanages because they could not support them.

As women pressured doctors for help, the medical practice of abortion, legal and illegal, expanded during the 1930s. Physicians granted, for the first time, that social conditions were an essential component of medical judgment in therapeutic abortion cases. Medical recognition of social indications reveals the ways in which political and social forces shaped medical thinking and practice. A handful of radical physicians, who looked to Europe as a model, raised the possibility of liberalizing the abortion law. . . .

If we move away from the dramatic narratives about abortion produced at inquests or in newspapers, which tell of the deaths and dangers of abortion, and step into the offices of physician-abortionists, a different story can be discerned. Abortion was not extraordinary, but ordinary. The proverbial "back-alley butcher" story of abortion overemphasizes fatalities and limits our understanding of the history of illegal abortion. Case studies of the "professional abortionists" and their practices in the 1930s provide a unique opportunity to analyze the experiences of the tens of thousands of women who went to physician-abortionists. Many women had abortions in a setting nearly identical to the doctors' offices where they received other medical care. These doctors specialized in a single procedure, abortion. They used standard medical procedures to perform safe abortions routinely and ran what may be called abortion clinics. Furthermore, abortion specialists were an integral part of regular medicine, as the network of physicians who referred patients to these physician-abortionists demonstrates. . . .

The Depression years make vivid the relationship between economics and reproduction. Women had abortions on a massive scale. Married women with children found it impossible to bear the expense of another, and unmarried women could not afford to marry. As young working-class women and men put off marriage during the Depression to support their families or to save money for a wedding, marriage rates fell drastically. Yet while they waited to wed, couples engaged in sexual relations, and women became pregnant. Many had abortions.[2]

During the Depression, married women were routinely fired on the assumption that jobs belonged to men and that women had husbands who supported them. Discrimination against married women forced single women to delay marriage and have abortions in order to keep their jobs. One such woman was a young teacher whose fiancé was unemployed. As her daughter recalled fifty years later, "She got pregnant. What were her choices? Marry, lose her job, and bring a child into a family with no means of support? Not marry, lose her job and reputation, and put the baby up for adoption or keep it?" As this scenario makes clear, she had no "choice." Furthermore, it points to the limitations of the rhetoric of "choice" in reproduction: Social forces condition women's reproductive options.[3] . . .

Medical studies and sex surveys demonstrated that women of every social strata turned to abortion in greater numbers during the Depression. Comparative studies by class and race appeared for the first time in the 1930s. Induced abortion rates among white, middle-and upper-class married women rose during the Depression years. The Kinsey Institute for Sex Research, led by Paul H. Gebhard, analyzed data from over five thousand married, white, mostly highly educated, urban women. The researchers found that "the depression of the 1930's resulted in a larger proportion of pregnancies that were artificially aborted." For every age group of women, born between 1890 and 1919, the highest induced abortion rate occurred during "the depth of the depression." White, married women were determined to avoid bearing children during the Depression: They reduced their rate of conception as well.[4] . . . The findings of Kinsey researchers suggest that aborting first pregnancies early in marriage might have been a growing trend, particularly among more educated, urban white women.[5]

Married black women, like their white counterparts, used abortion more during the Depression. . . . Dr. Charles H. Garvin, an esteemed black surgeon from Cleveland, commented in 1932 "that there has been a very definite increase in the numbers of abortions, criminally performed, among the married."[6] . . . In 1935, Harlem Hospital, which cared for mostly poor black patients, opened a separate ward, "The Abortion Service," to treat the women who came for emergency care following illegal abortions. . . .

A study of reproductive histories collected from forty-five hundred women at a New York clinic between 1930 and 1938 suggested that when class was controlled, working-class women, black and white alike, induced abortions at the same rate.[7] . . .

The key difference between black and white women was in their response to pregnancy outside of marriage, not their use of abortion. Unmarried white women who became pregnant were more likely to abort their pregnancies than were African American women in the same situation. Instead, more black women bore children out of wedlock and did so without being ostracized by their families and community. . . .

The tolerance of illegitimacy among African Americans was tempered by class. As African Americans advanced economically, they held their unwed daughters and sons to more rigid standards of chastity. Similarly, by the time the Kinsey Institute interviewed black women in the 1950s, there were clear class differences in the use of abortion by unmarried black women: Those with more education (and presumably more affluence) aborted at a higher rate than those with less education.[8]

. . . A study of working-class women in New York in the 1930s found almost identical abortion rates among Catholic, Jewish, and Protestant women.[9] However, researchers found striking differences in the reproductive patterns followed by women of different religious groups, a finding that seems to reflect class differences. Catholic and Jewish women tended to have their children earlier in their lives and began aborting unwanted pregnancies as they got older; Protestant women tended to abort earlier pregnancies and bear children later.[10] The Kinsey Report found for both married and unmarried white women, the more devout the woman, the less likely she was to have an abortion; the more religiously "inactive" a woman, the more likely she was to have an abortion.[11]

Access to physician-induced abortions and reliance upon self-induced methods varied greatly by class and race. Most affluent white women went to physicians for abortions, while poor women and black women self-induced them. Physicians performed 84 percent of the abortions reported by the white, urban women to Kinsey researchers. Fewer than 10 percent of the affluent white women self-induced their abortions, though black women and poor white women, because of poverty or discrimination in access to medical care, often did so. According to the Kinsey study on abortion, 30 percent of the lower-income and black women reported self-inducing their abortions.[12] . . .

Low-income women's and black women's greater reliance upon self-induced methods of abortion meant that the safety of illegal abortion varied by race and class. . . .

Since poor women and black women were more likely to try to self-induce abortions and less likely to go to doctors or midwives, they suffered more complications. . . . Women reported having no complications after their abortions in 91 percent of the abortions performed by doctors and 86 percent of those performed by midwives. In contrast, only 24 percent of the self-induced abortions were without complications.[13] . . .

As more women had abortions during the Depression, and perhaps more turned to self-induced measures because of their new poverty, growing numbers of women entered the nation's hospitals for care following their illegal abortions. The Depression deepened an earlier trend toward the hospitalization of women who had abortion-related complications in public hospitals. As childbirth gradually moved into the hospital, so too did abortion. . . . One intern at Cook County Hospital recalled that in 1928 she saw at least thirty or forty abortion cases in the month and a half she worked there; or, one woman a day and several hundred women a year entered the hospital because of postabortion complications. In 1934, the County Hospital admitted 1,159 abortion cases, and reported twenty-two abortion-related deaths that year.[14] . . .

Doctors and public health reformers began to realize the importance of illegal abortion as a contributor to maternal mortality. . . . [Obstetrician Frederick J.] Taussig estimated that approximately fifteen thousand women died every year in the United States because of abortion.[15] . . . In hospital wards, doctors saw women with septic infections, perforations of the uterus, hemorrhages, and mutilation of intestines and other organs caused by self-induced abortions or ineptly performed operations.

The hospital atmosphere . . . helped forge a liberal consensus within a section of the medical profession about the horrors of self-induced and poorly performed criminal abortions, together with an acceptance of performing abortions for needy patients or referring them to abortionists. . . .

Most cities had several physicians who "specialized" in abortion, and many small towns had at least one physician-abortionist. . . .

In the mid-1930s one businessman set up a chain of abortion clinics in cities on the West Coast. Doctors Gabler, Keemer, and Timanus, of Chicago, Detroit, and Baltimore respectively, were physician-abortionists who performed abortions for tens of thousands of women during the 1930s. The decades-long existence of these specialty practices points to the tolerance and accessibility of abortion during these years.

Physician-abortionists practiced in a legally and medically gray area. It was not always clear whether they performed illegal abortions or legal, therapeutic abortions. As physicians, the law allowed them to perform therapeutic abortions in order to preserve a woman's life, but abortion was illegal and frowned upon by the profession. What made physician-abortionists different from other doctors was the volume of abortions performed, often to the exclusion of other medical practice. As long as these physicians received referrals from other physicians, practiced safely, and avoided police interference, they might consider the abortions to be therapeutic. Yet any physician who regularly performed abortions also knew that the procedure was criminal and that he or she practiced on a fine line. . . .

It is difficult for the historian to gain access to patient records, and this is particularly true for an illegal procedure. Yet I have uncovered records of abortion patients and have reconstructed, for the first time, the daily practice of an underground abortion clinic and the characteristics of its clientele. Seventy patient records of women who had abortions at a Chicago clinic owned by Dr. Josephine Gabler have been preserved in legal documents. . . . The Gabler clinic (later run by Ada Martin) serves as a case study of a specialty practice and reveals the abortion experiences of many women who found physician-abortionists.[16]

Dr. Josephine Gabler was a major source of abortions for Chicago women and other Midwesterners in the 1930s. She graduated from an Illinois medical school in 1905 and received her Illinois medical license that year. She established herself as a specialist in abortion by the late 1920s, perhaps earlier. Over eighteen thousand abortions were performed at her State Street office between 1932 and 1941.[17] In other words, the clinic provided approximately two thousand abortions a year—about five a day, if it operated seven days a week. Dr. Gabler, and other doctors who worked at the State Street office, provided needed abortion services to women from the entire region, including patients from Illinois, Indiana, Michigan, and Wisconsin. . . .

The Gabler-Martin clinic demonstrates that doctors have been more responsive to the demands of their female patients—even demands for an illegal procedure—than previously suspected. Over two hundred doctors, including some of Chicago's most prominent physicians and AMA members, referred patients to Gabler and Martin for abortions.[18] . . .

When Mrs. Helen B. learned of her pregnancy in 1940, she wanted an abortion. She "finally persuaded" her doctor that she needed an abortion and was given Dr. Josephine Gabler's business card.[19] The use of business cards itself emphasizes the openness of abortion practice in this period. . . .

Gabler and Martin showed their appreciation for referrals—and encouraged their colleagues and allies to keep referring—by paying commissions to those who sent patients. Investigators reported that the payments were usually fifteen dollars each, which was about a quarter of the average fee for abortion. . . .

The other major path to an abortionist's office was through women's personal networks. An abortionist's name and address were critical information, which women shared with each other. In this sample, of the cases where the source of the referral is identifiable, almost a third of the patients found their way to the clinic through friends. . . . Every woman who went to 190 North State Street for an abortion became a potential source of information for others in the same predicament. . . .

In many ways, the experience of getting an abortion at the State Street clinic was like going into any other doctor's office for medical care. Referrals from physicians, note taking by a receptionist, women dressed in white uniforms, instruments and delivery tables, and the instructions for after-care were all typical in a doctor's office—and familiar to women who had previously delivered babies in hospitals. The women received anesthesia and, apparently, a dilation and curettage of the uterus—the same procedure they would have had if they had a legal, therapeutic abortion in the hospital.

Nonetheless, the criminality of abortion made its practice clandestine. Two safeguards designed to shield the people performing abortions made the procedures in Martin's office different from legal, hospital procedures: covering the eyes of patients in order to make identifying the physician-abortionist impossible and warning women not to go to anyone else if they experienced complications. The clinic did not abandon its clients if problems developed following the abortion, but they did not want them going to physicians or local hospitals who might alert authorities.

The majority of women in the State Street patient records were married when they had their abortions. . . . Over half of the married women (thirty-two women, or 57 percent) had children. Over a third of these women had children under two years old. Mothers seemed strongly motivated to avoid having two babies in diapers at once. . . .

A second, and large, group of the married women (twenty-four, or 43 percent) had no children at all. This is not what we would expect; we have learned that married women used birth control and abortion after they had children, not before. . . .

Could they represent a significant number of married couples who intended to have no children at all? Since the records do not say how long they had been married, it is possible that these were abortions of prebridal pregnancies. Perhaps some worried about extramarital affairs. Some may have been college students or married to students. Perhaps they needed an abortion because they could not risk losing their jobs. Probably most who had abortions in the early years of their marriages had children later. Class could shape reproduction in complicated ways. Working women and more affluent college women found it necessary to delay childbearing for different reasons and at different times.

The age range of the State Street patients reflected the diversity of women's reproductive patterns and needs. The ages of the women having abortions in this sample ranged from eighteen to forty-eight years. . . . Their average age was twenty-seven years, but over half were under twenty-five. In 1992, for comparison, most of the women who had abortions were unmarried and under twenty-five years old.[20] . . . The difference is that most of the women in the Martin case records ended their pregnancies within the context of marriage: 80 percent of the Gabler-Martin clinic patients were married; now, 80 percent are unmarried. Today, most of the women who have abortions do so when they are single and finishing high school or college and expect to bear children later.[21] . . .

It is difficult to determine the class of . . . the patients at 190 North State Street, but it seems to have been a mixed group. The records of this office show we cannot assume that working-class women were never able to get safe abortions from physicians. . . . Information about income or the occupation of the woman's husband, if married, was not included in the patient records, but the records show that at least a third of the women worked for wages. . . .

The racial composition of the women who relied upon the abortion services of Dr. Gabler is even more obscure. There is no racial information in the patient records. . . .

Gabler and Martin could provide illegal abortions openly because they paid for protection from the law. Bribery of police and prosecutors underpinned the abortion practice. We only know of the corruption of legal authorities in Chicago because police officer Daniel Moriarity tried to kill Martin in order to silence her.[22] . . .

The office at 190 North State Street where thousands of women obtained abortions from a skilled practitioner was not a rarity.[23] . . .

In Detroit, African American physicians might refer patients to Dr. Edgar Bass Keemer Jr. . . . Throughout his career as an abortionist, which lasted into the 1970s, Keemer served primarily poor women and black women. In thirty-five years, he performed over thirty thousand abortions.[24] . . .

In Baltimore, reputable physicians referred their patients to Dr. George Loutrell Timanus, one of two well-known physician-abortionists in [the city]. Dr. Timanus had a close relationship to Baltimore's white medical elite at Johns Hopkins University, where the faculty taught Timanus's techniques to their students and called him a friend. . . .

Doctors Gabler, Keemer, and Timanus represent a larger pattern of medical involvement in illegal abortion and an expansion of the medical provision of abortions during the 1930s. . . . [Their practices were not temporary, but established; they were not located in back alleys, but on main streets. Dr. Gabler had a business card; Dr. Timanus was listed in the phone book and his office had a sign in front.]

Thousands of women obtained abortions from physicians in conventional medical settings and suffered no complications afterwards. . . . A mixed group of patients—working-class and middle-class women, white and black—reached these trusted physicians. . . .

NOTES

1. "Unemployment," *Birth Control Review (BCR)* 5 (May 1931):131.
2. Lois Rita Helmbold, "Beyond the Family Economy: Black and White Working-Class Women

During the Great Depression," *Feminist Studies* 13 (Fall 1987):640–641; A. J. Rongy, *Abortion: Legal or Illegal?* (New York: Vanguard Press, 1933), p. 111.

3. Alice Kessler-Harris, *Out to Work: A History of Wage-Earning Women in the United States* (Oxford: Oxford University Press, 1982), pp. 256–257; quotations from typed letter from Charleston, IL 61920, April 20, 1985, "Silent No More" Campaign, National Abortion Rights Action League (NARAL), Chicago.

4. Paul H. Gebhard et al., *Pregnancy, Birth and Abortion* (New York: Harper and Brothers and Paul B. Hoeber Medical Books, 1958), pp. 113–114, 140, table 55. Since much of the data comes from the earlier Kinsey studies on sexuality and this report came out of his institute, hereafter I refer to this book in the text as the Kinsey report or study on abortion.

5. The percentage of first pregnancies aborted in this young generation was no more than 10 percent, but it was more than double the rate of earlier generations of women.

6. Charles H. Garvin, "The Negro Doctor's Task," *BCR* 16 (November 1932):270.

7. Endre K. Brunner and Louis Newton, "Abortions in Relation to Viable Births in 10,609 Pregnancies: A Study Based on 4,500 Clinic Histories," *American Journal of Obstetrics and Gynecology* 38 (July 1939):82–83, 88.

8. Gebhard et al., *Pregnancy, Birth and Abortion,* p. 162. Regina G. Kunzel also finds class difference among African-Americans in their use of maternity homes; Kunzel, *Fallen Women, Problem Girls: Unmarried Mothers and the Professionalization of Social Work, 1890–1945* (New Haven: Yale University Press, 1993), p. 73.

9. Brunner and Newton, "Abortions in Relation to Viable Births," pp. 85, 90.

10. Ibid., p. 87, fig. 4.

11. Gebhard et al., *Pregnancy, Birth and Abortion,* pp. 64–65, 114–118.

12. Ibid., pp. 194–195, 198.

13. Regine K. Stix, "A Study of Pregnancy Wastage," *Milbank Memorial Fund Quarterly* 13 (October 1935):362–363.

14. Dr. Gertrude Engbring in Transcript of *People* v. *Heissler,* 338 Ill. 596 (1930), Case Files, vault no. 44783, Supreme Court of Illinois, Record Series 901, Illinois State Archives, Springfield; Augusta Weber, "Confidential Material Compiled for Joint Commission on Accreditation, June 1964," box 5, "Obstetrics Department—Accreditation 1964," Office of the Administrator, Cook County Hospital Archives. An "Abortion Service" was opened at Harlem Hospital in 1935. Peter Marshall Murray

and L. B. Winkelstein, "Incomplete Abortion: An Evaluation of Diagnosis and Treatment of 727 Consecutive Cases of Incomplete Abortions," *Harlem Hospital Bulletin* 3 (June 1950):31.

15. Fred J. Taussig, "Abortion in Relation to Fetal and Maternal Welfare," *American Journal of Obstetrics and Gynecology,* p. 872.

16. This case study is based on patient records and other legal documents discovered in the Transcript of *People v. Martin,* 382 Ill. 192 (1943), Case Files, vault no. 51699, Supreme Court of Illinois, Record Series 901.

17. Supplemental Report, Statement of Gordon B. Nash, Assistant State's Attorney, April 23, 1942, in Transcript of *People v. Martin.*

18. Of the eighteen doctors named in the patient records, eleven could be identified. (Sometimes only a last name was included on the record.) All eleven were AMA members and eight were specialists of various types.

19. Mrs. Helen B. in transcript of *People v. Martin.*

20. "Abortion Surveillance: Preliminary Data— United States, 1992," *Morbidity and Mortality Weekly Report: CDC Surveillance Summaries* 43 (December 23, 1994):930, 932, table I.

21. Recent abortion data show the trend to delaying childbearing. Teenagers make up a smaller proportion of the women having abortions than in the past: in 1972, 33 percent of the women who had abortions were nineteen years old or less; in 1992, teenagers were only 20 percent of the women having abortions, and women twenty-five or older made up 45 percent of the women having abortions. "Abortion Surveillance," p. 932, table I.

22. As a police officer, Moriarity received a little less than $2,500 per year. Quotations in George Wright, "Tells Bribe Behind Killing," *Chicago Daily Tribune,* May 2, 1941, p. 1.

23. Other doctors who appear to have specialized in abortion in Chicago include Dr. William E. Shelton, who may have been involved with Martin ("Dr. William Eugene Shelton," *Daily Tribune,* September 27, 1928; "Loop Physician Held in Abortion Conspiracy Case," *Daily Tribune,* November 21, 1940); Dr. Joseph A. Khamis ("Doctor Accused Second Time as an Abortionist," *Daily Tribune,* August 18, 1942); Dr. Justin L. Mitchell (*People v. Mitchell,* 368 Ill. 399); and Dr. Edward Peyser (*People v. Peyser,* 380 Ill. 404). All newspaper clippings in Abortionists Files, Historical Health Fraud Collection, American Medical Association, Chicago.

24. Ed Keemer, *Confessions of a Pro-Life Abortionist* (Detroit: Vinco Press, 1980), pp. 13, 18, 27, 29, 89–93.

Margaret Sanger, "I resolved that women should have knowledge of contraception. . ."

The contrast between the high fertility of newly arriving immigrants and the low birth rate among old-stock Americans around the turn of the century prompted such leaders as Theodore Roosevelt to lament "race suicide" and to exhort women of the "proper sort" to perform their maternal functions in the self-less fashion dictated by time and tradition. Viewed through women's eyes, however, these population trends looked different, as this selection on the beginnings of the birth control movement dramatically illustrates. Although a few radicals such as Emma Goldman saw contraception as a means of liberating women by restoring to them control over their own bodies and thereby lessening their economic dependence on men, it was Margaret Higgins Sanger whose name would become most closely linked with the crusade for birth control.

The factors that propelled Sanger—a complex personality—to leadership were many. One of eleven children, she helped bury her mother, who died of tuberculosis. Young Margaret, however, was convinced that the sexual demands of her father (who lived to be eighty) were the real cause of her mother's death. A nursing career also shaped Sanger's thinking, as the following account suggests. Arrested under the Comstock Act (pp. 207–212) for publication of a newspaper advocating contraception, she fled in 1914 to England with her husband and three children. There she met the famous British psychologist and sex expert, Havelock Ellis, who further convinced her that sexual experience should be separated from reproduction, enabling couples to enhance the quality of their sexual relationship. Returning to New York, the Sangers continued their activities on behalf of birth control. The opening of the Brownsville clinic in 1916, recounted here, resulted in still further confrontation with authorities, including arrests. The hunger strike of Sanger's sister, Ethel Byrne, a nurse at the clinic, was followed by Sanger's own trial. Convicted of "maintaining a public nuisance," she was sentenced to thirty days in prison. When her lawyer asked for a suspended sentence in exchange for her promise not to break the law again, she announced, "I cannot promise to obey a law I do not respect." Ever the iconoclast and rebel, she gave talks to other inmates on sex hygiene when the prison guards were out of sight. Even after she was released, her attorney pursued an appeal. In January 1918, the New York Court of Appeals upheld her conviction, but interpreted the law in question broadly, allowing physicians to provide contraceptives to *married* women "to cure or prevent [venereal] disease." Sanger appealed unsuccessfully for the right of *nurses* to also provide contraceptives. Still, establishing the right of physicians to deliver birth control was a key breakthrough; it was the foundation of the birth control movement in the twentieth century, and would be a central element in the decision in *Roe v. Wade* (see pp. 658–661).

Excerpted from "Awakening and Revolt," "A 'Public Nuisance,'" and "Hunger Strike," chs. 3, 12, and 13 of *My Fight for Birth Control* by Margaret Sanger (New York: Farrar & Reinhart, 1931). Copyright © 1931 by Margaret Sanger. Reprinted by permission of Grant Sanger.

Margaret Sanger, following her conviction by the New York Court of Appeals in 1918. She and her supporters treated the outcome as a victory because the court allowed physicians to provide contraceptives to married women "to cure or prevent [venereal] disease." (Photograph reprinted by permission of Planned Parenthood Federation of America.)

Divorcing William Sanger in 1920, Sanger founded the American Birth Control League in 1921 (in 1942 it was transformed into the Planned Parenthood Federation of America). She soon married William Slee, a wealthy oil man whose resources would be a key source of support for her causes. These included the first doctor-staffed birth control clinic in the United States, a model for hundreds of clinics throughout the nation. Long before medical schools routinely taught the fitting of diaphragms, these clinics, staffed by physicians, made reliable contraceptive services widely available. In 1936 Sanger and her colleagues forced the courts to revisit the Comstock Act: a woman physician in New York ordered a package of diaphragms (also known as pessaries) from Japan; the Customs Bureau seized them as obscene articles. But the U.S. Court of Appeals for the Second Circuit ruled that objects ordered by physicians in good faith were exempted from the punishments of the law (*U.S v. One Package*, 86 F.2d 737).

Important financial aid would come in later years from the wealthy feminist Katherine McCormick, who shared Sanger's commitment to research in contraception. In the early 1950s, McCormick provided funds for experiments in endocrinology that led to the development of the birth control pill. At a time when few scientists thought an oral contraceptive was possible, the insistence of Sanger and McCormick that every woman had the right to control her own body helped bring about a major breakthrough in medical technology. In 1960, the year of Sanger's death, "the pill" became available to the public. The timing was propitious, for it coincided with a period of sexual liberation that, while proving in some respects to be a mixed blessing for women, also coincided with new recognition of the intensity of their sexual drive and capacity for sexual pleasure. (See Beth Bailey's essay, pp. 629–637.)

Although Sanger saw the development of an oral contraceptive as another victory in a long and difficult struggle for reproductive freedom, others viewed the birth control movement differently. Arguments that limiting family size could not only free women's energies for social reform but prevent the world's poor from producing children they were unable to care for met with opposition from some women in the early years of Sanger's crusade. Some feared that birth control would contribute to promiscuity; others feared it would deny women the dignity that was theirs by virtue of motherhood. The Roman Catholic Church was unrelenting in its opposition, maintaining that the use of contraceptives is a sin. Sanger is still being angrily attacked; her contribution to the lives of modern American women remains a matter of political debate. Birth control is not only a technical way of spacing and limiting children so as to benefit both mother and child but is part of a larger debate about the extent to which women should be able to control their own reproductive lives.

AWAKENING AND REVOLT

Early in the year 1912 I came to a sudden realization that my work as a nurse and my activities in social service were entirely palliative and consequently futile and useless to relieve the misery I saw all about me. . . .

It is among the mothers here that the most difficult problems arise—the outcasts of society with theft, filth, perjury, cruelty, brutality oozing from beneath.

Ignorance and neglect go on day by day; children born to breathe but a few hours and pass out of life; pregnant women toiling early and late to give food to four or five children, always hungry; boarders taken into homes where there is not sufficient room for the family; little girls eight and ten years of age sleeping in the same room with dirty, foul smelling, loathsome men; women whose weary, pregnant, shapeless bodies refuse to accommodate themselves to the husbands' desires find husbands looking with lustful eyes upon other women, sometimes upon their own little daughters, six and seven years of age.

In this atmosphere abortions and birth become the main theme of conversation. On Saturday nights I have seen groups of fifty to one hundred women going into questionable offices well known in the community for cheap abortions. I asked several women what took place there, and they all gave the same reply: a quick examination, a probe inserted into the uterus and turned a few times to disturb the

fertilized ovum, and then the woman was sent home. Usually the flow began the next day and often continued four or five weeks. Sometimes an ambulance carried the victim to the hospital for a curetage, and if she returned home at all she was looked upon as a lucky woman.

This state of things became a nightmare with me. There seemed no sense to it all, no reason for such waste of mother life, no right to exhaust women's vitality and to throw them on the scrap-heap before the age of thirty-five.

Everywhere I looked, misery and fear stalked—men fearful of losing their jobs, women fearful that even worse conditions might come upon them. The menace of another pregnancy hung like a sword over the head of every poor woman I came in contact with that year. The question which met me was always the same: What can I do to keep from it? or, What can I do to get out of this? Sometimes they talked among themselves bitterly.

"It's the rich that know the tricks," they'd say, "while we have all the kids." Then, if the women were Roman Catholics, they talked about "Yankee tricks," and asked me if I knew what the Protestants did to keep their families down. When I said that I didn't believe that the rich knew much more than they did I was laughed at and suspected of holding back information for money. They would nudge each other and say something about paying me before I left the case if I would reveal the "secret." . . .

I heard over and over again of their desperate efforts at bringing themselves "around"—drinking various herb-teas, taking drops of turpentine on sugar, steaming over a chamber of boiling coffee or of turpentine water, rolling down stairs, and finally inserting slippery-elm sticks, or knitting needles, or shoe hooks into the uterus. I used to shudder with horror as I heard the details and, worse yet, learned of the conditions *behind the reason* for such desperate actions.

... Each time I returned it was to hear that Mrs. Cohen had been carried to a hospital but had never come back, that Mrs. Kelly had sent the children to a neighbor's and had put her head into the gas oven to end her misery. Many of the women had consulted midwives, social workers and doctors at the dispensary and asked a way to limit their families, but they were denied this help, sometimes indignantly or gruffly, sometimes jokingly; but always knowledge was denied them. Life for them had but one choice: either to abandon themselves to incessant childbearing, or to terminate their pregnancies through abortions. Is it any wonder they resigned themselves hopelessly, as the Jewish and Italian mothers, or fell into drunkenness, as the Irish and Scotch? The latter were often beaten by husbands, as well as by their sons and daughters. They were driven and cowed, and only as beasts of burden were allowed to exist. . . .

They claimed my thoughts night and day. One by one these women, with their worried, sad, pensive and aging faces would marshal themselves before me in my dreams, sometimes appealingly, sometimes accusingly. I could not escape from the facts of their misery, neither was I able to see the way out of their problems and their troubles. . . .

Finally the thing began to shape itself, to become accumulative during the three weeks I spent in the home of a desperately sick woman living on Grand Street, a lower section of New York's East Side.

Mrs. Sacks was only twenty-eight years old; her husband, an unskilled worker, thirty-two. Three children, aged five, three and one, were none too strong nor sturdy, and it took all the earnings of the father and the ingenuity of the mother to keep them clean, provide them with air and proper food, and give them a chance to grow into decent manhood and womanhood.

Both parents were devoted to these children and to each other. The woman had become pregnant and had taken various drugs and purgatives, as advised by her neighbors. Then, in desperation, she had used some instrument lent to her by a friend. She was found prostrate on the floor amidst the crying children when her husband returned from work. Neighbors advised against the ambulance, and a friendly doctor was called. The husband would not hear of her going to a hospital, and as a little money had been saved in the bank a nurse was called and the battle for that precious life began.

... The three-room apartment was turned into a hospital for the dying patient. Never had I worked so fast, so concentratedly as I did to keep alive that little mother. . . .

... July's sultry days and nights were melted into a torpid inferno. Day after day, night after night, I slept only in brief snatches, ever too anxious about the condition of that feeble heart bravely carrying on, to stay long from the bedside of the patient. With but one toilet for the building and that on the floor below, everything had to be carried down for disposal, while ice, food and other necessities had to be carried three flights up. It was one of those old airshaft buildings of which there were several thousands then standing in New York City.

At the end of two weeks recovery was in sight, and at the end of three weeks I was preparing to leave the fragile patient to take up the ordinary duties of her life, including those, of wifehood and motherhood. . . .

But as the hour for my departure came nearer, her anxiety increased, and finally with trembling voice she said: "Another baby will finish me, I suppose."

"It's too early to talk about that," I said, and resolved that I would turn the question over to the doctor for his advice. When he came I said: "Mrs. Sacks is worried about having another baby."

"She well might be," replied the doctor, and then he stood before her and said: "Any more such capers, young woman, and there will be no need to call me."

"Yes, yes—I know, Doctor," said the patient with trembling voice, "but," and she hesitated as if it took all of her courage to say it, "what can I do to prevent getting that way again?"

"Oh ho!" laughed the doctor good naturedly, "You want your cake while you eat it too, do you? Well, it can't be done." Then, familiarly slapping her on the back and picking up his hat and bag to depart, he said: "I'll tell you the only sure thing to do. Tell Jake to sleep on the roof!"

With those words he closed the door and went down the stairs, leaving us both petrified and stunned.

Tears sprang to my eyes, and a lump came in my throat as I looked at that face before me. It was stamped with sheer horror. I thought for a moment she might have gone insane, but she conquered her feelings, whatever they may have been, and turning to me in desperation said: "He can't understand, can he?—he's a man after all—but you do, don't you? You're a woman and you'll tell me the secret and I'll never tell it to a soul."

She clasped her hands as if in prayer, she leaned over and looked straight into my eyes and beseechingly implored me to tell her something—something *I really did not know.* . . .

I had to turn away from that imploring face. I could not answer her then. I quieted her as best I could. She saw that I was moved by the tears in my eyes. I promised that I would come back in a few days and tell her what she wanted to know. The few simple means of limiting the family like *coitus interruptus* or the condom were laughed at by the neighboring women when told these were the means used by men in the well-to-do families. That was not believed, and I knew such an answer would be swept aside as useless were I to tell her this at such a time. . . .

The intelligent reasoning of the young mother—how to prevent getting that way again—how sensible, how just she had been— yes, I promised myself I'd go back and have a long talk with her and tell her more, and perhaps she would not laugh but would believe that those methods were all that were really known.

But time flew past, and weeks rolled into months. . . . I was about to retire one night three months later when the telephone rang and an agitated man's voice begged me to come at once to help his wife who was sick again. It was the husband of Mrs. Sacks, and I intuitively knew before I left the telephone that it was almost useless to go.

. . . I arrived a few minutes after the doctor, the same one who had given her such noble advice. The woman was dying. She was unconscious. She died within ten minutes after my arrival. It was the same result, the same story told a thousand times before—death from abortion. She had become pregnant, had

used drugs, had then consulted a five-dollar professional abortionist, and death followed.

The doctor shook his head as he rose from listening for the heart beat. . . . The gentle woman, the devoted mother, the loving wife had passed on leaving behind her a frantic husband, helpless in his loneliness, bewildered in his helplessness as he paced up and down the room, hands clenching his head, moaning "My God! My God! My God!"

The Revolution came—but not as it has been pictured nor as history relates that revolutions have come. . . .

After I left that desolate house I walked and walked and walked; for hours and hours I kept on, bag in hand, thinking, regretting, dreading to stop; fearful of my conscience, dreading to face my own accusing soul. At three in the morning I arrived home still clutching a heavy load the weight of which I was quite unconscious.

. . . As I stood at the window and looked out, the miseries and problems of that sleeping city arose before me in a clear vision like a panorama: crowded homes, too many children; babies dying in infancy; mothers overworked; baby nurseries; children neglected and hungry—mothers so nervously wrought they could not give the little things the comfort nor care they needed; mothers half sick most of their lives—"always ailing, never failing"; women made into drudges; children working in cellars; children aged six and seven pushed into the labor market to help earn a living; another baby on the way; still another; yet another; a baby born dead—great relief; an older child dies—sorrow, but nevertheless relief— insurance helps; a mother's death—children scattered into institutions; the father, desperate, drunken; he slinks away to become an outcast in a society which has trapped him.

. . . There was only one thing to be done: call out, start the alarm, set the heather on fire! Awaken the womanhood of America to free the motherhood of the world! I released from my almost paralyzed hand the nursing bag which unconsciously I had clutched, threw it across the room, tore the uniform from my body, flung it into a corner, and renounced all palliative work forever.

I would never go back again to nurse women's ailing bodies while their miseries were as vast as the stars. I was now finished with superficial cures, with doctors and nurses and social workers who were brought face to face with this overwhelming truth of women's needs and yet turned to pass on the other side. They must be made to see these facts. I resolved that women should have knowledge of contraception. They have every right to know about their own bodies. I would strike out—I would scream from the housetops. I would tell the world what was going on in the lives of these poor women. *I would* be heard. No matter what it should cost. *I would be heard. . . .*

I announced to my family the following day that I had finished nursing, that I would never go on another case—and I never have.

I asked doctors what one could do and was told I'd better keep off that subject or Anthony Comstock would get me. I was told that there were laws against that sort of thing. This was the reply from every medical man and woman I approached. . . .

A "PUBLIC NUISANCE"

The selection of a place for the first birth control clinic was of the greatest importance. No one could actually tell how it would be received in any neighborhood. I thought of all the possible difficulties: The indifference of women's organizations, the ignorance of the workers themselves, the resentment of social agencies, the opposition of the medical profession. Then there was the law—the law of New York State.

Section 1142 was definite. It stated that *no one* could give information to prevent conception to *anyone* for any reason. There was, however, Section 1145, which distinctly stated that physicians (*only*) could give advice to prevent conception for the cure or prevention of disease. I inquired about the section, and was told by two attorneys and several physicians that this clause was an exception to 1142 referring only to venereal disease. But anyway, as I was not a physician, it could not protect me. Dared I risk it?

I began to think of the doctors I knew. Several who had previously promised now refused. I wrote, telephoned, asked friends to ask other friends to help me find a woman doctor to help me demonstrate the need of a birth control clinic in New York. None could be found. No one wanted to go to jail. No one cared to test out the law. Perhaps it would have to be done without a doctor. But it had to be done; that I knew.

Fania Mindell, an enthusiastic young worker in the cause, had come on from Chicago to help me. Together we tramped the streets on that dreary day in early October, through a driving rainstorm, to find the best location at the cheapest terms possible . . .

Finally at 46 Amboy Street, in the Brownsville Section of Brooklyn, we found a friendly landlord with a good place vacant at fifty dollars a month rental; and Brownsville was settled on. It was one of the most thickly populated sections. It had a large population of working class Jews, always interested in health measures, always tolerant of new ideas, willing to listen and to accept advice whenever the health of mother or children was involved. I knew that here there would at least be no breaking of windows, no hurling of insults into our teeth; but I was scarcely prepared for the popular support, the sympathy and friendly help given us in that neighborhood from that day to this. . . .

With a small bundle of handbills and a large amount of zeal, we fared forth each morning in a house-to-house canvass of the district in which the clinic was located. Every family in that great district received a "dodger" printed in English, Yiddish and Italian. . . .

Women of every race and creed flocked to the clinic with the determination not to have any more children than their health could stand or their husbands could support. Jews and Christians, Protestants and Roman Catholics alike made their confessions to us, whatever they may have professed at home or in the church. Some did not dare talk this over with their husbands; and some came urged on by their husbands. Men themselves came after work; and some brought timid, embarrassed wives, apologetically dragging a string of little children. . . .

When I asked a bright little Roman Catholic woman what she would say to the priest when he learned that she had been to the Clinic, she answered indignantly: "It's none of his business. My husband has a weak heart and works only four days a week. He gets twelve dollars, and we can barely live on it now. We have enough children."

Her friend, sitting by, nodded a vigorous approval. "When I was married," she broke in, "the priest told us to have lots of children, and we listened to him. I had fifteen. Six are living. Nine baby funerals in our house. I am thirty-six years old now. Look at me! I look sixty."

As I walked home that night, I made a mental calculation of fifteen baptismal fees, nine funeral expenses, masses and candles for the repose of nine little souls, the physical suffering of the mother, and the emotional suffering of both parents; and I asked myself, "Was it fair? Is this the price of Christianity?" . . .

Ethel Byrne, who is my sister and a trained nurse, assisted me in advising, explaining, and demonstrating to the women how to prevent conception. As all of our 488 records were confiscated by the detectives who later arrested us for violation of the New York State law, it is difficult to tell exactly how many more women came in those days to seek advice; but we estimate that it was far more than five hundred. As in any new enterprise, false reports were maliciously spread about the clinic; weird stories without the slightest foundation of truth. We talked plain talk and gave plain facts to the women who came there. We kept a record of every applicant. All were mothers; most of them had large families.

It was whispered about that the police were to raid the place for abortions. We had no fear of that accusation. We were trying to spare mothers the necessity of that ordeal by giving them proper contraceptive information. . . .

The arrest and raid on the Brooklyn clinic was spectacular. There was no need of a large force of plain clothes men to drag off a trio of decent, serious women who were testing out a law on a fundamental principle. My federal arrest, on the contrary, had been assigned to intelligent men. One had to respect the dignity of their mission; but the New York city officials seem to use tactics suitable only for crooks, bandits and burglars. We were not surprised at being arrested, but the shock and horror of it was that a *woman,* with a squad of five plain clothes men, conducted the raid and made the arrest. A woman—the irony of it!

I refused to close down the clinic, hoping that a court decision would allow us to continue such necessary work. I was to be disappointed. Pressure was brought upon the landlord, and we were dispossessed by the law as a "public nuisance." In Holland the clinics were called "public utilities."

When the policewoman entered the clinic with her squad of plain clothes men and announced the arrest of Miss Mindell and myself (Mrs. Byrne was not present at the time and her arrest followed later), the room was crowded to suffocation with women waiting in the outer room. The police began bullying these mothers, asking them questions, writing down their names in order to subpoena them to testify against us at the trial. These women, always afraid of trouble which the very presence of a

policeman signifies, screamed and cried aloud. The children on their laps screamed, too. It was like a panic for a few minutes until I walked into the room where they were stampeding and begged them to be quiet and not to get excited. I assured them that nothing could happen to them, that I was under arrest but they would be allowed to return home in a few minutes. That quieted them. The men were blocking the door to prevent anyone from leaving, but I finally persuaded them to allow these women to return to their homes, unmolested though terribly frightened by it all.

. . . The patrol wagon came rattling through the streets to our door, and at length Miss Mindell and I took our seats within and were taken to the police station. . . .

HUNGER STRIKE

Out of that spectacular raid, which resulted in an avalanche of nation-wide publicity in the daily press, four separate and distinct cases resulted:

Mrs. Ethel Byrne, my sister, was charged with violating Section 1142 of the Penal Code, designed to prevent dissemination of birth control information.

Miss Fania Mindell was charged with having sold an allegedly indecent book entitled "What Every Girl Should Know" written by Margaret Sanger.

I was charged with having conducted a clinic at 46 Amboy Street, Brooklyn, in violation of the same section of the Penal Code.

Having re-opened the clinic, I was arrested on a charge of "maintaining a public nuisance," in violation of Section 1530 of the Penal Code.

The three of us were held for trial in the Court of Special Sessions, with bail fixed at $500 each. This meant that our cases would be decided by three judges appointed by the Mayor and not by a jury. . . .

My sister was found guilty, and on January 22 she was sentenced to thirty days in the Workhouse. A writ of habeas corpus as a means of suspending sentence during appeal was refused by Supreme Court Justice Callahan. She spent the night in jail.

Ethel Byrne promptly declared a hunger strike. I knew that she would not flinch. Quiet, taciturn, with a will of steel hidden by a diffident air, schooled by her long training as a professional nurse, she announced briefly that she would neither eat, drink, nor work until her release. Commissioner of Correction Burdette G. Lewis promptly announced that she would be permitted to see no one but her attorney.

While the newspapers were reporting—always on the front page—the condition of the hunger striker, plans were hastened for a monster mass meeting of protest, to be held in Carnegie Hall. Helen Todd acted as chairman, and Dr. Mary Halton was an additional speaker. The hall was crowded by a huge audience of all classes. The women patients of the Brownsville clinic were given places of honor on the platform. The salvos of applause which greeted me showed that intelligent opinion was strongly behind us, and did much to give me the courage to fight with renewed strength for the immediate release of Ethel Byrne.

This meeting was acclaimed by the press as a "triumph of women, for women, by women." The meeting was said to have struck the right note—that of being instructive and persuasive, instead of agitational.

In the meantime, Ethel Byrne's refusal to eat and drink was crowding all other news off the front pages of the New York papers. Her defiance was sharpening the issue between self-respecting citizens and the existing law, which was denounced on every street corner as hypocritical. In the subway crowds, on street-corners, everywhere people gathered, the case was discussed. "They are imprisoning a woman for teaching physiological facts!" I heard one man exclaim. . . .

"It makes little difference whether I starve or not," she replied, through her attorney, "so long as this outrageous arrest calls attention to the archaic laws which would prevent our telling the truth about the facts of life. With eight thousand deaths a year in New York State from illegal operations on women, one more death won't make much difference."

All this served to convince the now panic-stricken Mr. Lewis [Commissioner of Correction in charge of Blackwell's Island] that Mrs. Byrne was different, after all, from the alcoholics and drug addicts who had given him his previous experience, and with whom he had gallantly compared her. When she had gone 103 hours without food, he established a precedent in American prison annals. He ordered her forcibly fed. She was the first woman so treated in this country. . . .

The truth was that Mrs. Byrne was in a critical condition after being rolled in a blanket and having milk, eggs and a stimulant forced into her stomach through a rubber tube. I realized this as soon as I heard that she was "passive under the feeding." Nothing but loss of strength could have lessened the power of her resistance to such authority. Nothing but brutality could have reduced her fiery spirit to acquiescence. I was desperate; torn between admiration for what she was doing and misery over what I feared might be the result.

On January 31st, a committee headed by Mrs. Amos Pinchot, Jessie Ashley and myself went to Albany for the purpose of asking Governor Whitman to appoint a commission to investigate birth control and make a report to the state legislature. Governor Whitman, a wise, fair, intelligent executive and statesman, received us, and listened to our exposition of the economic and moral necessity for birth control; the medical theory behind its justification. He promised to consider appointing the commission. During the interview Miss Jessie Ashley introduced the subject of Mrs. Byrne's treatment on Blackwell's Island and the anxiety we felt about her condition. We tried to make him see the outrage committed by the state in making anyone suffer for so just a cause. The Governor offered Mrs. Byrne a pardon on condition that she would not continue to disseminate birth control information. . . .

When we left Albany that day, I had the promise of a provisional pardon for Mrs. Byrne, but best of all I had in my purse a letter from the Governor to the authorities at Blackwell's Island authorizing me to see her. I was shocked and horrified when, in the late afternoon of February 1st, I saw my sister. She was lying semi-conscious on a cot in a dark corner of the prison cell. . . .

There was not time to inform her of the conditions of her pardon, and moreover she was too ill to face the question. I still believe that I was right in accepting the conditions which the Governor imposed. There was no other course. I saw that she was dangerously ill, that nothing further was to be gained by her keeping on, and that her death would have been a terrible calamity. Her life was what mattered to me, regardless of her future activities. . . .

At any rate, by the time she was released the subject was a burning issue. Newspapers which previously had ignored the case, had to mention a matter important enough to bring the Governor of the State from Albany to New York.

PHOTO ESSAY: ADORNING THE BODY

How women manage their physical appearance is only in part a response to the aesthetics of changing fashions. What women wear and the spirit in which they wear it can code a range of changing judgments about their social role, their political views, and their understanding of their bodies. (Why men's fashion has shifted far more slowly is a question worth pondering.)

As you examine the images that follow, consider the extent to which women's clothing has linked them to the issues that are discussed in the documents and essays. What do you understand to be the relationships between women's bodies and their clothing in different periods of time? In different regions of the country? Among different classes of people?

What personal and political meaning do you find in your own clothing and the clothing that you see around you?

Fashions for June.

1. Long dresses dragged in muddy ground, signaling that the wearer was not expected to exert herself. By the mid-nineteenth century, as these dresses show, fashionable ball gowns featured wide, heavy skirts over petticoats and impossibly narrow waists. Wearing dresses like these required wearing corsets, often of whalebone, to hold the body rigid and constrict the breathing. ("Fashions for June," *Harper's New Monthly Magazine* 7, no. 37 [June 1853]: 143–44.)

2. Amelia Bloomer did not invent the short skirt and trousers that came to bear her name; known as the "Turkish style," it appeared here and there in the 1840s. Elizabeth Cady Stanton's cousin Elizabeth Miller wore it when she visited Seneca Falls. Stanton envied her ease of movement and began to wear it. Bloomer was the editor of a women's rights journal, the *Lily*, which supported the principle of dress reform. "It seemed proper that I should practise [*sic*] as I preached," she would write years later. "At the outset, I had no idea of fully adopting the style ... no thought that my action would create an excitement ... and give to the style my name and the credit due Mrs. Miller. This was all the work of the press. I stood amazed at the furor." Bloomer would wear the costume on her lecture tours throughout the country for the next six years or so; "I found the dress comfortable, light, easy and convenient, and well adapted to the needs of my busy life," she insisted. But Stanton gave up the dress within three years because she found that ridicule deflected attention from her serious arguments about women's right to education, the ballot, and a wide range of work and better pay.*

This was not the first time, nor would it be the last, that critics of women's political positions attacked women's dress rather than debate women's ideas directly. Can you think of occasions in recent years when criticism of women's fashion was also a criticism of women's behavior? (Amelia Bloomer in the "short dress," ca. 1852–1853. Courtesy of the Seneca Falls Historical Society, #1425; see http://cr.nps.gov/history/online_books/wori/shs4.htm)

---

*Dexter Bloomer, *The Life and Writings of Amelia Bloomer* (Boston: Arena, 1985), pp. 67–70.

WOMAN'S EMANCIPATION.
(BEING A LETTER ADDRESSED TO MR. PUNCH, WITH A DRAWING, BY A STRONG-MINDED AMERICAN WOMAN.)

3. Women who adopted the Bloomer costume quickly were subjected to withering scorn, as in this cartoon from *Harper's*, a widely circulated magazine whose editors were certain they had the correct position on what women ought to wear. (See "Fashions for June," p. 465.) What message about women does the cartoon convey? ("Women's Emancipation," *Harper's New Monthly Magazine* 3, no. 15 [Aug. 1851]: 424.)

4. By 1874 dress reform had more modest goals. At this meeting at the Freeman Place Chapel in Boston, Massachusetts, the speakers do not display the traditional Bloomer costume. Instead of short skirts and trousers, they emphasize the absence of whalebone stays on their undergarments, and hidden bloomers instead of petticoats. Note the dress and headwear of the attentive women in the pews.

Frank Leslie's Illustrated Newspaper was notably friendly to women's reform causes (see its coverage of suffragists before a congressional committee, pp. 258–259). When Frank Leslie died in 1881, his wife and collaborator, Miriam Squier Leslie, had her own name legally changed to Frank Leslie and continued his publishing enterprises for the rest of her life. When she died in 1914, she left her considerable fortune to Carrie Chapman Catt for use in the final stages of the suffrage campaign. (Sketched by E. R. Morse, "The Dress Reform Meeting in Boston," *Frank Leslie's Illustrated Newspaper* 38, no. 77 [June 20, 1874]: 209, 229. For more on the publishers, see Madeleine Stern, *Purple Passage: The Life of Mrs. Frank Leslie* [Norman: University of Oklahoma Press, 1953], and Lynne Vincent Cheney, "Mrs. Frank Leslie's Illustrated Newspaper," *American Heritage* 26, no. 6 [Oct. 1975].)

FRANK LESLIE'S ILLUSTRATED NEWSPAPER

NEW YORK, JUNE 20, 1874.

GETTING ON BROADWAY CAR

5. Street railways and long-distance railroads were among the benefits of the Industrial Revolution, but, as historian Barbara Welke writes, "[T]he physical act of jumping or stepping from train or streetcar to the ground was qualitatively different for women than the same act undertaken by able-bodied men. Women . . . [were] often burdened by children or by pregnancy." From the years in which the railroad was first invented until the 1920s, fashion details may have changed, but "women's long skirts swept across road and farmyard." Whether hoop skirt, bustle, or Gibson girl look, women's clothing was "long, dark, and cumbersome." At a time when men took pride in jumping on and off railroads and streetcars as they started to move or came to a stop, railroad and streetcar accident reports were "filled with stories of women falling because their skirts caught on a projection or were stepped on by another passenger as they alighted."* What dangers does this woman face? (Photograph courtesy of the Library of Congress, George Grantham Bain Collection, LC-USZ62-91532.)

---

*Barbara Young Welke, *Recasting American Liberty: Gender, Race, Law, and the Railroad Revolution, 1865–1920* (New York: Cambridge University Press, 2001), pp. 55–56. This photograph appears on page 58.

6. The woman on the left, a *mexicana* who perhaps belonged to a family that had settled in New Mexico almost three centuries earlier, is clearly skilled at carrying an *olla* full of water on her head. Photographed in Santa Fe in the mid- or late nineteenth century, she wears the looser, layered clothing long utilized by European women of the laboring classes. The image on the right, taken in a Tucson, Arizona, photography studio probably at the turn of the 1800s, is of a member of a prominent local Mexican American family. The young woman had the privilege of wearing at her wedding the elaborately tailored gown with train, feathered hat, and white gloves that were the height of fashion for elites in the dominant Anglo society.

The twinned practice of wearing an elegant white wedding gown, and staging an elaborate formal wedding was initially restricted to elite Britons and Americans (emulating Queen Victoria's 1840 wedding). By the early twentieth century, urban middle-class couples adopted the "white wedding." It became a widespread practice, supported by burgeoning commercial bridal and related enterprises, only after World War II.* (*Image on left*: Courtesy of the Palace of the Governors / New Mexico History Museum, division of New Mexico Department of Cultural Affairs, negative 3150. *Image on right*: Courtesy of the Arizona Historical Society, Tucson; image #73800, item in the Mexican Heritage Project, donation of Maria Urquides. We are grateful to Elizabeth "Betita" Martínez for identifying and pairing these images in her book, *500 Years of Chicana Women's History/Años de la Mujer Chicana* [New Brunswick, N.J.: Rutgers University Press, 2008], p. 43.)

---

*Katherine Jellison, introduction to *It's Our Day: America's Love Affair with the White Wedding*, 1945–2005 (Lawrence: University Press of Kansas, 2008).

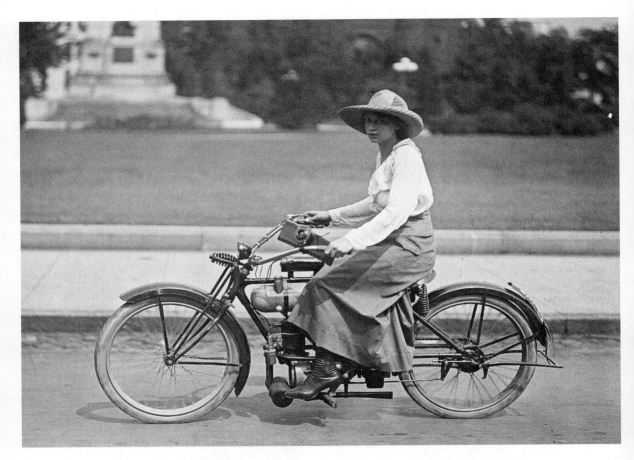

7. The bicycle offered women the opportunity to travel cheaply and independently in public space; it undermined long-standing assumptions about proper feminine behavior.* Note this woman's clothing and the camera she carries. Almost as soon as the bicycle with two wheels of the same size was invented, women embraced it enthusiastically. Susan B. Anthony observed that "the bicycle had done more to emancipate women than anything else in the world." The bicyclist chose where she would go at the rate she wished to go. On the bicycle, the corset had to be abandoned; shorter skirts, even divided skirts and long bloomers suddenly became a matter of necessity. "If women ride," wrote the reformer Frances E. Willard in 1895, "they must, when riding, dress more rationally than they have been wont to do. If they do this many prejudices as to what they may be allowed to wear will melt away. . . . [T]he comfortable, sensible and artistic wardrobe of the rider will make the conventional style of woman's dress absurd to the eye and unendurable to the understanding." How accurate was Willard's prediction? ("Woman on Bicycle," ca. 1917. Harris & Ewing, photographer. Courtesy of the Library of Congress, Prints and Photographs Division, Washington, D.C.)

---

*Frances E. Willard, *A Wheel Within a Wheel: How I Learned to Ride the Bicycle* (Chicago: Women's Temperance Union Publishing House, 1895), p. 39.

8. Congressman T. S. McMillan of Charleston, South Carolina, poses with Miss Ruth Bennett and Miss Sylvia Clavins, who are doing the Charleston on a railing; the U.S. Capitol looms behind them. The short skirts, short hair, and brash behavior marked the women as "flappers." Note the contrast between their clothes and those worn by suffragists demonstrating in front of the White House less than ten years before (see Photo Essay: "Women in Public," p. 261). What difference do you think this change of style made in the lives of women who adopted it? ("Charleston at the Capitol," ca. 1920s. Photo-print by National Photo Company. Courtesy of the Library of Congress, Prints and Photographs Division, Washington D.C.)

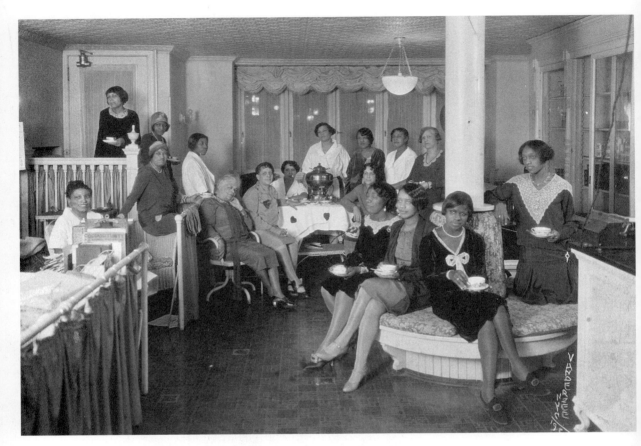

9. Women traditionally devised shampoos and cosmetics for themselves, in their own homes. In the early twentieth century, a number of women entrepreneurs, among them Elizabeth Arden, Helena Rubenstein, and Madam C. J. Walker, invented the concept of the commercial beauty product, made in factories and mass marketed. Walker, who was the daughter of former slaves, was born in 1867; she was probably the first woman self-made millionaire in the nation. In 1905 she developed a scalp-conditioning formula for African Americans. At its peak in the second decade of the century, her business employed some 3,000 people—in a factory in Indianapolis, in hair and manicure salons across the country, and as door-to-door saleswomen. Walker took pride in offering women well-paid alternatives to domestic labor, and in her support for African American philanthropies, especially the antilynching efforts of the NAACP and Bethune-Cookman College (for Bethune-Cookman, see pp. 329–331). She died in 1919. This photograph by the distinguished photographer James VanDerZee was taken in her New York salon and offices in 1929, a decade after Walker's death. How would you describe the hairstyles of these Harlemites, who sported the sophisticated urban look that Madam Walker's products and styling supported? (Courtesy of the Metropolitan Museum of Art, New York © Donna Mussenden VanDerZee.)

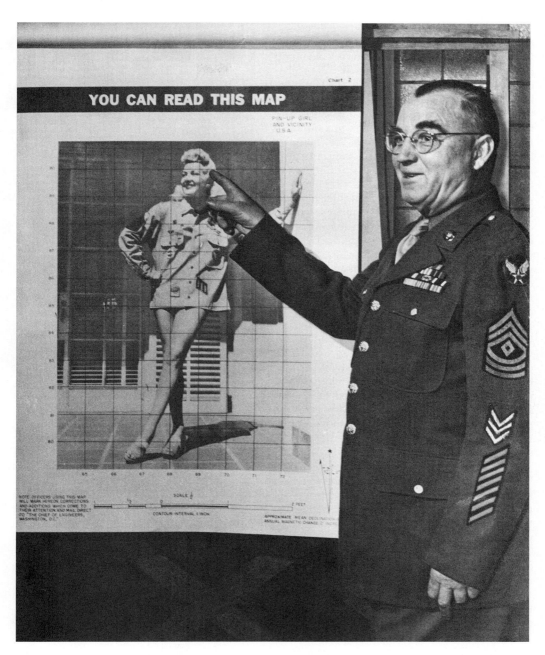

10. An Army Air Forces sergeant uses this image of the movie star Betty Grable (1916–73) to instruct military recruits in the skills of map reading during World War II. The original caption included this line: "The picture of the girl is divided into sections with lines, each of which is numbered, and by checking the lines on it, as on a real map, soldiers can locate any given spot—knowledge which in actual combat can mean the difference between life and death." What messages about women's bodies does this use of her photo—in this pose—convey? (Courtesy of Corbis). (For a subtle cultural analysis of the pinup, see Robert B. Westbrook, "'I Want a Girl Just Like the Girl Who Married Harry James': Women and the Problem of Political Obligation in World War II," *American Quarterly* 42 [Dec. 1990]: 587–614.) We are grateful to Robert Westbrook for identifying this photograph.

473

11. Barbie debuted in 1959 after much persistence and research by her creator, Ruth Handler. In the mid-1940s, Handler had founded a small company called Mattel, together with her husband and a partner who soon sold the Handlers his share. Initially housed in their southern California garage, Mattel produced picture frames but soon began to specialize in dollhouse furniture and toys. In 1955 and 1956, Handler had little success in convincing the company's male employees that there was a waiting market for adult-looking dolls aimed at prepubescent girls. She had noticed that her daughter Barbara, having outgrown baby dolls, enjoyed cutting out clothes and accessories from magazines to create adult paper dolls and assign them imaginary grown-up roles and professions. Handler was convinced that a three-dimensional adult doll would help girls become acquainted with the bodily changes they would experience during puberty. On a European family vacation, Handler came upon Lilli, a German-manufactured doll representing a buxom, blond young woman (Lilli had originated in a satirical, adult-oriented newspaper comic strip). The doll could be bought in various outfits, but the clothes were not sold separately. Mattel acquired the patent and rights for the doll, worked with Japanese

manufacturers to perfect the vinyl molding phase of production, and hired designers (including women) who embraced Handler's vision of a set of dolls for whom a wide wardrobe and accessories could be purchased.

The first Barbie measured 11.5 inches and was marketed as a "teen-age fashion model" and "a new kind of doll from real life." The purchaser chose between the blond and the brunette versions. *Barbie* (always written in a distinctive script) came in an attractive oblong box illustrated with alluring wardrobe possibilities; inside was a miniature catalog with more details. She cost three dollars. Note the designers' genius: whereas Lilli's earrings and shoes were molded and painted on, Barbie had bare feet and pierced ears, allowing for endless accessorizing options. The small-waisted, ever-smiling, preternaturally young doll soon made its way into the hands of millions of young girls, who were drawn to her long, malleable hair, her ever-expanding wardrobe, her supernatural womanly figure, and her "boyfriend" Ken and their coterie.*

During the 1970s, feminists began to ask challenging questions about the relationship between toys such as Barbie, body image, sexism, consumerism, and racial stereotypes. Many of these questions remain unresolved. To what extent do Barbie dolls teach young women to become consumers? Is it sufficient for Mattel simply to change the shade of Barbie's skin to appeal to children of various races and ethnicities? College health and wellness programs often use Barbie as a hook on their websites, pointing out, for example, that a real-life Barbie would be unable to walk given her top-heavy frame. What connections do you think exist between Barbie and eating disorders among adolescents? Between Barbie and the popularity of plastic surgery and tanning salons? If you played with Barbie dolls as a child, what types of scenes did you enact? How did you imagine adulthood through the lens of Barbie? (Photo by Joan Ashabraner. We are grateful to Joan Ashabraner for this image. For a provocative assessment of Barbie threaded with an interview with Ruth Handler, see Susan Stern's 1998 documentary, *Barbie Nation: An Unauthorized Tour* [videorecording, New Day Films].)

---

*Marco Tosca, *Barbie: Four Decades of Fashion, Fantasy, and Fun*, trans. Linda M. Eklund (New York: Harry N. Abrams, 1998), pp. 24–33.

12. From the 1600s onward, African American women felt pressure to adopt beauty regimens that made them appear "whiter." Light-skinned people, who often had straighter hair than dark-skinned African Americans, were granted more privileges on plantations during slavery. Throughout the nineteenth and twentieth centuries, many African Americans straightened their hair in order to appear respectable as they sought economic and social rights. By the 1960s, with the civil rights movement ever more visible and the black power movement on the rise, the emphasis on a look that bespoke respectability and conformity began to crumble. Many activist African Americans forged connections with their African past, adopting African styles of dress and hairstyles. Noted civil rights activist Angela Davis popularized the Afro hairstyle when she spoke across the United States. Here, Davis speaks at a street rally in Raleigh, North Carolina, on July 4, 1974. The Afro not only required a fraction of the care of previously popular hairstyles, but it also embodied the recognition that "black is beautiful." Some older African Americans, including religious people and civil rights activists, criticized the Afro as confrontational, fearing that it would limit African Americans' upward social mobility in white-controlled environments. Instead, the model spread to other ethnic groups, helping to make a wider range of hairstyles fashionable. However, as many recent memoirs and blogs by African-descended women have recounted, the "hair wars" in the black family and community have not ended; see the wry commentary of A'Lelia Bundles, who is a great-great granddaughter of Madam C. J. Walker. ("Hair Peace: A 5-Part Manifesto," *The Root*, Mar. 26, 2009, http://www.theroot.com/ views/ hair-peace-5-part-manifesto?). (Courtesy of Corbis.)

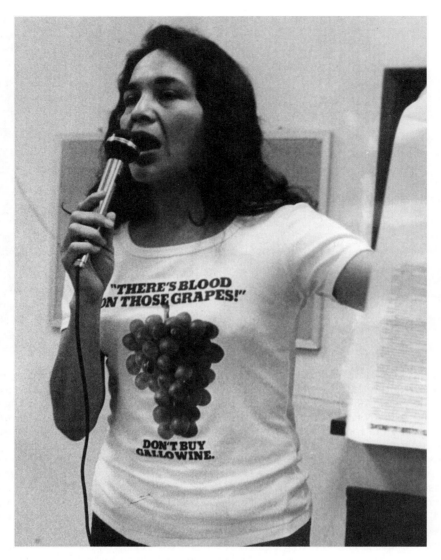

13. Dolores Huerta, a cofounder of the United Farm Workers of America, articulated the grievances of thousands of exploited Mexican and Mexican American farm laborers who toiled in California fields. In this 1973 photograph, Huerta is shown using not only her voice to denounce harsh living conditions and inadequate pay, but also powerful imagery on her T-shirt. Consider how clothing can serve both as a political signal and as a historical artifact. What information does Huerta's T-shirt convey? How might you use this photograph as a historical source? ("There's blood on those grapes!" Photograph by Chris Sanchez, likely taken during the Gallo strike, Livingston, California, 1973. Courtesy of the United Farm Workers Collection #273, Walter P. Reuther Library, Wayne State University.)

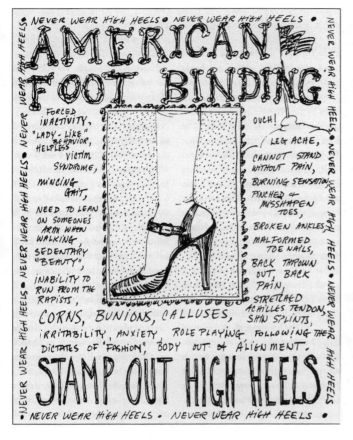

AMERICAN FOOT BINDING

NEVER WEAR HIGH HEELS • NEVER WEAR HIGH HEELS •

FORCED INACTIVITY, "LADY-LIKE" BEHAVIOR, HELPLESS victim SYNDROME, MINCING GAIT, NEED TO LEAN ON SOMEONE'S ARM WHEN WALKING, SEDENTARY "BEAUTY", INABILITY TO RUN FROM THE RAPISTS,

OUCH! LEG ACHE, CANNOT STAND WITHOUT PAIN, BURNING SENSATION, PINCHED & MISSHAPEN TOES, BROKEN ANKLES, MALFORMED TOE NAILS, BACK THROWN OUT, BACK PAIN, STRETCHED ACHILLES TENDON, SHIN SPLINTS,

CORNS, BUNIONS, CALLUSES, IRRITABILITY, ANXIETY, ROLE PLAYING, FOLLOWING THE DICTATES OF "FASHION", BODY OUT OF ALIGNMENT.

STAMP OUT HIGH HEELS

NEVER WEAR HIGH HEELS • NEVER WEAR HIGH HEELS •

14. Ever since patriot women boycotted elaborate and expensive British imports during the Revolutionary era as a way of expressing their political principles, resistance to fashion trends has been a recurring theme in women's clothing choices. Challenging the fashion industry, women's liberation activists rebelled against uncomfortable and binding clothing. If you view all the photos in this book depicting pre-1970s events (despite Amelia Bloomer and dress reformers), you will see that this rebellion was a very radical gesture. At mid-century, respectable professional dress required nylon stockings held up by girdles or garter belts, making breathing uncomfortable; narrow skirts that prevented running away from danger; and high heels that over the long run shortened muscles and created corns and bunions in the name of looking sexy. (Fifteen times as many women as men develop bunions requiring surgery.) Women who adopted looser, more comfortable clothing risked scorn and even the loss of their jobs. Until Title VII, it was not illegal to treat the display of beauty as a reasonable professional qualification for many lines of work, including flight attendants and executive secretaries. (See the concept of the Bona Fide Occupational Qualification [BFOQ] in the Civil Rights Act 1964, pp. 745–746.) It took two decades, from the mid-1970s to the mid-1990s, before flight attendants—who, it is estimated, walk as much as 225 miles up and down airplane aisles each year—were able to force most airlines to relax rules requiring them to wear shoes with 2 or 2 1/2-inch heels. (Male attendants could always wear loafers.)*

The "Stamp Out High Heels" poster was a grassroots expression of rebellion, addressing issues of health, safety, and cultural conformity. It augured a dramatic shift in sartorial choices. For example, the pants suit may seem dated now, but in the 1970s it was an important wedge for working women, especially in white-collar jobs. Over the past thirty years, the clothes acceptable for women to wear to work and in public have become very diverse—in style, color, fabric, and so on. This diversity, plus the informal, athletic look so prevalent in women's clothes and shoes, owes much to 1970s feminist activism. How many of the claims and slogans featured in the poster do you agree with? ("American Foot Binding: Stamp Out High Heels," poster, Houston, n.d. Courtesy Duke University Library Special Collections, ALFA Collection, Box 12. We are grateful to Rosalyn Baxandall and Linda Gordon, *Dear Sisters: Dispatches from the Women's Liberation Movement* [New York: Basic Books, 2000], p. 40, for identifying this image.)

---

*See Marc Linder, "Smart Women, Stupid Shoes, and Cynical Employers: The Unlawfulness and Adverse Health Consequences of Sexually Discriminatory Workplace Footwear Requirements for Female Employees," *Journal of Corporation Law* 22 (1996–97): 296–97, 308–12.

Cancer.
Sometimes you can put your finger on it.

One of the seven warning signals of cancer is a thickening or lump in the breast or elsewhere.

There are six more that you should be aware of. Indigestion or difficulty in swallowing. An obvious change in a wart or mole. A nagging cough or hoarseness. A change in bowel or bladder habits. A sore that does not heal. Unusual bleeding or discharge.

If you notice any one of these warning signals, there's only one thing to do. See your doctor.

We want to wipe out cancer in your lifetime. **Give to the American Cancer Society.**

15. Second-wave feminists urged women to take responsibility for their own well-being. As more was understood about breast cancer, it became clear that annual examinations by physicians were not enough to track its appearance; in the 1970s, as today, women are urged to examine their own bodies regularly. Over the years, unclothed women in art and advertising have presented their bodies to the male gaze; in a sharp departure from tradition, the model here is concerned with herself and her own health, encouraging women viewers to knowingly touch their own bodies as an act of self-preservation and self-empowerment. The advertisement appeared in the first issue of *Ms.* magazine. (Photo reprinted by the permission of The American Cancer Society, Inc. for historical purposes only. All rights reserved. See *Ms.* 1, no.1 [July 1972]: 35.)

16. Graduation ceremony at a large public university, May 2009. What meanings are conveyed by the footwear of these two women? (Photo by Tom Langdon.)

LABOR AND ACTIVISM

JACQUELYN DOWD HALL

Disorderly Women: Gender and Labor Militancy in the Appalachian South

By the 1920s, unionization had not taken hold in the former states of the Confederacy as it had in heavily industrialized areas of the Northeast and Midwest (see Annelise Orleck's essay, pp. 361–376). Moreover, working conditions had worsened as factory owners introduced new innovations designed to improve productivity. Southern textile mills, as employers of large numbers of poorly paid white women, were especially vulnerable to strikes. And indeed, this work force was white. Nearly all mill and factory work in the South was closed to African Americans until the 1960s.*

Jacquelyn Dowd Hall focuses on one of the many strikes exploding across the South in that tumultuous decade, exploring female activism in an essay that calls into question old stereotypes about southern workers as individualistic, docile, and "hard to organize." In this important study, Hall illuminates the distinctive style of collective action that the women of Elizabethton, Tennessee, employed and the self-concepts and family networks on which that style relied.

In what respects did working conditions resemble those confronting the young immigrant women in New York's garment district about whom Orleck wrote? What were the critical differences? Were the factors that inspired and sustained resistance similar? How does Hall view the actions of Trixie Perry and Texas Bill?

The rising sun "made a sort of halo around the crown of Cross Mountain" as Flossie Cole climbed into a neighbor's Model T and headed west down the gravel road to Elizabethton, bound for work in a rayon plant. Emerging from Stoney Creek hollow, the car joined a caravan of buses and self-styled "taxis" brimming with young people from dozens of tiny communities strung along the creek branches and nestled in the coves of the Blue Ridge Mountains of East Tennessee. The caravan picked up speed as it hit paved roads and crossed the Watauga River bridge, passing beneath a sign advertising the county seat's new-found identity as a "City of Power." By the time Cole reached the factory gate, it was 7:00 A.M., time to begin another ten-hour day as a reeler at the American Glanzstoff plant.[1]

The machines whirred, and work began as usual. But the reeling room stirred with anticipation. The day before, March 12, 1929, all but seventeen of the 360 women in the inspection room next door had walked off their jobs. Now they were gathered at the factory gate,

*Timothy Minchin, *Hiring the Black Worker: The Racial Integration of the Southern Textile Industry, 1960–1980* (Chapel Hill: University of North Carolina Press, 1999).

Excerpted from "Disorderly Women: Gender and Labor Militancy in the Appalachian South" by Jacquelyn Dowd Hall, in *Journal of American History* 73 (1986): 354–82. Copyright © 1986 by Jacquelyn Dowd Hall. Condensed and reprinted by permission of the author and publisher. Notes have been renumbered and edited.

refusing to work but ready to negotiate. When 9:00 A.M., approached and the plant manager failed to appear, they broke past the guards and rushed through the plant, urging their co-workers out on strike. By 1:40 P.M. the machines were idle and the plant was closed.

The Elizabethton conflict rocked Carter County and made national headlines. Before March ended, the spirit of protest had jumped the Blue Ridge and spread through the Piedmont. Gastonia, Marion, and Danville saw the most bitter conflicts, but dozens of towns were shocked by an unexpected workers' revolt.[2]

The textile industry has always been a stronghold of women's labor, and women were central to these events. They were noted by contemporaries, sometimes as leaders, more often as pathetic mill girls or as "Amazons" providing comic relief.[3] In historical renditions they have dropped out of sight. The result has been thin description: a one-dimensional view of labor conflict that fails to take culture and community into account.

Elizabethton, of course, is not unusual in this regard. Until recently, historians of trade unionism, like trade unionists themselves, neglected women, while historians of women concentrated on the Northeast and the middle class. There were few scholarly challenges to the assumption that women workers in general and southern women in particular were "hard to organize" and that women as family members exercised a conservative pull against class cohesion. Instances of female militancy were seen and not seen.[4] Because they contradicted conventional wisdom, they were easily dismissed.

Recent scholarship has revised that formulation by unearthing an impressive record of female activism. But our task is not only to describe and celebrate but also to contextualize, and thus to understand. In Elizabethton the preindustrial background, the structure of the work force and the industry, the global forces that impinged on local events—these particularities of time and place conditioned women's choices and shaped their identities. Equally important was a private world traditionally pushed to the margins of labor history. Female friendships and sexuality, cross-generational and cross-class alliances, the incorporation of new consumer desires into a dynamic regional culture—these too energized women's participation. Women in turn were historical subjects, helping to create the circumstances from which the strike arose and guiding by their actions the course the conflict took.

With gender at the center of analysis, unexpected dimensions come into view. Chief among them is the strike's erotic undercurrent, its sexual theme. The activists of Elizabethton belonged to a venerable tradition of "disorderly women," women who, in times of political upheaval, embody tensions that are half-conscious or only dimly understood.[5] Beneath the surface of a conflict that pitted workers and farmers against a new middle class in the town lay an inner world of fantasy, gender ideology, and sexual style.

The melding of narrative and analysis that follows has two major goals. The first is a fresh reading of an important episode in southern labor history, employing a female angle of vision to reveal aspects of the conflict that have been overlooked or misunderstood. The second is a close look at women's distinctive forms of collective action, using language and gesture as points of entry to a culture.

The Elizabethton story may also help to make a more general point. Based as it is on what Michel Foucault has termed "local" or "subjugated" knowledge, that is, perceptions that seem idiosyncratic, naive, and irrelevant to historical explanation, this study highlights the limitations of conventional categories.[6] The women of Elizabethton were neither traditionalists acting on family values nor market-oriented individualists, neither peculiar mountaineers nor familiar modern women. Their irreverence and inventiveness shatter stereotypes and illuminate the intricacies of working-class women's lives.

In 1925 the J. P. Bemberg Company of Barmen, Germany, manufacturer of high-quality rayon yarn by an exclusive stretch spinning process, began pouring the thick concrete floors of its first United States subsidiary. Three years later Germany's leading producer of viscose yarn, the Vereinigte Glanzstoff Fabriken, A.G., of Elberfeld opened a jointly managed branch nearby. A post-World War I fashion revolution, combined with protective tariffs, had spurred the American rayon industry's spectacular growth. As one industry publicist put it, "With long skirts, cotton stockings were quite in order; but with short skirts, nothing would do except sheer, smooth stockings. . . . It was on the trim legs of post-war flappers, it has been said, that rayon first stepped out into big business."

Dominated by a handful of European giants, the rayon industry clustered along the Appalachian mountain chain. By World War II, over 70 percent of American rayon production took place in the southern states, with 50 percent of the national total in Virginia and Tennessee alone.[7]

When the Bemberg and Glanzstoff companies chose East Tennessee as a site for overseas expansion, they came to a region that has occupied a peculiar place in the American economy and imagination. Since its "discovery" by local-color writers in the 1870s, southern Appalachia has been seen as a land "where time stood still." Mountain people have been romanticized as "our contemporary ancestors" or maligned as "latter-day white barbarians." Central to both images is the notion of a people untouched by modernity. In fact, as a generation of regional scholars has now made clear, the key to modern Appalachian history lies not in the region's isolation but in its role as a source of raw materials and an outlet for investment in a capitalist world economy.[8]

Frontier families had settled the fertile Watauga River Valley around Elizabethton before the Revolution. Later arrivals pushed farther up the mountains into the hollows carved by fast-falling creeks. Stoney Creek is the oldest and largest of those creek-bed communities. Here descendants of the original settlers cultivated their own small plots, grazed livestock in woods that custom held open to all, hunted and fished in an ancient hardwood forest, mined iron ore, made whiskey, spun cloth, and bartered with local merchants for what they could not produce at home.

In the 1880s East Tennessee's timber and mineral resources attracted the attention of capitalists in the United States and abroad, and an era of land speculation and railroad building began. The railroads opened the way to timber barons, who stripped away the forests, leaving hillsides stark and vulnerable to erosion. Farmers abandoned their fields to follow the march of the logging camps. Left behind, women and children did their best to pick up the slack.[9] But by the time Carter County was "timbered out" in the 1920s, farm families had crept upward to the barren ridge lands or grown dependent on "steady work and cash wages." Meanwhile, in Elizabethton, the county seat, an aggressive new class of bankers, lawyers, and businessmen served as brokers for outside developers, speculated in land, invested in homegrown factories, and looked

beyond the hills for their standards of "push, progress and prosperity."[10]

Carter County, however, lacked Appalachia's grand prize: The rush for coal that devastated other parts of the mountains had bypassed that part of East Tennessee. Nor had county farmers been absorbed into the cotton kingdom, with its exploitative credit system and spreading tenancy. To be sure, they were increasingly hard pressed. As arable land disappeared, farms were divided and redivided. In 1880 the average rural family had supported itself on 140 acres of land; by 1920 it was making do on slightly more than 52 acres. Yet however diminished their circumstances, 84.5 percent still owned their own land.[11] The economic base that sustained traditional expectations of independence, production for use, and neighborly reciprocity tottered but did not give way.

The coming of the rayon plants represented a coup for Elizabethton's aspiring businessmen, who wooed investors with promises of free land, tax exemptions, and cheap labor. But at first the whole county seemed to share the boomtown spirit. Men from Stoney Creek, Gap Creek, and other mountain hamlets built the cavernous mills, then stayed on to learn the chemical processes that transformed the cellulose from wood pulp and cotton linters (the short fibers that remain on cotton seeds after longer, spinnable fibers are removed) into "artificial silk." Women vied for jobs in the textile division where they wound, reeled, twisted, and inspected the rayon yarn. Yet for all the excitement it engendered, industrialization in Carter County retained a distinctly rural cast. Although Elizabethton's population tripled (from 2,749 in 1920 to 8,093 in 1930), the rayon workers confounded predictions of spectacular urban growth, for most remained in the countryside, riding to work on chartered buses and trains or in taxis driven by neighbors and friends.

Women made up approximately 37 percent of the 3,213 workers in the mills. Most were under twenty-one, but many were as young as twelve, or more commonly, fourteen. By contrast, the work force contained a large proportion of older, married men. Those men, together with a smaller number of teenage boys, dominated the chemical division, while young women processed the finished yarn.[12]

Whether married or single, town- or country-bred, the men who labored in the rayon plants followed in the footsteps of fathers, and sometimes grandfathers, who had combined farming with a variety of wage-earning occupations. To a greater extent than we might expect, young women who had grown up in Elizabethton could also look to earlier models of gainful labor. A search of the 1910 manuscript census found 20 percent (97/507) of women aged fourteen and over in paid occupations. The largest proportion (29.6 percent) were cooks and servants. But close behind were women in what mountain people called "public work": wage-earning labor performed outside a household setting. For rayon workers from the countryside it was a different story. Only 5.2 percent of adult women on Stoney Creek were gainfully employed (33/638). Nineteen of these were farmers. The rest—except for one music teacher—were servants or washerwomen.[13]

These contrasts are telling, and from them we can surmise two things. The first is that industrialization did not burst upon a static, conflict-free "traditional" world. The women who beat a path to the rayon plants came from families that had already been drawn into an economy where money was a key to survival. The second is that the timber industry, which attracted Carter County's men, undermined its agricultural base, and destroyed its natural resources, created few opportunities for rural women. No wonder that farm daughters in the mills counted their blessings and looked on themselves as pioneers.

Whether they sought work out of family need or for more individualistic reasons, these "factory girls" saw their jobs as a hopeful gamble rather than a desperate last resort, and they remembered the moment with astounding precision. "I'll never forget the day they hired me at Bemberg," said Flossie Cole. "We went down right in front of it. They'd come out and they'd say, 'You and you and you,' and they'd hire so many. And that day I was standing there and he picked out two or three more and he looked at me and he said, 'You.' It thrilled me to death." She worked 56 hours that week and took home $8.16.[14]

Such pay scales were low even for the southern textile industry, and workers quickly found their income eaten away by the cost of commuting or of boarding in town. When the strike came it focused on the issue of Glanzstoff women's wages, which lagged behind those at the older Bemberg plant. But workers had other grievances as well. Caustic chemicals

were used to turn cellulose into a viscous fluid that was then forced through spinnerets, thimble-shaped nozzles pierced with tiny holes. The fine, individual streams coagulated into rayon filaments in an acid bath. In the chemical division men waded through water and acid, exposed all day to a lethal spray. Women labored under less dangerous conditions, but for longer hours and less pay. Paid by the piece, they complained of rising production quotas and what everyone referred to as "hard rules."[15]

Women in particular were singled out for petty regulations, aimed not just at extracting labor but at shaping deportment as well. They were forbidden to wear makeup; in some departments they were required to purchase uniforms. Most galling of all was company surveillance of the washroom. According to Bessie Edens, who was promoted to "forelady" in the twisting room, "men could do what they wanted to in their own department," but women had to get a pass to leave the shop floor. "If we went to the bathroom, they'd follow us," Flossie Cole confirmed, "'fraid we'd stay a minute too long." If they did, their pay was docked; one too many trips and they lost their jobs.[16]

Complaints about the washroom may have had other meanings as well. When asked how she heard that a strike was brewing, Nettie Reece cited "bathroom gossip."[17] As the company well knew, the women's washroom, where only a forelady, not a male supervisor, could go, might serve as a communications center, a hub of gossip where complaints were aired and plans were formulated.

The German origins of the plant managers contributed to the tension. Once the strike began, union organizers were quick to play on images of an "imported Prussian autocracy." The frontier republicanism of the mountains shaded easily into post–World War I Americanism as strikers demanded their rights as "natural-born American citizens" oppressed by a "latter day industrialism." In that they had much in common with other twentieth-century workers, for whom the democratic values articulated during the war became a rallying cry for social justice at home. The nationality of the managers helped throw those values into sharp relief.[18]

The strike came on March 12, 1929, led by women in Glanzstoff inspection department, by what one observer called "girls in their teens [who] decided not to put up with the present conditions any longer." The county court immediately issued injunctions forbidding all demonstrations against the company. When strikers ignored the injunctions, the governor sent in the National Guard. The strikers secured a charter from the American Federation of Labor's United Textile Workers union (UTW). Meeting in a place called the Tabernacle, built for religious revivals, they listened to a Baptist preacher from Stoney Creek warn: "The hand of oppression is growing on our people. . . . You women work for practically nothing. You must come together and say that such things must cease to be." Each night more workers "came forward" to take the union oath.[19]

Meanwhile, UTW and Federal Conciliation Service officials arrived on the scene. On March 22 they reached a "gentlemen's agreement" by which the company promised a new wage scale for "good girl help" and agreed not to discriminate against union members. The strikers returned to work, but the conflict was far from over. Higher paychecks never materialized; union members began losing their jobs. On April 4 local businessmen kidnapped two union organizers and ran them out of town. Eleven days later the workers responded with what most observers agreed was a "spontaneous and complete walkout."[20]

This time the conflict quickly escalated. More troops arrived, and the plants became fortresses, with machine guns on the rooftops and armed guardsmen on the ground. The company sent buses manned by soldiers farther up the hollows to recruit new workers and escort them back to town. Pickets blocked narrow mountain roads. Houses were blown up; the town water main was dynamited. An estimated 1,250 individuals were arrested in confrontations with the National Guard.[21]

As far as can be determined, no women were involved in barn burnings and dynamitings—what Bessie Edens referred to as "the rough . . . stuff" that accompanied the second strike. Men "went places that we didn't go," explained Christine Galliher. "They had big dark secrets . . . the men did." But when it came to public demonstrations women held center stage. At the outset "hundreds of girls" had ridden down main street "in buses and taxis, shouting and laughing at people who watched them from windows and doorsteps." Now they blocked the road at Gap Creek and refused soldiers' orders that they walk twelve miles to jail in town. "And there was one girl that was awful tough in the bunch. . . . She

said, 'No, by God. We didn't walk out here, and we're not walking back!' And she sat her hind end down in the middle of the road, and we all sat down with her. And the law used tear gas on us! . . . And it nearly put our eyes out, but we still wouldn't walk back to town." In Elizabethton after picket duty, women marched down the "Bemberg Highway . . . draped in the American flag and carrying the colors"—thereby forcing the guardsmen to present arms each time they passed. Inventive, playful, and shrewd, the women's tactics encouraged a holiday spirit. They may also have deflected violence and garnered community support.[22]

Laughter was among the women's most effective weapons. But beneath high spirits the terms of battle had begun to change. Local organizers were hobbled by a national union that lacked the resources and commitment to sustain the strike. Instead of translating workers' grievances into a compelling challenge, the UTW pared their demands down to the bone. On May 26, six weeks after the strike began, the union agreed to a settlement that made no mention of wages, hours, working conditions, or union recognition. The company's only concession was a promise not to discriminate against union members. The workers were less than enthusiastic. According to one reporter, "It took nine speeches and a lot of question answering lasting two and a half hours to get the strikers to accept the terms."[23]

The press, for the most part, greeted the settlement as a workers' victory, or at least a satisfactory resolution of the conflict. Anna Weinstock, the first woman to serve as a federal conciliator, was credited with bringing the company to the bargaining table and was pictured as the heroine of the event. "SETTLED BY A WOMAN!" headlined one journal. "This is the fact that astounds American newspaper editors." "Five feet five inches and 120 pounds of femininity; clean cut, even features"—and so on, in great detail. Little was made of Weinstock's own working-class origins. She was simply a "new woman," come to the rescue of a backward mountain folk. The strikers themselves dropped quickly from view.[24]

From the outside, the conflict at Elizabethton looked like a straightforward case of labor-management strife. But it appeared quite different from within. Everyone interviewed put the blame for low wages on an alliance between the German managers and the "leading citizens" of the town. Preserved in the oral tradition is the story of how the "town fathers" promised the company a supply of cheap and unorganized labor. Bessie Edens put it this way: They told the company that "women wasn't used to working, and they'd work for almost nothing, and the men would work for low wages. That's the way they got the plant here." In this version of events the strike was part of a long-term struggle, with development-minded townspeople on one side and workers, farmers, and country merchants on the other.[25]

Workers' roots in the countryside encouraged resistance and helped them to mobilize support once the strike began. "These workers have come so recently from the farms and mountains ... and are of such independent spirit," Alfred Hoffman observed, "that they 'Don't care if they do lose their jobs' and cannot be scared." Asked by reporters what would happen if strike activity cost them their jobs, one woman remarked, "I haven't forgotten how to use a hoe," while another said, "We'll go back to the farm."[26] Such threats were not just bravado. High levels of farm ownership sustained cultural independence. Within the internal economy of families, individual fortunes were cushioned by reciprocity; an orientation toward subsistence survived side by side with the desire for cash and store-bought goods.

Stoney Creek farmers were solidly behind the sons and daughters they sent to the factories, as were the small shopkeepers who relied on farmers for their trade. In county politics Stoney Creekers had historically marshaled a block vote against the town. In 1929 Stoney Creek's own J. M. Moreland was county sheriff, and he openly took the strikers' side. A strike leader in the twisting room ran a country store and drove his working neighbors into town. "That's why he was pretty well accepted as their leader," said a fellow worker. "Some of them were cousins and other relations. Some of them traded at his store. Some of them rode in his taxi. All intertwined."[27]

The National Guard had divided loyalties. Parading past the plants, the strikers "waved to and called the first names of the guardsmen, for most of the young men in uniforms [were friends of] the men and girls on strike." Even when the local unit was fortified by outside recruits, fraternizing continued. Nettie Reece, like a number of her girlfriends, met her future husband that way; she saw him on the street and "knew that was mine right there." Some

guardsmen went further and simply refused to serve. "The use of the National Guard here was the dirtiest deal ever pulled," one protested. "I turned in my equipment when I was ordered to go out and patrol the road. I was dropped from the payroll two weeks later."[28]

In this context of family- and community-based resistance, women had important roles to play. Farm mothers nurtured the strikers' independence simply by cleaving to the land, passing on to their children a heritage at odds with the values of the new order and maintaining family production as a hedge against the uncertainties of a market economy. But the situation of farm mothers had other effects as well, and it would be a mistake to push the argument for continuity too far. As their husbands ranged widely in search of wage labor, women's work intensified while their status—now tied to earning power—declined. The female strikers of Elizabethton saw their mothers as resourceful and strong but also as increasingly isolated and hard pressed. Most important, they no longer looked to their mothers' lives as patterns for their own.[29]

The summer after the strike, Bessie Edens attended the Southern Summer School for Women Workers, a workers' education project in North Carolina, where she set the group on its ear with an impassioned defense of women's rights:

> It is nothing new for married women to work. They have always worked.... Women have always worked harder than men and always had to look up to the man and feel that they were weaker and inferior.... If we women would not be so submissive and take every thing for granted, if we would awake and stand up for our rights, this world would be a better place to live in, at least it would be better for the women.
>
> Some girls think that as long as mother takes in washings, keeps ten or twelve boarders or perhaps takes in sewing, she isn't working. But I say that either one of the three is as hard work as women could do. So if they do that at home and don't get any wages for it, why would it not be all right for them to go to a factory and receive pay for what they do?

Edens had been the oldest of ten children. She had dreamed of going to nursing school, but her poverty-stricken parents had opposed her plan. At fifteen, she had gone to work as a servant. "Then I'd come back when Momma had a baby and wait on her, and help if she needed me in any way." Asked fifty years later about a daughter's place on a hardscrabble farm, Edens replied: "The girls were supposed to do housework and work in the fields. They were supposed to be slaves."[30]

Bessie Edens was unusual in her articulation of a working-class feminism. But scattered through the life histories written by other students are echoes of her general themes. Read in the context of farm daughters' lives—their first-hand exposure to rural poverty, their yearnings for a more expansive world—these stories reflect the "structure of feeling" women brought to the rayon plants and then to the picket line and union hall.[31] Women such as Edens, it seems, sensed the devaluation of women's handicraft labor in the face of cheap consumer goods. They feared the long arm of their mothers' fate, resented their fathers' distant authority, and envied their brothers' exploits away from home. By opting for work in the rayon plants, they struck out for their own place in a changing world. When low wages, high costs, and autocratic managers affronted their dignity and dashed their hopes, they were the first to revolt.

The Elizabethton story thus presents another pattern in the female protest tradition. In coal-mining communities a rigid division of labor and women's hardships in company towns have resulted, paradoxically, in the notable militancy of miners' wives. By contrast, tobacco factories have tended to employ married women, whose job commitments and associational lives enable them to assume leadership roles in sustained organizing drives. In yet other circumstances, such as the early New England textile mills or the union insurgency of the 1920s and 1930s, single women initiated independent strikes or provided strong support for male-led, mixed-sex campaigns. Where, as in Elizabethton, people were mobilized as family and community members rather than as individual workers, non-wage-earning women could provide essential support. Once in motion, their daughters might outdo men in militancy, perhaps because they had fewer dependents than their male co-workers and could fall back more easily on parental resources, perhaps because the peer culture and increased independence encouraged by factory labor stirred boldness and inspired experimentation.[32]

The fact of women's initiative and participation in collective action is instructive. Even more intriguing is the gender-based symbolism of their protest style. Through dress, language, and gesture, female strikers expressed a complex cultural identity and turned it to their own rebellious purposes.

Consider, for instance, Trixie Perry and a woman who called herself "Texas Bill." Twenty-eight-year-old Trixie Perry was a reeler in the Glanzstoff plant. She had apparently become pregnant ten years before, had married briefly and then divorced, giving her son her maiden name. Her father was a butcher and a farmer, and she lived near her family on the edge of town. Trixie later moved into Elizabethton. She never remarried but went on to have several more children by other men. Texas Bill's background is more elusive. All we know is that she came from out of state, lived in a boardinghouse, and claimed to have been married twice before she arrived in town. These two friends were ringleaders on the picket line. Both were charged with violating the injunction, and both were brought to trial.[33]

Trixie Perry took the stand in a dress sewn from red, white, and blue bunting and a cap made of a small American flag. The prosecuting attorney began his cross-examination:

> "You have a United States flag as a cap on
>   your head?"
> "Yes."
> "Wear it all the time?"
> "Whenever I take a notion."
> "You are dressed in a United States flag,
>   and the colors?"
> "I guess so, I was born under it, guess I
>   have a right to."

The main charge was that Perry and her friend had drawn a line across the road at Gap Creek and dared the soldiers to cross it. Above all they were accused of taunting the National Guard. The defense attorney, a fiery local lawyer playing to a sympathetic crowd, did not deny the charges. Instead, he used the women to mock the government's case. Had Trixie Perry threatened a lieutenant? "He rammed a gun in my face and I told him to take it out or I would knock it out." Had she blocked the road? "A little thing like me block a big road?" What had she said to the threat of a tear gas bomb? "That little old fire cracker of a thing, it won't go off."[34]

Texas Bill was an even bigger hit with the crowd. The defense attorney called her the "Wild Man from Borneo." A guard said she was "the wildest human being I've ever seen." Texas Bill both affirmed and subverted her reputation. Her nickname came from her habit of wearing "cowboy" clothes. But when it was her turn to testify, she "strutted on the stand" in a fashionable black picture hat and a black coat. Besides her other transgressions, she was accused of grabbing a soldier's gun and aiming it at him. What was she doing on the road so early in the morning? "I take a walk every morning before breakfast for my health," Texas replied with what a reporter described as "an assumed ladylike dignity."[35]

Witnesses for the prosecution took pains to contradict Texas Bill's "assumed ladylike dignity." A guardsman complained that she called him a "'God damned yellow son-of-a-bitch,' and then branched out from that." Texas offered no defense: "When that soldier stuck his gun in my face, that did make me mad and I did cuss a little bit and don't deny it." Far from discrediting the strikers, the soldiers' testimony added to their own embarrassment and the audience's delight. In tune with the crowd, the defense attorney "enjoyed making the guards admit they had been 'assaulted' . . . by 16- and 18-year-old girls."[36]

Mock gentility, transgressive laughter, male egos on the line—the mix made for wonderful theater, and proved effective in court as well. The judge reserved maximum sentences for three especially aggressive men; all the women and most of the men were found not guilty or were lightly fined. In the end even those convictions were overturned by the state court of appeals.[37]

Trixie Perry and Texas Bill certainly donned the role of "disorderly woman." Since, presumably, only extraordinary circumstances call forth feminine aggression, women's assaults against persons and property constitute a powerful witness against injustice. At the same time, since women are considered less rational and taken less seriously than men, they may meet less resistance and be punished less severely for their crimes.[38]

But Trixie Perry and Texas Bill were not just out of line in their public acts; they also led unconventional private lives. It was this erotic subtext that most horrified officialdom and amused the courtroom crowd. The only extended discussion of the strike that appears in the city council minutes resulted in a resolution that read in part:

WHEREAS, it has come to [our] attention . . . that the moral tone of this community has been lowered by reason of men and women congregating in various houses and meeting-places in Elizabethton and there practicing lewdness all hours of the night, in defiance of morality, law and order. . . .

NOW, THEREFORE, BE IT RESOLVED, that the police force of the City arrest and place in the City Jail those who are violating the laws by practicing lewdness within the City of Elizabethton. . . .[39]

Union representatives apparently shared, indeed anticipated, the councilmen's concern. Worried by rumors that unemployed women were resorting to prostitution, they had already announced to the press that 25 percent of the strikers had been sent back to their hillside homes, "chiefly young single girls whom we want to keep off the streets." The townsmen and the trade unionists were thus united in drawing a line between good women and bad, with respectability being measured not only by chastity but by nuances of style and language as well.[40] In the heat of the trial, the question of whether or not women—as workers—had violated the injunction took second place to questions about their status as women, as members of their sex. Had they cursed? Had they been on the road at odd hours of the day or night? Was Texas Bill a lady or a "wild man from Borneo"? Fearing that "lewd women" might discredit the organizing drive, the organizers tried to send them home. To protect the community's "moral tone," the city council threatened to lock them up.

There is nothing extraordinary about this association between sexual misbehavior and women's labor militancy. Since strikers are often young single women who violate gender conventions by invading public space customarily reserved for men (and sometimes frequented by prostitutes)—and since female aggressiveness stirs up fears of women's sexual power—opponents have often undercut union organizing drives by insinuations of prostitution or promiscuity. Fearing guilt by association, "respectable" women stay away.[41]

What is impressive here is how Trixie Perry and Texas Bill handled the dichotomy between ladyhood and lewdness, good girls and bad. Using words that, for women in particular, were ordinarily taboo, they refused deference and signaled disrespect. Making no secret of their sexual experience, they combined flirtation with fierceness on the picket line and adopted a provocative courtroom style. And yet, with the language of dress—a cap made of an American flag, an elegant wide-brimmed hat—they claimed their rights as citizens and their place in the female community.

Moreover, that community upheld their claims. The defense attorney chose unruly women as his star witnesses, and the courtroom spectators enthusiastically cheered them on. The prosecuting attorney recommended dismissal of the charges against all the women on trial except Trixie Perry, Texas Bill, and a "hoodlum" named Lucille Ratliffe, on the grounds that the rest came from "good families." Yet in the court transcripts, few differences can be discerned in the behavior of good girls and bad. The other female defendants may have been less flamboyant, but they were no less sharp-tongued. Was Vivian King a member of the UTW? "Yes, and proud of it." Had she been picketing? "Yes, proud of that." What was a young married woman named Dorothy Oxindine doing on Gap Creek at five o'clock in the morning? "Out airing." Did Lena May Jones "holler out 'scab'"? "No, I think the statement made was 'I wouldn't be a scab' and 'Why don't you come and join our organization.'" Did she laugh at a soldier and tell him his gun wouldn't shoot? "I didn't tell him it wouldn't shoot, but I laughed at him . . . and told him he was too much of a man to shoot a lady."[42]

Interviewed over fifty years later, strike participants still refused to make invidious distinctions between themselves and women like Trixie Perry and Texas Bill. Bessie Edens was a settled, self-educated, married woman. But she was also a self-described "daredevil on the picket line," secure in the knowledge that she had a knife hidden in her drawstring underwear. To Edens, who came from a mountain hamlet called Hampton, the chief distinction did not lie between herself and rougher women. It lay between herself and merchants' wives who blamed the trouble on "those hussies from Hampton." When asked what she thought of Trixie Perry and Texas Bill, she answered simply, "There were some girls like that involved. But I didn't care. They did their part."[43]

Nettie Reece, who lived at home with parents who were "pretty particular with [their] daughters," shared Bessie Edens's attitude. After passing along the town gossip about Trixie Perry, she was anxious to make sure her meaning was not misconstrued. "Trixie was not a woman who sold her body," she emphasized. "She just had a big desire for sex. . . . And when she had a cause to fight for, she'd fight." Reece then went on to establish Perry's claim to a certain kind of respectability. After the strike Perry became a hard-working restaurant cook. She was a good neighbor: "If anybody got sick, she was there to wait on them." The children she bore out of wedlock did well in life, and they "never throwed [their mother] aside."[44]

Industrialization, as we know, changed the nature of work, the meaning of time. In Carter County it entailed a shift of economic and political power from the countryside to the town. At issue too were more intimate matters of fantasy, culture, and style.

Implicit in the conflict were two different sexual systems. One, subscribed to by union officials and the local middle class, mandated chastity before marriage, men as breadwinners, and women as housewives in the home. The other, rooted in a rural past and adapted to working-class life, recognized liaisons established without the benefit of clergy or license fees and allowed legitimacy to be broadly construed. It was unfamiliar with—or pragmatic about—prostitution. It circumscribed women's roles without investing in abstract standards of femininity. It was, in short, a society that might produce a Trixie Perry or defend "hussies from Hampton" against the snubs of merchants' wives.

This is not to say that the women of Elizabethton were simply acting on tradition. On the contrary, the strikers dressed the persona of the disorderly woman in unmistakably modern garb. Women's behavior on the witness stand presupposed a certain sophistication: A passing familiarity allowed them to parody ladyhood and to thumb a nose at the genteel standards of the town. Combining garments from the local past with fragments of an expansive consumer culture, the women of Elizabethton assembled their own version of a brash, irreverent Jazz Age style.

By the early 1920s radios and Model Ts had joined railroads and mail-order catalogs as conduits to the larger world. Record companies had discovered hill-country music and East Tennessee's first country-music stars were recording hits that transformed ballad singing, fiddle playing, and banjo picking into one of America's great popular-music sounds. The banjo itself was an Afro-American instrument that had come to the mountains with the railroad gangs. Such cultural interchanges multiplied during the 1920s as rural traditions met the upheavals of industrial life. The result was an explosion of musical creativity—in the hills of Tennessee no less than in New York City and other cosmopolitan centers.[45] Arriving for work in the rayon plants, young people brought with them the useable past of the countryside, but they quickly assimilated the speeded-up rhythms of a changing world.

Work-related peer groups formed a bridge between traditional loyalties and a novel youth culture. Whether married or single, living with parents or on their own, women participated in the strike in same-sex groups. Sisters boarded, worked, and demonstrated together. Girlfriends teamed up in groups or pairs. Trixie Perry and Texas Bill were a case in point. But there were others as well. Nettie Reece joined the union with her parents' approval but also with her whole school girl gang in tow. Ethel and M. C. Ashworth, ages eighteen and seventeen, respectively, came from Virginia to work in the plants. "Hollering and singing [in a] Ford touring car," they were arrested in a demonstration at Watauga Point. Ida and Evelyn Heaton boarded together on Donna Avenue. Evelyn Heaton was hit by a car on the picket line, swore out a warrant, and had the commander of the National Guard placed under arrest. After the strike she was black-listed, and Ida attended the Southern Summer School.[46]

The sudden gathering of young people in the town nourished new patterns of heterosociability, and the strike's erotic undercurrent surfaced not only in Trixie Perry's "big desire for sex" but also in the behavior of her more conventional peers. The loyalties of the national guardsmen were divided, but their sympathy was obvious, as was their interest in the female strikers. Most of the Elizabethton women were in their teens or early twenties, the usual age of marriage in the region, and the strike provided unaccustomed opportunities for courtship. Rather than choosing a neighbor they had known all their lives, under watchful parental eyes, women flirted on the picket lines or the shop floor. Romance and politics commingled in the excitement of the moment, flowering in a spectrum of behavior—from the outrageousness of Trixie Perry to a spate of marriages among other girls.

What needs emphasis here is the dynamic quality of working-class women's culture—a quality that is sometimes lost in static oppositions between modernism and traditionalism, individualism and family values, consumer and producer mentalities. This is especially important where regional history has been so thoroughly mythologized. Appalachian culture, like all living cultures, embraced continuity and discontinuity, indigenous and borrowed elements.[47] As surely as Anna Weinstock—or Alabama's Zelda Fitzgerald—or any city flapper, the Elizabethton strikers were "new women," making their way in a world their mothers could not have known but carrying with them values handed down through the female line.

Two vignettes may serve to illustrate that process of grounded change.

Flossie Cole's mother, known by everyone on Stoney Creek as "Aunt Tid," was Sheriff Moreland's sister, but that didn't keep her from harboring cardplayers, buckdancers, and whiskey drinkers in her home. Aunt Tid was also a seamstress who "could look at a picture in a catalog and cut a pattern and make a dress just like it." But like most of her friends, Cole jumped at the chance for store-bought clothes: "That first paycheck, that was it . . . I think I bought me some new clothes with the first check I got. I bought me a new pair of shoes and a dress and a hat. Can you imagine someone going to a plant with a hat on? I had a blue dress and black shoes—patent leather, honey, with real high heels—and a blue hat." Nevertheless, before Cole left home in the morning for her job in the rayon plant, Aunt Tid made sure that around her neck—beneath the new blue dress—she wore a bag of asafetida, a strong-smelling resin, a folk remedy to protect her from diseases that might be circulating in the town.[48]

Second, there is visual evidence: a set of sixteen-millimeter films made by the company in order to identify—and to blacklist—workers who participated in the union. In those films groups of smiling women traipse along the picket line dressed in up-to-date clothes.[49] Yet federal conciliator Anna Weinstock, speaking to an interviewer forty years later, pictured them in sunbonnets, and barefooted. "They were," she explained, "what we would normally call hillbillies": women who "never get away from their shacks."[50] This could be seen as the treachery of memory, a problem of retrospection. But it is also an illustration of the power of stereotypes, of how cultural difference is registered as backwardness, of how images of poverty and backwardness hide the realities of working-class women's lives.

The strike, as we know, was defeated. Participants were blacklisted. The Great Depression settled over the mountains, rekindling reliance on older ways of making do. Flossie Cole, for instance, had been new to factory labor, but she was no stranger to women's work. While her brothers had followed their father's lead to the coal mines, she had pursued the two most common occupations of the poorest mountain girls: agricultural labor and domestic service. "We would hire out and stay with people until they got through with us and then go back home. And when we got back home, it was workin' in the corn or wash for people." When Cole lost her job after the strike she went back to domestic service, "back to the drudge house," as she put it.[51]

Young women had poured eagerly into the rayon mills, drawn at least in part by the promise of independence, romance and adventure. As hard times deepened, such motives paled beside stark necessity. Two statistics make the point: The percentage of Carter County women who were gainfully employed held steady through the thirties. But by the end of the period a larger proportion than before worked as servants in other people's homes. When Flossie Cole went "back to the drudge house," she had plenty of company.[52]

Still, despite subsequent hardships, the spirit of the 1920s flickered on. Setting out to explore the strike through oral-history interviews, we expected to find disclaimers or silences. Instead, we heard unfaded memories and no regrets. "I knew I wasn't going to get to go back, and I didn't care," said Bessie Edens. "I wrote them a letter and told them I didn't care whether they took me back or not. I didn't! If I'd starved I wouldn't of cared, because I knew what I was a'doing when I helped to pull it. And I've never regretted it in any way. . . . And it did help the people, and it's helped the town and the country."[53] For those, like Edens, who went on to the Southern Summer School or remained active in the union, the strike was a pivot around which the political convictions and personal aspirations of a lifetime turned. For them, there were intangible rewards: a subtle deepening of individual power, a belief that they had made history and that later generations benefited from what they had done.

The strike, of course, made a fainter impression on other lives. Women's rebelliousness neither redefined gender roles nor overcame economic dependency. Their desire for the trappings of modernity could blur into a self-limiting consumerism. An ideology of romance could end in sexual danger or a married woman's burdensome double day. Still, the women of Elizabethton left a legacy. A norm of female public work, a new style of sexual expressiveness, the entry of women into public space and political struggles previously monopolized by men—all these pushed against traditional constraints even as they created new vulnerabilities. The farm daughters who left home for the rayon plants pioneered a new pattern of female experience, and they created for their post–World War II daughters an environment far different from the one they, in their youth, had known. It would be up to later generations to wrestle with the costs of commercialization and to elaborate a vision that embraced economic justice and community solidarity as well as women's liberation.

Notes

This study began as a collaborative endeavor with Sara Evans of the University of Minnesota, who helped to gather many of the interviews on which I have relied. Rosemarie Hester and Jennifer Dowd also joined me on trips to the mountains, and I benefited from their companionship, ideas, and research. I owe a special debt to Christopher Daly, Lu Ann Jones, Robert Korstad, James Leloudis, and Mary Murphy, with whom I have co-written *Like a Family: The Making of a Southern Cotton Mill World* (Chapel Hill, 1987).

1. Dan Crowe, *Old Town and the Covered Bridge* (Johnson City, Tenn., 1977), pp. 32, 71; Florence (Cole) Grindstaff interview by Jacquelyn Hall, July 10, 1981 (in Hall's possession).

2. For this strike wave, see Tom Tippett, *When Southern Labor Stirs* (New York, 1931); James A. Hodges, "Challenge to the New South: The Great Textile Strike in Elizabethton, Tennessee, 1929," *Tennessee Historical Quarterly* 23 (Dec. 1964):343–57; . . .

3. Contemporary observations include, *Knoxville News Sentinel*, May 17, 1929; Florence Kelley, "Our Newest South," *Survey*, June 15, 1929, pp. 342–44; . . .

4. Anne Firor Scott, "On Seeing and Not Seeing: A Case of Historical Invisibility," *Journal of American History* 71 (June 1984):7–8.

5. Natalie Zemon Davis, *Society and Culture in Early Modern France* (Stanford, 1975), pp. 124–51. . . .

6. Michel Foucault, *Power/Knowledge: Selected Interviews and Other Writings, 1972–1977*, trans. and ed. Colin Gordon (New York, 1980), p. 81.

7. Joseph Leeming, *Rayon: The First Man-Made Fiber* (Brooklyn, 1950), pp. 1–82; Jesse W. Markham, *Competition in the Rayon Industry* (Cambridge, Mass., 1952), pp. 1–38, 97, 186, 193, 209.

8. Bruce Roberts and Nancy Roberts, *Where Time Stood Still: A Portrait of Appalachia* (New York, 1970); William Goodell Frost, "Our Contemporary

Ancestors in the Southern Mountains," *Atlantic Monthly* 83 (March 1899):311; Arnold J. Toynbee, *A Study of History*, 2 vols. (New York, 1947), II: 312; . . .

9. For this preindustrial economy, and its transformation, see Eller, *Miners, Millhands, and Mountaineers*, pp. 3–38, 86–127. . . .

10. *Mountaineer*, Dec. 28, Dec. 31, 1887.

11. U.S. Department of the Interior, Census Office, *Report on the Productions of Agriculture as Returned at the Tenth Census* (June 1, 1880) (Washington, 1883), pp. 84–85, 132, 169; U.S. Department of Commerce, Bureau of the Census, *Fourteenth Census of the United States Taken in the Year 1920: Agriculture*, vol. VI, pt. 2 (Washington, [D.C.,] 1922), pp. 446–47.

12. Holly, "Elizabethton, Tennessee," pp. 123, 133–38, 156, 198; U.S. Congress, Senate, Committee on Manufactures, *Working Conditions of the Textile Industry in North Carolina, South Carolina, and Tennessee*, 71 Cong., 1 sess., May 8, 9, and 20, 1929, p. 95; Henry Schuettler interview by Hall, n.d. [1981] (in Hall's possession).

13. Thirteenth Census of the United States, 1910, Manuscript Population Schedule, Carter County, Tenn., district 7; ibid., district 15; ibid., district 10; ibid., district 12.

14. Grindstaff interview.

15. *Scraps of Work and Play*, Southern Summer School for Women Workers in Industry, Burnsville, N.C., July 11–Aug. 23, 1929, typescript, pp. 21–22, 24, box 111, American Labor Education Service Records (Martin P. Catherwood Library, New York State School of Industrial and Labor Relations, Cornell University, Ithaca, N.Y.); Bessie Edens interview by Mary Frederickson, Aug. 14, 1975, pp. 1–2, 31–32, Southern Oral History Program Collection, Southern Historical Collection (Wilson Library, University of North Carolina at Chapel Hill) [hereafter SOHP].

16. Edens interview, Aug. 14, 1975, p. 32; Grindstaff interview.

17. Nettie Reece [pseud.] interview by Hall, May 18 and 19, 1983 (in Hall's possession).

18. *Knoxville News Sentinel*, May 13, 1929; *American Bemberg Corporation* v. *George Miller, et al.*, East Tennessee District Supreme Court, Jan. 29, 1930, record of evidence, typescript, box 660 (Tennessee State Library and Archives, Nashville) [hereafter Record of Evidence]. . . .

19. *Knoxville News Sentinel*, Mar. 14, 1929; Christine (Hinkle) Galliher and Dave Galliher interview by Hall, Aug. 8, 1979, pp. 8–9, SOHP; Tom Tippett, "Southern Situation," speech typescript, meeting held at the National Board, May 15, 1929, p. 3, box 25, Young Women's Christian Association Papers, Sophia Smith Collection (Smith College, Northampton, Mass.); Tom Tippett, "Impressions of Situation at Elizabethton, Tenn., May 10, 11, 1929," typescript, p. 1, ibid.

20. *Knoxville News Sentinel*, Mar. 20, Mar. 29, 1929; "Instructions for Adjustment of Wage Scale for Girl Help," Mar. 15, 1929, Records of the Conciliation Service, RG 280 (National Archives); Committee of Striking Workers[,] Members of United Textile Workers of America to the Honorable Herbert Hoover, Apr. 16, 1929, ibid; "Preliminary Report of Commissioner of Conciliation," Apr. 16, 1929, ibid.

21. Dr. J. A. Hardin to Hon. H. H. Horton, May 16, 1929, box 12, Governor Henry H. Horton Papers

(Tennessee State Library and Archives); *Knoxville News Sentinel*, May 6, May 10, May 12, May 14, May 19, May 24, 1929.

22. Edens interview, Aug. 14, 1975, pp. 40, 49; Galliher interview, 33; *Knoxville News Sentinel*, Mar. 15, May 16, 1929.

23. *Knoxville News Sentinel*, May 27, 1929; Ina Nell (Hinkle) Harrison interview by Hall, Aug. 8, 1979, p. 2, SOHP; Mary Heaton Vorse, "Rayon Strikers Reluctantly Accept Settlement," press release, May 27, 1929, box 156, Mary Heaton Vorse Papers, Archives of Labor and Urban Affairs (Walter P. Reuther Library, Wayne State University, Detroit, Mich.).

24. "Rays of Sunshine in the Rayon War," *Literary Digest*, June 8, 1929, p. 12; *Charlotte Observer*, June 2, 1929; *Raleigh News and Observer*, May 24, 1929.

25. Edens interview, Aug. 14, 1975, pp. 43–44; Myrtle Simmerly interview by Hall, May 18, 1983 (in Hall's possession); Ollie Hardin interview by Hall and Sara Evans, Aug. 9, 1979 (in Hall's possession); Effie (Hardin) Carson interview by Hall and Evans, Aug. 6, 1979, p. 41, SOHP; Holly, "Elizabethton, Tennessee," 306–7.

26. James Myers, "Field Notes: Textile Strikes in the South," box 374, Archive Union Files (Martin P. Catherwood Library); *Raleigh News and Observer*, Mar. 15, 1929.

27. Hoffmann, "Mountaineer in Industry," 2–5; Robert (Bob) Moreland and Barbara Moreland interview by Hall, July 11, 1981 (in Hall's possession); *Knoxville News Sentinel*, Mar. 15, 1929; Honard Ward interview by Hall, n.d. [1981] (in Hall's possession).

28. *Knoxville News Sentinel*, May 15, 1929; Reece interview; . . .

29. For the argument that precisely because they are "left behind" by the economic developments that pull men into wage labor, woman-centered families may harbor alternative or oppositional values, see Mina Davis Caulfield, "Imperialism, the Family, and Cultures of Resistance," *Socialist Revolution* 4 (Oct. 1974):67–85; . . .

30. Bessie Edens, "Why a Married Woman Should Work," in *Scraps of Work and Play*, pp. 30–31; Edens interview, Aug. 14, 1975, pp. 14, 21, 34–35; Bessie Edens interview by Hall, Aug. 5, 1979 (in Hall's possession); Millie Sample, "Impressions," Aug. 1931, box 9, American Labor Education Service Records.

31. Mirion Bonner, "Behind the Southern Textile Strikes," *Nation*, Oct. 2, 1929, pp. 351–52; "Scraps From Our Lives," in *Scraps of Work and Play*, pp. 5–11; . . .

32. Corbin, *Life, Work, and Rebellion*, pp. 92–93; Louise A. Tilly, "Paths of Proletarianization: Organization of Production, Sexual Division of Labor, and Women's Collective Action," *Signs* 7 (Winter 1981): 400–17; . . .

33. *Elizabethton Star*, Nov. 14, 1953, Jan. 31, 1986; Reece interview; Carson interview, 25; Nellie Bowers interview by Hall, May 15, 1983 (in Hall's possession); *Knoxville News Sentinel*, May 17, May 18, 1929.

34. Record of Evidence.

35. *Knoxville News Sentinel*, May 17, 1929.

36. Ibid.; Record of Evidence.

37. *American Bemberg Corporation* v. *George Miller, et al.*, minute books "Q" and "R," Chancery Court minutes, Carter County, Tenn., July 22, 1929

(Carter County Courthouse, Elizabethton, Tenn.); *American Bemberg Corporation* v. *George Miller, et al.,* Court of Appeals, #1, Sept. 5, 1930 (Supreme Court and Courts of Appeal, State of Tennessee, Knoxville).

38. Davis, *Society and Culture in Early Modern France,* pp. 124–51; Laurel Thatcher Ulrich, *Good Wives* (New York, 1982), pp. 191–97.

39. Elizabethton City Council, Minutes, May 23, 1929, Minute Book, vol. 5, pp. 356–57 (City Hall, Elizabethton, Tenn.).

40. *Knoxville News Sentinel,* May 5, 1929; Myers, "Field Notes." . . .

41. See, for instance, Alice Kessler-Harris, "The Autobiography of Ann Washington Craton," *Signs* 1 (Summer 1976):1019–37.

42. *Knoxville News Sentinel,* May 18, 1929; Record of Evidence.

43. Edens interview, Aug. 5, 1979.

44. Reece interview, May 19, 1983.

45. Charles K. Wolfe, *Tennessee Strings: The Story of Country Music in Tennessee* (Knoxville, 1977), pp. 22–90; Barry O'Connell, "Dick Boggs, Musician and Coal Miner," *Appalachian Journal* 11 (Autumn-Winter 1983–84):48.

46. *Miller's Elizabethton, Tenn., City Directory,* 1930; Reece interview; Record of Evidence; *Knoxville News Sentinel,* May 16, May 17, 1929; . . .

47. David E. Whisnant, *All That Is Native and Fine: The Politics of Culture in an American Region* (Chapel Hill, 1983), p. 48.

48. Grindstaff interview; Moreland interview.

49. *Knoxville Journal,* Apr. 22, 1929; sixteen-millimeter film (1 reel), ca. 1929, Helen Raulston Collection, Archives of Appalachia (East Tennessee State University, Johnson City); sixteen-millimeter film (20 reels), ca. 1927–1928, Bemberg Industry Records (Tennessee State Library and Archives). . . .

50. Anna Weinstock Schneider interview by Julia Blodgett Curtis, 1969, pp. 161, 166, 172–3, 177, Anna Weinstock Schneider Papers, box 1 (Martin P. Catherwood Library).

51. Grindstaff interview.

52. Bureau of the Census, *Fifteenth Census of the United States: 1930. Population,* vol. III, pt. 2 (Washington, [D.C.], 1932), p. 909; U.S. Department of Commerce, Bureau of the Census, *Sixteenth Census of the United States: 1940. Population,* vol. II, pt. 6 (Washington, [D.C.], 1943), p. 616.

53. Edens interview, Aug. 14, 1975, p. 50. . . .

DEVRA ANNE WEBER
Mexican Women on Strike in 1933: The Structure of Memory

Did you ever wish you could travel back in time and ask someone directly about a historical event? Historians can't time travel, but they can interview people. When interviews are conducted in order to archive and make them accessible, this methodology is called oral history. What do you think are the strengths and weaknesses of using oral history? Whose history can we access if we incorporate oral history rather than primarily using written documents? How do we account for selective or faulty memory?

Devra Anne Weber's article analyzes why oral history is such a powerful methodology and how even mis-rememberings or inaccurate accounts of the past can still tell us quite a bit. She analyzes oral history accounts of Mexican American women who engaged in a cotton strike in California in the 1930s. As you read this article, think about how the oral history accounts give us different insights into the past.

Excerpted from "Mexican Women on Strike: Memory, History and Oral Narratives" by Devra Anne Weber in *Between Borders: Essay on Mexicana/Chicana History,* ed. Adelaida R. Del Castillo (Encino, Calif.: Floricanto Press, 1990), pp. 175–200. Reprinted by permission of the author and publisher. Notes have been edited and renumbered.

Oral histories, more than any other historical source, pivot around the central if complex relationship between memory and history. Flowing from this relationship is the source of the richness, immediacy, and unique value of oral histories. But it is just this relation to memory which can be both frustrating and challenging to historians and readers of history.

Oral histories are shaped by two simultaneous dialogues. One occurs between the individual and his or her own memory. The other occurs with the interviewer. The relationship with the interviewer determines how much will be shared or what will be shared or, perhaps, altered or fabricated. This is shaped by the questions asked, the class, ethnicity, and gender of the two people, and the subjective elements of sensitivity and compatibility which may bridge or accentuate differences between them. The individual's dialogue with his or her own memory determines the internal structuring of the individual consciousness and the oral history created by this. Yet memory, reflecting the complexity of human beings, can be contradictory and contentious, as well as reflective, insightful, articulate, and perceptive. Most importantly, memory is ultimately faithful only to an internal logic of consciousness.

Oral histories are a crucial source for exploring the history of Mexican women. Oral histories provide some answers to fundamental questions about life and work, culture and cultural change, women's perceptions, values and consciousness which are unavailable from more traditional sources. Yet there are problems with oral sources. One is the problem of memory: a frequent lament is that oral histories are factually inaccurate and thus a poor historical source. Another problem arises from how oral sources are used. In our enthusiasm over these sources which carry us out of dusty archives and into the world, oral histories are often used without critical analysis. They are often used in historical reassessments which aim, in part, to reconnect people with their own history. Yet we all act within a framework of institutional relations, struggles and divisions, change and process. As a result, using oral histories uncritically and without reevaluating the overall historical framework may ultimately reinforce what we are trying to change—peoples' alienation from their own past—by including them in a written history only to relegate them to anecdotal and colorful bystanders watching the traditionally conceived parade of historical process march by in front of them.[1]

This [essay] will explore how oral histories can be used, with their strengths and their weaknesses. This will touch upon the obvious—of how oral narratives can yield information about daily life and work. It will also address how oral histories can help in understanding the consciousness of these women and how, in this case, factual inaccuracies, frustrating as they are, follow an inherent logic which can be revealing of the internal meaning of these narratives and lead us to a greater understanding of peoples' interpretation of these events. [My research] draws on a series of oral histories with Mexican women who were cotton pickers in California's San Joaquin Valley during the 1930s and participated in the 1933 cotton strike by over 18,000 workers. [Here I] focus on the oral narrative of Rosaura Valdez.[2]

Mrs. Valdez, born near Torreon, Mexico, was not atypical of women who were in the strike. She came from Mexico, where her father had been a *sembrador*, a small farmer or sharecropper, eking out a livable but bleak existence. She had barely reached adolescence when the Mexican revolution broke out in 1910. With the exception of a rebellious sister-in-law, neither she nor her immediate family participated in the revolution.[3] As with many noncombatants, her memories of the revolution were not of the opposing ideologies nor issues, but of hunger, fear and death. Fleeing the revolution, the family crossed the border into Texas and three years later settled in the Los Angeles *colonia* of Maravilla. By 1933, she was 24, married, with two children and lived in a small San Joaquin Valley town.[4]

The agricultural industry in which she worked was, by 1933, California's major industry and cotton the most rapidly expanding crop in the states cornucopia. Cotton depended on Mexican labor, and highly capitalized, large cotton ranches of over 300 acres dominated the industry and hired the largest number of agricultural workers in the state. Approximately 20,000 workers picked the 208,000 acres of San Joaquin Valley cotton. Social relations were shaped by the size and the managerial structure on the ranches. Mexican workers migrated annually to the San Joaquin Valley to live on private labor camps which were rural versions of company towns. Here they lived in company owned housing, bought from company stores to which many remained in perpetual debt, and on the larger ranches sent their children to company schools. Their work and daily lives were supervised by a racially structured hierarchy dominated by Anglo managers and foremen: below them were Mexican contractors who recruited the workers, supervised work, and acted as the intermediary between workers and their English speaking employers.[5]

With the onslaught of the depression, agricultural prices fell and growers slashed wages. Workers, who had received $1.25 per a hundred pounds of cotton in 1926, were now receiving only 60 cents for the same amount in 1933. In response—and despite the threat of deportation—Mexican farm workers went on strike in crop after crop in California, convulsing the agricultural industry and sending tremors through the San Joaquin Valley. Encouraged by the erroneous belief that they were included in section 7A of the National Recovery Act of the New Deal which guaranteed the right of workers to bargain collectively, they shut down the agricultural heartland of the biggest industry of California. The wave of strikes began in May in southern California, around Los Angeles, and by August spread north into the San Joaquin Valley. While under the banner of the Cannery and Agricultural Workers Industrial Union (CAWIU), the strikes were conducted largely by Mexican workers and Mexican organizers. Extensive familial and social networks among the workers acted as conduits in spreading the strike and galvanizing workers to walk out. Thus the spread and success of the strikes depended as much, if not more, on the family and social networks of the Mexican workers as it did on the small but effective and ambitious union.

In October the strike wave crested in the cotton fields of the San Joaquin Valley when 18,000 cotton pickers went on strike. The strike brought picking to a standstill over one hundred miles of the California cotton belt. Growers evicted strikers from their ranch homes and the evicted strikers formed ad hoc camps on empty land. The largest camp was near the town of Corcoran where 3,500 strikers congregated. Strikers formed mobile picket lines which paraded in front of selected ranches where some workers still picked. Growers, panicked by the realization that anticipated new workers would not be forthcoming to pick their crop, retaliated by organizing groups of armed vigilantes who worked with local law enforcement to stop picketing and intimidate strikers.

Workers were beaten and within two weeks growers had shot and killed three strikers.

As the intensity of the conflict escalated, the strike became the unintentional testing ground for the New Deal's as yet unclear agricultural policy. The federal government sent in food to starving strikers. George Creel, an arbitrator with the National Recovery Administration, was sent in to settle the strike. But the strikers held out for over a month before a negotiated settlement between growers, and the California, United States, and Mexican governments reached a compromised wage of 75 cents per one hundred pounds.[6]

Mexicanas were a vital part of the strike, and about half of the strikers at Corcoran were women. They ran the camp kitchen, cared for the children, and marched on picket lines. They distributed food and clothing. Some attended strike meetings and a few spoke at the meetings. And it was the women who confronted Mexican strikebreakers. In short, women were an essential element to this strike but have been basically obscured from its history. Mrs. Valdez went on strike and was on the picket lines. She was not a leader, but one of the many women who made the strike possible.

Before launching into the content of the oral histories, a word is in order about the voice, the tone of oral histories. How information is conveyed is often as important as what is said, and can emphasize or contradict the verbal message. Conversation and social interaction are a major part of women's lives and gesture and voice are crucial to these communications. The verbal message, the "song" of a story, is especially important for people with a strong oral tradition. . . . Oral traditions are often also an art form, drama and literature. Oral histories are often dramatic and move with a grace and continuity which embodies analytical reflections to communicate an understanding of social relations and the complexities of human existence.

Mrs. Valdez structured her oral history in the form of stories or vignettes. Most sections had distinct beginnings and endings, interrupted only if I interjected a question. She developed characters, villains and heroes, hardship and tragedy (but little comedy). How this story was constructed and its characters developed embodied her assessment of the conflict.

As she told her story, the characters developed voices of their own, each with separate and distinct tones and cadence which reflected, perhaps to some extent, their personalities but moreover her assessment of them and their role in the drama. Strike breakers, for example, spoke in high-pitched and pleading voices: the listener understood immediately that they were measly cowards. The strikers voices were a clear contrast, as they spoke in sonorous, deep, and steady tones: they had the voice of authority, seemed to represent a communal voice, and verbalized what Mrs. Valdez considered community values.

Mrs. Valdez's sense of collective values, later expressed in the collective action, either by strikers as a whole or by women, was expressed in a collective voice. At times individuals spoke in her stories: the grower, Mr. Peterson; her contractor, "Chicho" Vidaurri; and the woman leader "la Lourdes." But more often people spoke in one collective voice which transcended the individual. This sense of community as told through the voices became a central feature of her narrative and permeated everything she said about the strike. Thus, in effect, a sense of unanimity permeated her story: an analysis of solidarity and clear cut division. In short, how she told the story underlined, accentuated and modified the meaning of the story itself.[7]

The "story" she told conveyed not only the "facts" as she remembered them but also conveyed nonverbal analysis. Mrs. Valdez's voice, gestures, and inflections conveyed both implications and meanings. She gestured with her arms and hands—a flat palm hard down on the table to make a point, both hands held up as she began again. Her "stories" had clear beginnings and often ended with verbal punctuations such as "and that's the way it was." She switched tenses around as in the heat of the story the past became the present and then receded again into the past. Vocal inflections carried a tonal counterpoint to her words as they jumped, vibrated, climbed, and then descended on the tone of her voice.

Mrs. Valdez's memories of the 1933 strike focused on two major concerns: providing and caring for her family and her role as a striker. How she structured these memories reveals something about her perceptions and her consciousness as a woman, a Mexican, and a worker. Her memories of the strike focused on the collectivity of Mexicans and, within this, the collectivity of Mexican women.

Mrs. Valdez's narrative suggests a sense of national identity which is an important underpinning to her narrative and reflects the importance of national cohesion against an historic background of Anglo-Mexican hostility. Mrs. Valdez vividly recounted the story of the United States' appropriation of Mexican land in 1848 and the Treaty of Guadalupe Hidalgo which ceded the area to the United States. She drew from stories of Mexican rebellion against U.S. rule in California and the nineteenth-century California guerrillas, Tiburcio Vasquez and Joaquin Murietta: the knowledge that Mexicans were working on the land which once belonged to Mexico increased her antagonism towards Anglo bosses. Mrs. Valdez may well have felt like Mrs. Martinez who, upon arriving at the valley, pointed out to her son and told him "Mira lo que nos arrebataron los bárbaros."[8]

The Mexican revolution of 1910 to 1920 influenced strikers in several ways. Only a few years away from the revolution, most Mexicans on strike had lived through the revolution and, some, the reverberations and conflicts which rocked Mexico in its wake. For many, such as Mrs. Valdez, their memories of the revolution were of hunger, death, and disruption. Yet the legacy of the revolution was important in several respects. The military experience was crucial in protecting the camp: often led by ex-military officers, Mexican veterans at the Corcoran camp formed a formidable armed security system which even the gun-happy growers shrank from attacking, and organized groups patrolled the roads to deter potential strikebreakers. Yet Mrs. Valdez remembers that the strike encouraged the recounting of stories of the revolution which were told, retold, and debated in the camp, punctuated by arguments between various factions of the revolution. The extent to which Mexicans employed the images and slogans of the revolution helped solidify a sense of community. Workers named the rough roads in the camp after revolutionary heroes and Mexican towns which suggested their common roots. Even Mrs. Valdez, whose individual memories of the revolution were primarily of the terror it held for her, shared in a collective memory of a national struggle and its symbols: Mrs. Valdez disdainfully compared the strikebreakers with the traitors who had "sold the head of Pancho Villa."

. . . Mrs. Valdez expressed a sense of collectivity among Mexicans. It needs to be pointed out that there were, in fact, many divisions among Mexicans: between different workers; between strikers and strikebreakers; between contractors and workers; between people from different areas of Mexico; and between people who had fought with different factions of the revolution or the Cristero movement in the 1920s. Yet working for Anglo bosses and the conflict of the strike emphasized an identification as Mexicans which overshadowed other divisions. This no doubt contributed to the recollection of many interviewed of an overall collectivity of Mexican strikers.

Mrs. Valdez's memories of the beginnings of the strike and the ensuing conflict with the grower suggest a sense of a collectivity as workers. On the Peterson ranch where Mrs. Valdez worked with her husband, the grower refused to meet strikers' demands for $1 for picking 100 pounds of cotton and workers walked out. The 150 workers who left the fields confronted their labor contractor ["Chicho"] Narciso Vidaurri. Mrs. Valdez recounted the confrontation between the interests of the workers, the grower and the contractor. All are represented with one voice.

> Chicho said, "You'd better go and work because if you don't go they're going to throw you out of the camp!"
>
> "So they throw us out! We're not afraid. But we won't pick any more unless they pay us to pick."
>
> Then he said, "He's (the grower, Peterson) not going to pay more and he wants the cabins vacated immediately in order to house other people who will pick."
>
> [Mrs. Valdez leaned forward and interjected her own comment into the dialogue:]
>
> But you think they could have gotten other people?! . . . When *everybody* was on strike? . . . Who would have picked?
>
> Then Chicho said, "Do what you think . . . If you want to work it's up to you. If you don't want to work, its up to you. The point is that those who won't work will be thrown out . . ."
>
> And the people said, "NONE OF US WILL WORK!!" Yes, that is what they said, "NONE OF US!!"
>
> Then old man Peterson asked him. "What did they say?" And he [Chicho] said, "They said no. That if one goes, they all go. That if one stays, they all stay. But they want more pay." . . . Peterson said, "No. No. They aren't going to be paid more."[9]

Within minutes, Peterson's men loaded the strikers' belongings onto trucks and dumped them onto the highway adjoining the ranch. The evicted strikers joined those evicted from other ranches on a plot of land on the outskirts of town. Within a week 3,500 strikers were camped at what became known as the Corcoran camp. The camp resembled a small town, larger than the adjacent town of Corcoran itself. Rows of cars attached to lean-tos formed rough roads in the camp, each corresponding to workers from a particular ranch. Workers formed a camp security force. The Circo Azteca, a small traveling circus unexpectedly stranded on the land, stayed through the strike and provided nightly entertainment and diversion. The camp became the hub of strike activity, the center for the CAWIU office on the west side of the San Joaquin Valley, the base for picket lines, a meeting place for daily strike meetings, and a visiting point, later, for government officials and the press.

Mrs. Valdez also remembered a collectivity of Mexican women. By 1933, Mexican women worked alongside men in the fields. They, as the men, were paid piece rates, 60 cents for each one hundred pounds of cotton picked. It required skill and experience to choose which bolls to pick and which to leave, to adroitly pick the bolls while avoiding twigs and dirt, and to pick rapidly enough to make money. Women picked, on the average, two hundred pounds per ten-hour day. Picking in the mile-long rows of cotton required strength, skill, and stamina:

> But let me describe to you what we had to go through. I'd have a twelve foot sack, about this wide. I'd tie the sack around my waist and the sack would go between my legs and I'd go on the cotton row, picking cotton and just putting it in there . . . So when we finally got it filled real good then we would pick up the [hundred pound] sack, toss [sic] it up on our shoulders, and then I would walk, put it up there on the scale and have it weighed, put it back on my shoulder, climb up a ladder up on a wagon and empty that sack in.[10]

Mrs. Valdez recounted the hardships which women faced in caring for their families: the houses without heat which contributed to disease; preparing food for her family without stoves, and cooking over fires in oil barrels. The issue of food played a central role in her memory. Getting enough food to eat could be a problem when wages were low, and the depression forced some women to forage for berries to eat. Others subsisted at times on flour and water. Food was an issue of survival. As in almost all societies, women were in charge of preparing the food and Mrs. Valdez's concern about food was repeated in oral histories with other women. While men recounted the depression and strike in terms of wages and conditions in general, women remembered these events in terms of food. This is not to say that men were oblivious or unconcerned. Rather it suggests that the woman's role in preparing food made this a central aspect of their consciousness and affected the way they perceived, remembered, and articulated the events of the strike.

Who Mrs. Valdez remembered as leaders is reflective of this sense of a community of women. When initially asked about leaders, Mrs. Valdez replied there were none. Later she named two, her labor contractor Chicho Vidaurri and Lourdes Castillo. Chicho she considered a leader, in the sense of someone you go to resolve problems, get help from, and use as a resource. This indeed fits, in many respects, the role that contractors played on the camps. But within the strike, Chicho was replaced in her memory by Lourdes Castillo. Lourdes is an interesting choice for several reasons.

Most obviously, Lourdes was a woman. But beyond that, Lourdes represented the transition which many Mexican women were undergoing during the process of the revolution, migration, and change in work. The Mexican revolution had convulsed Mexican families and, with it, the role of women. Women left alone to fend for themselves took care of farming [and] the family; [they] often migrated; and women sometimes fought on their own. The "soldaderas" were camp followers who went with men of all factions into battle. Most cooked, nursed, and provided sexual and emotional comfort. But some fought and were even executed in the course of battle. This image of "la soldadera," the woman fighting on behalf of the Mexican community as a whole, was praised as a national symbol of strength and resistance. Yet it was an ambivalent precedent. For while soldaderas may have fought in the revolution, in so doing they broke with traditional values. Thus while people praised the *image* of the *soldadera* within the context of an often mythified revolution, they were critical of the relative sexual freedom and independence which accompanied it. The term "soldadera" became double edged and, when used against individual women, was at times synonymous with "whore."

Ambivalence about independent women followed Mexicanas to the United States. The gender mores of the United States differed in some respects from rural Mexico. Some of these changes were cosmetic. Women bobbed their hair, adopted new dress, wore make up. But such changes reflected a changing gender division of labor. In the United States women began to work for wages. Often these were the younger, unmarried women who worked in canneries or garment factories unobserved by watchful male relatives.[11]

Some moved out of their family houses. And some women became financially independent, running bars and *cantinas,* often to support their children. Financial independence and a changing gender division of labor outside the house altered expectations of women's responsibilities and obligations. Women who adopted these new ways, either in appearance or through financial or social independence still risked . . . [disapproval from] segments of the community, male and female.

Lourdes Castillo was an attractive, single woman who lived in the town of Corcoran. She wore make up, bobbed her hair, and wore stylish dresses. Financially independent, she owned and ran the local bar. Lourdes became involved with the strike when union organizers asked her to store food for the camp in her cantina. Mrs. Valdez remembers that Lourdes was in charge of keeping a log of who entered and left the camp and spoke at meetings. She was also in charge of distributing food.[12] Thus Lourdes reflects women's concern about food. At the same time she epitomized the cultural transition of Mexican women and the changing gender roles from pre-revolutionary Mexico to the more fluid wage society of California. Within the context of the strike, it was precisely her financial independence which enabled her to perform this function of storing and distributing the food. Mrs. Valdez's enthusiastic memories of Lourdes perhaps suggest Mrs. Valdez's changing values for women, even if not directly expressed in her own life.

While Mrs. Valdez described the abysmal conditions under which women labored, the women were active, not passive, participants in the strike. Women joined the daily picket lines which paraded in front of the cotton fields where strikebreakers picked. Older women still sporting the long hair and rebozos of rural Mexico, younger women who had adapted the flapper styles of the United States, and young girls barely into their teens rode together in trucks to the picket lines where they badgered strikebreakers into leaving the fields. Their activities on the picket line led women to set up make shift child care centers to care for children, and they established a camp kitchen which fed men without families.

As the weeks wore on women expanded their role. When, after three weeks growers still refused to settle, the women organized and led confrontations with Mexican strikebreakers which resulted in pitched battles. Mrs. Valdez remembers that the women decided that they, not the men, would enter the fields to confront strikebreakers. They reasoned that strikebreakers would be less likely to physically hurt the women.[13]

In organized groups, the women entered the field to talk to strikebreakers. The women appealed to strikebreakers on the grounds of the community good to leave the fields and join the strike. They appealed on class and national grounds—as "poor people" and "Mexicanos" to join the strike. Those from the same regions or villages in Mexico sought out compatriots to appeal to them on the basis of more localized, and usually stronger, loyalties. Those who refused to join the strike were denounced as a disgrace. . . .

Few strikebreakers left the fields, and exhortations turned to threats. A strikebreaker who had the audacity to work after being fed by the striking women in the camp was threatened with a painful poisoning if he tried to touch the food again. Talking turned to armed conflict. Women who had come armed with lead pipes and knives, in expectation of using these more persuasive methods if verbal appeals were unheeded, went after the strikebreakers. One ripped a cotton sack with a knife, emptying its contents onto the ground. Others began to hit the strikebreakers with the pipes, their fists, or whatever was handy.

Although strikers had felt that the women would not be hurt, the male strikebreakers retaliated, and at least one woman was brutally beaten.

> The same women who were in the trucks, who were in the . . . picket line . . . these women went in and beat up all those that were inside (the fields) picking cotton . . . They tore their clothes. They ripped their hats and the [picking] sacks . . . And bad. Ohhh! It was ugly! It was an ugly sight. I was just looking and said "No. No." I watched the blood flowing from them.
>
> [She imitated the strikebreakers' voice in a high-pitched, pleading tone.] "Don't hit us. Leave them [other strikebreakers] alone. Don't hit them."
>
> [Her voice drops as the collective voice of the strikers speak.] "Let them be set upon," she says.

> "If we are going cold and hungry then you should too," she says. "They're cowards . . . sell outs. Scum," she said.
>
> [Her voice rises as the strikebreakers continue their plea.] "Because we live far away, we come from Los Angeles . . . We need to have money to leave . . ."
>
> "Yes," she says [her voice lowers and slows as it again becomes the voice of the strikers] "We also have to eat and we also have family," she says. "But we are not sell outs!"

Several points in this passage underline the importance of the collectivity of women in Mrs. Valdez's memory. Mrs. Valdez's statement that the women went in because, at least in this instance, it was more women's business, suggests a sense that women were acting on behalf of the community. For Mrs. Valdez, it also carried a suggestion that it was the role of women to do this and that the men had little to do with the decision or even opposed it. "Because women take more chances. The men always hold back because they are men and all. But the women, no. The men couldn't make us do anything. They couldn't make us do anything (to prevent us from going) and so we all went off in a flash." She also focuses, again, on food: the confrontation between the women and strikebreakers focused on feeding their families. At this juncture, the two strands of her narration come together. Her memories of the need for strikers to stay together collectiv[ely are] presented in relationship to the availability of food. Of course this underlines a harsh reality: strikebreakers chose to continue to work in order to feed their families in the face of the depression; and without food, strikers would eventually be forced back to work. In any case, her recollection suggests not only the reality of this confrontation, but what Mrs. Valdez understood as the central strike issues and the strength of her support of the strike. . . . Discussions about staying on strike, discussions about negotiations were all couched in relation to food or the lack of food. Thus her concerns as a woman are underscored by her concerns in the strike. Her interests as a Mexican worker were considered, weighed, and expressed within the context of her interest as a woman, mother, and wife.

For Mrs. Valdez, food remained central in her memory of the strike. As the strike wore on, conditions grew harsher in the Corcoran camp. Growers lobbed incendiaries over the fence at night. Food became hard to get and at least one child died of malnutrition. About two weeks into the strike, partially in response to growing public concern about the killing of several strikers, California Governor Rolph overrode NRA regulations which stipulated that relief was not to be given to strikers not under arbitration, and, over the protestations of local boards of supervisors, sent in trucks of milk and other food to the embattled camp. Mrs. Valdez remembers nothing about the role of federal, state, or local relief agencies, but she remembered the foods brought in: "rice, beans, milk. . . . " At a meeting where Lourdes was talking to strikers, the issue of food, or the lack of food, was juxtaposed against their stance in the strike.

> She [Lourdes] was telling them that they might have to go hungry for awhile.
> "But look," she said, " . . . they are bringing us food. We'll each get just a little, but we're not going to starve," she says. "But don't leave. But don't ANYBODY go to work. Even if a rancher comes and tells you 'come on, let's go,' don't anybody go," she says. "Look, even if it's a little bit, we're eating. But we aren't starving. They're bringing us food."
> [Mrs. Valdez interjected.] They brought us milk and everything. Yes everybody that was working [in the strikers camp] were told not to go with any rancher. They were told not to believe any rancher. But everyone had to stand together as one. Everyone had an equal vote [in what was decided] . . . equal.

The themes of unity and the importance of women were carried over into her recollection of the final negotiations.

> The Portuguese [a growers' representative] told [the strikers' representative] that the ranchers . . . were going to have a meeting at [the strikers' camp] with "la Lourdes."
> "Yes," he says, . . . "We're going to pay you so much. All of us are going to sign so that then all of you can return to your camps to work."
> "Yes," said [the strikers' representative.] "But not a cent less. No. We won't go until we have a set wage. Then all of us go. But if there is something more [if there is more trouble] NONE of us go. Not even ONE of us leave the camp."
> [Mrs. Valdez leaned back and summed it up] And all that . . . And that's the way it was. That's the way it was.

The strike was settled, the ranchers had been beaten, and wages went up. Mrs. Valdez continued:

> They paid $2.50 per hundred pounds . . . Yes. Yes . . . Look, they were paid well. They were paid well for the hundred pounds. Forty cents wasn't

money. Forty cents for the hundred pounds wasn't money. But $2.50, I believe that is . . . And then the following year, three dollars, and then after three and a half. And then four.

Mrs. Valdez's account of the strike and the role of women in it was revealing. What she remembered, how she structured her memories, and the meaning she gave to them, in short, her consciousness and perception of events, tell us more about why Mexicanas supported the strike than interviews with leaders might have. Without the perceptions of women such as Mrs. Valdez it would be more difficult to understand the dynamics of the strike and why people supported it for over a month. [What] Rosaura Valdez remembered [about] her life as a farmworker, life in the Corcoran, daily activities on the picket lines, and strike leaders [is] unrecorded in written accounts.

Even more to the point, she remembers (or recounts) a collectivity of spirit and action among the Mexican striking community. In her telling of the story workers speak in a collective voice and act as a united group. She remembers little or no dissent. In her account, *all* the workers on the Peterson ranch walked out together to join the strike, *all* the women were on the picket lines, and *all* the strikers voted unanimously to stay on strike. Growers were also a united group, spoke with one voice, and were presented as a collective opposition. The lines between worker and grower were clearly drawn. Mrs. Valdez credits the solidarity of the strikers for the strike's success. . . .

Mrs. Valdez also focused on a largely female collectivity. She remembered the hardships of Mexican women. For Mrs. Valdez, as other women, getting enough food for her family was a constant theme. Perhaps this is why, in part, Lourdes stands out so clearly in her memories. . . . Women also stand out most vividly in her memories of the strike and picket lines. In her description of the women's decision to enter the fields she also implies a judgment about men and women, and she praised the women's cohesion as a group.

Women's participation in the strike also changed their self perception and aspects of their relations with their husbands and the community. A large part of this was implicit. Mrs. Valdez praised women for their role in the confrontation and described them as "brave," "tough," and "mean." Even some men admiringly remembered women who were brave and, in a denial that this was a female role at all, who "could fight like a man." Yet this admiration was evidently short lived or at best ambivalent. All of the women interviewed admiringly described the actions of *other* women, but denied that they had taken part in the beatings. This included one woman who, according to all other informants, had beaten strikebreakers with a lead pipe.

For Mrs. Valdez, her active participation in the strike provided some compensation for the hurts of a philandering and abusive husband. She was contemptuous of her husband who, while a striker, did not go on picket lines and thus was not, by her estimation, a "real striker." By implication it was the people on the picket line, picket lines composed largely of women, who were the real strikers. She also remembered the strikebreakers as being males. Thus the confrontations between strikebreakers and strikers was, in her memory, also a confrontation between men and women. In her memory, she pictures these conflicts as between authoritative and strong women representing the community, and simpering, pleading men who were betraying the women and the community as a whole.[14] Mrs. Valdez stated flatly that the women were braver than the men and men played little part in her narrative. She remembered female leadership, female participation, female concerns, and a largely female victory. While other interviews and sources may disagree, her narrative suggests something about Mrs. Valdez's reality of the strike of 1933.

What Mrs. Valdez didn't say was both revealing and suggestive of the limitations of oral narratives in writing history. Mrs. Valdez either did not know about or did not recount several crucial factors in the strike. Mrs. Valdez, as many other strikers interviewed, knew nothing of the CAWIU per se, despite daily strike meetings and the small CAWIU office, marked by a handwritten sign in Spanish hung loosely over a wooden table in the middle of the camp.[15] This was not confined to the women, as several men also knew nothing of the union. Perhaps the union didn't reach the strikers, or seemed irrelevant. Understandably, she also didn't recognize the names of Anglo strike leaders mentioned in accounts.

The role of the New Deal and the negotiations of the governments—Mexican, United States, and Californian—play no part in her narrative. She didn't know about or didn't remember that the Mexican consul, Enrique Bravo, visited the camp and talked to an assembly of strikers. She didn't recount visits by government officials nor threats to deport strikers. And she recounted nothing about the negotiations which led to the eventual settlement of the strike. Her memory of the strike was, in looking at the entire history, thus limited. Her memory of the strike settlement was also factually inaccurate. The wage at the beginning of the season had been set at 60 cents per one hundred pounds. The final settlement of the strike resulted in a compromise wage of 75 cents per hundred pounds. Yet Mrs. Valdez remembers the original pay as 40 cents and the settlement wage as $2.50.

Thus her narrative could be criticized as both incomplete and inaccurate. Yet her narrative has an underlying logic which is faithful to the overall structure of her memory, of her reality. Why is her memory inaccurate? In part she may have simply not known of some of the events, an interesting point in itself. But, as in the case of the wages, there are points she would have known but which she remembers, or recounts, inaccurately. Perhaps she confuses the 1933 wage increase with the wage increases of the 1940s. Perhaps it was a lapse of memory and a confusion with other events which we don't have sufficient information to fully understand. Or perhaps she wanted to make it clear how successful the strike had been. This would have been in keeping with other parts of her interview. A main theme throughout the narrative, for instance, is her emphasis on the complete unity of the Mexican workers. Yet there is clear evidence of tension and discord: the confrontations with the strikebreakers, the initial dispute with her contractor, [and] her own marital battles with her husband. Yet although Mrs. Valdez may even remember this discord, what she either remembered or at least told me—as the history of the strike—was an overwhelming unity. Her narration of the high wages makes the same point: that the strike was successful. It was her *interpretation* of the strike which ultimately structured how she remembered the strike, organized her facts, and recounted the outcome to me. Her factual inaccuracies may say as much if not more about what the strike *meant* to her than a careful rendition of the facts.

Mrs. Valdez's memories of the strike were similar to those of other women I spoke with. Like her, the women did not know about or recall the union, conventional strike leadership, or the role of the governments in ending the strike. Yet they expressed similar assumptions about the collective nature of the strike. . . .

Oral narratives thus reflect peoples' memory of the past: they can be inaccurate, contradictory, and show the influence of the passage of time and the effects of alienation. As people become more alienated from the meaning of their history, they tend to individualize their lives and experiences. For example, Michael Frisch points out that in Studs Terkel's book *Hard Times,* many of the people interviewed perceived the devastating effects of the [Great D]epression not as evidence of systemic collapse but as a manifestation of personal failure.[16] Certainly there are exceptions, people who have developed an historical perspective on their own lives, work, and society.

We confront the same problem of alienation when using oral narratives. How oral narratives are understood reflects the consciousness of the reader. Used uncritically, they are open to misinterpretation and may reinforce rather than alleviate the separation from a meaningful past. This is especially true of people who have been ignored by written history. Readers may have no concept of the history of Mexican working women, for example, and lack an historical framework within which to situate and understand their narratives. The filters of cultural and class differences and chauvinism may also be obstacles. And some may embrace these narratives as colorful and emotional personal statements while ignoring Mexican women as reflective and conscious participants in history.

As valuable as oral testimonies are, they are not a complete history nor can they, by themselves, address the problems of historical amnesia. To do this, oral narratives need to be interpreted and placed within an historical framework encompassing institutional and social relations, struggle, and change. Yet within this they provide a unique and invaluable historical source. Used critically, oral narratives can reveal the transformations in consciousness and culture over time. They can be used to place self conscious and reflective people in the front of the parade of the historical process. And, perhaps, they can help return to us all a greater understanding of our lives by reuniting us with the meaning of our past.

Notes

1. For intriguing discussions of these questions see: Michael Frisch, "The Memory of History,"

Radical History Review 25 (October 1981); Michael Frisch, "Oral History and *Hard Times*: A Review Essay," *Red Buffalo,* vols. 1 and 2, n.d.; Ronald J. Grele, *Envelopes of Sound: The Art of Oral History,* 2nd ed. (Chicago: Precedent, 1981).

2. All of the names used are pseudonyms. Interview by author with Rosaura Valdez, Hanford, California, January 1982. All but one of the women I spoke with had been born and partially raised in Mexico. Although all have lived in the United States over fifty years, all but one identified themselves as Mexicanas by birth, culture and ethnicity. The one woman born and raised in the United States referred to herself interchangeably as Mexicana and Chicana.

3. The sister-in-law is an interesting, if fragmentary, part of Mrs. Valdez's memory. From Mrs. Valdez's account, the sister-in law left her husband (Mrs. Valdez's brother) to join a group of revolutionaries, as a *compañera* of one of them. When she returned to see her children, she threatened to have the entire family killed by her new lover. It was in the wake of this threat that the family fled to the United States.

4. She and her husband migrated every year to pick grapes with their labor contractor, Narciso "Chicho" Vidaurri, and then returned to the town of Corcoran where they lived and worked on the Peterson ranch for around six months of every year. Their limited migration pattern was not atypical, but they were slightly more stable than many of the workers who migrated from southern California and worked in more crops.

5. In California, any piece of cultivated land over a few acres is consistently called a ranch. By 1933, the overwhelming majority of Mexican workers in cotton did not migrate annually from Mexico. Most had settled in neighborhoods in the Los Angeles area or in the Imperial Valley, adjacent to the Mexican border. Others migrated from Texas. Some of the younger pickers were citizens.

6. Paul S. Taylor and Clark Kerr, "Documentary History of the Cotton Strike," in U.S. Congress, Senate, Subcommittee of the Committee on Education and Labor, *Hearings on S. Res. 266. Violations of Free Speech and the Rights of Labor,* Report no. 1150, 77th Cong., 2nd Sess. (Washington, D.C.: Government Printing Office, 1942) pt. 4. See also Cletus Daniel, *Bitter Harvest: A History of California Farmworkers, 1870–1941* (Ithaca: Cornell University Press, 1981).

7. For those of you who are pausing to question her analysis, I want to emphasize that this is her analysis. I would disagree with her analysis of solidarity, and the disputes among strikers would I think bear this out. Nevertheless, the point here is that even if her historical analysis is questionable, it tells us a great deal about her conception of the strike and perhaps her conception of what I should be told about it.

8. "Look at what the barbarians have stolen from us." Interview by author with Guillermo Martinez, Los Angeles, April 1982.

9. The original Spanish for all translations in this essay is available in the endnotes of the essay as originally published.

10. Interview by author with Lydia Ramos, Fresno, California, June 1981.

11. Mrs. Valdez, in describing her brother who kept an eye on her during a dance in Maravilla, near Los Angeles, said that he watched her "in the style of those on the other side." In other words, she was aware that this "watchful" behavior had its roots in the other side, in Mexico, and was different from the mores in the United States.

12. It is unclear whether Lourdes did keep the log. In a brief interview, Lourdes confirmed that she spoke at meetings and distributed food.

13. It is unclear exactly who made this decision. Roberto Castro, a member of the central strike committee, said the strike committee made the decision that women should enter the fields to confront strikebreakers because the women would be less likely to be hurt. The women remembered no such decision and said that the women made the decision. It is hard to ferret out the origins of the idea.

Even if the strike committee made the decision, the action was in keeping with spontaneous decisions by women which both antedated and followed this strike. Mexican women in Mexico City and other parts of the republic had taken part in bread riots in the colonial period. They had fought in the revolution. And in California, later strikes, both in the 1930s, but also as recently as the 1980s, were punctuated by groups of Mexican women invading the fields to confront strikebreakers both verbally and physically.

14. It is not clear if this was correct or not. Given the tensions of the strike, it is possible that only the men went out to pick [as strikebreakers].

15. This may have been due to several factors. The union was small and had few organizers in the Valley. These were English speaking and relied on Mexicans, some of whom did join the union, to contact workers. This should not discount the role of the CAWIU, however. The union was crucial as a rallying point, and linked the disparate groups together, helped organize picket lines, wrote leaflets and played a role in publicizing the strike and in the final negotiations.

16. Michael Frisch, "Oral History and *Hard Times*," p. 231.

GENDERING THE NATION-STATE

NANCY F. COTT

Equal Rights and Economic Roles: The Conflict over the Equal Rights Amendment in the 1920s

The vote achieved, former suffragists turned their attention to sex-based discrimination in the law. To some, the proper strategy, as in suffrage, seemed to be a constitutional amendment affirming equal rights; men and women would have to be treated under the law as equals and as individuals. In contrast, suffragists who had struggled to pass legislation shortening hours and improving working conditions for women in industry had achieved that goal only because the Supreme Court was prepared to regard women as a special class of workers in need of governmental protection because of their childbearing role. (See the discussion of *Muller v. Oregon* in Sklar's essay, p. 357.) An equal rights amendment (ERA) would invalidate sex-based labor laws, they feared, since comparable protection would not be extended to men. The ensuing debate was a critical one creating deep and lasting divisions. Unable to agree on a unified agenda for four decades, veterans of the first women's movement expended energy in internal conflict, thereby diluting their political effectiveness. Not surprisingly women's issues made little headway until the 1960s.

The debate over the ERA was critical not only because of its long-term consequences, but because it highlighted differing views within feminism of the social significance of gender and the meaning of equality. Does equality require that men and women have the "same" rights and be subject to the "same" treatment, or does equality require "different" treatment? How should the law treat the difference created by women's unique reproductive system? With these questions in mind, Nancy F. Cott carefully assesses the initial debate over the ERA, making clear the assumptions and limitations inherent in the arguments of each side.

Campaigning for ratification of the Equal Rights Amendment during the 1970s, feminists who found it painful to be opposed by other groups of women were often unaware that the first proposal of that amendment in the 1920s had likewise caused a bitter split between women's groups claiming, on both sides, to represent women's interests. The 1920s conflict itself echoed some earlier ideological and tactical controversies. One central strategic question for the women's rights movement in the late nineteenth century had concerned alliances: should proponents of "the cause of woman" ally with advocates for the rights for

Nancy F. Cott, "Historical Perspectives: The Equal Rights Amendment in the 1920s," in *Conflicts in Feminism*, ed. Marianne Hirsch and Evelyn Fox Keller (London and New York: Routledge, Chapman, and Hall, part of the Taylor & Francis Group, 1990), pp. 44–59. Reprinted by permission of the author and publisher. Notes have been edited.

freed slaves, with temperance workers, or labor reformers, or a political party, or none of them? At various times different women leaders felt passionately for and against such alliances, not agreeing on what they meant for the breadth of the women's movement and for the priority assigned to women's issues.[1] The 1920s contest over the equal rights amendment reiterated that debate insofar as the National Woman's Party, which proposed the ERA, took a "single-issue" approach, and the opposing women's organizations were committed to maintaining multiple alliances. But in even more striking ways than it recapitulated nineteenth-century struggles the 1920s equal rights conflict also predicted lines of fracture of the later twentieth-century women's movement. The advantages or compromises involved in "multi-issue" organizing are matters of contemporary concern, of course. Perhaps more important, the 1920s debate brought into sharp focus (and left for us generations later to resolve) the question whether "equal rights"—a concept adopted, after all, from the male political tradition—matched women's needs. The initial conflict between women over the ERA set the goal of enabling women to have the same opportunities and situations as men against the goal of enabling women freely to be different from men without adverse consequences. As never before in nineteenth-century controversies, these two were seen as competing, even mutually exclusive, alternatives.

The equal rights amendment was proposed as a legal or civic innovation but the intrafeminist controversy it caused focused on the economic arena. Indeed, the connection between economic and political subordination in women's relation to men has been central in women's rights advocacy since the latter part of the nineteenth century. In the Western political tradition, women were historically excluded from political initiatives because they were defined as dependent—like children and slaves—and their dependence was read as fundamentally economic. Nineteenth-century advocates, along with the vote, claimed women's "right to labor," by which they meant the right for women to have their labor recognized, and diversified. They emphasized that women, as human individuals no less than men, had the right and need to use their talents to serve society and themselves and to gain fair compensation. Influential voices such as Charlotte Perkins Gilman's at the turn of the

century stressed not only women's service but the necessity and warrant for women's economic independence. Gilman argued simultaneously that social evolution made women's move "from fireside to factory" inevitable, and also that the move ought to be spurred by conscious renovation of outworn tradition.

By the 1910s suffragists linked political and economic rights, and connected the vote with economic leverage, whether appealing to industrial workers, career women or housewives. They insisted on women's economic independence in principle and defense of wage-earning women in fact. Since the vast majority of wage-earning women were paid too little to become economically independent, however, the two commitments were not identical and might in practice be entirely at odds.[2] The purpose to validate women's existing economic roles might openly conflict with the purpose to throw open economic horizons for women to declare their own self-definition. These tensions introduced by the feminist and suffrage agitation of the 1910s flashed into controversy over the equal rights amendment in the 1920s.

The ERA was the baby of the National Woman's Party, yet not its brainchild alone. As early as 1914, a short-lived New York City group called the Feminist Alliance had suggested a constitutional amendment barring sex discrimination of all sorts. Like the later NWP, the Feminist Alliance was dominated by highly educated and ambitious women in the arts and professions, women who believed that "equal rights" were their due while they also aimed to rejuvenate and reorient thinking about "rights" around female rather than only male definition. Some members of the Feminist Alliance surely joined the NWP, which emerged as the agent of militant and political action during the final decade of the suffrage campaign.[3]

A small group (engaging perhaps 5 percent of all suffragists), the NWP grew from the Congressional Union founded by Alice Paul and Lucy Burns in 1913 to work on the federal rather than the state-by-state route to woman suffrage. Through the 'teens it came to stand for partisan tactics (opposing all Democrats because the Democratic administration had not passed woman suffrage) and for flamboyant, symbolic, publicity-generating actions— large parades, pickets in front of the White House, placards in the Congress, hunger-striking in jail, and more. It gained much of its energy from leftwing radical women who were attracted to its wholesale condemnation of gender inequality and to its tactical adaptations from the labor movement; at the same time, its imperious tendency to work from the top down attracted crucial financial and moral support from some very rich women. When the much larger group, the National American Woman Suffrage Association, moved its focus to a constitutional amendment in 1916, that was due in no little part (although certainly not solely), to the impact of the NWP. Yet while imitating its aim, NAWSA's leaders always hated and resented the NWP, for the way it had horned in on the same pro-suffrage turf while scorning the NAWSA's traditional nonpartisan, educative strategy. These resentments festered into deep and long-lasting personal conflicts between leaders of the two groups.

Just after the 19th Amendment was ratified in August of 1920, the NWP began planning a large convention at which its members would decide whether to continue as a group and, if so, what to work for. The convention, held six months later and tightly orchestrated by chairman Alice Paul, brushed aside all other suggestions and endorsed an ongoing program to "remove all remaining forms of the subjection of women," by means of the elimination of sex discrimination in law.[4] At the outset, NWP leaders seemed unaware that this program of "equal rights" would be much thornier to define and implement than "equal suffrage" had been. They began surveying state legal codes, conferring with lawyers, and drafting numerous versions of equal rights legislation and amendments at the state and federal levels.

Yet the "clean sweep" of such an approach immediately raised a problem: would it invalidate sex-based labor legislation—the laws regulating women's hours, wages, and conditions of work, that women trade unionists and reformers had worked to establish over the past thirty years? The doctrine of "liberty of contract" between employer and employed had ruled court interpretations of labor legislation in the early twentieth century, stymying state regulation of the wages and hours of male workers. State regulation for women workers, espoused and furthered by many women in the NWP, had been made possible only by differentiating female from male wage-earners on the basis of physiology and reproductive functions. Now members of the NWP had to grapple with the question whether such legislation was sex "discrimination," hampering women

workers in the labor market. Initially, there was a great deal of sentiment within the NWP, even voiced by Alice Paul herself, that efforts at equal rights legislation should not impair existing sex-based protective labor legislation. However, there was also contrary opinion, which Paul increasingly heeded; by late November 1921 she had come to believe firmly that "enacting labor laws along sex lines is erecting another handicap for women in the economic struggle." Some NWP affiliates were still trying to draft an amendment that would preserve special labor legislation, nonetheless, and continued to introduce equal rights bills with "safeguards" in some states through the following spring.[5]

Meanwhile women leaders in other organizations were becoming nervous and distrustful of the NWP's intentions. Led by the League of Women Voters (successor to the NAWSA), major women's organizations in 1920 formed a national lobbying group called the Women's Joint Congressional Committee. The LWV was interested in eliminating sex discrimination in the law, but more immediately concerned with the extension of sex-based labor legislation. Moreover, the LWV had inherited NAWSA's hostility to Alice Paul. The first president of the LWV, Maud Wood Park, still smarted from the discomfiture that NWP picketing tactics had caused her when she headed the NAWSA's Congressional Committee from 1916 to 1920.[6] Other leading groups in the Women's Joint Congressional Committee were no less suspicious of the NWP. The National Women's Trade Union League since the mid-1910s had concentrated its efforts on labor legislation to protect women workers. Florence Kelley, director of the National Consumers' League, had been part of the inner circle of the NWP during the suffrage campaign, but on the question of protective labor laws her priorities diverged. She had spent three decades trying to get state regulation of workers' hours and conditions, and was not about to abandon the gains achieved for women.[7]

In December 1921, at Kelley's behest, Paul and three other NWP members met for discussion with her and leaders of the League of Women Voters, the National Women's Trade Union League, the Woman's Christian Temperance Union, and the General Federation of Women's Clubs. All the latter objected to the new constitutional amendment now formulated by the NWP: "No political, civil or legal disabilities or inequalities on account of sex, or on account of marriage unless applying alike to both sexes, shall exist within the United States or any place subject to their jurisdiction." Paul gave away no ground, and all left feeling that compromise was unlikely. Each side already thought the other intransigent, though in fact debate was still going on within the NWP.[8]

By mid-1922 the National Consumers' League, the LWV, and the Women's Trade Union League went on record opposing "blanket" equal rights bills, as the NWP formulations at both state and federal levels were called. About the same time, the tide turned in the NWP. The top leadership accepted as definitive the views of Gail Laughlin, a lawyer from Maine, who contended that sex-based labor legislation was not a lamented loss but a positive harm. "If women can be segregated as a class for special legislation," she warned, "the same classification can be used for special restrictions along any other line which may, at any time, appeal to the caprice or prejudice of our legislatures." In her opinion, if "protective" laws affecting women were not abolished and prohibited, "the advancement of women in business and industry will be stopped and women relegated to the lowest, worst paid labor."[9] Since NWP lobbyists working at the state level were making little headway, a federal constitutional amendment appeared all the more appealing. In November 1923, at a grand conference staged in Seneca Falls, New York, commemorating the seventy-fifth anniversary of Elizabeth Cady Stanton's Declaration of Sentiments, the NWP announced new language: "Men and women shall have equal rights throughout the United States and every place subject to its jurisdiction." The constitutional amendment was introduced into Congress on December 10, 1923.[10]

In the NWP view, this was the logical sequel to the 19th Amendment. There were so many different sex discriminations in state codes and legal practices—in family law, labor law, jury privileges, contract rights—that only a constitutional amendment seemed effective to remove them. The NWP took the language of liberal individualism, enshrined in the catchphrase of "equal rights," to express its feminism. As Alice Paul saw it, what women as a gender group shared was their subordination and inequality to men as a whole; the legal structure most clearly expressed this subordination and inequality, and therefore was the

logical point of attack. The NWP construed this agenda as "purely feminist," that is, appealing to women as women, uniting women around a concern common to them regardless of the other ways in which they might differ. Indeed, at its founding postsuffrage convention the NWP leadership purposely bypassed issues it saw as less "pure," including birth control, the defense of black women's voting rights in the South, and pacifism, which were predictably controversial among women themselves.

The NWP posited that women could and would perceive self-interest in "purely" gender terms. Faced by female opponents, its leaders imagined a fictive or abstract unity among women rather than attempting to encompass women's real diversity. They separated the proposal of equal rights from other social and political issues and effects. Although the campaign for equal rights was initiated in a vision of inclusiveness—envisioned as a stand that all women could take—it devolved into a practice of exclusiveness. The NWP's "appeal for conscious sex loyalty" (as a member once put it) went out to members of the sex who could subordinate identifications and loyalties of class, ethnicity, race, religion, politics, or whatever else to a "pure" sense of themselves as women differentiated from men. That meant principally women privileged by the dominant culture in every way except that they were female.[11]

In tandem with its lobbying for an equal rights amendment, the NWP presented its opposition to sex-based labor legislation as a positive program of "industrial equality." It championed women wage-earners who complained of "protective" legislation as restrictive, such as printers, railroad conductors, or waitresses hampered by hours limitation, or cleaning women fired and replaced by men after the passage of minimum-wage laws. Only a handful of working-class women rose to support for the ERA, however.[12] Mary Anderson, former factory worker herself and since 1919 the director of the U.S. Women's Bureau, which was founded to guide and assist women workers, threw her weight into the fight against the amendment. Male trade unionists—namely leaders of the American Federation of Labor— also voiced immediate opposition to the NWP aims, appearing at the very first U.S. Senate subcommittee hearings on the equal rights amendment. Male unionists or class-conscious workers in this period put their faith in collective bargaining and did not seek labor legislation for themselves, but endorsed it for women and child workers. This differentiation derived partly from male workers' belief in women's physical weakness and veneration of women's "place" in the home, partly from presumptions about women workers being difficult to organize, and also from the aim to keep women from competing for men's jobs. Male unionists tended to view wage-earning women first as women—potential or actual wives and mothers—and only secondarily as workers. For differing reasons women and men in the labor movement converged in their support of sex-based legislation: women because they saw special protection necessary to defend their stake in industry and in union organizations, limited as it was; men to hold at bay women's demands for equal entry into male-controlled union jobs and organizations.[13]

The arguments against the equal rights amendment offered by trade unionists and by such women's organizations as the League of Women Voters overlapped. They assumed that an equal rights amendment would invalidate sex-based labor laws or, at least, destine them for protracted argument in the courts, where judges had shown hostility to any state regulation of employer prerogatives. They insisted that the greatest good for the greatest number was served by protective labor laws. If sex-based legislation hampered some—as the NWP claimed, and could be shown true, for instance, in the case of women linotypists, who needed to work at night—then the proper tactic was to exempt some occupations, not to eliminate protective laws whole. They feared that state welfare legislation in place, such as widows' pensions, would also be at risk. They contended that a constitutional amendment was too undiscriminating an instrument: objectionable sex discriminations such as those concerning jury duty, inheritance rights, nationality, or child custody would be more efficiently and accurately eliminated by specific bills for specific instances. Sometimes, opponents claimed that the ERA took an unnecessarily federal approach, overriding states' rights, although here they were hardly consistent for many of them were at the same time advocating a constitutional amendment to prohibit child labor.

Against the ERA, spokeswomen cited evidence that wage-earning women wanted and valued labor legislation and that male workers, too, benefitted from limits on women's hours

in factories where men and women worked at interdependent tasks. Before hours were legally limited, "we were 'free' and 'equal' to work long hours for starvation wages, or free to leave the job and starve!" WTUL leader Pauline Newman bitterly recalled. Dr. Alice Hamilton, pioneer of industrial medicine, saw the NWP as maintaining "a purely negative program, . . . holding down in their present condition of industrial slavery hundreds of thousands of women without doing anything to alleviate their lot."[14] Trade-unionist and Women's Bureau colleagues attacked the NWP's vision as callously class-biased, the thoughtless outlook of rich women, at best relevant to the experience of exceptional skilled workers or professionals. They regularly accused the NWP of being the unwitting tool (at best) or the paid servant of rapacious employers, although no proof of the latter was ever brought forward. They heard in the NWP program the voice of the ruling class and denounced the equal rights amendment as "class" legislation, by and for the bourgeoisie.[15]

Indeed, at the Women's Bureau Conference on Women in Industry in 1926, the NWP's opposition to sex-based labor legislation was echoed by the president of the National Association of Manufacturers, who declared that the "handful" of women in industry could take care of themselves and were not served by legislative "poultices." In this controversy, the positions also lent themselves to, and inevitably were colored by, male "allies" whose principal concerns dealt less with women's economic or legal protection or advancement than political priorities of their own. At the same conference the U.S. Secretary of Labor appointed by President Coolidge took the side of sex-based protective legislation, proclaiming that "The place fixed for women by God and Nature is a great place," and "wherever we see women at work we must see them in terms of motherhood." What he saw as the great danger of the age was the "increasing loss of the distinction between manliness and true femininity."[16]

Often, ERA opponents who supported sex-based labor legislation—including civic-minded middle-class women, social welfare reformers, government officials, and trade union men—appeared more concerned with workingwomen's motherhood than with economic justice. "Women who are wage earners, with one job in the factory and another in the home have little time and energy left to carry on the fight to better their economic status. They need the help of other women and they need labor laws," announced Mary Anderson. Dr. Hamilton declared that "the great inarticulate body of working women . . . are largely helpless, . . . [and] have very special needs which unaided they cannot attain. . . ."[17] Where NWP advocates had before their eyes women who were eager and robust, supporters of protective legislation saw women overburdened and vulnerable. The former claimed that protective laws penalized the strong; the latter claimed that the ERA would sacrifice the weak. The NWP looked at women as individuals and wanted to dislodge gender differentiation from the labor market. Their opponents looked at women as members of families— daughters, wives, mothers, and widows with family responsibilities—and believed that the promise of "mere equality" did not sufficiently take those relationships into account. The one side tacitly positing the independent professional woman as the paradigm, the other presuming the doubly burdened mother in industry or service, neither side distinguished nor addressed directly the situation of the fastest-growing sector of employed women, in white-collar jobs. At least half of the female labor force—those in manufacturing and in domestic and personal service—worked in taxing, menial jobs with long hours, unpleasant and often unhealthy conditions, very low pay, and rare opportunities for advancement. But in overall pattern women's employment was leaving these sectors and swelling in clerical, managerial, sales, and professional areas. White-collar workers were fewer than 18 percent of all women employed in 1900, but the proportion more than doubled by 1920 and by 1930 was 44 percent.[18]

The relation of sex-based legislation to women workers' welfare was more ambiguous and complicated than either side acknowledged. Such laws immediately benefitted far larger numbers of employed women than they hindered, but the laws also had a negative impact on women's overall economic opportunities, both immediately and in the long term. Sex segregation of the labor market was a very significant factor. In industries monopolizing women workers, where wages, conditions, and hours were more likely to be substandard, protective legislation helped to bring things up to standard. It was in more desirable crafts and trades more unusual for women workers, where

skill levels and pay were likely to be higher— that is, where women needed to enter in order to improve their earnings and economic advancement—that sex-based protective legislation held women back. There, as a contemporary inquiry into the issue said, "the practice of enacting laws covering women alone appears to discourage their employment, and thereby fosters the prejudice against them." The segregation of women into low-paid, dead-end jobs that made protective laws for women workers necessary, was thus abetted by the legislation itself.[19]

By 1925, all but four states limited workingwomen's hours; eighteen states prescribed rest periods and meal hours; sixteen states prohibited night work in certain occupations; and thirteen had minimum wage regulations. Such regulation was passed not only because it served women workers, but also because employers, especially large corporate employers, began to see benefits in its stabilization of the labor market and control of unscrupulous competition. Although the National Association of Manufacturers, fixed on "liberty of contract," remained opposed, large employers of women accepted sex-based labor legislation on reasoning about "protection of the race," or could see advantages for themselves in it, or both. A vice-president of Filene's, a large department store in Boston, for instance, approved laws regulating the hours, wages, and conditions of women employees because "economies have been effected by the reduction of labor turnover; by reduction of the number of days lost through illness and accidents; and by increase in the efficiency of the working force as well as in the efficiency of management." He appreciated the legislation's maintaining standards as to hours, wages, and working conditions "throughout industry as a *whole,* thus preventing selfish interests from indulging in unfair competition by the exploitation of women. . . ."[20]

While the anti-ERA side was right in the utilitarian contention that protective laws meant the greatest good to the greatest number of women workers (at least in the short run), the pro-ERA side was also right that such laws hampered women's scope in the labor market and sustained the assumption that employment advantage was not of primary concern to women. Those who advocated sex-based laws were looking at the labor market as it was, trying to protect women in it, but thereby contributing to the perpetuation of existing inequalities. They envisaged wage-earning women as veritable beasts of burden. That group portrait supplanted the prior feminist image of wage-earning women as a vanguard of independent female personalities, as equal producers of the world's wealth. Its advocates did not see that their conception of women's needs helped to confirm women's second-class position in the economy. On the other hand, the ERA advocates who opposed sex-based "protections" were envisioning the labor market as it might be, trying to ensure women the widest opportunities in that imagined arena, and thereby blinking at existing exploitation. They did not admit to the vulnerabilities that sex-based legislation addressed, while they overestimated what legal equality might do to unchain women from the economic stranglehold of the domestic stereotype.

Women on both sides of the controversy, however, saw themselves as legatees of suffragism and feminism, intending to defend the value of women's economic roles, to prevent economic exploitation of women and to open the doors to economic opportunity. A struggle over the very word feminism, which the NWP had embraced, became part of the controversy. For "us even to use the word feminist," contended Women's Trade Union League leader Ethel Smith, "is to invite from the extremists a challenge to our authenticity." Detractors in the WTUL and Women's Bureau called the NWP "ultra" or "extreme" feminists. Mary Anderson considered herself "a good feminist" but objected that "over-articulate theorists were attempting to solve the working women's problems on a purely feministic basis with the working women's own voice far less adequately heard." Her own type of feminist was moderate and practical, Anderson declared; the others, putting the "woman question" above all other questions, were extreme and abstract. The bitterness was compounded by a conflict of personalities and tactics dragged on from the suffrage years. Opponents of the ERA, deeply resenting having to oppose something called equal rights, maligned the NWP as "pernicious," women who "discard[ed] all ethics and fair play," an "insane crowd" who espoused "a kind of hysterical feminism with a slogan for a program."[21] Their critiques fostered public perception of feminism as a sectarian and impracticable doctrine unrelated to real life and blind to injustices besides sex inequality. By the end of the 1920s

women outside the NWP rarely made efforts to reclaim the term feminist for themselves, and the meaning of the term was depleted.

Forced into theorizing by this controversy, not prepared as philosophers or legal theorists, spokeswomen on either side in the 1920s were grappling with definitions of women's rights as compared to men's that neither the legal nor economic system was designed to accommodate. The question whether equality required women to have the same rights as men, or different rights, could not be answered without delving into definitions. Did "equality" pertain to opportunity, treatment, or outcome?[22] Should "difference" be construed to mean separation, discrimination, protection, privilege—or assault on the very standard that the male was the human norm?[23]

Opponents of the ERA believed that sex-based legislation was necessary because of women's biological and social roles as mothers. They claimed that "The inherent differences are permanent. Women will always need many laws different from those needed by men"; "Women as such, whether or not they are mothers present or prospective, will always need protective legislation"; "The working mother is handicapped by her own nature."[24] Their approach stressed maternal nature and inclination as well as conditioning, and implied that the sexual division of labor was eternal.

The NWP's approach, on the other hand, presupposed that women's differentiation from men in the law and the labor market was a particular, social-historical, and not necessary or inevitable construction. The sexual division of labor arose from archaic custom, enshrined in employer and employee attitudes and written in the law. The NWP approach assumed that wives and mothers as well as unencumbered women would want and should have open access to jobs and professions. NWP proponents imagined that the sexual division of labor (in the family and the marketplace) would change if women would secure the same rights as men and have free access to wage-earning. Their view made a fragile potential into a necessary fact. They assumed that women's wage-earning would, by its very existence, challenge the sexual division of labor, and that it would provide the means for women's economic independence—although neither of these tenets was necessarily being realized.

Wage-earning women's experience in the 1910s and 1920s, as documented by the Women's

Bureau, showed that the sexual division of labor was budged only very selectively and marginally by women's gainful employment. Most women's wages did not bring them economic independence; women earned as part of a plan for family support (as men did, though that was rarely stressed). Contrary to the NWP's feminist visions, in those places in the nation where the highest proportions of wives and mothers worked for pay, the sexual division of labor was most oppressively in place. To every child growing up in the region of Southern textile and tobacco mills, where wives and mothers worked more "jobs" at home and in the factory than any other age or status group—and earned less—the sexual division of labor appeared no less prescriptive and burdensome than it had before women earned wages.[25]

Critiques of the NWP and its ERA as "abstract" or "extreme" or "fanatical" represented the gap between feminist tenets and harsh social reality as an oversight of the NWP, a failure to adjust their sights. Even more sympathetic critics, such as one Southern academic, asked rhetorically, "Do the feminists see in the tired and haggard faces of young waitresses, who spend seventy hours a week of hard work in exchange for a few dollars to pay for food and clothing, a deceptive mask of the noble spirit within?" She answered herself, "Surely it is not an increasing army of jaded girls and spent women that pours every day from factory and shop that the leaders of the feminist movement seek. But the call for women to make all labor their province can mean nothing more. They would free women from the rule of men only to make them greater slaves to the machines of industry."[26] Indeed, the exploitation of female service and industrial workers at "cheap" wages cruelly parodied the feminist notion that gainful employment represented an assertion of independence (just as the wifely duties required of a secretary parodied the feminist expectation that wage-earning would challenge the sexual division of labor and reopen definitions of feminity). What such critics were observing was the distance between the potential for women's wage-earning to challenge the sexual division of labor, and the social facts of gender and class hierarchy that clamped down on that challenge.

Defenders of sex-based protective legislation, trying to acknowledge women's unique reproductive endowments and social obligations, were grappling with problems so difficult they would still be present more than half a century later. Their immediate resolution was to portray women's "difference" in merely customary terms. "Average American women prefer to make a home for husbands and children to anything else," Mary Anderson asserted in defense of her position. "They would rather fulfill this normal function than go into the business world."[27] Keeping alive a critique of the class division of wealth, protective legislation advocates lost sight of the need to challenge the very sexual division of labor that was the root of women's "handicap" or "helplessness." As compared to the NWP's emphasis on the historical and social construction of gender roles, advocates of sex-based protective legislation echoed customary public opinion in proposing that motherhood and wage-earning should be mutually exclusive. They easily found allies among such social conservatives as the National Council of Catholic Women, whose representatives testified against the ERA because it "seriously menaced . . . the unity of the home and family life" and contravened the "essential differences in rights and duties" of the two sexes which were the "result of natural law." Edging into plain disapproval of mothers of young children who earned, protective legislation supporters became more prescriptive, less flexible, than wage-earning mothers themselves, for whom cash recognition of their labor was very welcome. "Why should not a married woman work [for pay], if a single one does?" demanded a mill worker who came to the Southern Summer School for Women Workers. "What would men think if they were told that a married man should not work? If we women would not be so submissive and take everything for granted, if we would awake and stand up for our rights, this world would be a better place to live in, at least it would be better for the women. . . . "[28]

The onset of the Depression in many ways worsened the ERA controversy, for the one side thought protective legislation all the more crucial when need drove women to take any jobs available, and the other side argued that protective legislation prevented women from competing for what jobs there were. In the 1930s it became clear that the labor movement's and League of Women Voters' opposition to the equal rights amendment ran deeper than concern for sex-based legislation as an "entering wedge." The Fair Labor Standards Act of 1938 mandated wages and hours regulation for all workers, and the U.S. Supreme Court upheld it in 1941; but the labor movement and the LWV still opposed the ERA. Other major women's organizations, however—most importantly the National Federation of Business and Professional Women's Clubs and the General Federation of Women's Clubs—and the national platforms of both the Republican [Party] and the Democratic Party endorsed the ERA by 1944.[29]

We generally learn "winners'" history—not the history of lost causes. If the ERA passed by Congress in 1972 had achieved ratification by 1982, perhaps historians of women would read the trajectory of the women's movement from 1923 to the present as a steady upward curve, and award the NWP unqualified original insight. The failure of the ERA this time around (on new, but not unrelated, grounds) compels us to see the longer history of equal rights in its true complexity.[30] The ERA battle of the 1920s seared into memory the fact of warring outlooks among women while it illustrated the inevitable intermeshing of women's legal and political rights with their economic situations. If the controversy testified to the difficulty of protecting women in the economic arena while opening opportunities to them, even more fundamentally the debate brought into question the NWP's premise that the articulation of sex discrimination—or the call for equal rights—would arouse all women to mobilize as a group. What kind of a group were women when their occupational and social and other loyalties were varied, when not all women viewed "women's" interests, or what constituted sex "discrimination," the same way? The ideological dimensions of that problem cross-cut both class consciousness and gender identity. The debate's intensity, both then and now, measured how fundamental was the revision needed if policies and practices of economic and civic life deriving from a male norm were to give full scope to women—and to women of all sorts.

NOTES

1. An essential text on the mid-nineteenth-century split is Ellen Carol DuBois, *Feminism and Suffrage: The Emergence of an Independent Women's Movement, 1848–1869* (Ithaca, N.Y., 1978).

2. See Leslie Woodcock Tentler, *Wage-Earning Women: Industrial Work and Family Life in the U.S., 1900–1930* (New York, 1979), chap. 1, on industrially employed women's wages, keyed below subsistence.

3. On feminists in the final decade of the suffrage campaign, see Nancy F. Cott, *The Grounding of Modern Feminism* (New Haven, Conn., 1987), pp. 23–66.

4. For more detailed discussion of the February 1921 convention, see Nancy F. Cott, "Feminist Politics in the 1920s: The National Woman's Party," *Journal of American History* 71 (June 1984).

5. Paul to Jane Norman Smith, Nov. 29, 1921, folder 110, J. N. Smith Collection, Schlesinger Library (hereafter SL). See NWP correspondence of Feb.–Mar. 1921 in the microfilm collection "The National Woman's Party, 1913–1974" (Microfilm Corp. of America), reels #5–7 (hereafter NWP), and Cott, *Grounding*, pp. 66–74, 120–25.

In Wisconsin, prominent NWP suffragist Mabel Raef Putnam put together a coalition which successfully lobbied through the first state equal rights bill early in 1921. This legislation granted women the same rights and privileges as men *except for* "the special protection and privileges which they now enjoy for the general welfare."

6. Maud Wood Park, *Front Door Lobby*, ed. Edna Stantial (Boston, 1960), p. 23.

7. Historians' treatments of women's organizations' differing views on the ERA in the 1920s include J. Stanley Lemons, *The Woman Citizen: Social Feminism in the 1920s* (Urbana, Ill., 1973), pp. 184–99; William Chafe, *The American Woman: Her Changing Social, Economic and Political Roles* (New York, 1972), pp. 112–32; Susan Becker, *Origins of the Equal Rights Amendment: American Feminism between the Wars* (Westport, Conn, 1981), pp. 121–51; and Alice Kessler-Harris, *Out to Work: A History of Wage-Earning Women in the U.S.* (New York, 1982), pp. 194–95, 205–12. Fuller documentation of my reading of both sides can be found in Cott, *Grounding*, pp. 122–29.

8. "Conference on So-Called 'Equal Rights' Amendment Proposed by the National Woman's Party Dec. 4, 1921," ts. NWTUL Papers, microfilm reel 2.

9. NWP National Council minutes, Dec. 17, 1921, Feb. 14, 1922, Apr. 11, 1922, NWP #114. To the NWP inner circle Laughlin's point was borne out by a 1923 ruling in Wisconsin, where, despite the Equal Rights Bill, the attorney general declined to strike down a 1905 law which prohibited women from being employed in the state legislature. He likened the prohibition to an hours-limitation law, because legislative service required "very long and often unreasonable hours."

10. National Council Minutes, June 19, 1923, NWP #114. Before 1923, the ERA went through scores of drafts. Not until 1943 was the amendment introduced into Congress in the form "Equality of rights under the law shall not be denied or abridged by the United States or by any state on account of sex," modeled on the Nineteenth Amendment, which in turn was modeled on the Fifteenth Amendment.

11. Quotation from Edith Houghton Hooker, Editor's Note, *Equal Rights* (the NWP monthly publication), Dec. 22, 1928, p. 365. See Cott, *Grounding*, pp. 75–82.

12. The two most seen on NWP platforms were Josephine Casey, a former ILGWU organizer, suffrage activist, later a bookbinder, and Mary Murray, a Brooklyn Railway employee who had resigned from her union in 1920 to protest its acceptance of laws prohibiting night work for women.

13. Kessler-Harris, *Out to Work*, 200–5.

14. More extensive documentation of the debate can be found in the notes in Cott, *Grounding*, pp. 325–26.

15. Kessler-Harris, *Out to Work,* pp. 189–94, reveals ambivalent assessments of labor legislation by ordinary wage-earning women.

16. Printed release from the National Association of Manufacturers, "Defend American Womanhood by Protecting Their Homes, Edgerton Tells Women in Industry," Jan. 19, 1926, in folder 1118, and ts. speech by James Davis, U.S. Secretary of Labor, Jan. 18, 1926, in folder 1117, Box 71, Mary Van Kleeck Collection, Sophia Smith Collection, Smith College.

17. Mary Anderson, "Should There Be Labor Laws for Women? Yes," *Good Housekeeping,* Sept. 1925.

18. See Valerie K. Oppenheimer, *The Female Labor Force in the U.S.* (Westport, Conn., 1976), pp. 3, 149; Winifred Wandersee, *Women's Work and Family Values 1920–1940* (Cambridge Mass., 1981), pp. 85, 89.

19. Elizabeth F. Baker, "At the Crossroads in the Legal Protection of Women in Industry," *Annals of the American Academy of Political and Social Science* 143 (May 1929):277.

20. T. K. Cory to Mary Wiggins, Nov. 10, 1922, folder 378, Consumers' League of Mass. Coll., SL.

21. Ethel M. Smith, "What Is Sex Equality and What Are the Feminists Trying to Accomplish?" *Century Monthly Magazine* 118 (May 1929):96. . . . Mary Anderson, *Woman at Work: The Autobiography of Mary Anderson as Told to Mary N. Winslow* (Minneapolis, 1951), p. 168.

22. See Jean Bethke Elshtain, "The Feminist Movement and the Question of Equality," *Polity* 7 (Summer 1975):452–77.

23. This is the set of issues that preoccupied feminist lawyers in the 1980s. For a sense of the debate, see, e.g., Wendy Williams, "The Equality Crisis: Some Reflections on Culture, Courts, and Feminism," *Women's Rights Law Reporter* 7 (Spring 1982):175–200; and Joan Williams, "Deconstructing Gender," *Michigan Law Review* 87 (Feb. 1989):797–845.

24. Florence Kelley, "Shall Women Be Equal before the Law?" (debate with Elsie Hill), *Nation* 114 (Apr. 12, 1922):421.

25. Dolores Janiewski, *Sisterhood Denied: Race, Gender and Class in a New South Community* (Philadelphia: Temple University Press, 1985), pp. 30–32, 127–50.

26. Guion G. Johnson, "Feminism and the Economic Independence of Woman," *Journal of Social Forces* 3 (May 4, 1925):615.

27. Mary Anderson quoted in unidentified newspaper clipping, Nov. 25, 1925, in folder 349, Bureau of Vocational Information Collection, SL. Cf. Ethel Smith's objection that the NWP's feminism required that "men and women must have exactly the same things, and be treated in all respects as if they were alike," as distinguished from her own view that "men and women must each have the things best suited to their respective needs, which are not all the time, nor in all things, alike." Smith, "What Is Sex Equality?", p. 96.

28. National Council of Catholic Women testimony at U.S. Congress (House of Representatives) subcommittee of Committee on the Judiciary, hearings, 1925, quoted in Robin Whittemore, "Equality vs. Protection: Debate on the Equal Rights Amendment, 1923–1937" (M.A. thesis, Boston University, 1981), p. 19; mill worker quoted in Mary Frederickson, "The Southern Summer School for Women Workers," *Southern Exposure* 4 (Winter 1977):73. See also Maurine Greenwald, "Working-Class Feminism and the Family Wage Ideal: The Seattle Debate on Married Women's Right to Work, 1914–1920," *Journal of American History* 76 (June 1989):118–49.

29. For the history of the NWP in the 1930s and 1940s see Becker, *Origins of the Equal Rights Amendment.*

30. Jane L. Mansbridge's astute analysis, *Why We Lost the ERA* (Chicago, 1986), is essential reading on the failed 1970s campaign for ratification.

ALICE KESSLER-HARRIS
Designing Women and Old Fools: Writing Gender into Social Security Law

One historian has called the Social Security Act of 1935 "the most important single piece of social legislation in all American history . . . in terms of historical decisiveness and direct influence upon the lives of individual Americans."* It continues to sustain the modern welfare state, providing the basic foundation for old-age pensions and for unemployment insurance. Its conceptualization of how needy mothers and children could claim government assistance was not replaced for sixty years, and continues to haunt debates over welfare. (President Franklin Delano Roosevelt also hoped to include a national system of health care but could not find congressional support.)

The drive to design the legislation and shepherd it through Congress was led by Frances Perkins, secretary of labor and the first woman cabinet member. It was not easy; anything resembling charity was widely resented. Many compromises were made in order to get enough votes in Congress. Perhaps the most significant was the decision not to conceptualize benefits as entitlement to all citizens. Instead, benefits were linked to payroll taxes paid by employers and employees, who could conclude that they were getting back only what they had put in. The strategy left nearly half the working population—including those who were seasonally or marginally employed—not covered. In the short run, there was a deflationary effect, as money paid into the Social Security Administration was pulled out of circulation. By 1937, efforts to amend the law were under way.

Politicians, economists, and other experts struggled to reform the law. They worked, for the most part, in good faith; they understood themselves to be seeking fairness and equity. They spoke of "the people" or "the worker"; their words were general and generic. But, as historian Alice Kessler-Harris read the minutes of meetings and considered the conversations and arguments, she found that the words they chose inadvertently revealed that the reformers' ideas of fairness rested on their own assumptions about work, family, citizenship, gender, and race. Behind what they would have called "the common sense of the matter" lurked unspoken beliefs: that women are not serious or long-term workers and that African Americans were doomed to marginal employment.

---

*Kenneth S. Davis, *FDR, the New Deal Years, 1933–1937: A History* (New York: Random House, 1986), p. 437; see also David M. Kennedy, *Freedom from Fear: The American People in Depression and War, 1929–1945* (New York: Oxford University Press, 1999), pp. 257–73.

Excerpted from "Maintaining Self Respect" and "Questions of Equity," chs. 2 and 3 of *In Pursuit of Equity: Women, Men, and the Quest for Economic Citizenship in 20th-Century America* by Alice Kessler-Harris (New York: Oxford University Press, 2001). Reprinted by permission of the author and publisher. Notes have been edited and renumbered.

What were the bureaucrats and legislators trying to accomplish by reforming the social security law? What were they trying to avoid? How did the law
reflect their understandings of fairness? How did the new law reflect their
view of the appropriate relationship between men and women? Between husbands and wives? Between blacks and whites? between the citizen and the state?
Why were concepts that had lasted since the 1930s attacked at the beginning of
the 1970s?

[In the 1930s,] Americans moved from staunch opposition to federal government intervention in the lives of most men (but not women) to eager experiments with government mediation of every kind. Newly adopted social policies had many goals, but among the most dramatic were those connected with earning wages and keeping jobs. . . .

Achieving consensus on issues of who deserved employment and who could languish in uncompensated unemployment required some hard decisions, especially around questions of inclusion and exclusion. For the government to regulate working conditions and monitor benefits for those without jobs, legislators would have to agree on, and administrators determine, eligibility. Someone would have to decide who could be described as a "worker" and who didn't fit the picture; what jobs counted as work and what didn't; how many hours constituted full-time work and how few precluded the activity from being called "work" at all. Innovative programs and policies demanded clarifications and classifications, precisely placing individuals in their relationships to paid and unpaid activities of different sorts. Each categorization opened or closed a door to the status, social rights, and economic security that measured progress toward economic citizenship for someone. Not only did benefits and entitlements rest on symbols of belonging, but so, ultimately, did the identities of workers, as well as their self-respect, political participation, and a newly differentiated set of meanings for crucial concepts like breadwinning, manhood, and citizenship.

The social constraints that guided these decisions had many roots, including most crucially ideologies of race and of American freedom and liberty. Historians are only now beginning to understand the degree to which they reflected a fundamental consensus around issues of race. But the new policies were also deeply embedded in a widespread and widely shared set of assumptions about gender. The

Social Security Act of 1935 provides a case in point.

The pressing need of old people in the 1930s was for assistance or relief, not insurance. Advocates ranging from Abraham Epstein, whose American Association for Old Age Security proposed federal grants to the states, to Francis Townsend, whose plan to give everyone over sixty-five two hundred dollars a month to spend at will exceeded all others in popularity, stimulated the public to believe that the federal government could and should help the states solve this problem. Over this, there was little controversy. The very first title of the Social Security Act, Title I, provided states with matching grants to give relief to the needy aged and to care for unemployable old people. It replaced the mostly inadequate state-based programs with uniform federal standards and more generous grants than all but a handful of states had been able to provide. But Old Age Assistance came at a price: it subjected recipients to the indignities of means testing, fostering an unmanly spirit of dependency. . . .

Social insurance advocates sought to circumvent this anxiety with insurance rather than relief: They sought to prevent destitution and "obviate the necessity of public charity" by protecting family breadwinners against the potential hazards of industrial life. . . .

In the United States, the idea of government-subsidized insurance ran counter to the American grain, which reified independence and self-reliance. If there were to be any old age insurance program at all, its designers faced a formidable challenge: to remove aging workers from the labor force (which required that they be adequately supported) while affirming the dignity of pension recipients (which required that the program be self-supporting). To solve the labor force problem, policy makers imagined a program tied to work rather than to citizenship. Deciding which workers would be covered, however, created two classes of citizens: those who participated regularly in the kind of wage work where resolving unemployment seemed most important, and those who did not. In 1930, men made up the vast majority of gainfully employed persons (75 percent of the total); about 12 percent of this number were classified by the census as "Negro." But most African American men did not work in the core industrial sectors, where issues of unemployment and labor force stability mattered most. And while women made up a quarter of all wage earners, their tenuous rights to work led many to assume they had little commitment to wage labor. . . . Despite women's own efforts to seek jobs during the depression, public opinion resolutely condemned wage work for those with husbands and fathers who could support them. Through the depression years, less than 15 percent of married women earned wages. Consciously or not, policy makers imagined a program available to most white wage-earning men that would omit "as a matter of course" most African Americans, by virtue of their positions in the labor market, and most women, whose positions appeared derivative of their marital partners.

Efforts to preserve the dignity of beneficiaries participated in the same gendered imagination. In the battle over unemployment compensation, men fought to maintain a sense of themselves as self-sufficient, independent, free, and capable of providing for their families and especially for the dependent women within them. In the struggle for Old Age Insurance (which we now call Social Security), participants deployed gender in more subtle but equally aggressive ways, not only to promote a conception of fairness that relied on the language of male dignity and female dependence but to ensure adequate support for all the aged. Gendered constructs helped to soothe a public increasingly enamored of government-funded assistance (which seemed to some policy makers an appropriate and to others a short-sighted and short-term solution). And they provided the language of family normalcy that convinced reluctant policy makers who remained skeptical of the capacity of an insurance program to solve employment problems without depending on general taxation. Ultimately, gendered conceptions provided the keystone that maintained public confidence in the core old age program and justified its redistributive goals. By providing economic security

in particular ways and to particular people, old age insurance defined a new category of economic citizenship; at the same time . . . it fueled the desires of the excluded for fuller participation. . . .

No sooner had the Social Security Act been signed into law on August 14, 1935, than issues of adequacy began to surface. The bill provided for a 1 percent payroll tax, payable by employers, to be instituted in 1936 and matched by an equivalent contribution from every employee; benefits would not be payable until January 1942. The lag produced a surplus that, in a depression economy, threatened to exercise a deflationary effect. Most important, the exclusions written into the old age insurance provisions of the Social Security Act exempted nearly half the working population, evoking questions about its fairness as well as about its capacity to provide for the aged.[1] Because the program did not provide benefits to those who worked intermittently or for only a few years even when they worked in covered occupations, more than three-fifths of fully employed African Americans were denied coverage. Sixty percent of the excluded workers were female. . . . Probably as many as 85 percent of wage-earning black women were deprived of participation and benefits.[2]

At the same time, powerful popular support continued to build for the state-run, noncontributory old age assistance pensions that provided more generous benefits to the needy aged than those envisioned under Social Security for most contributors. . . . [These fueled] a sense of entitlement to old age pensions as a matter of justice. . . . Everyone knew that even when the insurance program started paying benefits in 1942, they would go at first to only three hundred thousand people, compared to the estimated two million needy elderly who would then be receiving noncontributory assistance.

. . . What was to be done? The solution seemed to be to spend the surplus. But how? And on whom? Despite the sharp and purposeful distinctions between adequacy and equity, the principle was violated by the very first set of amendments, which added old age insurance benefits for wives and widows who had not paid for them. No charitable impulse toward women motivated this act; no concern for their poverty inspired it. Rather, Congress added dependent wives and aged widows in order to shore up the legitimacy of a system in trouble. It did this by enhancing the benefits of already covered (mostly white) males to ensure extra income to those who had aged wives to support and extra insurance to those with young children who survived them. These amendments, adopted in 1939, reinforced the prerogatives, self-images, and citizenship rights of some males while reaffirming racialized conceptions of gender. They redefined equity to incorporate more adequate and appropriate provision for some men, infusing the American system of entitlements with the peculiar imbalance from which it has struggled to release itself since the early 1970s.

In the spring of 1937, the Senate Finance Committee pressured the Social Security Board into creating a federal Advisory Council to suggest remedies. In May, when the new Advisory Council, which J. Douglas Brown agreed to chair, was announced, it consisted of twenty-four members. Six represented employers; six came from the labor movement; and twelve were designated as "public" participants, most of them academics and businessmen. [The public members included three women.][3] . . .

Together with the Social Security Board and several congressional committees, the Advisory Council worked through the following year and a half to recommend basic changes. Their charge from Congress was clear: They had to recommend a permanent way of dealing with ballooning reserves. They were to do this by beginning old age insurance benefits earlier than the originally mandated January 1942 start-up date and by making them larger. They were to explore the possibility of extending benefits to the disabled, to survivors, and to excluded groups. In the end, the council sidestepped the challenge of significantly extending insurance to most of the excluded groups, including the disabled, domestic servants, and agricultural workers and chose to rely instead on a new and expensive package of benefits for aged wives and survivors to reduce the surplus.[4]

The discussions over these alternatives tell us something about how invisible assumptions about men and women informed an entire network of social policy. For when the council moved toward emphasizing expanding benefits to those already covered, it utilized gender to mediate the conflict between adequacy and equity—a conflict in which women played little role but issues of manliness and

womanliness assumed paramount importance. . . . The council, as its chairman, Douglas Brown, put it, had adopted "the principle of family protection."

The conversations within the Advisory Council and in Congress clarify the meaning of that principle. The council quickly agreed on pensions for fatherless children—an idea that already had popular support.[5] The Advisory Council adopted the notion rapidly because it promised to significantly reduce the numbers receiving means-tested assistance under both Title I (Old Age Assistance) and Title IV (Aid to Dependent Children) and strengthen the entire Social Security program by providing the illusion that their support was a product of insurance, the provenance of thoughtful and thrifty fathers. . . .

The Advisory Council relied on the same ideas of fairness to provide benefits for the widowed mothers of young children. These widows were to have benefits only as long as their children were young. The sums granted, and the restrictions on them, suggest that insurance for widowed mothers was conceived of as a matter of peace of mind for the husband. The widowed mother was to get three fourths of what her husband's pension would have been. The pension was granted as a matter of need, to enable "the widow to remain at home and care for the children."[6] It was to be reduced or eliminated if her earnings exceeded fifteen dollars a month (a tiny sum, even in 1939), thus encouraging her not to try to earn wages. In the likely event a widow's children reached eighteen before she reached sixty-five, the council recommended that all support end, to be resumed again when she became sixty-five, if in the meantime she had not remarried.[7] A young widow without children lacked any "rights" in her husband's contribution and got no benefits until and unless she grew old without remarrying.

Tying the dignity of men (defined by their capacity to provide) to the virtue of women (their willingness to remain dependent on men and to rear children) proved to be a continuing problem for young and old widows alike. The Social Security Board was fully cognizant of what it called the "widow's gap," noting at congressional hearings that "middle aged widows find it more difficult to become self-supporting." Still, . . . it deferred the annuity of an under-sixty-five widow until she reached that age, on the grounds that "there is some likelihood that the widow may reenter covered employment."[8] Its sympathies for widows whose children were grown could not overcome internalized portraits of the family that fully rationalized its position: "They are likely to have more savings than younger widows and many of them have children who are grown and able to help them until they reach 65 years of age."[9]

The conversations within the council and the provisions finally adopted suggest that old age insurance was never imagined in terms of fair treatment to women—a product of the joint efforts of a marriage partnership. Consistent with the notion of sustaining male provision for the family, and over the objections of some members of the Social Security Board, the council voted to eliminate any annuity to a widow who remarried lest it construct a system that, in the words of one member, constituted widows "a prize for the fellow that has looked for it."[10] It recommended a plan that gave a wife no rights at all in the husband's insurance in consequence of his contributions to it, though demanding that she forfeit everything if she remarried clearly violated the equity principle that promised a return for what had been put in. . . .

. . . Once a woman was no longer dependent on the earnings of a particular male (dead or alive), the council contended, his support for her should cease, "rendering the woman ineligible whether she is the widow of an annuitant or the widow of a worker who dies before 65."[11] As long as she remained dependent on him, the level of the surviving widow's benefits . . . would be tied to the earnings of the deceased male, feeding the illusion that families deprived of a father or husband would nevertheless conceive him in the abstract as a continuing provider. . . .

We have no need to guess at the gendered images that sustained these seemingly arbitrary decisions. They pop up everywhere. For example, halfway through its eighteen months of deliberations, the Advisory Council confronted the question of what allowance to provide to aged widows. Should it be half of what their provider-husbands would have received? Two thirds? Three quarters? After several hours of debate over what proportion of a husband's benefit might appropriately descend to his widow, one member thought to ask a question that had escaped scrutiny: "Why should you pay the widow less than the individual

himself gets if unmarried?" "She can look after herself better than he can," shot back the group's actuary.[12] But the question would not die. Two months later the Advisory Council returned to the issue. This time the chairman, prodded by one of its three female members, took up the defense. "A single woman" he suggested, can "adjust herself to a lower budget on account of the fact that she is used to doing her own housework whereas the single man has to go out to a restaurant."[13] By now, though, others had joined the fray. When the argument resumed at the next meeting, Douglas Brown tried to end it by painting a portrait everyone could accept. Lower rates for women made sense, he argued, his patience clearly worn thin,

> on the principle that it is more costly for the single man to live than for the single woman if she is able to avail herself of the home of the child. A woman is able to fit herself into the economy of the home of the child much better than the single man, that is, the grandmother helps in the raising of the children and helps in home affairs, whereas the aged grandfather is the man who sits out on the front porch and can't help much in the home.[14]

Such homely images shaped decisions that influenced the lives of almost everyone. They appeared at sporadic moments of unguarded conversation. Imagining women as irresponsible, the council voted to remove the original act's lump-sum death benefit to widows. "Such settlements," its minutes recorded, "are likely to be used for many other purposes long before her old age." Women could also be greedy and unprincipled. To avoid what it referred to as "deathbed marriages," the council adopted a clause requiring a pair to have been married and living together for at least a year before the husband died or reached sixty for his widow to be eligible for benefits on his account.[15] No benefits accrued to the woman who married a man over the age of sixty, unless she had lived with him for at least a year before he died.

The imagery became more complicated around the question of whether to increase benefits by providing more to every contributor or by enhancing the benefits of married men. Here the council clearly had in mind the normative 1930s household in which wives earned little or nothing, and it wanted to protect the economic well-being of the husbands who supported them. No one noted that its image failed to account for the more than 15 percent of white and at least 33 percent of African American households in which women earned regular wages. Rather, members noted that even the original bill had been criticized by social insurance advocates like Abraham Epstein for its failure to include additional benefits for men with aged wives.... Advisory Council staff members, including Wilbur Cohen and Isadore Falk, ... claimed that old age insurance would be perceived as more fair if it treated married men with greater generosity....

[After considering a number of suggestions for an aged wives' allowance, the Advisory Council] explicitly proposed "that the enhancement of early old-age benefits under the system be attained, not by increasing the amount of benefit now payable to an individual, but by the method of paying to a married annuitant on behalf of an aged wife a supplementary allowance equivalent to fifty percent of the husband's own benefit."[16] ...

None of the three women on the Advisory Council (Theresa McMahon, Elizabeth Wisner, and Josephine Roche, who seems to have been there only rarely) raised a question about gender equity or the rights of women. Neither did political activist and reformer, Mary Dewson, who attended council meetings as a member of the Social Security Board....

We can speculate that under the historical circumstances the proposals of the Advisory Council offered far more security to the families of covered workers than most women could expect to provide through earnings.... [I]nfluential women social reformers had long since accepted that providing security for the family was the most likely way to safeguard women.... With the exception of McMahon, the women engaged in the Advisory Council's deliberations had been involved in some part of the effort to develop state-run welfare systems, and all were more or less hostile to the efforts of more radical feminists to fight for women's individual rights.... In addition, at least some members of the women's reform network (including perhaps Dewson herself) had become convinced of the need to abandon an earlier strategy of seeking benefits for women only and to focus instead on an integrated system of security. Family benefits would encourage this direction.

If the suggestion to provide dependents' allowances for aging wives appealed to some because it recognized the family responsibilities of men, it appealed to others because it retained equity among covered men by maintaining a relationship between contributions and benefits. This strategy was essential to garnering the votes of southern racists....

[As one council member argued,] "It is impractical to have a level benefit in this country because of the differences between the colored workers of the south and the skilled workers of the north. A single flat figure for everybody would not work."[17] ... [It was important to the council that it not transgress the] relative expectations of income based on occupation or race....

In adopting the program, Congress accepted, with little debate, the relatively rigid definition of the family it demanded. For covered workers, the 1939 amendments provided benefits, without means tests, to fatherless children, widowed mothers of small children, and aged wives and widows. It did not extend benefits to the surviving children of covered women or to aged husbands, aged widowers, or widowed fathers of small children. Thus fatherless children might learn the sweet lesson of continuing parental support beyond the grave, and aging wives would continue to be dependent, though on phantom earnings. But motherless children and aged husbands without resources received quite another lesson in citizenship rights.[18] ...

Three million domestic workers (including two and a quarter million in private households) counted themselves among the women who learned bitter lessons. Like three and a half million agricultural workers, mostly male, they found themselves among the still "uncovered" workers when the 1939 amendments emerged from Congress.[19] In fact, as a group, they had received a slap in the face. Following the Advisory Council's recommendations, Congress incorporated more than a million seamen and bank employees into the old age insurance program. At the same time, it excluded an equal number of mostly female and largely African American workers by eliminating even the few who had crept under the wire. Three hundred thousand domestic workers in clubs, fraternities, and large households and about seven hundred thousand food-processing workers lost their coverage....

When Congress agreed to save the old age insurance system by changing its financing and using the funds generated annually to provide family protection, legislators altered expectations of the Social Security program

and provoked a set of new, vaguely anticipated pressures toward universal coverage.
Abandoning the idea that each generation of
recipients would build a reserve fund that
would support its own retirement in favor of a
pay-as-you-go system required each generation
of working people to subsidize the retirements
of its predecessors. The shift turned a program
that had originally been perceived primarily as
a labor regulation device meant to preserve the
dignity of workers who made way for the next
generation into something more clearly approx-
imating a promise of economic security freed of
its rigid requirement for an equitable return on
individual contributions. Adequate insurance
for families displaced individual equity as the
primary measure of fairness.

The inexorable logic of a system tilted
toward adequacy fueled the hopes of policy
makers and the excluded that old age insurance
could more quickly include everyone and effectively replace the costly and demeaning charity
offered by old age assistance. Advisory Council
member Paul Douglas warned his colleagues
that the changes made there raised the question
of why the council could not recommend an
"all-inclusive universal system": "If everybody
is in from the standpoint of benefits, then everybody is in from the standpoint of contributions,
and if there is to be a government subsidy . . .
for only the industrial part of the population, it
is going to be difficult to have the entire population pay taxes for benefits designed for only
half of the population."[20] As Douglas noticed,
by enhancing the value of social insurance for
some groups of relatively privileged wage earners without extending coverage to significant
numbers of additional workers, the program,
which was now called Old-Age and Survivors
Insurance (OASI), created two classes of citizens. For one of these, the "right to work" had
become a more valuable commodity, carrying
with it significant economic benefits and social
rights for which the other half was indirectly
paying. A large proportion of this other half
consisted of self-supporting women (black and
white) and African Americans of both sexes.

Afterward, the implications of these distinctions became clear. For one thing, some survivors benefited more than others. The family
benefits offered under contributory social insurance slowly removed most widows and
their children from the public assistance rolls.[21]
By 1960, OASDI (disability insurance was added
in 1941) covered 93 percent of widows with

children. Most of these were the dependents
of men who had held covered jobs, leaving
only a tiny number of children and their widowed mothers to rely on relief, or what quickly
became known as welfare. The result was to
produce an invidious distinction between
those said to have earned benefits as of right
and those for whom benefits remained a
matter of public charity. Both systems exercised some controls over the behavior of
mothers caring for children, restricting the
amount of income a mother could earn before
benefits were lost and removing benefits on
remarriage, but charitable provision subjected
women to stringent moral and supervisory
controls as well.[22] At the same time, the promise of more immediate and more reasonable
provenance for the aged, anchored in their
own virtue and thrift, successfully undermined public support for noncontributory old
age assistance schemes, which soon suffered
from derogatory labels. Because so many of
the poorest and least stable workers could not
collect Social Security benefits, these changes
also made racial exclusion more visible.

For another, women quickly learned the
costs of a gender-segregated labor market,
and black women learned the bitterest lessons
of all.[23] The poorest-paid workers, invariably
women and people of color, appeared to have
been multiply disadvantaged. As workers, they
would see their intermittent contributions captured by an insurance program that excluded
them, to be used to subsidize more stable workers. As consumers, they would pay higher prices
as employers factored their share of taxes into
the prices of goods and services. As citizens,
they were not only deprived of the dignity attached to a contributory program, but they were
compelled to support a dual system of noncontributory and contributory relief, producing the
apparent injustice of some receiving a demeaning "free" benefit while others received a due
return on their investment. . . .

The system's planners had anticipated
that some part of the contributions of intermittent workers would be captured and returned
to beneficiaries. In their imagination, these
workers were single women who would soon
marry or married women who, though they
worked intermittently, would ultimately reap
enhanced benefits earned by their husbands.
Policy makers frequently articulated these assumptions. With congressional concurrence,
the council agreed on the irrelevance of most

women's wage work with respect to this new citizenship right. "A married woman whether she works or no," it decided, "will receive an allowance because of her husband's earning." Its intent could not have been plainer. While "a single woman earns her own benefit rights," it concluded that "a married woman who works will not get advantage . . . of her own earnings, as in any case she will receive the 50% allowance for her husband."[24]

The actual situation was even worse. The council fully expected that married women would work occasionally and that their contributions, as well as the early contributions of single women who then married, would be absorbed by the system and help to sustain its financial health without necessarily yielding any direct benefit to the female contributor. There is no question that this was intentional, done, as Douglas Brown told the House Ways and Means Committee that affirmed the council's recommendations, "in order to control the cost of the system."[25] . . .

While some members of the council deplored its failure to provide equitable treatment to wives who earned wages, suggesting, for example, that "women who work all their lives should have a larger return than those who don't," most symbolically shrugged their shoulders along with Paul Douglas, who declared: "Of course, wives work too." Congress apparently concurred that wives who worked would simply have to sacrifice because, as one put it, "most wives in the long run will build up wage credits on their own account."[26] . . .

The 1939 council that designed this trade-off also aimed to discourage family members from taking advantage of the insurance program. Fearing inflated claims to benefits by women who falsely maintained they had worked for their husbands, Congress excluded "service performed by an individual in the employ of his spouse." . . . The issue of "forfeited" contributions had lasting resonance, for wives were not the only ones who forfeited their contributions. "Scrubwomen on their knees" fell victim, too, as well as all those who earned less than two hundred dollars a year from a single employer.[27] This hit African Americans particularly hard, as a special 1941 Senate report lamented when it deplored the unfairness to "contributors who fail to qualify because of insufficient employment or low wages. . . . Money thus forfeited by the dispossessed of the act will flow into the insurance

fund and from there it will be distributed to workers everywhere."[28]

The architects of the 1939 amendments surely never intended to harm poor women, but the particular ways in which their gendered imagination infused the legislation nevertheless produced negative consequences. In 1940, the male-breadwinner family remained the modal family. Only 15 percent of wives with husbands present earned wages. If countless numbers of others hid the incomes they earned by taking in sewing, laundry, and boarders, still, most white women and men gratefully accepted the derivative benefits offered to wives and widows. Not so for African American women. As the depression deepened throughout the 1930s, racial segregation made wage work an absolute necessity for many black women, regardless of their marital status. At the same time, gender segregation confined more and more women of color to domestic service jobs, most often in private households. Of the two and a quarter million private household workers in the United States in 1940, about 90 percent were women.[29] A little less than half were African Americans. In contrast, men made up 94 percent of agricultural workers. Yet viewed from the perspective of the prospective worker, the figures take on a different cast. Nearly a third of all black workers (1.6 million men and women) and two-thirds of black working women (compared to less than 18 percent of white women workers) were in domestic service.[30] Of the five and a half million African Americans in the labor force in 1935, fully two-thirds were excluded from old age insurance because they belonged to noncovered occupations. No constitutional impediments stood in the way of including them, especially after the Supreme Court sustained the Social Security Act on the grounds of the welfare clause. In contrast to agricultural workers, whom farm interests desperately wanted excluded, and unlike some other groups, such as nonprofits, retail clerks, and the self-employed, no large interest group lobbied to keep domestic workers out of the old age insurance provisions of the new law. Race alone united them.[31] . . .

. . . [The Committee on Economic Security] sent its proposal to Congress with domestic and agricultural workers included. They were eliminated again by the House Ways and Means Committee on the probably specious grounds that their contributions could not buy sufficient benefits and that in any event collecting their taxes and administering benefits would be costly.[32] Agitation to include both groups continued even as the Social Security Act made its way through Congress. Mary Anderson wrote hopefully that she expected, regardless of what happened to the unemployment provisions, that "all workers regardless of occupation will be eligible to share in the old age benefits of the Economic Security Bill."[33]

Her hopes, of course, did not materialize. . . . A racialized conception of gender created the double jeopardy of black women. The policy committees publicly cited putative administrative difficulties that stood in the way of enrolling workers employed in single-person workplaces; in private they admitted the difficulties of offending southern sensibilities. In public, legislators repeatedly sought to protect white housewives, whose ability to handle the paperwork they denigrated; at the same time, they labeled household workers as "girls" and fostered disrespect for the occupation. Over more than a decade, they deployed race to exaggerate the differences between household workers and their employers while seeking to attach to each the special attributes of gender. . . .

Providing benefits for domestics would offer tangible benefits to poorly paid workers, enhance the appearance of fairness, and solve some of the program's financial problems as well. Yet, for many years, pleas to extend coverage to domestic workers, including the recommendation of the Social Security Board, fell on deaf ears. What had made it possible to ignore domestics, argued a piece in the AFL's journal, *American Federationist,* in the fall of 1939, is that they were thought of as different. Ninety percent female, 45 percent African American, with greater proportions married, widowed, deserted, or divorced, and still working in their older years, they simply did not fit the profile of the stable industrial worker for whom social legislation was constructed.[34] Nor did they conform to the restricted images of womanhood within which the 1939 Advisory Council constructed its system of benefits. So they had been left out partly because they were different and mostly because "we have gotten into the habit of excluding them." . . .

Still, for most purposes, most members of Congress and officials of the Social Security Administration continued to support programs that radically distinguished between men and women as contributors. From the perspective of contributors, women's taxes continued to buy far less insurance protection than those of men. . . . From that of beneficiaries, men lacked the protections that their wives had. In 1961, Congress changed the law so that a wife's contributions covered aged husbands and widowers as well. Once again Congress insisted that they demonstrate financial dependency.

. . . The debate rendered voiceless a significant minority of women who believed that if they contributed at the same level as men, their contributions ought to buy their spouses and their children the same protection.

In the 1970s, these women found their voices. The rapidly rising numbers of wage-earning women and of women who did not marry, and the emergence of a dynamic and angry women's movement, soon rendered the discrepancies questionable and led some men and women to wonder if they were discriminatory. "The income security programs of this nation were designed for a land of male and female stereotypes," wrote Representative Martha Griffiths in 1973.[35] A series of court decisions confronted the issue, peaking on March 19, 1975, in the landmark decision of *Weinberger v. Wiesenfeld.* Eight justices of the U.S. Supreme Court (the ninth abstaining) agreed that Stephen Wiesenfeld, a widower and lone parent of an infant child, was entitled to Social Security benefits. Wiesenfeld claimed the benefits on the basis of contributions made by his wife, Paula, who had been a schoolteacher before she died in childbirth. But the Social Security Administration had turned him down: widows' benefits were available only to women. Now the Supreme Court demurred. "A father no less than a mother," said the Court, "has a constitutionally protected right to the companionship, care, custody, and management of children he has sired and raised."[36] On this basis, the Court struck down forty years of "archaic and overbroad generalizations," accepting the argument put forth in Wiesenfeld's defense that such generalizations unfairly discriminated against women because their contributions to Social Security did not buy as much as the contributions of men. Wisenfeld's lawyer, Ruth Bader Ginsburg, had done her part to draw a new image of gender to the Court's attention.

The Court's majority decision, written by Justice William J. Brennan, explicitly challenged assumptions about men's and women's wage-earning that underlay the Social Security

Act and anchored its old age insurance provisions. As late as 1971, an Advisory Council on Social Security had insisted that men rarely became homemakers after the death of a spouse and that, given their attachment to the workforce, widowed fathers did not require benefits to enable them to provide a home for their children. Acknowledging the truth of the generalization that men had been, and were more likely to be, the principal supporters of their families, Brennan nevertheless argued that this assumption did not "suffice to justify the denigration of efforts of women who do work and whose earnings contribute significantly to families' support." Dismissing the government's claim that benefits were unrelated to contributions, the Court held that statutory rights to benefits were directly "related to years worked and amount earned by a covered employee, and not to the need of the beneficiaries directly." Benefits had to be related to some reasonable classification; they could not be based solely on sex. Wiesenfeld's wife had not only been deprived of the security "a similarly situated male" would have received, she had been "deprived of a portion of her own earnings in order to contribute to the fund out of which benefits would be paid to others." As Justice Lewis Powell put it in a concurring opinion, the statute "discriminates against one particular category of family—that in which the female spouse is a wage-earner covered by social security."[37]

The decision in *Wiesenfeld* was followed by others. An aged widower was entitled to benefits on his wife's earnings whether or not he had been dependent on her, just as a widow was entitled to benefits earned by her husband, the Court declared two years later.[38] . . . With the Department of Health, Education, and Welfare and the Social Security Administration fighting every step, the Court methodically overturned a carefully structured set of images about women's roles in the family. Henceforth, the Court concluded, classifications by gender "must serve important governmental objectives."[39] Imaging women as nonworkers no longer met that test.

NOTES

1. Paul H. Douglas, *Social Security in the United States: An Analysis and Appraisal of the Federal Social Security Act* (New York: McGraw-Hill, 1936), estimates that 47 percent of those working would not come under the old age insurance features and thus would require old age assistance.

2. The most careful analysis of the data concludes that 86.69 percent of black female workers and 53.6 percent of black male workers were excluded; F. Davis, "The Effects of the Social Security Act upon the Status of the Negro," Ph.D. diss., University of Iowa, 1939, p. 99, n. 211, and 102, tables 21, 23.

3. "Social Security Advisory Council Is Appointed," typescript of press release, May 10, 1937, File 025: Advisory Council 1937, Box 10, Chairman's Files, RG47, NA2.

4. Typescript, I. S. Falk to the Advisory Council, November 5, 1937, "Benefits for Disabled Persons and Survivors, and Supplemental Allowances for Dependents," ibid., passim.

5. See, for example, Abraham Epstein, *Insecurity: A Challenge to America, a Study of Social Insurance in the United States and Abroad* (New York: Random House, 1938 [1933]), part 9.

6. Advisory Council on Social Security, *Final Report*, Senate Document no. 4, 76th Cong., 1st sess., December 10, 1938 (Washington, D.C.: GPO, 1939), p. 18; hereafter, Advisory Council, *Final Report*.

7. Advisory Council Minutes, April 29, 1938, morning session, pp. 8–10 and ff.

8. Advisory Council, *Final Report*, p. 17.

9. House, *Hearings on Social Security Act Amendments of 1939*, p. 6.

10. Advisory Council Minutes, April 29, 1938, second half of morning session, p. 9, A. L. Mowbray of the University of California, Berkeley, speaking.

11. Ibid., pp. 3, 40.

12. Ibid., February 19, 1938, afternoon session, p. 18. The actuary was William Williamson.

13. Ibid., April 29, 1938, first half of morning session, p. 41.

14. Ibid., April 29, 1938, second half of morning session, pp. 5–6.

15. Ibid., first half of morning session, pp. 37–38.

16. Typescript headed "Strictly Confidential," October 22, 1938, File 025, Box 138, Executive Director's Files, Advisory Council on Social Security, RG47, NARA.

17. Jill Quadagno, *The Transformation of Old Age Security: Class and Politics in the American Welfare State* (Chicago: University of Chicago Press, 1988), p. 39, and see ch. 6 on the influence of southern politicians on the old age assistance portion of the Social Security Act.

18. These amendments also included altering the fiscal plan to a pay-as-you-go system, paying benefits on the basis of a wage-averaging device rather than on the basis of accumulated benefits, and expanding the categories of agricultural and domestic workers excluded from coverage. See Edward D. Berkowitz, "The First Social Security Crisis," *Prologue* 15, no. 3 (1983):133–49, for a summary of their full contents.

19. These figures come from the testimony of Sumner Slichter, *Hearings on the Social Security Act Amendments of 1939*, p. 1512. Slichter estimated that eleven million self-employed farmers and others, and about a million employees of nonprofit corporations, also remained uncovered.

20. Advisory Council Minutes, February 19, 1938, afternoon session, p. 20.

21. Gwendolyn Mink, *The Wages of Motherhood: Inequality in the Welfare State, 1917–1942* (Ithaca: Cornell University Press, 1995), p. 175.

22. The best discussion of this issue is in ibid., chs. 6–7.

23. Edward J. McCaffery, *Taxing Women* (Chicago: University of Chicago Press, 1997), ch. 4.

24. Brown, Advisory Council Minutes, February 18, 1938, morning session, p. 14.

25. House, *Hearings on the Social Security Act Amendments of 1939*, p. 1218.

26. Testimony of Sen. Sheridan Downey of California, *Congressional Record—Senate*, July 13, 1939, p. 9012.

27. Downey, *Congressional Record—Senate*, July 13, 1939, p. 9012.

28. *Senate Resolution Preliminary Report, 1941*, p. 8.

29. Thus, though African Americans made up about 10 percent of the labor force, they constituted nearly half of the women in domestic service. Cf. Testimony of Margaret Plunkett, chief, Division of Legislation, Women's Bureau, Department of Labor, U.S. Congress, House, *Hearings before the Committee on Ways and Means, House of Representatives on Social Security Legislation, Amendments to the Social Security Act of 1946*, 79th Cong., 2nd sess. (Washington, D.C.: GPO, 1946), p. 542; hereafter, House, *Hearings on Amendments to the Social Security Act of 1946*. Plunkett also says that 6 percent of agricultural workers were women (p. 545).

30. Figures from Albion Hartwell, "The Need of Social and Unemployment Insurance for Negroes," *Journal of Negro Education* 5 (January 1936), pp. 79–87.

31. This argument appears in the testimony of Edgar G. Brown, director, National Negro Council, Washington, D.C., at U.S. Congress, House, *Hearings on Social Security Act Amendments of 1949*, p. 1878.

32. See the account of this incident in Edwin E. Witte, *The Development of the Social Security Act: A Memorandum on the History of the Committee on Economic Security and Drafting and Legislative History of the Social Security Act* (Madison: University of Wisconsin Press, 1962), pp. 152–53.

33. Mary Anderson, "The Plight of Negro Domestic Labor," *Journal of Negro Education* 5 (January 1936), p. 71.

34. Rae Needleman, "Are Domestic Workers Coming of Age," *American Federationist* 46 (October 1939), pp. 1070–75.

35. Martha W. Griffiths, "Sex Discrimination in Income Security Programs," *Notre Dame Lawyer* 49 (February 1974), p. 534.

36. *Weinberger v. Wiesenfeld*, 420 U.S. 636 (1975), p. 652.

37. Ibid., pp. 645, 647.

38. *Califano v. Goldfarb*, 97 S.Ct. 1021 (1977), p. 1023. Justice William J. Brennan for the Court.

39. *Califano v. Goldfarb*, p. 1028.

BLANCHE WIESEN COOK

Storms on Every Front: Eleanor Roosevelt and Human Rights at Home and in Europe

A woman of limitless energy, compassion, and humanitarian zeal, Eleanor Roosevelt was the most active and controversial First Lady in the nation's history. A fascinating figure, her ability to grow in understanding never ended. She began her adult life as a shy, insecure woman who had imbibed the racism and anti-Semitism of the privileged world to which she was born. She ended her life a feminist and a political champion of civil rights, civil liberties, social justice, and world peace—a woman whose activism was played out on a world stage.

The transformation was well under way by the 1920s. Indeed, it was accelerated when Franklin Delano Roosevelt was paralyzed by polio in 1921 and Eleanor began serving as his representative in the political arena. Long a political activist, she became a shrewd analyst of the political scene. When FDR became president, ER found herself in an increasingly complex political context. She could try to persuade the president in private conversation; she could also use public pulpits of her own. She was the only First Lady ever to write a long-running daily syndicated newspaper column, "My Day." She could choose (or refuse) speaking

Excerpted and revised by the author from ch. 27 of *Eleanor Roosevelt: The Defining Years, 1933–1938,* by Blanche Wiesen Cook (New York: Viking/Penguin, 1999). Published by permission of the author and publisher. Readers will find ch. 16, "A Silence Beyond Repair," a critical framework for this selection.

invitations, and use her opportunities to speak about issues that mattered to her. As the Nazi threat grew, ER found that the State Department insisted on her silence; she would have to find other ways of expressing her commitment to human rights.

Between 9 and 15 November [1938], Jewish homes, schools, hospitals, synagogues, businesses, and cemeteries were invaded, plundered, burned. Kristallnacht, the night of broken glass, was a week of contempt, abuse, destruction.

If anybody doubted the intent of Hitler's words, so clearly revealed in his writings, speeches, and previous outrages, those November days in Germany, Austria, and the Sudetenland shattered any illusion. The violence coincided with Armistice Day, 11 November, when the Allies ended World War I. The defeat of that war was for Hitler to be avenged with new blood, and unlimited terror.

The violence began on 28 October, when Germany expelled thousands of Polish Jews who had lived for decades within the historically changing borders of Germany. Nazis rounded up children and old people on the streets, emptied houses and apartment buildings, allowed people to take nothing with them except 10 marks ($4) and the clothes they wore, shoved them into waiting trucks and trains, and dumped them across the border onto the desolate flats of Poland's borderlands. More than ten thousand Jews were deported in this manner.

Among the deportees was the family of Zindel Grynszpan, whose seventeen-year-old son, Heschel, had previously fled the family home in Hanover to Paris. When he received a letter from his father recounting his family's ordeal, Heschel Grynszpan bought a gun and on 7 November walked to the German embassy in Paris to assassinate the ambassador. Ironically, he was detained by a minor official, Ernst vom Rath, who was himself under investigation by the Gestapo for his opposition to the increasing anti-Semitic violence, and shot him. This murder was the immediate excuse used to launch the well-orchestrated burnings, lootings, and round-ups known as Kristallnacht.

Then on 12 November, German Jews were fined a billion marks—$400 million—as penalty for the murder. This "money atonement" was astronomical and rendered it virtually impossible for most Jews to retain sufficient savings to emigrate. Yet another decree ordered the victims to pay for the repair and restoration of their former shops, buildings, and homes— from which they were permanently banished.

These fines had another, more sinister purpose. Hitler had announced: "If there is any country that believes it has not enough Jews, I shall gladly turn over to it all our Jews." Now, if they left, they left penniless. Moreover, most countries had closed their doors, and those who would accept Jews would not accept paupers.

It was a major challenge for FDR, whose policy was to do nothing to involve the United States in European affairs, but who wanted to respond somehow to the thousands of refugees who stood for hours before the U.S. embassy seeking asylum, only to be routinely turned away.

Within days, Jews were stripped of their remaining human rights. They were no longer permitted to drive cars, travel on public transportation, walk in parks, go to museums, attend theaters or concerts. Passports and visas were canceled. They were stateless and impoverished. Charged for the violence and fined for the damage, the Jewish community now owed the Reich, collectively, one billion Reichsmarks. For a time, they were not molested in their homes. But there was nothing to do, no work to be had; no place to pray; no recourse from agony. Many committed suicide; most tried to leave.

For all moral and political purposes, Kristallnacht was the terminal event. Civility in the heart of western Europe lay in ruins, surrounded by broken glass, bloodied streets, desecrated temples, burned Torahs, ripped books of prayer to the one shared God. Hitler's intentions were flagrant, and the whole world was invited to witness. Twenty thousand Jews were removed to concentration camps, which the Anglo-American press named: Dachau near Munich, Oranienburg-Sachsenhausen north of Berlin, Buchenwald near Weimar. . . .

ER's formerly private protests against bigotry were increasingly for public attribution. Although she had resigned in silence from the Colony Club for its discrimination against Elinor Morgenthau, she now canceled a speaking engagement at a country club in Lancaster, Pennsylvania, with a statement of distress that it excluded Jews.

While she counseled complete assimilation and urged Jews to "wipe out in their own consciousness any feeling of difference by joining in all that is being done by Americans" for justice and democracy, she also spoke on behalf of support for refugees in Palestine. . . . On 6 December 1938, ER appealed to fifteen hundred people assembled at the Hotel Astor under the auspices of a national committee for refugees chaired by William Green, president of the American Federation of Labor, to help promote the Léon Blum colony in Palestine for the settlement of one thousand Jewish refugee families. . . .

While ER called for demonstrations of "thought and example," little was done, or said, by FDR's administration to indicate official outrage at Hitler's violence. No message of protest warning of boycott or economic reprisal was sent. Yet history abounds in such protests on behalf of victimized peoples. In 1903 and 1906, Theodore Roosevelt protested against Jewish pogroms in Russia, after Jacob Schiff lobbied for an official U.S. condemnation of the massacre of Jews in Odessa. . . .

FDR sent no similar message to Germany.

FDR did respond to the pitiless carnage and massacre in China. In December 1937, Japan destroyed Nanking in a vicious episode of rape, horror, and death. Half the population, an estimated 300,000 people, were tortured and killed. Whether the details were immediately known to FDR, even of Japan's 12 December sinking of the U.S. gunboat *Panay*, remains controversial. But on 11 January 1938, FDR sent a memo to Cordell Hull and Admiral Cary T. Grayson, head of the American Red Cross. He called for additional relief funds for the "destitute Chinese civilians" and for medical aid. "I think we could raise $1,000,000 without any trouble at all." On 17 January, the U.S. Red Cross launched an appeal for aid to the Chinese people, initiated by FDR's formal request for such a drive.[1]

No similar appeal was made by FDR to the Red Cross on behalf of Europe's Jews.*

Since he was considered by many the best friend American Jews ever had, FDR's reactions to the European events of 1938 are unexplainable. . . . Except for Father Charles E. Coughlin, who hailed the violence against "Jewish-sponsored Communism," the press was unanimous in its condemnation. . . .

. . . FDR agreed to allow all German aliens on visitor visas to remain in the United States

for six months "and for other like periods so long as necessary." At the time there were between twelve thousand and fifteen thousand political refugees covered by his order, and "not all Jews, by any means," the president assured the press. "All shades of liberal political thought and many religions are represented."[2]

Anti-Semitism in FDR's State Department increased after Hitler's November atrocities. Breckenridge Long now dedicated himself to keeping refugees out of America. Curiously, FDR continually promoted Breckenridge Long, who had life-and-death control over visas and passports. Nevertheless, in 1938, for the first time, the United States filled its refugee quota.

ER and her asylum-seeking circle faced the urgent refugee crisis in a lonely political environment. Thousands of the earliest refugees who left in 1933 were still wandering Europe seeking safety and political asylum. After 31 January 1933, over 30 percent of Germany's 500,000 Jews had become refugees. After the March 1938 Anschluss, Germany's annexation of Austria, when the Nazis began to expel Austria's 190,000 Jews, the situation became critical. The flight of Czech Jews compounded the problem, and Kristallnacht ignited refugee panic.

FDR expanded his search for underpopulated and suitable lands upon which to place the world's unwanted Jews . . . but told his press conference that he had no intention of asking Congress to alter existing immigration quotas. . . .

During her own press conference, ER called for temporary emergency measures to do whatever was possible "to deal with the refugee problem, and at home, for renewed devotion to . . . the American way of life." Wary of her husband's strategies, she [rarely criticized] him directly. . . . "For ourselves, "[she said]," I hope we will do, as individuals, all we can to preserve what is a traditional right in this country—freedom for different races and different religions." . . .

[From 1938 to 1940, a committee of geographers, scholars, and members of the State Department explored the possibilities of sanctuary for Jews outside the United States, without success. ER was staggered by the contempt for human suffering expressed by the failure of

---

*During the 1940s, the International Red Cross deflected complaints about its neglect of Jewish needs, given the magnitude of the mounting tragedy, with the explanation that the Red Cross "could not interfere in the internal affairs of a belligerent nation." Blood plasma for U.S. troops was segregated into "white" and "colored," "Christian" and "Hebrew." It was not desegregated until 1954.

other nations to welcome refugees.] In the bitter time before the burning time there was hope for rescue country by country. But there was no official objection to Hitler's intention to remove Jews from Germany and all his new territories. ER increasingly bypassed State Department restrictions; she worked, often covertly, with private groups and individuals. She campaigned for a less restrictive refugee policy, pursued visas for individuals, and answered and passed on to government officials every appeal sent to her.

Revolted by world events, ER called for entirely new levels of action. Her speeches became more pointed and vigorous, and she spent more time in the company of radical activists, especially members of the American Youth Congress whose ardent views now coincided most completely with her own.

For ER, AYC leaders represented hope for the best of liberal America. Christian theology students, Jewish children of immigrants, black and white activists from the rural South and urban North imagined a nation united for progressive antifascist action.

A week after Kristallnacht, ER . . . defended the AYC at the annual luncheon of New York's branch of the American Association of University Women and spoke of the need for courage and fearlessness in perilous times. . . . ER's speech was bold: She rejected the current Red Scare tactics which branded the AYC communist and her a dupe or fool: Such name-calling had destroyed democracy in Europe, and she wanted democracy to survive here.

"People whose opinions I respect" had warned her not to attend the AYC convention.

> [But] I didn't think that those youngsters could turn me into a Communist, so I went just the same. . . .
>
> I listened to speeches which you and I could easily have torn to shreds. The Chinese listened while the Japanese spoke; the boy from India spoke with the British delegates. . . . Nobody hissed or left the room. I have been in lots of gatherings of adults who did not show that kind of respect. . . .

She spoke with many delegates, asked what they thought of the Soviet Union; she left convinced that there was interest in communism, but not domination by communists: "We who have training, and have minds that we know how to use must not be swept away" by fear and propaganda. The urgent problems before the United States and the world required scrutiny, debate, honest disagreement, democratic participation, not a wild and fearful flight from controversy. . . .

On 22 November 1938, ER embarked on a dangerous mission when she keynoted the radical biracial Southern Conference on Human Welfare, in Birmingham, Alabama. For the first time since the Civil War, Southern liberals were determined to face the race issue embedded within the region's struggling economy. Since 1890 there had been talk of a "New South," but always before, racial cruelties at the heart of peonage and poverty had been ignored in the interest of white supremacy. . . .

In the aftermath of Kristallnacht, there was a new level of commitment and urgency at the Birmingham meeting. Regional race and antiunion violence was behind the call for the SCHW, first conceived as a civil liberties conference by [pioneering progressive activists] Joseph Gelders and Lucy Randolph Mason. According to Virginia Durr, they wanted to deal with the "terrible things happening" to CIO organizers in Mississippi. Many people were beaten [and run out of town,] crosses were burned. . . .

While the South "led the world" in cotton, tobacco, paper, and other products, it was a disaster area. The average per capita income was half the nation's; the poll tax limited voting rights to 12 percent of the population in eight Southern states, including Virginia; the region's children were being undereducated. The South was hampered by backward and colonial customs; and its entrenched leaders wanted no changes.

The Southern Conference on Human Welfare determined to change the South and challenge segregation. Fifteen hundred delegates, black and white, sat anywhere they wanted Sunday night, 21 November 1938, in the city auditorium of downtown Birmingham. According to Virginia Durr: "Oh, it was a love feast. . . . Southern meetings always include a lot of preaching and praying and hymn singing. . . . The whole meeting was just full of love and hope. It was thrilling. . . . The whole South was coming together to make a new day."[3]

Somebody reported the integrated seating at the opening-night gala, and the next morning the auditorium was surrounded. . . . Every police van in the city and county was there. Policemen were everywhere, inside and out.

And there was Eugene "Bull" Connor "saying anybody who broke the segregation law of Alabama would be arrested." Tensions escalated; violence was in the air. The delegates complied and arranged themselves into separate sections.

ER, Mary McLeod Bethune, and Aubrey Williams arrived late that day, out of breath. ER "was ushered in with great applause," looked at the segregated audience—and took her seat on the black side. One of Bull Connor's police officers tapped ER on the shoulder and told her to move. . . .

As if to announce fascism would not triumph here, ER refused to "give in" and placed her chair between the white and black sections. Pauli Murray recalled that ER's demonstration of defiance and courage meant everything to the young people of the South, who now knew they were not alone. Although the national press did not report ER's brave action, the weekly *Afro-American* editorialized: "If the people of the South do not grasp this gesture, we must. Sometimes actions speak louder than words."[4]

ER was given a little folding chair and sat in the middle of whatever meeting hall or church she attended for the rest of the four-day meeting. She said she refused to be segregated, and carried the folding chair with her wherever she went. According to Durr: "Policemen followed us everywhere to make sure the segregation laws were observed, but they didn't arrest Mrs. Roosevelt."

ER's address to the SCHW stirred the packed auditorium:

We are the leading democracy of the world and as such must prove to the world that democracy is possible and capable of living up to the principles upon which it was founded. The eyes of the world are upon us, and often we find they are not too friendly eyes.

ER emphasized "universal education" in which "every one of our citizens, regardless of nationality, or race," might be allowed to flourish.[5] . . .

The 1938 SCHW adopted thirty-six resolutions, all of which involved the plight of African Americans, and eight of which directly concerned racial issues, including freedom for the four Scottsboro boys who remained in prison; availability of medical services by African American physicians in all public health facilities; more funding for public housing and

recreation facilities for African Americans; equal funding for graduate education in state-supported colleges; and—inspired by ER's demonstration—a resolution to support fully integrated SCHW meetings.

Perceived as "one of the gravest sins that a white southerner could commit," that direct assault against tradition created a furor. The antisegregation resolution divided the delegates, some of whom withdrew, and was branded communist, subversive, and un-American. On the other hand, it transformed national assumptions about the unspeakable: White supremacy, and its primary bulwark, segregation, were forevermore on the nation's agenda—put there by an integrated conference, led by Southern New Dealers.[6]

Traditional "race etiquette" was also challenged when Louise Charlton called on Mary McLeod Bethune to speak. (See Bethune, pp. 329–331.) According to Virginia Durr:

She said, "Mary, do you wish to come to the platform?" Mrs. Bethune rose. She looked like an African queen. . . . "My name is Mrs. Bethune." So Louise had to say, "Mrs. Bethune, will you come to the platform?" That sounds like a small thing now, but that was a big dividing line. A Negro woman in Birmingham, Alabama, was called Mrs. at a public meeting. . . .

Virginia Durr, wife of Clifford Durr, the assistant general counsel of the Reconstruction Finance Corporation, and sister-in-law of Justice Hugo Black, addressed the meeting to denounce the South's refusal to educate its people and the prevailing ignorance so general throughout the country. The reasons for an uninformed public, she declared, were propaganda and a controlled press dominated by Wall Street. She accused the National Manufacturers Association of being a "huge propaganda machine" intent on the "liquidation of organized labor." . . .

[A week after the SCHW], the Nazi press announced that Germany had embarked upon "the final and unalterably uncompromising solution" to the Jewish question. In the Gestapo's official paper, *Das Schwarze Korps*, on 24 November, the front-page feature announced that it should have been done immediately, brutally, and completely in 1933. But "it had to remain theory" for lack of the "military power we possess today."

Because it is necessary, because we no longer hear the world's screeching and because, after all, no power on earth can hinder us, we will now bring the Jewish question to its totalitarian solution.[7]

Two weeks after Kristallnacht, accepted without notable "screeching" from any government, Hitler felt sufficiently unrestrained to publish his intentions for all Jews caught in his widening web. First would come pauperization, isolation, ghettoization. They would all be marked for positive identification. Nobody would escape. Then, the starving, bedraggled remnant would become a scrounging, begging scourge. They would be forced to crime, would be an "underworld" of "politico-criminal subhumans," breeders of Bolshevism. At that stage "we should therefore face the hard necessity of exterminating the Jewish underworld. . . . The result will be the actual and definite end of Jewry . . . and its complete extermination."

While the announcement was made two years and eight months before it was actually implemented, the time to protest and resist was at hand. After it was reprinted in the U.S. and European press, many understood the implications of such crude words given the reality of the cruelties under way in Germany, Austria, and Czechoslovakia. Since Kristallnacht, race hatred had triumphed completely and Jews had been removed from all German institutions, doomed to a pariah existence in complete segregation. Jews could no longer dine with Gentiles—not in restaurants, not anywhere; nor could they buy food in the same stores. Nazis established separate stores where Jews were restricted in the purchase of life's staples—milk, bread.

Such laws cast a torchlight on American traditions. ER made the connections: brown shirts, white sheets; the twisted cross, the burning cross. Yet the internal affairs of a nation were deemed sacrosanct, nobody else's business. ER and other citizens no longer agreed with that diplomatic principle.

FDR remained virtually silent about human rights abuses, and did not end trade with Germany, but he began a vigorous rearmament program, emphasizing military planes and naval construction. Immediately after Kristallnacht, on 14 November, he reported to Josephus Daniels, his Wilson-era boss, that he was working on "national defense—especially mass production of planes." By December, he ordered the navy yards to run full-time, "two shifts or even three" wherever possible. It "is time to get action."

While ER approved of all defense programs, she also called for a worldwide educational crusade to address prejudice. . . . After the SCHW meetings, ER wrote her first articles specifically about Jews and race hatred. One, initially called "Tolerance," was for the *Virginia Quarterly* and attacked the kind of anticommunist hysteria that had resulted in fascist triumph and appeasement throughout so much of Europe. The other, which addressed the mounting hatred against Jews, was dated 25 November 1938. . . .

Untitled, ER's "Jewish article" called for a campaign of understanding to confront "the present catastrophe for Jew and Gentile alike. . . . In books . . . schools, newspapers, plays, assemblies we want incessant truth telling about these old legends that divide and antagonize and waste us."

As she struggled to understand "the kind of racial and religious intolerance which is sweeping the world today," ER rejected her former emphasis on assimilation. . . . Now ER assessed the historic hatred of Jews, their isolation, and forced ghettoization in the Middle Ages, and the ongoing contempt for Jews. . . . ER now pointed out that even when Jews attempted to assimilate they were condemned for "being too ostentatiously patriotic and of pushing themselves forward as nationals," as in Austria and Germany.

ER was also sensitive to the difficulties assimilated Jews faced among their coreligionists, who resented those who strayed from tradition. Never quite accepted into the majority culture, they were everywhere marginalized. . . . ER rejected ghettoization and deplored signs that appeared in many American neighborhoods that read "No Dogs or Jews Allowed."

Written from within the veil of her own stereotypes, ER concluded that the future was not up to the Jews.

> The Jew is almost powerless today. It depends almost entirely on the course of the Gentiles what the future holds. . . . If they perish, we perish sooner or later. . . .

She recalled that as a child her uncle Theodore Roosevelt once said "that when you are afraid to do a thing, that was the time to go and do it. Every time we shirk making up our minds or standing up for a cause in which we believe, we weaken our character and our ability to be fearless." . . .

ER challenged Americans to think and act politically, to engage in activist citizenship, to become their best selves. A sense of personal unimportance was encouraged by dictators. Democracy depended on "freedom from prejudice, and public awareness." It required education, economic security, and personal devotion, "a real devotion to freedom.... Freedom is something to guard jealously," but it can never be "freedom for me and not for you."

The bolder ER became, the tougher and more adamant her statements, the higher her public approval rating soared. On 16 January 1939, the *New York Times* published a poll taken by George Gallup regarding America's feelings about ER during 1938. The results were astounding. Two voters in every three voted in her favor (67 percent approved of her conduct, 33 percent disapproved).... According to the poll she had a greater approval rating than FDR.... Given the nature of the controversies ER engaged in and her challenge to work for the transformation of customs and traditions that subjected so many to poverty and powerlessness, America's response indicated a commitment to the very democracy she spoke about so earnestly. ER touched a nerve center in America, and the country would never be the same.

On 10 February 1938, ER [had] commemorated the seventy-fifth anniversary of the Emancipation Proclamation by asserting that while Abraham Lincoln took the "first step toward the abolition of slavery ... we still do tolerate slavery in several ways." Her words, addressed to nine thousand people at a meeting sponsored by the National Negro Congress, were electrifying:

There are still slaves of many different kinds, and today we are facing another era in which we have to make certain things become facts rather than beliefs.

As Europe fell to fascism, ER and her new network of youth and race radicals heralded the greatest changes in America since the betrayal of Reconstruction.

In her 8 December 1938 column, ER criticized liberals, smug partisans, and patriots for celebrating incomplete victories. . . .

As I listened [to speeches to promote the Leon Blum colony for refugees in Palestine] . . . I could not help thinking how much all human beings like to fool themselves. . . . [They] made us feel that . . . we were more virtuous and fortunate than any other people in the world. Of course, I concede this, and I feel for me it is true, for I have been free and fortunate all my life. While I listened, however, I could not help thinking of some of the letters which pass through my hands.

Are you free if you cannot vote, if you cannot be sure that the same justice will be meted out to you as to your neighbor, . . . if you are barred from certain places and from certain opportunities? . . .

Are you free when you can't earn enough, no matter how hard you work, to feed and clothe and house your children properly? Are you free when your employer can turn you out of a company house and deny you work because you belong to a union?

Her thoughts turned to refugees in this country, "of the little girl who wrote me not long ago: 'Why do other children call me names and laugh at my talk? I just don't live in this country very long yet.'" ER concluded:

There are lots and lots of things which make me wonder whether we ever look ourselves straight in the face and really mean what we say when we are busy patting ourselves on the back.

With grit, determination, and a very high heart, ER helped launch America's crusade for freedom in the fascist era. She was fortified every day by her new allies, her abiding partnership with FDR, love for the people in her life, and love of the world.

NOTES

1. FDR to Cordell Hull, Jan. 11, 1938, in *FDR: His Personal Letters, 1928–1945,* Elliott Roosevelt and Joseph P. Lash, eds. (Millwood, N.Y.: Kraus Reprint, 1970), IV, pp. 744–45; see also Iris Chang, *The Rape of Nanking: The Forgotten Holocaust of World War II* (New York: Penguin, 1997).

2. *New York Times,* Nov. 19, 1938.

3. Linda Reed, *Simple Decency and Common Sense: The Southern Conference Movement, 1938–1945* (Bloomington: Indiana University Press, 1991), pp. 15–16 and passim; Virginia Durr, *Outside the Magic Circle: The Autobiography of Virginia Durr* (Tuscaloosa: Univ. of Alabama Press, 1985).

4. Pauli Murray, *Song in a Weary Throat: An American Pilgrimage* (New York: Harper & Row, 1987), p. 113.

5. For ER's Nov. 22, 1938 speech at the SCHW, see Allida Black, ed., *Courage in a Dangerous World: The Political Writings of Eleanor Roosevelt* (New York: Columbia University Press, 1999).

6. Reed, pp. 46–48.

7. *New York Times,* Nov. 24, 1938; Arthur D. Morse, *While Six Million Died: A Chronicle of American Apathy* (New York: Random House, 1968); Michael Berenbaum, *The World Must Know* (Boston: Little Brown, 1993), p. 35.

WOMEN AND WAR

VALERIE MATSUMOTO

Japanese American Women During World War II

On no group of U.S. citizens did the war have greater impact than upon Japanese Americans. Fearful of a Japanese fifth column on American shores, military and civilian leaders urged Franklin Roosevelt to issue an executive order removing Americans of Japanese descent on the West Coast to relocation camps inland. Despite the fact that a vast majority of the nearly 120,000 Japanese Americans in the United States were citizens with the same rights and obligations as any other citizen, the president succumbed to pressure and issued Executive Order 9066 in February 1942, which ultimately resulted in the establishment of ten concentration camps, most of which were in remote areas of the West. Forced to leave their homes and businesses at great financial cost, both Japanese-born parents, the Issei, and their American-born children, the Nisei, faced the trauma of removal and the shame of implied disloyalty. Not until 1990 would the nation acknowledge the magnitude of its offense and begin providing financial redress for survivors of the camps.

The following essay explores what life in the camps was like for women and the efforts of younger ones to reconstruct a life after internment.

The life here cannot be expressed. Sometimes, we are resigned to it, but when we see the barbed wire fences and the sentry tower with floodlights, it gives us a feeling of being prisoners in a "concentration camp." We try to be happy and yet oftentimes a gloominess does creep in. When I see the "I'm an American" editorial and write-ups, the "equality of race etc."—it seems to be mocking us in our faces. I just wonder if all the sacrifices and hard labor on [the] part of our parents has gone up to leave nothing to show for it?

Letter from Shizuko Horiuchi,
Pomona Assembly Center, May 24, 1942

Overlying the mixed feelings of anxiety, anger, shame, and confusion [of the Japanese Americans who were forced to relocate] was resignation. As a relatively small minority caught in a storm of turbulent events that destroyed their individual and community security, there was little the Japanese Americans could do but shrug and say, "*Shikata ga nai*," or "It can't be helped," the implication being that the situation must be endured. The phrase lingered on many lips when the Issei, Nisei [second generation], and the young Sansei [third generation] children prepared for the move—which was completed by November 1942—to the ten permanent relocation camps organized by the War Relocation Authority: Topaz, Utah; Poston and Gila River, Arizona; Amache, Colorado; Manzanar and Tule Lake, California; Heart Mountain, Wyoming; Minidoka, Idaho; Denson and Rohwer, Arkansas.[1] Denson and Rohwer were located in the swampy lowlands of Arkansas;

Pledge of Allegiance, 1942.
Dorothea Lange had a keen eye for irony, as in this photograph of Japanese American girls in California a few weeks before they were deported to relocation camps. (Photograph courtesy of the National Archives.)

the other camps were in desolate desert or semi-desert areas subject to dust storms and extreme temperatures reflected in the nicknames given to the three sections of the Poston Camp: Toaston, Roaston, and Duston.

The conditions of camp life profoundly altered family relations and affected women of all ages and backgrounds. Family unity deteriorated in the crude communal facilities and cramped barracks. The unceasing battle with the elements, the poor food, the shortages of toilet tissue and milk, coupled with wartime profiteering and mismanagement, and the sense of injustice and frustration took their toll on a people uprooted, far from home.

The standard housing in the camps was a spartan barracks, about twenty feet by one

hundred feet, divided into four to six rooms furnished with steel army cots. Initially each single room or "apartment" housed an average of eight persons; individuals without kin nearby were often moved in with smaller families. Because the partitions between apartments did not reach the ceiling, even the smallest noises traveled freely from one end of the building to the other. There were usually fourteen barracks in each block, and each block had its own mess hall, laundry, latrine, shower facilities, and recreation room. . . . The even greater lack of privacy in the latrine and shower facilities necessitated adjustments in former notions of modesty. There were no partitions in the shower room, and the latrine consisted of two rows of partitioned toilets "with nothing in front of you, just on the sides."[2] . . . A married woman with a family wrote from Heart Mountain:

> Last weekend, we had an awful cold wave and it was about 20° to 30° below zero. In such a weather, it's terrible to try going even to the bath and latrine house. . . . It really aggravates me to hear some politicians say we Japanese are being coddled, for *it isn't so!!* We're on ration as much as outsiders are. I'd say welcome to anyone to try living behind barbed wire and be cooped in a 20 ft. by 20 ft. room. . . . We do our sleeping, dressing, ironing, hanging up our clothes in this one room.[3]

After the first numbness of disorientation, the evacuees set about making their situation bearable, creating as much order in their lives as possible. With blankets they partitioned their apartments into tiny rooms and created benches, tables, and shelves as piles of scrap lumber left over from barracks construction vanished; victory gardens and flower patches appeared. . . .

Despite the best efforts of the evacuees to restore order to their disrupted world, camp conditions prevented replication of their prewar lives. Women's work experiences, for example, changed in complex ways during the years of internment. Each camp offered a wide range of jobs, resulting from the organization of the camps as model cities administered through a series of departments headed by European American administrators. The departments handled everything from accounting, agriculture, education, and medical care to mess hall service and the weekly newspaper. The scramble for jobs began early in the assembly centers and camps, and all able-bodied persons were expected to work.

Even before the war many family members had worked, but now children and parents, men and women all received the same low wages. In the relocation camps, doctors, teachers, and other professionals were at the top of the pay scale, earning $19 per month. The majority of workers received $16, and apprentices earned $12. The new equity in pay and the variety of available jobs gave many women unprecedented opportunities for experimentation, as illustrated by one woman's account of her family's work in Poston:

> First I wanted to find art work, but I didn't last too long because it wasn't very interesting . . . so I worked in the mess hall, but that wasn't for me, so I went to the accounting department—timekeeping—and I enjoyed that, so I stayed there. . . . My dad . . . went to a shoe shop . . . and then he

was block gardener. . . . He got $16. . . . [My sister] was secretary for the block manager; then she went to the optometry department. She was assistant optometrist; she fixed all the glasses and fitted them. . . . That was $16.[4]

As early as 1942, the War Relocation Authority began to release evacuees temporarily from the centers and camps to do voluntary seasonal farm work in neighboring areas hard hit by the wartime labor shortage. The work was arduous, as one young woman discovered when she left Topaz to take a job plucking turkeys:

> The smell is terrific until you get used to it. . . . We all wore gunny sacks around our waist, had a small knife and plucked off the fine feathers.
>
> This is about the hardest work that many of us have done—but without a murmur of complaint we worked 8 hours through the first day without a pause.
>
> We were all so tired that we didn't even feel like eating. . . . Our fingers and wrists were just aching, and I just dreamt of turkeys and more turkeys.[5]

Work conditions varied from situation to situation, and some exploitative farmers refused to pay the Japanese Americans after they had finished beet topping or fruit picking. One worker noted that the degree of friendliness on the employer's part decreased as the harvest neared completion. Nonetheless, many workers, like the turkey plucker, concluded that "even if the work is hard, it is worth the freedom we are allowed." . . .

Like their noninterned contemporaries, most young Nisei women envisioned a future of marriage and children. They—and their parents—anticipated that they would marry other Japanese Americans, but these young women also expected to choose their own husbands and to marry "for love." This mainstream American ideal of marriage differed greatly from the Issei's view of love as a bond that might evolve over the course of an arranged marriage that was firmly rooted in less romantic notions of compatibility and responsibility. The discrepancy between Issei and Nisei conceptions of love and marriage had sturdy prewar roots; internment fostered further divergence from the old customs of arranged marriage. In the artificial hothouse of camp, Nisei romances often bloomed quickly. As Nisei men left to prove their loyalty to the United States in the 442nd Combat Team and the 100th Battalion, young Japanese Americans strove to grasp what happiness and security they could, given the uncertainties of the future. Lily Shoji, in her "Fem-a-lites" newspaper column, commented upon the "changing world" and advised Nisei women: "This is the day of sudden dates, of blind dates on the up-and-up, so let the flash of a uniform be a signal to you to be ready for any emergency. . . . Romance is blossoming with the emotion and urgency of war."[6]

In keeping with this atmosphere, camp newspaper columns like Shoji's in *The Mercedian, The Daily Tulean Dispatch's* "Strictly Feminine," and the *Poston Chronicle's* "Fashionotes" gave their Nisei readers countless suggestions on how to impress boys, care for their complexions, and choose the latest fashions. These evacuee-authored columns thus mirrored the mainstream girls' periodicals of the time. Such fashion news may seem incongruous in the context of an internment camp whose inmates had little choice in clothing beyond what they could find in the Montgomery Ward or Sears and Roebuck mail-order catalogues. These columns, however, reflect women's efforts to remain in touch with the world outside the barbed wire fence; they reflect as well women's attempt to maintain morale in a drab, depressing environment. "There's something about color in clothes," speculated Tule Lake columnist "Yuri"; "Singing colors have a heart-building effect. . . . Color is a stimulant we need—both for its effect on ourselves and on others."[7] . . .

RESETTLEMENT: COLLEGE AND WORK

Relocation began slowly in 1942. Among the first to venture out of the camps were college students, assisted by the National Japanese American Student Relocation Council, a nongovernmental agency that provided invaluable placement aid to 4,084 Nisei in the years 1942–46.[8] Founded in 1942 by concerned educators, this organization persuaded institutions outside the restricted Western Defense zone to accept Nisei students and facilitated their admissions and leave clearances. A study of the first 400 students to leave camp showed that a third of them were women.[9] Because of the cumbersome screening process, few other evacuees departed on indefinite leave before 1943. In that year, the War Relocation Authority tried to expedite the clearance procedure by broadening an army registration program aimed at Nisei males to include all adults. With this policy

change, the migration from the camps steadily increased.[10]

Many Nisei, among them a large number of women, were anxious to leave the limbo of camp and return "to normal life again."[11] . . . An aspiring teacher wrote: "Mother and father do not want me to go out. However, I want to go so very much that sometimes I feel that I'd go even if they disowned me. What shall I do? I realize the hard living conditions outside but I think I can take it."[12] Women's developing sense of independence in the camp environment and their growing awareness of their abilities as workers contributed to their self-confidence and hence their desire to leave. Significantly, Issei parents, despite initial reluctance, were gradually beginning to sanction their daughters' departures for education and employment in the Midwest and East. One Nisei noted: "[Father] became more broad-minded in the relocation center. . . . At first he didn't want me to relocate, but he gave in. . . . He didn't say I could go . . . but he helped me pack, so I thought, 'Well, he didn't say no.'"[13]

The decision to relocate was a difficult one. . . . Many internees worried about their acceptance in the outside world. The Nisei considered themselves American citizens, and they had an allegiance to the land of their birth. . . . But evacuation had taught the Japanese Americans that in the eyes of many of their fellow Americans, theirs was the face of the enemy. Many Nisei were torn by mixed feelings of shame, frustration, and bitterness at the denial of their civil rights. . . . "A feeling of uncertainty hung over the camp; we were worried about the future. Plans were made and remade, as we tried to decide what to do. Some were ready to risk anything to get away. Others feared to leave the protection of the camp."[14]

Thus, those first college students were the scouts whose letters back to camp marked pathways for others to follow. May Yoshino sent a favorable report to her family in Topaz from the nearby University of Utah, indicating that there were "plenty of schoolgirl jobs for those who want to study at the University."[15] Correspondence from other Nisei students shows that although they succeeded at making the dual transition from high school to college and from camp to the outside world, they were not without anxieties as to whether they could handle the study load and the reactions of the European Americans around them. One student at Drake University in Iowa wrote to her interned sister about a professor's reaction to her autobiographical essay, "Evacuation": "Today Mr.—, the English teacher that scares me, told me that the theme that I wrote the other day was very interesting. . . . You could just imagine how wonderful and happy I was to know that he liked it a little bit. . . . I've been awfully busy trying to catch up on work and the work is so different from high school. I think that little by little I'm beginning to adjust myself to college life."[16] . . . Lillian . . . Ota, a Wellesley student, reassured [her interned friends contemplating college:] "During the first few days you'll be invited by the college to teas and receptions. Before long you'll lose the awkwardness you might feel at such doings after the months of abnormal life at evacuation centers."[17] Although Ota had not noticed "that my being a 'Jap' has made much difference on the campus itself," she offered cautionary and pragmatic advice to the Nisei, suggesting the burden of responsibility these relocated students felt, as well as the problem of communicating their experiences and emotions to European Americans.

> It is scarcely necessary to point out that those who have probably never seen a nisei before will get their impression of the nisei as a whole from the relocated students. It won't do you or your family and friends much good to dwell on what you consider injustices when you are questioned about evacuation. Rather, stress the contributions of [our] people to the nation's war effort.[18] . . .

Armed with [such] advice and drawn by encouraging reports, increasing numbers of women students left camp.[19] . . . The trickle of migration from the camps grew into a steady stream by 1943, as the War Relocation Authority developed its resettlement program to aid evacuees in finding housing and employment in the East and Midwest. . . . [But] leaving camp meant [more changes.] Even someone as confident as Marii Kyogoku . . . found that reentry into the European American-dominated world beyond the barbed wire fence was not a simple matter of stepping back into old shoes. Leaving the camps—like entering them—meant major changes in psychological perspective and self-image.

> I had thought that because before evacuation I had adjusted myself rather well in a Caucasian society, I would go right back into my former frame of mind. I have found, however, that though the center became unreal and was as if it

had never existed as soon as I got on the train at Delta, I was never so self-conscious in all my life.

Kyogoku was amazed to see so many men and women in uniform and, despite her "proper" dining preparation, felt strange sitting at a table set with clean linen and a full set of silverware.

> I felt a diffidence at facing all these people and things, which was most unusual. Slowly things have come to seem natural, though I am still excited by the sounds of the busy city and thrilled every time I see a street lined with trees, I no longer feel that I am the cynosure of all eyes.[20] . . .

Many relocating Japanese Americans received moral and material assistance from a number of service organizations and religious groups, particularly the Presbyterians, the Methodists, the Society of Friends, and the Young Women's Christian Association. One such Nisei, Dorcas Asano, enthusiastically described to a Quaker sponsor her activities in the big city:

> Since receiving your application for hostel accommodation, I have decided to come to New York and I am really glad for the opportunity to be able to resume the normal civilized life after a year's confinement in camp. New York is really a city of dreams and we are enjoying every minute working in offices, rushing back and forth to work in the ever-speeding subway trains, counting our ration points, buying war bonds, going to church, seeing the latest shows, plays, operas, making many new friends and living like our neighbors in the war time. I only wish more of my friends who are behind the fence will take advantage of the many helpful hands offered to them.[21]

The Nisei also derived support and strength from networks—formed before and during internment—of friends and relatives. The homes of those who relocated first became way stations for others as they made the transition into new communities and jobs. In 1944, soon after she obtained a place to stay in New York City, Miné Okubo found that "many of the other evacuees relocating in New York came ringing my doorbell. They were sleeping all over the floor!"[22] Single women often accompanied or joined sisters, brothers, and friends as many interconnecting grapevines carried news of likely jobs, housing, and friendly communities. . . .

For Nisei women, like their non-Japanese sisters, the wartime labor shortage opened the door into industrial, clerical, and managerial occupations. Prior to the war, racism had excluded the Japanese Americans from most white-collar clerical and sales positions, and, according to sociologist Evelyn Nakano Glenn, "the most common form of nonagricultural employment for the immigrant women (Issei) and their American-born daughters (Nisei) was domestic service."[23] The highest percentage of job offers for both men and women continued to be requests for domestic workers. In July 1943, the Kansas City branch of the War Relocation Authority noted that 45 percent of requests for workers were for domestics, and the Milwaukee office cited 61 percent.[24] However, Nisei women also found jobs as secretaries, typists, file clerks, beauticians, and factory workers. By 1950, 47 percent of employed Japanese American women were clerical and sales workers and operatives; only 10 percent were in domestic service.[25] The World War II decade, then, marked a turning point for Japanese American women in the labor force. . . .

[Improved opportunities could not compensate for the] uprooting [of] communities and [the] severe psychological and emotional damage [inflicted upon Japanese Americans by internment.] The vast majority returned to the West Coast at the end of the war in 1945—a move that, like the initial evacuation, was a grueling test of flexibility and fortitude. Even with the assistance of old friends and service organizations, the transition was taxing and painful; the end of the war meant not only long-awaited freedom but more battles to be fought in social, academic, and economic arenas. The Japanese Americans faced hostility, crude living conditions, and a struggle for jobs. Few evacuees received any compensation for their financial losses, estimated conservatively at $400 million, because Congress decided to appropriate only $38 million for the settlement of claims.[26] It is even harder to place a figure on the toll taken in emotional shock, self-blame, broken dreams, and insecurity. One Japanese American woman still sees in her nightmares the watchtower searchlights that troubled her sleep forty years ago.

The war altered Japanese American women's lives in complicated ways. In general, internment and resettlement accelerated earlier trends that differentiated the Nisei from their parents. Although most young women, like their mothers and non-Japanese peers, anticipated a future centered on a husband and children, they had already felt the influence of mainstream middle-class values of love and marriage and quickly moved away from the pattern of arranged marriage in the camps. There, increased peer group activities and the relaxation of parental authority gave them more independence. The Nisei women's expectations of marriage became more akin to the companionate ideals of their peers than to those of the Issei.

As before the war, many Nisei women worked . . . , but the new parity in wages they received altered family dynamics. And though they expected to contribute to the family economy, a large number did so in settings far from the family, availing themselves of opportunities provided by the student and worker relocation programs. In meeting the challenges facing them, Nisei women drew not only upon the disciplined strength inculcated by their Issei parents but also upon firmly rooted support networks and the greater measure of self-reliance and independence that they developed during the crucible of the war years.

NOTES

1. Many of the Japanese community leaders arrested by the FBI before the evacuation were interned in special all-male camps in North Dakota, Louisiana, and New Mexico. Some Japanese Americans living outside the perimeter of the Western defense zone in Arizona, Utah, etc., were not interned.

2. Chieko Kimura, personal interview, Apr. 9, 1978, Glendale, Arizona.

3. Shizuko Horiuchi to Henriette Von Blon, Jan. 24, 1943, Henriette Von Blon Collection, Hoover Institution Archives ([hereafter] HIA).

4. Ayako Kanemura, personal interview, Mar. 10, 1978, Glendale, Arizona.

5. Anonymous, *Topaz Times*, Oct. 24, 1942, p. 3.

6. Lily Shoji, "Fem-a-lites," *The Mercedian*, Aug. 7, 1942, p. 4.

7. "Yuri," "Strictly Feminine," *The Daily Tulean Dispatch*, Sept. 29, 1942, p. 2.

8. From 1942 to the end of 1945 the Council allocated about $240,000 in scholarships, most of which were provided through the donations of the church and the World Student Service Fund. The average grant for student for was $156.73, which in that area was a major contribution towards the cost of higher education. Source: National Japanese American Student Relocation Council, Minutes of the Executive Committee Meeting, Philadelphia, Pennsylvania, Dec. 19, 1945.

9. Robert O'Brien, *The College Nisei* (Palo Alto: Pacific Books, 1949), pp. 73–74.

10. The disastrous consequences of the poorly conceived clearance procedure had been examined by Robert Wilson and Bill Hosokawa, *East to America: A History of the Japanese in the United States* (New York: Morrow, 1980), pp. 226–27, and Audrie Girdner and Anne Loftis, *The Great Betrayal: The Evacuation of the*

Japanese-Americans during World War II (New York: Macmillan, 1969), pp. 342–43.

11. May Nakamoto to Mrs. Jack Shoup, Nov. 20, 1943, Mrs. Jack Shoup Collection, HIA.

12. Toshiko Imada to Margaret Cosgrave Sowers, Jan. 16, 1943, Margaret Cosgrave Sowers Collection, HIA.

13. Ayako Kanemura, personal interview, Mar. 24, 1978, Glendale, Arizona.

14. Miné Okubo, *Citizen 13660* (New York: Columbia University Press, 1946), p. 66.

15. *Topaz Times*, Oct. 24, 2942, p. 3.

16. Masako Ono to Atsuko Ono, Sept. 28, 1942, Margaret Cosgrave Sowers Collection, HIA. Prior to the war, few Nisei had college experience: the 1940 census lists 674 second-generation women and 1,507 men who had attended or who were attending college.

17. Lillian Ota, "Campus Report," Trek (Feb. 1943), p. 33.

18. Ota, pp. 33–34.

19. O'Brien, p. 84.

20. Marii Kyogoku, *Resettlement Bulletin* (July 1943), p. 5.

21. Dorcas Asano to Josephine Duveneck, Jan. 22, 1944, Conard-Duveneck Collection, HIA.

22. Miné Okubo, *Miné Okubo: An American Experience,* exhibition catalogue (Oakland: Oakland Museum, 1972), p. 84.

23. Evelyn Nakano Glenn, "The Dialectics of Wage Work: Japanese American Women and Domestic Servants, 1905–1940," *Feminist Studies* 6, no. 3 (Fall 1980):412.

24. Advisory Committee of Evacuees, *Resettlement Bulletin* (July 1943), p. 3.

25. 1950 United States Census, Special Report.

26. Susan M. Hartmann, *The Home Front and Beyond, American Women in the 1940s* (Boston: Twayne Publishers, 1982), p. 126. There is some debate regarding the origins of the assessment of evacuee losses at $400 million. However, a recent study by the Commission on Wartime Relocation and Internment of Civilians has estimated that the Japanese Americans lost between $149 million and $370 million in 1945 dollars, and between $810 million and $2 billion in 1983 dollars. See the *San Francisco Chronicle*, June 16, 1983, p. 12.

RUTH MILKMAN
Gender at Work: The Sexual Division of Labor During World War II

As the nation, struggling with economic depression, began to fight its second world war in a single generation, unemployment lines quickly vanished. Manpower shortages meant that women would once again move into jobs in industry. They would experience new vocational opportunities; a lessening of discrimination based on marital status, age, and race; and public praise for their wartime contributions as workers. Using the techniques of advertising, the federal government publicized women's industrial work as patriotic support for the war by personifying the worker as "Rosie the Riveter." In short order, a catchy song circulated, written by Redd Evans and John Jacob Loeb:

All the day long, / Whether rain or shine, / She's a part of the assembly line.
She's making history, / Working for victory, / Rosie the Riveter

A witty Norman Rockwell painting for the cover of the popular magazine the *Saturday Evening Post* made it easy to visualize such a woman.*

*The cover appeared on May 29, 1943, several months after the song was published. A prizewinning documentary by Connie Field, *The Life and Times of Rosie the Riveter*, was made in 1980.

Excerpted from "Redefining 'Women's Work'" and "Demobilization and the Reconstruction of 'Woman's Place' in Industry," chs. 4 and 7 of *Gender at Work: The Dynamics of Job Segregation by Sex During World War II* by Ruth Milkman (Urbana: University of Illinois Press, 1987). Reprinted by permission of the author and the publisher. Notes have been renumbered and edited and figures omitted.

The potential provided by the war for refashioning gender roles was enormous, but the results were disappointing. The expectation was that once the men came home, women would happily exchange industrial tools for the broom and mop or new vacuum cleaner and the baby bottle. Polls showed that up to 85 percent of these women needed to continue working and expected that job seniority would entitle them to return after veterans had been absorbed in the work force.

The redefining of "men's jobs" and "women's jobs" precipitated by wartime mobilization and the rapid return to the prewar sexual division of labor is the subject of Ruth Milkman's study. Focusing especially on the auto and electronics industry, she provides unmistakable evidence of the persistence of occupational segregation at a time when the very survival of democracy was at stake. Note how job segregation demonstrates the double meaning of Milkman's title *Gender at Work*. What was the rationale for segregating jobs by sex? What evidence does Milkman provide to suggest that the designation of jobs as "male" or "female" was often arbitrary? Given management's assessment of women's job performance during the war, how does she explain the reversion to old patterns? What factors were involved? What explanation is offered for the fact that black men were able to hold on to wartime gains in industry whereas white and black women were not?

If it is true that occupational sex typing becomes even more important when women's labor force participation increases, what trends do you foresee for the postwar decades given the changes in the pattern of women's labor force participation noted by Milkman for the 1940s? How does job segregation help to explain the fact that women have yet to close the earnings gap with men when both are full-time workers (see this volume's introduction, p. 6)?

Conversion to war production involved redefinition of the entire employment structure. Some civilian automobile production jobs were also necessary for the production of tanks, aircraft, engines and ordnance; other war jobs were completely new. The changeover to war production in electrical manufacturing was less dramatic, but also involved shifts in the character and distribution of jobs. Thus, many of the war jobs that had to be filled (in both industries) were not clearly labeled as "women's" or "men's" work, at least at first. . . .

While the government had actively pressured some firms to hire women, it made no effort whatsoever to influence their placement within industry once management complied. The U.S. Employment Service routinely filled employer job openings that called for specific numbers of women and men. Although ceilings were imposed on the number of men who could be allocated to each plant, employers had a free hand in placing women and men in particular jobs within this constraint.[1] Although the unions sometimes contested the sexual division of labor after the fact, the initial job assignments were left entirely to management.

Women were not evenly distributed through the various jobs available in the war plants, but were hired into specific classifications that management deemed "suitable" for women and were excluded from other jobs. Some employers conducted special surveys to determine the sexual division of labor in a plant; probably more often such decisions were made informally by individual supervisors.[2] Although data on the distribution of women through job classifications in the wartime auto and electrical industries are sketchy, there is no mistaking the persistence of segregation by sex. A 1943 survey of the auto industry's Detroit plants, for example, found more than one-half of the women workers clustered in only five of seventy-two job classifications. Only 11 percent of the men were employed in these five occupations.[3]

Jobs were also highly segregated in the electrical industry during the war. A 1942 study of electrical appliance plants (most of which had already been converted to military

Frances Green, Peg Kirchner, Ann Waldner, and Blanche Osborne emerging from their four-engine, B-17 Flying Fortress.
See the painted lettering on the plane's nose for the name given it by these pilots, following a long-standing military tradition. They were among the 1,074 Women's Airforce Service Pilots (WASPs) who flew noncombat missions during World War II. Although 38 died in the line of duty, WASPs were not eligible for military insurance or GI benefits. At the end of the war, the WASPs were disbanded. Not until 1978 were the survivors offered veteran's status. In 2009, when barely 300 of the original 1,000 WASPs were still alive, the WASPs were awarded a Congressional Gold Medal. (Courtesy of the U.S. Army Museum.)

production when surveyed) found women, who were 30 percent of the workers, in only twenty-one job classifications, whereas men were spread across seventy-two of them. Nearly half of the women (47 percent) were employed in a single job category, and 68 percent were clustered in four occupations. Only 16 percent of the men were in these four job classifications.[4] . . .

Job segregation by sex was explicitly acknowledged in many war plants: Jobs were formally labeled "male" and "female." The two largest electrical firms, GE and Westinghouse, continued this practice until the end of the war. And in 45 percent of the auto plants with sexually mixed work forces responding to a survey conducted in mid-1944 by the UAW Women's Bureau, jobs were formally categorized as "male" or "female."[5] Available records suggest that sex segregation also existed elsewhere, even if it was not formally acknowledged. . . .

Segregation appears to be a constant across both industries during the war years.

However, in both industries there was considerable plant-to-plant variation in patterns of employment by sex. In the Detroit area, for example, there was a wide range in the proportion of women employed, even among plants manufacturing the same products. In April 1943, women were 29 percent of the workers at the GM Cadillac plant, which was producing engine parts, but women made up 59 percent of the work force at the Excello Corporation's Detroit plant, which made the same product. Similarly, although women were only 2 percent of the workers at Continental Motors, they were 27 percent of those at the Jefferson Avenue plant of the Hudson Motor Car Company. Both plants made aircraft motors.[6] In the electrical industry, too, there was considerable variation of this sort, even among plants owned by the same company and producing similar goods. . . .

Whatever the sexual division of labor happened to be at a given point in time, management always seemed to insist that there was no alternative. When a War Department representative visited an airplane plant where large numbers of women were employed, he was told that the best welder in the plant was a woman. "Their supervisors told me that their work is fine, even better than that of the men who were formerly on those jobs," he reported. "In another plant in the same area, I remarked on the absence of women and was told that women just can't do those jobs—the very same jobs. It is true, they can't do that type of work—as long as the employer refuses to hire and train them."[7]

Although the specifics varied, everywhere management was quick to offer a rationale for the concentration of women in some jobs and their exclusion from others. . . . "Womanpower differs from manpower as oil fuel differs from coal," proclaimed the trade journal *Automotive War Production* in October 1943, "and an understanding of the characteristics of the energy involved was needed for obtaining best results." Although it was now applied to a larger and quite different set of jobs, the basic characterization of women's abilities and limitations was familiar. As *Automotive War Production* put it:

> On certain kinds of operations—the very ones requiring high manipulative skill—women were found to be a whole lot quicker and more efficient than men. Engineering womanpower means realizing fully that women are not only different from men in such things as lifting power and arm reach—but in many other ways that pertain to their physiological and their social functions. To understand these things does not mean to exclude women from *the jobs for which they are peculiarly adapted,* and where they can help to win this war. It merely means using them as women, and not as men.[8]

The idiom of women's war work in the electrical industry closely paralleled that in auto. "Nearly every Westinghouse plant employs women, especially for jobs that require dexterity with tiny parts," reported an article in *Factory Management and Maintenance* in March 1942. "At the East Pittsburgh plant, for instance, women tape coils. The thickness of each coil must be identical to within close limits, so the job requires feminine patience and deft fingers. Another job that calls for unlimited patience is the inspection of moving parts of electric instruments. . . . " Repeatedly stressed, especially in auto, was the lesser physical strength of the average woman worker. "Woman isn't just a 'smaller man,'" *Automotive War Production* pointed out. "Compensations in production processes must be made to allow for the fact that the average woman is only 35 percent muscle in comparison to the average man's 41 percent. Moreover, industrial studies have shown that only 54 percent of woman's weight is strength, as against man's 87 percent, and that the hand squeeze of the average woman exerts only 48 pounds of pressure, against man's 81 pounds."[9]

Accompanying the characterization of women's work as "light" was an emphasis on cleanliness. "Women can satisfactorily fill all or most jobs performed by men, subject only to the limitations of strength and physical requirements," a meeting of the National Association of Manufacturers concluded in March 1942. "However . . . jobs of a particularly 'dirty' character, jobs that subject women to heat process or are of a 'wet' nature should not be filled by women . . . despite the fact that women could, if required, perform them."[10]

The emphasis in the idiom of sex-typing on the physical limitations of women workers had a dual character. It not only justified the sexual divison of labor, but it also served as the basis for increased mechanization and work simplification. "To adjust women's jobs to such [physical] differences, automotive plants have added more mechanical aids such as conveyors, chain hoists, and load lifters," reported *Automotive War Production.* A study by Constance

Green found job dilution of this sort widespread in electrical firms and other war industries in the Connecticut Valley as well. "Where ten men had done ten complete jobs, now . . . eight women and two, three, or possibly four men together would do the ten split-up jobs," she noted. "Most often men set up machines, ground or adjusted tools, and generally 'serviced' the women who acted exclusively as machine operators."[11]

Although production technology was already quite advanced in both auto and electrical manufacturing, the pace of development accelerated during the war period. Management attributed this to its desire to make jobs easier for women, but the labor shortage and the opportunity to introduce new technology at government expense under war contracts were at least as important. However, the idiom that constructed women as "delicate" and, although poorly suited to "heavy" work, amenable to monotonous jobs, was now marshaled to justify the use of new technology and work "simplification." At Vultee Aircraft, for example, a manager explained:

> It definitely was in Vultee's favor that the hiring of women was started when production jobs were being simplified to meet the needs of fast, quantity production. . . . Special jigs were added to hold small tools, such as drills, so that women could concentrate on employing more effectively their proven capacity for repetitive operations requiring high digital dexterity.
>
> Unlike the man whom she replaced, she as a woman, had the capacity to withstand the monotony of even more simplified repetitive operations. To have suspended the air wrench from a counterbalanced support for him would have served merely to heighten his boredom with the job. As for the woman who replaced him, she now handles two such counterbalanced, air-driven wrenches, one in each hand.[12] . . .

There was a contradiction in the management literature on women's war work. It simultaneously stressed the fact that "women are being trained in skills that were considered exclusively in man's domain" and their special suitability for "delicate war jobs."[13] These two seemingly conflicting kinds of statements were reconciled through analogies between "women's work" at home and in the war plants. "Note the similarity between squeezing orange juice and the operation of a small drill press," the Sperry Gyroscope Company urged in a recruitment pamphlet. "Anyone can peel potatoes," it

went on. "Burring and filing are almost as easy." An automotive industry publication praised women workers at the Ford Motor Company's Willow Run bomber plant in similar terms. "The ladies have shown they can operate drill presses as well as egg beaters," it proclaimed. "Why should men, who from childhood on never so much as sewed on buttons," inquired one' manager, "be expected to handle delicate instruments better than women who have plied embroidery needles, knitting needles and darning needles all their lives?"[14] The newsreel *Glamour Girls of '43* pursued the same theme: "Instead of cutting the lines of a dress, this woman cuts the pattern of aircraft parts. Instead of baking cake, this woman is cooking gears to reduce the tension in the gears after use. . . . "[15] In this manner, virtually any job could be labeled "women's work."

Glamour was a related theme in the idiom through which women's war work was demarcated as female. As if calculated to assure women—and men—that war work need not involve a loss of femininity, depictions of women's new work roles were overlaid with allusions to their stylish dress and attractive appearance. "A pretty young inspector in blue slacks pushes a gauge—a cylindrical plug with a diamond-pointed push-button on its side—through the shaft's hollow chamber," was a typical rendition.[16] Such statements, like the housework analogies, effectively reconciled woman's position in what were previously "men's jobs" with traditional images of femininity.

Ultimately, what lay behind the mixed message that war jobs were at once "men's" and "women's" jobs was an unambiguous point: Women *could* do "men's work," but they were only expected to do it temporarily. The ideological definition of women's war work explicitly included the provision that they would gracefully withdraw from their "men's jobs" when the war ended and the rightful owners returned. Women, as everyone knew, were in heavy industry "for the duration." This theme would become much more prominent after the war, but it was a constant undercurrent from the outset.

Before the war, too, women had been stereotyped as temporary workers, and occupational sex-typing had helped to ensure that employed women would continue to view themselves as women first, workers second. Now this took on new importance, because the reserves of "womanpower" war industries drew on included married women, even mothers of young children, in unprecedented numbers. A study by the Automotive Council for War Production noted that of twelve thousand women employed during the war by one large automotive firm in Detroit, 68 percent were married, and 40 percent had children. And a 1943 WPB study found that 40 percent of one hundred fifty thousand women war workers employed in Detroit were mothers. "With the existing prejudice against employing women over forty, the overwhelming majority of these women workers are young mothers with children under 16."[17]

This was the group of women least likely to have been employed in the prewar years. "In this time of pressure for added labor supply," the U.S. Women's Bureau reported, "the married women for the first time in this country's history exceeded single women in the employed group."[18] . . .

Some firms made deliberate efforts to recruit the wives and daughters of men whom they had employed before the war. A 1942 study by Princeton University's Industrial Relations Section reported on the reasons given by employers for this policy: "(1) It increases the local labor supply without affecting housing requirements; (2) it brings in new employees who are already acquainted with the company and who are likely to be as satisfactory employees as their male relatives; and (3) it may help to minimize postwar readjustment since wives of employed men are not looking for permanent employment."[19] Similarly, the Detroit Vickers aircraft plant had a policy of hiring "members of men's families who have gone to forces so that when these men come back there will be less of a problem in getting the women out of the jobs to give them back to the men."[20]

The dramatic rise in married women's employment during the war raised the longstanding tension between women's commitment to marriage and family and their status as individual members of the paid work force to a qualitatively different level. Before the war, the bulk of the female labor force was comprised of unmarried women; young wives with no children; and self-supporting widowed, divorced, and separated women. When married women and mothers went to work during the war, the occupational sex-typing that linked women's roles in the family and in paid work, far from disintegrating, was infused with new energy. . . .

DEMOBILIZATION AND THE RECONSTRUCTION OF "WOMAN'S PLACE" IN INDUSTRY

The war's end generated renewed upheaval in the sexual division of labor. As reconversion brought massive layoffs and then new hiring, the issue of women's position in industry came to the fore. . . . Would there be a return to the "traditional," prewar sexual division of labor as the mobilization-era ideology of "woman's place" in the war effort had promised? Or would the successful wartime deployment of women in "men's jobs" lead to a permanent shift in the boundaries between women's and men's jobs? Or—a third alternative—would completely new, postwar exigencies reshape, or even eliminate, the sexual division of labor?

Reversion to prewar patterns, which ultimately did occur, might appear to have been the only real possibility. Had not the nation been repeatedly assured that women's entrance into industry was a temporary adaptation to the extraordinary needs of war? . . . Such a view is consistent with the prevailing ideology of the demobilization period, but it obscures the significance of the war years themselves. Wartime conditions were indeed transitory, yet the extraordinary period between Pearl Harbor and V-J Day left American society permanently transformed. One legacy of the war years, from which no retreat would be possible, was the increase in female labor force participation. On an individual basis, to be sure, many women faced conflicting pressures after the war—to continue working for pay on the one hand, and to go back to the home on the other. Yet a permanent shift had occurred for women as a social group. Despite the postwar resurgence of the ideology of domesticity, by the early 1950s the number of gainfully employed women exceeded the highest wartime level. And as early as 1948, the labor force participation rate of married women was higher than in 1944, the peak of the war boom. The rise in female employment, especially for married women, would continue throughout the postwar period, and at a far more rapid rate than in the first half of the century. In this respect, far from being a temporary deviation, the war was a watershed period that left women's relationship to work permanently changed.[21]

The crucial issue, then, was not whether women would remain in the work force, but rather which women would do so and on what terms. What would the postwar sexual division of paid labor look like? Would women retain their wartime foothold in basic industries like auto and electrical manufacturing? To what extent would they be able to find work in fields that had been predominantly male before the war? For women who worked for pay, whether by choice or necessity, exclusion from "men's jobs" did not mean the housewifery first celebrated and later decried as the "feminine mystique." Instead, it meant employment in low-wage "female" jobs, especially clerical, sales, and service work—all of which expanded enormously in the postwar decades.

That the war brought a permanent increase in female employment made the demobilization transition particularly consequential. The opportunity was there for incorporating the dramatic wartime changes in women's position in industry into the fabric of a postwar order in which paid work would become increasingly central to women's lives. In the absence of any events affecting the labor market as fundamentally and cataclysmically as the war, there has been no comparable occasion for a wholesale restructuring of the sexual division of labor since the 1940s. The fact that the opportunity the wartime upheaval presented was lost had enormous implications for the entire postwar era.

Why, then, was the potential for an enduring transformation in the sexual division of labor not fulfilled in the 1940s? There are two standard explanations. One focuses on the postwar resurgence of domesticity, both as a practice and as an ideology, and suggests that women war workers themselves relinquished the "men's jobs" they held during the war—either because of the genuine appeal of traditional family commitments or because they were ideologically manipulated. The second explanation, in contrast, suggests that the key problem was the operation of union-instituted seniority systems, and their manipulation by male unionists, to exclude women and to favor returning male veterans in postwar employment.

. . . [B]oth these accounts of the postwar transition, while partially correct, are inadequate. . . . A large body of evidence demonstrates that management took the lead both in purging women from "men's jobs" after the war and in refusing to rehire them (except in traditionally "female" jobs) as postwar production resumed. Management chose this course despite the fact that most women war workers wanted to keep doing "men's work," and despite the fact that refusing to rehire women often violated seniority provisions in union contracts. . . .

I will offer a two-part explanation for management's postwar policy. First, in both auto and electrical manufacturing, the "traditional" sexual division of labor had a historical logic embodied in the structure of each industry, which remained compelling in the demobilization period. At one level, indeed, reconstructing the prewar sexual division of labor was a foregone conclusion from management's perspective. Wartime female substitution was an experiment that employers had undertaken unwillingly and only because there was no alternative. Despite the success with which women were integrated into "men's jobs," the war's end meant an end to the experiment, and management breathed a collective sigh of relief.

But that is only half of the story. The postwar purge of women from men's jobs also reflected management's assessment of labor's position on the issue. For one thing, the CIO's wartime struggles for equal pay for women workers, which narrowed sex differentials in wages considerably, made permanent female substitution less appealing than it might otherwise have been. Moreover, in the reconversion period, male workers displayed a great deal of ambivalence about the postwar employment rights of women war workers, even those with seniority standing. The CIO's official policy was to defend women's job rights in line with the seniority principle, but in practice there was substantial opposition to retaining women in "men's jobs." This, I will suggest, effectively reinforced management's determination to reconstruct the prewar sexual division of labor. . . .

MANAGERIAL POLICY TOWARD WOMEN WORKERS DURING THE WAR—AND AFTER

. . . Why was management so determined to oust women from the positions that they had occupied during the war? Women war workers wanted to keep their jobs, and union seniority policies did not stand in the way of hiring women, yet they were purged. The problem is all the more puzzling in light of contemporary evidence that management was highly satisfied with women war workers' abilities and performance. While initially employers had strenuously resisted replacing men with women in war industries, once having reconciled themselves to the inevitable, they seemed very pleased with the results. Moreover, because sex differentials in wages, although smaller than before, persisted during the war, one might expect management to have seriously considered the possibility of permanent female substitution on economic grounds.

There is no doubt that women's wartime performance proved satisfactory to management. Under the impact of the "manpower" crunch in the seven months following Pearl Harbor, the proportion of jobs for which the nation's employers were willing to consider women rose from 29 to 55 percent. And management praised women's industrial performance extravagantly during the mobilization period. "Women keep piling up evidence that they *can do,* and *do well,* a multitude of jobs," proclaimed the American Management Association in a 1943 report. "The distribution of basic aptitudes between the two sexes does not differ to any appreciable extent. . . . What is needed is *training*—training to develop latent aptitudes, to increase mechanical knowledge and skill, and to overcome any fear of the machine."[22] . . .

. . . In a 1943 National Industrial Conference Board survey of 146 executives, nearly 60 percent stated without qualification that women's production was equal to or greater than that of men on similar work. Similarly, a study by the Bureau of Employment Security of several California war plants found an increase in production per hour of workers of both sexes, and a lowering of costs per hour when women were employed, in every plant studied. The BES study also found that women were easier to supervise, and that labor turnover and accident rates decreased with the introduction of women.[23]

Many traditional management policies toward women workers were revised or eliminated with their successful incorporation into war industry. For example, physical segregation of the sexes was no longer deemed necessary; the belief "that men and women could work satisfactorily side by side" was held by the majority of executives questioned by the magazine *Modern Industry* as early as mid-1942. There were also many efforts to promote women to supervisory posts, especially at the lower levels, although women were almost never given authority over male workers, and there was a lingering conviction that women workers themselves preferred male bosses.[24]

Women workers' wartime performance, then, stood as evidence that they could be successfully incorporated into the industrial labor force. In addition, wage differentials between the sexes persisted during the war years—a consideration that one might expect to have enhanced management's interest in retaining women permanently in the postwar era. The unions, to be sure, had successfully contested sex discrimination in wages in many "equal pay for equal work" cases before the War Labor Board. But although sex differentials were narrowed as a result of these struggles, they were not eliminated. The Conference Board's composite earnings index for twenty-five manufacturing industries registered only a modest increase in the ratio of female to male average hourly earnings, from 61.5 percent in 1941 to 66.4 percent in 1945.[25] . . .

Still, because men and women rarely did "equal work" even during the war, the outcome of successful WLB equal pay cases was to narrow sex differentials in wages, not to eliminate them. And the Board's equal pay policy was not fully enforced, so that even when jobs were identical, or nearly so, women were often paid less than men. The Conference Board found differentials in starting rates paid to men and to "women hired for men's jobs" in nearly half the 148 plants that it surveyed in 1943, well after equal pay "for comparable quality and quantity of work" had become official WLB policy. Of the ninety-two plants in the survey that had systems of automatic progression in wage rates, twenty-five had sex differentials built into the progression systems despite the fact that the WLB had declared this practice improper.[26]

Similarly, a study of women's wages by the New York State Department of Labor found that 40 percent of the 143 plants surveyed had different starting rates for men and women on "men's jobs." When the state's investigators asked employers to account for such differences, most simply referred to "tradition," standard practice, prevailing wage rates, and custom. "It's also cheaper," said one manager.[27] . . .

There were some extra costs associated with the employment of women, to be sure, particularly in previously all-male plants. Women's absenteeism was generally higher than men's, especially if they were married and had domestic responsibilities, although employers succeeded in narrowing or even eliminating the gap in some plants.[28] UAW

President R. J. Thomas, summarizing the reasons auto industry employers were reluctant to hire women for postwar jobs, noted other costs associated with expanding or introducing female employment in a plant. "First is that as you know on most jobs equal rates are paid for equal jobs today," he pointed out. "Management doesn't want to pay women equal rates with men. Not only that but in many of these plants additional facilities have to be put in, such as toilet facilities to take care of women. More space has to be taken to give an opportunity of changing clothes and more safety measures have to be instituted. I think it is pretty well recognized that it is an additional expense to a management to have women."[29]

This is an accurate rendition of the reasons auto industry managers themselves adduced for their reluctance to employ women. Yet it is an inadequate explanation for managerial hostility toward female employment. The costs of maintaining special "facilities" for women were largely absorbed by the government during the war, and could hardly have been a major financial consideration in any event. Surely the savings associated with sex differentials in pay would outweigh any expense firms would incur in continuing to maintain such facilities. Indeed, if only the direct economic costs and benefits of female employment are taken into account, one would expect management to have consistently discriminated *in favor of* women and against men in postwar layoffs and rehiring. Particularly in view of the vigorous efforts of employers to increase labor productivity in the reconversion period, management should have preferred to retain women permanently in the "men's jobs" they had just demonstrated their ability to perform.[30]

Industrial employers chose the opposite course, however, defying not only the apparent imperatives of economic rationality, but also the stated preference of women war workers to keep their war jobs and the unions' official policy that layoffs and rehiring be done strictly by seniority. Rather than institutionalizing the wartime incorporation of women into male jobs, management returned to its prewar practices. . . .

THE ROOTS OF MANAGEMENT'S POSTWAR POLICY

In retrospect, then, management's determination to restore the status quo ante seems altogether irrational. Yet from the perspective of employers themselves at the time, it was a foregone conclusion. Management viewed the successful performance of women war workers as, at best, the fortunate outcome of an experiment in which it had participated with great trepidation and only because there was no alternative. To be sure, women had proved better workers than anyone had expected during the war. But now men's jobs were men's jobs once more. The ideology of sex-typing emerged triumphant again, defining the postwar order along prewar lines in both auto and electrical manufacturing.

In part, the explanation for management's postwar policy involves the logic of the sexual division of labor as it had first developed within the auto and electrical industries a half-century earlier. Not only did the traditions of sex-typing established then have a continuing influence in the post–World War II period, but the factors that had originally shaped those traditions remained salient. In auto, wage levels were still high relative to other industries and would continue to increase in the postwar decades. As in the prewar years, automotive management's efforts to boost productivity focused on tightening control over labor, not on reducing pay levels.[31] Under these conditions, female substitution had little to recommend it, and employers continued to indulge the conviction . . . that women simply were not suitable for employment in automotive production jobs.

In electrical manufacturing, too, prewar traditions of sex-typing persisted in the postwar [era]. But in this industry, the prewar sexual division of labor was historically rooted in a logic of feminization linked to labor-intensity and piecework systems. So why should the further extension of feminization during the war have been rolled back? Even in the case of the automobile industry, why was there a permanent departure from prewar tradition in regard to black employment while the sexual division of jobs persisted virtually unaltered? The historical, industry-specific logic of sex-typing seems to constitute only a partial explanation for management's postwar determination to reconstruct the prewar order.

It is tempting to look outside of the industrial setting to the arena of family and social reproduction in seeking a better solution to the conundrum of management's postwar policies. The interest of capital in reconstructing a family structure in which women are responsible for the generational and daily reproduction of the working class, one might argue, ruled out the permanent employment of women in the well-paid manufacturing jobs that they had during the war. In this view, if women—and more significantly, married women—were to be employed outside the home in ever-increasing numbers in the postwar era, it was crucial that they be confined to poorly paid, secondary jobs that would not jeopardize their primary allegiance to family.

The difficulty with this line of argument is in specifying how the presumed interest of collective capital in reconstituting traditional family forms was translated into the actual employer policies with respect to women workers that emerged in this period. The historical record offers no evidence that such familial considerations played a role in shaping managerial policy in the postwar transition.[32] Although the idea that "woman's place is in the home" was pervasive in the postwar period, it was seldom invoked by employers as a justification for restoring the prewar sexual division of jobs. Instead, management tended to define the issue in economic terms and, above all, by reference to women's physical characteristics and supposed inability to perform "men's jobs."

Although it would be extremely difficult to demonstrate that management policy was rooted in conscious concern over social reproduction, there is evidence for a different kind of explanation: that the postwar purge of women from "men's jobs" involved employers' assessment of the implications of their policies toward women for labor relations. The wartime struggles over equal pay indicated that the unions were committed to resisting any effort to substitute women for men in order to take advantage of their historically lower wages. If wage savings could not be garnered from substitution, or if they could only be garnered at substantial political cost, then why attempt to preserve the wartime sexual division of jobs after the war? In addition, given the widespread fear of postwar unemployment, management might reasonably have anticipated that unemployed male workers would be a source of potential political instability, given the working-class cultural ideal of the "family wage" and the obvious ambivalence of male unionists about women's postwar employment rights.

In short, management had good reason to believe that a wholesale postwar reorganization of the sexual division of labor, in defiance of the wartime assurances that women were in "men's jobs" only for the duration, could precipitate widespread resistance from labor. The unions were at the peak of their strength at this time, and at the war's end they were no longer constrained by the no-strike pledge. As one contemporary analyst noted, consideration of labor's reaction figured prominently in employers' postwar policies:

> Employers in plants where women had long been assigned to some jobs were disposed favorably to widening the fields of work open to women, unless the job dilutions had proved complicated and costly. In fact, union men declared that some companies, unless prevented by organized labor, would try to continue to use women on men's work because they could be hired at lower initial base pay, be upgraded more slowly, and would be throughout more docile. With the installation of mechanical aids, which using women had necessitated, already paid for out of war profits, management had frequently no particular reason to oppose keeping women on. . . . Yet most companies frankly admitted that, given full freedom of choice after the war, if only out of deference to prevailing male opinion in the shops, management would revert to giving men's jobs, so called, only to men. *And employers generally assumed that labor would permit no choice.*[33]

Understanding management's postwar policy in these terms helps explain why, in the auto case, women and blacks were treated differently. Despite their common history of exclusion from most auto jobs in the prewar era, the two groups stood in very different positions at the war's end. Organized feminism was at its nadir in the 1940s, and the labor movement's commitment to sexual equality was limited, so that management had little reason to fear that purging women from the industry would meet with substantial political opposition. In contrast, at least in the North, there was a large and vital black civil rights movement, which enjoyed substantial UAW support and from which management could expect vigorous protests if it pursued racially discriminatory employment policies.[34]

Only a few years earlier, when blacks were first hired in large numbers in Detroit's auto factories during the war mobilization, white workers had been vocal in their opposition, most notably in the numerous hate strikes which erupted in the plants and in the race riot of the summer of 1943.[35] But during the war, Detroit became a stronghold of the civil rights movement. The Motor City had the largest branch of the National Association for the Advancement of Colored People (NAACP) of any city in the nation, with a membership of twenty thousand by 1943, and the UAW had become a strong ally of the NAACP and other civil rights groups. While racial discrimination persisted in the auto industry in regard to promotion to the elite skilled trades, no one contested blacks' claims to semi-skilled jobs in the aftermath of the war.[36]

The sharp regional variation in racial patterns of hiring within the auto industry suggests the critical importance of the political dimension in shaping management's employment policies. Although the proportion of blacks in Detroit's auto plants rose dramatically in the 1940s and 1950s, reaching well over 25 percent of the production work force by 1960, in the nation as a whole the percentage of nonwhite auto workers grew much more modestly, from 4 percent in 1940 to only 9 percent in 1960. The national figures reflect the continuing practice of excluding blacks from employment in southern plants. As a manager at a GM plant in Atlanta told the *Wall Street Journal* in 1957, "When we moved into the South, we agreed to abide by local custom and not hire Negroes for production work. This is no time for social reforming and we're not about to try it."[37]

The situation of women auto workers was entirely different from that of northern blacks. Although the incorporation of women into the industry during the war had not provoked riots or hate strikes, this was primarily because female employment was explicitly understood to be a temporary expedient, "for the duration" only. After the war, women were expected to go "back to the home." There was no parallel expectation regarding black men. And while women war workers wanted to remain in the auto industry, as we have seen, their preferences (unlike blacks') lacked legitimacy. While black workers had the civil rights movement behind them, there was no mass feminist movement or even popular consciousness of women's job rights at this critical juncture, when the sexual division of labor that would characterize the postwar period was crystallizing. . . .

Notes

1. U.S. Senate Hearings, *Manpower Problems in Detroit*, 79th Cong. 1st sess., pp. 9–13 (Mar. 1945), pp. 13534, 13638; interview with Edward Cushman.

2. Reference to such a survey made "to determine those operations which were suitable for female operators" is made on pp. 2–3 of the Summary Brief Submitted by Buick Motor Division, Melrose Park, General Motors Corporation, "In the Matter of GMC–Buick, Melrose Park, Ill., and UAW-CIO," 14 June 1943, Walter Reuther Collection, WSU Archives, box 20, folder: "WLB, GM Women's Rates." A survey of this type was also conducted at the Ford Willow Run plant; see the section on "Training of Women" in *Willow Run Bomber Plant, Record of War Effort* (notebook), vol. 2, pt. 2, Jan.–Dec. 1942, p. 30, La Croix Collection, Accession 435, Ford Archives, Dearborn, Michigan, box 15.

3. Computed from data in U.S. Department of Labor, Bureau of Labor Statistics, Division of Wage Analysis, Regional Office no. 8-A, Detroit, Michigan, Dec. 3, 1943, serial no. 8-A-16 (mimeo), "Metalworking Establishments, Detroit, Michigan, Labor Market Area, Straight-Time Average Hourly Earnings, Selected Occupations, July, 1943." UAW Research Department Collection, WSU Archives, box 28, folder: "Wage Rates (Detroit) Bureau of Labor Statistics, 1943–45." . . .

4. Computed from data in "Earnings in Manufacture of Electrical Appliances, 1942," p. 532.

5. Regarding GE and Westinghouse, see U.S. National War Labor Board, *War Labor Reports*, vol. 28, pp. 677–78. . . .

6. See "Summary Employment Status Report for Michigan," Apr. 30, 1943, Records of the U.S. Employment Service, National Archives, Record Group 183, box 181, folder: "Michigan Statewide."

7. Press release of Office of Production Management, Labor Division, Dec. 5, 1941, UAW Research Department Collection, WSU Archives, box 32, folder: "Women Employment 1941."

8. "Engineers of Womanpower," *Automotive War Production* 2 (Oct. 1943):4–5 (emphasis added). . . .

9. "What Women Are Doing in Industry," *Factory Management and Maintenance* 100 (March 1942):63; "Provisions in Plants for Physical Differences Enable Women to Handle Variety of War Jobs," *Automotive War Production* 2 (Sept. 1943):7.

10. "Report of Two Special Meetings on Employing and Training Women for War Jobs," attended by executives from 85 N.A.M. companies from the East and Midwest, Mar. 27 and 30, 1942, in Records of the Automotive Council for War Production, Detroit Public Library, folder: "Manpower: Source Material: New Workers," p. 1.

11. "Provisions in Plants"; Constance Green, "The Role of Women as Production Workers in War Plants in the Connecticut Valley," *Smith College Studies in History* 28 (1946):32. . . .

12. W. Gerald Tuttle, "Women War Workers at Vultee Aircraft," *Personnel Journal* 21 (Sept. 1942):8–9.

13. "Women Work for Victory," *Automotive War Production* 1 (Nov. 1942):4; "Engineers of Womanpower," p. 4.

14. "There's a Job for You at Sperry . . . Today" (pamphlet), Records of UE District 4, UE Archives, University of Pittsburgh folder 877; "Hiring and Training Women for War Work," *Factory Management and Maintenance* 100 (Aug. 1942):73; "Engineers of Womanpower," p. 4.

15. The transcript of this newsreel was made available to me by the Rosie the Riveter Film Project, Emeryville, California.

16. "Engineers of Womanpower," p. 4.

17. "New Workers," *Manpower Reports* 10 (published by the Manpower Division of the Automotive Council for War Production), p. 4; Anne Gould, "Problems of Woman War Workers in Detroit," Aug. 20, 1943, Records of the War Production Board, National Archives, RG 179, box 203, folder: "035.606 Service Trades Divisions, WPB Functions," p. 2.

18. U.S. Department of Labor, Women's Bureau, Special Bulletin no. 20, *Changes in Women's Employment During the War* (1944), p. 18.

19. Helen Baker, *Women in War Industries* (Princeton: Princeton University Press, 1942), p. 15.

20. "Report of Mrs. Betty Sturges Finan on Cleveland Detroit Trip, Feb. 9–17 [1943] inclusive," pp. 3–4, Records of the War Manpower Commission, National Archives, Record Group 211, Series 137, box 977, folder. "Consultants—Betty Sturges Finan." See also "Report of Two Special Meetings," p. 6.

21. See U.S. Bureau of the Census, *Historical Statistics of the U.S.: Colonial Times to 1970* (1975), pp. 131, 133. This claim is considerably more modest than William Chafe's controversial thesis that the wartime changes in female labor force participation make the 1940s a key "turning point in the history of American women." See William H. Chafe, *The American Woman: Her Changing Social, Economic, and Political Role, 1920–1970* (New York: Oxford University Press, 1972), p. 195. . . .

22. Chafe, *The American Woman*, p. 137; American Management Association, Special Research Report no. 2, *Supervision of Women on Production Jobs: A Study of Management's Problems and Practices in Handling Female Personnel* (1943), pp. 8–10 (emphasis in the original).

23. National Industrial Conference Board, "Wartime Pay of Women in Industry," *Studies in Personnel Policy*, no. 58 (1943):27; "Woman's Place," *Business Week* (May 16, 1942):20–22. . . .

24. *Modern Industry*, July 15, 1942, summarized in *Management Review* 31 (Sept. 1942):303–4. Regarding the use of women as supervisors, see *Supervision of Women on Production Jobs*, pp. 24–27. . . .

25. Computed from data in *The Management Almanac 1946* (New York: National Industrial Conference Board, 1946), p. 77.

26. "Wartime Pay of Women in Industry," pp. 18–19. . . .

27. New York State Department of Labor, Division of Women in Industry, *Women's Wages on Men's Jobs* (1944), p. 26.

28. See New York State Department of Labor, Division of Women in Industry, *Absenteeism in New York State War Production Plants* (1943); National Industrial Conference Board, "The Problem of Absenteeism," *Studies in Personnel Policy*, no. 53 (1943); "Women Workers on War Production," *UAW Research Report* 3 (Mar. 1943):3. . . .

29. *Manpower Problems in Detroit*, pp. 13112–13.

30. See Howell John Harris, *The Right to Manage: Industrial Relations Policies of American Business in the 1940s* (Madison: University of Wisconsin Press, 1982), pp. 66–67, 91–93.

31. Ibid. This is Harris's main thesis.

32. Denise Riley, "The Free Mothers': Pronatalism and Working Women in Industry at the End of the Last War in Britain," *History Workshop* II (Spring 1981):59–118, presents the most convincing case for this argument in regard to the postwar transition for the British case, but she relies on evidence about state policy with virtually none directly from employers.

33. Green, "Role of Women as Production Workers," pp. 64–65 (emphasis added).

34. August Meier and Elliot Rudwick, *Black Detroit and the Rise of the U.A.W.* (New York: Oxford University Press, 1979).

35. Ibid.; Robert C. Weaver, *Negro Labor: A National Problem* (New York: Harcourt, Brace, and World, 1946).

36. Meier and Rudwick, *Black Detroit*, p. 113. See also Karen Anderson, "Last Hired, First Fired: Black Women Workers during World War II," *Journal of American History* 69 (June 1982), especially pp. 86–87, where white male workers' attitudes toward women and blacks are compared.

37. Both the employment figures and the quote are cited in Herbert R. Northrup, Richard L. Rowan, et al., *Negro Employment in Basic Industry*, Industrial Research Unit, Wharton School of Finance and Commerce, University of Pennsylvania (1970), pp. 65–75. The national employment figures are from the U.S. Census, and because (unlike the figures for Detroit) they include both production and nonproduction workers, they overstate the difference between Detroit and the nation as a whole, for the vast majority of nonproduction workers were white in this period. The quote is from the *Wall Street Journal*, Oct. 24, 1957.

V

A Transforming World

1945–2014

COLD WAR HETERONORMATIVITY

SUSAN K. CAHN
"Mannishness," Lesbianism, and Homophobia in U.S. Women's Sports

In the 1950s some women who identified as lesbians organized to gain constitutional protection, but their efforts were blocked, especially in New York City, where the local chapter of the Daughters of Bilitis was discovered to have subsequently been infiltrated with informants who were supplying names to the FBI and CIA. (The group was founded in San Francisco in the mid-1950s to work for social and civil rights for lesbians.) In an era when sexual conformity was seen as essential to national security, it is hardly surprising that *all* women who engaged in any same-sex activity were suspect. (See Margot Canaday's essay in this volume on the impact of sexuality investigations on women's military careers in the 1950s, pp. 678–689). Women athletes were particularly vulnerable.

In the following essay, Susan K. Cahn explores the suspicions and the reality behind those suspicions in women's athletics. Note the persistence of concerns about feminine sexuality, whether heterosexual or homosexual, throughout the history of women's sports. What measures did colleges and universities take to protect women's sports from charges of lesbianism? What was the price of such actions? Since those athletes who were lesbian could not afford to proclaim their sexual identity publicly, why does Cahn argue that athletics nonetheless afforded them social and psychic space to affirm their identity and find community? Do you agree?

In 1934, *Literary Digest* subtitled an article on women's sports, "Will the Playing Fields One Day Be Ruled by Amazons?" The author, Fred Wittner, answered the question affirmatively and concluded that as an "inevitable consequence" of sport's masculinizing effect, "girls trained in physical education to-day may find it more difficult to attract the most worthy fathers for their children."[1] The image of women athletes as mannish, failed heterosexuals represents a thinly veiled reference to lesbianism in sport. At times, the homosexual allusion has been indisputable, as in a journalist's description of the great athlete Babe Didrikson as a "Sapphic, Brobdingnagian woman" or in television comedian Arsenio Hall's more recent witticism, "If we can put a man on the moon, why can't we get one on Martina Navratilova?"[2] More frequently, however, popular commentary on lesbians in sport has taken the form of indirect references, surfacing through denials and refutations rather than open acknowledgment. When in 1955 an *Ebony* magazine article on African American track stars insisted that "off track, girls are entirely feminine. Most of them like boys, dances, club affairs," the reporter answered the implicit but unspoken charge that athletes, especially Black

Excerpted from "From the 'Muscle Moll' to the 'Butch' Ballplayer: Mannishness, Lesbianism, and Homophobia in U.S. Women's Sports" by Susan K. Cahn, in *Feminist Studies* 19, no. 2 (Summer 1993): 343–68. Reprinted by permission of the author and publisher. Notes have been edited and renumbered.

women in a "manly" sport, were masculine manhaters, or lesbians.[3]

The figure of the mannish lesbian athlete has acted as a powerful but unarticulated "bogey woman" of sport, forming a silent foil for more positive, corrective images that attempt to rehabilitate the image of women athletes and resolve the cultural contradiction between athletic prowess and femininity. As a stereotyped figure in U.S. society, the lesbian athlete forms part of everyday cultural knowledge. Yet historians have paid scant attention to the connection between female sexuality and sport.[4] This essay explores the historical relationship between lesbianism and sport by tracing the development of the stereotyped "mannish lesbian athlete" and examining its relation to the lived experience of mid-twentieth-century lesbian athletes.

I argue that fears of mannish female sexuality in sport initially centered on the prospect of unbridled heterosexual desire. By the 1930s, however, female athletic mannishness began to connote heterosexual failure, usually couched in terms of unattractiveness to men, but also suggesting the possible absence of heterosexual interest. In the years following World War II, the stereotype of the lesbian athlete emerged full blown. The extreme homophobia and the gender conservatism of the postwar era created a context in which longstanding linkages among mannishness, female homosexuality, and athletics cohered around the figure of the mannish lesbian athlete. Paradoxically, the association between masculinity, lesbianism, and sport had a positive outcome for some women. The very cultural matrix that produced the pejorative image also created possibilities for lesbian affirmation. Sport provided social and psychic space for some lesbians to validate themselves and to build a collective culture. Thus, the lesbian athlete was not only a figure of discourse but a living product of women's sexual struggle and cultural innovation.

The athletic woman sparked interest and controversy in the early decades of the twentieth century. In the United States and other Western societies, sport functioned as a male preserve, an all-male domain in which men not only played games together but also demonstrated and affirmed their manhood.[5] The "maleness" of sport derived from a gender ideology which labeled aggression, physicality, competitive spirit, and athletic skill as masculine attributes necessary for achieving true manliness. This notion found unquestioned support in the dualistic, polarized concepts of gender which prevailed in Victorian America. However, by the turn of the century, women had begun to challenge Victorian gender arrangements, breaking down barriers to female participation in previously male arenas of public work, politics, and urban nightlife. Some of these "New Women" sought entry into the world of athletics as well. On college campuses students enjoyed a wide range of intramural sports through newly formed Women's Athletic Associations. Off-campus women took up games like golf, tennis, basketball, swimming, and occasionally even wrestling, car racing, or boxing. As challengers to one of the defining arenas of manhood, skilled female athletes became symbols of the broader march of womanhood out of the Victorian domestic sphere into once prohibited male realms.

The woman athlete represented both the appealing and threatening aspects of modern womanhood. In a positive light, she captured the exuberant spirit, physical vigor, and brazenness of the New Woman. The University of Minnesota student newspaper proclaimed in 1904 that the athletic girl was the "truest type of All-American coed."[6] Several years later, *Harper's Bazaar* labeled the unsportive girl as "not strictly up to date," and *Good Housekeeping* noted that the "tomboy" had come to symbolize "a new type of American girl, new not only physically, but mentally and morally."[7]

Yet, women athletes invoked condemnation as often as praise. Critics ranged from physicians and physical educators to sportswriters, male athletic officials, and casual observers. In their view, strenuous athletic pursuits endangered women and threatened the stability of society. They maintained that women athletes would become manlike, adopting masculine dress, talk, and mannerisms. In addition, they contended, too much exercise would damage female reproductive capacity [interfering with menstruation and causing reproductive organs to harden or atrophy]. And worse yet, the excitement of sport would cause women to lose [sexual] control, . . . unleash[ing] nonprocreative, erotic desires identified with male sexuality and unrespectable women. . . . These fears collapsed into an all-encompassing concept of "mannishness," a term signifying female masculinity . . .

The public debate over the merits of women's athletic participation remained lively throughout the 1910s and 1920s. On all sides of the issue, however, the controversy about sports and female sexuality presumed heterosexuality. Neither critics nor supporters suggested that "masculine" athleticism might indicate or induce same-sex love. And when experts warned of the "amazonian" athlete's possible sexual transgressions, they linked the physical release of sport with a loss of hetero-sexual *control,* not of *inclination.*

In the 1930s, however, the heterosexual understanding of the mannish "amazon" began to give way to a new interpretation which educators and promoters could not long ignore. To the familiar charge that female athletes resembled men, critics added the newer accusation that sport-induced mannishness disqualified them as candidates for heterosexual romance. In 1930, an *American Mercury* medical reporter decried the decline of romantic love, pinning the blame on women who entered sport, business, and politics. He claimed that such women "act like men, talk like men, and think like men." The author explained that "women have come closer and closer to men's level," and, consequently, "the purple allure of distance has vamoosed."[8] . . . Although the charges didn't exclusively focus on athletes, they implied that female athleticism was contrary to heterosexual appeal, which appeared to rest on women's difference from and deference to men.

The concern with heterosexual appeal reflected broader sexual transformations in U.S. society. Historians of sexuality have examined the multiple forces which reshaped gender and sexual relations in the first few decades of the twentieth century. Victorian sexual codes crumbled under pressure from an assertive, boldly sexual working-class youth culture, a women's movement which defied prohibitions against public female activism, and the growth of a new pleasure-oriented consumer economy. In the wake of these changes, modern ideals of womanhood embraced an overtly erotic heterosexual sensibility. At the same time, medical fascination with sexual "deviance" created a growing awareness of lesbianism, now understood as a form of congenital or psychological pathology. The medicalization of homosexuality in combination with an antifeminist backlash in the 1920s against female autonomy and power contributed to a more fully articulated

taboo against lesbianism. The modern heterosexual woman stood in stark opposition to her threatening sexual counterpart, the "mannish" lesbian.[9]

By the late 1920s and early 1930s, with a modern lesbian taboo and an eroticized definition of heterosexual femininity in place, the assertive, muscular female competitor roused increasing suspicion. It was at this moment that both subtle and direct references to the lesbian athlete emerged in physical education and popular sport. Uncensored discussions of intimate female companionship and harmless athletic "crushes" disappear from the record, pushed underground by the increasingly hostile tone of public discourse about female sexuality and athleticism. Fueled by the gender antagonisms and anxieties of the Depression, the public began scrutinizing women athletes—known for their appropriation of masculine games and styles—for signs of deviance.

Where earlier references to "amazons" had signaled heterosexual ardor, journalists now used the term to mean unattractive, failed heterosexuals. Occasionally, the media made direct mention of athletes' presumed lesbian tendencies. A 1933 *Redbook* article, for example, casually mentioned that track and golf star Babe Didrikson liked men just to horse around with her and not "make love," adding that Babe's fondness for her best girlfriends far surpassed her affection for any man.[10] The direct reference was unusual; the lesbian connotation of mannishness was forged primarily through indirect links of association. . . .

Tentatively voiced in the 1930s, these accusations became harsher and more explicit under the impact of wartime changes in gender and sexuality and the subsequent panic over the "homosexual menace." In a post–World War II climate markedly hostile to nontraditional women and lesbians, women in physical education and in working-class popular sports became convenient targets of homophobic indictment.

World War II opened up significant economic and social possibilities for gay men and women. Embryonic prewar homosexual subcultures blossomed during the war and spread across the midcentury urban landscape. Bars, nightclubs, public cruising spots, and informal social networks facilitated the development of gay and lesbian enclaves. But the permissive atmosphere did not survive the war's end. Waving the banner of Cold War political and social conservatism, government leaders acted at the federal, state, and local levels to purge gays and lesbians from government and military posts, to initiate legal investigations and prosecutions of gay individuals and institutions, and to encourage local police crackdowns on gay bars and street life. The perceived need to safeguard national security and to reestablish social order in the wake of wartime disruption sparked a "homosexual panic" which promoted the fear, loathing, and persecution of homosexuals.[11]

Lesbians suffered condemnation for their violation of gender as well as sexual codes. The tremendous emphasis on family, domesticity, and "traditional" femininity in the late 1940s and 1950s reflected postwar anxieties about the reconsolidation of a gender order shaken by two decades of depression and war. As symbols of women's refusal to conform, lesbians endured intense scrutiny by experts who regularly focused on their subjects' presumed masculinity. Sexologists attributed lesbianism to masculine tendencies and freedoms encouraged by the war, linking it to a general collapsing of gender distinctions which, in their view, destabilized marital and family relations.[12]

Lesbians remained shadowy figures to most Americans, but women athletes—noted for their masculine bodies, interests, and attributes—were visible representatives of the gender inversion often associated with homosexuality. Physical education majors, formerly accused of being unappealing to men, were increasingly charged with being uninterested in them as well. The 1952 University of Minnesota yearbook snidely reported: "Believe it or not, members of the Women's Athletic Association are normal" and found conclusive evidence in the fact that "at least one . . . of WAA's 300 members is engaged."[13]

The lesbian stigma began to plague popular athletics too. . . . The career of Babe Didrikson, which spanned the 1920s to the 1950s, illustrates the shift. In the early 1930s the press had ridiculed the tomboyish track star for her "hatchet face," "door-stop jaw," and "button-breasted" chest. After quitting track, Didrikson dropped out of the national limelight, married professional wrestler George Zaharias in 1938, and then staged a spectacular athletic comeback as a golfer in the late 1940s and 1950s. Fascinated by her personal transformation and then, in the 1950s, moved by her battle with cancer, journalists gave Didrikson's comeback

extensive coverage and helped make her a much-loved popular figure. In reflecting on her success, however, sportswriters spent at least as much time on Didrikson's love life as her golf stroke. Headlines blared, "Babe Is a Lady Now: The World's Most Amazing Athlete Has Learned to Wear Nylons and Cook for Her Huge Husband," and reporters gleefully described how "along came a great big he-man wrestler and the Babe forgot all her man-hating chatter."[14] . . . The challenge for women athletes was not to conquer new athletic feats, which would only further reduce their sexual appeal, but to regain their womanhood through sexual surrender to men.

Media coverage in national magazines and metropolitan newspapers typically focused on the sexual accomplishments of white female athletes, but postwar observers and promoters of African American women's sport also confronted the issue of sexual normalcy. In earlier decades, strong local support for women's sport within Black communities and the racist gender ideologies that prevailed outside Black communities may have weakened the association between African American women athletes and "mannish" lesbianism. Historically, European American racial thought characterized African American women as aggressive, coarse, passionate, and physical—the same qualities assigned to manliness and sport.[15] Excluded from dominant ideals of womanhood, Black women's success in sport could therefore be interpreted not as an unnatural sexual deviation but, rather, as the natural result of their reputed closeness to nature, animals, and masculinity.[16] . . . Moreover, stereotypes of Black females as highly sexual, promiscuous, and unrestrained in their heterosexual passions further discouraged the linkage between mannishness and lesbianism. . . .

Although Black athletes may initially have encountered few lesbian stereotypes . . . circumstances in the broader society eventually pressed African American sport promoters and journalists to address the issue of mannish sexuality. The strong postwar association of sports with lesbianism developed at the same time as Black athletes became a dominant presence in American sport culture. . . . Therefore, while there was no particular correlation between Black women and lesbianism, the association of each with mannishness and sexual aggression potentially linked the two. . . . In the late 1950s, Black sport promoters and journalists joined others in taking up the question of sexual "normalcy." One Black newspaper in 1957 described tennis star Althea Gibson as a childhood "tomboy" who "in later life . . . finds herself victimized by complexes."[17] The article did not elaborate on the nature of Gibson's "complex," but lesbianism is inferred in the linkage between "tomboys" and psychological illness. This connotation becomes clearer by looking at the defense of Black women's sport. Echoing *Ebony's* avowal that "entirely feminine" Black female track stars "like boys, dances, club affairs," in 1962 Tennessee State University track coach Ed Temple asserted, "None of my girls have any trouble getting boy friends. . . . We don't want amazons."[18]

Constant attempts to shore up the heterosexual reputation of athletes can be read as evidence that the longstanding reputation of female athletes as mannish women had become a covert reference to lesbianism. By midcentury, a fundamental reorientation of sexual meanings fused notions of femininity, female eroticism, and heterosexual attractiveness into a single ideal. Mannishness, once primarily a sign of gender crossing, assumed a specifically lesbian-sexual connotation. In the wake of this change, the strong cultural association between sport and masculinity made women's athletics ripe for emerging lesbian stereotypes. This meaning of athletic mannishness raises further questions. What impact did the stereotype have on women's sport? And was the image merely an erroneous stereotype, or did lesbians in fact form a significant presence in sport? . . .

The image of the mannish lesbian athlete had a direct effect on women competitors, on strategies of athletic organizations, and on the overall popularity of women's sport. The lesbian stereotype exerted pressure on athletes to demonstrate their femininity and heterosexuality, viewed as one and the same. Many women adopted an apologetic stance toward their athletic skill. Even as they competed to win, they made sure to display outward signs of femininity in dress and demeanor. They took special care in contact with the media to reveal "feminine" hobbies like cooking and sewing, to mention current boyfriends, and to discuss future marriage plans.[19]

Leaders of women's sport took the same approach at the institutional level. In answer to portrayals of physical education majors and teachers as social rejects and prudes, physical educators revised their philosophy to place heterosexuality at the center of professional objectives. . . . Curricular changes implemented between the mid-1930s and mid-1950s institutionalized the new philosophy. In a paper on postwar objectives, Mildred A. Schaeffer explained that physical education classes should help women "develop an interest in school dances and mixers and a desire to voluntarily attend them."[20] To this end, administrators revised coursework to emphasize beauty and social charm over rigorous exercise and health. They exchanged old rationales of fitness and fun for promises of trimmer waistlines, slimmer hips, and prettier complexions. . . . Some departments also added co-educational classes to foster "broader, keener, more sympathetic understanding of the opposite sex."[21] Department heads cracked down on "mannish" students and faculty, issuing warnings against "casual styles" which might "lead us back into some dangerous channels."[22] They implemented dress codes which forbade slacks and men's shirts or socks, adding as well a ban on "boyish hair cuts" and unshaven legs.[23]

Popular sport promoters adopted similar tactics. Martialing sexual data like they were athletic statistics, a 1954 AAU poll sought to sway a skeptical public with numerical proof of heterosexuality—the fact that 91 percent of former female athletes surveyed had married.[24] Publicity for the midwestern All-American Girls Baseball League included statistics on the number of married players. . . . Behind the scenes, teams passed dress and conduct codes. For example, the All-American Girls Baseball League prohibited players from wearing men's clothing or getting "severe" haircuts.[25] That this was an attempt to secure the heterosexual image of athletes was made even clearer when league officials announced that AAGBL policy prohibited the recruitment of "freaks" and "Amazons."[26]

In the end, the strategic emphasis on heterosexuality and the suppression of "mannishness" did little to alter the image of women in sport. The stereotype of the mannish lesbian athlete grew out of the persistent commonsense equation of sport with masculinity. Opponents of women's sport reinforced this belief when they denigrated women's athletic efforts and ridiculed skilled athletes as "grotesque," "mannish," or "unnatural." Leaders of women's sport unwittingly contributed to the same set of ideas when they began to orient their programs around the new feminine heterosexual idea. As physical education policies and media campaigns worked to suppress lesbianism and marginalize athletes who did not conform to dominant standards of femininity, sport officials embedded heterosexism into the institutional and ideological framework of sport. The effect extended beyond sport to the wider culture, where the figure of the mannish lesbian athlete announced that competitiveness, strength, independence, aggression, and physical intimacy among women fell outside the bounds of womanhood. As a symbol of female deviance, she served as a powerful reminder to all women to toe the line of heterosexuality and femininity or risk falling into a despised category of mannish (non-women) women. . . .

[But] was the mannish lesbian athlete merely a figure of homophobic imagination, or was there in fact a strong lesbian presence in sport? When the All-American Girls Baseball League adamantly specified, *"Always appear in feminine attire . . .* MASCULINE HAIR STYLING? SHOES? COATS? SHIRTS? SOCKS, T-SHIRTS ARE BARRED AT ALL TIMES," and when physical education departments threatened to expel students for overly masculine appearance, were administrators merely responding to external pressure?[27] Or were they cracking down on women who may have indeed enjoyed the feel and look of a tough swagger, a short haircut, and men's clothing? And if so, did mannishness among athletes correspond to lesbianism, as the stereotype suggested? In spite of the public stigmatization, [is it probable that] some women may have found the activities, attributes, and emotions of sport conducive to lesbian self-expression and community formation?

As part of a larger investigation of women's athletic experience, I conducted oral histories with women who played competitive amateur, semiprofessional, and professional sports between 1930 and 1970. The interviews included only six openly lesbian narrators and thirty-six other women who either declared their heterosexuality or left their identity unstated.[28] Although the sample is too small to stand as a representative study, the interviews . . . and scattered other sources indicate that sport, particularly softball, provided an important site for the development of lesbian subculture

and identity in the United States.[29] Gay and straight informants alike confirmed the lesbian presence in popular sport and physical education. Their testimony suggests that from at least the 1940s on, sport provided space for lesbian activity and social networks and served as a path into lesbian culture for young lesbians coming out and searching for companions and community.

Lesbian athletes explained that sport had been integral to their search for sexual identity and lesbian companionship. Ann Maguire, a softball player, physical education major, and top amateur bowler from New England, recalled that as a teenager in the late 1950s,

> I had been trying to figure out who I was and couldn't put a name to it. I mean it was very— no gay groups, no literature, no characters on *Dynasty*—I mean there was just nothing at that time. And trying to put a name to it. . . . I went to a bowling tournament, met two women there [and] for some reason something clicked and it clicked in a way that I was not totally aware of.

She introduced herself to the women, who later invited her to a gay bar. Maguire described her experience at age seventeen:

> I was being served and I was totally fascinated by the fact that, oh god, here I am being served and I'm not twenty-one. And it didn't occur to me until after a while when I relaxed and started realizing that I was at a gay bar. I just became fascinated. . . . And I was back there the next night. . . . I really felt a sense of knowing who I was and feeling very happy. Very happy that I had been able to through some miracle put this into place.[30] . . .

For women like Maguire, sport provided a point of entry into lesbian culture.

The question arises of whether lesbians simply congregated in athletic settings or whether a sports environment could actually "create" or "produce" lesbians. Some women fit the first scenario, describing how, in their struggle to accept and make sense out of lesbian desire, sport offered a kind of home that put feelings and identities into place. For other women, it appears that the lesbian presence in sport encouraged them to explore or act on feelings that they might not have had or responded to in other settings. Midwestern baseball player Nora Cross remembered that "it was my first exposure to gay people. . . . I was pursued by the one I was rooming with, that's how I found out." She got involved with her roommate and lived "a gay lifestyle" as long as she stayed in sport. Dorothy Ferguson Key also noticed that sport changed some women, recalling that "there were girls that came in the league like this . . . yeah, gay," but that at other times "a girl came in, and I mean they just change. . . . When they've been in a year they're completely changed. . . . They lived together."[31]

The athletic setting provided public space for lesbian sociability without naming it as such or excluding women who were not lesbians. This environment could facilitate the coming-out process, allowing women who were unsure about or just beginning to explore their sexual identity to socialize with gay and straight women without having to make immediate decisions or declarations. Gradually and primarily through unspoken communication, lesbians in sport recognized each other and created social networks. Gloria Wilson, who played softball in a mid-sized midwestern city, described her entry into lesbian social circles as a gradual process in which older lesbians slowly opened up their world to her and she grew more sure of her own identity and place in the group.

> A lot was assumed. And I don't think they felt comfortable with me talking until they knew me better. Then I think more was revealed. And we had little beer gatherings after a game at somebody's house. So then it was even more clear who was doing what when. And then I felt more comfortable too, fitting in, talking about my relationship too—and exploring more of the lesbian lifestyle, I guess.[32]

In an era when women did not dare announce their lesbianism in public, the social world of popular sport allowed women to find each other as teammates, friends, and lovers. But if athletics provided a public arena and social activity in which lesbians could recognize and affirm each other, what exactly was it that they recognized? This is where the issue of mannishness arises. Women athletes consistently explained the lesbian reputation of sport by reference to the mannishness of some athletes. . . . Suspected lesbians were said to "act like a man, you know, the way they walked, the way they talked, the things they did."

Such comments could merely indicate the pervasiveness of the masculine reputation of athletes and lesbians. However, lesbian narrators also suggested connections, although more complicated and nuanced, between athletics, lesbianism, and the "mannish" or "butchy" style which some lesbians manifested. None reported any doubt about their own gender identification as girls and women, but they indicated that they had often felt uncomfortable with the activities and attributes associated with the female gender. They preferred boyish clothes and activities to the conventional styles and manners of femininity.

Several spoke of . . . their relief upon finding athletic comrades who shared this sensibility. Josephine D'Angelo recalled that as a lesbian participating in sport, "you brought your culture with you. You brought your arm swinging . . . , the swagger, the way you tilted or cocked your head or whatever. You brought that with you." She explained that this style was acceptable in sports: "First thing you did was to kind of imitate the boys because you know, you're not supposed to throw like a girl." Although her rejection of femininity made her conspicuous in other settings, D'Angelo found that in sport "it was overlooked, see. You weren't different than the other kids. . . . Same likeness, people of a kind."[33]

These athletes were clearly women playing women's sports. But in the gender system of U.S. society, the skills, movements, clothing, and competition of sport were laden with impressions of masculinity. Lesbianism too crossed over the bounds of acceptable femininity. Consequently, sport could relocate girls or women with lesbian identities or feelings in an alternative nexus of gender meanings, allowing them to "be themselves"—or to express their gender and sexuality in an unconventional way. This applied to heterosexual women as well, many of whom also described themselves as "tomboys" attracted to boyish games and styles. As an activity that incorporated prescribed "masculine" physical activity into a way of being in the female body, athletics provided a social space and practice for reorganizing conventional meanings of embodied masculinity and femininity. *All* women in sport gained access to activities and expressive styles labeled masculine by the dominant culture. However, because lesbians were excluded from a concept of "real womanhood" defined around heterosexual appeal and desire, sport formed a milieu in which they could redefine womanhood on their own terms. . . .

However, the connections among lesbianism, masculinity, and sport require qualification.

Many lesbians in and out of sport did not adopt "masculine" markers. And even among those who did, narrators indicated that butch styles did not occlude more traditionally "feminine" qualities of affection and tenderness valued by women athletes. Sport allowed women to combine activities and attributes perceived as masculine with more conventionally feminine qualities of friendship, cooperation, nurturance, and affection. Lesbians particularly benefited from this gender configuration, finding that in the athletic setting, qualities otherwise viewed as manifestations of homosexual deviance were understood as inherent, positive aspects of sport.[34] Aggressiveness, toughness, passionate intensity, expanded use of motion and space, strength, and competitiveness contributed to athletic excellence. With such qualities defined as athletic attributes rather than psychological abnormalities, the culture of sport permitted lesbians to express the full range of their gendered sensibilities while sidestepping the stigma of psychological deviance. For these reasons, athletics, in the words of Josephine D'Angelo, formed a "comforting" and "comfortable" place.[35]

Yet lesbians found sport hospitable only under certain conditions. Societal hostility toward homosexuality made lesbianism unspeakable in any realm of culture, but the sexual suspicions that surrounded sport made athletics an especially dangerous place in which to speak out. Physical educators and sport officials vigilantly guarded against signs of "mannishness," and teams occasionally expelled women who wore their hair in a "boyish bob" or engaged in obvious lesbian relationships. Consequently, gay athletes avoided naming or verbally acknowledging their sexuality. Loraine Sumner explained that "you never talked about it. . . . You never saw anything in public amongst the group of us. But you knew right darn well that this one was going with that one. But yet it just wasn't a topic of conversation. Never."[36] Instead, lesbian athletes signaled their identity through dress, posture, and look, reserving spoken communication for private gatherings among women who were acknowledged and accepted members of concealed communities.

Although in hindsight the underground nature of midcentury lesbian communities may seem extremely repressive, it may also have had a positive side. Unlike the bars where

women's very presence declared their status as sexual outlaws, in sport athletes could enjoy the public company of lesbians while retaining their membership in local communities where neighbors, kin, and coworkers respected and sometimes even celebrated their athletic abilities. The unacknowledged, indefinite presence of lesbians in sport may have allowed for a wider range of lesbian experience and identity than is currently acknowledged in most scholarship. For instance, among women who did not identify as lesbian but were sexually drawn to other women, sport provided a venue in which they could express their desires without necessarily having articulated their feelings as a distinct sexual identity. The culture of sport provided space for some women to create clearly delineated lesbian identities and communities, at the same time allowing other women to move along the fringes of this world, operating across sexual and community lines without a firmly differentiated lesbian identity.

Women in sport experienced a contradictory array of heterosexual imperatives and homosexual possibilities. The fact that women athletes disrupted a critical domain of male power and privilege made sport a strategic site for shoring up existing gender and sexual hierarchies. The image of the mannish lesbian confirmed both the masculinity of sport and its association with female deviance. Lesbian athletes could not publicly claim their identity without risking expulsion, ostracism, and loss of athletic activities and social networks that had become crucial to their lives. Effectively silenced, their image was conveyed to the dominant culture primarily as a negative stereotype in which the mannish lesbian athlete represented the unfeminine "other," the line beyond which "normal" women must not cross.

The paradox of women's sport history is that the mannish athlete was not only a figure of homophobic discourse but also a human actor engaged in sexual innovation and struggle. Lesbian athletes used the social and psychic space of sport to create a collective culture and affirmative identity. The pride, pleasure, companionship, and dignity lesbians found in the athletic world helped them survive in a hostile society. The challenge posed by their collective existence and their creative reconstruction of womanhood formed a precondition for more overt, political challenges to lesbian oppression which have occurred largely outside the realm of sport.

NOTES

1. Fred Wittner, "Shall the Ladies Join Us?" *Literary Digest* 117 (19 May 1934): 43.

2. Jim Murray, *Austin American Statesman* (n.d.), Zaharias scrapbook, Barker Texas History Center ([hereafter] BTHC), University of Texas, Austin; Arsenio Hall Show, 1988.

3. "Fastest Women in the World," *Ebony* 10 (June 1955): 28.

4. Helen Lenskyj, *Out of Bounds: Women, Sport, and Sexuality* (Toronto: Women's Press, 1986); Yvonne Zipter, *Diamonds Are a Dyke's Best Friend: Reflections, Reminiscences, and Reports from the Field on the Lesbian National Pastime* (Ithaca: Firebrand Books, 1988).

5. J. A. Mangan and Roberta J. Park, eds., *"Fair Sex" to Feminism: Sport and the Socialization of Women in the Industrial and Post-Industrial Era* (London: Frank Cays, 1987).

6. 1904–5 Scrapbooks of Anne Maude Butner, Butner Papers, University of Minnesota Archives, Minneapolis (UMA).

7. Violet W. Mange, "Field Hockey for Women," *Harper's Bazaar* 44 (Apr. 1910): 246; Anna de Koven, "The Athletic Woman," *Good Housekeeping* 55 (Aug. 1912): 150.

8. George Nathan, "Once There Was a Princess," *American Mercury* 19 (Feb. 1930):242.

9. This is an extremely brief and simplified summary of an extensive literature. For a good synthesis, see Estelle Freedman and John D'Emilio, *Intimate Matters: A History of Sexuality in America* (New York: Harper & Row, 1988), chaps. 8–10.

10. William Marston, "How Can a Woman Do It?" *Redbook* (Sept. 1933):60.

11. John D'Emilio, *Sexual Politics, Sexual Communities: The Making of a Homosexual Minority in the United States, 1940–1970* (Chicago: University of Chicago Press, 1983), pp. 9–53; Alan Berube, *Coming Out Under Fire: The History of Gay Men and Women in World War Two* (New York: Free Press, 1990).

12. Donna Penn, "The Meanings of Lesbianism in Post-War America," *Gender and History* 3 (Summer 1991):190–203; Wini Breines, "The 1950s: Gender and Some Social Science," *Sociological Inquiry* 56 (Winter 1986): 69–92.

13. Gopher Yearbook (1952), p. 257, UMA.

14. Paul Gallico, *Houston Post,* 22 Mar. 1960; Pete Martin, "Babe Didrikson Takes Off Her Mask," *Saturday Evening Post* 20 (Sept. 1947): 26–27.

15. Paula Giddings, *When and Where I Enter: The Impact of Black Women on Race and Sex in America* (New York: William Morrow, 1984), chaps. 1, 2, 4; Patricia Hill Collins, *Black Feminist Thought: Knowledge, Consciousness, and the Politics of Empowerment* (Boston: Unwin Hyman, 1990), chaps. 4, 8.

16. Elizabeth Lunbeck, "'A New Generation of Women': Progressive Psychiatrists and the Hypersexual Female," *Feminist Studies* 13 (Fall 1987): 513–43.

17. *Baltimore Afro-American,* 29 June 1957.

18. "Fastest Women in the World," pp. 28, 32; *Detroit News* 31 (July 1962): 1.

19. Patricia Del Rey, "The Apologetic and Women in Sport," in Carole Oglesby, ed., *Women and Sport* (Philadelphia: Lea & Febiger, 1978), pp. 107–11.

20. Mildred A. Schaeffer, "Desirable Objectives in Post-war Physical Education," *Journal of Health and Physical Education* 16 (Oct. 1945): 44–47.

21. "Coeducational Classes," *Journal of Health, Physical Education, and Recreation* 26 (Feb. 1955):18. For curricular changes, I examined physical education records at the universities of Wisconsin, Texas, and Minnesota, Radcliffe College, Smith College, Tennessee State University, and Hampton University.

22. Dudley Ashton, "Recruiting Future Teachers," *Journal of Health, Physical Education, and Recreation* 28 (Oct. 1957): 49.

23. The 1949–50 Physical Training Staff Handbook at the University of Texas stated, "Legs should be kept shaved" (p. 16). Box 3R213 of Department of Physical Training for Women Records, BTHC.

24. Roxy Andersen, "Statistical Survey of Former Women Athletes," *Amateur Athlete* (Sept. 1954):10–11.

25. All-American Girls Baseball League (AAGBL) 1951 Constitution, AAGBL Records.

26. Morris Markey, "Hey Ma, You're Out!" (n.d.), 1951 Records of the AAGBL; and "Feminine Sluggers," *People and Places* 8 (1952), AAGBL Records.

27. AAGBL 1951 Constitution, AAGBL Records.

28. The sample included forty-two women, ranging in age from their forties to their seventies, who had played a variety of sports in a range of athletic settings in the West, Midwest, Southeast, and Northeast. The majority were white women from urban working-class and rural backgrounds.

29. Zipter, *Diamonds Are a Dyke's Best Friend;* Lillian Faderman, *Odd Girls and Twilight Lovers: A History of Lesbian Life in Twentieth-Century America* (New York: Columbia University Press, 1991), pp. 154, 161–62.

30. Ann Maguire, interview with the author, Boston, 18 Feb. 1988.

31. Nora Cross (pseudonym), interview with the author, 20 May 1988; Dorothy Ferguson Key, interview with the author, Rockford, Ill., 19 Dec. 1988.

32. Gloria Wilson (pseudonym), interview with the author, 11 May 1988.

33. Josephine D'Angelo, interview with the author, Chicago, 21 Dec. 1988.

34. Joseph P. Goodwin, *More Man Than You'll Ever Be! Gay Folklore and Acculturation in Middle America* (Bloomington: Indiana University Press, 1989), p. 62.

35. D'Angelo interview.

36. Loraine Sumner, interview with the author, West Roxbury, Mass., 18 Feb. 1988.

JOYCE ANTLER
Imagining Jewish Mothers in the 1950s

The wartime alliance between the United States and the USSR melted quickly as the defeat of Germany was followed by a ruthless Soviet occupation of Eastern Europe. The use of the atomic bomb at Hiroshima and Nagasaki in the summer of 1945 was both indication of and cause for heightened mistrust, and failure to develop international control of atomic energy made it worse. By 1948 the former allies had become antagonists. The United States and major Western European nations joined in a mutual defense agreement that anticipated the North Atlantic Treaty Organization (NATO); the USSR and pro-Soviet regimes in Eastern Europe shaped what would eventually become the Warsaw Pact.

As historian William Chafe has observed, in this climate "legitimate concerns could easily spill into paranoia."[*] President Harry S Truman created a Federal Employee Loyalty Program, appointing a panel authorized to screen for sympathy toward "totalitarian, fascist or subversive" organizations. What counted as sympathy and what counted as subversive were left vague. The House Committee on Un-American Activities (HUAC) was uncompromising—investigating many who had only the vaguest connection with Communist organizations and demanding that witnesses not only account for their own activities but also name others with whom they had associated. If they refused to name others, they were held in contempt of Congress. The only alternative to naming friends and associates was to refuse to answer at all, citing the Fifth Amendment's protection against self-incrimination. When HUAC investigated Communist influence on the entertainment industry, even actors whose programs had no political content could be swept up, as Gertrude Berg would find.

When the Soviet Union tested its first atomic bomb in 1949, the American public was shaken. Early the following year, Klaus Fuchs, a British physicist, was convicted of spying for the Soviet Union. The FBI search for his American collaborators soon found Harry Gold, a Philadelphia chemist, who confessed to his own complicity, and David Greenglass, a machinist, who confessed and also implicated his brother-in-law, Julius Rosenberg. Shortly afterword, Julius's wife, Ethel, was also arrested on suspicion of conspiracy to commit espionage by passing atomic secrets to the Soviets. The evidence against them was fragile, drawn from alleged conversations for which there were no third-party witnesses. But the Rosenbergs' Communist sympathies were invoked at every turn in the trial; they were blamed for the vulnerability of the United States and for making feasible the Communist aggression in Korea. Both Rosenbergs protested their innocence; both were sentenced to death.

---

[*]William Chafe, *The Unfinished Journey: America Since World War II* (New York: Oxford University Press, 1986), p. 98.

Excerpted from ch. 8, with notes modified by the author, of *The Journey Home: Jewish Women and the American Century* by Joyce Antler (New York: Free Press, 1997). Reprinted with the permission of the author and the Free Press, a Division of Simon & Schuster, Inc. Copyright © 1997 by Joyce Antler. All rights reserved. Notes have been edited and renumbered. *Yoo Hoo, Mrs. Goldberg,* a documentary by Aviva Kempner, was released in 2009; see www.mollygoldbergfilm.org/home.php.

An extended series of unsuccessful legal appeals followed; the Rosenberg case became an international cause. The famous Spanish artist Pablo Picasso offered lithograph portraits of the couple as fund-raisers for the costs of their defense; there were mass rallies on their behalf in European and American cities. In June 1953, President Eisenhower refused a last plea for clemency; he explained his decision in a letter to his son John:

> I must say that it goes against the grain to avoid interfering in the case where a woman is to receive capital punishment. . . . [But] in this instance it is the woman who is the strong and recalcitrant character. The man is the weak one. . . . [I]f there would be any commuting of the woman's sentence without the man's then from here on the Soviets would simply recruit their spies from among women.[†]

Julius and Ethel Rosenberg were executed at Sing Sing prison, New York, on June 19, 1953. Nearly 50 years later, Ethel's brother, who had given damning testimony that she had typed spy notes, admitted to a reporter that he had lied on the witness stand to avoid implicating his own wife.[**]

Popular cultural ideas, including images of good mothers, seeped into the ways in which Ethel Rosenberg was judged by the media and the general public. Political anxieties about international relations made radio and television celebrities like Gertrude Berg cautious about the message they sent. And even after the entire European Jewish population had barely survived the Holocaust, Berg and Rosenberg's Jewishness made both vulnerable.

For most Americans, and not least for American Jews, the postwar period represented a paradoxical time in political as well as popular culture. Recovering from the Depression and World War II, Jews continued their move into the mainstream of American life, enjoying unprecedented economic prosperity and a great increase in opportunities for education, the professions, and business.

Yet troubling signs rippled the smooth surface of Jewish acculturation. Despite its decline, anti-Semitism remained a significant factor in American life, with almost sixty known anti-Semitic organizations operating in 1950. Also ominous was the association of American Jews in the public mind with the menace of communism, an association fostered by the trial and conviction of Ethel and Julius Rosenberg. Although the trial did not trigger the kind of virulent anti-Semitic tirades that many Jewish leaders had feared, the anxiety it caused among Jews suggested that they were

perhaps not as at home in America as they had believed.

The polar experiences of American Jews in the 1950s—their spectacular arrival in the American mainstream coupled with lingering fears of anti-Semitism and doubts about Jewish acculturation—are represented by two famous Jewish women of the time: the cherubic, smiling Molly Goldberg, the radio and TV sitcom heroine of the long-running series "The Goldbergs," and the taut, drawn, unsmiling Ethel Greenglass Rosenberg herself.

Although a fictional character, Molly Goldberg was played with such verisimilitude by Gertrude Berg—in fact an American-born, middle-class Jew—that the public easily confused the mythical Molly with her real-life impersonator. Berg, who created the character, lived a very different life from that of Molly Goldberg. Yet Molly/Gertrude was powerful in popular culture precisely because she ostensibly represented reality. Molly's character, tied

---

**Robert D. McFadden, "David Greenglass, Who Helped Seal the Rosenbergs' Doom, Dies at 92," *New York Times*, Oct. 15, 2014, p. A1 (New York edition).

†John Lewis Gaddis, *Strategies of Containment: A Critical Appraisal of Postwar American National Security Policy* (New York: Oxford University Press, 1982), p. 138, n. 31.

to Gertrude Berg, not only mobilized the cultural power of a "real" person but, in some sense, became a real person. In much the same way that Molly Goldberg enjoyed a reality independent of Gertrude Berg, so did the media representations of Ethel Greenglass Rosenberg come to dominate public perceptions of the real Ethel. Yet the flesh-and-blood Rosenberg differed as much from the media's Ethel as Gertrude did from Molly.[1]

Second-generation daughters of East European immigrant families, Gertrude Berg and Ethel Rosenberg exemplify the changing aspirations, and the changing representations, of Jewish women in the 1950s. Both women defied convention: Gertrude, by building a media career and directing and producing a long-running hit series, all the while managing her own household and family life; Ethel, by combining a staunch commitment to radical ideology with a conscientious, even obsessive, motherhood. For a generation or more, however, the cultural construction of "Molly" and "Ethel" has left little room for imagining the full historical matrix in which Gertrude and Ethel lived their lives. The potent alliance between media and politics that characterized the Red Scare years obliterated all but the masks of Molly and Ethel.[2]

Molly and Ethel were not the only representations of Jewish women in the politicized culture of the 1950s. Another archetypal middle-class Jewish woman of the decade was "Shirley," a type made famous by Herman Wouk in his 1955 novel, *Marjorie Morningstar*. Selling millions of copies and made into a successful movie starring the popular actress Natalie Wood, the book depicted the transformation of a young, ambitious, "emancipated" Jewish girl into a conventional suburban matron, a Shirley. Rebellious as a youth Marjorie/Shirley matured into "the respectable girl, the mother of the next generation, all tricked out to appear gay and girlish and carefree but with a terrible threatening dullness jutting through"; later Marjorie/Shirley became a regular synagogue goer, active in the Jewish organizations of the town," a model, in fact, of the many thousands of Jewish women who belonged to temple sisterhoods, Hadassah, the National Council of Jewish Women, and similar organizations. While Wouk treats Shirley sympathetically, Mrs. Patimkin, the Shirley-like Jewish mother in Philip Roth's 1959 novella, *Good-bye Columbus*, is portrayed as vain, empty-headed, materialistic. Her daughter,

Brenda, demonstrating the worst qualities of 1950s suburban Jewish affluence, joined Marjorie Morningstar as one in a series of indelible images of a new kind of Jewish heroine—assimilated, smoothly confident, flirtatious, beautiful, spoiled. Together with Ethel and Molly, these fictional representations would provide enduring images of Jewish American womanhood—mothers and daughters, protectors and princesses—that would wield more power and influence than their creators could ever have expected.[3]

Yet these images do not do justice to the varied experiences of Jewish women in postwar America. The activism demonstrated by such groups as the National Council of Jewish Women and the Emma Lazarus Federation of Jewish Women's Clubs (a left-wing group created after the Holocaust by a group of largely Yiddish-speaking women of the immigrant generation) belies the homogeneity of the period and demonstrates that "Molly," "Ethel," and "Shirley" were cultural constructs after all.

. . . "The Rise of the Goldbergs" was one of the most popular serials in radio's golden era, running from 1929 through 1946, and . . . 1949 to 1950. After 1931, the show aired nightly, for some years carried by both the CBS and NBC networks. In 1946, the show (known as "The Goldbergs") made the transition to television, running through 1955. It was revived in the early 1960s as "Mrs. G," a new series about Molly at college. Along the way there were also a comic strip, a syndicated column ("Mamatalks"), a published version of the show's early scripts, a cookbook, a hit Broadway play (*Me and Molly*), two films, and Berg's autobiography, *Molly and Me*. So identified was Gertrude Berg with Molly Goldberg that she signed autographs in the character's name. Yet it was Berg, the consummate professional, who wrote as well as starred in the show's five thousand-plus radio scripts as well as the later television programs.

During the second quarter of the twentieth century, Molly Goldberg became the quintessential representation of the American Jewish mother in popular culture. "Kind-hearted," "humane," "gentle," "gracious," "sympathetic," and "tender"—these were the words typically used in advertisements for the show—Molly Goldberg, like her creator Gertrude Berg, was nonetheless a woman of force and dominance. [Her] genius was to wed the iron qualities of traditional East European Jewish women with a charm and humor that counteracted the threat of their power. During the Depression, when a negative stereotype of the Jewish mother as materialistic and pushy began to appear in the works of Clifford Odets and other Jewish male writers, Berg's Molly had a more positive appeal.[4]

Molly's compassion and the comic elements in her character diverted attention from other, potentially troublesome traits. At best meddlesome and at worst nagging and controlling, Molly got her way in almost every show, but always for the purpose of helping others. Molly's speech, full of malapropisms, reflected her status as an immigrant whose eagerness to adopt American usages was greater than her knowledge: "Come sit on the table, dinner is ready . . . You'll swallow a cup, darling? . . . Throw an eye into the ice-box and give me an accounting. . . . "[5] Molly's generosity and the quaintness of her language—including the famous opening line of the show, "Yoo hoo Mrs. Bloom," which she yelled out the window to her tenement neighbor—endeared her to audiences.

No matter how exaggerated, caricatured, or sentimental the show's characters, to audiences they seemed believable and realistic. Writing in 1951, novelist Charles Angoff praised the show for its realistic representation of "virtually the whole panorama of middle-class Jewish-American life":

> There are the neighbors who borrow from and lend to one another, and who offer advice, whether asked or not . . . there are the sisters and cousins and aunts, with all their jealousies and bickerings and generosities and meddlings . . . the young folk who sometimes think they have "outgrown" their parents but who find that for comfort and counsel there are no substitutes . . . and there is Molly herself, whose heart bleeds for every unmarried girl and starving butcher and lonely grocer, and who is as quick as the proverbial lightning in concocting ideas to get the "right" girl and the "right" man together, to straighten out family squabbles, to help out a reformed thief, to get her own son to invite her to a college affair—in short, Molly the Mixer and the Fixer.

Together these characters presented "neurotic tensions, despair, ecstasy, conniving, kindliness, back-biting . . . the normal life of Bronx and Brooklyn and Manhattan and Chicago and Boston and Philadelphia and San Francisco Jews." Angoff concluded: "I have never heard anyone who knows Jewish life say that 'The Goldbergs' are not true to life. Molly Goldberg, indeed, is so basically true a character that I sometimes think she may become an enduring name in the national literature. She is the prototype of the Jewish mother during the past twenty-five years."[6]

A good part of the praise for "The Goldbergs" was due to its uplifting message about American family life and moral values. Berg once described the, show to a reporter, using Molly's lines: "Jake wants the children to have everything money can buy, and I want them to have everything money can't buy." This philosophical difference formed the core of the show's dramatic conflict, and despite the Goldbergs' upward mobility, it was always resolved in Molly's favor. Listeners found the message of "The Goldbergs" inspirational: ministers composed sermons around the program, and at least one Orthodox rabbi instructed congregants not to turn their radios off on Friday afternoon, so that they could listen to Molly on Shabbos evening "without breaking the law." During wartime, especially, the show received accolades as "a force for decency and the democratic way of life."[7]

Three points stand out regarding the Molly Goldberg character. First, Molly as a Jewish mother was an odd but lovable, generous woman who solved all the problems of her family, neighborhood, and community through her skillful "mixing-in." She was a voluble, talkative busybody, a *balaboste*, but one with a loving heart who could always be trusted to do the right thing.

The second point is that in spite of her ethnicity, which was always prominent (even when the use of dialect subsided), Molly and her children espoused assimilationist values. Over the decades, the audience saw the family leave their Bronx neighborhood, move to the suburbs, and send the children off to college. In this respect, "The Goldbergs" was an accurate representation of the Jewish middle-class's entry into the American mainstream. Despite the family's economic transformation, Molly herself changed very little. Even in the mid-1950s, she looked and sounded like a newly arrived immigrant; in this respect, Molly remained in a television time warp.[8]

The third point is that as the Goldbergs became America's surrogate family, Molly became everybody's mother, a woman who, *because* of her ethnicity (that is, her difference), represented the American ideal of brotherly love and interreligious cooperation. This point was borne out in the huge amount of fan mail Berg received and in the accolades from non-Jewish as well as Jewish organizations.

In order to achieve such wide acceptance in both mainstream and Jewish audiences, Berg made a conscious decision, as she told one reporter, not to bring in

> anything that will bother people . . . unions, politics, fundraising, Zionism, socialism, intergroup relations, I don't stress them. After all, aren't such things second to daily living? The Goldbergs are not defensive about their Jewishness, or especially aware of it. I keep things average. I don't want to lose friends.[9]

Like other situation comedies of the 1950s, "The Goldbergs" portrayed the family as a sea of domestic tranquillity—a "suburban middle landscape," according to one critic—isolated from problems in the larger society. Sitcoms were "Cold War comedies of reassurance," in which politics, "by its telling absence . . . was a contaminating force to be kept beyond the threshold of the private household." In shows like "Leave It to Beaver," "Father Knows Best," "The Adventures of Ozzie and Harriet," "The Donna Reed Show," "I Remember Mama," and "Make Room for Daddy/The Danny Thomas Show," television reinforced values of family togetherness—responsibility, maturity, adjustment, and "enlightened permissiveness."[10] In most of these comedies, it was not the maternal figure but the benevolent patriarch who navigated his family through the shoals of neighborhood life. Yet Molly Goldberg's affable, homespun wisdom, like that of the Norwegian mother in "I Remember Mama" (played by Peggy Wood), was no less authoritative than that of her male counterparts. As women in command of a vast repository of folk wisdom, Berg and Wood steered their families through the special challenges of modern American life, while demonstrating for the television audience that conflict could be easily managed and contained if "normal" family values were upheld.

But this is not the whole story. Gertrude Berg could eliminate controversy from her show, but not from her life. Philip Loeb, who played Molly's husband, Jake, on radio in the late 1940s and took the character to TV in 1949 was a victim of the blacklist in 1950. After a debate with her sponsors (who eventually pulled out), Gertrude Berg succumbed and fired Loeb in 1952; he committed suicide three years

later. Comedian Milton Berle reveals in his memoirs that in 1950, when Berg was "fighting the witch-hunters" who had "enough juice to hurt [her] in every way," his sponsors and NBC would not permit Berg to appear on his show, even though she had her own. . . . It is possible that Berg, a member of an actors' group that included many well-known left-wing artists such as Paul Robeson, was herself the target of a blacklist.[11]

The portrait of Molly Goldberg as the ideal Jewish mother of the 1950s may thus have clashed with the reality of Gertrude Berg's own politics; it certainly contrasted with the fact of her career. Married and the mother of two children, Berg had grown up writing skits to amuse the guests at her parents' summer hotel in the Catskills. Even after marriage and motherhood, she was determined to pursue her career as a writer, but the short stories she submitted to popular magazines all came back with rejection slips. Then came her breakthrough in a trial run of "Goldberg" scripts, written for radio. Almost immediately, Berg became a highly successful media entrepreneur. She was no Molly Goldberg, stay-at-home housewife, though she prided herself on her "normal" family life.

Berg's decision to eschew politics and what she described as "defensive" Jewishness reflected a common strategy of leading Jewish organizations of the period. In the late 1940s and the 1950s, these groups embarked on new ventures designed to counteract the forces of bigotry and enhance interreligious and interethnic harmony. Rather than responding exclusively to direct threats to American Jewry, they took action on a panoply of social and cultural concerns, including opposition to McCarthyism and the promotion of civil rights and the ideals of the welfare state. "The Goldbergs," with its exhortation to celebrate human brotherhood and its conscious disregard of difference, mirrored these objectives.

The example of compassionate concern that Molly Goldberg demonstrated to her Christian friends and neighbors was embodied in the postwar program of the National Council of Jewish Women. In 1947, the NCJW introduced a new initiative on "intercultural relations." The initiative, entitled "cultural democracy," exposed the flaws in the idea of the melting pot and championed the free expression of cultural differences. "Something good is lost when people are melted down to a uniform consistency," the NCJW asserted; it was the "diversity of [many] cultures which make the American society strong." According to the NCJW, the prophetic imperative to brotherhood and other Judaic teachings made "the universal concern for all people" a guide for American Jews. But the Council insisted that it was an American as well as a Jewish obligation to eradicate intolerance. . . .

Recognizing prejudice was . . . not sufficient to eradicate it. Council leaders argued that it was crucial to be "'good neighbors,' understanding and respecting our fellow citizens of different racial and religious backgrounds." For this purpose, chapters were instructed to work with other local groups on such issues as eliminating stereotypes and stimulating public interest in building better intercultural understanding. But it was equally important to develop a positive program of action, seeking "economic and social justice" for all people regardless of their race, religion, or national origin.[12] For this reason, the NCJW extended the project on interfaith harmony beyond such local issues as schools, housing, and citizenship to include broad questions of public policy, social legislation, and even international affairs, all of which it considered integral to intercultural work. During the 1950s, the NCJW promoted these objectives through public education and lobbying on behalf of such causes as immigration reform and civil rights.[13]

In 1952, the NCJW launched a related project, the Freedom Campaign, designed to educate the public to the importance of civil liberties and to encourage people in "speaking up for what they believe is right" while "respecting the beliefs of others." Declaring its staunch opposition to communism, the NCJW also declared war on Senator McCarthy and the House Un-American Activities Committee's "campaign of vilification" against "everyone who has ever held an original idea or participated in the activities of a minority group." . . . The Council formed a special alliance with the Young Women's Christian Association (YWCA) in this campaign.[14]

The common ground of racial and religious tolerance that guided NCJW's postwar intercultural effort was specifically acknowledged in 1961, when the council and the YWCA came together again to commemorate the fiftieth anniversary of both organizations' initial commitment to seek public policy protection for working women and children. . . . [They] issued a ten-point "Code of Personal Commitment," stressing opposition to prejudice, protection of individual liberties, and efforts toward world peace. "I will cultivate objectivity of thought / And will consider new and different points of view," the statement read. "I will recognize my common kinship with all / and remember that whatever happens to anyone happens to me."[15]

Despite the NCJW's freedom campaign and its dedication to protecting the rights of political dissidents and racial, religious, and ethnic minorities, the Council, like Gertrude Berg herself, had little to say about the Rosenberg case or Ethel Rosenberg as a Jewish woman.

Like Gertrude Berg, Ethel Rosenberg aspired to an artistic career, although it was as a singer and actress, rather than a writer, that she hoped to make her mark. An excellent student at Seward Park High School on Manhattan's Lower East Side, Ethel planned to attend college and took college preparatory courses. Graduating in 1931 at the height of the Depression, however, she felt lucky to obtain a clerical job with the National New York Shipping and Packing Company. The Clark House Players, an amateur theater group sponsored by a settlement house around the corner from her home, was the object of most of her enthusiasm over the next few years; she also took acting classes at the Henry Street Settlement and attended lectures by members of several experimental theater companies. At nineteen, Ethel was accepted into the prestigious Schola Cantorum, becoming the choir's youngest member; the group occasionally sang at the Metropolitan Opera House. The following year, singing an operatic solo at a benefit for the International Seamen's Union, Ethel met Julius Rosenberg, who claimed she had the most beautiful voice he had ever heard. They were married three years later.[16]

Ethel pursued her singing and acting interests only sporadically after her marriage. Her independent involvement in political action also declined. Before meeting Julius, she had helped to organize the Ladies Apparel Shipping Clerks Union at her company, serving as the only woman on a four-person strike committee that called a citywide action in which over 10,000 workers participated. Fired for her role in this strike, Ethel brought a complaint before the newly formed National Labor Relations Board; the case was later decided in her favor. By this time, she had found employment as a stenographer with Bell Textile Company. She left this job after Julius found work with the United States Signal Corps, turning her attention to volunteer activities. Among the groups she joined were the women's auxiliary of her husband's union—the Federation of Architects, Engineers, Chemists and Technicians (FAECT)—and, after the start of World War II, the Lower East Side Defense Council.

After the births of her sons—Michael in 1943 and Robert four years later—Rosenberg became increasingly absorbed in family matters. According to one neighbor, she was "literally a mother 24 hours out of 24."[17] But motherhood did not come as easily to Ethel as it did to Molly Goldberg and Gertrude Berg. Beset by physical ailments resulting from chronic scoliosis and the emotional strain of dealing with young children, she grew increasingly concerned about her parenting skills. Setting limits for her children—responding to them with both the generosity and the authority that she felt good parenting entailed—was especially problematic; the importance of these qualities was continually being emphasized in the pages of *Parents Magazine*, which Rosenberg read religiously, and in the vastly popular performances of Gertrude Berg. Seeking guidance, Rosenberg took a course on child psychology at the New School for Social Research and enlisted the help of a social worker at the Jewish Board of Guardians; soon afterward, she began to see a private psychiatrist. Though she deeply loved and respected Julius, he could not alleviate her anxieties about raising their sons. Despite their political radicalism, both accepted the gender role division that allotted breadwinning responsibilities to the husband and child rearing to the wife. "The good mother is the key to proper child rearing," Rosenberg wrote to her lawyer, Manny Bloch, after she had been arrested and imprisoned along with Julius on charges of conspiracy to commit espionage.[18]

In view of Rosenberg's faith in communism, her resorting to psychoanalysis and social work may seem surprising. But Rosenberg's worries as a mother apparently overshadowed any doubts she may have had about succumbing to such capitalist opiates. In the emphasis she placed on child rearing, Rosenberg was in fact not far removed from Molly Goldberg. Whether she read Gertrude Berg's advice column in the 1930s, or listened to any

of the Goldberg shows on radio or TV, is unknown, but her idea of what characterized the "good" mother certainly overlapped with Berg's portrayal of Molly as understanding, tolerant, generous—everything Rosenberg's own mother, Tessie Greenglass, was not.

Tessie Greenglass was an unhappy, troubled woman, disappointed in her husband's lack of ambition and inability to move the family out of poverty. Unlike the Goldbergs or the Bergs, the Greenglasses never realized their dream of American success; Tessie's frustrations with this failure were apparently visited on her only daughter. Favoring her three sons, especially the youngest, David, she treated Ethel with disrespect bordering on cruelty; certainly Ethel was abused emotionally (and sometimes physically, since Tessie used corporal punishment on all the children). Despite (or because of) Ethel's excellence at school and her good-girl demeanor at home, she was also the butt of her brothers' jealousy; she was very much the scapegoat of the entire family.[19]

When, years later, David Greenglass accused Ethel and Julius of masterminding the spy ring in which he was allegedly involved at Los Alamos, Rosenberg was not surprised that her mother accepted her brother's story rather than her own. But the extent of her mother's lack of support for her, and for her children, hurt Ethel Rosenberg enormously. When Tessie first visited Rosenberg in prison it was only to scream at her for harming David and to call her a "dirty Communist." After Rosenberg was transferred to solitary confinement at Sing Sing, Tessie did not visit her at all for two years; when she finally did it was only to urge her daughter to confess. Ethel Rosenberg responded angrily, but admitted to her lawyer that she would "still give anything in the world for one kind word from her." Tessie returned two months before Rosenberg's execution to insist again that she affirm her brother's account and admit her guilt. According to the prison official who was present, Rosenberg, enraged, called her mother a "witch" and "yelled and raved to such an extent that she was cautioned by the guard that the interview would be terminated unless she quieted down." That was the last time Rosenberg saw Tessie.[20]

No doubt Ethel Rosenberg's troubled relationship with her mother accounted in good part for her concerns about her own parenting. But her anxieties about her performance as a mother and her children's emotional well-being were also the product of cultural messages that she, like others with her background and aspirations, absorbed from the surrounding culture. Under the growing influence of child guidance specialists and behavioral psychologists, parenting in the late 1940s and early 1950s became more than ever a matter of expert counseling and knowledge rather than innate capability. During these years, the notion of motherhood as "pathology" was a staple in both the popular and scientific press, with all manner of experts holding mothers accountable for withdrawn, destructive, disturbed, and "deviant" children.[21] If Ethel Rosenberg blamed herself for child-rearing problems—however normal—she was merely reflecting the accepted wisdom. Rosenberg's faith in professional child guidance in fact illuminates why Molly Goldberg was so popular a figure in the postwar period. In representing an earlier time, when parents dominated their children's lives and truly "knew best," sitcoms like "The Goldbergs" provided nostalgic reassurance to a generation increasingly troubled about the viability of a harmonious family life in the context of a pluralistic society. Rosenberg's concern about her own family, and her employment of therapy for herself and counseling for the children, suggests how deeply a part of her generation she was.

In spite of her intense concerns about her children, Ethel Rosenberg's behavior during her trial convinced the jurors and the American public that she was guilty—not because of the evidence, but because she lacked "maternal feeling." That Rosenberg was arrested and tried as a "lever" to force her husband to talk is now well documented. Based wholly on the testimony of her brother David and his wife, Ruth, the case was "not too strong against Mrs. Rosenberg," as one prosecutor acknowledged privately. Such doubts continued after Ethel's conviction and remain today, even though Julius's guilt now appears certain. "Was your wife cognizant of your activities?" prosecutors asked Julius Rosenberg in a questionnaire submitted to him at the Sing-Sing Death House.[22] Given the paucity of evidence regarding her participation in the conspiracy, Ethel Rosenberg's appearance at the trial became all-important.

To the public Ethel Rosenberg's failure to break down under the pressure of her arrest and trial appeared to confirm that she cared more about ideology than about her offspring,

and was therefore guilty. Her denial of guilt, along with her repeated reliance on the Fifth Amendment, created the impression, according to one legal scholar, of a "cold, well-composed woman lacking 'normal' feminine characteristics." Because of her failure to lose her composure on the witness stand (both her husband [and] his co-defendant, Morton Sobell, appeared much more uneasy), Rosenberg seemed enigmatic, "unnatural." To the jury foreman she was a "steely, stoney, tight-lipped woman. She was the mastermind. Julius would have spoken if she would have permitted him. He was more human. She was more disciplined." According to another juror, she was certainly guilty—of being a bad mother: "I had two daughters at the time, and it bothered me how they would subject their children to such a thing. I just couldn't understand it."[23]

After the Rosenbergs were convicted and sentenced to death, the image of Ethel as an "unnatural" woman and mother blocked appeals for clemency. FBI director J. Edgar Hoover used the fact of Rosenberg's failure to talk with her own mother for two years as evidence of her evil nature; when Douglas Dillon, then ambassador to France, protested the severity of her sentence compared to those of convicted British spies Klaus Fuchs and Allan Nunn May, Hoover reported that when Tessie Greenglass urged Rosenberg to confess to spare her children, Rosenberg had rebuked her with the words, "Don't mention the children. Children are born every day of the week." Although he had previously opposed the execution of Ethel as well as Julius on the grounds that it would leave two young children orphaned, Hoover changed his mind after receiving the FBI's report that "Ethel was not a good mother after all." President Eisenhower used similar gender-based reasoning in his denial of clemency: "In this instance, it is the woman who is the strong and recalcitrant character, the man who is the weak one." He believed that as the unquestioned "leader in the spy ring," Ethel Rosenberg had renounced all rights to special treatment as a woman and mother of two young children.[24] She was the first American woman to be executed for the crime of conspiracy to commit espionage.

No greater contrast could exist than that between the Molly Goldberg ideal of the 1950s—friendly, garrulous, kindhearted, family-oriented, non-controversial, and nonpolitical—and the public image of Ethel Rosenberg: silent and mysterious, conspiratorial and political, dominating and evil. Blindly loyal to her husband at the cost of abandoning her own children, she seemed, above all—and perhaps most dangerously—a neglectful, uncaring mother. Many Americans who loved Molly Goldberg were deeply shocked by Ethel Rosenberg.

This portrait of Ethel Rosenberg, elaborated in the media, was especially troubling to Jews.[25] In contrast to the Goldbergs, with their seamless adjustment to American society, the Rosenbergs appeared as an alien couple linked to a foreign power; their rejection of mainstream American values, such as those espoused by the Goldbergs and other TV sitcom families, spoke to the dark underside of the American dream and enhanced the presumption of guilt. Moreover, in contrast to the wholesome Goldberg family ("Allow me to ask whether in Jewish families nothing ever goes wrong," one viewer wrote to ask. "Is it always 'Papa darling' and 'Mama darling'? . . . no wrangling, no quibbling?") the Rosenberg family was fatally divided between brothers and sister, mother and daughter.[26] In the early 1950s, when such a family was not yet labeled "dysfunctional," the Rosenbergs seemed not only abnormal but un-American. . . .

That the Molly Goldberg ideal coincided with the aspirations of the real Ethel Rosenberg was no more ironic than the fact that Ethel—a woman excessively concerned about mothering—was portrayed by government officials and the media as a cold, uncaring "monster" of a mother. Ethel's convincing stoicism in the face of her most enormous loss—that of her children—may have been her finest performance.

NOTES

1. For an extended discussion of Molly Goldberg in relation to Ethel Rosenberg, see my "A Bond of Sisterhood: Ethel Rosenberg, Molly Goldberg, and Radical Jewish Women of the 1950s," in Marjorie Garber and Rebecca L. Walkowitz, eds. *Secret Agents: The Rosenberg Case, McCarthyism, and Fifties America* (New York: Routledge, 1995): 197–214.
2. On the politicization of culture during the 1950s, see Stephen J. Whitfield, *The Culture of the Cold War* (Baltimore: Johns Hopkins University Press, 1991). On women's roles, see Elaine Tyler May, *Homeward Bound: American Families in the Cold War Era* (New York: Basic Books, 1988); Wini Breines, *Young, White, and Miserable: Growing Up Female in the Fifties* (Boston: Beacon, 1992); and Joanne Meyerowitz, ed. *Not June Cleaver: Women and Gender in Postwar America, 1945–1960* (Philadelphia: Temple University Press, 1994).

3. Herman Wouk, *Marjorie Morningstar* (Boston: Little Brown, 1955/1983), 172, 562; Philip Roth, *Goodbye Columbus and Five Short Stories* (Boston: Houghton Mifflin, 1959/1989).
4. B. G. Bienstock, "The Changing Image of the American Jewish Mother," in Virginia Tufte and Barbara Myerhoff, eds. *Changing Images of the Family* (New Haven: Yale University Press, 1979).
5. Charles Angoff, "'The Goldbergs' and Jewish Humor," *Congress Weekly* 18 (March 5, 1951): 13; "The Goldbergs March On," *Life* (April 25, 1949): 59; "The Goldbergs," script, Oct. 3, 1949, Gertrude Berg Papers, Special Collections, Syracuse University, Syracuse, N.Y.
6. Angoff, "The Goldbergs," 12–13. Gertrude Berg cited in Jack Long, "Her Family Is Her Fortune," *American*, n.d., Ill, Gertrude Berg Papers.
7. Joan Jacobs Brumberg, "Gertrude Berg," in Barbara Sicherman and Carol Hurd Green, eds., *Notable American Women—The Modern Period: A Biographical Dictionary* (Cambridge: Belknap Press of Harvard University Press, 1980), 73–74; Sulamith Ish-Kishor, "Interesting People: Gertrude Berg," *Jewish Tribune* (Oct. 10, 1930), 7.
8. Morris Freedman, "The Real Molly Goldberg," *Commentary* 21 (April 1954), 364; also see Donald Weber, *Haunted in the World: Jewish American Culture from Cahan to "The Goldbergs"* (Bloomington: Indiana University Press, 2005); and Glenn D. Smith, *Something on My Own: Gertrude Berg and American Broadcasting, 1929–1956* (Syracuse: Syracuse University Press, 2007).
9. Freedman, "The Real Molly Goldberg," 360.
10. Hal Himmelstein, *Television Myth and the American Mind* (New York: Praeger, 1984), 84–97; David Marc, *Comic Visions: Television Comedy and American Culture* (Boston: Unwin Hyman, 1989), 65; Darrell Y. Hamamoto, *Nervous Laughter : Television Situation Comedy and Liberal Democratic Ideology* (New York: Praeger, 1989), 24–25.
11. Milton Berle, *Milton Berle: An Autobiography* (New York: Delacorte Press, 1974), 293–94.
12. National Council of Jewish Women, "Cultural Democracy—Pattern for America" (mimeograph, Sept. 1947): 5, 4, 11, 9–10, 19, NCJW Papers, Library of Congress, Washington, D.C.
13. National Council of Jewish Women, Committee on Education and Social Action, *Spotlight*, Vols. 5–9, [1949–53], NCJW Papers.
14. *Spotlight*, Vols. 8–9.
15. National Council of Jewish Women and YWCA, Joint Statement, Dec. 6, 1961, NCJW Papers.
16. See Ilene Philipson, *Ethel Rosenberg: Beyond the Myths* (New Brunswick, N.J.: Rutgers University Press, 1988) and Carol Hurd Green, "Ethel Rosenberg," in Sicherman and Green, *Notable American Women*, 601–4.
17. Sheila M. Brennan, "Popular Images of American Women in the 1950s and Their Impact on Ethel Rosenberg's Trial and Conviction," *Women's Rights Law Reporter* 14, No. 1 (Winter 1992): 47.
18. Ethel Rosenberg to Emanuel Bloch, August 31, 1951–Sept. 6, 1951, in Robert Meeropol and Michael Meeropol, *We Are Your Sons: The Legacy of Ethel and Julius Rosenberg* (Boston: Houghton Mifflin, 1975), 101.
19. Philipson, *Ethel Rosenberg*, 28. The testimony of David Greenglass and especially his wife, Ruth

Greenglass, played a major role in convicting Ethel. In recent years, David admitted that he made up the story; see Sam Roberts, *Brother: The Untold Story of the Rosenberg Case* (New York: Random House, 2003). Filmmaker Ivy Meeropol, the granddaughter of Ethel and Julius, explores the Greenglass' involvement, and reflects on Ethel's family roles, in her moving documentary, *Heir to an Execution* (2004).

20. Philipson, 345.

21. See, for example, Barbara Ehrenreich and Deirdre English, *For Her Own Good: 150 Years of the Experts' Advice to Women* (New York: Doubleday, 1978), ch. 7.

22. Ronald Radosh and Joyce Milton, *The Rosenberg File: A Search for the Truth* (New York: Holt, Rinehart and Winston, 1973), 417.

23. Brennan, "Popular Images of American Women," 56–59.

24. Fuchs and May received fourteen- and ten-year terms, respectively. Brennan, "Popular Images," 60.

25. See Deborah Dash Moore, "Reconsidering the Rosenbergs: Symbol and Substance in Second Generation American Jewish Consciousness," *Journal of American Ethnic History* 8, No. 1 (Fall 1988): 21–37.

26. Cited by Donald Weber, "Situating Gertrude Berg: *The Goldbergs* and the Construction of Jewish American Identity, 1930–50," in Joyce Antler, ed., *Talking Back: Images of Jewish Women in American Popular Culture* (Hanover, N.H.: University Press of New England, 1998).

WOMEN'S COLD WAR ACTIVISM

DANIEL HOROWITZ
Betty Friedan and the Origins of Feminism in Cold War America

The years immediately after World War II were marked by a resurgent domesticity. The average age at marriage of women dropped sharply—by the end of the 1950s it was 20. Women's age at the birth of their first child also decreased precipitously; the number of children per family increased sharply. The proportion of women in college fell in comparison to men; many others dropped out of college to marry or because they saw no advantage in increased education.

In 1963 Betty Friedan published *The Feminine Mystique,* a searing indictment of the triviality and frustrations of postwar domesticity (pp. 606–610). She wrote in the voice of an author who located herself in the middle-class suburbs and whose ethnicity was unmarked. But as Daniel Horowitz explains in the essay that follows, Friedan's analysis emerged not only from her experience of suburban life, but also from her experience in left-wing politics and in the labor movement—experiences she did not mention in *The Feminine Mystique.* The execution of Ethel and Julius Rosenberg for spying in 1952 frightened many progressive Jewish organizations lest they be tainted as communist sympathizers; they would subsequently be inhospitable to reformers from the left. (For more about Ethel Rosenberg, see the essay by Joyce Antler on pp. 559–568.) Many elements of Cold War politics and culture may have contributed to the choices Friedan made as she developed her voice.

In 1951, a labor journalist with a decade's experience in protest movements described a trade union meeting where rank-and-file women talked and men listened. Out of these conversations, she reported, emerged the realization that the women were "fighters—that they refuse any longer to be paid or treated as some inferior species by their bosses, or by any male workers who have swallowed the bosses' thinking."[1] The union was the UE, the United Electrical, Radio and Machine Workers of America, the most radical American union in the postwar period and in the 1940s what historian Ronald Schatz . . . has called "the largest communist-led institution of any kind in the United States."[2] In 1952 that same journalist wrote a pamphlet, *UE Fights for Women Workers,* that the historian Lisa Kannenberg, unaware of the identity of its author, has called "a remarkable manual for fighting wage discrimination that is, ironically, as relevant today as it was in 1952." At the time, the pamphlet helped raise the consciousness of Eleanor Flexner, who in 1959 would publish *Century of Struggle,* the

Excerpted from Daniel Horowitz, "Rethinking Betty Friedan and *The Feminine Mystique*: Labor Union Radicalism and Feminism in Cold War America," *American Quarterly* 48 (March 1996): 1–42. Copyright © The American Studies Association. Reprinted with permission of the author and Johns Hopkins University Press. Notes have been renumbered and edited.

first scholarly history of American women. In 1953–54, Flexner relied extensively on the pamphlet when she taught a course at the Jefferson School of Social Science in New York on "The Woman Question." Flexner's participation in courses at the school, she later said, "marked the beginning of my real involvement in the issues of women's rights, my realization that leftist organizations—parties, unions—were also riddled with male supremacist prejudice and discrimination."[3] The labor journalist and pamphlet writer was Betty Friedan.

In 1973 Friedan remarked that until she started writing *The Feminine Mystique* (1963), "I wasn't even conscious of the woman problem." In 1976 she commented that in the early 1950s she was "still in the embrace of the feminine mystique."[4] Although in 1974 she revealed some potentially controversial elements of her past, even then she left the impression that her landmark book emerged only from her own captivity by the very forces she described. Friedan's portrayal of herself as so totally trapped by the feminine mystique was part of a reinvention of herself as she wrote and promoted *The Feminine Mystique*. Her story made it possible for readers to identify with its author and its author to enhance the book's appeal. However, it hid from view the connection between the union activity in which Friedan participated in the 1940s and early 1950s and the feminism she inspired in the 1960s. In the short term, her misery in the suburbs may have prompted her to write *The Feminine Mystique*; a longer term perspective makes clear that the book's origins lie much earlier—in her college education and in her experiences with labor unions in the 1940s and early 1950s.[5] . . . Friedan's life provides evidence of . . . continuity . . . between the struggle for justice for working women in the 1940s and the feminism of the 1960s. This connection gives feminism and Friedan, both long under attack for a lack of interest in working class and African American women, a past of which they should be proud. . . . Moreover, a new reading of *The Feminine Mystique* sheds light on the remaking of progressive forces in America, the process by which a focus on women and the professional middle and upper middle classes supplemented, in some ways replaced a focus on unions. Finally, an examination of *The Feminine Mystique* reminds us of important shifts in the ideology of the left: from an earlier economic analysis based on Marxism to one

developed in the 1950s that also rested on humanistic psychology, and from a focus on the impact of conditions of production on the working class to an emphasis on the effect of consumption on the middle class.

In print and in interviews, Friedan has offered a narrative of her life that she popularized after she became famous in 1963.[6] A full biography might begin in Peoria, where Bettye Naomi Goldstein was born February 4, 1921 and grew up with her siblings and their parents: a father who owned a jewelry store and a mother who had given up her position as a society editor of the local paper to raise a family.[7] My analysis of Friedan's political journey starts with her years at Smith College, although it is important to recognize Friedan's earlier sense of herself as someone whose identity as a Jew, a reader, and a brainy girl made her feel freakish and lonely.[8]

As an undergraduate, she has suggested, her lonely life took a turn for the better. "For the first time," she later remarked of her years in college, "I wasn't a freak for having brains." Friedan has acknowledged that she flourished at Smith, with her editorship of the student newspaper, her election to Phi Beta Kappa in her junior year, and her graduation *summa cum laude* among her most prominent achievements. She has told the story of how Gestalt psychology and Kurt Koffka (one of its three founders) were critical in her intellectual development.[9]

Friedan has described the years between her graduation from Smith in 1942 and the publication of her book twenty-one years later as a time when the feminine mystique increasingly trapped her. In her book and in dozens of speeches, articles, and interviews beginning in 1963, she mentioned a pivotal moment in her life, one that she felt marked the beginning of the process by which she succumbed. She told how, while in graduate school at Berkeley in the year after her graduation from college, the university's offer of a prestigious fellowship forced her to make a painful choice. Her first serious boyfriend, a graduate student who had not earned a similarly generous award, threatened to break off the relationship unless she turned down her fellowship. "I never could explain, hardly knew myself, why" she turned away from a career in psychology, she wrote in 1963. She decided to reject the fellowship because she saw herself ending up as an "old maid college teacher" in part because at Smith, she said, there were so few female professors who had husbands and children.[10] The feminine mystique, she insisted, had claimed one of its first victims.[11]

After leaving Berkeley, the copy on the dust jacket of *The Feminine Mystique* noted, Friedan did some "applied social-science research" and freelance writing for magazines. Friedan's biography in a standard reference book quotes her as saying that in the 1940s, "for conscious or unconscious reasons," she worked at "the usual kinds of boring jobs that lead nowhere."[12] This story continues in 1947 with her marriage to Carl Friedan, a returning vet who would eventually switch careers from theater to advertising and public relations. She has told of how she gave birth to three children between 1948 and 1956 and the family moved to the suburbs, with these experiences making her feel trapped. Friedan's picture of her years in the suburbs is not one of contentment and conformity.[13] Though she acknowledged her role in creating and directing a program that brought together teenagers and adult professionals, Friedan portrayed herself as someone who felt "freakish having a career, worried that she was neglecting her children."[14] In an oft-repeated story whose punch line varied, Friedan recounted her response to the census form. In the space where it asked for her occupation, she put down "housewife" but remained guilty, hesitant, and conflicted about such a designation, sometimes pausing and then adding "writer."[15]

Friedan laced *The Feminine Mystique* with suggestions of how much she shared with her suburban sisters. In the opening paragraph, she said that she realized something was wrong in women's lives when she "sensed it first as a question mark in my own life, as a wife and mother of three small children, half-guiltily, and therefore half-heartedly, almost in spite of myself, using my abilities and education in work that took me away from home." Toward the end of the paragraph, when she referred to "a strange discrepancy between the reality of our lives as women and the image to which we were trying to conform," she suggested that she experienced the feminine mystique as keenly and in the same way as her readers. Using the second person plural, she wrote that "all of us went back into the warm brightness of home" and "lowered our eyes from the horizon, and steadily contemplated our own navels." Her work on newspapers, she wrote in *The Feminine Mystique,* proceeded "with

no particular plan." Indeed, she claimed that she had participated as a writer in the creation of the image of the happy housewife.[16]

Friedan asserted she embarked on a path that would lead to *The Feminine Mystique* only when, as she read over the responses of her college classmates to a questionnaire in anticipation of their fifteenth reunion in 1957, she discovered what she called "The Problem That Has No Name," the dissatisfaction her suburban peers felt but could not fully articulate. When she submitted articles to women's magazines, Friedan said, editors changed the meaning of what she had written or rejected outright her suggestions for pieces on controversial subjects. Then at a meeting of the Society of Magazine Writers, she heard Vance Packard recount how he had written *The Hidden Persuaders* (1957) after *Reader's Digest* turned down an article critical of advertising. Friedan decided to write her book.[17]

In *"It Changed My Life": Writings on the Women's Movement* (1976), a book that included a 1974 autobiographical article, Friedan suggested some of what she had omitted from earlier versions of her life.[18] Perhaps responding to attacks on her for not being sufficiently radical, she acknowledged that before her marriage and for several years after she participated in radical activities and worked for union publications.[19] She and the friends with whom she lived before marrying considered themselves in "the vanguard of the working-class revolution," participating in "Marxist discussion groups," going to political rallies, and having "only contempt for dreary bourgeois capitalists like our fathers." Without getting much more specific, Friedan noted that right after the war she was "very involved, consciously radical. Not about women, for heaven's sake!" but about African Americans, workers, the threat of war, anti-communism, and "communist splits and schisms." This was a time, Friedan reported briefly, when, working as a labor journalist, she discovered "the grubby economic underside of American reality."[20]

"I was certainly not a feminist then—none of us," she remarked in the mid-1970s, "were a bit interested in women's rights." She remembered one incident, whose implications she said she only understood much later. Covering a strike, she could not interest anyone in the fact that the company and the union discriminated against women. In 1952, she later claimed, pregnant with her second child, she was fired from her job on a union publication and told that her second pregnancy was her fault. The Newspaper Guild, she asserted, was unwilling to honor its commitment to grant pregnancy leaves. This was, Friedan later remembered, as she mentioned her efforts to call a meeting in protest, "the first personal stirring of my own feminism, I guess. But the other women were just embarrassed, and the men uncomprehending. It was my own fault, getting pregnant again, a *personal* matter, not something you should take to the union. There was no word in 1949 for 'sex discrimination.'"[21]

Though in the 1970s Friedan suggested this more interesting version of her life in the 1940s and 1950s, she distracted the reader from what she had said. She began and ended the 1974 piece with images of domestic life. Even as she mentioned participation in Marxist discussion groups, she talked of how she and her friends read fashion magazines and spent much of their earnings on elegant clothes. Describing what she offered as a major turning point in her life, she told of how, after campaigning for Henry Wallace in 1948, all of a sudden she lost interest in political activity. The 1940s and 1950s were a period, she later asserted, when she was fully exposed to what she would label the feminine mystique as she learned that motherhood took the place of career and politics. She gave the impression of herself in the late 1940s as a woman who embraced domesticity, motherhood, and housework, even as she admitted that not everything at the time resulted from the feminine mystique.[22]

In her 1974 article Friedan filled her descriptions of the late 1940s and 1950s with a sense of the conflicts she felt over her new roles, as she surrendered to the feminine mystique with mixed emotions. She reported how wonderful was the time in Parkway Village, Queens, a period when she experienced the pleasure of a spacious apartment, edited the community newspaper, and enjoyed the camaraderie of young marrieds. Yet, having read Benjamin Spock's *Child and Baby Care,* she felt guilty when she returned to work after a maternity leave. With her move to a traditional suburb, she said, the conflicts intensified. She spoke of driving her children to school and lessons, participating in the PTA, and then, when neighbors came by, hiding "like secret drinking in the morning" the book she was working on.[23]

Accomplishing practical, specific tasks around the house and in local politics was "somehow more real and secure than the schizophrenic and even dangerous politics of the world revolution whose vanguard we used to fancy ourselves." Friedan remarked that by 1949 she realized that the revolution was not going to happen in the United States as she anticipated, in part because workers, like others, wanted kitchen gadgets. She reported that she found herself disillusioned with what was happening in unions, in Czechoslovakia, and in the Soviet Union, despite the fact that cries about the spread of Communism merely provided the pretext for attacks on suspected subversives. In those days, she continued, "McCarthyism, the danger of war against Russia and of fascism in America, and the reality of U.S. imperial, corporate wealth and power" combined to make those who once dreamed of "making the whole world over uncomfortable with the Old Left rhetoric of revolution." Using the first person plural as she referred to Margaret Mead's picture in *Male and Female* (1949) of women fulfilled through motherhood and domesticity, Friedan wrote, "we were suckers for that apple." It hardly occurred to any of those in her circle, who themselves now wanted new gadgets, that large corporations profited from marketing household appliances by "overselling us on the bliss of domesticity."[24]

The new information Friedan offered in 1974 did not dislodge the accepted understanding of how she became a feminist . . . [Yet] what the written record reveals of Friedan's life from her arrival at Smith in the fall of 1938 until the publication of *The Feminine Mystique* makes possible a story different from the one she has told. To begin with, usually missing from her narrative is full and specific information about how at college she first developed a sense of herself as a radical.[25] Courses she took, friendships she established with peers and professors, events in the United States and abroad, and her campus leadership all turned Friedan from a provincial outsider into a determined advocate of trade unions as the herald of progressive social change, a healthy skeptic about the authority and rhetorical claims of those in power, a staunch opponent of fascism, a defender of free speech, and a fierce questioner of social privilege expressed by the conspicuous consumption of some of her peers.[26]

What and with whom she studied points well beyond Gestalt psychology and Koffka.[27]

Though Friedan acknowledged the importance of James Gibson, she did not mention his activity as an advocate of trade unions.[28] Moreover, her statement that at Smith there were few role models is hard to reconcile with the fact that the college had a number of them; indeed she took courses from both James Gibson and Eleanor Gibson, husband and wife and parents of two children, the first of them born in 1940.[29] As a women's college, and especially one with an adversarial tradition, Smith may well have fostered in Friedan a feminism that was at least implicit—by enabling her to assume leadership positions and by encouraging her to take herself seriously as a writer and thinker.

In the fall of her junior year, Friedan took an economics course taught by Dorothy W. Douglas, Theories and Movements for Social Reconstruction. Douglas was well known at the time for her radicalism.[30] In what she wrote for Douglas, and with youthful enthusiasm characteristic of many members of her generation, Friedan sympathetically responded to the Marxist critique of capitalism as a cultural, economic, and political force.[31]

Friedan also gained an education as a radical in the summer of 1941 when, following Douglas's suggestion, she participated in a writers' workshop at the Highlander Folk School in Tennessee, an institution active in helping the CIO organize in the South. The school offered a series of summer institutes for fledgling journalists which, for 1939 and 1940 (but not 1941), the communist-led League of American Writers helped sponsor. For three years beginning in the fall of 1939, opponents of Highlander had sustained a vicious redbaiting attack, but a FBI investigator found no evidence of subversive activity.[32] In good Popular Front language, Friedan praised Highlander as a truly American institution that was attempting to help America to fulfill its democratic ideals. She explored the contradictions of her social position as a Jewish girl from a well-to-do family who had grown up in a class-divided Peoria, gave evidence of her hostility to the way her parents fought over issues of debt and extravagance, and described the baneful influence of the mass media on American life. Though she also acknowledged that her Smith education did "not lead to much action," she portrayed herself as someone whose radical consciousness relied on the American labor movement as the bulwark against fascism.[33]

At Smith Friedan linked her journalism to political activism. She served as editor-in-chief of the campus newspaper for a year beginning in the spring of 1941. The campaigns she undertook and the editorials she wrote reveal a good deal of her politics. Under Friedan's leadership, the newspaper's reputation for protest was so strong that in a skit a fellow student portrayed an editor, perhaps Friedan herself, as "a strident voice haranguing from a perpetual soap-box."[34] While at Smith, a Peoria paper reported in 1943, Friedan helped organize college building and grounds workers into a union.[35] Under her leadership, the student paper took on the student government for holding closed meetings, fought successfully to challenge the administration's right to control what the newspaper printed, campaigned for the relaxation of restrictions on student social life, censured social clubs for their secrecy, and published critiques of professors' teaching.[36] In response to an article in a campus humor magazine that belittled female employees who cleaned the students' rooms and served them food, an editorial supported the administration's censorship of the publication on the grounds that such action upheld "the liberal democratic tradition of the college."[37]

The editorials written on her watch reveal a young woman who believed that what was involved with almost every issue—at Smith, in the United States and abroad—was the struggle for democracy, freedom, and social justice. Under Friedan's leadership the editors supported American workers and their labor unions in their struggles to organize and improve their conditions. . . . The inequality of power in America, the editorial argued in good social democratic terms, "has to be admitted and dealt with if democracy is to have meaning for 95% of the citizens of this country."[38]

Above all, what haunted the editorials was the spread of fascism and questions about America's involvement in a world war. In April of 1941, the editors made it clear that the defeat of fascism was their primary goal and one that determined their position on questions of war or peace. In the fall of 1941, after the German invasion of the Soviet Union during the preceding summer, the editors increasingly accepted the inevitability of war even as they made it clear that they believed "fighting fascists is only one part of fighting fascism."[39] Some Smith students responded with redbaiting to the newspaper's anti-fascism and reluctance to support intervention wholeheartedly, accusing the editorial board of being dominated by communists, at a time when the Party reached its greatest membership in the years after Pearl Harbor while the United States and the Soviet Union were allies. Though one editor denied the charge of communist influence, like many newspapers at American colleges in these years, on the paper's staff were students attracted to the political analysis offered by radical groups. In the fall of 1940 one columnist argued against lumping communists and Nazis together, remarking that communism was not a "dark terror" but "a precarious scheme worked out by millions of civilized men and women."[40]

When America entered the war in December of 1941, the editors accepted the nation's new role loyally, albeit soberly. The central issue for them was how American students, especially female ones, could "contribute actively to the American cause." . . .

Friedan's experiences at Smith cast a different light on her decision to leave Berkeley after a year of graduate school. The editorials she and her peers had written immediately after Pearl Harbor revealed an impatience to be near the action. A 1943 article in the Peoria paper reported that Friedan turned down the fellowship because "she decided she wanted to work in the labor movement—on the labor press."[41] . . . Off and on from October 1943 until July 1946 she was a staff writer for the Federated Press, a left-wing news service that provided stories for newspapers, especially union ones, across the nation.[42] Here Friedan wrote articles that supported the aspirations of African Americans and union members. She also criticized reactionary forces that, she believed, were working secretly to undermine progressive social advances.[43] As early as 1943, she pictured efforts by businesses, coordinated by the National Association of Manufacturers (NAM), to develop plans that would enhance profits, diminish the power of unions, reverse the New Deal, and allow businesses to operate as they pleased.[44]

At Federated Press, Friedan also paid attention to women's problems. Right after she began to work there, she interviewed UE official Ruth Young, one of the clearest voices in the labor movement articulating women's issues. In the resulting article, Friedan noted that the government could not solve the problem of turnover "merely by pinning up thousands of glamorous posters designed to lure more women into industry." Neither women, unions, nor management, she quoted Young as saying, could solve problems of escalating prices or inadequate child care that were made even more difficult by the fact that "women still have two jobs to do." Action of the federal government, Friedan reported, was needed to solve the problems working women faced.[45]

She paid special attention to stories about protecting the jobs and improving the situation of working women, including married ones with children.

For about six years beginning in July, 1946, precisely at the moment when the wartime Popular Front came under intense attack, Friedan was a reporter for the union's paper *UE News*.[46] At least as early as 1943, when she quoted Young, Friedan was well aware of the UE's commitments to equity for women.[47]

. . . In 1949–50, union activists who followed the recommendations of the Communist Party . . . advocated the automatic granting of several years of seniority to all African Americans as compensation for their years of exclusion from the electrical industry. If the UE pioneered in articulating what we might call affirmative action for African Americans, then before and during World War II it advocated what a later generation would label comparable worth. Against considerable resistance from within its ranks, the UE also worked to improve the conditions of working-class women in part by countering a seniority system which gave advantage to men.[48] After 1949, with the UE out of the CIO and many of the more conservative union members out of the UE, women's issues and women's leadership resumed the importance they had in the UE during World War II, when it had developed, Ruth Milkman has written, a "strong ideological commitment to gender equality."[49]

Beginning in 1946, Friedan [also] witnessed the efforts by federal agencies, congressional committees, major corporations, the Roman Catholic Church, and the CIO to break the hold of what they saw as the domination of the UE by communists. The inclusion of a clause in the Taft-Hartley Act of 1947, requiring union officers to sign an anticommunist affidavit if they wished to do business with the National Labor Relations Board, helped encourage other unions to challenge the UE, whose leaders refused to sign.[50] Internecine fights took place within the UE, part of a longer term fight between radicals and anticommunists in its ranks. . . . Before long, . . . the UE was greatly weakened: in 1949, its connection with the CIO was severed and the newly-formed and CIO-backed IUE recruited many of its members. Membership in UE, numbering more than 600,000 in 1946, fell to 203,000 in 1953 and to 71,000 four years later.[51]

At *UE News,* from her position as a middle-class woman interested in the lives of the working class, Friedan continued to articulate a progressive position on a wide range of issues. She again pointed to concerted efforts, led by big corporations under the leadership of the NAM, to increase profits, exploit labor, and break labor unions.[52] In 1951, she contrasted the extravagant expenditures of the wealthy with the family of a worker who could afford neither fresh vegetables nor new clothes.[53] Friedan also told the story of how valiant union members helped build political coalitions to fight Congressional and corporate efforts to roll back gains workers made during the New Deal and World War II.[54] She drew parallels between the United States in the 1940s and Nazi Germany in the 1930s as she exposed the way HUAC [the House Committee on Un-American Activities, U.S. Congress] and big business were using every tactic they could to destroy the UE. Friedan hailed the launching of the Progressive Party in 1948.[55] She exposed the existence of racism and discrimination, even when they appeared among union officials and especially when directed against Jews and African Americans. Praising heroic workers who struggled against great odds as they fought monopolies, Friedan, probably expressing her hopes for herself, extolled the skills of a writer "who is able to describe with sincerity and passion the hopes, the struggle and the romance of the working people who make up most of America."[56]

Throughout her years at *UE News,* Friedan participated in discussions on women's issues, including the issue of corporations' systematic discrimination against women. Going to factories to interview those whose stories she was covering, she also wrote about working women, including African Americans and Latinas.[57] In the worlds Friedan inhabited in the decade beginning in 1943, as the historian Kathleen Weigand has shown, people often discussed the cultural and economic sources of women's oppression, the nature of discrimination based on sex, the special difficulties African American women faced, and the dynamics of discrimination against women in a variety of institutions, including the family.[58] Moreover, for the people around Friedan and doubtlessly for Friedan herself, the fight for justice for women was inseparable from the more general struggle to secure rights for African Americans and workers.[59] As she had done at the Federated Press, at *UE News* in the late 1940s and early 1950s she reported on how working women struggled as producers and consumers to make sure their families had enough to live on.[60]

Friedan's focus on working women's issues resulted in her writing the pamphlet, *UE Fights for Women Workers,* published by the UE in June of 1952.[61] She began by suggesting the contradiction in industry's treatment of women as consumers and as producers. "In advertisements across the land," Friedan remarked, "industry glorifies the American woman—in her gleaming GE kitchen, at her Westinghouse laundromat, before her Sylvania television set. Nothing," she announced as she insightfully explored a central contradiction women faced in the postwar world, "is too good for her—unless" she worked for corporations, including GE, or Westinghouse, or Sylvania.[62]

The central theme of the piece was how, in an effort to improve the pay and conditions of working women, the UE fought valiantly against greedy corporations that sought to increase their profits by exploiting women. Friedan discussed a landmark 1945 National War Labor Board decision on sex-based wage discrimination in favor of the UE. Remarking that *"fighting the exploitation of women is men's business too,"* she emphasized how discriminatory practices corporations used against women hurt men as well by exerting downward pressure on wages of all workers. To back up the call for equal pay for equal work and to fight against segregation and discrimination of women, she countered stereotypes justifying lower pay for women: they were physically weaker, entered the work force only temporarily, had no families to support, and worked only for pin money. She highlighted the "even more shocking" situation African American women faced, having to deal as they did with the "double bars" of being female and African American.[63] Friedan set forth a program that was, Lisa Kannenberg has noted, "a prescription for a gender-blind workplace."[64]

The conditions under which she left Federated Press and *UE News* are not entirely clear.

In May of 1946, during her second stint at Federated Press, she filed a grievance with the Newspaper Guild, saying she had lost her job in June of 1945 to a man she had replaced during the war. Later she claimed she was "bumped" from her position "by a returning veteran." There is evidence, however, that Friedan had to give up her position to a man who returned to the paper after two years in prison because he refused to serve in the military during what he considered a capitalists' war.[65] Friedan later claimed that she lost her job at the UE during her second pregnancy because the labor movement failed to honor its commitment to maternity leaves. Yet a knowledgeable observer has written that when the union had to cut the staff because of the dramatic drop in its membership, something that resulted from McCarthyite attacks, Friedan "offered to quit so another reporter," a man with more seniority, could remain at *UE News*.[66] Although her experience with unions may have provided a negative spur to her feminism, it also served as a positive inspiration. Friedan was indebted to the UE for major elements of her education about gender equity, sex discrimination, and women's issues.

The reason Friedan left out these years in her life story is now clear. Her stint at the *UE News* took place at the height of the anticommunist crusade, which she experienced at close quarters. When she emerged into the limelight in 1963, the issue of affiliation with communists was wracking SANE, SDS, and the civil rights movement. In the same years, HUAC was still holding hearings, the United States was pursuing an anti-communist war in Vietnam, and J. Edgar Hoover's FBI was wiretapping Martin Luther King, Jr., ostensibly to protect the nation against communist influence. Had Friedan revealed all in the mid-1960s, she would have undercut her book's impact, subjected herself to palpable dangers, and jeopardized the feminist movement, including the National Organization for Women (NOW), an institution she was instrumental in launching. Perhaps instead of emphasizing continuities in her life, she told the story of her conversion in order to heighten the impact of her book and appeal to white middle-class women. Or . . . Friedan may have come to believe a narrative that outlived the needs it originally fulfilled.

Until 1952, almost everything Friedan published as a labor journalist appeared under the name Betty Goldstein, though she had married in 1947. When she emerged as a writer for women's magazines in 1955, it was as Betty Friedan. Aside from indicating her marital status, the change in name was significant. It signaled a shift from an employee for a union paper who wrote highly political articles on the working class to a free-lance writer for mass circulation magazines who concentrated on the suburban middle class in more muted tones [and in the 1950s became a suburbanite herself. In 1957, the Friedans moved into an] eleven-room Victorian house, which they bought with the help of the GI Bill and some money Friedan inherited from her father.[67]

What Friedan wrote for mass circulation women's magazines [during those years] belies her claim that she had contributed to what she later attacked in *The Feminine Mystique*.

Sylvie Murray has demonstrated that Friedan drafted, but was unable to get into print, articles that fully celebrated women's political activism, expressed skepticism about male expertise, and described blue collar and lower middle-class families, not generic middle-class ones. Yet Friedan was able to sell articles that went against the grain of the Cold War celebration by criticizing middle-class conformity. . . . Friedan critiqued suburban life by drawing a dismal picture of those who conformed, by offering alternatives to conventional choices, and by exploring the strength of cooperative communities.[68] She drew portraits of American women that opposed the picture of the happy, suburban housewife who turned her back on a career in order to find satisfaction at home.[69] Friedan also portrayed women accomplishing important tasks as they took on traditionally feminine civic roles, thus implicitly undercutting the ideal of the apolitical suburban housewife and mother.[70]

In one particularly revealing piece, Friedan prefigured some of the issues she later claimed she only began to discover when she started to work on *The Feminine Mystique*. In "I Went Back to Work," published in *Charm* in April 1955, she wrote that initially she did not think highly of housework or of housewives and was guilty about what she was doing. Eventually she decided that her commitment to being a good mother was not "going to interfere with what I regarded as my 'real' life." Finding it necessary to be away from home for nine hours a day in order to work, she solved the problem of child care by hiring "a really good mother-substitute—a housekeeper-nurse." In the end, Friedan had no regrets about her decision or apparently about her privileged position. She believed her work outside the home improved her family's situation and acknowledged that her "whole life had always been geared around creative, intellectual work" and "a professional career."[71]

In what ways, then, was Friedan a captive of the feminine mystique? There is no question but that she was miserable in the suburbs. Her emphasis on her captivity may have expressed one part of her ambivalence. Yet, though she claimed that she shared so much with her suburban, white, middle-class sisters in the postwar world, during much of the two decades beginning in 1943 Friedan was participating in left-wing union activity, writing articles that went against the grain of Cold War ideology, and living in a cosmopolitan, racially integrated community. During most of the time between her marriage in 1947 and the publication of The Feminine Mystique, Friedan combined career and family life. As a woman who worked with her at Federated Press later noted, at the time Friedan and her female colleagues expected to have professional careers.[72] Caution about the predominantly suburban origins of her book is also in order because Friedan's move to suburban Rockland County in 1956 preceded by only a few months her initial work on the survey for her reunion that was so critical to The Feminine Mystique.[73]

To be sure, in the postwar world Friedan experienced at first hand the trials of a woman who fought against considerable odds to combine marriage, motherhood, and a career.[74] Yet in critical ways her difficulties did not stem from the dilemmas she described in her book: lack of career and ambition, a securely affluent household, and absence of a political sensibility. Friedan experienced psychological conflicts over issues of creativity in writing and motherhood.[75] Researching and writing her free-lance articles was a laborious process.[76] She had three young children, hardly felt comfortable in the suburbs, had no local institutions to provide a supportive environment for an aspiring writer, and continually faced financial difficulties. Her income from writing articles was unpredictable, a situation exacerbated by the pressure she was under to help support the household and justify the expenses for child care. Tension persisted between the Friedans over a wide range of issues, including

who was responsible for earning and spending the family's income. Moreover, she was in a marriage apparently marked by violence.[77]

Friedan was largely right when she said "all the pieces of my own life came together for the first time in the writing" of The Feminine Mystique. The skills as a journalist she had developed beginning as a teenager stood her in good stead as she worked to make what she had to say accessible to a wide audience. Her identity as a Jew and an outsider gave her a distinctive perspective on American and suburban life. Her years at Smith boosted her confidence and enhanced her political education. Her life as a wife and mother sensitized her to the conflicts millions of others experienced but could not articulate. Her education as a psychologist led her to understand the gestalt, the wholeness of a situation, and to advocate self-fulfillment based on humanistic psychology. Above all, her work as a labor journalist and activist provided her with the intellectual depth, ideological commitments, and practical experiences crucial to her emergence as a leading feminist in the 1960s.

Why did a woman who had spent so much energy advocating political solutions focus in The Feminine Mystique largely on adult education and self-realization and turn social problems into psychological ones? How did a woman who had fought to improve the lives of African Americans, Latinas, and working-class women end up writing a book that saw the problems of America in terms of the lives of affluent, suburban white women?[78]

Even at the time, at least one observer, Gerda Lerner, raised questions about what Friedan emphasized and neglected. Active in the trade union movement in the 1940s, present at the founding meeting of NOW, and after the mid-1960s one of the nation's leading historians of women, in February 1963 Lerner wrote Friedan. "I have just finished reading your splendid book and want to tell you how excited and delighted I am with it. . . . You have done for women," she remarked as she referred to the author who had warned about the destruction of the environment, "what Rachel Carson did for birds and trees." Yet, Lerner continued:

> I have one reservation about your treatment of your subject: you address yourself solely to the problems of middle class, college-educated women. This approach was one of the shortcomings of the suffrage movement for many years

and has, I believe, retarded the general advance of women. Working women, especially Negro women, labor not only under the disadvantages imposed by the feminine mystique, but under the more pressing disadvantages of economic discrimination. To leave them out of consideration of the problem or to ignore the contributions they can make toward its solution, is something we simply cannot afford to do. By their desperate need, by their numbers, by their organizational experience (if trade union members), working women are most important in reaching *institutional* solutions to the problems of women.[79]

The dynamics of Friedan's shifts in attention from working-class to middle-class women are not entirely clear. At some point after May 1953, when she followed the proceedings at the UE conference on the problems of women workers, Friedan turned away from working-class and African American women, something that undercut the power of *The Feminine Mystique*. An important question is whether the shift from her UE radicalism and focus on working-class women was a rhetorical strategy designed for the specific situation of *The Feminine Mystique* or part of a longer-term deradicalization. Until her personal papers are fully open and extensive interviewing is carried out, and perhaps not even then, we may not know the dynamics of this change.

NOTES

1. Betty Goldstein, "UE Drive on Wage, Job Discrimination Wins Cheers from Women Members," *UE News*, 16 Apr. 1951, 6. My interview of Friedan in 1987 first brought to my attention the possibility of this alternative story, as did the research my colleague, Helen L. Horowitz, carried out in the late 1980s. The appearance of the article by Joanne Meyerowitz in 1993, cited below, added an important piece of evidence. Because Friedan has denied me permission to quote from her unpublished papers and has not responded to my request that she grant me an opportunity to interview her or to have her respond to my questions, I have not been able to present as full and perhaps as accurate a story as I wished to do.

2. Ronald W. Schatz, *The Electrical Workers: A History of Labor at General Electric and Westinghouse, 1923–60* (Urbana, Ill., 1983), xiii.

3. Lisa Kannenberg, "The Impact of the Cold War on Women's Trade Union Activism: The UE Experience," *Labor History* 34 (spring-summer 1993): 318; Jacqueline Van Voris, interview with Eleanor Flexner, Northampton, Mass., 16 Oct. 1982, 70–71, Eleanor Flexner Papers, Schlesinger Library, Radcliffe College, Cambridge, Mass.

4. Betty Friedan, "Up From the Kitchen Floor," *New York Times Magazine*, 4 Mar. 1973, 8; Betty Friedan,

"It Changed My Life": Writings on the Women's Movement (New York, 1976), 304.

5. For evidence of the continuing importance of Friedan and her book, see, for example, Elaine T. May, *Homeward Bound: American Families in the Cold War Era* (New York, 1988), 209–17, 219.

6. For biographical information, in addition to what Friedan has said in print, I am relying on, among others, Kathleen Wilson, "Betty (Naomi) Friedan," *Contemporary Authors*, New Revision Series (New York, 1995) 45: 133–36; David Halberstam, *The Fifties* (New York, 1993), 592–98; Marilyn French, "The Emancipation of Betty Friedan," *Esquire* 100 (Dec. 1983): 510, 512, 514, 516, 517; Daniel Horowitz, interview of Betty Friedan, Santa Monica, Calif., 18 Mar. 1987. As late as 6 Nov. 1995, the date she sent me a letter denying me permission to quote from her unpublished papers, Friedan reiterated key elements of her story: I am grateful to Rachel Ledford for reporting to me on Friedan's 6 Nov. 1995 talk at the Smithsonian Institution, Washington, D.C. Ironically, two biographies aimed at children provide fuller stories than do other treatments (for instance, they are the only published sources I have been able to locate that make clear that Friedan worked for the UE): Sondra Henry and Emily Taitz, *Betty Friedan: Fighter for Women's Rights* (Hillside, N.J., 1990) and Milton Meltzer, *Betty Friedan: A Voice for Women's Rights* (New York, 1985).

7. This article is based on considerable but hardly exhaustive examination of the available written record. When other researchers examine the Friedan papers (including those to which access is restricted) and are able to carry out extensive interviews, they will be able to offer a fuller exploration of several issues, especially the shifts in Friedan's commitments as a radical at a time of great factionalism, when and how the feminine mystique did or did not trap her, how she interpreted the research on which *The Feminine Mystique* relied, and the pressures Friedan faced from her publisher to shape her 1963 book in certain ways.

8. An examination of what Friedan wrote for her high school paper reveals someone less lonely than she has often portrayed herself: see articles by Friedan in *Peoria Opinion* from the fall of 1936 until the spring of 1938.

9. Friedan, quoted in Wilkes, "Mother Superior," 140; Betty Friedan, *The Feminine Mystique* (New York, 1963), 12.

10. Friedan, *Feminine Mystique,* 70. On the paucity of role models at Smith, see Van Voris, Friedan interview.

11. Horowitz, interview.

12. Dust jacket of 1963 copy of *The Feminine Mystique,* author's possession.

13. Friedan, quoted in "Betty Friedan," *Current Biography Yearbook 1970*, ed. Charles Moritz (New York, 1971), 146; Betty Friedan, "New York Women: Beyond the Feminine Mystique," *New York Herald Tribune*, 21 Feb. 1965, 7–15, women's liberation, biographics, individuals, box 4, folder 31, clippings on Betty Friedan, Sophia Smith Collection, Smith College.

14. Tornabene, "Liberation," 138. See Betty Friedan, "The Intellectual Pied Pipers of Rockland County," unpublished paper, written in 1960–61, FP-SLRC, carton 9, folder 347, Friedan Collection,

Schlesinger Library, Radcliffe College, Cambridge, Mass. [hereinafter cited as BF-SLRC; unless otherwise noted, the references are to collection 71–62 . . . 81-M23].

15. Rollene W. Saal, "Author of the Month," *Saturday Review*, 21 Mar. 1964, women's liberation, biographies, individuals, box 4, folder 31, SSC-SC.

16. Friedan, *Feminine Mystique*, 9, 20, 66, 70, 186–87.

17. Horowitz, interview: Betty Friedan, "Introduction to the Tenth Anniversary Edition" of *Feminine Mystique* (New York, 1974), 1–5.

18. The 1974 article, which in the book was called "The Way We Were—1949," was originally published with some relatively unimportant differences, but with a more revealing title, as Betty Friedan, "In France, de Beauvoir Had Just Published 'The Second Sex,'" *New York* 8 (30 Dec. 1974–6 Jan. 1975): 52–55. In Horowitz, interview, which covered mainly the years up to 1963, Friedan discussed her move to a radical politics even as she emphasized captivity by the feminine mystique beginning in the Berkeley years. Though Friedan has revealed a good deal about her life, to the best of my knowledge she has not acknowledged in print the full range of reasons she left Berkeley, that she worked for the UE, her authorship of the 1952 pamphlet, and her leadership of the rent strike. Moreover, she has insisted that in the late 1940s and early 1950s, she had interest neither in a career nor in women's problems.

19. I am grateful to Judith Smith for helping me to think through this and other issues.

20. Friedan, *Changed My Life*, 6, 8–9.

21. Friedan, *Changed My Life*, 6, 9, 16; Halberstam, *Fifties*, 593; French, "Emancipation," 510. Horowitz, interview, dates the firing in 1952. In the immediate postwar years, the term "feminist" often referred to women who were Republicans, independent businesswomen, and professionals.

22. Friedan, *Changed My Life*, 5, 6–7, 8–9, 15, 16.

23. Friedan, *Changed My Life*, 14–16.

24. Friedan, *Changed My Life*, 12, 16.

25. Cohen, *Sisterhood*, 63 and Wilkes, "Mother Superior," 140 briefly draw a picture of Friedan as a college rebel but to the best of my knowledge, the politics of that rebellion have remained largely unknown.

26. This summary relies on unsigned editorials that appeared under Friedan's editorship, which can be found in *SCAN* [*Smith College Associated News*] from 14 Mar. 1941 to 10 Mar. 1942, p. 2. Although members of the editorial board held a wide range of opinions, I am assuming that as editor-in-chief Friedan had a significant role in shaping editorials.

27. For the article she published on the basis on her honors thesis, see H. Israel and B. Goldstein, "Operationism in Psychology," *Psychological Review* 51 (May 1944): 177–88.

28. See James J. Gibson, "Why a Union For Teachers?" *Focus* 2 (Nov. 1939): 3–7.

29. I am grateful to Margery Sly, Archivist of Smith College, for providing this information. She has also pointed out that teaching at Smith in Friedan's years were several married, female faculty members who had children and that Harold Israel and Elsa Siipola, two of Friedan's mentors, were married but without children.

30. In 1955 Douglas took the Fifth Amendment before HUAC as she was redbaited, accused of having been a member of a communist teachers union in the late 1930s. I am grateful to Margery Sly and Jacquelyn D. Hall for providing this information on Douglas. For Friedan's continued use of Marxist analysis, see Friedan, *It Changed My Life*, 110.

31. Bettye Goldstein, "Discussion of Reading Period Material," paper for Economics 319, 18 Jan. 1941, carton 1, folder 257, BF-SLRC, 1, 2, 4, 8.

32. John M. Glen, *Highlander: No Ordinary School, 1932–1962* (Lexington, Ky., 1988), 47–69.

33. Bettye Goldstein, "Highlander Folk School—American Future," unpublished paper, 1941, carton 6, folder 274, BF-SLRC; Goldstein, "Learning the Score," 22–24.

34. "Epilogue of Failure," *SCAN*, 10 Mar. 1942, 2.

35. "Betty Goldstein, Local Girl, Makes Good in New York," clipping from Peoria newspaper, probably 10 Dec. 1943 issue of *Labor Temple News*, carton 1, folder 86, BF-SLRC.

36. "Behind a Closed Door," *SCAN*, 3 Oct. 1941, 2; "Declaration of Student Independence," *SCAN*, 5 Dec. 1941, 1–2; "SCAN Protests Against Censorship," *SCAN*, 5 Dec. 1941, 1; "A Few Hours More," *SCAN*, 10 Oct. 1941, 2; "Review of Philosophy Courses," *SCAN*, 10 Mar. 1942, 2.

37. "The Tatler Suspension," *SCAN*, 7 Nov. 1941, 2; for the article in question see "Maids We Have Known and Loved," *Tatler*, Oct. 1941, 9, 21.

38. "Education in Emergency," *SCAN*, 15 Apr. 1941, 2; "The Right to Organize," *SCAN*, 21 Oct. 1941, 2; "Comment," *SCAN*, 14 Nov. 1941, 2; Filene's advertisement, *SCAN*, 21 Oct. 1941, 2.

39. "They Choose Peace," *SCAN*, 22 Apr. 1941, 2; for the minority opinion, see "The Case for Intervention," *SCAN*, 2 May 1941, 2; "War Against Fascism," *SCAN*, 24 Oct. 1941, 2. Placing the editorials written on Friedan's watch in the national context of student politics makes clear that after the Nazi-Soviet pact the student movement was more active and radical at Smith than elsewhere. On the national context see Robert Cohen, *When the Old Left Was Young: Student Radicals and America's First Mass Student Movement, 1929–1941* (New York, 1993), especially 315–37.

40. J. N., "The Red Menace," *SCAN*, 14 Oct. 1941, 2; Neal Gilkyson, "The Gallery," *SCAN*, 21 Oct. 1941, 2.

41. "Betty Goldstein, Local Girl," Meltzer, *Friedan*, 21 provides explanations for Friedan's decision that do not rely on the standard story.

42. For information on the Federated Press, see Doug Reynolds, "Federated Press," *Encyclopedia of the American Left*, ed. Mari Jo Buhle, Paul Buhle, and Dan Georgakas (New York, 1990), 225–27.

43. Editorials in clippings: carton 8, folder 328, BF-SLRC.

44. Betty Goldstein, "Big Business Getting Desperate, Promising Postwar Jobs," Federated Press, 19 Nov. 1943, carton 8, folder 328, BF-SLRC; Betty Goldstein, "NAM Convention Pro-War—For War on Labor, New Deal, Roosevelt," Federated Press, 14 Dec. 1943, carton 8, folder 328, BF-SLRC; Betty Goldstein, "Details of Big Business Anti-Labor Conspiracy Uncovered," Federated Press, 11 Feb. 1946, carton 8, folder 328, BF-SLRC.

45. Betty Goldstein, "Pretty Posters Won't Stop Turnover of Women in Industry," Federated Press,

26 Oct. 1943, and Ruth Young quoted in same, carton 8, folder 328, BF-SLRC.

46. Job application, 1951.

47. For information on women in the UE see Schatz, *Electrical Workers;* Ruth Milkman, *Gender at Work: The Dynamics of Job Segregation by Sex During World War II* (Urbana, 1987); Kannenberg, "Impact."

48. Schatz, *Electrical Workers,* 30, 89, 116–27, 129–30.

49. Milkman, *Gender at Work,* 77–78.

50. Zieger, *CIO,* 251.

51. This summary relies on Schatz, *Electrical Workers,* 167–240 (quotation, 181).

52. Betty Goldstein, "NAM Does Gleeful War Dance to Profits, Wage Cuts, Taft Law," *UE News,* 13 Dec. 1947, 4. What follows relies on the more than three dozen articles signed by Betty Goldstein in the *UE News* from the fall of 1946 until early 1952.

53. Betty Goldstein, "A Tale of 'Sacrifice': A Story of Equality in the United States, 1951," *March of Labor,* May 1951, 16–18, carton 8, folder 334, BF-SLRC.

54. Betty Goldstein, columns in *UE News,* 7 Dec. 1946, 9; 31 May 1947, 5, 8; 23 Aug. 1947, 4.

55. Betty Goldstein, columns in *UE News,* 12 May 1947, 5; 8 Nov. 1947, 6–7; 4 Sept. 1948, 6–7; 22 Aug. 1949, 4; 9 Jan. 1950, 5; 31 July 1948, 6–7.

56. B. G., review of Sinclair Lewis, *Kingsblood Royal, UE News,* 6 Sept. 1947, 7; B. G., review of the movie "Gentleman's Agreement," *UE News,* 22 Nov. 1947, 11; B. G., review of movie "Crossfire," *UE News,* 9 Aug. 1947, 8–9; Betty Goldstein, "CIO Sold Out Fight for FEPC, T-H Repeal, Rep. Powell Reveals," *UE News,* 17 Apr. 1950, 4; B. G., review of Fielding Burke, *Sons of the Stranger, UE News,* 24 Jan. 1948, 7.

57. These two sentences rely on James Lerner, interview. For treatments of the relationship between communism and women's issues, see Ellen K. Trimberger, "Women in the Old and New Left: The Evolution of a Politics of Personal Life," *Feminist Studies* 5 (fall 1979): 432–61.

58. Though she does not discuss Friedan's situation, the best treatment of the prominent role of women's issues in radical circles in the 1940s and 1950s is Weigand, "Vanguards."

59. Chinoy, interview.

60. Betty Goldstein, "Price Cuts Promised in Press Invisible to GE Housewives," *UE News,* 1 Feb. 1947, 7; Betty Goldstein, "Union Members Want to Know—WHO Has Too Much Money to Spend," *UE News,* 26 Mar. 1951, 8.

61. [Betty Goldstein], *UE Fights for Women Workers,* UE Publication no. 232, June 1952 (New York, 1952). To authenticate her authorship, I am relying on the following: Horowitz, interview; James Lerner, interview; Betty Friedan, postcard to author, late August, 1995; Meltzer, *Friedan,* 25.

62. [Goldstein], *UE Fights,* 5.

63. [Goldstein], *UE Fights,* 9–18, 26–27, 38.

64. Kannenberg, "Impact," 318.

65. Friedan, *Changed My Life,* 9; Mim Kelber, phone conversation with Daniel Horowitz, 16 Sept. 1995, identified the man as James Peck; obituary for James Peck, *New York Times* 13 July 1993, B7.

66. Meltzer, *Friedan,* 29.

67. To date these moves, I am relying on a number of sources, including Betty Friedan to Mrs. Clifford P. Cowen, 5 Aug. 1957, carton 7, folder, 313, BF-SLRC; Friedan, "New York Women"; "About the Author," in "New York Women"; "Friedan," *Current Biography,* 146; *Smith College Bulletin.*

68. Betty Friedan, "Two Are an Island," *Mademoiselle* 41 (July 1955): 88–89, 100–101; Betty Friedan, "Teenage Girl in Trouble," *Coronet* 43 (Mar. 1958): 163–68; Betty Friedan. "The Happy Families of Hickory Hill," *Redbook,* Feb. 1956, 39, 87–90; Sylvie Murray's "Suburban Citizens: Domesticity and Community Politics in Queens, New York, 1945–1960," Ph.D. diss., Yale University, 1994 ably contrasts the adversarial politics of Friedan's unpublished pieces with the milder tone of her published ones; on the difficulty of getting into print articles on women who were not middle-class, I am relying on Sylvie Murray, phone conversation with Daniel Horowitz, 9 Oct. 1995.

69. An influential book on the origins of 1960s feminism begins with a discussion of Friedan's magazine articles without seeing how they might connect parts of her career: Sara Evans, *Personal Politics: The Roots of Women's Liberation in the Civil Rights Movement and the New Left* (New York, 1979).

70. Betty Friedan, "Now They're Proud of Peoria," *Reader's Digest* 67 (Aug. 1955): 93–97.

71. Betty Friedan, "I Went Back to Work," *Charm,* Apr. 1955, 145, 200.

72. Kelber, conversation.

73. Parkway Village had some suburban characteristics and was marketed on the basis of its suburban qualities: Murray, conversation. Yet Friedan has made it clear that she was happy there: Friedan, *Changed My Life,* 14.

74. Especially crucial but nonetheless elusive is the period from May 1953, when she appears to have ended her union work, and 1955, when her first article appeared in a woman's magazine.

75. Friedan, "How to Find and Develop Article Ideas," 12–15 has some discussion of these conflicts.

76. This becomes clear through an examination of her files on her free-lance work, especially when compared with the files of Vance Packard in the same years.

77. Wilkes, "Mother Superior," 141. On violence in the marriage, see also Tornabene, "Liberation," 138; Cohen, *Sisterhood,* 17–18; Meyer, "Friedan," 608.

79. Gerda Lerner to Betty Friedan, 6 Feb. 1963, box 20a, folder 715, BF-SLRC; quoted with permission of Gerda Lerner. For information on Lerner's participation in the labor movement, the Congress of American Women, and at the founding meeting of NOW, I am relying on Daniel Horowitz, phone conversation with Gerda Lerner, 18 Oct. 1995; Amy Swerdlow, "The Congress of American Women: Left-Feminist Peace Politics in the Cold War," in *U.S. History as Women's History: New Feminist Essays,* ed. Linda K. Kerber, Alice Kessler-Harris, and Kathryn Kish Sklar (Chapel Hill, 1995), 306.

MICHELLE M. NICKERSON
Politically Desperate Housewives in Southern California

Betty Friedan became a feminist in reaction to her life as a middle-class house-wife who sought to be a journalist in 1950s America. Other housewives experienced a different sort of political awakening and emerged as energetic foot soldiers (or, shall we say mothers?) of conservatism.

Michelle Nickerson examines greater Los Angeles, with its spreading freeway system and booming economy, to ask what features of the Cold War era motivated middle-class white women to become energetic political actors, whether in women's clubs of the Republican Party or in homegrown groups, such as the Tuesday Morning Study Club and the Minute Women of the U.S.A. Publishing newsletters, attending lectures, gathering in reading groups, mobilizing voters, and protesting curriculum in the public schools they saw as dangerous, these women embraced the domestic as well as the political, and they poured their talents and skill into their volunteerism. A sense of divine mission, and a conviction that they "spoke the truth" to combat communism and other ills, united Catholic and Protestant women. "All politics is local" is a slogan that these historical subjects would heartily endorse. These activists saw their distinctive insights and effectiveness as stemming from their community watchfulness, common sense, and antielitism. And they would have agreed they were the "conservative sex" because the men in their lives, with salaried jobs, had far less time for political work.

How do you think the geographical location of these female activists shaped their politics? How do they compare to Betty Friedan or to Betty Jean Owens (in Danielle McGuire's essay that follows this one) or Phyllis Schlafly (pp. 610–614)? Be sure to check out the author's concluding question: is there such a thing as a "conservative feminist identity"?

Weary of war and relieved to be free of the Great Depression, Americans embraced family life with zeal in the 1950s. Women occupied a revered place in this revived domesticity that valorized homemaking and motherhood through television programming, film, and advertisements for appliances. Although the iconic 1950s housewife offers an abundance of insight into the ideals of the postwar generation, she obscures the countless ways that actual women attempted to live out those ideals. Operating among the legions of self-identified housewives who did not stay home in those years [was] a grassroots subculture of women that emerged mostly behind the scenes of the nascent conservative movement. These female activists on the right made the domestic ideology guiding their family, social, and civic lives into political careers by translating widespread cultural assumptions about female intuition into a basis for asserting authority in local affairs. . . . [This was an] animated, combative, and perfumed world of metropolitan politics. . . .

Important origins of the postwar right took root in such settings, where women shaped the conservative ascendancy with concerns, ideas, and issues that were drawn from

Excerpted, and slightly revised, from introduction, ch. 2, and conclusion of *Mothers of Conservatism: Women and the Postwar Right* by Michelle M. Nickerson (Princeton, N.J.: Princeton University Press, 2012). Reprinted by permission of the author and publisher. Notes have been edited and renumbered.

the fabric of their everyday lives. Capitalizing upon cultural assumptions about women and motherhood, they put themselves forward as representatives of local interests who battled bureaucrats for the sake of family, community, and God. Armed with a strong collective sense of where they and their local crusades fit into the global struggles against communism, they successfully overpowered school administrators, boards of education, and teachers in the name of local control and protection of parental authority. Female activists forced their priorities onto the larger agenda of the movement by anointing themselves spokespeople for parents, children, and local communities against the predatory interventionist state. . . .

[The back story lies in] the Great Depression. . . . The severe economic crisis invigorated the nation's appreciation for no-nonsense women with the wits to carry their families through the hard times. The new political woman of the 1930s was not the "angel of her home" housewife who volunteered to Americanize immigrants, rescue prostitutes, or save the nation from demon alcohol. She was an everywoman housewife, [often working-class,] who worked to keep her family and neighborhood intact— to maintain as much normalcy and security as possible. . . . Historian Temma Kaplan . . . sees "female consciousness," which relies upon assumptions about the "maternal duty to preserve life," as distinct from "feminist consciousness," which demands that women be given rights based on basic principles of equality.[1] . . .

. . . As the Depression wore on and World War II engulfed Europe and threatened to involve the United States, rage against Wall Street and landlords turned toward Washington as if financial and government leaders operated as one, centralized cabal. Indignation against economic elites shaded into anticommunist and anti-Semitic protest, attributing the nation's woes to New Deal bureaucrats as well as international Jewish bankers, eventually inflecting protests against U.S. entry into World War II with isolationist overtones. Feminine ideals contributed to a conservative political consciousness in formation. To be a "moral guardian" of society, in the minds of many women, meant to protect the nation from aliens, internationalism, and power-hungry bureaucrats in Washington. . . . Isolationist women found common cause in shared feelings of marginality, along with a sense of duty to family and community. Postwar women then updated its

political styles and culture for the conservatism of a new era.

Not until the early 1960s did American conservatism become a recognizable and self-conscious "movement," though its major ideological components, institutions, and political actors had been aligning since the end of World War II. While the Cold War and red scare of the 1950s revived anticommunism, critics of the New Deal welfare state . . . articulated economic arguments against centralized government. As the word "liberal," once associated with laissez-faire economic principles and small government as the means of realizing American egalitarianism, became linked during the Depression to federal growth and intervention on behalf of economic equality, proponents of small government formerly known as liberals claimed the designation "libertarian." . . . [Others] argued for a revival of faith and moral absolutes as the necessary antidotes for confronting recent scourges on the Western world, like genocide and totalitarianism. Anticommunism . . . gave conservatism the characteristics of a crusade around which adherents who disagreed about some things could rally. Conservatives gradually seized control of the GOP through important state battles, nominated conservative Barry Goldwater for president in 1964, and launched the political career of Ronald Reagan, who would complete the conservative revolution as president in the 1980s.[2] . . .

This study of women and conservatism examines how the anticommunist protest that scorched Southern California politics in the 1950s fueled a local conservative movement with broad national importance. [While] Orange County tends to win recognition as the epicenter of California conservatism, ... [I focus on the] more politically, racially, ethnically, and economically, diverse Los Angeles County, [which] figured centrally in this movement. . . . The growth of the defense industries, influx of migrants, rapidly changing demographics, expanded highway system, proliferation of suburbs, industrialization of those suburbs, and court rulings that chipped away at segregation fueled the metropolitan-based conservative movement. The sense of political community that made conservatism feel like a crusade in Southern California enveloped activists across greater Los Angeles. Southland activists built a movement that took advantage of their multinodal cityscape. Housewives who lived in

Pasadena drove cars over the hills to meetings in Encino and speaking engagements downtown. While living rooms in the newer suburbs proved comfortable for study groups, old Los Angeles venues like the First Congregational Church and Ambassador Hotel provided room, grandeur, and centralized locations appropriate for prominent lecturers. The new freeways made it easy for activists to attend each other's events and haul the cartons of the mimeographed literature they printed in their garages. The thirty-six different right-wing bookstores that opened across Southern California in the 1960s assisted each other like branches of the same regional bank, rather than competitors.[3] . . .

. . . [In] Southern California, community battles against school integration actually preceded the *Brown v. Board of Education* decision that mandated desegregation nationwide in 1954. California had been experimenting with integration and parents had been expressing their defiance of it for several years before the Warren Court handed down *Brown*. After the U.S. Court of Appeals for the Ninth Circuit in California upheld the *Mendez v. Westminster* ruling of 1946 that "segregation of Mexican youngsters found no justification in the laws of California," the [legislature] repealed segregationist statutes. School administrators then slowly crafted policies to bring their districts in line with the new mandates. . . . Conservative activists in greater Los Angeles worked in concert with activists all over the country, mainly in the South, to protect segregation in the public education system, an institution they recognized for its importance in maintaining racial order, [and] to forge a common anticommunist discourse of protest against the civil rights movement.[4]

Conservative women fought desegregation with the belief that their communities were under siege by political elites inciting turmoil that they, as women, needed to repel as housewives—the humblest, most self-sacrificial, and least pretentious members of American society. Women activists thus cultivated a gender consciousness, already in formation on the right, that valorized the local community as the fountainhead of American democracy. The links they made between feminine powerlessness and community powerlessness in the age of federal welfare and intervention isolated an amorphously defined centralized state as the most dangerous threat to freedom. Convinced

that progressive educators, civil rights activists, UNESCO [United Nations Educational, Scientific, and Cultural Organization], and the Supreme Court constituted a unified assault on community sovereignty . . . , they conflated problems of racial and bureaucratic outsiders.

Claiming a stake in these battles as representatives of the family—mothers and housewives protecting children, home life, and neighborhoods—women drew power from their class position and from [anticommunist] anxiety. . . . These female activists, in dialectic with conservative men, also cultivated an essentialist interpretation of women's political talents and duties, asserting that housewives and mothers were better suited than men to the work of anticommunist vigilance. Emphasizing that their flexible schedules gave them time to study communism, they argued that women were more politically aware than men, since husbands necessarily focused on the economic well-being of the family. [Indeed,] the economic status of female activists [was] vitally important, since a higher family income translated into political connections, an automobile, and funds for events, travel, or child care.

Los Angeles established a new paradigm of urban growth in the post–World War II era that facilitated transmission of conservative thought and activist culture. The region thrived over the 1950s from the billions of dollars of Pentagon defense contracts, which employed hundreds of thousands of workers in aircraft or missile manufacturing. Northrup, Lockheed, Douglas, and other companies . . . dispers[ed] their plants within and outside Los Angeles city limits. Manufacturers also built acres of single-family home communities for workers close to facilities. Long Beach to the south, Lakewood to the west, and the San Fernando Valley to the north bled urban and industrial sectors of the city into each other, creating new metropolitan economic and community relationships. Migrants, meanwhile, streamed in to fill jobs. Japanese and Mexican Americans arrived, but southerners represented the largest percentage of newcomers. . . . Millions of African Americans [went] to Los Angeles from the South during and after World War II. . . . [Another] exodus of white workers mainly from Texas, Arkansas, and Oklahoma start[ed] in the 1940s [and] infused the region with its own brand of religious culture and conservative politics.[5]

Map of Los Angeles County, 1963.

Mid-century Los Angeles also became a thought center for a Christian-inflected form of libertarianism. At the heart of these developments stood Spiritual Mobilization (SM), a non-profit religious organization that endeavored to rescue God's relationship with the individual. SM intercepted ideas and money streaming between East Coast and West Coast libertarians. Launched by a cadre of economic thinkers in Europe and the United States, libertarianism advocated minimal or no government intervention in economic affairs. . . . A spate of books published between 1943 and 1944 revived conservatives . . . with fresh inspiration. *The Road to Serfdom* by London School of Economics professor Friedrich Hayek, [a powerfully articulated polemic against governmental planning,] became the signature tome of the libertarian revival. . . . More popular than Hayek, however, Russian Jewish immigrant Ayn Rand published her ground-breaking utopian capitalist novel, *The Fountainhead,* in 1943.[6] . . .

. . . [By the 1950s] in the greater Los Angeles area, the political "right" [was] becoming a vast subculture with its own literature, radio broadcasts, workshops, home-based study groups, speaking circuits, and, by 1961, bookstores.

Anybody with enough time and money could rent a P.O. box, publish a newsletter, and circulate self-made leaflets, thus disseminating whatever literature they wished. A mother with two school-age children could do this as easily as a dentist or a clothing salesman, as long as she had the means. A mishmash discourse combining anticommunist, libertarian, and Christian ideas erupted on the local political scene. . . . Wealthy backers assisted with the proliferation of the materials, and not uncommon were partnerships between corporate leaders—men with money—and housewives—middle-class women with the time. . . .

. . . As conservative magazines, books, and speaking events proliferated in the mid-1950s, the ranks of conservative female activists grew. While ink dried on the first issues of the *National Review,* mimeograph machines across Los Angeles County spat out newsletters, many of them composed and printed by teams of housewives. When not clipping newspapers or poring over the political literature stacked on their credenzas, women attended lectures or gave their own prepared talks to audiences. They squeezed meetings, study, writing, and printing into daytime and nighttime hours between trips to the grocery store, meal preparation, and help with homework. Conservative women approached political work like other forms of civic work—as an extension of their household duties that fulfilled feminine responsibilities to the family and community.

Many activists developed their earliest feelings of political community and identity in Republican women's clubs. Since the 1920s, the GOP had been recruiting female voters by appealing to popular beliefs about the inherent differences between men and women. . . . [In earlier decades party leaders had fashioned] an "outsider" political style that emphasized women's moral superiority.[7] Officers framed involvement with the Republican Party in moralistic terms and conducted party work in settings familiar to women—homes, churches, and libraries. GOP women's clubs thus functioned as a feminine outlet to the traditionally masculine world of partisan politics. Democratic women's clubs offered the same menu of activities and relied on the similar politics of difference, but did not adhere to sex-segregated institutions in the party nearly as long, . . . pushing . . . for integration into the party's male-dominated power structure. . . . [In] the post–World War II era, Republican women's club literature emphasize[d] women's influence in the community, [and] stressed the importance of the warmth, sparkling personality, and overall positive attitude that it believed women could contribute to politics.

Reflecting the broader culture's celebration of domesticity, Republican club-women discourse of the 1950s and early 1960s also celebrated the American housewife. Literature, rituals, and speeches exhibited an optimistic view of how the nation's wives and mothers could harness their compassion, warmth, and femininity for the good of the party. The so-called "natural" political virtues of women, like moral superiority and mothering instincts, still found their way into the rhetoric of Republican leaders, yet its emphasis shifted to other attributes, namely feminine cheeriness and hospitality. "Organize your enthusiasm," commanded the president of the National Federation of Republican Women, "if you want to elect the nominee of the Republican national convention. . . . " Catherine Gibson assumed the office in the late fifties, stressing "neighbor-to-neighbor contacts."[8] Club leaders added new symbols to their campaign slogans, like the Republican "saleswomen," which invoked

both the growing importance of women to the retail industry as well as traits assumed to be intrinsically feminine, namely good manners and friendliness. Events designed for fun and sociability—teas, bridge games, fashion shows, and garden parties—became especially popular in this period. Club leaders extolled graciousness and affability as natural female qualities that could be marshaled for the benefit of the party.[9]

Though the ideal American housewife . . . ventured forth as a social and charitable community-builder, she also remained symbolically and spatially linked to the home. Activists opted increasingly to utilize their Formica kitchen tables, polyester living-room sectionals, and outdoor patio furniture for organizing-entertaining. These domestic settings provided a warm and nonintimidating atmosphere meant to promote the overlapping goals of political discussion and sociability. The National Federation of Republican Women encouraged women to use their homes through a variety of campaigns, including "Operation Coffee Cup." Launched during the 1956 Presidential campaign, the television broadcast presented Eisenhower and Nixon in conversation with different women's groups. The NFRW encouraged club leaders to watch alongside women guests to initiate discussion.[10] Indeed, study groups thrived in the home-centered atmosphere of postwar Republican women's clubs, especially as leaders took greater interest in promoting community relations skills among volunteers. One Republican women's study group met near the San Fernando Valley house of Jean Ward Fuller, who became president of the California Federation of Republican Women. . . . Her spacious abode, with housekeeper, in Encino helped to accommodate the sizeable number of clubwomen who hauled their bridge tables over to do mailings for political candidates. Her group, Fuller claimed, could turn out 60,000 pieces of mail within three days. "Everybody would bring their sandwiches," she recalled later, "and I'd have coffee for them and everybody would just work like beavers."[11]

Southern California became a hub of Republican clubwomen activism in the 1950s. Indeed, GOP women's clubs in California experienced their highest rate of growth in these years. In 1949, at 12,000, the California Federation of Republican Women became the sixth largest state federation in the nation, and by 1957 its ranks had swelled to 50,000 women. The Southern Division, always the strongest, included 123 clubs. . . . The San Fernando Valley, Glendale, San Marino, and Long Beach clubs represented its largest units. And in 1958 the National Federation of Republican Women boasted half a million members, while the Democratic National Committee counted only 100,000 women in female clubs.[12]

While the Republican women's clubs that met throughout Southern California's valleys politicized women, the Freedom Club, located in downtown Los Angeles, further encouraged militancy on the right. James Fifield's Freedom Club became a gathering place for conservatives, where like-minded suburbanites connected with each other as they eagerly imbibed the orations of speakers they admired. Established in 1950, the monthly series offered dinner, lectures, and discussion. With their hands busy with plates of jellied cranberry salad or turkey with gravy, participants listened and chatted about the evils of the income tax or mental health legislation. While Fifield's Spiritual Mobilization politicized clergymen, his Freedom Club politicized activists, especially female activists. Fifield attracted women to his ministry by appealing to both their sense of patriotism and their piety. Reared in a preacher's family, he acted on his familiarity with the ways that churches had historically relied on women to show spiritual devotion, inculcate religious values in children, and arrange church functions. Forceful women speakers like activist Phyllis Schlafly and foreign correspondent Freda Utley inspired housewives in the audience to shake off their timidity and push the boundaries of politeness on behalf of their families and the nation.[13]

A female right became visible and militant starting in 1950, as conservative women discovered and connected with each other in Republican women's clubs, the Freedom Club, and school board meetings. Indeed, debates about public education especially animated mothers after conservative parents successfully pressured school board members to fire the superintendent in one of the nation's finest school districts, Pasadena. Anticommunist attacks against the progressive education agenda of Superintendent Willard Goslin caused many mothers to look with new skepticism at the pedagogy employed by schoolteachers, making them wonder if leftist educators were trying to indoctrinate their children. A concerted campaign against UNESCO fueled such concerns, as critics of "internationalism" fought to ban educational materials published by the agency from Los Angeles schools.[14] The controversies surrounding Pasadena's superintendent and UNESCO inspired the formation of numerous organizations by women who came to see communist subversion as a grave problem and themselves and values they associated with femininity—vigilance, selflessness, carefulness, patience, and spirituality—as the solution. American Public Relations Forum, Pro-America, the Tuesday Morning Study Club, and Minute Women of the U.S.A., Incorporated, became the most active groups in the region.

"Politically desperate" to have their voices heard, they were by no means hysterical or pathological but rather approached their activist work with fervor and urgency. American Public Relations Forum, Pro-America, the Tuesday Morning Supper Club, and Minute Women of the U.S.A., Incorporated, became the most active groups in the region.

A housewife in Burbank by the name of Stephanie Williams founded American Public Relations Forum. Williams, a devout and fervent Catholic, joined a swelling number of parishioners who expanded the Los Angeles Catholic community after World War II with scores of churches that added hundreds of thousands of new members. As the church prospered and grew, the archdiocese exerted a conservative force on the political landscape mainly through Archbishop James McIntyre and its newspaper organ, *The Tidings*. Ordained the first Catholic cardinal from the American West in 1953, McIntyre sent priests to attend conservative political meetings, barred the sisters of the Immaculate Heart from teaching in the archdiocese after they stopped wearing the habit, and reformed other rules of discipline.[15] . . .

With the blessing of McIntyre, Williams formed the American Public Relations Forum, which gathered monthly in a few different locations. Forum meetings opened with a prayer, often featured a guest lecturer, and followed with a discussion. The organization coordinated correspondence campaigns by mailing its members bulletins regarding bills before Congress and by making cards available at gatherings so those present could write to their representatives together.[16] . . .

Minute Women of the U.S.A., which also operated from the San Fernando Valley, represented another popular choice for women who felt somewhat shy but wanted to do something about communism. The Southern

California unit worked in concert with the national organization, founded in 1949. . . . Minute Women were white, middle- and upper-class, between the ages of thirty and sixty, with school-age or grown children. In 1952 the organization boasted 50,000 members in forty-seven states. . . . Southern California claimed some of the strongest units, though the Minute Women's secrecy policy has kept their exact numbers unknown. . . . Newsletters represented the organization's lifeblood. Members rarely met but received mailings from the California chapter chairman and from the national leadership. . . . [17]

The Minute Women's anonymity might also have provided members with a sense of security or power at a time when secrecy yielded rewards. This was [after all] the McCarthy era; your cat could have been spying on you. Government officials, including J. Edgar Hoover, . . . encouraged women to look hard for communists in their midst . . . [because] the government was ill equipped to do so. Without enough agents in the FBI to find and thwart the red menace, Hoover asserted, private citizens needed to be eternally watchful. . . . Female activists took it upon themselves to adopt vigilance as their job, one they could do better than anyone else.

[At the same time] they knew that leftist opponents were infiltrating their ranks. The Community Relations Committee (CRC), a moderate civil rights organization affiliated with the Jewish National Committee, spied on conservatives. . . . Concerned about the threat posed by groups on the right like the Forum, the CRC regularly monitored their meetings and labeled typed manuscripts of minutes . . . "spy reports." . . . The culture of fear, mistrust, and secrecy touched activists across the political spectrum. [19]

The Tuesday Morning Study Club (TMSC) was formed a few years after the Forum and Minute Women in the rolling Linda Vista neighborhood of Pasadena. . . . Some Pasadena mothers, not content to play bridge, gathered instead in a backyard recreational space behind the lovely home of activist Marjorie Jensen. One Tuesday a month, in the Jensen "playhouse," as they called the small, simply crafted structure, TMSC meetings started with a guest speaker and ended with discussion. Early on, the gatherings tended to be small, sometimes including only seven women, but at the height of TMSC popularity in the late 1950s, attendance regularly reached 50 women or more. When

130 people arrived one day, filling the playhouse, yard, and back room of Jensen's house, the club began renting larger spaces. On those occasions when the TMSC invited prominent speakers to Pasadena, they reserved a conference room at the Huntington Hotel, where they could accommodate larger mixed-sex crowds for evening events. Almost all of the Tuesday Morning Study Club programs focused on education. Topics ranged from UNESCO to "State Curriculum and the 'New' Education," from "Civic Groups, Educating Toward World Citizenship," to "Indoctrination Through Literature." [20]

A mix of international, national, and local affairs filled the meeting agendas of the different conservative women's organizations. It was never necessary for any of these groups to announce that they were for women; the format, presentations, and rituals made that announcement. Men, in fact, attended meetings sometimes—they were generally welcome—but only rarely. . . . The ways in which group members talked about God [also] made these organizations female. . . . Most conservative women were Christian, though organizations did not tend to identify with particular churches or intensity of religious devotion. In Los Angeles, Catholic and Protestant women mixed quite comfortably in the conservative movement while antagonism characterized relations between the groups in the rest of the country. [21] . . . In Southern California, Catholic and Protestant women . . . cultivated political camaraderie not only from the fight against atheistic communism, but also from their common need to develop spiritual interpretations of the changing world around them. Activists from both faiths lamented the secularization of American society as well as numerous social problems that they attributed to that trend, from rising crime rates to juvenile delinquency to loosening sexual norms.

Conservative women contributed to the developing unity between Catholics and Protestants, not only by making all Christian women welcome in their meetings, but by cultivating a cross-denominational political style and culture. The American Public Relations Forum officially started its institutional life as a Catholic women's organization, but by the late 1950s the group listed two officers who were Protestant. . . . The Minute Women's membership policy welcomed women of all "faiths." The language of its literature suggests, though, that non-Christian women need not apply. From the rhetoric and practices of both groups emerged pan-Christian ideals of political femininity.

The American Public Relations Forum and Minute Women of the U.S.A. especially promulgated the idea that women had a divinely mandated role to fulfill in the defense of freedom. The Forum encouraged its members, first and foremost, to think about God with every political action they undertook, whether it involved the stroke of a pen or an uncomfortable confrontation with local school administrators. For God you could and should act unladylike. Though it was "nonsectarian" and included non-Catholic members, the group operated under the auspices of the Catholic Church. . . . Forum president Stephanie Williams reminded her members that while they toiled at their political tasks they must submit to God and pray. "We must place God as the senior of the family." . . . [22]

. . . The Forum and Minute Women fixat[ed] on a scripturally-defined understanding of the truth. "[S]peak the truth and shame the devil," declared the Minute Woman national president.[23] Her organization recognized, as one of its duties, protection of God's pronouncements—as well as those made by founding fathers—from the treachery of artful wordsmiths. Subversion, in their minds, stood for cunning. . . . Clipping newspapers and writing letters did not win glory, but did rescue facts from the chicanery of subversives. . . .

In oral history interviews with five women [active in the 1950s in the greater Los Angeles area], a common theme . . . was the [political] awakening. The activists tend[ed] to emphasize distinct moments when someone or a series of events made them alert, as they often put it, to how communism menaced their freedom. The process of becoming aware, in recollections, frequently followed a something-not-feeling-right period. Awakenings discourse thus presupposed that the political subjects lived for some time in the dark, and that most other Americans at the time continued to be oblivious. . . . Activists equated the acquisition of *vision* with political transformation. Indeed, this power of *sight*—to conquer one's enemy by shining light on his or her activities—became a powerful way for women to understand their unique political effectiveness. What others would describe as red-baiting, they interpreted as exposure of the truth.[24] . . .

The emphasis on awakenings resonated with the ways in which women talked about the political work that came to fill their days.

Never referring to conservatism as a "movement," activists instead remembered "patriotic" Americans rousing each other from a stupor and devoting themselves to saving the country. Subjects describe their involvement as if they had no serious interest in politics until the light had been turned on for them. . . . Although activists betrayed a shared love for the movement's labor in their oral histories, they almost never said outright that they joined organizations for any fulfillment of a personal need. . . . [They] instead privileged the gravity of dangers that created the political work for them. Activists, in other words, liked to talk about work—hard work—without calling it "work." . . . [T]he vigor of the conservative movement owes much to this labor of middle- and upper-class women who might have enjoyed professional "careers" given their backgrounds, but would not likely legitimize professional "career" employment as a choice for women. . . .

In their relentless defense of community-level decision making, [conservative] women [of the Cold War era] stoked populist outrage. . . . In campaigns against progressive educators, programs, and federal funding, they denounced administrators as elitist outsiders who aimed to use children for social experiments designed at far-away Ivy League institutions. To stem the problems they associated with social decline in the United States, they advocated for stronger parental and clerical influence in the lives of children. Although many of the women involved in these battles were born, raised, and college-educated in other parts of the country, [in Southern California] they developed an insider-outsider dichotomy—a sharp community boundary line between them on the inside and their opponents on the outside. This housewife populism contributed to the conservative movement's identification with the everyman, real people, and middle America. Women on the right also spoke out as taxpayers, linking the interests of property holders and families in an alliance against state intervention.

Among the most important lessons to be drawn from this history of conservative women concerns their ability to manage ideological ambiguity. [We find such ambiguity in many social and political movements. For example, women's] right to vote was won in the 1910s with a careful balance between seemingly contradictory arguments for sameness and difference. Women demanded the ballot

on the basis of universal, democratic, egalitarian ideals stemming from the Enlightenment—
on the principle that they should have the same
rights as men. Yet they also argued that womanly virtues made them worthy of the vote,
that their feminine instincts for morality, spirituality, and purity would uplift the corrupt
world of politics. . . . [In the 1970s] Equal Rights
Amendment opponents . . . valorized full-time
motherhood, yet worked as full-time activists.
[A third example are] religious conservatives
who decry every form of state intervention
except those that serve to enforce their Christian ideals. [All] exhibit what [some] . . . describe as "cognitive dissonance." [The most
interesting question to ask of conservative
Southern California women activists, as of
other political actors, is:] How did [they] resolve and deploy such dissonance for their
own political purposes?

The endurance of housewife populism
stands as a testament to the power of this ambiguity. A distinguishing characteristic of the
post-1970 "new right" was the vehemence of
its attacks against "women libbers." Make no
mistake: this "backlash" was real. . . . Like the
feminists they attacked, conservative women
participated in an organic process of reviving,
reformulating, and building upon traditions
started by political foremothers. The "pro-
family" agenda of the late twentieth century
included familiar advocacy on behalf of parental authority over the state. Bridging multiple
generations of women, housewife populism
coursed through the defensive, maternal, com-
munitarian rhetoric of these new-right women.
In campaigns against abortion and the Equal
Rights Amendment, activists represented themselves as champions of real, ordinary people
battling a rarified class of secular elites so en-
tombed in the trappings of their privilege that
they lost touch with the most basic principles of
morality. They also introduced stronger Christian elements into the feminine political styles
of earlier generations.

A driving theme of the anti-ERA campaign . . . was the danger of "losing of one's
children" to educators and government officials who meddled in the relationships between parents, sons, and daughters. Critiques
of "forced equality" adapted female traditions
of antistatist protest for the new battles,
equating the ERA with other unwanted state
interventions into the family, including
government-sponsored desegregation. One

woman accused ERA ratificationists of trying
to "desexegrate" society. . . . Phyllis Schlafly,
whose *Eagle Forum* established a long and continuing pattern of attacking the United Nations, World Health Organization, and other
international organizations for threatening
U.S. sovereignty, now targets "globalism," described by Schlafly as socialism enforced
through global regulatory structures like the
World Trade Organization. Housewife populism marshals women against globalism
today much as it did to mobilize them against
communism in the 1950s and 1960s.[25]

Opposition to the Equal Rights Amendment also assumed the populist inflections
that Cold War conservatives added to political discourse. Antiratificationists represented
themselves as "the people in arms." . . . [26] The
fearsome and deeply entrenched antielitism in
conservative political culture of the Cold War
era endured, fueling the popular notion that
feminist demands for "rights" and "equality"
would improve the lives of privileged women
only. Regular wives and mothers, on the other
hand, needed the armor of patriarchy and sex-
based protectionist legislation that, opponents
believed, the Equal Rights Amendment would
undo. . . .

After Barack Obama won election in 2008,
[conservative] populist style carried over into
the Tea Party movement, an alliance of organizations and bloggers that emerged in opposition to government-sponsored economic
stimulus, health-care reform, and numerous
other grievances. . . . The movement has served
as a conduit for [new versions of] housewife
populist outrage. . . . [In 2010] polls indicated
that women represented 45 to 55 percent of the
membership and an even greater share of the
leadership positions. Six of the eight Tea Party
Patriots board members who also serve as national coordinators for the movement [were]
women; [and so were] fifteen of the twenty-five
state coordinators. At a summer 2010 gathering
of the abortion-opposing organization Susan B.
Anthony List, [Sarah] Palin identified the wom-
en's empowerment trend on the right as a "conservative feminist identity."[27]

Conservative feminists? . . . As oxymoronic
as the expression . . . appears, its logic lies in
the tribute that conservative women should
properly pay [to a wide variety of self-identified
feminists, such as Alice Paul, bell hooks, and
Kate Millett.] Conservative women have been
able to hold public office because of feminist

pressure for antidiscrimination legislation that opened doors for women in education, the professions, the business world, and politics—legislation that antifeminist women opposed vigorously. The Susan B. Anthony List illustrates how the process of creating a conservative feminist consciousness is, indeed, a project of cognitive dissonance, selective memory, and mythmaking.

NOTES

1. Temma Kaplan, "Female Consciousness and Collective Action: the Case of Barcelona, 1910–1918," *Signs* 7, no. 3 (Spring 1982), 545–66.

2. On the evolution of conservatism in the 1950s and 1960s, see, for example, Donald Critchlow, *Phyllis Schlafly and Grassroots Conservatism: A Woman's Crusade* (Princeton, N.J.: Princeton University Press, 2005), 5–7; George H. Nash, *The Conservative Intellectual Movement in America Since 1945* (reprint, Wilmington, Del.: Intercollegiate Studies Institute, 1996; orig. pub. 1975); and Elizabeth Tandy Shermer, "Origins of the Conservative Ascendancy: Barry Goldwater's Early Senate Career and the De-legitimatization of Organized Labor," *Journal of American History* 95 (Dec. 2008), 678–709.

3. On women and postwar conservatism, see Lisa McGirr, *Suburban Warriors: The Origins of the New American Right* (Princeton, N.J.: Princeton University Press, 2001); Mary Brennan, *Wives, Mothers, and the Red Menace: Conservative Women and the Crusade Against Communism* (Boulder: University of Colorado Press, 2008). On California, see Kurt Schuparra, *Triumph of the Right: The Rise of the California Conservative Movement, 1945–1966* (Armonk, N.Y.: M. E. Sharpe, 1998).

4. Vicki Ruiz, "Nuestra América: Latino History as American History," *Journal of American History* 93 (Dec. 2006), 670; *Mendez et al. v. Westminster School District of Orange County*, 64 F. Supp. 544 (C.D. Cal. 1946).

5. Greg Hise, *Magnetic Los Angeles: Planning the Twentieth-Century Metropolis* (Baltimore: Johns Hopkins University Press, 1997); Josh Sides, *L.A. City Limits: African American Los Angeles from the Great Depression to the Present* (Berkeley: University of California Press, 2003); and Darren Dochuk, *From Bible Belt to Sunbelt: Plain-Folk Religion, Grassroots Politics, and the Rise of Evangelical Conservatism* (New York: Norton, 2010), esp. xv–xx.

6. F. A. Hayek, *The Road to Serfdom* (Chicago: University of Chicago Press, 1944); Jennifer Burns, *Goddess of the Market: Ayn Rand and the American Right* (New York: Oxford University Press, 2009); Nash, *Conservative Intellectual Movement*, 3.

7. Michael McGerr, "Political Style and Women's Power, 1830–1930," *Journal of American History* 77 (Dec. 1990), 864–85; Catherine Rymph, *Republican Women: Feminism and Conservatism from Suffrage through the Rise of the New Right* (Chapel Hill: University of North Carolina Press, 2006), 5–6.

8. Jean Ward, "Organize Your Enthusiasm . . . ," *Los Angeles Examiner*, Nov. 14, 1959, Regional History Collection, University of Southern California.

9. Mrs. Vernon W. Janney, Report of the Los Angeles County Federation of Republican Women's Clubs: Annual Convention (Jan. 25, 1956), National Federation of Republican Women records (hereafter, NFRW), Dwight D. Eisenhower Library, Abilene, KS, 1; "New GOP Fashion Set by Women," *Los Angeles Times*, Mar. 5, 1956, p. 2; "Fashion Lunch Planned by GOP in Long Beach," ibid., Mar. 6, 1956, p. B3; Letter to Mrs. Peter Gibson, Sep. 16, 1957, NFRW.

10. Rymph, *Republican Women*, 138–39.

11. Jean Ward Fuller, "Organizing Women: Careers in Volunteer Politics and Government Administration," an oral history conducted Oct. 1977 by Miriam Stein, Regional Oral History Office, Bancroft Library, University of California, Berkeley, 35–37.

12. Jacqueline R. Braitman, "Legislated Parity: Mandating Integration of Women into California Political Parties, 1930s–1950s," in *We Have Come to Stay: American Women and Political Parties, 1880–1960*, ed. Melanie Gustafson, Kristie Miller, and Elisabeth Israels Perry (Albuquerque: University of New Mexico Press, 1999), 180; Mrs. Robert W. Malcauley to Mrs. Paul Jasper, 1949, NFRW; Program, California Federation of Republican Women, *Tenth Biennial Convention* (Santa Barbara, Calif., 1957); California Federation of Republican Women, *The Federation*, Sept. 1954, *Scrapbook*; Fuller, "Organizing Women," 101–102; Jo Freeman, *A Room at a Time: How Women Entered Party Politics* (Lanham, Md.: Rowman and Littlefield, 2000), 158.

13. *Freedom Club Bulletin* (Nov. 20, 1856), and ibid., 8, no. 5 (April 1, 1958), both in Marie Koenig Personal Collection; ibid., 18, no. 2 (Nov. 7, 1967), 1, Social Protest Collection, Bancroft Library; Community Relations Committee, "Report on Reverend Fifield Dinner Meeting—Freedom Clubs—First Congregational Church, April 15, 1952," Community Relations Committee Collection (hereafter, CRC), Urban Archives Center, California State University, Northridge.

14. Glen Warren Adams, "The UNESCO Controversy in Los Angeles, 1951–1953: A Case Study of the Influence of Right-Wing Groups on Urban Affairs" (Ph.D. diss., University of Southern California, 1970); David Hulburd, *This Happened in Pasadena* (New York: MacMillan, 1951).

15. McGirr, *Suburban Warriors*, 107; "Religion: The Immaculate Heart Rebels," *Time*, Feb. 16, 1970.

16. Community Relations Committee, American Public Relations Forum Meeting ["spy report"], May 2, 1952, CRC.

17. "Minute Women Band to Fight Reds and Pink," *Chicago Daily Tribune*, May 6, 1950, p. 4F. Personal Collection of Marie Koenig; Don Carlton, *Red Scare!: Right-wing Hysteria, Fifties Fascism and Their Legacy in Texas* (Austin: Texas Monthly Press, 1985), 111–34; Timothy G. Turner, "Minute Women Leader Begins L.A. Campaign," *Los Angeles Times*, Feb. 7, 1952, CRC. One chapter in Texas had its own male auxiliary, but those were few.

18. J. Edgar Hoover, *Masters of Deceit: The Story of Communism in American and How to Fight It* (New York: Henry Holt and Co., 1958), 310.

19. See the voluminous "spy reports" of the Community Relations Committee, CRC.

20. Marjorie Jensen, taped interview with author, Pasadena, Calif., July 15, 2002, 6–7; Tuesday Morning Study Club, *Program and Directory*, 4–5.

21. Robert Wuthnow, *The Restructuring of American Religion: Society and Faith Since World War II* (Princeton, N.J.: Princeton University Press, 1988), 72–75, 93.

22. Community Relations Committee, "American Public Relations Forum, Inc." [report of Aug. 15, 1952 meeting], 1, CRC.

23. Minute Women of the U.S.A., Inc., newsletter, Apr. 1954, 1, Marie Koenig Personal Collection.

24. Jensen, interview; Jane Crosby, taped interview with author, San Juan Capistrano, Calif., Feb. 26, 2001; Marie Koenig, taped interview with author, Pasadena, Calif., Apr. 5, 2001; Florence Ranuzzi and Mary Cunningham, taped interview with author, Tehachapi, Calif., Feb. 11, 2001; Marion Miller, *I Was a Spy: The Story of a Brave Housewife* (New York: Bobbs-Merrill Co., 1960).

25. Donald G. Mathews and Jane Sherron DeHart, *Sex, Gender, and the Politics of the ERA: A State*

and the Nation (New York: Oxford University Press, 1990), 156–57, 172; "Globalism: Enemy of the Middle Class," *The Phyllis Schlafly Report* (Feb. 2007), http://www.eagleforum.org/psr/2007/feb07/psrfeb07.html (last accessed Mar. 25, 2011).

26. Mathews and DeHart, *Sex, Gender, and the Politics of the ERA*, 173.

27. Hanna Rosin, "Is the Tea Party a Feminist Movement?" *Slate*, May 12, 2010; Amy Gardner, "Palin Pushes Abortion Foes to Form 'Conservative Feminist Identity,'" *Washington Post*, May 15, 2010, http://www.washingtonpost.com/wp-dyn/content/article/2010/05/15/AR2010051500002.html (last accessed July 15, 2010).

DANIELLE L. McGUIRE
Sexual Violence and the Long Civil Rights Movement

What role did African American women play in the civil rights movement? Our understanding of the civil rights movement, like other historical events, has changed over time. A previous focus on charismatic leaders, like Martin Luther King, Jr., has expanded to include female organizers—Rosa Parks, Fannie Lou Hamer, Ella Baker, and Diane Nash—as well as the rank and file, many of whom were women.

In addition, scholars now call for a "long civil rights" perspective that expands the chronology beyond the 1954–1965 period, bookended by the 1954 *Brown v. Board of Education* desegregation decision and the 1965 Voting Rights Act. The black freedom struggle can be dated at least back to the interracial labor movements of the 1930s or even to the resistance movements against slavery. It can go forward in time to encompass the black power movement and beyond.

Danielle L. McGuire argues powerfully that sexual violence against black women has inspired much civil rights campaigning. In addition to political equality, desegregation, and access to jobs, civil rights activists demanded respect and bodily autonomy for black women. She insists that it is important, though painful, to face—to see—the violence directed toward black women, because only then can we understand the individual and collective grounding of resistance. The story she tells here centers on college students: Betty Jean Owens and her friends returning from a dance, and the student body of Florida A&M, a historically black university. Would the students' rallying cry, "It Was Like All of Us Had Been Raped," be an effective organizing tool on campuses today? *

*Jacquelyn Dowd Hall, "The Long Civil Rights Movement and the Political Uses of History," *Journal of American History* 91 (March 2005): 1233–63. For more on the contemporary vexation over sexual assault on or near college campuses, see pp. 750–751.

Excerpted from " 'It Was Like All of Us Had Been Raped:' Sexual Violence, Community Mobilization, and the African American Freedom Struggle" by Danielle L. McGuire, *Journal of American History* 91 (Dec. 2004): 906–31. Reprinted with permission of the author and publisher. Notes have been edited and renumbered.

On Saturday, May 2, 1959, four white men in Tallahassee, Florida, made a pact, one of their friends testified in court later, to "go out and get a nigger girl" and have an "all night party." That evening, they armed themselves with shotguns and switchblades and crept up behind a car parked alongside a quiet road near Jake Gaither Park. At about 1:00 A.M. on May 3, Patrick Scarborough pressed a sixteen-gauge shotgun against the driver's nose and ordered Richard Brown and his companions out of the car. Dressed in formal gowns and tuxedoes, the four African Americans—all students at Florida A&M University who had spent the evening dancing at the Green and Orange Ball—reluctantly stepped out of the car. Scarborough forced the two black men to kneel, while his friend David Beagles held the two black women at knifepoint. When Betty Jean Owens began to cry, Beagles slapped her and told her to "shut up" or she "would never get back home." Waving his gun, Scarborough ordered Richard Brown and his friend Thomas Butterfield back in the car and told them to leave. As Brown and Butterfield began to move toward the car and then slowly drove away, Edna Richardson broke free and ran to the nearby park, leaving Betty Jean Owens alone with their attackers. Beagles pressed the switchblade to Owens's throat and growled, "We'll let you go if you do what we want," then forced her to her knees, slapped her as she sobbed, and pushed her into the backseat of their blue Chevrolet; the four men drove her to the edge of town, where they raped her seven times.[1]

Analyses of rape play little or no role in most histories of the civil rights movement, even as stories of violence against black and white men—from Emmett Till to Andrew Goodman, Michael Schwerner, and James Chaney—provide gripping examples of racist brutality.[2] Despite a growing body of literature that focuses on the roles of black and white women and the operation of gender in the movement, sexualized violence—both as a tool of oppression and as a political spur for the movement—has yet to find its place in the story of the African American freedom struggle.[3] Rape, like lynching and murder, served as a tool of psychological and physical intimidation that expressed white male domination and buttressed white supremacy. During the Jim Crow era, women's bodies served as signposts of the social order, and white men used rape and rumors of rape not only to justify violence against black men but to remind black women that their bodies were not their own.

African American women frequently retaliated by testifying about their brutal experiences. I argue that, from Harriet Jacobs to Ida B. Wells to the women of the present, the refusal of black women to remain silent about sexualized violence was part of a long-standing tradition. Black women described and denounced their sexual misuse, deploying their voices as weapons in the wars against white supremacy. Indeed, their public protests often galvanized local, national, and even international outrage and sparked campaigns for racial justice and human dignity. When Betty Jean Owens spoke out against her assailants, and when the local black community mobilized in defense of her womanhood in 1959, they joined in this tradition of testimony and protest.

The arrest, trial, and conviction of Owens's white rapists by an all-white jury marked a dramatic change in the relations between this tradition of testimony and a tradition of silence that Darlene Clark Hine has termed the "culture of dissemblance."[4] The verdict not only broke with southern tradition but fractured the philosophical and political foundations of white supremacy by challenging the relationship between sexual domination and racial inequality. For perhaps the first time since Reconstruction, southern black communities could imagine state power being deployed in defense of their respectability as men and women. As a result, the 1959 Tallahassee rape case was a watershed event that remains as revealing now as it was important then.

The sexual exploitation of black women had its roots in slavery. Slave owners, overseers, and drivers took advantage of their positions of power and authority to rape slave women, sometimes in the presence of their husbands or families. White slave owners' stolen access to black women's bodies strengthened their political, social, and economic power, partly because colonial laws made the offspring of slave women the property of their masters. After the fall of slavery, when African Americans asserted their freedom during the interracial experiment in democracy that briefly characterized Reconstruction, former slaveholders and their sympathizers used violence and terror to reassert control over the social, political, and economic agency of freedpeople. At the heart of this violence, according to Gerda Lerner, rape became a "weapon of terror" to dominate the bodies and minds of African American men and women.[5]

"Freedom," as Tera Hunter notes, "was meaningless without ownership and control over one's own body." During Reconstruction and Jim Crow, sexualized violence served as a "ritualistic reenactment of the daily pattern of social dominance," and interracial rape became the battleground upon which black men and women fought for ownership of their own bodies. Many African American women who were raped or assaulted by white men fought back by speaking out. Frances Thompson told a congressional committee investigating the 1866 Memphis race riot that seven armed white men broke into her house on a Tuesday afternoon, "drew their pistols and said they would shoot us and fire the house if we did not let them have their way with us." Four of the men raped Frances, while the other three choked and raped sixteen-year-old Lucy Smith and left her close to death. In 1871, Harriet Simril testified in front of a congressional committee investigating Ku Klux Klan terror during Reconstruction that she was beaten and "ravished" by eight men in South Carolina who broke into her house to force her husband to "join the democratic ticket." Essic Harris, appearing before the same committee, reported that "the rape of black women was so frequent" in the postbellum South that it had become "an old saying by now." Ferdie Walker, who grew up during the height of segregation in the 1930s and 1940s in Fort Worth, Texas, remembered being "scared to death" by a white police officer who often exposed himself to her while she waited at the bus stop when she was only eleven years old. The sexual abuse of black women, she recalled, was an everyday occurrence. "That was really bad and it was bad for *all black girls*," she recalled.[6]

John H. McCray, editor of the South Carolina *Lighthouse and Informer*, reported that it was "a commonplace experience for many of our women in southern towns . . . to be propositioned openly by white men." He said, "You can pick up accounts of these at a dime a dozen in almost any community." African American women that I interviewed in Birmingham, Alabama, in March 2003 echoed Ferdie Walker's and McCray's comments. Nearly all of them testified about being sexually abused or intimidated by white men—particularly bus drivers, police officers, and employers.[7]

The acclaimed freedom fighter Fannie Lou Hamer knew that rape and sexual violence was a common occurrence in the segregated South. . . . Hamer's grandmother, Liza Bramlett, spoke often of the "horrors of slavery," including stories about "how the white folks would do her." . . . Twenty of the twenty-three children Bramlett gave birth to were products of rape. Hamer grew up with the clear understanding that a "black woman's body was never hers alone." If she was at all unclear about this lesson, the forced hysterectomy she received in 1961 and the brutal beating she received in the Winona, Mississippi, jail in 1963 left little room for confusion. After being arrested with other Student Nonviolent Coordinating Committee (SNCC) activists for desegregating a restaurant, Hamer received a savage and sexually abusive beating by the Winona police. "You bitch," one officer yelled, "we going to make you wish you was dead." He ordered two black inmates to beat Hamer with "a long wide blackjack," while other patrolmen battered "her head and other parts of her body." As they assaulted her, Hamer felt them repeatedly "pull my dress over my head and try to feel under my clothes." She attempted to pull her dress down during the brutal attack in order to "preserve some respectability through the horror and disgrace." Hamer told this story on national television at the Democratic National Convention in 1964 and continued to tell it "until the day she died," offering her testimony of the sexual and racial injustice of segregation.[8]

By speaking out, whether it was in the church, the courtroom, or a congressional hearing, black women used their own public voices to reject the stereotypes used by white supremacists to justify economic and sexual exploitation, and they reaffirmed their own humanity. Additionally, African American women's refusal to remain silent offered African American men an opportunity to assert themselves as *men* by rallying around the protection of black womanhood. Many other men, however, remained silent since speaking out was often dangerous, if not deadly. Most important, women's testimonies were a political act that exposed the bitter ironies of segregation and white supremacy, helped to reverse the shame and humiliation rape inflicts, and served as catalysts in mobilizing mass movements.[9]

Only after local and national groups were organized, black women's testimony began to spark public campaigns for equal justice and protection of black womanhood. In this respect, World War II served as a watershed for African Americans—especially in the South. Black women's testimony and the willingness of black leaders to protect black womanhood must be viewed as part of these resistance movements. For example, in Montgomery, Alabama, the organizational infrastructure that made the Montgomery bus boycott possible in 1955 stemmed in part from decades of black women's activism and a history of gendered political appeals to protect black women from sexual assault. The majority of leaders active in the Montgomery Improvement Association in 1955 cut their political teeth demanding justice for black women who were raped in the 1940s and early 1950s.[10]

In 1944, the kidnapping and gang rape of Mrs. Recy Taylor by six white men in Abbeville, Alabama, sparked what the *Chicago Defender* called "the strongest campaign for equal justice to Negroes to be seen in a decade." Taylor, a twenty-four-year-old African American woman, was walking home from the Rock Hill Holiness Church near Abbeville on September 3 when a carload of six white men pulled alongside her, pointed a gun at her head, and ordered her to get into the car. They drove her to a vacant patch of land where Herbert Lovett pointed his rifle at Taylor and . . . held her at gunpoint while each of the white men took turns "ravishing" her. After the men raped her, Lovett blindfolded her, pushed her into the car, and dropped her off in the middle of town. That night, Recy Taylor told her father, her husband, and Deputy Sheriff Lewey Corbitt the details of her harrowing assault.[11]

Within a few weeks, the Committee for Equal Justice for Mrs. Recy Taylor formed and was led on a local level by Rosa Parks, E. D. Nixon, Rufus A. Lewis, and E. G. Jackson (editor of the *Alabama Tribune*), all of whom later became pivotal figures in the Montgomery bus boycott. By utilizing the political infrastructure designed to defend the Scottsboro boys a decade earlier and employing the rhetoric of democracy sparked by World War II, Parks, Nixon, and their allies secured the support of national labor unions, African American organizations, women's groups, and thousands of individuals who demanded that Gov.

Chauncey Sparks order an immediate investigation and trial. "The raping of Mrs. Recy Taylor was a fascist-like, brutal violation of her personal rights as a woman and as a citizen of democracy," Eugene Gordon, a reporter for the *New York Daily Worker*, wrote in a pamphlet about the case; "Mrs. Taylor was not the first Negro woman to be outraged," he argued, "but it is our intention to make her the last. White-supremacy imitators of Hitler's storm troopers [will] shrink under the glare of the nation's spotlight." Gordon closed by universalizing the rape: "The attack on Mrs. Taylor was an attack on all women. Mrs. Taylor is a Negro . . . but no woman is safe or free until all women are free."[12] Few African Americans were surprised when the Henry County Grand Jury twice failed to indict the white men—despite the governor's belief that they were, in fact, guilty. Still, Recy Taylor's testimony launched a national and international campaign for equal justice that must not be ignored.[13]

Five years later, African Americans in Montgomery, Alabama, rallied to the defense of a twenty-five-year-old black woman named Gertrude Perkins. On March 27, 1949, Perkins was walking home when she was arrested for public drunkenness and attacked by two white police officers in uniform. After forcing her into their squad car, they drove her to the edge of town and raped her repeatedly at gunpoint. Afterwards, they threw her out of their car and sped away. Somehow, she found the strength to stagger into town, where she went directly to Rev. Solomon Seay Sr.'s house. Awaking him, she told him the details of her brutal assault through sobs and tears. "We didn't go to bed that morning," remembered Seay; "I kept her at my house, carefully wrote down what she said, and later had it notarized." Seay sent Perkins's horror story to the syndicated columnist Drew Pearson, who let the whole country know what happened in his daily radio address before Montgomery's white leaders knew what hit them.[14]

The leaders of the local Interdenominational Ministerial Alliance, the Negro Improvement League, and the National Association for the Advancement of Colored People (NAACP), led by E. D. Nixon and the Reverend Mr. Seay, joined together to form the Citizens Committee for Gertrude Perkins. Mary Fair Burks and her newly formed Women's Political Council may have been involved since one of their early goals was to "aid victims of rape." Although the community mobilized on behalf of Perkins, a grand jury failed to indict the assailants a few weeks later, despite running the full process of "the Anglo-Saxon system of justice." Still, Joe Azbell, editor of the *Montgomery Advertiser*, thought Gertrude Perkins, who bravely spoke out against the men who raped her, "had as much to do with the bus boycott and its creation as anyone on earth." The Perkins protest did not occur in isolation. In February 1951, Rufus A. Lewis . . . led a boycott of a grocery store owned by Sam E. Green, a white man, who was accused of raping his black teenage babysitter while driving her home. Lewis, a World War II veteran and football coach at Alabama State University, organized other veterans and members of the Citizens' Coordinating Committee in the successful campaign to close the store and bring Green to trial.[15]

The 1955 Montgomery bus boycott itself can be viewed as the most obvious example of the African American community coming to the rescue of a black woman, Rosa Parks, though not because of rape. When Parks sat down in a bus's "no-man's land" and was arrested for refusing to give up her seat to a white man, Montgomery blacks found the *perfect* woman to rally around. "Humble enough to be claimed by the common folk," Taylor Branch notes, Rosa Parks was "dignified enough in manner, speech, and dress to command the respect of the leading classes." Rosa Parks fit the middle-class ideals of "chastity, Godliness, family responsibility, and proper womanly conduct and demeanor" and was the kind of woman around which all the African Americans in Montgomery could rally. It is clear that her symbolic role as icon of virtuous black womanhood was decisive in Montgomery. Rev. Martin Luther King Jr.'s first speech at Holt Street Baptist Church stressed this point. "And since it had to happen," the young preacher told the crowd, "I'm happy it happened to a person like Mrs. Parks. Nobody can doubt the height of her character; nobody can doubt the depth of her Christian commitment."[16]

By selecting Rosa Parks as the symbol of segregation instead of other, less exemplary black women who had been arrested on buses earlier in 1955, black leaders in Montgomery embraced the "politics of respectability" . . . as a matter of political necessity amidst the burning white backlash that the 1954 Supreme

Court decision in *Brown v. Board of Education* sparked. The White Citizens' Councils, a kind of uptown Ku Klux Klan, led the movement for massive resistance to school integration by relying heavily on sexual scare tactics and white fears of racial amalgamation.[17] . . .

. . . [The strategies of emphasizing] respectability and . . . [maintaining] silence [about] black sexuality, [has meant that] . . . violence toward black women has not been as "vividly and importantly retained in our collective memory" . . . as the lynching of and violence against black men. . . . Over the past two decades, historians have sharpened their focus on the gendered meanings of respectability, but they have lost sight of the role rape and the threat of sexual violence played in the daily lives of African American women as well as within the larger black freedom struggle.[18] Yet throughout the Jim Crow South African American women such as Recy Taylor in 1944, Gertrude Perkins in 1949, and Betty Jean Owens in 1959 refused to shield their pain in secrecy, thereby challenging the pervasiveness of the politics of respectability. Following in the footsteps of their Reconstruction-era counterparts, they testified about their assaults, leaving behind critical evidence that historians must find the courage to analyze. . . .

When the four armed white men in Tallahassee forced Thomas Butterfield and Richard Brown to get into their car and drive away, leaving Betty Jean Owens and Edna Richardson at the mercy of their assailants, the two black men did not abandon them but drove around the corner and waited. As the blue Chevrolet disappeared down the street, Brown and Butterfield hurried back to the scene. Edna Richardson, the black woman who was able to get away, saw her friends from her hiding spot, called out to them, and then ran to the car. Hoping to save Owens, the Florida A&M students rushed to the local police station to report the crime.[19]

Similar situations in other southern towns had typically left African Americans without police aid. The officer on duty that night in Tallahassee was Joe Cooke Jr., a nineteen-year-old intern from the all-white Florida State University. Much to the surprise of the three black students, he agreed to look for Owens and her assailants. After a lengthy search, one of the students finally spotted the blue Chevrolet and shouted, "That's it!" It was just after 4:00 A.M.

Deputy Cooke turned on his flashers and drove alongside the car. Attempting to escape, the kidnappers led Cooke "twisting and turning through the dark streets of Tallahassee at speeds up to 100 miles per hour." . . . Finally, [the driver, William] Collinsworth pulled the car to the curb, grabbed his shotgun, and got out of the car. Deputy Cooke drew his pistol and ordered all four to line up against the car or, he threatened, "I will shoot to kill."[20]

As they waited for assistance from Cooke's supervisor, they heard muffled screams coming from the car. Richard Brown and Deputy Cooke peered through the rear window and saw Betty Jean Owens, bound and gagged, lying on the backseat floorboards. Brown tried to help her out of the car, but, as her feet touched the ground, she collapsed. Cooke drove Betty Jean Owens and her friends to the local colored hospital at Florida A&M while Deputy Sheriff W. W. Slappey arrested the four white men and drove them to the jailhouse.[21]

Laughing and joking on the way to the police station, the four white men apparently did not take their arrest seriously, nor did they think they had done anything wrong. Collinsworth, for example, worried less about the charges against him than about the safety of his car. Deputy Sheriff Slappey revealed his disgust when he handed the men over to Sheriff Raymond Hamlin Jr. "They all admitted it," Slappey said; "they didn't say why they did it and that's all I'm going to say about this dirty business." William Collinsworth, David Beagles, Ollie Stoutamire, and Patrick Scarborough confessed in writing to abducting Betty Jean Owens at gunpoint and having "sexual relations" with her. When Sheriff Hamlin asked the men to look over their statements and make any necessary corrections, David Beagles, smiling, bent over the table and made one minor adjustment before he and his friends were hustled off to jail.[22]

If the four white men did not take their arrests seriously, students at Florida A&M University flew into a rage. Many of them were veterans of the Tallahassee bus boycott in 1957, a Montgomery-inspired campaign that highlighted the trend in students' preference for direct action rather than the more respectable and slower litigation favored by the NAACP throughout the 1940s and 1950s. When the students heard news of the attack on Owens and the subsequent arrest of four white men, a small group planned an armed march to city hall to let city officials know that they were willing to protect black womanhood the same way whites "protected" white womanhood—with violence or at least a show of force. Mainstream student leaders persuaded them that an armed march was "the wrong thing to do" and patched together a "Unity" demonstration on Sunday, May 3, only twelve hours after Betty Jean Owens was admitted to the hospital and the four white men were taken to jail.[23]

Fifteen hundred students filled Lee Auditorium, where Clifford Taylor, president of the Student Government Association, said he "would not sit idly by and see our sisters, wives, and mothers desecrated." Using language white men in power could understand, student leaders professed their "belief in the dignity, respect, and protection of womanhood" and announced that they would petition the governor and other authorities for a "speedy and impartial trial."[24]

Early the next day, a thousand students gathered in the university's grassy quadrangle with signs, hymns, and prayers aimed at the national news media, which sent out stories of the attack across the country. The students planned to show Tallahassee and the rest of the nation that white men could no longer attack black women without consequence. Student protesters held signs calling for "Justice"; other posters declared, "It could have been YOUR sister, wife, or mother." Some students linked the attack in Tallahassee to larger issues related to the black freedom struggle: two students held up a poster depicting scenes from Little Rock, Arkansas, which read, "My God How Much More of This Can We Take."[25]

It was the deeply personal violation that rape inflicts, however, that gave the students their focus. Patricia Stephens Due remembered feeling helpless and unsafe. She recalled, "we all felt violated, male and female. It was like all of us had been raped." The student leader Buford Gibson, speaking to a crowd, universalized the attack when he said, "You must remember it wasn't just one Negro girl that was raped—it was all of Negro womanhood in the South."[26] By using Betty Jean Owens as a black Everywoman, Gibson challenged male students to rise up in protest and then placed the protection of black womanhood in their hands. Gibson's exhortation inspired students at Florida A&M to maintain their nonviolent demonstration, unlike white men who historically used the protection of white womanhood to inspire mob violence against black men. . . .

Accelerating media coverage, student-led protests, and a threat to boycott classes at Florida A&M forced Judge W. May Walker to call members of the grand jury into special session in Tallahassee on May 6, 1959. Over two hundred black spectators, mostly students, squeezed into the segregated balcony at the Leon County Courthouse to catch a glimpse of Betty Jean Owens and her attackers before they retreated into the secret hearing. Still undergoing hospital treatment for injuries inflicted during the attack and for "severe depression," Owens was accompanied to the court-house by a nurse, the hospital administrator, and her mother.[27]

Gasps and moans emanated from the balcony when, after two hours behind closed doors, William Collinsworth, David Beagles, Patrick Scarborough, and Ollie Stoutamire emerged, calmly faced the judge, and pleaded innocent to the charge of rape, making a jury trial mandatory. African Americans in the balcony roared with disapproval. Dr. M. C. Williams, a local black leader, shouted, "four colored men would be dead if the situation had been reversed. It looks like an open and shut case." Defense attorneys for Collinsworth and Scarborough argued for a delay, insisting that public excitement threatened a fair trial, but Judge Walker ignored their objections. For the first time in Florida history, a judge sent the white defendants charged with raping an African American woman back to jail to await their trial. . . . [28]

Justice was the last thing the black community expected. In the thirty-four years since Florida began sending convicted rapists to the electric chair instead of the gallows, the state had electrocuted thirty-seven African Americans charged with raping white women. Before this, Florida led the country in per capita lynchings, even surpassing such notoriously violent states as Mississippi, Georgia, and Louisiana. From 1900 to 1930, white Floridians lynched 281 people, 256 of whom were African American. Throughout its history, Florida never executed or lynched a white man for raping a black woman. . . . [29]

News that four white men would actually face prosecution for raping a black woman plunged both whites and blacks into largely unfamiliar territory. . . . According to the *Pittsburgh Courier*, the arraignment made the "arguments for white supremacy, racial discrimination, and segregation fall by the wayside" and the arguments against school desegregation

seem "childishly futile." "Time and again," another newspaper editor argued, "Southern spokesmen have protested that they oppose integration in the schools only because it foreshadows a total 'mingling of the races.' The implication is that Negroes are hell-bent for intimacy, while whites shrink back in horror." "Perhaps," the writer argued, "as Lillian Smith and other maverick Southerners have suggested, it is not quite that simple."[30]

While prominent members of the white community expressed their shock and horror at the rape, they continued to stumble into old narratives about race and sex. The indictment helped incite age-old fears of miscegenation and stereotypes of the so-called black beast rapist. . . . White women around Tallahassee began to speak openly about their "fear of retaliation," while young white couples avoided parking "in the country moonlight lest some Negroes should be out hunting in a retaliatory mood." Reflecting this fear as well as the larger concern with social equality, Florida legislators, like other lawmakers throughout the South, passed a series of racist bills designed to segregate children in schools by sex in order to circumvent the *Brown v. Board of Education* decision and "reduce the chances of interracial marriage."[31] The extent to which the myth of the black beast rapist was a projection of white fears was never clearer than when the gang rape of a black woman conjured up terror of *black-on-white* rape. The fact that the black community rallied around Betty Jean Owens and her womanhood threatened white male power—making the myth of the black savage a timely political tool. . . .

Ella Baker, director of the Southern Christian Leadership Conference (SCLC), felt that the evidence in the Tallahassee case was so strong that "not even an all white Florida jury could fail to convict." Reminding whites of their tendency to mete out unequal justice toward black men, she warned, "with memories of Negroes who have been lynched and executed on far less evidence, Negro leaders from all over the South will certainly examine every development in this case. . . . What will Florida's answer be?" The *New York Amsterdam News* called for equal justice, noting that the "law which calls for the death sentence does not say that Negro rapists should be punished by death and white rapists should be allowed to live." . . . [32]

Martin Luther King Jr., at the annual SCLC meeting in Tallahassee a few days after the indictment, praised the student protesters for giving "hope to all of us who struggle for human dignity and equal justice." But he tempered his optimism with political savvy, calling on the federal government to force the country to practice what it preached in its Cold War rivalry with the Soviet Union. "Violence in the South can not be deplored or ignored," King declared, directing his criticism at President Dwight D. Eisenhower; "without effective action, the situation will worsen." King exploited a political context in which America's racial problems were increasingly an international issue. The British Broadcasting Corporation (BBC) broadcast segments of the Florida A&M University student speeches condemning the rape and racial injustice, while newspapers throughout Europe closely watched the case unfold. "It is ironical that these un-American outrages occur as our representatives confer in Geneva to expand democratic principles . . . it might well be necessary and expedient," King threatened, "to appeal to the conscience of the world through the Commission on Human Rights of the United Nations." This international angle was a strategy shared by mainstream integrationists, leftist radicals, and black nationalists alike. Audley "Queen Mother" Moore, leader of the Universal Association of Ethiopian Women, Inc., petitioned the United Nations Human Rights Commission in person to end the "planned lynch terror and willful destruction of our people." She tied issues of race, gender, sex, and citizenship together by demanding Justice Department assistance for Betty Jean Owens's rape case, an FBI investigation of a [recent lynching in Mississippi], and basic voting rights.[33]

On June 11, 1959, at least four hundred people witnessed Betty Jean Owens face her attackers and testify on her own behalf. Owens approached the witness box with her head bowed. She wore a white embroidered blouse and a black-and-salmon checked skirt with gold earrings. The African American press had cast her in the role of respectable womanhood by characterizing her as a God-fearing, middle-class college co-ed "raised in a hardworking Christian household" with parents devoted to the "simple verities of life that make up the backbone of our democracy." Unlike white women, who were often able to play the role of "fair maiden" before a lynch mob worked its will on their alleged attackers, Betty

Jean Owens had to tell her story knowing that the four white men who raped her might go unpunished. Worse, Owens had to describe the attack in front of hundreds of white people in a segregated institution that inherently denied her humanity.[34] Though it may seem unnecessary, even lurid, to bear witness to the details of her testimony today, it is crucial that we hear the same testimony that the jurors heard. Owens's willingness to identify those who attacked her and to testify against them in public broke the institutional silence surrounding the centuries-long history of white men's sexual violation of black women, made a white southern judge and jury recognize her womanhood and dignity, and countered efforts to shame or stereotype her as sexually unchaste. As a result, her testimony alone is a momentous event.

Owens remained strong as state prosecutor William Hopkins asked her to detail the attack from the moment she and her friends left the Florida A&M dance. This she did powerfully and emotionally. "We were only parked near Jake Gaither Park for fifteen minutes," she said, when "four white men pulled up in a 1959 blue Chevrolet." She identified Patrick Scarborough as the man who pressed the shotgun into her date's nose and yelled, "Get out and get out now." When Owens began to cry, David Beagles pressed a "wicked looking foot long knife" to her throat and forced her down to the ground. . . . Owens testified that Beagles pushed her into the car and then "pushed my head down in his lap and yelled at me to be quiet or I would never get home." "I knew I couldn't get away," she stated; "I thought they would kill me if I didn't do what they wanted me to do."[35]

She continued with the horrid details. . . . Owens testified that the men eagerly watched one another have intercourse with her the first time around but lost interest during the second round. "Two of them were working on taking the car's license plate off," she said, "while the oldest one" offered her some whiskey. "I never had a chance to get away," she said quietly; "I was on the ground for two or three hours before the one with the knife pushed me back into the car." After the men had collectively raped her seven times, Ollie Stoutamire and Beagles blindfolded her with a baby diaper and pushed her onto the floorboards of the car, and they all drove away. When she heard the police sirens and felt the car stop, she pulled the blindfold down and began yelling for help.

After police ordered the men out of the car, Owens recalled, "I was so scared and weak and nervous that I just fell on the ground and that is the last thing I remember."[36]

Betty Jean Owens then described the physical injuries she sustained from the attack. "One arm and one leg," she said, "were practically useless" to her for several days while she was at the hospital. A nurse had to accompany her to the grand jury hearing a few days after the attack, and she needed medication for severe depression. She also had a large bruise on her breast where the bodice stay from her dress dug into her skin as the four men pressed their bodies into hers. Asking her to identify some of the exhibits, Hopkins flipped open the switchblade used the night of the attack, startling some of the jurors. Immediately the four defense attorneys jumped up and vehemently called for a mistrial, arguing that "by flashing the knife Mr. Hopkins tried to inflame the jury and this prejudiced their clients' constitutional rights to a fair trial." Judge Walker denied their motion, signaling Hopkins to continue. When asked whether she consented, Owens clearly told Hopkins and the jury, "No sir, I did not."[37]

Defense attorneys grilled Owens for more than an hour, trying to prove that she consented because she never struggled to get away and that she actually enjoyed the sexual encounter. "Didn't you derive any pleasure from that? Didn't you?" the attorney Howard Williams yelled repeatedly. He kept pressing her, "Why didn't you yell or scream out?" "I was afraid they would kill me," Owens said quietly. She showed signs of anger when Williams repeatedly asked if she was a virgin in an attempt to characterize her as a stereotypical black jezebel. Owens retained her composure, refused to answer questions about her chastity, and resisted efforts to shame her. The defense made a last-ditch effort to discredit Owens by arguing that, if the young men had actually raped her and threatened her life, she would have sustained more severe injuries.[38]

Proceeding with the state's case, William Hopkins called the doctors, both black and white, who examined Owens after the attack. They told the jury that they found her in a terrible condition and that she "definitely had sexual relations" that caused the injuries that required a five-day hospital stay. Richard Brown, Thomas Butterfield, and Edna Richardson took the stand next. They all corroborated Owens's testimony. . . . When the prosecution finally

rested its case at 8:30 P.M. on June 11, defense attorneys moved for a directed verdict of acquittal, claiming the state failed to prove anything except sexual intercourse. Judge Walker vigorously denied the motion and insisted the defense return the next day to present their defense.

Amid a sea of people in the tiny courtroom, David Beagles, an eighteen-year-old high school student, sat rigidly on the stand, pushing a ring back and forth on his finger as he answered questions from his attorney. His mother buried her head in her arms as she listened to her son tell the jury his side of the story. Beagles testified that he had a knife and William Collinsworth had a shotgun. The four of them were out "looking around for Negroes who had been parking near Collinsworth's neighborhood and bothering them." When they came upon the Florida A&M students, Beagles admitted holding the switchblade but then said he put it away when he saw they were dressed in formal wear. He admitted that they ordered Brown and Butterfield to drive away but insisted that he "asked the girls to get into the car." He denied the rape, arguing that Owens consented and even asked them to take her "back to school to change her dress." Under cross-examination, Beagles admitted that he "pushed her, just once . . . not hard," into the car, that he said, "If you do what we want you to, we'll let you go," and that he blindfolded her with a diaper after the attack. Defense attorney Howard Williams then asked Judge Walker to remove the jury as Beagles detailed the confession he made the night of the crime. Williams argued that when police officers arrested the young men, they "were still groggy from a night of drinking," making their confessions inadmissible. Under Hopkins's cross-examination, however, Beagles admitted that he was not pressured to say anything, that his confession was voluntary, and that he actually looked over the written statement and made an adjustment.[39]

Patrick Scarborough, who admitted that he was married to a woman in Texas, testified that he had intercourse with Owens twice but emphatically denied using force. When Hopkins questioned him, Scarborough admitted that Owens pleaded, "please don't hurt me," but he insisted that she offered "no resistance." He denied kissing her at first and then said he kissed her on the neck while he had sex with her.[40]

Defense attorneys [tried a series of contra-dictory approaches to win over the jury. First, they] focused on discrediting Owens instead of defending their clients because the prosecution repeatedly drew self-incriminating informa-tion from them.... [Then they] tried to use each man's ignorance to prove his innocence, highlighting their low IQ's and poor educa-tions. When that failed, they detailed the dys-functional histories of each defendant, as though to diminish the viciousness of the crime by offering a rationale for the men's depravity. Character witnesses for William Collinsworth, for example, described his sordid home life and drinking problem. Nearly every member of Collinsworth's family took the stand, spilling sorrowful stories about their poverty and dysfunction.... His wife, Pearlie, told the jury through sobs and tears that he was "not him-self when he was drunk," but when he was sober "you couldn't ask for a better husband." On the stand, she failed to mention what her letter to the judge had made explicit: that her husband regularly beat her.[41] ...

Finally, the defense appealed to the jury's prejudices. Collinsworth blamed his actions on the "Indian blood" pulsing through his veins; the Pensacola psychiatrist Dr. W. M. C. Wilhoit backed him up when he argued, "It is a known fact that individuals of the Indian race react violently and primitively when psy-chotic or intoxicated." When Collinsworth added alcohol to his "Indian blood," Wilhoit argued, "he was unable to discern the nature and quality of the crime in question." The at-torney for Ollie Stoutamire, city judge John Rudd, blamed "outside agitators." The defend-ants are "being publicized and ridiculed to sat-isfy sadists and people in other places," Rudd yelled during closing arguments. "Look at that little skinny, long legged sixteen-year-old boy. Does he look like a mad rapist who should die ... should we kill or incarcerate that little boy be-cause he happened to be in the wrong place at the wrong time?"[42]

In their summations to the jury, defense attorneys S. Gunter Toney and Harry Michaels followed Rudd's lead. Michaels insisted that "the crime here is insignificant ... the pressure, clamor, and furor are completely out of propor-tion." Pointing to Scarborough, Michaels told the jury, "his motives, intentions, and designs that night were wholesome, innocent and decent." The fact that Owens could "have easily walked ten feet into the woods where nobody

could find her," Michaels said, proved she con-sented. Waving her gold and white gown in front of the jury, he pointed out that it was "not soiled or torn," which he said proved no brutal-ity was involved. Finally, he called for an ac-quittal, arguing that the jury could not possibly convict on the basis of "only one witness—the victim, and confessions that admitted only one fact—sexual intercourse." Sitting in the segre-gated balcony, Charles U. Smith, a sociologist at Florida A&M University, said he gasped when he heard Howard Williams yell, "Are you going to believe this nigger wench over these four boys?"[43]

In his summation, prosecuting attorney William Hopkins jumped up, grabbed the shot-gun and Betty Jean Owens's prom dress, and appealed to the jury for a conviction.

> Suppose two colored boys and their moron friends attacked Mrs. Beagles' daughter ... had taken her at gunpoint from a car and forced her into a se-cluded place and regardless of whether they se-cured her consent or not, had intercourse with her seven times, leaving her in such a condition that she collapsed and had to be hospitalized?

Betty Jean Owens, he said, "didn't have a chance in the world with four big boys, a loaded gun and a knife. She was within an inch of losing her life ... she was gang-raped SEVEN times." "When you get to the question of mercy," he told the jury, "consider that they wouldn't even let that little girl whimper."[44]

Restless spectators, squeezed into every corner of the segregated courthouse, piled back into their seats when jurors emerged after three hours of deliberation with a decision. An addi-tional three hundred African Americans held a silent vigil outside. A. H. King, the jury fore-man and a local plantation owner, slowly read aloud the jury's decision for all four defendants: "guilty with a recommendation for mercy." The recommendation for mercy saved the four men from the electric chair and, according to the *Baltimore Afro-American*, "made it inescapably clear that the death penalty for rape is only for colored men accused by white women...." Judge Walker deferred sentencing for fifteen days, cleared the courtroom, and sent the four white men to Raiford prison.[45]

African Americans who attended the trial quietly made their way home after the bitter-sweet verdict. Betty Jean Owens's mother told reporters that she was "just happy that the jury upheld my daughter's womanhood."

Rev. A. J. Reddick, former head of the Florida NAACP, snapped, "If it had been Negroes, they would have gotten the death penalty." "Florida," he said, "has maintained an excellent record of not veering from its pattern of never executing a white man for the rape of a Negro," but he acknowledged that the conviction was "a step forward." Betty Jean Owens showed a similar ambivalence in an interview by the New York Amsterdam News. "It is something," she said; "I'm grateful that twelve white men believed the truth, but I still wonder what they would have done if one of our boys raped a white girl."[46]

Florida A&M students, who had criticized Butterfield and Brown for failing to protect black womanhood a week earlier, were visibly upset after the trial. In fact, letters to the editors of many African American newspapers condemned the two men and all black men for failing to protect "their" women. Mrs. C. A. C. in New York City felt that all Negro men were "mice" and not worthy of respect because "they stand by and let the white men do anything they want to our women." She then warned all black men that they "would never have freedom until [they] learn to stand up and fight." In a letter to the Baltimore Afro-American, a black man accepted her challenge: "unless we decide to protect our own women," he argued, "none of them will be safe." Some African American women felt they should protect themselves. A white woman sent her black maid home one day after she came to work with a knife, "in case any white man came after her," reported the Tallahassee Democrat. Still, many felt that "someone should have burned."[47]

Despite their anger at the unequal justice meted out, some African Americans in the community considered the guilty verdict a victory. The Reverend C. K. Steele Jr., head of the Tallahassee chapter of the SCLC, said it showed progress, reminding others that four white men "wouldn't have even been arrested twenty years ago." The Reverend Leon A. Lowery, state president of the Florida NAACP, saw a strategy in the mercy recommendation. He thought that it could help "Negroes more in the long run" by setting a precedent for equal justice in future rape cases. After Judge Walker handed down life sentences to the four white men, some African Americans in Tallahassee applauded what they felt was a significant step in the right direction; many others, however, exhibited outrage. Roy Wilkins openly praised

the verdict as a move toward equal justice but acknowledged in a private letter the "glaring contrast that was furnished by the Tallahassee verdict." . . . Editors of the Louisiana Weekly called the trial a "figment and a farce" and insisted that anyone who praised the verdict "confesses that he sees nothing wrong with exacting one punishment for white offenders and another, more severe for others."[48]

Any conviction was too much for some whites who felt that sending four white men to jail for raping a black woman upset the entire foundation of white supremacy. Many believed the guilty verdict was the result of a Communist-inspired NAACP conspiracy, which would ultimately lead to miscegenation. Letters to Judge Walker featured a host of common fears and racist stereotypes of black men and women. Fred G. Millette reminded the judge that a conviction "would play into the hands of the Warren Court, the NAACP, and all other radical enemies of the South . . . even though the nigger wench probably had been with a dozen men before." Mrs. Laura Cox wrote to Judge Walker that she feared this case would strengthen desegregation efforts, posing a direct threat to white children who might attend integrated schools. "If the South is integrated," she argued, "white children will be in danger because the Negroes carry knives, razors, ice picks, and guns practically all the time." Petitioning Judge Walker for leniency, Mrs. Bill Aren reminded him to remember that "Negro women like to be raped by the white men" and that "something like this will help the Supreme Court force this low bred race ahead, making whites live and eat with him and allow his children to associate with the little apes, grow up and marry them."[49] . . .

While the verdict was likely the confluence of localized issues—a politically mobilized middle-class African American community, the lower-class status of the defendants (who were politically expendable), Florida's status as a "moderate" southern state dependent on northern tourism, and media pressure—it had far-reaching consequences.[50] The Tallahassee case focused national attention on the sexual exploitation of black women at the hands of white men, leading to convictions elsewhere that summer. In Montgomery, Alabama, Grady F. Smith, a retired air force colonel, was sentenced to fourteen months of hard labor for raping a seventeen-year-old African American girl. In Raleigh, North Carolina, Ralph Lee Betts, a thirty-six-year-old white man, was sentenced to life imprisonment for kidnapping and molesting an eleven-year-old African American girl. And in Burton, South Carolina, an all-white jury sent a white marine named Fred Davis to the electric chair—a first in the history of the South—for raping a forty-seven-year-old African American woman. In each case, white supremacy faltered in the face of the courageous black women who testified on their own behalf.[51]

Betty Jean Owens's grandmother recognized the historic and political significance of the verdicts. "I've lived to see the day," she said, "where white men would really be brought to trial for what they did." [Newspaper editor] John McCray . . . realized the importance of guilty verdicts. "This forced intimacy," he argued, "goes back to the days of slavery when our women were the chattel property of white men." For McCray, the life sentences indicated a new day: "Are we now witnessing the arrival of our women? Are they at long last gaining the emancipation they've needed?"[52]

McCray's connection between the conviction of white men for raping black women and black women's emancipation raises important questions that historians are just beginning to ponder. How did the daily struggle to gain self-respect and dignity, rooted in ideas of what it meant to be men and women, play out in the black freedom struggle? It is not just a coincidence that black college students, struggling for their own identity and independence, sparked the sit-in movement soon after Betty Jean Owens was brutally raped. In Tallahassee, Patricia Stephens Due, who felt that the rape symbolized an attack on the dignity and humanity of all African Americans, organized the city's first Congress of Racial Equality (CORE) chapter just six weeks after Owens's trial. Florida A&M CORE members launched an uneventful sit-in campaign that fall, but, like other black students throughout the South, successfully desegregated local lunch counters, theaters, and department stores in the spring of 1960. The students later led the "jail, no bail" tactic popularized by SCLC and SNCC.[53] While the rape alone may not have been the galvanizing force that turned students into soldiers for freedom, the sexual and racial dynamics inherent in this case speak to larger themes in the African American freedom struggle.

The politics of respectability—Betty Jean Owens's middle-class background, her college education, and her chastity—may have enabled African Americans on the local and national level to break through the "culture of dissemblance" and speak out against her rape. But it was the convergence of the politics of respectability, Owens's testimony, and African Americans' growing political influence on the national and international stage in the late 1950s that made the legal victory possible. Still, the long tradition of black women's testimony, stretching back to slavery and Reconstruction, makes it clear that some elements of the Tallahassee case were not aberrations. The testimonies and trials of Betty Jean Owens, Gertrude Perkins, and Recy Taylor, to name just a few, bear witness to these issues, forcing historians to reconsider the individual threads that make up the fabric of African American politics. Black women not only dissembled where it was necessary but testified where it was possible. Not only silence but often protest surrounded the sexualized violence against African American women. If we are fully to understand the role of gender and sexuality in larger struggles for freedom and equality, we must explore these battles over manhood and womanhood, frequently set in the context of sexualized violence, that remain at the volatile core of the modern civil rights movement.

NOTES

1. *New York Amsterdam News,* June 20, 1959, p. 37. Trezzvant W. Anderson, "Rapists Missed Out on First Selection," *Pittsburgh Courier,* June 20, 1959, p. 3; "Four Convicted in Rape Case," *Tallahassee Democrat,* June 14, 1959, p. 7. "I Was Scared," *Pittsburgh Courier,* June 20, 1959, p. 1. "Four Begin Defense in Trial on Rape," *New York Times,* June 13, 1959, p. A13. See also criminal case file #3445, *State of Florida v. Patrick Gene Scarborough, David Ervin Beagles, Ollie Odell Stoutamire, and William Ted Collinsworth,* 1959 (Leon County Courthouse, Tallahassee, Fla.) (copy in author's possession). Thanks to the Leon County Courthouse for sending me the file. Because the original trial transcript is no longer available, I have had to rely on newspaper reports, particularly those in African American newspapers: the *Baltimore Afro-American,* the *Louisiana Weekly,* the *New York Amsterdam News,* the *Pittsburgh Courier,* and the South Carolina *Lighthouse and Informer.*

2. The murders of Emmett Till in 1955 and Andrew Goodman, Michael Schwerner, and James Chaney in 1963 are considered pivotal moments in the civil rights movement. Their stories are given prominent attention in the PBS *Eyes on the Prize* series and Hollywood films such as the 1988 thriller *Mississippi Burning.* For monographs on these murders, see, for example, Nicolaus Mills, *Like a Holy Crusade: Mississippi 1964—The Turning Point of the Civil Rights Movement in America* (Chicago, 1992); and

Stephen J. Whitfield, *A Death in the Delta: The Story of Emmett Till* (Baltimore, 1991).

3. Historians have only recently begun to explore how gender and sexuality affected the civil rights movement. On the ways women changed the civil rights movement and how it changed their lives as well, see, for example, Vicki L. Crawford, Jacqueline Anne Rouse, and Barbara Woods, eds., *Women in the Civil Rights Movement: Trailblazers and Torchbearers, 1941–1965* (New York, 1990); and Belinda Robnett, *How Long? How Long? African-American Women in the Struggle for Civil Rights* (New York, 1997). Recent works place black and white women and their long-standing traditions of community organizing and resistance in the forefront of the movement; see, for example, Charles M. Payne, *I've Got the Light of Freedom: The Organizing Tradition and the Mississippi Freedom Struggle* (Berkeley, 1995); and Barbara Ransby, *Ella Baker and the Black Freedom Movement: A Radical Democratic Vision* (Chapel Hill, 2003).

4. Darlene Clark Hine, "Rape and the Inner Lives of Black Women in the Middle West: Preliminary Thoughts on a Culture of Dissemblance," *Signs,* 14 (Summer 1989), 912–20.

5. Gerda Lerner, ed., *Black Women in White America: A Documentary History* (New York, 1972), 172.

6. Tera W. Hunter, *To 'Joy My Freedom: Southern Black Women's Lives and Labors after the Civil War* (Cambridge, Mass., 1997), 34. Winthrop Jordan, *White over Black: American Attitudes toward the Negro, 1550–1812* (Chapel Hill, 1968), 141. Frances Thompson quoted in Lerner, ed., *Black Women in White America,* 174–75; Harriet Simril quoted ibid., 183–85. Essic Harris quoted in Elsa Barkley Brown, "Negotiating and Transforming the Public Sphere: African American Political Life in the Transition from Slavery to Freedom," *Public Culture,* 7 (1994), 112n8; Ferdie Walker quoted in William Chafe, Raymond Gavins, and Robert Korstad, eds., *Remembering Jim Crow: African Americans Tell about Life in the Segregated South* (New York, 2001), 9–10.

7. John H. McCray, "South's Courts Show New Day of Justice," *Baltimore Afro-American,* July 11, 1959. Theralene Beachem interview by McGuire, March 19, 2003, audiotape (in McGuire's possession); Gloria Dennard interview by McGuire, March 19, 2003, audiotape, ibid.; Linda S. Hunt interview by McGuire, March 19, 2003, audiotape, ibid.; Mrs. Lucille M. Johnson interview by McGuire, March 16, 2003, audiotape, ibid.

8. Chana Kai Lee, *For Freedom's Sake: The Life of Fannie Lou Hamer* (Urbana, 1999), 9, 10, 78–81. Though over a half century old, two of the best articulations of the sexual subtext of segregation that exist are John Dollard, *Caste and Class in a Southern Town* (Madison, 1937); and Lillian Smith, *Killers of the Dream* (New York, 1949). See also Kay Mills, *This Little Light of Mine: The Life of Fannie Lou Hamer* (New York, 1993).

9. See Deborah Gray White, *Too Heavy a Load: Black Women in Defense of Themselves, 1894–1994* (New York, 1999), 60–66. John Lewis Adams, "Arkansas Needs Leadership': Daisy Bates, Black Arkansas, and the National Association for the Advancement of Colored People" (M.A. thesis, University of Wisconsin, Madison, 2003). Thanks to John Adams for sharing his research with me. On "reversing the shame," see

Temma Kaplan, "Reversing the Shame and Gendering the Memory," *Signs,* 28 (Autumn 2002), 179–99. Jo Ann Robinson, *The Montgomery Bus Boycott and the Women Who Started It: The Memoir of Jo Ann Gibson Robinson,* ed. David J. Garrow (Knoxville, 1987), 37.

10. On the impact of World War II, see, for example, Timothy B. Tyson, "Wars for Democracy: African American Militancy and Interracial Violence in North Carolina during World War II," in *Democracy Betrayed: The Wilmington Race Riot of 1898 and Its Legacy,* ed. David Cecelski and Timothy B. Tyson (Chapel Hill, 1998), 254–75; and Harvard Sitkoff, "Racial Militancy and Interracial Violence in the Second World War," *Journal of American History,* 58 (Dec. 1971), 661–81. My research indicates that African Americans throughout the South used World War II as a wedge to publicize southern injustice, especially sexual violence by white men. Between 1942 and 1950, African American women accused white men of rape, testified about their assaults, and sparked community mobilization efforts in a number of southern towns, often securing convictions, mostly on minor charges with small fines assessed.

11. Fred Atwater, "$600 to Rape Wife? Alabama Whites Make Offer to Recy Taylor Mate," *Chicago Defender,* n.d., clipping, Recy Taylor case, folder 2, Administrative Files, Gov. Chauncey Sparks Papers, 1943–1947 (Alabama Department of Archives and History, Montgomery); N. W. Kimbrough and J. V. Kitchens, "Report to Governor Chauncey Sparks," Dec. 14, 1944, ibid.; John O. Harris, N. W. Kimbrough, and J. V. Kitchens to Gov. Chauncey Sparks, "Supplemental Report, December 27, 1944," ibid. See also "Grand Jury Refuses to Indict Attackers," *Pittsburgh Courier,* Feb. 24, 1945, folder 3, ibid.; "This Evening," *Birmingham News,* Feb. 21, 1945, ibid.; and "Second Grand Jury Finds No Bill in Negro's Charges," *Dothan Eagle,* Feb. 15, 1945, ibid.

12. On Scottsboro's political infrastructure, see Dan T. Carter, *Scottsboro: A Tragedy of the American South* (New York, 1971); and James Goodman, *Stories of Scottsboro* (New York, 1994). Over thirty national labor unions and many more locals supported Recy Taylor. See "Press release," Feb. 3, 1945, folder 4, box 430, Earl Conrad Collection (Cayuga Community College Library, Auburn, N.Y.). Other organizations that played an active role in Recy Taylor's defense include the Southern Conference for Human Welfare, the National Council of Negro Women, the Southern Negro Youth Congress, the National Negro Congress, the International Labor Defense, and the Birmingham and Montgomery branches of the NAACP: "Partial Sponsor List," Dec. 28, 1944, ibid.; Earl Conrad, Eugene Gordon, and Henrietta Buckmaster, "Equal Justice under Law," pamphlet draft, ibid.

13. See Kimbrough and Kitchens, "Report to Governor Chauncey Sparks"; Harris, Kimbrough, and Kitchens to Sparks, "Supplemental Report." See also "Grand Jury Refuses to Indict Attackers," *Pittsburgh Courier,* Feb. 24, 1945; "Dixie Sex Crimes against Negro Women Widespread," *Chicago Defender,* n.d., Scrapbook Collection, Conrad Collection; "Alabama Rapists Came from Church to Join White Gang in Sex Crime," *Chicago Defender,* March 24, 1945, ibid.; and "Alabama Has No Race Problem, Claims Official," *Chicago Defender,* n.d., ibid.

14. See *Montgomery Advertiser*, April 5, 1949, p. 8A; April 6, 1949, p. 1B; April 7, 1949, p. 2A; S. S. Seay, *I Was There by the Grace of God* (Montgomery, 1990), 130–31. "Drew Pearson Changes Mind; Criticizes City," *Montgomery Advertiser*, May 3, 1949, p. 1A; ibid., May 21, 1949, p. 1A; "Anglo-Saxon System of Justice," ibid., May 22, 1949, p. 2B.

15. "Rape Cry against Dixie Cops Fall on Deaf Ears," *Baltimore Afro-American*, April 9, 1949, p. 1; Stewart Burns, ed., *Daybreak of Freedom: The Montgomery Bus Boycott* (Chapel Hill, 1997), 7; Joe Azbell quoted in "Cradle of the Confederacy," transcript, *Will the Circle Be Unbroken*, Southern Regional Council Web site (March 1997; not currently available; printout in McGuire's possession). Rufus A. Lewis story in Townsend Davis, *Weary Feet, Rested Souls: A Guided History of the Civil Rights Movement* (New York, 1998), 34.

16. Taylor Branch, *Parting the Waters: America in the King Years, 1954–1963* (New York, 1988), 130 (first and last quotations). Marissa Chappell, Jenny Hutchinson, and Brian Ward, "'Dress modestly, neatly . . . as if you were going to church'; Respectability, Class, and Gender in the Montgomery Bus Boycott and the Early Civil Rights Movement," in *Gender in the Civil Rights Movement*, ed. Peter J. Ling and Sharon Monteith (New York, 1999), 87.

17. Black leaders in Montgomery decided against using the arrests of Claudette Colvin, an unwed pregnant teenager, and Mary Louise Smith, the daughter of a local drunk, as test cases for desegregating the buses; see Branch, *Parting the Waters*, 123–28; Lynn Olson, *Freedom's Daughters: The Unsung Heroes of the Civil Rights Movement from 1830–1970* (New York, 2001), 94–95. Neil R. McMillen, *The Citizens' Council: Organized Resistance to the Second Reconstruction, 1954–1964* (Urbana, 1994), 184, 186.

18. Brown, "Negotiating and Transforming the Public Sphere," 146. Historians of the modern day civil rights movement are beginning to build upon work that chronicled the ways respectability, dignity, and manhood and womanhood shaped the strategies and goals of the middle- and working-class black activists during Reconstruction and the Progressive Era; see, for example, Glenda Gilmore, *Gender and Jim Crow: Women and the Politics of White Supremacy in North Carolina, 1896–1920* (Chapel Hill, 1999); and Evelyn Brooks Higginbotham, *Righteous Discontent. The Women's Movement in the Black Baptist Church, 1880–1920* (Cambridge, Mass., 1993).

19. "Deputy Tells of Confessions," *Tallahassee Democrat*, June 12, 1959.

20. Saunders, "Report on Tallahassee Incident."

21. "Deputy Tells of Confessions," *Tallahassee Democrat*, June 12, 1959. Original reports stated that Owens was "bound and gagged," but she later testified that she was only blindfolded; after she pulled the blindfold down, she appeared to have been gagged.

22. "Four Whites Seized in Rape of Negro," *New York Times*, May 3, 1959, p. A45.

23. On the Tallahassee bus boycott, see Glenda Alice Rabby, *The Pain and the Promise: The Struggle for Civil Rights in Tallahassee, Florida* (Athens, Ga., 1999), 9–46. Robert M. White, "The Tallahassee Sit-ins and CORE: A Nonviolent Revolutionary Sub-movement" (Ph.D. diss., Florida State University, 1964), 65.

24. White, "Tallahassee Sit-ins and CORE," 65.

25. "Rapists Face Trial," *Famuan*, 27 (May 1959), 1, 3; "Negroes Ask Justice for Co-ed Rapists," *Atlanta Constitution*, May 4, 1959, p. 2; "Four Whites Seized in Rape of Negro," *New York Times*, May 3, 1959, p. A45; ibid., May 5, 1959, p. A23; "Mass Rape of Co-ed Outrages Students," *Louisiana Weekly*, May 9, 1959, p. 1; *L'Osservatore Romano*, June 12, 1959; *Herald Tribune–London*, June 13, 1959; "Jury to Take Up Rape of Negro Co-ed," *Atlanta Constitution*, May 5, 1959, p. 5.

26. Patricia Stephens Due telephone interview by McGuire, March 4, 1999 (notes in McGuire's possession).

27. "4 Indicted in Rape of Negro Co-ed," *New York Herald Tribune*, May 7, 1959, p. 5; Moses Newson, "Leaves Hospital to Give Testimony," *Pittsburgh Courier*, May 16, 1959, pp. 1–2.

28. M. C. Williams quoted in "Packed Court Hears Not Guilty," *Pittsburgh Courier*, May 16, 1959, pp. 1–2; "Judge Instructs July Here," *Tallahassee Democrat*, May 6, 1959, p. 1; "Sobbing Co-ed Bares Ordeal," *Baltimore Afro-American*, May 16, 1959, p. 1; "Indictment for Rape," criminal case file #3445, *Florida v. Scarborough, Beagles, Stoutamire, and Collinsworth*; "Four Plead Not Guilty to Rape," *Tallahassee Democrat*, n.d., clipping, folder 4, box 912, W. May Walker Papers (Special Collections, Robert Manning Strozier Library, Florida State University, Tallahassee).

29. Statistics are from David R. Colburn and Richard K. Scher, *Florida's Gubernatorial Politics in the Twentieth Century* (Gainesville, 1995), 13.

30. "Another Dixiecrat Headache," *Pittsburgh Courier*, June 20, 1959; "The Other Story," n.d., clipping, folder 1, box 912, Walker Papers.

31. William H. Chafe, "Epilogue from Greensboro, North Carolina," in *Democracy Betrayed*, ed. Cecelski and Tyson, 281–82. "Senate to Get Racial Measures," *Tallahassee Democrat*, June 14, 1959, p. 1; "Pent Up Critique on the Rape Case," ibid., May 14, 1959.

32. Ella Baker quoted in *Pittsburgh Courier*, May 30, 1959, p. 3; see also Ransby, *Ella Baker and the Black Freedom Movement*, 210. "Enforce the Law," *New York Amsterdam News*, May 9, 1959.

33. "King Asks Ike to Go to Mississippi," *Baltimore Afro-American*, May 23, 1959. "Report from Europe," *Baltimore Afro-American*, May 23, 1959. For the impact of the Cold War on civil rights, see, for example, Mary L. Dudziak, *Cold War Civil Rights: Race and the Image of American Democracy* (Princeton, 2000); and Thomas Borstelmann, *The Cold War and the Color Line: American Race Relations in the Global Arena* (Cambridge, Mass., 2001). "Appeal to U.N. to Stop Race Violence," *Louisiana Weekly*, May 9, 1959, p. 1.

34. *Tallahassee Democrat*, May 4, 1959. On the "fair maiden," see Jacquelyn Dowd Hall, "'Not That Sort of Woman': Race, Gender, and Sexual Violence during the Memphis Riot of 1866," in *Sex, Love, Race: Crossing Boundaries in North American History*, ed. Martha Hodes (New York, 1999), 267–93.

35. "I Was Scared," *Pittsburgh Courier*, June 20, 1959; see also "Did Not Consent," *Tallahassee Democrat*, June 11, 1959; "Rape Co-eds Own Story," *New York Amsterdam News*, June 20, 1959, p. 1; *Atlanta Constitution*, June 12, 1959; "Negro Girl Tells Jury of Rape by Four," *New York Times*, June 12, 1959, p. A16. Coverage of Owens's testimony was nearly identical in newspapers cited.

36. "Did Not Consent," *Tallahassee Democrat,* June 11, 1959; ibid.; ibid.; "I Was Scared," *Pittsburgh Courier,* June 20, 1959, p. 1; "Did Not Consent," *Tallahassee Democrat,* June 11, 1959; ibid.; see also *Charlotte Observer,* June 12, 1959, p. 1A.

37. "Did Not Consent," *Tallahassee Democrat,* June 11, 1959; "I Was Scared," *Pittsburgh Courier,* June 20, 1959; "State's exhibits" (knife) in criminal case file #3445, *Florida v. Scarborough, Beagles, Stoutamire, and Collinsworth,* 1959.

38. "Rape Co-eds Own Story," *New York Amsterdam News,* June 20, 1959, p. 1; "I Was Scared," *Pittsburgh Courier,* June 20, 1959, p. 1; see also "Four Begin Defense in Trial on Rape," *New York Times,* June 13, 1959, p. A13.

39. Anderson, "Rapists Missed Out on First Selection," *Pittsburgh Courier,* June 20, 1959, p. 3; "Four Begin Defense in Trial on Rape," *New York Times,* June 13, 1959, p. A13; Howard Williams quoted in "Rape Defendants Claim Consent," *Tallahassee Democrat,* June 13, 1959.

40. "Negro Co-ed Gave Consent, Rape Defendants Tell Jury" *Atlanta Constitution,* June 13, 1959.

41. William Hopkins quoted in "Four Convicted in Rape Case; Escape Chair; 2 hr 45 min Verdict Calmly Received in Court," *Tallahassee Democrat,* June 14, 1959, p. 1; Pearlie Collinsworth and friends quoted in "Rape Defendants Claim Consent," ibid., June 13, 1959; Maudine Reeve's history of Ted Collinsworth, "State's exhibit #15," criminal case file #3445, *Florida v. Scarborough, Beagles, Stoutamire, and Collinsworth,* 1959; letter from Mrs. W. T. Collinsworth, "State's exhibit #16," ibid.

42. W. M. C. Wilhoit's testimony in "Motion for Leave to File Notice of Defense of Insanity," May 28, 1959, criminal case file #3445, *Florida v. Scarborough, Beagles, Stoutamire, and Collinsworth,* 1959. "Four Begin Defense in Trial on Rape," *New York Times,* June 13, 1959, p. A13; John Rudd quoted in "Four Guilty of Raping Negro; Florida Jury Votes Mercy," ibid., June 14, 1959, p. A1.

43. "Four Guilty of Raping Negro; Florida Jury Votes Mercy," *New York Times,* June 14, 1959, p. A1. Charles U. Smith interview by Jackson Lee Ice, 1978, in Jackson Lee Ice Interviews, Florida Governors Manuscript Collection (Special Collections, Strozier Library); verified in Charles U. Smith telephone interview by McGuire, March 9, 1999 (notes in McGuire's possession).

44. "Precedent Seen in Rape Trial," *Tampa Tribune,* June 15, 1959; *Tallahassee Democrat,* June 14, 1959, p. 1.

45. "Verdict," June 14, 1959, criminal case file #3445, *Florida v. Scarborough, Beagles, Stoutamire, and* Collinsworth, 1959. "Guilty as Charged," *Baltimore Afro-American,* June 20, 1959.

46. Sitton, "Negroes See Gain in Conviction of Four for Rape of Co-ed," *New York Times,* June 15, 1959, p. A1; "I'm Leaving Dixie," *New York Amsterdam News,* June 20, 1959.

47. Apparently students at Florida A&M ostracized Thomas Butterfield and Richard Brown for failing to protect Betty Jean Owens and Edna Richardson; students thought they ought to have shown some "physical resistance" rather than run away from the "point of a knife and gun": "I'm Leaving Dixie," *New York Amsterdam News,* June 20, 1959. "Hits Negro Men," ibid., June 6, 1959, p. 8. "Williams Was Right," *Baltimore Afro-American,* June 27, 1959; "Four Convicted in Rape Case," *Tallahassee Democrat,* June 14, 1959, p. 7; "I'm Leaving Dixie," *New York Amsterdam News,* June 20, 1959.

48. Sitton, "Negroes See Gain in Conviction of Four for Rape of Co-ed," *New York Times,* June 15, 1959, p. A1. "Negroes Say They Will Use Tallahassee Case as Precedent in Rape Trials," *Tampa Tribune,* June 15, 1959; "This Is Not Equal Justice," *Louisiana Weekly,* July 4, 1959.

49. Fred G. Millette to Judge W. May Walker, June 15, 1959, box 912, folder 1, Walker Papers; Mrs. Laura Cox to Judge Walker, June 15, 1959, ibid.; Mrs. Bill Aren to Judge Walker, June 15, 1959, ibid.

50. See Tom Wagy, *Governor LeRoy Collins of Florida: Spokesman of the New South* (University, Ala., 1985); and Steven F. Lawson, "From Sit-in to Race Riot: Businessmen, Blacks, and the Pursuit of Moderation in Tampa, 1960–1967," in *Southern Businessmen and Desegregation,* ed. Elizabeth Jacoway and David R. Colburn (Baton Rouge, 1982), 257–81.

51. Cases cited in Kimberly R. Woodard, "The Summer of African-American Discontent," unpublished paper, Duke University, 1992 (in McGuire's possession). See also "Death to Be Demanded in Rape Case," *Baltimore Afro-American,* July 4, 1959; John H. McCray, "Marine Doomed to Electric Chair in S.C. Rape Case," ibid., July 11, 1959, p. 1; Clarence Mitchell, "Separate but Equal Justice," ibid.; "Girlfriend Turns in Rape Suspect," ibid., Aug. 1, 1959; Trezzvant Anderson, "Negroes Weep as Georgia White Is Acquitted," *Pittsburgh Courier,* Sept. 2, 1959.

52. "The Tallahassee Case: A Turning Point in South," *New York Amsterdam News,* July 18, 1959; John H. McCray, "South's Courts Show New Day of Justice," *Baltimore Afro-American,* June 11, 1959.

53. Richard Haley, "Report on Events in Tallahassee, October 1959–June 1960," folder 7, box 10, series 5, Congress of Racial Equality Papers (Wisconsin Historical Society, Madison).

Betty Friedan, "The problem that has no name"

In the late 1950s, Elvis Presley monopolized the top of the rock and roll charts. The Beatles would not arrive until 1964. But by 1960 African American girl groups, led by the Shirelles and the Supremes, were elbowing for the top place, and in December 1960, the top song was the Shirelles hit, "Will You Love Me Tomorrow?" As their most astute analyst, Susan Douglas, has written, they had emerged from the black gospel tradition; they were not voices of social complacency or homogenized commercialism (such as Doris Day's hit "How Much is that Doggie in the Window?"). Their music was "revolutionary . . . [It] conveyed both a moral authority and a spirited hope for the future." They questioned men's reliability:

Tonight you're mine completely
You give your love so sweetly
Tonight the light of love is in your eyes
But will you love me tomorrow?

Is this a lasting treasure
Or just a moment's pleasure?
Can I believe the magic of your sighs . . .

As their songs "gave voice to girls' changing attitudes toward sex," and claimed the power to make their own choices, girl groups of the period sang "that they, as a generation, would not be trapped."*

Mothers who worried about their daughters had their own set of frustrations. They were not much better than their daughters at articulating their discomfort and malaise. It was 1963 when Betty Friedan, identifying herself as a suburban housewife, did the job for them, exposing the triviality and frustrations of a resurgent domesticity.

Friedan's indictment, a brief portion of which appears here, was the subject of much controversy. Women who found the gratification associated with child care and housework vastly overemphasized applauded Friedan's forceful articulation of their own dissatisfactions. Other women objected vehemently, insisting that, as wives and mothers and perhaps community activists, they enjoyed a lifestyle that not only benefited both their families and communities but also provided them personally with freedom, pleasure, and a sense of self-worth. (Among Friedan's critics was Phyllis Schlafly, whose criticism of the women's liberation movement appears in the next selection.)

Among the thousands of letters that Friedan received was one from Gerda Lerner, then a 43-year-old mother and graduate student studying history at Columbia University. (Lerner's essay on the continuing relevance of the 1848 Seneca

Falls Declaration of Sentiments appears on pp. 221–227). "I have just finished reading your splendid book," Lerner wrote; "and want to tell you how excited and delighted I am . . . I am sure it will unsettle a great many smug certainties, cause a lot of healthy doubts, and, I hope, will stir up controversy. . . . The more controversy, the better, for the sooner people will begin to think of new solutions. You have done for women what Rachel Carson has done for birds and trees."**

But Lerner was not uncritical. Her life as a Jewish refugee from Nazis (she had been briefly imprisoned in Vienna) had sensitized her to the marginalized, and she had found friends and colleagues among black women ever since arriving in the United States. Now she wrote:

> I have one reservation . . . you address yourself solely to the problems of middle-class, college-educated women. . . . Working women, especially Negro women, labor not only under the disadvantages imposed by the feminine mystique, but under the more pressing disadvantages of economic discrimination. To leave them out of consideration of the problem or to ignore the contributions they can make toward its solution, is something we simply cannot afford to do. . . . It is my belief, that one of the most insidious results of the feminine mystique is that it led women to believe that their problems could be solved on the basis of the individual family. This is, in fact, a serious retrogression, for American women learned before the turn of the century that community solutions to their problems were more . . . far-reaching than the best individual solutions. I have in mind . . . a system of social reforms (daycare centers, maternity benefits . . .), which would bring our social services up to a standard already taken for granted in many European and Scandinavian countries.

How are we to explain such different responses to Friedan's book–in some cases instant agreement, in others instant rejection, and then the complex response articulated by Lerner? Is "the problem" that Friedan identifies a universal one?

The problem lay buried, unspoken, for many years in the minds of American women. It was a strange stirring, a sense of dissatisfaction, a yearning that women suffered in the middle of the twentieth century in the United States. Each suburban wife struggled with it alone. As she made the beds, shopped for groceries, matched slipcover material, ate peanut butter sandwiches with her children, chauffeured Cub Scouts and Brownies, lay beside her husband at night, she was afraid to ask even of herself the silent question—"Is this all?"

For over fifteen years there was no word of this yearning in the millions of words written about women, for women, in all the columns, books and articles by experts telling women their role was to seek fulfillment as wives and mothers. Over and over women heard in voices of tradition and of Freudian sophistication that they could desire no greater destiny than to glory in their own femininity. Experts told them how to catch a man and keep him, how to breast-feed children and handle their toilet training, how to cope with sibling rivalry and adolescent rebellion; how to buy a dishwasher, bake bread, cook gourmet snails, and build a swimming pool with their own hands; how to dress, look, and act more feminine and make marriage more exciting; how to keep their husbands from dying young and their sons from growing into delinquents. They were taught to pity the neurotic, unfeminine, unhappy women who wanted to be poets or physicists or presidents. They learned that truly feminine women do not want careers, higher education, political rights—the independence and the

---

*This interpretation is offered in Susan Douglas, *Where the Girls Are: Growing Up Female with the Mass Media* (New York: Times Books, 1994), ch. 4.

**Gerda Lerner to Betty Friedan, Feb. 6, 1963, in Folder 715, Box 57, Betty Friedan Papers, MC 575, Schlesinger Library, Radcliffe Institute, Harvard University. Reprinted by permission of Stephanie Lerner Lapidus. For digital images of the two-page, typed letter, see http://schlesingerlibrary.omeka.net/items/show/55. Biologist Rachel Carson's *Silent Spring*, an indictment of the human illness and environmental damages caused by pesticides, was published in Sept. 1962, but initially was serialized in *The New Yorker* in the previous months. It garnered much attention and enormous sales.

opportunities that the old-fashioned feminists fought for. Some women, in their forties and fifties, still remembered painfully giving up those dreams, but most of the younger women no longer even thought about them. A thousand expert voices applauded their femininity, their adjustment, their new maturity. All they had to do was devote their lives from earliest girlhood to finding a husband and bearing children.

By the end of the 1950s, the average marriage age of women in America dropped to 20, and was still dropping, into the teens. Fourteen million girls were engaged by 17. The proportion of women attending college in comparison with men dropped from 47 percent in 1920 to 35 percent in 1958. A century earlier, women had fought for higher education; now girls went to college to get a husband. By the mid-fifties, 60 percent dropped out of college to marry, or because they were afraid too much education would be a marriage bar. Colleges built dormitories for "married students," but the students were almost always the husbands. A new degree was instituted for the wives—"Ph.T." (Putting Husband Through).

Then American girls began getting married in high school. And the women's magazines, deploring the unhappy statistics about these young marriages, urged that courses on marriage, and marriage counselors, be installed in the high schools. Girls started going steady at twelve and thirteen, in junior high. Manufacturers put out brassieres with false bosoms of foam rubber for little girls of ten. And an advertisement for a child's dress, size 3–6x, in the *New York Times* in the fall of 1960, said: "She Too Can Join the Man-Trap Set."

By the end of the fifties, the United States birthrate was overtaking India's. The birth-control movement, renamed Planned Parenthood, was asked to find a method whereby women who had been advised that a third or fourth baby would be born dead or defective might have it anyhow. Statisticians were especially astounded at the fantastic increase in the number of babies among college women. Where once they had two children, now they had four, five, six. Women who had once wanted careers were now making careers out of having babies. So rejoiced *Life* magazine in a 1956 paean to the movement of American women back to the home.

In a New York hospital, a woman had a nervous breakdown when she found she could not breast-feed her baby. In other hospitals, women dying of cancer refused a drug which research had proved might save their lives: Its side effects were said to be unfeminine. "If I have only one life, let me live it as a blonde," a larger-than-life-sized picture of a pretty, vacuous woman proclaimed from newspaper, magazine, and drugstore ads. And across America, three out of every ten women dyed their hair blonde. They ate a chalk called Metrecal, instead of food, to shrink to the size of the thin young models. Department-store buyers reported that American women, since 1939, had become three and four sizes smaller. "Women are out to fit the clothes, instead of vice-versa," one buyer said.

Interior decorators were designing kitchens with mosaic murals and original paintings, for kitchens were once again the center of women's lives. Home sewing became a million-dollar industry. Many women no longer left their homes, except to shop, chauffeur their children, or attend a social engagement with their husbands. Girls were growing up in America without ever having jobs outside the home. In the late fifties, a sociological phenomenon was suddenly remarked: A third of American women now worked, but most were no longer young and very few were pursuing careers. They were married women who held part-time jobs, selling or secretarial, to put their husbands through school, their sons through college, or to help pay the mortgage. Or they were widows supporting families. Fewer and fewer women were entering professional work. The shortages in the nursing, social work, and teaching professions caused crises in almost every American city. Concerned over the Soviet Union's lead in the space race, scientists noted that America's greatest source of unused brainpower was women. But girls would not study physics: It was "unfeminine." A girl refused a science fellowship at Johns Hopkins to take a job in a real-estate office. All she wanted, she said, was what every other American girl wanted—to get married, have four children, and live in a nice house in a nice suburb.

The suburban housewife—she was the dream image of the young American women and the envy, it was said, of women all over the world. The American housewife—freed by science and labor-saving appliances from the drudgery, the dangers of childbirth, and the illnesses of her grandmother. She was healthy, beautiful, educated, concerned only about her husband, her children, her home.

She had found true feminine fulfillment. As a housewife and mother, she was respected as a full and equal partner to man in his world. She was free to choose automobiles, clothes, appliances, supermarkets; she had everything that women ever dreamed of.

In the fifteen years after World War II, this mystique of feminine fulfillment became the cherished and self-perpetuating core of contemporary American culture. Millions of women lived their lives in the image of those pretty pictures of the American suburban housewife, kissing their husbands good-bye in front of the picture window, depositing their station wagons full of children at school, and smiling as they ran the new electric waxer over the spotless kitchen floor. They baked their own bread, sewed their own and their children's clothes, kept their new washing machines and dryers running all day. They changed the sheets on the beds twice a week instead of once, took the rug-hooking class in adult education, and pitied their poor frustrated mothers, who had dreamed of having a career. Their only dream was to be perfect wives and mothers; their highest ambition to have five children and a beautiful house, their only fight to get and keep their husbands. They had no thought for the unfeminine problems of the world outside the home; they wanted the men to make the major decisions. They gloried in their role as women, and wrote proudly on the census blank: "Occupation: housewife."

For over fifteen years, the words written for women, and the words women used when they talked to each other, while their husbands sat on the other side of the room and talked shop or politics or septic tanks, were about problems with their children, or how to keep their husbands happy, or improve their children's school, or cook chicken or make slipcovers. Nobody argued whether women were inferior or superior to men; they were simply different. Words like "emancipation" and "career" sounded strange and embarrassing; no one had used them for years. When a Frenchwoman named Simone de Beauvoir wrote a book called *The Second Sex*, an American critic commented that she obviously "didn't know what life was all about," and besides, she was talking about French women. The "woman problem" in America no longer existed.

If a woman had a problem in the 1950s and 1960s she knew that something must be wrong with her marriage, or with herself.

Other women were satisfied with their lives, she thought. What kind of a woman was she if she did not feel this mysterious fulfillment waxing the kitchen floor? She was so ashamed to admit her dissatisfaction that she never knew how many other women shared it. If she tried to tell her husband, he didn't understand what she was talking about. She did not really understand it herself. For over fifteen years women in America found it harder to talk about this problem than about sex. Even the psychoanalysts had no name for it. When a woman went to a psychiatrist for help, as many women did, she would say, "I'm so ashamed," or "I must be hopelessly neurotic." "I don't know what's wrong with women today," a suburban psychiatrist said uneasily. "I only know something is wrong because most of my patients happen to be women. And their problem isn't sexual." Most women with this problem did not go to see a psychoanalyst, however. "There's nothing wrong really," they kept telling themselves. "There isn't any problem."

But on an April morning in 1959, I heard a mother of four, having coffee with four other mothers in a suburban development fifteen miles from New York, say in a tone of quiet desperation, "the problem." And the others knew, without words, that she was not talking about a problem with her husband, or her children, or her home. Suddenly they realized they all shared the same problem, the problem that has no name. They began, hesitantly, to talk about it. Later, after they had picked up their children at nursery school and taken them home to nap, two of the women cried, in sheer relief, just to know they were not alone.

Gradually I came to realize that the problem that has no name was shared by countless women in America. As a magazine writer I often interviewed women about problems with their children, or their marriages, or their houses, or their communities. But after a while I began to recognize the telltale signs of this other problem. I saw the same signs in suburban ranch houses and split-levels on Long Island and in New Jersey and Westchester County; in colonial houses in a small Massachusetts town; on patios in Memphis; in suburban and city apartments; in living rooms in the Midwest. Sometimes I sensed the problem, not as a reporter, but as a suburban housewife, for during this time I was also bringing up my own three children in Rockland County, New York. I heard echoes of the problem in

college dormitories and semi-private maternity wards, at PTA meetings and luncheons of
the League of Women Voters, at suburban
cocktail parties, in station wagons waiting for
trains, and in snatches of conversation overheard at Schrafft's. The groping words I heard
from other women, on quiet afternoons when
children were at school or on quiet evenings
when husbands worked late, I think I understood first as a woman long before I understood their larger social and psychological
implications.

Phyllis Schlafly, "The thoughts of one who loves life as a woman . . ."

Not all well-educated, white middle-class family women with energy and ability to spare reacted to the resurgent domesticity of the Cold War years as did
Betty Goldstein Friedan. Phyllis Stewart Schlafly is a case in point. The two
women had much in common. Separated in age by only three years, both were the
first child born to their respective families, the Goldsteins, who were Jewish, and
the Stewarts, who were Roman Catholic. Both grew up during the Depression
years in Illinois and were valedictorians of their high school classes. Both attended women's colleges, Goldstein choosing prestigious Smith College in Massachusetts and Stewart attending College of the Sacred Heart in Maryville,
Illinois, before transferring to Washington University in St. Louis. Excelling in
college, both entered graduate school, Goldstein studying for an M.A. in psychology at the University of California, Berkeley, Stewart earning an M.A. in political
science at Radcliffe College and Harvard University. (She would later return to
Washington University for a law degree.)

Both went on to interesting jobs, Stewart as a congressional researcher in
Washington, Goldstein as a journalist in New York City. Both subsequently married, Stewart choosing John Fred Schlafly, Jr., a lawyer and fellow conservative,
and Goldstein choosing Carl Friedan, a theatrical producer and later an advertising executive. Both women had children, Schlafly six and Friedan three, whom
they reared in suburbia along with the millions of other middle-class families
caught up in the resurgent domesticity of the postwar years.

Energetic and intelligent, neither found domesticity sufficient. Friedan continued to write, as did Schlafly, who also became a community volunteer, Republican Party activist, and, in 1952, a congressional candidate, winning her primary
but losing in the general election. In the early 1960s, both published first books
that became best-sellers—Friedan *The Feminine Mystique* and Schlafly *A Choice Not
an Echo*, a political endorsement of conservative Arizona senator Barry Goldwater,
the Republican presidential candidate in 1964.

Yet despite these similarities, the personal became political for these two
women in ways that would lead them in sharply divergent directions in the years
ahead. Friedan's name would become synonymous with a resurgent feminism,
Schlafly's with antifeminism. Friedan, as a founder and the first president of the
National Organization for Women (NOW), would champion equal rights for

---

Excerpted from the preface and "Understanding the Difference" of *The Power of the Positive Woman* by Phyllis
Schlafly (New Rochelle, N.Y.: Arlington House, 1977), pp. 9–28. Copyright © 1977 by Phyllis Schlafly. Reprinted
by permission of Crown Publishers, Inc.

women. (For more about the shaping of Friedan's career, see the essay by Daniel Horowitz, pp. 569–580.) Schlafly, creator and author of the *Phyllis Schlafly Report*, would devote her extraordinary energy as well as formidable organizational and speaking skills to defeat of the Equal Rights Amendment (ERA) (see p. 746–747). Equality between the sexes, she insisted, would harm rather than help women.

While Schlafly's states' rights stance partially explains her opposition to using the federal government on behalf of sexual equality, more is involved, as is evident in the following document.

The cry of "women's liberation" leaps out from the "lifestyle" sections of newspapers and the pages of slick magazines, from radio speakers and television screens. Cut loose from past patterns of behavior and expectations, women of all ages are searching for their identity—the college woman who has new alternatives thrust upon her via "women's studies" courses, the young woman whose routine is shattered by a chance encounter with a "consciousness-raising session," the woman in her middle years who suddenly finds herself in the "empty-nest syndrome," the woman of any age whose lover or lifetime partner departs for greener pastures (and a younger crop).

All of these women, thanks to the women's liberation movement, no longer see their predicament in terms of personal problems to be confronted and solved. They see their own difficulties as a little cog in the big machine of establishment restraints and stereotypical injustice in which they have lost their own equilibrium. Who am I? Why am I here? Why am I just another faceless victim of society's oppression, a nameless prisoner behind walls too high for me to climb alone? . . .

For a woman to find her identity in the modern world, the path should be sought from the Positive Women who have found the road and possess the map, rather than from those who have not. In this spirit, I share with you the thoughts of one who loves life as a woman and lives love as a woman, whose credentials are from the school of practical experience, and who has learned that fulfillment as a woman is a journey, not a destination.

Like every human being born into this world, the Positive Woman has her share of sorrows and sufferings, of unfulfilled desires and bitter defeats. But she will never be crushed by life's disappointments, because her positive mental attitude has built her an inner security that the actions of other people can never fracture. To the Positive Woman, her

particular set of problems is not a conspiracy against her, but a challenge to her character and her capabilities.

The first requirement for the acquisition of power by the Positive Woman is to understand the differences between men and women. Your outlook on life, your faith, your behavior, your potential for fulfillment, all are determined by the parameters of your original premise. The Positive Woman starts with the assumption that the world is her oyster. She rejoices in the creative capability within her body and the power potential of her mind and spirit. She understands that men and women are different, and that those very differences provide the key to her success as a person and fulfillment as a woman.

The women's liberationist, on the other hand, is imprisoned by her own negative view of herself and of her place in the world around her. . . . Someone—it is not clear who, perhaps God, perhaps the "Establishment," perhaps a conspiracy of male chauvinist pigs—dealt women a foul blow by making them female. It becomes necessary, therefore, for women to agitate and demonstrate and hurl demands on society in order to wrest from an oppressive male-dominated social structure the status that has been wrongfully denied to women through the centuries. . . . Confrontation replaces cooperation as the watchword of all relationships. Women and men become adversaries instead of partners. . . . Within the confines of the women's liberationist ideology, therefore, the abolition of this overriding inequality of women becomes the primary goal.

This goal must be achieved at any and all costs—to the woman herself, to the baby, to the family, and to society. Women must be made equal to men in their ability *not* to become pregnant and *not* to be expected to care for babies they may bring into the world. This is why women's liberationists are compulsively involved in the drive to make abortion and

Phyllis Schlafly demonstrated the domestic ideal by posing cooking her husband's breakfast the morning after her victory in the 1952 Republican congressional primary. She would lose her bid for a congressional seat but continue to be active as a party volunteer. In 1964, she was a strong supporter of Republican presidential candidate Barry Goldwater, and the author of one of the most effective pieces of his campaign literature, A Choice Not an Echo. *The first printing sold more than 600,000 copies and made her national reputation; there were two more printings before Election Day. In 1967, she lost her bid for the presidency of the National Federation of Republican Women (NFRW). In the early 1970s, the NFRW endorsed the ERA. Independently, Schlafly mobilized women behind conservative issues like free enterprise and support for nuclear weapons development. When she began to publicize her opposition to the ERA, the circulation of* The Phyllis Schlafly Report *bounced quickly from 3,000 to 35,000 and continued to grow. Her organization, the Eagle Forum, took the lead in developing opposition to the ERA and to feminism generally. (*St. Louis Globe-Democrat *photo. Courtesy of the Collections of the St. Louis Mercantile Library at the University of Missouri–St. Louis. Caption courtesy of Catherine Rymph.)*

child-care centers for all women, regardless of religion or income, both socially acceptable and government-financed. . . .

If man is targeted as the enemy, and the ultimate goal of women's liberation is independence from men and the avoidance of pregnancy and its consequences, then lesbianism is logically the highest form in the ritual of women's liberation. . . .

The Positive Woman will never travel that dead-end road. It is self-evident to the Positive Woman that the female body with its baby-producing organs was not designed by a conspiracy of men but by the Divine Architect of the human race. Those who think it is unfair that women have babies, whereas men cannot, will have to take up their complaint with God because no other power is capable of changing that fundamental fact. . . . The Positive Woman looks upon her femaleness and her fertility as part of her purpose, her potential, and her power. She rejoices that she has a capability for creativity that men can never have.

The third basic dogma of the women's liberation movement is that there is no difference between male and female except the sex organs, and that all those physical, cognitive, and emotional differences you *think* are there, are merely the result of centuries of restraints imposed by a male-dominated society and sex-stereotyped schooling. The role imposed on women is, by definition, inferior, according to the women's liberationists. . . .

There are countless physical differences between men and women. The female body is 50 to 60 percent water, the male 60 to 70 percent water, which explains why males can dilute alcohol better than women and delay its effect. The average woman is about 25 percent fatty tissue, while the male is 15 percent, making women more buoyant in water and able to swim with less effort. Males have a tendency to color blindness. Only 5 percent of persons who get gout are female. Boys are born bigger. Women live longer in most countries of the world, not only in the United States where we have a hard-driving competitive pace. Women excel in manual dexterity, verbal skills, and memory recall. . . .

Does the physical advantage of men doom women to a life of servility and subservience? The Positive Woman knows that she has a complementary advantage which is at least as great—and, in the hands of a skillful woman, far greater. The Divine Architect who gave men a superior strength to lift weights also gave women a different kind of superior strength. . . . A Positive Woman cannot defeat a man in a wrestling or boxing match, but she can motivate him, inspire him, encourage him, teach him, restrain him, reward him, and have power over him that he can never achieve over her with all his muscle. How or whether a Positive Woman uses her power is determined solely by the way she alone defines her goals and develops her skills.

The differences between men and women are also emotional and psychological. Without woman's innate maternal instinct, the human race would have died out centuries ago. . . . The overriding psychological need of a woman is to love something alive. A baby fulfills this need in the lives of most women. If a baby is not available to fill that need, women search for a baby-substitute. This is the reason why women have traditionally gone into teaching and nursing careers. They are doing what comes naturally to the female psyche. The schoolchild or the patient of any age provides an outlet for a woman to express her natural maternal need. . . . The Positive Woman finds somebody on whom she can lavish her maternal love so that it doesn't well up inside her and cause psychological frustrations. Surely no woman is so isolated by geography or insulated by spirit that she cannot find someone worthy of her maternal love. . . .

One of the strangest quirks of women's liberationists is their complaint that societal restraints prevent men from crying in public or showing their emotions, but permit women to do so, and that therefore we should "liberate" men to enable them, too, to cry in public. The public display of fear, sorrow, anger, and irritation reveals a lack of self-discipline that should be avoided by the Positive Woman just as much as by the Positive Man. Maternal love, however, is not a weakness but a manifestation of strength and service, and it should be nurtured by the Positive Woman. . . .

Another silliness of the women's liberationists is their frenetic desire to force all women to accept the title *Ms* in place of *Miss* or *Mrs.* If Gloria Steinem and Betty Friedan want to call themselves *Ms* in order to conceal their marital status, their wishes should be respected. But most married women feel they worked hard for the *r* in their names; and they don't care to be gratuitously deprived of it. . . .

Finally, women are different from men in dealing with the fundamentals of life itself. Men are philosophers, women are practical, and 'twas ever thus. Men may philosophize about how life began and where we are heading; women are concerned about feeding the kids today. No woman would ever, as Karl Marx did, spend years reading political philosophy in the British Museum while her child starved to death. Women don't take naturally to a search for the intangible and the abstract. . . . Where man is discursive, logical, abstract, or philosophical, woman tends to be emotional, personal, practical, or mystical. Each set of qualities is vital and complements the other. Among the many differences explained in [Amaury] de Riencourt's book, [*Sex and Power in History*], are the following:

> Women tend more toward conformity than men—which is why they often excel in such disciplines as spelling and punctuation where there

is only one correct answer, determined by social authority. Higher intellectual activities, however, require a mental independence and power of abstraction that they usually lack, not to mention a certain form of aggressive boldness of the imagination which can only exist in a sex that is basically aggressive for biological reasons.

To sum up: The masculine proclivity in problem solving is analytical and categorical; the feminine, synthetic and contextual.... Deep down, man tends to focus on the object, on external results and achievements; woman focuses on subjective motives and feelings. If life can be compared to a play, man focuses on the theme and structure of the play, woman on the innermost feelings displayed by the actors.

De Riencourt provides impressive refutation of two of the basic errors of the women's liberation movement: (1) that there are no emotional or cognitive differences between the sexes, and (2) that women should strive to be like men.... An effort to eliminate the differences by social engineering or legislative or constitutional tinkering cannot succeed, which is fortunate, but social relationships and spiritual values can be ruptured in the attempt....

RETHINKING FAMILY AND SEX

JOANNE MEYEROWITZ
Christine Jorgensen and the Story of How Sex Changed

In 1952, Christine Jorgensen made the front-page of newspapers around the world. Jorgensen, an Army veteran, underwent medical procedures to transform from being a man to a woman. Examining the publicity about Jorgensen, and tracing the media attention to transsexuals back to the 1930s, Joanne Meyerowitz argues that a modern transsexual identity was created partly through the media. Some readers identified with and sought the advice of those who had sex changes. Before the mid-twentieth century, these surgical procedures had taken place only in Europe.

Why did Jorgensen become a celebrity in the 1950s? How does her treatment in the media mirror and differ from other press interest in transsexuals? How does transsexuality raise questions about what it means to be a woman? What characteristics makes one a woman? What does it mean to identify as a woman?

On December 1, 1952, the *New York Daily News* announced the "sex change" surgery of Christine Jorgensen. The front-page headline read: "Ex-GI Becomes Blonde Beauty: Operations Transform Bronx Youth," and the story told how Jorgensen had traveled to Denmark for "a rare and complicated treatment." For years, Jorgensen, born and reared as a boy, had struggled with what she later described as an ineffable, inexorable, and increasingly unbearable yearning to live her life as a woman. In 1950 she sailed to Europe in search of a doctor who would alter her bodily sex. Within months she found an endocrinologist who agreed to administer hormones if she would in return cooperate with his research. Over the next two years she took massive doses of estrogen and underwent two major surgeries to transform her genitals. At the end of 1952 the *New York Daily News* transformed her obscure personal triumph into mass media sensation.

The initial scoop immediately escalated to a frenzy. In the first two weeks of coverage, according to *Newsweek*, the three major wire services sent out 50,000 words on the Christine Jorgensen story. Reporters cast Jorgensen, who was young and conventionally beautiful, as the personification of glamour, akin to a Hollywood starlet on the rise. They followed her every move in Copenhagen and hounded her parents at their home in the Bronx. In the winter of 1953 Jorgensen returned to the United States and surrendered to her celebrity. In the summer she launched a successful nightclub act that kept her name on marquees and her body in spotlights for the rest of the decade.[1]

Jorgensen was more than a media sensation, a stage act, or a cult figure. Her story opened debate on the visibility and mutability of sex. It raised questions that resonated with force in the 1950s and engage us still today. How do we determine who is male and who is female,

Excerpted and slightly revised by the author from *How Sex Changed: A History of Transsexuality in the United States* by Joanne Meyerowitz (Cambridge, Mass.: Harvard University Press, 2002), 1–5, 95–97, 286; and "Sex Change and the Popular Press: Historical Notes on Transsexuality in the United States, 1930–1955," by Joanne Meyerowitz, in *GLQ: A Journal of Lesbian and Gay Studies* 4, no. 2 (1998): 159–187. Reprinted by permission of the author and publishers. Notes have been edited and renumbered.

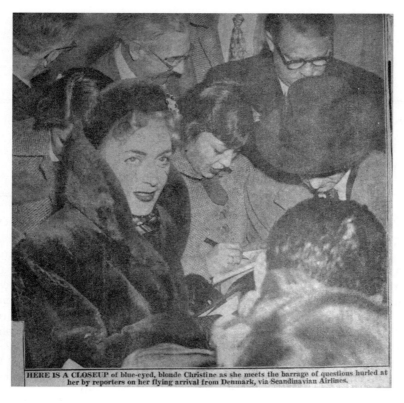

HERE IS A CLOSEUP of blue-eyed, blonde Christine as she meets the barrage of questions hurled at her by reporters on her flying arrival from Denmark, via Scandinavian Airlines.

Christine Jorgensen is met by the press on the day she returns to New York, after surgery in Denmark. New York Daily Mirror, *Feb. 13, 1953. (Image courtesy of the Kinsey Institute for Research in Sex, Gender, and Reproduction.)*

and why do we care? Can humans actually change sex? Is sex less apparent than it seems? As a narrative of boundary transgression, the Jorgensen story fascinated readers and elicited their surprise, and as an unusual variant on a familiar tale of striving and success, it inspired them. It opened possibilities for those who questioned their own sex and offered an exoticized travelogue for armchair tourists who had never imagined that one could take a journey across the sex divide. In the post–World War II era, with heightened concerns about science and sex, the Jorgensen story compelled some readers to spell out their own versions of the boundaries of sex, and it convinced others to reconsider the categories they thought they already knew. In response, American doctors and scientists began to explore the process of defining sex.

In the mid-twentieth century, sex was already high on the American cultural agenda. For decades Americans of all sorts had found themselves inundated with news, research, stories, opinions, and imperatives about the multiple meanings of "sex." The study of sex hormones and sex chromosomes had removed the biology of sex from the visible realm of genitals to the microscopic gaze, and the uncertainty of it all eventually set the International Olympic Committee, among others, on an elusive quest to decide who counts as a woman and who counts as a man. The growing numbers of women in the labor force and the early twentieth-century women's movement had put issues of sex equality and sex difference at the forefront of political life, and the emergence of gay and lesbian subcultures had created visible spots of sexual variation within the urban landscape. Meanwhile the mass media had made sex a mainstay of the visual culture, and popular versions of Freud and other sexologists had given sex a recognized role in the modern discourse of psychology. The new ideal of "consenting adults" had positioned sex as a key component of liberal freedom, while older ideals still made moving targets of anyone who strayed from expectations that sex belonged in marriage. In broad outline and narrow, American society had "sexualized" in the first half of the century.[2]

And the vocabulary of sex had begun to change. At the dawn of the century the word *sex* covered a range of phenomena. In popular and scientific formulations, sex signified not only female and male but also traits, attitudes, and behaviors associated with women and men and with erotic acts. In various attempts to delineate the components of sex, some observers tried to sort the sex "characteristics." They separated "primary sexual features," found in the genitals and gonads, from "secondary" features, seen in breasts, beards, and other physical differences that usually appeared after puberty, from "tertiary" features, as evidenced in erotic drives, from "fourth-order" features, manifest in traits, mannerisms, and even occupations and clothes. Or they distinguished "anatomical" sex, the sex of the body, from "functional" sex, the ways men and women thought and behaved.[3] Despite a few dissenters, most observers adhered to a biological determinism. The desires and practices known as masculine and feminine seemed to spring from the same biological processes that divided female and male. All came bundled together within the broad-ranging concept of "sex."

By midcentury this concept had begun to break down. Various experts used different terms to distinguish one meaning of sex from another. Anthropologist Margaret Mead chose *sex roles* to describe the culturally constructed behaviors expected of women and men. Sex researcher Alfred C. Kinsey adopted the term *sexual behavior* to outline a range of erotic practices. And the "sex" of the body no longer provided adequate explanation of either "sex roles" or "sexual behavior." By the end of the century the earlier understanding of sex had given way to three categories of inquiry and analysis: "biological sex" referred to chromosomes, genes, genitals, hormones, and other physical markers, some of which could be modified and some of which could not; "gender" represented masculinity, femininity, and the behaviors commonly associated with them; and "sexuality" connoted the erotic, now sorted into a range of urges, fantasies, and behaviors. Once seen as outgrowths of a primary sex division, "gender" and "sexuality" no longer seemed to spring directly from the biological categories of female and male. In fact some scholars envisioned sex, gender, and

sexuality as constructed categories constantly defined and redefined in social, cultural, and intellectual processes and performances.[4] They thus directly rejected the older belief in a universal, unchanging biological sex that dictated both the behavior of women and men and their sexual desires.

Jorgensen's story and the history of transsexuality are central parts of this reconceptualization of sex in the twentieth century. The notion that biological sex is mutable, that we define and redefine it, that we can divide it into constituent parts, such as chromosomes, hormones, and genitals, and modify some of those parts, that male and female are not opposites, that masculinity and femininity do not spring automatically from biological sex, that neither biological sex nor gender determines the contours of sexual desire—these were significant shifts in American social and scientific thought. . . . [These shifts] occurred piecemeal through vociferous conflict and debate, and because not everyone accepted them, they laid the groundwork for ongoing contests over the meanings of biological sex, the sources of gender, and the categories of sexuality. . . .

Jorgensen was not the first transsexual, nor was the publicity accorded her the first media coverage of sex-change surgery. Cross-gender identification, the sense of being the other sex, and the desire to live as the other sex all existed in various forms in earlier centuries and other cultures. The historical record includes countless examples of males who dressed or lived as women and females who dressed or lived as men.[5] Transsexuality, the quest to transform the bodily characteristics of sex via hormones and surgery, originated in the early twentieth century. By the 1910s European scientists had begun to publicize their attempts to transform the sex of animals, and by the 1920s a few doctors, mostly in Germany, had agreed to alter the bodies of a few patients who longed to change their sex.

In Europe, the medical practice of sex change arose less as a result of new technology than as a result of new understandings of sex. . . . [T]he scientists and doctors who endorsed sex-change surgery posited a universal mixed-sex condition, in which all males had female features and all females male features. This theory of universal bisexuality directly challenged a[n earlier] . . . vision of binary sex that saw female and male as distinct, immutable, and opposite. With this novel conception of sex, a few doctors began to use hormones and surgery to enable a few people who pleaded for bodily change to move toward the female or male ends of a perceived continuum.

In the United States the public discourse on transsexuals came first through popular culture, then through science and medicine, and eventually through the courts. It also came from the people who hoped to change their sex. They were a diverse group with a wide array of political views. They were [neither] "dupes of gender," who tampered with their bodies in the name of gender ideology, [n]or conscious radicals, who purposefully [wished to] . . . destabilize traditional norms.[6] Many . . . expressed the desire to live as men or women, and not as something other or in between . . . Like everyone else, they articulated their sense of self with the language and cultural forms available to them. They were neither symbols . . . nor heroes or villains engaged in mythic battles to further or stifle progress. They were instead ordinary and extraordinary human beings who searched for workable solutions to pressing personal problems. In so doing they investigated, debated, promoted, and accelerated new definitions of sex, gender, and sexuality.[7]

B.C. (BEFORE CHRISTINE)

. . . Surgical attempts at changing sex first won publicity in the early 1910s when Eugen Steinach, a physiologist in Vienna, attracted international acclaim for his "transplantation" experiments on rats and guinea pigs. In 1912, Steinach published "Arbitrary Transformation of Male Mammals into Animals with Pronounced Female Sex Characteristics and Feminine Psyche," followed in 1913 by "Feminization of Males and Masculization of Females." The articles, soon scientific classics, demonstrated that castrated infant male guinea pigs implanted with ovaries developed certain characteristics associated with females and that castrated infant female guinea pigs implanted with testes developed characteristics of males. Steinach claimed to have found the specific impacts of "male" and "female" hormones, thus placing his research in the larger turn-of-the-century scientific project that attempted to locate a biological sexual essence in gonadal secretions. His research also suggested the possibility of medically transforming sex. As he put it, "The implantation of the gonad of the opposite sex transforms the original sex of an animal." His work directly influenced Magnus Hirschfeld, Harry Benjamin, and other sexological scientists.[8]

. . . A few records of surgery for humans [exist in this period for the United States. They involved] removal of body parts such as testicles, uteri, and breasts, [thus] a form of intervention that did not require advanced medical technology. Alberta Lucille Hart, a [young] physician in Oregon, pursued surgery as a means of changing sex. As a child, Hart, reared as a girl, considered himself a boy, and as an adult he wore masculine collars, ties, hats, and shoes along with the requisite skirts. In 1917, at the age of twenty-six, Hart persuaded psychiatrist J. Allen Gilbert to recommend hysterectomy. The surgery required medical justification, in this case the relief of painful menstruation. In the quest for surgery, Hart also employed a form of eugenic reasoning, advising "sterilization" for "any individual" with "abnormal inversion." . . . After surgery, haircut, and change of attire, Hart "started as a male with a new hold on life," and as Alan Lucill Hart he had successful careers as a radiologist and a novelist.[9]

Although we have isolated examples of early surgery in the United States, the quest for sex change seems to have been more widely acknowledged in Europe. . . . By the 1920s, Germany stood at the forefront of the human sex change experiments, with Magnus Hirschfeld's Institute for Sexual Science in Berlin at center stage. Hirschfeld encountered female-to-male "transvestites" who requested mastectomy and preparations for beard growth and males-to-females who sought castration, elimination of facial hair, and "apparatus for making the breasts bigger." For Hirschfeld, hermaphrodites, androgynes, homosexuals, and transvestites constituted distinct types of sexual "intermediates," natural variations that all likely had inborn, organic bases. He considered transvestism "a harmless inclination" and advocated the social acceptance of transvestites. He listened seriously to the desire to change sex expressed by some of the subjects he studied, and he began to recommend surgery. In 1931, German physician Felix Abraham, who worked at the Institute, published the first scientific report on modern transsexual surgery, an article on the male-to-female genital transformation (*Genitalumwandlung*) of two "homosexual transvestites." The illustrated account of surgery included castration, amputation of the penis, and creation of an artificial vagina. Abraham believed that countless other patients wanted similar operations.[10]

Word of the sex change experiments in Germany reached a wider public in the early

1930s when the press reported on Danish artist Einar Wegener, who became Lili Elbe. The operations began with castration in Berlin, following psychological tests conducted by Hirschfeld at the Institute for Sexual Science. Later, in Dresden, doctors removed the penis and allegedly also transplanted human ovaries. Elbe died from heart failure in 1931 after a final operation, an attempt to create a "natural outlet from the womb." Before her death, the story broke in Danish and German newspapers and soon thereafter appeared in book form in both Danish and German.[11] . . .

At least one American, Florence Winter (a pseudonym), born around 1900, investigated the medical possibilities for female-to-male sex change in Europe. She went to Germany, probably in the 1920s, "to find solutions to her problems of homosexuality and transvestism." In Chicago, she had felt "isolated from her kind," but in Berlin she found others like her through association with Hirschfeld's Institute. She underwent "years of analysis before she could overthrow her guilt feelings about herself." Hirschfeld himself agreed to arrange her sex change surgery. "However, when he warned her that after the operations she would not be either a man or a woman, she backed out." Perhaps Hirschfeld meant that Winter would not have reproductive capacities, or perhaps be referred to the crude technology of phalloplasty that could not create a functioning penis. In any case, after living for "a long time" as a man, Winter left Europe at the outbreak of World War II and returned to Chicago, where she lived again as a lesbian.[12]

While few Americans, it seems, traveled to Europe for sex changes, more began to learn through the mass media of new possibilities for medical intervention. . . . In 1933, Dutton published the first English translation of the Lili Elbe story, *Man into Woman: An Authentic Record of a Change of Sex.* The book presented its subject as an occasional cross-dresser whose female personality had come to predominate. More dubiously, it also depicted her as a hermaphrodite with "stunted and withered ovaries" as well as testicles. The book included an introduction by British sexologist Norman Haire, who informed readers of Steinach's transplantation experiments on animals but considered it "unwise to carry out, even at the patient's own request, such operations" as those performed on Elbe.[13] . . .

These and other stories of sex changes attempted to lure American readers with shocking accounts of unusual behavior, rare biological problems, and astonishing surgical solutions. Such stories often appeared on the margins of the mainstream press, in sensational magazines, tabloid newspapers, or publications like *Sexology* that presented the science of sex to a popular audience. They covered cases of cross-gender behavior, intersexuality, homosexuality, and transvestism, sometimes without distinguishing among them, and frequently depicted them all as interrelated pathologies in need of medical cure. They occasionally mentioned "sex reversals" of the "purely psychical" kind but presented them as homosexuality that did not qualify for surgery. Sometimes they reported metamorphoses wherein a woman or man, perhaps with a glandular disturbance, underwent spontaneous changes in bodily sex and gendered behavior during late adolescence or adulthood. (A typical headline read, "Boy Prisoner Slowly Changing into a Girl.") More generally, though, the articles mentioned surgery but failed to specify what it entailed. They depicted sex change surgery as unveiling a true but hidden physiological sex and thus tied the change to a biological mooring that justified surgical intervention. These stories often reinforced stereotypes of gender and sexuality by locating the sources of gendered and erotic behavior in the sex of the physical body. In this binarist vision of sex, science could and should correct nature's tragic "rare blunders," creating an unambiguous male or female sex from a condition of ambiguity.[14]

In the second half of the 1930s, these features appeared in widely reported accounts of European women athletes who became men. In 1935, twenty-three-year-old Belgian cycling champion Elvira de Bruyne changed sex and began to live as Willy. About a year later, British shot-put and javelin champion Mary Edith Louise Weston underwent two operations and adopted the name Mark, and Czechoslovakian runner Zdenka Koubkova became Zdenek Koubkov through what one report termed "a delicate surgical operation." Because he came to New York in 1936, the American press covered Koubkov's case extensively. Considered female at his birth in 1913, Koubkov grew up as "an utterly masculine youth" who resisted feminine clothes and domestic training. As he aged, "the feeling of masculinity began to assert itself," and he longed for women sexually, "his imagination inflamed by reading French novels." He competed as a woman in the 1932 Olympics, setting a world record in the 800-meter event, but in his early twenties "a great light dawned," and he realized he was a man. Four months after a procedure described only as a "flick of a surgeon's scalpel," Koubkov came to New York to perform in a *tableau vivant* in the French Casino, a Broadway club. He ran on a treadmill, chasing a woman, foreshadowing Christine Jorgensen's later staged performances of gender.[15] In part, the press attention reflected discomfort with women athletes and confirmed popular opinions that athletic women were, if not actually men, at least suspiciously mannish. But the stories also provided further publicity for the possibility of changing sex.[16] . . .

[Some physicians] tried to dissuade readers [from imagining that] "we are on the threshold of new discoveries which will enable any individual to be changed to the sex he or she prefers."[17] . . . Despite the warning, . . . the publicity accorded to sex change surgery caught the attention of individuals who identified possibilities in it for themselves. *Sexology* published several letters from readers in search of information. In 1934, one letter writer explained: "I have a peculiar complex—I believe it is called 'Eonism.' That is, I desire to dress as a woman. . . . The fact is I have an even stronger desire, and that is—I wish I were a woman. . . . I am interested in the Steinach operation in regard to change of sex. I would like more information." In 1937, a "Miss E. T." from Nebraska asked: "Is it possible through a surgical operation, or several operations, to change a female into a male? I have read something—not very informative—about such things having been done. . . . Could you give me any idea of the method, and also of the cost?" In "They Want to Change Sexes" (1937), *Sexology* acknowledged that press reports on European athletes had "stirred" some of its readers, who now asked "whether it is possible, and if so, how and where." The magazine summarized a handful of letters (both male-to-female and female-to-male). The fragmentary presentation of the letters makes it impossible to know to what extent readers used the popular narratives to plot stories about themselves, but one letter suggests some readers might have fitted the stories of intersexuality to their own wants. A woman who described herself as "nothing feminine" but "apparently of [the female] sex" asked: "If it were true that I have both male and female organs of reproduction, would it not be advisable to undergo what operations are necessary to become the male I wish to be? Can you refer me to a competent surgeon who would be interested in my case?"[18]

The magazine did not offer the information that letter writers sought and tried instead to discourage them. In response to one male-to-female inquiry, the editor acknowledged that the letter writer could have "the operation of complete castration" and thereafter live as a woman but warned that surgery would create a "completely sexless creature." The editor stated bluntly to a female-to-male correspondent, "There is no operation whereby a *normal female* can be changed to a normal male, or a normal male into normal female. The operations you have read of were performed on 'hermaphrodites.'" Through the 1940s, *Sexology* continued to advise such readers, whom it sometimes called "inverts" or "homosexuals," that doctors performed such surgery for cases of intersexuality only. Nevertheless, it continued to run stories about men who became women and women who became men, and letter writers continued to ask for sex change operations.[19]

Dr. David O. Cauldwell, *Sexology*'s question-and-answer department editor, coined the English-language term transsexual. In a 1949 article, he chose the phrase "psychopathia transexualis" . . . to describe the case of "Earl," who asked Cauldwell "to find a surgeon" who would remove breasts and ovaries, "close the vagina," and construct "an artificial penis." Cauldwell acknowledged that a surgeon could perform such operations, but he refused to endorse them, stating that the artificial penis would have "no material use" and "no more sexual feeling than a fingernail." Furthermore, he considered it "criminal" for a doctor to remove healthy glands and tissues.[20]

What distinguished this article from earlier ones was the definition of "psychopathia transexualis" as an independent sexological category. Cauldwell dissociated this request for surgery from cases of intersexuality and glandular disorder. To Cauldwell, a psychiatrist, transsexuals were "products, largely of unfavorable childhood environment." And although Earl was sexually drawn to women, the article also distinguished transsexuals from homosexuals. The caption to an accompanying surreal illustration (of a double-headed man/woman binding his/her breasts) read, "Many individuals have an irresistible desire to have their sex changed surgically. . . . These persons are not necessarily homosexuals." Cauldwell elaborated in a 1950 pamphlet, *Questions and Answers on the Sex Life and Sexual Problems of Trans-Sexuals.* The pamphlet's subheading summarized the key points: "Trans-sexuals are individuals who

Sept. **1937**

SEXOLOGY

THE MAGAZINE
OF

SEX SCIENCE

ILLUSTRATED

CONTENTS

TRUTHFUL AND EDUCATIONAL

KNOWLEDGE OF SELF

THE DOORWAY TO

$3.— A YEAR

As Joanne Meyerowitz explains, "from the 1930s on, the popular magazine Sexology *carried articles on sex changes, including the article 'They Want to Change Sexes' in this September 1937 issue." (Image Courtesy of the Kinsey Institute for Research in Sex, Gender, and Reproduction.)*

are physically of one sex and apparently psychologically of the opposite sex. Trans-sexuals include heterosexuals, homosexuals, bisexuals and others. A large element of transvestites have trans-sexual leanings."[21] In this way, Cauldwell separated gender, described as psychological sex, from biological sex and sexuality. Cross-gender identification and the request for surgery were not necessarily linked either to intersexed conditions or to same-sex desire.

In constructing his definition, Cauldwell relied on the letters of those he now called "trans-sexuals." He had a voluminous correspondence—in part as a *Sexology* editor but even more as the author of numerous pamphlets on sex published in the popular Blue Book series of Haldeman-Julius Publications, a counter-cultural "freethinking" press.[22] In the pamphlet on transsexuals, Cauldwell quoted extensively from letters he had received. Some letter writers already expressed a sense of the surgical possibilities, and sometimes they explained their knowledge with direct reference to what they had read in magazines, newspapers, and sexological writings. A thirty-three-year-old male-to-female cross-dresser who had lived as a woman for fourteen years wrote: "Everything leads to the fact that I have developed a burning desire to be made into a woman. I've read of a number of such instances. The reports were in the daily press and must have been true." Cauldwell expressed annoyance with the persistent requests for surgery. He blamed medicine for creating "fantastic hopes" and popular magazines for publishing "tales of magic cures and magical accomplishments of surgeons."[23]

Indeed, by midcentury, some popular American magazines, especially of the sensational bent, no longer insisted that sex change surgery was for intersexed conditions only. One article stated: "With hormones plus surgery, there's little doubt that, in the not far future . . . doctors can take a full grown normal adult and—if he or she desires it—completely reverse his or her sex." Another granted: "The fact that sex is mutable has been illustrated in definite instances of men who have been physiologically turned to women and women to men."[24] Doctors could, as the magazines claimed, alter the bodily sex characteristics of nonintersexed patients, but in the United States they still generally refused to do so. While the popular literature increasingly broached the possibility of surgically altering sex, even a sympathetic doctor could not arrange the operations.

Endocrinologist Harry Benjamin—born, reared, and trained in Germany—came to the United States in 1913 and established himself as an expert on aging and prostitution. . . . Benjamin saw himself as "a maverick or an outsider," an advocate for sexual freedom who did not have the same hesitancy to intervene on behalf of transgendered patients that American-born doctors often exhibited. As an endocrinologist, he placed greater faith in hormone treatments and glandular surgery than in attempts at psychotherapeutic cures. A friend and follower of both Steinach and Hirschfeld, he assumed that cross-gender identification had some physiological cause and saw transsexuals as desperate patients in need of his medical help.[25]

In 1949 Benjamin met a patient, referred [to him] by Kinsey, who was desperate to change sex. Val Barry (a pseudonym), who already lived as a woman, had spent most of her childhood as a girl. In 1948, at the age of twenty-two, she entered a hospital in her home state of Wisconsin for psychiatric examination. Like many other transgendered individuals, she had read a variety of works on sex and sexology, including *Man into Woman*, and she now expressed the "desire to be changed surgically." She "refused to consider any other alternative," including any "brain surgery" that might eliminate her "desire to remain a female mentally." More than thirty hospital staff members met to discuss her case and recommended castration and plastic surgery, but the state attorney general's office "ruled against the operations as constituting mayhem," a strange interpretation of statutes descended from British common law forbidding the maiming of potential soldiers.[26]

In May 1949, Barry wrote to Benjamin for help. After reading her medical history, Benjamin promised to write to Germany to find out what the law stipulated there. In the meantime, he advised female hormones and also raised the possibility of "x-ray castration" as well as "x-ray treatment of your face to remove the hair growth." In the summer of 1949, at his office in San Francisco, he began to administer hormones to Barry and to search for surgeons in the United States. He contacted district attorney (later governor) Edmund G. Brown about the legality of castration in California. Initially, Brown did not envision any legal obstacles to sex-change surgery, but after consulting another lawyer he sent Benjamin a discouraging memorandum. . . . Soon after, psychiatrists at the Langley Porter Clinic in San Francisco refused to endorse the surgery, and a surgeon in Chicago, initially sympathetic, also failed to help.[27] It was not until 1953, after the publicity about Jorgensen, that Barry finally had her surgery in Sweden.

A.D. (AFTER DENMARK)

In 1952 and 1953, the coverage of Christine Jorgensen far exceeded any previous reporting on sex changes. Jorgensen rose to the rank of celebrity in the mainstream press as well as in tabloid, pulp, and countercultural publications. Aside from their more extensive dissemination, though, the initial stories on Jorgensen generally replicated the key features found in earlier accounts of sex change. They announced a startling bodily change, referred to surgery but usually failed to specify what it encompassed, and attempted to tie the change of sex to an intersexed condition. Reporters consulted American doctors, most of whom assumed that Jorgensen was a pseudohermaphrodite with internal female gonads but external male characteristics. For one Associated Press story, "Thousands Do Not Know True Sex," a reporter went to the American Medical Association convention and interviewed doctors, who immediately associated sex change surgery with such intersexed conditions. In other reports, journalists found doctors who reported cases of pseudohermaphroditism that they considered similar to Jorgensen's. Urologist Elmer Hess of Erie, Pennsylvania, told of "Hundreds of Boy-Girl Operations." Another doctor claimed to have "performed five operations similar to" Jorgensen's, cases in which "the actual sex had been disguised and was simply released." *Time* magazine soon assessed these reports as the "expert opinion" of doctors who "pooh-poohed the story as anything new . . . far from a medical rarity . . . [with] similar cases in hospitals all over the U.S. right now."[28]

Nonetheless, there was from the beginning a hint that the Jorgensen story might be different. In the first week of publicity, G. B. Lal, the science editor of *American Weekly* (a nationally distributed Sunday newspaper supplement), suggested that Jorgensen "was physically speaking, adequately a male, yet somehow felt the urge to be a woman." Such a situation "would call for drastic alterations—such as no doctor would perform in this country." Lal then referred to Harry Benjamin and cases of "transvestism" but immediately retreated to a discussion of intersexed conditions. "We may assume," Lal wrote, "still without knowing the facts, that Jorgensen was a case of sex confusion—what is known as pseudo-hermaphroditism, in which one's inborn real sex is hidden." As in earlier cases, the muddled reporting attracted transgendered readers who wondered about the journalists' claims. In early December, shortly after the story broke, Louise Lawrence, a full-time male-to-female cross-dresser in San Francisco, wrote to Benjamin: "This case, I think, has received more publicity even than Barbara [Richards Wilcox]'s ten years ago." She could not, though, "make any concrete decision regarding it because there have actually been no absolute facts given." Still, she wondered why Jorgensen would have traveled to Denmark for "a case of hermaphroditism" that "could be handled in this country very easily. . . . From the papers, it seems that such cases are being handled all over the country."[29]

As the publicity continued, the press began to publish new details that gradually undermined the initial reports. In mid-February, *American Weekly* orchestrated Jorgensen's return to New York to coincide with the publication of its exclusive five-part series, Jorgensen's "The Story of My Life," "the only authorized and complete account of the most dramatic transformation of modern times." The series adopted a first-person confessional formula that personalized the coverage and invited readers to sympathize with Jorgensen's ordeal. As *American Weekly* later reported, it saw the story "not as a sensationalized bit of erotica, but as the courageous fight of a desperately unhappy person with the fortitude to overcome a seemingly hopeless obstacle." With the help of a veteran reporter, Jorgensen emphasized the "feminine qualities" she had manifested as the lonely boy George, including a teenage romantic attraction to a male friend. To explain her problem, Jorgensen did not adopt the metaphor, common by the 1960s, of a woman "trapped" in a male body.[30] Instead, she referred to herself as "lost between sexes," a phrase that implied a physical condition as much as a psychological one. As in earlier stories of sex change, she presented her problem as a biological disturbance, in this case a "glandular imbalance," and as a spiritual longing to become "the woman [she] felt sure Nature had intended." But Jorgensen veered away from earlier accounts when she described her doctors, her diagnosis, and what her treatment entailed. In Denmark, endocrinologist

Christian Hamburger (a student of Steinach) had agreed to treat her free of charge. Hamburger had reassured her that she was not, as she feared, a homosexual but rather had a "condition called transvestism" and might (but did not necessarily) have female "body chemistry" and female "body cells." Over the course of two years, she had undergone hormone treatments, psychiatric examination, "removal of sex glands," and plastic surgery."[31]

Before and after the series, entrepreneurial journalists realized that Jorgensen attracted readers. She caught the public imagination in part because her story embodied tensions central to the postwar culture. In the atomic age, Jorgensen's surgery posed the question of whether science had indeed triumphed over nature. In an era of overt cultural contests over changing gender roles, the press stories on Jorgensen enabled a public reinscription of what counted as masculine and what counted as feminine. At the same time, though, they also incited the fantasy of boundary transgression, with convincing evidence of how a person might present a masculine persona on one day and a feminine one on another. As homosexuality became increasingly visible and as homophobic reaction intensified, Jorgensen brought the issue into the mainstream news with the confession of her preoperative longing for a male friend. But she also confounded the category as she distinguished a depathologized version of cross-gender identification (in which she loved a man because she understood herself as a heterosexual woman) from a still-pathologized version of same-sex desire. And all along, she demonstrated an affinity for the media that kept her in the public eye. She reinforced her popularity by adopting a feminine style that played on the postwar cult of "blond bombshell" glamor. At least one author has speculated that Jorgensen, despite her expressed surprise, leaked her own story to the press. Whether she did or not, she eventually courted the attention to boost her career on the stage.[32]

The unremitting interest allowed a public hashing out of what Jorgensen represented, especially after the *American Weekly* series provided a more detailed account. Journalists soon began to question Jorgensen's status as "100 per cent woman." By mid-March, they asserted that Jorgensen was "neither hermaphroditic nor pseudo-hermaphroditic": she had "no vestiges of female organs or female reproductive glands." Following these leads, the *New York Post* ran a six-part exposé, "The Truth about 'Christine'

Jorgensen," that was reprinted in other cities. Based on interviews with Danish doctors, reporter Alvin Davis claimed that Jorgensen was "physically . . . a normal male" before her treatment, and now a castrated male, with no added female organs. (Jorgensen did not undergo vaginoplasty until 1954.) Davis classified Jorgensen as a transvestite, hinted at homosexuality, and referred to her disrespectfully with male pronouns. He contrasted American doctors' outrage at what they saw as mutilating surgery with Danish doctors' advocacy of the operations.[33] In the wake of the [alleged] exposé, *Time* declared, "Jorgensen was no girl at all, only an altered male," and *Newsweek* followed suit. In the mainstream American press, an intersexed person had a legitimate claim to female status, but a male-to-female "transvestite," even surgically and hormonally altered, apparently did not. Jorgensen's doctors in Denmark seemed to confirm the exposé in the *Journal of the American Medical Association,* in which they described Jorgensen's case as one of "genuine transvestism." Pulp magazine sensation followed. *Modern Romances,* for example, ran "Christine Jorgensen: Is She *Still* a Man?" Another pulp called the case "Sex-Change Fraud."[34]

Not surprisingly, these reports upset Jorgensen. She had not represented herself as a pseudohermaphrodite, although she clearly preferred organic explanations that presented her problem as a biological disorder, often described as a hormonal imbalance. She followed her Danish doctors who, in accord with Hirschfeld and others, saw cross-gender identification not as psychopathology but as a somatic condition. Her emphasis on biological causes helped cleanse her cross-gender identification of the taint of sin or weakness and underscored how deeply she felt the need for surgery. Mostly, though, she bridled at the insinuation that she "had perpetrated a hoax" when calling herself a woman, and she resented the disrespectful tone and "pseudo-scientific commentary" of some of the reports. Ultimately, the stories did little to damage her popularity. Shortly after the exposés, a crowd of "more than 2000" met her at the Los Angeles airport. Journalists continued to follow her every move—her nightclub tour, her interview with Alfred Kinsey, her romances with men. While occasional reports portrayed her as an oddity or a joke, in general the press continued to treat her as a woman and a star.[35]

In any case, the European version of sex change as treatment for "transvestites" had finally hit America. News reports alerted transgendered readers that transformative surgery might take place without a claim to an intersexed condition. San Francisco cross-dresser Louise Lawrence appreciated the *Post* exposé. "I can see how it would disturb [Jorgensen]," she wrote, "but I still think it is the fairest explanation yet published."[36] Stories of other transsexuals soon established that Jorgensen was not alone. In 1954, the press reported on Americans Charlotte McLeod and Tamara Rees, MTFs who had surgery in Denmark and Holland, respectively, and also on Roberta Cowell in England. The openly gay and wildly eccentric San Francisco millionaire John Cabell ("Bunny") Breckenridge announced that he, too, planned to undergo sex change surgery. In these post-Jorgensen cases, the press rarely claimed that the surgery had any connection to an intersexed condition.

From the beginning, the Jorgensen story had tremendous impact on its readers. Letter writers flooded Jorgensen with requests for advice. In her 1967 autobiography, Jorgensen referred to "some twenty thousand letters" in the first few months of publicity. Because of her celebrity, letters addressed simply to "Christine Jorgensen, United States of America" reached their destination. Some letters came from admirers or critics, but a "briefcase full" came from people who identified with Jorgensen and expressed "a seemingly genuine desire for alteration of sex." In Denmark, Christian Hamburger also reported hundreds of letters requesting surgery. In less than a year after Jorgensen entered the public domain, Hamburger received "765 letters from 465 patients who appear to have a genuine desire for alteration of sex." Of the 465 letter writers, 180 wrote from the United States. Within the United States, other doctors reported themselves "besieged by would-be castrates pleading for the Danish 'cure.'"[37]

As in the 1930s and 1940s, some readers of the popular press saw themselves in the stories about sex change. With Jorgensen, though, the sheer magnitude of coverage, depth of detail, and public accounting of what the surgery entailed provided a more highly informative how-to story. An unprecedented number of readers identified with Jorgensen, who in turn used her access to the media to encourage them. "The letters that say 'Your story is my story; please help,'" she wrote, "make me willing to bare the secrets of my confused childhood and youth in the hope that they will bring courage, as well as understanding, to others." The exposés that provided the diagnosis of transvestism

also helped transgendered readers who were not visibly intersexed to find their own stories within Jorgensen's. In various cities, some of these readers paid homage by collecting press clippings about Jorgensen. Louise Lawrence, for example, compiled a carefully constructed Jorgensen scrapbook, now housed in the archives of the Kinsey Institute. These clipping collections, several of which still exist today, offer tangible testimony to Jorgensen's popularity and the impact of the press on isolated readers.[38]

For some such readers, Jorgensen stood jointly as revelation, role model, and public defender of the cause. One MTF remembered her overwhelming sense of "being a freak." Before reading about Jorgensen, she had understood herself variously (and uncomfortably) as "effeminate, homosexual, a transvestite, a narcissist, a masturbator, ... a would-be castrate, a potential suicide, and a paranoid." Then:

> The Jorgensen case appeared in all the newspapers and changed my life.... Suddenly, like a revelation, I knew WHO and WHAT I was—and something COULD BE DONE ABOUT IT! Christ only knows how much time I spent poring over every last item about Christine I could lay my hands on. Not Christ but Christine, I thought, was my Saviour! Now everything about me made perfect sense, I knew what had to be done, and I had some real HOPE of being able to live a normal life *as a woman*! Talk about your shock of recognition! Man, this was IT![39]

For others, the "shock of recognition" provoked more ambivalent feelings. Stephen Wagner (a pseudonym) ... focused on one sentence in one of the stories in the *Chicago Sun-Times*: "They may have the physical form of one sex and think, act and feel like the opposite." "This seems to describe me to the dot," he wrote. He recognized Jorgensen immediately as "a normal man," not a pseudohermaphrodite, and tortured himself with the thought that he could not gain access to the surgery she had managed to obtain. "When I read about Christine's case," he wrote, "I got terribly upset. I was really very frantic." On the East Coast, Albert Savon (a pseudonym) had a similar reaction: "Life ... was bearable, at least it was until the Jorgensen story came out. From then on, I have suffered, because *her* life parallels mine so closely! It is *me* twenty years younger.... Her story is my story.... I need help, I need relief and I need it soon." On the West Coast, Barbara and Lauren Wilcox were interested in Jorgensen "from the point of view of, 'when and where will the operation be made available to Barbara.'"[40]

In the wake of the Jorgensen story, FTMs were only a small minority of the letter writers seeking surgery, Of the 180 Americans who asked Christian Hamburger about sex change surgery, only thirty-nine sought female-to-male operations. Commentators of the era believed that MTFs far outnumbered FTMs.[41] The lesser response of FTMs might have reflected economic and technological inequities. Those who lived and worked as women were less likely to have the economic means to finance medical intervention, and FTMs in general were less likely to pursue a surgical solution that still could not produce a functioning penis. As Hamburger acknowledged, the media probably had some influence as well. The publicity accorded to Jorgensen helped mark transsexuality as a male-to-female phenomenon, a distinct reversal from the 1930s when stories of female-to-male sex changes predominated in the popular press.... Some FTMs, though, did see themselves immediately in Jorgensen's story. In a later account, Mario Martino described his reaction at the age of fifteen when he first read press accounts on Jorgensen: "Over and over I read the news stories I'd secreted in my room.... At last I had hope. *There were people like me.*"[42]

The stories of sex change also had wider appeal. Jorgensen, in particular, inspired nontransgendered correspondents.... Over and over again, [they] identified with her and sympathized with her struggle. They placed her story in the context of their own lives and their own beliefs. She had overcome obstacles, and so could they. "My problem," one man wrote, "seems so insignificant to the hell you had to wade through ... You've really made me wake up." Like Helen Keller, she served for some readers as a model of how the human will might triumph over adversity. A number of letters adopted religious language to express the inspirational lessons they drew. No doubt the name Christine, derived from Christ, helped some readers cast Jorgensen in religious form. Jorgensen's story, one woman said, "reminds me of the suffering Christ had to go through so we might have salvation." Others referred to Jorgensen's surgery as an example of miracles. "I have seen in Christine," one man wrote, "a miracle of God." ... Jorgensen's story also served as a model for struggles for human rights. "I am a Negro," a woman wrote Jorgensen's parents, and "find many obstacles that must be overcome." Jorgensen, too, she said, "belonged to a minority group but she [broke] through its

limitations. If more people would face the brunt of the battle I am sure we would all live in a much more pleasant world." ... The letters indicate that Jorgensen's attempt to portray her particular battle as a more common story of human striving had struck a resonant chord.[43]

The publicity showered on Jorgensen did not bring direct relief to those who identified with her. Overwhelmed with sex change requests, Danish officials forbade operations for foreigners. Jorgensen and Hamburger began to refer correspondents to Harry Benjamin, who offered paternalist sympathy, hormone treatment, and the diagnosis "transsexual," but not surgery. Benjamin helped a few male-to-female patients arrange operations through [a] urologist ... in Los Angeles for a brief period in the 1950s, and sent others to Holland and Mexico for surgery. But many avowed transsexuals, especially poorer ones, had no access to surgery.[44]

It was not until the late 1960s that more American surgeons began to perform sex reassignment surgery. Nonetheless, the ground had shifted. By the mid-1950s the mass media were reporting constantly on sex change. Christine Jorgensen had agreed tacitly to serve as an icon for those who wanted to change sex and also for nontransgendered people who looked to her as a model of persistence, faith, and hope. With ambition and a sense of her mission, she perpetuated her popularity and kept herself on stage. Although she could not control the media, she asserted her presence, and she refused to let the press define her. She told a story that humanized her and defended her right to pursue her own happiness, and she pushed the public to acknowledge her status as a woman.[45]

Jorgensen also pushed American doctors and scientists to redefine their terms. By the mid-1950s they began to adopt the term *transsexual* and to enter into heated debates about the merits of surgical intervention. An American scientific literature on transsexuality, which had not existed before Jorgensen made the news, soon engaged the older European literature that had originated in Germany. American doctors and scientists [in coming decades would return over and over again] to the unanswered questions, "What is a woman and what is a man?"

In all of ... [these developments], Jorgensen could have been the exception that proved the rule, but instead she became the exception that undermined the rules. It could have been said, for example, that we are all distinctly male or female except for a few people like Christine Jorgensen; instead, transsexuals, doctors, and journalists argued repeatedly that no one is one hundred percent male or one hundred percent female. It could have been argued that sex cannot be changed; instead, various observers reconceived sex as the sum of constituent parts, some of which could be altered and some of which could not. It could have been claimed that gender is part of biological sex, except in the case of handful of people like Jorgensen; instead, researchers debated the sources of gender and saw in transsexuality "an opportunity to study the whole problem of how human beings normally get their sense of being a male or a female."[46] It could have been stated (and sometimes it was) that Jorgensen was a gay crossdresser; instead, a prevailing view gradually emerged that transsexuality differed from homosexuality and transvestism. In sum, in the context of her day, with the concepts of sex, gender, and sexuality already in flux, Jorgensen showed her public how sex changed, a process that continues today.

NOTES

1. "Ex-GI becomes Blonde Beauty," New York Daily News, Dec. 1, 1952, 1; "Christine and the News," Newsweek, Dec. 15, 1952, 64.

2. See, for example, John D'Emilio and Estelle B. Freedman, Intimate Matters: A History of Sexuality in America, 2d ed. (Chicago: University of Chicago Press, 1997); Paul Robinson, The Modernization of Sex, 2d ed. (Ithaca: Cornell University Press, 1989); Sharon R. Ullman, Sex Seen: The Emergence of Modern Sexuality in America (Berkeley: University of California Press, 1997); Jonathan Ned Katz, The Invention of Heterosexuality (New York: Dutton, 1995).

3. Magnus Hirschfeld, Transvestites: The Erotic Drive to Cross Dress, trans. Michael A. Lombardi-Nash (1910; reprint, Buffalo: Prometheus, 1991), 219, 226; Gregorio Marañon, The Evolution of Sex and Intersexual Conditions (London: George Allen and Unwin, 1932), 24.

4. Margaret Mead, Male and Female: A Study of the Sexes in a Changing World (New York: William Morrow, 1949); Alfred C. Kinsey, Sexual Behavior in the Human Male (Philadelphia: W. B. Saunders, 1948). For important recent formulations, see, for example, Judith Butler, Gender Trouble: Feminism and the Subversion of Identity (New York: Routledge, 1990); Anne Fausto-Sterling, Sexing the Body: Gender Politics and the Construction of Sexuality (New York: Basic Books, 2000).

5. See Richard Green, "Mythological, Historical, and Cross-Cultural Aspects of Transsexualism," in Transsexualism and Sex Reassignment, ed. Richard Green and John Money (Baltimore: Johns Hopkins Press, 1969), 13–22; Vern L. Bullough, "Transsexualism in History," Archives of Sexual Behavior 4:5 (1975), 561–71; Leslie Feinberg, Transgender Warriors: Making History from Joan of Arc to RuPaul (Boston: Beacon, 1996).

6. Bernice Hausman, Changing Sex: Transsexualism, Technology, and the Idea of Gender (Durham, N.C.: Duke University Press, 1995), 140.

7. In the popular lingo used today, transsexuals are a subset of "transgendered" people, an umbrella term for those with various forms and degrees of crossgender practices and identifications. "Transgendered" includes, among others, some people who identify as "butch" or masculine lesbians, as "fairies," "queens," or feminine gay men, and as heterosexual crossdressers as well as those who identify as transsexual. The categories are not hermetically sealed, and to a certain extent the boundaries are permeable. The same person might identify as a butch lesbian at one point in life and as an FTM (female-to-male) transsexual at another. Transsexuals today are understood to differ from homosexuals, who rarely wish to change their sex. The longing to change the sex of one's body does not necessarily correspond with any set pattern of erotic behavior or sexual desire. Some transsexuals identify themselves as (and engage in behavior recognized as) homosexual, bisexual, or asexual. Transsexuals are also understood to differ from transvestites or crossdressers, who dress in the clothes of the other sex but do not necessarily hope to change the sex of their bodies. By the definitions most commonly used today, transsexuals are not intersexed, a term used to describe the people who used to be called "hermaphrodites" and "pseudohermaphrodites," people with various physical conditions in which the genitals or reproductive organs do not fit into the standard category of female or male. All these terms have histories.

8. Eugen Steinach, Sex and Life: Forty Years of Biological and Medical Experiments (New York: Viking, 1940) 66. On Steinach, see Harry Benjamin, "Eugen Steinach, 1861–1944: A Life of Research," Scientific Monthly 61 (1945): 427–42; Sexual Anomalies and Perversions: A Summary of the Work of the Late Dr. Magnus Hirschfeld, Compiled as a Humble Memorial by His Pupils (London: Francis Aldor, 1944 [1938]), 172–77.

9. J. Allen Gilbert, "Homo-Sexuality and Its Treatment," Journal of Nervous and Mental Disease 52 (October 1920): 297–322, quotations on 321. In Gilbert's article, Hart is referred to as "H." Jonathan Katz's sleuthing uncovered Hart's identity. See Jonathan Katz, Gay American History: Lesbians and Gay Men in the U.S.A.: A Documentary Anthology (New York: Crowell, 1976), 419.

10. Sexual Anomalies and Perversions, 179, 218; Magnus Hirschfeld, Transvestites: The Erotic Drive to Cross Dress (New York: Prometheus Books, 1991[1910]), 235; Felix Abraham, "Genitalumwandlung an zwei männlichen Transvestiten," Zeitschrift für Sexualwissenschaft und Sexualpolitik 18 (10 September 1931): 223–26, quotation on 223.

11. Niels Hoyer, ed., Man into Woman: An Authentic Record of a Change of Sex (New York: Dutton, 1933), 284. On Elbe's death and the involvement of Hirschfeld and the Institute, see Preben Hertoft and Teit Ritzau, Paradiset er ikke til salg: Trangen til at vaere begge koen (Paradise is not for sale: the desire to be both sexes) (Denmark: Lindhardt og Ringhof, 1984), 82–83.

12. S. W. [pseud.], letter to Alfred C. Kinsey, 14 Dec. 1947, Correspondence file: S. W., Kinsey Institute for Research in Sex, Gender, and Reproduction, Indiana University, Bloomington, Ind. (hereafter, KI).

13. Hoyer, *Man into Woman*, 178, xi–xii. The claim to hermaphroditism is hard to believe. By the late 1930s, the reigning expert in the field, Hugh Hampton Young, found only twenty medically confirmed cases of hermaphroditism; not one of them had, as the story of Lili Elbe suggested, two ovaries in the pelvis and two testes in the scrotum. See Hugh Hampton Young, *Genital Abnormalities, Hermaphroditism and Related Adrenal Diseases* (Baltimore: Williams and Wilkins, 1937), 200–201.

14. "Man in Woman's Body," *Your Body*, September 1937, 12–15, quotation on 15. "Boy Prisoner Slowly Changing into a Girl," n.p., n.d. [ca. 1936]; "When Science Changed a Man into a Woman!" n.d. [ca. 1934], 2: both in "Order Book" scrapbook, box 1/1 scrapbooks, Virginia Prince Collection, California State University at Northridge (hereafter, VPC).

15. Gordon Kahn, "['Bad-Old'] Days of Newly-Made Man," *New York Daily Mirror*, n.d. [ca. 1936]; Kahn, "Boy Ex-Girl 'Corsetiere,'" ibid., n.d. [ca. 1936]; "Former Girl Athlete Arrives, Now a Man"; Kahn, "Once Girl, He Talks of Loves," ibid., n.d. [ca. 1936]; and Kahn, "Koubkov Met Love at Track," ibid., n.d. [ca 1936], all in "Order Book" scrapbook, box 1/1 scrapbooks, VPC.

16. See, for example, Brett Riley, "Are Sexual Changes Possible?" n.d. [late 1930s or 1940s], box 1/4 clippings, VPC.

17. Jacob Hubler, "Science Turns Girl into Boy," *Sexology* 2:3 (Nov. 1934): 158.

18. Letter to the editor, "Dissatisfaction with Sex," *Sexology* 1:12 (Aug. 1934), 810; Letter to the editor, "Changing Sex," *Sexology* 5:4 (Dec. 1937), 265; "They Want to Change Sexes," *Sexology* 5:1 (Sept. 1937), 32.

19. "Dissatisfaction with Sex," 810; "Changing Sex," 265. For articles, see "Woman into Man," *Sexology* 10:8 (March 1944), 484–85; David O. Cauldwell, "A Man Becomes a Woman," *Sexology* 13:2 (Sept. 1946), 73–79, and 13:3 (Oct. 1946), 149–52. For letters to the editor, see "Homosexuality," *Sexology* 9:6 (Nov. 1942), 390, 392; "'Man into Woman'?" *Sexology* 13:1 (Aug. 1946), 59–60; "Man into Woman," *Sexology* 13:5 (Dec. 1946), 312; and "Desire to Be of the Opposite Sex," *Sexology* 15:1 (Aug. 1948), 53.

20. David O. Cauldwell, "Psychopathia Transexualis," *Sexology* (Dec. 1949), 276, 278.

21. Ibid., 280, 274; David O. Cauldwell, *Questions and Answers on the Sex Life and Sexual Problems of Trans-Sexuals* (Girard, Kans.: Haldeman-Julius Publicans, 1950), front cover, 11.

22. Jim Kepner, "Excavating Lesbian and Gay History," *ONE/IGLA Bulletin* 2 (spring/summer 1996): 9.

23. Cauldwell, *Questions and Answers*, 13, 24.

24. Gene St. Ledges, "Can Science Switch Sexes?" *Whisper* (Jan. 1950), box 1/4 clippings, VPC; "Would You Change Your Sex?" *Glance* (March 1950), box 1/1 scrapbooks, ibid.

25. Tom Buckley, "Transsexuality Expert, 90, Recalls 'Maverick' Career," *New York Times*, Jan. 11, 1975, B1. On Benjamin's career in the United States, see Harry Benjamin, "Reminiscences," *Journal of Sex Research* 6:1 (Feb. 1970): 3–9.

26. "Medical Report on V. B.," July 19, 1948, pp. 1–3; V. B. to Harry Benjamin, May 19, 1949, both in V.B. folder, box 3, Series IIC, Harry Benjamin Collection, KI (hereafter, HBC). On the mayhem statute, see Robert Veit Sherwin, "The Legal Problem in Transvestism,"

American Journal of Psychotherapy 8 (April 1954), 243–244. By all accounts, no surgeon engaged in sex reassignment was ever prosecuted under the mayhem statute. More generally, surgeons hesitated to engage in sex change surgery for other reasons; they worried, for example, about their reputations in the medical community, and they also feared liability suits. By the late 1960, doctors and lawyers had ceased using the mayhem statutes as an excuse to refuse sex reassignment surgery.

27. Harry Benjamin, letter to V. B., May 31. 1949; Harry Benjamin, letter to Edmund G. Brown, Nov. 22, 1949, both in V. B. folder, box 3, Series IIC, HBC; Berdeen Frankel Meyer, "Case Summary and Closing Note," Oct. 2, 1950, 8, in ibid.

28. Alton Blakeslee, "Thousands Do Not Know True Sex," *New York Daily News*, Dec. 7, 1952, C6; Jack Geiger, "Sex Surgery Specialist Reports Hundreds of Boy-Girl Operations," n.d. [ca. 2 Dec. 1952], Christine Jorgensen scrapbook, Louise Lawrence Collection, KI (hereafter, LLC); "Doctor Tells of Five Sex Operations," *New York Daily News*, Dec. 18, 1952, C4; "The Great Transformation," *Time*, Dec. 15, 1952, 59.

29. G. B. Lal, "MD's and Public to Eagerly Follow Christine's Life," *New York Journal-American*, Dec. 7, 1952, 18L; Louise Lawrence, letter to Harry Benjamin, Dec. 9, 1952, TRNSV notebook, LLC.

30. Christine Jorgensen, "The Story of My Life," *American Weekly*, Feb. 15, 1953, 5, 9; "How AW Got and Prepared Christine Story," *Editor and Publisher*, March 28, 1953, 62. See Gert Hekma, "'A Female Soul in a Male Body': Sexual Inversion as Gender Inversion in Nineteenth-Century Sexology," in *Third Sex, Third Gender: Beyond Sexual Dimorphism in Culture and History*, ed. Gilbert Herdt (New York: Zone Books, 1996), 213–39.

31. Christine Jorgensen, "The Story of My Life," *American Weekly*, Feb. 22, 1953, 4, 6; March 8, 1953, 8, 9.

32. Susan Stryker, "Transsexuality: The Postmodern Body and/as Technology," *Exposure: The Journal of the Society for Photographic Education* 30 (1995): 38–50; Dallas Denny, "Black Telephones, White Refrigerators: Rethinking Christine Jorgensen," in Denny, ed. *Current Concepts in Transgender Identity* (New York: Garland Publishing, 1998), 35–44.

33. "Christine Discounted as 100 Pct. Woman by Her Copenhagen Doctor," *San Francisco Call-Bulletin*, Feb. 18, 1953, Christine Jorgensen scrapbook, Louise Lawrence Collection, KI; "AMA Studies Christine–Some U.S. Doctors Say She's Not a Woman Still," *San Francisco Chronicle*, March 11, 1953, in ibid.; Alvin Davis, "The Truth about 'Christine' Jorgensen," *New York Post*, pt. 1, April 6, 1953.

34. "The Case of Christine," *Time*, April 20, 1953, 82; "Boy or Girl?" *Newsweek*, May 4, 1953, 91; Christian Hamburger, Georg Stürup, and E. Dahl-Iversen, "Transvestism: Hormonal, Psychiatric, and Surgical Treatment," *Journal of the American Medical Association* 152 (May 1953): 396; Robert King, "Christine Jorgensen: Is She *Still* a Man?" *Modern Romances*, Aug. 1953, in ONE/International Gay and Lesbian Archives (ONE/IGLA), University of Southern California, Los Angeles, file: Christine Jorgensen; "Sex-Change Fraud," *Exclusive*, Feb. 1955, vertical file: Christine Jorgensen, KI.

35. Christine Jorgensen, *Christine Jorgensen: A Personal Autobiography* (New York: Paul S. Eriksson, 1967),

207, 209; "2000 in L.A. Greet Christine," *Los Angeles Herald and Express*, May 7, 1953, Christine Jorgensen scrapbook, LLC. For a different interpretation of the media's treatment of Jorgensen, see David Harley Serlin, "Christine Jorgensen and the Cold War Closet," *Radical History Review* 62 (Spring 1995): 136–65.

36. Louise Lawrence to Harry Benjamin, April 22, 1953, TRNSV notebook, LLC.

37. Jorgensen, *Christine Jorgensen*, 189, 217; Christian Hamburger, "The Desire for Change of Sex as Shown by Personal Letters from 465 Men and Women," *Acta Endocrinologica* 14 (1953): 361–76, quotation on 363; Davis, "The Truth about 'Christine' Jorgensen," *New York Post*, April 9, 1953.

38. Jorgensen, "Story of My Life," *American Weekly*, Feb. 15, 1953, 7. In addition to Louise Lawrence's scrapbook, see the various scrapbooks and clipping collections in the Virginia Prince Collection. Special thanks to Joseph Agnew for lending me the "Christine" scrapbook from Chicago in his private possession.

39. R.E.L. Masters, *Sex-Drive People: An Autobiographical Approach to the Problem of the Sex-Dominated Personality* (Los Angeles: Sherbourne, 1966), 229–32.

40. S. W. to Alfred C. Kinsey, Dec. 8, 1952, Correspondence file S. W., KI; S. W. to Harry Benjamin, July 2, 1954, S. W. folder, Box 8, Series IIC, HBC; A. S. [pseud.], letter probably to Harry Benjamin [ca. March 1954], A. D. folder, ibid.; Louise Lawrence to Harry Benjamin, April 6, 1953, TRNSV notebook, LLC.

41. On ratios of MTFs and FTMs, see Ira B. Pauly, "Male Psychosexual Inversion: Transsexualism," *Archives of General Psychiatry* 13 (Aug. 1965): 179. The ratios offered by various doctors in the 1950s and early 1960s ranged from 6:1 to 2:1. In general, the published ratios have declined over time, and some today now posit an equal number of FTMs and MTFs. In the 1950s, though, MTFs clearly predominated in the doctors' estimates, and some mid-century sexologists considered transvestism and transsexualism, like fetishism, largely, if not wholly, "male" conditions. Among the broader population of transgendered people, were there in fact more MTFs than FTMs? If so, why? These larger questions remain unanswered.

42. Hamburger, "The Desire for Change of Sex," 364; Mario Martino, with Harriet, *Emergence: A Transsexual Autobiography* (New York: Crown Publishers, 1979), 40. For a lengthier discussion of the contemporary marking of transsexuality as male to female, see Marjorie Garber, *Vested Interests: Cross-Dressing and Cultural Anxiety* (New York: Routledge, 1992), ch. 4.

43. H. S. to Christine Jorgensen [c. 1953], Christine folder; Barbara Williams to George and Florence Jorgensen, Dec. 1, 1952, loose, both in Letters Box, Christine Jorgensen Papers, Royal Danish Library, Copenhagen.

44. Harry Benjamin, "Transvestism and Transsexualism," *International Journal of Sexology* 7 (Aug. 1953), 13; and see the collected correspondence in HBC.

45. Jorgensen died on May 3, 1989, at the age of sixty-two.

46. Frederic G. Worden and James T. Marsh, "Psychological Factors in Men Seeking Sex Transformation: A Preliminary Report," *Journal of the American Medical Association* 157:15 (April 9, 1955), 1292.

BETH L. BAILEY
Prescribing the Pill: The Coming of the Sexual Revolution in America's Heartland

In this fascinating bit of historical detective work, Beth Bailey explodes the myth that the advent of the oral contraceptive in 1960 ushered in the Sexual Revolution, freeing women—especially those who were unmarried—to engage in sex without fears of unwanted pregnancies. Bailey tells a different story, one in which use of the new contraceptive is closely linked to concerns about overpopulation and poverty. By narrowing her focus to Lawrence, Kansas, home to the University of Kansas, she provides a clear view of the complex process by which college women gained access to the pill.

Why does Bailey refer to this process as "elite-managed, gradual change"? At what point did young women demand access on their own behalf? Why were

Excerpted from "Prescribing the Pill," ch. 4 of *Sex in the Heartland* by Beth L. Bailey (Cambridge, Mass.: Harvard University Press, 1999). Reprinted with permission of the author and publisher. Notes have been renumbered and edited.

their voices virtually mute throughout the 1960s, even though Bailey provides clear evidence that their behavior was changing? Is this silencing on the part of heterosexual young women related in any way to the silencing that Betty Friedan or lesbian athletes imposed on themselves in the postwar era?

American women went "on the pill" in the 1960s. The oral tablets that most Americans called simply "the pill" were approved for contraceptive use by the FDA in 1960. By early 1969, eight and a half million women were using the pill; their numbers had grown by about one million each year from 1961.[1] Every day for three weeks out of their monthly menstrual cycle, millions of women popped the tiny tablet through the foil package that fit into the daisy-wheel container that somewhat resembled a compact—if one didn't know better. The high hormonal doses of the early oral contraceptives had pronounced side effects, which mimicked pregnancy: breast tenderness, weight gain, some nausea. But the pill was more than 99 percent effective, in no way dependent on the direct cooperation of the woman's partner, and completely separate from the act of sexual intercourse. A great many women were willing to accept some side effects in exchange for freedom from fear of pregnancy. By giving women greater control over their sexual and reproductive lives, this new contraceptive technology helped change the meaning and experience of sex in America.

The great majority of the women who went on the pill in its early years, however, were not the young single women who lived "the revolution." Most were married. . . . Nonetheless, by the mid-1960s the pill symbolized the revolution in sex. . . . In America, talk of the sexual revolution inevitably turned to talk of the pill, and discussions of the pill often centered on its possible effects on America's sexual mores.

Largely because of its symbolic role, the pill frequently appears in discussions (both then and now) as a sort of *deus ex machina*, bringing about the sexual revolution. In 1968 a no less distinguished figure than Pearl S. Buck, writing for the mass market in *Reader's Digest*, linked a crisis in sexual morality to the pill: "It is a small object—yet its potential effect upon our society may be even more devastating than the nuclear bomb."[2] . . . [But Buck's analogy to the bomb] overlooks a key fact. The pill was not simply a new technology available in the free marketplace of postwar America. It had to be prescribed by a physician.

Doctors, then as now, controlled access to oral contraceptives. And at that time only a small minority of physicians would prescribe birth control pills to women who were not married. Most believed, along with a large majority of the American public, that it was wrong for unmarried women to have sex. Thus, before the pill could play any significant role in the sexual behavior of America's unmarried youth, something had to change. Unmarried women—in large numbers—had to have access to oral contraceptives. How did single women get the pill?

Once again, revolutionary change in Americans' sexual mores and behavior was made possible inadvertently. . . . The pill did not become available to single women because they raised their voices and demanded the right to sexual freedom and control of their own bodies. Instead, it became available to them as a by-product of two political movements that were at the heart of sixties liberalism and its attempts to ameliorate the difficult social problems that plagued America and the world.

One of these movements was driven by concern about population growth, both international and domestic, which reached near-panic proportions in the United States during the 1960s and early 1970s. The other, Lyndon Johnson's Great Society, used federal funds and programs to attack the causes and consequences of poverty and racism in the United States. Neither set of efforts, by any stretch of the imagination, was intended to foster a sexual revolution. However, these two movements helped make the pill available to single women, in large part by providing rationales for prescribing contraceptives that did not employ a language of morality. . . .

[In Kansas, population control advocates urged the state senate to] vote on legislation allowing public agencies to distribute information about contraceptives to Kansas citizens. Senate Bill 375 stemmed largely from the intense lobbying efforts of Patricia Schloesser, M.D., head of the state division of maternal and child services, who was motivated by a frightening vision of unrestrained world population growth. . . . [T]he senate voted unanimously in favor of the measure. The house vote the following April, however, was close enough to require a roll call. . . . While it was now legal for public institutions to offer birth control and contraceptive information to citizens of Kansas, the legislature had offered no . . . funding. Without money for birth control services, the change in law had little practical impact. . . .

Among the most vocal and vehement advocates of birth control in Kansas was the director of Lawrence's public health department, Dr. Dale Clinton. . . . Like Dr. Schloesser, Clinton believed that the world population explosion was a greater threat to public health than any contagious disease or environmental hazard. . . . In 1959 the professional organization for public health workers, the 20,000-member American Public Health Association (APHA), had adopted a resolution that called for attention, at "all levels of government," to "the impact of population change on health." And in 1963 the APHA called population growth "one of the world's most important health problems" and began lobbying government officials for action.[3]

[While the population advocates pressed for maximum dissemination of both information about contraceptives and the contraceptives themselves, the Johnson administration pursued a similar strategy as part of a very different objective.] President Johnson pledged in his state of the union address "to seek new ways to use our knowledge to help deal with the explosion in world population and the growing scarcity of world resources." In April [1965], Senator Gruening of Alaska introduced a bill that led to the funding of birth control programs through the Department of Health, Education, and Welfare. Earlier, the Office of Economic Opportunity (OEO) had funneled some money to family planning programs under the "local option" policy that allowed community groups to initiate welfare programs. (Initially the OEO did not allow its funds to be used for contraceptives for unmarried women; that restriction was lifted in 1966.)[4] The federal government's decisions to spend taxpayers' money on public family planning programs were not based on concern about women's reproductive health or a wish to promote sexual freedom. Rather, the funding was a result of the confluence of alarm about the "population problem" and increased federal involvement in programs intended to alleviate the effects of poverty in the United States. Limiting the number of children born to poor women (or allowing poor women to avoid

unplanned and unwanted pregnancies) was a priority for these programs.

The political implications of linking Johnson's Great Society (with its strong focus on poverty) and population control were as apparent at the time as they are today. In the early twentieth century, many advocates of birth control had worked closely with the eugenics movement, which sought to limit childbearing among people the eugenicists deemed genetically and racially inferior and so preserve the dominance of white, Anglo-Saxon Americans. Those uncomfortably close links between the birth control movement and the eugenics movement were not so far in the past. . . .

The politics of the Johnson administration's "war on poverty" and welfare programs were complicated at best, and those who attempted to implement policies struggled with opposition from widely divergent sources. In the case of birth control, the administration faced both the suspicions of targeted groups such as poor African Americans *and* voters' reservations about the costs of burgeoning social welfare programs. . . . The American Association of Public Health consistently focused on the dangers of world population growth, an argument that was more compelling to Americans who rejected the idea of "benefits" for the poor and underprivileged. But throughout the 1960s, authors also attempted to demonstrate that contraception for America's poor was fully in keeping with "broadly democratic principles of equal opportunity for all." Birth control, one prominent activist wrote in an attempt to shift the grounds for suspicion, should not be the "special privilege" of the "well-to-do."[5]

Many Americans, however, drew connections between birth control and antipoverty programs that were exactly what government agencies had tried to avoid. For example, when *Good Housekeeping* sampled its 20,000-member "consumer panel" in 1967 on the question "Should Birth Control Be Available to Unmarried Women," its editors discovered that the negative responses (significantly, a strong majority) were based on "moral" arguments, while the affirmative responses were "practical." An Arizona woman wrote: "It would eliminate many dollars in child-welfare payments." A more vehement response came from a woman in the Midwest, who supported birth control for unmarried women because "I deeply resent having to deprive my family of privileges I cannot afford because I have to pay support for others not of my choosing."[6] . . .

Once the Kansas legislature made funding available, Dr. Clinton moved quickly and Lawrence's health department began to offer contraceptive services—something fewer than 20 percent of local health departments in the United States did at that time. Clinton, however, was decidedly uninterested in the professional debate about birth control for the indigent and the related directives. Though the framework provided by state (and eventually federal) guidelines indicated an implicit, but clear, association of these programs with services for the poor, Clinton made it equally clear that his birth control clinic was not "indigent-oriented," nor did he consider it the appropriate site for clinical medicine. He did not intend to focus on the poor, and he did not mean to provide women (of any income level) with health care. Instead, he intended to combat the scourge of unrestrained population growth by offering contraceptives to any and all.

. . . Kansas's laws restricting birth control, in effect from 1870 through 1963, had applied only to public agencies. Even before 1963 a married woman in Lawrence had ready access to birth control if she could afford a private doctor. When the pill became available for contraceptive purposes in 1960, Lawrence doctors had begun prescribing it to married women. . . .

As private doctors in Lawrence were already meeting the needs of their patients, the health department, naturally, would draw from a different constituency. Married women who could afford private doctors were more or less out of the pool. Who was left? Those for whom medical fees were too expensive. . . .

There was also another constituency, one that the state and federal governments had not intended to target: unmarried women. And because of the University of Kansas and Haskell Indian Junior College, Lawrence had a disproportionately high number of young, unmarried women. The Kansas legislature had mandated access to contraceptive information and services only for *married* women 18 years and older. Parental permission was required for women under 18, no matter what their marital status. But the legislature also provided a back door to access: Any woman might receive contraceptives at a public clinic if she was "referred to said center by a licensed physician." Clinton interpreted this law in the broadest terms. He was a licensed physician, legally

authorized to make such referrals. Thus, as he made clear in newspaper interviews and public talks, any woman who wanted birth control might receive her referral at the clinic itself, at the time of her appointment. With virtually no exceptions, women seeking contraceptives at the health department came away with the pill.

[At the University of Kansas,] the question was whether the University Health Service should prescribe the pill to unmarried women students. This debate . . . centered [on] issues of morality. It was precipitated by a 1966 forum on the topic: "Should unmarried undergraduates be given birth control information and/or materials through Watkins Hospital [the student health service]?"

The panelists were three: Rev. Simmons, the campus minister who had helped form the family planning clinic [affiliated with Planned Parenthood] and who focused on sexuality counseling and birth control in his ministry at KU; Father Falteisch, chairman of the moral theology department at St. Louis University and a Roman Catholic priest; and Dr. Raymond Schwegler, director of KU's student health service. According to coverage by the *University Daily Kansan,* Simmons argued that population control was desperately needed. Father Falteisch agreed, and suggested that the Church was moving toward accepting the "responsible use" of contraceptives as legitimate, though not for the unmarried. In the context of 1966 America and their respective churches, both men of the cloth took liberal to progressive positions. The hard line, however, came from the man of medicine.

The *Kansan* described Dr. Schwegler, then about 60 years old, as a "small, white-haired man" with a soft voice, but he certainly never minced words. Watkins would not, Schwegler insisted, give contraceptives to unmarried students "under any circumstances." "I know this is old fashioned, mid-Victorian, and the *Kansan* will cut us to ribbons," he is quoted in the *Kansan* as saying, "but I don't want to do it and my staff backs me completely." Rev. Simmons pushed, arguing that unless premarital intercourse was grounds for expulsion, Schwegler's policy was unfair. Schwegler replied: "We'd have trouble keeping the student population up [if we expelled students for premarital intercourse]. But Watkins will not contribute to the recreational activities of the campus." When a student asked about the possibility of a "rebel doctor," Schwegler deemed it impossible: "All the doctors are handpicked—by me." He continued: "If I had somebody over there who I thought was as far out as some of the teaching faculty, I'd fire him. I want a conservative hospital that can be respected."[7]

The 1966 forum on birth control prompted a flood of letters to the *Kansan*. The letters contained no dire predictions about the earth's future if population growth continued uncontrolled. Instead, students used a language of morality to dispute Schwegler's stance. . . .

The first response to Schwegler published in the *Kansan* was . . . from a graduate student from Iola, Kansas. . . . Noting that the health service did provide the pill to married women, he argued that by so doing the administration had defined the issue as moral, not medical. Thus, he said, the question was, "Who should make the moral decision, the university or the students themselves?" Another graduate student (from Gettysburg, South Dakota) questioned "the irresponsible use of the concept 'morality' as employed primarily by the 'anti-pill' proponents." Morality, he insisted, existed only in a situation in which there was "opportunity for choice." Without "free access" to contraceptives, students were not making a moral—or immoral—choice about premarital intercourse. Instead, their choices were constrained by fear or coercion.

The "anti-pill" faction was represented by only one letter. The writer, a male sophomore from Nebraska, argued that because the university was a "public servant," it must follow the "doctrines of the society." He warned that premarital sex would be likely to increase if single women could get the pill, for without fear of pregnancy, "restraining factors would be few and far between." Reaching for an analogy, he asked: "If the possibility of punishment for murder were eliminated," would there not be "a substantial increase in the number of murders committed every year?" . . .

What was largely missing in this flurry of letters was a statement embracing sexual freedom—an affirmative voice. . . . [M]ost of the writers shifted the focus away from sex in making their arguments. . . . While their central claim—that the university should provide contraceptives to unmarried women students— was quite radical, their arguments were not. These were not yet the voices of revolution.

In the forum and in the ensuing debate, there were no arguments centering around the rights of women to control their own bodies. In fact, only two women participated in this public debate, and their names do not appear, effaced in the signatures "Mr. and Mrs. James Cooley" and "Mr. and Mrs. Angus Wright." . . . Why didn't women speak out in the paper? After all, the debate was about women's choices—it was not men who might go "on the pill."

Women did not write because the stakes for them were so high. Discussions about morality and the pill in the larger society did not center on the morality of existential choice, but on the immorality of premarital sex. In the February 1967 *Good Housekeeping* poll on unmarried women and the pill, respondents made comments such as: "I truly pity a generation growing up with the morals of alley cats"; and "Making birth control available to unmarried girls to me would mean lowering our moral standards and destroying our culture." These women were not policymakers or experts. . . . [T]heir voices represent a different sort of authority. These are the voices of mothers—mothers of the sort whose daughters went to state colleges in the Midwest. The *Kansan* was a student paper, but news of a daughter's making public claims about her right to birth control was very likely to travel fast and to travel home.

. . . Writings in the *Journal of the American College Health Association, School and Society*, and the *Journal of School Health* at the time were equally emphatic about the evils of premarital sex. . . . The director of the Princeton health service . . . warned against prescribing contraceptives to unmarried women, as "the student's unconscious mind might interpret such prescriptions as a signal from 'authority' giving permission for sexual freedom."[8] [A] physician at the Ohio State University health service . . . made an unfortunate analogy to sex: "It is all a bit like cars: Some choose a new one and break it in with loving care; others buy from a used car lot—it is just as nice and shiny but you are not sure what problems the previous drivers have left you."[9]

Mass-circulation magazines and professional journals would not have devoted so much space to debates over premarital sex if there had been no audience for them. . . . Nonetheless, these are essentially prescriptive discourses. What of the students themselves?

In the spring semester of 1964 the "Roles of Women" committee of the Associated Women Students (AWS) surveyed its constituency. Presented with descriptions of behavior ("using race as one basis for choosing your associates"; "showing disrespect for those in authority"; "wearing short shorts in town"; "feeling very angry with someone"), students were asked to judge each item. Categories were "morally or ethically right," "generally acceptable," "generally unacceptable," and "morally or ethically wrong." The instructions emphasized that each student should indicate what was right or wrong "for *you*." More than 1,900 women completed the survey.

Questions about sex provoked the strongest responses. Significantly higher percentages of women students disapproved of "mixed swimming parties in the nude" than of using an exam "which has been illegally obtained." . . . [M]ost of the respondents (77 percent of the freshmen and 68 percent of the seniors) rated premarital sex with a fiancé as "morally or ethically wrong," not merely as "generally unacceptable." Even stronger was the students' disapproval of sexual intercourse when the couple was not engaged to be married. A striking 91 percent of both freshmen and seniors labeled it unacceptable or wrong. Only 2 percent of each group deemed premarital sex for those who were not engaged "morally or ethically right."

. . . In 1967 a student union forum offered three professors addressing the question "Is Free Love a Bargain?" . . . This forum was dominated by a professor of English, who accused the audience of coming in search of "some rationalization for the sex you've indulged in." . . . [In] such a climate, with the threat of moral condemnation from peers and authorities alike, few students wished to make public their private decisions about sex.

In 1967, following the "Is Free Love a Bargain?" forum, an unmarried woman finally wrote to the editor of the campus newspaper, claiming her right to both sex and the pill: "I take the pill because I'd rather express my love than repress it. I'm not promiscuous, but once in a while I meet a 'special' guy. I've seen too many girls on campus totally disregard school for several weeks as they suffer anxiety over a missed menstrual period. . . . If a girl takes one chance a year, that's enough to warrant taking the pill." . . . Her letter, which had begun, "I'm a woman and I'm glad," employed a feminist language, emphasizing women's right and capacity to choose. It was a powerful and affirmative statement. But it was unsigned. An editor's note below the letter read: "Contrary to established editorial page policy, we are printing this letter without signature." All letters, no matter how controversial their claims, required signature—except this one. A woman's

claiming her right to sex and the pill was understood as a whole different category of risk.

That this woman remained anonymous and was allowed to do so by the *Kansan* editorial board in violation of its policy, that women's voices were so conspicuously silent in the previous year's debate on the pill, that 91 percent of the women students surveyed *said* they believed premarital sex to be "ethically or morally wrong"—all this is strong evidence that it wasn't only the prescriptive voices of adults denying the legitimacy of the culture of youth. Even within student culture, there was a gulf between public claims and private behavior. For the women of KU were having sex. And they were, in increasing numbers, on the pill.

Actually getting the pill could be complicated, however. When a young, single woman sought a prescription for contraceptives in the 1960s, she was making a statement about her sexual status. Virgins didn't need birth control pills unless they did not plan to remain virgins much longer. . . . When a single woman went to a doctor to request any sort of contraceptive device, she risked refusal, embarrassment, even lectures on morality and appropriate behavior. Some women bought cheap rings and tried to pass them off as wedding bands. Others claimed they were coming in for a "premarital exam," with the wedding pending. Still others complained of menstrual cramps or heavy bleeding and came away with the pill, prescribed to "regulate" their periods. But many doctors, especially those in small towns and university communities, saw through such pretexts and often treated young women with suspicion. Single women were not guaranteed, by law or custom, access to birth control.

As women learned through informal networks, alternative newspapers, and the completely mainstream *Journal World,* the quickest, cheapest, and least complicated place to get birth control pills in Lawrence was the public health department. The university student health service refused to "contribute to the recreational activities of the campus," in its director's colorful words, and many students worried about having such information about their sex lives in what were, after all, official university records at the health service. . . . [The Planned Parenthood–affiliated] clinic was open only two nights a month, and simply could not serve large numbers of women. . . .

The number of women obtaining oral contraceptives at the public health department grew dramatically from year to year, and the vast majority of the new patients each year were KU students. The patient load closely followed the academic year. In 1971, for example, there were only 44 new patients in August, but in September, with the beginning of the fall semester, there were 300. That year the Lawrence-Douglas County health department served 8,529 birth control patients and dispensed or prescribed almost 38,000 months of pills.... The pill was a wonder drug not simply because of its effectiveness for women but also because of its possible convenience for those who prescribed it. Women went to the health department and walked out a few minutes later "on the pill." Stories of young women who were offered virtual armloads of free pills and told to pass them on to their friends still circulate today....

The Planned Parenthood–affiliated clinic took a very different approach. Prescription of the pill was contingent upon not only a physical examination but also a time-consuming process of education and counseling.... The clinic, which had opened in early 1967, closed its doors permanently on the first day of 1970. Though it had been founded to serve low-income residents of Lawrence, the president of its sponsoring group explained, it had been used almost exclusively by KU students (she did not say whether they were married or single). Many of the volunteers were frustrated by what they saw as a misdirection of resources, and upon closing the clinic the directors sent a letter to Dr. Schwegler at the student health service and to the chancellor arguing that the university must take responsibility for its students' birth control needs instead of allowing students to overwhelm community resources needed by and for a different population.[10]

... In 1970, after the closing of the Planned Parenthood clinic, a student group approached top-level administrators about the health service's birth control policies. The administrators responded sympathetically, promising that two upcoming vacancies at Watkins would be filled with doctors who would prescribe the pill without using marital status or "morality" as criteria. This never happened.... In 1970, 53 percent of American college health services offered no gynecological care to women students, and 72 percent did not prescribe contraceptives (to single *or* married students).[11]

Thus far, the story of the pill in Lawrence, Kansas, has been one of elite-managed, gradual change.... Until the 1970s, Lawrence's youth also fit into this model.... While thousands of young women went on the pill during the 1960s, public acknowledgment of that private behavior lagged behind. [Although the] pill may have been revolutionary in its results, it was not especially revolutionary in its introduction.

In the early 1970s the women's movement captured the pill, in both its symbolic and its physical manifestations. Women in Lawrence—and not only young women—interrupted the process of gradual change within the paradigms of population control and sexual morality and offered, instead, revolutionary claims about gender equality, cultural authority, and sexual freedom.

By 1972 any woman in Lawrence—married or unmarried—could obtain birth control pills, free if necessary. This had been true, and widely known, for at least five years. But it wasn't simply access to the pill that was at stake. It was the nature of the access, and the meaning attributed to it, that angered some women. In 1972 two different groups of women in Lawrence challenged the medical men who controlled access to the pill.[12] Though the two groups used different methods and different vocabularies ... both made claims based on the rights and needs of women themselves and not on those of the larger society. In so doing they stepped outside the discourses of morality and of the population problem and centered the debate over access to the pill in a discourse on women, rights, and freedom.

... KU's dean of women, Emily Taylor, was a NOW-style feminist who lobbied for political legislation and university policies supporting equal rights for women. Her office had supported a form of liberal feminism on campus, including a commission on the status of women, and had served as a center of action for some women students and administrators throughout her tenure.

On the other end of the continuum, women in Lawrence's large and diverse counterculture had begun to draw connections between the oppression of minorities and the oppression of women. The women of *Vortex* (the most important underground newspaper) published a women's issue in 1970, and soon afterward the *Lavender Luminary*, a lesbian paper, appeared. W.I.T.C.H. (Women's International Terrorist Conspiracy from Hell) emerged briefly as a local group. Consciousness-raising groups formed. In Lawrence, women were talking with other women about their lives, and those conversations would have repercussions in the world they inhabited.

[In February 1972,] a lecture by radical feminist Robin Morgan inspired these two groups of women to unite as the February Sisters. They took over a university building to voice their demands for full health care for women students, a federally funded child care center on campus, an end to discriminatory employment practices at KU, more women in high-level administrative positions, an affirmative action program, and a department of women's studies. . . . When the Sisters emerged from the building early the next morning, they had won commitments from the administration on a substantial portion of their demands, including the women's health program.

[The Sisters] couched their argument in language echoing the American tradition of rights and freedoms. "We, the February Sisters," their proposal for a human sexuality clinic began, in an invocation of the U.S. Constitution. Arguing that "control of her reproductive functions is a fundamental right of every woman," the Sisters insisted: "The University cannot view the action proposal . . . as a request for additional privileges, but rather as a demand to recognize right [sic] which have been neglected."[13]

It was not simply the right to access these women claimed. . . . More important, these women were rejecting the frameworks of sexual morality and population control that had governed access to contraceptives for more than a decade. The February Sisters condemned the ways that many Americans used concepts of sexual morality to deny women's autonomy and dignity—a fairly obvious and expected critique—but also criticized the efforts of population control groups. . . . These women understood that rationales for contraception based on population control, no less than those based on morality, left room for comments like the one made by the irritated director of student health, Dr. Schwegler, who said that he did so many pelvic exams he sometimes felt like he worked in a whorehouse. The February Sisters and their allies meant to provide a new framework for prescribing the pill that centered around the needs of women themselves and left no room for such demeaning and disrespectful remarks.[14]

After the actions of the February Sisters in February 1972, Watkins student health center officially began prescribing the pill to unmarried women. Somewhat ironically, the following month the Supreme Court ruled that women could not be denied contraceptives on the basis of marital status.

The struggles over the pill in Lawrence were not yet over, however. Even though Watkins offered contraceptives, students still sought the quick access to birth control and the relative anonymity offered by Dr. Clinton's clinic at the public health department. . . . In August 1972, however, the Kansas State Department of Health cut off funding for Clinton's birth control program. The state agency received its funding from the Department of Health, Education, and Welfare (HEW), and it came with federal mandates [that] committed doctors to follow a specified procedure in prescribing the pill, including performing a complete physical exam, pap smear, visual exam for cancer, tuberculin test, hemoglobin, and urinalysis. Clinton . . . refused to perform these tests. . . . Comprehensive medical services for the indigent were not his mandate, he insisted, and he would continue to provide birth control as before, funding it through donations from patients, not to exceed $1 per woman each month. Dr. Schwegler, the director of KU's student health service, who was also serving as chairman of the public health committee, told the *Journal World* that he was "irritated as a private citizen" over the state health department's action. Clinton prevailed with Lawrence's Board of Health, and his refusal stood. Though the local clinic lost a $12,000 federal grant, it was soon running a $10,000 surplus from donations by birth control patients.[15]

Young women who took the pill Clinton prescribed had sex without fear of pregnancy. They obtained the pill simply by request, without the demeaning act of lying about an impending marriage or the purchase of a cheap gold ring at a drugstore. They were, by and large, grateful. By prescribing the pill, Dr. Clinton inadvertently facilitated the sexual revolution in Lawrence and changed the lives of thousands of young women and their partners. . . .

NOTES

1. Elizabeth Rose Siegel Watkins, in "On the Pill: A Social History of Oral Contraceptives in America, 1950–1970" (Ph.D. diss., Harvard University, 1996), pp. 130–131.

2. Pearl S. Buck, "The Pill and the Teen-Age Girl," *Reader's Digest* 92 (April 1968):111, quoted in Watkins, "On the Pill," p. 138.

3. Donald Harting and Leslie Corsa, "The American Public Health Association and the Population Problem," *American Journal of Public Health* 59 (Oct. 1969):1927–29. For a history of population control initiatives, see James Reed, *From Private Vice to Public Virtue* (New York: Basic Books, 1978).

4. Leslie Corsa, "Public Health Programs in Family Planning," *American Journal of Public Health* 56 (Jan. 1966, supplement); Reed, *From Private Vice*, p. 378; Watkins, "On the Pill," pp. 141–142. For statistics on federal funding see "Family Planning Services," Hearing before the Subcommittee on Public Health and Welfare of the Committee on Interstate and Foreign Commerce, House of Representatives, serial no. 91–70 (Washington: GPO, 1970), pp. 190–193.

5. Mary Calderone, "Health Education for Responsible Parenthood: Preliminary Considerations," *American Journal of Public Health* (Jan. 1964): 1735–40.

6. "Should Birth Control Be Available to Unmarried Women?" *Good Housekeeping*, Feb. 1967, p. 14.

7. Will Hardesty, "Birth Control Practices Debated," *University Daily Kansan (UDK)*, Nov. 4, 1966.

8. Willard Dalrymple, M.D., "A Doctor Speaks of College Students and Sex," *Journal of the American College Health Association* 15 (Feb. 1967):286.

9. W. Roy Mason Jr., M.D., "Problems of Married College Students: Health Education Implications," ibid., 14 (April 1966):273–274. Frances K. Harding, M.D., "The College Unmarried Population Explosion," *Journal of School Health* 35 (Dec. 1965):450–457.

10. "Over-Interest Closes County Clinic," *UDK*, Feb. 3, 1970; "Birth Control Clinic Closes," *UDK*, Feb. 5, 1970.

11. The student request was in conjunction with the Commission on the Status of Women at KU, sponsored by the dean of women's office. Information here is from "February Sisters Position Statement on a Health Care Program for Women," Addendum II, in Lorna Zimmer personal files, Lawrence, Kan.; "Women—February First Movement," Women's Studies Program Archives, KU (WSPA); Judy Browder, "Women's Decade of History," WSPA; "Campus Problems for Consideration," Council on Student Affairs files, University of Kansas Archives.

12. There was at least one woman physician in Lawrence, and she had been quoted in the *UDK* refusing to prescribe contraceptives to unmarried women. But in this controversy the divisions that appeared publicly were strictly along gender lines.

13. "February Sisters Position Statement on a Health Care Program for Women," in Zimmer files.

14. Judy Henry, "Groups Urge Birth Control," *UDK*, April 4, 1971. Browder, "Women's Decade," and transcript of "February Sisters Panel Discussion," 1987, statement by Mary Coral, in WSPA.

15. "State Drops Birth Control Funding Here," *Lawrence Daily Journal World (JW)*, Sept. 22, 1972; "Birth Control Funding Possible," *JW*, Sept. 27, 1972; Tim Pryor, "Health Agency Says Changes Due," *JW*, Jan. 10, 1973; Toby MacIntosh, "Policy on Pills is Controversial," *JW*, Feb. 9, 1973.

JI-YEON YUH
Korean Military Brides: Cooking American, Eating Korean

How do transnational and multiracial families navigate cultural differences? In the aftermath of the Korean War, U.S. military personnel stationed in Asia married "native" women. These marriages were part of a broader trend. American military men going abroad socialized and sometimes married foreign women in many countries.

Couples who wanted to marry across national borders faced challenges. First, they had to seek permission from the U.S. soldier's senior officer, and the U.S. military generally discouraged these unions. The armed forces promoted commercialized sexual interactions by helping establish red-light districts and rest-and-recreation sites. But marriage was more problematic. Racially discriminatory immigration laws were being reversed in the aftermath of World War II

Excerpted from the introduction and ch. 4 of *Beyond the Shadow of Camptown: Korean Military Brides in America* by Ji-Yeon Yuh (New York: New York University Press, 2002). Reprinted by permission of the author and publisher. Notes have been renumbered and edited.

and during the Cold War and the civil rights movement. Even so, it was not until 1967 that the Supreme Court ruling in *Loving v. Virginia* made antimiscegenation laws unconstitutional. Beyond these regulations and laws, interracial and international couples met with many social and cultural challenges.

Ji-Yeon Yuh's essay explores some of these difficult dynamics in Korean-American families in the United States through an examination of foodways—the social and cultural practices associated with producing, preparing, and consuming food. For Yuh and her interview subjects, food is intimate and symbolic. The culinary desires and practices of a wide range of immigrant families reveal profound longings for cultural connection as well as deep conflicts concerning cultural identity.

A young Asian woman in Western clothing steps off a boat and is greeted with flowers by middle-aged Americans. She is a Korean war bride meeting her in-laws for the first time, announces the narrator, who then intones a platitude about embarking on a new American life.[1]

Images similar to this grainy scene from a Korean War-era government newsreel could also be found in popular American magazines such as *Life* and *Time* during the 1940s and 1950s. For the most part, these numerous depictions of war brides featured smiling young women waving from ships as they arrived in the United States to join their American soldier husbands. At the dawning of the so-called American Century, these women, who had left behind all that was familiar for an American man, were seen by the American public as proof positive of America's superiority. The very term "war brides" emphasizes the women's dependence on men and their link to war, conferring an identity on them as human war booty. There were even "war bride ships" that took entire groups of young women from Europe to America to join their husbands.

But despite the burgeoning sense of American superiority that came with victory in World War II, there was some doubt among the general public as to the wisdom of American men marrying foreign women, and couples were made to jump through quite a few bureaucratic hoops before gaining the necessary permission to marry. It was, however, generally assumed and expected that the women were eager to become Americans, both out of wifely love and admiration for the American way of life.[2]

When the brides in question were Asian, these expectations were simultaneously tempered by a keener suspicion and bolstered by a stronger confidence. The generally held view at the time was that women from such alien cultures would not make suitable wives for American men and would likely have great difficulty really becoming American. Their choice of America, however, validated America's confidence in itself as the greatest country on earth. In the early years, legal barriers to Asian immigration greatly restricted the number of Asian war brides permitted to enter America. A series of laws culminating in the 1924 Immigration Act prohibited [most] Asians from immigrating and the War Brides Act of 1945 made no provision that allowed for an exception in the case of Asian women who married American soldiers. It was not until the immigration laws were revised in 1952 that the prohibition against Asian immigration was lifted. Until then, Asian war brides—primarily those from Japan, but also a few from Korea—were allowed to immigrate only through special acts of Congress that established temporary windows of opportunity through which American soldiers could bring home their Asian wives.[3]

Despite suspicions as to their ability to do so, Asian war brides were fully expected to Americanize as quickly as possible. After all, they were now married to American men. That their new lives as Americans were structured by racial, cultural, and gender ideologies privileging white male authority and mainstream American culture is made explicit in the 1952 movie, *Japanese War Bride*. The heroine's troubles are linked to her friendship with Japanese American neighbors. She achieves happiness only by rejecting Japanese Americans and ensconcing herself within a nuclear family household headed by her white American husband. This kind of cinematic portrayal of the expectations that Asian war brides had to meet was based on real-life experiences. A survey of Korean war brides in the 1970s, for example, revealed that their primary conflict was with in-laws who demanded that they renounce

Korean culture, even restricting their contact with fellow Koreans.[4]

For war brides, then, becoming American meant discarding one's culture and forsaking relationships with ethnic kin in order to cleave to the culture of a husband and serve as housewife and mother within an all-American family. In other words, war brides were expected to fulfill a role defined by others. In the case of Asian war brides this was further complicated by the particular suspicions, stereotypes, and racism that Americans directed at Asians.

Between 1950 and 1989 nearly a hundred thousand Korean war brides immigrated to the United States. . . . Until recently, few Koreans or Americans really knew who these women were. They existed as stereotypes at the fringes of consciousness. For Koreans, they were women of questionable character who had married American soldiers because such marriage was their only escape from poverty. For Americans, they were foreigners whom red-blooded American men had inexplicably married. . . . For second-generation Korean Americans, they were the women sitting alone, without husbands, during church service and fellowship, the ones they'd ignore because everyone else did. Their presence has barely been acknowledged and their histories have been marginalized. But their presence is significant and Korean women continue to marry American soldiers every year.[5]

Korean women met and married American soldiers in the historical context of U.S. military domination over South Korea that preceded the 1950–53 Korean War and extends into the present. Thus for Korean war brides, as well as for most other Asian war brides, the term "war bride" is misleading. The majority of Korean war brides married their soldier husbands during times of suspended armed conflict, that is, during times of relative peace, not war.[6] Their marriages are a direct result of ongoing U.S. military troop deployments in South Korea since 1945. U.S. military domination is what made these marriages possible and it has also had far-ranging effects on the tenor of Korean-American marriages. For this reason, . . . I call these women "military brides."

Korean military brides were born and raised in a country that went from being a Japanese colony to being sundered in two by the superpower rivalry between the United States and the Soviet Union. They come from a nation-state, South Korea, that has served the needs of

U.S. national security in the name of anticommunism and defense against North Korea, often at the expense of its own citizens. South Korea has been politically, militarily, and economically subordinated to the United States since before its inception in 1948. . . . [7]

Military brides, like most South Koreans, are in constant negotiation with American cultural hegemony, accepting some of its demands and constraints while seeking to reject others. The neoimperialist relationship between South Korea and the United States has shaped the ways in which these women have experienced and encountered America, as well as the ways in which they are positioned within their families and American society as a whole. Korean military brides have been on the front line of Korea-U.S. cultural and social contact for the past half-century.

. . . As women, they have been shaped by Korean gender ideology to view marriage and motherhood as the ultimate feminine goals. But as women who have married non-Koreans and as women who—regardless of their social background—are stained by presumed association with U.S. military camptowns and prostitution simply because they married an American soldier, they are left standing outside the bounds of both respectable Korean womanhood and authentic Koreanness. Thus military brides are constantly defending their respectability as well as their Korean identity. . . .

[This essay explores one aspect of] the women's attempts to be both good Korean women and good American wives, highlight[ing] food as a form of cultural expression. The stories presented in these pages are based primarily on oral history interviews and fieldwork conducted over a three-year period. The women and families I interviewed and observed were found through personal contacts throughout the Korean immigrant community. The women I met led me to other women, who led me to three regional associations of military brides and a Korean church composed of military brides and their families. I attended meetings and fund-raising dinners held by the associations and became a member of the church for two years, participating in church life. . . . [8]

Throughout my research, I was acutely aware of my outsider-insider status. I too am a Korean woman but I am not a military bride and I'm usually not of the same generation as the women I interviewed for this book. Like them, I'm an immigrant Korean woman, but unlike them, I came as a child rather than as an adult. I am a racial and ethnic minority in America, as they are, but I'm also fluent in English. That fluency has allowed me many privileges, including an advanced education, higher social status, and greater earning power. . . .

Studying the lives and history of Korean military brides has profound ramifications for American history, Asian history, and Asian American history. The history I tell of Korean military brides reveals a history of American involvement in Korea and Korean involvement with America seen from "way, way, way down below."[9] The linkages I make—between the imperialist nature of Korea-U.S. relations and husband-wife dynamics, between pressures to Americanize and Orientalist images of Asian women and family relations—demonstrate that even the most personal of relationships are deeply rooted in and shaped by historical and social circumstances. In this history, I trace the contours of an everyday resistance not against strangers or social superiors in public spaces, but against family intimates in private spaces. It shows us the hollowness of American multiculturalism even as it shows us the ways in which military brides contest that particular hegemony. And it offers us a glimpse of the transformative potential of imagining and locating community beyond the nation.

In the United States, where people of different cultures, races, and ethnicities have encountered each other since the beginning, food is a signifier of difference and identity. It is a terrain where ethnicity is contested, denigrated, and affirmed. It is an arena of struggle between Americanization and adherence to native cultural ways, where the demands are often either-or, but the lives lived are more often constructed from pieces of both.[10]

The experiences of Korean military brides with food mirror their broader experiences as interculturally and interracially married immigrant women. As military brides learned to cook and eat American foods, they enacted a process of assimilation that was demanded of them by husbands, in-laws, and even children who had the weight of the dominant American culture behind them. The marginalization and stigmatization of Korean food within their households represent their cultural isolation within their own families. The incorporation of "palatable" Korean foods into American meals illustrated their own incorporation into

their American families, their Korean culture and identity literally consumed as cultural accessories in a process that cultural critic bell hooks has called "consumer cannibalism."[11] At the same time, their perseverance in cooking and eating Korean food and their insistence on maintaining a Korean identity testifies to the limits of the United States' ongoing project of Americanization.

Historian Donna Gabaccia's study of American foodways, *We Are What We Eat*, celebrates the incorporation of ethnic foods into mainstream American culture, drawing a picture of a harmonious and peaceful America full of what she calls multiethnics, people of different backgrounds who eat foods from different backgrounds. In her picture, conflict between native-born Americans and immigrants as expressed in "food fights"—particularly during the first half of the twentieth century— is a thing of the past. No longer do Americans turn up their noses at different foods and try to Americanize the eating habits of immigrants. Instead, they enthusiastically adopt new foods introduced by new immigrants. Eating a mélange of ethnic foods has become the American thing to do. Marriage across cultural and ethnic boundaries is one way, she suggests, that multiethnic peoples and foods are produced.[12]

The experiences of military brides, however, illustrate that "food fights" are not yet over; they are simply conducted more quietly and with less fanfare than in the past. Military brides' narratives reveal that a matrix of power relations surrounds the choice of what foods are cooked and eaten in the families that have resulted from interracial and intercultural marriages.

The first part of the story is that of the deprivation that began with the physical absence of Korean food. Korean military brides who immigrated to the United States in the decades of the 1950s and 1960s, a time when the proverbial land of plenty was basking in unprecedented economic wealth, told me that "here, there was nothing to eat." For these women, accustomed to the tastes and smells of Korean food, American food was not food at all. Like the overwhelming majority of Korean immigrants—indeed, like most immigrants from any country—they craved the foods of their homeland. Women who immigrated in later decades experienced few of the difficulties of their predecessors, for Korean food could be found relatively easily at stores and restaurants catering to the burgeoning

Korean immigrant population. Many of them had already experienced American food in Korea, where hamburgers and pizza, along with McDonald's and KFC, became well known to urban dwellers beginning in the 1980s. Nevertheless, these women also spoke of missing Korean food, for not everything Korean could be found everywhere in America.

The very absence of Korean food in the midst of a bounty of American food is itself a powerful force for Americanization, for immigrants are faced with a choice between eating the food that is available or starving. The choice is obvious. The women ate American food. But their consumption of American food was not necessarily a sign of their Americanization. Even though they ate it, they did not necessarily like it. The women not only longed for Korean food, they also searched for it, invented ways to replicate it, and gave it an emotional loyalty they never developed for the American food they ate out of necessity. . . .

For the military brides who arrived during the 1950s and 1960s, a time when immigration from Korea and other Asian countries was still legally restricted and Korean communities were small and mostly limited to Hawaii and California, the biggest shock was the food. Suddenly, every meal became a painful reminder of having left home. Not only did the absence of Korean food intensify their feelings of homesickness and loneliness, but it also caused physical problems: American food was so unpalatable that eating was difficult and hunger was a constant companion.

One woman, who arrived by boat in 1951 with her soldier husband, said that the most difficult thing during her first years in the United States was craving Korean food, but having to eat American food. Like many other Koreans, she found American food to be heavy, greasy, and bland. The smell and taste of butter, used in so many American foods, was distasteful. "[A]t that time," said Mrs. Mullen, "I was very homesick, and the most difficult thing was food, eating, yes. It was difficult, back then."

The craving for Korean food was so strong that even her dreams were all about food:

> Food, Korean food, very very . . . I think about it, I dream about it, in my dreams there is no Korean food, or I am eating Korean food, or Korean food appears, this is what I dream about. When I first came, what I survived on was, well, rice was, you know, but I survived on *American pickle*. And

spaghetti, that's what I survived on. It was terrible, I wanted so badly to eat [Korean] food, it was terrible. Oh, I suffered very very much.

. . . Pickles and spaghetti, however, weren't enough to sustain her.[13] Mrs. Mullen noted in a later conversation that she lost weight during those first years in America. This appears to [have been] common among military brides of her generation. . . .

Craving for Korean food was accompanied by homesickness and a loneliness that resulted from the absence of other Koreans in their lives. Both Mrs. Mullen and Mrs. Crispin spoke in the same breath about missing Korean food and missing Korean people. . . . For Mrs. Crispin as well, missing Korea and missing Korean food were intertwined:

> Back then, I was always thinking about Korea, in Korea this is delicious and that is delicious. . . . So when we [she and other Koreans] sit and talk, the talk starts with food and ends with food. In Korea the pears are delicious and so are the apples, and so are the fried pancakes and so on. We talk about this the whole time and then go home, after just smacking our lips the whole time. We were lonesome for people, very lonesome, but back then eating was a big shock as well. The food just wasn't to our taste.

The opportunity to eat Korean food came with meeting other Korean people, illustrating the connection between food and companionship. For Mrs. Mullen, that opportunity came through the first Korean woman she met in America, a woman from Seoul. The friend would sometimes go shopping in New York—a distance of some four hours by car—for Korean food. The two women would then cook and eat Korean food together. . . .

. . . The lack of Korean food was compounded by the inability to cook Korean food. Like many other military brides I interviewed, both Mrs. Mullen and Mrs. Crispin had never learned to cook Korean food. So even though some of the ingredients necessary to make Korean food, such as soy sauce, soybean curd, and Korean vegetables could be found at grocery stores in urban Chinatowns, many women were unable to duplicate the tastes of home.[14] . . .

Red pepper paste and soybean paste, two crucial seasonings in Korean food, were virtually impossible to find during those early years. Unlike soy sauce, they were not available in Chinatown stores, for they are not part of any tradition of Chinese cooking. But the women were inventive and passed their inventions on to each other. Mrs. Crispin learn[ed]to make imitation red pepper paste, [drying] "the heels from loaves of bread, and pour[ing] soy sauce over it. {laughs} When the bread became all soggy, [you] would sprinkle crushed red pepper and mix it all up. And then you call that red pepper paste and eat it!" The taste was not the same as the real stuff, of course. It could not be used for making stews, only as a condiment for rice. . . .

. . . [M]any of the later arrivals also spoke about food when they talked about missing home and being lonely. . . . One woman noted that no matter how prevalent Korean food has become in America, it can't compare with the prevalence of American food. In Korea, she pointed out, one can find Korean food anywhere and everywhere, and the variety is seemingly endless. But even in the so-called multicultural 1990s in America, one still has to know exactly where to look to find Korean food and the repertoire available in Korean restaurants is depressingly standardized and bland.

. . . Many of the military brides I interviewed stated that Korean food in America just doesn't taste as good as Korean food in Korea. . . . [When] Mrs. Crispin described the pears [she loved in Korea,] it was Korea she was always thinking about, not Korean food. It wasn't Korean food that tastes good and which they missed, it was food in Korea. Location was important.

. . . In short, Korean food in America just isn't the same as Korean food in Korea. . . . The issue here is displacement. Displaced from its home, the food apparently loses a certain something. The women's craving for Korean food is linked to a longing for a return home, to a time before . . . [they became] strangers in a strange land.

Throughout the first half of the twentieth century, immigrant and ethnic women were subject to native-born American women's attempts to Americanize immigrant families by teaching the women how to cook and eat American food. It was an urgent project, for Americans feared that America would be "swallowed by foreigners" unless they were properly Americanized. The fact that America at that time was more a conglomeration of regional cultures than a unified national culture made America seem vulnerable to foreign influence and thus endowed the project with greater urgency. . . .

It was also a zero-sum project, for—in keeping with the prevailing sentiment that immigrants must shed their old identities in order to become American—it was not enough to add American food to one's diet. One also had to subtract or substantially alter the familiar foods of home. It was also an endeavor that disguised its fundamental ethnocentricity and nativism under the progressive banner of good health, science, and economical housekeeping. Asian and southern European women were told to feed their families more milk for proper nutrition. Italian women were told not to cook meat, cheese, beans, and macaroni together because the combination allegedly hindered digestion. Mexican women were told to use less tomato and pepper to make blander foods that were purportedly easier to digest and kinder to the kidneys, and were urged to stop the allegedly unsanitary practice of dipping with tortillas into the same pot at the dinner table. And everyone was urged to eat plain, bland, thrifty foods such as mashed potatoes and baked beans.[15]

In these admonitions to immigrant women by American women home economists, nutritionists, and other professionals can be seen several strong and interconnected ideas about food. One is the gendered conceptualization of food preparation as the women's domain; another is the endowment of food with cultural properties, such that what one eats and how it is eaten become markers of group identity.[16] What one ate clearly marked one as either a backward, ignorant immigrant or an educated, modern American. Furthermore, the belief that educating immigrant women would lead to educating and thus Americanizing their entire immigrant families rests on assumptions about women as the bearers of culture and thus the mediating force for Americanization. Although these Americanization-through-food projects fizzled as fears of immigrant hordes receded during the 1940s and 1950s and disparate regions became increasingly bound within a "national culture" disseminated through the mass media and mass commerce, the underlying assumptions about food, gender, and Americanization have remained very much in force.

Thus Korean military brides found themselves subject to pressures to Americanize . . . primarily from husbands, children, and mothers-in-law—people difficult, even dangerous, to ignore precisely because they were intimate family members. There is remarkable consistency in the women's narratives regardless of the time period in question. A woman who came in the 1990s was just as likely as a woman who came in the 1950s to face demands that she cook primarily, or even only, American food. The one difference is that the husbands and in-laws of women who arrived in later decades seem to have been more open to incorporating selected items of Korean food into the household repertoire. This seems connected to a general revival of interest in ethnic foods, however, and is not related to any desire to allow Korean women to maintain their Korean identity.

Although they married Korean women, most husbands do not seem to have been interested in a Korean wife complete with all the cultural trappings of customs, food, and language. . . . [T]hey were looking for women with the traditional feminine values of submissiveness and deference to male authority, and believed that Asian women had such characteristics. They wanted wives who would serve them roast beef and potatoes, with English and a smile. . . . [17]

Expressed in the language of teaching a new wife or new daughter-in-law how to please her husband and adjust to her new environment, the racial and cultural power dynamics of Americanization were effectively hidden in the gender dynamics of marriage. In this matrix of intersecting and overlapping power relations—between mainstream American culture and a "foreign," minority culture, between a neoimperialist United States and a neocolonial Korea, between American men and Korean women, between husband and wife, between primary breadwinner and dependent—Korean women were almost always at a disadvantage. Their acceptance of gender roles often led them into compliance, making overt expressions of Americanization on the part of husbands or in-laws unnecessary. But in acceding to these pressures, as did most of the women I encountered, they were not necessarily undergoing a willing or total Americanization. Rather, their compliance was part of the complex negotiation in which they alternately resisted and complied. . . .

As married women, they took for granted the expectation that it was their duty to cook for their husbands and that this meant cooking what husbands liked to eat. . . . Learning to cook American food, an experience that one woman described as universal for Korean military brides, was one that set them apart from their other immigrant compatriots in an important way. Most Korean immigrants were not interested in learning how to cook non-Korean foods, but instead focused on recreating Korean dishes in an American immigrant setting.[18] For military brides, however, learning to cook American food became one of their primary tasks as they learned how to become good American wives.

. . . [In] the families of Korean military brides, . . . since most American husbands prefer to eat American food, and some even dislike Korean food intensely, whatever Korean cooking ability the wives may possess is virtually useless. In accordance with the husbands' preferences, family meals are characterized by the presence of American food and the absence of Korean food. The wives must either eat American food with their husbands, or eat Korean food alone. Their biracial children also tend to prefer American food. Her son, Mrs. Peterson reported, doesn't like to eat rice, stating that he is an American boy and therefore must eat bread. This seven-year-old boy has already singled out food as a marker of identity, refusing to eat food that he considers foreign to his sense of self. The male prerogative of the husband coupled with the cultural dominance of America leave little room for Korean food at the dining tables of these intercultural and interracial families. Food is a marker of difference and of the accompanying power inequities of which every meal is a potential reminder. . . . Thus, unlike other immigrant women, military brides become the transmitters not of their own familiar cultures, but of the foreign cultures of their husbands. . . .

. . . Despite their own distaste for most American food, learning to cook it was so important that many women considered this task to be at the center of their adjustment to American life. This was also true of military brides who arrived in later years and had few problems eating American food. None of the women I interviewed had ever cooked American food before they married their American husbands, and they all said that they spent a great deal of time and effort learning how to cook to suit their husbands' tastes. Those who could not cook Korean food, or cooked it poorly by their own estimation, noted regretfully that they had had no chance to learn because they were preoccupied with cooking American food for their families. For these women, learning to cook

American food had the result of blocking their acquisition of Korean cooking skills. An important expression of culture and self, food, thus changed dramatically for these women as a result of intermarriage and subsequent migration to the husband's country.

At the same time, every woman I interviewed expressed pride in her ability to cook American food. Several women, such as Mrs. Goldin, said they cooked American food better than Americans, and many noted that their husbands complimented them on their cooking. This pride in meeting the expectations of their husbands and in acquiring new skills cannot be easily dismissed. It can be read as a partial, if problematic, resistance to the denial of Korean identity that their participation in the daily mealtime rituals of family production entails. They may be suppressing their Korean identity, but they are actively building a new life around their American husbands. By learning to cook American food and fulfilling the roles of mother and wife, they were also living up to the traditional ideal of Korean womanhood, which dictates self-sacrifice for the sake of the family.[19] Thus, learning to cook American food and the denial of ethnic self which that entails can be read as an ironic affirmation of their Korean womanhood, a merger of their struggle to be both good American wives and good Korean women. . . .

. . . The kitchens of these military brides were filled with food products common to middle-class Americans across the nation, from A-1 steak sauce and Heinz ketchup to Oscar Mayer bologna, Kraft American Cheese, and Quaker Instant Oatmeal. This was true regardless of the specific ethnic background of their husbands. Their comments and their kitchens demonstrate that while America may not have a national cuisine, it certainly has national food habits that are readily discernible by newcomers. . . . These foodways are closely linked to commercialized, processed, and prepared foods whose brands are household names and can be found everywhere from the supermarket to the neighborhood corner grocery.[20]

In addition to salads, bacon, lettuce, and tomato sandwiches, and steak, many women also learned to cook dishes reflecting their husbands' particular cultural backgrounds. Mrs. Weinberg, who came in 1969 with her Jewish American husband, learned to cook blintzes, potato latkes, and chicken soup, among other dishes. With pride, and some self-conscious laughter for complimenting herself, Mrs. Weinberg said that she had become quite a good cook. Mrs. Goldin, who said she can cook American food better than many Americans, learned to cook soul food for her African American husband. Mrs. Bugelli, who arrived in 1959, learned to cook Italian food, including all kinds of Italian cakes and cookies, for her Italian American husband and his two sons. . . . Despite the presence of ethnic foods, however, standard or mainstream American food seemed to predominate. . . . Asked whether American food or Jewish food was eaten more often in her home, Mrs. Weinberg replied that Jewish food was eaten occasionally, especially at Passover, but that most meals were "just American."[21] . . .

Based on observations of her own family's eating habits and preferences, sociologist Mary Douglas has aptly observed that meals have structures. . . . Korean meals are structured around a bowl of rice and several side dishes. There are no courses and everything is served at once. The side dishes usually include a bowl of soup or a pot of stew, and always include *kimchi*. Only rice and soup are served in individual portions; other side dishes are served each in its own dish placed at the center of the table. Diners use their own chopsticks or spoons to take mouthfuls of the side dishes. Many of the side dishes, including different varieties of *kimchi*, are prepared in advance and eaten slowly over a period of several days or even several months. Some side dishes actually require advance preparation, since several days or weeks are needed to produce the desired flavor. Eating the same side dishes meal after meal is common.[22]

The structure of American meals, on the other hand, is [typically] a main dish accompanied by two supporters. Families that put together a full dinner usually have a main course (1a) and a first course and dessert (2b). Soup or salad is often served as the first course. The main course usually consists of meat or fish (1a) accompanied by two side dishes (2a) served on the same plate. If rice is served, not only is it unlikely to be Korean-style rice, but it appears as a side dish, not the meal's center. Everything is individually served, and diners do not dip their eating utensils into the same bowls or plates of food. Eating the same thing twice in a row is usually considered to be eating leftovers. Dessert, a common ending to middle-class American meals, has no equivalent in Korean meals. . . .

[And yet, in some families,] Korean foods [were] incorporated into other American food rituals [besides formal meals]. Mrs. Orellana, who arrived in 1991, expressed surprise that her husband, their preschool son, and her parents-in-law enjoyed eating seasoned *keem,* thin sheets of dried laver. *Keem* is a common side dish at Korean meals, where it is eaten wrapped around a spoonful of rice. She then noted that while they also like rice, they never ate *keem* with rice. . . . Instead, to her surprise, they ate the seasoned *keem* like a snack while talking or watching TV, . . . a snack akin to potato chips. . . . [Here,] a Korean food is accepted by the American family, but on their own terms. . . .

This is not to say, however, that the families do not identify the foods as Korean. They do. They are aware that they are eating Korean *keem* and not American potato chips, [or] Korean barbecued beef and rice, not American steak and potatoes. These Korean foods are incorporated into a larger American structure of meals and food habits so that rather than the foods "Koreanizing" American meals, the [practice] "Americanizes" the foods even as they are labeled "Korean." It is one of the steps toward Americanization that various other ethnic foods—pizza, corn chips, tacos, hot dogs, and bagels come to mind—have taken in the course of American history.[23] The new foods serve to enrich, not transform, American culture, and eating them does not necessarily turn Americans into multiethnics.

The interest in Korean food seems linked to a general surge of interest in ethnic foods that began in the 1960s and soared in the 1980s. Mrs. Orellana's mother-in-law, for example, took an interest in foods from different cultures and bought a Korean cookbook in preparation for meeting her new daughter-in-law in 1991. Another woman, who arrived in 1989, said her sister-in-law commented that having a Korean in the family made life more interesting because it allowed them to be close to a different culture. Although friendly interest is preferable to hostility, this does not necessarily place the Korean cultures of the women on par with the American cultures of the husbands

and in-laws. The husbands and in-laws can choose whether or not to learn about Korean culture and eat Korean food, that is, they can choose whether or not to make their lives more interesting, but the women do not have similar freedom of choice regarding American culture. Nor does their acquisition of American culture serve to strip it of context and transform it into a consumer item for pleasure and cultural enrichment. When the husbands, children, and in-laws of military brides consume selected items of Korean food, this is not necessarily evidence of biculturality or multiethnicity. Especially in households that otherwise devalue and stigmatize the Korean culture of the wife and mother, it is just as likely to be a shallow gesture that appropriates bits and pieces of Korean culture for a variety that adds "spice" to American life.[24] . . .

[A] pattern of eating American food with their husbands and Korean food when alone was common among military brides I met. . . . Those who insisted on eating Korean food daily often found themselves cooking two sets of meals, serving one and then eating the other alone. Rather than a family affair eaten together that symbolizes and reaffirms the unity of the family, . . . meals became individual affairs eaten separately that symbolized the internal cultural dissonance within the family. . . .

. . . [Mrs. Peterson reported that her husband] didn't mind her cooking and eating Korean food. He rarely complained about the smell of Korean food, she said, except once in a while when she cooked *doenjang* stew or *kimchi* stew. This was a common refrain among women who cooked Korean food at home: even if he doesn't eat it, at least he doesn't complain much about the smell when I do. The feeling seemed to be that they were among the lucky ones. . . .

Those who were unable to keep Korean food at home spoke of attending Korean functions where food was served, simply to eat some Korean food as well as to see some Korean faces, or of calling up other military brides and getting themselves invited over for a Korean lunch. Some women told me that one of the most enjoyable aspects of going to Korean churches was the food. Gatherings of military brides, such as the monthly meetings of military bride organizations, invariably include Korean food. Even their fund-raising dinners—aimed at a mixed audience of Koreans and Americans—usually feature Korean food. Every military bride who spoke with me about participating in such organizations noted that the chance to eat Korean food was a major attraction. . . .

Although they maintain their families through the cooking and serving of meals that suppresses their Korean culture and identity, and although they live under constant awareness of the marginalization of their cultures, military brides do retain their identities as Korean women. They negotiate through and around the suppression and marginalization, finding ways to express their Korean selves and to eat the foods they crave. Even if, like Mrs. Mullen, they rarely eat these foods, their views of the tastiness of Korean food versus American food tend to favor Korean food. They speak as if it were natural that they should concede the family territory to American food but reserve a slice of personal space for Korean food, for themselves. Eating Korean food is a way of expressing Korean identity, of partaking of ethnic community, of being connected to kin, hometown, and fellow immigrants. The women spoke of a strong need for the comforts of the familiar, for affirmation of self, and for emotional sustenance. Eating Korean food and retaining their loyalties to it appear to be a way of meeting these needs and keeping body and soul together . . .

The women at New York's Rainbow Center, a women's collective of and for Korean military brides, know that food is more than just food. They have experienced its healing powers. Many of the women who come to the Rainbow Center come after suffering years of abuse. As a result, some have emotional and mental problems. When center women know that a new woman is due to arrive, they make sure that the house is redolent with the fragrance of Korean food. The new arrivals are treated to meal after meal of Korean food: *doenjang* stew, *kimchi* stew, *kimchi*, and lots of rice. The dominant language at the center is Korean, the atmosphere is familial, and the kitchen is filled with Korean food and Korean eating utensils. In this deliberately Korean atmosphere, said the center's founder and director, the Rev. Geumhyun Yeo, the women slowly come back to life. During some twenty years of working with military wives, she said, she came to realize that many of the emotional and mental problems that troubled military brides are linked to their deprivation

of Korean food and Korean companionship. Surrounding them with these things is therefore an essential part of the Rainbow Center's program of resuscitating abused military brides, she said.[25]

While preparing our dinner after our formal oral history session, Mrs. Crispin talked about the different ways of cooking seaweed soup, which was on our menu for the evening. Asking me how my mother cooked it, she said that she usually first sautéed the seaweed and dried anchovies in sesame oil, then added hot water and simmered it until done. My aunt, I replied, usually used bits of beef instead of dried anchovies, while my vegetarian mother used neither but added only a different variety of seaweed that is used primarily to make broth. Women from the coastal regions of Korea used fresh clams and other shellfish, Mrs. Crispin noted, recalling her childhood years spent in those regions. She then sighed a little and said, "It's more than just fun to talk about this, don't you think?" Noting that she had lived in the United States for so long that it seemed like home, she said that times like this, cooking and eating Korean food with another Korean woman, even a stranger like myself, gave her an indescribable feeling. Searching for words to express herself, she said, "Maybe something like drinking water after being thirsty for a really long time."

Notes

1. Seen in the documentary *Women Outside*, by Hye-Jung Park and J. T. Takagi (Third World Newsreel, 1996).

2. For example, "War Brides Arriving in U.S.," *Life*, February 18, 1946, p. 27.

3. Chinese American men in the armed forces also brought home Chinese women as brides. As citizens of China, an American ally during World War II, these women were exempt from immigration restrictions against Asians; about six thousand Chinese war brides came under the War Brides Act. This influx of women helped even skewed gender ratios in Chinese American communities. See Sucheng Chan, *Asian Americans: An Interpretive History* (Philadelphia: Temple University Press, 1991), p. 140. Apparently, few of the Chinese war brides married non-Chinese Americans.

4. *Japanese War Bride*, 91 min., directed by King Vidor.

5. Daniel B. Lee, "Korean Women Married to Servicemen," in *Korean American Women Living in Two Cultures*, ed. Young In Song and Ailee Moon (Los Angeles: Academia Koreana, Keimyung-Baylo University Press, 1997), pp. 94–123.

6. The Korean War ended with a truce, not a peace treaty, and thus the United States remains officially at war on the Korean peninsula despite the absence of outright armed conflict. This is why South Korea is categorized as a combat zone by the U.S. military and soldiers posted there are given hardship pay.

7. See Bruce Cumings, *The Origins of the Korean War*, 2 vols. (Princeton: Princeton University Press, 1981 and 1990), and, Cumings, *Korea's Place in the Sun: A Modern History* (New York: W. W. Norton, 1997).

8. All interviews for this study were conducted in Korean and translated into English by the author. All names of military brides are pseudonyms, and some identifying traits have been changed as necessary to protect confidentiality.

9. I first heard this phrase during a talk Robin D. G. Kelley gave at the University of Pennsylvania in 1993–94 about southern blacks, resistance, and the civil rights movement.

10. Roland Barthes, "Toward a Psychosociology of Contemporary Food Consumption," in *Food and Culture*, ed. Carole Counihan and Penny Van Esterik (New York: Routledge, 1997), p. 21. The ideal of Americanization, one that posits a white America and things white American as superior, has remained strong throughout the twentieth century. One important measure of Americanization has been food.

11. bell hooks, "Eating the Other: Desire and Resistance," in *Eating Culture*, ed. Ron Scapp and Brian Seitz (Albany: State University of New York Press, 1998), 181–200.

12. Donna Gabaccia, *We Are What We Eat* (Cambridge, Mass.: Harvard University Press, 1998).

13. Spaghetti became a popular foreign dish among many Koreans, perhaps because it contains garlic and because noodles topped with sauce is a familiar form of food to Koreans.

14. It is common for Korean women to know only the rudimentary basics of cooking when they marry and to learn how to cook as young wives under the direction of their mothers-in-law. For military brides, marriage to an American can thus mean that they never learn to cook Korean food.

15. Gabaccia, *We Are What We Eat*, pp. 122–48. See also George Sanchez, "'Go after the Women': Americanization and the Mexican Immigrant Woman, 1915–1929," in *Unequal Sisters: A Multicultural Reader in U.S. Women's History*, ed. Vicki L. Ruiz and Ellen Carol Dubois (New York: Routledge, 1990), pp. 284–97.

16. See, for example, Marjorie L. DeVault, *Feeding the Family: The Social Organization of Caring as Gendered Work* (Chicago: University of Chicago Press, 1991); Jacqueline Burgoyne and David Clarke, "You Are What You Eat: Food and Family Reconstitution," in *The Sociology of Food and Eating*, ed. Anne Murcott (Aldershot, England: Gower Publishing House, 1983); and M. Ekstrom, "Class and Gender in the Kitchen," in *Palatable Worlds: Sociocultural Food Studies*, ed. E. L. Furst, R. Prattala, M. Ekstrom, L. Holm, and U. Kjaernes (Oslo: Solum Forlag, 1991).

17. Ji-Yeon Yuh, *Beyond the Shadow of Camptown: Korean Military Brides in America* (New York: New York University Press, 2002), ch. 3.

18. Min Pyong Gap et al., *Migug Sok-eu Hangugin (Koreans in America)* (Seoul: Yurim Munhwa Sa, 1991), pp. 179–80.

19. See Laurel Kendall and Mark Peterson, ed., *Korean Women: View from the Inner Room* (New Haven, Conn.: East Rock Press, 1983) Sandra Mattielli, ed., *Virtues in Conflict: Tradition and the Korean Woman Today* (Seoul: Royal Asiatic Society. Korea Branch, 1977); Yung-Chung Kim, ed. and trans., *Women of Korea*, by the Committee for the Compilation of the History of Korean Women (Seoul: Ewha Women's University Press, 1976); and Alternative Culture, ed., *Jubu: Geu Makhim-gwa Teu-im (Housewife: That Closing and Opening)* (Seoul: Alternative Culture Press, 1990).

20. Sidney Mintz, *Tasting Food, Tasting Freedom* (Boston: Beacon Press, 1996), has observed that America does not have a cuisine per se but a distinctive way of eating characterized by fast food, instant food, frozen food, canned food, and other ready-to-eat and easy-to-prepare edibles.

21. One study of white Americans shows that while eating the foods of one's own ethnic background (Italian, Polish, etc.) is the most common ethnic-related activity (reported by 47 percent of respondents), such foods are eaten less than once a month by the majority of these respondents; Richard D. Alba, *Ethnic Identity: The Transformation of White America* (New Haven, Conn.: Yale University Press, 1990), pp. 79–80, 85–86. See also Mary C. Waters, *Ethnic Options: Choosing Identities in America* (Berkeley: University of California Press, 1990).

22. Mary Douglas, "Deciphering a Meal," in *Food and Culture*, ed. Carole Counihan and Penny Van Esterik (New York: Routledge, 1997), pp. 36–54. My description of the structure of Korean meals is based on my life experience eating meals in middle-class Korean families in Korea and in America, plus discussions with other Korean women about what constitutes a proper Korean meal. Fancy Korean meals served in restaurants vary in structure, and some include courses.

23. Gabaccia, *We Are What We Eat*, discusses the incorporation of ethnic food items into American culture.

24. On the superficial incorporation of aspects of foreign cultures other than food, see Kristin L. Hoganson, *Consumer's Imperium: The Global Production of American Domesticity, 1865–1920* (Chapel Hill: University of North Carolina Press, 2007).

25. Similarly, Indochinese and Hmong immigrant women speak of eating their native foods as a means of healing the illnesses and emotional traumas that come from the stress of cultural change. See Donna Gabaccia, *From the Other Side: Women, Gender, and Immigrant Life in the U.S., 1820–1990* (Bloomington: Indiana University Press, 1994), p. 121.

LISA LEVENSTEIN

Hard Choices at 1801 Vine: African American Women, Child Support, and Domestic Violence in Postwar Philadelphia

Drawing lines between the deserving and the undeserving, the worthy poor and the unworthy poor, the independent and the dependent—along with the stigmatizing of the dependent—has been an enduring part of our history. In this essay, Lisa Levenstein explores the efforts of working-class African American women to claim public protection against domestic violence and to seek economic support in the years after World War II. Examining the records of the Philadelphia Municipal Court, she finds that poverty and domestic violence were inextricably entangled in ways that public officials often found difficult to appreciate. The straightforward claims of women citizens for entitlements that the law provided— Aid to Families with Dependent Children, for example—all too easily were translated by judges and social workers into reproach: blame of fathers who could not support their children, blame of women who could not "hold" a husband, blame of mothers who could not care for their children and simultaneously hold a full-time job. Yet African American women continued to turn to the Philadelphia Municipal Court, where they had some real success in persuading judges to recognize their claims and meet their needs.

For their part, legal officials began with the assumption that the wage levels sufficient to enable a single male earner to support his wife and children—the "family wage"—were universally available. They tended to discount the racial discrimination that excluded many African Americans from the secure work force. What other assumptions does Levenstein find that court officials were likely to make when they assessed the charges made by African American women? What risks did African American women take when they turned to the courts? What did they want court officials to understand?

In a Philadelphia criminal courtroom on November 18, 1947, Judge Gay Gordon called Janice Carson, an African American woman in her early twenties, to testify in an assault and battery case that she had brought against her husband. When questioned, Mrs. Carson told the court that she and Vince Carson had had a rocky marriage with constant domestic violence both before and after he served in the army during World War II. The most recent incident had occurred after she told Vince that

she was pregnant with their second child: He "beat me and he struck me. . . . He was choking me and he knocked me against a radiator, and the night after that I had a miscarriage."

When Vince Carson took the stand, he admitted that he had beaten Janice. However, he stated that the incident had occurred during an argument "about her allowance" and that he had hit her in self-defense. "She slapped me first," he testified, "and I just lost thy head and slapped her—" "Your Honor, I never struck

Excerpted and slightly revised by the author from ch. 2 of *A Movement Without Marches: African American Women and the Politics of Poverty in Postwar Philadelphia* by Lisa Levenstein (Chapel Hill: University of North Carolina Press, 2009). Reprinted by permission of the author and publisher. Notes have been edited and renumbered.

him first," interrupted Mrs. Carson. "Everyone knows he fights me." At this point, Judge Gordon intervened in the dispute. "You talk too much," he told Mr. Carson. The judge proceeded to call Mr. Carson a "brute," told him that the "seeds of murder" were planted in his home, and warned him that he would end up in the electric chair one day.

After a few more questions, Judge Gordon turned to Mrs. Carson and asked, "Madam, what do you want me to do with him?" Mrs. Carson explained that although she had separated from Mr. Carson, she still needed his financial support because she had been in poor health since the miscarriage and could not seek employment to support herself and her son. She asked for a "peace bond," a type of bail that would give Mr. Carson freedom and allow him to look for a job as long as he did not beat her. The judge told Mrs. Carson that Mr. Carson belonged in jail, but that he would grant the peace bond. The day after his release, Vince Carson attacked his wife, tore her clothing, and beat her up.[1]

In the years after World War II, working-class African American women like Janice Carson turned to the Philadelphia Municipal Court for economic support and protection from domestic violence ... The legal system was geared toward preserving two-parent families and limiting the parent financial support that the government provided to poor single mothers through the Aid to Dependent Children (ADC) program. However since judges strongly believed that men needed to fulfill their roles as breadwinners and owed women physical protection and financial support, women could harness the court's biases to work in their favor. Most women won their cases, often obtaining either a small amount of money or limited protection from domestic violence.

Of all the public institutions in the city, it was in the municipal court that the intimate connections between poverty and domestic abuse became most clearly visible. During years when civil rights activists focused on violence outside the home, and well before middle-class feminists would interpret spousal abuse as a political issue, working-class African American women placed the issue of domestic violence squarely on the public stage. Like Mrs. Carson, many viewed their need for protection from violence as integrally linked to their need for financial assistance and struggled because the municipal court separated charges of assault from charges for support. They had to choose between freedom from violence and freedom from hunger, even though gaining one often meant sacrificing the other.

... Instituted in early twentieth-century cities throughout the country, municipal courts worked under the assumption that common crimes should be addressed in a comprehensive manner that promoted individual and social rehabilitation. The Philadelphia Municipal Court had been created by the state legislature in 1913 in response to agitation by white middle-class social reformers. ... Although ... it was a court of record and had the power to imprision offenders, like most twentieth-century municipal courts, it sought not only to punish, but also to assist, educate, and discipline its clients. Legal authorities conducted thorough investigations of their clients' life circumstances and provided medical testing, counseling, and other social services. To provide specialized attention to different types of cases, the court was divided into five divisions: civil, criminal, domestic relations, juvenile, and misdemeanant. ...[2]

African American women's legal dealings usually took place in the courthouse that handled domestic and juvenile cases, which they referred to by its address as "1801 Vine." Marcelle Blackwell, who grew up in postwar Philadelphia, described 1801 Vine as the "most famous address in the city of Philadelphia" because of the frequency of women's visits.[3] Opened in 1940, on the eighteenth block of Vine Street, a wide, central thoroughfare for municipal buildings in Philadelphia, its architecture exuded a formality that distinguished it from most other public institutions in the city. The imposing limestone structure had a colonnaded front. Grand front doors opened onto an expansive main hallway with high ceilings, chandeliers, murals, and terrazzo floors. ... A series of murals throughout the building symbolized the "uplifting" work that the court envisioned itself performing—reuniting families and rehabilitating juvenile delinquents.

... Legal rituals underscored the court's function as an institution that enforced the rule of law. Although most trials were conducted without juries, women had to swear before signing petitions or testifying in front of judges, and their statements were carefully recorded by court employees. They interacted mainly with middle-class, often college-educated, interviewers and probation officers who were the foot soldiers of the court's efforts to collect and organize personal and demographic information about clients. . . . In the mid-1950s, African Americans comprised less than one-quarter of the city's population, but black women were half of the plaintiffs in nonsupport cases and two-thirds of the plaintiffs in assault and battery cases. Although African American and white women both experienced domestic violence and nonsupport, black women had less access to alternative resources than did white women and were more likely to take legal action against men.

Women who pressed charges in the municipal court confronted judges whose outlooks exemplified some of the limitations of postwar liberalism in meeting their needs. In the 1950s, the court had fourteen judges, elected by city voters to ten-year terms. All of the judges who worked in the domestic relations court were white men, usually Democrats from Italian American, Polish American, or Jewish backgrounds.[4] Although many of them were active in a range of civic organizations and known for their humanitarianism, they felt little sympathy for the plight of struggling African Americans. Most believed that two-parent families with male breadwinners were superior to other family forms. They looked down on unmarried mothers, particularly those who received welfare, and expressed contempt for fathers who could not adequately support their wives and childen.

Most women who approached the municipal court sought child support or protection from domestic violence. Their suits took three main forms. Unmarried women's suits against the fathers of their children for financial support, called fornication and bastardy, were handled in the women's criminal division, making it ambiguous exactly who legal officals believed should be on trial.[5] In the 1950s, on average, nearly two thousand women pressed these charges each year. The domestic relations court handled married women's financial support cases, usually in the form of nonsupport charges against their husbands. These cases numbered over four thousand each year. . . . Finally, assault and battery charges brought by women against violent men were handled in the criminal division until 1952, when the domestic relations division took control of their adjudication.[6] The court usually handled over six hundred of these cases each year. Although women did not press charges of assault as often as they pressed charges of nonsupport, the large number of assault cases challenges

feminist scholarship that has portrayed this period as a time when women rarely used the legal system to prosecute domestic violence.[7]

The rulings in women's assault and battery cases varied widely because judges did not have formal procedures in place for dealing with them. Prior to 1952, the municipal court sent abused women to the magistrates' courts for an initial hearing. Some women settled their cases with the magistrates, securing warnings, peace bonds, and occasionally jail sentences for their husbands. Those not satisfied with the magistrates' hearings could pay a $10 fee to obtain a warrant for their husbands' arrest and press assault and battery charges in the criminal division of the municipal court. During the criminal trials, municipal court judges almost always tried to reconcile couples. However, when reconciliation proved impossible, judges used their own discretion to settle the disputes, finding some men not guilty and requiring others to post peace bonds or go to jail.

. . . The legal system did not address or help remedy the connections between poverty and domestic abuse: women who were financially dependent on their husbands were more vulnerable to abuse, and abuse could reinforce women's poverty by injuring and isolating them. If women with abusive husbands chose to seek support orders, they were left without protection from violence. If they pressed criminal charges and their husbands ended up in jail, they were left without financial support. Faced with this impossible choice, some abused women who relied on men's financial support sought a compromise: They pressed assault charges and then asked judges to give their husbands a warning or put them on probation, hoping that this would allow men to continue earning money while helping curb subsequent episodes of violence. As Mrs. Carson's case illustrates, this strategy could backfire by making men so furious that they continued the abuse.

Nonsupport . . . cases had far more predictable outcomes. Married women seeking to press nonsupport charges met with an interviewer, usually a woman, who recorded detailed information about their cases and their backgrounds. The interviewer then contacted women's husbands and requested their presence in court. Probation officers investigated men's places of employment to verify their wages and sometimes conducted home visits to inspect couples' living arrangements. Seven to ten days after the women's initial contact with the court, most men came in for their meetings with interviewers. Interviewers spoke individually with the men and then met with the couples together in one or more joint conferences. No matter what interviewers learned about the men's and women's relationships, they tried to convince couples to reconcile. Most women refused and insisted on filing a formal petition for a trial. The cases then joined a line of hundreds of other similar cases waiting for a trial, a backlog caused by the large numbers of women pressing nonsupport charges and the limited number of judges assigned to the cases. On average, it took ten to fourteen weeks before women received hearings. The trials themselves usually lasted less than five minutes because judges were under tremendous pressure to move quickly. Even when men painted unflattering portraits of women's behavior by complaining about their promiscuity, failure to perform domestic chores, or excessive nagging, court policy was formulated so that judges almost always ruled in women's favor and awarded them financial support.[8]

Fornication and bastardy cases, which concerned unmarried couples, involved similar procedures, but were usually settled more quickly. To secure benefits, women had to press charges within two years of the conception of a child. Because the couples were not married, interviewers did not try to persuade them to reconcile. Instead, during the initial meetings and fieldwork inquiries, court workers pressured men to admit paternity and agree to pay child support. Most men recognized that they had a slim chance of winning their cases, acknowledged that they had fathered the child, and agreed to comply with a support order. Fewer than one in ten cases went to trial, and the mothers who testified were usually awarded financial support.

The legal priorities that undergirded the policies favoring reconciliation and men's support of women and children reflected judges' commitment to the family-wage system and to preventing women's dependence on the state. Family-wage ideology envisioned men earning a wage that was sufficient to support a wife and children at home. This ideal was unattainable for most working class African Americans; men could rarely obtain stable, well-paying jobs, and many women with young children were gainfully employed. State authorities

recognized that African American women held jobs because African American men's wages were insufficient, but they did not believe that women should be the primary breadwinners for their families or head their own households. Judges claimed that households with married couples and male breadwinners were morally superior to those headed by single mothers. They also preferred two-parent households for fiscal reasons because most married women did not qualify for welfare. The court's Annual Reports noted that interviewers tried to "effect a reconciliation . . . and a reestablishment of wholesome family relationships" to save "the community many millions of dollars" in welfare payments.[9] In cases in which reconciliations proved impossible, judges promoted support orders in order to diminish women's welfare checks. . . .

Women often faulted the court for failing to ensure that they received adequate financial assistance. Many criticized the judges' practice of calculating support orders according to men's wages, which typically awarded them one-third of men's pay. Since most men who came before the court held low-wage jobs, most women received very small stipends. Jessie Redd observed, "When you take a man into court you hardly get enough to pay a babysitter."[10] The fact that the court was notoriously slow and inefficient in delivering support checks on time exacerbated the problem. . . . Even more troubling for many women was the court's failure to compensate them for the high rates of male noncompliance. In 1960, 70 percent of the support orders in effect were not being paid.[11]

To address the problem of noncompliance, judges advocated changing men's behavior, a solution that did not take into account many working-class men's precarious economic circumstances. Annual Reports attributed men's default to willful neglect, charging that men found "devious and sundry" ways to "escape their family obligations." . . . This approach did not take into account how unemployment and low-wage jobs made it difficult for many men—especially African American men—to support families. . . . When there was a sharp increase in the cost of living just after World War II, many men returned to court to get their support orders decreased. That many women returned to have their orders increased for the very same reason illustrates a fundamental problem with court policies that made poor women and children directly dependent on poor men for their livelihood.[12]

Many men charged that they suffered from the court's financial support policies. Those who had remarried, lost their jobs, or had to care for parents or other family members usually found support orders financially burdensome. Particularly in cases involving unmarried mothers, the court's policy of ruling in favor of women was so entrenched that men had little chance of being found innocent even if they did not believe that they had fathered the child. Throughout the postwar period, legal officials engaged in periodic crackdowns on delinquent accounts in which field-workers tracked down men and sometimes even arrested them at their places of employment. Authorities experimented with jail terms and garnished wages; in 1959, 463 men were jailed for nonpayment of support orders. Judges justified the crackdowns by emphasizing that men's avoidance of child support resulted in increased welfare payments to women, claiming that it was "the state and not the wife—who suffers when the husband fails to meet the court order." By laying part of the blame for welfare expenditures on unpaid support orders, judges suggested that African American men contributed to the immorality and fiscal irresponsibility that they associated with ADC.[13]

Working-class African American women insisted that they, not the state, were the victims of men's noncompliance. Thousands of women lived in precarious situations, never assured of receiving financial support because the legal and welfare system forced them to depend on men's irregular contributions. Arlene Starks remarked: "Maybe the next week I'll get a check. Maybe the following week I'll get a check. Now the next two weeks I don't get no check. See, that keeps me off base all the time." Court policies stipulated that men had to default on four consecutive payments before women could issue a complaint at the Department of Accounts. After women reported the nonpayment, probation officers often instructed them to track down men themselves to find the reason for the defaults. . . .

Throughout the 1950s, nearly seven thousand women returned to court each year to complain of men's noncompliance. Many women needed their small support checks so desperately that they returned five to fifteen times over the course of several years when men refused or were unable to pay.[14]

Even when women managed to get their husbands back into court, they did not always receive compensation for missed payments. Several years after Corrine Elkins pressed charges, her husband stopped paying his support order. When she took him back to court, "he was $4,800 in arrears." To Mrs. Elkins's dismay, "The judge dismissed $2,000 of it. He said, 'Well, just get rid of $2,000 of it, and you owe $2,800, and you can pay $5.00 extra each week.'" Knowing that this ruling would have little effect on her husband's behavior, Mrs. Elkins said that she "came to the conclusion, you've got to do things yourself, girl" and started putting in more overtime, working twelve to sixteen hours a day, six or seven days each week. With her arduous schedule and decent city job, Mrs. Elkins could get by without her missed support payments. Most poor mothers could not.[15]

When the court advocated policies that ensured women's financial dependence on men, why did it fail so consistently in enforcing them? First, enforcement procedures were expensive since, as women knew from experience, it could take weeks to track down men and verify their wages. By forcing women to find and discipline men themselves, the court saved money. . . . Second, because welfare administrators decreased women's ADC checks after they pressed nonsupport charges, the state conserved money simply by issuing a support order, regardless of whether or not judges enforced it. Third, as historian Anna R. Igra has argued, in an era in which the "taint of corruption . . . adhered to state spending," the court's financial support policies performed an important symbolic function. By strongly advocating support orders, public authorities . . . could demonstrate both their desire to conserve state monies and their adherence to social norms concerning men's responsibilities to their wives and children.[16]

In most cases, women made carefully calculated decisions about their use of the court. Taking legal action was an ordeal, requiring regular visits to court, several interviews, and a great deal of paperwork. Those with small children found the process particularly difficult. Bell Jackson described a typical visit: "My children and I spent almost six hours in court. I took them at 9:30 that morning and we didn't get out until 3:00 that afternoon . . . I spent my last money getting there, and all that time.

And what happened? Nothing, except we discussed why he wasn't staying with us and how come we broke up, which I've been over a lot of times." Prior to initiating such frustrating procedures, women took stock of their circumstances and tried to decide whether the assistance they could receive from the court was worth the costs.[17] . . .

Most ADC recipients tried to avoid going to court because they risked losing money by pressing charges. The fathers of their children usually could not keep up with support orders, and since welfare caseworkers subtracted the dollar amount of support orders from their ADC checks and rarely provided compensation when men defaulted, taking legal action was a potential financial burden, not a help. Women on decent terms with the fathers of their children generally preferred to receive full welfare grants with no court order, supplemented "under the table" with informal gifts from men.

Some women tried to avoid getting involved with the court because of the humiliation that frequently accompanied the process of taking legal action. Pursuing assistance from the court was never publicly maligned in the way that seeking welfare was, but it was still tarnished by its association with low-income Philadelphians. When Hazel Weinberg, a Jewish woman, went to court to press nonsupport charges, she did not return after her first visit because the interviewers were rude and condescending and she found the process "degrading." Many African American women dreaded testifying in court because the judges were well-known for publicly condemning their reliance on ADC and claiming that they neglected their children. Whether or not they received welfare, all black women felt vulnerable to judges' wrath. Joan Park, a financially secure working-class African American woman, explained that she "wouldn't be caught dead in court" because she considered herself an upstanding member of her community and did not want to subject herself to the indignities involved in pursuing legal action.[18]

The women who decided to press nonsupport charges frequently had financial troubles that led them to believe that even a meager court order would make a positive difference in their lives. . . . Ada Morris, a welfare recipient, explained the importance of her small support check to her livelihood: "I sit down on the first of the month . . . and I count my money

up—to who I owe. . . . My rent comes first. My gas comes next. My food bill . . . comes next. . . . If I don't get nothing from him—well, I can't pay." For women like Mrs. Morris, who struggled each month to make ends meet, even a small stipend made a difference.[19]

Women who pressed domestic abuse charges tended to come from slightly more financially stable homes than those who pursued nonsupport charges and considered their need for physical protection to be their most pressing concern. They were rarely middle-class, but they were often not completely impoverished either. Although some very poor abused women like Mrs. Carson pressed assault charges, others were either deterred by the $10 fee (until 1952, when the fee was waived) or prioritized financial support over protection from violence. . . .

Most abused women decided to avoid legal action completely. Some lived in an acute state of terror with extremely violent and volatile husbands. They were unable or unwilling to leave their marriages and feared that pressing charges would only make the abuse worse. Charlotte Elkins decided to "hang in there" with her husband while "getting my butt beat" for thirteen years because of the "mental abuse" that accompanied his physical violence. She stated that her husband's verbal and physical assaults made her feel worthless and convinced her that she would be unable to survive on her own. Many women who did not go to court resisted the abuse in other ways, escaping to friends' and relatives' houses, attempting to protect their children, and fighting back. Catherine Sanderson recalled standing up to her husband when he beat her. "I sure would . . . hit him back," she explained. "He wasn't my father." Corrine Elkins never fought back until the night that she decided to leave her husband: "He came home . . . and got crazy, and I went for the kitchen knife . . . and . . . really tried" to kill him.[20]

When women made decisions about their pursuit of legal action, they considered their responsibility for children, access to alternative resources, employment opportunities, and experiences of domestic violence. They also took into account a wide range of facts about their husbands and boyfriends: how much money men made, whether they were abusive or unfaithful, and how involved they were with their children. Most women only pressed financial support charges against men who had jobs because they knew that unemployed men did not have any money to give them.

While legal authorities assumed that all African American men who did not provide for their families were irresponsible, African American women had a different and more nuanced definition of nonsupport. Recognizing that racial discrimination made it difficult for the most dedicated husband and father to earn enough to support his wife and children, they did not condemn all men who failed to provide them with financial resources. Instead, most African American women reserved charges of nonsupport for cases in which men deliberately withheld funds from their families, complaining about men squandering their wages on alcohol, other women, or luxury items, instead of rent, food, and clothing for their families. For some married women, the discovery that their husbands had been cheating on them further galvanized them to press nonsupport charges. Unmarried women sometimes responded similarly when they learned that their boyfriends had wives. In other cases, unmarried women may have only had casual contact with the father of their children and pressed charges in court because they had nothing to lose.[21] . . .

Many women who maintained cordial relationships with the fathers of their children found that even the threat of legal action provided them with considerable leverage when negotiating financial support. Because of the strength of their community information networks, women and men who had never set foot in court knew from other people's experiences that women would almost always win financial support cases. Men understood that they would be saddled with a court order and subjected to humiliating treatment from legal authorities, and women knew that men would be angry and would rarely pay regularly. Many women decided that, rather than alienate men by pressing charges, they were better off having men feel indebted to them for not pursuing legal action. The undesirability of legal action gave some leverage to women like Beverly Jordan, who was separated with one child and worked in a coat factory in postwar Philadelphia. Every year, Mrs. Jordan was laid off for two to three months during slow seasons around Christmas and Easter. When this occurred, she would phone her ex-husband and ask for money for food and for her daughter's Christmas present, threatening to take him to court if he did not comply. . . .

In women's dealings with the court, they frequently challenged legal authorities' attempts to collect detailed personal information. Interviewers sought to compile extensive files documenting women's backgrounds and grievances, while field-workers investigated men's earnings and employment records and made home visits to ask about children's school attendance and inspect women's living conditions. Unmarried mothers had to provide detailed descriptions of their relationships with the fathers of their children, the date of the sexual intercourse that produced the child, and accounts of their previous sexual experiences. Many women refused to give court interviewers full access to their private lives, falsifying information or refusing outright to answer questions that they deemed too personal. . . .

One of the only times that interviewers and judges did not attempt to challenge or pry into women's decisions about their private lives was when women withdrew their assault and battery charges against their husbands, which occurred in approximately one-third of all abuse cases. On the witness stand, these women usually minimized the abuse and told judges that they had changed their minds and did not want to press charges. Even when women testified that their husbands had "busted my head open" or stabbed them with knives, if they stated that they wanted to return home with their husbands, judges made no attempt to dissuade them. Most judges feared that if couples separated or the men received jail sentences, the wives would seek public assistance.[23] . . .

. . . Working-class African American women faced problems at every level of the criminal justice system but still refused to give up on the municipal court. Most African Americans in Philadelphia believed that the police department and the courts were racially prejudiced institutions. Yet, building on decades of African American legal assertiveness, women sought to harness a system that they viewed as racist to work on their behalf. Had black women testified against white men, judges' racial prejudices might have served as more of a deterrent to their use of the court. However, since most African American women pressed charges against African American men, they knew that the verdicts would usually be in their favor. Although women did not receive very much money or physical protection from their legal victories, most of them faced such severe problems and had so few alternative sources of support that even the small amount of assistance they secured from the court made a difference. Mrs. Elkins recalled, "In those days, the women didn't really have too much going for them. Except 1801 Vine."

Notes

1. Case 447, November 18, 1947, Philadelphia City Archives, Philadelphia, PA [hereafter PCA].

2. Clarence B. Shenton, *History and Functions of the Municipal Court of Philadelphia* (Philadelphia: Thomas Skelton Harrison Foundation, 1930), 66, 80–81; *Philadelphia Municipal Court Annual Reports* [hereafter *PMC-AR*], 1949, A19.

3. All interviews were conducted by the author in Philadelphia, PA, between July 1, 1999 and June 27, 2000. Audiotapes are in author's possession. M.B.M. interview.

4. The juvenile division had the court's only black judge, Juanita Kidd Stout, the first African American woman appointed to a court of record in the nation.

5. In the 1940s, Pennsylvania, Maryland, and Massachusetts courts considered fornication and bastardy a criminal action. In eight states, the courts did not allow unmarried women to prosecute the fathers of their children for support at all. Other states heard these cases but dealt with them in civil court. Not until 1963 did the Philadelphia courts begin to hear the cases as civil rather than criminal proceedings.

6. *PMC-AR, 1959,* 318; *PMC-AR, 1964,* 221. Although a few cases of nonsupport each year were brought by husbands against wives, their numbers were very small.

7. Ruth Rosen, *The World Split Open: How the Modern Women's Movement Changed America* (New York: Viking, 2000), 186. Linda Gordon found that poor women's complaints about domestic abuse in social service agencies increased in the 1930s and 1940s, but her account suggests that they rarely approached the legal system; see Linda Gordon, *Heroes of Their Own Lives: The Politics and History of Family Violence: Boston, 1880–1960* (New York: Viking, 1988), 250–60, 280–81.

8. "Municipal Court Judges Decries 'Assembly-Line Justice,'" *Philadelphia Evening Bulletin* [hereafter *PEB*], February 17, 1957, 1, 6; *PMC-AR, 1950,* 132, 135;

"Court Backlog Boosts Aid to Unwed Mothers Here," *PEB*, May 15, 1959, 34.

9. First quotation in *PMC-AR, 1954,* 153; second quotation in *PMC-AR, 1957,* 197.

10. Quoted in "Unwed Mothers Speak Their Piece," *Philadelphia Afro-American*, January 31, 1959, 3.

11. "Court Slashes Backlog in Distributing Support Cases," *Philadelphia Inquirer*, January 4, 1959, 14; "In Municipal Court Holidays Bring Added Work . . . Held-up Checks," *Philadelphia Independent*, December 28, 1958, 3; *PMC-AR, 1960,* 21–211.

12. "Wanted: Solomon with an Adding Machine as HCL Plagues Estranged Couples," *PEB*, August 28, 1946, 14.

13. *PMC-AR, 1959,* 196; "Bonnelly Acts to Clear Up Support Cases," *PEB*, March 8, 1959, 3.

14. Starks quoted in Gail Levy and Judith Shouse, "A Concept of Alienation: A New Approach to Understanding the AFDC Recipient," (Master of Social Service Thesis, Bryn Mawr College, 1965), 54; *PMC-AR, 1960,* 210–211; *PMC-AR, 1961,* 215. Similarly in early twentieth-century New York, see Anna R. Igra, "Likely to Become a Public Charge: Deserted Women and the Family Law of the Poor in New York City," *Journal of Women's History* 11:4 (2000): 59–81.

15. C. E. interview. Similarly, see G.J. interview.

16. Anna R. Igra, *Wives Without Husbands: Marriage, Desertion, and Welfare in New York, 1900–1935* (Chapel Hill: University of North Carolina Press, 2007), 44, 97, 122, quotation on 44; Igra, "Likely to Become a Public Charge," 73. On postwar public assistance policy, see *PMC-AR, 1953,* A23; *PMC-AR, 1957,* 201.

17. Quoted in Levy and Shouse, "Concept of Alienation," 81.

18. H. C. interview; J. P. interview.

19. Quoted in Levy and Shouse, "Concept of Alienation," 23.

20. Sanderson quoted in C. S. interview; Elkins quoted in C. E. interview.

21. *PMC-AR, 1944,* A62–A63; *PMC-AR, 1949,* 261; *PMC-AR, 1934,* 276–77; *PMC-AR, 1939,* 1, 310–12; *PMC-AR, 1950,* 173; *PMC-AR, 1957,* 237.

22. M.B.M. interview; J.E.J, interview; Van Dyke interview.

23. *PMC-AR, 1953,* 166. For "busted my head open," see Case 127, February 18, 1948, PCA. For knife wounds, see Case 631 and Case 632, May 22, 1957, PCA. It is not clear from the records whether these cases involved African Americans or whites.

DOCUMENTS

Kay Weiss, "With doctors like these for friends, who needs enemies?"

Bubbling up in the 1950s and 1960s came critiques of physicians not only from female patients and medical students but also from health care workers at every level. Gynecologists and obstetricians who treated women on matters relating to sexual activity, abortion, and childbirth received the severest scrutiny. Many were patronizing, moralistic, and infantilizing in their treatment of female patients. Critics emphasized that the problem was not just the personal shortcomings of individual doctors. Nor was it merely the result of their training. At the heart of the problem was a fundamental devaluation of women that led physicians to feel that it was their responsibility to make health care decisions for their female patients, since women were simply not competent to participate in informed decisions regarding their own health. Medical scientists under the imprimatur of the National Institutes of Health, operating under their own masculinist bias, tested drugs on men and mistakenly assumed the results would apply to women, whom they didn't bother to include in the tests.

Many of these early critiques, like the one that follows, were published and distributed through women's movement networks. In calling for women to take greater responsibility for their own health care, they were forerunners of the classic *Our Bodies, Ourselves*. The book had its origins in 1969 in the discussion of a small group of Boston women who felt frustrated about doctors whom they considered "condescending, paternalistic, judgmental, and non-informative."* (See if you can find the table of contents of the most recent edition [2011] or an older edition online. Try to imagine what it would have been like to encounter the text and illustrations in the chapters on sexuality and birth control in 1971.)

While these early indictments, including the one that follows, may have verged on exaggeration, they also provide a window into psychotherapy in the age of the feminine mystique. It should come as no surprise that feminists would challenge a sexist psychiatric and psychological establishment that recommended treatment for any woman who displayed mental and physical symptoms suggesting she was not behaving as a "mature adult" who found sexual fulfillment in vaginally induced orgasm and personal fulfillment in marriage and maternity.

In your own experience with the medical community, have most of the problems about which young women complained a quarter of a century ago been remedied as both sexes have come to take greater responsibility for their medical treatment and as more physicians are women? What vestiges linger?

---

*The Boston Women's Health Book Collective, *The New Our Bodies, Ourselves* (New York: Simon & Schuster, 1984), quoted from the preface of the original edition, xvii.

Kay Weiss, "What Medical Students Learn," KNOW pamphlet #310, Pittsburgh, 1975; reprinted in *Dear Sisters: Dispatches from the Women's Liberation Movement*, ed. Rosalyn Baxandall and Linda Gordon (New York: Basic Books, 2000), pp. 118–120.

One of the cruelest forms of sexism we live with today is the unwillingness of many doctors to diagnose people's diseases with equality. The education of doctors can explain this. [Consider the messages in] the recently revised text *Obstetrics and Gynecology* (1971, 4th edition), which is used this year [1975] in 60 of the nation's medical schools.

SHE'S A CHILD

In *Obstetrics and Gynecology,* women are child-like, helpless creatures with animal-like or "instinctive" natures, who can't get through intercourse, pregnancy, labor or child-raising without "enlightened" physician intervention. The woman in childbirth is just a child herself. Her doctor, even if he is a novice and she is an old pro, is a fount of knowledge while she is "anxious," "fearful," afraid of "getting messy" and may feel "ashamed" and "guilty." The medical student is taught to believe that many symptoms of illness in pregnancy (excessive nausea, headache) are really a result of her "fear of pregnancy" rather than any physical condition he (all medical students and physicians are "he" in *Obstetrics and Gynecology*) need test for. . . .

SHE LOVES RAPE

Many gynecology texts reveal a greater concern with the patient's husband than with the patient herself and tend to maintain sex-role stereotypes in the interest of men and from a male perspective. But *Obstetrics and Gynecology* clearly spells out the attitudes that other texts only imply:

> The normal sexual act . . . entails a masochistic surrender to the man . . . there is always an element of rape.
>
> The traits that compose the core of the female personality are feminine narcissism, masochism, and passivity.
>
> Every phase of a woman's life is influenced by narcissism. Women then love in a different way from men. The woman falls in love with the idea of being loved; whereas the man loves an object for the pleasure it will give. She says, "I am valuable, important, etc. because he loves me. . . . " This type of narcissism finds expression in . . . her interest in clothes, personal appearance, and beauty. Too much feminine narcissism without masochism produces a self-centered woman.

> The idea of suffering is an essential part of her life.

SHE FEELS LIKE AN ANIMAL

Women are described in the text alternately as psychopathic and idiotic: "She is likely to feel that she is animal-like . . . to think of the vagina as a 'dirty cavity.' Black patients will think that the source of sexual desires is in the uterus; white patients think that it is in the ovaries. . . . Orgasm represents the woman's ability to accent her own feminine role in life. . . . Menstruation symbolizes her role in life. . . . "

The medical student is persuaded by the authors that women with dysmenorrhea (menstrual dysfunctions including painful uterine contractions) have no organic disease they need test for; these women simply have "personality disorders," "emotional difficulty in the home," or "neurotic predispositions." They need "sex education" and "mental hygiene" . . . if not "intensive psychotherapy." . . . A brief concession is made to the possible physical causes for menstrual pain, but the authors then quickly return to the problem of diagnosis:

> It is important to ascertain how crippling the symptom and how much emotional gain the patient is deriving from it. For example, does the whole household revolve around whether or not the mother is having menstrual cramps? . . .
>
> The adult woman who presents this symptom very often is resentful of the feminine role. Each succeeding period reminds her of the unpleasant fact that she is a woman. . . .

SHE NEEDS A PSYCHIATRIST

. . . Frigidity is defined as "occasional failure to obtain orgasm," placing 99 percent of women in the category of abnormal. If pleasure is only felt from clitoral stimulation, she may be referred to a psychiatrist. . . . Her frigidity may develop because she "resents her husband's preoccupation with his work or his recreational activities." The physician, a "parental figure," should "discover the problem in the patient's personality" and "encourage her to mature sexually."

Twenty-seven gynecology texts written over the past three decades were reviewed by Diana Scully and Pauline Bart in the *American Journal of Sociology* in January 1973. . . . No text Scully and Bart examined incorporated

Kinsey's 1953 findings that orgasm without stimulation "is a physical and physiological impossibility for nearly all females" or Masters and Johnson's 1966 findings that portions of the vagina have no nerve endings and lack sensation and that although orgasm is felt in the vagina, the feeling derives from stimulation of clitoral nerves.

With doctors like these for friends, who needs enemies?

Roe v. Wade, 1973; Planned Parenthood of Southeastern Pennsylvania v. Casey, 1992; Carhart v. Gonzales, 2007; Recent Developments

---

The Comstock Act of 1873 was echoed by a series of anticontraception and anti-abortion laws throughout the country. By 1900, James Mohr observes, "Every state in the Union had an antiabortion law of some kind on its books . . . except Kentucky, where the state courts outlawed the practice anyway."* (See Leslie Reagan's essay, pp. 451–456.)

In 1962 the ethics of abortion became a pressing problem when it was revealed that thalidomide, a drug extensively used in Europe and occasionally in the United States, resulted in the birth of thousands of babies with phocomelia (deformed or missing arms and legs). Sherri Finkbine, an Arizona woman who had taken the drug, demanded a legal abortion. Although her own doctors supported her, the county medical society refused to approve the procedure, and, lacking confidence that she and her doctors would be granted immunity from prosecution, she fled to Sweden, where abortion was legal. Believing that other women should not have to discover the dangers of thalidomide the way she did, Sherri Finkbine told her story to local newspapers, and the news traveled quickly across the nation.

Her plight, and her challenge to hospital practice, helped to shift public opinion, both within the medical profession, which would subsequently be instrumental in advocating liberalization of abortion legislation, and among women's groups, which began to articulate dismay that women were generally denied access to safe abortion services. Estimates of the number of illegal abortions performed each year before 1973 range from 200,000 to 1,200,000; it is estimated that at least 200 women died each year as a result. Abortion was virtually the only medical procedure to which middle-class women did not have access. The issue was less intense for black women's groups; working-class minority women lacked a wide range of medical services, and abortion was only one among many which they needed. Thus, at the beginning of the reinvigorated women's movement of the late 1960s, black and white women were divided about the place that access to legal abortion should hold in their list of priorities for legal change.

Some physicians, like those who had approved Sherri Finkbine's request for a therapeutic abortion, sought to liberalize antiabortion laws, arguing that medical practitioners were best situated to judge when an abortion was appropriate. They were joined by a grassroots movement of women throughout the country who argued that current abortion statutes undermined their own constitutional right to equal protection of the laws. It was not equal protection, they insisted, when women with financial resources—like Sherri Finkbine—could find safe abortions and poor women could not, nor when women could not make their own

---

*James C. Mohr, *Abortion in America: The Origins and Evolution of National Policy, 1800–1900* (New York: Oxford University Press, 1978), pp. 229–30.

fundamental decisions whether to carry and bear a child. The severe social stigma to which unmarried pregnant women were subjected deprived them of dignity.

Before the *Roe* decision was handed down, a number of expansions of reproductive rights were made on the state level. In Connecticut over 800 women, joined as plaintiffs in a case popularly known as "Women versus Connecticut," convinced the state supreme court to declare the state's severe law unconstitutional; in 1969 the California Supreme Court held the California abortion law unconstitutional because it violated "the fundamental right of the woman to choose whether to bear children," citing the U.S. Supreme Court's decisions in *Griswold* (see pp. 671–672) and *Loving* (see pp. 669–670). Women activists also filed lawsuits in New Jersey, Rhode Island, Pennsylvania, and Massachusetts. In Iowa the Young Women's Christian Association supported abortion reform as early as 1966; women legislators took the lead in introducing reform bills, and a statewide organization largely composed of women—the Iowa Association for Medical Control of Abortion—lobbied vigorously for reform.** In 1970, Alaska, Hawaii, the state of Washington, and New York, legalized abortion. (In New York, the measure passed the lower house by a single vote; the Assemblyman who gave it predicted accurately that he would lose his seat.)

Faith groups divided on the issue. For many Catholics, opposition to abortion reform was of a piece with opposition to the death penalty. As members of Americans United for Life put it in 1972, "those who argue for the unborn child's right to life are arguing not only for the unborn child, but for the civil right to life of every human being–the mentally ill, the aged, the genetically incompetent, the idle, the useless." Clergy of a wide range of Protestant denominations and Reform and Conservative Rabbis, on the other hand, organized the Clergy Consultation Service in 1967, a nationwide network providing reliable information for women seeking safe abortions before the procedure was legal. (Recent studies show that close to 30 percent of women now obtaining abortions identify as Catholic; over 35 percent identify as Protestant.)†††

Texas law continued to prohibit abortion except for the purpose of saving the mother's life. In 1970, Norma McCorvey, a single pregnant woman, known as Jane Roe to protect her privacy, brought a class action suit challenging the constitutionality of that law as a violation of her right to liberty as guaranteed by the due process clause of the Fourteenth Amendment.

The Supreme Court's 7–2 decision in *Roe v. Wade* marked a sharp change from long-established practice. As the opening lines of the majority decision make clear, the justices were aware they were making a sensitive and important decision. There were two dissents; one, by Justice William Rehnquist, characterized the desire for abortion by a healthy woman as a matter of her "convenience."

On what constitutional grounds does Justice Blackmun base the Supreme Court's reasoning? Where does he find the right of privacy? (See the Fourteenth

**Amy Kesselman, "Women Versus Connecticut: Conducting a Statewide Hearing on Abortion," in *Abortion Wars: A Half Century of Struggle*, ed. Rickie Solinger (Berkeley: University of California Press, 1998), pp. 42–67; *People v. Dr. Leon Belous*, 458 P.2d 194 (1969); James C. Mohr, "Iowa's Abortion Battles of the Late 1960s and Early 1970s: Long-term Perspectives and Short-term Analyses," *Annals of Iowa* 50, no. 1, 3rd ser. (Summer 1989): 63–89. Selections from Americans United for Life , the Clergy Consultation Service, and many opponents and supporters of reform are included in Linda Greenhouse and Reva B. Siegel, *Before* Roe v. Wade: *Voices that Shaped the Abortion Debate Before the Supreme Court's Ruling* (New York: Kaplan, 2010). The 2nd edition (New Haven: Yale Law School, 2012), with a new afterword, is available free as a downloadable PDF at http://documents.law.yale .edu/sites/default/files/BeforeRoe2ndEd_1.pdf.

†††Fact Sheet: Induced Abortion in the United States, July 2014, Guttmacher Institute http://www.guttmacher .org/pubs/fb_induced_abortion.html.

Amendment, p. 289, and inspect the Bill of Rights—the first ten amendments to the U.S. Constitution, readily available on-line). What limits does the Court place on the exercise of that right?

ROE V. WADE, 1973

MR. JUSTICE HARRY A. BLACKMUN
DELIVERED THE OPINION OF THE COURT:

We forthwith acknowledge our awareness of the sensitive and emotional nature of the abortion controversy, of the vigorous opposing views, even among physicians, and of the deep and seemingly absolute convictions that the subject inspires. One's philosophy, one's experiences, one's exposure to the raw edges of human existence, one's religious training, one's attitudes toward life and family and their values, and the moral standards one establishes and seeks to observe, are all likely to influence and to color one's thinking and conclusions about abortion.

In addition, population growth, pollution, poverty, and racial overtones tend to complicate and not to simplify the problem.

Our task, of course, is to resolve the issue by constitutional measurement, free of emotion and of predilection. We seek earnestly to do this. . . .

The principal thrust of the appellant's attack on the Texas statutes is that they improperly invade a right, said to be possessed by the pregnant woman, to choose to terminate her pregnancy. Appellant would discover this right in the concept of personal "liberty" embodied in the Fourteenth Amendment's Due Process Clause; or in personal, marital, familial and sexual privacy said to be protected by the Bill of Rights . . . or among those rights reserved to the people by the Ninth Amendment. . . .

It perhaps is not generally appreciated that the restrictive criminal abortion laws in effect in a majority of States today are of relatively recent vintage. Those laws, generally proscribing abortion or its attempt at any time during pregnancy except when necessary to preserve the pregnant woman's life, are not of ancient or even of common-law origin. Instead, they derive from statutory changes effected, for the most part, in the latter half of the nineteenth century. . . . At common law, at the time of the adoption of our Constitution, and throughout the major portion of the nineteenth century . . . a woman enjoyed a substantially broader right to terminate a pregnancy than she does in most states today. . . .

When most criminal abortion laws were first enacted, the procedure was a hazardous one for the woman. This was particularly true prior to the development of antisepsis. . . . Abortion mortality was high. . . . Modern medical techniques have altered this situation. Appellants . . . refer to medical data indicating that abortion in early pregnancy, that is, prior to the end of the first trimester, although not without its risk, is now relatively safe. Mortality rates for women undergoing early abortions, where the procedure is legal, appear to be as low as or lower than the rates for normal childbirth. Consequently, any interest of the State in protecting the woman from an inherently hazardous procedure . . . has largely disappeared. . . . The State has a legitimate interest in seeing to it that abortion, like any other medical procedure, is performed under circumstances that insure maximum safety for the patient. . . .

The Constitution does not explicitly mention any right of privacy. In a line of decisions, however . . . the Court has recognized that a right of personal privacy, or a guarantee of certain areas or zones of privacy, does exist under the Constitution. . . . This right . . . whether it be founded in the Fourteenth Amendment's concept of personal liberty . . . or . . . in the Ninth Amendment's reservation of rights to the people, is broad enough to encompass a woman's decision whether or not to terminate her pregnancy. . . . We . . . conclude that the right of personal privacy includes the abortion decision, but that this right is not unqualified and must be considered against important state interests in regulation. . . .

. . . the State does have a important and legitimate interest in preserving and protecting the health of the pregnant woman . . . and . . . it has still *another* important and legitimate interest in protecting the potentiality of human life. These interests are separate and distinct. Each grows in substantiality as the woman approaches term, and, at a point during pregnancy, each becomes "compelling."

With respect to the State's important and legitimate interest in the health of the mother, the "compelling" point, in the light of present medical knowledge, is at approximately the end of the first trimester. This is so because of the now-established medical fact . . . that until the end of the first trimester mortality in abortion may be less than mortality in normal childbirth. It follows that . . . for the period of pregnancy prior to this "compelling" point, the attending physician, in consultation with his patient, is free to determine, without regulation by the State, that in his medical judgment, the patient's pregnancy should be terminated.

. . . For the stage subsequent to approximately the end of the first trimester, the State, in promoting its interest in the health of the mother, may, if it chooses, regulate the abortion procedure in ways that are reasonably related to maternal health.

For the stage subsequent to viability, the State in promoting its interest in the potentiality of human life may, if it chooses, regulate, and even proscribe, abortion except where it is necessary, in appropriate medical judgment, for the preservation of the life or health of the mother.

Our conclusion . . . is . . . that the Texas abortion statutes, as a unit, must fall. . . .

Roe v. Wade, 410 U.S. 113 (1973).

In the years before 1973, when abortion was generally illegal, commonly performed in the private offices of doctors and unlicensed practitioners without emergency medical support, and generally without anesthesia, death from abortion was substantial. In 1985, it was estimated that only two deaths occurred from illegal abortion and only six deaths resulted from legal abortion.

Another large question remains: How does "equal protection of the laws" apply to reproductive rights and access to abortion? Justice Blackmun grounded *Roe v. Wade* in a right of privacy, balanced against a compelling state interest in the health of the fetus in the late stages of pregnancy. Because only women become pregnant, and because there is no obvious parallel to pregnancy in male experience, arguments about abortion are less easily made on the simple equal treatment grounds that served women's rights activists so well in *Frontiero v. Richardson* (see pp. 752–753) and other similar cases. It has been left to Justice Ruth Bader Ginsburg (and Justices William Brennan, William O. Douglas, and Thurgood Marshall before her) to give abortion rights an equal-protection context: pregnancy is woman-specific. Is pregnancy leave vacation time? Is it sick leave? Is the denial of insurance benefits for work loss resulting from a normal pregnancy sex discrimination? Or does the commitment to equal protection require the law to make it possible for women to be both parents and workers on the same terms as men? In 1974, dissenting in *Geduldig v. Aiello* (17 U.S. 484), Justices Brennan, Douglas, and Marshall insisted that California's failure to cover pregnancy-related disabilities threatened "to return men and women to a time when 'traditional' equal protection analysis sustained legislative classifications that treated differently members of a particular sex solely because of their sex." They cited three of Ginsburg's benchmark cases: *Muller, Goesaert,* and *Hoyt.* They, like Ginsburg in her arguments on behalf of the Women's Rights Project (see pp. 752–753), believed that the thinking that undergirded those earlier rulings was antiquated. (For Muller, see p. 357; for Goesaert, pp. 699–700; and for Hoyt, pp. 741–742.)

In writing the majority decision, Justice Blackmun observed "this right is not unqualified and must be considered against important state interests in regulation." The state, he went on to say, has a "legitimate interest in protecting the health of the pregnant woman . . . and it has still another important and legitimate interest in protecting the potentiality of human life." The interest in protecting the pregnant woman's health is to be balanced against a "compelling state interest" in the health of the fetus in the late stages of pregnancy.

In the 1980s, a number of states tested what boundaries would be considered reasonable limits on the abortion rights sustained in *Roe.* In 1980, the Supreme Court upheld the "Hyde Amendment" by which Congress refused to fund even medically necessary abortions for indigent women (*Harris v. McRae,* 448 U.S. 297). This decision was not the focus of massive public protest, and it was replicated in the laws of many states. An effort to defeat the Hyde Amendment failed in Congress in 1993, but some states did revise their practice, covering some abortions for indigent women, usually in the case of rape or incest.

Missouri legislators developed further the position that the state could deny any form of public support or facilities for the performance of abortions. A 1986 law prohibited the use of public employees and facilities to perform or assist abortions not necessary to save the life of the mother and also prohibited the use of public funds for counseling a woman in abortion decisions not necessary to save her life. It included a preamble that claimed that the life of each human being begins at conception and a provision that required that medical tests of fetal viability—tests whose efficacy was disputed—be performed before any abortion on a fetus estimated to be twenty weeks or more in gestation. Since 97 percent of all late abortions (done at an estimated sixteen-week gestational age) were performed at a single hospital in Kansas City that, although private, received public aid and was located on public property, the practical impact of the law was great.

In deciding *Webster v. Reproductive Health Services* in July 1989, by a 5–3 vote, the Supreme Court majority claimed that the conclusions of *Roe* had not been changed.*** Missouri law left a pregnant woman free to terminate her pregnancy so long as neither public funds nor facilities were used for it; this was, the Court majority said, a "value judgment" favoring childbirth over abortion. But the majority raised a general question about *Roe*. "[T]he rigid Roe framework," wrote Chief Justice Rehnquist in the majority opinion, "is hardly consistent with the notion of a Constitution cast in general terms, as ours is, and usually speaking in general principles, as ours does. The key elements of the *Roe* framework—trimesters and viability—are not found in the text of the Constitution or in any place else one would expect to find a constitutional principle . . . the result has been a web of legal rules that . . . [resemble] a code of regulations rather than a body of constitutional doctrine." Justice Anthony Scalia concurred, adding that in his view, *Roe* should have been overturned; abortion is, he thought, a field in which the Court "has little proper business since the answers to most of the cruel questions posed are political and not juridical." He was appalled at efforts to bring the pressure of public opinion to bear on the decisions of the Court, notably the March on Washington of some 200,000 people that had been sponsored by pro-choice groups shortly before the *Webster* case was argued in April 1989.

Justice Harry A. Blackmun, who had written the Court's opinion in *Roe*, now wrote a bitter dissent for the minority. He denied that Rehnquist's opinion left *Roe* "undisturbed." Rather it challenged a large body of legal precedent that had established a "private sphere of individual liberty," which although not explicitly specified in the Constitution had long been taken to have been implied by the Fourth Amendment guarantee against unreasonable searches. The right to privacy had been invoked in the 1960s when the Court protected the sale and use of birth control devices; the *Webster* decision, Blackmun feared, bypassed "the true jurisprudential debate underlying this case: . . . whether and to what extent . . . a right to privacy extends to matters of childbearing and family life, including abortion." Justice John Paul Stevens argued that the preamble's claim that life begins at conception was a religious view, and to write it into law was to ignore First Amendment requirements for the separation of church and state. Finally, Blackmun argued that the state had a distinct interest in maintaining public health, and that

---

***William L. Webster, Attorney General of Missouri v. Reproductive Health Services*, 109 S. Ct. 3040 (1989).

as safe and legal abortions became more difficult to get, an increase in deaths from illegal abortions could be predicted. "For today," he concluded, "the women of this Nation still retain the liberty to control their destinies. But the signs are evident and very ominous, and a chill wind blows."

The Court's decision in *Webster* left many questions open. If states could deny public funds for abortions, what other limitations was it reasonable for state legislatures to impose? Was it reasonable to require a waiting period? Was it reasonable to require minors to get the consent of one parent? of both parents?

In 1988 and 1989 Pennsylvania amended its Abortion Control Act of 1982 extensively, requiring a twenty-four-hour waiting period and the provision of "certain information" twenty-four hours before the abortion is performed. Minors were required to have the consent of one parent, and married women to have notified their husbands, although it was possible for a court to waive that requirement and all requirements could be waived in the event of a "medical emergency." Because most of the justices had made public substantial reservations about the decision in *Roe*, it seemed to many observers not unreasonable to predict that the Court would uphold the entire Pennsylvania statute and, possibly, overturn *Roe v. Wade*. Instead, a plurality organized by Justices Sandra Day O'Connor, Anthony Kennedy, and David Souter, joined by Harry Blackmun and John Paul Stevens, wrote a complex opinion that began with a ringing affirmation of *Roe*. But O'Connor, Kennedy, and Souter also made it clear that they shared Rehnquist's skepticism of the trimester framework of *Roe*. How does the plurality think the principle of equal protection of the laws should be applied in abortion decisions?

Note the comments on coverture at the end of the plurality opinion; why did court find it useful to refer to *Bradwell v. Illinois* (pp. 292–294) and *Hoyt v. Florida* (pp. 741–742)? The final statement in the selection marks the first explicit recognition by the Court of the end of coverture. Why do the dissenting justices think *Roe* should be overturned?

PLANNED PARENTHOOD OF SOUTHEASTERN PENNSYLVANIA V. CASEY, 1992

JUSTICES O'CONNOR, KENNEDY, SOUTER: (WITH WHOM JUSTICES BLACKMUN AND STEVENS JOIN)

Liberty finds no refuge in a jurisprudence of doubt. Yet 19 years after our holding that the Constitution protects a woman's right to terminate her pregnancy in its early stages . . . that definition of liberty is still questioned. . . . After considering the fundamental constitutional questions resolved by *Roe*, principles of institutional integrity, and the rule of *stare decisis* [the principle that decisions of previous courts should be let stand unless there is overwhelming reason to change them], we are led to conclude this: the essential holding of *Roe v. Wade* should be retained and once again reaffirmed. . . . Constitutional protection of the woman's decision to terminate her pregnancy

derives from the Due Process Clause of the Fourteenth Amendment. It declares that no State shall "deprive any person of life, liberty, or property, without due process of law." . . . It is a premise of the Constitution that there is a realm of personal liberty which the government may not enter. We have vindicated this principle before. Marriage is mentioned nowhere in the Bill of Rights and interracial marriage was illegal in most States in the 19th century, but the Court was no doubt correct in finding it to be an aspect of liberty protected against state interference by the substantive component of the Due Process Clause in *Loving v. Virginia* 388 U.S. 1 (1967). . . .

Men and women of good conscience can disagree, and we suppose some always shall disagree, about the profound moral and spiritual implications of terminating a pregnancy, even in its earliest stage. Some of us as individuals find abortion offensive to our most basic principles of morality, but that cannot control our decision. Our obligation is to define the liberty of all, not to mandate our own moral code. . . .

Our law affords constitutional protection to personal decisions relating to marriage, procreation, contraception, family relationships, child rearing, and education. . . . These matters, involving the most intimate and personal choices a person may make in a lifetime, choices central to personal dignity and autonomy, are central to the liberty protected by the Fourteenth Amendment. At the heart of liberty is the right to define one's own concept of existence, of meaning, of the universe, and of the mystery of human life. Beliefs about these matters could not define the attributes of personhood were they formed under compulsion of the State. The woman's right to terminate her pregnancy before viability is the most central principle of *Roe* v. *Wade*. It is a rule of law and a component of liberty we cannot renounce.

On the other side of the equation is the interest of the State in the protection of potential life. The *Roe* Court recognized the State's "important and legitimate interest in protecting the potentiality of human life." . . . That portion of the decision in *Roe* has been given too little acknowledgment and implementation by the Court in its subsequent cases. . . . Though the woman has a right to choose to terminate or continue her pregnancy before viability, it does not at all follow that the State is prohibited from taking steps to ensure that this choice is thoughtful and informed. Even in the earliest stages of pregnancy, the State may enact rules and regulations designed to encourage her to know that there are philosophic and social arguments of great weight that can be brought to bear in favor of continuing the pregnancy to full term. . . . We reject the trimester framework, which we do not consider to be part of the essential holding of *Roe*. . . . Measures aimed at ensuring that a woman's choice contemplates the consequences for the fetus do not necessarily interfere with the right recognized in *Roe* . . . not every law which makes a right more difficult to exercise is, ipso facto, an infringement of that right. . . .

. . . We . . . see no reason why the State may not require doctors to inform a woman seeking an abortion of the availability of materials relating to the consequences to the fetus. . . . Whether the mandatory 24-hour waiting period is . . . invalid because in practice it is a substantial obstacle to a woman's choice to terminate her pregnancy is a closer question. [We

do not agree with the District Court] that the waiting period constitutes an undue burden. . . . [From Part D: We have already established the precedent, and] we reaffirm today, that a State may require a minor seeking an abortion to obtain the consent of a parent or guardian, provided that there is an adequate judicial bypass procedure. . . .

. . . Pennsylvania's abortion law provides, except in cases of medical emergency, that no physician shall perform an abortion on a married woman without receiving a signed statement from the woman that she has notified her spouse that she is about to undergo an abortion. The woman has the option of providing an alternative signed statement certifying that her husband is not the man who impregnated her; that her husband could not be located; that the pregnancy is the result of spousal sexual assault which she had reported [or that she fears bodily harm from him]. A physician who performs an abortion on a married woman without receiving the appropriate signed statement will have his or her license revoked, and is liable to the husband for damages.

. . . In well-functioning marriages, spouses discuss important intimate decisions such as whether to bear a child. But there are millions of women in this country who are the victims of regular physical and psychological abuse at the hands of their husbands. . . . Many may have a reasonable fear that notifying their husbands will provoke further instances of child abuse [or psychological abuse]. . . .

. . . [A]s a general matter . . . the father's interest in the welfare of the child and the mother's interest are equal. Before birth, however, the issue takes on a very different cast. It is an inescapable biological fact that state regulation with respect to the child a woman is carrying will have a far greater impact on the mother's liberty than on the father's. [That is why the Court has already ruled that when the wife and husband disagree on the abortion decision, the decision of the wife should prevail.]

. . . There was a time, not so long ago, when a different understanding of the family and of the Constitution prevailed. In *Bradwell v. Illinois* [pp. 292–294], three Members of this Court reaffirmed the common-law principle that "a woman had no legal existence separate from her husband." . . . Only one generation has passed since this Court observed that "woman is still regarded as the center of home and family life," with attendant "special responsibilities" that precluded full and independent legal status under the Constitution (*Hoyt v. Florida* [pp. 741–742]). These views, of course, are no longer consistent with our understanding of the family, the individual, or the Constitution.... [The Pennsylvania abortion law] embodies a view of marriage consonant with the common-law status of married women but repugnant to our present understanding of marriage and of the nature of the rights secured by the Constitution. Women do not lose their constitutionally protected liberty when they marry.

CHIEF JUSTICE REHNQUIST, WITH WHOM JUSTICE WHITE, JUSTICE SCALIA, AND JUSTICE CLARENCE THOMAS JOIN:

The joint opinion ... retains the outer shell of *Roe v. Wade* ... but beats a wholesale retreat

from the substance of that case. We believe that *Roe* was wrongly decided, and that it can and should be overruled consistently with our traditional approach to *stare decisis* in constitutional cases. We would ... uphold the challenged provisions of the Pennsylvania statute in their entirety.... [B]y foreclosing all democratic outlet for the deep passions this issue arouses, by banishing the issue from the political forum that gives all participants, even the losers, the satisfaction of a fair hearing and an honest fight, by continuing the imposition of a rigid national rule instead of allowing for regional differences, the Court merely prolongs and intensifies the anguish.

We should get out of this area, where we have no right to be, and where we do neither ourselves nor the country any good by remaining.

The U.S. Supreme Court began its opinion in *Casey* by scorning "a jurisprudence of doubt." In 2000 it reaffirmed its support of the principles of *Roe v. Wade*, and struck down another state abortion statute, this one a Nebraska law forbidding a specific procedure for late term abortion that physicians called "Dillation and Evacuation" and opponents called "partial birth abortion" *(Stenberg v. Carhart*, 530 U.S. 914 [2000]). But within a few years, Congress overrode that decision by passing a federal "partial birth abortion ban." The four Nebraska physicians who had challenged the state statute now challenged the federal version—not least on the grounds that it did not contain an exception for the health of the mother. Now the U.S. Supreme Court denied their challenge despite the strong opposition of the American College of Obstetricians and Gynecologists, which found the procedure necessary and proper in certain cases.

In *Carhart v. Gonzales* (550 U.S. 124 [2007]), the Supreme Court agreed with Congress that the procedure was distinctively "brutal and inhumane," and that Congress and the Court could bar it "in furtherance of its legitimate interests in regulating the medical profession." Although the majority, in an opinion written by Justice Anthony Kennedy, acknowledged that "we find no reliable data to measure the phenomenon," it announced that "it seems unexceptionable to conclude some women come to regret their choice to abort the infant life they once created and sustained.... Severe depression and loss of esteem can follow." For the mother's own good, he wrote that "[t]he law need not give abortion doctors unfettered choice in the course of their medical practice...." Justice Kennedy acknowledged early on that "the principles set forth in the joint opinion in *Planned Parenthood of Southeastern Pa. v. Casey* ... did not find support from all those who join [in this] opinion," but he asserted that they reaffirmed "*Roe*'s essential holding."

The principle of equal protection lurks within every abortion argument. The failure to ground the decriminalization of abortion in equal protection and to specify the end of coverture (married women's legal subordination to husbands) has had major consequences. Nowhere is the argument that access to abortion is a matter of equal protection made more eloquently than in Ruth Bader Ginsburg's

Planned Parenthood of Southeastern Pennsylvania v. Casey, 505 U.S. 833 (1992).

dissent, in which she was joined by justices Stevens, Souter and Breyer. Ginsburg took the unusual step of reading her emphatic dissent from the bench. She began by restating *Roe*'s promise, emphasizing not only "the right of the woman to choose to have an abortion before viability and to obtain it without undue interference from the State," but also that the State's "legitimate interests . . . in protecting . . . the life of the fetus that may become a child" were limited by its interests "in protecting *the health of the woman*" [her emphasis]. The Court, Ginsburg asserted, was now "retreating from prior rulings that abortion restrictions cannot be imposed absent an exception safeguarding a woman's health." She was deeply critical of the reasoning on which Congress had based the "partial birth abortion ban" statute: "Congress claimed that there was a medical consensus that the banned procedure is never necessary . . . and that 'there is no credible medical evidence that partial-birth abortions are safe or are safer than other abortion procedures.' But the congressional record includes . . . statements from nine professional associations, including the American College of Obstetricians and Gynecologists, the American Public Health Association, and the California Medical Association, attesting that intact D&E carries meaningful safety advantages over other methods . . . the physicians who testified that intact D&E is never necessary to preserve the health of a woman had slim authority for their opinions. They had no training for, or personal experience with the intact D&E procedure. . . . " Relying on misleading information, "the Court deprives women of the right to make an autonomous choice, even at the expense of their safety."

As the Court had recognized in *Casey* fifteen years before, Ginsburg observed, "at stake in cases challenging abortion restrictions is a woman's 'control over her [own] destiny.'" She ended by quoting and commenting on the lines from the *Hoyt* decision that had been rejected by the Court in *Casey*:

> "There was a time, not so long ago, when women were regarded as the center of home and family life, with attendant special responsibilities that precluded full and independent legal status under the Constitution." In the *Casey* decision, the Court made clear that these views "are no longer consistent with our understanding of the family, the individual, or the Constitution." Women, it is now acknowledged, have the talent, capacity, and right no participate equally in the economic and social life of the Nation. Their ability to realize their full potential, the Court [had] recognized, is intimately connected to "their ability to control their reproductive lives" Thus, legal challenges to undue restrictions on abortion procedures do not seek to vindicate some generalized notion of privacy; rather they center on a woman's autonomy to determine her life's course, and thus to enjoy equal citizenship stature.

RECENT DEVELOPMENTS

The legalization of abortion improved women's health care. After 1973, states assumed responsibility for ensuring that qualified physicians in licensed facilities performed the procedure. Medical complications from abortions plummeted. But resistance to recognizing access to abortion—a medical procedure that men do not need—as a matter of equal protection (men confront no similar law limiting their choice of medical procedures) continued and strengthened. The decision in *Carhart* was evidence of the success with which opponents of legal abortion reform worked to expand what can be understood as the state's "legitimate interest . . . in regulation." Women who need access to a constitutionally protected medical procedure now face, in state after state, mandatory waiting periods that increase the physical dangers of the procedure; parental consent or notification requirements that constrain young women who have reason to fear their own parents, especially women who are victims of incest; mandatory pre-abortion sonograms accompanied by "counseling" by medical staff who are required to describe the fetus as a "baby." Under the federal Affordable Care Act of 2013, health plans cannot be required to include abortion coverage.

The legalization of abortion was accompanied by a paradox: when the procedure was legitimized and made safer by the state, extremists in the antiabortion movement imperiled the health and safety of abortion providers. Between 1977 and 1993, abortion providers reported 543 cases of vandalism, 113 cases of arson, and 166 death threats to federal authorities.

By 1993, antiabortion violence reached a fevered pitch: clinics across the United States reported a one-hundred percent increase in hate mail and harassing phone calls over the previous year, while the number of bomb threats nearly doubled and death threats against abortion providers increased by nearly tenfold. In March 1993, Dr. David Gunn was shot and killed outside of a Pensacola, Florida, clinic. Five months later, Shelley Shannon, an antiabortion extremist, shot Dr. George Tiller in both arms outside of his Wichita, Kansas, clinic, where he was one of a handful of physicians nationwide who performed third-trimester abortions. In 2009, less than two years after the Supreme Court's decision in *Carhart v. Gonzales*, Tiller became the eighth abortion clinic employee and the fourth physician to be murdered by an antiabortion extremist when Scott Roeder shot and killed the physician inside of his church.

Many women had a harder time finding abortion providers by the first decade of the twenty-first century than they had in the 1970s. Between 1992 and 2000, the number of abortion providers in the United States declined by 11 percent. Rural states, including Georgia, Kansas, Kentucky, and Missouri lost more than 50 percent of their providers during this period. And in 2009, the year Dr. Tiller was murdered, 87 percent of counties in the United States lacked a single abortion provider. One out of every three women lived in a county without abortion services.

Since 2009 there has been a dramatic increase in state-level provisions restricting access to abortion and physicians' ability to provide safe abortion services. Some states now ban abortions starting at 20 weeks—the point at which tests to determine the health of the pregnancy are available—rather than the usual ban at viability, which is about 24 weeks. Some states require abortion providers to have admitting privileges in nearby hospitals. (Generally hospitals require physicians to admit a minimum number of patients in order to maintain these privileges, a requirement that is rarely possible for clinic-based physicians to meet.) Both the American Medical Association and the American Congress of Obstetricians and Gynecologists have opposed these restrictions. In 2013, 27 states had at least four types of major abortion restrictions. The risks associated with abortion increase with the length of pregnancy.[†]

Such restrictions have had major impact. Five states (all of them large, geographically, with significant rural populations) have only one abortion clinic: Arkansas, Mississippi, North Dakota, South Dakota, and Wyoming. In some cases, statutes have passed forcing them to close; these statutes are being appealed. In 2014, a federal district court in North Dakota found unconstitutional a state law that would have banned abortion once a fetal heartbeat could be detected—an event that normally occurs at around six weeks of pregnancy, before some women are even aware of their condition. The decision is being appealed.[††] Women in rural areas have particular difficulty getting abortions. When the last clinic in the Texas Rio Grande Valley closed, women had to travel 250 miles to the nearest city clinic—facing extra costs of gas, lodging, and child care.

In June 2014, the U.S. Supreme Court unanimously overturned a Massachusetts law that prohibited protestors from coming within 35 feet of an abortion clinic; the statute was designed to create a "buffer zone" for patients and staff.[†††] Cities and states had begun to enact buffer zone laws in the 1990s, after it had become commonplace for antiabortion activists to harass patients and after

---

[†]"Fact Sheet: Induced Abortion in the United States, July 2014," Guttmacher Institute, http://www.guttmacher .org/pubs/fb_induced_abortion.html. See the points under "Law and Policy."

[††]For more about women's work in the anti-abortion movement, see Karissa Haugeberg, *Women to the Rescue: Leaders, Martyrs, and Foot Soldiers in the Campaign to End Abortion* (Urbana: University of Illinois Press, forthcoming). A useful and regularly updated guide to state policies on reproductive health is conveniently found on a website maintained by the Guttmacher Institute: http://www.guttmacher.org/statecenter/spibs/index.html.

[†††]*McCullen v. Coakley,* U.S. Sup. Ct. Docket 12-1334, 2014.

extremists had begun to bomb clinics and to shoot physicians. Courts have generally overturned these measures on the grounds that they violate activists' First Amendment right to free speech. Pro-choice activists have countered that patients seeking abortions deserve the types of buffer zone protections afforded to voters, students, and Supreme Court justices as they enter polling sites, schools, and the U.S. Supreme Court.

The Affordable Care Act (ACA) does not require health plans to cover abortion except in the case of rape, incest, or endangerment of life; and forbids the use of federal funding for abortion coverage. It does include all medically authorized forms of contraception, as part of a wide range of essential health benefits, some specific to women's "preventive health" services, such as annual check-ups, pap smears, and mammograms. Religiously affiliated employers—generally understood to be nonprofit institutions like schools and hospitals—who had religious reservations to birth control were permitted to opt-out of coverage, and employees who wished coverage for contraception were assured a route to private or federal coverage. (Most private insurance companies found the prospect of subsidizing contraceptives appealing because it is less expensive to pay for birth control than to provide health care coverage for dependent children.)

Hobby Lobby, a family-owned arts-and-crafts chain, filed suit against the Department of Health and Human Services, charging that the ACA requirement of no-cost access to contraception violated the Religious Freedom Restoration Act of 1993 by forcing them to pay for products that violated their religious beliefs. The corporation objected to contraception, and it claimed that some of the common forms of birth control—the "morning-after" pill and two kinds of intrauterine devices (IUDs)—should be understood not as preventative but as "abortifacients" because they prevent the implantation of a fertilized egg in the uterus. In June 2014, in a 5–4 decision, the U.S. Supreme Court ruled in favor of Hobby Lobby, finding that the birth control requirement was a substantial burden on the owners' religious freedom (*Burwell v. Hobby Lobby Stores*, Docket No. 13-354).

The dissenters—the three women members and Justice Stephen Breyer—joined in a dissent written by Justice Ginsburg, reaching back to the *Casey* decision to stress that "the ability of women to participate equally in the economic and social life of the nation has been facilitated by their ability to control their reproductive lives." Women's need for coverage of their expenses was real: Ginsburg cited a recent Institute of Medicine report that "women are consistently more likely than men to report a wide range of barriers to receiving . . . medical tests and treatments." A few days later, the court temporarily exempted a Christian college from some administrative regulations governing its own employees and students' access to contraception. As we go to press, the line between access to abortion and access to birth control may be blurring.

What difference would it have made if, in 1973, the majority in *Roe* had grounded its defense of women's right to choose not in privacy rights but in equal protection and equal rights claims? Consider that *Roe v. Wade* granted women, in consultation with their physicians, the right to abortion, but did not guarantee women access to the procedure. How might we create policies that ensure that all women have the ability to obtain safe medical care? And how might we protect the health and safety of clinic employees while preserving the First Amendment rights to free speech of anti-abortion activists?

A Challenge for Our Readers: Become an Historian! As the 40th anniversary of Roe passes, activists of the 1960s—on both sides of the debate—are now in their 70s and 80s. Activists of the 1950s are in their 90s. The time available to us is short. Most have never been interviewed; many are hungry to place their experience on the historical record. Some have kept in their possession the records of the small groups of which they were a part, yet they are not aware that their collected materials and their recollections may be welcomed by historical societies and college- and university-based archives. Local newspapers—many now digitized—can be searched. The papers of some state legislators have been archived; often they are filed by topic, and thus one can identify materials by searching under "abortion." Many of these collections include letters from constituents on both sides of the question, urging action. Some of these letters are heartbreaking; all are interesting. (Archivists will generally ask researchers to sign an agreement not to publish the names of the authors.)

Catholic bishops were early to organize challenges to abortion reform; the role of Catholic clergy and of nuns in our towns and counties deserves its own history.

Although the Clergy Consultation Service on Abortion originated in New York City, chapters flourished throughout the country. Identifying participants in these campaigns in your town or county or state—and interviewing them about their memories of their work—could make significant contributions to recapturing the history of the fight over abortion reform. Partisan alignments after *Roe* took longer to develop than many appreciate, and varied greatly from one region or county to another. *Roe*'s 40th anniversary is both a warning about rapidly fading memories and an opportunity to capture a history that still shapes American lives and politics.

Rethinking Marriage: Loving v. Virginia, 1967; Griswold v. Connecticut, 1965; Defense of Marriage Act, 1996; Goodridge v. Massachusetts Department of Public Health, 2003; Recent Developments

---

Although marriage is generally understood to be the most private of matters, it has been subjected to regulation by colonies and the states since the founding era. Even when marriage ceremonies take a religious form, marriage in the United States has always been regulated by civil laws. States rely on marriages to maintain stable households, legitimate and care for children, and minimize public support for the vulnerable. States set and enforce the terms of marriage—including who can and cannot marry, what marital rights and obligations are, and the terms for ending it in divorce. States set the rules of inheritance—that is, the transmission of property from one generation to the next within marital families. Throughout much of American history, states enforced the rules of coverture that gave husbands expansive powers over their wives' bodies, property, and choices.

The national government has also been deeply involved in defining which marriages would be legally recognized. It has enacted laws in areas ranging from polygamy, to immigration policy, to the family structures that would be eligible for social security and aid to dependent children. As World War II ended, pressures for legislative change grew. American military personnel successfully claimed the right to bring spouses into the United States more easily than established quotas permitted. Federal laws that made Asians ineligible for citizenship proved embarrassing when China was a U.S. ally during World War II; the exclusion of Chinese was ended in 1943. American military personnel stationed in Japan during the occupation repeatedly challenged the rule that Asians were ineligible for citizenship. Acts passed in 1945 and 1946, which cautiously facilitated the entry of foreign fiancées and spouses regardless of race, were responses to this situation. And the joint income tax, devised in 1948, offered substantial advantages to married couples that unmarried individuals did not (and still do not) enjoy.*

The democratic, inclusive rhetoric of a war against fascism made American practices of segregation increasingly anomalous and an international embarrassment. Among the civil rights that increasing numbers of citizens claimed was the right to marry the person of their choice despite state laws defining interracial marriage between whites and others as miscegenation. (Generally, these statutes

---

*Carolyn Jones, "Split Income and Separate Spheres: Tax Law and Gender Roles in the 1940s," *Law and History Review*, 6 (Fall 1988): 259–310.

permitted interracial marriage among other groups.) At the close of World War II, the laws of thirty states barred interracial marriage. Challenges built state by state. Although the California Supreme Court struck down that state's miscegenation statute in 1948[†] and thirteen other legislatures repealed their laws, bans continued to be enforced with serious penalties in sixteen other states.

Virginia's law made it illegal for "any white person in the state to marry any save a white person, or a person with no other admixture of blood than white and American Indian." (The link between whiteness and Native Americans was arranged in order to include all those white Virginians who proudly claimed descent from Pocahontas.) In 1958, two Virginians, Mildred Jeter, who was black, and Richard Loving, who was white, married in a ceremony in Washington, D.C. When they returned to Virginia to live, they were indicted for violating Virginia's ban on interracial marriages. They were found guilty and sentenced to one year in jail, which would be suspended if they left the state and did not return for twenty-five years. The aptly named Lovings moved to Washington, D.C., and challenged the conviction; eventually their case reached the U.S. Supreme Court. Richard Loving said to his attorney, "Tell the Court I love my wife, and it is just unfair that I can't live with her in Virginia."

How did the state of Virginia defend its practice? On what grounds did the Supreme Court declare the miscegenation law illegal? How did the Court describe "freedom to marry"?

LOVING V. VIRGINIA, 1967

CHIEF JUSTICE EARL WARREN WROTE
THE OPINION FOR A UNANIMOUS COURT:

. . . the State [of Virginia] argues that the meaning of the Equal Protection Clause [of the Fourteenth Amendment, see p. 247] . . . is only that state penal laws containing an interracial element as part of the definition of the offense must apply equally to whites and Negroes in the sense that members of each race are punished to the same degree. Thus the State contends that, because its miscegenation statutes punish equally both the white and the Negro participants in an interracial marriage, these statutes, despite their reliance on racial classifications, do not constitute an invidious discrimination based upon race. . . .

Because we reject the notion that the mere "equal application" of a statute containing racial classifications is enough to remove the classifications from the Fourteenth Amendment's proscription of all invidious racial discriminations, we do not accept the State's contention. . . . There is patently no legitimate overriding purpose independent of invidious racial discrimination which justifies this classification. The

fact that Virginia prohibits only interracial marriages involving white persons demonstrates that the racial classifications must stand on their own justification, as measures designed to maintain White Supremacy. . . . There can be no doubt that restricting the freedom to marry solely because of racial classification violates the central meaning of the Equal Protection Clause.

These statutes also deprive the Lovings of liberty without due process of law in violation of the Due Process Clause of the Fourteenth Amendment. The freedom to marry has long been recognized as one of the vital personal rights essential to the orderly pursuit of happiness by free men.

Marriage is one of the "basic civil rights of man," fundamental to our very existence and survival. To deny this fundamental freedom on so unsupportable a basis as the racial classifications embodied in these statutes . . . is surely to deprive all the State's citizens of liberty without due process of law. . . . Under our Constitution, the freedom to marry or not marry, a person of another race resides with the individual and cannot be infringed by the state.

These convictions must be reversed. It is so ordered.

[†]*Perez v. Sharp*, 32 Cal 2d. 711 (1948).

Loving v. Virginia, 388 U.S. 1 (1967).

Meanwhile, debate over the appropriate limits of contraceptives—dating at least from the Comstock Act (see p. 212)—continued in the postwar era. Long after they were legal in other states, Connecticut continued to forbid their use. Seeking to test the statute, the Planned Parenthood League (PPL) of Connecticut established a center in New Haven where a physician offered counsel and prescriptions to married couples. It opened on November 1, 1961; within 10 days it had served 75 patients. But on the tenth day, detectives arrived to arrest its volunteer physician, Dr. C. Lee Buxton, who was the chairman of the Yale Medical School's department of obstetrics and gynecology, and Estelle Griswold, the executive director of the PPL. They were quickly convicted and fined. They appealed their conviction. When their case reached the U.S. Supreme Court, they won on a 7–2 decision.

Note the discussion of marital privacy in Justice Douglas's opinion. Why did Justice Stewart disagree?

GRISWOLD V. CONNECTICUT, 1965

JUSTICE WILLIAM O. DOUGLAS WROTE THE MAJORITY OPINION:

. . . The association of people is not mentioned in the Constitution nor in the Bill of Rights . . . [but] specific guarantees in the Bill of Rights have penumbras, formed by emanations from those guarantees that help give them life and substance. Various guarantees create zones of privacy.

The right of association contained in the penumbra of the First Amendment is one. . . . The Third Amendment in its prohibition against the quartering of soldiers "in any house" in time of peace without the consent of the owner is another facet of that privacy. The Fourth Amendment explicitly affirms the "right of the people to be secure in their persons, houses, papers, and effects, against unreasonable searches and seizures." . . . We deal with a right of privacy older than the Bill of Rights— older than our political parties, older than our school system. Marriage is a coming together for better or for worse, hopefully enduring, and intimate to the degree of being sacred. It is an association that promotes a way of life, not causes; a harmony in living, not political faiths, a bilateral loyalty, not commercial or social projects. Yet it is an association for as noble a purpose as any involved in our prior decisions.

JUSTICE BYRON WHITE, CONCURRING

In my view this Connecticut law as applied to married couples deprives them of "liberty" without due process of law . . . the liberty entitled to protection under the Fourteenth Amendment includes the right "to marry, establish a home and bring up children." . . . These [prior] decisions affirm that there is a "realm of family life which the state cannot enter" without substantial justification.

JUSTICE POTTER STEWART, DISSENTING

Since 1879 Connecticut has had on its books a law which forbids the use of contraceptives by anyone. I think this is an uncommonly silly law. As a practical matter, the law is obviously unenforceable . . . as a philosophical matter, I believe the use of contraceptives in the relationship of marriage should be left to personal and private choice, based upon each individual's moral, ethical and religious beliefs. . . . But we are not asked in this case to say whether we think this law is unwise, or even asinine. We are asked to hold that it violates the United States Constitution. And that I cannot do. . . .

What provision of the Constitution, then, does make this state law invalid? The Court says it is the right of privacy "created by several fundamental constitutional guarantees." With all deference I can find no such general right of privacy in the Bill of Rights, in any other part of the Constitution. . . . It is the essence of judicial duty to subordinate our own personal views, our own ideas of what legislation is wise and what is not. If, as I should surely hope, the law before us does not reflect the standards of the people of Connecticut, the people of Connecticut can freely exercise their true Ninth and Tenth Amendment rights to persuade their elected representatives to repeal it. That is the constitutional way to take this law off the books.

Griswold v. Connecticut, 381 U.S. 479 (1965). See Mary L. Dudziak, "Just Say No: Birth Control in the Connecticut Supreme Court Before Griswold v. Connecticut," Iowa Law Review 75 (May 1990): 915–39.

Griswold v. Connecticut limited its decision to married couples, recognizing for them a zone of privacy in their intimate relations into which the state could not intrude. Not until 1972 did the Supreme Court rule that unmarried people also have a right to contraceptives. That decision, as historian Nancy F. Cott has observed, "pronounced a historic reversal, since it denied the state's right to distinguish between citizens of differing marital status." The Court recognized "the right of the individual, married or single, to be free from unwarranted governmental intrusion into matters so fundamentally affecting a person as the decision whether to bear or beget a child."* That decision made state practice congruent with the sexual revolution that characterized American society in the 1960s and 1970s, sustained by new developments in contraceptive technology, notably the widely available birth control pill. (See Beth Bailey's essay on the pill, pp. 629–637.) Nearly fifty years later, access to contraception again became a subject for litigation, and new questions were opened by the Supreme Court decision in *Burwell v. Hobby Lobby Companies* (June 2014, see pp. 668.)

But the Supreme Court was not prepared to recognize intimate privacy for same-sex couples. From the 1970s to early twenty-first century, gay men and lesbians challenged criminal sodomy laws, usually written in generic terms but enforced only against gay couples, which denied intimate privacy. In 1986 the Atlanta police, acting on a tip, entered the apartment of Michael Hardwick and found him in bed with another man. When they were arrested for violating Georgia's sodomy statutes, they claimed—unsuccessfully—that their constitutional right to equal protection of the laws had been violated. Chief Justice Warren Burger observed, "Decisions of individuals relating to homosexual conduct have been subject to state intervention throughout the history of Western civilization." The vote in this case (*Bowers v. Hardwick*, 478 U.S. 186 [1986]), was 5-4; voting with the majority was Justice Lewis Powell, who stated publicly several years later that the decision was one he regretted.

In the aftermath of *Bowers v. Hardwick*, gay men and lesbians argued with increasing conviction that they were marked as criminals for behavior covered by the protections of privacy when engaged in by heterosexuals. They argued that they too fulfilled one of the major social reasons for the practice of marriage—the choice of committed relationships rather than transient ones. Lesbians and gay men also identified ways in which the status of marriage gave privileges and rights to heterosexual couples, including tax advantages in the form of joint-income tax returns; the ability to share health insurance coverage (often paid for in part by employers); and rights related to the acquisition and inheritance of property, awards of child custody, and companionship as next of kin when partners were hospitalized or dying. And they resented the stigma of being marked as criminals.

By the late twentieth century, these claims developed a dynamism of their own. The number of states that had laws criminalizing sodomy declined substantially, and virtually none enforced these laws against private, consensual, heterosexual conduct. The European Court of Human Rights sustained the right of homosexual adults to engage in intimate, consensual conduct. As this book goes to press, same-sex marriages are valid in 16 nations, including Argentina, Belgium, Brazil, Canada, Denmark, France, Iceland, Netherlands, New Zealand, Norway, Portugal, Spain, South Africa, Sweden, United Kingdom (including Scotland), and Uruguay.

In 1993, the Hawaii Supreme Court held that although it was not prepared to say that the claim of gay men and lesbians to same-sex marriage was a fundamental

---

Eisenstadt v. Baird, 405 U.S. 438 (1972). Nancy F. Cott, *Public Vows: A History of Marriage and the Nation* (Cambridge, Mass.: Harvard University Press 2000) pp. 198–99.

right "rooted in the traditions and collective conscience of our people," it did agree that by limiting the rights and benefits that were associated with marriage to heterosexual couples, the state had established a sex-based classification, reserving "a multiplicity of rights and benefits" for a single class of people, and therefore presumed to be unconstitutional unless it could be justified by "compelling state interests." The logic of the decision established twenty years before in *Frontiero v. Richardson* (see pp. 752–753) that illegality must turn on the act, not the gender of the actor—opened the door to claims on behalf of same-sex partnerships. In 2000, Vermont extended the rights and protections of marriage to same-sex couples who had established a "civil union."

In 2003, the U.S. Supreme Court heard arguments in *Lawrence v. Texas*, a case with many similarities to *Bowers*. Acting on what turned out to be a false report of a disturbance, Houston police entered John Lawrence's apartment and found him in bed with Tyron Garner. Lawrence and Garner challenged the Texas law that criminalized private homosexual intimacy. Writing for the majority in a sweeping 6–3 decision, Justice Anthony Kennedy placed the matter in the center of constitutional understandings of liberty: "As the Constitution endures, persons in every generation can invoke its principles in their own search for greater freedom." The protection against intrusion should be broadly understood; liberty is traditionally the protection from unwarranted government intrusions into a dwelling or other private places. In our tradition the state is not omnipresent in the home. Liberty is also the right to "an autonomy of self that includes freedom of thought, belief, expression, and certain intimate conduct. [This case] involves liberty of the person both in its spatial and more transcendent dimensions. . . . To say that the issue in *Bowers* was simply the right to engage in certain sexual conduct demeans the claim [of John Lawrence] . . . just as it would demean a married couple were it to be said marriage is simply about the right to have sexual intercourse . . . [this] personal relationship . . . is within the liberty of persons to choose without being punished as criminals."

The Court explicitly overturned *Bowers*. It recognized that the decision in *Bowers* had relied on historical misunderstandings and overstatements. The Court was persuaded that laws directed specifically against homosexual conduct are of a relatively recent vintage; in the nineteenth century, laws against sodomy criminalized heterosexual as well as homosexual conduct and were enforced generally only when the activity was public or involved a minor or the victim of assault. "It was not until the 1970s that any state singled out same-sex relations for criminal prosecution." And the Court pointed to changing international understandings: "the right the petitioners seek has been accepted as an integral part of human freedom in many other countries."*

Many people, however, were deeply dismayed by these moves toward treating marriage as malleable. Polls in 2000 showed strong popular support for the extension of health insurance, Social Security benefits, and insurance rights to same-sex partners. But strong majorities—as high as two-thirds—opposed "marriage." Hawaii voters, who supported the extension of benefits, also overwhelmingly supported a constitutional amendment to bar same-sex marriages. Predicting that once a single state recognized same-sex marriage, gay and lesbian couples would travel there to solemnize their relationship and then return to their home states to live (much as couples had made use of Nevada's "quickie" divorce laws in the 1940s and 1950s), Congress quickly passed the Defense of Marriage Act in 1996. It was a brief statute with two major parts.

Lawrence v. Texas, 539 U.S. 558 (2003).

AN ACT TO DEFINE AND PROTECT THE INSTITUTION OF MARRIAGE, 1996

... No State, territory or possession of the United States, or Indian tribe, shall be required to give effect to any public act, record, or judicial proceeding of any other State, territory possession or tribe respecting a relationship between persons of the same sex that is treated as a marriage under the laws of such other State, territory, possession or tribe, or a right or claim arising from such relationship . . .

In determining the meaning of any Act of Congress, or of any ruling, regulation, or interpretation of the various administrative bureaus and agencies of the United States, the word "marriage" means only a legal union between one man and one woman as husband and wife, and the word "spouse" refers only to a person of the opposite sex who is a husband or a wife.

U.S. Statutes at Large, 110:2419

DOMA, as the Defense of Marriage Act came to be known, was echoed by a successful movement to enact similar state statutes and to amend state constitutions. The movement strengthened over the next decade. Within a decade, 29 states had constitutional provisions that restricted marriage to heterosexuals; another thirteen states had laws that did the same. Supporters argued that restricting marriage to heterosexual couples respected the long history of an unchanging institution. They also argued that such marriages sustain children–both biological and adopted–better than same-sex partnerships. The following paragraphs track the mounting challenges to Defense of Marriage Acts, first at the state level, then in the U.S. Supreme Court.

Challenges to limiting marriage to heterosexuals also grew in number and in intensity. In November 2003, the Supreme Judicial Court of Massachusetts decided by a 4–3 vote that barring same-sex couples from "access to the protections, benefits and obligations of civil marriage" "arbitrarily" deprives them "of membership in one of our community's most rewarding and cherished institutions. That exclusion is incompatible with the constitutional principles of respect for individual autonomy and equality under law" and "violates the Massachusetts Constitution." To those who would offer civil unions as the equivalent of marriage, and who thought that the constitutional claim was merely a semantic quibble over language, Chief Justice Margaret Marshall and her colleagues in the majority invoked the decision of the U.S. Supreme Court in *Brown v. Board of Education*: a separate but equal institution is inherently unequal.

GOODRIDGE V. MASSACHUSETTS DEPARTMENT OF PUBLIC HEALTH, 2003

CHIEF JUSTICE MARSHALL:

Marriage is a vital social institution. The exclusive commitment of two individuals to each other nurtures love and mutual support; it brings stability to our society. For those who choose to marry, and for their children, marriage provides an abundance of legal, financial, and social benefits. In return it imposes weighty legal, financial, and social obligations. The question before us is whether, consistent with the Massachusetts Constitution, the Commonwealth may deny the protections, benefits, and obligations conferred by civil marriage to two individuals of the same sex who wish to marry. We conclude that it may not. The Massachusetts Constitution affirms the dignity and equality of all individuals. It forbids the creation of second-class citizens. In reaching our conclusion we have given full deference to the arguments made by the Commonwealth. But it has failed to identify any constitutionally adequate reason for denying civil marriage to same-sex couples.

We are mindful that our decision marks a change in the history of our marriage law. . . .

In Massachusetts, civil marriage is, and since pre-Colonial days has been, precisely what its name implies: a wholly secular institution. No religious ceremony has ever been required to validate a Massachusetts marriage . . . Civil marriage anchors an ordered society by encouraging stable relationships over transient ones. It is central to the way the Commonwealth identifies individuals, provides for the orderly distribution of property, ensures that children and adults are cared for and supported whenever possible from private rather than public funds, and tracks important epidemiological and demographic data.

Marriage also bestows enormous private and social advantages on those who choose to marry . . . the decision whether and whom to marry is among life's momentous acts of self-definition. . . . The benefits accessible only by way of a marriage license are enormous . . . "hundreds of statutes" are related to marriage and to marital benefits. With no attempt to be comprehensive, we note that some of the statutory benefits conferred by the Legislature on those who enter into civil marriage include, as to property: joint Massachusetts income tax filing; tenancy by the entirety (a form of ownership that provides certain protections against creditors and allows for the automatic descent of property to the surviving spouse without probate); extension of the benefit of the homestead protection (securing up to $300,000 in equity from creditors) to one's spouse and children; automatic rights to inherit the property of a deceased spouse who does not leave a will. . . .

Where a married couple has children, their children are also directly or indirectly, but no less auspiciously, the recipients of the special legal and economic protections obtained by civil marriage . . . [including] the greater ease of access to family-based State and

Federal benefits that attend the presumptions of one's parentage.

It is undoubtedly for these concrete reasons, as well as for its intimately personal significance, that civil marriage has long been termed a "civil right." See, e.g., *Loving v. Virginia*. . . .

The Department [of Health] . . . argues that broadening civil marriage to include same-sex couples will trivialize or destroy the institution of marriage as it has historically been fashioned. Certainly our decision today marks a significant change in the definition of marriage as it has been inherited from the common law, and understood by many societies for centuries. But it does not disturb the fundamental value of marriage in our society.

Here, the plaintiffs seek only to be married, not to undermine the institution of civil marriage. They do not want marriage abolished. They do not attack the binary nature of marriage, the consanguinity provisions, or any of the other gate-keeping provisions of the marriage licensing law. Recognizing the right of an individual to marry a person of the same sex will not diminish the validity or dignity of opposite-sex marriage, any more than recognizing the right of an individual to marry a person of a different race devalues the marriage of a person who marries someone of her own race. If anything, extending civil marriage to same-sex couples reinforces the importance of marriage to individuals and communities. That same-sex couples are willing to embrace marriage's solemn obligations of exclusivity, mutual support, and commitment to one another is a testament to the enduring place of marriage in our laws and in the human spirit.

The *Goodridge* decision set off, one historian observed, "a rolling act of civil disobedience" as mayors in San Francisco, Portland, Oregon, and other cities issued marriage licenses. But the decision was also met with a firestorm of protest: every one of these non-Massachusetts marriages was nullified by state courts while at the same time DOMA statutes and constitutional amendments seemed to block same-sex marriage in other jurisdictions. The issue continued to be hotly debated throughout the nation in state and federal elections. Civil unions were embraced in Vermont. Prompted by a 2006 state supreme court ruling in New Jersey that same-sex couples are entitled to the same benefits and protections as opposite-sex couples, the legislature authorized civil unions. New Hampshire, Maine, and Vermont legalized same-sex marriage in 2009.

Goodridge v. Massachusetts Department of Public Health, 798 N.R. 2d 941 (Mass. 2003).

In April 2009, the Iowa Supreme Court became the first court to overturn a DOMA statute unanimously, ruling that limiting marriage to heterosexuals is a violation of the Iowa state constitution's equal protection clause and the constitutional separation of powers.* To rule otherwise, they said, would be a denial of the court's "constitutional mandate to protect the free exercise of religion in Iowa," and also its general responsibility to "proceed as civil judges, far removed from the theological debate of religious clerics." They observed that they were instructed by the Iowa Code § 595A.1 that "provides that 'Marriage is a civil contract' and then regulates that civil contract . . . we give respect to the views of all Iowans on the issue of same-sex marriage—religious or otherwise—by giving respect to our constitutional principles. These principles require that the state recognize both opposite-sex and same-sex civil marriage." The court invoked its own strong history of sustaining civil rights: roughly a century before the U.S. Supreme Court made its rulings, public school segregation, the denial of equal access to public accommodations, and the definition of interracial marriage as miscegenation had all been declared to be denials of equal protection of the laws in Iowa. And the court took note of Iowa's recognition of women's equality: it was the first state to admit a woman to the practice of law and to its public university on the same terms as male students.Whatever position supporters or opponents take, the terms of marriage are now increasingly recognized as not only a private matter but also a civil rights issue. In October 2008, the Connecticut Supreme Court ruled that equal protection of the law requires equal access to marriage. The California Supreme Court had made a similar ruling a few months before, but California voters interrupted with an initiative (Proposition 8 on the fall 2008 state ballot) to add a state constitutional amendment barring such marriage, and in the spring of 2009, the California Supreme Court ruled that the initiative was a valid exercise of the voters' right to amend the Constitution.

Meanwhile, the American Foundation for Equal Rights initiated a challenge to Proposition 8 in the *federal* courts, on behalf of Kristin Perry and Sandra Stier, and another same-sex couple who had been denied marriage licenses, claiming that they had been denied the equal protection of the law promised in the Fourteenth Amendment. The trial in *Perry v. Schwarzenegger* was held in the U.S. District Court for the Northern District of California in January, 2010. The first two witnesses to testify at length against Proposition 8 were historians. Nancy Cott, author of *Public Vows: A History of Marriage and the Nation* (2000), whose essay on equal rights appears on pp. 503–512 of this book, testified that the history of marriage has changed over time and that it has been a secular, not religious, institution in the United States. George Chauncey, author of *Gay New York: Gender, Urban Culture, and the Making of the Gay Male World, 1890–1940* (1994), testified to the long history of discrimination against gay men and lesbians in the United States. It is rare that historians are asked to testify at such length; their testimony can be followed on the transcripts posted by the Equal Rights Foundation (http://www .equalrightsfoundation.org/our-work/hearing-transcripts. Start with page 181 of Day 1 for Cott's testimony; page 356 for Chauncey's).

Arnold Schwarzenegger, the governor of the State of California declined to support Proposition 8; its defense was conducted by private attorneys. In the summer of 2010, Judge Vaughn R. Walker ruled that Proposition 8 was an unconstitutional denial of the equal protection and due process guaranteed by the Fifth and Fourteenth Amendments to the Constitution. The case, now called *Hollingsworth v.*

Varnum v. Brien, 763 N. W. 2d 862 (Iowa 2009).

Perry, was appealed to the U.S. Supreme Court. In June 2013, the Court upheld Judge Walker's decision, on the technical ground that as private citizens, the sponsors of Proposition 8 did not have standing to challenge Judge Walker's decision.

By 2012, same-sex couples could marry in more than a dozen states, among them New York. They were entitled to the benefits offered by state law. But DOMA meant that federal law did not recognize their marriages; they were not entitled to any of the many federal benefits, including the rules of inheritance. Edith Windsor launched the challenge that ended up in the U.S. Supreme Court. She and Thea Spyer had met in New York City in 1966 and had a loving relationship thereafter. When New York gave same sex couples the right to register as domestic partners, in 1993, they did so. When Canada recognized same-sex marriage in 2007, they traveled there to marry. Speyer died in February 2009, leaving her entire estate to Windsor. The Internal Revenue Service ruled that Windsor was not a "surviving spouse" and did not qualify for the marital exemption from the federal estate tax. Windsor paid $363,053 in estate taxes and sued on the grounds that she had been denied the Fifth Amendment's guarantee of due process and therefore equal protection of the laws.

In June 2013–on the same day that it handed down its decision on Proposition 8—the U.S. Supreme Court ruled for Edith Windsor. While deferring to the authority of individual states to set the rules for civil marriage, it held that DOMA "singles out a class of persons . . . , [instructing] all federal officials, and indeed all persons with whom same-sex couples interact, including their own children, that their marriage is less worthy than the marriages of others. . . . [N]o legitimate purpose overcomes the purpose and effect to disparage and to injure those whom the State, by its marriage laws, sought to protect in personhood and dignity."**

Technically, the Windsor decision applied only to people in states where same-sex marriage was recognized. There, married same-sex couples would not be subjected to two different tax regimes or excluded from the benefits of the 1,000 federal laws that apply to married couples. But the eloquent decision prompted same-sex couples in many other states to ask: "if marriage is included in the equal protection of the laws in New York or California or Iowa, why isn't it included in my own state?" Many acted on that question, joining in litigation to overturn state bans. Polls show rapidly changing public opinion, especially among people under age 30. A March 2014 Washington Post-ABC News poll found 59 percent to 34 percent in favor—a result that crossed party lines and reversed the results of a poll 10 years earlier.[††]

When we published the previous edition of *Women's America*, same-sex marriage was legal in a half-dozen states. As this book goes to press, same-sex marriage is legal in 31 states and the District of Columbia. The situation remans fluid. For reasonably up-to-date summaries of the rapidly changing marriage laws in the various states, consult the website of the National Conference of State Legislatures: http://www.ncsl.org/research/human-services/same-sex-marriage.aspx.

The impact of striking down DOMA has repercussions beyond marriage law. DOMA was struck down because its purpose, according to the Court, was to "impose inequality" on a class of individuals based on their sexual orientation. This could apply in many contexts.

**U.S. v. Windsor*, 133 S. Ct. 2675 (2013). The vote was 5–4; the majority opinion was delivered by Justice Anthony Kennedy. For an elegant history of marriage laws, see the historians' brief, Brief on the Merits for Historians, Am. Historical Ass'n et al. as Amici Curiae Supporting Respondents, *United States v. Windsor*, 133 S. Ct. 2675 (2013) (No. 12-307).

[††]Dana Milbank, "The Politics of Same-Sex Marriage Are Swiftly Changing," *Washington Post*, May 30, 2014.

GENDER AND THE ARMED FORCES

MARGOT CANADAY
Finding a Home in the Army: Before "Don't Ask, Don't Tell"

The military has traditionally been a male realm. Women's exclusion from arms-bearing on behalf of the state has been a major marker of the ambivalence of their citizenship. Margot Canaday shows that the years in the late 1940s and 1950s when women joined the armed forces as soldiers on a permanent, not temporary, basis coincided with a campaign to identify and target lesbians for exclusion. Yet, given the long-standing cultural acceptance of life-long, intimate friendships between women (see Carroll Smith-Rosenberg's and Leila J. Rupp's essays in this volume), lesbians were more difficult for military officials to detect than gay male soldiers. Canaday tells the story of the lengthy, wide-ranging investigations that ensued, along with the resistance strategies used by women service members. One of her surprising conclusions is that state repression can prompt individuals to "see" and articulate an important, latent aspect of their sense of self, and thus can help produce historically complex identities such as "lesbian."

Why did military leaders seek to exclude lesbians from the armed forces? How did they go about identifying lesbians? Note the wide-ranging impact of these investigations. How do these lesbian witch-hunting campaigns during the Cold War compare with the "Don't Ask, Don't Tell" policy (1993–2011) and with evolving military policies on sexuality?

While Alfred Kinsey's 1953 study of female sexuality is usually remembered for shattering several mid-twentieth-century myths about women's sexual behavior, the volume also contained several important observations about the American state, especially concerning the regulation of homosexuality among women. The relationship between the state and female homosexuality, Kinsey concluded in *Sexual Behavior in the Human Female*, was not a well-developed one. The state had, in fact, a long history of indifference to homosexuality among women. . . . Kinsey's survey of . . . recent enforcement of sex law in New York City revealed three cases from the 1940s or 1950s in which women had been arrested for homosexuality. "But all of these cases were dismissed, although there were some tens of thousands of arrests and convictions of males charged with homosexual activity" during those same years.[1]

Kinsey's assertion about government indifference to lesbianism is accurate even when applied in contexts beyond the state-level regulation of sexual behavior that he surveyed. In the early years of the twentieth century, . . . the federal government's concern with sexually degenerate aliens included effeminate men and male sodomists, but focused on neither mannishness nor same-sex eroticism among women. While World War I vice investigators

Excerpted from ch. 5 of *The Straight State: Sexuality and Citizenship in Twentieth-Century America* by Margot Canaday (Princeton, N.J.: Princeton University Press, 2009). Reprinted by permission of the author and publisher. Notes have been edited and renumbered.

occasionally identified "female pervertors" in and around military bases, . . . such revelations seemed to have little impact on local, state, or federal policing, which remained directed at men. . . . In his study of gays and lesbians during the Second World War, Allan Bérubé argues that lesbians were often invisible to military authorities and women were rarely discharged for homosexuality. Even during the massive 1950s' purge of homosexuals from the civil service, women (who comprised 40 percent of the federal workforce) were far less likely to be targeted than men. "Of the initial ninety-one homosexuals fired from the State Department," historian David Johnson writes, "only two were women."[2]

Yet while generally true, Kinsey's conclusion about state indifference to lesbianism does not hold in at least one time and place: the early Cold War military. Here one finds a state that did not ignore, conflate, or subsume lesbianism, but was instead focused upon it. Although women made up just 1 percent of the force during the late 1940s and early 1950s, the military's efforts to purge soldiers suspected of homosexuality targeted women especially. Military officials maintained that homosexuality among women was more disruptive to morale and discipline than homosexuality in men, and they attributed a far higher rate of homosexual activity to female than male personnel. . . . [3]

As with earlier moments of increased federal attention to homoerotic practices and desires, the process of state-building itself stimulated growing federal interest in homosexuality among military women. The coming of the Cold War . . . gave an enduring "cast to the transmutations of World War II"—especially the increased size of the bureaucratic state, which remained "intact." The postwar boom in military spending expanded the economy generally, paving the way for greater numbers of women to enter the civilian labor force. Cold War expansion also created a lasting need for women inside the military. When Congress authorized a permanent peacetime force that was at least five times its 1939 size, it simultaneously provided for a stable nucleus of women who would attend to the military's growing clerical, administrative, and other needs. Legislation that permanently integrated women into the regular forces was passed in 1948.[4]

Homosexuality mattered most to state officials in the places where citizenship was defined, and if women's military service was becoming less peripheral, then so was their perversion. The Cold War military thus reveals [a] . . . federal arena in which the increasingly salient opposition between citizenship and homosexuality was forged. . . . Women's proximity to first-class citizenship helps to explain why the focus on lesbianism first became apparent inside the Cold War military, but other factors were at work. The federal regulation of homosexuality among women also depended on the crystallization of a binaristic conception of homosexuality and heterosexuality, which . . . developed gradually in the years before World War II, and then hardened during and immediately after the war. By the late 1940s and early 1950s, many Americans (and certainly most state officials) believed that individuals were either heterosexual or homosexual, and that "normal" men and women were those who had sexual relations with persons of the opposite sex. As a result of this broad-ranging conceptual shift, . . . men and women who were identified as homosexual were seen as fundamentally similar kinds of people, and this paved the way for a military policy that applied to both men and women "irrespective of sex."[5]

In drafting new guidelines after the war, military officials were adamant that a single policy would be used to deal with homosexuality among both sexes. Under that policy, women, like men, could be discharged for either committing homosexual acts or possessing homosexual tendencies. Yet . . . , the policy was implemented in ways that suggested gender difference. Unsure of how to define a homosexual act between women, military authorities often relied on the provision barring soldiers who had homosexual "tendencies" to eliminate women who were physically intimate with other women. Moreover, officials not only believed that sex among women was less easily defined than sex between men, but that women were more private in their sexual lives. As a result, and in contrast to the way that investigations of homosexuality among men often centered around the commission of an act, women's romantic attachments, social networks, and emotional ties were all scrutinized for evidence that a woman possessed homosexual tendencies. . . .

As relationships (rather than relations) became the focus of state policing, antilesbian investigations took on an unprecedented size. Such investigations encompassed not simply the parties to an alleged sexual encounter, but an expansive web of friends and acquaintances that sometimes extended far beyond a single base or unit. These ordeals—which represented a huge expansion of the state's investigatory power—were a manifestation of the military's own ambivalence about the women who served in the military after the war. In contrast to the women whose World War II service was understood as a heroically brief interlude before marriage, this later cohort signed up not to meet a temporary emergency but, rather as part of a permanent nucleus of women within the armed services. Because they were seen as choosing the military (as opposed to marriage) for a career, these soldiers were automatically suspect, considered overly ambitious and unlikely to be satisfied with the things that "normal" women wanted. The way that these soldiers were policed, then, was related to why they were policed: antilesbian investigations aimed not only to remove a few women from the service, but to employ the threat of lesbianism to secure the subordination of women soldiers as a class. Policing this vast network of relationships enabled military officials to touch the lives of virtually every woman in a unit under investigation, warning each not only to monitor her own relationships with other women on her base, but to avoid appearing too driven or exercising too much authority as well. The exclusion of women believed to be lesbians was, in short, closely related to the inclusion of women in the service in general. Lesbianism was constituted by military authorities to help maintain gender hierarchy after women's integration eliminated a historic barrier between male and female service. . . .

Albeit in a temporary capacity, women first served in the U.S. military in significant numbers during the Second World War. Approximately 350,000 women enlisted during those years in the WAC or its equivalent in the other branches of the armed services (the WAVES, WAF, WASP, or SPARS).[6] Women were drawn to the military for a variety of reasons—it offered excitement and independence, as well as a chance to serve the country. A portion of those who enlisted were also attracted by the emotional and perhaps sexual dimensions of working and living with other women. Some of these women continued in the military a lesbian life they had led before the war; some had their first romantic or sexual experiences with women after they enlisted. As long as they did

not attract public attention, the military generally ignored "romantic friendships" among women. But women who drew suspicion of lesbianism to their unit—usually butch, often working-class women—presented a greater problem for military authorities. Such women were only rarely subject to formal regulations barring homosexuality, but . . . they might be discharged for unsuitability (or for such general offenses as public drunkenness or insubordination), if they even made it past the initial screening procedures that "focused on class background, education, personality, and behavior. . . ."[7] "During the war," WAC commander Mary Hallaren remembered, "we skirted the homosexual problem." . . . Similarly, WAC psychiatrist Margaret Craighill described homosexuality as a "serious problem" for men during the war, but "much less of a problem than . . . expected" for women.[8]

Such attitudes stand in stark relief to those expressed in the years after the war. Women's entry into the armed services paralleled a broader movement of women into the labor market overall during these years, and women in the military generally performed the same kind of clerical work as their counterparts in the civil service. But while many working women pushed up against the conservative gender ideology of the era, only women in the service threatened the special relationship between men, soldiering, and martial citizenship. . . . Widespread concern about lesbianism among women in the military actually preceded the 1950s' "lavender scare" in the federal government. What one journalist referred to as the military's "project lesbian" instead coincided with congressional debates on women's integration in 1947 and 1948. During those hearings, military and congressional leaders argued that the services would only be able to meet recruitment goals for female personnel if women were given the opportunity to build a lasting career in the military. Official interest in lesbianism arose in tandem with the military's growing need for women.[9]

It was, for example, as Congress was making plans for women's permanent entry into the service in 1947 that the army drafted instructions for investigating homosexuality among female soldiers. . . . In 1948, as integration was enacted, the military established the WAC Training Center at Fort Lee, and in response to what it then described as an extraordinarily high rate of homosexuality among women, included lectures on homo-sexuality in the curriculum for enlistees. . . . Leadership courses for noncommissioned of-ficers and officer refresher courses introduced around the same time included segments on how to detect and handle abnormal conduct among female personnel. The approach was, the WAC director wrote, to bring homosexu-ality among women out from "behind a veil of silence and mystery."[10] . . .

Some months later Lieutenant General Lutes reported to WAC director Hallaren that "the indications continue to grow that a condi-tion of homosexuality is widespread in the army." Despite the outbreak of war with Korea—which might have encouraged officials to look the other way—150 enlisted women and officers were implicated, Lutes told Hallaren, in investigations into homosexuality in the Fourth Army. In 1951, a memo from the commanding officer of the Military District of Washington described the situation in more alarming tones. "The number of sexual perverts in the WAC who are assigned to this command is a matter of grave concern to me," he wrote. "This situa-tion is steadily growing worse, although I have been cognizant of it for some time and have used every means at my disposal to cope with it." The command had already separated two officers and transferred four more; nine en-listed women had been undesirably discharged for homosexuality. Beyond that, the general claimed to have conclusive evidence that an-other thirteen WAC soldiers were perverts and stated that eleven others were under suspicion. The general's memo prompted a high-level meeting with seven other commanders a month later. The numbers themselves were not unusual, but reflected a broader pattern. Inves-tigations conducted at any given base during these years regularly involved up to twenty women and sometimes several times that number.[11]

The army's postwar focus on homosexual-ity among women existed with equal or greater intensity in the navy, air force, and marines. When he took command of his office, for in-stance, the head of the air force's special investi-gations unit did not believe the rumors concerning homosexuality among air force women because they were so incredible. He soon found that the "situation was actually more fantastic than the rumors." . . . A 1952 report on the women's marine detachment at El Toro, California, observed that homosexuality

among the women there was considered to be a "definite problem" that probably existed at other bases as well.[12] Yet it was the navy's 1957 Crittenden report that most clearly articulated that homosexuality was a special problem among women. The report noted that "homo-sexual activity of female members of the mili-tary has appeared to be more disruptive of morale and discipline . . . than similar male ac-tivity," and it posited a higher rate of homosex-uality for women than men in the navy.[13] . . .

To understand the military's broadest purposes in regulating homosexuality, it is necessary to look at its most precise targets. Antilesbian repression in the military was *broadly* powerful against all women because it was *individually* devastating against a smaller number. How, then, was homosexuality in women defined, how was it policed in specific women, and how did those individuals who were directly targeted resist such policing? . . .

. . . Homosexuality in women might consist of anything, Fort McClellan psychiatrists stated, from the "bus station pick up . . . to a close emotional relationship extending over a period of years with no more than . . . casual physical contact."[14] As this broad range suggests, the ambiguity of homosexuality in women in-creased its scope.

Part of the confusion as to what comprised female homosexuality resulted from a greater cultural tolerance for homosocial intimacy be-tween women than between men. Acts that were "indicative of homosexuality in the male" were thought "normal [in] the female." Women might, the Crittenden Board reported, "kiss and embrace . . . and live together and occupy the same bed without any connotation of ho-mosexuality," while "similar acts on the part of males would immediately be branding." In a military context, where women had to adapt to male behavioral norms, such circumstances meant that "normal female propensities" might be misinterpreted as homosexual acts. "It is very difficult to know where to draw the line on anything of this kind," commented WAC director Hallaren.[15]

But military officials did not attribute the high rate of homosexuality among women solely to such misinterpretation. Rather, as the WAC director conceded of the women in her branch, there might be "some fact among the fancy." Indeed, widespread acceptance of the expression of affection between women could conceal actual homosexuality in the service. Relationships among women, army psychiatrists wrote, could be "more easily covered" than relationships among men. A homosexual act between two women "leaves no physical evidence of its commission," an army manual on female homosexuality noted, "and seldom if ever is committed in the presence of an innocent person." Relatedly, the Crittenden Board noted that female homosexuality was difficult to detect because women were "more secretive" and "more seclusive" than men.[16] Because women were thought more likely to engage in sex in private, and because military officials were unclear about how to define sexual activity between women even when it was witnessed, the regulation of female homosexuality could not rest primarily on homosexual acts.

. . . The navy acted first to update its guidelines on homosexuality for the postwar period, releasing in July 1949 a policy instructing military officials to consider homosexuality among personnel, whether "male or female." The navy policy then guided the work of a Department of Defense (DOD) committee charged with creating a uniform policy for all branches of the service. The DOD committee—in what was a harbinger of rising homophobia throughout the federal government—firmly broke with World War II policies that permitted some personnel charged with homosexuality to be rehabilitated and returned to the service. "Prompt separation of homosexuals from the military is mandatory," the DOD policy of October 1949 read. The committee, which included a representative from the WAC to cover "women's interests," wrote women into the hardening opposition between homosexuality and martial citizenship. Homosexuals were not to be allowed to serve in any capacity, these officials mandated, and "the character of separation" would be, moreover, "without distinction as to sex."[17]

. . . The new policy established three classes of homosexual offenders. Class I homosexuals, as with the World War II–era policy, were violent offenders who were to be court-martialed. Class II homosexuals, also a carryover from the war years, were to be undesirably discharged for consensual homosexual acts. Finally, the new policy inaugurated the category of the Class III homosexual, who had homosexual "tendencies," and was to be either generally or undesirably discharged.[18]

To be clear, the idea that a person could have homosexual tendencies was not entirely new—during World War II the term referred to a soldier (generally male) who declared himself homosexual but had committed no in-service acts.[19] But the new policy's denotation of such persons as a separate class indicated a growing emphasis on the category of tendencies by the end of the 1940s. "The only major change prescribed by [the DOD policy]," wrote Under Secretary of the Navy Dan Kimball, "is the establishment of the Class III category of personnel."[20]

As deployed by the new guidelines, the concept of tendencies paved the way for more aggressive policing, capturing, as one air force captain put it, "the complexity of the homosexual problem." . . . With women, the category could designate (a physically) unexpressed homosexuality . . . [and it] helped military officials cope with the fact that, despite their best efforts, they still did not understand how homosexuality in women was expressed. The concept of tendencies absolved military officials of the responsibility of drawing a line between sex and what was considered normal female intimacy. In so doing, the designation of the Class III homosexual enabled military officials to extend the apparatus they used to police women far beyond sexual acts. The label of tendencies not only penalized mannish women for "the way they walk[ed], talk[ed], or dress[ed]," but also brought a sprawling web of women's friendships and associations under state surveillance.[21] Military authorities, in short, had begun to identify a new set of attributes as evidence of homosexuality, revealing the power of the state to not only regulate but constitute identity as well. . . .

How, then, did military police and administrative discharge boards enforce the DOD's policy on homosexuality against individual women? Military discharge files for *male* soldiers from the early 1950s follow remarkably clear patterns. Most cases involved two or perhaps four men, who either admitted or were observed in acts of sodomy or fellatio. (Often the admissions followed being caught by other men in their units.) The investigation, while undoubtedly painful to those accused, was a contained and relatively straightforward inquiry: Did two men engage in sexual relations together? How, when, and where? Who saw it?[22] When male soldiers were processed as Class III (for tendencies), the investigation still generally revolved around the commission of acts, albeit ones with fewer witnesses. In one case, for example, . . . a male soldier wrote a letter to the president stating that he was a homosexual and asking for help to cope with his condition. After this admission, the army commenced an investigation into the soldier's homosexual tendencies. . . . The soldier received a general discharge for homosexual tendencies "after the investigation disclosed that [the accused] committed acts."[23]

Policing homosexuality among women was not as clear-cut. While military police sometimes encountered two women hugging and kissing in cars on base, and were aware that many of the women "[went] steady" together, military authorities did not expect to observe acts between women that could clearly be identified as homosexuality. When they did, they were not well equipped to deal with such situations. In one episode from 1952, a military police officer (MP) spotted one WAC member performing oral sex on another in the front seat of a parked car. He watched for about thirty seconds, before the two women (having recognized the MP vehicle behind them) drove off. Although he had identified the two women, he did not make a report because, as he admitted subsequently, "I wouldn't know how." He further explained that "there never were any orders given to me to cover anything like that."[24] . . .

One could conclude, based on the way that these MPs responded to the two WAC soldiers, that military authorities were uninterested in policing sexual activity between women. But that was not the case. Military authorities sought evidence of physical involvement between women suspected of being lesbians. Yet MPs simply did not expect that women would routinely engage in homosexual acts where they could be observed. "It was just one of those things you read about and hear about," declared one of the MPs who had spotted the two women together in the car, "but never *see*."[25] Accordingly, in most cases the policing of women relied more on interrogation, through which investigators induced women to confess and corroborate sexual activity with other women, sometimes quite successfully. . . .

. . . [H]omosexual tendencies were also attributed to women who exhibited gender inversion, or as one military guide to homosexuality among women put it, "the wearing of the clothes and the desire to assume the role of the opposite sex." . . . [For example,] one recruit

testified, Williams was a "queer one" . . . who had "masculine ways." She would announce her presence in the barracks by calling out, "There's a man in the house!" She wore mannish clothes, "combed her hair in a mannish way," and women appeared to be drawn to her. She had, the investigation revealed, "magnetism."[26]

The investigator's mention of recruit Williams's apparent ability to attract women demonstrates that in identifying the attributes of homosexuality in women, military officials were attuned to not only sexual activity and gender traits but also women's relationships with one another. Indeed, the bonds between women were commonly scrutinized for evidence of homosexual tendencies—an assessment that rested on intimacy as much as sex. Moreover, including relationships within their scope meant that investigations among women often took on an enormous scale. An investigation that began with evidence of a single homosexual incident might lead to every woman in a unit being called in for questioning. As women were pressured to name their associates, investigations thus expanded to massive proportions involving a complex web of women, sometimes spreading across several bases in different regions of the country. . . .

In contrast to investigations involving male soldiers, then, a focus on relationships and associations could supplement or even supplant questions about sexual activity when women were the subjects of official scrutiny. One such large-scale probe at Fort Meyer, Virginia, began when one woman admitted to her commanding officer that she was a homosexual and had "performed acts of cunnilingus." A comparable admission by a male soldier most likely would have resulted in his discharge and that of his sex partner(s). The scope of the WAC investigation's final report was much broader: "Baker has told Armstrong, that she, Baker, loves Duffy. It is known that Duffy visits Baker at Ft. Meyer, and vice versa." Mitchell and Tracey were "co-owners of a Nash two-door sedan automobile," and the investigating officer explained, "this partnership was consummated to strengthen their friendship." These two women also exchanged Christmas presents; two others, Abel and McNeil, exchanged letters. Hale and Taylor were constantly together, and "Hale wears a ring of Taylor's." Warren and Schneider had also exchanged rings, and so had Baker and Simonides, which "undoubtedly hurt Edwards." Baker knew "Edwards to be extremely jealous of Simonides." But the latter woman also dated Jones. Edwards wanted to exchange rings with Jones, but "Jones denied this offer for fear of consequences which had developed after having exchanged rings with Simonides." And on and on it went.[27]

Military authorities did not just police sexual acts or gender traits; they policed a culture of women. That broad focus involved, despite official "consensus" that one policy on homosexuality govern both sexes, the development of an entirely separate and quite elaborate methodology for investigating homosexuality among women. This methodology borrowed extensively from loyalty and other anticommunist investigations (which also uncovered a network among women, although one allegedly connected by political ideology rather than sexual desire). One manual described army procedure to handle the "widespread condition" of "female homosexuality": in addition to "scientific" interrogation, unit commanders were instructed to set up a cross-reference file (with information from the FBI and civil vice squads as well as military intelligence agencies); "secure a . . . roster of the unit concerned [and] a list of all automobiles owned or operated by suspects"; "secure and maintain informant-informer systems"; "arrange for mail cover"; and finally, that the most valuable information would come "through surveillance, the secretive and continuous watching of persons, vehicles, and places." Should such surveillance reveal female homosexuals, commanders were instructed to "plan and conduct a detailed search of their personal effects, automobiles, and any known 'off post' residences, for the purposes of obtaining correspondence, literature, or pictures of a homosexual nature."[28]

In carrying out their duties, agents went through wastepaper baskets looking for notes. They conducted "shakedowns" of the barracks, searching for letters, photographs, and books with lesbian themes.[29] They set up wiretaps and took polygraphs. Investigators planted informants within units to report on the complicated textures of women's lives together. They uncovered evidence of lesbian weddings, and noted which women had arrived in men's formal wear. Agents recorded the names of women who lived with "notorious homosexuals," as well as those who expressed tolerance for or curiosity about such women. They knew which soldiers did not date the men on base, and they kept a record of which women gave each other

gifts, shared a bank account, participated in a business venture, traveled together, or did each other's grocery shopping.[30] "They knew the times I was [with a lover], the buses that I took, how long I stayed, my mode of transportation home, [and] what I wore," one woman in the air force recalled of the painful investigation she experienced. "They knew every damn move I made. It was mind shattering."[31]

Such intensive techniques were in some measure the result of the military's belief that homosexual acts among women were more obscured and less clear-cut than similar acts between men. They were also a result of fierce misogyny. Simply put, there is little evidence in the documentary record that male soldiers went through anything like what their female counterparts did. "The methods used by these investigators," one WAC major wrote in a complaint to the inspector general, were "calculated to embarrass and humiliate the women involved." The major described how investigators searched the belongings of a woman "not even 20 years of age" by opening "the woman's box of Tampax" and going "to the extreme of ripping the tissue paper from each of them." She asked, "What could possibly have been gained by this action except to perpetrate an indignity on this young woman in front of her Commanding Officer?" . . . Women were picked up for questioning at all hours, held under guard, and not allowed telephone calls or visitors. . . . And the interrogation itself was a humiliating experience that could approximate psychological rape. One woman, for example, was asked if she was not "missing a lot of fun" because she had never had intercourse with a man. "You are the same as a little girl that didn't like cake because she had never had any," the investigating officer chided her.[32]

Women investigated for homosexuality went through ordeals that could last months. It was "psychological warfare," one WAF member recalled of her investigation by the air force's Office of Special Intelligence. "They opened my mail . . . they'd look under my mattress . . . they'd get me up in the middle of the night for questioning." She recalled being questioned once or twice each day for four months. "They'd come to the mess hall and get me in the middle of a meal. They knew no bounds." But the worst part was the isolation. "There was no way I could tell [my lover] what was happening and explain to her that my whole relationship with her was something of value, not some tawdry

affair." Other women on base avoided this soldier too, "for fear of their own careers."[33] . . .

When her discharge finally came—an undesirable, not a general one—it was soul destroying. "I left that base feeling like a real
piece of shit." Fired twice when employers
learned of her discharge, "for the next six years,
I felt like a real loser. . . . I had no ego left, no
self-image, no confidence, no surety-of-self."
For years, the WAF member "never told a soul
about it." Evidence suggests that other women
were equally tormented by these witch
hunts. . . . "I have steadily lost weight," [one]
WAC member stated, "[and] I have had to go on
'sick call' for a nervous condition caused by
this aggravation." Some women committed
suicide. The scale of these investigations, moreover, made even those who were not targeted
feel vulnerable. "If you were so accused, how
would you prove your innocence?" one WAC
major asked herself, in the midst of a destructive investigation in her unit. She concluded
that this was a "precarious and untenable position to occupy. How does one prove the absence of tendencies?"[34] . . .

. . . Yet while soldiers rarely fought their
discharges in the federal courts, it was not unusual for military women to refuse to be discharged administratively and to demand a
court-martial proceeding. Perhaps women did
so out of desperation. What better career
option than the military existed in the early
1950s for working-class women who wanted to
avoid marriage and family, or who did not conform to conventional gender stereotypes? "I
went into the service to be a career woman . . .
and I'd have stayed there," remembered one
woman who was devastated by losing everything "that was air force" right down to her
boots. "I request that I be allowed to stay in
the army [to] prove that I can be a good soldier," another wrote. Alternatively, women
may also have demanded trial by court-martial because they were politically savvy, insisting that the military prove a case that was
often based on tenuous evidence regarding
emotional ties and loose associations (rather
than well-documented accounts of homosexual acts). While military regulations allowed
the secretary of each branch to administratively remove a soldier without a court-martial
who refused a discharge for homosexuality, in
practice a demand for a court-martial could
derail the entire process. Officials sometimes
just dropped a case, in other words, when a

discharge was refused and conviction by court-
martial seemed unlikely.[35] . . .

[Some] women refused to pathologize their
sexuality during the investigatory process. One
soldier, for instance, described her relationship
as "beautiful" and told investigators that her
"life in the future [would] be centered around
[her] relationship." Another woman told investigators that she did not consider her homosexual activity to be unnatural. Perhaps most
remarkably, one woman wrote in a detailed
confession for the Criminal Investigation Division, "I am not ashamed of what I have done,
for it was something which has been born
with me."[36]

As such declarations indicate, state repression was productive of identity in complicated
ways—women's attempts to manage the antilesbian apparatus within the military frequently led them to articulate a lesbian identity
in much sharper terms. "The patient declares
that she has been homosexual all her life," one
psychiatrist reported, but "did not realize [it]
until . . . the investigation into this problem at
Ft. Lee stimulated her interest." . . . "Knowing
about [homosexuality] now," one woman informed authorities during an investigation at
her base, "I look back into my childhood and
feel that I have been gay all my life."[37] . . .

Here . . . [we see] how involved the conversation was between the regulator and the regulated, how much women themselves worked
with the state to produce the category of lesbianism. It was, to be sure, a forced and unpleasant
collaboration, but also extremely far-reaching in
that it did not just affect the women who had
begun to think of themselves as homosexual,
the women who literally and figuratively *found
themselves* in front of military boards. From the
beginning, the lesbian witch hunt had a much
broader audience and purpose. . . .

As a few DOD officials pointed out during
these years, the most "undesirable" personnel
could have been purged—without such intensive and far-reaching investigations. . . . Perhaps the point of the investigation[s] was not
removal as much as submission—to train
those who survived the purge, in other words,
to be junior partners in the military marriage
that . . . [leaders] envisioned. Military officials
were uneasy not only about . . . lesbians [being]
well represented [among the women who
chose military careers]. They worried as well
about maintaining gender hierarchy as formal

barriers separating men's and women's service fell.

Prior to the Women's Integration Act, women's service was always differentiated from men's in such a way as to highlight its lesser character, to set it apart from the kind of sacrifice that produced first-class citizenship. Women's service was auxiliary, quasi-auxiliary, or temporary. After 1948, only the provision keeping women out of combat demarcated women's service as different—a distinction that was becoming less and less meaningful in the nuclear age. . . .

The extent of official concern about maintaining women's subordination in the postintegration period . . . is perhaps nowhere more obvious than in the hostility directed at women officers across the service branches, and the way in which lesbian baiting worked especially to rein in those marked as deviant by their own career ambitions. (The vitriol directed at women officers, usually older women, was also expressed via concerns about the potentially harmful impact of having menopausal women in the service.)[38] So a psychiatrist noted the "drive" of one officer under investigation for homosexuality. She desired independence, the psychiatrist said, positing that her homosexuality was the result of "competitive feelings toward men." Moving up the ranks was itself a sign that an officer bore watching. One navy memo, for instance, noted that female homosexuals achieved "rapid advancement" because they worked hard to "compensate for or to avoid suspicion of [their] sexual weakness."[39]

Women officers were regularly blamed when lesbianism was seen as flourishing within their commands. It was women officers who allegedly opened the floodgates to lesbian recruits, or who turned a blind eye on sexual misconduct because "there but for the grace of God go I." Sometimes such complaints were registered by enlisted women, perhaps as a way of turning the tables on an authority figure.[40] But it was the male command structure that viewed women officers with the most animosity. "I cannot depend on WAC officers to command even a small detachment," one general wrote in a scathing memo on perversion among women. He advocated that both the WAC Training Center and WAC units over a certain size be placed under the control of male officers. It was also proposed that "male officer inspection teams make periodic inspection of all WAC installations," during the course of

which enlisted women be granted confidential interviews to discuss their concerns on the subject of "leadership" and "homosexuality."[41]

For enlisted women as well but especially for officers, the closer women moved to power, to first-class citizenship, the more homosexuality seemed to matter.[42] Indeed, the air force was the first service to feature coeducational officer training and a single gender-integrated officer promotion list. It was also "far ahead of the army in investigating and discharging female homosexual personnel." The extent to which the air force carried both gender integration and lesbian persecution only makes clearer their interconnection across the service branches. Women knew at what cost their own ambition came . . . and how carefully they had to manage it. Perhaps this was part of what led the women service directors (all unmarried) to personally fight congressional legislation that would have allowed them each to obtain a rank higher than colonel. "They were afraid of appearing 'grasping.'" It was similarly what motivated these same women to stop saying, as their counterparts had during World War II, that female personnel could "replace" men, and instead talk about how well female soldiers "complemented" male personnel.[43] . . .

The way that women's integration intensified antilesbian repression makes citizenship seem like a zero-sum game: as one group wins, another must lose. A parallel observation may be made with respect to racial integration, which was also occurring as the armed forces adopted increasingly homophobic policies more generally.[44] Yet while this substitutionist logic dominates the rhetoric of citizenship, one need not probe far beneath it to see that every new inclusion was deeply sedimented by past exclusion. Women's integration, in short, did not neuter the tradition of martial citizenship, which remained male. To preserve gender hierarchy in citizenship, though, the state had needed to constitute lesbianism. The incredibly broad way it did so meant that so many women were touched during the course of any given investigation that it was not individual women who were policed, but women in the service as a class.

Notes

1. Alfred C. Kinsey, *Sexual Behavior in the Human Female* (Philadelphia: Saunders, 1953), 484–85. See also "The Consenting Adult Homosexual and the Law: An Empirical Study of Enforcement and

Administration in Los Angeles County," *UCLA Law Review* 13 (1966): 740.

2. Allan Bérubé, *Coming Out Under Fire: The History of Gay Men and Women in World War II* (New York: Plume, 1991), 28; David K. Johnson, *The Lavender Scare: The Cold War Persecution of Gays and Lesbians in the Federal Government* (Chicago: University of Chicago Press, 2004), 12. Elizabeth Lunbeck notes that male homosexuality has almost always been more condemned by sexologists than lesbianism. See Elizabeth Lunbeck, *The Psychiatric Persuasion: Knowledge, Gender, and Power in Modern America* (Princeton, NJ: Princeton University Press, 2003), 410–11.

3. Crittenden Report, 40, box 16, World War II Project Records, Gay, Lesbian, Bisexual, and Transgender Historical Society, San Francisco.

4. Bruce D. Porter, *War and the Rise of the State: The Military Foundations of Modern Politics* (New York: Free Press, 1994), 286–91; Alice Kessler-Harris, *Out to Work: A History of Wage Earning Women in the United States* (Oxford: Oxford University Press, 1982), 303; Women's Armed Services Act of 1948, Public Law 80-625, *U.S. Statutes at Large* 62 (1948) 368. Two weeks after the enactment of women's integration, Harry S. Truman authorized the nation's first-ever peacetime draft (the Selective Service Act of 1948). Jeanne Holm, *Women in the Military: An Unfinished Revolution* (Novato, CA: Presidio Press, 1992), 129.

5. Hubert E. Howard to the Secretary of the Army, the Secretary of the Navy, the Secretary of the Air Force, "Discharge of Homosexuals from the Armed Services," October 11, 1949, decimal 250.1, box 100, Assistant Secretary of Defense decimal file 1949–1950, Records of the Secretary of Defense, RG 330, National Archives, College Park, MD.

6. Most of the evidence for this chapter is from army records, because records are most available for that branch of the service. The Records of the Secretary of the Air Force at the National Archives, for example, have only been declassified recently. Because all branches were under the DOD after 1947, however, relatively uniform policies guided all branches, and wherever possible, I have included evidence from the air force and navy.

7. Leisa D. Meyer, "The Myth of Lesbian (In)visibility: World War II and the Current Gays in the Military Debate," in *Queer American History*, ed. Alida M. Black (Philadelphia: Temple University Press, 2001), 272; Leisa D. Meyer, *Creating G.I. Jane: Sexuality and Power in the Women's Army Corps* (New York: Columbia University Press, 1996), 156, 161, and chapter 7 generally.

8. Memorandum from Colonel Mary Hallaren to Major General G. E. Byers, "The Homosexual Problem," January–February 1950, box 86, Background Papers, Women's Army Corps 1945–1978, Records of the Army Chief of Staff, RG 319. Margaret Craighill, "Psychiatric Aspects of Women Serving in the Army," *American Journal of Psychiatry* 104 (1947–1948): 228.

9. On women's work in the military, see Holm, *Women in the Military*, especially 113, 175. On domestic ideology during the 1950s, see especially Elaine Tyler May, *Homeward Bound: American Families in the Cold War Era* (New York: Basic Books, 1988). Sam Crown, "Do Lesbians Dominate Our WAC?" *SIR* (March 1956): 20, in vertical file "Homosexuals in the

Military," Kinsey Institute, Indiana University, Bloomington. Janann Sherman, "'They Either Need These Women or They Do Not': Margaret Chase Smith and the Fight for Regular Status for Women in the Military," *Journal of Military History* 54 (January 1990): 72.

10. Memo from R. L. Howze, "Investigation of WAC Personnel," October 14, 1947, decimal 321, box 843, "WAC Project," G-1 (Personnel) decimal file 1946–1948, War Department General Staff, RG 165. Memorandum from Colonel Mary Hallaren to Major General G. E. Byers on "the Homosexual Problem."

11. Lt. General L. Lutes to Colonel Mary A. Hallaren, November 22, 1950, decimal 333.9, "Fourth Army," box 1012, decimal file July 1950–June 1951, Records of the Inspector General, RG 159, National Archives, College Park, MD. Memorandum from Major General Thomas W. Herren, March 26, 1951, "Unsatisfactory Control," decimal 250.1, box 967, G-1 (Personnel) decimal file 1951–1952, Records of the Army Chief of Staff, RG 319; Memorandum from Colonel W. T. Moore, Chief, Personnel Actions Branch, April 24, 1951, "Homosexuality," decimal 250.1, box 967, G-1 (Personnel) decimal file 1951–1952, Records of the Army Chief of Staff, RG 319.

12. Major Robin Elliott to Colonel Lewis and General Lutes, "Air Force Investigation," November 20, 1950, decimal 333.9, "Fourth Army," box 1012, decimal file July 1950–June 1951, Records of the Inspector General, RG 159. Lt. Bowdre L. Carswell to Chief of the Bureau of Medicine and Surgery, October 22, 1952, file no. P13-1, box 503, Administrative Division General Correspondence 1952–1955, Bureau of Medicine and Surgery, RG 52, National Archives, College Park, MD.

13. The Crittenden Board was a special committee assembled by the navy in 1957 to study homosexuality in the military. Crittenden Report, 40–41, box 16, World War II Project Records. Because the services did not break down overall discharge statistics by gender, there is not hard statistical evidence available to back up this claim. Approximately 4,380 cases of perversion were handled by the armed services from January 1947 to October 1950. Another estimated 10,000 cases were handled by the armed services from November 1950 to December 1955. Louis Jolyon West, William T. Doidge, and Robert L. Williams, "An Approach to the Problem of Homosexuality in the Military Service," *American Journal of Psychiatry* 115 (November 1958): 400.

14. M. D. Hogan and R. E. Anderson to CG, Third Army, "Fort McClellan, Mental Hygiene Consultations Service Report," September 14, 1956, box 64, Background Papers, Women's Army Corps 1945–1978, Records of the Army Chief of Staff, RG 319.

15. Crittenden Report, 40–41; Colonel Mary Hallaren, Interview by Colonel Donald Hargrove and Lt. Colonel Milton Little, March 7, 1977, box 86, Background Papers, Women's Army Corps 1945–1978, Records of the Army Chief of Staff, RG 319.

16. Mary Hallaren to Marion B. Kenworthy, April 17, 1950, "WAC Conference June 1950" folder, box 26, Marion Kenworthy Papers, Rare Book and Manuscript Library, Columbia University, New York. Hogan and Anderson to CG, Third Army, "Fort McClellan, Mental Hygiene Consultations Service Report"; "Female Homosexuality," 1950,

decimal 333.9, "Fourth Army," box 1012, decimal file July 1950–June 1951, Records of the Inspector General, RG 159; Crittenden Report, 40–41.

17. Elmer Wohl to Ralph Stohl, "Study to Revise Regulations for the Handling of Homosexuals in the Armed Services for Both Sexes," June 20, 1949, decimal 730, box 153, Assistant Secretary of Defense, decimal file 1949–1950, Records of the Secretary of the Defense, RG 330; Hubert E. Howard to the Secretary of the Army, Secretary of the Navy, and Secretary of the Air Force, "Discharge of Homosexuals from the Armed Services," October 11, 1949, decimal 250.1, box 100, Assistant Secretary of Defense decimal file 1949–1950, Records of the Secretary of Defense, RG 330; file M-46, box 1481, Assistant Secretary of Defense Subcommittee Studies 1948–1951, Records of the Secretary of Defense, RG 330; Manfred S. Guttmacher, *Sex Offenses: The Problem, Causes, and Prevention.*(New York: W. W. Norton, 1951), 132–33; Bérubé, *Coming Out Under Fire*, 260–62.

18. File M-46, box 1481, Assistant Secretary of Defense Subcommittee Studies 1948–1951, Records of the Secretary of Defense, RG 330.

19. Bérubé, *Coming Out Under Fire*, 141–48. From 1945 to 1947, the army made honorable discharges available to soldiers with homosexual tendencies who had committed no homosexual acts in the service. In 1947, the policy changed such that a soldier who had tendencies but had committed no acts would be given either an undesirable discharge or a general discharge.

20. Kimball to Chairman of the Personnel Policy Board, "Discharge of Homosexuals from the Armed Services," December 16, 1949, file M-46, box 1481, Assistant Secretary of Defense Subcommittee Studies 1948–1951, Records of the Secretary of Defense, RG 330.

21. Colonel Robert R. Gideon Jr. to Director of the Staff, "Preliminary Survey of Separation Procedures for Homosexuals in the Armed Forces," March 15, 1949, file M-46, box 1481, Assistant Secretary of Defense Subcommittee Studies 1948–1951, Records of the Secretary of Defense, RG 330. Hogan and Anderson to CG, Third Army, "Fort McClellan, Mental Hygiene Consultations Service Report."

22. See the thirty-two discharge files for homosexuality involving men, decimal 220.8, boxes 3592–93, Classified decimal file 1948–1950, Records of the Adjutant General, RG 407; decimal 220.8, boxes 3776–78, Classified decimal file 1950–1951, Records of the Adjutant General, RG 407.

23. ——— Case, decimal 220.8, box 3776, Classified decimal file 1950–1951, Records of the Adjutant General, RG 407. In order to protect the privacy of individuals who may still be living, I have omitted surnames in case file citations. (Most case files involve investigations of multiple women.) The surnames that appear in the text are pseudonyms. I have not changed the names of individuals (in the citations or text) in court cases because of the public nature of those documents.

240. ——— Case, decimal 220.8, box 3776, Classified decimal file 1950–1951, Records of the Adjutant General, RG 407.

25. Ibid. (emphasis added).

26. "Female Homosexuality," decimal 333.9, "Fourth Army," box 1012, decimal file July 1950–June

1951, Records of the Inspector General, RG 159.

——— Case, decimal 220.8, box 3593, Classified decimal file 1948–1950, Records of the Adjutant General, RG 407.

27. ——— Case, decimal 220.8, box 3776, Classified decimal file 1950–1951, Records of the Adjutant General, RG 407.

28. ——— Case, decimal 220.8, box 3776, Classified decimal file 1950–1951, Records of the Adjutant General, RG 407. On women's networks and the way they were uncovered during loyalty investigations, see Landon R. Y. Storrs, "Red Scare Politics and the Suppression of Popular Front Feminism: The Loyalty Investigation of Mary Dublin Keyserling," *Journal of American History* 90 (September 2003): 508–9.

29. The 1950 pulp novel *Women's Barracks*— which sold three million copies and was singled out during a congressional investigation in 1952 into pornographic materials—must have enjoyed considerable circulation among military women. See Martin Meeker, *Contacts Desired: Gay and Lesbian Communities and Community, 1940s–1970s* (Chicago: University of Chicago Press, 2006), 87, 118.

30. For these investigatory techniques, see cases involving homosexuality among women in decimal 220.8, boxes 3592–93, Classified decimal file 1948–1950, Records of the Adjutant General, RG 407; decimal 220.8, boxes 3776–78, Classified decimal file 1950–1951, Records of the Adjutant General, RG 407.

31. Interview with Loretta "Ret" Coller, in Mary Ann Humphrey, *My Country, My Right to Serve: Experiences of Gay Men and Women in the Military, World War II to the Present* (New Yorker: HarperCollins, 1990), 13.

32. Complaint to Inspector General from Major Florence M. Packard, June 18, 1957, decimal 333, "Ft. McPherson," box 2283, Confidential decimal file July 1957–June 1958, Records of the Inspector General, RG 159. Letter to Senator Wayne Morse, decimal 333.5, "Ft. McClellan," box 2375, Confidential decimal file July 1958–June 1959, Records of the Inspector General, RG 159. ——— Case, decimal 220.8, box 3778, Classified decimal file 1950–1951, Records of the Adjutant General, RG 407.

33. Interview with Coller, in Humphrey, *My Country, My Right to Serve*, 13–14.

34. Ibid., 16–17. B. L. to Senator Spessard L. Holland, decimal 201.23, box 2281, Confidential decimal file July 1957–June 1958, Records of the Inspector General, RG 159. On suicide, see Allan Bérubé and John D'Emilio, "The Military and Lesbians during the McCarthy Years," *Signs: Journal of Women in Culture and Society* 9 (Summer 1984): 775. Complaint to Inspector General from Major Florence M. Packard, June 18, 1957, decimal 333, "Ft. McPherson," box 2283, Confidential decimal file July 1957–June 1958, Records of the Office of the Inspector General, RG 159.

35. It is unclear as to how women knew to do this; it seems plausible that word traveled among women being investigated from base to base. Interview with Coller, in Humphrey, *My Country, My Right to Serve*, 11–12. ——— Case, decimal 220.8, box 3592, Classified decimal file, 1948–1950, Records of the Adjutant General, RG 407. *Fannie Mae Clackum v. United States*, 296 F.2d 226 (Ct. Cl. 1960), trial records at the National Archives.

36. "Beautiful," "not ashamed": —— Case, decimal 220.8, box 3777, Classified decimal file 1950–1951, Records of the Adjutant General, RG 407. —— Case, decimal 220.8, box 107, decimal file 1953–1954, Records of the Adjutant General, RG 407.

37. —— Case, decimal 220.8, box 3777, Classified decimal file 1950–1951, Records of the Adjutant General, RG 407.

38. Menopausal women were discussed during hearings on women's integration. See Sherman, "They Either Need These Women or They Do Not," 69. The irony is, of course, that they, along with lesbians, were a perfect solution to the military's pregnancy problem.

39. —— Case, decimal 220.8, box 3777, Classified decimal file 1950–1951, Records of the Adjutant General, RG 407. Lt. Bowdre L. Carswell to Chief of the Bureau of Medicine and Surgery, "Prophylactic Measures for Control of Homosexuality among Women Personnel of the Armed Services," October 22, 1952, file no. P13-1, box 503.

40. Resume of Proceedings, June 27, 1957, decimal 333, "Ft. McPherson," box 2283, Confidential decimal file July 1958–June 1958, Records of the Inspector General, RG 159; Hogan and Anderson to CG, Third Army, "Fort McClellan, Mental Hygiene Consultations Service Report." ——Case, decimal 201.36, box 52, General Correspondence 1939–1947, Records of the Inspector General, RG 159.

41. Memorandum from Major General Thomas W. Herren, March 26, 1951, "Unsatisfactory Control," and Colonel T. J. Hartford, "Recommendations regarding WAC Enlistment and Utilization," March 29, 1951, decimal 250.1, box 967, G-1 (Personnel) decimal file 1951–1952, Records of the Army Chief of Staff, RG 319; Hogan and Anderson to CG, Third Army,

"Fort McClellan, Mental Hygiene Consultations Service Report."

42. This point would not have been lost on Kinsey, whose study of female sexuality attributed overall state indifference to lesbianism to women's lack of social and cultural power. Kinsey, *Sexual Behavior in the Human Female*, 485.

43. Linda Witt, Judith Bellafaire, Britta Granrud, and Mary Jo Binker, *"A Defense Weapon Known to Be of Value": Servicewomen of the Korean War Era* (Hanover, N.H.: University Press of New England, 2005), 36, 8, 93. Lt. General Lutes to Colonel Mary A. Hallaren, Nov. 22, 1950, decimal 333.9, "Fourth Army," box 1012. Colonel Mary A. Hallaren (army), Colonel Mary Jo Shelly (air force), Colonel Katherine Towle (marines), and Captain Joy Bright Hancock (navy) were all unmarried at this time.

44. In 1945, military officials suggested the increasing separation of policies on race and sexuality in a statement that there was "less reported homosexuality among colored troops then [sic] white"; and again, in a claim in 1957 that homosexuality "could not be correlated with any other characteristic." Lt. Colonel Lewis H. Loeser, "The Sexual Psychopath in the Military Service: A Study of 270 Cases," *American Journal of Psychiatry* 102 (July 1945): 100; Crittenden Report, 11, box 16, World War II Project Records. Also intriguing is an enormous witch hunt in 1947 concerning fifty African American WAC soldiers at Camp Beale, California. Because the service feared "probable publicity concerning racial discrimination," the women were "surplused" rather than being given undesirable discharges for lesbianism. ——Case, decimal 201.36, box 52, General Correspondence 1939–1947, Records of the Inspector General, RG 159.

ELIZABETH L. HILLMAN

The Female Shape of the All-Volunteer Force

During the Vietnam War, President Johnson and other officials referred to our "boys in uniform" without apology to the women who also served in that war. By the twenty-first century, however, when President George W. Bush deployed U.S. troops to fight the war on terror in Afghanistan and Iraq, these troops were always referred to by government officials and members of the media as "our brave men and women in uniform." In the span of 30 short years, the participation of women in the military rose dramatically; since early 2009, women have comprised roughly 15 percent of the armed forces. No longer invisible, servicewomen are now consistently acknowledged as critical members of the U.S. military.

In this essay, Elizabeth Hillman explains how women came to figure crucially in recruitment, and how the military has responded to this dramatic demographic shift within its ranks. What factors account for the "feminization" of the armed services? Why have military leaders supported affirmative action? What have been the benefits and the costs of women's enhanced presence in the U.S. military? Why have many women found military service appealing? What dangers have they experienced from their own colleagues in the U.S. military? How do military policies related to race, gender, and sexual orientation relate to one another?

Because of the numbers and influence of women in the ranks, the U.S. military took on a distinctively female shape in the last decades of the twentieth century. In every service, at nearly every rank and grade, in virtually every unit and at every installation, servicewomen reported for duty alongside men. As early as the 1970s, military and political leaders knew that the military could not meet its personnel needs without drawing on the female labor force. And the need for women in uniform has not let up since. The tremendous demand for military resources in the post-Vietnam era, coupled with women's push for equal opportunity, has drawn women into the military in transformative numbers. In spite of the resistance of military institutions, the post-Vietnam armed forces have become "feminized" in many key respects. "Female" issues such as promoting healthy families, ending sexual harassment, and preventing sexualized torture command the attention of military task forces and congressional committees. "Feminine" skills including compromise, negotiation, and communication are among the skills most critical to successful peacekeeping operations and even to military interrogation. And women themselves are essential cogs in the military manpower machine.

But this new gender balance, this "feminization," has caught military and political leaders off guard. The United States has not reconceived military service as a civic duty of and career opportunity for both women and men, nor has it made the military workplace safe for women. Instead, military and civilian leaders have restricted women's opportunities and reinvented a "warrior" culture of aggression and male coming-of-age.[1] Despite the integration of women and racial minorities into most of the armed forces, the U.S. military remains one of the only American institutions that can legally discriminate on the basis of sex.

In the last three decades, observers in and out of uniform have debated the wisdom and consequences of women's military service. But none can dispute the new gender demographics of the post-Vietnam U.S. military. Those demographics reveal a startling and largely ignored truth: with the end of forcible service for men, women rescued the all-volunteer force from devastating shortfalls in the number and quality of recruits. As the Vietnam War ended, the Selective Service Act was allowed to expire. When the last draft call went out in 1973, women made up less than 2 percent of the U.S. military. Ten years later, the female presence in the ranks had increased five times over. By September 2005, women were 16 percent of the American armed forces.[2] Without them, the military would have suffered not only a shortage of personnel, but also a striking drop in the education levels and test scores of new recruits.

Much as the officials and consultants of the Vietnam era failed to appreciate the degree to which women and racial minorities would become essential military personnel, the architects of the early twenty-first century military transformation have failed to reckon with the consequences of women's heightened military participation. One of the lessons that the military has forgotten since the Vietnam War is that women saved the all-volunteer force. That rescue came at great cost—to servicewomen, to the military, and to the United States.

THE ALL-VOLUNTEER FORCE: WOMEN AS SAVING GRACE

In 2003, the University of Michigan won a battle in the courts to preserve its ability to consider race in student admissions decisions. It won by arguing that diversity was a compelling objective of state educational policy.[3] A turning point in that case was the amicus curiae [friend of the court] brief signed by twenty-nine retired generals and admirals, including notable military leaders such as Admiral William T. Crowe, chairman of the Joint Chiefs of Staff from 1985 to 1989; General Norman Schwarzkopf, commander of allied forces in the Gulf War of 1991; and General Wesley Clark, supreme allied commander in Europe from 1997 to 2000. Their brief, quoted at some length in Justice Sandra Day O'Connor's opinion for the Supreme Court, stressed the negative consequences of racial disparities in the Vietnam-era armed forces and declared that affirmative action was essential to maintaining a diverse, well-qualified military. That amicus brief was a direct outgrowth of the military's role as a model of successful racial integration. Active-duty as well as retired military leaders routinely invoke the rhetoric of equal opportunity in the strongest possible language.[4] The armed forces of the early twenty-first century embrace diversity as a positive good as thoroughly and publicly as any American institution.

But thirty years ago, the experts who were asked to prepare the nation for the end of conscription did not see diversity as a possibility, much less a goal. During the Vietnam War, the Department of Defense had relied on forced service, not volunteers, to fill many of the least desirable and most dangerous military occupations. The risks and hardships of serving in the Army's ground forces rather than in the more technical, less martial forces of the air and sea services persuaded many young men to enlist in the Navy or Air Force rather than wait for a draft notice and end up in the infantry. After the war, military planners and civilian government officials underestimated the degree to which the end of the draft would also end this incentive to volunteer. They also misjudged the extent of American youth's disenchantment with military service. As a result, they anticipated almost no change in the gender or racial demographics of military service in a volunteer military.[5]

The most influential expert assessment was the report prepared by the Gates Commission in 1970. Chartered by President Nixon to develop a plan to end the draft and named for its chair, Thomas S. Gates, a former secretary of defense, the commission unanimously recommended that conscription be ended. The commission's report ignored women entirely, mentioning female service only in the context of alternatives to a volunteer force. Instead, the report stressed the importance of increasing military pay, describing "the first indispensable step" toward a successful volunteer force as removing "the present inequity in the pay" of servicemen. This emphasis on financial incentives reflected the influence of commissioners such as economists Alan Greenspan and Milton Friedman, but the commission's failure to discuss even the possible recruitment of

women was nonetheless a remarkable omission.[6] Military leaders knew—and had known since at least World War II, when more than 350,000 women served in military uniforms—that women could be relied upon to fill gaps in military staffing. A 1966 Pentagon task force had studied the use of women to meet the personnel needs of the war in Vietnam, and in 1967 Congress had lifted the 2 percent ceiling on female enlistments.[7] In addition, the commissioners themselves had identified the structural factors—the evolution in military occupations and the skills that those occupations required—that soon led to many more women in uniform. The commission noted the trend toward more technical and bureaucratic military jobs, documenting how the proportion of military occupations involving ground combat had fallen from 25 percent in 1945 to 10 percent by 1974. This meant that an increasing number of military positions could be filled by servicewomen without even reaching the question as to whether women should be subjected to combat situations. The commission also identified the quality of recruits as a major concern for an all-volunteer force, a problem that could logically be addressed by broadening the potential pool of recruits to include women. But the commission failed to connect the dots when it came to women. The demographics of the commission itself were part of the problem: only one of fifteen commissioners, and none of the thirty-one senior staff and research leads, was a woman.[8]

The experts' botched forecast was apparent almost immediately. As soon as the draft ended, the numbers and quality indicators of male volunteers fell and the Department of Defense scrambled to recruit women. By 1972, Secretary of Defense Melvin R. Laird was establishing a task force, to prepare contingencies for the use of women if the draft ended, and by 1978, the Carter administration was explicitly directing the Pentagon to increase the number of servicewomen.[9] A 1977 Brookings Institution study recommended recruiting women because it was less expensive and would reduce the pressure for more men.[10] Fifteen years after the draft ended, the number of women in uniform had increased from 1.5 percent to more than 9 percent. Women's scores on military aptitude tests shored up the military's quality indicators as well as its overall numbers.[11] In fiscal years 1974 to 1976, for example, 88 percent of the women who joined the Army were high school graduates, as compared to only 52 percent of the men; in the first decade of the volunteer force, 92 percent of all women enlistees had high school diplomas, compared to only 70 percent of male enlistees. One scholar bluntly wrote, "It is widely acknowledged that women were the saving grace of the volunteer concept during the 1970s."[12]

After the 1970s, women continued to enlist in larger numbers than initially expected, spurred in part by changes in military personnel policies. In order to attempt to recruit more men, the military increased pay and benefits and recognized the need to support military families and service members' dependents. These changes in military policy created economic and social incentives that made recruiting and retention of skilled, reliable servicemen possible. But they also made a military career more attractive to women, especially those who lacked significant economic opportunities in the civilian sector. The military eliminated restrictions on assignments that prevented women from serving in many military occupations and relaxed restrictions that forced pregnant women to be discharged and limited the number of dependent children of recruits. These trends combined to make the armed forces a viable career choice for those seeking economic security and educational support. By the late 1990s, the number of military personnel who served for more than four years had increased significantly, one of many indicators of an increasingly career-oriented force.[13]

This sea change in military demographics made women the fastest-growing segment of veterans in the early twenty-first century. In 1983, Congress established a Secretary of Veterans' Affairs Advisory Committee on Women Veterans. In 1994, a Center for Women Veterans was established in the Department of Veterans Affairs after legislation championed by Representative Maxine Waters of California.[14]

In addition to missing the gender implications of the volunteer force, government planners also underestimated the rate at which African Americans would enlist in a volunteer military. The percentage of African Americans in the military nearly doubled in the first decade after the end of the draft. This concurrent increase in minority and female participation led to a dramatic rise in the number of African American women in the service; by 1986, black women were 43 percent of Army enlisted women and 30 percent of the entire female force.[15] In 2005, women constituted 16 percent

of the military workforce and 48 percent of the overall civilian workforce. African American women, however, accounted for 28 percent of the female military presence despite being only 13 percent of the female civilian labor force. In the Army, this overrepresentation of African American women was especially pronounced: black women made up 39 percent of female Army personnel on active duty in 2004.[16] In recent years, the Congressional Black Caucus Veterans Braintrust has paid particular attention to the needs of the fast-growing population of African American female veterans. In many respects, African American women were at the center of the demographic transformation triggered by the end of the Vietnam War. Their experience crystallizes the role and treatment of women in the volunteer force: they helped to save the volunteer army by enlisting in disproportionately high numbers but their opportunities for military success were circumscribed by discrimination and harassment.

WOMEN VOLUNTEERS: FITS, STARTS, AND PROGRESS

Once in uniform, women were assigned, evaluated, and promoted in ways that reflected cultural assumptions about female capability. Military laws and policies structured the work environments of servicewomen and reinforced a gender hierarchy that affected civilian as well as military women. Within that hierarchy, sexual harassment and assault became a feature of the military workplace and threatened the lives and health of women around domestic and foreign military bases. Because the volunteer force needed female servicemembers, and because women needed the career stability and economic opportunities that military service offered, the ranks of servicewomen steadily grew. But the emphasis on male authority and aggressiveness that predominated in many quarters of military service left women unprotected from discrimination and abuse. Women made great strides toward becoming full participants in military service. Their success, however, came against a backdrop of continued restrictions and a repetitious debate about whether or not they belonged in the service at all.

When the Vietnam War ended, servicewomen had already won the support of many commanders and political leaders. The Defense Department Advisory Committee on Women in the Services, established by Secretary of Defense George C. Marshall in 1951 to aid in the recruitment of women during the Korean War, monitored the progress of women's service and recommended solutions to recurring problems.[17] The promotion and recruiting restrictions that had prevented women from either attaining high rank or reaching a significant proportion of the force were already gone, and by 1972, the Air Force, Army, and Navy Reserve Officer Training Corps (ROTC) programs were all open to women.[18] Admiral Elmo Zumwalt, the Navy's maverick chief of naval operations from 1970 to 1974, opened many previously closed naval occupational specialties to women during his tenure. The Air Force led the way in accommodating women's reproductive lives by allowing women with children to enlist and permitting waivers of the Department of Defense's automatic discharge policy for pregnant women. Civil courts, responding to new pressure for civil rights and expanding notions of legal equality, had also begun to push the armed forces to treat women fairly. Sharron Frontiero, who served in the Air Force, found that her male colleagues automatically got dependents' benefits for their wives, but in order for her to get dependent's allowances for her husband, she had to prove that she provided more than 50 percent of his financial support. She challenged this practice, and in 1973, the Supreme Court struck down sex discrimination in the distribution of military benefits.[19] Still, in 1972, just before the draft ended, only 42,000 women served in the military, and more than 90 percent were assigned to jobs classified as medical, dental, or clerical in nature.[20]

The advent of the volunteer force brought sharp increases not only in servicewomen's numbers (more than 100,000 women were serving in 1976 and more than 150,000 by 1979) but also in their opportunities. By 1976, the percentage of women in those "feminine" military classifications had dropped to 60 percent, and by 1983, it was down to 55 percent, with increasing numbers of women assigned to fields such as intelligence, supply, and equipment repair.[21] Congress opened the elite national service academies to women in 1976, and the courts continued to nudge the military in the direction of equitable gender policies, holding in 1976 that the Marine Corps' policy of mandatory discharge of pregnant Marines violated the Constitution and ordering the Navy to open additional ships to women in 1978.[22] By

2005, women accounted for about one-sixth of the active and reserve forces. They were most outnumbered in Marine Corps, where female marines were but 5 percent of the force, but they made up nearly a quarter of both Army and Air Force reserves.[23]

Progress toward equal opportunity across gender lines was not a steady march, however. As the number of servicewomen grew, gender-based restrictions on military assignments remained in place. Military leaders limited the changes wrought by women's military presence by preserving some positions as male-only. They argued that the risks involved, the physical capabilities required, or the military facilities available (such as berthing capacity on ships) would make women's presence in these positions a detriment to military effectiveness. This debate centered on the issue of the appropriateness and practicability of assigning women only to noncombat jobs. Proponents of women in combat argued that the restrictions protected masculine privilege, not female bodies, while opponents pointed to the history of male participation in war fighting and the vital importance of bonding ("unit cohesion") in guaranteeing performance under fire. The Supreme Court upheld the all-male Selective Service system in 1981 on the grounds that women were not eligible for combat, demonstrating the importance of this military personnel policy.[24]

The patchwork of combat exclusion rules that evolved as Congress and the president negotiated with the services revealed widespread resistance to the full inclusion of female service members. Identifying combat positions was not a simple task; some military occupational specialties were opened, closed, and reopened to women as opinions shifted about their suitability for women. Lawrence J. Korb, a scholar of military affairs and an assistant secretary of defense from 1981 to 1985, once described the "combat-exclusion policy" as "the worst of all possible worlds for female military personnel" because it limited women's advancement but failed to protect them from the risks of dangerous service. The arguments for and against permitting women to serve in combat positions were endlessly recycled during the first three decades of the volunteer force.[25]

Still, the trend was clearly in the direction of opening doors to women. Most military jobs are now performed by both men and women. In 1988, the Department of Defense opened about 30,000 new positions to service women by setting a single standard (called the "risk rule") to be used in evaluating sex-based restrictions on assignments. The service of military women in the invasion of Panama in 1989 and the Persian Gulf War in 1990 and 1991 led to more pressure to lift sex-based restrictions on assignments. Combat aviation opened to women in 1993, and a 1994 policy change rescinded the "risk rule" in favor of a ban on the assignment of women to units below the brigade level with a primary mission of engaging in direct ground combat. Servicewomen have acted as peacekeepers in Haiti, enforced no-fly zones in Iraq, flown combat missions in Kosovo, died in terrorist attacks on the USS *Cole* in 2000 and at the Pentagon in 2001, and been wounded alongside men in Afghanistan and Iraq in the first U.S. wars of the twenty-first century.[26]

Thirty years into the volunteer force, women shoulder the burdens of military duty but have yet to ascend to the highest ranks of military institutions. In 2005, there were 43 female flag or general officers as compared to 874 male such officers, a female representation of less than five percent, and only one woman stood among the 173 men at the two highest grades. The wide gap between women's representation at the top and the bottom of the military hierarchy reflects more than the time lag between accession to duty and late-career promotions.[27]

The vestiges of the combat exclusion policy keep women off the fastest tracks to military promotion. In 2005, sex-based restrictions on women's assignments placed 15 to 20 percent of military positions off-limits for women, most of them in the infantry and special forces. Women are excluded from 178 enlisted specialties (5 percent of all available specialties) and 17 officer specialties (1 percent of those available). Servicewomen remain concentrated in health care and administrative occupations. Although these combat exclusions cannot eliminate female casualties, they have placed disproportionately more servicemen than women in harm's way. Even in the ongoing war in Iraq, which has brought female military casualties and deaths to the front pages of U.S. newspapers, servicewomen account for only 1 percent of deaths and 2 percent of the wounded.[28] For those who served short terms in the conscript army of the Vietnam War, avoiding combat had been a way to stay alive; for those who make careers in the volunteer military, avoiding combat is still a safer way to

go, but it has also become a professional liability. Women are "underrepresented in tactical operations, the area that yields two-thirds of the general and flag officers of the Services." Women are also a smaller percentage of service academy graduates than men, partly because so many women are directly commissioned as nurses but also because women's presence at the academies has been carefully monitored by officials unwilling to permit too many women to populate the ranks of elite cadets and midshipmen. Women of all races have lower promotion and retention rates than men, though the data vary across race lines. White women tend to leave the military before attaining high rank, while African American women—notwithstanding a widespread perception among white servicemen that minorities are favored in selection for promotions—are promoted at lower rates than the members of any other demographic category. Every service except the Air Force still includes photographs in the packets considered by promotion boards, furthering the perception that race and gender are taken into account—as pluses or minuses in the promotion process.[29]

Family responsibilities also contribute to women's underrepresentation at the highest levels of military service. Although most senior servicemen are married, husbands—and children—are scarce for women at high ranks as compared to men. At the relatively senior ranks of O–5 and O–6 (that is, lieutenant colonels and colonels in the Army, Air Force, and Marine Corps and commanders and captains in the Navy), 90 percent of men but only 55 percent of women are married. Ninety-four percent of military spouses are women. Even with such relatively low rates of marriage, servicewomen routinely identify family issues such as child care among their primary concerns about continued military service.[30]

Women's family responsibilities were of great concern to those who opposed the integration of women into the military infrastructure. But fears about women missing too much time for medical reasons and maternity, including pregnancy-related disabilities, have proven unfounded. Most studies of gender differences in performance point out that men miss more time for disciplinary matters such as drug and alcohol abuse than women miss for medical leave. After all, the demands of family push servicemen as well as women away from the sacrifices that a military career requires.[31]

THE VOLUNTEER FORCE TODAY

Women's military opportunities have opened up dramatically since the Vietnam War, and women were critical in keeping the volunteer army afloat after the draft ended. But women's appearance in the volunteer military was not enough to meet the armed forces' relentless need for more people, more expertise, and more money. Servicewomen mitigated, but did not end, the constant pressure to recruit. The military's failure to promote gender equity in assignment and promotion policies and its inability to build a culture in which women were valued and respected as much as men have created additional problems for the volunteer force. Though the gender transformation of the volunteer military answered the question of whether women should serve, doubts about the proper extent of that service have persisted in American public discourse. In the post-9/11 military, the debate continues over women's military participation, even in the face of rising demands for military personnel and declining success in recruiting.[32]

Thirty years into the volunteer military, the United States has invested enormous resources in recruiting military personnel. In fiscal year 2003, the Department of Defense spent $455 million on special incentives such as enlistment bonuses, college funds, and loan repayments. In addition to these incentive programs, the United States has repeatedly increased military pay since the Vietnam era, responding to studies that stressed higher pay as a primary means of recruiting high-quality personnel. These financial incentives are necessary because current military personnel policies prohibit so many potential recruits from enlisting. According to the Department of Defense, at least half of U.S. youth between the ages of 16 and 21 are not qualified to enlist, mostly because of "physical and mental deficits" such as asthma, obesity, illegal drug use, or the use of prescription antidepressants. Potential recruits are also disqualified for failure to meet educational, aptitude, or moral character standards (measured by criminal convictions and evidence of "asocial behavior"). A recruit can also be disqualified for having too many children; if unmarried, no dependent children are allowed, and if married, a recruit may have no more than two dependent children. Waivers to these requirements are permitted and are more likely during times of greatest need; in 2005, the GAO reported that

waivers for physical disabilities appeared to be increasing, while waivers for character failings were declining. The military's policy prohibiting service by men and women who are unable—or refuse—to hide their gay or lesbian sexual orientation also limits the pool of available military recruits. The constant need for more personnel both taxes resources and undermines morale.[33]

The twenty-first-century U.S. military also faces an uphill battle in retaining high-quality personnel because of the conditions under which many service members work and live. One recent study described the strain that the post-9/11 military actions have placed on the volunteer military as "unprecedented" because of lengthy, frequent deployments and "exposure to nontraditional, hostile combat conditions." These conditions have contributed to declining interest among male high school students in military service, a shift that is especially evident among African American young men since fiscal year 2002. As a result of these trends, the military has little choice but to recruit women to help to fill its ranks.[34]

The women who heed the call to join, as well as the civilian women who live or work with service members, must reckon with not only limits on advancement but also a climate of sexual harassment, assault, and violence.[35] Some of the abuse endured by military and civilian women at the hands of servicemen takes place at home, where the stresses of military life can explode into family violence. The pressures of military service are often worst at the bottom of the military hierarchy, where financial pressures are greatest and where the wives of young enlistees often find their career opportunities limited by their husbands' service. Military families often face "separations, serious financial pressures, isolation from family and peer support systems, and frequent moves," all of which increase the risk of family violence. Military training and combat experience may also increase the risk of domestic violence. The Department of Defense has responded to public outcry and congressional mandates by establishing programs to discourage and track spousal and child abuse in military families, but the problem is far from resolved.[36]

Abuse of women also takes place in military workplaces, partly because of continued resistance to the integration of the volunteer force. Women and racial minorities struggle with being excluded, tested, and harassed more often than white men, who still dominate the ranks, constituting 58 percent of the 2005 military. Servicewomen routinely hear denigrating comments about female capabilities, rebuff unwanted sexual advances, are physically harassed, and must face down assumptions that they are promoted because of, not in spite of, their gender and/or race. The parade of military sexual harassment and assault scandals in the 1990s and first few years of the 2000s demonstrated that sexualized abuse had become a part of military service.[37] Servicewomen are also disproportionately censured under the "don't ask/don't tell" policy, and fear of being called a lesbian deters women from reporting unwanted sexual advances and assaults. The military's zero-tolerance response to this epidemic of abuse has led some servicemen to avoid allegations of sexual harassment by avoiding women entirely, a reaction that further isolates servicewomen and limits their advancement. As a 2005 task force on sexual harassment and assault at the U.S. service academies described the situation: "Although progress has been made, hostile attitudes and inappropriate actions toward women, and the toleration of these by some . . . continue to hinder the establishment of a safe and professional environment."[38]

Even with the help of women enlistees, the volunteer force faces constant challenges to meet its personnel needs. Despite their willingness to serve, women have not been able to rescue the U.S. military from the threat posed by the end of conscription, nor have they changed its fundamental nature. Their service has not ended the insular nature of military service, lessened the rigidity of military culture, or restored the luster of military service to attract and keep the best and brightest. They have not transformed the military's social and political order into the entrepreneurial, risk-taking environment that Secretary of Defense Donald Rumsfeld called for. And neither has their presence forestalled the sexual violence so often committed by U.S. service members.

Perhaps the most telling example of the success and limits of the gender integration of the volunteer force is the appearance of women at the center of the first major military scandal of the twenty-first century. Although the sexual harassment and torture of detainees in the post-9/11 wars was perpetrated by both women and men, the public faces of the American torturers indisputably belonged to two Army women, a private and a general: the derisive smile and dangling cigarette of Specialist Lynndie R. England, a young female enlistee photographed while pointing at naked detainees, and the stern visage of Brigadier General Janis Karpinski, the Army Reserve officer in charge of the prison at Abu Ghraib during the most publicized incidents of prisoner abuse.[39] Other women were also key figures in the debacle, including dozens of enlisted military police and nonmilitary interrogators. Lieutenant Colonel Diane E. Beaver, the staff judge advocate for a joint task force at Guantanamo Bay, wrote a key legal brief recommending the use of more aggressive interrogation techniques in 2002. Major General Barbara Fast, the highest-ranking woman to serve in Iraq, was the intelligence chief for the U.S. military ground commander and oversaw the interrogation centers at Abu Ghraib during 2003 and 2004. Not all of these women were punished for their roles in the scandal, but several were, most notably Karpinski, who was reprimanded and demoted, and England, who was sentenced to three years' confinement and dishonorably discharged. Servicewomen's successful integration into the intelligence, military police, and legal career fields put them at the center of detainee operations in Iraq and made them relatively easy to blame for the military's maltreatment of detainees and mismanagement of detention facilities.[40]

Whoever bears ultimate responsibility for the crimes that took place in American detention facilities in the post-9/11 wars, Lynndie England has joined the rogues' gallery of U.S. service members punished for their failures in wartime. That gallery used to be exclusively male, featuring the troubled Eddie Slovik, executed during World War II for desertion; the unfortunate Claude Batchelor, a trumpet player turned infantryman who was court-martialed after the Korean War for collaborating with Communists while imprisoned in North Korea; and the notorious William Calley, convicted but barely punished for leading the horrifying massacre at My Lai. The addition of women to such a dubious military legacy suggests that women bear the impossible burdens of wartime service no more nobly or easily than men.

POSTSCRIPT, 2014

The U.S. military's policies with respect to gender and sexual orientation continue to evolve, and the military continues to depend on women to perform its missions around the world in the first decades of the twenty-first century. After a long campaign of advocacy and litigation by activists for equal rights, the military's "don't ask, don't tell" regime came to an end in 2011 when Congress, the executive branch, and the military agreed to end sexual orientation discrimination in the military. Meanwhile, women comprised a relatively constant fraction, about 15 percent, of military personnel and continued to be most commonly assigned to medical and administrative specialities. Policy restrictions limit women's participation in "combat" arms, though the Obama administration has promised to lift the ban on women in combat by 2016, and women remained a small fraction of the military's highest ranks. In April 2014, servicewomen were less than 7 percent of the military's generals and admirals, and only one woman appeared among 37 four-star flag officers. In 2008, Ann E. Dunwoody became the first woman nominated to the rank of four-star general. The Air Force's Janet C. Wolfenbarger ascended to four stars in 2012 and the Navy's Michelle J. Howard became the first four-star female admiral in 2014. Hence, women have broken nearly every barrier in the armed forces yet are still far scarcer in the higher ranks compared to their representation among rank-and-file service members.[41]

Sexual assault in the military became a primary concern of Congress in 2012 with the release of reports about high numbers of sexual assaults against service members, several high-profile scandals, and a privately produced and widely distributed documentary about military sexual assault, *The Invisible War*. President Barack Obama spoke out against military sexual assault, and Congress created an independent panel in 2013 to both assess the effectiveness of military responses to sexual assault and consider pending and prospective legislation intended to address the problem. Whether this external pressure for change will hasten the advent of gender equality and an end to sexual violence in the military remains to be seen.[42]

NOTES

1. See Judith A. Youngman, "Whatever Happened to the Citizen Soldier?" in *Women in Uniform: Exploding the Myths, Exploring the Facts* (Washington, DC: Women's Research and Education Institute, 1998); Laura Miller, "Not Just Weapons of the Weak: Gender Harassment as a Form of Protest for Army Men," *Social Psychology Quarterly* 60 (1997), pp. 32–51.

2. *Military Personnel: Reporting Additional Service member Demographics Could Enhance Congressional Oversight*, General Accounting Office Report to Congressional Requesters, September 2005 (hereafter GAO report), pp. 10–11; see also chart, p. 38.

3. *Grutter v. Bollinger*, 539 U.S. 306 (2003).

4. Defense Equal Opportunity Council, *Report of the Task Force on Discrimination and Sexual Harassment*, vol. I, Washington, DC, May 1995, p. i.

5. Martin Binkin and Mark J. Eitelberg, "Women and Minorities in the All-Volunteer Force," in *The All-Volunteer Force After a Decade: Retrospect and Prospect*, ed. William Bowman et al. (New York: Pergamon-Brassey's, 1986), p. 74.

6. *The Report of the President's Commission on an All-Volunteer Force* (New York: Collier/Macmillan, 1970).

7. Binkin and Eitelberg, "Women and Minorities in the All-Volunteer Force," p. 82.

8. *The Report of the President's Commission on an All-Volunteer Force*, pp. 43, 18. The only female commissioner was Dr. Jeanne Noble, a professor of education and vice president of the National Council of Negro Women, who in 1962 had become one of the first African American women to receive tenure at New York University.

9. Binkin and Eitelberg, "Women and Minorities in the All-Volunteer Force," p. 83.

10. Carolyn Becraft, "Women and the Military: Bureaucratic Policies and Politics," in *Women in the Military*, ed. E. A. Blacksmith (New York: H. W. Wilson, 1992), p. 9.

11. Lawrence Korb, "The Pentagon's Perspective," in *Who Defends America? Race, Sex, and Class in the Armed Forces*, ed. Edwin Dorn (Washington, DC: Joint Center for Political Studies, 1989), pp. 24–25.

12. Martin Binkin, *America's Volunteer Military: Progress and Prospects* (Washington, DC: Brookings Institution, 1984), pp. 7–8, 48.

13. Office of the Under Secretary of Defense Personnel and Readiness, *Career Progression of Minority and Women Officers* (Washington, DC: 1998) (hereafter *Career Progression* report), p. 10.

14. See the research compiled by the Women's Research and Education Institute, available at www .wrei.org, which uses Bureau of Labor Statistics to document the rising number of women veterans.

15. Binkin and Eitelberg, "Women and Minorities in the All-Volunteer Force," p. 82; *Who Defends America?*, p. 48.

16. GAO report, pp. 3, 42.

17. Laura L. Miller, "Feminism and the Exclusion of Army Women from Combat," in *Women in the Military*, ed. Rita James Simon (New Brunswick, NJ: Transaction, 2001), p. 109. See also the DACOWITS website at http://www.dtic.mil/dacowits (visited July 29, 2006).

18. For a chronology of significant dates, see Captain Lory Manning, *Women in the Military: Where They Stand*, 5th ed. (Washington, DC: Women's Research and Education Institute, 2005), pp. 4–9.

19. *Frontiero v. Richardson*, 411 U.S. 677 (1973). (See pp. 752–753.)

20. Binkin and Eitelberg, "Women and Minorities in the All-Volunteer Force," p. 85.

21. It is important to remember that these aggregate figures describe a volunteer military that was not a monolith but instead a collection of service branches and subcultures. The almost entirely

male Marine Corps shares little in mission or tradition, for instance, with the technocratic Air Force, which is nearly one-fifth female.

22. *Crawford v. Cushman*, 538 F.2d 1114 (1976); *Owens* et al. *v. Brown*, 455 F.Supp. 291 (1978).

23. GAO report, p. 38.

24. *Rostker v. Goldberg*, 453 U.S. 57 (1981).

25. Becraft, "Women and the Military," pp. 11–15; Korb, "The Pentagon's Perspective," p. 25. For a useful overview of the issues surrounding women in combat, see *Female Soldiers: Combatants or Noncombatants*, ed. Nancy Loring Goldman (Westport, CT: Greenwood Press, 1982). In 2005, the arguments looked much the same as in 1982. See, e.g., "G.I. Jane, Again," *National Review* 57, no. 10 (June 6, 2005), pp. 22–24 (Army's restrictions on women in combat and debating the efficacy of such restrictions); "Women Already See Combat," *USA Today*, May 25, 2005; M.C. Devilbiss, *Women and Military Service: A History, Analysis, and Overview* (Maxwell Air Force Base, AL: Air University Press, 1990); Linda Grant DePauw, *Battle Cries and Lullabies* (Norman: University of Oklahoma Press, 1998).

26. On the integration of women into combat aviation, see Captain Alice W. W. Parham, "The Quiet Revolution: Repeal of the Exclusionary Statutes in Combat Aviation—What We Have Learned from a Decade of Integration," 12 *William and Mary Journal of Women and the Law* 377 (2006); Korb, "The Pentagon's Perspective," p. 25.

27. Department of Defense, *Active Duty Military Personnel*, September 30, 2005, available at the Office of the Secretary of Defense (OSD) website, http://www.defenselink.mil/osd/; Susan Hosek et al., *Minority and Gender Differences in Officer Career Progression* (Santa Monica, CA: Rand, 2001), pp. 2–3.

28. GAO report, pp. 38–39, 45, 121.

29. *Career Progression* report, pp. viii, 24, 18, 58, 75–76.

30. Karen Houppert, *Home Fires Burning: Married to the Military—for Better or Worse* (New York: Ballantine, 2005), p. xix.

31. Korb, "The Pentagon's Perspective," p. 25. See also Elizabeth Lutes Hillman, *Defending America: Military Culture and the Cold War Court-Martial* (Princeton, NJ: Princeton University Press, 2005), pp. 70–79.

32. See, e.g., Rowan Scarborough, "Iraq War Muddles Role of Women," *Washington Times*, October 17, 2005, p. A4; Jodi Wilgoren, "A Nation at War: Women in the Military: A New War Brings New Role for Women," *New York Times*, March 28, 2003, p. Bl; Rowan Scarborough, "Army Affirms Its Ban on Women in Combat," *Washington Times*, January 19, 2005, p. A1.

33. The Gates Commission report was the first such study; the most recent is the Government Accounting Office's *Military Personnel: DOD Needs to Improve the Transparency and Reassess the Reasonableness, Appropriateness, Affordability, and Sustainability of Its Military Compensation System*, GAO-05-798 (Washington, DC: July 19, 2005), which points out that military pay is but 70 percent of comparable civilian pay scales; GAO report, pp. 4, 68–76.

34. James Hosek, Jennifer Kavanaugh, and Laura Miller, *How Deployments Affect Service Members* (Santa Monica, CA: Rand, 2006), p. xiii; GAO report, pp. 80, 67, 4; "Problem for Navy: Too Few Hands on Deck," *New York Times*, February 2, 1999, pp. Al, 17.

35. Notwithstanding this grim picture, the primary targets of military sexual violence are civilian rather than military women. Cynthia Enloe's work reveals the stark dimensions of the military's long and tragic history of participating in human sex trafficking and prostitution around the world. Cynthia Enloe, *Does Khaki Become You? The Militarization of Women's Lives* (Boston: South End Press, 1983), pp. 18–45; *Bananas, Beaches, and Bases: Making Feminist Sense of International Politics* (Berkeley: University of California Press, 1990), pp. 81–90; *The Morning After: Sexual Politics at the End of the Cold War* (Berkeley: University of California Press, 1993), pp. 142–160. In the ongoing war in Iraq, the secondary targets of sexual violence seem to be the male enemy, particularly captured irregulars thought to be terrorists and considered "high-value" detainees.

36. See, e.g., Margaret C. Harrell, *Invisible Women: Junior Enlisted Army Wives* (Santa Monica, CA: Rand, 2000); James Hosek et al., *Married to the Military: The Employment and Earnings of Military Wives Compared with Those of Civilian Wives* (Santa Monica, CA: Rand, 2002), and *Battle Cries on the Homefront: Violence in the Military Family*, ed. Peter J. Mercier and Judith D. Mercier (Springfield, IL: Charles C. Thomas, 2000). See also http://www.vva.org/Committees/WomenVeterans/MilesFoundationSAMM.htm Accessed 20 October 2014.

37. GAO report, p. 40; *Career Progression* report, chapter 7; see Linda Bird Francke, *Ground Zero: The Gender Wars in the Military* (New York: Simon & Schuster, 1997).

38. See Aaron Belkin and Geoffrey Bateman, eds., *Don't Ask/Don't Tell: Debating the Gay Ban in the Military* (Boulder.CO: Lynne Rienner, 2003); Human Rights Watch, *Uniform Discrimination: The "Don't Ask, Don't Tell" Policy of the U.S. Military* (January 2003), http://www.hrw.org/reports/2003/usa0103/ (accessed July 24, 2006) (especially the section titled "Impact on Women"); Servicemembers Legal Defense Network statistics on the disproportionately high discharge rate for servicewomen accused of being lesbians, http://www.sldn.org/binarydata/SLDN_ARTICLES/pdf_file/351 .pdf (accessed July 10, 2006); *Report of the Defense Task Force on Sexual Harassment and Violence at the Military Service Academies* (Washington, DC: Department of Defense, June 2005), executive summary.

39. See, e.g., Karen J. Greenberg and Joshua L. Dratel, eds., *The Torture Papers: The Road to Abu Ghraib* (New York: Cambridge University Press, 2005).

40. James W. Smith III, "A Few Good Scapegoats: The Abu Ghraib Courts-Martial and the Failure of the Military Justice System," 27 *Whittier Law Review* 671 (2006).

41. Military personnel statistics for 2014 are drawn from the Defense Manpower Data Center: https://www.dmdc.osd.mil/appj/dwp/dwp_reports.jsp (accessed Jun. 19, 2014).

42. Materials on military sexual assault appear at the website of the Response Systems Panel, http://responsesystemspanel.whs.mil/ and *The Invisible War* is described at http://invisiblewarmovie.com/ (accessed Jun. 19, 2014).

Goesaert v. Cleary, 1948

In response to the worries of returning World War II veterans over finding well-paying jobs in the postwar recession, Michigan's legislature passed a statute prohibiting any woman from serving liquor as a bartender in cities of more than 50,000 unless she was "the wife or daughter of the male owner" of a licensed liquor establishment. (Women could, however, be hired as waitresses.) The statute was justified on the grounds that the presence of a man behind the bar shielded women from drunken violence; we can see it as another version of the protective legislation that had been upheld in *Muller v. Oregon* (1908) (see p. 357).

Valentine Goesaert's husband had recently died. She and her daughter Margaret wanted to continue to operate their family's tavern in Dearborn, Michigan. They were joined by 26 other women bar owners and barmaids who claimed their right to equal protection guaranteed by the Fourteenth Amendment. Their legal expenses were partially paid for by the Michigan Barmaids Association; their attorney, Anne R. Davidow, had graduated from law school in time to vote in 1920, and had represented the leaders of the United Auto Workers Union. The Federal District Court for Michigan denied their claim, observing that the legislature had not been unreasonable: "[T]he legislature may have reasoned that a graver responsibility attaches to the bartender who has control of the liquor supply than to the waitress who merely receives prepared orders of liquor from the bartender for service at a table." The Goesaerts appealed to the U.S. Supreme Court, where they lost again. The decision was 6–3. Note the reasoning of the dissenters as well as the majority.

JUSTICE FELIX FRANKFURTER, WRITING FOR THE MAJORITY:

[The question is: can Michigan forbid females generally] from being barmaids and at the same time make an exception in favor of the wives and daughters of the owners of bars? . . . Beguiling as the subject is, it need not detain us long. To ask whether or not the Equal Protection of the Laws Clause of the Fourteenth Amendment barred Michigan from making the classification the State has made between wives and daughters of owners of liquor places and wives and daughters of non-owners, is one of those rare instances where to state the question is in effect to answer it.

We are to be sure, dealing with a historic calling. We meet the alewife, sprightly and ribald, in Shakespeare, but centuries before him she played a role in the social life in England. . . . The Fourteenth Amendment did not tear history up by the roots, and the regulation of the liquor traffic is one of the oldest and

---

Goesaert v. Cleary, 335 U.S. 464, 69 S.Ct. 198 (1948). For a history of this case, based in part on oral histories, see Amy Holtman French, "Mixing It Up: Michigan Barmaids Fight for Civil Rights," *Michigan Historical Review* 40 (Spring 2014): 1–20. The principle of *Goesaert* was not undermined until 1971, when the California Supreme Court upheld the right of women to tend bar in *Sail'er Inn, Inc. v. Kirby*, 5 Cal. 3d 1 (1971). *Sail'er Inn* was argued by a very recent law school graduate, Wendy Webster Williams, using a brief written by two law students, Mary Dunlap and Margaret Kemp.

most untrammeled of legislative powers. Michigan could, beyond question, forbid all women from working behind a bar. This is so despite the vast changes in the social and legal position of women. The fact that women may now have achieved the virtues that men have long claimed as their prerogatives and now indulge in vices that men have long practiced, does not preclude the States from drawing a sharp line between the sexes, certainly in such matters as the regulation of the liquor traffic. . . . The Constitution does not require legislatures to reflect sociological insight, or shifting social standards, any more than it requires them to keep abreast of the latest scientific standards.

While Michigan may deny to all women opportunities for bartending, Michigan cannot play favorites among women without rhyme or reason. The Constitution in enjoining the equal protection of the laws upon States precludes irrational discrimination as between persons or groups of persons in the incidence of a law. But the Constitution does not require situations "which are different in fact or opinion to be treated in law as though they were the same." . . . Michigan evidently believes that the oversight assured through ownership of a bar by a barmaid's husband or father minimizes

hazards that may confront a barmaid without such protecting oversight. . . . [If it is reasonable,] as we think it is, Michigan has not violated its duty to afford equal protection of the laws. We cannot cross-examine . . . the mind of Michigan legislators nor question their motives . . . we cannot give ear to the suggestion that the real impulse behind this legislation was an unchivalrous desire of male bartenders to try to monopolize the calling. . . .

JUSTICE WILEY RUTLEDGE, DISSENTING:

. . . This statute arbitrarily discriminates between male and female owners of liquor establishments. A male owner, although he himself is always absent from his bar, may employ his wife and daughter as barmaids. A female owner may neither work as a barmaid herself nor employ her daughter in that position, even if a man is always present in the establishment to keep order. This inevitable result. . . . belies the assumption that the statute was motivated by a legislative solicitude for the moral and physical well-being of women who, but for the law, would be employed as barmaids. Since there could be no other conceivable justification for such discrimination against women owners of liquor establishments, the statute should be held invalid as a denial of equal protection.

"We were the first American women sent to live and work in the midst of guerrilla warfare. . ."

The American ships and planes that went to Vietnam carried women as well as men. There were approximately 10,000 military women and more than 13,000 Red Cross women, as well as smaller numbers of women foreign service officers, staff of the U.S. Agency for International Development, and employees of the united service organizations (USO). In 1980, Congress authorized a memorial to be built "in honor and recognition of the men and women of the Armed Forces of the United States who served in Vietnam." The competition for the design of the memorial was won by twenty-one-year-old Maya Lin, an undergraduate architecture student at Yale. The memorial stands today in Washington, visited by millions of people each year. They leave offerings as at a shrine: flowers, photographs, mementos.

The design of the memorial—whose black granite walls bear the names of 58,000 Americans who died, including eight women—was controversial from the

U.S. Senate Committee on Energy and Natural Resources, *Vietnam Women's Memorial*. Hearing before the Subcommittee on Public Lands, National Parks, and Forests to consider S. 2042, February 23, 1988, 100th Cong., 2nd Sess.

beginning. Many veterans groups insisted on a more traditional, representational design. In 1984 an additional statue that depicted three soldiers was placed in a grove of trees nearby. When the additional statue failed to include the figure of a woman, women veterans began to urge the addition of another statue honoring the women who had served.

In 1988 Congress authorized a statue recognizing women, to be constructed on federal property at the Vietnam Veterans Memorial from funds (like those of the other memorials) raised from private donations. The comments that follow were made at hearings conducted by Senator Dale Bumpers of Arkansas, chair of the Senate Subcommittee on Public Lands, National Parks, and Forests.

Each of the veterans had complex memories of their experience in Vietnam, 20 years before. How do the women explain the meaning of their service? How is Robert Doubek's testimony affected by concerns about class, race, and gender?

Karen Johnson's testimony addresses the issue of whether men and women have an equal obligation to serve in the military. Do you think men and women have an equal obligation to serve in the military in time of war, as Karen Johnson believes? Does that obligation extend to service in combat? Does the exclusion of women from combat suggest that American society attaches greater value to women's lives than men's? What other factors might also be relevant in explaining the exclusion of women from combat? (For more on these issues, see Elizabeth Hillman's essay, above. For the perspectives of peace and antiwar activists in both North America and Vietnam, see Judy Tzu-Chun Wu's essay, pp. 719–730.)

STATEMENT OF DONNA-MARIE BOULAY, CHAIRMAN, VIETNAM WOMEN'S MEMORIAL PROJECT

Mr. Chairman, people who serve in wars have unique experiences. War was never meant to be. War makes death. Day after day, even hour after hour, we lived and worked amidst the wounded, the dead, and the dying.

I arrived in Vietnam at the end of February 1967. A few days later I was assigned to triage for the first time. The medevac helicopters brought twelve soldiers into our emergency room. Ten were already dead. Two were bleeding to death.

Mr. Chairman, our daily duty was to care for the badly wounded, the young men whose legs had been blown off, whose arms had been traumatically amputated, whose bodies and faces had been burned beyond recognition.

We eased the agony of a young marine, his legs amputated, his wounds dangerously infected. We worked hard to stop the bleeding of a sailor who had been shot in his liver. He died three days after, in immense pain.

We cared for a young Army lieutenant from New York named Pat who had been admitted with a badly mangled leg and later evacuated to Japan, like many of the other seriously wounded soldiers we treated. I do not know whether Pat's leg was saved. I hope so. Pat was a good soldier.

Mr. Chairman, "Pat" is not short for "Patrick." Pat is a nurse. Patty was a nurse. She was stationed at the 24th Evacuation Hospital in Long Binh.

We were the first American women sent to live and work in the midst of guerrilla warfare. The month-long Tet offensive was especially frightening. The Viet Cong blew up the ammunition dump down the street, causing a wall in our unit to collapse on some patients.

VC snipers shot at us. The North Vietnamese Army artillery roared throughout the nights. Those of us not at work huddled in our bunkers, wondering if we would survive until dawn.

At work, listening to the thundering sounds around us, we tried to keep our hands from shaking, the fear out of our voices and off of our faces, so that the wounded would not see or hear it.

Women served in Vietnam in many capacities. We served as personnel specialists, journalists, clerk-typists, intelligence officers, and nurses. There was no such thing as a generic woman soldier, as there was no such thing as a generic male soldier. Men served as mechanics, engineers, pilots, divers, and infantrymen.

The design of the men's statue at the Veterans Memorial was selected, according to Frederick

Hart, the sculptor, because they "depict the bonds of men at war and because the infantry bore the greatest burden."

Mr. Chairman, we are proposing that the design for the women's statue be that of a nurse who served in Vietnam. The statue of a nurse is so compatible with the existing trio of figures because the nurses' experience so closely parallels the experience of the infantrymen—the intensity, the trauma, the carnage of war.

The statue design which we are proposing is an easily recognizable symbol of healing and hope, consistent with the spirit and the experience of the Vietnam Veterans Memorial. . . .

STATEMENT OF KAREN K. JOHNSON, LITTLE ROCK, AR

I was born in Petersburg, Virginia. My father was in the military. He was killed in France on November the 11th, 1944.

I was raised in Oklahoma. I graduated from college in 1964 and explored the military as a career and joined the Army in 1965.

My family was very patriotic because of the trials and tribulations that we had to go through because of being raised without a father. Considering that everyone in my family had experienced all that patriotism, when I said that I was going to join the Army it was not a new thought, even though I was the first woman to have joined.

My family felt that all Americans owed their country any sacrifice needed for the national good, regardless of their race or sex, that patriotism should be a blind emotion, and it should be accepted by our country without any thought or qualm as to who offered such patriotism.

Consequently, after I served in Germany from 1966 to 1968, when my country asked me to go overseas again to Vietnam, I went. I served in Vietnam from July of 1970 to March of 1972, for a total of 20 months in country.

When I tell people these facts, they always ask me, was I a nurse, that I did not see any combat, and that I must have volunteered. When I tell them that I was awarded a Bronze Star, they ask me what for.

For 18 years I have answered these questions with several long-winded explanations which were really an apology for my Vietnam service, because I was not a nurse and I was not a combat soldier, and there were many others who had served who the public much better understood their service in their traditional roles.

I have kept silent on what I did in Vietnam because it was easier than making the apologies or trying to educate my listener. I know now that I have done many Vietnam veterans a great disservice by my silence. Thanks to the support of the Arkansas Vietnam Veterans, my husband and my grandchildren, I have made my last apology, felt my last twinge of embarrassment, and I will not remain silent to the detriment of my comrades in arms.

I am a veterans' veteran and I am proud of it. I was not a nurse. I saw very little fullfledged combat, and when my country called I went willingly. I see no disgrace in answering such a call or in volunteering to serve in the United States Army.

I served as the Command Information Officer of the United States Army, Vietnam Headquarters, located at Long Binh. However, my job entailed finding out what Army troops were doing, photographing those troops, writing news reports, and printing the internal publications to keep the troops informed.

I could not do that from Long Binh. I traveled all over Vietnam. Wherever there were Army troops, I went, too. I have flown in attack helicopters, been shot at in jeeps, and I went over the Hay Van Pass in several convoys.

Whatever it took to get the news out to the troops is what I and my staff did, and we did it very well. "Uptight Magazine," one of our publications, was awarded the Thomas Jefferson Award for the outstanding military publication in its field, an award that was given to me by "Time Magazine."

Our office published a twice-daily news bulletin, a weekly Long Binh paper, the weekly "Army Reporter," "Uptight Magazine Quarterly"; and "Tour 364," the history of the war, was updated every six months so that troops rotating home had a written history of their service. We were also responsible for the free distribution of "Stars and Stripes" to ensure that every U.S. military personnel serving in Vietnam had daily access to a newspaper.

There were a lot of obstacles to resolve to make all of this happen. My staff made it happen every day for 20 months, in 12 hour shifts, seven days a week, including Christmas, when we worked harder because we were responsible for making Operation Jingle Bells work so that the troops could see Bob Hope.

I am here today to tell you that I am very proud of that staff, and especially of Spec. 5 Steven Henry Warner, who gave his life so the American soldier could be the best informed and most motivated soldier in the world. I do not believe they would want me to apologize for our service or the fact that Steve Warner gave his life as a journalist and not as a combat soldier.

If there is any apology owed, it is the one I owe my staff for not standing up for them for the last 18 years because I did not like the questions my admission to being a Vietnam veteran elicited because I was a woman, something not well understood by the American public.

Their service and mine should be given equal recognition with all who served, not diminished because of the non-traditional position I held.

I come before you today to ask you to legislate equal dignity for the women who served their country by answering the call to arms. The Vietnam Women's Memorial would do much to give women veterans a new sense of self-respect and it will make a strong public statement that bias, prejudice, or ignorance of the sacrifices that women veterans have made for their country will no longer be tolerated.

Today the flag that covered my father's casket when he was put to final rest in 1948 lies in front of me, because I have always wanted him to be proud of me, his only child. And I believe he would be proudest of me today when I say, after 18 long years of silence: I was an American soldier; I answered my country's call to arms; and I am an American veteran, a title I should be able to share with equal dignity with all who have served before me and will serve after me. . . .

STATEMENT OF ROBERT W. DOUBEK . . .

Mr. Chairman, my name is Robert W. Doubek of Washington, D.C. I am a Vietnam veteran. I am employed in the private sector. I was a founder of the Vietnam Veterans Memorial Fund. I served as its Executive Director and Project Director. I was responsible for building the memorial. I did the work. In recognition of my achievement, I was nominated for a Congressional Gold Medal which was a bill passed by the Senate on November 14, 1985.

The fact is that women are not represented by the Vietnam Veterans Memorial. The fact is also that the memorial does not represent anyone. It is not a legislative body. It is a symbol of honor, and as such, it is complete as a tribute to all who served their country in the Vietnam War.

It is a basic rule of common sense that mandates that something which is not broken should not be fixed. The genius of the wall is its equalizing and unifying effect. All veterans are honored, regardless of rank, service branch, commission, sex, or any other category. The names of the eight women casualties take their rightful places of honor. To ensure that this fact is never overlooked, the inscription on the first panel of the wall states that the memorial is in honor of the men and women of the Armed Forces. The reason I know this is because I was instrumental in drafting the inscription.

In 1982, politics required that we add a figurative sculpture as a more specific symbol of the Vietnam veteran. Even with the heroic and dangerous service rendered by other combatants such as Air Force and Navy pilots, Navy swiftboat crews, and the life saving efforts of nurses, helicopter pilots and medics, there was only one possible choice of what category would be literally depicted to symbolize the Vietnam veteran, and that could only be the enlisted infantrymen, grunts. They account for the majority of names on the wall; they bore the brunt of the battle. The fact is all grunts were men.

The addition of a statue of a woman or of any other category, for that matter, would reduce the symbolism of the existing sculpture from honoring or symbolizing the Vietnam veterans community as a whole to symbolizing only enlisted infantrymen. This in turn would open a Pandora's box of proliferating statuary toward the goal of trying to depict every possible category. The National Park Service has already received requests for a statue to literally depict Native Americans and even for scout dogs, and in fact, I want to say that the figure for Native American casualties was 225.

The addition of a statue solely on the basis of gender raises troubling questions about proportion. Is gender of such overriding importance among veterans that we should have a specific statue to women who suffered eight casualties, and none for the Navy which suffered over 2,500, nor for the Air Force which suffered over 2,400? Is gender of such importance to outweigh that some 90 percent of the women who served in Vietnam in the military were officers [nurses were commissioned officers], while over 87 percent of all casualties were enlisted? ... Approval ... would set the precedent that strict literal depiction of both genders is an absolute requirement of all military related memorials. What about the new Navy memorial? Will Congress mandate an additional figure at the Iwo Jima Memorial?

STATEMENT OF COL. MARY EVELYN BANE, USMC (RETIRED), ARLINGTON, VA

Mr. Chairman, my name is Mary Evelyn Bane. I live in Arlington, Virginia, and I have lived in the Washington metropolitan area for a total of almost 19 nonconsecutive years. I retired in 1977 from a 26-year career in the United States Marine Corps in the grade of colonel. I never served in Vietnam, only a few women Marines did, and they were in Saigon, but I was in active service during the entire period of the war there. My career was in personnel management and, like most Marine officers, I had a variety of assignments and experiences, including two tours at our famous or infamous Parris Island training recruits, and an assignment with the Joint Staff in France. All of my male Marine colleagues did serve in Vietnam, many of them more than once, and some of their names are on the Vietnam Veterans Memorial.

I am opposed to the installation of a statue of a woman at the site of the VVM for both artistic and philosophical reasons, artistically, because it is at odds with the design as well as the theme of the memorial . . . [and] philosophically simply because I am a woman. This may seem unfathomable to the statue's proponents, but perhaps I can explain. From the beginning of my chosen career in what most will agree is a macho outfit, I tried hard to be the best Marine I was capable of being. When I was commissioned, fewer than 1 percent of the officers in the Marine Corps were female. Women were assigned to women's billets, and restricted to a handful of occupational specialties considered appropriate for women. Over the years, through the combined efforts of many, many people, of which I am happy to say I am one, the concept of how women could and should serve their country has changed. The huge increase in the military's population required by the Vietnam War hastened the changes.

Nevertheless, in 1973 when I, then a lieutenant colonel, was assigned as the Marine Corps member of a Department of Defense ad hoc group studying the recruitment and processing of non-prior service personnel, the Civil Service GS-15 chair of the group complained to the Commandant of the Marine Corps that he had not appointed a real Marine.

My point here is that sex is an accident of birth. I chose to be a Marine and worked hard at it, and spent a career combatting discrimination based on sex. I feel every service person should be recognized for what he or she accomplished as a soldier, sailor, Marine or airman. The Vietnam Veterans Memorial recognizes American military members for their service in Vietnam, irrespective of sex, rank, service, race, or occupational specialty. To single out one of these criteria for special recognition in the form of a statue on the site of the Vietnam Veterans Memorial would not only violate the integrity of the design, but would be discriminatory.

FEMINISMS

ROSALYN BAXANDALL AND LINDA GORDON
The Women's Liberation Movement

How did the women's liberation movement transform American society? Rosalyn Baxandall and Linda Gordon seek to dispel myths about the feminist movement of the 1960s and 1970s and to document what they describe as "the largest social movement in the history" of the United States.

As you read the essay, think about the following questions: What motivated women to become part of the women's liberation movement? What did the movement accomplish—and when? Where do you see evidence of backlash? What challenges remain?

The women's liberation movement, as it was called in the 1960s and 1970s, or feminism, as it is known today, reached into every home, school, and business, into every form of entertainment and sport. Like a river overflowing its banks and seeking a new course, it permanently altered the landscape. Some think its impact has been excessive and others—like us—believe that much more progress toward sex equality is needed. But all agree that it has left an indelible mark on women, men, and children everywhere. Women's liberation was the largest social movement in the history of the U.S. . . .

. . . Widespread misconceptions [exist] about the movement. . . . These exist not because the public is foolish or hostile to feminism. In fact, 1998 Roper polls found that 51 percent of Americans believe feminists have been helpful to women, 53 percent that feminists are "in touch with the average American woman," 65 percent that black feminists help the black community. The misimpressions derive in part from widely published misinformation. Indeed, it is hard to imagine an historical event as widespread and powerful as the women's liberation movement that has been so poorly documented and reported. . . .

Part of this problem is the movement's success. Its achievements—the broad range of work women now do, the equal treatment they expect, the direct way women express themselves—have become the very air we breathe, so taken for granted as to be invisible. . . . Furthermore, the largest grassroots part of the women's movement is difficult to study precisely because it was so big, so decentralized, so varied, and often left few records. It is hardly surprising that most of what has been written has focused on the main national feminist organization, the National Organization for Women, and its leaders, such as Gloria Steinem and Betty Friedan, because this aspect of the movement was more centralized, less outrageous, more focused—and kept better records. . . .

There are deeper reasons, too, for the lack of reliable studies and the perpetuation of false stereotypes. Despite the huge changes in our society brought about by the women's movement, feminism's fundamental ideas are still controversial—indeed, they are at the root of the hottest debates of our times: abortion rights, contraception for teenagers, welfare, women in the armed forces, gay marriage,

Excerpted from the introduction of *Dear Sisters: Dispatches From The Women's Liberation Movement*, by Rosalyn Baxandall and Linda Gordon (New York: Basic Books, 2000; orig. publ. 1995). Reprinted by permission of the authors and publisher.

affirmative action. The media—and not only conservative sources—often portray the women's movement through unrepresentative anecdotes and outright falsehoods. . . . In turn, such poor journalism arises in part from the lack of scholarly research upon which reporters can draw.

Three biases from three different perspectives infuse the misinformation about women's liberation: an overtly hostile, conservative perspective that demonizes the movement as acting against nature, even doing the work of the devil; the perspective of those feminist activists who, disappointed by the movement's incomplete success, consider it a failure; and a trivializing view of the movement as a lifestyle rather than politics, as personal self-transformation rather than social change, as a digression from traditional politics. These biases give rise to widespread myths about women's liberation. Depen-ding on one's particular bias, women's libbers:

- were privileged, white young women who had neither knowledge about nor concern for working-class women or women of color.
- rejected motherhood and considered children only a burden.
- ignored bread-and-butter economic issues and focused only on sex, violence, and personal issues.
- drew energy away from movements aimed at correcting major social and economic problems, such as militarism, racism, and poverty, and prevented the formation of strong coalitions or united efforts.
- hated being women and rejected everything feminine, from bras and long hair to shaved legs and high heels.
- were man-haters who tried to belittle and compete with men, often rejecting them entirely and becoming lesbians.
- were losers, bitter because men rejected them.
- were humorless and prudish, quick to take offense.
- were spoiled, self-centered, and self-pitying women who whined about life's difficulties and exaggerated the discrimination against women.

Like most myths, some of these contain kernels of truth. Yes, feminists did reject confining clothing such as high heels and girdles. (See p. 477.) Many stopped dieting and curling,

straightening, processing, dyeing, shaving, plucking their hair. Yes, feminists wanted help raising children—from husbands and organized day care—as more and more women joined the workforce. Yes, feminists were angry at men who beat them, harassed them, belittled them, and kept them in inferior and dead-end jobs. Yes, women's liberation was particularly strong among college-educated young women. Yes, in order to be heard, especially because women had a history of being timid, soft-spoken, and ignored, feminists sometimes shouted and oversimplified.

But some of these myths contain not a grain of truth. Feminists never rejected motherhood; rather, they sought to improve its conditions. . . . All [feminists] had sons, brothers, fathers, male friends, or coworkers whom they loved. Far from being losers, feminists were typically the most achieving and self-confident of women. Feminist humor was so popular it became mainstream—think of Lily Tomlin and Nicole Hollander. Anything but prudes, feminists dedicated themselves to liberating women's sexuality. They were doers, not complainers. They identified discrimination for the purpose of trying to change it.

SOCIAL ROOTS OF WOMEN'S LIBERATION

Women's liberation was a movement long overdue. By the mid-1950s a majority of American women found themselves expected to function as full economic, social, and political participants in the nation while still burdened with handicaps. As wage-earners, as parents, as students, as citizens, women were denied equal opportunity and, often, even minimal rights and respect. Many women experienced sharp conflict among the expectations placed on them—education, employment, wife- and motherhood. Looking back at the beginning of the twenty-first century, we can see feminism as a necessary modernizing force and, not surprisingly, one which rapidly became global. Within the U.S., the movement gained widespread support so quickly because it met real needs, because the great majority of women stood to benefit from reducing discrimination, harassment, and prejudice against them. A movement that might at first have seemed to promise to rationalize the current political and economic system by integrating women into it quickly took off—as many social movements do—into uncharted territory, exposing the degree to which basic social structures had rested on a traditional gender system. . . .

How did an apparently arch-conservative decade like the 1950s produce a movement so radical? To answer that we have to look beneath a veneer that concealed discomforts and discontents. The period between the end of World War II and the birth of women's liberation at the end of the 1960s has usually been described as an era of prosperity, stability, and peace, leading to the conclusion that it was also an era of satisfaction and little change. An intensely controlled and controlling official and commercial culture seemed to provide evidence for that conclusion. The domestic correlate of the Cold War and the Korean War was the hysterical anticommunism that stigmatized nonconformity, including that related to family, sex, and gender. Anxiety about the Soviet threat made family stability seem critical and linked women's domestic roles to the nation's security. . . . Historian Elaine Tyler May [has] observed that the concept of containment, first used to characterize the U.S. policy of preventing Soviet expansion, could characterize equally well the stifling of female ambitions, the endorsement of female subordination, and the promotion of domesticity by Cold War gender culture. Resistance to these norms was un-American, and that label became a heavy club with which to beat misfits and dissidents. . . .

Cold War culture demanded sexual as well as political and gender conformity. The witch hunts targeted not only alleged communists but also homosexuals, and drove many people out of their employment. Films and magazines depicted the lesbian as a moral threat, a symbol of decay, chaos, and predatory evil. Vice control units of local police departments, along with private moral crusade organizations like the American Society for Social Hygiene and public health officials, routinely rounded up those engaged in "immoral" sexual activities. Psychiatrists labeled homosexuals and discontented women alike as sick and in need of rehabilitation.

Girls grew up in this Cold War era barred from wearing blue jeans or sneakers to school, required to sit with their knees together and to set their hair in pin curls. Nothing in the culture encouraged them to become strong or competitive. Girls grew to hate athletics and dread physical education in school, where they were required to wear unfashionable tunics or bloomers. Girls were not encouraged to fantasize about careers, about what they would "become" when they grew up. They were expected to break a date with a girlfriend if a boy asked for a date. They watched movies and TV in which married couples slept in twin beds and mothers were full-time housewives. The people of color on TV were stereotypes, comic or worse: step-and-fetch-it black servants, marauding Apaches, or fat lazy Mexicans. Rape, illegitimacy, abortion—some of women's real problems—were among many tabooed subjects, whispered about but rarely seriously or openly discussed.

But this official feminine-mystique culture obscured an unofficial but probably more widespread reality that was, ironically, designated as deviant. A small band of historians has been uncovering the story of what turns out to be the majority of American women who did not, and often could not, conform. . . . In contrast to official norms, women's labor-force participation climbed rapidly throughout the fifties and by 1954 women's employment had equaled that during World War II. Most women displaced from well-paid, industrial jobs at the war's end did not return to domesticity but found work in traditionally female low-paying jobs in the expanding service and clerical sectors. As has long been true in American history, African American women and poor women of all colors had particularly high rates of employment, so that the domesticity myth was in part a racist assumption that elite white norms were universal. Women in "pink collar" employment swelled the membership of unions, such as the Hotel Employees and Restaurant Employees and the National Federation of Telephone Workers. And these working women were not only young and single: By 1960, 30 percent of married women were employed, and 39 percent of mothers with school-age children were in the labor force. By 1955, 3 million women belonged to unions, constituting 17 percent of union members. In unions in which women made up a significant part of the membership, they wielded considerable power, especially at the local level.

The number of married women seeking employment rose fastest in the middle class. Women benefited from an enormous expansion in higher education after World War II. Government investment in universities after the war had multiplied educational opportunity, especially in public institutions. In 1940, 26 percent of American women completed college; in 1970, 55 percent. These relatively privileged American women faced a particular dilemma: educated with men and often achieving, despite discrimination, the same levels of knowledge, discipline, and sophistication as the men of their social class, they were still expected to forego professional or intellectual pursuits after college to become full-time housewives and mothers. Those who resisted this directive and sought employment, through choice or economic necessity, usually found themselves limited to clerical or low-level administrative jobs.

In part as a response to this restriction, many women . . . defied the limits of domesticity through community and political activism. Even in the suburbs, where women seemed to be conforming to the "feminine mystique" by staying home with small children, many were active in churches, schools, libraries, and parks. New forms of organizing appeared: In 1956, for example, the first all-female La Leche group met to encourage breast feeding. Other groups, alarmed by Rachel Carson's studies of the dangers of pesticides like DDT, had the audacity to challenge official science. Women Strike for Peace, composed largely of left-wing women, attacked military spending priorities, raised an alarm about strontium-90 fallout in milk, and directly challenged the Cold War and American military buildup by contesting U.S. government propaganda about the threat of Soviet expansionism. . . . Conservative women, while paying official homage to the ideal of women's domesticity, were organizing in the Ku Klux Klan, White Citizen's Councils, John Birch Society, and Republican Party.

Some forms of deviance from the official domestic norms were more private. At the edges of mainstream culture a counterculture began to emerge in the early 1950s, reflecting a mood of depression, alienation, and anger at the shallowness of dominant standards. True, the "beat" poets and artists were mainly male, but they attracted female groupies who preferred this alternative masculinity and identified with the rejection of respectability and conformity. Beatnik women, dressed in black with heavy black eye makeup and uncurled hair, hung around coffeehouses in New York and San Francisco. Rebelling against consumerism and conformity, yearning for something more genuine, some embraced Zen Buddhism

and existentialism. Even popular commercial culture was riddled with contradictions, ambivalence, competing voices, and transgressions. . . .

Only now, as the women's movement can be seen in historical context, have historians looked back again and noticed the complexity of the cultural messages. In addition to emphasizing femininity and domesticity, many women's magazines featured and honored women who made a mark beyond their homes. Magazine articles glorified housewives, but they also offered tips to women managing wage work along with housework and openly praised participation in community activism and politics. Readers met, for example, Dorothy McCullough Lee, who cultivated the image of a pale, frail housewife but as mayor of Portland singlehandedly defeated the heavyweights of organized crime; Louise Williams, mother of two, a great cook but an even better mechanic at American Airlines; and Babe Didrikson Zaharias, a champion golfer and pole vaulter who continued competing despite cancer. *Reader's Digest* placed Mary McLeod Bethune among the world's greatest living women, despite the fact that she was the highest-ranking African American in the New Deal and had been accused of being a communist by McCarthy. Honoring women's work and public activity was especially pronounced in black journalism: magazines like *Ebony* and *Jet* promoted marriage and motherhood but also professional and artistic achievement. . . .

Dissidence in the 1950s was, of course, particularly pronounced in youth culture. . . . Nowhere was the youth rebellion as intense or as contagious as in music, and the transcendence of race segregation was the proximate cause. The officially dominant 1950s white sound (Peggy Lee, Jo Stafford, Rosemary Clooney, and Pat Boone) combined inane lyrics, like "How Much Is That Doggie in the Window," with soothing melodies, bland orchestration, and ballad rhythms. Yet this is the decade that produced rock and roll, a revolution in popular music. The term was first applied to black rhythm and blues by Alan Freed, the white disk jockey who promoted black music to white audiences. The breakthrough singer was Elvis Presley, the "white boy who could sing black." Not only did whites start to buy records by black artists, but they also attended huge concerts where for the first time white and black youth mingled and danced. In Los Angeles, for example, racially mixed rock concerts were busted up by the police. Conservatives considered rock and roll the music of the devil, dangerous, degenerate, mongrel, oversexualized, and in a way they were right: it is difficult to overestimate the impact of rock and roll on the men and women who moved from the inchoate, half-conscious alienation of rebels without a cause to the organized radical movements that began with the civil rights movement.

POLITICAL ROOTS OF WOMEN'S LIBERATION

From the vantage point of the [twenty-first] century, the women's liberation movement appears extravagant, immoderate, impatient, as well as young and naive. It was all those and more, but how one weighs its radicalism, positively or negatively, and how one measures its naivete depend on understanding its historical context. Fifty years later our culture has been so transformed, the expectations of young women so altered, that it is hard to grasp the unique combination of anger and optimism that made second-wave feminism so determined to change so much so fast.

Women coming into adulthood at the end of the 1960s, both middle- and working-class, faced an economy that was producing an ever larger number of jobs; ... [also,] women had unprecedented access to education. But many were disappointed in the jobs they could get. They went from being the equals or even the superiors of men in educational achievement to working as secretaries or "administrative assistants" for the same class of men. Although they faced discrimination in their colleges and universities, they also encountered professors who recognized and challenged their intelligence. Yet their studies, no matter how rigorous, offered them no way to escape the cultural imperative that directed them toward marriage and family as their fundamental and often exclusive source of identity and satisfaction.

If economic and educational abundance opened windows for the women who began women's liberation in 1968, the passionate new social activism of the 1950s and 1960s opened doors and invited women in. But these movements, like the economy as a whole, also sent women a double message. Whenever there have been progressive social change movements in modern history, women's movements have arisen within them, and for similar reasons: in the crucible of activism for civil rights,

for peace, for the environment, for free speech, for social welfare, women have been valued participants who gained skills and self-confidence. At the same time they have been thwarted, treated as subordinates, gophers, even servants, by the men in charge—including men who considered themselves partisans of democracy and equality. Within these movements women learned to think critically about social structures and ideologies, to talk the language of freedom and tyranny, democracy and domination, power and oppression. Then they applied these concepts to question their own secondary status. It is precisely this combination of raised aspirations and frustration that gives rise to rebellion.

... By the 1960s, there was a sense of unity among progressive campaigns for social justice; in fact, they came to be collectively called "the movement," a singular designation. Reflecting the relative prosperity of the period, its mood was optimistic, even utopian. Its members came largely from the middle class, but working-class people also participated. The movement was as critical of commercialization, conformity, and moral hypocrisy as of poverty. Its guiding principle was to challenge received wisdom and hierarchical authority. Quintessentially a movement of young people, it was correspondingly impatient and preferred direct action to political process. In dress, in sexual behavior, in its favorite intoxicants, and above all in its beloved music, it distinguished itself sharply from grown-ups.

By the mid-1960s, the more ideologically Left currents within the movement were called the New Left, because they differed fundamentally from the older Lefts: communism, socialism, and New Deal progressivism. At least a decade earlier, the civil rights movement had been the first to break with conventional politics, helped by its high proportion of student activists, ability to stimulate mass participation, decentralized and pluralist organization, and commitment to direct but nonviolent action. Like all mass movements, the civil rights movement had no defined beginning, although the 1955 Montgomery bus boycott announced to the country that something big was happening. Thousands of African Americans were challenging three hundred years of apartheid, demonstrating unprecedented discipline, solidarity, and bravery against brutal retaliation. Their courage forced racist viciousness into the open; journalists and their cameras then brought into living rooms the high-power water hoses turned on peaceful protesters, the grown men who spat on first-graders, the dogs who charged at protesters singing gospel hymns. The news brought a heightened appreciation of the possibility of making change from the bottom up. In contrast to the bitter liberal-versus-conservative national division in the 1980s and 1990s, the civil rights struggles seemed to galvanize, at least among the most articulate citizenry, broad majority approval for social change in the direction of greater democracy and equality. (There may have been a "silent majority" that did not approve.) While any individual battle might be won or lost, it seemed to supporters that their cause was unstoppable, so great was the groundswell of desire for the long-overdue racial equality and respect.

. . . Civil rights was, at first, preeminently a black movement, but it was also the first of a series of youth movements that would transform American culture. Civil rights generated youth protest throughout the country, producing a political culture marked by antiauthoritarianism, direct action, and anger at the constraints of respectability. Particularly in the South, many whites from religious backgrounds were drawn into the movement through the student division of the YWCA, which was far more committed to interracial activity than the YMCA. The drama of the attack on segregation drew some northern and western young blacks and whites to the South to help, while others were inspired to contest inequality where they lived. Young whites emulated African American activists in many ways: they adopted the blue jeans that Student Nonviolent Coordinating Committee (SNCC) workers wore in identification with poor southern farmers and workers; their artistic sensibility was permanently revolutionized by black music—blues and rock and roll—and their images of heroism and virtue were modeled after the nonviolent resistance of SNCC volunteers who refused to run or defend themselves from beatings.

In the late 1950s, another kind of rebellion was developing, primarily among the more privileged whites: a cultural rebellion. Discovering and inventing unconventional art, music, and poetry; exploring a variety of intoxicants; and signaling defiance in the way they dressed, adherents of this new cultural revolution soon grew visible enough to draw mainstream media attention. The press created popular icons—"flower children" and "hippies"—whose values resembled those of the earlier 1950s beatnik rebels. The influence of this lifestyle dissent can be measured by how quickly it was picked up by commercial interests and sold back to a broader public: the new fashion included beards, long straight hair, psychedelic design, granny dresses, and beads. Handmade, patched, and embroidered clothing and jeans once bought at Sears Roebuck or Goodwill were soon being mass-produced in Hong Kong and sold in department stores. For its most zealous participants, counterculture iconoclasm and adventurousness meant such an extreme rejection of the work ethic, temperance, and discipline that it horrified many observers, including some in the movement. Excessive use of drugs, promiscuous sexuality, and irresponsibility were sometimes destructive to participants, some of whom later rebounded into conventionality. Women suffered particular exploitation, as the counterculture's gender ideology reaffirmed that of the conventional culture, but now with a twist, lauding "free" and "natural" heterosexual relations between women who were sexually open and "giving" and men who could not be tied down. Women were to be earth mothers, seeking fulfillment by looking after men and children, while guys needed freedom from marital or paternal responsibilities in order to find and express themselves.

This cultural rebellion had transformative potential and gave rise to some serious political challenges. When civil rights and the counterculture intersected on campuses, the result was a college students' movement for free speech that would ultimately create the New Left and women's liberation. The first major student revolt, at the University of California at Berkeley in 1964, arose in reaction to the administration's attempt to prevent students from recruiting civil rights volunteers on campus. This protest movement spread to campuses late in the 1960s throughout the U.S., producing a series of protests against *in loco parentis* rules that treated students like children.

Campus protests soon expanded to include national issues and nonstudents. Sensitized to injustice and convinced of the potential of grassroots activism by what they learned from civil rights, more and more Americans began to see the Vietnam War as immoral and undemocratic. In the name of stopping communism, the U.S. was defending a fla-grantly corrupt regime that had canceled elec-tions when it seemed likely to lose to a popular, nationalist liberation movement that promised land reform in the interests of the poor peas-antry. The most powerful nation in the world was attacking a tiny nation that had demon-strated not the slightest aggression toward Americans. The U.S. employed some of the cru-elest weapons and tactics yet developed: shoot-ing down unarmed peasants because of fear that they might be supporting the liberation movement; bulldozing villages; spraying herbi-cides from planes to deprive the guerrilla fight-ers of their jungle cover; dropping napalm, a jellied gasoline antipersonnel weapon that stuck to the skin and burned people alive. . . . Americans routinely witnessed these atrocities on the evening news. American soldiers of color and of the working class were killed and injured in disproportionate numbers. Hun-dreds of young men began resisting or dodg-ing the draft while scores of soldiers deserted and defied orders. So widespread, vocal, and convincing were the protests at home, includ-ing several massive national demonstrations, that by its end the Vietnam War became the only war in U.S. history to be opposed by a ma-jority of the population.

The Vietnamese revolution was part of a wave of nationalist struggles of Third World countries against Western imperial domina-tion, and these also influenced American do-mestic politics. Many of these emerging nations and movements took socialist forms, as Third World nationalists observed that the introduction of capitalism increased inequal-ity and impoverishment. But many of these newly independent countries fell under Soviet domination as the price of the aid they so des-perately needed, and leading parts of the American New Left, already angry at the stul-tifying domestic culture of the Cold War, ne-glected to subject Soviet control to the same critique. U.S. interventions against commu-nism, both military and covert, had the ironic effect of making the New Left less critical of Soviet and Chinese communism than it might have been otherwise.

Before Vietnam, the Cuban revolution of 1959 had seized the developing New Left im-agination. Cubans overthrew the Batista dicta-torship and brought to power a group of daring reformers committed, at first, not only to economic justice but also to educational,

cultural, and political democracy. Influential New Leftists, including many future femi-nists, traveled to Cuba in the 1960s, volunteer-ing to work in the sugar harvests, and their enthusiasm for Cuba's valiant struggle led them to overestimate its independence from the U.S.S.R., just as the anti–Vietnam War move-ment romanticized Vietnam (and overlooked its lack of democracy). The New Left's in-creasing identification with anti-imperialist and nationalist struggles around the world caused it to subordinate its early emphasis on freedom and democracy.

. . . In this context of international mobili-zation, American radicals associated civil rights struggles in the U.S. with anti-imperialism. Blacks and other nonwhite groups identified themselves as a Third World within the U.S., victims of internal colonialism. (Some feminist groups would argue that women were another colonized people.)

Activism spread throughout the U.S., creat-ing civil rights movements among other racial/ ethnic groups, including Chicanos, Asian Americans, Native Americans; movements to protect the environment; a movement for the rights of the disabled; and renewed labor strug-gles for a fair share of the prosperity. Among whites there soon arose a national student or-ganization that was to become central to the white New Left, Students for a Democratic Soci-ety (SDS), established in 1962. With a member-ship reaching about 100,000 at its peak in the late 1960s, and with many times that number of students—including high school students— who considered themselves a part of the move-ment, SDS changed the attitudes of a considerable part of a generation. New Leftists and counter-culture activists created institutions that spread progressive ideas still further: radical book-stores, a few national magazines, and many local underground newspapers. These were produced by amateurs working in scruffy of-fices, offering critical perspectives on every-thing from U.S. foreign policy to the local police to the latest films. Many of these underground newspapers combined words and graphics in innovative ways, inspired in part by the street art of 1968 in France where the *beaux arts* stu-dents had considerable influence.

Although the movement (civil rights and the New Left) had no unified ideology—its members included anarchists, social demo-crats, Marxist-Leninists, black nationalists—it bequeathed identifiable legacies to feminism.

Most important among these were anti-authoritarianism and irreverence. Favorite buttons and T-shirts read "Question Authority" and "Never Trust Anyone Over 30." . . . The movement's message was: look beneath formal legal and political rights to find other kinds of power, the power of wealth, of race, of violence.

. . . Some women began in the mid-1960s to examine power relations in areas that the movement's male leaders had not considered relevant to radical politics. The women's preliminary digging uncovered a buried deposit of grievances about men's power over women within the movement. Women in civil rights and the New Left were on the whole less victimized, more respected, and less romanticized than they were in the mainstream culture or the counterculture. Despite women's passionate and disciplined work for social change, however, they remained far less visible and less powerful than the men who dominated the meetings and the press conferences. Women came into greater prominence wherever there was grassroots organizing, as in voter registration in the South and the SDS community projects in northern cities. Throughout the civil rights and the student movements, women proved themselves typically the better organizers, better able than men to listen, to connect, to reach across class and even race lines, to empower the previously diffident, to persevere despite failure and lack of encouragement. Still, the frustrations and humiliations were galling. In every organization women were responsible for keeping records, producing leaflets, telephoning, cleaning offices, cooking, organizing social events, and catering to the egos of male leaders, while the men wrote manifestos, talked to the press, negotiated with officials, and made speeches. This division of labor did not arise from misogyny or acrimony. It was "natural" and had always been so, until it began to seem not natural at all.

THE RISE OF SECOND-WAVE FEMINISM

Although women's liberation had foremothers, the young feminists of the late 1960s did not usually know about this heritage because so little women's history had been written. Feminist historians have now made us aware that a continuing tradition of activism stretched from "first-wave" feminism, which culminated in winning the right to vote in 1920, to the birth of the "second wave" in 1968. Some women of unusual longevity bridged the two waves. Florence Luscomb, who had traveled the state of Massachusetts speaking for woman suffrage during World War I, also spoke for women's liberation in Boston in the early 1970s. Within many progressive social movements, even at the nadir of the conservative 1950s, there were discontented women agitating against sex discrimination and promoting female leadership. Within the Communist and Socialist Parties there had been women's caucuses and demands to revise classic socialist theory to include sex inequality. . . . Some women spanned the older progressive causes and the new feminism—Ella Baker, Judy Collins, Ruby Dee, Eleanor Flexner, Fanny Lou Hamer, Flo Kennedy, Coretta Scott King, Gerda Lerner, Amy Swerdlow.

Liberal women had continued to be politically active between feminism's two waves. They were mainly Democrats but there were some Republicans, such as Oveta Culp Hobby, who became the first secretary of the Department of Health, Education and Welfare, established in 1953. In 1961 this women's political network persuaded President Kennedy, as payback for their support in the close election of 1960, to establish a Presidential Commission on the Status of Women. It was chaired by Eleanor Roosevelt, embodying continuity with first-wave feminism and the New Deal, and Women's Bureau head Esther Peterson served as vice-chair. Kennedy may have expected this commission to keep the women diverted and out of his hair. But the commission produced substantive recommendations for a legislative agenda and set in motion a continuing process. Its report, issued in 1963, called for equal pay for *comparable* work (understanding that equal pay for *equal* work would not be adequate because women so rarely did the same work as men), as well as child care services, paid maternity leave, and many other measures still not achieved. Determined not to let its momentum stall or its message reach only elite circles, the commission built a network among women's organizations, made special efforts to include black women, and got Kennedy to establish two ongoing federal committees. Most consequentially, it stimulated the creation of state women's commissions, created in every state by 1967. The network that formed through these commissions enabled the creation of the National Organization for Women (NOW) in 1966.

NOW's history has been often misinterpreted, especially by the radical women's liberationists, who denounced it, as the radicals of SNCC criticized their elders and the New Left criticized the Old Left, as stodgy and "bourgeois." At first NOW included more working-class and minority leadership than women's liberation did. Many of its leaders identified strongly with civil rights and defined NOW as pursuing civil rights for women. Former Old Leftist Betty Friedan and black lawyer and poet Pauli Murray were centrally involved in the East, while in the Midwest, labor union women . . . were prime movers. NOW's first headquarters was provided by the UAW. NOW concentrated heavily on employment issues, . . . and NOW's membership was composed largely of employed women. NOW refused to endorse reproductive rights, which the majority considered too controversial, but it rejected the idea that gender was immutable and called for "equitable sharing of responsibilities of home and children and of the economic burdens of their support." This position marked a decisive break with earlier women's rights agitation, which had primarily accepted the traditional division of labor—breadwinner husbands and housewives—as inevitable and desirable. And this position was to give rise to tremendous advances in feminist theory in the next decades.

NOW represented primarily adult professional women and a few male feminists, and at first it did not attempt to build a mass movement open to all women. Although only thirty women had attended its founding conference, and 300 its second conference, NOW demonstrated political savvy in creating the impression that it spoke for a mass power base. It had no central office of its own for three years—networking among a relatively small group did not require one. Its members used their professional and political skills to exert pressure on elected officials.

NOW concentrated on lobbying, using its ties to the few women in influential positions in government; its program focused on governmental action against sex discrimination. Its members met with the attorney general, the secretary of labor, the head of the Civil Service Commission. Its board of directors read like entries from a "Who's Who" of professional women and their male supporters. Its initial impetus was anger that the Equal Employment Opportunity Commission (EEOC) was not enforcing the sex-discrimination provisions of the Civil Rights Act of 1964, and it got immediate results: in 1967 President Johnson issued Executive Order 11375, prohibiting sex discrimination by federal contractors. In the same year NOW forced the EEOC to rule that sex-segregated want ads were discriminatory (although newspapers ignored this ruling with impunity for years). NOW's legal committee, composed of four high-powered Washington lawyers, three of them federal employees, brought suits against protective legislation that in the name of protecting women's fragility in fact kept them out of better jobs. . . .

Women's liberation derided NOW's perspective and tactics as "liberal"—not in the 1990s pejorative sense, coined by the Right, of permissive, but in the 1960s sense, used by the Left, as legalistic and compromising. When a mass women's movement arose, it was not liberal but radical in the sense of seeking out the roots of problems and working for structural change at a level more fundamental than law. It wanted not just to redistribute wealth and power in the existing society, but to challenge the sources of male dominance: the private as well as the public, the psychological as well as the economic, the cultural as well as the legal. Given this radical agenda it was hard for women's liberation to become a player in the political process, and it tended to make purist and moralistic judgments of those who chose to work within the system.

The mass women's movement arose independently of NOW and the government commissions, and its members had a different style: they were younger, typically in their twenties, and less professional. Most importantly, it generated groups consisting of women only. The new women's liberation movement insisted that women needed a woman-only space in which they could explore their grievances and define their own agenda. They observed that women frequently censored not only what they said but even what they thought when men were around. Arriving directly from male-dominated, grassroots social-justice movements, these women longed for a space where they could talk freely with other women. First in Chicago, then in several other cities such as Gainesville, Florida; Chapel Hill, North Carolina; Washington, D.C.; and New York City, women's liberation groups formed in 1967 and 1968. At a 1968 antiwar demonstration in Washington organized by the Jeannette Rankin Brigade, 500 women gathered as a women's liberation counter-conference and then spread the movement to other towns and cities. In August 1968 twenty of them met in Sandy Springs, Maryland, to plan a larger conference. Everyone present was disturbed by the fact that they were all white. But identifying this problem did not mean they could solve it: when over 200 women from thirty-seven states and Canada met in Chicago at Thanksgiving, black women's groups were not represented, because they had not been invited or because they were not interested.

The first women's liberation groups were founded by veteran activists, but soon women with no previous movement experience joined. The decentralization of the movement was so great . . . that different geographic locations developed different agendas and organizational structures. In Iowa City, a university town, the movement began with college students and concentrated much of its energies on publishing a newspaper, *Ain't I a Woman?* In Gainesville, Florida, another university town, the movement originated in civil rights networks. In several large cities—Baltimore, Chicago, Boston, Los Angeles—single citywide organizations brought different groups together; in New York City an original group, New York Radical Women, gave birth to several smaller groups with divergent ideologies. Small-town feminists had to hang together despite their differences, while in big cities there was room to elaborate various political positions. Different cities had different ideological personalities: Washington, D.C., was best known for The Furies, a lesbian separatist group, while Chapel Hill, North Carolina, was noted for its socialist-feminist orientation.

The movement developed so widely and quickly that it is impossible to trace a chronology, impossible to say who led, what came first, who influenced whom. This lack of a clear narrative, and the sense that participants across great distances were making some of the same breakthroughs simultaneously, are characteristic of all mass social movements. . . .

WOMEN'S LIBERATION DEVELOPS

The movement's characteristic form of development was consciousness-raising (CR), a form of structured discussion in which women connected their personal experiences to larger structures of gender. . . . These discussion groups, usually small, sprung up starting in 1968–70 throughout the country among women of all ages and social positions. They were simultaneously supportive and transformative. Women formed these groups by the hundreds, then by the thousands. In Cambridge/Boston where a core group offered to help other women form CR groups, a hundred *new* women attended weekly for several months. The mood was exhilarating. Women came to understand that many of their "personal" problems—insecurity about appearance and intelligence, exhaustion, conflicts with husbands and male employers—were not individual failings but a result of discrimination. The mood became even more electric as women began to create collective ways of challenging that discrimination. At first there was agitprop: spreading the word through leaflets, pamphlets, letters to newspapers; pasting stickers onto sexist advertisements; verbally protesting being called "girl" or "baby" or "chick"; hollering at guys who made vulgar proposals on the streets. Soon action groups supplemented and, in some cases, replaced CR groups. Women pressured employers to provide day care centers; publicized job and school discrimination; organized rape crisis hot lines; opened women's centers, schools, and credit unions; built unions for stewardesses and secretaries; agitated for women's studies courses at colleges; published journals and magazines.

Soon different groups formulated different theoretical/political stands. But the clarity and discreteness of these positions should not be exaggerated; there was cross-fertilization, none was sealed off from others, the borderlines and definitions shifted, and there were heated debates *within* tendencies. Liberal feminists were at first associated with NOW and similar groups, although these tended to merge with women's liberation by the end of the 1970s. Those who remained committed to a broad New Left agenda typically called themselves socialist feminists (to be distinguished from Marxist feminists, who remained convinced that Marxist theory could explain women's oppression and were not committed to an autonomous women's movement). Socialist feminists weighed issues of race and class equally with those of gender and tried to develop an integrated, holistic theory of society. Radical feminists, in contrast, prioritized sexual oppression, but by no means ignored other forms of domination.

Our research suggests that the radical/social-ist opposition was overstated, but small theoretical differences seemed very important at the time because the early feminists were in the process of developing new political theory, not yet making political alliances to achieve concrete objectives. A few separatists, often but not exclusively lesbians, attempted to create self-sustaining female communities and to withdraw as much as possible from contact with men. By the late 1970s, some women had become cultural feminists, celebrating women's specialness and difference from men and retreating from direct challenges to sexist institutions; they believed that change could come about through building new exemplary female communities. But despite this proliferation of ideological groupings, most members of women's liberation did not identify with any of these tendencies and considered themselves simply feminists, unmodified.

Racial/ethnic differences were more significant. Feminists of different racial/ethnic groups established independent organizations from the beginning and within those organizations created different feminisms: black, Chicana, Asian American, Native American. Feminists of color emphasized the problems with universalizing assumptions about women and with identifying gender as a category autonomous from race and class. . . . [F]eminists of color were not more unanimous than white feminists—there were, for example, black liberal feminists, black socialist feminists, black radical feminists, black cultural feminists. These complexities do not negate the fact that feminists of color experienced racism within the women's movement. The majority of feminists, white women from middle-class backgrounds, were often oblivious to the lives of women from minority and working-class families. Feminists of color faced the additional problems that certain women's issues, such as reproductive rights, had been historically tainted by racism; and that feminist criticisms of men were experienced differently, often as betraying racial solidarity when the men were themselves victims of racism.

Lesbians sometimes created separate feminist groups. . . . As lesbians became more open and vocal, they protested the heterosexual assumptions of straight feminists, but they also experienced discrimination from the male-dominated gay movement. For the most part lesbians continued to be active in women's liberation and made important contributions to feminist theory. Lesbians even led campaigns of primary concern to heterosexual women, such as campaigns for reproductive rights.

At the beginning of the movement, feminists tended to create multi-issue organizations, which in turn created committees to focus on single issues, such as day care, rape, or running a women's center. One of the fundamental tenets of early feminist theory was the interconnectedness of all aspects of women's oppression. As political sophistication grew and activists grasped the difficulties of making sweeping changes, feminists settled for piecemeal, fragmented activism. By the mid-1970s feminist politics often occurred in single-issue organizations focused on, for example, reproductive rights, employment discrimination, health, domestic violence, female unions, women's studies. Single-issue politics de-emphasized theory, which reduced divisions; it had the advantage of making coalitions easier but . . . made the movement less radical and more practical. Single-issue politics also lessened the movement's coherence as its activists became specialized and professionalized.

ORGANIZATIONAL PRINCIPLES OF WOMEN'S LIBERATION

In sharp opposition to its liberal feminist sisters in NOW, women's liberation preferred radical decentralization. . . . Women, whose voices had been silenced and whose actions had been directed by others, were loath to have anyone telling them what to think or do. They understood that central organization would produce principles, programs, and priorities they would be required to follow. They also sensed that a movement growing at such velocity could not be contained by central organizations, which would only inhibit creative growth. Without formal rules of membership, any group of women could declare themselves a women's liberation organization, start a newspaper or a women's center, issue a manifesto. The resulting diversity then made it all the harder to keep track of, let alone unify, the many groups.

Not only was there no formal structure bringing groups together, there was very little structure within groups, and this was, again, by choice. Feminists . . . were often hostile in principle to formal procedures, which they saw as arbitrary and not organic. This attitude was part of the feminist critique of the public/private distinction, and it was a way of making the public sphere accessible to women who were traditionally more experienced with a personal, familial form of conversing. In small meetings, especially in the consciousness-raising groups that were the essence of women's liberation, the informal "rapping" style was nurturant, allowing women to speak intimately and risk self-exposure, and therefore to come up with rich new insights into the workings of male dominance. When there were large meetings and/or sharp disagreements, the sessions often became tediously long, unable to reach decisions, and even chaotic. As a result, small groups of women or strong-minded and charismatic individuals sometimes took charge, and others, exhausted by the long aimless discussions, grudgingly relinquished power to these unelected leaders.

Women's liberation faced a major dilemma with respect to leadership. Its search for direct democracy led the movement to revere the principle of "every woman a leader" and to imagine that collectives could speak with one voice. Consequently the movement empowered thousands of women who had never dreamt they could write a leaflet, speak in public, talk to the press, chair a meeting, assert unpopular points of view, or make risky suggestions. The emphasis on group leadership meant that many important statements were unsigned, written anonymously or collectively, or signed with first names only, indicating the degree to which theory and strategy were being developed democratically. But the bias against leadership hindered action, decision-making, and coherent communication beyond small groups. More problematically, the movement did create leaders, but they were frequently unacknowledged and almost always unaccountable because they were essentially self-appointed rather than chosen by the members. This led to widespread, sometimes intense resentment of leaders. The hostility, usually covert, sometimes escalated to stimulate open attacks, as women publicly criticized or "trashed" leaders in meetings. One result was that individuals who had worked hard and made personal sacrifices felt betrayed and embittered. Another was that women's liberation groups became vulnerable to takeovers by highly organized sectarian groups (mainly the Marxist-Leninist sects) or obstruction by

disturbed individuals who could not be silenced. Perhaps the most deleterious result was that many women became reluctant to assert leadership and thus deprived the movement of needed talent. The leadership problem involved the movement's denial of internal inequalities, its refusal to recognize that some women were more articulate and self-confident; had more leisure time, connections, and access to power; or were simply more forceful personalities. These inequalities mainly derived, as the feminists' own analysis showed, from the class and race hierarchy of the larger society. This is an example of utopian hopes becoming wishful thinking: feminists so badly wanted equality that they pretended it was already here.

Despite decentralization and structurelessness, women's liberation created a shared culture, theory, and practice. In an era before e-mail, even before xeroxing, printed publications were vital and feminists spent a significant proportion of their energy, resources, and ingenuity producing them. Mimeographed pages stapled together into pamphlets were the common currency of the early years of the movement, and soon a few feminist publishing houses, such as KNOW in Pittsburgh, Lollipop Inc. in Durham, and the Feminist Press in New York, were printing and selling feminist writings for prices ranging from a nickel to a quarter. These were widely discussed, debated, and answered in further publications. . . . By the mid-1970s over 500 feminist magazines and newspapers appeared throughout the country, such as *Women: A Journal of Liberation* from Baltimore, *It Ain't Me Babe* from the San Francisco Bay Area, *Off Our Backs* from Washington, D.C., *Everywoman* from Los Angeles. . . .

Unlike *Ms.*, a mass-circulation advertisement-supported liberal feminist magazine established in 1972, women's liberation publications struggled along without funds or paid staff. . . . Many articles were signed simply "Susan" or "Randy," or not signed at all, because the movement was hostile to the idea of intellectual private property. The papers sometimes forgot to print dates of publication, addresses, and subscription information. Women worked hard at producing these publications but, unfortunately, less hard at financing and distributing them, so many were irregularly published and short-lived. Nevertheless, it was in these homespun rags that you could find the most creative and cutting-edge theory and commentary.

WHAT WOMEN'S LIBERATION ACCOMPLISHED

. . . [Specific] achievements arose from [women's liberation] campaigns, [but] most transformations only revealed themselves later. Social change, after all, happens slowly. Judicial and legislative victories include the legalization of abortion in 1973, federal guidelines against coercive sterilization, rape shield laws that encourage more women to prosecute their attackers, affirmative action programs that aim to correct past discrimination—but not, however, the Equal Rights Amendment, which failed in 1982, just three states short of the required two-thirds. There are many equally important but less obvious accomplishments: not only legal, economic, and political gains, but also changes in the way people live, dress, dream of their future, and make a living. In fact, there are few areas of contemporary life untouched by feminism. As regards health care, for example, many physicians and hospitals have made major improvements in the treatment of women; about 50 percent of medical students are women; women successfully fought their exclusion from medical research; diseases affecting women, such as breast and ovarian cancer, now receive more funding thanks to women's efforts. Feminists insisted that violence against women, previously a well-kept secret, become a public political issue; made rape, incest, battering, and sexual harassment understood as crimes; and got public funding for shelters for battered women. These gains, realized in the 1980s and 1990s, are the fruits of struggles fought in the 1970s.

Feminist pressure generated substantial changes in education: curricula and textbooks have been rewritten to promote equal opportunity for girls, more women are admitted and funded in universities and professional schools, and a new and rich feminist scholarship in many disciplines has won recognition. Title IX, passed in 1972 to mandate equal access to college programs, has worked a revolution in sports. Consider the many women's records broken in track and field, the expanding number of athletic scholarships for women, professional women's basketball, and the massive popularity of girls' and women's soccer.

Campaigning to support families, feminists organized day care centers, developed standards and curricula for early childhood education, demanded day care funding from government and private employers, fought for parental leave from employers and a decent welfare system. They also struggled for new options for women in employment. They won greater access to traditionally male occupations, from construction to professions and business. They joined unions and fought to democratize them, and they succeeded in organizing previously nonunion workers such as secretaries, waitresses, hospital workers, and flight attendants. As the majority of American women increasingly need to work for wages throughout their lives, the feminist movement tried to educate men to share in housework and child raising. Although women still do the bulk of the housework and child rearing, it is common today to see men in the playgrounds, the supermarkets, and at the PTA meetings.

Feminism changed how women look and what is considered attractive, although the original feminist impulse toward simpler, more comfortable, and less overtly sexual clothing is being challenged by another generation of women at the turn of the century. As women's-liberation influence spread in the 1970s, more and more women refused to wear the constricting, uncomfortable clothes that were required in the 1950s—girdles, garter belts, and stockings; tight, flimsy, pointed, and high-heeled shoes; crinolines and cinch belts; tight short skirts. Women wearing pants, loose jackets, walking shoes, and no makeup began to feel attractive and to be recognized by others as attractive. By the 1980s, however, younger women began to feel that feminist beauty standards were repressive, even prudish, and developed a new, more playful, ornate, and multicultural fashion sensibility that may signal a "third wave" of feminism. Women's newfound passion for athletics has made a look of health and strength fashionable, sometimes to an oppressive degree as women feel coerced to reach a firm muscular, spandex thinness. At the same time, a conservative antifeminist backlash is also influencing fashion, trying to reestablish an allegedly lost femininity. The politics of feminism is being fought out on the fashion front.

Other aspects of the culture also reveal feminism's impact. Finally some older movie actresses, such as Susan Sarandon, Olympia Dukakis, and Meryl Streep, are recognized as desirable, and women entertainers in many media and art forms are rejecting simplistic, demeaning, and passive roles, despite the reemergence of misogynist and hypersexualized entertainments. Soap operas, sitcoms, even cop shows now feature plots in which lesbianism, abortion, rape, incest, and battering are portrayed from women's perspectives. . . . The way we speak has been altered: new words have been coined—"sexist" and "Ms." and "gender"; many Americans are now self-conscious about using "he" to mean a human, and text-books and even sacred texts are being rewritten in inclusive language. Women now expect to be called "women" instead of "ladies" or "girls."

Some of the biggest transformations are personal and familial, and they have been hotly contested. Indeed, even from a feminist perspective not all of them are positive. Women's relationships with other women are more publicly valued and celebrated and lesbianism is more accepted. . . . Most women today enter marriage or other romantic relationships with the expectation of equal partnership; since they don't always get this, they seem more willing to live as single people than to put up with domineering or abusive men. Conservatives argue that the growth of divorce, out-of-wedlock childbirth, and single motherhood is a sign of social deterioration, and certainly the growing economic inequality in the U.S. has rendered many women and especially single mothers and their children impoverished, depressed, and angry. But, feminists retort, is being poor in a destructive marriage really better than being poor on one's own? Even the growth of single motherhood reflects an element of women's choice: in different circumstances both poor and prosperous women are refusing to consider a bad marriage the price of motherhood, and are giving birth to or adopting children without husbands. . . . There is a growing sentiment that families come in a variety of forms.

By the mid-1970s an antifeminist backlash was able to command huge funding from right-wing corporate fortunes, fervent support from religious fundamentalists, and considerable media attention. The intensity of the reaction is a measure of how threatened conservatives were by popular backing for women's liberation and the rapid changes it brought about. Even with their billions of dollars, their hundreds of lobbyists and PR men, their foundations and magazines dishing out antifeminist misinformation, as compared to the puny amounts of money and volunteer labor available to women's liberation, the striking fact is that public opinion has not shifted much. Polls show overwhelming support for what feminism stands for: equal rights, respect, opportunity, and access for women.

That there is still a long way to go to reach sexual equality should not prevent us from recognizing what has been achieved. If there is disappointment, it is because women's liberation was so utopian, even apocalyptic, emerging as it did in an era of radical social movements and grand optimism. Unrealistic? Perhaps. But without utopian dreams, without anger, without reaching for the moon and expecting to get there by express, the movement would have achieved far less. In fact, without taking risks, feminists would never have been able to imagine lives of freedom and justice for women.

Feminism is by no means dead. Feminist groups continue to work on specific issues such as reproductive rights, rape, violence against women, sweatshops, sexism in the media, union organizing, and welfare rights. Nevertheless, the mass social movement called women's liberation did dissolve by the end of the 1970s. This is not a sign of failure. All social movements are short-lived because of the intense personal demands they make; few can sustain the level of energy that they require at their peak of activity. Moreover, as people age, most put more energy into family, employment, and personal life. Equally important, women's liberation could not survive outside the context of the other progressive social movements that nurtured hope and optimism about social change. As the Left declined, the right-wing backlash grew stronger. It did not convert many feminists to conservatism but it moved the mainstream far to the right. Given this change in mainstream politics, it is all the more striking that so few feminist gains have been rolled back and many have continued and even increased their momentum. Although the word "feminist" has become a pejorative term to some American women, most women (and most men as well) support a feminist program: equal education, equal pay, child care, freedom from harassment and violence, shared housework and child rearing, women's right to self-determination. . . .

JUDY TZU-CHUN WU
The Vietnam War and Global Sisterhood

We see some of the complexity of women's activism in the 1960s in the women and peace activists who gathered at the two Indochinese Women's Conferences (IWCs) held in Canada in 1971. (The meetings were held north of the 49th parallel because Canada was officially neutral during the U.S. war in Vietnam. Both U.S. draft resisters and representative of North Vietnam could enter Canada.) Here, an unprecedented number of North American women, many for the first time, encountered female leaders from Southeast Asia. All believed that citizen diplomacy might succeed in advancing peace at a time when governments appeared to balk at substantive negotiations. From Vietnam came representatives of two women's unions, one based in North Vietnam and one in South Vietnam. The westerners were well aware of their guests' deep experience in resisting colonialism and fighting for national liberation. Here were women who had been guerrilla fighters, organized all-women brigades, and endured many losses. Some, like Nguyen Thi Binh, had held high political offices. Their search for self-determination on many fronts held great appeal for North American women who came from different activist strands, including long-time peace advocates whose predecessors are described in Leila J. Rupp's essay (pp. 393–404); recently awakened women's liberationists; and newly empowered Third World women like Marii Hasegawa and Betita Martinez.

What were the differences in experience and in approach to political work between Vietnamese and North American women that emerge from Judy Tzu-Chun Wu's research? As you contemplate political alliances across national borders in today's "globalizing" world, what lessons are found in Wu's conclusions about the global sisterhood achieved in the IWCs?

In April 1971, approximately one thousand female activists from throughout North America gathered in Vancouver and Toronto, Canada, to attend the Indochinese Women's Conferences (IWCs). The U.S. and Canadian women originated from large metropolitan centers, small towns, and even rural communities to meet a delegation of women from North and South Vietnam as well as Laos. . . . The 1971 IWCs, represented the first opportunities for large numbers of North American women to have direct contact with their Asian "sisters."

The IWCs illuminate how women literally and symbolically crossed borders in order to build an international antiwar movement. As such, the organizing of the conferences and the experiences of those who attended shed light on the process of building "global sisterhood." Critics of the idea have argued that the call for female international solidarity represents another form of Western domination, this time by well-intentioned champions of women's rights who see themselves as the saviors of oppressed women in non-Western societies. The IWCs provide an opportunity to rethink global sisterhood in two ways.[1]

First, the conferences highlight the political multiplicity of North American women and the complex process of negotiation that occurred to foster an international peace movement. There were three North American sponsors of the IWCs: "old friends" or more "traditional" women's peace organizations; "new friends" or women's liberation activists;

Excerpted from ch. 7 of *Radicals on the Road: Internationalism, Orientalism, and Feminism During the Vietnam Era* by Judy Tzu-Chun Wu (Ithaca, N.Y.: Cornell University Press, 2013). Reprinted by permission of the author and publisher. Notes have been edited and renumbered.

and "Third World" women or women of color
in North America. Within each group, the
women ascribed to a variety of political viewpoints. Engaging in an international movement
did not unify women in the West. In fact, the
IWCs provided a forum to air and accentuate
differences between North American women,
particularly along the lines of ideology, race,
sexuality, and nationality. Fractured by these
differences, women from North America did
not dominate the political agenda at the IWCs.
Instead, they looked to women from Southeast
Asia for leadership and inspiration. Thus, the
IWCs reveal the political variety among women
in the West and how these conflicts can ironically foster the growth of a global women's antiwar movement.

Second, while critics of global sisterhood
emphasize the power and misperceptions of
Western women, a focus on the Southeast Asian
women demonstrates how women from outside the West deployed female internationalism. During the U.S. war in Vietnam, the
Women's Union of North Vietnam and the
Women's Union for the Liberation of South
Vietnam (collectively referred to [here] as the
VWUs, Vietnam Women's Unions) played integral roles in fostering a global women's peace
movement. Through meetings, correspondence, and the circulation of print as well as
visual media, the VWUs actively nurtured
American women's interest in U.S. foreign
policy and military activity in Southeast Asia.
The Vietnamese believed that all human beings,
and especially all women, could share a sense of
commonality and purpose. To promote an international peace movement, Vietnamese
women cultivated a belief in global sisterhood,
projecting and cultivating a female universal-
ism that simultaneously critiqued and transcended racial and cultural divides. It was not
just an ideology imposed by the West but was
promoted by women from the East as well.

The IWCs resulted from a longer history
of North American and Southeast Asian
women politically engaging with one another.
They developed personal and political connections through face-to-face meetings that took
place in Eastern and Western Europe, Asia,
Cuba, Africa, Australia, and Canada. These
conversations and partnerships in turn helped
to shape the political content of Vietnamese
antiwar appeals, which eventually circulated
beyond the individuals involved to influence
activist media portrayals of the U.S. war in

Vietnam. In this campaign to promote a worldwide antiwar movement, the VWUs established relationships with individual women
and with female organizations from a variety
of political spectrums and backgrounds. The
North American sponsors of the IWC—old
friends, new friends, and Third World women—
reveal the diversity of individuals engaged in
fostering female internationalism.

The term "old friends" referred to the U.S.-
based Women Strike for Peace (WSP), the
Canadian Voice of Women (VOW), and the
Women's International League for Peace and
Freedom (WILPF), headquartered in Switzerland but with national sections throughout the
world. These organizations were designated old
not because of the age of their constituency, although all three did attract largely middle-aged
to elderly women. Rather, the organizations
were considered old friends because of the history of friendship that these North American
women established with Vietnamese women.
For example, WSP's contact with the VWU extended back to 1965, when two WSP members
were among the first Americans to visit Hanoi
after the commencement of U.S. bombing of
North Vietnam. That same year, a ten-person
delegation from WSP met with representatives
from North and South Vietnam in Jakarta, Indonesia, to affirm women's unique abilities to cross
Cold War barriers and foster peace.[2] These political and personal relationships continued to
develop as WSP sent international delegations
to Europe, Canada, Cuba, and North Vietnam
throughout the remainder of the war.

Although differences existed among WSP,
VOW, and WILPF, they could be characterized
as maternalist peace organizations. For example, WSP originated in 1961 from the efforts of
predominantly middle-class and middle-raged
white women to protect their families from nuclear annihilation. As historian and former
WSP activist Amy Swerdlow explained:

> On 1 November 1961 an estimated fifty thousand
> women walked out of their kitchens and off their
> jobs, in an unprecedented nationwide strike for
> peace. As a radioactive cloud from a series of Rus-
> sian atom bomb tests passed over American cities
> and the United States threatened to retaliate with
> its own cycle of nuclear explosions, the striking
> women sent delegations to their elected offi-
> cials. . . . They demanded that their local officials
> pressure President John Kennedy on behalf of all
> the world's children, to end nuclear testing at once
> and begin negotiations for nuclear disarmament.

This initial strike eventually led committed women to form Women Strike for Peace. The members of the organization ... had "wide-ranging professional identities," yet they chose to publicly identify themselves as "housewives and mothers." These women proclaimed their right to condemn the threat of global and nuclear warfare based on the desire to protect their own and other people's families. They embraced gender difference to define a special role for women on the global stage.[3]

[The Canadian group] VOW, founded just a year before WSP in 1960, was similarly inspired by a belief in women's unique abilities and responsibilities to foster peace. Following the failure of the 1960 Paris summit on disarmament between the United States and the Soviet Union, thousands of women across Canada decided to form VOW. They presented themselves as "respectable" and as maternal, "protectors of the world's children." One of the founding members and an eventual president of the group, Muriel Duckworth, explained that "Voice of Women founders had the idea of women as lifegivers," mothers who could not support acts of aggression and violence.[4]

The roots of this maternalist form of peace politics can be traced back to Victorian and Progressive era notions of gender difference as opposed to more modern beliefs in gender sameness. In fact, WILPF, the third organizational member among the old friends, was founded before American women achieved suffrage and in the context of World War I. Created under the leadership of Jane Addams, WILPF advocated for equal political rights for women because members believed that women had a propensity to promote peace. As suffragist and pacifist Carrie Chapman Catt explained, "War is in the blood of men"; inversely, peace was believed to be in the blood of women.[5]

This maternalist and gender essentialist justification for women's engagement in international politics held particular significance in the early Cold War period. In the midst of the Red Scare, critics of U.S. foreign policies were easily dismissed and ridiculed as communist sympathizers and political ideologues. In fact, members of WSP, VOW, and WILPF all endured anticommunist attacks. By proclaiming the political responsibilities of motherhood, these women presented themselves as "common-sense" or nonideological activists. They sought to defuse global conflict and promote peace in order to protect "all the world's children."[6]

With their similarities, the three organizations frequently collaborated with one another and shared ideas for promoting peace. Representatives of each group corresponded with one another and participated in each other's conferences and activities. The organizations also overlapped in membership. In addition, for all three groups, traveling across geopolitical borders and having face-to-face meetings with their nations' enemies were important strategies for their efforts to defuse global conflict. . . . Representatives of WSP, following a series of exchanges with Vietnamese women, cosponsored with their Asian counterparts the historic Conference of Concerned Women to End the War. The conference was held in Paris in the spring of 1968, just a few weeks before the formal peace talks began. In attendance were representatives from countries involved in the war, including Japan, Britain, Australia, New Zealand, West Germany, and Canada. One American participant recalled the impact of the meeting: "I have always been convinced that the women who come in contact with the Vietnamese women come back home changed. They seem to march to the beat of another drummer. They have a new sense of urgency. Now I know why. It has happened to me. When you are actually faced with the 'enemy' and realize that American sons and husbands are killing them—it's too much to bear."[7]

After attending the emotionally charged Paris conference, Kay MacPherson, president of VOW, visited Hanoi for the first time. She did so with a sense of trepidation as well as determination. Aware that she would travel in the midst of an ongoing bombing campaign by the United States, MacPherson wrote, "In case I get to Hanoi and end up with a bomb on top of me I want to put down one or two thoughts before hand. . . . Not many people are invited to go to Hanoi, though many wish to go. To have earned the trust of the Vietnam women is a very great honour. . . . We cannot treat such an honour lightly, nor, however reluctant I felt, would I dream of refusing to go." Following MacPherson's journey to Southeast Asia, VOW sponsored a reciprocal visit by representatives of the North and South Vietnam Women's Unions to Canada in the summer of 1969. Members of WSP, including Jane Spock—wife of Dr. Benjamin Spock—attended this gathering. In fact, they staged a protest against the war on the Fourth of July as they crossed the U.S.-Canada border at Niagara Falls.[8] This

1969 exchange directly inspired the subsequent 1971 IWCs.

The members of WSP, VOW, and WILPF recognized the power of face-to-face communication with Vietnamese women and sought to provide similar opportunities for other individuals. Aware of their own demographic base, they made various attempts to involve younger and nonwhite activists. Cora Weiss, a leader in WSP as well as in the peace movement overall, played arguably the most central role in arranging American delegations to Hanoi during the U.S. war in Vietnam. . . . [Weiss] protested against the Red Scare during her college years at the University of Wisconsin, Madison. While in the home state of Senator Joe McCarthy, she petitioned for his recall of in a campaign called Joe Must Go. She also met her husband in college. Peter Weiss, a survivor of the Holocaust, joined with Cora as they participated in the civil rights movement and in support of African decolonization. During the war, Cora, who is fluent in French, went to Paris several times to meet with Vietnamese representatives. She also helped to organize the 1969 and 1971 women's conferences in Canada. She traveled to Vietnam a total of five times, the first time in December 1969 after the first Canada conference and the last time in 1978. . . . [9]

Weiss traveled to North Vietnam and organized the trips of others because she believed in the power of "citizen diplomacy." On her initial journey in 1969, she discussed with Vietnamese representatives the importance of facilitating communication between American POWs and their families. In keeping with the maternalist outlook of other old friends, Weiss was motivated by a sense of compassion for the soldiers and their families. In addition, she recognized the political impact such humanitarian gestures would have. During the late 1960s and early 1970s, President Nixon and the U.S. administration focused on American POWs and soldiers missing in action to justify extending the war. Weiss and other antiwar activists sought to defuse this issue by facilitating communication for and the release of U.S. POWs. After her first trip in 1969, Weiss established the Committee of Liaison with Servicemen Detained in North Vietnam, which organized monthly visits to Hanoi to serve as mail carriers for American POWs and their families. On her second trip to Hanoi in 1972, Weiss negotiated with the North Vietnamese to release three POWs as a gesture of goodwill.

The regularly scheduled trips, sponsored by the Committee of Liaison, not only delivered mail and packages to U.S. soldiers but also provided an opportunity to expose dedicated peace activists to wartime conditions in Hanoi. In composing the membership of these monthly delegations, Weiss invited individuals from diverse racial, generational, and gender backgrounds to expand the range of people who otherwise would not have the opportunity to travel to North Vietnam. These journeys invariably reaffirmed and further motivated the travelers' engagement in the antiwar movement.[10]

The women from North and South Vietnam who cultivated and encouraged international contact with women from the West also articulated a unique gender role for women in the struggle for peace and national liberation. They represented women's organizations in their respective regions. The Women's Union of North Vietnam, based in Hanoi, traced its history back to the founding of the Indochinese Communist Party in 1930. The Women's Union for the Liberation of South Vietnam was founded in 1960, along with the National Liberation Front (NLF). The phrase "women's liberation" in the Western context referred to activists who sought to identify and subvert the workings of patriarchy. The VWUs conceived of women's liberation primarily through the lens of anticolonial struggles for national liberation. Because of the long history of political repression and anticolonial warfare, Vietnamese women had assumed a variety of political, military, economic and cultural roles. Consequently, they had a wider array of life experiences than did most of their Western counterparts. Yet, interestingly, the Vietnamese women also conveyed the arguments for peace in the name of protecting their families.

Nguyen Thi Binh, who was present at the 1965 Jakarta meeting with WSP as well as the 1968 Paris Women's Conference, became one of the most recognizable Asian female figures in Western women's political circles. Like WSP members, she came from a relatively elite and educated background. The granddaughter of nationalist leader Phan Chu Trinh and the daughter of a civil servant under the French, Binh became a political activist in the 1950s when she led a series of student protests against the French and the United States in Saigon. Imprisoned for three years for these activities, she helped to found the NLF and the Women's Union for the Liberation of South Vietnam after her release. Unlike most WSP members, who were denied formal political power, Binh became an authorized leader as the foreign minister of the Provisional Revolutionary Government. WSP historian Amy Swerdlow noted the unequal status of the American and Asian women who met at international gatherings. While WSP publicly identified itself as consisting of "nonprofessional housewives, . . . the women who represented North and South Vietnam presented themselves as workers, students, professionals, and artists."[11]

Despite the disjuncture in status, Vietnamese women like Binh used a language of sisterhood and motherhood to establish a common connection with their old friends. In a fifteen-minute film produced in 1970 and intended for an American female audience, Binh explained:

> I am so happy as a South Vietnamese woman and mother to have the opportunity to speak to you. . . . May I express my sincere thanks to the Women Strike for Peace for its contribution to the anti-war movements and its sympathy and support to our people, particularly the South Vietnamese women. . . . Our aspirations for peace are all the more ardent for over 25 consecutive years now, our compatriots, we women included, have never enjoyed a single day of peace. Let me tell you that in my own family, several members have been killed while some others are still jailed by the Saigon regime. I myself have had not much time to live with my husband and my children. The moments my son and daughter were allowed to be at my side have become so rare and therefore so precious to them.[12]

Her emphasis on the destructive impact of warfare on family life reflected the actual experiences of women in Vietnam. Her appeal also resonated effectively with maternalist activists in the West who stressed the sanctity of motherhood and home life. . . .

VWU initiated multiple international gatherings to facilitate personal contact with Western women. In addition, VWU circulated print materials to communicate how Vietnamese women both suffered from but also heroically resisted colonialism and military aggression. During the U.S. war in Vietnam, the VWU published a periodical in English and French titled *Women of Viet Nam*. They also shared copies of Vietnamese Studies no. 10, a booklet called *Vietnamese Women* (*VW*). This 1966 English-language publication was presented to U.S. visitors, both at international gatherings and during their travels to Vietnam. The portrayal of Vietnamese women in this work, numbering over three hundred pages, appealed to the political ideologies and sympathies of women from a variety of generations and backgrounds in the West.

[The book] *VW* consisted of eight sections, with chapters having titles such as "The Vietnamese Woman, Yesterday and Today," as well as more intimate and localized portrayals of either individual women or women from particular villages or regions. The overall effect was to personalize and humanize women in North and South Vietnam by providing a narrative of personal and social uplift through four historical stages: (1) Vietnamese women's lives under patriarchal as well as colonial oppression under French rule beginning in the mid- to late nineteenth century; (2) Vietnamese women's efforts to challenge traditional gender roles through involvement in national liberation movements, first against the French and then against the United States; (3) the transformation of Vietnamese women's lives through socialist reconstruction projects in the North after the end of the First Indochina War against the French in 1954; and (4) finally, how the opportunities for improving Vietnamese women's lives continue to be threatened by American imperialism and the Second Indochina War, which was being fought against the United States and the South Vietnamese government. Somewhat predictably, the publication argued that the oppression of Vietnamese women, particularly for the vast majority who were members of the peasantry, was centrally connected to class and national oppression. For Vietnamese women to achieve liberation and equality, then, they had to struggle not only against patriarchal family and societal norms but also for national independence and socialist revolution. The way this political message was conveyed, particularly through intimate portraits, appealed to Western women in various ways.

For maternalist peace activists who subscribed to "traditional" gender roles and justified their political interventions as part of their responsibilities as mothers and housewives, the destructive impact of war on heteronormative family life in Vietnam resonated most strongly. Numerous stories in *VW* emphasize how war separates, sometimes permanently, husbands and wives as well as mothers and children. The tragedy of war, then, was conveyed through heteronormative and maternal loss. One folksong quoted in *VW* expressed this longing of a young woman in North Vietnam and her fiancé who had departed to fight in the South: "Our destinies are bound together, I will wait for you / Even if I should have to wait a thousand years."[13]

Protecting their families and loved ones against colonialism and war required Vietnamese women to engage in or support acts of rebellion and violence. In their publications and in face-to-face meetings, they frequently quoted the traditional saying, "When the enemy comes, even the women must fight." They also cited historic examples of Vietnamese women who battled against foreign invasion, such as the Trung sisters, credited with leading the first national liberation struggle against Chinese domination in 40 AD. This Vietnamese female warrior tradition, which could be regarded as a transgression of traditional gender roles, was framed as a heteronormative or maternalist act of agency. For example, the publication *VW* featured a poem by Minh Khai, a famous revolutionary against the French who wrote on her prison cell before she was executed:

> A rosy-cheeked woman, here I am fighting side by side with you men!
> On my shoulders, weighs that hatred which is common to us.
> The prison is my school, its mates my friends.
> The sword is my child, the gun my husband.[14]

In this poem, instruments of violence are equated with members of a heteronormative family. The evocation of the sword as a child and the gun as a husband justifies the embrace of these objects as a means to fulfill traditional familial responsibilities. Given colonial and wartime conditions that do not allow for peaceful existence of kinship units, the female warrior bears the responsibility of defending her home and homeland in order to become a wife and mother. . . .

Maternalist activists in the West embraced pacifism.[15] However, they could understand the fierce desire to step outside of accepted gender practices in the name of protecting their families. After all, to help end the war and stop nuclear annihilation, members of WSP, VOW, and WILPF also left the confines of the home to travel, lobby, and stage protests. Rather than condemning the Vietnamese women for fighting to save their loved ones, Western women peace activists demanded that the U.S. government end the war. As one slogan adopted by WSP pleaded: "Not Our Sons, Not Their Sons."

The model of revolutionary womanhood that Vietnamese women offered resonated differently for the new friends who cosponsored the IWCs. This designation generally referred to a younger generation of women who became politically active through the civil rights, New Left, and eventually the women's and sexual liberation movements. In contrast to the old friends who claimed their roles as housewives and mothers to justify their political interventions, the new friends sought to fundamentally challenge male domination over women. They demanded equal opportunities and rights for women in the legal and political system as well as the workplace. They identified inequalities in the home, naming the "second shift" that women worked as primary caregivers and housekeepers as well as the limited rights of women in marriage and divorce. They questioned the reproduction of gender roles through child rearing practices and socialization. They protested the sexual objectification and violence directed toward women and their bodies. And they challenged heteronormativity by claiming lesbianism as a sexual and political practice.

Although the individuals referred to as "new friends" differed and disagreed with one another, they collectively constituted members of the so-called second wave of feminism. (The first wave [is said to have] crested with the attainment of suffrage in 1920, while the second wave is associated with women's activism of the 1960s and 1970s.) . . . For them, the experiences of Vietnamese women offered a range of possibilities [for] discover[ing] new political roles and identities.

For liberal feminists seeking access and equality for women in the realm of work and politics, the experiences of Vietnamese women provided insight into the social reconstruction of gender roles. The *VW* booklet notes, "It is easy to inscribe the 'liberation of women' in the programme of a political party, it is much more difficult to get it into legislation, and more difficult still to integrate it into the customs and manners of the time." Significantly, the publication did not regard women in the West as the vanguard of change, stating instead that "at present, women in all Western countries are still asking for equal salary and wages with men. . . . And they are not to get it very soon." Strikingly, the authors regarded women in the West as being engaged in a similar struggle and perhaps even falling behind the so-called

Third World. Because North Vietnam was in the process of constructing a new society, *VW* documented at length the rights and advances women had achieved under the Democratic Republic of Vietnam, such as suffrage, equal pay, and women holding prominent positions of political and economic leadership. At the same time, the publication also frankly acknowledged barriers to greater gender equity, conveying both advances and challenges through individual stories and charts with clear quantitative data.[17]

While the Vietnamese focus on women integrating the public arena might appeal to liberal feminists in the West, other aspects of the Vietnamese analysis resonated more strongly with women's liberation activists in the United States.[18] These individuals sought to identify and subvert the workings of patriarchy in all realms of life, not just in the public sphere of work and politics but also in the private sphere of personal, familial, and sexual relationships. For these women, the Vietnamese provided functioning examples of female communities. They organized all-women economic production teams, guerrilla units, and even regular military battalions, while leading hybridized and improvised family structures in the midst of war. Although products of emergency circumstances, these practices nevertheless offered empowering demonstrations of how women, through separatist institutions, could transform the society around them.

The VWU often used biographical examples of heroic women to offer political instruction. This "emulation campaign" was primarily directed toward the largely peasant constituency in Vietnam. One of the prominently featured women was Nguyen Thi Dinh, a cofounder of the NLF and president of the Women's Union for the Liberation of South Vietnam. Unlike Nguyen Thi Binh, who came from a relatively elite family, Dinh was a peasant. Born in 1920, she began dedicating herself to fighting French colonialism at the age of fifteen. She eventually became a guerrilla fighter and a general in the People's Liberation Army. Like many other women engaged in the struggle for national liberation, described by the Vietnamese as "longhaired warriors," Dinh suffered imprisonment and separation from her husband and child, as well as the death of her loved ones. Dinh's life story as a female revolutionary leader engaged in armed struggle inspired new friends in the West who were

trying to understand how they might fundamentally change their society. In addition, the Vietnamese use of the personal to offer political instruction corresponded strongly to one of the key mantras of the U.S. women's liberation movement: the personal is political.[19]

Some "new friend" feminists had the opportunity to learn from Vietnamese women through direct contact. Vivian Rothstein, who was a student activist at Berkeley before her involvement in the women's liberation movement in Chicago, met with Vietnamese women in Eastern Europe and then in North Vietnam in 1967. As a member of Students for a Democratic Society, she had been invited to participate in a significant gathering of antiwar activists in Bratislava, Czechoslovakia, in September 1967. Thirty-eight Americans attended the meeting, including representatives from religious pacifist organizations, the civil rights movement, the liberal and progressive media, and faculty and student antiwar activists. In Bratislava, they met with Vietnamese spokespersons from the North and the South, including Nguyen Thi Binh and other representatives of the VWU.[20]

Rothstein recalled that the Vietnamese women whom she met insisted on having women-only discussions with American representatives. This was unusual for her. She tended to work in mixed-gender settings as a student activist. . . . However, the women from South Vietnam wanted to convey how the war had a unique impact on women. Rothstein recalled that they discussed how militarization fostered the growth of prostitution in South Vietnam. In addition, they provided examples of how American soldiers threatened and utilized rape as well as sexual mutilation as military tactics. Shaken and moved by these meetings, Rothstein requested an audiotape version of their presentation so that she might share their "appeal to the American women."[21]

During the conference in Bratislava, Rothstein received an invitation from the VWU to visit North Vietnam. The trip to Eastern Europe was the first time she had left the United States, so traveling to Hanoi, which was then being bombed, was a "huge, terrifying" experience. Nevertheless, the journey profoundly touched Rothstein. In North Vietnam, she observed how the VWU inspired and mobilized women to protect and transform their society. The VWU had chapters at various levels, ranging from local villages to the national level and operating in schools, workplaces, health clinics, and government units. In all of these settings, the unions trained women for political leadership and advocated for their collective interests. VWU representatives conveyed to Rothstein "how important it was to organize the women . . . and how powerful American women could be" as well. When Rothstein returned to the United States, she went back to the "little women's group" that she had participated in before she left. Inspired by her experiences in Czechoslovakia and North Vietnam, Rothstein proposed the formation of the Chicago Women's Liberation Union, a group modeled on the VWU.

Just as American activists learned from the Vietnamese, their hosts were eager to learn from the visitors. Charlotte Bunch-Weeks, a women's liberation activist based in the Washington, DC, area, traveled to Vietnam as part of a multiracial and mixed-sex group in 1970. . . .

Like other travelers to North Vietnam, Bunch-Weeks returned with a deeper commitment to ending the war. She remembers one particularly profound exchange she had with a Buddhist nun [outside of Vinh] south of Hanoi, where the countryside, villages, and towns that had been repeatedly bombed . . . [At] a Buddhist pagoda, which was only partly standing, their host, "a small, thin, quiet Buddhist nun in [a] brown habit," showed them around.

> Suddenly she leaned toward us, grew very intense, and grasped our hands. She said that she had been waiting many years to talk with American women. She was convinced that if the women of the US knew what was really happening in her country, they would make it stop. She told of her experience, of how children came crying to her for their mothers, but she knew their mothers had been killed. Finally she said, "We the women, must unite to stop this war. We must unite to stop the terrible things that are happening in this world. I would like you to take that message back to the women of America."[22]

Accepting this mandate, Bunch-Weeks returned to the United States and shared her experiences through talks and writings, which circulated in women's liberation and antiwar publications. She also cofounded the Women and Imperialism Collective in the Washington, DC, area and proposed to launch the National Women's Anti-War Program. Along with Cora Weiss, Bunch-Weeks served on the steering committee of the New Mobilization Committee to End the War in Vietnam (the new Mobe). The first Mobe or National Mobilization Committee to End the War in Vietnam had organized a series of national protests, including a large rally of over one hundred thousand in Washington, DC, in 1967, the follow-up March on the Pentagon, and the protests at the 1968 Democratic National Convention in Chicago. The new Mobe formed in 1969 and coordinated a series of local and national protests that culminated in two national moratoriums, general strikes to force the Nixon administration to end the war. Held on 15 October and 15 November of that year, the second moratorium attracted over half a million people to Washington, DC. The strong showing sought to challenge Nixon's 3 November appeal to the "silent majority" of Americans whom he believed supported his policies. The new Mobe continued its efforts into the spring of 1970 as Nixon's secret bombings and invasion of Cambodia, a neutral country, were made public.

Although Weiss and Bunch-Weeks played leadership roles in the new Mobe, they both recognized the limited authority and respect that women had within the male-dominated antiwar movement. Even though women performed crucial organizing work, their ideas and voices tended to be marginalized and at times publicly denigrated. To address these issues from within the movement, Bunch-Weeks, Weiss, and other female members on Mobe's national staff and steering committee formed a women's caucus. Their group identified three main goals: (1) "combating male supremacy" in the antiwar movement, (2) developing "ideological and programmatic clarity about how the struggle for the liberation of women is related to the struggles against racism and imperialism," and (3) connecting the "spring actions of the Mobe to their own oppression as women."[23] The Women and Imperialism Collective as well as the Women's Caucus provided opportunities for female activists to organize with other women and to develop a feminist analysis of war and imperialism. . . .

Vivian Rothstein, Charlotte Bunch-Weeks, and other women's liberation activists who met with Vietnamese representatives in Asia and other parts of the world became key organizers of the IWCs. Their face-to-face encounters inspired U.S. women profoundly. Alice Wolfson of the Washington, DC, Women and Imperialism Collective shared her impressions after a 1970 planning meeting for the IWCs that was held in Budapest, Hungary:

We have just had our first formal meeting with the Vietnamese & Cambodians. They are incredible out of sight people. Yesterday, when I first met them, I filled up with tears & wanted to take them in my arms & say "I'm sorry." . . . No matter how much you read & how much you know in your head what a monster imperialism is, it comes home to you with an emotional force that seems physical, meeting women who live under the threat of death. It seems impossible to think that I could ever, even for a minute, contemplate withdrawing or dropping out.[24]

By organizing the IWCs, women's liberation activists had the opportunity to recreate their political intimacy with Southeast Asian women for larger numbers of women who did not have the privilege or opportunity to travel to Asia and other parts of the world.

The final group of cosponsors of the IWCs were Third World women. These individuals from racially oppressed groups in North America identified their status in the West as being akin to the status of Third World peoples globally. Understanding themselves as internal colonial subjects, they expressed solidarity among themselves based on similar experiences of disfranchisement and marginalization within the United States. In addition, they allied with people in the Third World who were fighting for self-determination and national liberation from colonialism and neocolonialism. Given this identification with Third World people both domestically and abroad, women of color tended to distance themselves from the predominantly white old and new friends. Instead, racialized women in the "First World" turned to one another and to women in the Third World for political inspiration.

Both the old and new friends recognized that their groups consisted predominantly of white women. Consequently, they attempted to work with nonwhite women. WSP and WILPF cultivated contacts with Coretta Scott King and other African American women at a time when great pressures were being placed on male civil rights leaders to avoid making public statements about Vietnam.[25] In addition, both organizations also attracted women of Asian ancestry. Aline Berman, a Chinese American, attended the Jakarta and Paris meetings as a WSP representative. . . . In addition, Marii Hasegawa, a Japanese American, served as president of the U.S. Section of WILPF during the late 1960s and early 1970s.

The presence of women of Asian ancestry in mainstream women's peace organizations

stemmed from these groups' engagement with domestic racism and international pacifism. Hasegawa explained that WILPF was "one of the few organizations which had passed a resolution against the concentration camps in which Japanese and their citizen children were held in WWII" by the U.S. government.[26] To assist Japanese American internees seeking to resettle outside of the designated internment zones on the West Coast, WILPF supported a hostel in Philadelphia where Hasegawa found a place to stay after she left camp. . . .

The category of Third World women [for the most part was composed of] women who became active during the late 1960s in racially based liberation movements. These activists identified as black, Asian American, Chicana or Mexican American, Puerto Rican, and indigenous or Native. For these individuals, the Vietnamese analysis of women's oppression as resulting from a confluence of patriarchy, colonialism, and capitalism held particular appeal. In the mid- to late 1960s and into the 1970s, women of color in the global North began to articulate an intersectional analysis.[27] Rather than seeing themselves only in terms of their race, gender, or class, they began to understand how multiple systems of social hierarchy operated simultaneously to shape their lives. Consequently, they turned to one another and to women in the Third World for political inspiration.

Like other antiwar activists, women of color also traveled to Vietnam. In 1970, . . . Betita Martinez visited North Vietnam. She believes that she was the first Mexican American to journey there. In fact, she went on the same delegation as Charlotte Bunch-Weeks and was asked to describe the movement that she was engaged in building in New Mexico. Martinez grew up in Washington, DC, a member of an international and multiracial family. Her father, a dark-skinned Mexican, worked for Mexico's embassy, and her mother, a fair-skinned Scotch-Irish, worked for the Swiss embassy. Growing up in the racially polarized, black-white city of Washington, DC, Martinez found it difficult to socially locate herself as a multiracial person of Latino/a heritage. She recalled, "The composition of the neighborhood was either . . . black or white, or both, because that's the way Washington, DC, was. There was no Latinos around the street back then. It was a very lonely thing."[28]

In that environment, Martinez developed both a racial identification with African

Americans and a global consciousness against Western colonialism. She inherited her father's dark skin and was treated as if she was black. Martinez recalled, "The girl next door was not allowed to play with me by her parents because I was too dark ... and we passed for black often on the buses and got sent to the back of the bus." ... During the late 1950s and early 1960s, Martinez became invested in supporting the civil rights movement. As a writer and editor based in New York City at the time, [in reaction to] the 1963 church bombing in Birmingham, Alabama, which killed four black girls, she decided to volunteer for the Student Nonviolent Coordinating Committee (SNCC). [After] work[ing] Mississippi for the 1964 Summer Project, she coordinated the New York office, where she raised funds and mobilized support for civil rights activities in the South. She also edited an important collection of letters about Mississippi Freedom Summer under the name of Elizabeth Sutherland.[29] ...

Martinez's interest in Latino/a issues persisted, though, and her ethnic consciousness eventually emerged. She traveled to Cuba repeatedly, the first time after the 1959 revolution, and eventually published a book in 1967 about her observations of their new society. Also that year, she decided to relocate from New York City to New Mexico. ... Eventually, Martinez started an influential Chicano/a newspaper, *El Grito del Norte*. ...

When Martinez traveled to Vietnam in 1970, her sense of commonality with the Vietnamese, particularly the women, was due not only to gender but also to a comparable colonized status. Because of the heavy bombing campaign ordered by President Nixon at the time, the plane that she and Bunch-Weeks traveled on to Hanoi "landed on a totally dark airstrip in a totally dark airport." Martinez's reflections, though, ... focused on the positive, [indeed indomitable] spirit of the Vietnamese people. ... Martinez observed how the vast majority of Vietnamese people were peasants, a status similar to the agricultural background of many Chicano/as of New Mexico. In addition, the Vietnamese were demanding the right to determine their political future, just like what the Chicano/a movement and other liberation movements in the United States and globally were demanding.[30] ...

After returning from Hanoi, Martinez ... focused on sharing her insights with the Chicano/a community. She wrote articles in *El*

Grito del Norte and also gave public presentations. She was one of the featured speakers at the Chicano National Moratorium. Held in Los Angeles on 29 August 1970, the moratorium was part of a nearly two-year effort to mobilize Chicano/as against the Vietnam War. Similar to African Americans, Mexican Americans tended to have lower socioeconomic status as well as fewer opportunities for career advancement and college admissions. Consequently, Chicanos tended to be overrepresented in the military. Chicano/a activists like Martinez encouraged other members of their communities to question why they were fighting in the war. They formed the only "minority-based anti-war organization, called the National Chicano Moratorium Committee." The National Moratorium attracted an estimated twenty thousand to thirty thousand protesters, including elderly and children; it was the "largest anti-war march by any specific ethnic or racial group in U.S. history." The event was brutally disrupted by the Los Angeles police force. Approximately 150 were injured that day, and three were killed.[31]

Despite this aborted attempt, Martinez found other ways to encourage Chicano/as to understand the issues of the war. She was not able to replicate her own experiences of traveling to Vietnam. The people with whom she interacted in New Mexico lacked the financial means to do so. Also, some expressed reservations that their journey might taint them as communists. However, Chicanas from New Mexico did travel to Vancouver for the IWC. There they met with women from Southeast Asia and other women of color, including other Mexican, Mexican American, and indigenous activists from throughout North America.[32] ...

Maternal peace activists, second-wave feminists, and women of color all developed profound political connections with Southeast Asian women. These alliances across national, cultural, and ideological boundaries provide an opportunity to reexamine global sisterhood in two significant ways. First, rather than regarding women in the Third World as oppressed recipients of Western benevolence and feminist rescue, it is important to emphasize the agency of Vietnamese women in initiating international partnerships and to recognize their role as political mentors for women in the West. In other words, global sisterhood as a political strategy was not just imposed by the West but also crafted and promoted by women in the Global South.

Second, international sisterhood does not depend upon a monolithic, universal analysis of gender oppression that transcends time and space. Rather, the political messages that Vietnamese women conveyed through face-to-face meetings and the circulation of print and visual media suggest that a rich and diverse array of discourses could be transmitted and debated between women of varying backgrounds. . . . [This message was a balm to North American organizers and attendees of the IWCs in Canada, whose efforts at unity were plagued by volatile factionalism.] In contrast, as Vivian Rothstein noted following her travels to North Vietnam, what impressed her was the emphasis that the VWU placed on organizing a "majoritarian" movement. This approach focused on building broad political agreements and coalitions.[33] Literally engaged in a struggle for life and death, the women of Vietnam cultivated the widest possible range of allies.

Global sisterhood, then, was not intended to propose a rigid universal theory for understanding women's oppression. Rather, the VWU sought to involve women of varying backgrounds and political beliefs to engage in ideas with one another and to learn from each other's life experiences. Vietnamese women did want women from the West to help them end the war. Yet the women from Southeast Asia believed that they had a reciprocal and perhaps even greater ability to inspire the political imagination of women in the First World. The Indochinese Women's Conferences of 1971 represented a continuation of these efforts to build a global antiwar movement among diverse sisters.

NOTES

1. Inderpal Grewal, *Transnational America: Feminisms, Diasporas, Neoliberalisms* (Durham, N.C.: Duke University Press, 2005); Chandra Mohanty, "Under Western Eyes: Feminist Scholarship and Colonial Discourses," *Feminist Review* 30 (Autumn 1988): 61–88; Leila J. Rupp, *Worlds of Women: The Making of an International Women's Movement* (Princeton: Princeton University Press, 1997); and Wu, "Rethinking Global Sisterhood: Peace Activism and Women's Orientalism," *No Permanent Waves: Recasting Histories of U.S. Feminism*, ed. by Nancy A. Hewitt (New Brunswick, N.J.: Rutgers University Press, 2010), pp. 193–220.

2. Amy Swerdlow, *Women Strike for Peace: Traditional Motherhood and Radical Politics in the 1960s* (Chicago: University of Chicago, 1993), pp. 214–215.

3. Ibid., p. 15; Andrea Estepa, "Taking the White Gloves Off: Women Strike for Peace and 'the Movement,' 1967–73," in Stephanie Gilmore, *Feminist Coalitions: Historical Perspectives on Second-Wave Feminism in the United States* (Urbana: University of Illinois Press, 2008), p. 87.

4. Jill Vickers, "The Intellectual Origins of the Women's Movements in Canada," in *Challenging Times: The Women's Movement in Canada and the United States*, ed. by Constance Backhouse and David H. Flaherty (Montreal: McGill-Queen's University Press, 1992), pp. 53–55; and Candace Loewen, "Making Ourselves Heard: 'Voice of Women' and the Peace Movement in the Early Sixties," in *Framing Our Past: Canadian Women's History in the Twentieth Century*, ed. by Sharon Anne Cook, Lorna R. McLean, and Kate O'Rourke (Montreal: McGill-Queen's University Press, 2001), p. 248. Duckworth: quoted in Judy Rebick, *Ten Thousand Roses: The Making of a Feminist Revolution* (Toronto: Penguin Canada, 2005), p. 3.

5. Quoted in Harriet Hyman Alonso, *Peace as a Women's Issue: A History of the U.S. Movement for World Peace and Women's Rights* (Syracuse, N.Y.: Syracuse University Press, 1993), p. 86. WILPF was officially founded in 1919; the organization evolved from the U.S. Women's Peace Party, which was established in 1915.

6. Estepa, "Taking the White Gloves Off," p. 88.

7. "Paris," *Memo* 6:4 (March 1968): 2;"To Canadian Press Representatives, London," 15 May 1968, Vol. 3, file Hanoi Trip, Voice of Women (VOW) Fonds, MG 28 Series I 218, Library and Archives Canada; Ethel Taylor, "Conference: Paris, April 23–26," *Memo* 6:5 (May–June 1968): 6.

8. Kay MacPherson, "October 9th 1967, Cambridge," Vol. 3, file Hanoi Trip, VOW Fonds; Cora Weiss, "The Face of the Enemy," *Memo* (Fall 1969), pp. 4–7.

9. Swerdlow, *Women Strike for Peace*, p. 222.

10. Mary Hershberger, *Traveling to Vietnam: American Peace Activists and the War* (Syracuse: Syracuse University Press, 1998); Cora Weiss, Interviews with Author, New York City, 7 and 8 April 2006, and 4 May 2006. Also see Swerdlow, *Women Strike for Peace*, and James W. Clinton, "Cora Weiss," in *The Loyal Opposition: Americans in North Vietnam, 1965–1972* (Niwot: University Press of Colorado, 1995).

11. Sandra C. Taylor, *Vietnamese Women at War: Fighting for Ho Chi Minh and the Revolution* (Lawrence: University Press of Kansas, 1999), p. 123; Swerdlow, *Women Strike for Peace*, p. 216.

12. "Madame Nguyen Thi Binh Speaking to American Women," Text of Film, Oct. 1970, p. 1, Series A, 2, Box B, 2, Women Strike for Peace Records, DG 115, Swarthmore College Peace Collection (SCPC), Swarthmore, Penn.

13. *Vietnamese Women*, Vietnam Studies No. 10 (Hanoi: Xunhasaba, 1966) p. 42.

14. Ibid., p. 33.

15. For an analysis of how Women Strike for Peace emphasized a maternalist construction of Vietnamese female identity to foster a common politics based on pacifism, see "Collaborative Efforts to End the War in Viet Nam: The Interactions of Women Strike for Peace, the Vietnamese Women's Union, and the Women's Union of Liberation, 1965–1968," *Peace and Change*, 37, no. 3 (July 2012): 339–365

16. For critiques of the wave metaphor, see Nancy A. Hewitt, ed., *No Permanent Waves: Recasting*

Histories of U.S. Feminism (New Brunswick, N.J.: Rutgers University Press, 2010).

17. *Vietnamese Women*, pp. 3, 307.

18. Agatha Beins examines how women's movement periodicals created political meaning and fostered a sense of community among activists, placing strong emphasis on the representations of Vietnamese women in American women's movement periodicals; Beins, "Free Our Sisters, Free Ourselves! Locating U.S. Feminism through Feminist Publishing" (Ph.D. Dissertation, Rutgers University, 2011); Beins, "Radical Others: Women of Color and Revolutionary Feminism" (unpublished manuscript, 2011).

19. Taylor, *Vietnamese Women at War*.

20. Hershberger, *Traveling to Vietnam*, p. 139.

21. Vivian Rothstein, Telephone Interview with Author, 9 March, 2007 (this paragraph and the next).

22. Charlotte Bunch-Weeks and Frank Joyce, "North Vietnam: A Photo Essay," *Motive* (February 1971): 18, 20.

23. Jan Fenty and Charlotte Bunch-Weeks, "Women and the Anti-War Movement," Box 1, folder 33, Charlotte Bunch Papers, Schlesinger Library, Radcliffe Institute, Harvard University, Cambridge, Mass.

24. Alice Wolfson to "Companeras," n.d., pp. 1–2, Box 1, folder 34, Charlotte Bunch Papers.

25. Hershberger, *Traveling to Vietnam*; and Joyce Blackwell, *No Peace without Freedom: Race and the Women's International League for Peace and Freedom, 1915–1975* (Carbondale: Southern Illinois University Press, 2004).

26. "New President, Board Elected," *Peace and Freedom* 31, no. 7 (July 1971): 1. See also Judy Tzu-Chun Wu, "Journeys for Peace and Liberation: Third World Internationalism and Radical Orientalism during the U.S. War in Viet Nam," *Pacific Historical Review* 76:4 (November 2007): 575–584

27. Frances Beale, "Double Jeopardy: To Be Black and Female," *Sisterhood is Powerful: An Anthology of Writings from the Women's Liberation Movement*, ed. By Robin Morgan (New York: Vintage Books, 1970), pp. 382–396; Benita Roth, *Separate Roads to Feminism: Black, Chicana, and White Feminist Movements in America's Second Wave* (New York: Cambridge University Press, 2003); Cynthia A. Young, *Soul Power: Culture, Radicalism, and the Making of a U.S. Third World Left* (Durham, N.C.: Duke University Press, 2006).

28. Betita Martinez, Telephone Interview with author, 7 Dec. 2006. Also see Lorenza Oropeza, *¡Raza Sí! ¡Guerra No!: Chicano Protest and Patriotism during the Viet Nam War Era* (Berkeley: University of California Press, 2005).

29. Martinez, telephone interview. In the predominantly black-white environment of SNCC, Martinez felt more comfortable using a non-Latino name. In the movement, she was known as "Liz," not Betita. She also chose Sutherland rather than Martinez as her surname, because "in my mother's past there was this Duchess of Sutherland . . . the chief lady in waiting to the queen."

30. "Viet Nam War—Why? Their People . . . Our People . . . ," *El Grito del Norte*, 29 August 1970. Betita Martinez also reported on the treatment of ethnic minorities in Viet Nam, who had the right to bilingual education.

31. Oropeza, *¡Raza Sí! ¡Guerra No!*, p. 6.

32. "Chicanas Meet Indo-Chinese," *El Grito Del Norte*, 5 June 1971, p. K.

33. Rothstein, telephone interview. For more analysis of the IWCs, see Judy Tzu-Chun Wu, *Radicals on the Road: Internationalism, Orientalism, and Feminism During the Vietnam Era* (Ithaca, N.Y.: Cornell University Press, 2013), chs. 8–9.

The Personal Is Political

Many documents—manifestos, handbills, mimeographed newsletters, posters with artwork, meeting minutes—survive, recording the thoughts and actions of groups who identified themselves with the women's liberation or who campaigned for reform. As we urge in our discussion of the abortion wars of recent decades (pp. 658–669), the activism of the 1960s and 1970s is a ripe area for individuals or groups to investigate what happened on your campus and in your town, and to record and preserve materials in concert with librarians, women's centers, and academic programs. Ask your family members, teachers, and friends who came of age in the sixties and seventies what they were reading, debating, and producing in those years! Encourage them to preserve journals, diaries , photographs, programs from concerts and gatherings, and material souvenirs (buttons, hats, t-shirts, etc.).

One good starting point for the broad range of calls-to-action issued in the period are the selected documents we present below. Many others are readily available online. We call your attention to a few "classics":

- "The Redstockings Manifesto," issued in New York City on July 7, 1969, on the Women's Liberation Movement Archives for Action: http://www.redstockings.org/index.php?option=com_content&view=article&id=76&Itemid=59.
- Pat Mainardi, "The Politics of Housework," ca. 1970: a hilarious and powerful critique of many men's learned helplessness, following up on Crystal Eastman's 1920 manifesto, "Now We Can Begin" (pp. 380–382), on the CWLU Herstory website archive: http://www.uic.edu/orgs/cwluherstory/CWLUArchive/polhousework.html.
- Radicalesbians, "The Woman-Identified Woman," 1970, on Documents from the Women's Liberation Movement, Duke University Library: http://library.duke.edu/rubenstein/scriptorium/wlm/womid/.

Carol Hanisch, *A Critique of the Miss America Protest, 1968*

Women of Betty Friedan's and Phyllis Schlafly's generation were divided as to whether they saw domesticity as sufficient to their personal fulfillment or if there truly was "a problem that had no name," and, if so, what it involved. Many young women, who had joined in the protest movements of the 1960s, had no such doubts. The group who gathered in Atlantic City in 1968 to protest the Miss America Pageant instantly caught the eye of the national and world media. Contrary to myth, no bras were burned. Instead, demonstrators hurled what they called "items of female torture" into a large "Freedom Trash Can," including false

Reprinted by permission of the author, who has condensed the original document—"A Critique of the Miss America Protest" © 1968—especially for *Women's America*. The original document is reproduced online, accompanied by a 2003 radio interview with Hanisch about the protest: www.carolhanisch.org/CHwritings/MissACritique.html.

eyelashes, hair curlers, girdles, high-heel shoes, Toni home permanents (a sponsor of the pageant), *Playboy* and *Good Housekeeping* magazines, and even some bras. The protesters called for the end of beauty competitions, the pressure to conform to false beauty standards and buy related products, and the elevation of appearance over more important human qualities.

Were the concerns of the 1968 protesters valid? Are they relevant to today's women? In what sense are they among the body issues Brumberg introduces in "Fasting Girls" (pp. 420–428)? Why does Hanisch consider some of the actions employed by her sister protesters counterproductive? What was the message of the protest that she believed they failed to get across?

The protest of the Miss America Pageant in Atlantic City told the nation that a new feminist movement is afoot in the land.

Due to the tremendous coverage in the mass media, millions of Americans now know there is a Women's Liberation Movement. The action brought many new members into our group and many requests from women outside the city for literature and information. A recurrent theme was, "I've been waiting so long for something like this."

But no action taken in the Women's Liberation struggle will be all good or all bad. We must analyze each step to see what was effective, what was not, and what was downright destructive.

At this point in our struggle, our actions should be aimed primarily at doing two interrelated things: (1) awakening the latent consciousness of women about our own oppression, and (2) building sisterhood. With these in mind, let us examine the Miss America protest.

The idea for the protest came out of the method used first in New York Radical Women of analyzing women's oppression by analyzing our own experiences, called consciousness-raising. One night at a meeting we were watching *Schmearguntz*, a feminist movie which contains flashes of the Miss America Pageant. I found myself remembering the powerful feelings the pageant had evoked in me as a child, an adolescent, and a college student. When I proposed the action to our group, we decided to go around the room with each woman telling how she felt about the pageant. We discovered that many of us who had always put down the contest still watched it. Others had consciously identified with it.

From our communal thinking came the concrete plans for the action. The original planning group agreed that the main point in the demonstration would be that all women are hurt by beauty competition—Miss America as well as ourselves. We opposed the pageant in our own self-interest, e.g., the self-interest of all women.

Yet one of the biggest mistakes of the whole pageant was our anti-womanism. A spirit of every woman "doing her own thing" began to emerge as women not in the original meetings came to the planning meetings. Some just went ahead and did what they wanted to do, even though it was something we had decided against. Because of this egotistic individualism, a definite strain of anti-womanism was presented to the public to the detriment of the action.

Posters that read "Up against the Wall, Miss America," "Miss America Sells It," and "Miss America Is a Big Falsie" hardly raised any woman's consciousness and really harmed the cause of sisterhood. Miss America and all beautiful women came off as our enemy instead of as our sisters who suffer with us.

A more complex situation developed around the decision of a few women to use an "underground" disruptive tactic. The group approved this activity only after its adherents said they would do it anyway as an individual action. We learned there is no such thing as "individual action" in a movement. There is, at this time, no real need to do "underground" actions anyway. We need to reach as many women as possible as quickly as possible with a clear message that has the power of our person behind it. Women need to see other women standing up together and saying these things. That's why draping a women's liberation banner over the balcony and yelling our message was much clearer than spraying a smelly chemical in the audience. The problem of how to enforce group decisions is one we haven't solved.

Another way we came off as anti-woman was our lack of clarity. We didn't say clearly enough that we women are all *forced* to play the Miss America role—not by beautiful women but by men who we have to act that way for, and by a system that has so well institutionalized male supremacy for its own ends. This was not very clear in our guerrilla theater. Women chained to a replica, red, white, and blue bathing-suited Miss America could have been misinterpreted as our blaming beautiful women. Also, crowning a live sheep Miss America sort of said that beautiful women *are* sheep. However, the action did say to some that women are *viewed as* auction-block, docile animals. The grandmother of one of the participants really began to understand the action when she was told about the sheep, and she ended up joining the protest.

There is as great a need for clarity in our language as there is in our actions. The leaflet that was distributed as a press release and flyer was too long, too wordy, too complex, too hippy-yippee-campy. Instead of an "in" phrase like "Racism with Roses," we could have just called the pageant "racist" and everybody would have understood our opposition on that point.

We should avoid the temptation to say everything there is to say about what is wrong with the world and thereby say nothing that a new person can really dig into and understand. Women's liberation itself is revolutionary dynamite. When other issues are interjected, we should clearly relate them to our oppression as women.

We tried to carry the democratic means we used in planning the action into the actual doing of it. We didn't want leaders or spokesmen. It makes the movement not only *seem* stronger and larger if everyone is a leader, but it actually *is* stronger if not dependent on a few. And, of course, many voices are more powerful than one. We must learn how to fight against the media's desire to make leaders— and some women's desire to appoint themselves spokesmen.

The Miss America protest was a zap action, which means using our presence as a group to make women's oppression into a social issue. In such actions we speak to men as a group as well as to women. It is a rare opportunity to talk to men in a situation where they can't talk back. (Men must learn to listen.) Our power of solidarity, not our individual intellectual exchanges will change men.

The reaction of many of the women we talked to about the protest was, "But I'm not oppressed" or "I don't care about Miss America." If more than half the television viewers in the country watch the pageant, somebody cares! While much of the Left was putting us down for attacking something so "silly and unimportant" or "reformist," the Right saw us as a threat and yelled such things as "Go back to Russia" and "Mothers of Mao" at the picket line. Ironically enough, what the Left/Underground press seemed to like best about our action was what was really our worst mistake—our anti-woman signs.

Surprisingly and fortunately, some of the mass media ignored our mistakes and concentrated on our best points. To quote the *Daily News*, "Some women who think the whole idea of such contests is degrading to femininity, took their case to the people. . . . During boardwalk protest, gals say they're not anti-beauty, just anti-beauty contest." Shana Alexander wrote in a *Life* magazine editorial that she "wished they'd gone farther."

The best slogan for the action came up afterward, when Ros Baxandall blurted out on the David Susskind television show that "Every day in a woman's life is a walking Miss America Contest!" But we shouldn't wait for the perfect slogan; we should go ahead to the best of our understanding.

Jennie V. Chávez, Women of the Mexican American Movement, 1972

Jennie Chávez, like thousands of young women of color, joined liberation movements in the 1960s and 1970s. In this account of her experience in the Chicano movement, Chávez describes the resistance she faced when, recognizing the double oppression of Mexican American women, she organized "Las Chicanas."

Excerpted from "Women of the Mexican American Movement" by Jennie V. Chávez, in *Chicana Feminist Thought: The Basic Historical Writings,* ed. Alma M. Garcia (New York: Routledge, 1998), pp. 36–39. Copyright © 1972 Conde Nast Publications. All rights reserved. Originally published in *Mademoiselle*, April 1972. Reprinted by permission.

What insights does she have into power relationships between Mexican Americans and Anglos as well as between men and women within her own ethnic group? Note her disdain for the consumer goods that signal middle-class status. What evidence is there to suggest that Chávez and her Chicana generation had been affected by the sexual revolution of the 1960s? How did males in the movement respond to women asserting themselves? To what does Chávez attribute their machismo? Note the links between Chávez's La Familia and Vicki Ruiz's insights into the family oligarchy experienced by teenagers in the Southwest earlier in the century (pp. 428–435).

As one of the first members of the United Mexican American Students [UMAS] when it got started in 1969 on the UNM [University of New Mexico] campus, I was given special attention, being fairly attractive and flirtatious. But as soon as I started expounding my own ideas the men who ran the organization would either ignore my statement or make a wisecrack about it and continue their own discussion. This continued for two years until I finally broke away because of being unable to handle the situation. I turned to student government. There I was considered a radical racist Mexican militant, yet with the Chicano radicals I was considered a sellout. I was caught in the middle, wanting to help but with neither side allowing me.

The summer of 1970, after the Cambodia crisis, I traveled extensively, "getting my head together," [and formed] Las Chicanas the following December. [The result was that I] caught more shit than I knew existed from both males and females in the movement. Some felt I was dividing the existing UMAS; some were simply afraid of displeasing the men. Some felt that I was wrong and my ideas were "white," and still others felt that their contribution to La Causa or El Movimiento was in giving the men moral support from the kitchen. It took two months of heartbreak on both sides for the organization to be recognized as valid. Now, however, because a few women were willing to stand strong against some of the macho men who ridiculed them, called them white and avoided them socially, the organization has become one of the strongest and best-known in the state.

It has taken what I consider a long time for [Chicanas] to realize and to speak out about the double oppression of the Mexican-American woman. Chicanas traditionally, have been tortilla-makers, baby-producers, to be touched but not heard. In order to someday obtain those middle-class goods (which in my eyes oppress more people than they liberate from "drudgery")

our women have not only been working at slave jobs for the white society as housemaids, hotel maids and laundry workers, but have tended also to the wants of a husband and many children—many children because contraceptives have been contrary to the ethnic idea of La Familia (with all its socio-political economic implications).

As the social revolution for all people's freedoms has progressed, so Chicanas have caught the essence of freedom in the air. The change occurred slowly. Mexican-American women have been reluctant to speak up, afraid that they might show up the men in front of the white man—afraid that they may think our men not men. Now, however, the Chicana is becoming as well-educated and as aware of oppression, if not more so, as the Mexican-American male.

The women are changing their puritanical mode of dress, entering the professions of law, business, medicine and engineering. They are no longer afraid to show their intellect, their capabilities and their potential. More and more they oppose the Catholic Church, to which a large majority of our ethnic group belongs, challenging its sexual taboos as well as the idea that all Catholic mothers must be baby-producing factories, and that contraceptives are a sin.

Out of the workshop on "Sex and La Chicana" at the first National Mujeres Por la Raza conference in Houston, Texas, [in 1971] came the following resolutions: (1) that Chicanas should develop a more healthy attitude toward sex and get rid of the misconceptions about its "evil," thus allowing ourselves to be as aggressive as men; (2) that we object to the use of sex as a means of exploiting women and for commercial purposes; (3) that no religious institution should have the authority to sanction what is moral or immoral between a man and a woman.

As the new breed of Mexican-American women, we have been, and probably will continue to be, ridiculed by our men for attempting the acrobatics of equality. We may well be ostracized by La Familia for being vendidos, sell-outs to the "white ideas" of late marriage, postponing or not wanting children and desiring a vocation other than tortilla-rolling, but I believe that this new breed of bronze womanhood, as all women today, will be a vanguard for world change.

Naturally, there are liberated Chicanos who respect and treat women as equals, but they are so few that at this point I still have to generalize. Mexican-American men, as other men of oppressed groups, have been very reluctant to give up their machismo [exaggerated assertion of masculinity] because it has been a last retention of power in a society which dehumanizes and mechanizes them. But now they are comprehending the meaning of carnalismo (brotherhood) in the feminine gender as well . . . a new revolution within a revolution has begun.

Editorial Staff of Rodan, *Asian Women as Leaders*, 1971

L ike their Chicana sisters, Asian American women fought against old stereotypes and encountered new ones when they tried to exercise leadership in the Asian American movement. They too found that male allies were prone to male chauvinism and that as women they had to deal with racism, sexism, and imperialism simultaneously.

On the basis of this document compare the stereotypes that exist about women of both ethnic groups in the larger culture. What vision of the future and what strategies do the anonymous authors advocate?

American society is broken up into different levels based on economic income, education, politics, color, and sex. Each level has a prescribed set of rules for action and interplay—roles that are enforced by the levels above. At the bottom of these varying gradations are women of color. Third World women face domination by both racism and sexism (discrimination based on sex). Both racism and sexism are means by which American society controls and oppresses everyone. Everyone is forced to conform to the values and roles established by the dominant group in order to "succeed." For the Asian movement to progress, it must have a clear understanding of sexism, racism, and imperialism; and deal with them simultaneously.

For Asian women in general, the stereotypes or roles have been of two major kinds: either docile, submissive Oriental dolls who will cater to the whims of any man; or the Suzie Wong, sexpot, exotic bitch-body. Between these two are the efficient secretary, sexy stewardess, the good housekeeper and domestic, the girl any guy would like to marry.

Women in the Asian movement find that these stereotypes are still hovering over their heads. Not only these but new stereotypes, too: i.e., Asian men have tried to define for "their women" what it means to be "heavy." Men in the Asian movement also find themselves tied down to stereotypes. Perhaps they may feel that to be a MAN one must have authority and responsibility. In the same light, they will frown on women who take on a lot of responsibility (and the authority that goes along with it), labelling them as "unfeminine." Women then tend to fear this loss of "femininity" and so they do the clerical work and the cleaning up, activities for which intellect is not essential or expected. Women may also fulfill these jobs because they do them best: And why do they do them the best? Because women are never encouraged to do anything else; women's potential abilities as a leader are left untapped and undeveloped. She loses her confidence in being able to handle such responsibility.

The sisters who have achieved a position of authority in the movement are a minority and are still trapped by the stereotypes that society has created. It is a struggle for women to attain the top leadership positions. Women who "make it" into such positions have had to reject the stereotypes already imposed upon them. But because the new definition of "the Asian woman" has not yet evolved, women find themselves in a "limbo." Some find themselves being labelled as Bitches—women who speak out loudly and strongly; who are authoritarian, who boss people around, and command some form of respect. Some must resort to being overly diligent and efficient to prove themselves as worthy of the same leadership positions as the men. Others gain respect by appearing to accomplish work in a multitude of projects but actually only complete a few tasks. And still others attain their leadership positions as token gestures. Some women can gain respect only by putting up with put-downs on other women, i.e., "you're not one of those bird-brained little girls," or "You're as strong as a man!"

Once women do get into leadership positions, they find that their ideas are usurped by the men, who then take credit for the idea as being their own. Women are often heard but not listened to. Many times, the woman must play her old role in order to get things done: "Oh, please, can you help me carry this. It's much too heavy for little old me. . . . "

How can these problems be solved? People must recognize that women are half of the working force in the movement against oppression, exploitation, and imperialism. They are half of the working force in creating the new revolutionary lifestyle. Men and women in the movement must therefore begin to live the ideals and goals they are working for. To do this, they must not let chauvinist acts slide by. People cannot work together effectively if there are hidden tensions or if people let little annoyances build up inside themselves. They must deal with racism or imperialism. They must be able to develop as human beings, not subject to categorizations and stereotypes. Developing as people confident in themselves, in their ideas, they will not be afraid of criticism; they will see the need for criticism, and self-criticism, in order to move forward. The struggle is not men against women nor women against men, but it is a united front striving for a new society, a new way of life.

> If I go forward,
> Follow me.
> Push me if I fall behind.
> If I betray you,
> If they take me,
> Avenge me then in kind.

Combahee River Collective, *The Combahee River Collective Statement,* 1977

The Combahee River Collective, a black feminist group founded in Boston in 1974, took its name from a guerrilla action planned and led by Harriet Tubman during the Civil War that freed more than 750 South Carolina slaves. The group, which consisted of battle-scarred veterans of the civil rights, New Left, and early women's movements, had done some hard thinking before writing this statement. In it, they stated what they believed to be the limitations of their white feminist sisters as well as their own problems in organizing black feminists.

What were the Collective's specific criticisms of other feminists—radical, liberal, as well as lesbian separatists? Why did they think that black feminism was (and is) so threatening to the black community, especially to black males who identified with black nationalism? What do you regard as their most important insights?

Excerpted from The Combahee River Collective Statement in *Home Girls: A Black Feminist Anthology,* ed. Barbara Smith (Latham, N. Y.: Kitchen Table: Women of Color Press, 1983), pp. 272–82. The original document was dated April 1977. Reprinted by permission of Barbara Smith.

We are a collective of Black feminists who have been meeting together since 1974. During that time we have been involved in the process of defining and clarifying our politics, while at the same time doing political work within our own group and in coalition with other progressive organizations and movements. The most general statement of our politics at the present time would be that we are actively committed to struggling against racial, sexual, heterosexual, and class oppression, and see as our particular task the development of integrated analysis and practice based upon the fact that the major systems of oppression are interlocking. The synthesis of these oppressions creates the conditions of our lives. As Black women we see Black feminism as the logical political movement to combat the manifold and simultaneous oppressions that all women of color face. . . .

1. THE GENESIS OF CONTEMPORARY BLACK FEMINISM

Before looking at the recent development of Black feminism, we would like to affirm that we find our origins in the historical reality of Afro-American women's continuous life-and-death struggle for survival and liberation. Black women's extremely negative relationship to the American political system (a system of white male rule) has always been determined by our membership in two oppressed racial and sexual castes. As Angela Davis points out in "Reflections on the Black Woman's Role in the Community of Slaves," Black women have always embodied, if only in their physical manifestation, an adversary stance to white male rule and have actively resisted its inroads upon them and their communities in both dramatic and subtle ways. There have always been Black women activists—some known, like Sojourner Truth, Harriet Tubman, Frances E. W. Harper, Ida B. Wells Barnett, and Mary Church Terrell, and thousands upon thousands unknown—who have had a shared awareness of how their sexual identity combined with their racial identity to make their whole life situation and the focus of their political struggles unique. Contemporary Black feminism is the outgrowth of countless generations of personal sacrifice, militancy, and work by our mothers and sisters.

A Black feminist presence has evolved most obviously in connection with the second wave of the American women's movement beginning in the late 1960s. Black, other Third World, and working women have been involved in the feminist movement from its start, but both outside reactionary forces and racism and elitism within the movement itself have served to obscure our participation. In 1973, Black feminists, primarily located in New York, felt the necessity of forming a separate Black feminist group. This became the National Black Feminist Organization (NBFO).

Black feminist politics also have an obvious connection to movements for Black liberation, particularly those of the 1960s and 1970s. Many of us were active in those movements (Civil Rights, Black nationalism, the Black Panthers), and all of our lives were greatly affected and changed by their ideologies, their goals, and the tactics used to achieve their goals. It was our experience and disillusionment within these liberation movements, as well as experience on the periphery of the white male left, that led to the need to develop a politics that was anti-racist, unlike those of white women, and anti-sexist, unlike those of Black and white men.

There is also undeniably a personal genesis for Black feminism, that is, the political realization that comes from the seemingly personal experiences of individual Black women's lives. Black feminists and many more Black women who do not define themselves as feminists have all experienced sexual oppression as a constant factor in our day-to-day existence. As children we realized that we were different from boys and that we were treated differently. For example, we were told in the same breath to be quiet both for the sake of being "ladylike" and to make us less objectionable in the eyes of white people. As we grew older we became aware of the threat of physical and sexual abuse by men. However, we had no way of conceptualizing what was so apparent to us, what we *knew* was really happening.

Black feminists often talk about their feelings of craziness before becoming conscious of the concepts of sexual politics, patriarchal rule, and most importantly, feminism, the political analysis and practice that we women use to struggle against our oppression. The fact that racial politics and indeed racism are pervasive factors in our lives did not allow us, and still does not allow most Black women, to look more deeply into our own experiences and, from that sharing and growing consciousness, to build a politics that will change our lives and inevitably end our oppression. Our development must also be tied to the contemporary economic and political position of Black people. The post–World War II generation of Black youth was the first to be able to minimally partake of certain educational and employment options, previously closed completely to Black people. Although our economic position is still at the very bottom of the American capitalistic economy, a handful of us have been able to gain certain tools as a result of tokenism in education and employment which potentially enable us to more effectively fight our oppression.

2. WHAT WE BELIEVE

Above all else, our politics initially sprang from the shared belief that Black women are inherently valuable, that our liberation is a necessity not as an adjunct to somebody else's but because of our need as human persons for autonomy. This may seem so obvious as to sound simplistic, but it is apparent that no other ostensibly progressive movement has ever considered our specific oppression as a priority or worked seriously for the ending of that oppression. Merely naming the pejorative stereotypes attributed to Black women (e.g., mammy, matriarch, Sapphire, whore, bulldagger), let alone cataloguing the cruel, often murderous, treatment we receive, indicates how little value has been placed upon our lives during four centuries of bondage in the Western hemisphere. We realize that the only people who care enough about us to work consistently for our liberation are us. Our politics evolve from a healthy love for ourselves, our sisters, and our community, which allows us to continue our struggle and work.

This focusing upon our own oppression is embodied in the concept of identity politics. . . . We reject pedestals, queenhood, and walking ten paces behind. To be recognized as human, levelly human, is enough.

We believe that sexual politics under patriarchy is as pervasive in Black women's lives as are the politics of class and race. We also often find it difficult to separate race from class from sex oppression because in our lives they are most often experienced simultaneously. We know that there is such a thing as racial-sexual oppression which is neither solely racial nor solely sexual, e.g., the history of rape of Black women by white men as a weapon of political repression.

Although we are feminists and Lesbians, we feel solidarity with progressive Black men and do not advocate the fractionalization that white women who are separatists demand. Our situation as Black people necessitates that we have solidarity around the fact of race, which white women of course do not need to have with white men, unless it is their negative solidarity as racial oppressors. We struggle together with Black men against racism, while we also struggle with Black men about sexism.

We realize that the liberation of all oppressed peoples necessitates the destruction of the political-economic systems of capitalism and imperialism as well as patriarchy. We are socialists because we believe that work must be organized for the collective benefit of those who do the work and create the products, and not for the profit of the bosses. . . .

A political contribution which we feel we have already made is the expansion of the feminist principle that the personal is political. In our consciousness-raising sessions, for example, we have in many ways gone beyond white women's revelations because we are dealing with the implications of race and class as well as sex. Even our Black women's style of talking/testifying in Black language about what we have experienced has a resonance that is both cultural and political. We have spent a great deal of energy delving into the cultural and experiential nature of our oppression out of necessity because none of these matters has ever been looked at before. . . . An example of this kind of revelation/conceptualization occurred at a meeting as we discussed the ways in which our early intellectual interests had been attacked by our peers, particularly Black males. We discovered that all of us, because we were "smart" had also been considered "ugly," i.e., "smart-ugly." "Smart-ugly" crystallized the way in which most of us had been forced to develop our intellects at great cost to our "social" lives. The sanctions in the Black and white communities against Black women thinkers is comparatively much higher than for white women, particularly ones from the educated middle and upper classes.

As we have already stated, we reject the stance of Lesbian separatism because it is not a viable political analysis or strategy for us. It leaves out far too much and far too many people, particularly Black men, women, and children. We have a great deal of criticism and loathing for what men have been socialized to be in this society: what they support, how they act, and how they oppress. But we do not have the misguided notion that it is their maleness, per se—i.e., their biological maleness—that makes them what they are. As Black women we find any type of biological determinism a particularly dangerous and reactionary basis upon which to build a politic. We must also question whether Lesbian separatism is an adequate and progressive political analysis and strategy, even for those who practice it, since it so completely denies any but the sexual sources of women's oppression, negating the facts of class and race.

3. PROBLEMS IN ORGANIZING BLACK FEMINISTS

During our years together as a Black feminist collective, we have experienced success and defeat, joy and pain, victory and failure. We have found that it is very difficult to organize around Black feminist issues, difficult even to announce in certain contexts that we *are* Black feminists. We have tried to think about the reasons for our difficulties, particularly since the white women's movement continues to be strong and to grow in many directions. In this section we will discuss some of the general reasons for the organizing problems we face and also talk specifically about the stages in organizing our own collective.

The major source of difficulty in our political work is that we are not just trying to fight oppression on one front, or even two, but instead to address a whole range of oppressions. We do not have racial, sexual, heterosexual, or class privilege to rely upon, nor do we have even the minimal access to resources and power that groups who possess any one of these types of privilege have.

The psychological toll of being a Black woman and the difficulties this presents in reaching political consciousness and doing political work can never be underestimated. There is very low value placed upon Black women's psyches in this society, which is both racist and sexist. . . . If Black women were free, it would mean that everyone else would have to be free, since our freedom would necessitate the destruction of all the systems of oppression.

Feminism is, nevertheless, very threatening to the majority of Black people because it calls into question some of the most basic assumptions about our existence, i.e., that sex should be a determinant of power relationships. Here is the way male and female roles were defined in a Black nationalist pamphlet from the early 1970s:

> . . . The man is the head of the house. He is the leader of the house/nation because his knowledge of the world is broader, his awareness is greater, his understanding is fuller and his application of this information is wiser. . . . Women cannot do the same things as men—they are made by nature to function differently. Equality of men and women is something that cannot happen even in the abstract world.[1] . . .

The material conditions of most Black women would hardly lead them to upset both economic and sexual arrangements that seem to represent some stability in their lives. Many Black women have a good understanding of both sexism and racism, but because of the everyday constrictions of their lives, cannot risk struggling against them both.

The reaction of Black men to feminism has been notoriously negative. They are, of course, even more threatened than Black women by the possibility that Black feminists might organize around our own needs. They realize that they might not only lose valuable and hardworking allies in their struggles but that they might also be forced to change their habitually sexist ways of interacting with and oppressing Black women. Accusations that Black feminism divides the Black struggle are powerful deterrents to the growth of an autonomous Black women's movement. . . .

4. BLACK FEMINIST ISSUES AND PROJECTS

During our time together we have identified and worked on many issues of particular relevance to Black women. The inclusiveness of our politics makes us concerned with any situation that impinges upon the lives of women, Third World, and working people. We are of course particularly committed to working on those struggles in which race, sex, and class are simultaneous factors in oppression. We might, for example, become involved in workplace organizing at a factory that employs Third World women or picket a hospital that is cutting back on already inadequate health care to a Third World community, or set up a rape crisis center in a Black neighborhood. Organizing around welfare and daycare concerns might also be a focus. The work to be done and the countless issues that this work represents merely reflect the pervasiveness of our oppression.

Issues and projects that collective members have actually worked on are sterilization abuse, abortion rights, battered women, rape, and health care. We have also done many workshops and educationals on Black feminism on college campuses, at women's conferences, and most recently for high school women.

One issue that is of major concern to us and that we have begun to publicly address is racism in the white women's movement. As Black feminists we are made constantly and painfully aware of how little effort white women have made to understand and combat their racism, which requires among other things that they have a more than superficial comprehension of race, color, and Black history and culture. Eliminating racism in the white women's movement is by definition work for white women to do, but we will continue to speak to and demand accountability on this issue.

In the practice of our politics we do not believe that the end always justifies the means.

Many reactionary and destructive acts have been done in the name of achieving "correct" political goals. As feminists we do not want to mess over people in the name of politics. We believe in collective process and a nonhierarchical distribution of power within our own group and in our vision of a revolutionary society. We are committed to a continual examination of our politics as they develop through criticism and self-criticism as an essential aspect of our practice. . . .

As Black feminists and Lesbians we know that we have a very definite revolutionary task to perform and we are ready for the lifetime of work and struggle before us.

NOTE

1. Mumininas of Committee for Unified Newark, Mwanamke Mwananchi (The Nationalist Woman), Newark, NJ, 1971, pp. 4–5.

Gender Equality and the Law

Hoyt v. Florida, 1961; Taylor v. Louisiana, 1975

S ome members of the founding generation had believed that service on juries is a more significant aspect of citizenship than voting; voting, after all, is complete in a moment, while service on juries requires extended periods of time, debate, and deliberation among the jurors, and ultimately the exercise of judgment, which can result in important consequences—including the death sentence—for an accused fellow citizen. The Constitution promises an "impartial" jury drawn from "the district wherein the crime shall have been committed." The conditions of impartiality are not spelled out; the Constitution promises neither "a jury of one's peers," nor one drawn from a "cross-section" of the community. It is tradition that has linked the concept of the jury with "peers," neighbors, and the community in which the crime is committed and from which the jury is chosen.

When women achieved the vote in Wyoming in 1869, it seemed to follow that they could hold office and serve on juries but, after only a few years, the objection of male voters and officeholders was so severe that the law was changed to exclude them.

In some states, the achievement of jury service followed painlessly on the heels of suffrage. In Iowa, Michigan, Nevada, and Pennsylvania, where statutes defined competent jurors as "all qualified electors . . . of good moral character, sound judgment, and in full possession of the senses of hearing and seeing, and who can speak, write and read the English language," the admission of women to the electorate automatically defined them as competent jurors. When these interpretations were tested in state courts, judges usually upheld them. Not all state courts, however, thought it was obvious that "electors" could be properly construed to mean women as well as men. In 1925 the Illinois Supreme Court ruled that because only men had been voters in 1874 when the jury statute had been passed, the terms "legal voters" and "electors" referred only to male persons. Not until 1939 did the Illinois state legislature permit women to serve on juries.

In most states, new statutes were required. By 1923, 18 states and the territory of Alaska had arranged for women to serve on juries. But then the momentum ran out; subsequently the issue had to be debated afresh in each state. A few states continued to exclude women completely, but most developed some form of "voluntary" jury service, in which women could be called to serve but could easily decline. In Florida, no women at all served on juries until 1949, when the legislature passed a law providing that women who wished to be eligible could go to their county courthouses and register their willingness to have their names placed in the *venire*, the randomly selected pool from which jurors are selected.

When Gwendolyn Hoyt came to trial in Tampa in 1957, charged with manslaughter for killing her husband, only 218 women of the more than 46,000 women voters in Hillsborough County had registered to serve; the jury commissioner placed only 10 of those women's names in a pool of 10,000 names. It was no surprise that she was tried—and found guilty—by an all-male jury. It took the six-man jury only 25 minutes to convict Hoyt of second-degree murder; on January 20, 1958, she was sentenced to imprisonment at hard labor for 30 years.

Hoyt appealed, first to the Florida Supreme Court, and then to the U.S. Supreme Court, which heard the case in 1961. Hoyt claimed temporary insanity, brought on by her suspicions of her husband's infidelity, his rejection of her offer of reconciliation, and her own vulnerability to epilepsy. She believed that women would understand her distress better than would men. But with so few women's names in the large jury pool, women had virtually no chance of being chosen.

Hoyt and her lawyers did *not* claim that a fair jury was required to have women as members. Instead, they claimed that a fair jury would have been drawn at random from a list of names from which women had not been excluded. Hoyt believed that in order to enjoy the *right* to a trial by a jury of her peers, other women would have to be *obliged* to serve on juries.

HOYT V. FLORIDA, 1961

Mr. Justice John Marshall Harlan:

At the core of appellant's argument is the claim that the nature of the crime of which she was convicted peculiarly demanded the inclusion of persons of her own sex on the jury. She was charged with killing her husband . . . in the context of a marital upheaval involving, among other things, the suspected infidelity of appellant's husband, and culminating in the husband's final rejection of his wife's efforts at reconciliation. It is claimed, in substance, that women jurors would have been more understanding or compassionate than men in assessing the quality of appellant's act and her defense of "temporary insanity." No claim is made that the jury as constituted was otherwise afflicted by any elements of supposed unfairness.

. . . [T]he right to an impartially selected jury assured by the Fourteenth Amendment . . . does not entitle one accused of crime to a jury tailored to the circumstances of the particular case, whether relating to the sex or other condition of the defendant, or to the nature of the charges to be tried. It requires only that the jury be indiscriminately drawn from among those eligible in the community for jury service, untrammelled by any arbitrary and systematic exclusions. . . . The result of this appeal must therefore depend on whether such an exclusion of women from jury service has been shown.

. . . Florida's [law] does not purport to exclude women from state jury service. Rather, the statute "gives to women the privilege to serve but does not impose service as a duty." It accords women an absolute exemption from jury service unless they expressly waive that privilege. . . . [W]e [cannot] . . . conclude that Florida's statute is . . . infected with unconstitutionality. Despite the enlightened emancipation of women from the restrictions and protections of bygone years, and their entry into many parts of community life formerly considered to be reserved to men, woman is still regarded as the center of home and family life. We cannot say that it is constitutionally impermissible for a State, acting in pursuit of the general welfare, to conclude that a woman should be relieved from the civil duty of jury service unless she herself determines that such service is consistent with her own special responsibilities.

II

. . . Finding no substantial evidence whatever in this record that Florida has arbitrarily undertaken to exclude women from jury service . . . we must sustain the judgment of the Supreme Court of Florida.

Justices Warren, Black, and Douglas, concurring:

We cannot say from this record that Florida is not making a good faith effort to have women perform jury duty without discrimination on the ground of sex. Hence we concur in the result, for reasons set forth in Part II of the Court's opinion.

Hoyt v. Florida, 368 U.S. 57 (1961).

Women line up to register for jury duty at the Hall of Records, New York City, 1937.
When New York State passed a voluntary jury service law for women in 1937, hundreds of women lined up to register. The New York World Telegram *treated the story as cute: "Women jurors registering in the Hall of Records, and do they like it!" The caption—"They augur no good for love slayers"—predicted that women jurors would not join in the common practice of light sentences for men who had wounded or killed their wives' lovers. Dorothy Kenyon, a feminist attorney who had fought for 15 years for mandatory jury service, welcomed the new statute as a first step: "This gives a new lease of life to the jury system." In the 1960s, Kenyon and Pauli Murray would lead the efforts of the American Civil Liberties Union to establish equitable jury service throughout the nation. (Courtesy of the Library of Congress.)*

Note that these three justices are careful to uphold the decision of the lower court only "for reasons set forth in Part II of the Court's opinion." What is the difference between the argument in part I and part II? Did granting women the power to avoid jury duty hurt Hoyt's right to a fair trial? If men and women are equal, does a virtually all-male jury *pool* undermine equality? If men and women are equal, does an all-male *jury* undermine equality? Why do you think Justices Warren, Black, and Douglas wrote a separate concurring opinion? To what extent was the Court's opinion based on arguments from equality? On arguments from difference?

When Ruth Bader Ginsburg began to work on the ACLU's Women's Rights Project (see *Frontiero v. Richardson*, pp. 752–753), she was committed to persuading the Supreme Court to reverse its decisions on several major cases that had sustained sex discrimination; one of those cases was *Hoyt*. Not until 1975, in a case arising in Louisiana, a state in which women were still required to file a written declaration of their desire to be subject to jury service, was *Hoyt* reversed by the Supreme Court. Billy Taylor, convicted of rape and kidnapping, successfully appealed his conviction on the grounds that women had been systematically excluded from the jury pool. His lawyers drew an analogy between his experience and the Court's decision three years before that a white man was entitled to have a jury from which blacks had not been systematically barred. The majority opinion upheld Taylor's claim. It made extensive use of an opinion written by Justice William O. Douglas in 1946, relating to jury selection practices in federal courts. What did Douglas mean when he said that "two sexes are not fungible"? Do you agree?

TAYLOR V. LOUISIANA, 1975

MR. JUSTICE BYRON R. WHITE:

The Louisiana jury-selection system does not disqualify women from jury service, but in operation its conceded systematic impact is that only a few women, grossly disproportionate to the number of eligible women in the community, are called for jury service. In this case, no women were on the venire from which the petit jury was drawn. . . .

The State first insists that Taylor, a male, has no standing to object to the exclusion of women from his jury. . . . Taylor was not a member of the excluded class; but there is no rule that claims such as Taylor presents may be made only by those defendants who are members of the group excluded from jury service. In [1972] . . . a white man [successfully] challenged his conviction on the ground that Negroes had been systematically excluded from jury service. . . .

We are . . . persuaded that the fair-cross-section requirement is violated by the systematic exclusion of women, who in the judicial district involved here amounted to 53 percent of the citizens eligible for jury service. . . . This very matter was debated in *Ballard v. U.S.* [1946]. . . . The . . . view that an all-male panel drawn from various groups in the community would be as truly representative as if women were included, was firmly rejected:

> . . . who would claim that a jury was truly representative of the community if all men were intentionally and systematically excluded from the panel? The truth is that the two sexes are not fungible; a community made up exclusively of one is different from a community composed of both; the subtle interplay of influence one on the other is among the imponderables. . . . The exclusion of one may indeed make the jury less representative of the community than would be true if an economic or racial group were excluded. [Justice William O. Douglas, 1946]

. . . It is untenable to suggest these days that it would be a special hardship for each and every woman to perform jury service . . . it may be burdensome to sort out those who should be exempted from those who should serve. But that task is performed in the case of men, and the administrative convenience in dealing with women as a class is insufficient justification for diluting the quality of community judgment represented by the jury in criminal trials.

Taylor v. Louisiana, 419 U.S. 522 (1975).

The decision in *Taylor* addressed only the problem of who is included in the panels from whom jurors are chosen. Not until 1994 did the Supreme Court rule that the Fourteenth Amendment's equal protection clause prohibits the use of peremptory jury challenges on the basis of gender. Overturning a paternity suit in which a woman challenged virtually all the men in the jury pool, leaving an all-female jury to decide on her claims for child support, the majority held "that gender, like race, is an unconstitutional proxy for juror competence and impartiality."[*]

[*]J.E.B. v. Alabama, 511 U.S. 127 (1994). For a full treatment of the history of women and jury service, see Linda K. Kerber, *No Constitutional Right to Be Ladies: Women and the Obligations of Citizenship* (New York: Hill & Wang, 1998), ch. 4.

Civil Rights Act, Title VII, 1964

The Civil Rights Act of 1964 was a comprehensive law of enormous significance. It was a complex statute, 28-printed pages long and divided into 11 major sections, or titles. Title I dealt with voting rights; Title III with the desegregation of public facilities; Title V established a Commission on Civil Rights. Title VII defined a long list of practices that would be forbidden to employers and labor unions; obliged the federal government to undertake an "affirmative" program of equal employment opportunity for all employees and job applicants; and created an Equal Employment Opportunity Commission (EEOC) to monitor compliance with the law.

Title VII was notable in that it outlawed discrimination on the basis of sex as well as race. Sex was added to the categories "race, color, religion and national origin" by Congressman Howard Smith, a conservative Democrat from Virginia, who was a vigorous opponent of civil rights legislation. He introduced his motion after urging from Republican supporters of the National Woman's Party, who had been lobbying for an equal rights amendment whether or not it would undermine protective labor legislation, and who wanted to equate discrimination on the basis of race with discrimination on the basis of sex. The debate on Smith's motion was filled with misogyny; Smith joked that his amendment would guarantee the "right" of every woman to a husband. But it passed, supported by conservative members who were more comfortable voting for a civil rights bill if there was something in it for white women.

The EEOC, which began to operate in the summer of 1965, anticipated that virtually all of its complaints would come from blacks. The commission was surprised to discover that 25 percent of the complaints received during the first year were from women from a range of racial and ethnic backgrounds, many African American. In the course of responding to these complaints, both the commission and the courts were driven to a more subtle analysis of female job categories and work patterns. Section 703(e) 1 required that employers wishing to restrict a job category to one sex had to show that being male or female was a "bona fide occupational qualification"; it was not enough to say that men or women had traditionally filled any given job.

In the decade that followed, most states developed their own versions of Title VII, establishing laws that prohibited sex discrimination in employment. The federal statute was amended in 1972 and again in 1978; on both occasions the EEOC was given substantial additional powers and responsibilities. The three major areas of EEOC activity are (1) furnishing assistance to comparable state agencies, (2) furnishing advice to employers and labor unions about compliance, and (3) enforcing compliance by conciliation and legal action. In 1978 Congress passed the Pregnancy Discrimination Act, which amplified the definition of sex to include pregnancy, childbirth, or related medical conditions. EEOC has been willing to view sexual harassment as a form of sex discrimination but has not endorsed the concept of comparable worth.

U.S. Statutes at Large 78 (1964): 253–66. For a discussion of the circumstances of the passage of Title VII, see Jo Freeman, "How 'Sex' Got into Title VII: Persistent Opportunism as a Maker of Public Policy," Law and Inequality 9 (1991): 163–84.

Sec. 703.(a) It shall be an unlawful employment practice for an employer—

(1) to fail or refuse to hire or to discharge any individual, or otherwise to discriminate against any individual with respect to his compensation, terms, conditions, or privileges of employment, because of such individual's race, color, religion, sex, or national origin; or

(2) to limit, segregate, or classify his employees in any way which would deprive or tend to deprive any individual of employment opportunities or otherwise adversely affect his status as an employee, because of such individual's race, color, religion, sex, or national origin.

(b) It shall be an unlawful employment practice for an employment agency to fail or refuse to refer for employment, or otherwise to discriminate against, any individual because of his race, color, religion, sex, or national origin, or to classify or refer for employment any individual on the basis of his race, color, religion, sex, or national origin.

(c) It shall be an unlawful employment practice for a labor organization—

(1) to exclude or to expel from its membership, or otherwise to discriminate against, any individual because of his race, color, religion, sex, or national origin;

(2) to limit, segregate, or classify its membership, or to classify or fail or refuse to refer for employment any individual, in any way which would deprive or tend to deprive any individual of employment opportunities, or would limit such employment opportunities or otherwise adversely affect his status as an employee or as an applicant for employment, because of such individual's race, color, religion, sex, or national origin; or

(3) to cause or attempt to cause an employer to discriminate against an individual in violation of this section. . . .

(e) Notwithstanding any other provision of this title, (1) it shall not be an unlawful employment practice for an employer to hire and employ employees, for an employment

agency to classify, or refer for employment any individual, for a labor organization to classify its membership or to classify or refer for employment any individual, or for an employer, labor organization, or joint labor-management committee controlling apprenticeship or other training or retraining programs to admit or employ any individual in any such program, on the basis of his religion, sex, or national origin in those certain instances where religion, sex, or national origin is a bona fide occupational qualification reasonably necessary to normal operation of that particular business or enterprise. . . .

Sec. 705.(a) There is hereby created a Commission to be known as the Equal Employment Opportunity Commission, which shall be composed of five members, not more than three of whom shall be members of the same political party, who shall be appointed by the President by and with the advice and consent of the Senate. . . .

(g) The Commission shall have power—

(1) to cooperate with and, with their consent, utilize regional, State, local, and other agencies, both public and private, and individuals; . . .

(3) to furnish to persons subject to this title such technical assistance as they may request to further their compliance with this title or an order issued thereunder;

(4) upon the request of (i) any employer, whose employees or some of them, or (ii) any labor organization, whose members or some of them, refuse or threaten to refuse to cooperate in effectuating the provisions of this title, to assist in such effectuation by conciliation or such other remedial action as is provided by this title;

(5) to make such technical studies as are appropriate to effectuate the purposes and policies of this title and to make the results of such studies available to the public;

(6) to refer matters to the Attorney General with recommendations for intervention in a civil action brought by an aggrieved party under section 706, or for the institution of a civil action by the Attorney General under section 707, and to advise, consult, and assist the Attorney General on such matters. . . .

Equal Rights Amendment, 1972

An equal rights amendment, with wording slightly different from that passed by Congress in 1972, was sponsored in 1923 by the National Woman's Party. It seemed to party members the logical corollary to suffrage. But that amendment was vigorously opposed by the League of Women Voters and other progressive reformers, lest it undermine the protective legislation for which they had fought so hard. A key question raised was what impact the amendment, if passed, would have on a military draft.

An equal rights amendment was introduced regularly in Congress virtually every year thereafter, but it received little attention until after World War II. In 1950 and 1953, it was passed by the Senate but ignored by the House.

By 1970 much protective legislation had been applied to both men and women. It was possible to support an equal rights amendment without risking the undoing of labor law reforms. The hope that the Supreme Court would apply the Fourteenth Amendment's "equal protection of the laws" clause to cases involving discrimination on the basis of sex as firmly as it applied the clause to cases involving racial discrimination had not been fulfilled. When the current Equal Rights Amendment was introduced in 1970, it was endorsed by a wide range of organizations, some of which had once opposed it; these organizations included groups as disparate as the United Automobile Workers and the Woman's Christian Temperance Union. Its main sponsor in the House was Martha Griffiths of Michigan; in the Senate, Birch Bayh of Indiana.

The ERA was passed by Congress on March 22, 1972, and sent to the states for ratification. There was much initial enthusiasm; within two days six states had ratified. But the pace of ratification slowed after 1975, and only 35 of the needed 38 states had ratified it by 1978. (Four state legislatures voted to rescind ratification, although the legality of that move was open to question.) In October 1978 Congress extended the deadline for ratification to June 30, 1982; the extension expired with no additional ratifications. The amendment was reintroduced in Congress in 1983 but has not been passed. Compare the language here to that of the Fifteenth Amendment (p. 289) and Title VII of the 1964 Civil Rights Act (pp. 745–746).

Section 1. Equality of rights under the law shall not be denied or abridged by the United States or by any State on account of sex.

Section 2. The Congress shall have the power to enforce, by appropriate legislation, the provisions of this article.

Section 3. The amendment shall take effect two years after the date of ratification.

Title IX, Education Amendments of 1972

In 1972, women received 9 percent of the M.D. degrees awarded by universities in the United States, 7 percent of the law degrees, and 15 percent of the doctoral degrees. Women were 2 percent of college varsity athletes. It was common practice to encourage women students into specialties marked as appropriate for women: teaching rather than scientific research, for example, or nursing rather than medicine. It was estimated that colleges offered athletic scholarships to 50,000 men, while women athletes received fewer than 50. It was usual practice for the travel expenses of men's athletic teams to be paid for from student fees (paid by both women and men), while women's teams received 0.5 percent of schools' athletic dollars. Women's teams often had to raise their own travel funds, sometimes from bake sales and raffles. Title IX of the Education Amendments to the Civil Rights Act, passed in 1972, was brief but far-reaching.

No person in the United States shall, on the basis of sex, be excluded from participation in, be denied the benefits of, or be subjected to discrimination under any education program or activity receiving Federal financial assistance. . . .

Each Federal department and agency which is empowered to extend Federal financial assistance to any education program or activity, by way of grant, loan, or contract . . . is authorized and directed to effectuate the provisions of . . . this title with respect to such program or activity by issuing rules, regulations, or orders of general applicability which shall be consistent with achievement of the objectives of the statute. . . .

Title IX has proven to be a powerful tool in the fight for gender equity because it affects a wide range of educational opportunities and services. Title IX forbids sex discrimination in admissions policies (outlawing the common practice of using separate standards for men and women); in career training and vocational programs (which had previously been largely segregated by sex); and in employment. Title IX also forbids discrimination against pregnant or parenting students and requires schools to provide an environment that is free of sexual harassment.

Until recently, the most widely discussed consequence of Title IX has been its transformative effect on high school and undergraduate athletic programs. In the years since the passage of Title IX, the number of women participating in National Collegiate Athletic Association (NCAA) intercollegiate athletics has risen from approximately 32,000 in 1971 to roughly 203,600 in 2012–13, an increase of over 600 percent. (The number of men in intercollegiate athletics has also risen at the rate of 53 percent, from 173,000 to 265,600 athletes.) At the high school level, the change is even more striking: over three million girls have participated in high school sports in each of the last seven years, compared with fewer than 300,000 in 1971–72, an increase of nearly 1,000 percent. (During the same time period, high school boys' participation in sports has risen by approximately 15 percent.) Thus, contrary to the widespread misperception that Title IX has decreased the opportunities for males to participate in sports, the number of male athletes has continued to increase and, most significantly, so has the funding for men's sports. At Division I schools (with major football and basketball teams), although the number of men's teams has declined, the amount of money spent on men's athletics is still almost twice as much as the money spent on women's athletics. Between 1995–96 and 2004–5, Division I schools increased their spending on men's football by approximately $2.45 million per team, while the average funding increase for women's teams (except basketball) was about $135,000 per team.

Title IX is enforced by the Department of Education's Office of Civil Rights. Enforcement has been gradual. Not until 1975 were there full federal regulations applying to secondary schools and colleges and universities, and these have continued to evolve over time. The Title IX regulations governing athletic programs require that the total amount of athletic financial assistance awarded to men and women be proportionate to their respective participation rates in intercollegiate athletic programs. They require that male and female athletes receive equivalent— not identical—benefits, treatment, services, and opportunities. Title IX does *not* require that all teams be coeducational, nor that the same number of teams be provided for men and women, nor that men's teams be cut in order for the institution to come into compliance with the law.

In 2002, the U.S. secretary of education established the Commission on Opportunity in Athletics. At issue were the measures of fairness. After more than a year of intense public debate, the commission announced its wholehearted support for the goal of gender equity in sports, while suggesting that schools be

By the turn of the twenty-first century, diversity in admissions and more equitable funding for women's athletics had made new opportunities for women to hone their skills and overcome challenges, as these players at the University of California attest. (Photo courtesy of the Department of Athletics, University of California, Santa Barbara.)

offered more flexible terms of establishing their compliance with Title IX. The Department of Education relies on a "three-prong test" established in 1979, requiring schools to show either that the ratio of male and female athletes is about equal to the ratio of all male and female undergraduates; that they have a "history and continuing practice" of expanding opportunities for women; or that they are "fully and effectively accommodating the interests and abilities" of women on campus. More than three-quarters of colleges and universities are in comfortable compliance with Title IX, having added women's teams and continued to support men's teams. It is Division I schools, which reserve substantial numbers of slots for revenue-producing sports (even at the expense of cutting men's minor sports), that have found it most difficult to meet Title IX's expectations.

Recent reports confirm several arguments that women have made about Title IX's effects on intercollegiate sports programs. Both men's and women's participation levels in college athletics have increased since the passage of Title IX. College and universities have responded to Title IX by increasing women's participation rather than decreasing men's participation. Men's sports continue to receive funding and athletic opportunities out of proportion to their representation in the college population; 57 percent of undergraduates are women, yet they receive only 43 percent of the athletic participation opportunities. In addition, the NCAA's 2012-13 report on sports participation shows that male athletic participation in intercollegiate sports—both the numbers of athletes and the number of teams—has reached an all-time high.

Argument continues about what constitutes equitable treatment. Is it fair for men to hold the majority of athletic scholarships (an imbalance largely due to the size of men's football and basketball teams)? Is it fair for a university to support a women's varsity rowing team but not a men's varsity rowing team? What is the proper relationship between women's sports and men's sports? Between women's sports and men's "minor" sports? Perhaps most significantly, what is the wise relationship between expenditures on athletics and expenditures on academic programs?

TITLE IX AND SEXUAL ASSAULT

Students and their parents have used Title IX to fight sexual harassment at school and during school-sponsored activities. One of the earliest cases was brought against Yale University in 1977 by a group of female students who argued that harassment of students by professors—and the absence of procedures for students to file effective formal complaints—is a violation of Title IX. In 1999 the Supreme Court responded to the appeal of the fifth-grade girl who had been subjected to explicit sexual teasing by a classmate. He attempted to touch her breasts and genital area, he told her "I want to get into bed with you," and he rubbed his body against her in the hallway. Her grades plummeted as she lost the ability to concentrate on her studies. Although she and her mother complained repeatedly to teachers and the principal, no action was taken. The Court ruled that school districts may be liable for damages when administrators are indifferent to repeated and known acts of student-to-student sexual harassment, during school hours and on school grounds (*Davis v. Monroe County Board of Education*, 119 S.Ct. 1661). The case raised the question of responsibility of schools to provide a harassment-free environment (see *Meritor Savings Bank v. Mechelle Vinson et al.*, pp. 754–756).

In 1990, the Jeanne Clery Act, named for a 19-year old freshman who was raped and murdered in her Lehigh University dormitory room in 1986, required colleges and universities to report crimes committed on campus. In 2010 it was strengthened, requiring institutions to issue timely warnings about crimes that pose an ongoing danger. The law also requires annual public campus security reports that include three years' worth of crime statistics; the statistics must include both forcible and non-forcible sex offenses. The resulting reports were stunning in what they revealed about the frequency of rape and the laxity of punishment. The example of Christy Bronzkala, whose lawsuit against Virginia Tech after her rape by a football player triggered a test of the Violence Against Women Act (VAWA), is exemplary; the players were briefly suspended, but Bronzkala left the university. (For VAWA, see pp. 756–758.) Few schools have expelled violators of campus behavior codes. When victims brought their complaints to police, they regularly encountered disbelief and humiliation. Even today, victims often feel that they have to choose between the dread of facing their assaulters in classes and on campus or transferring to another or dropping out of school.

By 2014, women student activists had forced the question. They organized public protests; they deployed social media to link activists on many campuses; they used student newspapers to publicize the violence they endured; they encouraged one another to file complaints with the Department of Education and the Office of Civil Rights under the Clery Act and Title IX. Through a new organization, "End Rape on Campus," they waged a sophisticated lobbying campaign. They gained the support of members of Congress—among them, Senators Kristin Gillibrand and Claire McCaskill, who had already challenged the military for its weak response to sexual violence. Among the students who filed complaints with the Office of Civil Rights were Annie E. Clark and Andrea Pino of the University of North Carolina and Emma Sulkowicz of Columbia University—all profiled in articles in the *New York Times*. In May 2014 the Department of Education issued a finding that supported a student's complaint that Tufts University had delayed

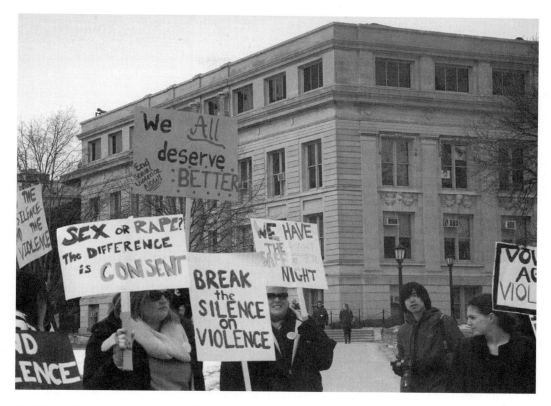

In 2014, college students organized many public demonstrations addressing sexual violence on campuses, like this one at the University of Iowa on February 24. Photographer: James Soukup. (Courtesy of the Daily Iowan.)

investigating her assault and had not protected her from her assailant; the university refused the settlement proposed by the Department of Education and thus risked losing all federal funding.*

As this book goes to press, a White House task force has concluded that one in five female students are assaulted during their college years but only 12 percent of rapes are reported. The Department of Education has announced that it is investigating 55 colleges and universities for their failures to provide a "prompt and equitable response" to complaints of sexual harassment and violence, as Title IX requires. The list included some of the nation's most distinguished public and private institutions. All over the country, women student activists continue to publicize the records of their own universities; at some they are appearing at recruitment tours to warn prospective students about the dangers they face.†

What has been the history of Title IX enforcement and of sexual assault on your campus? Is your college among the 55 singled out for investigation? What programs to increase awareness of sexual violence and to prevent it are in place, and which to your mind are most effective? What have been the responses of students, men as well as women, to the reinvigorated movement for women's safety?**

*See www.endrapeoncampus.org; "Behind Focus on College Assaults, a Steady Drumbeat by Students," *New York Times*, April 29, 2014; "Fight Against Sexual Assaults Holds Colleges to Account," ibid., May 3, 2014.

† See www.notalone.gov.

**This note was prepared with information from reports and press releases issued in 2007, 2008, and 2013 by the National Collegiate Athletic Association (NCAA), the National Federation of State High School Associations (NFHS), the Women's Sports Foundation, the National Coalition for Women and Girls in Education, and the ACLU Women's Rights Projects, which are available on their websites.

Frontiero v. Richardson, 1973

Sharron A. Frontiero was an Air Force officer who was dismayed to discover that she could not claim dependent's benefits for her husband on the same terms that her male colleagues could for their wives. She and her husband brought suit, claiming that statutes requiring spouses of female members of the uniformed services to receive more than half of their support from their wives to be considered dependents, while all spouses of male members were treated as dependents, violated the due process clause of the Fifth Amendment and the equal protection clause of the Fourteenth Amendment.

Until 1971, the Supreme Court had never ruled that discrimination on the basis of sex was a violation of the equal protection clause of the Fourteenth Amendment. So long as a legislature had a "reasonable" basis for making distinctions between men and women, discriminatory laws were upheld. Between 1971 and 1975, in a stunning series of decisions, the Supreme Court placed the burden of proof that discrimination on the basis of sex was reasonable on those who tried to discriminate. Ruth Bader Ginsburg was a thirty-eight-year-old law professor working with the American Civil Liberties Union (ACLU) in 1971 when the Court accepted her argument that an Idaho law requiring that fathers, rather than mothers, always be preferred as executors of their children's estates was unconstitutional (*Reed v. Reed*, 404 U.S. 71 [1971]).

The ACLU set up a Women's Rights Project in 1972 with Ginsburg at its head to follow up on the implications of the *Reed* decision. Ginsburg wrote the brief and managed the argument in *Frontiero;* it was one of a brilliant series of cases that she argued in the early 1970s. With her colleagues, she helped persuade the Court that a wide range of discriminatory practices were illegal. Her career as a litigator would lead to her appointment as a judge on the U.S. Court of Appeals in 1980 and, in 1993, to her appointment to the U.S. Supreme Court.

The Supreme Court ruled in favor of the Frontieros in a complex decision that used statistical information about woman's place in the work force in a manner reminiscent of the Brandeis Brief (see Sklar, p. 357). Speaking for three of his colleagues Justice William J. Brennan, Jr., prepared a historically based argument, explaining the distance American public opinion had traveled since the *Bradwell* case (see pp. 292–294). He drew analogies between discrimination on the basis of race, which the court subjected to strict scrutiny, and discrimination on the basis of sex.

In concurring with Brennan's opinion, three justices observed that although they agreed with the Frontieros in this particular case, they were not yet persuaded that sex ought to be regularly treated as a "suspect category." Only when—or if—the Equal Rights Amendment were passed could the Court be sure that the public agreed that discrimination on the basis of sex ought to be evaluated as critically as discrimination on the basis of race. Note that the facts in *Frontiero* relate to discrimination against the husband of the wage earner, not directly against a woman. It is the family of the wage earner that is discriminated against. A similar case, also argued by Ginsburg, is *Weinberger v. Weisenfeld* (420 U.S. 636 [1975]), in which the husband of a dead woman successfully demanded survivor's benefits equal to those available to widows. Ginsburg and her colleagues stressed that both men and women benefited from gender-blind equal treatment under the law.

MR. JUSTICE WILLIAM J. BRENNAN, JR., DELIVERED THE OPINION OF THE COURT:

The question before us concerns the right of a female member of the uniformed services to claim her spouse as a "dependent." . . .

At the outset, appellants contend that classifications based upon sex, like classifications based upon race, alienage, and national origin, are inherently suspect and must therefore be subjected to close judicial scrutiny. We agree. . . .

There can be no doubt that our Nation has had a long and unfortunate history of sex discrimination. Traditionally, such discrimination was rationalized by an attitude of "romantic paternalism" which, in practical effect, put women, not on a pedestal, but in a cage. Indeed, this paternalistic attitude became so firmly rooted in our national consciousness that, 100 years ago, a distinguished Member of this Court was able to proclaim. . . . "The natural and proper timidity and delicacy which belongs to the female sex evidently unfits it for many of the occupations of civil life." . . .

It is true, of course, that the position of women in America has improved markedly in recent decades. Nevertheless, it can hardly be doubted that, in part because of the high visibility of the sex characteristic, women still face pervasive, although at times more subtle, discrimination in our educational institutions, in the job market, and perhaps most conspicuously, in the political arena. . . .

Moreover, since sex, like race and national origin, is an immutable characteristic determined solely by the accident of birth, the imposition of special disabilities upon the member of a particular sex because of their sex would seem to violate "the basic concept of our system that legal burdens should bear some relationship to individual responsibility. . . ." And what differentiates sex from such nonsuspect statuses as intelligence or physical disability, and aligns it with the recognized suspect criteria, is that the sex characteristic frequently bears no relation to ability to perform or contribute to society. . . .

. . . over the past decade, Congress has itself manifested an increasing sensitivity to sex-based classification. In Tit[le] VII of the Civil Rights Act of 1964, for example, Congress expressly declared that no employer, labor union, or other organization subject to the provisions of the Act shall discriminate against any individual on the basis of "race, color, religion, *sex*, or national origin." Similarly, the Equal Pay Act of 1963 provides that no employer covered by the Act "shall discriminate . . . between employees on the basis of sex." . . .

With these considerations in mind, we can only conclude that classifications based upon sex, like classifications based upon race, alienage, or national origin, are inherently suspect, and must therefore be subjected to strict judicial scrutiny. Applying the analysis mandated by that stricter standard of review, it is clear that the statutory scheme now before us is constitutionally invalid. . . .

MR. JUSTICE LEWIS F. POWELL, JR., WITH WHOM THE CHIEF JUSTICE AND MR. JUSTICE HARRY A. BLACKMUN JOIN, CONCURRING IN THE OPINION:

I agree that the challenged statutes constitute an unconstitutional discrimination against servicewomen . . . but I cannot join the opinion of Mr. Justice Brennan, which would hold that all classifications based upon sex . . . are "inherently suspect and must therefore be subjected to close judicial scrutiny." . . . The Equal Rights Amendment, which if adopted will resolve the substance of this precise question, has been approved by the Congress and submitted for ratification by the States. If this Amendment is duly adopted, it will represent the will of the people accomplished in the manner prescribed by the constitution. . . . It seems to me that this reaching out to pre-empt by judicial action a major political decision which is currently in process of resolution does not reflect appropriate respect for duly prescribed legislative processes.

Frontiero v. Richardson, 411 U.S. 677 (1973).

Meritor Savings Bank v. Mechelle Vinson et al., 1986

The term "sexual harassment" was unknown before the mid-1970s. One legal scholar has written, "the term was invented by feminist activists, given legal content by feminist litigators and scholars, and sustained by a wide-ranging body of scholarship generated largely by feminist academics." Another legal scholar observes "[f]or the first time in history, women have defined women's injuries in a law."*

Consider Part 1 of Section 703 of Title VII of the Civil Rights Act of 1964 (p. 746). The authors of the statute were defining economic injuries, and for more than a decade the Equal Employment Opportunity Commission supported only economic claims of sex discrimination. But working women had long put up with behavior that, beginning in the 1970s, they began to say was also sex discrimination: supervisors who referred to all women as "whores," whether or not in joking tones; workplaces that had cheesecake or frankly pornographic calendars on the walls; and, worst of all, covert or explicit pressure to have sex with supervisors or employers for fear of losing their jobs if they refused.

Legal scholar Catharine MacKinnon gave names to two forms of sexual harassment: (1) "quid pro quo": when sexual submission to a supervisor becomes, either implicitly or explicitly, a condition of employment; and (2) "offensive working environment": when the conduct of a supervisor, co-employee, or client unreasonably interferes with an individual's work or creates an intimidating and hostile workplace. By the late 1970s, many behaviors that men had described as flirting, and that women had "put up with" because they saw no alternative, could be named and challenged. In 1980, the EEOC published an official set of guidelines describing behavior it would challenge as sexual harassment, even if the actors claimed they were merely flirting or "joking around."

In 1986, a unanimous Supreme Court for the first time formally recognized sexual harassment as a violation of Title VII. Catharine MacKinnon was one of the attorneys for Mechelle Vinson, an African American woman who had been hired in 1974 as a teller-trainee by a vice president of Meritor Savings Bank and was steadily promoted for four years until she became assistant branch manager. During those four years, she had a sexual relationship with the man (Mr. Taylor) who had hired her. . . . However, when she tried to decline his attentions, he exposed himself to her and forcibly raped her.

Vinson claimed that she had been the victim of both "quid pro quo" and offensive environment forms of sexual harassment. Vinson told the court "that because she was afraid of Taylor she never reported his harassment to any of his supervisors and never attempted to use the bank's complaint procedure." But when she was fired for what the bank claimed was excessive use of sick leave, she sued the bank, claiming sexual harassment and asking for punitive damages. The

---

*Martha Chamallas, "Writing About Sexual Harassment: A Guide to the Literature," *UCLA Women's Law Journal* 4 (1993): 37–38; Catharine MacKinnon, *Feminism Unmodified: Discourses on Life and Law* (Cambridge, Mass.: Harvard University Press, 1987), p. 105; Vicki Schultz, "Reconceptualizing Sexual Harassment," *Yale Law Journal* 107 (1998): 1683–1805.

bank claimed that "any sexual harassment by Taylor was unknown to the bank and engaged in without its consent or approval."

A unanimous Court agreed with Vinson. What analogies do they see with race discrimination? Why do they hold Meritor Bank guilty as well as Mr. Taylor? Taylor argued that Vinson wore sexually provocative clothing. How much responsibility do you think the victim of sexual harassment should be expected to take for avoiding the harassment?

JUSTICE WILLIAM REHNQUIST:

This case presents important questions concerning claims of workplace "sexual harassment" brought under Title VII of the Civil Rights Act of 1964 ... [Vinson] argues ... that unwelcome sexual advances that create an offensive or hostile working environment violate Title VII. Without question, when a supervisor sexually harasses a subordinate because of the subordinate's sex, that supervisor "discriminate[s]" on the basis of sex. [Meritor Bank] does not challenge this proposition. It contends instead that in prohibiting discrimination with respect to "compensation, terms, conditions, or privileges" of employment, Congress was concerned with what petitioner describes as "tangible loss" of "an economic character," not "purely psychological aspects of the workplace environment."

We reject petitioner's view. First, the language of Title VII is not limited to "economic" or "tangible" discrimination. The phrase "terms, conditions, or privileges of employment" evinces a congressional intent "to strike at the entire spectrum of disparate treatment of men and women" in employment. . . . As the Court of Appeals for the Eleventh Circuit wrote . . . in 1982: "Sexual harassment which creates a hostile or offensive environment for members of one sex is every bit the arbitrary barrier to sexual equality at the workplace that racial harassment is to racial equality. Surely a requirement that a man or woman run a gauntlet of sexual abuse in return for the privilege of being allowed to work and make a living can be as demeaning and disconcerting as the harshest of racial epithets."

. . . [W]e reject the . . . view that the mere existence of a grievance procedure and a policy against discrimination, coupled with respondent's failure to invoke that procedure, must insulate petitioner from liability. . . . the bank's grievance procedure apparently required an employee to complain first to her supervisor, in this case Taylor. Since Taylor was the alleged perpetrator, it is not altogether surprising that respondent failed to invoke the procedure and report her grievance to him. . . . [W]e hold that a claim of "hostile environment" sex discrimination is actionable under Title VII. . . .

Meritor Savings Bank v. Mechelle Vinson et al., 477 U.S. 57 (1986).

A wave of attention to sexual harassment in the workplace took place after the fall of 1991, when hearings on the nomination of Clarence Thomas to the Supreme Court were interrupted by the charges of Anita Hill that he had sexually harassed her a decade earlier. Ironically, their encounter had taken place within the EEOC itself, where Thomas had been director and Hill had been a lawyer on his staff. In response, Thomas charged that he was himself victimized by the media attention. Adrienne Davis and Stephanie Wildman observe, "in a stunning sleight of hand, [Thomas] managed to convince all involved, including the Senate, that white racism, rather than a Black woman, had accused him of harassment."* Thomas's nomination to the Supreme Court was confirmed by the Senate.

Over the years since the *Meritor* decision, increasing numbers of workers have filed sexual harassment complaints, and a massive body of doctrine has developed on the details of the law's protection. In 1998 the Supreme Court ruled

*Adrienne D. Davis and Stephanie M. Wildman, "The Legacy of Doubt: Treatment of Sex and Race in the Hill-Thomas Hearings," *Southern California Law Review* 65 (1992): 1367.

that harassment based on an employee's homosexuality could constitute sex discrimination, and that male-on-male harassment could be a cause of action (*Oncale v. Sundowner Offshore Services, Inc.*). The definition of an "offensive working environment" remains under debate. Legal theorist Vicki Schultz has proposed:

> Many of the most prevalent forms of harassment are actions that are designed to maintain work—particularly the more highly rewarded lines of work—as bastions of masculine competence and authority. Every day, in workplaces all over the country, men uphold the image that their jobs demand masculine mastery by acting to undermine their female colleagues' perceived (or sometimes even actual) competence to do the work. The forms of such harassment are wide-ranging. They include characterizing the work as appropriate for men only; denigrating women's performance or ability to master the job; providing patronizing forms of help in performing the job; withholding the training, information, or opportunity to learn to do the job well; engaging in deliberate work sabotage; . . . isolating women from the social networks that confer a sense of belonging . . . much of the time, harassment assumes a form that has little or nothing to do with sexuality but everything to do with gender.[†]

Have you or your family members or friends encountered some of these forms of harassment, or others?

Violence Against Women Act, 1994, 2000, 2005, 2013

The Violence Against Women Act (VAWA) was part of the comprehensive Violent Crime Control and Law Enforcement Act, passed in 1994. It was pathbreaking in establishing a new right: "All persons within the United States shall have the right to be free from crimes of violence motivated by gender." Congress was persuaded that the states fail to treat violent assaults against women as seriously as they treat other forms of violent assault. As one member of the Senate observed, "Typically we do not ask whether the victim of a barroom brawl is a real victim; we do not comment that the victim deserved to be hit; we do not inquire whether there was resistance or whether the victim said 'no' persistently enough."

VAWA provided funding to states for criminal law enforcement against perpetrators of violence. It also created (based on the commerce clause of the Fourteenth Amendment) a new federal civil rights remedy for victims of violence resulting from "animus based on the victim's gender." It defined domestic violence and sexual assault as potential infractions of the victim's civil rights. It overrode the inadequate remedies that persist in many states (for example, several states exempted cohabiting companions from rape laws). A victim of a violent crime motivated by the victim's gender was permitted to bring a civil lawsuit in federal or state court, seeking money damages or an injunction.

(a) PURPOSE.—Pursuant to the affirmative power of Congress to enact this subtitle under section 5 of the Fourteenth Amendment to the Constitution, as well as under section 8 of Article I of the Constitution, it is the purpose of this subtitle to protect the civil rights of victims of gender motivated violence and to promote public safety, health, and activities affecting interstate commerce by establishing a Federal civil rights cause of action for victims of crimes of violence motivated by gender.

(b) RIGHT TO BE FREE FROM CRIMES OF VIOLENCE.—All persons within the United States shall have the right to be free

[†]Schultz, p. 1687.

from crimes of violence motivated by gender (as defined in subsection (d)).

(c) CAUSE OF ACTION.—A person (including a person who acts under color of any statute, ordinance, regulation, custom, or usage of any State) who commits a crime of violence motivated by gender and thus deprives another of the right declared in subsection (b) shall be liable to the party injured, in an action for the recovery of compensatory and punitive damages, injunctive and declaratory relief, and such other relief as a court may deem appropriate.

(d) DEFINITIONS.—For purposes of this section—

(1) the term "crime of violence motivated by gender" means a crime of violence committed because of gender or on the basis of gender, and due, at least in part, to an animus based on the victim's gender; and

(2) the term "crime of violence" means—

(A) an act or series of acts that would constitute a felony against the person or that would constitute a felony against property if the conduct presents a serious risk of physical injury to another, and that would come within the meaning of State or Federal offenses described in section 16 of title 18, United States Code, whether or not these acts have actually resulted in criminal charges, prosecution, or conviction and whether or not those acts were committed in the special maritime, territorial, or prison jurisdiction of the United States; and

(B) includes an act or series of acts that would constitute a felony described in subparagraph (A) but for the relationship between the person who takes such action and the individual against whom such action is taken.

U.S. Statutes at Large, 110:2419.

Not long after VAWA was passed, Christy Brzonkala charged that she had been raped by two college football players in her dorm during her first semester at Virginia Polytechnic Institute. The athletes were not suspended from school, even though they had boasted about what they'd done and had been found guilty of "abusive conduct" by the university's judicial committee. Virginia Tech sentenced one of the players to two semesters' suspension, but upon appeal the provost set the suspension aside, calling it excessive punishment.

Brzonkala dropped out of school, fearing its dangers, and sued Virginia Tech, claiming damages equal to what the school earned from the Sugar Bowl, in which the athletes played. She lost. In May 2000, the U.S. Supreme Court upheld an appeals court ruling that Congress had reached too far in its interpretation of a right to regulate interstate commerce. The Court invalidated the part of the VAWA that permitted victims of rape, domestic violence, and other crimes "motivated by gender" to sue their attackers in federal court.*

Congress acted quickly: Within a few months it had reauthorized all but the contested section of VAWA. It provided more than $3 billion to fight violence against women: (1) $1 billion over five years to help prosecutors track down domestic abusers; (2) $875 million to expand shelters for battered women; (3) $95 million over two years to protect foreign women brought into the country by the international sex trade; and (4) $140 million to stop violent crimes against women on college campuses. The amount of money required is itself an indictment of the extent to which gender-motivated crimes, international trafficking in women, and the conditions on college campuses are major threats to women. VAWA was reauthorized and expanded in 2013, after a long legislative battle. (Every woman in Congress, regardless of party, voted for it.). The new legislation expands federal programs to assist local communities with law enforcement and it protects gay, bisexual, or transgender victims from domestic and sexual abuse. Recognizing

U.S. v. Morrison, 529 U.S. 598 (2000).

that Native American women have a higher likelihood of being sexually assaulted than any other group, VAWA 2013 also permits Native American women who are assaulted on reservations to press charges against non-Indians in tribal courts. (Generally tribal courts do not have jurisdiction over defendants who do not live on tribal land.) The White House Task Force to Protect Students from Sexual Assault, established in 2014, is charged with adding teeth—giving force to the safeguards promised not only by VAWA but also by Title IX and the Jeanne Clery Act (see p. 750).

BORDERS AMONG US

PIERRETTE HONDAGNEU-SOTELO
Domésticas Demand Dignity

Anti-immigration rhetoric is pervasive in U.S. political discourse today. In some ways, the arguments against immigrants echo nativist sentiment at the turn of the twentieth century, which culminated in the passage of exclusion and restriction laws. However, there are some differences as well. Over a hundred years ago, the largest number of immigrants came from eastern and southern Europe. In contrast, immigrants in recent decades are more likely to come from Latin America and Asia. In addition, while immigrants during the last century tended to be predominantly male, women are migrating in equal and sometimes even greater numbers. In fact, some of the fears about immigrants center on women, whose existing or future children are thought of as acting as an unwanted drain on the shrinking social services available.

Pierrette Hondagneu-Sotelo examines why women are migrating in greater numbers in the context of a globalized economy in which factories, capital, and workers increasingly cross national borders. She focuses on the mounting demand for service and domestic workers, as more middle-class American women seek paid employment outside their homes, and on the difficulty of recognizing work done inside a home as labor. In Los Angeles, most recently it has been Central American immigrant women whose poorly paid labor has helped maintain affluent homes and communities. The author's interviews with domestic workers and her research on their pay, working conditions, and migration, work, and family histories reveal much about both continuities and variations in the situations of domestic workers over the past three centuries. What are some of the dilemmas facing care and domestic workers that you have witnessed or are aware of?

Today, a substantial number of domestic workers provide care to the increasing numbers of the aged, infirm, and housebound, most of who are also women. Home health care is among the fastest growing and least well paid occupations; more and more have been joining unions. Some successes in organizing domestic workers and enacting legislation have challenged the view that the labor movement in the United States is dying. In fall 2013 and summer 2014, the governors of California and Massachusetts signed Domestic Workers' Bills of Rights into law, following similar statutes in New York and Hawaii. And in September 2013, the Obama administration put into place rules extending the Fair Labor Standards Act (FLSA) to home health workers. The difficulties of implementing these steps

Excerpted from the prefaces and Chaps. 2 and 8 of *Doméstica: Immigrant Workers Cleaning and Caring in the Shadows of Affluence* by Pierrette Hondagneu-Sotelo (Berkeley: University of California Press, 2007; orig. pub. 2001). Reprinted by permission of the author and publisher. Notes have been edited and renumbered.

are illustrated in the continuing legal challenges faced by unions and their state government partners.* Moving forward, what do you think are some solutions to the problems that Hondagneu-Sotelo depicts?

We live in the age of migration. Around the world, at least 185 million people, and perhaps as many as 200 million, reside in countries other than those where they were born. Why are so many people leaving their countries of origin? The legacies of colonialism, neocolonialism, imperialism, civil wars, imperial wars, uneven development, and the contemporary shock effects of neoliberalism [meaning policies such as deregulation, free trade, and government down-sizing] and political shifts have laid the structure for today's global migration. Meanwhile, innovations in technology, particularly in transportation and communications, have facilitated this vast human movement. International migration occurs through legal, quasi-legal, and illegal channels. It is important to recognize, however, that in many cases, deliberate labor-recruitment programs have helped to activate and maintain international labor migration. These are generally inaugurated for employer interests in the receiving society, and they are facilitated by receiving-state government, and sometimes bilateral, agreements. Such programs rely on the state to condone a particular type of legal migration predicated on the denial of migrants' basic human, labor, and civil rights.

Not long ago, migrants were mainly men. In fact, the international labor migration of men was a key feature of industrialization. During peak periods of modernization and industrialization, the industrial state relied on the recruitment and importation of men—usually men from poorer, often colonial societies—to do "men's work." Chinese, Filipino, Japanese, Irish, Italian, and Mexican men, for instance, all took turns as recruits who were brought in to build the infrastructure of an industrializing America. These migrants built canals and railroads, dug deep in mines, stoked factory furnaces, laid irrigation pipes, and provided the labor for large-scale agribusiness. In some

instances, family members were allowed to join them, but in many cases, especially those involving immigrant groups perceived as non-white, dependent family members were denied admission to the migrant-receiving societies. Women and children were perceived as burdens who would consume resources, and they were also seen to be demographically and racially undesirable as permanent members of the society. For these reasons, the reproduction of families and communities was forbidden. In many instances, government legislation enforced these prohibitions on the permanent incorporation of workers and their families. It was labor, not human beings, that was being recruited. The Bracero Program, which issued nearly five million temporary labor contracts to Mexican agricultural laborers in the United States between 1942 and 1964, and the Guest Worker Program, which relied on Turkish and Algerian men to rebuild cities and toil in the factories of Europe after World War II, are the exemplars of these modern systems, in which labor recruitment relied not only on men, but on subordinated men who were subjected to meticulous rules and regulations and to rigorous, dehumanizing bodily inspections.

Today, industry and manufacturing are no longer the primary fulcrums driving labor migration. . . . In a globalized world, factories migrate to places overseas that offer cheaper labor. High-tech and highly educated professionals have now joined the international migration, as have legions of migrant domestic workers. . . . Consequently, in some sites, we are seeing an oversupply of male migrant labor and the saturation of labor markets for working men. . . . In places as diverse as Italy, the Middle East, Taiwan, and Canada, Filipina migrant women working as caregivers and cleaners far out-number Filipino migrant men. . . . In Los Angeles newly arrived Latina

---

*For example, see the June 2014 U.S. Supreme Court ruling against the fee structure supporting Service Employees International Union (SEIU Illinois) home health care workers, who by unionizing and working as personal assistants in the Illinois Home Services Program were able to nearly double their pay and gain health insurance; *Harris v. Quinn*, decided June 30, 2014. For changes in the home care sector and a history of organizing efforts, see Eileen Boris and Jennifer Klein, *Caring for America: Home Health Workers in the Shadow of the Welfare State* (New York: Oxford University Press, 2012).

immigrant women find jobs much more easily than their husbands and brothers, because of the steady demand for live-in domestic workers.

. . . Many of the newly industrialized Asian nations, such as Taiwan, Hong Kong, and Singapore, as well as Middle Eastern oil-rich nations, such as Saudi Arabia, Kuwait, and the United Arab Emirates, rely on state-legislated projects to recruit migrant domestic workers. The migrant domestic workers employed in these societies hail from poorer nations that are desperate to capture migrant remittances for foreign exchange, and to diffuse the social and political pressures created by unemployment. Consequently, nations such as the Philippines, Indonesia, Sri Lanka, and Thailand actively promote the out-migration of women into global domestic worker labor markets.

The nation-states from which domestic workers migrate have responded to these pressures in varied ways. The Philippines not only facilitates the out-migration of Filipina women as domestic workers, but it honors the return migrant *domésticas* as "heroes," to emphasize their contributions to building and sustaining the Philippine nation. The Philippines does make some effort to intervene on behalf of the domestic workers, but when Filipino diplomats and labor attachés attempt to impose fair labor standards in the countries where Filipinas go, they often discover that their bargaining power is weak, especially in contexts where migrant women are arriving from other, competing countries. Meanwhile, nations such as Bangladesh act in a more paternalistic, patriarchal way, attempting to thwart abuses by prohibiting the out-migration of women as foreign domestic workers. By contrast, Mexico—the nation that sends by far the most immigrants to the United States, a fair number of whom wind up working as *domésticas*—remains curiously silent on the incorporation of Mexican women as workers in private American homes.

When nation-states collaborate on contract-labor programs for domestic workers, the regulations are usually geared toward the control and submission of these workers, and not toward ensuring their rights. . . . [In some countries] migrant domestic workers may be required to remain with one employer for the duration of their contract period, regardless of the treatment they might receive. If they are unhappy with their job, they may not seek out another one, remaining stuck in a feudal-like situation. Some must sign oaths promising

loyalty and docility. Other rules specify how they may dress and wear their hair, and prohibit makeup or lipstick. The confiscation of passports by employers is common. Domestic workers may also be subjected to medical surveillance designed to ensure they are not pregnant, and may be prohibited from leaving the homes where they work except for perhaps a few hours on one afternoon a week. Some are subjected to beatings or sexual abuse, but have no escape or access to legal recourse. . . .

Just as slavery produced runaway slaves, many times these conditions result in "runaway maids." In the worst-case scenarios, these sorts of institutional conditions have resulted in the tragic deaths of migrant domestic workers, as in Singapore and Kuwait. Human rights advocates around the globe have raised their voices against such abuses, but the institutionalized violation of domestic workers' human rights has not received as much public attention and action as has been directed toward thwarting the illegal trafficking of women and girls.

In [some] countries, such as the United States, laws and regulations do not tie migrant domestic workers to their. . . . Moreover, there are labor-protection laws on the books, and legal and community advocates working for enforcement of those rules. For domestic workers and agricultural workers, who were historically excluded from these pacts, the reach of these laws has been limited. Labor activists, legislators, and domestic workers themselves, however, continue to push for change, as they did in 2006, when they tried to change California legislation to allow overtime labor protections for live-in domestic workers and for personal attendants. [The change was enacted in 2013.] Latina immigrant domestic workers in the United States hold a range of legal statuses, from those who are undocumented to those who are naturalized U.S. citizens. . . . Unlike their global peers working on temporary contract programs, many immigrant domestic workers in the United States already live with their own families in immigrant communities in American cities, but a massive legalization program would allow them to further improve their labor prospects and better support their families. . . .

While the social trends that create the international flow of migrant domestic workers are diverse, the result is the same: families in the wealthy nations get women from poor nations to do the dirty domestic work, while families from the poor nations lose their mothers and wives. Is this simply a continuation of imperialism? As Barbara Ehrenreich and Arlie Hochschild have astutely noted, rich nations increasingly assume "a role like that of the old-fashioned male in the family—pampered, entitled, unable to cook, clean or find his socks." The poor nations, like the traditional woman, remain mired in domestic work and subservience. As for the migrant female domestic workers, who is left at home to do the care for them? This is a big moral question, one with social, political, and economic consequences. . . . [1]

Meanwhile, it is important to listen to the voices and experiences of the domestic workers themselves. Not all immigrant domestic workers are exploited. In fact, many of them remind us that they are valuable contributors to two societies, the one they left behind and the one in which they work. They value their jobs, and when employers and society offer them social recognition and fair labor conditions, they take satisfaction from their work and their earnings.

Can we conceive of a Los Angeles where there is, as the title of a short film puts it, "A Day without a Mexican"?[2] In fact, as I learned while chatting with domestic workers at parks and bus stops, this is an exercise regularly indulged in by Mexican, Salvadoran, and Guatemalan women who work in middle-class and upper-middle-class homes throughout Los Angeles. "If we called a three-day strike," nannies say to their peers, "How many days would it take before we shut it all down?" Not only would households fall into a state of chaos, but professionals, managers, and office workers of all sorts would find themselves unable to perform their own jobs. Latina domestic workers debate this scenario with humor—some arguing that it might take two days, others chiming in with four. They know that in their job, a general strike is unlikely. Yet their strident humor is bolstered by the resurgence of militant unionism among Latino immigrant janitors and hotel and restaurant employees and by collective organizing among gardeners, day laborers, and drywallers in California. Significantly, their running dialogue speaks to a shared recognition of their own indispensability. In their own conversations, they reclaim what their job experiences often deny them: social recognition and dignity. . . .

Private paid domestic work, in which one individual cleans and cares for another individual or family, poses an enormous paradox. In the United States today, these jobs remain effectively unregulated by formal rules and contracts. Consequently, even today they often resemble relations of servitude that prevailed in earlier, precapitalist feudal societies. These contemporary work arrangements contradict American democratic ideals and modern contractual notions of employment. [My research] reveals how these fundamental tensions in American social life are played out in private homes, between the women who do the work and those who employ them.

Paid domestic work is widely recognized as part of the informal "shadow" or "under the table" economy. Although wage and hour regulations do cover the job, scarcely anyone, employee or employer, knows about them. Government regulations remain ineffective, and there are no employee handbooks, unions, or management guidelines to help set wages or job duties or to stipulate how the work should be performed. The jobs are done in isolated, private, widely dispersed households, and typically involve negotiations between two individuals—usually women from radically different backgrounds. . . . Relying on primary information gathered in the mid- to late 1990s from more than two hundred people in Los Angeles (in-depth interviews with 68 individuals, a survey of 153 Latina domestic workers, and ethnographic observations in various settings), I examine how the practices and concerns of both employers and employees shape how paid domestic work occurs today.

There are many lived dramas in America today, and among the least visible and most deeply felt are those that unfold behind carefully manicured lawns and residential facades. [I] highlight the voices, experiences, and views both of the Mexican and Central American women who care for other people's children and homes and of the women in Los Angeles who employ them. The study of paid domestic work thus offers a key window through which we can view contemporary relations between women whose social positions are in stark contrast: between poor women and affluent families; between foreign-born, immigrant women and U.S.-born citizens; and between members of the growing, but still economically and racially subordinate, Latino communities and the shrinking population of white suburban residents, many of whom feel increasingly anxious about these demographic developments. Differences of class, race, nationality, and citizenship characterize the study's participants, yet this is an occupation in which the chasm of social differences plays out in physical proximity. Unlike the working poor who toil in factories and fields, domestic workers see, touch, and breathe the material and emotional world of their employers' homes. They scrub grout, coax reluctant children to nap and eat their vegetables, launder and fold clothes, mop, dust, vacuum, and witness intimate and otherwise private family dynamics. Inside the palatial mansion, the sprawling ranch-style home, or the modest duplex, they do these activities over and over again. . . .

Domestic work was the single largest category of paid employment for all women in the United States during the late nineteenth and early twentieth centuries, in large part because other opportunities were not available. Although the timing of exit varies by race and region, by the mid-twentieth century the doors to retail, clerical, and professional jobs were opening for many working women, and single and married women walked out of their homes and into formal-sector employment. Paid domestic work declined, a trend leading some commentators to predict the occupation's demise. But instead in the late twentieth century new domestic demands arose and new recruits were found, now crossing the southern border to reach the doorstep of domestic work. The work of cleaning houses and caring for children gradually left the hands of wives and mothers and entered the global marketplace. In the process, it has become the domain of disenfranchised immigrant women of color. . . .

I am the daughter of a Latina woman who, like many modestly educated women in mid-twentieth-century Latin America, migrated from the countryside to the city to work as a live-in nanny/house-keeper. Eventually, employment in her native Chile for the American family of an Anaconda copper mining engineer was her ticket to California, bought with indentured labor. When the family that brought her to the United States refused to pay her, she found live-in domestic jobs with other well-to-do American families before eventually marrying my father, a French gardener whom she met on the job. . . .

Today, my husband and I do laundry, cook, and clean daily, but we also pay a Salvadoran woman to clean our house. Every other Thursday she drives from her apartment near downtown Los Angeles to our suburban home to sweep and mop the hardwood floors, vacuum the carpets, dust the furniture, and scrub, wipe, and polish the bathrooms and kitchen to a blinding gleam. I love the way the house looks after she's done her job; but like many of the employers that I interviewed for this study, I remain deeply ambivalent about the glaring inequalities exposed by this arrangement—and exposed in a particularly visible and visceral way. Capitalist manufacturing misery abounds in this world; but when I purchase Nike shoes or Gap jeans, my reliance on child labor in Mauritania or Pakistan, or on Latina garment workers who toil in sweatshops just a stone's throw away from my office at USC, remains conveniently hidden and invisible in the object of consumption. I take possession of a new item, and no one but the cashier stares back at me. By contrast, my privileges and complicity in a worldwide system of inequalities and exploitation are thrown into relief by the face-to-face relations between me and the woman who cleans my house.

When colleagues and students in my classes have discussed these issues, some of them have argued passionately and compellingly that we cannot have a just society until everyone cleans up and picks up after themselves, regardless of their race, sex, or immigration or class status. They might be right (and I'm certainly in favor of men and boys learning to do their fair share), but I think an abolitionist program smacks of the utopian, not the feasible. Domestic work should not fall disproportionately on the shoulders of any one group (such as Filipina, or Latina, or Caribbean immigrant women); but putting an end to domestic employment is not the answer. Upgrading the occupation, a change ushered in by systemic regulation and by public recognition that this seemingly private activity is a job—one that creates particular obligations in both employees and employers—is our best chance for salvaging paid domestic work, for increasing the opportunities of those who do the work and of their families, and for reclaiming the dignity and humanity of both employees and employers.

Since 1990, . . . I have worked toward that end with a group of women under the auspices of the Coalition for Humane Immigrant Rights of Los Angeles (CHIRLA). The project began as an information and outreach program organized by immigrant rights attorneys, community organizers, and myself, but today it is a full-fledged, dues-collecting membership organization called the Domestic Workers' Association (DWA), which is part of CHIRLA. Similar organizations have sprouted up in other cities around the country, and they have long been common in Latin America. . . . All research is partial, situated and shaped by who we are. My multiple social locations—as the daughter of a former domestic worker, as a current employer, and as an advocate—have certainly shaped my approach and my emphases. . . .

Most Latina immigrant women who do paid domestic work in Los Angeles had no prior experience working as domestics in their countries of origin. Of the 153 Latina domestic workers that I surveyed at bus stops, in ESL classes, and in parks, fewer than 10 percent reported having worked in other people's homes, or taking in laundry for pay, in their countries of origin. This finding is perhaps not surprising, as we know from immigration research that the poorest of the poor rarely migrate to the United States; they simply cannot afford to do so.[3]

Some of the Latina immigrant women who come to Los Angeles grew up in impoverished squatter settlements, others in comfortable homes with servants. In their countries of origin, these women were housewives raising their own children, or college students, factory workers, store clerks, and secretaries; still others came from rural families of very modest means. Regardless of their diverse backgrounds, their transformation into housecleaners and nanny/housekeepers occurs in Los Angeles. . . .

Who are these women who come to the United States in search of jobs, and what are those jobs like? Domestic work is organized in different ways. [Here] I describe live-in [jobs] and housecleaning jobs, and profile some of the Latina immigrants who do them and how they feel about their work. . . . [I also discuss] why it is that Latina immigrants are the primary recruits to domestic work [and what wage and hour regulations apply. I then offer a short history of efforts to organize domestic workers in the United States, and, finally, suggest some steps forward.] . . .

[Live-ins:] It is the rare California home that offers separate maid's quarters, but that doesn't stop families from hiring live-ins; nor

does it stop newly arrived Latina migrant workers from taking jobs they urgently need. When live-ins cannot even retreat to their own rooms, work seeps into their sleep and their dreams. There is no time off from the job, and they say they feel confined, trapped, imprisoned.

"I lose a lot of sleep," said Margarita Gutiérrez, a twenty-four-year-old Mexicana who worked as a live-in nanny/housekeeper. At her job in a modest-sized condominium in Pasadena, she slept in a corner of a three-year-old child's bedroom. Consequently, she found herself on call day and night with the child, who sometimes went several days without seeing her mother because of the latter's schedule at an insurance company. Margarita was obliged to be on her job twenty-four hours a day; and like other live-in nanny/housekeepers I interviewed, she claimed that she could scarcely find time to shower or brush her teeth. "I go to bed fine," she reported, "and then I wake up at two or three in the morning with the girl asking for water, or food." After the child went back to sleep, Margarita would lie awake, thinking about how to leave her job but finding it hard to even walk out into the kitchen. Live-in employees like Margarita literally have no space and no time they can claim as their own.

Working in a larger home or staying in plush, private quarters is no guarantee of privacy or refuge from the job. Forty-four-year-old Elvia Lucero worked as a live-in at a sprawling, canyon-side residence, where she was in charge of looking after twins, two five-year-old girls. On numerous occasions when I visited her there, I saw that she occupied her own bedroom, a beautifully decorated one outfitted with delicate antiques, plush white carpet, and a stenciled border of pink roses painstakingly painted on the wall by the employer. It looked serene and inviting, but it was only three steps away from the twins' room. Every night one of the twins crawled into bed with Elvia. Elvia disliked this, but said she couldn't break the girl of the habit. And the parents' room lay tucked away at the opposite end of the large (more than 3,000 square feet), L-shaped house.

Regardless of the size of the home and the splendor of the accommodations, the boundaries that we might normally take for granted disappear in live-in jobs. They have . . . "no clear line between work and non-work time," and the line between job space and private space is similarly blurred.[4] Live-in nanny/

housekeepers are at once socially isolated and surrounded by other people's territory; during the hours they remain on the employers' premises, their space, like their time, belongs to another. The sensation of being among others while remaining invisible, unknown and apart, of never being able to leave the margins, makes many live-in employees sad, lonely, and depressed. Melancholy sets in and doesn't necessarily lift on the weekends.

Rules and regulations may extend around the clock. Some employers restrict the ability-of their live-in employees to receive telephone calls, entertain friends, attend evening ESL classes, or see boyfriends during the workweek. Other employers do not impose these sorts of restrictions, but because their homes are located on remote hillsides, in suburban enclaves, or in gated communities, their live-in nanny/housekeepers are effectively kept away from anything resembling social life or public culture. A Spanish-language radio station, or maybe a *telenovela,* may serve as their only link to the outside world.

Food—the way some employers hoard it, waste it, deny it, or just simply do not even have any of it in their kitchens—is a frequent topic of discussion among Latina live-in nanny/housekeepers. These women are talking not about counting calories but about the social meaning of food on the job. Almost no one works with a written contract, but anyone taking a live-in job that includes "room and board" would assume that adequate meals will be included. But what constitutes an adequate meal? Everyone has a different idea, and using the subject like a secret handshake, Latina domestic workers often greet one another by talking about the problems of managing food and meals on the job. Inevitably, food enters their conversations.

No one feels the indignities of food more deeply than do live-in employees, who may not leave the job for up to six days at a time. For them, the workplace necessarily becomes the place of daily sustenance. In some of the homes where they work, the employers are out all day. When these adults return home, they may only snack, keeping on hand little besides hot dogs, packets of macaroni and cheese, cereal, and peanut butter for the children. Such foods are considered neither nutritious nor appetizing by Latina immigrants, many of whom are accustomed to sitting down to meals prepared with fresh vegetables, rice, beans, and meat. In some employers' homes, the cupboards are literally bare. . . .

Food scarcity is not endemic to all of the households where these women work. In some homes, ample quantities of fresh fruits, cheeses, and chicken stock the kitchens. Some employer families readily share all of their food, but in other households, certain higher-quality, expensive food items may remain off-limits to the live-in employees, who are instructed to eat hot dogs with the children. One Latina live-in nanny/housekeeper told me that in her employers' substantial pantry, little "do not touch" signs signaled which food items were not available to her; and another said that her employer was always defrosting freezer-burned leftovers for her to eat, some of it dating back nearly a decade. . . .

The issue of food captures the essence of how Latina live-in domestic workers feel about their jobs. It symbolizes the extent to which the families they work for draw the boundaries of exclusion or inclusion, and it marks the degree to which those families recognize the live-in nanny/housekeepers as human beings who have basic human needs. When they first take their jobs, most live-in nanny/housekeepers do not anticipate spending any of their meager wages on food to eat while on the job, but in the end, most do—and sometimes the food they buy is eaten by members of the family for whom they work.

Although there is a wide range of pay, many Latina domestic workers in live-in jobs earn less than minimum wage for marathon hours: 93 percent of the live-in workers I surveyed in the mid-1990s were earning less than $5 an hour (79 percent of them below minimum wage, which was then $4.25), and they reported working an average of sixty-four hours a week. Some of the most astoundingly low rates were paid for live-in jobs in the households of other working-class Latino immigrants, which provide some women their first job when they arrive in Los Angeles. Carmen Vasquez, for example, had spent several years working as a live-in for two Mexican families, earning only $50 a week. By comparison, her current salary of $170 a week, which she was earning as a live-in nanny/housekeeper in the hillside home of an attorney and a teacher, seemed a princely sum.[5] . . .

Once they experience it, most women are repelled by live-in jobs. The lack of privacy, the mandated separation from family and friends, the round-the-clock hours, the food issues, the low pay, and especially the constant loneliness prompt most Latina immigrants to seek other job arrangements. Some young, single women who learn to speak English fluently try to move up the ranks into higher-paying live-in jobs. As soon as they can, however, the majority attempt to leave live-in work altogether. Most live-in nanny/housekeepers have been in the United States for five years or less. . . . Like African American women earlier in the century, who tired of what the historian Elizabeth Clark-Lewis has called "the soul-destroying hollowness of live-in domestic work," most Latina immigrants try to find other options.[6]

Until the early 1900s, live-in jobs were the most common form of paid domestic work in the United States, but through the first half of the twentieth century they were gradually supplanted by domestic "day work." Live-in work never completely disappeared, however, and in the last decades of the twentieth century, it revived with vigor, given new life by the needs of American families with working parents and young children—and . . . by the needs of newly arrived Latina immigrants, many of them unmarried and unattached to families. When these women try to move up from live-in domestic work, they see few job alternatives. Often, the best they can do is switch to another form of paid domestic work, either as live-out nanny/housekeeper or as a weekly housecleaner. When they do such day work, they are better able to circumscribe their work hours, and they earn more money in less time.[7] . . .

[House cleaners:] Like many working mothers, every weekday morning Marisela Ramírez awoke to dress and feed her preschooler, Tomás, and drive him to school (actually, a Head Start program) before she herself ventured out to work, navigating the dizzying array of Los Angeles freeways. Each day she set off in a different direction headed for a different workplace. On Mondays she maneuvered her way to Pasadena, where she cleaned the stately home of an elderly couple; on Tuesdays she alternated between cleaning a home in the Hollywood Hills and a more modest-sized duplex in Glendale; and Wednesdays took her to a split-level condominium in Burbank. You had to keep alert, she said, to remember where to go on which days and how to get there!

By nine o'clock she was usually on the job, and because she zoomed through her work she was able to finish, unless the house was extremely dirty, by one or two in the afternoon. After work, there were still plenty of daylight hours left for Marisela to take Tomás to the park . . . before she started dinner. Working as a housecleaner allowed Marisela to be the kind of wife and mother she wanted to be. Her job was something she did, she said, "because I have to"; but unlike her peers who work in live-in jobs, she enjoyed a fairly regular family life of her own, one that included cooking and eating family meals, playing with her son, bathing him, putting him to bed, and then watching *telenovelas* in the evenings with her husband and her sister. On the weekends, family socializing took center stage, with *carne asadas* in the park; informal gatherings with her large Mexican family, which extended throughout Los Angeles; and music from her husband, who worked as a gardener but played guitar in a weekend *ranchera* band.

Some might see Marisela Ramírez as just another low-wage worker doing dirty work, but by her own account—and gauging by her progress from her starting point—she had made remarkable occupational strides. Marisela had begun working as a live-in nanny/housekeeper in Los Angeles when she was only fifteen years old. Ten years later, the move from live-in work to housecleaning had brought her higher hourly wages, a shorter workweek, control over the pace of work, and flexibility in arranging when she worked. Cleaning different houses was also, she said, less boring than working as a nanny/housekeeper, which entailed passing every single day "in just one house, all week long with the same routine, over and over."

For a while she had tried factory work, packaging costume jewelry in a factory warehouse located in the San Fernando Valley, but Marisela saw housecleaning as preferable on just about every count. "In the factory, one has to work very, very fast!" she exclaimed. "And you can't talk to anybody, you can't stop, and you can't rest until it's break time. When you're working in a house, you can take a break at the moment you wish, finish the house when you want, and leave at the hour you decide. And it's better pay. It's harder work, yes," she conceded, "but it's better pay."

"How much were you earning at the factory?" I asked.

"Five dollars an hour; and working in houses now, I make about $11, or even more. Look, in a typical house, I enter at about 9 A.M., and I leave at 1 P.M., and they pay me $60. It's much better [than factory work]." Her income varied, but she could usually count on weekly earnings of about $300. By pooling these together with her husband's and sister's earnings, she was able to rent a one-bedroom bungalow roofed in red tile, with a lawn and a backyard for Tomás's sandbox and plastic swimming pool. In Mexico, Marisela had only studied as far as fifth grade, but she wanted the best for Tomás. Everyone doted on him, and by age four he was already reading simple words. . . .

Breaking into housecleaning is tough, often requiring informal tutelage from friends and relatives. Contrary to the image that all women "naturally" know how to do domestic work, many Latina domestic workers discover that their own housekeeping experiences do not automatically transfer to the homes where they work. As she looked back on her early days in the job, Marisela said, "I didn't know how to clean or anything." . . . Erlinda Castro, a middle-aged woman who had already run her own household and raised five children in Guatemala, . . . recalled . . . : "Learning how to use the chemicals and the liquids" in the different households was confusing, and, as friends and employers instructed her on what to do, she began writing down in a little notebook the names of the products and what they cleaned. Some women learn the job by informally apprenticing with one another, accompanying a friend or perhaps an aunt on her housecleaning jobs. . . .

Housecleaning represents . . . the "modernization" of paid domestic work. Women who clean different houses on different days sell their labor services in much the same way that a vendor sells a product to various customers.[8] The housecleaners themselves see their job as far preferable to that of a live-in or live-out nanny/housekeeper. They typically work alone, during times when their employers are out of the home; and because they are paid "by the job" instead of by the hour, they don't have to remain on the job until 6 or 7 P.M., an advantage much appreciated by women who have families of their own. Moreover, because they work for different employers on different days, they are not solely dependent for their livelihood on one boss whom they see every single day. Consequently, their relationships with their employers are less likely to become highly charged and conflictual; and if problems do arise, they can leave one job

without jeopardizing their entire weekly earnings. . . .

Housecleaners also see working independently and informally as more desirable than working for a commercial cleaning company. "The companies pay $5 an hour," said Erlinda Castro, whose neighbor worked for one, "and the women have to work their eight hours, doing up to ten, twenty houses a day! One does the vacuuming, the other does the bathroom and the kitchen, and like that. It's tremendously hard work, and at $5 an hour? Thank God, I don't have to do that." Two of the women I interviewed, one now a live-out nanny/housekeeper and the other a private housecleaner, had previously worked for cleaning services, and both of them complained bitterly about their speeded-up work pace, low pay, and tyrannical bosses.

Private housecleaners take enormous pride in their work. When they finish their job, they can see the shiny results, and they are proud of their job autonomy, their hours, their pay, and, most important, what they are able to do with their pay for themselves and for their families. Yet housecleaning brings its own special problems. Intensive cleaning eventually brings physical pain, and sometimes injury. "Even my bones are tired," said fifty-three-year-old Lupe Vélez; and even a relatively young woman like Celestina Vigil at age thirty-three was already reporting back problems that she attributed to her work. While most of them have only fleeting contact with their employers, and many said they work for "good people," just about everyone has suffered, they said, "inconsiderate persons" who exhort them to work faster, humiliate them, fail to give raises, add extra cleaning tasks without paying extra, or unjustly accuse them of stealing or of ruining a rug or upholstery. And the plain old hard work and stigma of cleaning always remain, as suggested by the answer I got when I asked a housecleaner what she liked least about her job. "The least?" she said, with a wry smile. "Well, that you have to clean." . . .

As Mexican and Central American immigrant women move into live-out and housecleaning jobs, their family lives change. With better pay and fewer hours of work, they become able to live with their own family members. Among those I surveyed, about 45 percent of the women doing [live-out] day work were married, but only 13 percent of the live-ins were married. Most women who have husbands and children with them in Los Angeles do not wish to take live-in jobs; moreover, their application for a live-in job is likely to be rejected if they reveal that they have a husband, a boyfriend, or children living in Los Angeles. . . . Live-out nanny/housekeepers often face this family restriction too, as employers are wary of hiring someone who may not report for work when her own children come down with the flu.

Their subminimum wages and long hours make it impossible for many live-in workers to bring their children to Los Angeles; other live-ins are young women who do not have children of their own. [A] substantial proportion of Latina domestic workers in Los Angeles whose children stay in their countries of origin are in the same position as . . . the Filipinas who predominate in domestic jobs in many cities around the globe. This is what I label "transnational motherhood." . . . Today, international labor migration and the job characteristics of paid domestic work, especially live-in work, virtually impose transnational motherhood on many Mexican and Central American women who have children of their own.[9] . . .

Why today are Central American women hugely overrepresented in these jobs in Los Angeles in comparison with Mexicans (whose immigrant population is of course many times larger)? In the survey I conducted of 153 Westside Latina domestic workers, 75 percent of the respondents were from Central America; of those, most were from El Salvador and Guatemala. And in census counts, Salvadoran and Guatemalan women are, respectively, twelve times and thirteen times more likely than the general population to be engaged in private domestic work in Los Angeles. Numerous studies paint a similar picture in other major U.S. cities, such as Washington, D.C., Houston, and San Francisco; one naturally wonders why this should be so.[10] . . .

Mexican migration to the United States goes back over a hundred years, initially driven by labor recruitment programs designed to bring in men to work in agriculture. Since the late 1960s, it has shifted from a primarily male population of temporary or sojourner workers to one that includes women and entire families; these newcomers have settled in rural areas, cities, and suburbs throughout the United States, but disproportionately in California. Many Mexican women who migrated in the 1970s and 1980s were accompanied by their families and were aided by rich social networks; the latter helped prevent the urgency that leads new immigrants to take live-in jobs. . . . When Mexican women arrive in the United States, many of them enjoy access to well-developed, established communities whose members have long been employed in various industries, particularly agriculture, construction, hotels, food-processing plants, and garment factories. . . . Their social networks give Mexican women greater variety in their employment options; paid domestic work is only one of their alternatives.[11]

Salvadoran and Guatemalan women migrating to the United States have done so under different circumstances than Mexican women. For Central Americans coming to *el norte*, there was no long-standing labor program recruiting men who could then bring, or encourage the migration of, their wives and daughters. . . . More significantly, Salvadoran and Guatemalan women and men left their countries in haste, often leaving their children behind, as they fled the civil wars, political violence, and economic upheaval of the 1980s. Theirs are immigrant communities that subsisted without legal status for nearly two decades, grew rapidly, and remain very poor. . . .

Family structures and marriage patterns may have also contributed to the preponderance of Central American women in paid domestic work. El Salvador has traditionally had one of the lowest marriage rates in the hemisphere, especially among the urban poor, where common-law marriages and legacies of internal and intra–Central America labor migration— mostly for work on coffee plantations—have encouraged the formation of female-headed households. Thus Salvadoran women have been more likely to migrate on their own and accept live-in jobs. . . . [12]

The experience of Central American women might also be compared to that of Asian immigrant women, who have been entering the United States at increasing rates. The latter are an extremely heterogeneous group, but on average—and this is particularly true of Chinese, Indian, and Filipina women—they arrive with much higher levels of education, better English language skills, and more professional credentials than do their Latina peers. They are also more likely to have legal status; and members of some groups, especially Korean immigrant women, enjoy access to jobs in family businesses and ethnic enclaves.[13] At the same time, the generally poorer and less-educated women from Vietnam, Laos, and Cambodia have been able to withstand periods of underemployment and unemployment because they are officially sanctioned political refugees and therefore enjoy access to welfare and resettlement assistance from the federal government. While some individual Asian immigrant women are working in paid domestic work, they have not developed social networks that channel them into this niche.

It is particularly striking that Filipina immigrants predominate in this occupation elsewhere around the globe, but not in the United States. Worldwide, about two-thirds of Filipina migrants in countries as different as Italy, Canada, Hong Kong, Taiwan, Singapore, Saudi Arabia, and Jordan, do paid domestic work; but in the United States, their high levels of education and fluent English enable most of them to enter higher status occupations that require more skills than does domestic work. In 1990, 71 percent of the Filipinas in the United States were working in managerial, professional, technical/sales, and administrative support jobs, and only 17 percent were employed in service jobs. They are disproportionately concentrated in the health professions, the result of formal recruitment programs designed to fill U.S. nursing shortages. Experience in the health professions leads many Filipinas to take jobs in elder care. . . . [14]

During the period that I was researching this book, I attended funerals for three children of Latina domestic workers. Two perished in an apartment blaze with their mother, victims of suspected arson, and another fell to her death from the balcony of a public housing project while her mother was at work. To my mind, the deaths of these three young children were neither accidents of fate nor the result of parental abuse, but rather tragedies of poverty. If their mothers, who worked as domestics, had earned higher wages, they could have afforded safer housing, and these children might still be alive.

These deaths are among the most glaring costs of the way paid domestic work is done today in Los Angeles. The more mundane costs to the domestic workers—the loss of dignity, respect, and self-esteem; the inability to even live with their children; and the daily hardships of raising families on poverty-level wages—do not command the same attention, but they are, nevertheless, social prices. When

working people who earn the legal minimum wage cannot bring home enough money to keep a family of three above official poverty levels, Latina domestic workers who earn *below* minimum wage are in big trouble.[15]

As we have seen, the arrangements of paid domestic work give rise to many problems, largely because paid domestic work is not treated as bona fide employment and because the women who do it—in Los Angeles, Latina immigrant women—are among the most disenfranchised members of society. . . . [Are] these problems are remediable? . . .

Most people involved in domestic work, employers as well as employees, still do not know that wage and hour regulations cover paid domestic work. The reason for their ignorance is obvious: virtually no attempt has been made by the government or media to educate domestic workers and employers about these laws. . . . Among the most basic labor protections [on the books] are those regarding wages and hours; these are codified in the federal Fair Labor Standards Act (FLSA), which was enacted in the wake of the Great Depression. Based on a model of industrial wage employment, the FLSA initially excluded private household workers; but in 1974 . . . Congress amended the act to guarantee private domestic workers the right to receive minimum wages and overtime pay.[16] The amendment covered a range of domestic occupations, including the jobs of butlers, cooks, housekeepers, and maids. Accordingly, domestic employees who work more than eight hours in one workweek are entitled to receive the minimum wage. Various legal precedents . . . have established that undocumented immigrant workers are also covered under the FLSA. It would seem, then, that basic legal protection with respect to wages is already in place.

There are two significant limitations in this federal legislation, however. First, domestic employees who work as personal attendants— for example, baby-sitters, caregivers to young children, or companions of the elderly and infirm—are explicitly *excluded* from the right to earn minimum wage and overtime pay; only those domestic employees who can show that they devote at least 20 percent of their work time to housekeeping duties are covered. Thus, while our society may pay great lip service to the value of caring for people, especially for the young, the elderly, and the ill, those who do private care work are not granted the same legal rights as those who clean and care for material possessions. Indeed, this legislative divide suggests that those responsible for caring for other human beings are not recognized as workers at all. . . .

A second and far more serious weakness of the FLSA is that live-in employees are completely exempt from overtime coverage. Accordingly, domestic workers who reside in the households where they work have no right under federal law to overtime pay. The legislation seems to encode the assumption that live-in domestic work is closer to being "just like one of the family" than to wage employment. . . . California laws, however, to some extent remedy the FLSA, regulating deductions for room and board and mandating overtime pay for some domestic workers.

A third weakness of the statutes already on the books lies outside the law itself: when it comes to paid domestic work, there is effectively no enforcement of these laws, or even encouragement of compliance. . . . [For] five Southern California counties, twenty agents are charged with the monumental task of investigating and enforcing labor practices among a population of millions. Given their scarcity of resources, labor investigators naturally focus on work sites such as factories or farms that affect more than one employee. Moreover, investigating infractions of wage and hours in a home raises far more sensitive issues of privacy than does searching a factory.

State wage and hours laws complement the federal Fair Standards Labor Act. Some states (usually those with relatively high costs of living) mandate higher hourly wages than federal law. Others specifically expand the labor rights of paid domestic workers. New York, for example, extends overtime protections to live-in workers. Still other states, among them Alaska, Delaware, Hawaii, Idaho, and Kansas, exclude domestics from state minimum wage laws and from other protections, leaving them only the inadequate protection of the FLSA. More than half the states also exclude paid domestic workers from the protection of civil rights laws, which are intended to guard against discrimination, and some state laws exempt domestic employers from compliance with occupational safety and health regulations. . . .

Formal organizations and collective efforts focused on improving domestic workers' jobs have been rare in the United States, but

they are not impossible undertakings. Virtually every Latin American nation has active domestic workers' associations and unions, and since 1988 many of them have met in inter–Latin American congresses.[19] In recent years, as Latina and Caribbean immigrants have swelled the numbers of women in the occupation in the United States, a plethora of innovative, community-based associations for Latina domestic workers, each one slightly different in form and focus, have sprouted on the East and West Coasts.[17]

Efforts to organize domestic workers in the United States began in the first half of the twentieth century, but those early groups were concerned less with advocacy for the domestic workers than with vocational training for them, so they might better serve employers. The most notable exception in this regard is the National Committee on Household Employment (NCHE), which initially grew out of a 1928 Young Women's Christian Association–sponsored conference on domestic workers' wages and job hours, held in Washington, D.C. The white middle-class women of the YWCA were more reformers than union organizers. At one point, Eleanor Roosevelt served as honorary chair. . . . The group at first tried to mediate between white housewives who wanted a supply of well-trained help and black women workers who wanted better wages and limited hours. Although its members sincerely desired to remedy abuses in the occupation, the NCHE remained, in this early phase, a primarily white, middle-class, employers' organization, adamantly opposed to the imposition of written contracts and regulations.[18]

After the NCHE reorganized in 1964 under the leadership of the National Council on Negro Women, it began affiliating with and receiving support from other groups. During this period, the NCHE became a more militant advocate, organized by and for African American paid domestic workers. It worked to publicize the poor working conditions and lack of labor regulations in the occupation, to establish training programs to standardize job skills, and to open contracting centers for job placement. Training programs were implemented in eight cities between 1967 and 1971, assisted by mediators who helped individual domestic employees bargain with individual employers. The NCHE's biggest concrete achievement came in 1974, when domestic workers were finally included in the Fair Labor Standards Act.[19] . . .

Although personal attendants (baby-sitters, nannies, and attendants to the elderly and infirm who do not clean) still lack minimum wage rights, the 1974 victory was significant. The NCHE has faded away, but it had a lasting impact on private domestic work.[20]

Organizing labor is not easy in any industry, and the obstacles to efforts in domestic work are particularly daunting. One of the biggest impediments is that many women who work as housecleaners and housekeeper/nannies find it difficult to see themselves as workers, for reasons that include the stigma attached to the job, its location in a private residence, and the tasks themselves—which are associated with women's "natural" expressions of love and caring. . . . Besides the job's low status, its low pay and the limits on upward mobility within the occupation also persuade many Latina domestic workers, especially young women, that they should leave it altogether. Often these women find that their alternative sources of employment are no more attractive; but regardless of whether they actually leave or not, their ambivalence about staying in domestic work lessens the likelihood that they will put their energy into collective organizing to make the occupation better.

Those who do seek to organize and upgrade domestic work find their efforts hindered by spatial and legal constraints. Because the work sites are spread through residential neighborhoods, there is no obvious place in which to begin organizing—no garment district or factory gates for organizers to target with leaflets and recruitment efforts. Moreover, paid domestic workers are not covered by the National Labor Relations Act of 1935 (NLRA), which declares that "The term employee shall include any employee . . . but shall not include any individual employed . . . in the domestic service of any family or person at his home" (section 152, provision 3). Domestic workers have no legal rights to organize, and therefore no protection from termination if they begin to organize. . . .

[What can be done?] Many wonder why Latina immigrants who are dissatisfied with their jobs don't simply look for other types of work in Los Angeles; or failing that, why they don't just "go home." Aren't they ambitious? Don't they aspire to something better? Some Latina domestic workers do try to leave the occupation, but they find the alternatives scarce. Among the most common and easily accessible jobs for them are informal vending, janitorial work, and factory work, often in the garment sector. But garment industry jobs in Los Angeles have deteriorated in recent years. Of the estimated 120,000 garment workers in Los Angeles, the majority are Latina immigrant women and many of them now earn less than the state minimum wage at jobs that present serious health and safety problems.[21] And as more immigrant women have turned to vending, competition has increased and shaved already slim profits even further. . . . Even Latina domestic workers who have all of their legal papers, who have years of experience in the United States, who have received some higher education, and who are totally bilingual have few options. The kinds of jobs they might get as cosmetologists, secretaries, or bank tellers, they say, would require high investment in work clothes and would still bring in low earnings . . .

The bad news is this: there are no ladders of upward mobility leading out of paid domestic work today, as there were for European immigrant women in the early twentieth century. We live in a society that is increasingly characterized by an occupational hourglass, without a booming industrial sector for Latina domestic workers or their husbands to latch onto in the United States. While some of them hope to retire in El Salvador or Mexico, their possibilities for sustainable employment in their countries of origin have lessened with globalization, the North American Free Trade Agreement, and the economic aftermath of civil wars.

Many Latina domestic workers would like to have better jobs, but their options and their opportunities for advancement are slim. Upgrading their current occupation is one solution to their dilemma. How to achieve that, however, is less clear. . . . Nearly all nanny/housekeepers and housecleaners work without written contracts. States could also take inspiration from New York State, which in 1997 (through the efforts of Latina immigrant workers) passed what is reputed to be the toughest wage enforcement law in the country, the Unpaid Wages Prohibition Act.[22]

Strengthening the formal employment standards is not enough, however. Widespread compliance with those standards will require a program of public education and outreach directed at middle-class and upper-middle-class employers, as well as enforcement of the laws

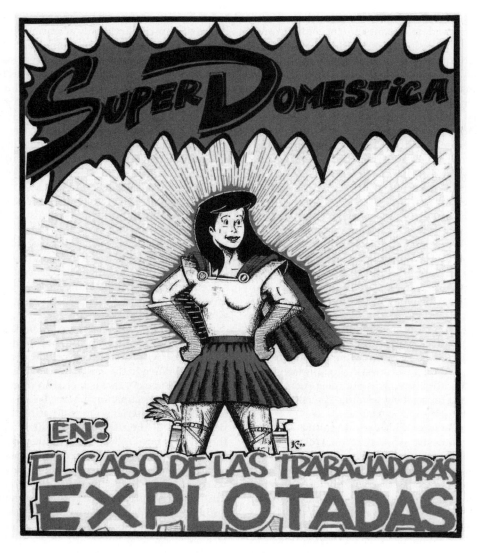

Cover for the novela graphic, Super Doméstica, *published by the Coalition for Human Immigrant Rights of Los Angeles (CHIRLA), artwork by Kelvin Manzanares. Reprinted with permission of the artist and publisher. The Domestic Workers' Association in Los Angeles had its start in 1990 as an advocacy program under the wing of CHIRLA. Organizers created and distributed free, inexpensive booklets—novelas—with captioned pictures, aimed at informing domestic workers about wage and hour rights, safety issues, and more.* Super Doméstica, *as Pierrette Hondagneu-Sotelo explains, "featured the story of a house-keeper who successfully learns to negotiate with her demanding employer." Domestic workers who were activists embraced the icon, "taking turns dressing" as the superhero "when the group marched together in political rallies or protests or in neighborhood parades. . . . Political marches took on a festive aspect, and the costume—a red cape, a short skirt showing a spray bottle of cleanser and a feather duster attached to her thighs, and yellow rubber gloves on both hands—made the Domestic Workers' Association increasingly visible and drew many inquiries. The Super Doméstica icon was also featured on the organization's first T-shirts" and starred in a community theater work created by organization members. When a few critics charged that the icon "represented an unrealistic, sexist, idealized physical figure," DWA women responded, "She's a Super Hero!" The icon echoes the figure "Super Barrio, a caped and masked priest in Mexico City who organized protests in squatter settlements."*

that apply to them. Employers . . . must learn to act as employers with particular obligations rather than as consumers of domestic services. . . . Improving the occupation will also require collective organizing by and for domestic workers. In spite of the many obstacles that Latina domestic workers face in undertaking such a project, . . . they *are* organizing in major cities around the country. The Domestic Workers' Association in Los Angeles, just one example of these associations, provides a site for domestic workers to give and receive social recognition, to seek job advice, and to pursue new occupational skills (e.g., how to do CPR, serve at a seder, or file income taxes); and when necessary, it helps its members pursue claims for back wages. . . . When the members of the Domestic Workers' Association listed their job demands, dignity and respect topped the list. [These] aspects of the job, unlike wages and hours, cannot be legislated. . . . Organizations aiming at improving the terms of paid domestic work, might take a page from strategies used in the garment organizing campaigns of the 1990s, which targeted consumers and consumers' consciences with their "No Sweat" labels and National Day of Conscience.[23] Domestic workers could similarly target their employers.

Indeed, the employers have good reason to change: they and their family members who are cared for by Latina nannies will benefit greatly if the occupation is upgraded. They stand to gain better child care and other domestic services, greater length of service by those they employ, and perhaps even a fuller sense of humanity. We might ask ourselves what kind of society we wish to create for ourselves and our children. Do we wish to continue current arrangements, whereby many Latina and Caribbean immigrant women in nanny/housekeeper jobs must forfeit their own family and community lives, leaving their own young children in their countries of origin? Is transnational motherhood and a form of domestic apartheid what we want? Should the costs of care be borne so disparately? Or can we imagine and design domestic jobs so that, like other forms of employment, these can accommodate and allow for employees' own social and family lives? While we cannot legislate caring about employees, we can strive for public education and social acknowledgment that paid domestic work is work, that it is an integral part of how our society is organized today, and that the Latina immigrant women who do the work are people with their own families, communities, and concerns.

NOTES

1. Barbara Ehrenreich and Arlie Russell Hochschild, eds., *Global Woman: Nannies, Maids, and Sex Workers in the New Economy* (New York: Henry Holt, 2002), 11.

2. *A Day Without a Mexican* (2004), 100 minutes, directed by Sergio Arau. For a comparison of the economic status of Mexican immigrants and Mexican Americans in Los Angeles, see Vilma Ortiz, "The Mexican-Origin Population: Permanent Working Class or Emerging Middle Class?" in *Ethnic Los Angeles*, ed. Roger Waldinger and Mehdi Bozorgmehr (New York: Russell Sage Foundation, 1996), 247–77.

3. Mary Romero, *Maid in the U.S.A.* (New York: Routledge, 1992).

4. Evelyn Nakano Glenn, *Issei, Nisei, Warbride: Three Generations of Japanese American Women in Domestic Service* (Philadelphia: Temple University Press, 1986), 141. In drawing on my interviews, pseudonyms are used for all employees and employers.

5. Many Latina domestic workers do not know the amount of their hourly wages; and because the lines between their work and nonwork tend to blur, live-in nanny/housekeepers have particular difficulty calculating them. Consider a prototypical live-in who works 5 days a week, from 7 A.M. until 9 P.M., with 1.5 hours off during the children's nap time. Her on-duty work hours would total 64.5 hours per week. The weekly pay of live-in nanny/housekeepers surveyed ranged from $130 to $400, averaging $242. Dividing this figure by 64 yields an hourly wage of $3.80. None of the live-ins were charged for room and board—but 86 percent said they brought food with them to their jobs. The majority reported being paid in cash.

6. Elizabeth Clark-Lewis, *Living In, Living Out: African American Domestics in Washington, D.C., 1910–1940* (Washington, D.C.: Smithsonian Institution Press, 1994), 123.

7. In many urban regions of the United States, the shift to day work accelerated during World War I, so that live-out arrangements eventually became more prevalent. See David M. Katzman, *Seven Days a Week: Women and Domestic Service in Industrializing America* (Urbana: University of Illinois Press, 1981), and Phyllis Palmer, *Domesticity and Dirt: Housewives and Domestic Servants in the United States, 1920–1945* (Philadelphia: Temple University Press, 1989). Elsewhere, and for different groups of domestic workers, these transitions happened later; see Glenn, *Issei, Nisei, Warbride*, 143.

8. Romero, *Maid in the U.S.A.*

9. Pierette Hondagneu-Sotelo and Ernestine Avila, "'I'm Here, But I'm There': The Meanings of Latina Transnational Motherhood," *Gender and Society* 11 (1997), 548–71; Judith Rollins, *Between Women: Domestics and Their Employers* (Philadelphia: Temple University Press, 1985); Glenn, *Issei, Nisei, Warbride*; Romero, *Maid in the U.S.A.*; Mary Romero, "Who Takes Care of the Maid's Children? Exploring the Costs of Domestic Service," in *Feminism and Families*,

ed. Hilde L. Nelson (New York: Routledge, 1997), 63–91.

10. On the census data, see David E. Lopez, Eric Popkin, and Edward Telles, "Central Americans: At the Bottom, Struggling to Get Ahead," in *Ethnic Los Angeles*, 279–304. For other cities, see Terry A. Repak, *Waiting on Washington: Central American Workers in the Nation's Capital* (Philadelphia: Temple University Press, 1995); and Jacqueline Maria Hagan, *Deciding to be Legal: A Maya Community in Houston* (Philadelphia: Temple University Press, 1994).

11. According to the PUMS (Public Use Microdata Sample) Census data, about 70 percent of Central American women between the ages of 24 and 60 in Los Angeles County are in the labor force, while only 56 percent of their Mexican peers are. Among this same group, 71 percent of Mexican immigrant women but only 56 percent of their Central American peers are married and living with a spouse. To put it more starkly, 28 percent of Mexican immigrant women and 43 percent of Central American women report living with family members or adults other than their spouses.

12. Some studies estimate that as many as 50 percent of poor households in San Salvador were formed by "free unions" rather than marriage by law. This pattern is related not just to migration but also to urban poverty, as there is no need to secure inheritance rights when there is no property to share. See Isabel Nieves, "Household Arrangements and Multiple Jobs in San Salvador," *Signs* 5 (1979), 130–50; and Repak, *Waiting on Washington*. For a comparative study, see Katharine Donato, "Understanding U.S. Immigration: Why Some Countries Send Women and Others Send Men," in *Seeking Common Ground: Multidisciplinary Studies of Immigrant Women in the United States*, ed. Donna Gabaccia (Westport, Conn.: Praeger, 1992), 159-84.

13. On Korean immigrant business owners, see Pyong Gap Min, *Caught in the Middle: Korean Communities in New York and Los Angeles* (Berkeley: University of California Press, 1996).

14. D. Mar and M. Kim, "Historical Trends," in *The State of Asian Pacific America: Economic Diversity, Issues, and Policies*, ed. Paul Ong (Los Angeles: LEAP American Pacific American Public Policy Institute and UCLA Asian American Studies Center, 1994). Between 1966 and 1985 nearly 25,000 Filipina nurses came to work in the United States, and another 10,000 came between 1989 and 1991. Filipinas who were formally recruited through government programs then informally recruited their friends and former nursing school classmates; Paul Ong and Tania Azores, "Health Professionals on the Front Line," in ibid., 139–63. Interviews conducted with 26 Filipina domestic workers in Los Angeles reveal that many have college diplomas and [yet] are working in homes because they are older and face age discrimination; they tend to earn more as care providers for the elderly ($425 per week) and as nanny/housekeepers ($350 per week) than do Latina immigrants in these same jobs. See Rhacel Salazar Parreñas, "Migrant Filipina Domestic Workers and the International Division of Reproductive Labor," *Gender and Society* 14:4 (Aug. 2000), 560–80.

15. Robert Pollin, "Living Wage Gives a Boost to Demand," *Los Angeles Times*, April 1, 1999, B9; Pollin, *The Living Wage: Building a Fair Economy* (New York: Free Press, 1998).

16. National Organization for Women, *Out of the Shadows: Strategies for Expanding State Labor and Civil Rights Protections for Domestic Workers* (New York: NOW Legal Defense and Education Fund, 1997), Appendix A: The Fair Labor Standards Act. See also Linda Martin and Kerry Seagrave, *The Servant Problem: Domestic Workers in North America* (Jefferson, N.C.: McFarlands, 1985); Rollins, *Between Women*.

17. Katharine A. Schmidt, "Domestic Workers Note Abuse, Low Pay," *Santa Monica Outlook*, Nov. 5, 1991, A1, A3; Tracy Wilkinson, "To Protect Those Who Must Serve," *Los Angeles Times*, Feb. 2, 1992, A1, A12; Doreen Carvajal, "For Immigrant Maids, Not a Job but Servitude," *New York Times*, Feb. 25, 1995, C1, C19. In 1988 domestic workers belonging to unions in 11 countries met in Bogota, Colombia, to form the Confederation of Household Workers in the Caribbean and Latin America (CONLATRAHO). In March 1999 they held their inter-American meetings in Mexico City with organized domestic workers from the United States, including representatives from the Domestic Workers' Association of CHIRLA. See the essays by Thelma Galvez and Rosalba Todoro, Mary Goldsmith, Magdelena Leon, and Suzana Prates in *Muchachas No More: Household Workers in Latin America and the Caribbean*, ed. Elsa M. Chaney and Mary Garcia Castro (Philadelphia: Temple University Press, 1989).

18. On early organizing efforts and on the NCHE, see Palmer, *Domesticity and Dirt*; Romero, *Maid in the U.S.A.*; and Phyllis Palmer, "Housework and Domestic Labor: Racial and Technological Change," in *My Troubles Are Going to have Trouble with Me*, ed. Karen Brodkin Sacks and Dorothy Remy (New Brunswick, N.J.: Rutgers University Press, 1984), 80–91.

19. The 1974 amendment passed partly because of a vociferous bloc of women representatives in Congress (Shirley Chisholm, Marjorie S. Holt, Leonor K. Sullivan, Yvonne Brathwaite Burke, Patsy T. Mink, Julia Butler Hansen, Edith Green, Martha W. Griffiths, Ella T. Grasso, Bella S. Abzug, Elizabeth Holtzman, Barbara Jordan, and Patrica Schroeder). Their rhetoric framed the amendment as part of a national initiative to fight poverty: they wished to include domestic workers under the FLSA so that domestic workers would be kept above poverty levels and off public assistance; H.R. Res. No. 93-913, 93d Cong., 2d sess. 2842–2844; see their letter quoted in NOW, *Out of the Shadows*, 2.

20. The decline of the NCHE and the entry of Latina and Caribbean immigrant women into U.S. domestic work coincided with the exodus from the occupation of African American women (especially young women) after the civil rights era. Many U.S.-born women of color left private household work for jobs in cafeterias, offices (as janitors), hotels, and restaurants, jobs that one scholar refers to as "public reproductive work"; Evelyn Nakano Glenn, "From Servitude to Service Work: Historical Continuities in the Racial Division of Women's Work," *Signs* 18 (1992), 1–43. The United Domestic Workers Alliance was another important worker-based effort aimed at organizing workers in private homes. It began in San Diego, inspired by César

Chávez and the UFW. Later, it pursued collective bargaining for home care workers who care for the elderly in private homes. [For more on the UDWA, see Eileen Boris and Jennifer Klein, *Caring for America: Home Health Workers in the Shadow of the Welfare State* (New York: Oxford University Press, 2012), 143–48, 207–208, 212.]

21. On wage levels, see Nancy Cleeland, "Garment Jobs: Hard, Bleak, and Vanishing," *Los Angeles Times*, March 11, 1999, A1, A14–16. On the numbers of

garment workers and the rise of the sweatshop apparel industry, see Edna Bonacich and Richard P. Appelbaum, *Behind the Label: Inequality in the Los Angeles Apparel Industry* (Berkeley: University of California Press, 2000).

22. Jennifer Gordon, "Immigrants Fight the Power," *The Nation*, Jan. 3, 2000, 16–20.

23. See Andrew Ross, ed., *No Sweat: Fashion, Free Trade, and the Rights of Garment Workers* (New York: Verson, 1997).

ASHRAF ZAHEDI
Muslim American Women After 9/11

The date September 11, 2001, has become a defining moment in U.S. history. On that day, four airplanes crossing U.S. territory were hijacked by al-Qaeda terrorists. Two of the planes flew into and collapsed the twin towers of the World Trade Center. Another targeted the Pentagon, and a fourth was brought down by passengers before it could be used as a weapon. In response, the government launched a global war on terrorism, targeting al-Qaeda, the organization responsible for the attacks.

Critics have noted that the war on terrorism has often been conflated with war on Islam. The term Islamaphobia has been coined to describe this intense fear and hatred of Muslims and Muslim culture. In addition, non-Muslims, such as Sikhs, have been mistaken for Muslims and targeted for violence.

Ashraf Zahedi's essay explores how Muslim women in the United States have navigated this fraught political landscape. Zahedi, a sociologist, interviewed women of diverse ethnic, racial, and national backgrounds as part of her research. She also draws on images of Muslim women in the mainstream media and in political discourse, and she tells us about women's leadership roles in several American Muslim organizations. Skewering the classic European assumption that veiled Muslim women are passive, uneducated, and monolithically oppressed, Zahedi underscores the variability in contemporary veiling practices. More importantly, we see the wide range of issues about which Muslim women are concerned. As with all the essays and documents in this book, think about how you could use her findings to contradict misinformation and spark constructive dialogue.

The events of 11 September 2001 are clearly marked as transformative events in the history of the United States of America. These events shattered Americans' sense of security and heightened their anxiety. While the majority of Americans feared potential future terrorist attacks, Muslim Americans not only feared such

attacks but also feared attacks from their fellow Americans.

Unfortunately, this was not an unfounded fear. Many Americans associated Muslim Americans with the attackers who happened to be Muslims. Public frustration and misplaced anger, in many cases, have led to violence against

Excerpted from "Muslim American Women in the Post-11 September Era" by Ashraf Zahedi in *International Feminist Journal of Politics* 13, no. 2 (June 2011): 183–203. Reprinted with permission of the author and publisher. Notes have been edited.

Muslim men and women or those perceived as Muslims, such as Sikh men wearing turbans and beards. They have been chased, attacked verbally and attacked physically, resulting in a number of deaths, Among Muslim women, those wearing headscarves or the hijab were the most identifiable Muslims and got the brunt of the hate and harassment.

Concerned with the negative public perception of Islam and Muslims, some Muslim women have retreated to their own communities. Other women, however, have chosen to engage non-Muslims and serve as public educators. They have used public spaces available to them to explain their religion, affirm their membership in American society, and assert their identities as Muslim, American and women. This has been a major shift from keeping a low socio-political profile, as had been the case before 11 September, to demonstrating their integration in American society and claiming their place in civic and political spaces.

This [essay] seeks to explain the socio-political dimension of "Otherization" of Muslim women and examines the impact of the 11 September events on their lives. These events paradoxically posed challenges to their civil rights as American citizens while serving to present them with opportunities to engage with Americans at large and move from the margin to the mainstream. Their efforts in engaging Americans, however, have been hampered by discriminatory anti-Muslim sentiments including racial profiling and hate crimes. Their efforts have also been eclipsed by two opposing discourses on Muslim women, Orientalism and Islamic fundamentalism, which essentialize the image and meaning of Muslim womanhood. Despite the odds, Muslim American women have been taking an active role in simultaneously challenging and changing the singular image imposed on them by Orientalists and fundamentalists alike and carving a space for themselves as Muslim American women.

Following 11 September, many Muslims and ethnic minorities experienced racial profiling, hatred and hate crimes; however, the focus of this article is hijab-wearing immigrant Muslim American women. Although African-American Muslim women observe the hijab as well, their head covers and style of wearing the hijab draw on African tradition and reflect their African-American identity. Often they do not cover their ears and necks while hijab-wearing immigrant Muslim women do. The difference in

style of hijab signifies their different ethnic identity. Hijab-wearing first- and second-generation immigrant Muslim women are more likely to be associated with Islam and foreignness. What is more, African-American Muslims and immigrant Muslims have different ethno-racial histories and are divided on ethnicity, race, social class, and claims of Islamic authenticity and American nativism. While both groups have experienced ethnic, racial and religious discrimination, . . . "after 9/11 it was better to be African Americans than immigrant Muslims." African-Americans were regarded more as Americans and less as Muslims while the opposite was true for immigrant Muslim Americans.[1] Thus the latter have been the subject of mistrust and misplaced anger following 11 September. With these differences in mind, I have chosen to focus on immigrant Muslim women, both the first generation and second generation born in the United States.

. . . I have drawn on different research methods. . . . I have consulted the reports of Muslim civic and community organizations, attended Muslims' public events, reviewed academic literature, and interviewed twenty-four first- and second-generation immigrant Muslim women. The interviews were semi-structured and conducted individually. In conducting this research, I have drawn upon my training as a sociologist, my religious background as a Muslim woman and my relations with Muslim organizations.

I have changed interviewees' names to protect their identities. These women belong to diverse ethnic, racial, and national backgrounds. Their national origins are: Pakistan; India; Bangladesh; Syria; Palestine; Sudan; Eritrea; and Montenegro (former Yugoslavia). The interviewees were mostly middle class and college educated, as these are often the characteristics of the members of formal community and civic organizations. Their age ranged from 23 to 50 and all except two of them wear the hijab. They work for Muslim organizations in different capacities: as staff, attorney and board members. . . .

Muslims have had a long history in the United States. Amber Haque believes that the "first Muslims may have arrived in the Americas as early as 1178, when Chinese Muslim sailors landed on the West Coast." Of the estimated 6 to 10 million African slaves who came to the United States in later centuries, about 30 percent of them were Muslims. Arab Muslims migrated to America between 1870 and World War II. They came from Greater Syria (Syria, Lebanon, the Palestinians, Israel, Jordan and possibly Iraq), which was under Ottoman rule. Since World War II, and particularly after the long-standing national origin quota was repealed and the Immigration Act of 1965 was adopted, Muslim migration to the United States has increased significantly. Political upheavals, wars, and revolutions have expedited Muslims' migration from all over the world.[2]

American Muslims enjoy a great diversity. According to the Council on American-Islamic Relations, "The three major ethnic groups in the Muslim community are South Asian (32 percent), Arabs (26 percent) and African American (20 percent)." The remaining Muslims come from Africa and Europe. Of the estimated 6 to 7 million Muslim Americans, 36 percent were born in the United States and 64 percent were born in eighty different countries around the world. They are indeed a microcosm of the Muslim world. They have higher levels of education than average Americans and thus enjoy higher incomes and are professionally and economically integrated.[3]

Despite Muslims' long presence in the United States and their diversity in terms of ethnicity, race, national origin, social class, and gender, the American public tends to view them as homogenized and as an undifferentiated distinct religious community. Some Muslims have been in the United States for generations but are still viewed as outsiders . . . and as the perpetual "Other."[4]

Much like the Europeans, the Americans' perceptions of the Muslim Other were shaped by the ideology of the Crusades Wars, which promoted the superiority of Christianity. Christian missionaries were important players in shaping these perceptions by providing "the lens through which" people of the West saw Muslims.[5] Americans' views of Muslims had also been influenced by the European colonial constructs of the colonized as less civilized people who led inferior religious and social lives compared to the Europeans: these constructs justified Europe's civilizing mission. . . .

The United States inherited the European Orientalist legacy and over time constructed its own. Scores of scholars have examined this construct and how Orientalism has made its way into American culture. Nineteenth-century American literature (novels, travel books,

missionary reports and books and political writings) has contributed to the making of American Orientalism. These literary works have been, to varying degrees, tainted by the authors' Orientalist views and ideological biases portraying the people of the so-called Orient, including Muslims, as inferior and unworthy others. Many travel writers . . . "focused on the picturesqueness and exoticism of the 'backward' Eastern races." The much-celebrated Mark Twain whose books were widely read viewed Muslims as "a people by nature and training filthy, brutish, ignorant, unprogressive [and] superstitious."[6]

Through text and images, the widely circulated magazine, *National Geographic*, contributed to the construct of American Orientalism by depicting African, Asians, Arabs, and Muslims as backward. The film industry has also been a significant player in the dissemination of Orientalist ideology. . . . Hollywood popular movies and television sitcoms have caricaturized Muslims, continuously casting their Muslim characters as villains, violent and fanatical. . . .[7]

What is more, Orientalist ideology is reflected in political writings and the view of many American political writers and politicians, . . . [often shaping] US foreign policy toward Muslim countries. Sharing this mindset, the American mass media have constructed a negative image of Muslims and justified unfair American policies in the region. Moreover, they have characterized the national aspirations and political struggles of the people of the Muslim world as violent acts of terrorism. In short, they have demonized the political forces critical of the United States.[8]

Unfortunately, the events of 11 September and the religious background of the attackers have intensified negative perceptions about Muslims. Now Muslims are associated with terrorism, and Islam as a belief system is blamed. Islam is generally perceived as archaic, barbaric, irrational and a "religion of violence and aggression that supports terrorism."[9]

Muslim women have shared the socio-political characterization of "Other" imposed on them. Yet, the Otherization of Muslim women has had a gender dimension as well. The Muslim female body, covered by the veil, serves as context for Otherization. Western perceptions of the veil and the social meaning they have assigned to it have led westerners to view the veil as symbolic of Muslim women's oppression. They have reduced the multifaceted oppression of women in the Islamic world to the veil and concealment of the female body.

Although the veil is often associated with Islam, research indicates that veiling, as a status symbol, was practiced in Persia and the Byzantine before the advent of Islam. The practice of veiling, as a form of modesty, was observed in some Jewish and Christian communities as well. Early Muslims appropriated the veil as a result of their exposure to the cultures of conquered countries.[10]

In most contemporary Muslim countries, the practice of veiling has limited application and many observant Muslim women wear head scarves along with loose clothing, the hijab. Only two Muslim countries have mandatory veil (Saudi Arabia) and hijab (Iran); yet in the western mind, the image of Muslim women has been tied to the singular image of the veil. Western perceptions of the veil, as will be discussed, continue to essentialize Muslim women. In the veil or hijab, Muslim women are perceived as passive, oppressed and at the mercy of the male members of their family. Like many Muslim women throughout the world, Muslim American women challenge this portrayal.

Muslim American women, like other Americans, were devastated by the human tragedy of 11 September. They joined the search and rescue efforts; they donated money and blood. They mourned the death and destruction. They affirmed their loyalty to America, condemned acts of terror and reached out to other Americans; yet the legal system that was supposed to protect them worked to their disadvantage.

Drawing on public support for civil rights limitations for Muslims and building on the existing feeling of Otherization of Muslims, the House and Senate, without much critical discussion, passed the USA-Patriot Act (Uniting and Strengthening America by Providing Appropriate Tools Required to Intercept and Obstruct Terrorism Act of 2001). The Patriot Act expanded the power of the US government. This expansion of power allowed the government, in the name of security, to wire tap Muslims' conversations, seize their property, and freeze their bank accounts.[11]

In the politically and emotionally charged environment of post-11 September, some directed their frustration and anger toward Muslims. According to the FBI, the number of hate crimes against Muslims rose from twenty-eight in 2000 to 481 in 2001, a seventeen fold increase. Hate crimes caused the deaths of Muslim and

Sikh men. The Council on American-Islamic Relations, a Muslim civil rights organization, reported 1,717 incidents of "backlash discrimination against Muslims" between 11 September 2000 and February 2001. Hate incidents ranged from verbal assault to damage to property to vandalism of mosques and Muslim organizations.[12]

Hijab-wearing women received the brunt of hate incidents in the first few years after 11 September. As a result, some women stayed home, others went out only in groups or in the company of non-Muslims. Muslim organizations and mosques developed safety tips for women and children. . . . While sharing the national pains of 11 September, they also had to endure the pain of being suspects, thereby carrying multiple burdens. Many women's husbands, fathers, brothers and sons were detained based on the Patriot Act.[13] . . . These women had to deal with the emotional, legal, political and financial impacts of their male relatives' detention. In the climate of hyper-patriotism, their troubles did not get much public attention. Rather, the public scene was saturated with images and symbols of American unity: American flags were displayed everywhere— houses, shops, buildings and even cars. Some people wore t-shirts with the American flag on the front and patriotic phrases on the back. Assortments of merchandise with flags or patriotic slogans flooded the market. In that political climate, some Americans did not view Muslim Americans as belonging to America and challenged their American-ness. Many Muslims shared conflicting feelings like those of Noor, one of the interviewees for this research: "I recall particularly the level of anger that existed, and the way in which American patriotism felt like an assault on ethnic and religious minorities. The number of flags waving everywhere was on the one hand reassuring, but on the other felt like a political statement against immigrants and non-Christian Americans."

Ironically, the hijab that was supposed to bring Muslim women anonymity brought unwanted attention. As Noor remarked, "Every day since 9/11 has reminded me vividly that I will never be anonymous again." A large number of the Muslim women I interviewed experienced stares, dirty looks, verbal attack, name-calling, harassment, and hate incidents. In the hijab, they were, as Noor put it, a "moving target." Twenty-two out of twenty-four interviewees indicated that they were yelled at, chased or tail-gated on high-ways, and told to "go back to your country." Some men spat on women's head-scarves or tried to pull them off.... "Some people tried to light the tips of the scarves with a match to set them on fire."[14] Women I interviewed recalled unpleasant experiences: "I was verbally harassed by a carload of college-aged guys while I was at an ATM machine, and I've been told to go back to my country more times than I can remember," said Noor. "The worse thing for me has been people yelling out of passing cars," ... remarked Sarah. ...

... [Due to the] many incidents of hate and discrimination target[ing] women in the hijab, discussions ensued in mosques, Islamic organizations, and on the Internet over the viability of wearing the hijab and the safety of Muslim women. A fatwa or religious decree was issued [by the Muslim Women's League] according to which it was permissible for women to remove their hijab: "If a Muslim woman senses a possibility of danger to herself, adjusting her attire to minimize the chances of physical attack is a logical and Islamically permissible precaution that falls squarely within the Fiqh [Islamic jurisprudence] principles of necessity and hardship."Muslim leaders validated "Muslim women wearing non-obvious alternative attire such as hats in public."[15]

Interestingly, the harassment of women wearing the hijab had different outcomes. Some took off the hijab; others, however, were more determined to exert their religious identity. Karima, for example, chose to take off her hijab: "Hijab is supposed to provide you with safety; it no longer did, so I removed my hijab," she remarked. Actually, many did, but with much hesitation and with a sense of being disempowered by the hostile political environment. At the same time, other women chose to wear the hijab. Shabana pointed out, "Other Muslim women felt empowered and started wearing the hijab shortly after 9/11." Mahbooba resisted the temptation to take off her hijab: "Even my husband thought at one point that I should [remove my hijab]; however, I refused to give up my Islamic identity." For women such as Mahbooba, the hijab symbolizes their choice of self-presentation and assertion of their identity.

Fortunately, Muslim Americans' experiences with the American public have not been all negative: many non-Muslim Americans, driven by a strong sense of justice and morality, extended their support to Muslim Americans. One of the highly praised expressions of solidarity with Muslim women was the Scarf Campaign. Jennifer Schock came up with this idea as "a simple gesture of solidarity with Muslim women"; she invited non-Muslim women to wear headscarves for a day. She wanted to convey to Muslim women that they are "not alone." Schock's Scarf Campaign created an opportunity for interaction and dialogue between Muslims and non-Muslims. On 8 October 2001, non-Muslim women donned scarves in many cities through out the United States. They gathered in churches, mosques, community centers, and schools to show their solidarity with Muslim women.[16]

Many Muslim American organizations and individuals shared stories of support and sympathy from their neighbors, community members, and interfaith groups: they have received cards, phone messages, and flowers. Across the county, non-Muslim women volunteered to chaperone Muslim women to shopping, medical appointments, and schools to pick up their children. Zarina echoed the appreciation expressed by many Muslim women: "I was pleasantly surprised by the number of average Americans who reached out to us to let us know they stood with us and they were not falling prey to the climate of fear that was quickly taking over the country."

During these trying times, Muslim women established strong ties with other women with whom they otherwise may not have socialized. These newly found friendships have been very important to Muslim women. Noor put it nicely: "The deep and meaningful and dear friendship I have developed with many Christian and Jews and atheists have had a profound impact on my life, my perception of myself, my community and my faith. I wouldn't trade this enhanced self-awareness for anything."

Yet hate incidents continue to be documented. Although ten years have passed since 11 September 2001, anti-Muslim sentiments remain high due to the American led wars in Afghanistan and Iraq. Displaced anger in the wake of the unsuccessful wars and large numbers of American war casualties has continued to target Muslim Americans. Nevertheless, Muslim American women have continued to speak at interfaith gatherings, appear on television, take part in radio programs, and provide training for corporations, health care providers, and law enforcement authorities. Despite their efforts, a singular, one-dimensional image continues to be projected on them by Orientalists and Islamic fundamentalists. . . .

The predominant image that outsiders have of Muslim women is one swathed in the veil/hijab. This constructed singular image has overshadowed the racial, ethnic, national, and cultural diversity of Muslim women. Their entire existence has been reduced to their public attire. Yet not all Muslims agree on the Islamic mandate of this attire and draw on Quranic verses to support their position. Many Islamic scholars, such as Leila Ahmed Asma Barlas, and Riffat Hassan, contest the universal use of the hijab and thus do not observe it.[17]

Muslim women choosing the hijab or the veil have emotional, socio-political, and religious rationales for this. The hijab can be functional, providing safety and generating respect. Observing the hijab can serve to gain access to resources and opportunities. Some women use the hijab as a means of "negotiating with patriarchy" and appropriate it to their own advantage. Observing the hijab can secure conservative families' consent, allowing their female members to get an education and seek employment, which in turn can lead to the empowerment of Muslim women. Wearing the hijab can serve as a symbol of political and cultural resistance against the West, as has been the case in Egypt, Turkey and Iran. Some women may use the hijab to challenge the tyranny of fashion and the sexualization of the female body. And last, but not least, wearing the hijab can be based on Muslim women's strong beliefs and their piety.[18]

Muslim women challenge the singular meaning that westerners assign to the hijab and their perception of the veil/hijab as a univocal symbol of women's oppression. As Yasmeen remarked, "Muslim women are viewed as illogical for choosing or complying with a religion that is viewed as oppressive towards women." All interviewees expressed their disappointment with many western feminists for their limited understanding of the hijab and Islam and their views of Muslim women as oppressed victims who need to be saved.

Saving Muslim women has served as an integral part of Orientalist/colonial ideologies. Many scholars have therefore challenged the notion of the Christian West saving supposedly oppressed Muslim women. The scholars ask, "do Muslim women need saving?" And what are Muslim women saved from? Inherent to the concept of saving is the given-ness of the power play: the superiority of the savior and the inferiority of the subjects in need of saving. . . . This form of western "compassion" effectively creates a hierarchy between women and assigns positive meanings to the lives of western women and negative meanings to Muslim ones. Dichotomous notions such as "veiled/unveiled, Islamic/secular, Western/non-Western, and free/unfree" both signify and legitimize this hierarchy.[19]

Despite their criticism of Orientalist feminism and the lack support from American feminists following the tragedy of 11 September, some of the Muslim women I interviewed expressed their willingness to work with American feminists. "While I obviously don't agree with all the premises and goals of western feminism, I do feel there are common challenges. We can stand together against [these challenges] as long as we have clear understanding of Islam's goals for women," Iman remarked. Noor agreed: "I have not worked with [American feminists] nor have they reached out to me . . . I am not opposed to working with them because there is value to exchanging ideas and experiences in order to enhance mutual understanding."

Yet, many interviewees pointed out that they do not share some western feminists' prioritizing of gender over other forms of inequality. Much like other women of color, these women support "the basic premise of universal gender equality but reject the prioritization of gender over race and class." They are engaged in multiple sites of struggle and gender is a part of their struggle. Overall, interviewees expressed a preference for working with third-wave feminists who incorporate the issues of race, ethnicity, nationality, sexuality, and social class in their gender analysis.[20]

. . . Although some Muslim women are inclined to work with western feminists, others have a limited knowledge of western feminism, its struggles, and its achievements. Jahan's statement that "western feminism does not appeal to me" and Fatama's remark that "I have all the rights in Islam and do not need western feminism" . . . [obscure the possibility that there might be] much to be learned from western feminism. It seems that some Muslim women, while objecting to the essentializing of Muslim women by westerners, do not hesitate to essentialize western feminists. . . . Western feminists are viewed as anti-family, anti-men, self-centered, and consumed with sexual liberation. These Muslim women's views are influenced by misinformation propagated by conservative forces, secular and religious, of their own communities.[21] . . .

Mainstream western feminists, for their part, will benefit from jettisoning their notion of saving Muslim women and freeing them from oppression. Women's oppression is not a creation of Islam; it is an aspect of patriarchy shared by other religions that have not completed the process of reformation. Islamic reformation has been truncated as a result of western domination and resistance to it. Resistance to foreign domination has diverted national attention to external threats and effectively masked domestic forms of gender oppression. . . .

Many western feminists are driven by their empathy for Muslim women as oppressed women, yet, . . . empathy "does not necessarily lead to insight."[22] Women's oppression has socio-economic, political, and cultural bases and manifests itself in different forms and degrees. Assigning meaning to the female body, covered or concealed, as a site of liberation or oppression is misleading and serves to prevent Muslim women's alliances with women of the West. Liberation and oppression are multilayered and dynamic. Understanding the complexity, . . . is essential for women's alliances. What is more, western women can make an important contribution to the status of Muslim women by demanding that their own governments pursue fair socio-economic and political policies in Muslim societies. By doing so, they can disarm Muslim forces, secular and religious, that have undermined women's rights in the guise of protecting Muslim women. One such force is Islamic fundamentalists.

Islamic fundamentalists aim to construct a singular image of Muslim women. In line with other forms of religious fundamentalism—whether Jewish, Christian, or Hindu—Islamic fundamentalism's agenda for women is framed in the language of care and protection. Control of women is an important element of fundamentalist movements. This control, fundamentalists claim, is for women's good and they have carefully selected self-serving religious texts to support their claim. Fundamentalists tend to refer to religious texts rigidly and literally and to project their interpretation of religious texts as the sole truth: final and unchangeable. Although Islamic fundamentalists tend to favor "puritan and literalist trends

within the Islamic ideological, social, and political traditions," not all of them adhere to extremism and violence. Nevertheless, all Islamic fundamentalists claim to have a monopoly on the truth about Islam and the status of women in Islam. Their truth, however, has been shaped by a patriarchal mindset and misogynist practices. Islamic fundamentalists have constructed one image of Muslim womanhood that is in sharp contrast with multiple images and identities of Muslim women and their varied life experiences.[23]

Muslim women scholars criticize fundamentalists' vision and definition of women and challenge their interpretation of Islamic texts. Azizah Al-Hibri believes that Muslims are bound only by the Qur'an and not its patriarchal interpretations. These scholars argue in favor of historicizing and contextualizing the religious texts; ijtihad, . . . [or adopting] critical thinking that corresponds to the changing times, is central to their arguments . . . Ijtihad "involves a process of recontextualizing the Qur'an through new modes of reading none of which can exhaust it meanings. Verses of the Qur'an fundamentalists rely on so heavily need to be historicised and contextualized rather than blindly followed." Riffat Hassan makes a similar statement: "In every age the Qur'an had to be reread and recontextualized."[24] Islamic fundamentalists, however, stand firm against reform in Islam and, correspondingly, against any change in the status of Muslim women. They have used harsh words for Muslim women who challenge them, accusing them of being agents of western colonialism and working against Islamic societies. . . . Fundamentalists' ideal of authentic Islamic culture can only exist outside history. As the Islam of the seventh century entered different regions and built on existing cultures and traditions, many Islamic cultures emerged. Muslim women of these varying regions and cultures have different views about their Islamic culture and the notion of authenticity. Yet, this belief in authenticizing Muslim women has been shared by some fundamentalist members of Muslim American communities and has impacted gender relations within Muslim American organizations.[25]

Muslim American organizations have played a major role in reaching out to the American public and presenting a peaceful image of Islam and Muslim communities. Embedded in the image of Islam has been the image of hijab-wearing women. The hijab and the status of Muslim women have been of great interest to the American public and Muslim organizations have created opportunities for Muslim women's engagement with non-Muslims. Although the primary interest of these organizations has been the defense of Islam, the attire of these women has kept gender in the spotlight.

Faced with a barrage of questions about the status of women in Islam, many Muslim women have increased their knowledge of Islam and different interpretations of the Qur'an. Some acknowledge that certain beliefs and attitudes have had a negative impact on the social standing of women in the family and society; they often attribute these negative outcomes to pre-Islamic customs and cultures. These women believe the Qur'an has granted equal status to men and women, but that the male interpretations of the Qur'an and Hadith (the sayings and deeds of Prophet Muhammad) have led to social and economic disadvantages for women. They have been revisiting Islamic laws with a new vigor, analyzing the Qur'an, and extracting verses that support gender equality. With knowledge of Islam and dedication to the faith, Muslim American women have been serving as public educators.

As my interviewees and I have observed, Muslim American organizations have experienced an increase in women's participation after 11 September. These women, moved by their own agency and the desire to depict an accurate picture of a true Islam, have been engaged at every level of civic activity, some becoming the public face of their organizations. However, although there has been a significant increase in Muslim women's civic participation, the majority of these women have been volunteers and not part of a decision-making body. Even those in paid positions often lack organizational authority. Like other organizations, secular and religious, glass ceilings have been at play in Muslim American organizations. The interplay of gender, financial resources, and politics has kept many women out of the boardrooms. Since major donors to Muslim organizations are often men, they tend to support the board membership of men and prefer men for important organizational positions. Some women who have experienced this glass ceiling have chosen to form their own organizations. In small women-run organizations such as the Muslim Women's League and Muslim Women's Lawyers for Human Rights,

women do fill the boardrooms and exercise organizational authority. . . .

. . . The increased number of women board members of local chapters of the Council on American-Islamic Relations (CAIR), and the recent election of Ingrid Mattson, a hijab-wearing Canadian-American Muslim convert, to the presidency of one of the largest Muslim organization in the USA, the Islamic Association of North American (ISNA), testify to changing tides. The glass ceiling may be broken [once] but the question remains: is Mattson in a position to advance gender issues? Wafa, [one interviewee,] believed Mattson "cannot afford to focus on women. She cannot alienate the others [men]. She is the first woman and needs to succeed to be politically effective (given the conservative framework of the ISNA)." . . .

While some smaller organizations such as the Muslim Women's League, Muslim Women Lawyers for Human Rights, and the American Society for Muslim Advancement have both hijab-wearing and non-hijab-wearing women on the board, women in hijab are still the dominant image of Muslim woman in larger Muslim organizations. Although non-hijab-wearing women staff these organizations, the two prominent Muslim organizations, CAIR and ISNA, have only hijab-wearing women officially representing them. Hijab-wearing Noor [commented].

> Who gets to speak for Islam and Muslims with credibility and authority and truth has become only more complex since 9/11, particularly for women. Many mainstream Muslim leaders and organizations have been hesitant at least, and downright oppositional at worst, to the possibility of a non-hijab-wearing Muslim women speaker representing Islam. This symbol of modesty has become more and more a construction of Muslim womanhood—and has therefore placed a difficult question before Muslim women in public roles on behalf of the community . . . women feel obligated to wear hijab because of their public role.

In a way, the hijab, . . . "has become the litmus test of a Muslim women's piety" and those not "covering their hair and throat are judged as women" who have not reached the ideal "level of devotion to God." Some Muslim American organizations have promoted the hijab as an essential aspect of Muslim women's image and identity. Non-hijab-wearing Muslim women are highly critical of this singular image of Muslim women: they believe, as Saba said, that "beliefs are personal and private and should not be publicly displayed. I do not want to wear my beliefs outside. I am a Muslim but hijab does not define me or my beliefs." They would like to see multiple images of Muslim women being allowed to surface at the high levels of Muslim American organizations.[26]

In the post-11 September era, Muslim American women have played an important role in shaping public perception of Islam and women in Islam. They are in a position to redefine the meaning of women in Islam, thereby shaping the meaning of American Islam. American Islam, in turn, has the potential to inspire the quest for reform in Islam worldwide. The amazing diversity of Muslim American women allows them to be culturally connected to all parts of the world and yet be truly Americans. Their unique position as Muslims and as believers in American values—liberty, personal rights, and democracy—provides them with a great opportunity to be agents of change both in the United States and, by extension, the world over.

NOTES

1. Sherman A. Jackson, *Islam and the Blackamerican: Looking toward the Third Resurrection* (Oxford: Oxford University Press, 2005); Jamillah Karim, *American Muslim Women: Negotiating Race and Gender with the Ummah* (New York: New York University Press, 2008), 40.

2. Amber Haque, "Islamophobia in North America: Confronting the Menace," in Barry Van Dreil, ed., *Confronting Islamophobia in Educational Practice* (Oakhill, Va.: Trentham Books, 2004), 1–18, quotation on 4. On post-1870 migration, see Michael W. Suleiman, ed., *Arabs in America: Building a New Future* (Philadelphia, Penn.: Temple University Press, 1999), 2.

3. Council on American-Islamic Relations (CAIR), "Western Muslim Minorities: Integration and Disenfranchisement," Policy Bulletin, April 26, 2–3. Available at http://www.cair.com/Portals/0/pdf/policy_bulletin_integration_in_the_West.pdf (accessed Oct. 19, 2009).

4. Sam Afridi, "Muslims in America: Identity, Diversity, and the Challenge of Understanding," Carnegie Corporation of New York, 2001, 2. Available at http://carnegie.org/fileadmin/Media/Publications/PDF/muslims.pdf.

5. Yvonne Yazeck Haddad, Jane I. Smith, and Kathleen M. Moore, *Muslim Women in America: The Challenge of Islamic Identity Today* (Oxford: Oxford University Press, 2006), 24.

6. Twain quoted in Douglas Little, *American Orientalism* (Chapel Hill: University of North Carolina Press, 2002), 13. On Orientalism in the U.S. and elsewhere, see Edward Said, *Orientalism* (New York: Vintage, 1979); Malini Johar Schueller, "Orientalism," in Janet Gabler-Hover and Robert Sattelmeyer, eds., *American History through Literature, 1820–1920*

(New York: Charles Scribner's Sons, 2006), 839; and Amira Jarmakani, *Imagining Arab Womanhood: The Cultural Mythology of Veils, Harems, and Belly Dancers in the U.S.* (New York: Palgrave Macmillan, 2008).

7. Little, *American Orientalism*, 10; Haddad et al., *Muslim Women in America*, 22. A few examples of popular movies are *The Sheik* (1921), *Aladdin* (1992), *Executive Decision* (1996), *The Siege* (1998), and *Rules of Engagement* (2000).

8. Little, *American Orientalism*; Zachary Lockman, *Contending Visions of the Middle East: The History and Politics of Orientalism* (Cambridge: Cambridge University Press, 2004); Suad Joseph, "Against the Grain of the Nation: The Arab," in Suleiman, *Arabs in America*, 257–71.

9. Haque, "Islamophobia in North America," 3.

10. Practice of veiling: John L. Esposito, ed., *The Oxford Encyclopedia of the Modern Islamic World*, 4 vols. (New York: Oxford University Press, 1995), 2:108; Guity Nashat, "Women in Pre-Islamic and Early Islamic Iran," in Guity Nashat and Lois Beck, eds., *Women in Iran from the Rise of Islam to 1800* (Urbana: University of Illinois Press, 2003), 38.

11. Louise Cainkar, "The Impact of the September 11 Attacks and Their Aftermath on Arab and Muslim Communities in the United States," *Global Security and Cooperation (GSC) Quarterly* 13 (Summer–Fall 2004): 1.

12. Human Rights Watch, "'We Are Not the Enemy': Hate Crimes Against Arabs, Muslims, and Those Perceived to Be Arab or Muslim after September 11" (Nov. 14, 2002), available at http://www.hrw.org/sites/default/files/reports/usa1102.pdf.

13. See the Council on American-Islamic Relations (CAIR) website: http://www.cair.com/american-muslims/67-cair-muslim-community-safety-kit.html.

14. Scarves on fire: Sandy Banks, "Donning Scarves in Solidarity," *Los Angeles Times*, Sept. 25, 2001.

15. Muslim Women's League, "Muslim Dress in Dangerous Times" (2001), available at http://www.mwlusa.org/topics/Sept11/hijab_dangerous_times.htm (accessed 19 Oct. 2009).

16. Chris L. Coryn, James M. Beale, and Krista M. Myers, "Response to September 11: Anxiety, Patriotism, and Prejudice in the Aftermath of Terror," *Current Research in Social Psychology* 9:12 (Dec. 2004): 165–84. Scarf campaign: Banks, "Donning Scarves."

17. Leila Ahmed, *Women and Gender in Islam: Historical Roots of a Modern Debate* (New Haven, Conn.: Yale University Press, 1992); Asma Barlas, *"Believing Women" in Islam: Unreading Patriarchal Interpretations of the Qur'an* (Austin: University of Texas Press, 2002); Riffat Hassan, "Interview with Dawn Newspaper of Pakistan Regarding the Role of Religion and Status of Women in Pakistan, January 2003," in Fawzia Afzah-Khan, ed., *Shattering the Stereotypes: Muslim Women Speak Out* (Northampton, Mass.: Olive Branch Press, 2005), 184–91.

18. Arlene Elowe Macleod, *Accommodating Protest: Working Women, the New Veiling, and Change in Cairo* (New York: Columbia University Press, 1991); Fadwa El Guindi, *Veil: Modesty, Privacy and Resistance* (Oxford: Berg, 1999); Faegheh Shirazi, *The Veil Unveiled: The Hijab in Modern Culture* (Gainesville: University Press of Florida, 2001); Saba Mahmood, *Politics of Piety: The Islamic Revival and the Feminist Subject* (Princeton, N.J.: Princeton University Press,

2004); Ashraf Zahedi, "Contested Meaning of the Veil and Political Ideologies of Iranian Regimes," *Journal of Middle East Women's Studies* 3 (March 2007), 75–98; Deniz Kandiyoti, "Bargaining with Patriarchy," *Gender and Society* 2:3 (Sept. 1988): 274–90; Lila Abu-Lughod, "Do Muslim Women Really Need Saving? Anthropological Reflections on Cultural Relativism and Its Others," *American Anthropologist* 104 (March 2002): 787.

19. Shahnaz Khan, *Muslim Women: Crafting North American Identity* (Gainesville: University Press of Florida, 2000), 5; Abu-Lughod, "Do Muslim Women Really Need Saving?" 783, 788; Mahmood, *Politics of Piety*, 189; Haddad, et al., *Muslim Women in America*, 146; Minoo Moallem, *Between Warrior Brother and Veiled Sister: Islamic Fundamentalism and the Politics of Patriarchy in Iran* (Berkeley: University of California Press, 2005), 16.

20. Carolyn Rouse, *Engaged Surrender: African American Women and Islam* (Berkeley: University of California Press, 2004), 143.

21. Shahrzad Mojab, "The Politics of Theorizing 'Islamic Feminism': Implications for International Feminist Movements," WLUML (Women Living under Muslim Laws) Dossier 23–24 (July 2001), available at http://www.wluml.org/node/344.

22. Corinne Fowler, "Journalists in Feminist Clothing: Men and Women Reporting Afghan Women during Operation Enduring Freedom, 2001" *Journal of International Women's Studies* 8:2 (Jan. 2007): 13.

23. Marie-Aimee Hélie-Lucas, "What Is Your Tribe? Women's Struggles and the Construction of Muslimness," in Courtney W. Howland, ed., *Religious Fundamentalisms and the Human Rights of Women* (New York: Palgrave Macmillan, 2001), 22; Nira Yuval-Davis, "The Personal is Political: Jewish Fundamentalism and Women's Empowerment," in ibid., 34; Lily Zakiyah Munir, "Islamic Fundamentalism and Its Impact on Women" (March 2003), available at http://www.law.emory.edu/ihr/acessay.html; Jasmin Zine, "Between Orientalism and Fundamentalism: Muslim Women a Feminist Engagement," in Krista Hunt and Kim Rygiel, eds., *(En)Gendering the War on Terror: War Stories and Camouflaged Politics* (Aldershot, Eng.: Ashgate, 2006), 28.

24. Azizah Al-Hibri, "Muslim Women's Rights in the Global Village: Challenges and Opportunities," in Afzal-Khan, *Shattering the Stereotypes*, 161; Barlas, *"Believing Women" in Islam*, 60; Hassan, "Interview with Dawn Newspaper," 191.

25. Gwendolyn Zoharah Simmons, "Are We Up to the Challenge? The Need for a Radical Re-Ordering of the Islamic Discourse on Women," in Omid Safi, *Progressive Muslims: On Justice, Gender, Pluralism* (Oxford: Oneworld, 2003), 243.

26. Haddad et al., *Muslim Women in America*, 39, 40.

Wilma Mankiller and Michael Wallis, A Chief and Her People

Wilma Mankiller (1945–2010) served from 1985–1995 as the first female principal chief of the Cherokee Nation, the second-largest indigenous group in the United States. She received Ms. magazine's Woman of the Year for 1987, the Presidential Medal of Freedom in 1988, and was inducted in the National Women's Hall of Fame in 1993. In an obituary published by Ms. magazine, Mankiller was described as making "great strides to improve health, education, housing, utilities management, and tribal government during her time as chief. She also devoted much of her time to civil rights work, focusing largely on women's rights."*

The introduction to Mankiller's autobiography, written collaboratively by Mankiller and historian-biographer-reporter Michael Wallis provides an overview of Mankiller's life. It introduces the land and the community that inspired her political activism. The excerpt and the rest of the autobiography also highlight how Mankiller's commitments and achievements as a female indigenous political leader were shaped by a longer history. Mankiller felt that her life was intertwined with the forced removal of the Cherokee Nation (through the Trail of Tears) from the U.S. Southeast to the central plains in the 1830s. Mankiller's ownership of land traced back to the 1887 Dawes Severalty Act, which promised allotments of land in exchange for indigenous people giving up sovereignty, communal living, and reservations. The Cherokee were able to prevent tribal termination, but they faced steady pressure to assimilate culturally. These pressures intensified after World War II through the Termination Policy (1953–1968), which sought once again to relocate native people, this time to urban centers such as San Francisco, Los Angeles, and Minneapolis. Mankiller's parents moved the family to San Francisco when she was 10. The ghettoization and poverty that "urban Indians" faced in cities as well as on reservations led to the emergence of an American Indian Movement during the 1960s. Inspired by black liberation and Third World liberation movements of that time, the movement attracted Wilma Mankiller, then a young mother. Her relocation back to Cherokee lands in Oklahoma and her political ascendancy represent the culmination of this longer history of oppression and resistance.

Wilma Mankiller's election to principal chief also resonated with an even longer history of indigenous women. Historian Theda Perdue argues that prior to European contact, Cherokee women held great authority and power. Women farmed, controlling a steady food supply for their communities. Kinship, clans,

*"First Woman Cherokee Chief Mankiller Dies," April 13, 2010, http://www.msmagazine.com/news/uswirestory.asp?ID=12346.

Excerpted from the introduction to Mankiller: A Chief and Her People by Wilma Mankiller and Michael Wallis (New York: St. Martin's Griffin, 1993), xxvii–xxvi. Reprinted by permission of Michael Wallis and the publisher.

and households were based on female lineage, which meant women were decision-makers and authority figures. Women also held political power. These gender structures were challenged by European and American contact. Anglo-Americans tended to recognize only male-led political systems and patriarchal nuclear family structures. The Cherokee Nation, particularly the women, resisted these western gender norms but some aspects were adopted.[†] The election of Wilma Mankiller resurrects, in some ways, the precontact and eighteenth-century practice of female political leadership. (For more on these issues, see Kathleen M. Brown's essay, pp. 12–23.) How do you see her twentieth-century leadership in comparison with the "public mothers" that Lucy Murphy describes (pp. 161–168)? What are the similarities and differences between Mankiller and a figure like Hillary Clinton?

Dawn arrives in the countryside of northeastern Oklahoma, warm and familiar like an old pal who's come calling. . . . Before too long the front door slowly opens and Wilma Mankiller—the woman of the house—emerges. She is barefoot and wears a brightly colored dress. Her dark hair is still damp from a morning shampoo. She sits on a kitchen chair on the narrow porch and sips a mug of coffee. . . .

The surrounding forests and hills conceal the animal life native to this eastern region of Oklahoma. . . . This is the place on earth that Wilma Mankiller loves best. She is surrounded by 160 acres of ancestral property, allotted to her paternal grandfather, John Mankiller, when Oklahoma became a state in 1907. The land is located in Adair County, within hollerin' distance of the Cherokee County line. Named for a prominent Cherokee family, Adair County is the heart of the area first settled by Cherokees in the late 1830s. The county still claims a higher percentage of Native American population than any other in the United States. . . . Here, a person's wealth and worth are measured in other ways besides bank accounts and worldly goods.

In generations past, the Cherokee people came to this area to rebuild their nation after the westward trek from their beloved homelands in the mountainous South. Herded by federal soldiers, the Cherokees took a path in 1838–39 that became known as the Trail of Tears.

At Tahlequah, the seat of Cherokee County in the eastern foothills of the Ozarks, where their bitter journey ended, the Cherokees built new homes and some of the first schools west of the Mississippi for the education of both men and women. They also reestablished an intricate government in Indian Territory, including a system of courts of law. Although oral historians assert that the tribe possessed a written language long before, the Cherokees put to good use the eighty-five-character syllabary developed by Sequoyah over a twelve-year period prior to the Trail of Tears, to publish Oklahoma's first newspaper in both Cherokee and English.[*]

. . . It is country where conversation centers on farming, hunting, weather, football and, forever and always, politics. Not just mainstream party politics, such as candidates for county commissioner or sheriff or the U.S. Senate, but also tribal politics—the critical issue of Cherokee leadership.

Much of the talk at the gas stations, bait shops, and convenience stores scattered along the country roads is about Wilma Mankiller. This is only natural, since she serves as the principal chief of the Cherokee Nation of Oklahoma. The Cherokees represent the second-largest tribe in the United States, after the Dine (Navajo) Nation. Mankiller is the first female to lead a major Native American tribe. With an enrolled tribal population worldwide of more than 140,000, an annual budget of more than $75 million, and more than 1,200 employees spread across 7,000 square miles, her responsibilities as chief are the same as a head of state and the chief executive officer of a major corporation.

Although it is the land of rugged males who, for the most part, prefer to see fellow "good ol' boys" run for political office, it is difficult to find anyone from the Cherokee ranks, including some of Mankiller's former political foes, who can find fault with the performance of her administration. It was not always that

[†]Theda Perdue, *Cherokee Women: Gender and Cultural Change, 1700–1835* (Lincoln: University of Nebraska Press, 1998).

way. In the beginning, there were many problems and obstacles. Often, those were mean times. There were some Cherokees who didn't wish to be governed by a female. Wilma Mankiller had her share of enemies. Her automobile tires were slashed. There were death threats. Chief Mankiller was admittedly an unlikely politician. But gradually she won acceptance. In time, most of her constituents became quite comfortable with her. Now when disagreements occur, they are based on issues rather than gender.

Wilma Mankiller shares her home and life with her husband, Charlie Soap, and Winterhawk, his son from a former marriage. Her two daughters, Felicia and Gina, and their children often stop by to visit, as do other family members and friends. Mankiller's widowed mother lives just down the road.

In the winter, Mankiller's house is warmed by a stove fed by the constant supply of firewood cut from the surrounding forest. Native American art, including masks, baskets, and pottery as well as Cherokee, Kiowa, and Sioux paintings, adorns the shelves and walls. Colorful blankets drape the chair backs and couches. Framed family photographs are scattered about tabletops. On a living room shelf is a small bust of Sam Houston, the revered Texas statesman and folk hero called "the Raven" by the Cherokees who adopted him. Cases hold Mankiller's beloved books, mostly volumes of poetry, novels, biographies, and histories. The works of her favorite authors, including Gloria Steinem, Alex Haley, and Alice Walker, are mixed with the writings of Vine Deloria, Joy Harjo, Robert Conley, Chaucer, Tolstoy, and Milton.

As comfortable as the house is, Mankiller also loves being outside on the land. She tends to the garden and sometimes she walks, trailed by one or two of the family dogs, to a nearby spring where past generations of Mankillers fetched fresh water and gathered mint and watercress.

The nearest community—with just a small grocery–gas station and a school—is called Rocky Mountain. The land where Mankiller and her family reside is known as Mankiller Flats. Born at Hastings Indian Hospital in Tahlequah in 1945, she was raised at Mankiller Flats from her first days. She spent her early years there, with her parents and eight of her ten brothers and sisters. The land is important to Mankiller. It was allotted to her grandfather, and now she and her family maintain it. The land is an important part of their heritage, and they preserve it for future generations.

But of primary importance to Mankiller—the woman who overcame tremendous personal crises—are the thousands of people she serves and her mission to bring self-sufficiency to them. Mankiller felt honored to become her tribe's chosen leader, but she readily adds that she did not seek the responsibility. Indeed, she thought she had reached her pinnacle in tribal government in 1983, when she became her tribe's first female deputy chief.

"Prior to my election, young Cherokee girls would never have thought that they might grow up to be chief," she says. Mankiller had been asked to run as deputy chief by Ross Swimmer, a quarter-blood Indian lawyer and former bank president, who assumed leadership of the Cherokee Nation in 1975. Swimmer convinced Mankiller that, if elected, she could effect greater change in the rural Cherokee communities where she worked.

When Swimmer, a staunch Republican, resigned in 1985 to go to Washington to head the Bureau of Indian Affairs, it was his deputy, a liberal Democrat, who took over. Mankiller was left with a tribal council which more than likely would not have chosen her to take Swimmer's place had it not been for the Cherokee Constitution mandating that the deputy chief move to the higher post when the chief resigns.

In a historic tribal election in July 1987, Mankiller won the coveted post in her own right, and political success brought an unprecedented worldwide interest in both her and the Cherokee Nation. In 1991—winning with an 83 percent majority—she was reelected for four more years.

"We are a revitalized tribe," says Mankiller. "After every major upheaval, we have been able to gather together as a people and rebuild a community and a government. Individually and collectively, Cherokee people possess an extraordinary ability to face down adversity and continue moving forward. We are able to do that because our culture, though certainly diminished, has sustained us since time immemorial. The Cherokee culture is a well-kept secret."

Since becoming chief of her people, Mankiller has become a visible force in America. Named *Ms.* magazine's Woman of the Year in 1987, she has been awarded many honorary degrees and citations, and makes numerous national media appearances and public presentations on behalf of her tribe. But the hardworking chief is much the same unaffected person she always has been. She is at her best when in the halls of Congress quietly advocating better health care, improved housing, or more jobs for the Cherokee people.

Her father, the late Charley Mankiller, was a full-blooded Cherokee, and her mother, Irene, is of Dutch-Irish descent. "We traced our family name back to the eastern part of the country, where the Cherokees lived in great numbers," says Mankiller. "As best we can tell, our name is an old Cherokee military title. It was usually given to a person who was in a position of safeguarding a Cherokee village."

Cherokee culture thrived for hundreds of years in the southeastern United States until the tribe was pushed westward out of its homelands. Among those who survived the Trail of Tears were some of Mankiller's paternal ancestors. They were part of the tribe that regrouped to make Tahlequah its capital and embarked on what historians today call the Cherokees' "Golden Age." This was, in spite of the removal, a time of prosperity, marked by the development of businesses, schools, and a flourishing culture. In those days, people helped each other more and maintained a greater sense of interdependence.

Nonetheless, this prosperity did not last. The years of good fortune and revival after the shameful removal ended with tribal division over the Civil War. At the war's end in 1865, the Cherokees—many of whom had not taken a side—were treated like defeated southerners. Eventually, poverty replaced affluence as a predominant theme as more and more Cherokee land was taken to make room for other tribes who were also forced to leave their homes and move into Indian Territory.

By 1907, the federal government had dismantled the tribal government, ignored the Cherokee Constitution, and divided up the land in individual allotments. It was at that time that Wilma Mankiller's family received its share of property in the wooded hills. In that remote setting, where she and her siblings were raised, the family grew strawberries and other crops for a living. There was no indoor plumbing, so the Mankiller children hauled water about a quarter of a mile to their home.

"I remember when we bartered with neighbors and ate what we grew," she says. "Those days helped me so much. I was raised with a sense of community that extended beyond my family."

When she was ten years old, Mankiller's entire family was moved to California as participants in the federal government's relocation program. "It was part of the national Indian policy of the 1950s," she explains. "The government wanted to break up tribal communities and 'mainstream' Indians, so it relocated rural families to urban areas. One day I was living in a rural Cherokee community, and a few days later I was living in California and trying to deal with the mysteries of television, neon lights, and elevators. It was total culture shock."

The Mankiller family eventually became acclimated to California. Mankiller attended school and met her first husband, a well-to-do Ecuadoran. They had two daughters, Felicia in 1964 and Gina in 1966 It was during the turbulent 1960s, while starting her family, that Mankiller began to raise her political consciousness. Her concern for Native American issues was fully ignited by 1969 when a band of university students occupied the abandoned prison on Alcatraz Island in San Francisco Bay. They wanted to attract attention to issues affecting them and their tribes. Mankiller answered the call. Out of that historic experience, an activist was born.

"In most ways I was a typical housewife at that time," recalls Wilma, "but when Alcatraz occurred, I became aware of what needed to be done to let the rest of the world know that Indians had rights too. Alcatraz articulated my own feelings about being an Indian. It was a benchmark. After that, I became involved."

She attended sociology classes at San Francisco State College and took on Native American issues with a fervor. Mankiller worked as a volunteer for five grueling years with the Pit River Tribe in California on treaty-rights issues, helping to establish a legal defense fund for the battle to reclaim the tribe's ancestral lands. She also devoted much of her time to Native American preschool and adult education programs and directing a dropout prevention program for Native American youngsters.

In 1974, Mankiller divorced her husband of eleven years. "He wanted a traditional housewife. I had a stronger desire to do things in the community than at home." Two years later, she returned to Oklahoma with her daughters. "I was delighted to be back on our ancestral homelands," she recalls. "I wanted to come home and raise my kids and build a house on my land."

She managed all that and more. In 1979, after almost three years of helping to procure important grants and launch critical rural services for the tribe, Mankiller enrolled in graduate courses at the nearby University of Arkansas. Late one morning in the fall of 1979, while returning home from class on a two-lane country road, Mankiller was seriously injured in a freak automobile accident which resulted in a fatality. An oncoming car, which had pulled into her lane to pass, collided head-on with Mankiller's station wagon. Unbelievably, the young woman driving the other vehicle, who was killed, was Mankiller's close friend. When Mankiller regained consciousness in the hospital, her face was crushed and her ribs and legs were broken. It was one of several brushes with death. After avoiding the amputation of her right leg, she endured seventeen operations and was bedridden for months. During the long healing process, Mankiller never allowed herself to become discouraged or to sink into despair.

"That accident in 1979 changed my life," she says. "I came very close to death, felt its presence and the alluring call to complete the circle of life. I always think of myself as the woman who lived before and the woman who lives afterward. I was at home recovering for almost a year, and I had time to reevaluate." For Mankiller, it proved to be a deep spiritual awakening when she adopted what she referred to as "a very Cherokee approach to life—what our tribal elders call 'being of good mind.'"

Then in November 1980, just a year after the tragic accident, Mankiller was diagnosed with myasthenia gravis, a chronic neuromuscular disease that causes varying weakness in the voluntary muscles of the body. Treatment required surgery to remove the thymus gland and a program of drug therapy. In December 1980—just barely out of the hospital—she was back on the job. She needed only one month to recover from her illness. Although a regimen of drugs followed, work seemed to be the best medicine of all.

"I thought a lot about what I wanted to do with my life during that time," says Mankiller. "The reality of how precious life is enabled me to begin projects I couldn't have otherwise tackled."

In 1981, she spearheaded the tribe's most ambitious and lauded experiment to that date—the Bell Community Revitalization Project. With hundreds of thousands of dollars in federal and private funds and with their own labor, the residents of a poverty-stricken community named Bell in eastern Oklahoma remodeled dilapidated housing, constructed new homes, and laid a sixteen-mile pipeline that brought running water to many homes for the first time. Beyond the physical improvements, the volunteers from the Bell community did the work themselves, while developing a strong bond and gaining a sense of control over their own lives.

The national publicity that followed made the Bell Project a model for other Native American tribes eager for self-sufficiency. This work also established Mankiller as an expert in community development, and brought her to the attention of Cherokee Chief Swimmer.

The election to deputy chief occurred two years later, and in 1985, when Swimmer resigned from office, Mankiller became principal chief. Still, she did not feel she had a mandate until 1987 when she was elected on her own, even though from the very start she never slowed down.

"In order to understand how I operate, it is necessary to remember that I come from an activist family," says Mankiller. "My father was involved in union organizing, community service, and liked to discuss political issues. With a background like that, you naturally get involved in the community."

Her terms of office have produced countless highlights: a dramatic increase in tribal revenue and services; the attraction of new businesses to eastern Oklahoma, where many Cherokees live; the garnering of more than $20 million in construction projects, including new clinics, the procurement of funding for innovative programs to help Cherokee women on welfare develop microenterprises, the establishment of an $8 million Job Corps training center; and dozens of other projects, ranging from an extensive array of services for children to revitalization of the Cherokee judicial system. Other initiatives Mankiller has spearheaded include a new tribal tax commission, an energy-consulting firm, a pilot self-government agreement with the federal government, and an agreement with the Environmental Protection Agency.

In October 1986, Wilma married her old friend Charlie Soap, a full-blooded Cherokee and the former director of the tribal development program. Mankiller and Soap met while working together on the Bell Project. Known as a quiet but effective "Cherokee powerhouse,"

Soap has focused his effort on development projects for several low-income Cherokee communities. . . . When Soap recites his personal heroes, his wife tops the list. When Mankiller names her heroes, Soap is her first choice. "He is the most secure male I have ever met," says Mankiller. "He is not threatened by strong women. He is supportive of women, of women's causes, and of me and my work."

Mankiller's love of family and her people paid off in major dividends again, in 1990, when she was faced with yet another physical dilemma. Recurrent kidney problems resulted in the need for a kidney transplant. Her oldest brother, Don Mankiller, consented to serve as the donor, and the operation was a success. During her convalescence, she had many long talks with Charlie Soap and other members of her family before ultimately deciding to run for yet another term as chief.

"It was a big decision," says Mankiller, who admits that it finally came down to the fact that she believed too much unfinished work remained. Her mission was not completed. With her reelection in 1991, the Cherokee people returned Mankiller to office with a landslide vote.

But all the honorary degrees and successful tribal development projects do not begin to measure the influence that Mankiller has had in so many diverse circles of America. First and foremost are her stewardship of the Cherokees, and the pride she has instilled in thousands of Native American people. She has shown—in her typically ebullient and joyous way—not what Cherokees or other native people can learn from European Americans, but what

whites can learn from native people. In fact, without the knowledge of the interconnectedness of all living things and the spirituality that Native American culture so powerfully possesses, many white Americans are beginning to understand that they have much to learn from native wisdom, culture, and spirituality.

Spirituality is then key to the public and private aura of Wilma Mankiller, a leader who has indeed become known as much for her able leadership of the Cherokee Nation as for her spiritual presence among all Americans A woman rabbi who serves as the head of a large synagogue in New York City commented that Mankiller was a significant spiritual force in the nation. One would imagine that a rabbi in Manhattan and an Indian chief in Oklahoma would have little in common, but it is clearly Mankiller's way of life—her religion, so to speak—that has formed bonds with spiritual leaders throughout the country.

No less significant has been Mankiller's reputation among women and women's groups. A woman who proudly describes herself as a feminist, a leader who is concerned with women's issues worldwide, Mankiller is ironically a female leader who has been as comfortably embraced by men as by women. Most of the attacks directed against her in those early days of campaigning because of her gender, because she threatened the male Cherokee status quo, have subsided. She has become a leader who can play easily to a multitude of audiences—from the cover of *Ms.* to the cover of *Parade*—in an effortless way that few others have been able to duplicate. Perhaps it truly is her innate love of all people that breaks down so many doors.

Hillary Clinton, "Women's Rights Are Human Rights," 1995

The United Nations Charter of 1948 committed the UN to promote and encourage respect for human rights "without distinction as to race, sex, language and religion." A Commission on Human Rights, with a Subcommission on the Status

Women's Rights are Human Rights" (speech, First Lady Hillary Clinton, United Nations Fourth World Conference on Women, Plenary Session, Beijing, China, September 5, 1995). A full video and audio file of this speech, along with the unabridge text, is available at http://www.americanrhetoric.com/speeches/hillaryclintonbeijingspeech.htm.

*Sequoyah, who was born in about 1776, was the son of Wut-Teh (the daughter of a Cherokee chief) and a Virginia fur trader, Nathaniel Gist. During the War of 1812, Sequoyah enlisted under Andrew Jackson to fight against the British. In the war's aftermath, he spent 12 years working on a written language for Cherokee, introducing it in 1821. For a chart of the syllabary, see hhttp://www.nlm.nih.gov/nativevoices/timeline/270.html

of Women, was constructed as part of the UN's Economic and Social Council (ECOSOC); shortly afterward, the subcommission broke off to be an independent Commission on the Status of Women (CSW), reporting directly to the Economic and Social Council. Whether constituted as subcommission or commission, members found it almost impossible to get the attention of ECOSOC or to persuade the UN that women's infirmities really deserved international attention. The shrill insistence of the Soviet Union that it had already solved all of women's problems meant that it was almost impossible to make critical assessments of women's status independently of Cold War rivalries.

Yet the CSW did engage in significant advocacy, even though the press paid almost no attention to it and most male politicians, inside and outside the UN, were dismissive. For example, that some of the language of the Universal Declaration of Human Rights is gender-neutral is due to CSW insistence. At the time of its founding, nearly one-third of UN member nations did not allow women to vote; the CSW moved its 1950 meeting to Lebanon to call international attention to the denial of democracy there and elsewhere. French women could not vote until 1945, and women in French Algeria not until 1958, on the eve of their own independence; Swiss women did not get the right to vote or stand for election until 1971. In 2011, King Abdullah of Saudi Arabia granted women the right to vote but only in municipal elections. (As we go to press, they still lack the right to drive.) In Lebanon, where all men over 21—whatever their education—are required to vote, women over 21 may now choose to vote, but only if they have an elementary education, which is not required of men.)* The CSW identified and sought to publicize weaknesses in women's literacy, education, employment, and the integrity of their citizenship. By 1979 the UN adopted—at the CSW's urging—a Convention on the Elimination of All Forms of Discrimination Against Women (CEDAW), which recognizes women's rights in family life—the right to freedom from domestic violence, for example—and in the public sector—rights to equal education, work, and health care. The United States participated in drafting the convention and President Jimmy Carter signed it within its first year. But the Senate has not ratified this convention, and as this volume goes to press, the United States remains one of only seven nations that have refused to do so. (The others include Sudan, Somalia, and Iran.)

Identifying 1975–85 as the UN Decade for Women, the UN convened three major international conferences—1975 in Mexico City, 1980 in Copenhagen, and 1985 in Nairobi. All three generally focused on economic development. A fourth was held a decade later, in 1995 in Beijing, on the heels of the UN Conference on Human Rights held at Vienna in 1993, at which it had been clear that it was not easy to find international consensus on women's entitlements. The declaration that emerged from Vienna specified that "the human rights of women and of the girl-child are an inalienable, integral, and indivisible part of universal human rights"; it named as a target "gender-based violence and all forms of sexual harassment and exploitation, including those resulting from cultural prejudice and international trafficking"; but it omitted provisions on reproductive rights because they had run afoul of religious arguments about what constituted freedom.**

At Beijing, as at the conferences that had preceded it, the number of official delegates was swamped by the enormous numbers of women who surrounded

---

*Data on women's voting from CIA *World Factbook*, available at https://www.cia.gov/library/publications/the-world-factbook/fields/2123.html.

**Vienna Declaration and Programme of Action*, UN World Conference on Human Rights, June 14–25, 1993, A/Conf 157/23, Sec. I, par. 18.

the conference with meetings of their own. These meetings were sponsored by hundreds of women's nongovernmental organizations (NGOs), notably from underdeveloped countries which demanded improvements in the status of women that could be measured by international law. The conference itself was an expression of post–Cold War confidence, and the invitation to Hillary Clinton, wife of the then president of the United States, to offer a major speech recognized the international power of the United states and Clinton's own long-standing commitment to women's rights. The speech was expected to attract international attention.

In her memoir, Clinton describes the care she and her "speech team"—which included Madeleine Albright, then the U.S. permanent representative to the United Nations (President Bill Clinton would appoint her secretary of state in 1997)—lavished on the wording. "Although I had delivered thousands of speeches, I was nervous," Hillary Clinton wrote.

> I felt passionately about the subject, and I was speaking as a representative of my country. . . . If nothing came out of the conference, it would be viewed as another missed opportunity to galvanize global opinion on behalf of . . . the cause of women's rights. . . . I wanted the speech to be simple, accessible and unambiguous in its message that women's rights are not separate from, or a subsidiary of, human rights. . . . Pushing the envelope in this speech meant being clear about the injustice of the Chinese government's behavior. The Chinese leadership had blocked non–governmental organizations from holding their NGO forum at the main conference in Beijing. They forced NGOs devoted to causes ranging from prenatal care to microlending to convene at a makeshift site in the small city of Huairou, forty miles north, where there were few accommodations or facilities. Although I didn't mention China or any other country by name, there was little doubt about the egregious human rights violators to whom I was referring.[†]

Fourteen years later, President Barak Obama would appoint Hilary Clinton Secretary of State. In 2011 she launched the Women's Nationality Initiative, collaborating with the United Nations High Commission on Refugees to encourage change in the laws of the 29 nations that now prevent women from acquiring, retaining, or transmitting citizenship to their children or their foreign spouses, a situation that results in widespread statelessness. (For the existence of similar rules in the United States in the first half of the twentieth century, see *Mackenzie v. Hare*, pp. 413–415.)

As you read this speech, note the women's vulnerabilities that are named. Compare the list that Hillary Clinton constructs with the demands for reform in the 1848 Seneca Falls Declaration of Sentiments. What has changed? What has remained the same? Review the UN Declaration of Human Rights at http://www.un.org/en/documents/udhr/. Do you think it is useful to describe women's rights as human rights? What difference does it make? Does the impact or emphasis of Clinton's speech seem to change in any way when you listen to the audio version?

I would like to thank the Secretary General for inviting me to be part of this important United Nations Fourth World Conference on Women. This is truly a celebration—a celebration of the contributions women make in every aspect of life: in the home, on the job, in the community, as mothers, wives, sisters, daughters, learners, workers, citizens and leaders.

It is also a coming together, much the way women come together every day in every country. . . . Whether it is while playing with our children in the park, or washing clothes in a

[†]Hillary Rodham Clinton, *Living History* (New York: Simon & Schuster, 2003), pp. 303–5.

river, or taking a break at the office water cooler, we come together and talk about our aspirations and concerns. And time and again, our talk turns to our children and our families. However different we may appear, there is far more that unites us than divides us. We share a common future, and we are here to find common ground so that we may help bring new dignity and respect to women and girls all over the world, and in so doing bring new strength and stability to families as well.

By gathering in Beijing, we are focusing world attention on issues that matter most in our lives—the lives of women and their families: access to education, health care, jobs and credit, the chance to enjoy basic legal and human rights and to participate fully in the political life of our countries.

There are some who question the reason for this conference. . . . There are some who wonder whether the lives of women and girls matter to economic and political progress around the globe. . . .

The great challenge of this conference is to give voice to women everywhere whose experiences go unnoticed, whose words go unheard. Women comprise more than half the world's population, 70% of the world's poor, and two-thirds of those who are not taught to read and write. We are the primary caretakers for most of the world's children and elderly. Yet much of the work we do is not valued—not by economists, not by historians, not by popular culture, not by government leaders.

At this very moment, as we sit here, women around the world are giving birth, raising children, cooking meals, washing clothes, cleaning houses, planting crops, working on assembly lines, running companies, and running countries. Women also are dying from diseases that should have been prevented or treated. They are watching their children succumb to malnutrition caused by poverty and economic deprivation. They are being denied the right to go to school by their own fathers and brothers. They are being forced into prostitution, and they are being barred from the bank lending offices and banned from the ballot box.

Those of us who have the opportunity to be here have the responsibility to speak for those who could not. As an American . . . I want to speak up for mothers who are fighting for good schools, safe neighborhoods, clean air, and clean airwaves; for older women, some of them widows, who find that, after raising their families, their skills and life experiences are not valued in the marketplace; for women who are working all night as nurses, hotel clerks, or fast food chefs so that they can be at home during the day with their children; and for women everywhere who simply don't have time to do everything they are called upon to do each and every day.

Speaking to you today, I speak for them, just as each of us speaks for women around the world who are denied the chance to go to school, or see a doctor, or own property, or have a say about the direction of their lives, simply because they are women. . . . We need to understand there is no one formula for how women should lead our lives. That is why we must respect the choices that each woman makes for herself and her family. Every woman deserves the chance to realize her own God-given potential. But we must recognize that women will never gain full dignity until their human rights are respected and protected.

Our goals for this conference, to strengthen families and societies by empowering women to take greater control over their own destinies, cannot be fully achieved unless all governments—here and around the world—accept their responsibility to protect and promote internationally recognized human rights. The international community has long acknowledged and recently reaffirmed at Vienna that both women and men are entitled to a range of protections and personal freedoms, from the right of personal security to the right to determine freely the number and spacing of the children they bear. No one should be forced to remain silent for fear of religious or political persecution, arrest, abuse, or torture.

Tragically, women are most often the ones whose human rights are violated. Even now, in the late 20th century, the rape of women continues to be used as an instrument of armed conflict. Women and children make up a large majority of the world's refugees. And when women are excluded from the political process, they become even more vulnerable to abuse. I believe that now, on the eve of a new millennium, it is time to break the silence. It is time for us to say here in Beijing, and for the world to hear, that it is no longer acceptable to discuss women's rights as separate from human rights.

These abuses have continued because, for too long, the history of women has been a history of silence. Even today, there are those who are trying to silence our words. But the voices of this conference . . . must be heard loudly and clearly: It is a violation of *human* rights when babies are denied food, or drowned, or suffocated, or their spines broken, simply because they are born girls; . . . when women and girls are sold into the slavery of prostitution for human greed—and the kinds of reasons that are used to justify this practice should no longer be tolerated; . . . when women are doused with gasoline, set on fire, and burned to death because their marriage dowries are deemed too small; . . . when individual women are raped in their own communities and when thousands of women are subjected to rape as a tactic or prize of war; . . . when a leading cause of death worldwide among women ages 14 to 44 is the violence they are subjected to in their own homes by their own relatives; . . . when young girls are brutalized by the painful and degrading practice of genital mutilation; . . . [and] when women are denied the right to plan their own families, and that includes being forced to have abortions or being sterilized against their will.

If there is one message that echoes forth from this conference, let it be that human rights are women's rights and women's rights are human rights once and for all. And among those rights are the right to speak freely—and the right to be heard.

Women must enjoy the rights to participate fully in the social and political lives of their countries, if we want freedom and democracy to thrive and endure. . . .

In my country, we recently celebrated the 75th anniversary of Women's Suffrage. It took 150 years after the signing of our Declaration of Independence for women to win the right to vote. It took 72 years of organized struggle, before that happened, on the part of many courageous women and men. It was one of America's most divisive philosophical wars. But it was a bloodless war. Suffrage was achieved without a shot being fired. . . . We have seen peace prevail in most places for a half century. We have avoided another world war. But we have not solved older, deeply-rooted problems that continue to diminish the potential of half the world's population.

. . . As long as discrimination and inequities remain so commonplace everywhere in the world, as long as girls and women are valued less, fed less, fed last, overworked, underpaid, not schooled, subjected to violence in and outside their homes—the potential of the human family to create a peaceful, prosperous world will not be realized.

Let this conference be our—and the world's—call to action. Let us heed that call so we can create a world in which every woman is treated with respect and dignity, every boy and girl is loved and cared for equally, and every family has the hope of a strong and stable future. . . .

God's blessing on you, your work, and all who will benefit from it.

INDEX